FREE WITH NEW COPIES OF THIS TEXTBOOK*

Start using myBusinessCourse Today: www.mybusinesscourse.com

myBusinessCourse is a web-based learning and assessment program intended to complement your textbook and faculty instruction.

Student Benefits

- **eLectures**: These videos review the key concepts of each Learning Objective in each chapter.
- **Guided examples**: These videos provide step-by-step solutions for select problems in each chapter.
- **Auto-graded assignments**: Provide students with immediate feedback on select assignments. (**with Instructor-Led course ONLY**).
- **Quiz and Exam preparation**: myBusinessCourse provides students with additional practice and exam preparation materials to help students achieve better grades and content mastery.

You can access myBusinessCourse 24/7 from any web-enabled device, including iPads, smartphones, laptops, and tablets.

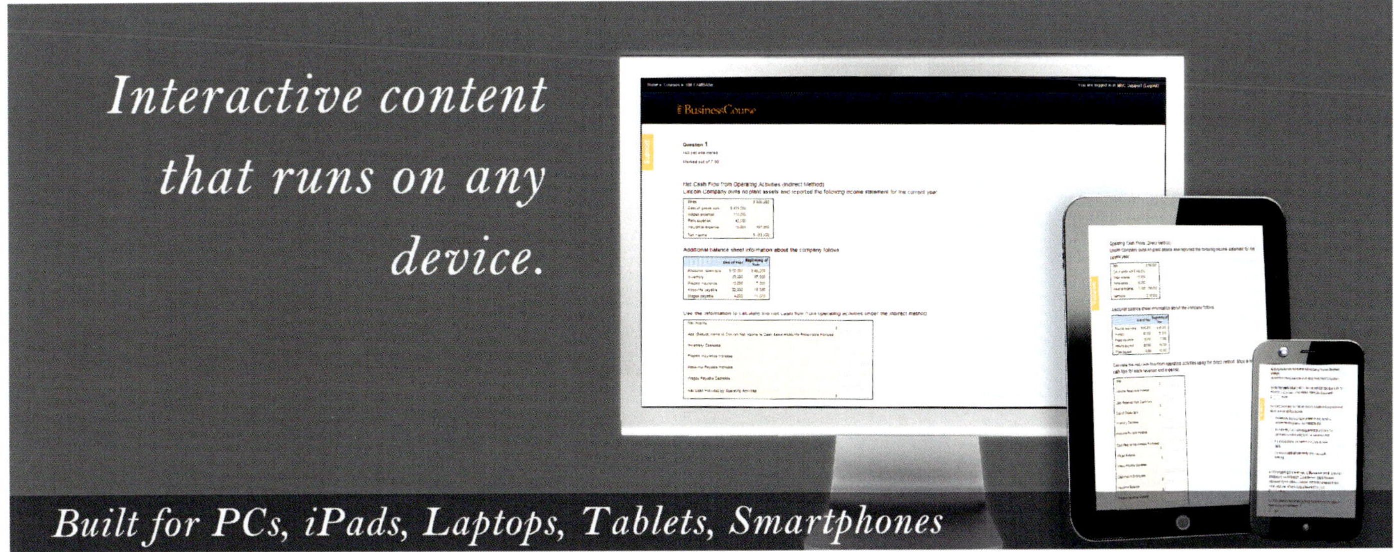

***Each access code is good for one use only.** If the textbook is used for more than one course or term, students will have to purchase additional myBusinessCourse access codes. In addition, students who repeat a course for any reason will have to purchase a new access code. If you purchased a used book and the protective coating that covers the access code has been removed, your code may be invalid.

Access to myBusinessCourse is free ONLY with the purchase of a new textbook.

SIXTH EDITION

Financial Accounting

MICHELLE L. HANLON
Massachusetts Institute of Technology

ROBERT P. MAGEE
Northwestern University

GLENN M. PFEIFFER
Chapman University

THOMAS R. DYCKMAN
Cornell University

To my husband, Chris, and to our children, Clark and Josie.

—MLH

To my wife, Peggy, and our family, Paul and Teisha, Michael and Heather, and grandchildren Sage, Caillean, Rhiannon, Corin, Connor, and Harrison.

—RPM

To my wife, Kathie, and my daughter, Jaclyn.

—GMP

To my wife, Ann, and children, Daniel, James, Linda, and David; and to Pete Dukes, a friend who is always there.

—TRD

Photo credits:

Chapter 1: iStock.com/BestForLater91
Chapter 2: shutterstock.com/QualityHD
Chapter 3: gettyimages/Jose Luis Pelaez Inc
Chapter 4: shutterstock.com/David Tonelson
Chapter 5: gettyimages/Joe Raedle/Staff
Chapter 6: iStock.com/NicolasMcComber
Chapter 7: JAM Photography
Chapter 8: P&G
Chapter 9: iStock.com/helen89
Chapter 10: gettyimages/Justin Sullivan/Staff
Chapter 11: gettyimages/Bloomberg/Contributor
Chapter 12: iStock.com/Purplexsu

Cambridge Business Publishers

FINANCIAL ACCOUNTING, Sixth Edition, by Michelle L. Hanlon, Robert P. Magee, Glenn M. Pfeiffer, and Thomas R. Dyckman.

Student Edition ISBN: 978-1-61853-311-1

Bookstores & Faculty: To order this book, contact the company via email **customerservice@cambridgepub.com** or call 800-619-6473.

Students: To order this book, please visit the book's website and order directly online.

Printed in Canada.
10 9 8 7 6 5 4 3 2

About the Authors

The combined skills and expertise of Michelle Hanlon, Bob Magee, Glenn Pfeiffer, and Tom Dyckman create the ideal team to author this exciting financial accounting textbook. Their combined experience in award-winning teaching, consulting, and research in the area of financial accounting and analysis provides a powerful foundation for this pioneering textbook.

Michelle L. Hanlon is the Howard W. Johnson Professor at the MIT Sloan School of Management. She earned her doctorate degree at the University of Washington. Prior to joining MIT, she was a faculty member at the University of Michigan. Professor Hanlon has taught undergraduates, MBA students, Executive MBA students, and Masters of Finance students. She is the winner of the 2013 Jamieson Prize for Excellence in Teaching at MIT Sloan. Professor Hanlon's research focuses primarily on the intersection of financial accounting and taxation. She has published research studies in the *Journal of Accounting and Economics,* the *Journal of Accounting Research, The Accounting Review*, the *Review of Accounting Studies*, the *Journal of Finance*, the *Journal of Financial Economics*, the *Journal of Public Economics*, and others. She has won several awards for her research and has presented her work at numerous universities and conferences. Professor Hanlon has served on several editorial boards and currently serves as an editor at the *Journal of Accounting and Economics*. Professor Hanlon is a co-author on two other textbooks—*Intermediate Accounting* and *Taxes and Business Strategy*. She has testified in front of the U.S. Senate Committee on Finance and the U.S. House of Representatives Committee on Ways and Means about the interaction of financial accounting and tax policy and international tax policy. She served as a U.S. delegate to the American-Swiss Young Leaders Conference in 2010 and worked as an Academic Fellow at the U.S. House Ways and Means Committee in 2015.

Robert P. Magee is Keith I. DeLashmutt Professor Emeritus of Accounting Information and Management at the Kellogg School of Management at Northwestern University. He received his A.B., M.S. and Ph.D. from Cornell University. Prior to joining the Kellogg faculty in 1976, he was a faculty member at the University of Chicago's Graduate School of Business. For academic year 1980–81, he was a visiting faculty member at IMEDE (now IMD) in Lausanne, Switzerland.

Professor Magee's research focuses on the use of accounting information to facilitate decision-making and control within organizations. He has published articles in *The Accounting Review,* the *Journal of Accounting Research*, the *Journal of Accounting and Economics*, and a variety of other journals. He is the author of *Advanced Managerial Accounting* and co-author (with Thomas R. Dyckman and David H. Downes) of *Efficient Capital Markets and Accounting: A Critical Analysis*. The latter book received the Notable Contribution to the Accounting Literature Award from the AICPA in 1978. Professor Magee has served on the editorial boards of *The Accounting Review,* the *Journal of Accounting Research*, the *Journal of Accounting and Economics* and the *Journal of Accounting, Auditing and Finance*. From 1994–96, he served as Editor of *The Accounting Review*, the quarterly research journal of the American Accounting Association. He received the American Accounting Association's Outstanding Accounting Educator Award in 1999 and the Illinois CPA Society Outstanding Educator Award in 2000.

Professor Magee has taught financial accounting to MBA and Executive MBA students. He has received several teaching awards at the Kellogg School, including the Alumni Choice Outstanding Professor Award in 2003.

Glenn M. Pfeiffer is the Warren and Doris Uehlinger Professor of Business at the George L. Argyros School of Business and Economics at Chapman University. He received his M.S. and Ph.D. from Cornell University after he earned a bachelors degree from Hope College. Prior to joining the faculty at the Argyros School, he held appointments at the University of Washington, Cornell University, the University of Chicago, the University of Arizona, and San Diego State University.

Professor Pfeiffer's research focuses on accounting and capital markets. He has investigated issues relating to lease accounting, LIFO inventory liquidation, earnings per share, management compensation, corporate reorganization, and technology investments. He has published articles in *The Accounting Review*, *Accounting Horizons*, the *Financial Analysts Journal*, the *International Journal of Accounting Information Systems*, the *Journal of High Technology Management Research*, the *Journal of Economics*, the *Journal of Accounting Education*, and several other academic journals. In addition, he has published numerous case studies in financial accounting and reporting.

Professor Pfeiffer teaches financial accounting and financial analysis to undergraduate, MBA, and Law students. He has also taught managerial accounting for MBAs. He has won several teaching awards at both the undergraduate and graduate levels.

Thomas R. Dyckman is Ann Whitney Olin Professor Emeritus of Accounting and Quantitative Analysis at Cornell University's Johnson Graduate School of Management. In addition to teaching accounting and quantitative analysis, he has taught in Cornell's Executive Development Program. He earned his doctorate degree from the University of Michigan. He is a former member of the Financial Accounting Standards Board Advisory Committee and the Financial Accounting Foundation, which oversees the FASB. He was president of the American Accounting Association in 1982 and received the association's *Outstanding Educator* Award for the year 1987. He also received the AICPA's *Notable Contributions to Accounting Literature Award* in 1966 and 1978.

Professor Dyckman has extensive industrial experience that includes work with the U.S. Navy and IBM. He has conducted seminars for Cornell Executive Development Program and Managing the Next Generation of Technology, as well as for Ocean Spray, Goodyear, Morgan Guaranty, GTE, Southern New England Telephone, and Goulds Pumps. Professor Dyckman was elected to The Accounting Hall of Fame in 2009.

Professor Dyckman has coauthored eleven books and written over 50 journal articles on topics from financial markets to the application of quantitative and behavioral theory to administrative decision making. He has been a member of the editorial boards of *The Accounting Review,* the *Journal of Finance and Quantitative Analysis,* the *Journal of Accounting and Economics,* the *Journal of Management Accounting Research,* and the *Journal of Accounting Education.*

Preface

Welcome to the sixth edition of *Financial Accounting* and, to adopters of the first five editions, thank you for the great success those editions have enjoyed. We wrote this book to equip students with the accounting techniques and insights necessary to succeed in today's business environment. It reflects our combined experience in teaching financial accounting to college students at all levels. For anyone who pursues a career in business, the ability to read, analyze, and interpret published financial reports is an essential skill. *Financial Accounting* is written for future business leaders who want to understand how financial statements are prepared and how the information in published financial reports is used by investors, creditors, financial analysts, and managers. Our goal is to provide the most engaging, relevant, and accessible textbook available.

TARGET AUDIENCE

Financial Accounting is intended for use in the first financial accounting course at either the undergraduate or graduate level; one that balances the preparation of financial statements with their analysis and interpretation. This book accommodates mini-courses lasting only a few days as well as extended courses lasting a full semester.

Financial Accounting is real-world oriented and focuses on the most salient aspects of accounting. It teaches students how to read, analyze, and interpret financial accounting data to make informed business decisions. To that end, it consistently incorporates **real company data**, both in the body of each chapter and throughout the assignment material.

REAL DATA INCORPORATED THROUGHOUT

Today's business students must be skilled in using real financial statements to make business decisions. We feel strongly that the more exposure students get to real financial statements, the more comfortable they become with the variety in financial statements that exists across companies and industries. Through their exposure to various financial statements, students will learn that, while financial statements do not all look the same, they can readily understand and interpret them to make business decisions. Furthermore, today's students must have the skills to go beyond basic financial statements to interpret and apply nonfinancial disclosures, such as footnotes and supplementary reports. We expose students to the analysis and interpretation of real company data and nonfinancial disclosures through the use of focus companies in each chapter, the generous incorporation of footnotes, financial analysis discussions in nearly every chapter, and an abundance of assignments that draw on real company data and disclosures.

Focus Companies for Each Chapter

Each chapter's content is explained through the accounting and reporting activities of real companies. Each chapter incorporates a "focus company" for special emphasis and demonstration. The enhanced instructional value of focus companies comes from the way they engage students in real analysis and interpretation. Focus companies were selected based on student appeal and the diversity of industries.

Chapter 1	Nike	**Chapter 7**	Home Depot
Chapter 2	Walgreens	**Chapter 8**	Procter & Gamble
Chapter 3	Walgreens	**Chapter 9**	Verizon
Chapter 4	CVS Health Corporation	**Chapter 10**	Delta Air Lines
Chapter 5	PepsiCo	**Chapter 11**	Pfizer
Chapter 6	Microsoft Corporation	**Chapter 12**	Alphabet, Inc.

Footnotes and Management Disclosures

We incorporate footnote and other management disclosures, where appropriate, throughout the book. We explain the significance of the footnote and then demonstrate how to use the disclosed information to make managerial inferences and decisions. A representative sample follows.

Footnote Disclosures and Interpretations

In its balance sheets, Microsoft reports current accounts receivable, net of allowance for doubtful accounts, of $26,481 million at June 30, 2018, and $22,431 million at June 30, 2017. In its MD&A (Management Discussion and Analysis), the company provides the following information.

The allowance for doubtful accounts reflects our best estimate of probable losses inherent in the accounts receivable balance. We determine the allowance based on known trouble accounts, historical experience, and other currently available evidence.

Activity in the allowance for doubtful accounts was as follows:

(In millions)			
Year Ended June 30,	**2018**	**2017**	**2016**
Balance, beginning of period	$361	$409	$289
Charged to costs and other	134	58	175
Write-offs	(98)	(106)	(55)
Balance, end of period	$397	$361	$409

Allowance for doubtful accounts included in our consolidated balance sheets:

June 30,	**2018**	**2017**	**2016**
Accounts receivable, net allowance for doubtful accounts	$377	$345	$392
Other long-term assets	20	16	17
Total	$397	$361	$409

Financial Analysis Discussions

Each chapter includes a financial analysis discussion that introduces key ratios and applies them to the financial statements of the chapter's focus company. By weaving some analysis into each chapter, we try to instill in students a deeper appreciation for the significance of the accounting methods being discussed. One such analysis discussion follows.

ANALYZING FINANCIAL STATEMENTS

Analysis Objective

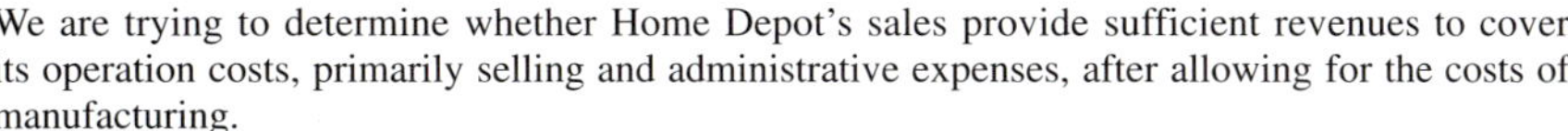

We are trying to determine whether Home Depot's sales provide sufficient revenues to cover its operation costs, primarily selling and administrative expenses, after allowing for the costs of manufacturing.

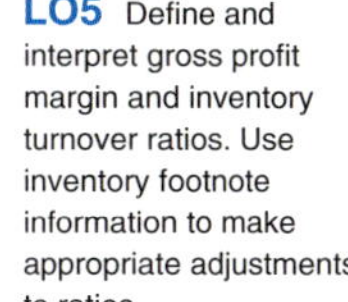

LO5 Define and interpret gross profit margin and inventory turnover ratios. Use inventory footnote information to make appropriate adjustments to ratios.

Analysis Tool Gross Profit Margin (GPM) Ratio

$$\textbf{Gross profit margin} = \frac{\textbf{Sales revenue} - \textbf{Cost of goods sold}}{\textbf{Sales revenue}}$$

Applying the Gross Profit Margin Ratio to Home Depot

$$2015: \frac{(\$88,519 - \$58,254)}{\$88,519} = 0.342 \text{ or } 34.2\%$$

$$2016: \frac{(\$94,595 - \$62,282)}{\$94,595} = 0.342 \text{ or } 34.2\%$$

$$2017: \frac{(\$100,904 - \$66,548)}{\$100,904} = 0.340 \text{ or } 34.0\%$$

Assignments that Draw on Real Data

It is essential for students to be able to apply what they have learned to real financial statements. Therefore, we have included an abundance of assignments in each chapter that draw on recent, real data and disclosures. These assignments are readily identified by an icon in the margin that usually includes the company's ticker symbol and the exchange on which the company's stock trades. A representative example follows.

LO3

Abbott Laboratories NYSE :: ABT
Bristol-Myers Squibb Company NYSE :: BMY
Johnson & Johnson NYSE :: JNJ
GlaxoSmithKline plc (ADR) NYSE :: GSK
Pfizer Inc. NYSE :: PFE

P5-45. Comparing Profitability Ratios for Competitors
Selected income statement data for Abbott Laboratories, Bristol-Myers Squibb Company, Johnson & Johnson, GlaxoSmithKline plc, and Pfizer, Inc. is presented in the following table:

(millions)	Abbott Laboratories	Bristol-Myers Squibb	Johnson & Johnson	Glaxo Smith Kline plc	Pfizer
Sales revenue	$27,390	$19,258	$76,450	£30,186	$52,546
Cost of sales	12,337	6,066	25,354	10,342	11,240
SG&A expense	9,117	4,687	21,420	9,672	14,784
R&D expense	2,235	6,411	10,554	4,476	7,657
Interest expense	904	196	934	734	1,270
Net income	477	975	1,300	2,169	21,355

REQUIRED

a. Compute the profit margin (PM) and gross profit margin (GPM) ratios for each company. (As a British company, GlaxoSmithKline plc has a statutory tax rate of 19.25% in 2017. Assume a tax rate of 35% for the others.)

b. Compute the research and development (R&D) expense to sales ratio and the selling, general and administrative (SG&A) expense to sales ratio for each company.

c. Compare the relative profitability of these pharmaceutical companies.

BALANCED APPROACH

As instructors of introductory financial accounting, we recognize that the first financial accounting course serves the general business students as well as potential accounting majors. *Financial Accounting* embraces this reality. This book **balances financial reporting, analysis, interpretation**, and **decision making** with the more standard aspects of accounting such as **journal entries**, **T-accounts**, and the **preparation of financial statements**.

3-Step Process: Analyze, Journalize, Post

One technique we use throughout the book to maintain a balanced approach is the incorporation of a 3-step process to analyze and record transactions. **Step 1** analyzes the impact of various transactions on the financial statements using the financial statement effects template. **Step 2** records the transaction using journal entries, and **Step 3** requires students to post the journal entries to T-accounts.

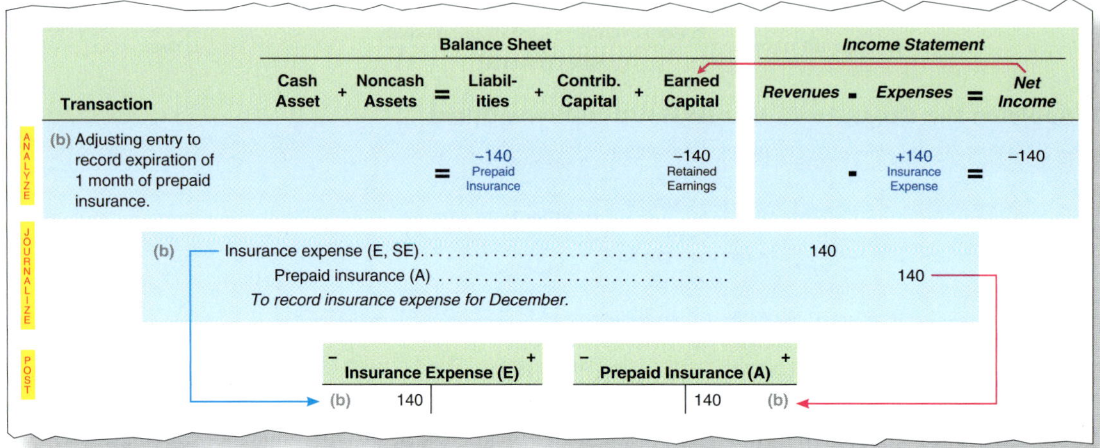

The template captures each transaction's effects on the four financial statements: the balance sheet, income statement, statement of stockholders' equity, and statement of cash flows. For the balance sheet, we differentiate between cash and noncash assets to identify the cash effects of transactions. Likewise, equity is separated into the contributed and earned capital components (the latter includes retained earnings as its major element). Finally, income statement effects are separated into revenues, expenses, and net income (the updating of retained earnings is denoted with an arrow line running from net income to earned capital). This template provides a convenient means to represent financial accounting transactions and events in a simple, concise manner for assessing their effects on financial statements.

INNOVATIVE PEDAGOGY

Business Insights

Students appreciate and become more engaged when they can see the real-world relevance of what they are learning in the classroom. We have included a generous number of current, real-world examples throughout each chapter in Business Insight boxes. The following is a representative example:

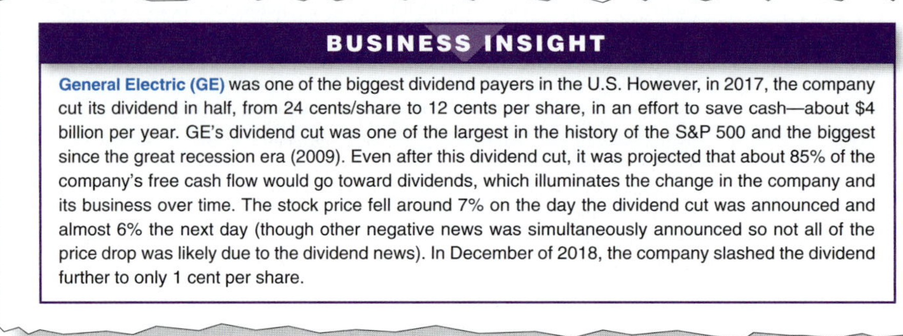

BUSINESS INSIGHT

General Electric (GE) was one of the biggest dividend payers in the U.S. However, in 2017, the company cut its dividend in half, from 24 cents/share to 12 cents per share, in an effort to save cash—about $4 billion per year. GE's dividend cut was one of the largest in the history of the S&P 500 and the biggest since the great recession era (2009). Even after this dividend cut, it was projected that about 85% of the company's free cash flow would go toward dividends, which illuminates the change in the company and its business over time. The stock price fell around 7% on the day the dividend cut was announced and almost 6% the next day (though other negative news was simultaneously announced so not all of the price drop was likely due to the dividend news). In December of 2018, the company slashed the dividend further to only 1 cent per share.

Decision Making Orientation

One primary goal of a financial accounting course is to teach students the skills needed to apply their accounting knowledge to solving real business problems. With that goal in mind, **You Make the Call** boxes in each chapter encourage students to apply the material presented to solving actual business scenarios.

YOU MAKE THE CALL

You are the Division Manager You are the division manager for a main operating division of your company. You are concerned that a declining PPE turnover is adversely affecting your division's profitability. What specific actions can you take to increase PPE turnover? [Answers on page 395]

Mid-Chapter and Chapter-End Reviews

Financial accounting can be challenging—especially for students lacking business experience or previous exposure to business courses. To reinforce concepts presented in each chapter and to ensure student comprehension, we include mid-chapter and chapter-end reviews that require students to recall and apply the financial accounting techniques and concepts described in each chapter. Each review has a corresponding Guided Example video, available to students in myBusinessCourse (our online learning and homework system).

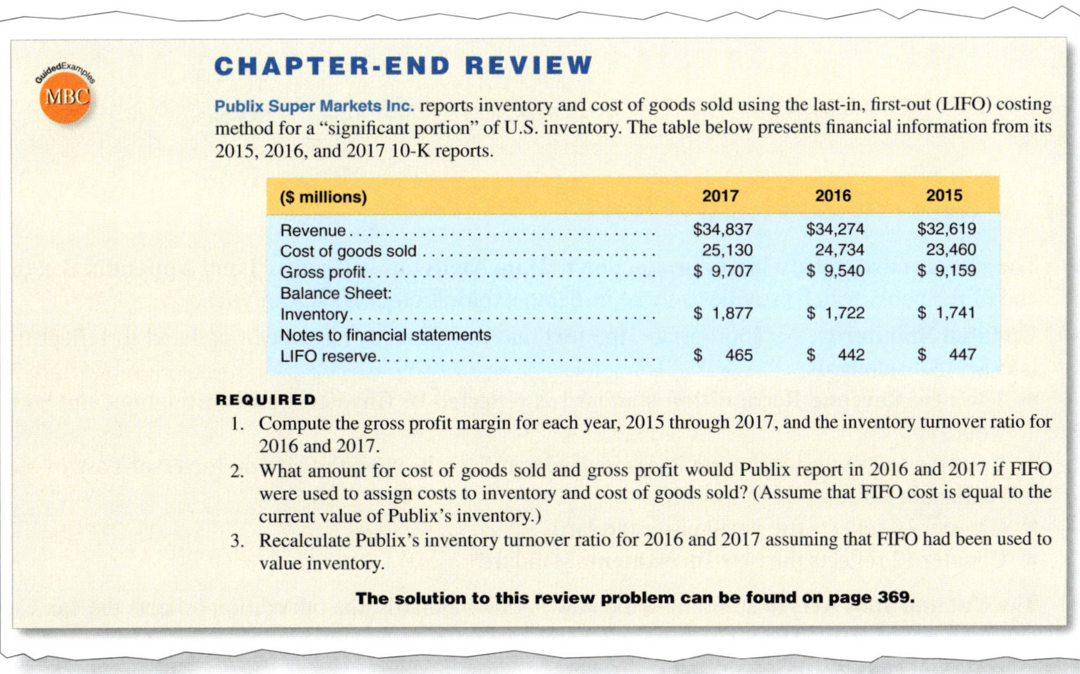

CHAPTER-END REVIEW

Publix Super Markets Inc. reports inventory and cost of goods sold using the last-in, first-out (LIFO) costing method for a "significant portion" of U.S. inventory. The table below presents financial information from its 2015, 2016, and 2017 10-K reports.

($ millions)	2017	2016	2015
Revenue	$34,837	$34,274	$32,619
Cost of goods sold	25,130	24,734	23,460
Gross profit	$ 9,707	$ 9,540	$ 9,159
Balance Sheet:			
Inventory	$ 1,877	$ 1,722	$ 1,741
Notes to financial statements			
LIFO reserve	$ 465	$ 442	$ 447

REQUIRED

1. Compute the gross profit margin for each year, 2015 through 2017, and the inventory turnover ratio for 2016 and 2017.
2. What amount for cost of goods sold and gross profit would Publix report in 2016 and 2017 if FIFO were used to assign costs to inventory and cost of goods sold? (Assume that FIFO cost is equal to the current value of Publix's inventory.)
3. Recalculate Publix's inventory turnover ratio for 2016 and 2017 assuming that FIFO had been used to value inventory.

The solution to this review problem can be found on page 369.

Research Insights for Business Students

Academic research plays an important role in the way business is conducted, accounting is performed, and students are taught. It is important for students to recognize how modern research and modern business practice interact. Therefore, we periodically incorporate relevant research to help students understand the important relation between research and modern business.

RESEARCH INSIGHT

Accounting Conservatism and Cost of Debt Research indicates that companies applying more conservative accounting methods incur a lower cost of debt. Research also suggests that while accounting conservatism can lead to lower-quality accounting income (because such income does not fully reflect economic reality), creditors are more confident in the numbers and view them as more credible. Evidence also implies that companies can lower the required return demanded by creditors (the risk premium) by issuing high-quality financial reports that include enhanced footnote disclosures and detailed supplemental reports.

FLEXIBILITY FOR COURSES OF VARYING LENGTHS

Many instructors have approached us to ask about suggested chapter coverage based on courses of varying length. To that end, we provide the following table of possible course designs:

	15 Week Semester-Course	10 Week Quarter-Course	6 Week Mini-Course	1 Week Intensive-Course
Chapter 1	Week 1	Week 1	Week 1	Day 1
Chapter 2	Week 2 & 3	Week 2	Week 1 & 2	
Chapter 3	Week 3 & 4	Week 3 & 4	Week 2 & 3	Day 2
Chapter 4	Week 5 & 6	Week 4 & 5	Optional	Optional
Chapter 5	Week 6 & 7	Optional	Optional	Optional
Chapter 6	Week 7 & 8	Week 6	Week 3	Day 3
Chapter 7	Week 9	Week 7	Week 4	Day 4
Chapter 8	Week 10	Week 8	Week 5	
Chapter 9	Week 11 & 12	Week 9	Week 6	Day 5
Chapter 10	Week 12 & 13	Week 10	Week 6 (optional)	Skim
Chapter 11	Week 14	Optional	Optional	Optional
Chapter 12	Week 15	Optional	Optional	Optional

NEW IN THE 6TH EDITION

- The authors have added a brief introduction to **Data Analytics** in Chapter 1 and **Appendix B** at the end of the book, which provides a more in-depth exploration of Data Analytics.
- **Updated Standards:** As appropriate, the text and assignments have been updated to reflect the latest FASB standards:
  - The new **Revenue Recognition** standard is reflected in Chapter 6 and throughout the book where appropriate
  - Inventory coverage in Chapter 7 was revised to reflect the new standard on **lower-of-cost-or-net realizable value**
  - Chapter 10 reflects the new **Lease** standard
  - Chapter 12 reflects the new **Investments** standard
- **Tax Cut and Jobs Act:** In addition to the new FASB standards, the 6th edition reflects the Tax Cut and Jobs Act of 2017. The tax section in Chapter 10 reflects the new tax law.
- **CVS Health Corporation** replaced Golden Enterprises as the focus company of Chapter 4.
- **Microsoft** replaced Cisco as the focus company of Chapter 6.
- The parent company of Google, **Alphabet**, is now the focus company of Chapter 12.
- In addition to the chapter-specific changes, there have been several changes that span the entire book. Some of these global changes include:
  - Updated numbers for examples, illustrations, and assignments that use real data
  - Updated footnotes and other nonfinancial disclosures
  - Updated excerpts from the business and popular press
  - Numerous assignments in each chapter have been revised or replaced with new assignments

- **myBusinessCourse:** myBusinessCourse (MBC) is a complete learning and assessment program that accompanies the textbook and contributes to student success in this course. MBC has been expanded to include more assignments and resources. In addition, the Guided Examples and eLectures have been revised and improved.

TECHNOLOGY THAT IMPROVES LEARNING AND COMPLEMENTS FACULTY INSTRUCTION

myBusinessCourse is an online learning and assessment program intended to complement your textbook and faculty instruction. Access to **myBusinessCourse** is FREE ONLY with the purchase of a new textbook, but can be purchased separately.

MBC is ideal for faculty seeking opportunities to augment their course with an online component. MBC is also a turnkey solution for online courses. The following are some of the features of MBC.

95% students who used MBC, responded that MBC helped them learn accounting.*

Increase Student Readiness

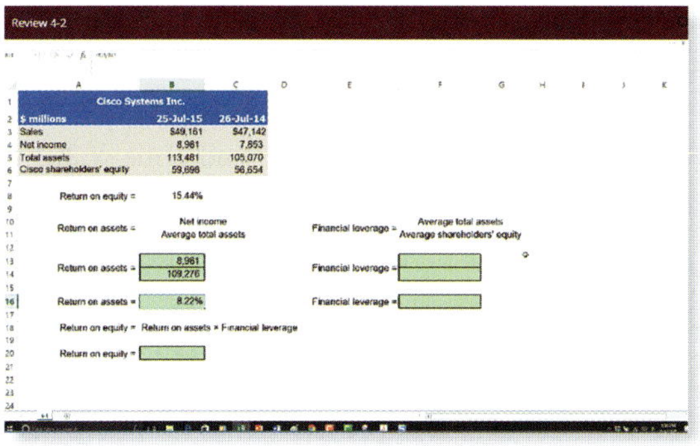

- **Demos** apply each chapter's learning objectives and concepts to a problem. Consistent with the text and created by the authors, these videos are ideal for remediation and online instruction.
- **Reviews** are narrated video demonstrations created by the authors that show students how to solve the Review problems from the textbook.
- Immediate feedback with **auto-graded homework**.
- **Test Bank** questions that can be incorporated into your assignments.
- Instructor **gradebook** with immediate grade results.

Make Instruction Needs-Based

- Identify where your students are struggling and customize your instruction to address their needs.
- Gauge how your entire class or individual students are performing by viewing the easy-to-use gradebook.
- Ensure your students are getting the additional reinforcement and direction they need between class meetings.

86% of students said they would encourage their professor to continue using MBC in future terms.*

Provide Instruction and Practice 24/7

- Assign homework from your Cambridge Business Publishers' textbook and have MBC grade it for you automatically.
- With our Videos, your students can revisit accounting topics as often as they like or until they master the topic.
- Make homework due before class to ensure students enter your classroom prepared.
- For an additional fee, upgrade MBC to include the eBook and you have all the tools needed for an online course.

Integrate with LMS

myBusinessCourse integrates with many learning management systems, including **Canvas**, **Blackboard**, **Moodle**, **D2L**, **Schoology**, and **Sakai**. Your gradebooks sync automatically.

* These statistics are based on the results of two surveys in which 2,330 students participated.

ADDITIONAL RESOURCES

Financial Accounting Bootcamp

This interactive tutorial is intended for use in programs that either require or would like to offer a tutorial that can be used as a refresher of topics introduced in the first financial accounting course. It is designed as an asynchronous, interactive, self-paced experience for students. Available Learning Modules (You Select) follow.

1. Introducing Financial Accounting (approximate completion time 2 hours)
2. Constructing Financial Statements (approximate completion time 4 hours)
3. Adjusting Entries and Completing the Accounting Cycle (approximate completion time 4 hours)
4. Reporting and Analyzing Cash Flows (approximate completion time 3.5 hours)
5. Analyzing and Interpreting Financial Statements (approximate completion time 3.5 hours)
6. Excel and Time-Value of Money Basics (approximate completion time 2 hours)

This is a separate, saleable item. Contact your sales representative to receive more information or email customerservice@cambridgepub.com.

Companion Casebook

Cases in Financial Reporting, 8th edition by Michael Drake (Brigham Young University), Ellen Engel (University of Illinois—Chicago), D. Eric Hirst (University of Texas—Austin), and Mary Lea McAnally (Texas A&M University). This book comprises 27 cases and is a perfect companion book for faculty interested in exposing students to a wide range of real financial statements. Each case deals with a specific financial accounting topic within the context of one (or more) company's financial statements. Each case contains financial statement information and a set of directed questions pertaining to one or two specific financial accounting issues. This is a separate, saleable casebook (ISBN 978-1-61853-122-3). Contact your sales representative to receive a desk copy or email customerservice@cambridgepub.com.

For Instructors

Solutions Manual: Created by the authors, the *Solutions Manual* contains complete solutions to all the assignment material in the text.

PowerPoint: The PowerPoint slides outline key elements of each chapter.

Test Bank: The Test Bank includes multiple-choice items, matching questions, short essay questions, and problems.

Website: All instructor materials are accessible via the book's Website (password protected) along with other useful links and marketing information. www.cambridgepub.com

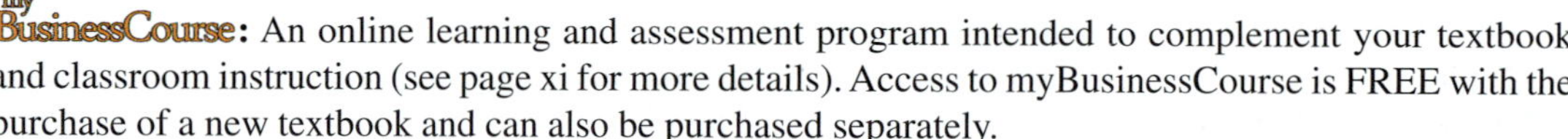

myBusinessCourse: An online learning and assessment program intended to complement your textbook and classroom instruction (see page xi for more details). Access to myBusinessCourse is FREE with the purchase of a new textbook and can also be purchased separately.

For Students

Student Solutions Manual: Created by the authors, the student Solutions Manual contains solutions to the even numbered assignments in the textbook. This is a **restricted** item that is only available to students after their instructor has authorized its purchase.

Website: Practice quizzes and other useful links are available to students free of charge on the book's Website.

myBusinessCourse: An online learning and assessment program intended to complement your textbook and faculty instruction (see page xi for more details). This easy-to-use program grades assignments automatically and provides you with additional help when your instructor is not available. Access is free with new copies of this textbook (look for the page containing the access code towards the front of the book).

ACKNOWLEDGMENTS

This book has benefited greatly from the valuable feedback of focus group attendees, reviewers, students, and colleagues. We are extremely grateful to them for their help in making this project a success.

Ajay Adhikari, *American University*
Hank Adler, *Chapman University*
Pervaiz Alam, *Kent State University*
Kris Allee, *University of Arkansas*
Bob Allen, *University of Utah*
Beverley Alleyne, *Belmont University*
Elizabeth Arnold, *Citadel*
Frances Ayres, *University of Oklahoma*
Paul Bahnson, *Boise State University*
Jan Barton, *Emory University*
Progyan Basu, *University of Maryland*
James Benjamin, *Texas A&M University*
Anne Beyer, *Stanford University*
Robert Bowen, *University of San Diego*
Kimberly Brickler-Ulrich, *Lindenwood University*
Rada Brooks, *University of California, Berkeley*
Helen Brubeck, *San Jose State University*
Jacqueline Burke, *Hofstra University*
Bruce Busta, *St. Cloud State University*
Richard J. Campbell, *University of Rio Grande*
Judson Caskey, *UCLA*
Sumantra Chakravarty, *California State—Fullerton*
Paul Chaney, *Vanderbilt University*
Craig Chapman, *Northwestern University*
Sean Chen, *Furman University*
Hans Christensen, *University of Chicago*
Paul Clikeman, *University of Richmond*
Daniel Cohen, *Texas A&M University*
John Core, *MIT*
Erin Cornelsen, *University of South Dakota*
Steve Crawford, *University of Houston*
Somnath Das, *University of Illinois, Chicago*
Angela Davis, *University of Oregon*
Mark Dawkins, *University of Georgia*
David DeBoskey, *San Diego State University*
Mark DeFond, *University of Southern California*
Bruce Dehning, *Chapman University*
Bala G. Dharan, *Rice University*
Timothy Dimond, *Northern Illinois University*
Joe Dulin, *University of Oklahoma*
Reed Easton, *Seton Hall University*
Ellen Engel, *University of Illinois Chicago*
Bud Fennema, *Florida State Univeristy*
Tom Fields, *Washington University*
Mark Finn, *Northwestern University*
Linda Flaming, *Monmouth University*
Elizabeth Foster, *College of William & Mary*
Micah Frankel, *California State—East Bay*
George Geis, *University of California, Los Angeles*
Hubert Glover, *Drexel University*
Nancy Goble, *University of Southern California*
Rajul Gokarn, *Clark Atlanta University*
Jeff Gramlich, *University of Southern Maine*
Wayne Guay, *University of Pennsylvania*
Umit Gurun, *University of Texas, Dallas*
Rebecca Hann, *University of Maryland*
David Harvey, *University of Georgia*
Rayford Harwell, *California State—East Bay*
Susan Hass, *Simmons College*
Joseph Hatch, *Lewis University*
Haihong He, *California State—Los Angeles*
Kenneth Henry, *Florida International University*
Eric Hirst, *University of Texas, Austin*
Jeffrey Hoopes, *UNC at Chapel Hill*
Robert Hoskin, *University of Connecticut*
Ying Huang, *University of Texas at Dallas*
Marsha Huber, *Otterbein College*
Richard E. Hurley, *University of Connecticut*
Robert L. Hurt, *California State—Pomona*
Marianne L. James, *California State—Los Angeles*
Ross Jennings, *University of Texas*
Chris Jones, *George Washington University*
Januj Juneja, *San Diego State*
Jane Kennedy, *University of San Diego*
Irene Kim, *George Washington University*
Michael Kimbrough, *University of Maryland*
Allison Koester, *Georgetown University*
Kalin Kolev, *Yale University*
Gopal Krishnan, *George Mason University*
Benjamin Lansford, *Rice University*
Zawadi Lemayian, *Washington University*
Annette Leps, *Johns Hopkins University*
Alina Lerman, *Yale University*
Xu Li, *University of Texas, Dallas*
Thomas Lin, *University of Southern California*
Brad Lindsey, *Utah State University*
Thomas J. Linsmeier, *University of Wisconsin*
Jiangxia Liu, *Valparaiso University*
Frank Longo, *Centenary College*
Barbara Lougee, *University of San Diego*
Luann Lynch, *University of Virginia, Darden*
Jason MacGregor, *Baylor University*
Bill Magrogan, *University of South Carolina*
Lois Mahoney, *Eastern Michigan University*
Daphne Main, *Loyola University New Orleans*
Cathy Margolin, *Brandman University*
Maureen Mascha, *University of Wisconsin, Oshkosh*
Dawn Matsumoto, *University of Washington*
Katie Maxwell, *University of Arizona*
John McCauley, *San Diego State University*
Bruce McClain, *Cleveland State University*
Harvey McCown, *California State—Bakersfield*
Katie McDermott, *University of Virginia*
Marc McIntosh, *Augsburg College*
Jeff McMillan, *Clemson University*
Greg Miller, *University of Michigan*
Jeffrey Miller, *Augusta University*
Jeffrey Miller, *University of Notre Dame*
Marilyn Misch, *Pepperdine University, Malibu*
Stephen Moehrle, *University of Missouri—KC*

Matt Munson, *Chapman University*
Mark Myring, *Ball State University*
Sandeep Nabar, *Oklahoma State University*
James Naughton, *Northwestern University*
Karen Nelson, *TCU*
Christopher Noe, *MIT*
Walter O'Connor, *Fordham University*
Jose Oaks, *University of Connecticut*
Shailendra Pandit, *University of Illinois, Chicago*
Simon Pearlman, *California State—Long Beach*
Marietta Peytcheva, *Lehigh University*
Brandis Phillips, *North Carolina A&T State*
Kristen Portz, *St. Cloud State University*
Richard Price, *Utah State University*
S.E.C. Purvis, *University of Nevada, Reno*
Kathleen Rankin, *Chatham University*
Lynn Rees, *Texas A&M University*
Susan Riffe, *Southern Methodist University*
Leslie Robinson, *Dartmouth College*
Paulette Rodriguez, *University of Texas*
Darren Roulstone, *Ohio State University*
Debra Salbador, *Virginia Tech*
Anwar Y. Salimi, *California State—Pomona*
Haresh Sapra, *University of Chicago*
Robert Scharlach, *University of Southern California*
Steve Sefcik, *University of Washington*
Timothy Shields, *Chapman University*
Scott Showalter, *North Carolina State University*
Nemit Shroff, *MIT*
Andreas Simon, *California Polytechnic*
Robert Singer, *Lindenwood University*
Parveen Sinha, *Chapman University*
David Smith, *University of Nebraska Lincoln*
Eric So, *MIT*
Kathleen Sobieralski, *University of Maryland*
Gregory Sommers, *Southern Methodist University*
Sri Sridharan, *Northwestern University*
Vic Stanton, *University of California, Berkeley*
Jack Stecher, *Carnegie Mellon University*
Doug Stevens, *Georgia State University*
Toby Stock, *Ohio University*
Phillip Stocken, *Dartmouth College*
William Stout, *University of Louisville*
Shyam Sunder, *University of Arizona*
Andrew Sutherland, *MIT*
Robert J. Swieringa, *Cornell University*
Thomas Tallerico, *Dowling College*
Mary Tarling, *Aurora University*
Robin Tarpley, *George Washington University*
Nicole Thibodeau, *Willamette University*
Patti Tilley, *Frostburg State University*
Rodrigo Verdi, *MIT*
Robert Walsh, *University of Dallas*
Isabel Wang, *Michigan State University*
Rick Warne, *George Mason University*
Catherine Weber, *University of Houston*
Joe Weber, *MIT*
Lourdes White, *University of Baltimore*
Donna Whitten, *Purdue University North Central*
Rahnl Wood, *Northwest Missouri State University*
Jia Wu, *University of Massachusetts, Dartmouth*
Jason Xiao, *University of Pennsylvania*
Jennifer Yin, *University of Texas, San Antonio*
Susan Young, *Fordham University*
Stephen Zeff, *Rice University*
Yuping Zhao, *University of Houston*
Jian Zhou, *University of Hawaii at Manoa*

In addition, we are extremely grateful to George Werthman, Lorraine Gleeson, Jocelyn Mousel, Katie Jones-Aiello, Dana Zieman, Jill Sternard, Marnee Fieldman, Debbie McQuade, Terry McQuade, and the entire team at Cambridge Business Publishers for their encouragement, enthusiasm, and guidance.

Michelle Hanlon *Robert Magee* *Glenn Pfeiffer* *Thomas Dyckman*

May 2019

Brief Contents

Contents

Chapter 3 Adjusting Accounts for Financial Statements 100

Chapter 4 Reporting and Analyzing Cash Flows 156

Chapter 5 Analyzing and Interpreting Financial Statements 218

Chapter 6 Reporting and Analyzing Revenues, Receivables, and Operating Income 270

THE HOME DEPOT

verizon wireless

DELTA
DELTA
DELTA

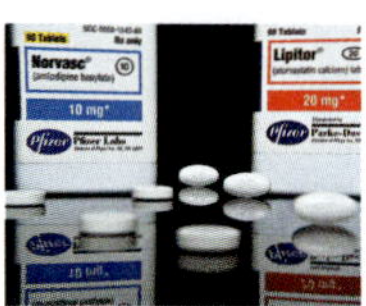
Norvasc
Lipitor

Chapter 12 Reporting and Analyzing Financial Investments 580

Appendix A Compound Interest and the Time-Value of Money 638

Appendix B Data Analytics (Available Online)

1 Introducing Financial Accounting

Learning Objectives *identify the key learning goals of the chapter.*

A **Focus Company** *introduces each chapter and illustrates the relevance of accounting in everyday business.*

LEARNING OBJECTIVES

1. Identify the users of accounting information and discuss the costs and benefits of disclosure. (p. 4)
2. Describe a company's business activities and explain how these activities are represented by the accounting equation. (p. 7)
3. Introduce the four key financial statements including the balance sheet, income statement, statement of stockholders' equity, and statement of cash flows. (p. 11)
4. Describe the institutions that regulate financial accounting and their role in establishing generally accepted accounting principles. (p. 17)
5. Compute two key ratios that are commonly used to assess profitability and risk—return on equity and the debt-to-equity ratio. (p. 21)
6. Appendix 1A: Explain the conceptual framework for financial reporting. (p. 26)

NIKE
www.Nike.com

Phil Knight majored in accounting and was a member of the track team at the University of Oregon.

A few years after graduation, Knight teamed up with his former track coach, Bill Bowerman, to form a business called Blue Ribbon Sports to import, sell, and distribute running shoes from Japan. Blue Ribbon Sports, or BRS as it came to be known, was started on a shoestring—Knight and Bowerman each contributed $500 to start the business. A few years later, BRS introduced its own line of running shoes called Nike. It also unveiled a new logo, the now familiar Nike swoosh. Following the overwhelming success of the Nike shoe line, BRS officially changed its company name to Nike, Inc. Currently, the company is worth more than $120 billion. Knight is the former CEO and the Chairman, Emeritus of Nike, Inc.

Today, Nike, Inc. has sales in almost every country on the planet and, in the year ended May, 2018, Nike had total revenues of $36 billion and income of $1.9 billion. Nike owes much of its success to marketing prowess and innovative design and development of new products. The swoosh, along with advertising campaigns featuring taglines such as "just do it," have made the company and its products instantly recognizable to consumers all over the world. Endorsements by the most recognizable icons in sports, including Serena Williams, Michael Jordan, Tiger Woods, Maria Sharapova, Tom Brady, LeBron James, and Mike Trout, add to Nike's brand recognition.

In recent years, Nike has expanded its product lines beyond the traditional offerings of athletic shoes, athletic apparel, and sports equipment to include eyewear, watches such as the *Nike+ Sportwatch GPS*, and *Fuelband*, a wearable wristband which tracks energy output. In recent years, Nike has further expanded its product offering by acquiring other companies such as Converse, an established athletic shoe company; Hurley International, a leading designer and distributor of surf, skate, and snowboarding apparel and footwear; and Umbro, specializing in soccer equipment, footwear, and apparel.

But as CEO Mark Parker recognizes, Nike needs to stay on its toes as newcomers **Under Armour** and **Quiksilver** challenge for customers. Nike also cannot ignore **Adidas**. As Nike's main competitor, it is nearly two-thirds of Nike's size in terms of sales. Perhaps this situation, along with new product developments, explains Nike's future marketing commitments that reached $10 billion as of the end of the fiscal year ended May 2018.

How does someone take a $1,000 investment and turn it into a company whose stock is worth more than $120 billion? Well, Nike's success is not an accident. Along the way, Nike management made countless decisions that ultimately led the company to where it is today. Each of these decisions involved identifying alternative courses of action and weighing their costs, benefits, and risks in light of the available information.

Comparison of 5-Year Cumulative Total Return for Nike, Inc., The S&P 500 Index, and The Dow Jones U.S. Footwear Index (Assumes an investment of $100 on May 31, 2013)

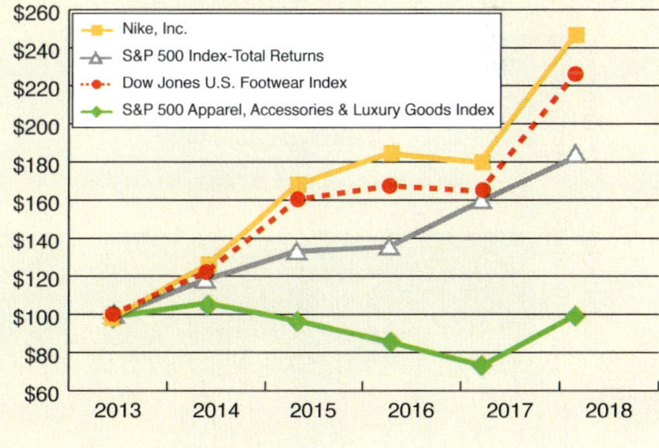

Accounting is the process of identifying, measuring, and communicating financial information to help people make *economic* decisions. People use accounting information to facilitate a wide variety of transactions, including assessing whether, and on what terms, they should invest in a firm, seek employment in a business, or continue purchasing its products. Accounting information is crucial to any successful business, and without it, most businesses would not even exist.

This book explains how to create and analyze financial statements, an important source of accounting information prepared by companies to communicate with a variety of users. We begin by introducing transactions between the firm and its investors, creditors, suppliers, employees, and customers. We continue by demonstrating how accounting principles are applied to these transactions to create the financial statements. Then, we "invert" the process and learn how to analyze the firm's financial statements to assess the firm's underlying economic performance. Our philosophy is simple—we believe it is crucial to have a deep understanding of financial accounting to become critical readers and users of financial statements. Financial statements tell a story—a business story. Our goal is to understand that story, and apply the knowledge gleaned from financial statements to make good business decisions.

Sources: Nike.com; Nike, Inc. 10-K Report for the year ended May 31, 2018; *Business Week* (October 2007, August 2009); *Portland Business Journal* (October 2007); *Fortune* (February 2012). For more on Phil Knight and Nike's history, see the book *Shoe Dog* (published by Scribner).

CHAPTER ORGANIZATION

Chapter Organization *Charts visually depict the key topics and their sequence within the chapter.*

Introducing Financial Accounting

Demand for Accounting Information	Business Activities	Financial Statements	Financial Reporting Environment	Financial Statement Analysis
• Who Uses Financial Accounting Information? • Costs and Benefits of Disclosure	• Planning Activities • Investing Activities • Financing Activities • Operating Activities	• Balance Sheet • Income Statement • Statement of Stockholders' Equity • Statement of Cash Flows • Financial Statement Linkages	• Generally Accepted Accounting Principles • Regulation and Oversight • Role of the Auditor • A Global Perspective • Conceptual Framework (Appendix 1A)	• Profitability Analysis • Credit Risk Analysis

eLecture *icons identify topics for which there are instructional videos in* **myBusinessCourse** *(MBC). See the Preface for more information on MBC.*

1

LO1 Identify the users of accounting information and discuss the costs and benefits of disclosure.

DEMAND FOR ACCOUNTING INFORMATION

Accounting can be defined as the process of recording, summarizing, and analyzing financial transactions. While accounting information attempts to satisfy the needs of a diverse set of users, the accounting information a company produces can be classified into two categories (see **Exhibit 1.1**):[1]

- **Financial accounting**—designed primarily for decision makers outside of the company
- **Managerial accounting**—designed primarily for decision makers within the company

EXHIBIT 1.1 Information Needs of Decision Makers Who Use Financial and Managerial Accounting

	Decision Makers	Decisions	Information
Financial Accounting	• Investors and analysts • Creditors • Suppliers and customers	• Buy or sell stock? • Lend or not? • Purchase/sell goods or not?	• Sales and costs • Cash in and out • Assets and liabilities
Managerial Accounting	• Top management • Marketing teams • Production and operations	• Develop new strategy? • Launch a new product or not? • Manage operations	• Product sales and costs • Department performance reports • Budgets and quality reports

Financial accounting reports include information about company profitability and financial health. This information is useful to various economic actors who wish to engage in contracts with the firm, including investors, creditors, employees, customers, and governments. Managerial accounting information is not reported outside of the company because it includes proprietary information about the profitability of specific products, divisions, or customers. Company managers use managerial accounting reports to make decisions such as whether to drop or add products or divisions, or whether to continue serving different types of customers. This text focuses on understanding and analyzing financial accounting information.

[1] Businesses also have to compute a measure of income for income tax purposes in order to file tax returns in the jurisdictions that require them to file. This book is not about taxation, but we cover the accounting for income taxes in Chapter 10.

Who Uses Financial Accounting Information?

Demand for financial accounting information derives from numerous users including:

- Shareholders and potential shareholders
- Creditors and suppliers
- Managers and directors
- Financial analysts
- Other users

FYI *features provide additional information that complements the text.*

Shareholders and Potential Shareholders Corporations are the dominant form of business organization for large companies around the world, and corporate shareholders are one important group of decision makers that have an interest in financial accounting information. A **corporation** is a form of business organization that is characterized by a large number of owners who are not involved in managing the day-to-day operations of the company.[2] A corporation exists as a legal entity that issues **shares of stock** to its owners in exchange for cash and, therefore, the owners of a corporation are referred to as *shareholders* or **stockholders**.

FYI Shareholders of a corporation are its owners; although managers can own stock in the corporation, most shareholders are not managers.

Because the shareholders are not involved in the day-to-day operations of the business, they rely on the information in financial statements to evaluate management performance and assess the company's financial condition.

In addition to corporations, sole proprietorships, partnerships, and limited liability companies are also common forms of business ownership. A **sole proprietorship** has a single owner who typically manages the daily operations. Small family-run businesses, such as corner grocery stores, are commonly organized as sole proprietorships. A **partnership** has two or more owners who are also usually involved in managing the business. Many professionals, such as lawyers and CPAs, organize their businesses as partnerships. Many new businesses today start up as a limited liability company (LLC). An LLC allows for limited liability for the owners similar to a corporation, while at the same time allowing for more flexibility and other features that are similar to a partnership.

Most corporations begin as small, privately held businesses (sole proprietorships, partnerships, or an LLC). As their operations expand, however, they require additional capital to finance their growth. One of the principal advantages of a corporation over the other organizational forms of doing business is the ability to raise large amounts of cash by issuing (selling) stock. For example, as Nike grew from a small business with only two owners into a larger company, it raised the funds needed for expansion by selling shares of Nike stock to new shareholders. In the United States, large corporations can raise funds by issuing stock on organized exchanges, such as the **New York Stock Exchange (NYSE)** or **NASDAQ** (which is an acronym for the National Association of Securities Dealers Automated Quotations system). Corporations with stock that is traded on public exchanges are known as *publicly traded corporations* or simply *public corporations*. The raising of capital from a large group of outside shareholders leads to what is known as the separation of ownership and control. For example, as Nike sold more stock, the CEO (Knight) owned a smaller amount of the shares. In cases of such separation, which exists at most publicly traded firms, the information flow from the managers to the shareholders is very important.

Financial statements and the accompanying footnotes provide information on the risk and return associated with owning shares of stock in the corporation, and they reveal how well management has performed. Financial statements also provide valuable insights into future performance by revealing management's plans for new products, new operating procedures, and new strategic directions for the company as well as for their implementation. Corporate management provides this information because the information reduces uncertainty about the company's future prospects which, in turn, increases the market price of its shares and helps the company raise the funds it needs to grow.

Creditors and Suppliers Few businesses rely solely on shareholders for the cash needed to operate the company. Instead, most companies borrow from banks or other lenders known as **creditors**. Creditors are interested in the potential borrower's ability to repay. They use financial

FYI Financial statements are typically required when a business requests a bank loan (unless the business is very small, then tax returns will often suffice).

---

[2] Most countries have business forms that are similar in structure to those of a U.S. corporation, though they are referred to by different names. For example, while firms that are incorporated in the United States have the extension "Inc." appended to their names, similar firms in the United Kingdom are referred to as a Public Limited Company, which has the extension "PLC."

accounting information to help determine loan terms, loan amounts, interest rates, and collateral. In addition, creditors' loans often include contractual requirements based on information found in the financial statements.

Suppliers use financial information to establish credit sales terms and to determine their long-term commitment to supply-chain relationships. Supplier companies often justify an expansion of *their* businesses based on the growth and financial health of their customers. Both creditors and suppliers rely on information in the financial statements to monitor and adjust their contracts and commitments with a company.

Managers and Directors Financial statements can be thought of as a financial report card for management. A well-managed company earns a good return for its shareholders, and this is reflected in the financial statements. In most companies, management is compensated, at least in part, based on the financial performance of the company. That is, managers often receive cash bonuses, shares of stock, or other *incentive compensation* that is linked directly to the information in the financial statements.

FYI The Sarbanes-Oxley Act requires issuers of securities to disclose whether they have a code of ethics for the senior officers.

Publicly traded corporations are required by law to have a **board of directors**. Directors are elected by the shareholders to represent shareholder interests and oversee management. The board hires executive management and regularly reviews company operations. Directors use financial accounting information to review the results of operations, evaluate future strategy, and assess management performance.

Both managers and directors use the published financial statements of *other companies* to perform comparative analyses and establish performance benchmarks. For example, managers in some companies are paid a bonus for financial performance that exceeds the industry average.

BUSINESS INSIGHT

Court cases involving corporations such as **Enron**, **Tyco**, and **WorldCom** (now **MCI**) have found executives, including several CEOs, guilty of issuing fraudulent financial statements. These executives have received substantial fines and, in some cases, long jail sentences. These trials have resulted in widespread loss of reputation and credibility among corporate boards.

Financial Analysts Many decision makers lack the time, resources, or expertise to efficiently and effectively analyze financial statements. Instead, they rely on professional financial analysts, such as credit rating agencies like **Moody's** investment services, portfolio managers, and security analysts. Financial analysts play an important role in the dissemination of financial information and often specialize in specific industries. Their analysis helps to identify and assess risk, forecast performance, establish prices for new issues of stock, and make buy-or-sell recommendations to investors.

Other Users of Financial Accounting Information External decision makers include many users of accounting information in addition to those listed above. For example, ***prospective employees*** often examine the financial statements of an employer to learn about the company before interviewing for or accepting a new job.

Labor unions examine financial statements in order to assess the financial health of firms prior to negotiating labor contracts on behalf of the firms' employees. ***Customers*** use accounting information to assess the ability of a company to deliver products or services and to assess the company's long-term reliability.

Government agencies rely on accounting information to develop and enforce regulations, including public protection, price setting, import-export, taxation, and various other policies.[3] Timely and reliable information is crucial to effective regulatory policy. Moreover, accounting information is often used to assess penalties for companies that violate various regulations.

[3] A company's tax returns are distinctly different from its financial statements. Tax returns are prepared for tax authorities in order to comply with income tax rules. The financial statements are prepared to provide information to investors, creditors, and other decision makers outside of the business.

Costs and Benefits of Disclosure

The act of providing financial information to external users is called **disclosure**. As with every decision, the benefits of disclosure must be weighed against the costs of providing the information.

One reason companies are motivated to disclose financial information to external decision makers is that it often lowers financing and operating costs. For example, when a company applies for a loan, the bank uses the company's financial statements to help determine the appropriate interest rate. Without adequate financial disclosures in its financial statements, the bank is likely to demand a higher interest rate or perhaps not make the loan at all. Thus, in this setting, a benefit of financial disclosure is that it reduces the company's cost of borrowing.

While there are benefits from disclosing financial information, there are also costs. Besides the obvious cost of hiring accountants and preparing the financial statements, financial disclosures can also result in costs being imposed by competitors. It is common practice for managers to scrutinize the financial statements of competitors to learn about successful products, new strategies, innovative technologies, and changing market conditions. Thus, disclosing too much information can place a company at a competitive disadvantage. Disclosure can also raise investors' expectations about a company's future profitability. If those expectations are not met, they may bring litigation against the managers.

There are also political costs that are potentially associated with accounting disclosure. Highly visible companies, such as defense contractors and oil companies, are often the target of scrutiny by the public and by government officials. When these companies report unusually large accounting profits, they are often the target of additional regulation or increased taxes.

Stock market regulators impose disclosure standards for publicly traded corporations, but the nature and extent of the required disclosures vary substantially across countries. Further, because the requirements only set the minimum level of disclosure, the quantity and quality of information provided by firms will vary. This variation in disclosure ultimately reflects differences among companies in the benefits and costs of disclosing information to the public.

You Make The Call *requires you to assume various roles within a business and use your accounting knowledge to address an issue. Solutions are at the end of the chapter.*

YOU MAKE THE CALL

You are a Product Manager There is often friction between investors' needs for information and a company's desire to safeguard competitive advantages. Assume that you are the product manager for a key department at your company and you are asked for advice on the extent of information to disclose in the annual report on a potentially lucrative new product that your department has test marketed. What considerations affect the advice you provide and why? [Answer on page 30]

BUSINESS ACTIVITIES

LO2 Describe a company's business activities and explain how these activities are represented by the accounting equation.

2

Businesses produce accounting information to help develop strategies, attract financing, evaluate investment opportunities, manage operations, and measure performance. Before we can attempt to understand the information provided in financial statements, we must understand these business activities. That is, what does a business actually do? For example:

- Where does a company such as Nike find the resources to develop new products and open new retail stores?
- What new products should Nike bring to market?
- How much should Nike spend on product development? On advertising? On executive compensation?
- How does Nike's management determine if a product is a success?

Questions such as these define the activities of Nike and other companies.

Exhibit 1.2 illustrates the activities of a typical business. All businesses *plan* business activities, *finance* those activities, *invest* resources in those activities, and then engage in *operating* activities. Companies conduct all these activities while confronting a variety of *external forces,* including competition from other businesses, government regulation, economic conditions and market forces, and changing preferences of customers. The financial statements provide information that helps us understand and evaluate each of these activities.

EXHIBIT 1.2 Business Activities

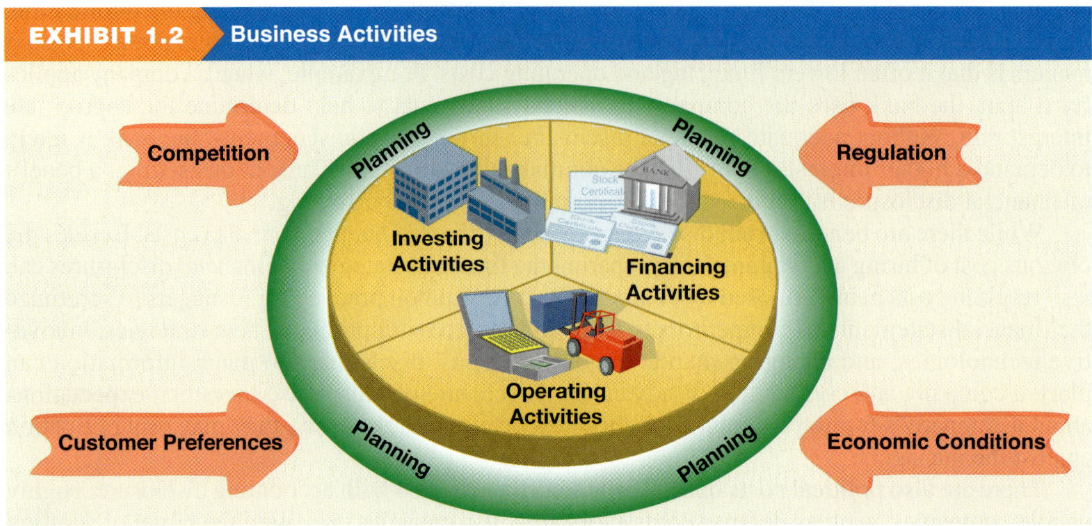

Planning Activities

Excerpts from recent financial statements are used to illustrate and reinforce concepts.

A company's goals, and the strategies adopted to reach those goals, are the product of its **planning activities**. Nike, for example, states that its mission is "To bring inspiration and innovation to every athlete in the world" adding "If you have a body, you are an athlete." However, in its 2018 annual report to shareholders, for the year ended May 2018, Nike management suggests another goal that focuses on financial success and earning a return for the shareholders.

> Our goal is to deliver value to our shareholders by building a profitable global portfolio of branded footwear, apparel, equipment, and accessories businesses. Our strategy is to achieve long-term revenue growth by creating innovative, "must have" products, building deep personal consumer connections with our brands and delivering compelling consumer experiences through digital platforms and at retail.

As is the case with most businesses, Nike's primary goal is to create value for its owners, the shareholders. How the company plans to do so is the company's **strategy**.

A company's *strategic* (or *business*) *plan* describes how it plans to achieve its goals. The plan's success depends on an effective review of market conditions. Specifically, the company must assess both the demand for its products and services, and the supply of its inputs (both labor and capital). The plan must also include competitive analyses, opportunity assessments, and consideration of business threats. The strategic plan specifies both broad management designs that generate company value and tactics to achieve those designs.

Most information in a strategic plan is proprietary and guarded closely by management. However, outsiders can gain insight into planning activities through various channels, including newspapers, magazines, and company disclosures. Understanding a company's planning activities helps focus accounting analysis and place it in context.

Key Terms are highlighted in bold, red font.

Investing Activities

Investing activities consist of acquiring and disposing of the resources needed to produce and sell a company's products and services. These resources, called **assets**, provide future benefits to the company. Companies differ on the amount and mix of these resources. Some companies require buildings and equipment while others have abandoned "bricks and mortar" to conduct business through the Internet.

Some assets that a company invests in are used quickly. For instance, a retail clothing store hopes to sell its spring and summer merchandise before purchasing more inventory for the fall and winter. Other assets are acquired for long-term use. Buildings are typically used for several decades. The relative proportion of short-term and long-term investments depends on the type of business and the strategic plan that the company adopts. For example, Nike has relatively few long-term assets because it outsources most of the production of its products to other companies.

The graph in **Exhibit 1.3** compares the relative proportion of short-term and long-term assets held by Nike and seven other companies, several of which are featured in later chapters. Nike has adopted a business model that requires very little investment in long-term resources. A majority of its investments are short-term assets. In contrast, **Verizon**, **PepsiCo**, and **Procter & Gamble** all rely heavily on long-term investments. These companies hold relatively small proportions of short-term assets. This mix of long-term and short-term assets is described in more detail in Chapter 2.

Real Companies *and* **Institutions** *are highlighted in bold, blue font.*

EXHIBIT 1.3 Relative Proportion of Short-Term and Long-Term Assets

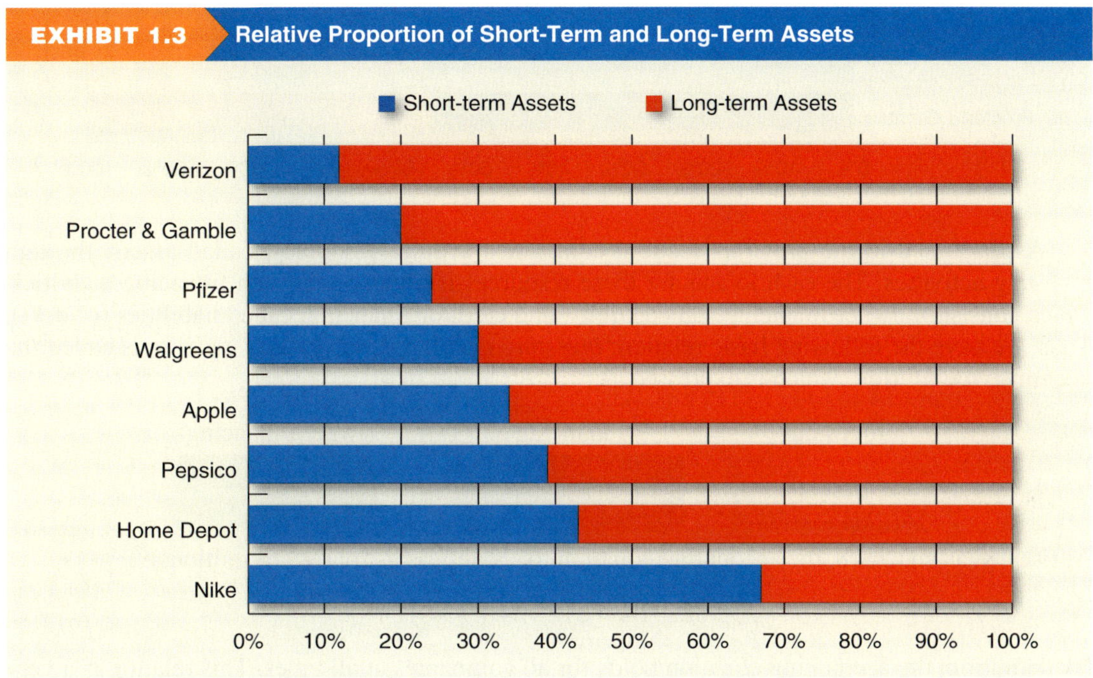

Financing Activities

Investments in resources require funding, and **financing activities** refer to the methods companies use to fund those investments. *Financial management* is the planning of resource needs, including the proper mix of financing sources.

Companies obtain financing from two sources: equity (owner) financing and creditor (nonowner) financing. *Equity financing* refers to the funds contributed to the company by its owners along with any income retained by the company. One form of equity financing is the cash raised from the sale (or issuance) of stock by a corporation. *Creditor* (or debt) *financing* is funds contributed by nonowners, which create *liabilities*. **Liabilities** are obligations the company must repay in the future. One example of a liability is a bank loan. We draw a distinction between equity and creditor financing for an important reason: creditor financing imposes a legal obligation to repay, usually with interest, and failure to repay amounts borrowed can result in adverse legal consequences such as bankruptcy. In contrast, equity financing does not impose an obligation for repayment.

Exhibit 1.4 compares the relative proportion of creditor and equity financing for Nike and other companies. PepsiCo uses liabilities to finance 75% of its resources. In contrast, **Walgreens Boots Alliance, Inc.**, relies more heavily on its equity financing, receiving 45% of its financing from creditors. Nike has the lowest proportion of creditor financing in this sample of companies with just 42% of its assets financed by nonowners.

EXHIBIT 1.4 Relative Proportion of Credit and Equity Financing

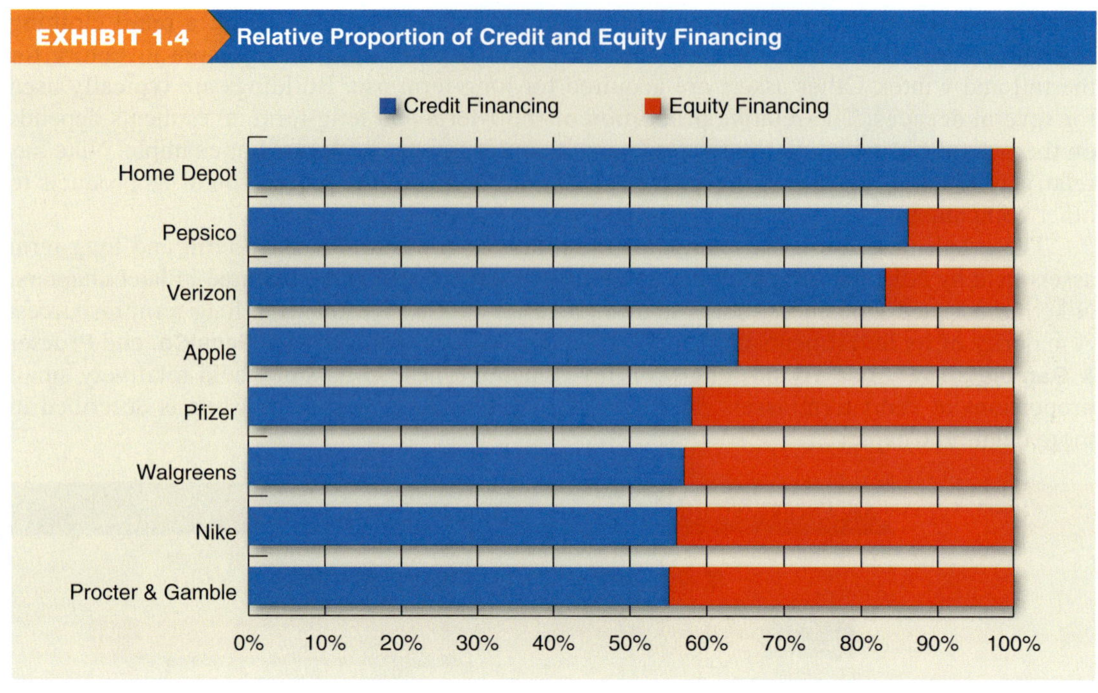

Infographics *are used to convey difficult concepts and procedures.*

As discussed in the previous section, companies acquire resources, called assets, through investing activities. The cash to acquire these resources is obtained through financing activities, which consist of owner financing, called equity, and creditor financing, called liabilities (or debt). Thus, we have the following basic relation: *investing equals financing*. This equality is called the **accounting equation**, which is expressed as:

Investing	=	Financing	+	Owner Financing
Assets	=	**Liabilities**	+	**Equity**

At fiscal year-end 2018, the accounting equation for Nike was as follows ($ millions):

$$\$22,536 = \$12,724 + \$9,812$$

By definition, the accounting equation holds for all companies at all times. This relation is a very powerful tool for analyzing and understanding companies, and we will use it often throughout the text.[4]

Operating Activities

Operating activities refer to the production, promotion, and selling of a company's products and services. These activities extend from a company's input markets, involving its suppliers, and to its output markets, involving its customers. Input markets generate *operating expenses* (or *costs*) such as inventory, salaries, materials, and logistics. Output markets generate *operating revenues* (or *sales*) from customers. Output markets also generate some operating expenses such as for marketing and distributing products and services to customers. When operating revenues exceed operating expenses, companies report *operating income*, also called *operating profit* or *operating earnings*. When operating expenses exceed operating revenues, companies report operating losses.

Revenue is the increase in equity resulting from the sale of goods and services to customers. The amount of revenue is determined *before* deducting expenses. An **expense** is the cost incurred to generate revenue, including the cost of the goods and services sold to customers as well as the

[4] There are securities that do not neatly fit into either "debt" or "equity" classification, but rather have characteristics of both. These are known as debt-equity hybrid securities. Their existence does not alter the conceptual idea that assets are financed with debt and equity. A detailed discussion of these is beyond the scope of this textbook, but we describe these briefly in the chapters on debt and equity. For most ratio analysis in this introductory-level textbook, we include all these types of securities as either debt or equity for the sake of simplicity.

cost of carrying out other business activities. **Income**, also called *net income*, equals revenues minus expenses, and is the net increase in equity from the company's activities.

For fiscal year 2018, Nike reported revenues of over $36 billion, yet its reported income was a fraction of that amount—just over $1.9 billion.

Business Insights *offer recent examples from the business news and popular press.*

BUSINESS INSIGHT

Each year, *Fortune* magazine ranks the 500 largest corporations in the United States based on total revenues. For 2018, which is based on fiscal 2017 financial results, Nike ranked 89th on the *Fortune 500* list with revenues of just over $34 billion. The company also ranked 56th in profits, with net income of approximately $4.2 billion. For comparison, the largest corporation was **Wal-Mart Stores**, with revenues of more than $500 billion and almost $9.9 billion in net income (ranking number 20 in terms of profit). (Source: http://fortune.com/fortune500/list)

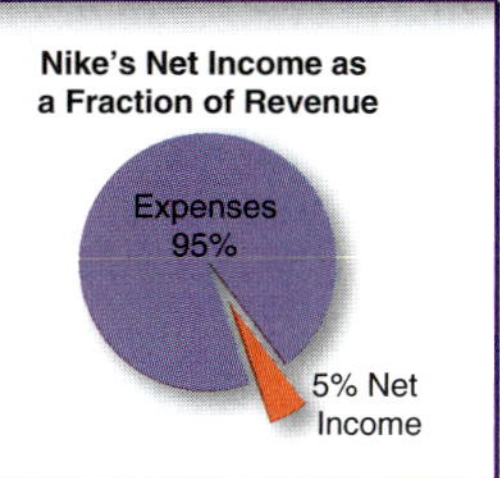

FINANCIAL STATEMENTS

eLectures MBC

LO3 Introduce the four key financial statements including the balance sheet, income statement, statement of stockholders' equity, and statement of cash flows.

Four financial statements are used to periodically report on a company's business activities. These statements are:

- **balance sheet**, which lists the company's investments and sources of financing using the accounting equation;
- **income statement**, which reports the results of operations;
- **statement of stockholders' equity**, which details changes in owner financing;
- **statement of cash flows**, which details the sources and uses of cash.

Exhibit 1.5 shows how these statements are linked across time. A balance sheet reports on a company's position at a point in time. The income statement, statement of stockholders' equity, and the statement of cash flows report on performance over a period of time. The three statements in the middle of **Exhibit 1.5** (period-of-time statements) link the balance sheet from the beginning of a period to the balance sheet at the end of a period.

EXHIBIT 1.5 Financial Statement Links Across Time

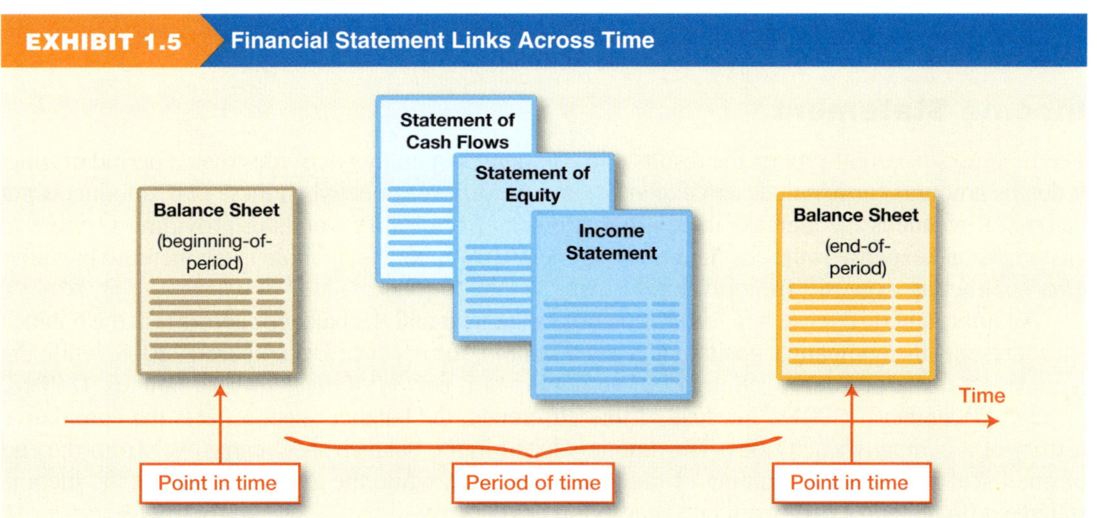

A one-year, or annual, reporting period is common, which is called the *accounting*, or *fiscal year*. Semiannual, quarterly, and monthly reporting periods are also common. *Calendar-year* companies have a reporting period that begins on January 1 and ends on December 31. **Pfizer**, **Google**, and **Verizon** are examples of calendar-year companies. Some companies choose a fiscal year ending

FYI The heading of each financial statement includes who, what, and when.

on a date other than December 31. Seasonal businesses, such as retail stores, often choose a fiscal year that ends when sales and inventories are at their lowest level. For example, **Home Depot**, the retail home improvement store chain, ends its fiscal year on the Sunday closest to February 1, after the busy holiday season. Nike has a May 31 fiscal year. The heading of each statement identifies the: (1) company name, (2) statement title, and (3) date or time period of the statement.

Balance Sheet

FYI The balance sheet is also known as the statement of financial position and the statement of financial condition.

A **balance sheet** reports a company's financial position at a point in time. It summarizes the result of the company's investing and financing activities by listing amounts for assets, liabilities, and equity. The balance sheet is based on the accounting equation, also called the *balance sheet equation*: Assets = Liabilities + Equity.

Nike's balance sheet for fiscal year 2018, which ended May 31, 2018, is reproduced in a reduced format in **Exhibit 1.6** and reports that assets are $22,536 million, liabilities are $12,724 million, and equity is $9,812 million, where owner financing is the sum of contributed capital of $6,387 million, retained earnings of $3,517 million, and other equity of $(92) million. Thus, the balance sheet equation holds true for Nike's balance sheet: assets equal liabilities plus equity.

Real financial data *for focus companies illustrate key concepts of each chapter.*

EXHIBIT 1.6 Balance Sheet ($ millions)

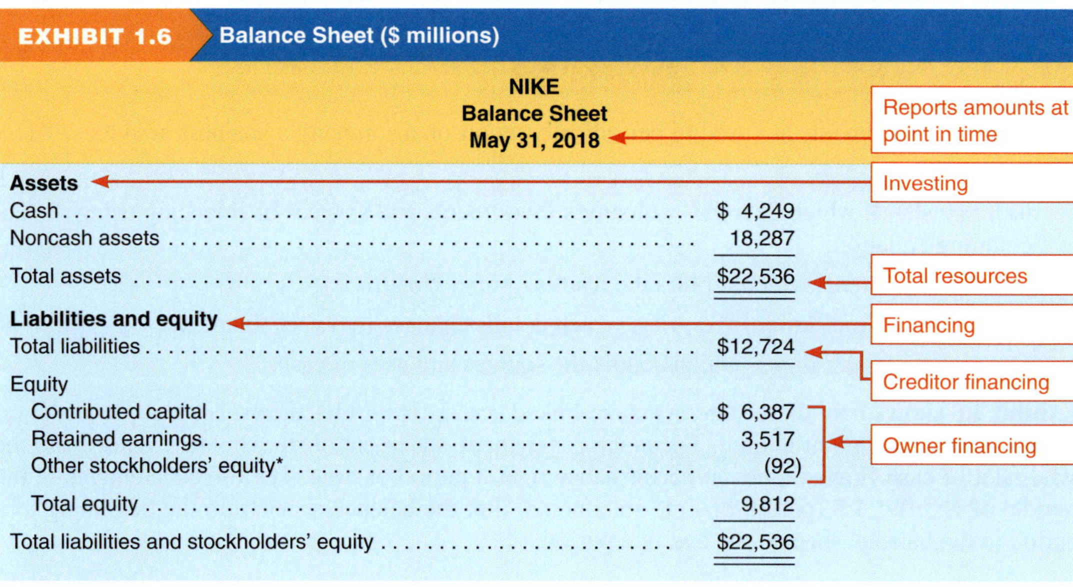

NIKE
Balance Sheet
May 31, 2018

Assets	
Cash	$ 4,249
Noncash assets	18,287
Total assets	$22,536
Liabilities and equity	
Total liabilities	$12,724
Equity	
Contributed capital	$ 6,387
Retained earnings	3,517
Other stockholders' equity*	(92)
Total equity	9,812
Total liabilities and stockholders' equity	$22,536

* Other stockholders' equity includes accumulated other comprehensive income. Other components of stockholders' equity are discussed in Chapter 11.

Income Statement

FYI The income statement is also known as statement of income, statement of earnings, statement of operations, and statement of profit and loss.

The **income statement** reports the results of a company's operating activities over a period of time. It details amounts for revenues and expenses, and the difference between these two amounts is net income. Revenue is the increase in equity that results from selling goods or providing services to customers and expense is the cost incurred to generate revenue. Net income is the increase in equity *after* subtracting expenses from revenues.

An important difference between the income statement and the balance sheet is that the balance sheet presents the company's position at a *point in time*, for instance December 31, 2018, while the income statement presents a summary of activity over a *period of time*, such as January 1, 2018, through December 31, 2018. Because of this difference, the balance sheet reflects the cumulative history of a company's activities. The amounts listed in the balance sheet carry over from the end of one fiscal year to the beginning of the next fiscal year, while the amounts listed in the income statement do not carry over from one year to the next.

Refer to Nike's income statement for the fiscal year ended May 31, 2018, shown in reduced format as **Exhibit 1.7**. It reports that revenues = $36,397 million, expenses = $34,464 million, and net income = $1,933 million. Thus, revenues minus expenses equals net income for Nike.

For manufacturing and merchandising companies, the **cost of goods sold** is an important expense that is typically disclosed separately in the income statement immediately following revenues. It is also common to report a subtotal for gross profit (also called gross margin), which is revenues less the cost of goods sold. The company's remaining expenses are then reported below gross profit. Nike's income statement is presented in this reduced format in **Exhibit 1.8**.

FYI The term "gross" refers to an amount before subtractions, such as Gross Sales. An exception is made for the term Gross Profit (Gross Margin), defined as Sales less Cost of Goods Sold (Cost of Sales). When items are subtracted from a gross amount, the term "net" is generally used, as in the case of Net Sales (Gross Sales less returns and other items) or Net Income (Sales less all expenses).

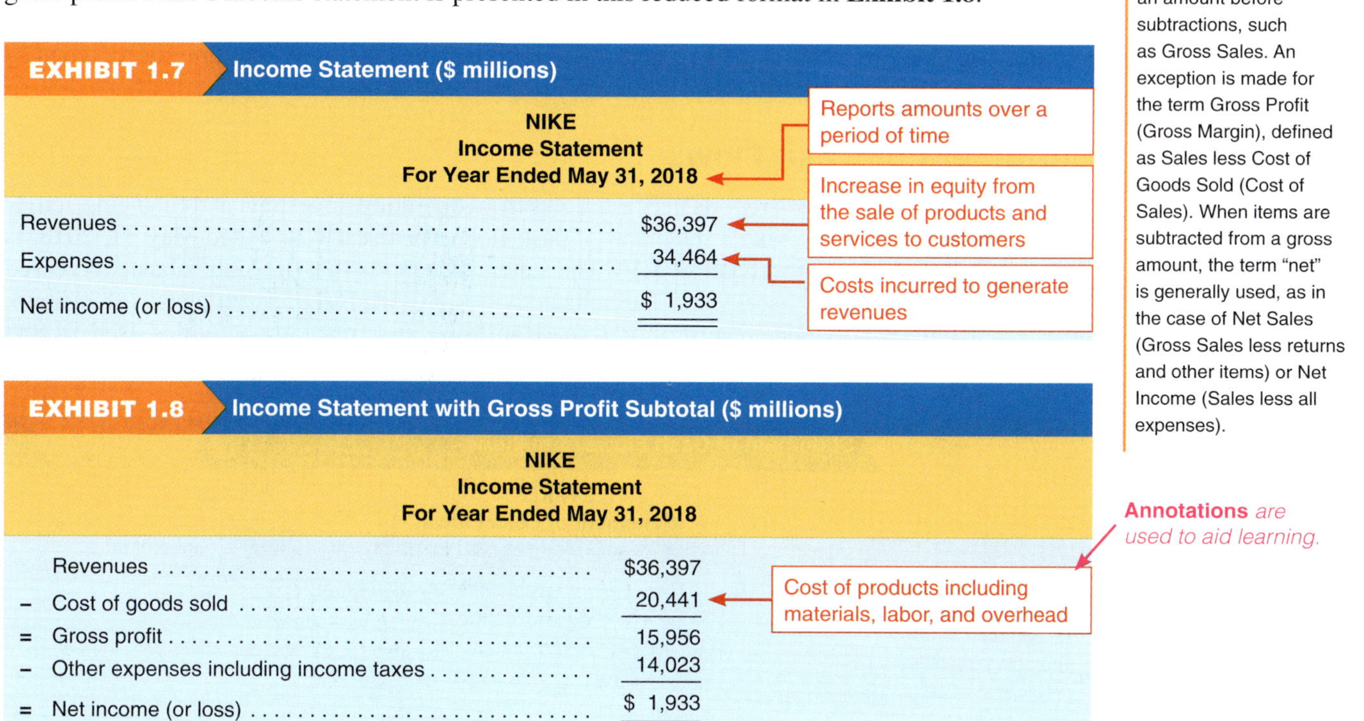

EXHIBIT 1.7 Income Statement ($ millions)

NIKE
Income Statement
For Year Ended May 31, 2018

Revenues	$36,397
Expenses	34,464
Net income (or loss)	$ 1,933

EXHIBIT 1.8 Income Statement with Gross Profit Subtotal ($ millions)

NIKE
Income Statement
For Year Ended May 31, 2018

	Revenues	$36,397
–	Cost of goods sold	20,441
=	Gross profit	15,956
–	Other expenses including income taxes	14,023
=	Net income (or loss)	$ 1,933

Annotations are used to aid learning.

Statement of Stockholders' Equity

The **statement of stockholders' equity**, or simply *statement of equity*, reports the changes in the equity accounts over a period of time. Nike's statement of stockholders' equity for fiscal year ended May 31, 2018, is shown in reduced format as **Exhibit 1.9**. During the year ended May 31, 2018, Nike's equity changed due to share issuance and income reinvestment. The exhibit details and classifies these changes into three categories:

- Contributed capital (includes common stock and additional paid-in capital)
- Retained earnings (includes cumulative net income or loss, and deducts dividends)
- Other stockholders' equity

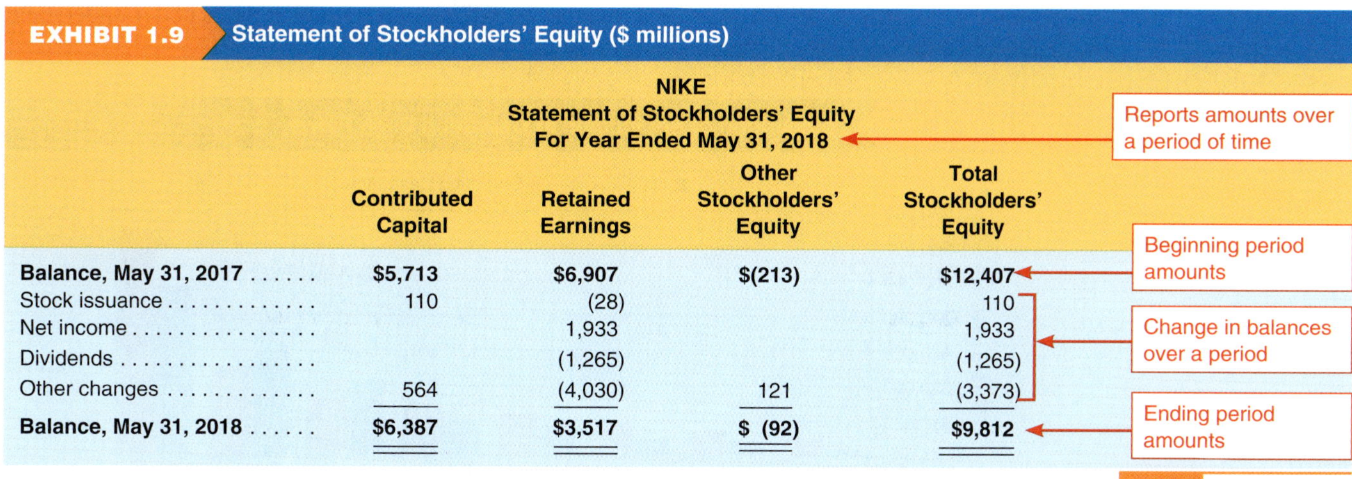

EXHIBIT 1.9 Statement of Stockholders' Equity ($ millions)

NIKE
Statement of Stockholders' Equity
For Year Ended May 31, 2018

	Contributed Capital	Retained Earnings	Other Stockholders' Equity	Total Stockholders' Equity
Balance, May 31, 2017	**$5,713**	**$6,907**	**$(213)**	**$12,407**
Stock issuance	110	(28)		110
Net income		1,933		1,933
Dividends		(1,265)		(1,265)
Other changes	564	(4,030)	121	(3,373)
Balance, May 31, 2018	**$6,387**	**$3,517**	**$ (92)**	**$9,812**

FYI Dividends are reported in the statement of equity, and not in the income statement.

Contributed capital represents the net amount received from issuing stock to shareholders (owners). **Retained earnings** (also called *earned capital*) represents the income the company has earned since its inception, minus the dividends it has paid out to shareholders. Thus, retained earnings equals the amount of income retained in the company. The change in retained earnings links consecutive balance sheets through the income statement. Nike's retained earnings decreased from $6,907 million at May 31, 2017, to $3,517 million at May 31, 2018. This decrease is explained by net income of $1,933 million, less dividends of $1,265 million and other reductions of $4,058 million. The category titled "other changes" refers to changes in equity that are not recorded in income and is discussed in Chapter 11.

Statement of Cash Flows

FYI Cash is critical to operations because it is necessary for purchasing resources and paying bills.

The **statement of cash flows** reports net cash flows from operating, investing, and financing activities over a period of time. Nike's statement of cash flows for fiscal year ended May 31, 2018, is shown in a reduced format in **Exhibit 1.10**. The statement reports that the cash balance increased by $441 million during the fiscal year. Operating activities provided $4,955 million (a cash inflow), investing activities provided $276 million (a cash inflow), and financing activities used $4,835 million (a cash outflow). These changes reduced Nike's ending balance of cash to $4,249 million.

EXHIBIT 1.10 Statement of Cash Flows ($ millions)

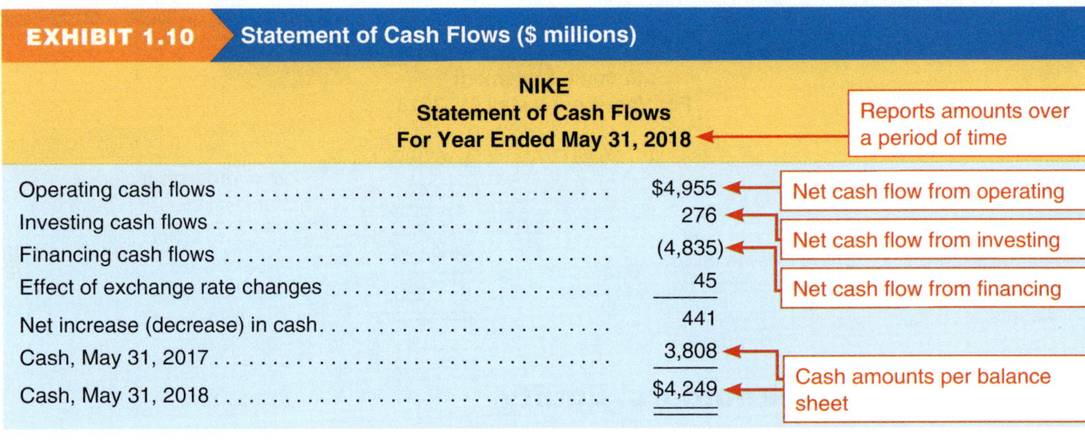

NIKE
Statement of Cash Flows
For Year Ended May 31, 2018 ← Reports amounts over a period of time

Operating cash flows	$4,955	← Net cash flow from operating
Investing cash flows	276	← Net cash flow from investing
Financing cash flows	(4,835)	← Net cash flow from financing
Effect of exchange rate changes	45	
Net increase (decrease) in cash	441	
Cash, May 31, 2017	3,808	← Cash amounts per balance sheet
Cash, May 31, 2018	$4,249	← Cash amounts per balance sheet

FYI Common formatting for U.S. financial statements includes:
- Dollar sign next to first and last amount listed in a column
- Single underline before a subtraction or addition; double underline after a major total
- Assets listed in order of liquidity, which is nearness to cash
- Liabilities listed in order of due dates

Operating cash flow is the amount of cash generated from operating activities. This amount usually differs from net income due to differences between the time that revenues and expenses are recorded, and the time that the related cash receipts and disbursements occur. For example, a company may report revenues for goods sold to customers this period, but not collect the payment until next period. Consistent with most companies, Nike's operating cash flows of $4,955 million do not equal its net income of $1,933 million. **Exhibit 1.11** compares net income and operating cash flows for Nike and several other companies. The exhibit shows that there is large variation across companies in the amount of net income and operating cash flows.

Both cash flow and net income are important for making business decisions. They each capture different aspects of firm performance and together help financial statement users better understand and assess a company's past, present, and future business activities.

EXHIBIT 1.11 Comparison of Net Income to Operating Cash Flows

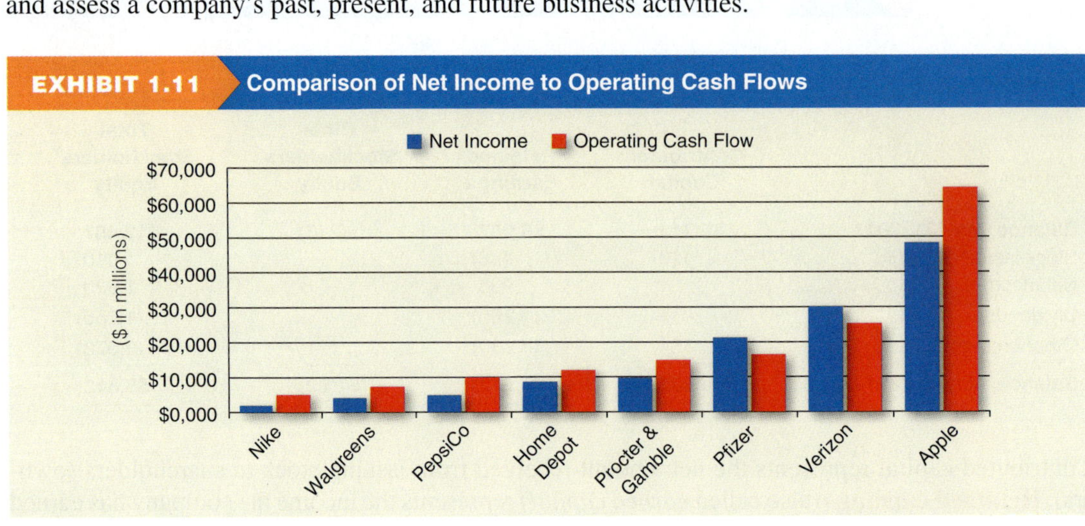

Financial Statement Linkages

A central feature of the accounting system is the linkage among the four primary statements, referred to as the *articulation* of the financial statements. Three of the key linkages are:

- The statement of cash flows links the beginning and ending cash in the balance sheet.
- The income statement links the beginning and ending retained earnings in the statement of stockholders' equity.
- The statement of stockholders' equity links the beginning and ending equity in the balance sheet.

Exhibit 1.12 demonstrates these links using Nike's financial statements from **Exhibits 1.6** through **1.10**. The left side of **Exhibit 1.12** presents Nike's beginning-year balance sheet for fiscal year 2018 (which is the same as the balance sheet for the end of fiscal year 2017) and the right side presents Nike's year-end balance sheet for fiscal year 2018. These balance sheets report Nike's investing and financing activities at the beginning and end of the fiscal year, two distinct points in time. The middle column of **Exhibit 1.12** presents the three financial

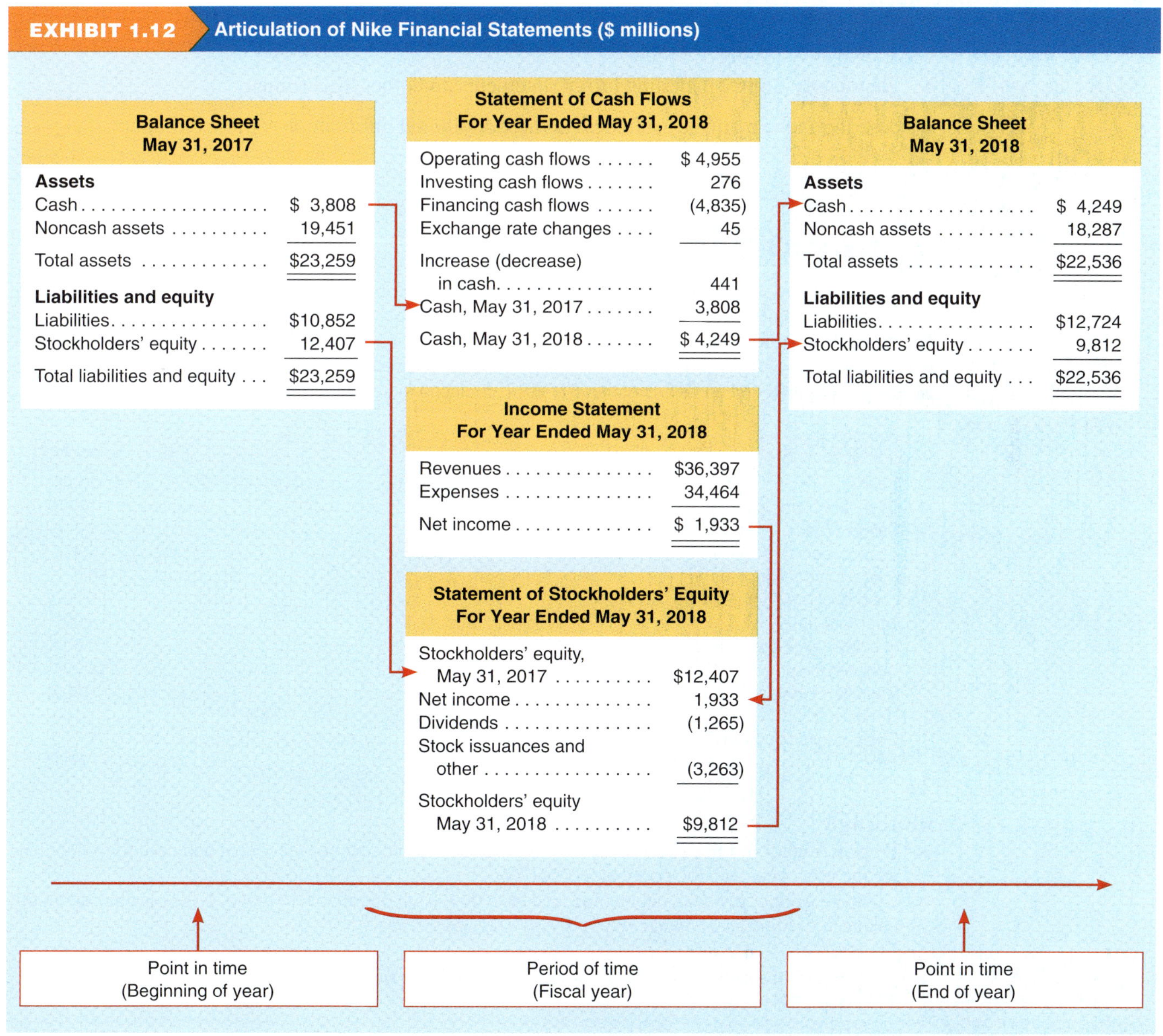
EXHIBIT 1.12 Articulation of Nike Financial Statements ($ millions)

Balance Sheet May 31, 2017	
Assets	
Cash	$ 3,808
Noncash assets	19,451
Total assets	$23,259
Liabilities and equity	
Liabilities	$10,852
Stockholders' equity	12,407
Total liabilities and equity	$23,259

Statement of Cash Flows For Year Ended May 31, 2018	
Operating cash flows	$ 4,955
Investing cash flows	276
Financing cash flows	(4,835)
Exchange rate changes	45
Increase (decrease) in cash	441
Cash, May 31, 2017	3,808
Cash, May 31, 2018	$ 4,249

Income Statement For Year Ended May 31, 2018	
Revenues	$36,397
Expenses	34,464
Net income	$ 1,933

Statement of Stockholders' Equity For Year Ended May 31, 2018	
Stockholders' equity, May 31, 2017	$12,407
Net income	1,933
Dividends	(1,265)
Stock issuances and other	(3,263)
Stockholders' equity May 31, 2018	$9,812

Balance Sheet May 31, 2018	
Assets	
Cash	$ 4,249
Noncash assets	18,287
Total assets	$22,536
Liabilities and equity	
Liabilities	$12,724
Stockholders' equity	9,812
Total liabilities and equity	$22,536

statements that report Nike's fiscal year 2018 business activities over time: the statement of cash flows, the income statement, and the statement of stockholders' equity. The three key linkages shown in **Exhibit 1.12** are:

- The statement of cash flows explains how operating, financing, and investing activities increased the cash balance by $441 million, from the $3,808 million reported in the beginning-year balance sheet, to the $4,249 million reported in the year-end balance sheet.
- The net income of $1,933 million reported in the income statement is added to retained earnings in the statement of stockholders' equity.
- The statement of stockholders' equity explains how total equity of $12,407 million, reported in the beginning-year balance sheet, becomes total equity of $9,812 million, reported in the year-end balance sheet.

Information Beyond Financial Statements

FYI An analysis of a firm's activities requires extensive study of its footnotes and the MD&A.

Important information about a company is communicated to various decision makers through reports other than financial statements. These reports include the following:

- Management Discussion and Analysis (MD&A)
- Independent Auditor Report
- Financial statement footnotes
- Regulatory filings, including proxy statements and other SEC filings

We describe and explain the usefulness of these additional information sources throughout the book.

Review Problems *are self-study tools that require the application of accounting. To aid learning, solutions are provided at the end of the chapter.*

MID-CHAPTER REVIEW

Guided Example *icons denote the availability of a demonstration video in* **myBusinessCourse** *(MBC)—see the Preface for more on MBC.*

Based in Germany, **Adidas** is one of **Nike**'s primary competitors. It markets athletic shoes and apparel under the Adidas and Reebok brands. It also sells Solomon ski equipment as well as TaylorMade and Adams golf equipment. Adidas' financial statements are reported in euros, the currency of the European Union. The statements are also prepared using International Financial Reporting Standards (IFRS). The following information is from the company's December 31, 2017, financial statements (€ millions):

	2017
Cash	€ 1,598
Cash flow from operations	1,648
Sales revenue	21,218
Stockholders' equity	6,435
Cost of goods sold	10,514
Cash flow used for financing	(769)
Total liabilities	8,087
Net other expenses	9,604
Noncash assets	12,924
Cash flow used for investing	(680)
Net income	1,100
Cash, beginning of year	1,510
Effect of exchange rates on cash	(111)

REQUIRED

a. Prepare Adidas' balance sheet at December 31, 2017, and its income statement and cash flow statement for the fiscal year ended December 31, 2017.

b. Compare Adidas' revenue, net income, and cash flow from operations to that of Nike (as reported in this chapter). Assume an exchange rate of €1.00 = $1.35.

The solution to this review problem can be found on pages 39–40.

FINANCIAL REPORTING ENVIRONMENT

LO4 Describe the institutions that regulate financial accounting and their role in establishing generally accepted accounting principles.

Learning Objectives *are repeated at the start of the section covering that topic.*

4

Information presented in financial statements is of critical importance to external decision makers. Financial statements affect the prices paid for equity securities and interest rates attached to debt securities. To the extent that financial performance and condition are accurately communicated to business decision makers, debt and equity securities are more accurately priced. By extension, financial reporting plays a crucial role in efficient resource allocation within and across economies. Accounting information contributes to the efficient operation of securities markets, labor markets, commodity markets, and other markets.

To illustrate, imagine the consequences of a breakdown in the integrity of financial reporting. The Enron scandal provides a case in point. At the beginning of 2001, **Enron** was one of the more, if not the most, innovative and respected companies in the United States. With revenues of over $100 billion and total company value of over $60 billion, it was the fifth largest U.S. corporation based on market value. In October 2001, the company released its third quarter earnings report to the public. Although operating earnings were higher than in previous years, the income statement contained a $1 billion "special charge." Financial analysts began investigating the cause of this charge and discovered that it was linked to related-party transactions and questionable accounting practices. Once it became clear to the capital markets that Enron had not faithfully and accurately reported its financial condition and performance, people became unwilling to purchase its securities. The value of its debt and equity securities dropped precipitously and the company was unable to obtain the cash needed for operating activities. By the end of 2001, Enron was bankrupt!

The Enron case illustrates the importance of reliable financial reporting. Accountants recognize the importance of the information that they produce and, as a profession, they agree to follow a set of standards for the presentation of financial statements and the disclosure of related financial information. In the following paragraphs, we discuss these standards, or *principles*, as well as the institutional and regulatory environment in which accountants operate.

Generally Accepted Accounting Principles

Decision makers who rely on audited financial statements expect that all companies follow similar procedures in preparing their statements. In response to these expectations, U.S. accountants have developed a set of standards and procedures called **generally accepted accounting principles (GAAP)**. GAAP is not a set of immutable laws. Instead, it is a set of standards and accepted practices, based on underlying principles, that are designed to guide the preparation of the financial statements. GAAP is subject to change as conditions warrant. As a result, specific rules are altered or new practices are formulated to fit changes in underlying economic circumstances or business transactions.

Some people mistakenly assume that financial accounting is an exact discipline—that is, companies select the proper standard to account for a transaction and then follow the rules. The reality is that GAAP allows companies considerable discretion in preparing financial statements. The choice of methods often yields financial statements that are markedly different from one company to another in terms of reported income, assets, liabilities, and equity amounts. In addition, financial statements depend on numerous estimates. Consequently, even though two companies may engage in the same transactions and choose the same accounting methods, their financial statements will differ because their managements have made different estimates about such things as the amount to be collected from customers who buy on credit, the length of time that buildings and equipment will be in use, and the future costs for product warranties.

Accounting standard setters walk a fine line regarding choice in accounting. On one hand, they are concerned that management discretion in preparing financial statements will lead to abuse by those seeking to influence the decisions of those who rely on the statements. On the other hand, they are concerned that companies are too diverse for a "one size fits all" financial accounting system. Ultimately, GAAP attempts to strike a balance by imposing constraints on the choice of accounting procedures, while allowing companies some flexibility within those constraints.

YOU MAKE THE CALL

You are a Financial Analyst Accountants, business leaders, and politicians have long debated the importance of considering the **economic consequences** of accounting standards (GAAP). Should accounting standards be designed to influence behavior and affect social or economic change considered by, say, a government body or other interested group? Alternatively, should such standards be designed simply to provide relevant and reliable information on which economic decisions can be made by others with a reasonable degree of confidence? What do you believe the objectives of financial reporting should be? [Answers on page 30.]

Regulation and Oversight

Following the U.S. stock market crash of 1929, the United States Congress passed the Securities Acts of 1933 and 1934. These acts were passed to require disclosure of financial and other information about securities being offered for public sale and to prohibit deceit, misrepresentations, and other fraud in the sale of securities. The 1934 Act created the **Securities and Exchange Commission (SEC)** and gave it broad powers to regulate the issuance and trading of securities. The act also provided that companies with more than $10 million in assets and whose securities are held by more than 500 owners must file annual and other periodic reports, including a complete set of financial statements.

While the SEC has ultimate authority over financial reporting by companies in the United States, it has ceded the task of setting accounting standards to a professional body, the **American Institute of Certified Public Accountants (AICPA)**. Over the years, this process has resulted in three standard-setting organizations.

Currently, accounting standards are established by the **Financial Accounting Standards Board (FASB)**. The FASB is a seven-member board that has the primary responsibility for setting financial accounting standards in the United States. In 2009, the FASB codified the standards into the FASB Accounting Standards Codification. This is now the single source of authorative, non-governmental U.S. GAAP.

BUSINESS INSIGHT

Accounting can be complicated—but rule-makers are trying to make it a little simpler. The Financial Accounting Standards Board, which sets accounting rules for U.S. companies, launched the FASB Simplification Initiative in 2014. The objective of the initiative is to make financial reporting a little less complex and reduce costs for companies and their accountants, while at the same time maintaining or improving the quality of information reported.

The projects are relatively narrow, straightforward changes in accounting that clearly would help reduce complexity and that the board expects to be able to make relatively quickly, without the years of work that often accompany major revisions in accounting rules.

"Complexity in accounting can be costly to both investors and companies," FASB Chairman Russ Golden said. The simplification initiative, which FASB began in June 2014, "is focused on identifying areas that we can address quickly and effectively, without compromising the quality of information provided to investors."

Besides setting standards for financial accounting, the FASB has developed a framework to form the basis for future discussion of proposed standards and serve as a guide to accountants for reporting information that is not governed by specific standards. A summary of this *Conceptual Framework* is presented in Appendix 1A at the end of this chapter.

In the wake of the Enron, Tyco, AOL, Global Crossing, Halliburton, Xerox, Adelphia, Bristol-Myers Squibb, and WorldCom scandals, concerns over the quality of corporate financial reporting led Congress to pass the **Sarbanes-Oxley Act** in 2002. The goal of this act—sometimes referred to as SOX—was to increase the level of confidence that external users, particularly investors, have in the financial statements. To accomplish this objective, SOX imposed a number of requirements to strengthen audit committees and improve deficient **internal controls** by:

- increasing management's responsibility for accounting information,
- increasing the independence of the auditors,

- increasing the accountability of the board of directors,
- establishing adequate internal controls to prevent fraud.

SOX requires that the chief executive officer (CEO) and the chief financial officer (CFO) of a publicly traded corporation personally sign a statement attesting to the accuracy and completeness of financial statements. The prospect of severe penalties is designed to make these managers more vigilant in monitoring the financial accounting process. In addition, SOX established the **Public Company Accounting Oversight Board (PCAOB)** to approve auditing standards and monitor the quality of financial statements and audits.

SOX has had an impact on financial disclosures. A report by Glass, Lewis and Co. indicates that the number of publicly traded companies restating their financial reports increased to 1,295 in 2005, which is one restatement for every 12 reporting companies. That's triple the total in 2002 when SOX was passed.

The Sarbanes-Oxley Act is not without critics. Many small companies complain that the additional reporting and auditing requirements established in the act are prohibitively costly. In response to this criticism, the JOBS Act of 2012 relaxed the SOX reporting requirements for companies with less than $1 billion in sales. Of even greater concern is the criticism that the penalties imposed on management for misstatements or errors are too severe. Some argue that managers have become less forthcoming in their disclosures and more conservative in choosing accounting methods and making accrual estimates to avoid the possibility of heavy fines or criminal charges.

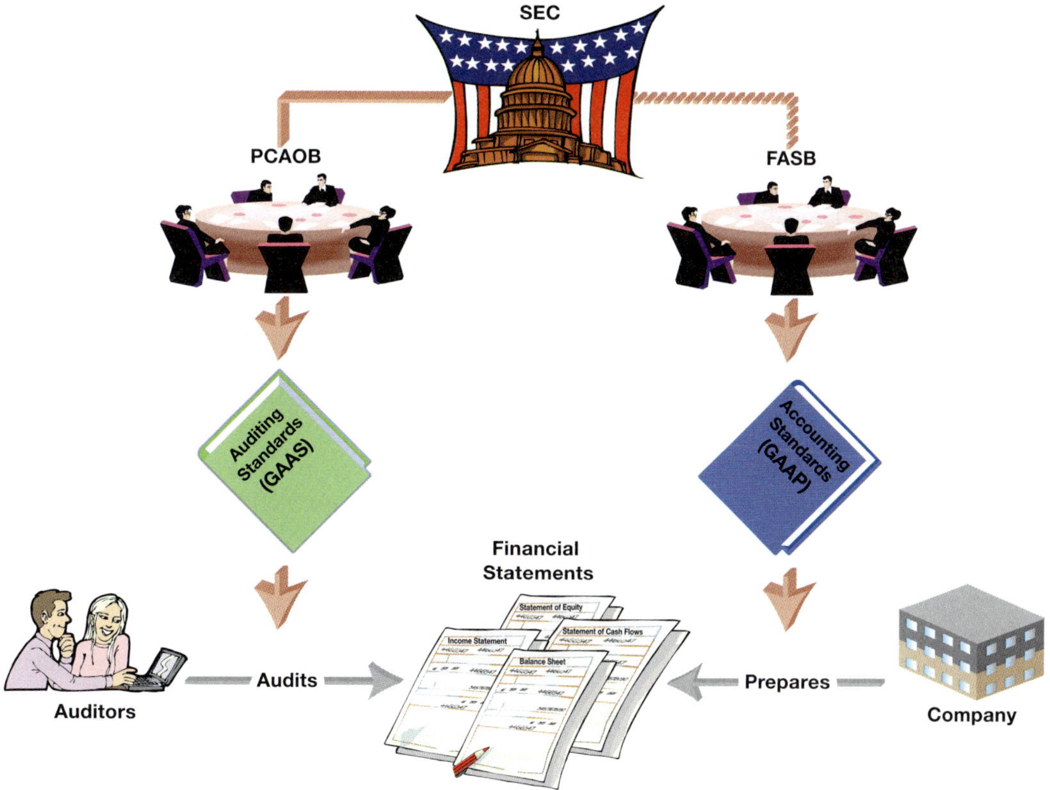

Role of the Auditor

What prevents a company from disclosing false or misleading information? For one thing, the financial statements are prepared by management, and management must take responsibility for what is disclosed. Management's reputation can be severely damaged by false disclosures when subsequent events unfold to refute the information. This situation can adversely affect the firm's ability to compete in capital, labor, and consumer markets. It can also lead to litigation and even criminal charges against management.

Even though management must personally attest to the accuracy and completeness of the financial statements, markets also demand assurances from independent parties. Therefore, the financial statements of publicly traded corporations must be **audited** by an *independent audit firm*. The auditors provide an opinion as to whether the statements *present fairly* and *in all material respects* a company's financial condition and the results of its operations.

The audit opinion is not a guarantee. Auditors only provide reasonable assurance that the financial statements are free of material misstatements. Even so, auditors provide a valuable service. Auditors effectively ensure that the information contained in the financial statements is reliable, thus increasing the confidence of outside decision makers in the information they use to make investment, credit, and other decisions. Therefore, creditors and shareholders of privately held corporations often demand that the financial statements be audited as well.

Public corporations are required to establish audit committees whose purpose is not to audit but, rather, to appoint the audit firm and assure that what is learned in the audit is disclosed to the firm's directors and shareholders.

YOU MAKE THE CALL

You are a Member of the Board of Directors Until recently accounting firms were permitted to earn money for consulting activities performed for clients they audited. Do you see any reason why this might not be an acceptable practice? Do you see any advantage to your firm from allowing such activity? [Answer on page 30.]

A Global Perspective

Businesses increasingly operate in global markets. Consumers and businesses with access to the Internet can purchase products and services from anywhere in the world. Products produced in one country are often made with parts and materials imported from many different countries. Businesses outsource parts of operations to other countries to take advantage of better labor markets in those countries. Capital markets are global as well. Corporations whose securities trade on the New York Stock Exchange may also trade on exchanges in London, Toronto, Tokyo, or Hong Kong.

Because countries have a variety of laws and customs, accounting principles and practices can vary considerably from one country to the next. Over time, many companies based in countries other than the United States chose to present financial statements that conformed to U.S. GAAP because they believed that doing so provided them better access to investors in the U.S. capital markets. Many other companies prepare financial statements following GAAP of the country in which they are based.

The globalization of capital markets, combined with the diversity of international accounting principles, led to an effort to increase comparability of financial information across countries. The **International Accounting Standards Board (IASB)** oversees the development of accounting standards outside the United States. Over 100 countries, including those in the European Union, require the use of **International Financial Reporting Standards (IFRS)** developed by the IASB. The intention is to unify all public companies under one global set of reporting standards. The remaining major capital markets without an IFRS mandate are the U.S. (with no current plans to adopt), Japan (where voluntary adoption is permitted), and China (where standards are substantially converged and the country has plans to adopt).

Early in the 2000s, the Financial Accounting Standards Board (FASB) and the IASB committed to developing the highest-quality standards useable for both domestic and cross-border financial reporting and to assure the standards would (a) be fully compatible as soon as practicable and (b) maintain that compatibility. Statements prepared under IFRS and U.S. GAAP are quite similar, yet important differences remain. For example, balance sheets prepared under IFRS often classify assets in reverse order of liquidity to those prepared under GAAP. Thus, intangible assets are listed first and cash last on the balance sheet. Both approaches require the same basic set of four financial statements, with explanatory footnotes. We shall examine some of the more important differences under a Global Perspective heading as they arise in future chapters. Websites maintained by the larger accounting firms as well as both the FASB and IASB provide considerable information.

Because it is international in its scope, the IASB has no legal authority to impose accounting standards on any country. However, by working with standard setters within countries, such as the FASB within the United States, the IASB is working to reduce diversity in financial reporting practice. Despite the push for comparability, not everyone is convinced that IFRS will improve the usefulness of accounting information. As one observer put it, "There is a real risk of a veneer of comparability that hides a lot of differences." A number of countries—over 30 at last count—have reserved the right to adopt exceptions to IFRS when they deem them to be appropriate. Perhaps this helps explain why the SEC on July 13, 2012, declined to recommend IFRS for adoption by the United States.

Global Perspectives *examine issues related to similarities and differences in accounting practices of the U.S. and other countries.*

A GLOBAL PERSPECTIVE

Prior to 2007, foreign-based companies wishing to sell securities in the United States were required to reconcile their financial statements to be consistent with U.S. GAAP. However, in June 2007, the SEC adopted a rule that allows foreign companies using international accounting standards to stop reconciling their financial statements to American rules. While this change made it easier for U.S. investors to purchase securities from around the world, a *New York Times* article referred to a "Tower of Babel in Accounting." The article raises concerns about the difficulty of comparing companies when their financial statements are based on diverse reporting standards. The situation is complicated by the fact that a number of developing countries have reserved the right to adopt exceptions to IFRS when deemed appropriate.

Each chapter includes a section on **Analyzing Financial Statements** *to emphasize the use of accounting information in making business decisions.*

ANALYZING FINANCIAL STATEMENTS

LO5 Compute two key ratios that are commonly used to assess profitability and risk—return on equity and the debt-to-equity ratio.

5

The financial statements provide insights into the financial health and performance of a company. However, the accounting data presented in these statements are difficult to interpret in raw form. For example, knowing that Nike's net income was $1,933 million in the fiscal year ended May 2018 is, by itself, not very useful. Similarly, knowing the dollar amount of liabilities does not tell us whether or not Nike relies too heavily on creditor financing.

Financial analysts use a number of tools to help interpret the information found in the financial statements. They look at trends over time and compare one company to another. They calculate ratios using financial statement information to summarize the data in a form that is easier to interpret. Ratios also allow us to compare the performance and condition of different companies even if the companies being compared are dramatically different in size. Ratios also help analysts spot trends or changes in performance over time.

Throughout the book, we introduce ratios that are commonly used by financial analysts and other users who rely on the financial statements. Our goal is to develop an understanding of how to effectively use the information in the financial statements, as well as to demonstrate how these statements are prepared. In this chapter we introduce one important measure of **profitability** and one measure of financial **risk**.

Profitability Analysis

Profitability reveals whether or not a company is able to bring its product or service to the market in an efficient manner, and whether the market values that product or service. Companies that are consistently unprofitable are unlikely to succeed in the long run.

A key profitability metric for stockholders and other decision makers is company return on equity. This metric compares the level of net income with the amount of equity financing used to generate that income.

Analysis Objective

We are trying to determine Nike's ability to earn a return for its stockholders.

Analysis Tool Return on Equity

$$\textbf{Return on equity} = \frac{\textbf{Net income}}{\textbf{Average stockholders' equity}}$$

Applying the Return on Equity Ratio to Nike

$$\textbf{2015: } \frac{\$3{,}760}{[(\$12{,}258 + \$12{,}707)/2]} = 0.301 \text{ or } 30.1\%$$

$$\textbf{2016: } \frac{\$4{,}240}{[(\$12{,}407 + \$12{,}258)/2]} = 0.344 \text{ or } 34.4\%$$

$$\textbf{2017: } \frac{\$1{,}933}{[(\$9{,}812 + \$12{,}407)/2]} = 0.174 \text{ or } 17.4\%$$

Guidance Taken over time, ROE ratios that are over 10% and preferably increasing suggest the company is earning reasonable returns. For firms that are in more risky businesses, such as renewable power, even larger returns on equity would be appropriate, while firms in less risky endeavors, such as large food chains, would not be expected to generate as large returns. (Note the years for Nike are fiscal years ended May of 2016, 2017, and 2018.)

Nike in Context

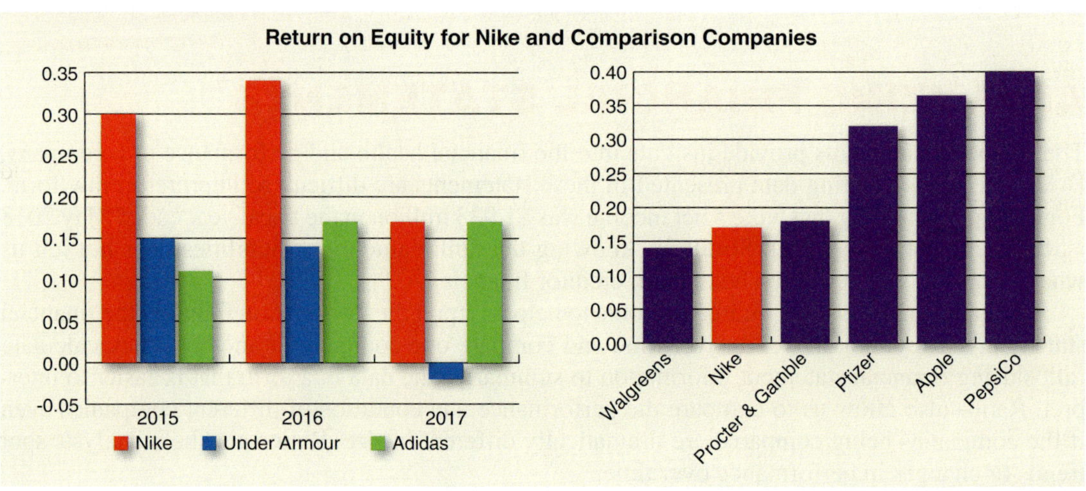

Takeaways Over the time period covered by our calculations and by the graph, it is clear that Nike has done very well earning returns for its stockholders. Not only have returns been over 15% but the trend is one of generally increasing profitability until fiscal 2018 (we discuss part of the reason for 2018 below). Whether Nike can return to increasing returns and continue to do well is less clear. Several new companies have entered the market and Nike will need to continue developing new products to preserve its market leadership.

Other Considerations As with all ratios, care in their interpretation is essential. First, we need to be careful about comparing companies that operate in different product markets.

Second, regulation, such as applicable tax laws, can be different across countries and over time. In December of 2017 the U.S. enacted a new tax law known as the **Tax Cuts and Jobs Act (TCJA)**. (We discuss the TCJA in more detail in Chapter 10.) Many companies, including Nike, had to account for some of the provisions of the TCJA in the year that contained December 2017—for Nike this is the year that ended May 31, 2018. Nike's tax expense increased significantly, lowering net income. This is part of the explanation of the decrease in ROE in 2018 computed above.[5] These are one-time charges and how the TCJA will fully affect U.S. companies going forward is not yet known.

[5] At a high level for now, the TCJA decreased the U.S. corporate statutory tax rate to 21% (from a graduated rate that topped out at 35%). However, the TCJA also required taxation of prior foreign earnings that many companies had not accrued U.S. tax on previously. This was the case for Nike and it had to accrue a significant amount of U.S. tax (what Nike labels a transition tax in its report) leading to the higher tax expense for 2018. As a ballpark estimation, if we assume the same tax expense as in 2017 for Nike (and adjust earnings and equity accordingly), the ROE would have been 21.5% for 2018.

Third, firms with different customer or supplier demographics can also produce different conclusions. Furthermore, different management policies toward assets and liabilities have their own unique effect on ratios across firms. For example, the conversion of inventories to sales can be subject to slowdowns that affect companies differently, within the same industry.

Fourth, these measures can be altered by management decisions designed solely for cosmetic effects such as improving current earnings or an important ratio. Thus, delaying inventory orders or filling sales orders early can lead to increasing net income and ROE in current periods to the detriment of future periods.

Finally, differences in the fiscal year-end of companies can influence a comparison of ROE ratios. If one company's fiscal year ends in May and another company's fiscal year ends in December, economic conditions may change between May and December, creating differences in ROE that are not due to differences in the operations of the two companies.

Credit Risk Analysis

In addition to measuring profitability, analysts also frequently analyze the level of risk associated with investing in or lending to a given company. The riskier an investment is, the greater the return demanded by investors. For example, a low-risk borrower is likely to be able to borrow money at a lower interest rate than would a high-risk borrower. Similarly, there is a risk-return trade-off in equity returns. Investments in risky stocks are expected to earn higher returns than investments in low-risk stocks, and stocks are priced accordingly. The higher expected rate of return is compensation for accepting greater uncertainty in returns.

FYI Return cannot be evaluated without considering risk; the greater the risk of any decision, the greater the expected return.

Many factors contribute to the risk a company faces. One important factor is a company's *long-term solvency*. **Solvency** refers to the ability of a company to remain in business and avoid bankruptcy or financial distress. One such measure is the **debt-to-equity (D/E) ratio**.

Analysis Objective

We are interested in determining the ability of a company to make the necessary interest and principal payments on its debt.

Analysis Tool Debt-to-Equity

$$\textbf{Debt-to-equity ratio} = \frac{\textbf{Total liabilities}}{\textbf{Total stockholders' equity}}$$

Applying the Debt-to-Equity Ratio to Nike

$$\textbf{2015:}\ \frac{\$9{,}138}{\$12{,}258} = 0.75$$

$$\textbf{2016:}\ \frac{\$10{,}852}{\$12{,}407} = 0.88$$

$$\textbf{2017:}\ \frac{\$12{,}724}{\$9{,}812} = 1.30$$

Guidance Solvency is closely related to the extent a company relies on creditor financing. As the amount of creditor financing increases, the possibility of bankruptcy also increases. Short of bankruptcy, a company that has borrowed too much will occasionally find that the required interest payments are hurting the company's cash flow. The debt-to equity ratio is an important measure used by analysts and others to assess a company's ability to make the necessary interest and principal payments on its debt. (Note the years above are the fiscal years ended May of 2016, 2017, and 2018).

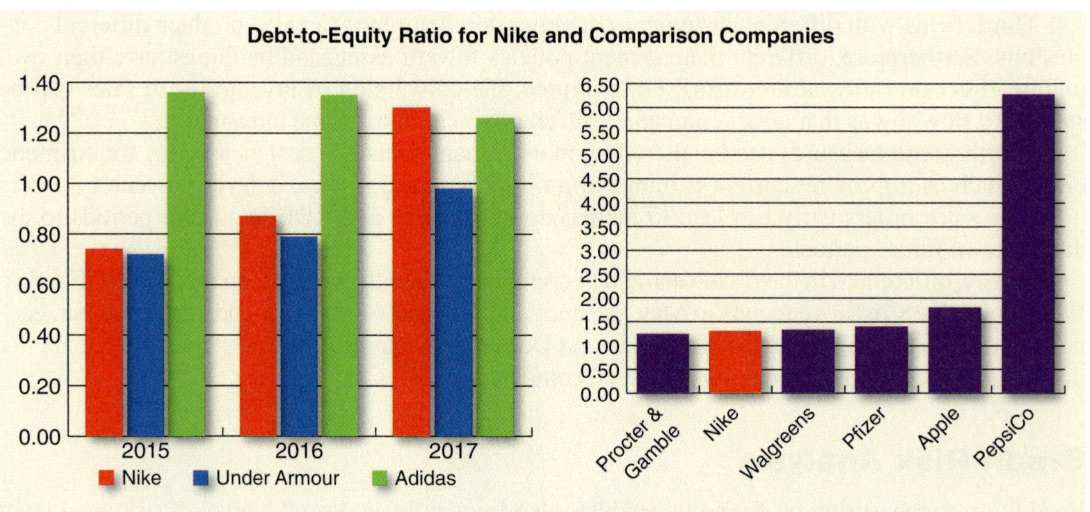

A debt-to equity ratio of one indicates that the company is using equal parts of debt and equity financing. Nike's debt-to-equity ratio has increased steadily since at least 2012, when it was 0.49.

The appropriate D/E ratio level depends on the nature of the business and will differ appreciably as can be seen in the chart above. Typically, firms with large long-term commitments often reflected in fixed assets will find it appropriate to raise more capital through borrowing. The amount of debt relative to equity will also mirror the risk tolerance of the firm's management. If management believes it can earn a return above the debt interest cost, borrowing will increase the expected return to the owners.

Takeaways Nike's D/E ratio has increased slightly over the three years presented. Nike's liabilities have been steadily increasing. Yet, stockholders' equity has not increased at the same pace, and in fact it declined considerably in 2018. Indeed, by 2017, Nike has a higher D/E ratio than its closest competitors.

Other Considerations Comparisons with other companies in similar lines of business, such as Under Armour and Adidas, are always appropriate. New competitors, such as Quiksilver, could also prove insightful to examine in regards to strategic decisions. In Chapter 9, we will explore the accounting for liabilities in more depth. Balance sheets do not always recognize all obligations of a firm, and a careful reader will examine the footnotes to get a more complete picture of financial health in such comparisons. Nike might also consider increasing its debt level if profitable opportunities exist. The company has been, and remains, very successful, but new entrants are emerging indicating there is additional business to be had.

The graph shows that Nike has a similar and somewhat relatively lower D/E ratio when compared to the other companies we show. Procter & Gamble has a lower D/E but Apple and Pepsi have higher D/Es.

There are other measures of profitability and risk that will be introduced in later chapters. Collectively, these ratios, when placed in the context of the company's business activities, help to provide a clear picture of the *drivers* of a company's financial performance and the factors affecting its financial condition. Understanding these performance drivers and their impact on the financial health of a company is key to effectively using the information presented in the financial statements.

Technology and Accounting

New technological innovations arise frequently, and they often increase the capabilities of businesses and make them more efficient. Recently, data analytics and blockchain technology have emerged as two prominent business-changing innovations. Many companies, including **Amazon** and **Google**, use data analysis throughout their organizations to make business decisions. **Data analytics** can broadly be defined as the process of examining large sets of data with the goal of discovering useful information from patterns found in the data. Business people employing data analytics can glean important insights from large data sets and identify opportunities for growth and operational efficiency. Data analysis has many applications and you will encounter it in many disciplines beyond accounting.

Blockchain was made famous as the underpinning technology used for digital currencies, such as **Bitcoin** and **Ethereum**. **Blockchain** is a distributed digital ledger that provides a secure means, for approved parties, to view recorded transactions. This technology has wide-ranging implications for business and is expected to greatly affect the way accountants perform audits.

Understanding what data analytics and blockchain technology are and how they are used is the first step towards developing marketable skills in each area, so we have included examples of each at various points in the book. In addition, **Appendix B** at the end of this book provides a more detailed discussion of data analytics.

ORGANIZATION OF THE BOOK

In the pages that follow Chapter 1, we will explore the financial accounting model and how it reflects an organization's activities and events. Chapters 2 and 3 are focused on building the balance sheet and the income statement from transactions and a set of required adjustments. This process requires a structure for "bookkeeping" and also an understanding of the basic rules of the accounting language. When do we recognize revenue? When do we recognize an asset? We will look at these questions in a relatively simple setting.

In Chapter 4, we will construct the statement of cash flows. The balance sheet, income statement, and statement of cash flows are all built on the same underlying set of information, and they are each designed to give a different perspective on what's going on in the company. Chapter 5 shows how managers and investors organize financial information using ratios and how managers and investors use those ratios to compare companies and to make forecasts of the future.

While the first five chapters build the financial statement structure and its interpretation, the latter seven chapters are more topical. Accounting is not a cut-and-dried process, and financial reports can be affected by a variety of management decisions. So these seven chapters explore more sophisticated settings and analyses. We will find that financial reports rely on management estimates of future events, and that sometimes management has the freedom to choose accounting methods that affect income and assets. And, when accounting practices don't allow reporting discretion, management's choice of transactions can make financial reports look more favorable.

Becoming an effective user of financial information requires an understanding of how the financial reports fit together and a willingness to explore the footnote material to look for useful information. As we progress through *Financial Accounting* together, we will show you how to become a sophisticated reader of financial reports by looking at real companies and real financial statement information.

CHAPTER-END REVIEW

Adidas, a major competitor of Nike, markets athletic shoes and apparel under the Adidas and Reebok brands. It also sells Solomon ski equipment and TaylorMade golf equipment. The following information is from Adidas' 2017 financial statements (Adidas' financial statements are reported in Euros, the currency of the European Union):

(millions)	Adidas
Net income (loss) (2017)	€1,100
Stockholders' equity (2017 year-end)	6,435
Stockholders' equity (2016 year-end)	6,455
Total liabilities (2017 year-end)	8,087

REQUIRED

a. Calculate the 2017 return on equity (ROE) ratio for Adidas.
b. Calculate the 2017 debt-to-equity ratio for Adidas.
c. Compare the profitability and risk of Adidas to that of Nike.

The solution to this review problem can be found on page 40.

6

LO6 Explain the conceptual framework for financial reporting.

APPENDIX 1A: Conceptual Framework for Financial Reporting

The Financial Accounting Standards Board (FASB) has worked in conjunction with the International Accounting Standards Board (IASB) to develop a conceptual framework for financial reporting. The conceptual framework consists of a system of interrelated objectives that, if met, would help to identify desirable reporting standards. The FASB and the IASB expect that the two Boards will most directly benefit from the conceptual framework by using the framework as a common foundation in the development of future standards. Both the IASB and the FASB issued new or amended conceptual frameworks in 2018. In addition, the FASB issued a new Chapter 8: *Notes to Financial Statements* (Statement of Financial Accounting Concepts No. 8). Chapter 8 is primarily about presentation and disclosure. FASB states that the intent is to aid the Board in identifying disclosures to be considered when setting disclosure requirements. The chapter is also intended to help the FASB improve its procedures and promote consistent decision making when determining disclosure requirements.

In this appendix, we focus on the objective for financial reporting as stated in the conceptual framework, as well as the characteristics of financial reporting that determine the degree of success in meeting that objective.

Objective of Financial Reporting

The objective of financial reporting is ***to provide information that is useful to present and potential equity investors, as well as lenders and other creditors, in making decisions about providing resources to the entity.*** The objective suggests that the information that is presented in financial statements is produced to 1) help the firm raise financing by providing information to equity investors and creditors about the financial health and performance of the firm, and 2) to provide ongoing information to those deciding whether to buy, sell, or hold equity and debt securities (including whether to settle loans and other types of credit). Information that is intended for investors and creditors may also be useful to other users of the financial statements.

This objective may be met by providing information for the assessment of the amount, timing, and uncertainty of future (net) cash flows to the firm, which enables investors and creditors to assess the amount, timing, and uncertainty of the cash flows which they will receive. The objective of financial reporting is not to provide a value of a firm, but to provide information for users' own assessments of value.

Qualitative Characteristics of Useful Financial Information

The conceptual framework identifies ***relevance*** and ***faithful representation*** as two fundamental qualitative characteristics of financial information that are necessary to fulfill the objective described in the previous section. As the conceptual framework states, "Neither a faithful representation of an irrelevant phenomenon, nor an unfaithful representation of a relevant phenomenon, helps users make good decisions." In addition, the conceptual framework identifies several enhancing qualitative characteristics that affect the usefulness of relevant and faithfully represented information. These qualitative characteristics and their relationship to the basic objective are depicted in **Exhibit 1A.1** and discussed below.

EXHIBIT 1A.1 Conceptual Framework

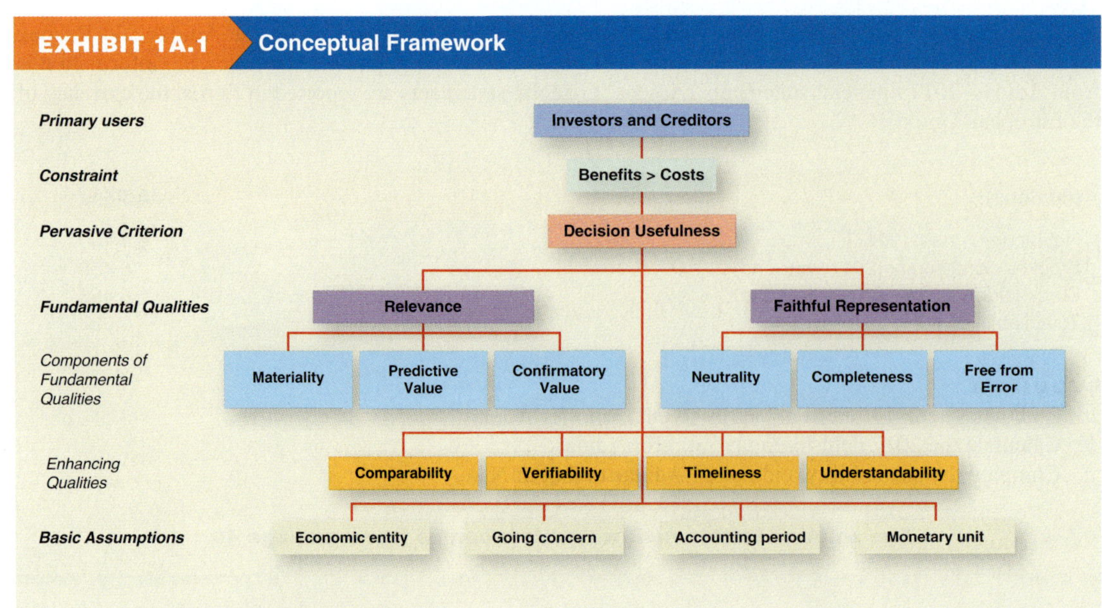

Relevance To be relevant, accounting information must have the ability to make a difference in a decision. Such information may be useful in making predictions about future performance of a company or in providing confirmatory feedback to evaluate past events.

MATERIALITY Materiality refers to whether a particular amount is large enough or important enough to affect the judgment of a reasonable decision maker. In practice, materiality is typically judged by the relative size of an item (e.g., relative to total assets, sales revenues, or net income).

PREDICTIVE VALUE Financial information has predictive value if it can be used as an input in the decision processes employed by users to predict future outcomes. The information does not have to be a prediction or forecast itself, but if it can be used by others in making predictions, it has predictive value.

CONFIRMATORY VALUE Financial information has confirmatory value if it provides feedback about previous evaluations.

Faithful Representation In addition to being relevant, financial information must report the economic events that it purports to report. Financial reports describe where an organization is at a point in time and how it arrived at that location from a previous one. To a traveler, a map would provide a faithful representation if the traveler can use the map to discern his or her actual location.

Information is a perfectly faithful representation if it is ***complete***, ***neutral***, and ***free from error***. The objective stated in the conceptual framework does not expect to achieve such perfection, but the requirement of faithful representation for information provides a measuring stick for standard-setters when considering alternative reporting standards.

COMPLETENESS Financial information is complete if it enables the user to understand all the dimensions of an economic phenomenon. Achieving such completeness may require disclosure of additional numerical information (an asset's historical cost and its fair value) or descriptive information (ongoing litigation).

NEUTRALITY While lack of bias is desirable in any reporting system, the effects of financial reports on management and investors create significant incentives to report outcomes and to choose disclosures that portray the firm in a favorable light. In choosing accounting standards, standard-setters aspire to reduce the ability of organizations to bias financial reports and to give financial statement users the ability to identify those biases when they occur.

FREE FROM ERROR Free from error means there are no errors or omissions in the description of the phenomenon and that the process used to produce the reported information has been selected and applied with no errors in the process. A common misconception about accounting is that it consists solely of a historical record of a firm's economic activities. It is such a record, but it is also dependent on management's forecasts of the future. Financial reports are very dependent on forecasts of the future, and forecasts of the future are almost always wrong (though we hope not by much). In this context, "free from error" means that any estimates are described clearly as such, with an explanation of the estimating process.

Enhancing Qualitative Characteristics

For financial information that is relevant to investors and faithfully represents an economic phenomenon, the conceptual framework describes several additional qualitative characteristics that—when present—enhance the usefulness of that information.

Comparability Accounting information should enable users to identify similarities and differences between sets of economic phenomena. For instance, the financial statements of different companies should be presented in a way that allows users to make comparisons across companies concerning their activities, financial condition, and performance. In addition, the information supplied to decision makers should exhibit conformity from one reporting period to the next with unchanging policies and procedures. Companies can choose to change accounting methods, and sometimes they are required to do so by standard-setters. However, such changes make it difficult to evaluate financial performance over time. Accounting changes should be rare and supported as the better means of reporting the organization's financial condition and performance.

Verifiability Verifiability means that consensus among independent observers could be reached that reported information is a faithful representation. An independent auditor should be able to examine the economic events and transactions underlying the financial statements and reach conclusions that are similar to those of management concerning how these events are measured and reported.

Timeliness Financial reporting information must be available to decision makers before it loses its capacity to influence decisions.

Understandability Modern organizations engage in a wide variety of transactions, and this complexity can make it difficult for a general user of the financial statements to assess the amount, timing, and uncertainty of the organization's future cash flows. The conceptual framework endeavors to take into consideration the reporting requirements for "users who have a reasonable knowledge of business and economic activities and who review and analyze the information diligently."

The Cost Constraint

Financial reporting requirements impose costs on companies. There are the costs of gathering, processing, and verifying the information, as well as the costs of publicly disclosing information to competitors. These costs are ultimately borne by the companies' investors and should be justified by the benefits of the information produced.

Additional Underlying Basic Assumptions

While not a part of the conceptual framework, four assumptions underlie the preparation of financial statements. Knowing these assumptions is helpful in understanding how the statements are prepared and in interpreting the information reported therein. These assumptions include:

Separate Economic Entity For accounting purposes, the activities of a company are considered independent, distinct, and separate from the activities of its stockholders and from other companies.

Going Concern Companies are assumed to have continuity in that they can be expected to continue in operation over time. This assumption is essential for valuing assets (future benefits) and liabilities (future obligations).

Accounting Period While continuity is assumed, company operations must be reported periodically, normally each fiscal year. Interim reporting periods, such as quarterly or monthly reports, allow companies to supplement the annual financial statements with more timely information.

Monetary Unit The unit of measure is the monetary unit of the country in which the firm's accounting reports are issued. The dollar is the monetary unit in the United States.

YOU MAKE THE CALL

You are the Bank Loan Officer Hertz, the rental car firm, has a fleet of relatively new automobiles that it rents to customers for usually short periods. Suppose that Hertz applied to your bank for a loan and offered their fleet of cars as collateral. Would you, as the loan officer, be satisfied with the value shown on Hertz's balance sheet as a measure of the fleet's value? If not, what value would you prefer and how might you estimate that value? [Answers on page 30.]

Summary *offers key bullet point takeaways for each Learning Objective.*

SUMMARY

LO1 Identify the users of accounting information and discuss the costs and benefits of disclosure. (p. 4)

- There are many diverse decision makers who use financial information.
- The benefits of disclosure of credible financial information must exceed the costs of providing the information.

LO2 Describe a company's business activities and explain how these activities are represented by the accounting equation. (p. 7)

- To effectively manage a company or infer whether it is well managed, we must understand its activities as well as the competitive and regulatory environment in which it operates.
- All corporations *plan* business activities, *finance* and *invest* in them, and then engage in *operations.*

- Financing is obtained partly from stockholders and partly from creditors, including suppliers and lenders.
- Investing activities involve the acquisition and disposition of the company's productive resources called assets.
- Operating activities include the production of goods or services that create operating revenues (sales) and expenses (costs). Operating profit (income) arises when operating revenues exceed operating expenses.

Introduce the four key financial statements including the balance sheet, income statement, statement of stockholders' equity, and statement of cash flows. (p. 11) **LO3**

- The four basic financial statements used to periodically report the company's progress are the balance sheet, the income statement, the statement of stockholders' equity, and the statement of cash flows. These statements articulate with one another.
- The balance sheet reports the company's financial position *at a point* in time. It lists the company's asset, liability, and equity items, and it typically aggregates similar items.
- The income statement reports the firm's operating activities to determine income earned, and thereby the firm's performance *over a period* of time.
- The stockholders' equity statement reports the changes in the key equity accounts *over a period* of time.
- The statement of cash flows reports the cash flows into and out of the firm from its operating, investing, and financing sources *over a period* of time.

Describe the institutions that regulate financial accounting and their role in establishing generally accepted accounting principles. (p. 17) **LO4**

- Generally Accepted Accounting Principles (GAAP) are established standards and accepted practices designed to guide the preparation of the financial statements.
- While the Securities and Exchange Commission (SEC) has ultimate authority over financial reporting by companies in the United States, it has ceded the task of setting accounting standards to the accounting profession.
- The Financial Accounting Standards Board (FASB) has the primary responsibility for setting financial accounting standards in the United States.
- The Sarbanes-Oxley Act established the Public Company Accounting Oversight Board (PCAOB) to approve auditing standards and monitor the quality of financial statements and audits.
- International Financial Reporting Standards (IFRS) are set by the International Accounting Standards Board (IASB).
- IFRS are an attempt to achieve a greater degree of commonality in financial reporting across different countries.

Compute two key ratios that are commonly used to assess profitability and risk—return on equity and the debt-to-equity ratio. (p. 21) **LO5**

- **Return on equity (ROE)**—a measure of profitability that assesses the performance of the firm relative to the investment made by stockholders (equity financing)
- Return on equity (ROE) is an important profitability metric for stockholders.

$$\text{ROE} = \frac{\text{Net income}}{\text{Average stockholders' equity}}$$

- **Debt-to-equity ratio (D/E)**—a measure of long-term solvency that relates the amount of creditor financing to the amount of equity financing
- The debt-to-equity ratio is an important measure of long-term solvency, a determinant of overall company risk.

$$\text{D/E} = \frac{\text{Total liabilities}}{\text{Total stockholders' equity}}$$

Appendix 1A: Explain the conceptual framework for financial reporting. (p. 26) **LO6**

- The conceptual framework includes, among other things, a statement of the *objectives* of financial reporting along with a discussion of the *qualitative characteristics* of accounting information that are important to users.

GUIDANCE ANSWERS . . . YOU MAKE THE CALL

You are a Product Manager There are at least two considerations that must be balanced—namely, the disclosure requirements and your company's need to protect its competitive advantages. You must comply with all minimum required disclosures. The extent to which you offer additional disclosures depends on the sensitivity of the information; that is, how beneficial it is to your existing and potential competitors. Another consideration is how the information disclosed will impact your existing and potential investors. Disclosures such as this can be beneficial in that they convey the positive investments that are available to your company. Still, there are many stakeholders impacted by your decision and each must be given due consideration.

You are a Financial Analyst This question has received a lot of discussion from both sides under the title "Economic Consequences." On one side are those who maintain that accounting rules should not only reflect a rule's economic consequences but should be designed to facilitate the attainment of a specific economic goal. One example is the case where the oil industry lobbied for an accounting rule that they and others believed would increase the incentive to explore and develop new oil deposits.

Those on the other side of the argument believe that accounting should try to provide data that is objective, reliable, and free from bias without considering the economic consequences of the decisions to be made. They believe that accounting rule makers have neither the insight nor the public mandate to attempt forecasts of the economic effects of financial reporting. Decisions that will affect the allocation of resources or that affect society's social structure should be made only by our elected representatives. While there are substantive points on both sides, we believe that it is the job of accounting rule makers to work toward the objective of financial reporting that reflects economic reality, subject to practical measurement limitations.

You are a Member of the Board of Directors In order to perform a thorough audit, a company's auditors must gain an intimate knowledge of its operations, its internal controls, and its accounting system. Because of this familiarity, the accounting firm is in a position to provide insights and recommendations that another consulting firm might not be able to provide. However, the independence of the auditor is critical to the credibility of the audit and there is some concern that the desire to retain a profitable consulting engagement might lead the auditors to tailor their audit opinions to "satisfy the customer." Contrary to this concern, however, research finds that there is no evidence that auditors provide more optimistic audit reports for the companies they consult for. Rather, it appears that litigation and/or reputation concerns are reasonably effective in keeping auditors honest. Nevertheless, recent legislation in the United States now prohibits auditors from performing consulting services for their audit clients.

You are the Bank Loan Officer The value shown on Hertz's books will be the purchase price, though perhaps reduced for the time the fleet has been in use. However, the bank would want to know the current market value of the fleet, not its book value, and the bank would then adjust this market value. The current market value of a single car can be found in used-car market quotes. If the bank ultimately becomes the owner of the fleet, it will need to sell the cars, probably a few at a time through wholesalers. Therefore, the adjusted market value and the book value are likely to differ for several reasons, including:

1. Hertz would have been able to buy the fleet at a reduced value due to buying in large volume regularly (market value lower than used-car quotes).
2. Hertz is likely to have kept the cars in better condition than would the average buyer (market value higher than used-car quotes).
3. The bank would reduce the value by some percentage due to the costs associated with disposing of the fleet (including the wholesaler's discount) and the length of the bank loan (reduction to the value as otherwise determined).

KEY RATIOS

$$\text{Return on equity (ROE)} = \frac{\text{Net income}}{\text{Average stockholders' equity}} \qquad \text{Debt-to-equity (D/E)} = \frac{\text{Total liabilities}}{\text{Total stockholders' equity}}$$

Key Terms *are listed for each chapter with references to page numbers within the chapter.*

KEY TERMS

Data analytics (p. 24)
Debt-to-equity (D/E) ratio (p. 23)
Disclosure (p. 7)
Economic consequences (p. 18)
Expense (p. 10)
Financial accounting (p. 4)
Financial Accounting Standards Board (FASB) (p. 18)
Financing activities (p. 9)
Generally accepted accounting principles (GAAP) (p. 17)
Income (p. 11)
Income statement (p. 11, 12)
Internal controls (p. 18)
International Accounting Standards Board (IASB) (p. 20)
International Financial Reporting Standards (IFRS) (p. 20)
Investing activities (p. 8)
Liabilities (p. 9)
Managerial accounting (p. 4)
Operating activities (p. 10)
Partnership (p. 5)
Planning activities (p. 8)
Profitability (p. 21)
Public Company Accounting Oversight Board (PCAOB) (p. 19)
Retained earnings (p. 13)
Revenue (p. 10)
Risk (p. 21)
Sarbanes-Oxley Act (p. 18)
Securities and Exchange Commission (SEC) (p. 18)
Shares of stock (p. 5)
Sole proprietorship (p. 5)
Solvency (p. 23)
Statement of cash flows (p. 11, 14)
Statement of stockholders' equity (p. 11, 13)
Stockholders (p. 5)
Strategy (p. 8)
Suppliers (p. 6)
Tax Cuts and Jobs Act (TCJA) (p. 22)

Assignments with the MBC logo in the margin are available in myBusinessCourse. See the Preface of the book for details.

Multiple Choice questions with answers are provided for each chapter.

MULTIPLE CHOICE

1. Which of the following is a potential cost of the public disclosure of accounting information?
   a. Loss of competitive advantage caused by revealing information to competitors.
   b. Potential increased regulation and taxes due to reporting excessive profits in politically sensitive industries.
   c. Raising and then failing to meet the expectations of investors.
   d. All of the above are potential costs of disclosure.
2. Banks that lend money to corporations are considered
   a. creditors.
   b. stockholders.
   c. both *a* and *b* above.
   d. neither *a* nor *b* above.
3. Which of the following financial statements reports the financial condition of a company at a point in time?

   a. the balance sheet
   b. the income statement
   c. the statement of cash flows
   d. the statement of stockholders' equity
4. Which of the following is *not* one of the four basic financial reports?
   a. the balance sheet
   b. the income statement
   c. the statement of stockholders' equity
   d. the notes to the financial statements
5. Which of the following expressions is a correct statement of the accounting equation?
   a. Equity + Assets = Liability
   b. Assets – (Liabilities + Equity) = 0
   c. Liabilities – Equity = Assets
   d. Liabilities + Assets = Equity

Multiple Choice Answers
1.d 2.a 3.a 4.d 5.b

Homework icons indicate which assignments are available in myBusinessCourse (MBC). This feature is only available when the instructor incorporates MBC in the course.

Superscript A denotes assignments based on Appendix 1A.

QUESTIONS

Q1-1. What are the three major business activities of a company that are motivated and shaped by planning activities? Explain each activity.

Q1-2. The accounting equation (Assets = Liabilities + Equity) is a fundamental business concept. Explain what this equation reveals about a company's sources and uses of funds and the claims on company resources.

Q1-3. Companies prepare four primary financial statements. What are those financial statements and what information is typically conveyed in each?

Q1-4. Does a balance sheet report on a period of time or at a point in time? Also, explain the information conveyed in that report. Does an income statement report on a period of time or at a point in time? Also, explain the information conveyed in that report.

Q1-5. Warren Buffett, CEO of Berkshire Hathaway, and known as the "Sage of Omaha" for his investment success, has stated that his firm is not interested in investing in a company whose business model he does not understand through reading its financial statements. Would you agree? Name several information items (3 or 4) reported in financial statements that corporate finance officers would find particularly relevant in considering whether to invest in a firm.

Q1-6. Does a statement of cash flows report on a period of time or at a point in time? Also, explain the information and activities conveyed in that report.

Q1-7. Explain what is meant by the articulation of financial statements.

Q1-8. The trade-off between risk and return is a fundamental business concept. Briefly describe both risk and return and their trade-off. Provide some examples that demonstrate investments of varying risk and the approximate returns that you might expect to earn on those investments.

Q1-9. Why might a company voluntarily disclose more information than is required by GAAP?

Q1-10. Financial statements are used by several interested stakeholders. Develop a listing of three or more potential external users of financial statements and their applications.

Q1-11. What ethical issues might managers face in dealing with confidential information?

Q1-12. Return on equity (ROE) is an important summary measure of financial performance. How is it computed? Describe what this metric reveals about company performance.

Q1-13. Business decision makers external to the company increasingly demand more financial information on business activities of companies. Discuss the reasons why companies have traditionally opposed the efforts of regulatory agencies like the SEC to require more disclosure.

Q1-14. What are generally accepted accounting principles and what organization presently establishes them?

Q1-15. What are International Financial Reporting Standards (IFRS)? Why are IFRS needed? What potential issues can you see with requiring all public companies to prepare financial statements using IFRS?

Q1-16. What is the primary function of the auditor? To what does the auditor attest in its opinion?

Q1-17.[A] What are the objectives of financial accounting? Which of the financial statements satisfies each of these objectives?

Q1-18.[A] What are the two fundamental qualitative characteristics and the six enhancing qualitative characteristics of accounting information? Explain how each characteristic improves the quality of accounting disclosures.

MINI EXERCISES

LO2 Homework MBC

Macy's, Inc.
NYSE :: M

M1-19. Financing and Investing Relations, and Financing Sources
Total assets of Macy's, Inc. equals \$19,381 million and its equity is \$5,661 million. What is the amount of its liabilities? Does Macy's receive more financing from its owners or nonowners, and what percentage of financing is provided by its owners?

LO2 Homework MBC

Coca-Cola Company
NYSE :: KO

M1-20. Financing and Investing Relations, and Financing Sources
Total assets of The Coca-Cola Company equals \$87,896 million and its liabilities equal \$68,919 million. What is the amount of its equity? Does Coke receive more financing from its owners or nonowners, and what percentage of financing is provided by its owners?

LO2 Homework MBC

Hewlett-Packard
NYSE :: HPE
General Mills
NYSE :: GIS
Harley-Davidson
NYSE :: HOG

M1-21. Applying the Accounting Equation and Computing Financing Proportions
Use the accounting equation to compute the missing financial amounts (a), (b), and (c). Which of these companies is more owner-financed? Which of these companies is more nonowner-financed?

($ millions)	Assets	=	Liabilities	+	Equity
Hewlett-Packard Enterprise Company . . .	\$55,493.0		\$34,219.0		\$ (a)
General Mills	30,624.0		(b)		6,141.1
Harley-Davidson	(c)		8,128.4		1,844.3

M1-22. Identifying Key Numbers from Financial Statements
Access the most recent 10-K for Apple Inc., at the SEC's EDGAR database for financial reports (www.sec.gov). What are Apple's dollar amounts for assets, liabilities, and equity at September 29, 2018? Confirm that the accounting equation holds in this case. What percent of Apple's assets is financed from creditor financing sources?

LO3

Apple Inc.
NASDAQ :: AAPL

M1-23. Verifying Articulation of Financial Statements
Access the fiscal 2017 10-K for Nike at the SEC's EDGAR database of financial reports (www.sec.gov). Using its consolidated statement of stockholders' equity, prepare a table similar to **Exhibit 1.9** showing the articulation of its retained (reinvested) earnings for the year ended May 31, 2017. Was Nike more or less profitable in 2018 compared to 2017?

LO3

Nike
NYSE :: NKE

M1-24. Identifying Financial Statement Line Items and Accounts
Several line items and account titles are listed below. For each, indicate in which of the following financial statement(s) you would likely find the item or account: income statement (IS), balance sheet (BS), statement of stockholders' equity (SE), or statement of cash flows (SCF).

LO3

a. Cash asset
b. Expenses
c. Noncash assets
d. Contributed capital
e. Cash outflow for land
f. Retained earnings
g. Cash inflow for stock issued
h. Cash outflow for dividends
i. Net income

M1-25. Ethical Issues and Accounting Choices
Assume that you are a technology services provider and you must decide whether to record revenue from the installation of computer software for one of your clients. Your contract calls for acceptance of the software by the client within six months of installation before payment is due. Although you have not yet received formal acceptance, you are confident that it is forthcoming. Failure to record these revenues will cause your company to miss Wall Street's earnings estimates. What stakeholders will be affected by your decision and how might they be affected?

LO1

LOs link assignments to the Learning Objectives of each chapter.

M1-26. Internal Controls and Their Importance
The Sarbanes-Oxley legislation requires companies to report on the effectiveness of their internal controls. What are internal controls and their purpose? Why do you think Congress felt it to be such an important area to monitor and report?

LO4

EXERCISES

E1-27. Applying the Accounting Equation and Assessing Financing Contributions
Determine the missing amount from each of the separate situations (a), (b), and (c) below. Which of these companies is more owner-financed? Which of these companies is more creditor-financed?

LO2

Motorola Solutions
NYSE :: MSI
Kraft Foods
NASDAQ :: KHC
Merck & Co.
NYSE :: MRK

($ millions)	Assets	=	Liabilities	+	Equity
a. Motorola Solutions, Inc.	$ 8,208		$?		$ (1,742)
b. The Kraft Heinz Company	?		53,958		66,034
c. Merck & Co., Inc.	87,872		53,303		?

E1-28. Financial Information Users and Uses
Financial statements have a wide audience of interested stakeholders. Identify two or more financial statement users that are external to the company. Specify two questions for each user identified that could be addressed or aided by use of financial statements.

LO1

E1-29. Applying the Accounting Equation and Financial Statement Articulation
Answer the following questions. (*Hint*: Apply the accounting equation.)

LO2, 3

Intel
NASDAQ :: INTC
JetBlue Airways
NASDAQ :: JBLU

a. Intel Corporation had assets equal to $123,249 million and liabilities equal to $54,230 million for a recent year-end. What was the total equity for Intel's business at year-end?

b. At the beginning of a recent year, JetBlue Airways Corporation's assets were $9,323 million and its equity was $4,013 million. During the year, assets increased $458 million and liabilities decreased $363 million. What was its equity at the end of the year?

c. At the beginning of a recent year, The Walt Disney Company's liabilities equaled $49,637 million. During the year, assets increased by $2,809 million, and year-end assets equaled $98,598 million. Liabilities decreased $4,944 million during the year. What were its beginning and ending amounts for equity?

Walt Disney Company
NYSE :: DIS

Ticker symbols are provided for companies so one can easily obtain additional information.

LO3

E1-30. Financial Statement Relations to Compute Dividends

Colgate-Palmolive
NYSE :: CL

Colgate-Palmolive Company reports the following balances in its retained earnings.

($ millions)	2017	2016
Retained earnings	$20,531	$19,922

During 2017, Colgate-Palmolive reported net income of $2,024 million.

a. Assume that the only changes affecting retained earnings were net income and dividends. What amount of dividends did Colgate-Palmolive pay to its shareholders in 2017?

b. This dividend amount constituted what percent of its net income?

LO3

E1-31. Calculating Gross Profit and Preparing an Income Statement

Colgate-Palmolive
NYSE :: CL

In 2017, Colgate-Palmolive Company reported sales revenue of $15,454 million and cost of goods sold of $6,099 million. Its net income was $2,024 million. Calculate gross profit and prepare an income statement using the format illustrated in **Exhibit 1.8**.

LO2, 5

E1-32. Applying the Accounting Equation and Calculating Return on Equity and Debt-to-Equity Ratio

Alphabet, Inc.
NASDAQ :: GOOG

At the end of 2017, Alphabet, Inc., reported stockholders' equity of $152,502 million and total assets of $197,295 million. Its balance in stockholders' equity at the end of 2016 was $139,036 million. Net income in 2017 was $12,662 million.

a. Calculate Alphabet, Inc., return on equity ratio for 2017.

b. Calculate its debt-to-equity ratio as of December 31, 2017. (*Hint:* Apply the accounting equation to determine total liabilities.)

LO2, 5

E1-33. Applying the Accounting Equation and Computing Return on Equity and Debt-to-Equity Ratio

Daimler AG
OTC :: DDAIF

At the end of 2017, Daimler AG, reported stockholders' equity of €64,023 million and total assets of €255,605 million. Its stockholders' equity at the end of 2016 was €57,950 million. Net income in 2017 was €10,525 million.

a. Calculate Daimler's return on equity ratio for 2017.

b. Calculate Daimler's debt-to-equity ratio as of December 31, 2017.

LO1, 4

E1-34. Accounting in Society

Financial accounting plays an important role in modern society and business.

a. What role does financial accounting play in the allocation of society's financial resources?

b. What are three aspects of the accounting environment that can create ethical pressure on management?

LO6

E1-35.[A] Basic Assumptions, Principles, and Terminology in the Conceptual Framework

Match each item in the left column with the correct description in the right column.

_____ 1. Relevance
_____ 2. Verifiability
_____ 3. Going concern
_____ 4. Materiality
_____ 5. Monetary unit
_____ 6. Representational faithfulness
_____ 7. Accounting period
_____ 8. Comparability
_____ 9. Timeliness
_____ 10. Economic entity

a. Refers to whether or not a particular amount is large enough to affect a decision.

b. The activities of a business are considered to be independent and distinct from those of its owners or from other companies.

c. Accounting information should enable users to identify similarities and differences between sets of economic phenomena.

d. Financial reporting information must be available to decision makers before it loses its capacity to influence decisions.

e. Information is useful if it has the ability to influence decisions.

f. Consensus among measures assures that the information is free of error.

g. Accounting information should reflect the underlying economic events that it purports to measure.

h. The financial reports are presented in one consistent monetary unit, such as U.S. dollars.

i. A business is expected to have continuity in that it is expected to continue to operate indefinitely.

j. The life of a business can be divided into discrete accounting periods such as a year or quarter.

PROBLEMS

P1-36. Applying the Accounting Equation and Calculating Ratios

LO2, 5

Procter & Gamble
NYSE :: PG

The following table contains financial statement information for The Procter & Gamble Company ($ millions) for the fiscal years ended in June of each year:

Year	Assets	Liabilities	Equity	Net Income
2016	$127,136	$69,153	$?	$10,508
2017	?	64,628	54,178	15,326
2018	118,310	?	51,326	9,750

REQUIRED

a. Compute the missing amounts for assets, liabilities, and equity for each year.

b. Compute return on equity for 2017 and 2018. Let's assume that the median ROE for Fortune 500 companies is about 15%. How does P&G compare with this median?

c. Compute the debt-to-equity ratio for 2017 and 2018. Let's assume that the median debt-to-equity ratio for the Fortune 500 companies is 1.8. How does P&G compare to this median?

P1-37. Formulating Financial Statements from Raw Data

LO2, 3

General Mills
NYSE :: GIS

Following is selected financial information from General Mills, Inc., for its fiscal year ended May 27, 2018 ($ millions):

Cash and cash equivalents	$ 399.0
Net cash from operations	2,841.0
Sales.	15,740.4
Stockholders' equity	6,492.4
Cost of goods sold	10,312.9
Net cash from financing	5,445.5
Total liabilities	24,131.6
Other expenses, including income taxes	3,264.5
Noncash assets	30,225.0
Net cash from investing	(8,685.4)
Net income	2,163.0
Effect of exchange rate changes on cash	31.8
Cash, beginning year	766.1

REQUIRED

a. Prepare an income statement, balance sheet, and statement of cash flows for General Mills, Inc.

b. What portion of the financing is contributed by owners?

P1-38. Formulating Financial Statements from Raw Data

LO2, 3

Abercrombie & Fitch
NYSE :: ANF

Following is selected financial information from Abercrombie & Fitch for its fiscal year ended February 3, 2018 ($ millions):

Cash asset	$ 675.6
Cash flows from operations	285.7
Sales.	3,492.7
Stockholders' equity	1,252.5
Cost of goods sold	1,408.8
Cash flows from financing	(74.8)
Total liabilities	1,073.2
Other expenses, including income taxes	2,073.4
Noncash assets	1,650.1
Cash flows from investing.	(106.8)
Net income	10.5
Effect of exchange rate changes on cash	24.3
Cash, beginning year	547.2

REQUIRED

a. Prepare an income statement, balance sheet, and statement of cash flows for Abercrombie & Fitch.

b. Determine the owner and creditor financing levels.

LO3 **P1-39. Preparing Comparative Financial Statements from Raw Data**

Tilly's, Inc.
NYSE :: TLYS

Following is selected financial information for Tilly's, Inc.

($ thousands)	Feb. 3, 2018	Jan. 28, 2017
Cash and cash equivalents	$ 53,202	$ 78,994
Cash flow from operations	32,708	48,509
Cost of goods sold	401,529	400,493
Total liabilities	129,686	101,286
Total assets	290,111	290,506
Cash flow from financing	(17,622)	1,123
Sales revenue	576,899	568,952
Cash flow from investing	(40,878)	(21,658)
Other expenses, including income taxes	160,670	157,049

REQUIRED

Prepare balance sheets, income statements and cash flow statements for the years ended February 3, 2018 and January 28, 2017.

LO3 **P1-40. Preparing Comparative Financial Statements from Raw Data**

Tesla, Inc.
NASDAQ :: TSLA

Following is selected financial information for Tesla, Inc.

($ millions)	Dec. 31, 2017	Dec. 31, 2016
Cash and cash equivalents	$ 3,367.9	$ 3,393.2
Cash flow from operations	(60.7)	(123.8)
Cost of goods sold	9,536.3	5,400.9
Total liabilities	23,420.8	17,126
Total assets	28,655.4	22,664.1
Cash flow from financing	4,414.9	3,744.0
Sales revenue	11,758.8	7,000.1
Cash flow from investing	(4,419.0)	(1,416.4)
Other expenses, including income taxes	4,183.9	2,274.2
Effect of exchange rate changes on cash	39.5	(7.4)

REQUIRED

Prepare balance sheets, income statements and cash flow statements for the years ended December 31, 2017 and 2016.

LO3 **P1-41. Formulating a Statement of Stockholders' Equity from Raw Data**

Crocker Corporation began calendar-year 2019 with stockholders' equity of $100,000, consisting of contributed capital of $70,000 and retained earnings of $30,000. During 2019, it issued additional stock for total cash proceeds of $30,000. It also reported $50,000 of net income, of which $25,000 was paid as a cash dividend to shareholders.

REQUIRED

Prepare the December 31, 2019, statement of stockholders' equity for Crocker Corporation.

LO3 **P1-42. Formulating a Statement of Stockholders' Equity from Raw Data**

DP Systems, Inc., reports the following selected information at December 31, 2019 ($ millions):

Contributed capital, December 31, 2018 and 2019	$ 550
Retained earnings, December 31, 2018	2,437
Cash dividends, 2019	281
Net income, 2019	859

REQUIRED

Use this information to prepare its statement of stockholders' equity for 2019.

LO2, 3, 5 **P1-43. Analyzing and Interpreting Return on Equity**

Nokia
NYSE :: NOK

Nokia Corp. manufactures, markets, and sells phones and other electronics. Stockholders' equity for Nokia are €16,218 million in 2017 and €20,975 million in 2016. In 2017, Nokia reported a loss of €(1,458) million on sales of €23,147 million.

REQUIRED

a. What is Nokia's return on equity for 2017?

b. Nokia's total assets were €41,024 million at the end of 2017. Compute its debt-to-equity ratio.

c. What are total expenses for Nokia in 2017?

P1-44. Presenting an Income Statement and Computing Key Ratios

LO3, 5

Best Buy
NYSE :: BBY

Best Buy Co., Inc., reported the following amounts in its February 3, 2018, and January 28, 2017, financial statements.

($ millions)	2018	2017
Sales revenue	$42,151	$39,403
Cost of sales	32,275	29,963
Net income (loss)	1,000	1,228
Total assets	13,049	13,856
Stockholders' equity	3,612	4,709

REQUIRED

a. Prepare an income statement for Best Buy for the year ended February 3, 2018, using the format illustrated in **Exhibit 1.8**.

b. Calculate Best Buy's return on equity for the year ended February 3, 2018.

c. Compute Best Buy's debt-to-equity ratio as of February 3, 2018.

P1-45. Preparing Income Statements and Computing Key Ratios

LO3, 5

Facebook, Inc.
NASDAQ :: FB

Facebook, Inc. reported the following amounts in its 2017 and 2016 financial statements.

($ millions)	Dec. 31, 2017	Dec. 31, 2016
Total assets	$84,524	$64,961
Total liabilities	10,177	5,767
Retained earnings	33,990	21,670
Revenue	40,653	27,638
Operating expenses	20,450	15,211
Other expenses, including income taxes	4,269	2,210

REQUIRED

a. Prepare income statements for Facebook for 2017 and 2016. Use the format illustrated in **Exhibit 1.8**.

b. Compute Facebook's return on equity ratio for 2017 and 2016. Facebook's stockholders' equity at the end of 2015 was $4,899 million.

c. Compute Facebook's debt-to-equity ratio for 2017 and 2016.

CASES AND PROJECTS

C1-46. Preparing Comparative Income Statements and Computing Key Ratios

LO3, 5

Starbucks Corporation
NASDAQ :: SBUX

Starbucks Corporation reported the following data in its 2018 and 2017 10-K reports.

($ millions)	Sept. 30, 2018	Oct. 1, 2017
Total assets	$24,256.4	$14,365.6
Total liabilities	22,980.6	8,908.6
Sales revenue	24,719.5	22,386.8
Cost of goods sold	10,174.5	9,034.3
Other expenses, including income taxes	10,027	10,467.6

REQUIRED

a. Prepare income statements for Starbucks for the years ended September 30, 2018, and October 1, 2017. Use the format illustrated in **Exhibit 1.8**.

b. Compute Starbucks' return on equity ratio for 2018 and 2017. Starbucks stockholders' equity at October 2, 2016, was $5,890.7 million.

c. Compute Starbucks' debt-to-equity ratio for 2018 and 2017.

d. In 2018, Starbucks reported a lawsuit is in process where plaintiffs allege that Starbucks did not inform customers about the chemical acrylamide in their products (as required by California law). Starbucks did not record a liability (and expense), stating that the loss was possible but not probable. What would Starbucks' ROE have been if it had accrued a $3,700 million litigation liability (and expense)? What effect did this one-time charge have on the company's return on equity ratio? (*Hint:* Compute the ratio and include the litigation charge in other expenses, reduce stockholders' equity, and compare to the ratio computed in *b.*) Ignore tax effects.

e. Starbucks disclosed information about the pending litigation in the footnotes to its 2017 financial statements (before the case was settled). Discuss the costs and benefits of disclosing this information in its 2017 annual report.

LO2, 3, 5
The Gap
NYSE :: GPS
Nordstrom
NYSE :: JWN

C1-47. Computing and Interpreting Key Ratios and Formulating an Income Statement
Data from the financial statements of The Gap, Inc., and Nordstrom, Inc., are presented below.

($ millions)	The Gap	Nordstrom
Stockholders' equity, 2017	$ 3,144	$ 977
Stockholders' equity, 2016	2,904	870
Total assets, 2017	7,989	8,115
Total assets, 2016	7,610	7,858
Revenue, 2017	15,855	15,478
Cost of goods sold, 2017	9,789	9,890
Net income, 2017	848	437

REQUIRED

a. Compute the return on equity ratio for The Gap and Nordstrom for 2017. Which company earned the higher return for its shareholders?

b. Compute the debt-to-equity ratio for each company as of 2017. Which company relies more on creditor financing?

c. Prepare a 2017 income statement for each company using the format in **Exhibit 1.8**. For each firm, compute gross profit as a percentage of sales revenue.

d. Based on your answers to questions *a*, *b*, and *c*, compare these two retail companies. What might be the cause of any differences in the ratios that you computed?

LO5

JetBlue Airways
NASDAQ :: JBLU
Southwest Airlines
NYSE :: LUV

C1-48. Computing and Interpreting Key Ratios
Data from the financial statements of JetBlue Airways and Southwest Airlines are presented below.

($ millions)	JetBlue Airways	Southwest Airlines
Total liabilities, 2017	$1,108	$13,973
Total liabilities, 2016	1,444	14,845
Total assets, 2017	9,781	25,110
Total assets, 2016	9,323	23,286
Revenue, 2017	7,015	21,171
Net income, 2017	1,147	3,488

REQUIRED

a. Compute the return on equity ratio for JetBlue and Southwest for 2017. Which company earned the higher return for its shareholders?

b. Compute the debt-to-equity ratio for each company as of December 31, 2017. Which company relies more on creditor financing?

c. For each firm, compute net income as a percentage of revenue in 2017.

d. Based on your answers to questions *a*, *b*, and *c*, compare these two competitors. What might be the cause of any differences in the ratios that you computed?

LO1, 3, 5

C1-49. Interpreting Financial Statement Information
Paula Seale is negotiating the purchase of an extermination firm called Total Pest Control. Seale has been employed by a national pest control service and knows the technical side of the business. However, she knows little about accounting data and financial statements. The sole owner of the firm, Meg Krey, has provided Seale with income statements for the past three years, which show an average net income of $72,000 per year. The latest balance sheet shows total assets of $285,000 and liabilities of $45,000. Seale brings the following matters to your attention and requests advice.

1. Krey is asking $300,000 for the firm. She has told Seale that because the firm has been earning 30% on its investment, the price should be higher than the net assets on the balance sheet (net assets equals total assets minus total liabilities).
2. Seale has noticed no salary for Krey on the income statements, even though she worked half-time in the business. Krey explained that because she had other income, the firm only paid

$18,000 in cash dividends to Krey (the sole shareholder). If she purchases the firm, Seale will hire a full-time manager for the firm at an annual salary of $36,000.

3. Krey's tax returns for the past three years report a lower net income for the firm than the amounts shown in the financial statements. Seale is skeptical about the accounting principles used in preparing the financial statements.

REQUIRED

a. How did Krey arrive at the 30% return figure in point 1? If Seale accepts Krey's average annual net income figure of $72,000, what would Seale's percentage return be, assuming that the net income remained at the same level and that the firm was purchased for $300,000?

b. Should the dividend to Krey affect the net income reported in the financial statements? What will Seale's percentage return be if she takes into consideration the $36,000 salary she plans to pay a full-time manager?

c. Could there be legitimate reasons for the difference between net income shown in the financial statements and net income reported on the tax returns, as mentioned in point 3? How might Seale obtain additional assurance about the propriety of the financial statements?

C1-50. Management, Auditing, and Ethical Behavior **LO1, 4**

Jackie Hardy, CPA, has a brother, Ted, in the retail clothing business. Ted ran the business as its sole owner for 10 years. During this 10-year period, Jackie helped Ted with various accounting matters. For example, Jackie designed the accounting system for the company, prepared Ted's personal income tax returns (which included financial data about the clothing business), and recommended various cost control procedures. Ted paid Jackie for all these services. A year ago, Ted markedly expanded the business; Ted is president of the corporation and also chairs the corporation's board of directors. The board of directors has overall responsibility for corporate affairs. When the corporation was formed, Ted asked Jackie to serve on its board of directors. Jackie accepted. In addition, Jackie now prepares the corporation's income tax returns and continues to advise her brother on accounting matters.

Recently, the corporation applied for a large bank loan. The bank wants audited financial statements for the corporation before it will decide on the loan request. Ted asked Jackie to perform the audit. Jackie replied that she cannot do the audit because the code of ethics for CPAs requires that she be independent when providing audit services.

REQUIRED

a. Why is it important that a CPA be independent when providing audit services?

b. Which of Jackie's activities or relationships impair her independence?

SOLUTIONS TO REVIEW PROBLEMS

Mid-Chapter Review

SOLUTION

a.

ADIDAS
Balance Sheet (€ millions)
December 31, 2017

Cash	€ 1,598	Total liabilities	€ 8,087
Noncash assets	12,924	Stockholders' equity	6,435
Total assets	€14,522	Total liabilities and stockholders' equity	€14,522

ADIDAS
Income Statement (€ millions)
For Year Ended December 31, 2017

Sales revenue	€21,218
Cost of goods sold	10,514
Gross profit	10,704
Other expenses	9,604
Net income (loss)	€ 1,100

ADIDAS Statement of Cash Flows (€ millions) For Year Ended December 31, 2017	
Cash flow from operations	€1,648
Cash flow from investing	(680)
Cash flow from financing	(769)
Effect of exchange rates on cash	(111)
Net increase (decrease) in cash	88
Cash, beginning of year	1,510
Cash, end of year	€1,598

b. Adidas reported revenues of €21,218 million (which is approximately equivalent to $28,644 million) compared to Nike's $36,397 million. Adidas reported net income of €1,100 million ($1,485 million) compared to Nike's $1,933 million. Adidas' operations produced cash flow of €88 million ($119 million) while Nike's cash flow from operations was $441 million. Hence, based on revenues, Nike is a larger company indicated by its substantially larger sales revenue. Its total assets of $22,536 million are also greater than Adidas' total assets of €14,522 million (or $19,605 million). Nike's operating cash flows and income are also larger than those of Adidas.

Chapter-End Review

SOLUTION

a. $\text{ROE} = \frac{1{,}100}{[(6{,}435 + 6{,}455)/2]} = 0.171 \text{ or } 17.1\%$

b. $\text{Debt-to-equity} = \frac{8{,}087}{6{,}435} = 1.26$

c. One additional benefit to using ratios to analyze financial information is that ratios can be computed for amounts denominated in any currency. Thus, we can compare Adidas and Nike without translating euros into dollars. Adidas' ROE of 17.1% is almost identical to Nike's of 17.4%. This means that both companies earned a very similar return for their stockholders in 2017.

Adidas' debt-to-equity ratio is 1.26 compared to Nike's 1.30. This means that Nike relies slightly more on debt, but again the companies are quite similar. A similar debt-to-equity ratio indicates a similar level of risk associated with an investment in either company.

Constructing Financial Statements

LEARNING OBJECTIVES

1. Describe and construct the balance sheet and understand how it can be used for analysis. (p. 44)
2. Use the financial statement effects template (FSET) to analyze transactions. (p. 49)
3. Describe and construct the income statement and discuss how it can be used to evaluate management performance. (p. 53)
4. Explain revenue recognition, accrual accounting, and their effects on retained earnings. (p. 54)
5. Illustrate equity transactions and the statement of stockholders' equity. (p. 60)
6. Use journal entries and T-accounts to analyze and record transactions. (p. 62)
7. Compute net working capital, the current ratio, and the quick ratio, and explain how they reflect liquidity. (p. 71)

WALGREENS
www.walgreens.com

More than a hundred years have passed since Charles R. Walgreen, Sr. purchased his first pharmacy in 1901. In that time, the company that bears his name has grown remarkably. As of August 31, 2017, **Walgreens Boots Alliance, Inc.**, operated over 12,000 locations in 50 states and 11 countries; it had 385,000 employees.

Even with the company's recent success, Walgreens faces a number of challenges. The economic changes of the recent past have made consumers more cautious and cost-conscious. Pharmacy sales constitute two-thirds of Walgreens' sales, and almost all of those are paid for by a third party. The success of that business depends significantly on factors like the growth of generic pharmaceuticals, legislative changes such as the Affordable Care Act, and the relationships with Pharmacy Benefit Managers. Furthermore, Walgreens faces rising costs for pharmaceuticals and increasing competition from other drugstore chains like **CVS Health Corp.** and discount retailers like **Wal-Mart Stores, Inc.**

These factors, however, have not prevented Walgreens from reporting profits continuously for the last five years. Chief Executive Officer, Gregory D. Wasson, seems to have found a strategy for profitable growth by slowing the rate of new store openings and turning its focus to cost control and operating efficiencies.

Walgreens increased its geographic footprint with its 2014 acquisition of **Alliance Boots GmbH**, an international health and beauty group. Subsequent

to August 31, 2014, the merged companies have reorganized into Walgreens Boots Alliance, Inc. The company is poised to increase sales substantially with the purchase of almost 2,000 Rite-Aid Stores in late 2017.

As we discovered in Chapter 1, companies like Walgreens prepare financial statements annually. These financial statements allow investors and creditors to assess the impact of changing economic conditions on the company's financial health and performance.

This chapter will introduce and explain financial statements using Walgreens as its prime example. The chapter also introduces some key accounting procedures such as transaction analysis, journal entries, and posting. The general ledger, key accounting assumptions, and basic accounting definitions are also introduced.

Sources: "In the beginning . . . " Walgreens history on the corporate Website; Walgreens Boots Alliance, Inc., and Subsidiaries 2017 10-K annual report; *Fortune* magazine, *Wall Street Journal*, *Chicago Tribune, Bloomberg News* Websites.

CHAPTER ORGANIZATION

Constructing Financial Statements

Reporting Financial Condition	Reporting Financial Performance	Reporting on Equity	Journalizing and Posting Transactions	Financial Statement Analysis
• Assets • Liabilities • Equity • Recording Balance Sheet Transactions • Financial Statement Effects Template	• Revenue Recognition • Accrual Accounting • Retained Earnings • Recording Income Statement Transactions	• Recording Equity Transactions • Statement of Stockholders' Equity	• T-Account • Debit and Credit System • Journal Entry • Analyze, Journalize, and Post	• Net Working Capital • Current Ratio • Quick Ratio

In Chapter 1, we introduced the four financial statements—the balance sheet, the income statement, the cash flow statement, and the statement of stockholders' equity. In this chapter and in Chapter 3, we turn our attention to how the balance sheet and income statement are prepared. The statement of cash flows is discussed in detail in Chapter 4, and the statement of stockholders' equity is discussed in detail in Chapter 11.

1 **LO1** Describe and construct the balance sheet and understand how it can be used for analysis.

REPORTING FINANCIAL CONDITION

The balance sheet reports on a company's financial condition and is divided into three components: assets, liabilities, and stockholders' equity. It provides us with information about the resources available to management and the claims against those resources by creditors and shareholders. At the end of August 2017, Walgreens reports total assets of $66,009 million, total liabilities of $37,735 million, and equity of $28,274 million. Drawing on the **accounting equation**, Walgreens' balance sheet is summarized as follows ($ millions).

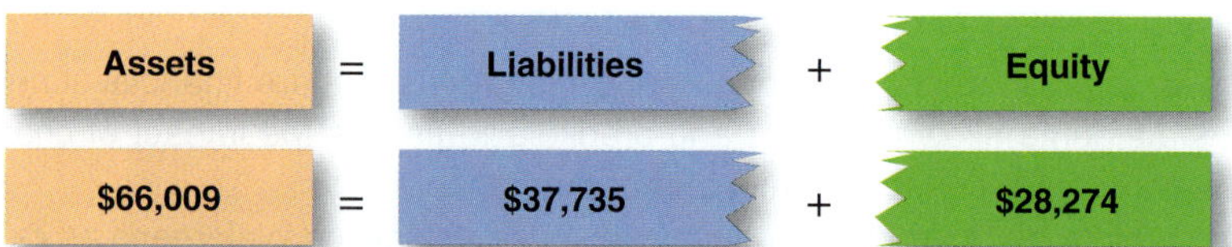

The balance sheet is prepared at a *point in time.* It is a snapshot of the financial condition of the company at that instant. For Walgreens, the above balance sheet amounts were reported at the close of business on August 31, 2017. Balance sheet accounts carry over from one period to the next; that is, the ending balance from one period becomes the beginning balance for the next period.

Walgreens' summarized 2017 and 2016 balance sheets are shown in **Exhibit 2.1**. These balance sheets report the assets and the liabilities and shareholders' equity amounts as of August 31, the company's fiscal year-end. Walgreens had $66,009 million in assets at the end of August 31, 2017, with the same amount reported in liabilities and shareholders' equity. Companies report their audited financial results on a yearly basis.[1] Many companies use the calendar year as their fiscal year. Other companies prefer to prepare their yearly report at a time when business activity is at a low level. Walgreens is an example of the latter reporting choice.

Assets

An **asset** is a resource owned or controlled by a company and expected to provide the company with future economic benefits. When a company incurs a cost to acquire future benefits, we say

[1] Companies also report quarterly financial statements, and these are reviewed by the independent accountant, but not audited.

EXHIBIT 2.1 Walgreens' Balance Sheet

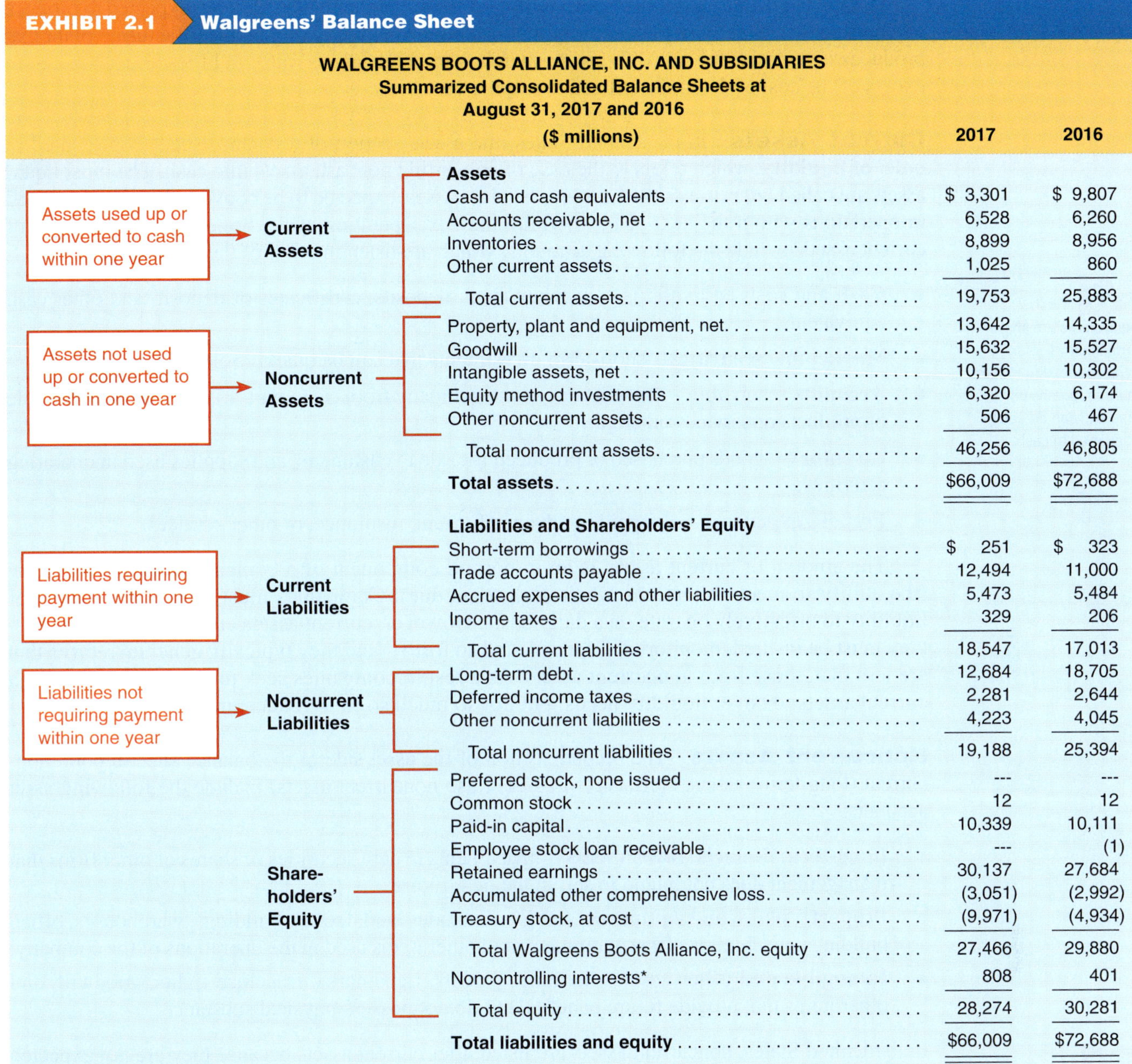

WALGREENS BOOTS ALLIANCE, INC. AND SUBSIDIARIES
Summarized Consolidated Balance Sheets at August 31, 2017 and 2016
($ millions)

	2017	2016
Assets		
Cash and cash equivalents	$ 3,301	$ 9,807
Accounts receivable, net	6,528	6,260
Inventories	8,899	8,956
Other current assets	1,025	860
Total current assets	19,753	25,883
Property, plant and equipment, net	13,642	14,335
Goodwill	15,632	15,527
Intangible assets, net	10,156	10,302
Equity method investments	6,320	6,174
Other noncurrent assets	506	467
Total noncurrent assets	46,256	46,805
Total assets	$66,009	$72,688
Liabilities and Shareholders' Equity		
Short-term borrowings	$ 251	$ 323
Trade accounts payable	12,494	11,000
Accrued expenses and other liabilities	5,473	5,484
Income taxes	329	206
Total current liabilities	18,547	17,013
Long-term debt	12,684	18,705
Deferred income taxes	2,281	2,644
Other noncurrent liabilities	4,223	4,045
Total noncurrent liabilities	19,188	25,394
Preferred stock, none issued	---	---
Common stock	12	12
Paid-in capital	10,339	10,111
Employee stock loan receivable	---	(1)
Retained earnings	30,137	27,684
Accumulated other comprehensive loss	(3,051)	(2,992)
Treasury stock, at cost	(9,971)	(4,934)
Total Walgreens Boots Alliance, Inc. equity	27,466	29,880
Noncontrolling interests*	808	401
Total equity	28,274	30,281
Total liabilities and equity	$66,009	$72,688

*** Noncontrolling interests arise from the practice of consolidating subsidiaries that are controlled, but not wholly owned. Chapters 11 and 12 provide a brief introduction to this topic.**

that cost is capitalized and an asset is recorded. An asset must possess two characteristics to be reported on the balance sheet:

1. It must be owned or controlled by the company.
2. It must possess probable future benefits that can be measured in monetary units.

The first requirement, that the asset must be owned or controlled by the company, implies that the company has legal title to the asset or has the unrestricted right to use the asset. This requirement presumes that the cost to acquire the asset has been incurred, either by paying cash, by trading other assets, or by assuming an obligation to make future payments.

The second requirement indicates that the company expects to receive some future benefit from ownership of the asset. Benefits can be the expected cash receipts from selling the asset or from selling products or services produced by the asset. Benefits can also refer to the receipt of other noncash assets, such as accounts receivable or the reduction of a liability (e.g., when assets are given up to settle debts). It also requires that a monetary value can be assigned to the asset.

Companies acquire assets to yield a return for their shareholders. Assets are expected to produce revenues, either directly (e.g., inventory that is sold) or indirectly (e.g., a manufacturing plant that produces inventories for sale). To create shareholder value, assets must yield resources that are in excess of the cost of the funds utilized to acquire the assets.

Current Assets In the United States, the assets section of a balance sheet is presented in order of **liquidity**, which refers to the ease of converting noncash assets into cash. The most liquid assets are called **current assets**. Current assets are assets expected to be converted into cash or used in operations within the next year, or within the next operating cycle. Some typical examples of current assets include the following accounts, which are listed in order of their liquidity:

FYI Cash equivalents are short-term, highly liquid investments that mature in three months or less and can be easily converted to cash.

- **Cash** and **cash equivalents**—currency, bank deposits, certificates of deposit, and other cash equivalents;
- **Marketable securities**—short-term investments that can be quickly sold to raise cash;
- **Accounts receivable**—amounts due to the company from customers arising from the past sale of products or services on credit;
- **Inventory**—goods purchased or produced for sale to customers, and supplies used in operating activities;
- **Prepaid expenses**—costs paid in advance for rent, insurance, or other services.

The amount of current assets is an important component of a company's overall liquidity (the ability to meet obligations when they come due). Companies must maintain a degree of liquidity to effectively operate on a daily basis. However, current assets are expensive to hold—they must be insured, monitored, financed, and so forth—and they typically generate returns that are less than those from noncurrent assets. As a result, companies seek to maintain just enough current assets to cover liquidity needs, but not so much so as to reduce income unnecessarily.

Noncurrent Assets The second section of the asset side of the balance sheet reports noncurrent (long-term) assets. **Noncurrent assets** (also noncurrent assets) include the following asset accounts:

- **Long-term financial investments**—investments in debt securities or shares of other firms that management does not intend to sell in the near future;
- **Property, plant, and equipment (PPE)**—includes land, factory buildings, warehouses, office buildings, machinery, office equipment, and other items used in the operations of the company;
- **Intangible and other assets**—includes patents, trademarks, franchise rights, goodwill, and other items that provide future benefits, but do not possess physical substance.

In the United States, noncurrent assets are listed after current assets because they are not expected to expire or be converted into cash within one year.

FYI Excluded assets often relate to self-developed, knowledge-based assets, like organizational effectiveness and technology. This is one reason that knowledge-based industries are so difficult to analyze. Yet, excluded assets are presumably reflected in company market values. This fact can explain why the firm's market capitalization (its share price multiplied by the number of shares) is often greater than the book value shown on the balance sheet.

Measuring Assets Physical (tangible) assets that are intended to be used, such as inventory and property, plant, and equipment, are reported on the balance sheet at their **historical cost** (with adjustments for depreciation in some cases). Historical cost refers to the original acquisition cost. The use of historical cost to report asset values has the advantage of **reliability**. Historical costs are reliable because the acquisition cost (the amount of cash paid to purchase the asset) can be objectively determined and accurately measured. The disadvantage of historical costs is that some assets can be significantly undervalued on the balance sheet. For example, the land in Anaheim, California, on which Disneyland was built more than 50 years ago, was purchased for a mere fraction of its current fair value.

Some assets, such as marketable securities, are reported at current value or **fair value**. The current value of these assets can be easily obtained from online price quotes or from reliable sources such as **The Wall Street Journal**. Reporting certain assets at fair value increases the **relevance** of the information presented in the balance sheet. Relevance refers to how useful the information is to those who use the financial statements for decision making. For example, marketable securities are intended to be sold for cash when cash is needed by the company to pay its obligations. Therefore, the most relevant value for marketable securities is the amount of cash that the company would receive if the securities were sold.

Only those asset values that have probable future benefits are recorded on the balance sheet. For this reason, some of a company's most important assets are often not reflected among the reported assets of the company. For example, the well-recognized Walgreens logo does not appear as an asset on the company's balance sheet. The image of Mickey Mouse and that of the Aflac Duck are also absent from **The Walt Disney Company**'s and **Aflac Incorporated**'s balance sheets. Each of these items is referred to as an unrecognized intangible asset. These intangible assets and others, such as the Coke bottle silhouette, the Kleenex name, or a well-designed supply chain, are measured and reported on the balance sheet only when they are purchased from a third party (usually in a merger). As a result, *internally created* intangible assets, such as the Mickey Mouse image, are not reported on a balance sheet, even though many of these internally created intangible assets are of enormous value.

Liabilities and Equity

Liabilities and equity represent the sources of capital to the company that are used to finance the acquisition of assets. **Liabilities** represent the firm's obligations for borrowed funds from lenders or bond investors, as well as obligations to pay suppliers, employees, tax authorities, and other parties. These obligations can be interest-bearing or non-interest-bearing. **Equity** represents capital that has been invested by the shareholders, either directly via the purchase of stock (when issued by the company), or indirectly in the form of earnings that are reinvested in the business and not paid out as dividends (retained earnings). We discuss liabilities and equity in this section.

The liabilities and equity sections of Walgreens' balance sheets for 2017 and 2016 are reproduced in the lower section of **Exhibit 2.1**. Walgreens reports $37,735 million of total liabilities and $28,274 million of equity as of its 2017 fiscal year-end. The total of liabilities and equity equals $66,009—the same as the total assets—because the shareholders have the residual claim on the company.

A liability is a probable future economic sacrifice resulting from a current or past event. The economic sacrifice can be a future cash payment to a creditor, or it can be an obligation to deliver goods or services to a customer at a future date. A liability must be reported in the balance sheet when each of the following three conditions is met:

1. The future sacrifice is probable.
2. The amount of the obligation is known or can be reasonably estimated.
3. The transaction or event that caused the obligation has occurred.

When conditions 1 and 2 are satisfied, but the transaction that caused the obligation has not occurred, the obligation is called an **executory contract** and no liability is reported. An example of such an obligation is a purchase order. When a company signs an agreement to purchase materials from a supplier, it commits to making a future cash payment of a known amount. However, the obligation to pay for the materials is not considered a liability until the materials are delivered. Therefore, even though the company is contractually obligated to make the cash payment to the supplier, a liability is not recorded on the balance sheet. However, information about purchase commitments and other executory contracts is useful to investors and creditors, and the obligations, if material, should be disclosed in the footnotes to the financial statements. In its annual report, Walgreens reports open inventory purchase orders of $1,944 million at the end of fiscal year 2017.

Current Liabilities Liabilities on the balance sheet are listed according to maturity. Obligations that are due within one year or within one operating cycle are called **current liabilities**. Some examples of common current liabilities include:

- **Accounts payable**—amounts owed to suppliers for goods and services purchased on credit. Walgreens uses another common name for this account—trade accounts payable.
- **Accrued liabilities**—obligations for expenses that have been recorded but not yet paid. Examples include accrued compensation payable (wages earned by employees but not yet paid), accrued interest payable (interest on debt that has not been paid), and accrued taxes (taxes due).
- **Short-term borrowings**—short-term debt payable to banks or other creditors.

- **Deferred (unearned) revenues**—an obligation created when the company accepts payment in advance for goods or services it will deliver in the future. Sometimes also called advances from customers or customer deposits.
- **Current maturities of long-term debt**—the current portion of long-term debt that is due to be paid within one year.

Noncurrent Liabilities **Noncurrent liabilities** (also noncurrent liabilities) are obligations to be paid after one year. Examples of noncurrent liabilities include:

FYI Borrowings are often titled **Notes Payable**. When a company borrows money, it normally signs a promissory note agreeing to pay the money back (including interest)—hence, the title notes payable.

- **Long-term debt**—amounts borrowed from creditors that are scheduled to be repaid more than one year in the future. Any portion of long-term debt that is due within one year is reclassified as a current liability called *current maturities of long-term debt.*
- **Other long-term liabilities**—various obligations, such as warranty and deferred compensation liabilities and long-term tax liabilities, that will be satisfied at least a year in the future. These items are discussed in later chapters.

Detailed information about a company's noncurrent liabilities, such as payment schedules, interest rates, and restrictive covenants, are provided in the footnotes to the financial statements.

BUSINESS INSIGHT

How Much Debt Is Reasonable? In August 2017, Walgreens reports total assets of $66,009 million, liabilities of $37,735 ($18,547 current + $19,188 noncurrent) million, and equity of $28,274 million. This means that Walgreens finances 57% of its assets with borrowed funds and 43% with shareholder investment. Liabilities represent claims for fixed amounts, while shareholders' equity represents a flexible claim (because shareholders have a residual claim). Companies must monitor their financing sources and amounts because borrowing too much increases risk, and investors must recognize that companies may have substantial obligations (like Walgreens' inventory purchase commitment) that do not appear on the balance sheet.

Stockholders' Equity Equity reflects capital provided by the shareholders of the company. It is often referred to as a *residual interest.* That is, stockholders have a claim on any assets that are not needed to meet the company's obligations to creditors. The following are examples of items that are typically included in stockholders' equity:

Contributed Capital

- **Common stock**—the capital received from the primary owners of the company. Total common stock is divided into shares. One share of common stock represents the smallest fractional unit of ownership of a company.[2]
- **Additional paid-in capital**—amounts received from the common shareholders in addition to the par value or stated value of the common stock.
- **Treasury stock**—the amount paid for its own common stock that the company has reacquired, which reduces contributed capital.

Earned Capital

- **Retained earnings**—the accumulated earnings that have not been distributed to stockholders as dividends.
- **Accumulated other comprehensive income or loss**—accumulated changes in equity that are not reported in the income statement; discussed in Chapters 11 and 12.

The equity section of a balance sheet consists of two basic components: contributed capital and earned capital. **Contributed capital** is the net funding that a company has received from issuing and reacquiring its equity shares. That is, the funds received from issuing shares less any funds paid

[2] Many companies' common shares have a par value, but that value has little economic significance. For instance, Walgreens' shares have a par value of $0.01 per share, while the market price of the stock is about $65 at the time of this writing. In most cases, the sum of common stock (at par) and additional paid-in capital represents the value of stockholders' contributions to the business in exchange for shares.

to repurchase such shares. In 2017, Walgreens' equity section reports $28,274 million in equity. Its contributed capital is a $380 million ($12 million in common stock plus $10,339 million in [additional] paid-in capital minus $9,971 million in treasury stock).

Earned capital is the cumulative net income (and losses) retained by the company (not paid out to shareholders as dividends). Earned capital typically includes retained earnings and accumulated other comprehensive income or loss. Walgreens' earned capital is $27,086 million ($30,137 million in retained earnings minus $3,051 million in accumulated other comprehensive loss). Other comprehensive income is discussed in Chapters 11 and 12.

RETAINED EARNINGS There is an important relation for retained earnings that reconciles its beginning and ending balances as follows:

Beginning retained earnings
+ Net income (or – Net loss)
– Dividends
= Ending retained earnings

This relation is useful to remember, even though there are other items that sometimes impact retained earnings. We revisit this relation after our discussion of the income statement and show how it links the balance sheet and income statement.

FYI **Equity** is a term used to describe owners' claims on the company. For corporations, the terms **shareholders' equity** and **stockholders' equity** are also used to describe owners' claims. We use all three terms interchangeably.

MID-CHAPTER REVIEW 1

Assume Schaefer's Pharmacy, Inc., has the following detailed accounts as part of its accounting system. Enter the letter of the balance sheet category A through E in the space next to the balance sheet items numbered 1 through 20. Enter an **X** in the space if the item is not reported on the balance sheet.

A. Current assets
B. Noncurrent assets
C. Current liabilities
D. Noncurrent liabilities
E. Equity

_____ 1. Accounts receivable
_____ 2. Short-term notes payable
_____ 3. Land
_____ 4. Retained earnings
_____ 5. Intangible assets
_____ 6. Common stock
_____ 7. Repairs expense
_____ 8. Equipment
_____ 9. Treasury stock
_____ 10. Investments (noncurrent)
_____ 11. Rent expense
_____ 12. Cash
_____ 13. Buildings
_____ 14. Accounts payable
_____ 15. Prepaid rent
_____ 16. Borrowings (due in 25 years)
_____ 17. Marketable securities
_____ 18. Inventories
_____ 19. Additional paid-in capital
_____ 20. Unearned revenue

The solution to this review problem can be found on page 93.

Analyzing and Recording Transactions for the Balance Sheet

LO2 Use the financial statement effects template (FSET) to analyze transactions.

The balance sheet is the foundation of the accounting system. Every event, or transaction, that is recorded in the accounting system must be recorded so that the following accounting equation is maintained:

Assets = Liabilities + Equity

We use this fundamental relation throughout the book to help us assess the financial impact of transactions. This is our "step 1" when we encounter a transaction. Our "steps 2 and 3" are to journalize those financial impacts and then post them to individual accounts to emphasize the linkage from entries to accounts (steps 2 and 3 are explained later in this chapter).

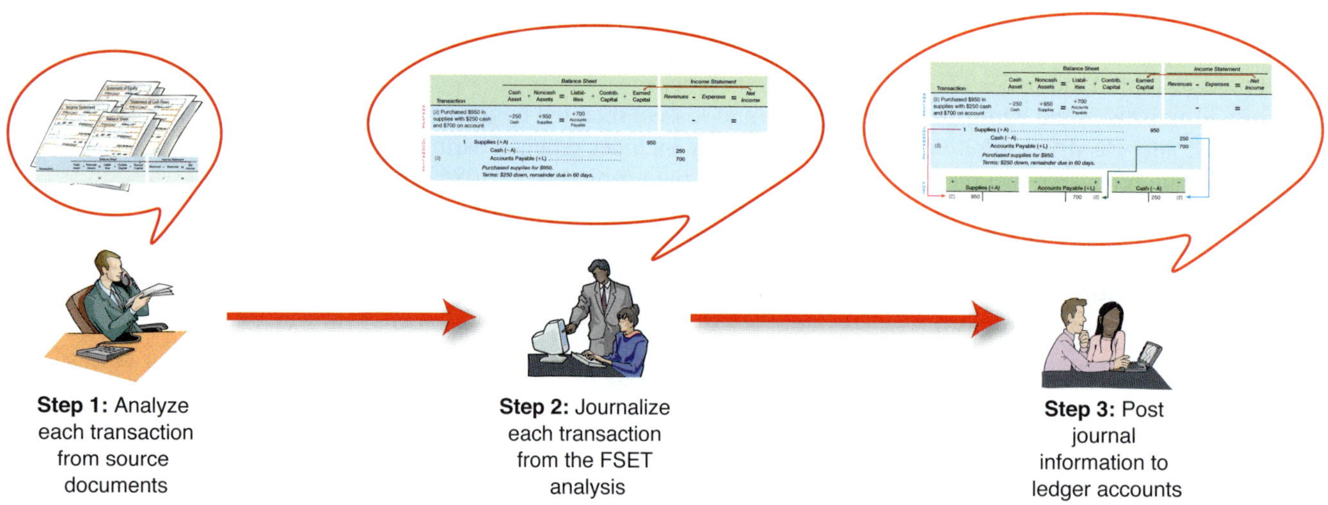

Financial Statement Effects Template To analyze the financial impacts of transactions, we employ the following **financial statement effects template (FSET)**.

	Balance Sheet									Income Statement				
Transaction	**Cash Asset**	+	**Noncash Assets**	=	**Liabil-ities**	+	**Contrib. Capital**	+	**Earned Capital**	***Revenues***	-	***Expenses***	=	***Net Income***
				=							-		=	

The template accomplishes several things. First and foremost, it captures the transaction that must be recorded in the accounting system. That "recording" function is our focus for the next several pages. But accounting is not just recording financial data; it is also the reporting of information that is useful to financial statement readers. So, the template also depicts the effects of the transaction on the four financial statements: balance sheet, income statement, statement of stockholders' equity, and statement of cash flows. For the balance sheet, we differentiate between cash and noncash assets so as to identify the cash effects of transactions. Likewise, equity is separated into the contributed and earned capital components (the latter includes retained earnings as its major element). Finally, income statement effects are separated into revenues, expenses, and net income (the updating of retained earnings is denoted with an arrow line running from net income to earned capital). This template provides a convenient means to demonstrate the relationships among the four financial statements and of representing financial accounting transactions and events in a simple, concise manner for analyzing, journalizing, and posting.

The Account An **account** is a mechanism for accumulating the effects of an organization's transactions and events. For instance, an account labeled "Merchandise Inventory" allows a retailer's accounting system to accumulate information about the receipts of inventory from suppliers and the delivery of inventory to customers.

Before a transaction is recorded, we first analyze the effect of the transaction on the accounting equation by asking the following questions:

- What accounts are affected by the transaction?
- What is the direction and magnitude of each effect?

To maintain the equality of the accounting equation, each transaction must affect (at least) two accounts. For example, a transaction might increase assets and increase equity by equal amounts. Another transaction might increase one asset and decrease another asset, while yet another might decrease an asset and decrease a liability. These *dual effects* are what constitute the **double-entry accounting system**.

The account is a record of increases and decreases for each important asset, liability, equity, revenue, or expense item. The **chart of accounts** is a listing of the titles (and identification codes) of all accounts for a company.[3] Account titles are commonly grouped into five categories: assets, liabilities, equity, revenues, and expenses. The accounts for Natural Beauty Supply, Inc. (introduced below), follow:

Assets

110 Cash
120 Accounts Receivable
130 Other Receivables
140 Inventory
150 Prepaid Insurance
160 Security Deposit
170 Fixtures and Equipment
175 Accumulated Depreciation—Fixtures and Equipment

Liabilities

210 Accounts Payable
220 Interest Payable
230 Wages Payable
240 Taxes Payable
250 Unearned Revenue
260 Notes Payable

Equity

310 Common Stock
320 Retained Earnings

Revenues and Income

410 Sales Revenue
420 Interest Revenue

Expenses

510 Cost of Goods Sold
520 Wages Expense
530 Rent Expense
540 Advertising Expense
550 Depreciation Expense—Fixtures and Equipment
560 Insurance Expense
570 Interest Expense
580 Tax Expense

Each transaction entered in the template must maintain the equality of the accounting equation, and the accounts cited must correspond to those in its chart of accounts.

Transaction Analysis Using FSET To illustrate the effect of transactions on the accounting equation and, correspondingly, the financial statements, we consider the business activities of Natural Beauty Supply, Inc., Natural Beauty Supply was established to operate as a retailer of organic beauty and health care products, though the owners hoped that they also would become a wholesale provider of such products to local salons. The company began business on November 1, 2018. The following transactions occurred on the first day of business:

(1) Nov. 1 Investors contributed $20,000 cash to launch Natural Beauty Supply, Inc. (NBS), in exchange for 10,000 shares of NBS stock.

(2) Nov. 1 NBS borrowed $5,000 cash from a family member of the company's founders by signing a note. The $5,000 must be paid back on November 30 with interest of $50.

(3) Nov. 1 NBS arranged to rent a storefront location and began to use the property. The landlord requires payment of $1,500 at the end of each month. NBS paid a $2,000 security deposit that will be returned at the end of the lease.

(4) Nov. 1 NBS purchased, on account (i.e., to be paid later), and received $17,000 of inventory consisting of natural soaps and beauty products.

Let's begin by analyzing the financial statement effects of the first transaction. At the beginning of its life, Natural Beauty Supply has accounts that show no balances, so the financial statements would be filled with zeroes. In the company's very first transaction, shareholders invested $20,000 cash in Natural Beauty Supply, and the company issued 10,000 shares of common stock, which increased equity (contributed capital). This transaction is reflected in the following financial statements effects template.

[3] Accounting systems at large organizations have much more detail in their account structures than we use here. The account structure's detail allows management to accumulate information by responsibility center or by product line or by customer.

	Balance Sheet					Income Statement		
Transaction	Cash Asset +	Noncash Assets =	Liabil-ities +	Contrib. Capital +	Earned Capital	Revenues −	Expenses =	Net Income
(1) Issue stock for $20,000 cash.	+20,000 Cash	=		+20,000 Common Stock		−	=	

Assets (cash) and equity (common stock) increased by the same amount, and the accounting equation remains in balance (as it always must).

In the second transaction, Natural Beauty Supply borrowed cash by signing a note (loan agreement) with a family member. This transaction increased cash (an asset) and increased notes payable (a liability) by the same amount. The notes payable liability recognizes the obligation to repay the family member.

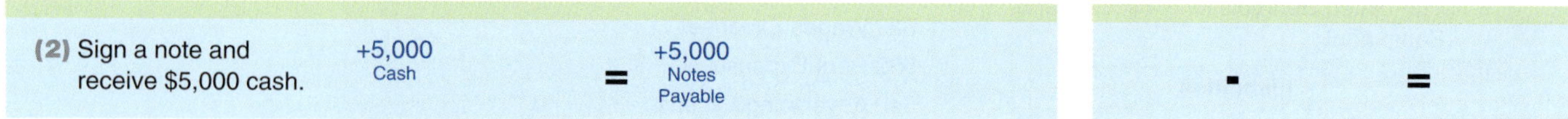

Transaction	Cash Asset +	Noncash Assets =	Liabilities +	Contrib. Capital +	Earned Capital	Revenues −	Expenses =	Net Income
(2) Sign a note and receive $5,000 cash.	+5,000 Cash	=	+5,000 Notes Payable			−	=	

At this point, Natural Beauty Supply would not record anything for the interest that will eventually be paid. Interest expense occurs with the passage of time, and at the moment of borrowing on November 1, there is no interest obligation to be recognized.

Also on November 1, 2018, Natural Beauty Supply arranged for rental of a location and paid a security deposit which it expects to be returned at a future date. This transaction decreased cash (an asset) and increased security deposits (another asset). We'll assume that Natural Beauty Supply hopes to move to a more upscale location within a year, so the security deposit is considered a current asset.

Transaction	Cash Asset +	Noncash Assets =	Liabilities +	Contrib. Capital +	Earned Capital	Revenues −	Expenses =	Net Income
(3) Sign rental agreement and pay $2,000 security deposit.	−2,000 Cash	+2,000 Security Deposit =				−	=	

Like the case of interest expense, Natural Beauty Supply would make no entry for rent expense on November 1, because the obligation to pay for the use of the location occurs with the passage of time.

Finally, Natural Beauty Supply purchased and received $17,000 of inventory on credit. This transaction increased inventory (an asset) by $17,000 and increased accounts payable (a liability) by $17,000, recognizing the obligation to the supplier. This transaction is recorded as follows:

Transaction	Cash Asset +	Noncash Assets =	Liabilities +	Contrib. Capital +	Earned Capital	Revenues −	Expenses =	Net Income
(4) Purchase $17,000 inventory on account.		+17,000 Inventory =	+17,000 Accounts Payable			−	=	

To summarize, the description of each transaction appears in the first column of the template. Then the financial statement effects of that transaction are recorded with a + or a – in the appropriate columns of the template. Under each number, the account title within that column of the balance sheet or income statement is entered. So far, Natural Beauty Supply's activities have not affected the revenue or expense accounts of the income statement.

After each transaction, the equality of the accounting equation is maintained. If we so choose, we can prepare a balance sheet at any time, reflecting the transactions up to that point in time. At the end of the day on November 1, 2018, Natural Beauty Supply's balance sheet appears as follows:

NATURAL BEAUTY SUPPLY, INC. Balance Sheet November 1, 2018			
Assets		**Liabilities and Equity**	
Cash	$23,000	Notes payable	$ 5,000
Inventory	17,000	Accounts payable	17,000
Security deposit	2,000	Total current liabilities	22,000
Total current assets	42,000	**Equity**	
		Common stock	20,000
Total assets	$42,000	Total liabilities and equity	$42,000

MID-CHAPTER REVIEW 2

Assume that Schaefer's Pharmacy, Inc., enters into the following transactions. Record each of the following transactions in the financial statement effects template.

a. Issued common stock for $20,000 cash.
b. Purchased inventory costing $8,000 on credit.
c. Purchased equipment costing $10,000 for cash.
d. Paid suppliers $3,000 cash for part of the inventory purchased in *b*.

The solution to this review problem can be found on page 94.

REPORTING FINANCIAL PERFORMANCE

LO3 Describe and construct the income statement and discuss how it can be used to evaluate management performance.

While balance sheets provide useful information about the structure of a company's resources and the claims on those resources at a point in time, they provide little sense of recent movement or trajectory. The retained earnings balance represents the amount earned (but not paid out in dividends) over the entire life of the company. Looking at the difference between points in time doesn't provide a complete picture about what happened between those points in time. For that perspective, we need the income statement to see whether our business activities generated more resources than they used. For instance, Walgreens' retained earnings increased by $2,453 million over fiscal year 2017, but that amount does not convey the volume of activity that occurred to accomplish it.

Walgreens' fiscal year summarized 2017 Statement of Earnings is shown in **Exhibit 2.2**. Walgreens reported net earnings of $4,101 million on revenues of $118,214 million, or about $0.035 of each revenue dollar ($4,101 million/$118,214 million). The remaining $0.965 of that revenue dollar relates to costs incurred to generate the revenues, such as the costs of products sold and equipment used, wages, advertising and promotion, interest and taxes. Interpretation of this $0.035 amount requires further analysis, as shown in Chapter 5, but we can compare it to previous amounts of $0.036 in fiscal year 2016, and $0.041 in fiscal year 2015.

FYI The income statement is also called the statement of earnings or the statement of operations or the profit and loss statement. Walgreens uses all three terms (profit, income, and earnings) in **Exhibit 2.2**.

To analyze an income statement, we need to understand some terminology. **Revenues** result in increases in **net assets** (assets minus liabilities) that are caused by the company's transferring goods or services to customers. **Expenses** result from decreases in net assets (assets minus liabilities) that are caused by the company's revenue-generating activities, including costs of products and services sold, operating costs like depreciation, wages and advertising, nonoperating costs like interest on debt and, finally, taxes on income. The difference between revenues and expenses is **net income** when revenues exceed expenses, or **net loss** when expenses exceed revenues. The connection to the balance sheet can be seen in that reporting net income means that revenues exceeded expenses, which in turn means that the company's business activities increased its net assets.

Operating expenses are the usual and customary costs that a company incurs to support its main business activities. These include cost of goods sold expense, selling expenses, depreciation expense, amortization expense, and research and development expense. Not all of these expenses are recognized in the period in which cash is disbursed. For example, depreciation expense is recognized in the time period during which the asset is used, not in the period when it was first acquired in exchange for cash. In contrast, other expenses, such as compensation expense, are recognized in

FYI The terms revenues and sales are often used interchangeably.

3

EXHIBIT 2.2 Walgreens' Income Statement

WALGREENS BOOTS ALLIANCE, INC. AND SUBSIDIARIES
Summarized Consolidated Statement of Earnings
Year ended August 31, 2017
($ millions)

Net sales	$118,214
Cost of sales	89,052
Gross profit	29,162
Selling, general and administrative expenses	23,740
Equity earnings in AmerisourceBergen	135
Operating income	5,557
Interest (expense) income, net	(693)
Other (expense) income	(11)
Earnings before income tax provision	4,853
Income tax provision	760
Post tax earnings from other equity method investments	8
Net earnings	4,101
Net earnings attributable to noncontrolling interests*	(23)
Net earnings attributable to Walgreens Boots Alliance, Inc.	$ 4,078

*Noncontrolling interests arise from the practice of consolidating subsidiaries that are controlled, but not wholly owned. Chapters 11 and 12 provide a brief introduction to this topic.

the period when the services are performed, which is often before cash is actually paid to employees. Walgreens' operating expenses in 2017 were $112,792 million ($89,052 million + $23,740 million).[4]

Nonoperating revenues and expenses relate to the company's financing and investing activities, and include interest revenue and interest expense. Business decision makers and analysts usually segregate operating and nonoperating activities as they offer different insights into company performance and condition. Walgreens' income statement reports net nonoperating expenses in 2017 of $704 million ($693 million + $11 million), followed by tax expense of $760 million.

It is helpful to distinguish income from continuing operations from nonrecurring items. Many readers of financial statements are interested in forecasting future company performance and focus their analysis on sources of operating income that are expected to *persist* into the future. Nonrecurring revenues and expenses are unlikely to arise in the future and are largely irrelevant to predictions of future performance. Consequently, many decision makers identify transactions and events that are unlikely to recur and separate them from operating income in the income statement. These nonrecurring items are described in greater detail in Chapter 6.

Accrual Accounting for Revenues and Expenses

4 **LO4** Explain revenue recognition, accrual accounting, and their effects on retained earnings.

The income statement's ability to measure a company's periodic performance depends on the proper timing of revenues and expenses. Revenue should be recorded when the company has transferred goods or services to customers, in an amount that reflects how much the company expects to be entitled from the transfer—even if there is not an immediate increase in cash. This is called **revenue recognition**, a topic that receives more detailed attention in Chapter 6. Expenses are recognized when assets are diminished (or liabilities increased) as a result of earning revenue or supporting operations, even if there is no immediate decrease in cash. This is called **expense recognition**. **Accrual accounting** refers to this practice of recognizing revenues when earned through the company's operations and recognizing expenses as the assets used and obligations incurred in carrying out those operations.

An important consequence of accrual accounting for revenues and expenses is that the balance sheet depicts the resources of the company (in addition to cash) and the obligations which the company must fulfill in the future. Accrual accounting is required under U.S. GAAP and IFRS because it is considered to be the most useful information for making business decisions and evaluating business performance. (That is not to say that information on cash flows is not important—but it is conveyed by the statement of cash flows discussed in Chapter 4.)

[4] Walgreens also reports $135 million in Equity earnings in AmerisourceBergen, a company in which Walgreens invested. The operations of AmerisourceBergen are similar enough to Walgreens' operations that they include this as a component of operating income.

Walgreens' net sales in 2017 were $118,214 million. **Cost of goods sold** (cost of sales) is an expense item in the income statements of manufacturing and merchandising companies. It represents the cost of products that are delivered to customers during the period. The difference between revenues (at selling prices) and cost of goods sold (at purchase price or manufacturing cost) is called **gross profit**. Gross profit for merchandisers and manufacturers is an important number as it represents the remaining income available to cover all of the company's overhead and other expenses (selling, general and administrative expenses, research and development, interest, and so on). Walgreens' gross profit in 2017 is calculated as total net revenues less cost of sales, which equals $29,162 million ($118,214 million – $89,052 million).

The principles of revenue and expense recognition are crucial to income statement reporting. To illustrate, assume a company purchases inventories for $100,000 cash, which it sells later in that same period for $150,000 cash. The company would record $150,000 in revenue when the inventory is delivered to the customer, because at that point, the company has fulfilled its responsibilities in the exchange with the customer. Also assume that the company pays $20,000 cash for sales employee wages during the period. The income statement is designed to tell how effective the company was at generating more resources than it used, and it would appear as follows (ignoring income taxes for the moment):

Revenues	$150,000
Cost of goods sold	100,000
Gross profit.	50,000
Wages expense	20,000
Net income (earnings)	$ 30,000

In this illustration, there is a correspondence between each of the revenues/expenses and a cash inflow/outflow within the accounting period. Net income was $30,000 and the increase in cash was $30,000.

However, that need not be the case under accrual accounting. Suppose that the company sells its product on **credit** (also referred to as *on account*) rather than for cash. Does the seller still report sales revenue? The answer is yes. Under GAAP, revenues are reported when a company has earned those sales at delivery. Earned means that the company has done everything required under the sales agreement—no material contingencies remain. The seller reports an accounts receivable asset on its balance sheet, and revenue can be recognized before cash collection.

Credit sales mean that companies can report substantial sales revenue and assets without receiving cash. When such receivables are ultimately collected, no further revenue is recorded because it was recorded earlier when the revenue recognition criteria were met. The collection of a receivable merely involves the decrease of one asset (accounts receivable) and the increase of another asset (cash), with no resulting increase in net assets.

Next, consider a different situation. Assume that the company sells gift cards to customers for $9,500. Should the $9,500 received in cash be recognized as revenue? No. Even though the gift cards were sold and cash was collected, there has been no transfer of goods or services to the customer. The revenue from gift cards is recognized when the product or service is provided. For example, revenue can be recognized when a customer purchases an item of merchandise using the gift card for payment. Hence, the $9,500 is then recorded as an increase in cash and an increase in *gift card liabilities*, a liability, with no resulting increase in net assets.

The proper timing of revenue recognition suggests that the expenses incurred in earning that revenue be recognized in the same fiscal period. Thus, if merchandise inventory is purchased in one period and sold in another, the cost of the merchandise should be retained as an asset until the items are sold. It would not be proper to recognize expense when the inventory was purchased or the cash was paid. Accurate income determination requires the proper timing of revenue and expense recognition, and the exchange of cash is *not* the essential ingredient.

We have already seen that when a company incurs a cost to acquire a resource that produces benefits in the future (for example, merchandise inventory for future sale), it recognizes an asset. That asset represents costs that are waiting to be recognized as expenses in the future, when these assets are used to produce revenue or to support operations. When inventory is delivered to a customer, we recognize that the asset no longer belongs to the selling company. The inventory asset is decreased, and cost of goods sold is recognized as an expense.

FYI Purchase of inventories on credit or on account means that the buyer does not pay the seller at the time of purchase. The buyer reports a liability (accounts payable) on its balance sheet that is later removed when payment is made. The seller reports an asset (accounts receivable) on its balance sheet until it is removed when the buyer pays.

FYI Sales on credit will not always be collected. The potential for uncollectable accounts introduces additional risk to the firm.

FYI **Cash accounting** recognizes revenues only when received in cash and expenses only when paid in cash. This approach is not acceptable under GAAP.

The same principle applies when employees earn wages for work in one period, but are paid in the next period. Wages expense must be recognized when the liability (obligation) is *incurred*, regardless of when they are paid. If the company in the illustration doesn't pay its employees until the following reporting period, it recognizes a wages payable liability of $20,000 and, because this decreases net assets, it would recognize a wage expense of the same amount.

When wages are paid in the next reporting period, both cash and the wages payable liability are decreased. No expense is reported when the wages are paid, because the expense is recognized when the employees worked to generate sales in the prior period.

Accrual accounting principles are crucial for reporting the income statement revenues and expenses in the proper period, and these revenues and expenses provide a more complete view of the inflows and outflows of resources (including cash) for the firm. Was an outflow of cash supposed to produce benefits in the current period or in a future period? Was an inflow of cash the result of past operations or current operations? The accrual accounting model uses the balance sheet and income statement to answer such questions and to enable users of financial statements to make more timely assessments of the firm's economic performance.

However, accrual accounting's timeliness requires management to estimate future events in determining the amount of expenses incurred and revenue earned. The precise amount of cash to be received or disbursed may not be known until a later date. In the case of wages, the amount of the accrual is known with certainty. In other cases (e.g., incentive bonuses), it may not and thus require an estimate.

Retained Earnings

Net income for the period is added to the company's retained earnings, which, in turn, is part of stockholders' equity. The linkage between the income statement and the beginning- and end-of-period balance sheets, which we called articulation in Chapter 1, is achieved by tying net income to retained earnings because net income is, by definition, the *change* in retained earnings resulting from business activities during an accounting period. This link is highlighted by the red arrow at the top of the financial statement effects template (FSET).[5] There are typically other adjustments to retained earnings. The most common adjustment is for dividend payments to stockholders. **Exhibit 2.3** provides the annual adjustments to retained earnings for Walgreens.

EXHIBIT 2.3 Walgreens' Retained Earnings Reconciliation

WALGREENS BOOTS ALLIANCE, INC. AND SUBSIDIARIES
Year Ended August 31, 2017
($ millions)

Retained earnings, August 31, 2016	$27,684
Add: Net earnings attributable to Walgreens Boots Alliance, Inc.	4,078
	31,762
Less: Cash dividends declared	1,625
Retained earnings, August 31, 2017	$30,137

Analyzing and Recording Transactions for the Income Statement

Earlier, we introduced the financial statement effects template as a tool to illustrate the effects of transactions on the balance sheet. In this section, we show how this template is used to analyze transactions that may affect the current period's income statement. To do so, we extend our illustration of Natural Beauty Supply (NBS) to reflect the following events in 2018:

(5) Nov. 2 NBS paid $670 to advertise in the local newspaper for November.

(6) Nov. 18 NBS paid $13,300 cash to its suppliers in partial payment for the earlier delivery of inventory.

[5] In the FSET, we show that each transaction that affects the income statement also impacts retained earnings. This approach is useful for *analyzing* the effect of the transaction on both the income statement and balance sheet. However, the impact of net income on retained earnings is *recorded* only once each accounting period, after all of the revenues and expenses have been recorded. This recording procedure is explained later in this chapter and in Chapter 3.

(7) Nov. — During the month of November, NBS sold and delivered products to retail customers. The customers paid $7,000 cash for products that had cost NBS $4,000.

(8) Nov. — During the month of November, sales and deliveries to wholesale customers totaled $2,400 for merchandise that had cost $1,700. Instead of paying cash, wholesale customers are required to pay for the merchandise within ten working days.

(9) Nov. — NBS employed a salesperson who earned $1,400 for the month of November and was paid that amount in cash.

(10) Nov. 24 NBS received an order from a wholesale customer to deliver products in December. The agreed price of the products to be delivered is $700 and the cost is $450.

(11) Nov. 25 NBS introduced holiday gift certificates, which entitle the recipient to a one-hour consultation on the use of NBS's products. $300 of gift certificates were sold for cash, but none were redeemed before the end of November.

(12) Nov. 30 NBS received $1,450 in partial payment from customers billed in (8).

(13) Nov. 30 NBS repaid the loan and interest in (2).

(14) Nov. 30 NBS paid $1,680 for a twelve-month fire insurance policy. Coverage begins on December 1.

(15) Nov. 30 NBS paid $1,500 to the landlord for November rent.

In the fifth transaction, Natural Beauty Supply gave cash in return for advertising for the month of November. This payment does not create a benefit for future periods, so it does not create an asset. Nor does the payment discharge an existing obligation. Therefore, it decreases NBS's net assets (assets minus liabilities). The purpose of this decrease in net assets is to generate revenues for the company, so it is reported as an expense in the income statement.

We begin by entering the decrease in cash and an increase in expenses. (The minus sign in front of expenses insures that the accounting equation still holds.) Recording the expense allows the income statement to keep track of the flows of assets and liabilities that result from the company's operations.

	Balance Sheet					*Income Statement*		
Transaction	Cash Asset +	Noncash Assets =	Liabil-ities +	Contrib. Capital +	Earned Capital	*Revenues* −	*Expenses* =	*Net Income*
(5) Pay $670 cash for November advertising.	−670 Cash						+670 Advertising Expense	

However, the FSET goes further than recording the accounting entry. It also depicts the effects of the expense on net income and of net income on retained earnings. So, the complete FSET description of transaction (5) is as follows. The FSET uses color to differentiate between the accounting entry (in blue) and the resulting effect on income and retained earnings (in black).

Transaction	Cash Asset	Noncash Assets	Liabilities	Contrib. Capital	Earned Capital	Revenues	Expenses	Net Income
(5) Pay $670 cash for November advertising.	−670 Cash				−670 Retained Earnings		+670 Advertising Expense	−670

In the sixth transaction, Natural Beauty Supply made a partial payment of $13,300 in cash to the suppliers who delivered inventory on November 1. This transaction decreases cash by $13,300 and decreases the accounts payable liability by $13,300. The income statement is not affected by this payment. The cost of merchandise is reflected in the income statement when the merchandise is sold, not when it is paid for (as we will see shortly).

Transaction	Cash Asset	Noncash Assets	Liabilities	Contrib. Capital	Earned Capital	Revenues	Expenses	Net Income
(6) Pay $13,300 cash in partial payment to suppliers from transaction 4.	−13,300 Cash		−13,300 Accounts Payable					

In transaction seven, Natural Beauty Supply sold and delivered products to customers who paid $7,000 in cash. NBS's transfer of products to customers results in the recognition of revenue in the income statement and an increase in net assets (cash) on the balance sheet. As in transaction 5, the FSET also depicts the impact of these sales on net income and on the retained earnings balance.

	Balance Sheet					Income Statement		
Transaction	Cash Asset +	Noncash Assets =	Liabil-ities +	Contrib. Capital +	Earned Capital	Revenues −	Expenses =	Net Income
(7a) Sell $7,000 of products for cash.	+7,000 Cash	=			+7,000 Retained Earnings	+7,000 Sales Revenue	−	= +7,000

At the same time, NBS must recognize that these sales transactions involved an exchange, and cash was received while inventory costing $4,000 was delivered. Transaction (7b) recognizes that NBS no longer has this inventory and that this decrease in net assets produces an expense called cost of goods sold. In this way, the income statement portrays the increases in net assets (revenues) and the decreases in net assets (expenses like cost of goods sold and advertising) from the company's operating activities. (Again, the minus sign in front of all expenses insures that the accounting equation remains balanced.)

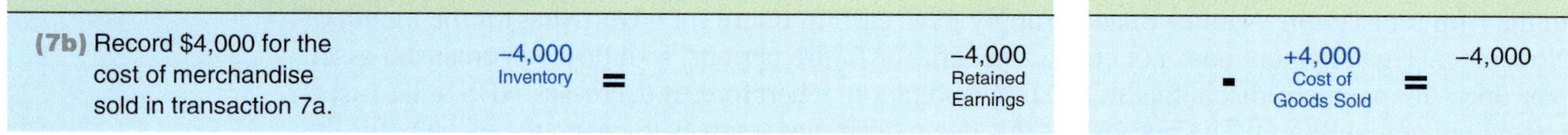

Transaction	Cash Asset	Noncash Assets	Liabilities	Contrib. Capital	Earned Capital	Revenues	Expenses	Net Income
(7b) Record $4,000 for the cost of merchandise sold in transaction 7a.		−4,000 Inventory =			−4,000 Retained Earnings	−	+4,000 Cost of Goods Sold =	−4,000

The eighth transaction is very similar to the previous one, except that Natural Beauty Supply's customers will pay for the products ten days after they were delivered. Should NBS recognize revenue on these sales? The products have been delivered, so the revenue has been earned.[6] Therefore, NBS should recognize that it has a new asset—accounts receivable—equal to $2,400, and that it has earned revenue in the same amount. As above, NBS would also record cost of goods sold to recognize the cost of inventory delivered to the customers.

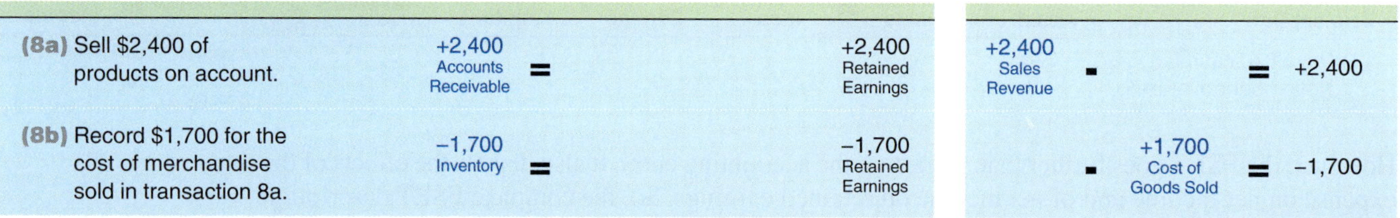

Transaction	Cash Asset	Noncash Assets	Liabilities	Contrib. Capital	Earned Capital	Revenues	Expenses	Net Income
(8a) Sell $2,400 of products on account.		+2,400 Accounts Receivable =			+2,400 Retained Earnings	+2,400 Sales Revenue −	=	+2,400
(8b) Record $1,700 for the cost of merchandise sold in transaction 8a.		−1,700 Inventory =			−1,700 Retained Earnings	−	+1,700 Cost of Goods Sold =	−1,700

The ninth entry records wage expense. In this case, wages were paid in cash. Cash is decreased by $1,400, and this decrease in net assets results in a recognition of wages expense in the income statement (with resulting decreases in net income and retained earnings).

Transaction	Cash Asset	Noncash Assets	Liabilities	Contrib. Capital	Earned Capital	Revenues	Expenses	Net Income
(9) Record $1,400 in wages to employees.	−1,400 Cash	=			−1,400 Retained Earnings	−	+1,400 Wages Expense =	−1,400

Transaction ten involves a customer order for products to be delivered in December. This transaction is an example of an *executory contract*, which does not require a journal entry (just like Walgreens' open purchase orders for inventory described earlier). NBS has not earned revenue, because it has not yet delivered the products.

[6] In Chapter 6, we consider the possibility that a customer might not pay the receivable. For the time being, we assume that the receivables' collectability is assured.

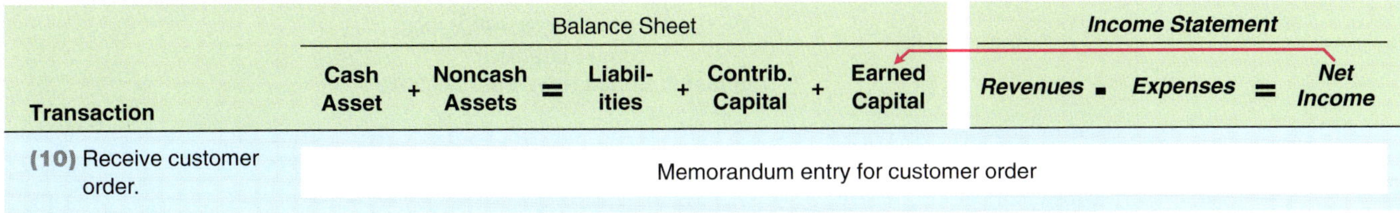

Transaction	Cash Asset	+ Noncash Assets	= Liabilities	+ Contrib. Capital	+ Earned Capital	Revenues	− Expenses	= Net Income
				Balance Sheet			Income Statement	
(10) Receive customer order.	Memorandum entry for customer order							

In transaction eleven, Natural Beauty Supply sold gift certificates for $300 cash, but none were redeemed. In this case, NBS has received cash, but revenue cannot be recognized because no goods or services have been transferred to the customers. Rather, NBS has accepted an obligation to provide services in the future when the gift certificates are redeemed. This obligation is recognized as a liability titled unearned revenue.

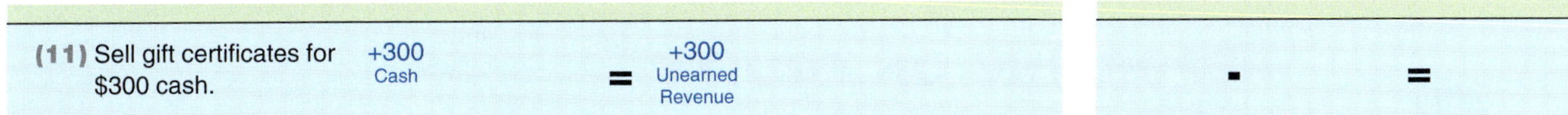

Transaction	Cash Asset	+ Noncash Assets	= Liabilities	+ Contrib. Capital	+ Earned Capital	Revenues	− Expenses	= Net Income
(11) Sell gift certificates for $300 cash.	+300 Cash		+300 Unearned Revenue					

In transaction twelve, NBS received $1,450 cash as partial payment from customers billed in transaction eight. Cash increases by $1,450 and accounts receivable decreases by $1,450. Recall that revenues are recorded when earned (transaction 8), not when cash is received.

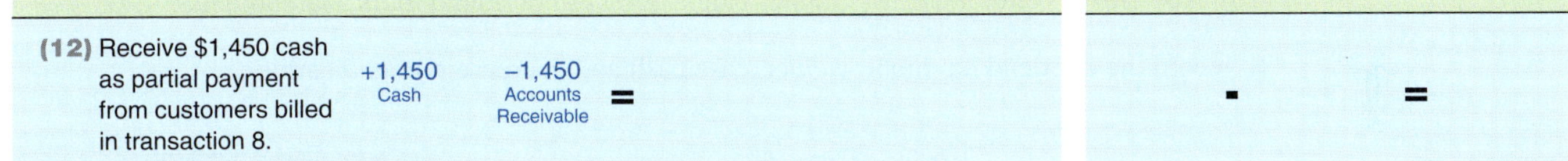

Transaction	Cash Asset	+ Noncash Assets	= Liabilities	+ Contrib. Capital	+ Earned Capital	Revenues	− Expenses	= Net Income
(12) Receive $1,450 cash as partial payment from customers billed in transaction 8.	+1,450 Cash	−1,450 Accounts Receivable						

In transaction thirteen on November 30, Natural Beauty Supply paid back the family member who had loaned money to the business. The cash payment was the agreed-upon $5,050 ($5,000 principal and $50 interest). The repayment of the principal does not change the net assets of NBS; cash goes down by $5,000 and the note payable liability goes down an equal amount. However, the payment of $50 interest does cause the net assets to decrease, and this net asset decrease creates an interest expense in the income statement.

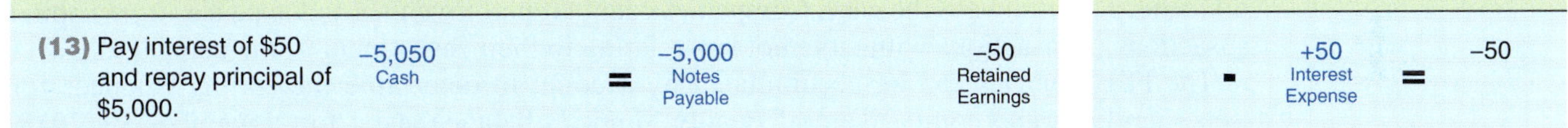

Transaction	Cash Asset	+ Noncash Assets	= Liabilities	+ Contrib. Capital	+ Earned Capital	Revenues	− Expenses	= Net Income
(13) Pay interest of $50 and repay principal of $5,000.	−5,050 Cash		−5,000 Notes Payable		−50 Retained Earnings		+50 Interest Expense	−50

In the fourteenth transaction, NBS paid an annual insurance premium of $1,680 for coverage beginning December 1. NBS will receive the benefits of the insurance coverage in the future, so insurance expense will be recognized in those future periods. At this time, a noncash asset titled prepaid insurance is increased by $1,680, and cash is decreased by the same amount.

Transaction	Cash Asset	+ Noncash Assets	= Liabilities	+ Contrib. Capital	+ Earned Capital	Revenues	− Expenses	= Net Income
(14) Pay $1,680 for one-year insurance policy.	−1,680 Cash	+1,680 Prepaid Insurance						

In the last transaction of the month of November, Natural Beauty Supply paid $1,500 cash to the landlord for November's rent. This $1,500 reduction of net assets is balanced by rent expense in the income statement.

Transaction	Cash Asset	+ Noncash Assets	= Liabilities	+ Contrib. Capital	+ Earned Capital	Revenues	− Expenses	= Net Income
(15) Pay $1,500 rent for November.	−1,500 Cash				−1,500 Retained Earnings		+1,500 Rent Expense	−1,500

We can summarize the revenue and expense entries of these transactions to prepare an income statement for Natural Beauty Supply for the month ended November 30, 2018.

NATURAL BEAUTY SUPPLY, INC. Income Statement For Month Ended November 30, 2018	
Sales revenue	$9,400
Cost of goods sold	5,700
Gross profit	3,700
Wages expense	1,400
Rent expense	1,500
Advertising expense	670
Operating income	130
Interest expense	50
Net income	$ 80

REPORTING ON EQUITY

Analyzing and Recording Equity Transactions

LO5 Illustrate equity transactions and the statement of stockholders' equity.

5

Earlier we recorded the effect of issuing common stock on the balance sheet of Natural Beauty Supply. To complete our illustration, we illustrate one final equity transaction—a dividend payment.

(16) Nov. 30 Natural Beauty Supply paid a $50 cash dividend to its shareholders.

To record the dividend payment, we decrease cash and decrease retained earnings.

	Balance Sheet									*Income Statement*				
Transaction	**Cash Asset**	+	**Noncash Assets**	=	**Liabil-ities**	+	**Contrib. Capital**	+	**Earned Capital**	***Revenues***	−	***Expenses***	=	***Net Income***
(16) Pay $50 cash dividend to shareholders.	−50 Cash			=					−50 Retained Earnings		−		=	

No revenue or income is recorded from a stock issuance. Similarly, no expense is recorded from a dividend. This is always the case. Companies cannot report revenues and expenses from capital transactions (transactions with stockholders relating to their investment in the company).

The FSET entries can be accumulated by account to determine the ending balances for assets, liabilities and equity. Natural Beauty Supply's balance sheet for November 30, 2018, appears in **Exhibit 2.4**. The balance in retained earnings is $30 (net income of $80 less the cash dividend of $50).

EXHIBIT 2.4 Natural Beauty Supply's Balance Sheet

NATURAL BEAUTY SUPPLY, INC. Balance Sheet November 30, 2018			
Assets		Liabilities	
Cash	$ 8,100	Accounts payable	$ 3,700
Accounts receivable	950	Unearned revenue	300
Inventory	11,300	Total current liabilities	4,000
Prepaid insurance	1,680	Equity	
Security deposit	2,000	Common stock	20,000
Total current assets	24,030	Retained earnings	30
		Total equity	20,030
Total assets	$24,030	Total liabilities and equity	$24,030

Statement of Stockholders' Equity

The statement of stockholders' equity is a reconciliation of the beginning and ending balances of selected stockholders' equity accounts. The statement of stockholders' equity for Natural Beauty Supply for the month of November is in **Exhibit 2.5**.

EXHIBIT 2.5 Natural Beauty Supply's Statement of Stockholders' Equity

NATURAL BEAUTY SUPPLY, INC.
Statement of Stockholders' Equity
For Month Ended November 30, 2018

	Contributed Capital	Earned Capital	Total Equity
Balance, November 1, 2018	$ 0	$ 0	$ 0
Common stock issued	20,000	—	20,000
Net income	—	80	80
Cash dividends	—	(50)	(50)
Balance, November 30, 2018	**$20,000**	**$30**	**$20,030**

This statement highlights three main changes to Natural Beauty Supply's equity during November.

1. Natural Beauty raised $20,000 in equity capital during the month.
2. Natural Beauty Supply earned net income of $80. That is, its business activities increased the company's net assets by $80 during the month.
3. Natural Beauty Supply declared a $50 cash dividend.

At this point, we can make the important observation that the various financial statements are not the result of independent processes. That is, the process of constructing the income statement is intimately tied to the process of constructing the balance sheet. When we think about the fact that revenues reflect how much the company expects to receive from its delivery of goods to customers, while expenses measure the outflow of assets and increases in liabilities resulting from earning revenues and supporting operations, it should be apparent that an error on the income statement will, in all likelihood, lead to an error in the balance sheet. Understanding the connections among the various statements is a key step in becoming an effective reader of financial information.

YOU MAKE THE CALL

You are an Analyst Walgreens reported a balance in retained earnings of $30,137 million at August 31, 2017. This amount compares to $27,684 million one year earlier at the end of 2016. In 2017, Walgreens reported net income of $4,078 million. Why did the company's retained earnings go up by less than reported net income? [Answer on page 74.]

MID-CHAPTER REVIEW 3

Part 1. Assume that Schaefer's Pharmacy, Inc.'s records show the following amounts at December 31, 2018. Use this information, as necessary, to prepare its 2018 income statement (ignore income taxes).

Cash	$ 3,000	Cash dividends	$ 1,000
Accounts receivable	12,000	Revenues	45,000
Office equipment	32,250	Cost of goods sold	20,000
Inventory	26,000	Rent expense	5,000
Land	10,000	Wages expense	8,000
Accounts payable	7,500	Utilities expense	2,000
Common stock	45,750	Other expenses	4,000

continued

continued from previous page

Part 2. Assume that Schaefer's Pharmacy, Inc., reports the following selected financial information for the year ended December 31, 2018.

Retained earnings, Dec. 31, 2018 . . .	$30,000	Dividends	$ 1,000
Net income	$ 6,000	Retained earnings, Dec. 31, 2017 . . .	$25,000

Prepare the 2018 calendar-year retained earnings reconciliation for this company.

Part 3. Use the listing of accounts and figures reported in part 1 along with the ending retained earnings from part 2 to prepare the December 31, 2018, balance sheet for Schaefer's Pharmacy, Inc.

The solution to this review problem can be found on pages 94–95.

JOURNALIZING AND POSTING TRANSACTIONS

6

LO6 Use journal entries and T-accounts to analyze and record transactions.

The financial statement effects template is a useful tool for illustrating the effects of a transaction on the balance sheet, income statement, statement of stockholders' equity, and statement of cash flows. However, when representing individual transactions or analyzing individual accounts, the accounting system records information in journal entries (step 2) that are collected in individual accounts. This section introduces the basics of that system. It also introduces the T-account as a useful tool for learning debits and credits and for representing accounts in the ledger (step 3).

T-Account

Accountants commonly use a graphic representation of an account called a **T-account**, so named because it looks like a large T. The typical form of a T-account is:

Account Title	
Debits **(Dr.)** Always the left side	Credits **(Cr.)** Always the right side

FYI Recall that an account is a record of increases and decreases in asset, liability, equity, revenue, or expense items.

One side of the T-account is used to record increases to the account and the other side is used to record decreases.

Accountants record individual transactions using the journal entry. A **journal entry** is an accounting entry in the financial records (journals) of a company. The journal entry is the *bookkeeping* aspect of accounting. Even if we never make a journal entry for a company, we still interact with accounting and finance professionals who do, and who will use this language. Further, journal entries and T-accounts can help in reconstructing transactions and interpreting their financial effects.

Debit and Credit System

FYI Debit and credit are accounting terms meaning left and right, respectively.

Accountants describe increases and decreases in accounts using the terms **debit** and **credit**. The left side of each account is the debit side (abbreviated Dr.) and the right side of each account is the credit side (abbreviated Cr.). In some accounts, increases are recorded on the debit (left) side of the account and decreases are recorded on the credit (right) side of the account. In other accounts, just the opposite is true—increases are credits and decreases are debits. An easy way to remember what the words debit and credit reflect is to visualize a balance sheet in "T" account form with assets on the left and liabilities and equity on the right as follows:

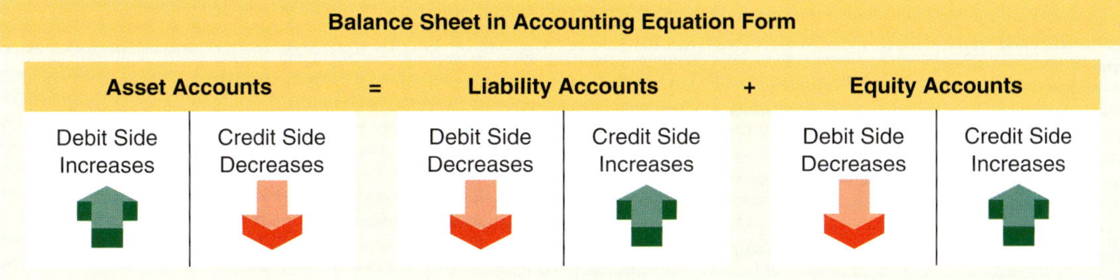

FYI In our everyday speech, the words "debit" and "credit" are often imbued with value connotations. For example, "To her credit, she took responsibility for the incident." But there are no value connotations within the accounting system. Every good event is recorded with both a debit and a credit, and the same is true for every bad event.

Thus, assets are assigned a *normal debit balance* because they are on the left side. Liabilities and equity are assigned a *normal credit balance* because they are on the right side. So, to reflect an increase in an asset, we debit the asset account. To reflect an increase in a liability or equity account, we credit the account. Conversely, to reflect a decrease in an asset account, we credit it. To reflect a decrease in a liability or equity account, we debit it. (There are exceptions to these normal balances; one case is accumulated depreciation, which is explained in Chapter 3.)

The balance sheet must always balance (assets = liabilities + equity). So too must total debits equal total credits in each journal entry. There can, however, be more than one debit and one credit in an entry. These so-called **compound entries** still adhere to the rule: *total debits equal total credits for each entry*. This important relation is extended below to show the *expanded accounting equation* in T-account form with the inclusion of debit (Dr.) and credit (Cr.) rules. Equity is expanded to reflect increases from stock issuances and revenues, and to reflect decreases from dividends and expenses.

FYI The rule that total debits equal total credits for each entry is known as double-entry accounting, or the duality of accounting.

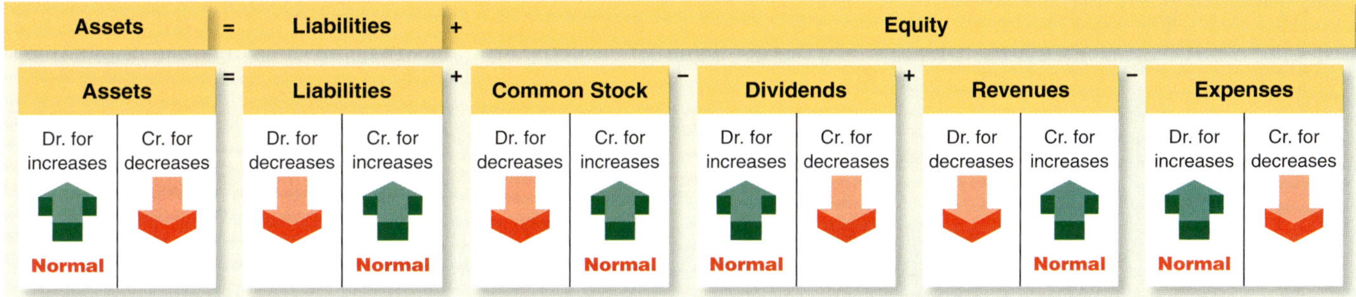

Income (revenues less expenses) feeds directly into retained earnings. Also, anything that increases equity is a credit and anything that decreases equity is a debit. So, to reflect an increase in revenues (which increases retained earnings and, therefore, equity), we credit the revenue account, and to reflect an increase in an expense account (which reduces retained earnings and, therefore, equity), we debit it.

To summarize, the following table reflects the use of the terms debit and credit to reflect increases and decreases to the usual balance sheet and the income statement relations.

FYI The **normal balance** of any account is on the side on which increases are recorded.

Accounting Relation		Debit	Credit
Balance sheet	Assets (A)	Increase	Decrease
	Liabilities (L)	Decrease	Increase
	Equity (SE)	Decrease	Increase
Income statement	Revenue (R)	Decrease	Increase
	Expense (E)	Increase	Decrease

T-Account with Debits and Credits

To illustrate use of debits and credits with a T-account, we use the Cash T-account for NBS transactions 1, 2, 3, and 4 (see page 51). There is a beginning balance of $0 on the left side (which is also the ending balance of the previous period). Increases in cash have been placed on the left side of the Cash T-account and the decreases have been placed on the right side. Transactions (1) and (2) increased the cash balance, while transaction (3) decreased it. Transaction (4) does not involve cash.

The ending balance of cash is $23,000. An account balance is determined by totaling the left side and the right side monetary columns and entering the difference on the side with the larger total. The T-account is an extremely simple record that can be summarized in terms of four elements: beginning balance, additions, deductions, and the ending balance.

+	Cash (A)		−
Beg. bal.	0		
(1)	20,000	2,000	(3)
(2)	5,000		
End. bal.	23,000		

Dates and other related data are usually omitted in T-accounts, but it is customary to *key* entries with a number or a letter to identify the similarly coded transaction. The number or letter is keyed to the journal entry (discussed next) that identifies the transaction involved. The type and number of accounts used by a business depend on the complexity of its operations and the degree of detail demanded by managers.

The Journal Entry

FYI We denote the transaction's effect on assets, liabilities, equity, revenues, and expenses in parentheses for each journal entry.

The journal entry records each transaction (step 2) by summarizing the debits and credits. To illustrate the use of journal entries and T-accounts (step 3), assume that Walgreens: (1) Paid employees $1,200 cash wages, recognizing that amount as an expense, and (2) Paid $9,500 cash to acquire equipment. The journal entries and T-accounts reflecting these two transactions follow. The T-accounts can be viewed as an abbreviated representation of the company *ledger,* which is a listing of all accounts and their dollar balances.

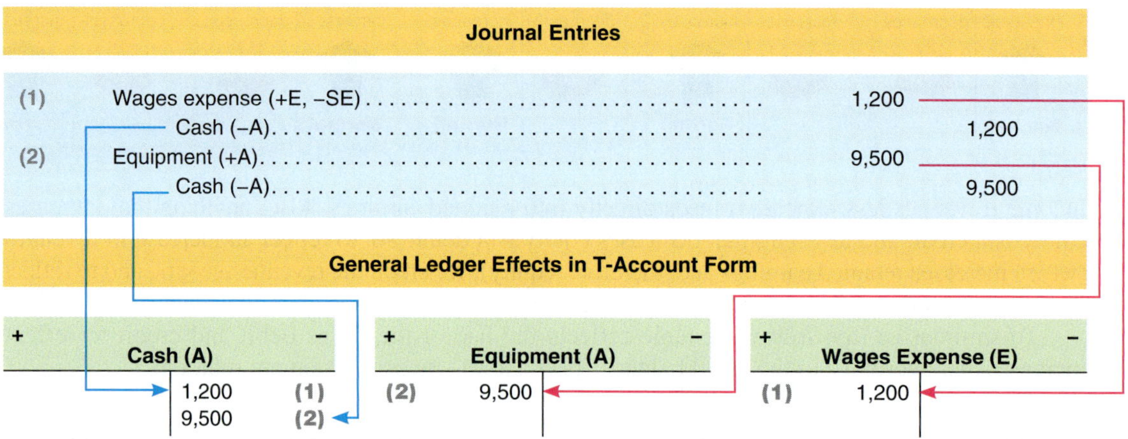

For journal entries, debits are recorded first followed by the credits. Credits are commonly indented. The dollar amounts are entered in both the debit (left) column and credit (right) column. In practice, recordkeepers also enter the date. An alternative presentation is to utilize the abbreviation *Dr* to denote debits and *Cr* to denote credits that precede the account title. We use the first approach in this book.

Analyze, Journalize, and Post

To illustrate the use of journal entries and T-accounts to record transactions, we return to Natural Beauty Supply and reexamine the same transactions recorded earlier in the financial statement effects template. The following layout illustrates our 3-step accounting process of analyzing, journalizing, and posting.

Balance Sheet
Income Statement
Transaction
Cash Asset + Noncash Assets = Liabil-ities + Contrib. Capital + Earned Capital
Revenues - Expenses = Net Income
ANALYZE
(1) Issue stock for $20,000 cash.
+20,000 Cash = +20,000 Common Stock
JOURNALIZE
(1) Cash (+A) . . . 20,000
Common stock (+SE) . . . 20,000
Issue 10,000 shares of common stock.
POST
+ Cash (A) −
(1) 20,000
− Common Stock (SE) +
20,000 (1)
ANALYZE
(2) Sign a note and receive $5,000 cash.
+5,000 Cash = +5,000 Notes Payable
JOURNALIZE
(2) Cash (+A) . . . 5,000
Notes payable (+L) . . . 5,000
Borrow $5,000 on a one-month, 12% (per annum) note.
POST
+ Cash (A) −
(2) 5,000
− Notes Payable (L) +
5,000 (2)
ANALYZE
(3) Sign rental agreement and pay $2,000 security deposit.
−2,000 Cash +2,000 Security Deposit =
JOURNALIZE
(3) Security deposit (+A) . . . 2,000
Cash (−A) . . . 2,000
Pay $2,000 rental security deposit.
POST
+ Security Deposit (A) −
(3) 2,000
+ Cash (A) −
2,000 (3)
ANALYZE
(4) Purchase $17,000 inventory on account.
+17,000 Inventory = +17,000 Accounts Payable
JOURNALIZE
(4) Inventory (+A) . . . 17,000
Accounts payable (+L) . . . 17,000
Purchase inventory on account.
POST
+ Inventory (A) −
(4) 17,000
− Accounts Payable (L) +
17,000 (4)

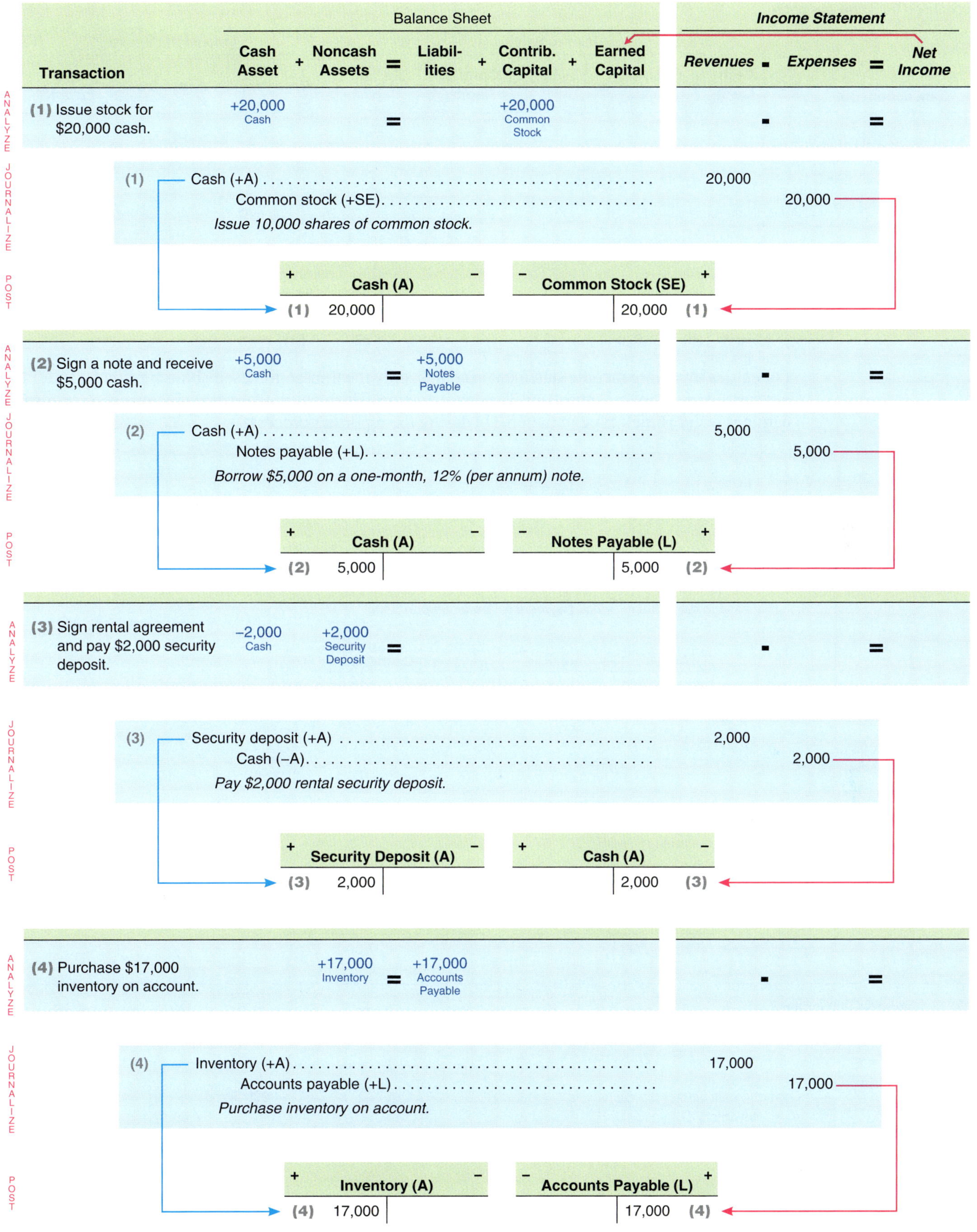

continued

continued from previous page

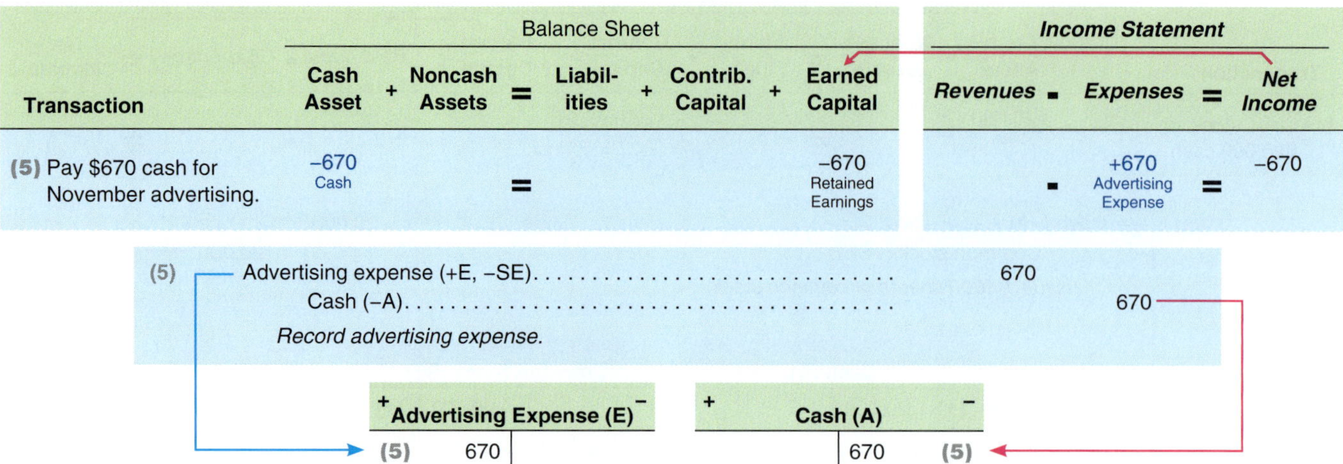

Transaction	Cash Asset	+	Noncash Assets	=	Liabil-ities	+	Contrib. Capital	+	Earned Capital	Revenues	−	Expenses	=	Net Income
(5) Pay $670 cash for November advertising.	−670 Cash			=					−670 Retained Earnings		−	+670 Advertising Expense	=	−670

ANALYZE

JOURNALIZE

		Debit	Credit
(5)	Advertising expense (+E, −SE)	670	
	Cash (−A)		670
	Record advertising expense.		

POST

+ Advertising Expense (E) −		+ Cash (A) −	
(5) 670			670 (5)

For entries involving income statement accounts, only the transaction itself (**blue type** in the FSET) is recorded in the journal entry and T-account posting. The resulting effects on income and retained earnings occur (**black type** in the FSET) during the reporting process.

ANALYZE

Transaction	Cash Asset	+	Noncash Assets	=	Liabil-ities	+	Contrib. Capital	+	Earned Capital	Revenues	−	Expenses	=	Net Income
(6) Pay $13,300 cash in partial payment to suppliers from transaction 4.	−13,300 Cash			=	−13,300 Accounts Payable						−		=	

JOURNALIZE

		Debit	Credit
(6)	Accounts payable (−L)	13,300	
	Cash (−A)		13,300
	Pay cash to suppliers in partial payment for previous purchase.		

POST

− Accounts Payable (L) +		+ Cash (A) −	
(6) 13,300			13,300 (6)

ANALYZE

Transaction	Cash Asset	+	Noncash Assets	=	Liabil-ities	+	Contrib. Capital	+	Earned Capital	Revenues	−	Expenses	=	Net Income
(7a) Sell $7,000 of products for cash.	+7,000 Cash			=					+7,000 Retained Earnings	+7,000 Sales Revenue	−		=	+7,000

JOURNALIZE

		Debit	Credit
(7a)	Cash (+A)	7,000	
	Sales revenue (+R, +SE)		7,000
	Sell products for cash.		

POST

+ Cash (A) −		− Sales Revenue (R) +	
(7a) 7,000			7,000 (7a)

ANALYZE

Transaction	Cash Asset	+	Noncash Assets	=	Liabil-ities	+	Contrib. Capital	+	Earned Capital	Revenues	−	Expenses	=	Net Income
(7b) Record $4,000 for the cost of merchandise sold in transaction 7a.			−4,000 Inventory	=					−4,000 Retained Earnings		−	+4,000 Cost of Goods Sold	=	−4,000

JOURNALIZE

		Debit	Credit
(7b)	Cost of goods sold (+E, −SE)	4,000	
	Inventory (−A)		4,000
	Record cost of merchandise sold as expense.		

POST

+ Cost of Goods Sold (E) −		+ Inventory (A) −	
(7b) 4,000			4,000 (7b)

continued

continued from previous page

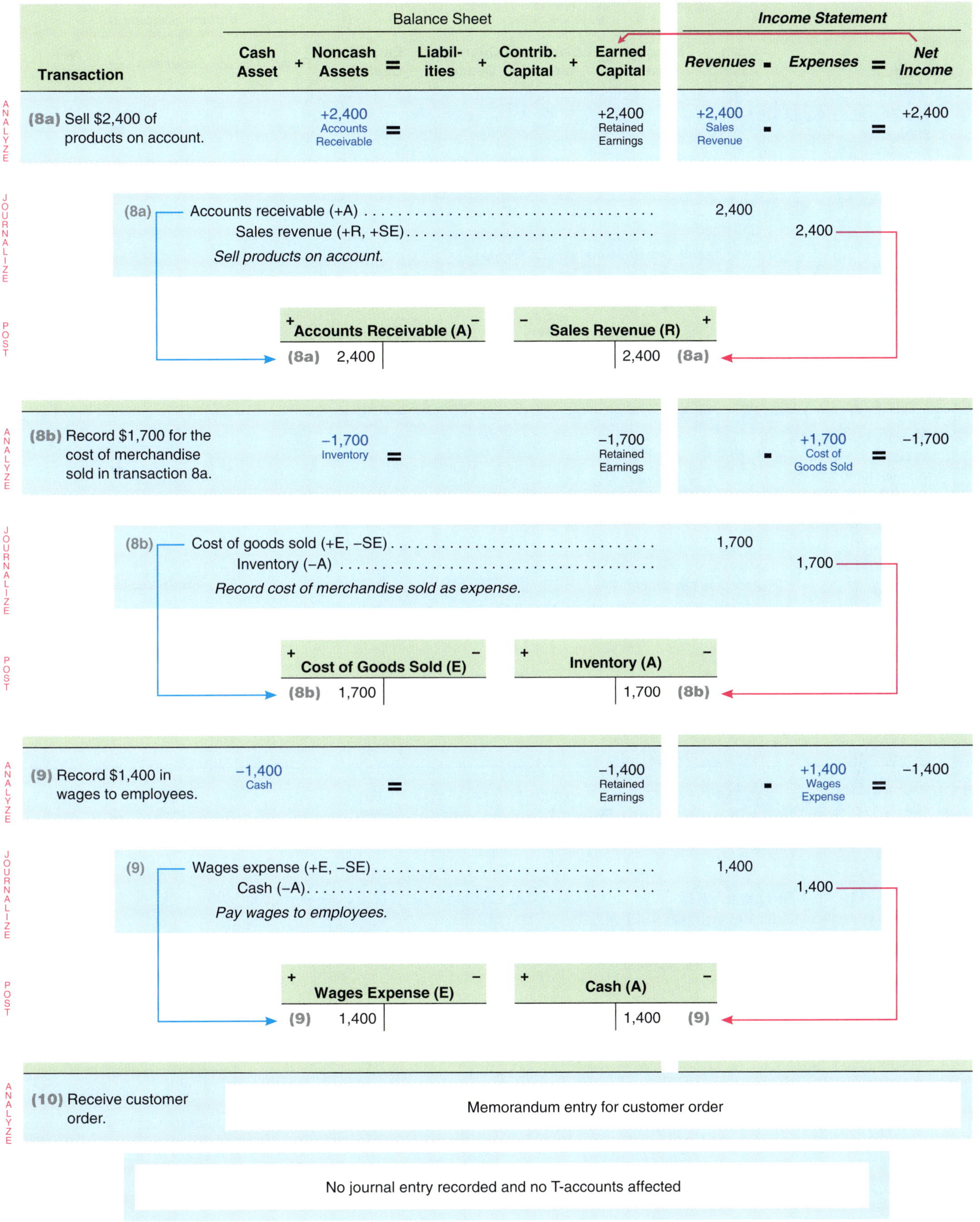

	Transaction	Cash Asset	+	Noncash Assets	=	Liabil-ities	+	Contrib. Capital	+	Earned Capital	Revenues	−	Expenses	=	Net Income
ANALYZE	**(8a)** Sell $2,400 of products on account.			+2,400 Accounts Receivable	=					+2,400 Retained Earnings	+2,400 Sales Revenue	−		=	+2,400

JOURNALIZE

		Dr.	Cr.
(8a)	Accounts receivable (+A)	2,400	
	Sales revenue (+R, +SE)		2,400
	Sell products on account.		

POST

+ Accounts Receivable (A) −	
(8a) 2,400	

− Sales Revenue (R) +	
	2,400 (8a)

	Transaction	Cash Asset	+	Noncash Assets	=	Liabil-ities	+	Contrib. Capital	+	Earned Capital	Revenues	−	Expenses	=	Net Income
ANALYZE	**(8b)** Record $1,700 for the cost of merchandise sold in transaction 8a.			−1,700 Inventory	=					−1,700 Retained Earnings		−	+1,700 Cost of Goods Sold	=	−1,700

JOURNALIZE

		Dr.	Cr.
(8b)	Cost of goods sold (+E, −SE)	1,700	
	Inventory (−A)		1,700
	Record cost of merchandise sold as expense.		

POST

+ Cost of Goods Sold (E) −	
(8b) 1,700	

+ Inventory (A) −	
	1,700 (8b)

	Transaction	Cash Asset	+	Noncash Assets	=	Liabil-ities	+	Contrib. Capital	+	Earned Capital	Revenues	−	Expenses	=	Net Income
ANALYZE	**(9)** Record $1,400 in wages to employees.	−1,400 Cash			=					−1,400 Retained Earnings		−	+1,400 Wages Expense	=	−1,400

JOURNALIZE

		Dr.	Cr.
(9)	Wages expense (+E, −SE)	1,400	
	Cash (−A)		1,400
	Pay wages to employees.		

POST

+ Wages Expense (E) −	
(9) 1,400	

+ Cash (A) −	
	1,400 (9)

ANALYZE

(10) Receive customer order. — Memorandum entry for customer order

No journal entry recorded and no T-accounts affected

continued

continued from previous page

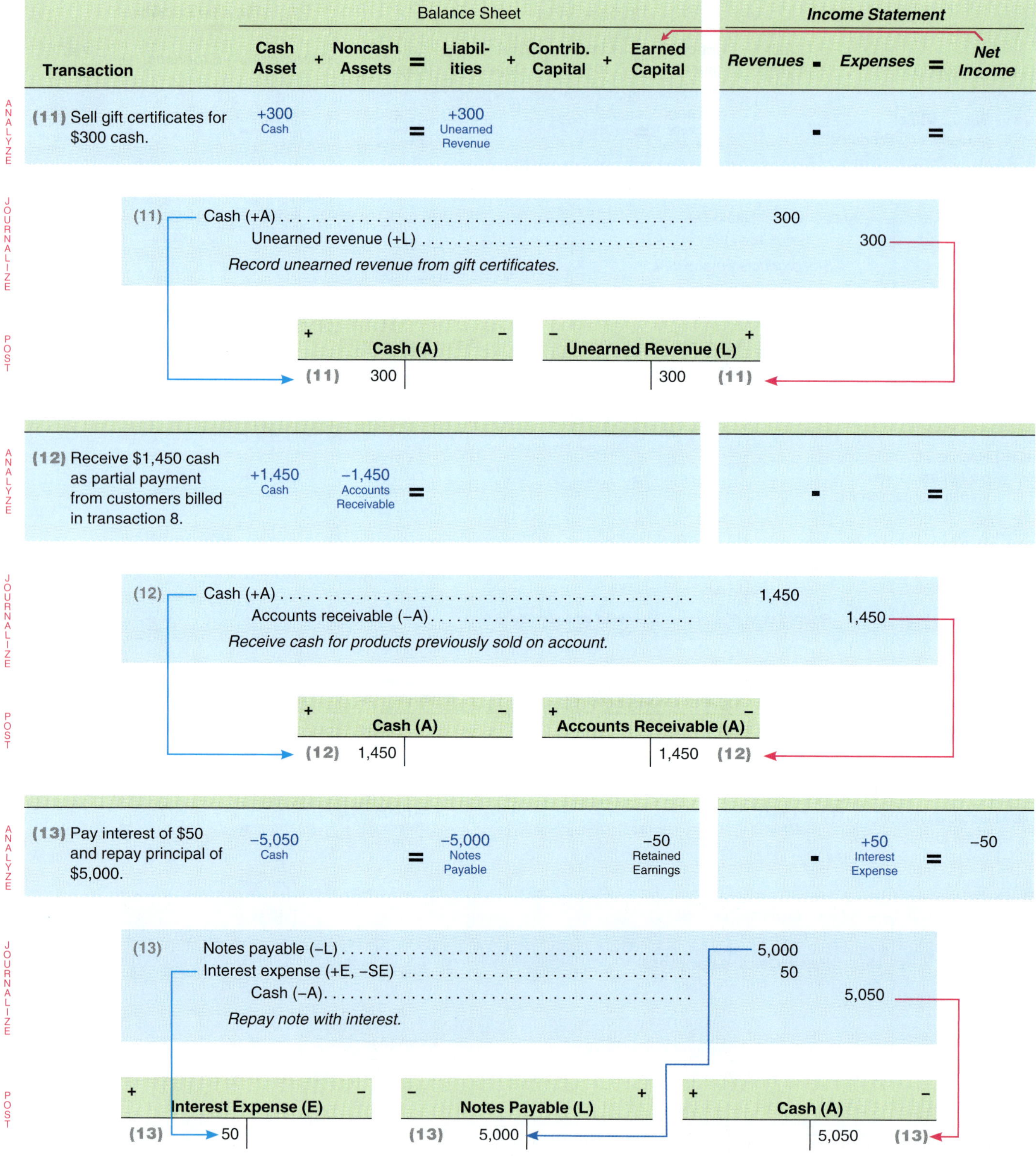

continued

continued from previous page

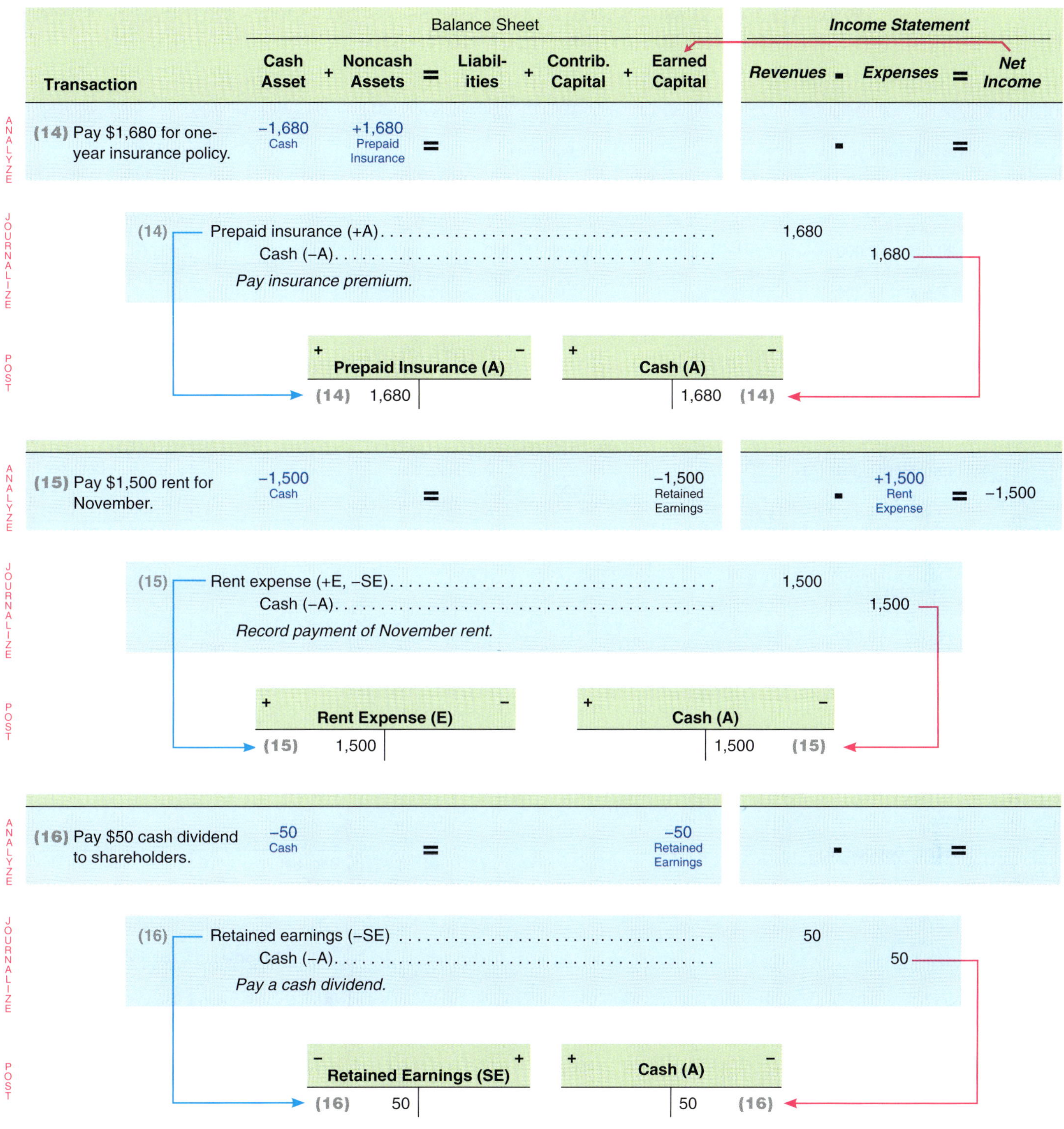

As shown above, each of the journal entries is posted to the appropriate T-accounts, which represent the general ledger. The complete general ledger reflecting each of these sixteen transactions follows, reflecting how the balance sheet and income statement are produced by the same underlying process. The dashed line around the six equity accounts indicates those that are reported in the income statement before becoming part of retained earnings. Each balance sheet T-account starts with an opening balance on November 1 (zero in this case), and the ending balances are the starting balances for December. Income statement T-accounts do not have an opening balance, for reasons we explore in Chapter 3.

As always, we see that: Assets = Liabilities + Equity. Specifically, $24,030 assets ($8,100 + $950 + $11,300 + $1,680 + $2,000) = $4,000 liabilities ($3,700 + $300) + $20,030 equity ($20,000 – $50 + $9,400 – $5,700 – $1,400 – $1,500 – $670 – $50).

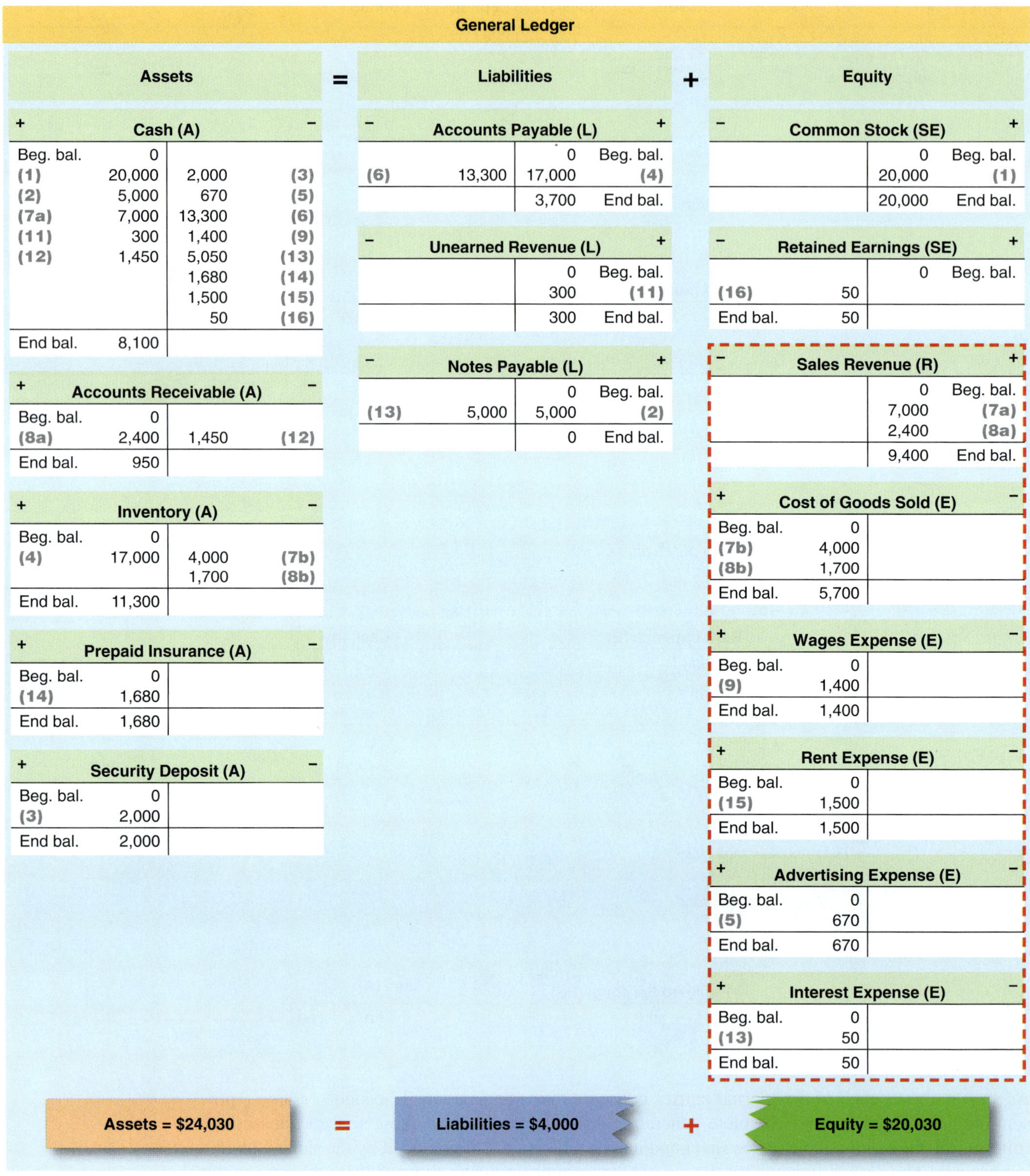

General Ledger

Assets = Liabilities + Equity

Assets

+	Cash (A)		–
Beg. bal.	0		
(1)	20,000	2,000	(3)
(2)	5,000	670	(5)
(7a)	7,000	13,300	(6)
(11)	300	1,400	(9)
(12)	1,450	5,050	(13)
		1,680	(14)
		1,500	(15)
		50	(16)
End bal.	8,100		

+	Accounts Receivable (A)		–
Beg. bal.	0		
(8a)	2,400	1,450	(12)
End bal.	950		

+	Inventory (A)		–
Beg. bal.	0		
(4)	17,000	4,000	(7b)
		1,700	(8b)
End bal.	11,300		

+	Prepaid Insurance (A)		–
Beg. bal.	0		
(14)	1,680		
End bal.	1,680		

+	Security Deposit (A)		–
Beg. bal.	0		
(3)	2,000		
End bal.	2,000		

Liabilities

–	Accounts Payable (L)		+
		0	Beg. bal.
(6)	13,300	17,000	(4)
		3,700	End bal.

–	Unearned Revenue (L)		+
		0	Beg. bal.
		300	(11)
		300	End bal.

–	Notes Payable (L)		+
		0	Beg. bal.
(13)	5,000	5,000	(2)
		0	End bal.

Equity

–	Common Stock (SE)		+
		0	Beg. bal.
		20,000	(1)
		20,000	End bal.

–	Retained Earnings (SE)		+
		0	Beg. bal.
(16)	50		
End bal.	50		

–	Sales Revenue (R)		+
		0	Beg. bal.
		7,000	(7a)
		2,400	(8a)
		9,400	End bal.

+	Cost of Goods Sold (E)		–
Beg. bal.	0		
(7b)	4,000		
(8b)	1,700		
End bal.	5,700		

+	Wages Expense (E)		–
Beg. bal.	0		
(9)	1,400		
End bal.	1,400		

+	Rent Expense (E)		–
Beg. bal.	0		
(15)	1,500		
End bal.	1,500		

+	Advertising Expense (E)		–
Beg. bal.	0		
(5)	670		
End bal.	670		

+	Interest Expense (E)		–
Beg. bal.	0		
(13)	50		
End bal.	50		

Assets = $24,030 = Liabilities = $4,000 + Equity = $20,030

eLectures MBC

LO7 Compute net working capital, the current ratio, and the quick ratio, and explain how they reflect liquidity.

7

ANALYZING FINANCIAL STATEMENTS

Analysis Objective

We are trying to determine if Walgreens has sufficient funds to pay its short-term debts as they come due. To accomplish this task, we employ several measures of liquidity. We introduce three such measures below to assess liquidity.

Analysis Tool Net Working Capital

Net working capital = Current assets − Current liabilities

Applying Net Working Capital to Walgreens

2015: \$19,657 − \$16,557 = \$3,100
2016: \$25,883 − \$17,013 = \$8,870
2017: \$19,753 − \$18,547 = \$1,206

Guidance A company's net working capital is determined primarily by the time between paying for goods and employee services and the receipt of cash from sales for cash or on credit. This cycle is referred to as the firm's **cash operating cycle** (see **Exhibit 2.6**). The cash operating cycle can provide additional resources through trade credit financing. For example, inventory is typically bought on credit with terms that allow payment to be deferred for 30 to 90 days without penalty. The delay in payment allows the cash to be invested, thereby increasing the cash to be used in the following operating cycle. Of course, the reluctant supplier of the credit strives to reduce this payment delay, for example, through discounts for early payment.

A company's net working capital is a broad measure including all current assets even though some of them—inventories for one—require time to turn them into cash. Later in the book, we will discover that the accounting for some components of working capital, like inventory, needs to be adjusted with information found in the footnotes.

EXHIBIT 2.6 Operating Cycle

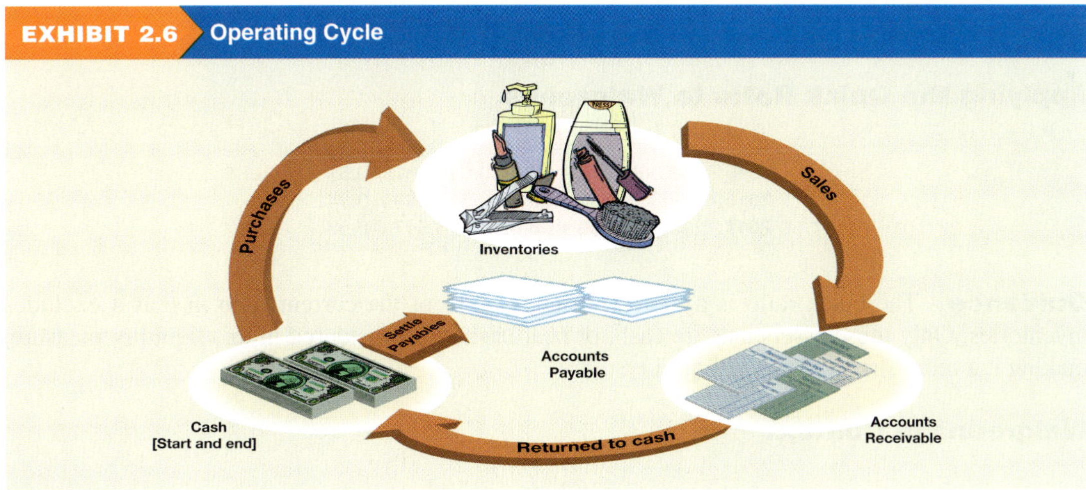

Analysis Tool Current Ratio

$$\textbf{Current ratio} = \frac{\textbf{Current assets}}{\textbf{Current liabilities}}$$

Applying the Current Ratio to Walgreens

2015: $19,657/$16,557 = 1.19
2016: $25,883/$17,013 = 1.52
2017: $19,753/$18,547 = 1.07

Guidance The current ratio is just a different form of net working capital and as such simply provides a different viewpoint. Current ratios exceeding one indicate a positive net working capital. However, for firms that find difficulty in predicting sales and collections, a higher current ratio is desirable, as discussed in Chapter 5. Companies generally prefer a current ratio greater than one but less than two. The ratio allows us to discern whether the company is likely to have difficulty meeting its short-term obligations. The current ratio has additional value as a ratio because net working capital depends on the size of the company. This is useful when comparing companies as below.

Walgreens in Context

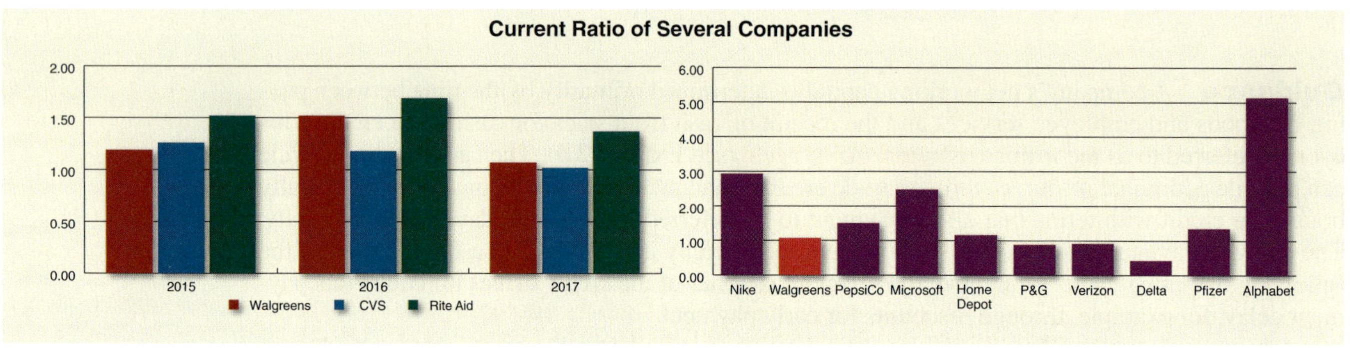

Analysis Tool Quick Ratio

$$\text{Quick ratio} = \frac{\text{Cash} + \text{Short-term securities} + \text{Accounts receivable}}{\text{Current liabilities}}$$

Applying the Quick Ratio to Walgreens

2015: ($3,000 + $0 + $6,849)/$16,557 = 0.59
2016: ($9,807 + $0 + $6,260)/$17,013 = 0.94
2017: ($3,301 + $0 + $6,528)/$18,547 = 0.53

Guidance The quick ratio is a more restrictive form of the current ratio in that it excludes inventories. Only those assets that are cash, or near cash, are considered in this liquidity measure, making it a more stringent test of liquidity.

Walgreens in Context

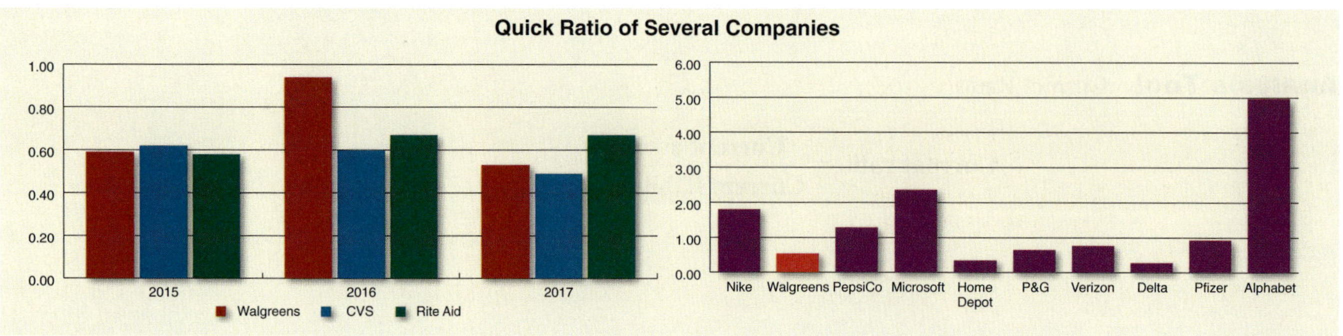

Takeaways Over the three-year period covered by our calculations, we can conclude that Walgreens is in a relatively strong position with respect to liquidity. Its net working capital, while declining in fiscal 2017 has remained positive. Our conclusions are bolstered by comparing Walgreens with two of its major competitors, **CVS Health Corp.** and **Rite Aid Corporation**. In 2017, all three companies are quite similar on liquidity measures even though quite different in size. CVS is about 1.6 times the size of Walgreens while Rite Aid is less than one-third the size based on revenues.

Other Considerations While the ratios above tell us about retail pharmacy chains, other companies with different operating cycles are likely to exhibit different values at optimal levels of activity. Thus grocery stores will have few current assets but consistent large operating cash inflows that ensure sufficient liquidity despite current ratios less than one. Additionally, companies that efficiently manage inventories, receivables, and payables can also operate with current ratios below one. **Wal-Mart**, for example, uses its strong market power to extract extended credit terms from suppliers while simultaneously enforcing short payment periods on customers. In Chapter 10, we explore how many technology and pharmaceutical companies have adopted tax strategies that accumulate large amounts of assets that appear to be liquid, but which could be significantly reduced if brought back to the United States.

CHAPTER-END REVIEW

GuidedExamples MBC

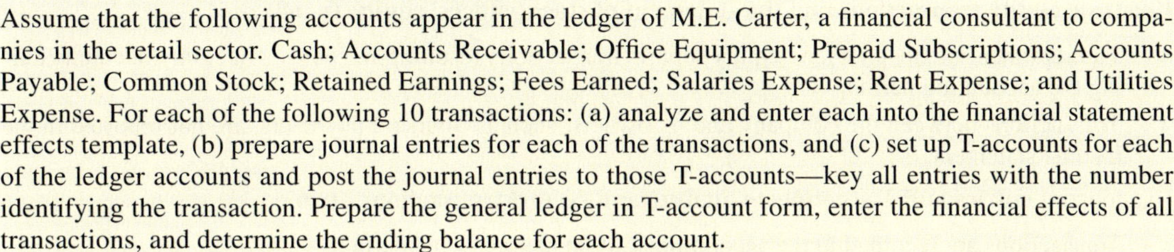

Assume that the following accounts appear in the ledger of M.E. Carter, a financial consultant to companies in the retail sector. Cash; Accounts Receivable; Office Equipment; Prepaid Subscriptions; Accounts Payable; Common Stock; Retained Earnings; Fees Earned; Salaries Expense; Rent Expense; and Utilities Expense. For each of the following 10 transactions: (a) analyze and enter each into the financial statement effects template, (b) prepare journal entries for each of the transactions, and (c) set up T-accounts for each of the ledger accounts and post the journal entries to those T-accounts—key all entries with the number identifying the transaction. Prepare the general ledger in T-account form, enter the financial effects of all transactions, and determine the ending balance for each account.

(1) M.E. Carter started the firm by contributing $19,500 cash to the business in exchange for common stock.
(2) The firm purchased $10,400 in office equipment on account.
(3) Paid $700 cash for this period's office rent.
(4) Paid $9,600 cash for subscriptions to online financial databases covering the next three periods.
(5) Billed clients $11,300 for services rendered.
(6) Made $6,000 cash payment on account for the equipment purchased in transaction 2.
(7) Paid $2,800 cash for assistant's salary for this period.
(8) Collected $9,400 cash from clients previously billed in transaction 5.
(9) Received $180 invoice for this period's utilities; it is paid early in the next period.
(10) Paid $1,500 cash for dividends to shareholders.

The solution to this review problem can be found on pages 95–98.

SUMMARY

Describe and construct the balance sheet and understand how it can be used for analysis. (p. 44) **LO1**

- Assets, which reflect investment activities, are reported (in order of their liquidity) as current assets (expected to be used typically within a year) and noncurrent (or plant) assets.
- Assets are reported at their historical cost and not at market values (with a few exceptions) and are restricted to those that can be reliably measured.
- Not all assets are reported on the balance sheet; a company's self-developed intellectual capital, often one of its more valuable assets, is one example.

- For an asset to be recorded, it must be owned or controlled by the company and carry future economic benefits.
- Liabilities and equity are the sources of company financing; ordered by maturity dates.

LO2 Use the financial statement effects template (FSET) to analyze transactions. (p. 49)

- The FSET captures the effects of transactions on the balance sheet, income statement, statement of stockholders' equity, and the statement of cash flows.
- Income statement effects are separated into revenues, expenses, and net income. The updating of retained earnings is denoted with an arrow line running from net income to earned capital.

LO3 Describe and construct the income statement and discuss how it can be used to evaluate management performance. (p. 53)

- The income statement presents the revenues, expenses, and net income recognized by the company during the accounting period.
- Net income (or loss) is the increase (decrease) in net assets that results from business activities.
- Net income is determined based on the use of accrual accounting.

LO4 Explain revenue recognition, accrual accounting, and their effects on retained earnings. (p. 54)

- Revenues must be recognized only when goods or services have been transferred to the customer.
- Expenses should be recognized as assets are used or liabilities incurred in order to earn revenues or carry out other operating activities.

LO5 Illustrate equity transactions and the statement of stockholders' equity. (p. 60)

- The statement of stockholders' equity reports transactions resulting in changes in equity accounts during the accounting period.
- Transactions between the company and its owners, such as dividend payments, are not reported in the income statement.

LO6 Use journal entries and T-accounts to analyze and record transactions. (p. 62)

- Transactions are recorded in the accounting system using journal entries.
- Journal entries are posted to a general ledger, represented by "T-accounts."
- Accountants use "debits" and "credits" to record transactions in the accounts.

LO7 Compute net working capital, the current ratio, and the quick ratio, and explain how they reflect liquidity. (p. 71)

- Net working capital: an indicator of a firm's ability to pay its short-term debts computed as the difference between current assets and current liabilities.
- Current ratio (CR): A measure of liquidity indicating the degree of coverage of current liabilities by current assets.
- Quick ratio (QR): A measure of the ability to cover current liabilities using only cash and cash equivalents (such as money market accounts), short-term securities, and accounts receivable.

GUIDANCE ANSWERS . . . YOU MAKE THE CALL

You are an Analyst In 2017, Walgreens paid cash dividends of $1,625 million. The net income and dividend payments account for the change in retained earnings ($30,137 million – $27,684 million = $4,078 million – $1,625 million). On occasion, companies pay dividends in excess of their earnings (or pay dividends even when earning losses), resulting in a decrease in retained earnings over the period.

KEY RATIOS

Net working capital = Current assets – Current liabilities

$$\text{Current ratio} = \frac{\text{Current assets}}{\text{Current liabilities}} \qquad \text{Quick ratio} = \frac{\text{Cash} + \text{Short-term securities} + \text{Accounts receivable}}{\text{Current liabilities}}$$

KEY TERMS

Account (p. 50)
Accounting equation (p. 44)
Accounts payable (p. 47)
Accounts receivable (p. 46)
Accrual accounting (p. 54)
Accrued liabilities (p. 47)
Accumulated other comprehensive income or loss (p. 48)
Additional paid-in capital (p. 48)
Asset (p. 44)
Cash (p. 46)
Cash accounting (p. 55)
Cash equivalents (p. 46)
Cash operating cycle (p. 71)
Chart of accounts (p. 51)
Common stock (p. 48)
Compound entries (p. 63)
Contributed capital (p. 48)
Cost of goods sold (p. 55)
Credit (p. 55, 62)
Current assets (p. 46)
Current liabilities (p. 47)
Current maturities of long-term debt (p. 48)
Debit (p. 62)
Deferred (unearned) revenues (p. 48)
Double-entry accounting system (p. 50)
Earned capital (p. 49)
Equity (p. 47, 49)
Executory contract (p. 47)
Expense recognition (p. 54)
Expenses (p. 53)
Fair value (p. 46)
Financial statement effects template (FSET) (p. 50)
Gross profit (p. 55)
Historical cost (p. 46)
Intangible and other assets (p. 46)
Inventory (p. 46)
Journal entry (p. 62)
Liabilities (p. 47)
Liquidity (p. 46)
Long-term debt (p. 48)
Long-term financial investments (p. 46)
Marketable securities (p. 46)
Net assets (p. 53)
Net income (p. 53)
Net loss (p. 53)
Noncurrent assets (p. 46)
Noncurrent liabilities (p. 48)
Nonoperating revenues and expenses (p. 54)
Normal balance (p. 63)
Notes payable (p. 48)
Operating expenses (p. 53)
Other long-term liabilities (p. 48)
Prepaid expenses (p. 46)
Property, plant, and equipment (PPE) (p. 46)
Relevance (p. 46)
Reliability (p. 46)
Retained earnings (p. 48)
Revenue recognition (p. 54)
Revenues (p. 53)
Shareholders' equity (p. 49)
Short-term borrowings (p. 47)
Stockholders' equity (p. 49)
T-account (p. 62)
Treasury stock (p. 48)

Assignments with the MBC logo in the margin are available in myBusinessCourse. See the Preface of the book for details.

MULTIPLE CHOICE

Multiple Choice Answers
1. d 2. a 3. c 4. b 5. d

1. Which of the following conditions must exist for an item to be recorded as an asset?
a. Item is not owned or controlled by the company.
b. Future benefits from the item cannot be reliably measured.
c. Item must be a tangible asset.
d. Item must be expected to yield future benefits.

2. Company assets that are excluded from the company financial statements
a. are presumably reflected in the company's stock price.
b. include all of the company's intangible assets.
c. are known as intangible assets.
d. include investments in other companies.

3. If an asset declines in value, which of the following must be true?
a. A liability also declines.
b. Equity also declines.
c. Either a liability or equity also declines or another asset increases in value.
d. Neither *a* nor *b* can occur.

4. Which of the following is true about accrual accounting?
a. Accrual accounting requires that expenses always be recognized when cash is paid out.
b. Accrual accounting is required under GAAP.
c. Accrual accounting recognizes revenue only when cash is received.
d. Recognition of a prepaid asset (e.g., prepaid rent) is not an example of accrual accounting.

5. Which of the following options accurately identifies the effects a cash sale of an iPhone has on Apple's accounts?

a. Accounts receivable increases, sales revenue increases, cost of goods sold increases, and inventory decreases.

b. Cash increases, sales revenue increases, cost of goods sold decreases, and inventory decreases.

c. Accounts receivable increases, sales revenue increases, cost of goods sold decreases, and inventory decreases.

d. Cash increases, sales revenue increases, cost of goods sold increases, and inventory decreases.

QUESTIONS

Q2-1. The balance sheet consists of assets, liabilities, and equity. Define each category and provide two examples of accounts reported within each category.

Q2-2. Two important concepts that guide income statement reporting are the revenue recognition principle and the expense recognition principle. Define and explain each of these two guiding principles.

Q2-3. GAAP is based on the concept of accrual accounting. Define and describe accrual accounting.

Q2-4. What is the statement of stockholders' equity? What information is conveyed in that statement?

Q2-5. What are the two essential characteristics of an asset?

Q2-6. What does the concept of liquidity refer to? Explain.

Q2-7. What does the term *current* denote when referring to assets?

Q2-8. Assets are recorded at historical costs even though current market values might, arguably, be more relevant to financial statement readers. Describe the reasoning behind historical cost usage.

Q2-9. Identify three intangible assets that are likely to be excluded from the balance sheet because they cannot be reliably measured.

Q2-10. How does the quick ratio differ from the current ratio?

Q2-11. What three conditions must be satisfied to require reporting of a liability on the balance sheet?

Q2-12. Define net working capital. Explain how increasing the amount of trade credit can reduce the net working capital for a company.

Q2-13. On December 31, 2018, Miller Company had $700,000 in total assets and owed $220,000 to creditors. If this corporation's common stock totaled $300,000, what amount of retained earnings is reported on its December 31, 2018, balance sheet?

MINI EXERCISES

LO1

M2-14. Determining Retained Earnings and Net Income Using the Balance Sheet
The following information is reported for Kinney Corporation at the end of 2018.

Accounts receivable	$ 23,000	Retained earnings	$?
Accounts payable	11,000	Supplies inventory	9,000
Cash	8,000	Equipment	138,000
Common stock	110,000		

a. Compute the amount of retained earnings reported at the end of 2018.

b. If the amount of retained earnings at the beginning of 2018 was $30,000, and $12,000 in cash dividends were declared and paid during 2018, what was its net income for 2018?

LO1

M2-15. Applying the Accounting Equation to the Balance Sheet
Determine the missing amount in each of the following separate company cases.

	Assets	Liabilities	Equity
a.	$200,000	$85,000	$?
b.	?	32,000	28,000
c.	93,000	?	52,000

M2-16. Applying the Accounting Equation to the Balance Sheet

LO1

Determine the missing amount in each of the following separate company cases.

	Assets	Liabilities	Equity
a.	$375,000	$105,000	$?
b.	?	43,000	11,000
c.	878,000	?	422,000

M2-17. Applying the Accounting Equation to Determine Unknown Values

LO1 Homework MBC

Determine the following for each separate company case:

a. The stockholders' equity of Jensen Corporation, which has assets of $450,000 and liabilities of $326,000.

b. The liabilities of Sloan & Dechow, Inc., which has assets of $618,000 and stockholders' equity of $165,000.

c. The assets of Clem Corporation, which has liabilities of $400,000, common stock of $200,000, and retained earnings of $185,000.

M2-18. Analyzing Transaction Effects on Equity

LO2, 4, 5 Homework MBC

Would each of the following transactions increase, decrease, or have no effect on equity?

a. Paid cash to acquire supplies.

b. Paid cash for dividends to shareholders.

c. Paid cash for salaries.

d. Purchased equipment for cash.

e. Shareholders invested cash in business in exchange for common stock.

f. Rendered service to customers on account.

g. Rendered service to customers for cash.

M2-19. Identifying and Classifying Financial Statement Items

LO1, 3, 4 Homework MBC

For each of the following items, identify whether they would most likely be reported in the balance sheet (B) or income statement (I).

a.	Machinery	_____	*e.*	Common stock	_____	*i.*	Taxes expense	_____
b.	Supplies expense	_____	*f.*	Factory buildings	_____	*j.*	Cost of goods sold	_____
c.	Prepaid advertising	_____	*g.*	Receivables	_____	*k.*	Long-term debt	_____
d.	Advertising expense	_____	*h.*	Taxes payable	_____	*l.*	Treasury stock	_____

M2-20. Computing Net Income

LO3, 4

Healy Corporation recorded service revenues of $100,000 in 2018, of which $70,000 were for credit and $30,000 were for cash. Moreover, of the $70,000 credit sales, it collected $20,000 cash on those receivables before year-end. The company also paid $60,000 cash for 2018 wages.

a. Compute the company's net income for 2018.

b. Suppose you discover that employees had earned an additional $10,000 in wages in 2018, but this amount had not been paid. Would 2018 net income change? If so, by how much?

M2-21. Classifying Items in Financial Statements

LO1, 3, 5 Homework MBC

Next to each item, indicate whether it would most likely be reported on the balance sheet (B), the income statement (I), or the statement of stockholders' equity (SE).

a.	Liabilities	_____	*d.*	Revenues	_____	*g.*	Assets	_____
b.	Net income	_____	*e.*	Stock issuance	_____	*h.*	Expenses	_____
c.	Cash	_____	*f.*	Dividends	_____	*i.*	Equity	_____

LO1, 3, 4, 5

M2-22. Classifying Items in Financial Statements

For each of the following items, indicate whether it is most likely reported on the balance sheet (B), the income statement (I), or the statement of stockholders' equity (SE).

a.	Accounts receivable	_____	*e.*	Notes payable	_____
b.	Prepaid rent	_____	*f.*	Supplies expense	_____
c.	Net income	_____	*g.*	Land	_____
d.	Stockholders' equity	_____	*h.*	Supplies	_____

LO1, 3, 4, 5

M2-23. Classifying Items in Financial Statements

For each of the following items, indicate whether it is most likely reported on the balance sheet (B), the income statement (I), or the statement of stockholders' equity (SE).

a.	Cash (year-end balance)	_____	*e.*	Dividends	_____
b.	Advertising expense	_____	*f.*	Accounts payable	_____
c.	Common stock	_____	*g.*	Inventory	_____
d.	Printing fees earned	_____	*h.*	Equipment	_____

LO1, 5

L Brands, Inc.
NYSE :: LB

M2-24. Determining Company Performance and Retained Earnings Using the Accounting Equation

Use your knowledge of accounting relations to complete the following table for L Brands, Inc. (All amounts in $ millions.)

Fiscal year ending	January 28, 2017	February 3, 2018
Beginning retained earnings (deficit)	$ (258)	$(727)
Net income (loss)	?	983
Dividends paid	(1,268)	?
Other net changes in retained earnings	(359)	(321)
Ending retained earnings (deficit)	$ (727)	$(751)

LO1, 4

M2-25. Analyzing the Effect of Transactions on the Balance Sheet

Following the example in *a* below, indicate the effects of transactions *b* through *i* on assets, liabilities, and equity, including identifying the individual accounts affected.

a. Rendered legal services to clients for cash
ANSWER: Increase assets (Cash)
Increase equity (Service Revenues)

b. Purchased office supplies on account

c. Issued additional common stock in exchange for cash

d. Paid amount due on account for office supplies purchased in *b*

e. Borrowed cash (and signed a six-month note) from bank

f. Rendered legal services and billed clients

g. Paid cash to acquire a desk lamp for the office

h. Paid cash to cover interest on note payable to bank

i. Received invoice for this period's utilities

LO1, 4

M2-26. Analyzing the Effect of Transactions on the Balance Sheet

Following the example in *a* below, indicate the effects of transactions *b* through *i* on assets, liabilities, and equity, including identifying the individual accounts affected.

a. Paid cash to acquire a computer for use in office
ANSWER: Increase assets (Office Equipment)
Decrease assets (Cash)

b. Rendered services and billed client

c. Paid cash to cover rent for this period

d. Rendered services to client for cash

e. Received amount due from client in *b*

f. Purchased an office desk on account
g. Paid cash to cover this period's employee salaries
h. Paid cash to cover desk purchased in *f*
i. Declared and paid a cash dividend

M2-27. Constructing a Retained Earnings Reconciliation from Financial Data **LO1, 5**

Following is financial information from **Johnson & Johnson** for the year ended December 31, 2017. Prepare the 2017 fiscal-year retained earnings reconciliation for Johnson & Johnson ($ millions).

Johnson & Johnson
NYSE :: JNJ

Retained earnings, Jan. 1, 2017	$70,418	Dividends	$8,943
Net earnings	1,300	Retained earnings, Dec. 31, 2017	?
Other retained earnings changes	$ (2,615)		

M2-28. Analyzing Transactions to Compute Net Income **LO3, 4**

Guay Corp., a start-up company, provided services that were acceptable to its customers and billed those customers for $350,000 in 2018. However, Guay collected only $280,000 cash in 2018, and the remaining $70,000 of 2018 revenues were collected in 2019. Guay employees earned $200,000 in 2018 wages that were not paid until the first week of 2019. How much net income does Guay report for 2018? For 2019 (assuming no new transactions)?

M2-29. Analyzing Transactions Using the Financial Statement Effects Template **LO1, 2, 4**

Report the effects for each of the following independent transactions using the financial statement effects template. If no entry should be made, answer "No entry."

	Balance Sheet									Income Statement				
Transaction	Cash Asset	+	Noncash Assets	=	Liabilities	+	Contrib. Capital	+	Earned Capital	Revenues	−	Expenses	=	Net Income
a. Issue common stock for $20,000 cash.				=							−		=	
b. Pay $2,000 rent in advance.				=							−		=	
c. Purchase computer equipment for $7,000 cash.				=							−		=	
d. Purchase and receive $13,000 of inventory on account (i.e., pay supplier later)				=							−		=	
e. Pay supplier of inventory in part (d)				=							−		=	

M2-30. Analyzing Transactions Using the Financial Statement Effects Template **LO1, 2**

Report the effects for each of the following independent transactions using the financial statement effects template. If no entry should be made, answer "No entry."

	Balance Sheet									Income Statement				
Transaction	Cash Asset	+	Noncash Assets	=	Liabilities	+	Contrib. Capital	+	Earned Capital	Revenues	−	Expenses	=	Net Income
a. Borrow €19,000 from local bank.				=							−		=	
b. Pay €3,000 insurance premium for coverage for following year.				=							−		=	
c. Purchase vehicle for €32,000 cash.				=							−		=	

continued

continued from previous page

Transaction	Balance Sheet: Cash Asset	+	Noncash Assets	=	Liabilities	+	Contrib. Capital	+	Earned Capital	Income Statement: Revenues	−	Expenses	=	Net Income
d. Purchase and receive €2,500 of office supplies on account (i.e., pay supplier later).				=							−		=	
e. Place order for €1,000 of additional supplies to be delivered next month.				=							−		=	

LO1, 2, 3, 4, 5

M2-31. Analyzing Transactions Using the Financial Statement Effects Template
Report the effects for each of the following independent transactions using the financial statement effects template. If no entry should be made, answer "No entry."

Transaction	Balance Sheet: Cash Asset	+	Noncash Assets	=	Liabilities	+	Contrib. Capital	+	Earned Capital	Income Statement: Revenues	−	Expenses	=	Net Income
a. Receive merchandise inventory costing $9,000, purchased with cash.				=							−		=	
b. Sell half of inventory in (a) for $7,500 on credit.				=							−		=	
c. Place order for $5,000 of additional merchandise inventory to be delivered next month.				=							−		=	
d. Pay employee $4,000 for compensation earned during the month.				=							−		=	
e. Pay $7,000 rent for use of premises during the month.				=							−		=	
f. Receive full payment from customer in part (b).				=							−		=	

LO6

M2-32. Journalizing Business Transactions
Refer to the transactions in M2-31. Prepare journal entries for each of the transactions (*a*) through (*f*).

LO6

M2-33. Posting to T-Accounts
Refer to the transactions in M2-31. Set up T-accounts for each of the accounts referenced by the transactions and post the amounts for each transaction to those T-accounts.

EXERCISES

LO1, 7

E2-34. Constructing Balance Sheets and Computing Working Capital
The following balance sheet data are reported for Beaver, Inc., at May 31, 2019.

Accounts receivable	$18,300	Accounts payable	$ 5,200
Notes payable	20,000	Cash	12,200
Equipment	55,000	Common stock	42,500
Supplies	16,400	Retained earnings	?

Assume that on June 1, 2019, only the following two transactions occurred.

June 1 Purchased additional equipment costing $15,000, giving $2,000 cash and a $13,000 note payable.
Declared and paid a $7,000 cash dividend.

a. Prepare its balance sheet at May 31, 2019.
b. Prepare its balance sheet at June 1, 2019.
c. Calculate its net working capital at June 1, 2019. (Assume that Notes Payable are noncurrent.)

E2-35. Applying the Accounting Equation to Determine Missing Data LO1, 3, 5 Homework MBC

For each of the four separate situations *1* through *4* below, compute the unknown amounts referenced by the letters *a* through *d* shown.

	1	2	3	4
Beginning				
Assets	$28,000	$12,000	$28,000	$ (d)
Liabilities	18,600	5,000	19,000	9,000
Ending				
Assets	30,000	26,000	34,000	40,000
Liabilities	17,300	(b)	15,000	19,000
During Year				
Common Stock Issued	2,000	4,500	(c)	3,500
Revenues	(a)	28,000	18,000	24,000
Expenses	8,500	21,000	11,000	17,000
Cash Dividends Paid	5,000	1,500	1,000	6,500

E2-36. Preparing Balance Sheets, Computing Income, and Applying the Current and Quick Ratios LO1, 5, 7 Homework MBC

Balance sheet information for Lang Services at the end of 2018 and 2017 is:

	December 31, 2018	December 31, 2017
Accounts receivable	$22,800	$17,500
Notes payable	1,800	1,600
Cash	10,000	8,000
Equipment	32,000	27,000
Supplies	4,700	4,200
Accounts payable	25,000	25,000
Stockholders' equity	?	?

a. Prepare its balance sheet for December 31 of each year.
b. Lang Services raised $5,000 cash through issuing additional common stock early in 2018, and it declared and paid a $17,000 cash dividend in December 2018. Compute its net income or loss for 2018.
c. Calculate the current ratio and quick ratio for 2018.
d. Assume the industry average is 1.5 for the current ratio and 1.0 for the quick ratio. Comment on Lang's current and quick ratios relative to the industry.

E2-37. Constructing Balance Sheets and Determining Income LO1, 3, 5 Homework MBC

Following is balance sheet information for Lynch Services at the end of 2018 and 2017.

	December 31, 2018	December 31, 2017
Accounts payable	$ 6,000	$ 9,000
Cash	23,000	20,000
Accounts receivable	42,000	33,000
Land	40,000	40,000
Building	250,000	260,000
Equipment	43,000	45,000
Mortgage payable	90,000	100,000
Supplies	20,000	18,000
Common stock	220,000	220,000
Retained earnings	?	?

a. Prepare balance sheets at December 31 of each year.

b. The firm declared and paid a cash dividend of $10,000 in December 2018. Compute its net income for 2018.

LO1, 7 Homework MBC

E2-38. Constructing Balance Sheets and Applying the Current and Quick Ratios
The following balance sheet data are reported for Brownlee Catering at September 30, 2019.

Accounts receivable	$17,000	Accounts payable	$24,000
Notes payable	12,000	Cash	10,000
Equipment	34,000	Common stock	27,500
Supplies inventory	9,000	Retained earnings	?

Assume that on October 1, 2019, only the following two transactions occurred:

October 1 Purchased additional equipment costing $11,000, giving $3,000 cash and signing an $8,000 note payable.
Declared and paid a cash dividend of $3,000.

REQUIRED

a. Prepare Brownlee Catering's balance sheet at September 30, 2019.

b. Prepare the company's balance sheet at the close of business on October 1, 2019.

c. Calculate Brownlee's current and quick ratios on September 30 and October 1. (Assume that Notes Payable are noncurrent.)

d. The October 1, 2019, transactions have decreased Brownlee's current and quick ratios, reflecting a decline in liquidity. Identify two transactions that would increase the company's liquidity.

LO1, 3, 4 Homework MBC

E2-39. Constructing Financial Statements from Transaction Data
Baiman Corporation commences operations at the beginning of January. It provides its services on credit and bills its customers $30,000 for January sales to be collected in February. Its employees also earn January wages of $12,000 that are not paid until the first of February. Complete the following statements for the month-end of January.

Income Statement		Balance Sheet	
Sales	$	Cash	$ 8,000
Wages expense		Accounts receivable	
Net income (loss)	$	Total assets	$
		Wages payable	$
		Common stock	8,000
		Retained earnings	
		Total liabilities and equity	$

LO1, 3 Homework MBC

Procter & Gamble
NYSE :: PG

E2-40. Classifying Balance Sheet and Income Statement Accounts
Following are selected accounts for The Procter & Gamble Company for June 30, 2017.

($ millions)	Amount	Classification
Net sales	$65,058	
Income tax expense	3,063	
Retained earnings	96,124	
Net earnings	15,411	
Property, plant & equipment (net)	19,893	
Selling, general & administrative expense	18,568	
Accounts receivable	4,594	
Total liabilities	64,268	
Stockholders' equity	56,138	
Net earnings from continuing operations	10,194	

a. Indicate the appropriate classification of each account as appearing in either its balance sheet (B) or its income statement (I).

b. Using the data, compute the amount that Procter & Gamble reported for total assets.

E2-41. Classifying Balance Sheet and Income Statement Accounts and Computing Current Ratio

LO1, 3, 7

Shoprite Holdings Ltd
JSE :: SHP

Shoprite Holdings Ltd is an African food retailer listed on the Johannesburg Stock Exchange. The following accounts are selected from its annual report for the fiscal year ended July 2, 2017. The amounts below are in millions of South African rand.

(rand millions)	Amount	Classification
Sales of merchandise	R 141,000	
Depreciation and amortisation	2,176	
Reserves (Retained earnings)	18,838	
Property, plant and equipment	18,407	
Cost of goods and services	107,174	
Trade and other payables	17,414	
Total assets	55,723	
Total equity	27,749	
Employee benefits expense	10,498	
Total noncurrent assets	24,572	
Total noncurrent liabilities	1,492	

a. Indicate the appropriate classification of each account as appearing in either its balance sheet (B) or its income statement (I).

b. Using the data, compute Shoprite's total liabilities at July 2, 2017.

c. Calculate Shoprite's current ratio as of July 2, 2017.

E2-42. Classifying Balance Sheet and Income Statement Accounts and Computing Quick Ratio

LO1, 3, 7

El Puerto de Liverpool
OTCMKTS :: ELPQF

El Puerto de Liverpool (Liverpool) is a large retailer in Mexico. The following accounts are selected from its annual report for the fiscal year ended December 31, 2017. The amounts below are in thousands of Mexican pesos.

(pesos thousands)	Amount	Classification
Total revenue	$122,168,279	
Retained earnings	82,963,786	
Inventory	18,486,423	
Administration expenses	33,549,108	
Total assets	168,266,121	
Long-term debt	33,358,545	
Financing costs	7,137,563	
Total current assets	67,351,290	
Total stockholders' equity	90,082,378	
Prepaid expenses	1,913,794	
Total noncurrent liabilities	38,849,994	

a. Indicate the appropriate classification of each account as appearing in either its balance sheet (B) or its income statement (I).

b. Determine Liverpool's total liabilities and current liabilities as of December 31, 2017.

c. Calculate Liverpool's quick ratio as of December 31, 2017. (Assume that Liverpool only has five types of current assets—cash, marketable securities, accounts receivable, inventory, and prepaid expenses.)

E2-43. Classifying Balance Sheet and Income Statement Accounts and Computing Debt-to-Equity

LO1, 3

Kimberly-Clark
NYSE :: KMB

Following are selected accounts for Kimberly-Clark Corporation for 2017.

($ millions)	Amount	Classification
Net sales	$18,259	
Cost of goods sold	11,706	
Retained earnings	6,730	
Net income	2,319	
Property, plant & equipment, net	7,436	
Marketing research and general expenses	3,227	
Accounts receivable, net	2,315	
Total liabilities	14,269	
Total stockholders' equity	882	

a. Indicate the appropriate classification of each account as appearing in either its balance sheet (B) or its income statement (I).

b. Using the data, compute its amounts for total assets and for total expenses.

c. Compute Kimberly-Clark's debt-to-equity ratio. (Debt-to-equity was defined in Chapter 1.)

LO1, 2, 3, 4 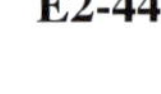

E2-44. Analyzing Transactions Using the Financial Statement Effects Template

Record the effect of each of the following independent transactions using the financial statements effects template provided. Confirm that Assets = Liabilities + Equity for each transaction.

	Balance Sheet									*Income Statement*				
Transaction	**Cash Asset**	+	**Noncash Assets**	=	**Liabil-ities**	+	**Contrib. Capital**	+	**Earned Capital**	***Revenues***	-	***Expenses***	=	***Net Income***
(1) Receive €50,000 in exchange for common stock.				=							-		=	
(2) Borrow €10,000 from bank.				=							-		=	
(3) Purchase €2,000 of supplies inventory on credit.				=							-		=	
(4) Receive €15,000 cash from customers for services provided.				=							-		=	
(5) Pay €2,000 cash to supplier in transaction 3.				=							-		=	
(6) Receive order for future services with €3,500 advance payment.				=							-		=	
(7) Pay €5,000 cash dividend to shareholders.				=							-		=	
(8) Pay employees €6,000 cash for compensation earned.				=							-		=	
(9) Pay €500 cash for interest on loan in transaction 2.				=							-		=	
Totals				=							-		=	

LO2, 6 

E2-45. Recording Transactions Using Journal Entries and T-Accounts

Use the information in Exercise 2-44 to complete the following.

a. Prepare journal entries for each of the transactions (1) through (9).

b. Set up T-accounts for each of the accounts used in part *a* and post the journal entries to those T-accounts. (The T-accounts will not have opening balances.)

LO1, 7 

E2-46. Constructing Balance Sheets and Intrepreting Liquidity Measures

The following balance sheet data are reported for Bettis Contractors at June 30, 2019.

Accounts payable	$ 8,900	Common stock	$100,000
Cash	14,700	Retained earnings	?
Supplies	30,500	Notes payable	30,000
Equipment	98,000	Accounts receivable	9,200
Land	25,000		

Assume that during the next two days only the following three transactions occurred:

July 1 Paid $5,000 cash toward the notes payable owed.
 2 Purchased equipment for $10,000, paying $2,000 cash and an $8,000 note payable for the remaining balance.
 2 Declared and paid a $5,500 cash dividend.

a. Prepare a balance sheet at June 30, 2019.
b. Prepare a balance sheet at July 2, 2019.
c. Calculate its current and quick ratios at June 30, 2019. (Notes Payable is a noncurrent liability.)
d. Assume the industry average is 3.0 for the current ratio and 2.0 for the quick ratio. Comment on Bettis's current and quick ratios relative to the industry.

E2-47. Analyzing Transactions Using the Financial Statement Effects Template LO1, 2, 3, 4
Record the effect of each of the following independent transactions using the financial statement effects template provided. Confirm that Assets = Liabilities + Equity.

	Balance Sheet									*Income Statement*				
Transaction	Cash Asset	+	Noncash Assets	=	Liabil-ities	+	Contrib. Capital	+	Earned Capital	*Revenues*	−	*Expenses*	=	*Net Income*
(1) Receive $20,000 cash in exchange for common stock.				=							−		=	
(2) Purchase $2,000 of inventory on credit.				=							−		=	
(3) Sell inventory for $3,000 on credit.				=							−		=	
(4) Record $2,000 for cost of inventory sold in 3.				=							−		=	
(5) Collect $3,000 cash from transaction 3.				=							−		=	
(6) Acquire $5,000 of equipment by signing a note.				=							−		=	
(7) Pay wages of $1,000 in cash.				=							−		=	
(8) Pay $5,000 on a note payable that came due.				=							−		=	
(9) Pay $2,000 cash dividend.				=							−		=	
Totals				=							−		=	

E2-48. Recording Transactions Using Journal Entries and T-Accounts LO6
Use the information in Exercise 2-47 to complete the following.

a. Prepare journal entries for each of the transactions 1 through 9.
b. Set up T-accounts for each of the accounts used in part *a* and post the journal entries to those T-accounts. (The T-accounts will not have opening balances.)

PROBLEMS

LO1, 3

Comcast Corporation
NASDAQ :: CMCSA
Apple Inc.
NASDAQ :: AAPL
Nike, Inc.
NYSE :: NKE
Target Corporation
NYSE :: TGT
Harley-Davidson, Inc.
NYSE :: HOG

P2-49. Comparing Operating Characteristics Across Industries

Review the following selected income statement and balance sheet data for fiscal years ending in 2017.

($ millions)	Sales	Cost of Sales	Gross Profit	Net Income	Assets	Liabilities	Equity
Comcast Corporation....	$ 84,526	$ 25,384	$59,142	$22,900	$186,949	$117,500	$ 69,449
Apple Inc.	229,234	141,048	88,186	48,351	375,319	241,272	134,047
Nike Inc................	34,350	19,038	15,312	4,240	23,259	10,852	12,407
Target Corporation......	71,879	51,125	20,754	2,934	38,999	27,290	11,709
Harley-Davidson Inc.	4,915	3,262	1,653	522	9,973	8,129	1,844

REQUIRED

a. Compare and discuss how these companies finance their operations.

b. Which companies report the highest ratio of income to assets (net income/total assets)? Suggest a reason for this result.

c. Which companies have the highest estimated ROE? Is this result a surprise? Explain.

LO1, 3

Hewlett-Packard Company
NYSE :: HPQ

P2-50. Comparing Operating Characteristics Within an Industry

Selected data from Hewlett-Packard Company at October 31, 2017, follow.

($ millions)	Sales	Cost of Sales	Gross Profit	Net Income	Assets	Liabilities	Equity
Hewlett-Packard.......	$52,056	$42,478	$9,578	$2,526	$32,913	$36,321	$(3,408)

REQUIRED

Apple inc.
NASDAQ :: AAPL

a. Using the data for Apple Inc. in P2-49, compare and discuss the two companies on the basis of how they finance their operations.

b. Which company reports the higher ratio of income to assets (net income/total assets)? Suggest a reason for this result.

c. Which firm has the higher gross margin (gross profit as a percentage of sales)? What factors might account for the difference?

LO1, 3

Verizon Communications Inc.
NYSE :: VZ

P2-51. Comparing Operating Characteristics Within an Industry

Review the following selected income statement and balance sheet data for Verizon Communications Inc. as of December 31, 2017.

($ millions)	Sales	Cost of Sales	Gross Profit	Net Income	Assets	Liabilities	Equity
Verizon Communications Inc. ...	$126,034	$29,409	$96,625	$30,550	$257,143	$212,456	$44,687

REQUIRED

Comcast Corporation
NASDAQ :: CMCSA

a. Using the data for Comcast Corporation in P2-49, compare and discuss how Verizon and Comcast finance their operations.

b. Which company reports the higher ratio of income to assets (net income/total assets)? Suggest a reason for this result.

c. Which company is likely better able to raise capital? Explain.

LO1, 7

P2-52. Comparing Operating Structure Across Industries

Review the following selected income statement and balance sheet data from the fiscal years ending in 2017 and 2018.

($ millions)	Current Assets	Non-current Assets	Total Assets	Current Liab.	Non-current Liab.	Total Liab.	Equity
3M*	$ 14,277	$ 23,710	$ 37,987	$ 7,687	$ 18,678	$ 26,365	$ 11,622
Abercrombie & Fitch**	1,265	1,061	2,326	508	566	1,074	1,252
Apple†	128,645	246,674	375,319	100,814	140,458	241,272	134,047

* Manufacturer of consumer and business products

** Retailer of name-brand apparel at premium prices

† Computer company

3M Company NYSE :: MMM
Abercrombie & Fitch Co. NYSE :: ANF
Apple Inc. NYSE :: AAPL

REQUIRED

a. Compare and discuss how these companies finance their operations.

b. Which company has the greatest net working capital? Which company has the highest current ratio? Do you have any concerns about any firm's net working capital position? Explain.

P2-53. Preparing a Balance Sheet, Computing Net Income, and Understanding Equity Transactions

LO1, 5

At the beginning of 2018, Barth Company reported the following balance sheet.

Assets		Liabilities	
Cash	$ 4,800	Accounts payable	$12,000
Accounts receivable	14,700	Equity	
Equipment	10,000	Common stock	47,500
Land	50,000	Retained earnings	20,000
Total assets	$79,500	Total liabilities and equity	$79,500

REQUIRED

a. At the end of 2018, Barth Company reported the following assets and liabilities: Cash, $8,800; Accounts Receivable, $18,400; Equipment, $9,000; Land, $50,000; and Accounts Payable, $7,500. Prepare a year-end balance sheet for Barth. (*Hint:* Report equity as a single total.)

b. Assuming that Barth did not issue any common stock during the year but paid $12,000 cash in dividends, what was its net income or net loss for 2018?

c. Assuming that Barth issued an additional $13,500 common stock early in the year but paid $21,000 cash in dividends before the end of the year, what was its net income or net loss for 2018?

P2-54. Analyzing and Interpreting the Financial Performance of Competitors

LO1, 3

Abercrombie & Fitch Co. NYSE :: ANF
Nordstrom, Inc. NYSE :: JWN

Abercrombie & Fitch Co. and **Nordstrom, Inc.**, are major retailers that concentrate in the higher-end clothing lines. Following are selected data from their 2017 fiscal-year ended February 3, 2018, financial statements:

($ millions)	ANF	JWN
Total liabilities and equity	$2,326	$ 8,115
Net income	11	437
Net sales	3,493	15,137
Total liabilities	1,074	7,138

REQUIRED

a. What is the total amount of assets invested in (1) ANF and (2) JWN? What are the total expenses for each company (1) in dollars and (2) as a percentage of sales?

b. What is the return on equity (ROE) for (1) ANF and (2) JWN? ANF's total equity at the beginning of 2017 is $1,252 million and JWN's beginning 2017 equity is $870 million. (ROE was defined in Chapter 1.)

P2-55. Analyzing Balance Sheet Numbers from Incomplete Data and Interpreting Liquidity Measures

LO1, 7

Kimberly-Clark Corp NYSE :: KMB

Selected balance sheet amounts for **Kimberly-Clark Corp**, a consumer products company, for four recent years follow:

($ millions)	Current Assets	Non-current Assets	Total Assets	Current Liabilities	Non-current Liabilities	Total Liabilities	Equity
2014	$?	$9,967	$15,526	$6,226	$8,301	$14,527	$?
2015	5,426	?	14,842	6,349	?	?	40
2016	5,115	9,487	?	?	8,639	?	117
2017	?	9,940	15,151	5,858	?	14,269	?

REQUIRED

a. Compute the missing balance sheet amounts for each of the four years shown.

b. What types of accounts would you expect to be included in current assets? In noncurrent assets?

c. Calculate Kimberly-Clark's working capital and current ratio for 2016 and 2017.

d. Assume that the industry average is 2.0 for the current ratio. Comment on Kimberly-Clark's liquidity measures relative to the industry.

LO1, 7
Sears Holdings Corp.
NASDAQ :: SHLD

P2-56. Analyzing and Interpreting Balance Sheet Data and Interpreting Liquidity Measures
Selected balance sheet amounts for **Sears Holdings Corp.**, a retail company, for four recent fiscal years follow:

($ millions)	Current Assets	Non-current Assets	Total Assets	Current Liabilities	Non-current Liabilities	Total Liabilities	Equity
2014	$5,863	$7,322	$?	$5,595	$8,535	$14,130	$?
2015	?	5,292	11,337	?	7,855	13,293	?
2016	4,996	?	9,362	4,681	?	13,186	(3,824)
2017	3,812	3,450	?	4,915	?	10,985	?

REQUIRED

a. Compute the missing balance sheet amounts for each of the four years shown.

b. What asset category do you expect to constitute the majority of the company's current assets?

c. Calculate SHLD's current ratio for fiscal years 2014 and 2017.

d. Recent popular press articles have described SHLD's declining sales and deteriorating financial condition. What indications of financial deterioration do you see in the balance sheet numbers?

LO1, 2, 3, 4

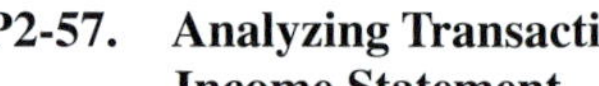

P2-57. Analyzing Transactions Using the Financial Statement Effects Template and Preparing an Income Statement
On December 1, 2018, R. Lambert formed Lambert Services, which provides career and vocational counseling services to graduating college students. The following transactions took place during December, and company accounts include the following: Cash, Accounts Receivable, Land, Accounts Payable, Notes Payable, Common Stock, Retained Earnings, Counseling Services Revenue, Rent Expense, Advertising Expense, Interest Expense, Salary Expense, and Utilities Expense.

1. Raised $7,000 cash through common stock issuance.
2. Paid $750 cash for December rent on its furnished office space.
3. Received $500 invoice for December advertising expenses.
4. Borrowed $15,000 cash from bank and signed note payable for that amount.
5. Received $1,200 cash for counseling services rendered.
6. Billed clients $6,800 for counseling services rendered.
7. Paid $2,200 cash for secretary salary.
8. Paid $370 cash for December utilities.
9. Declared and paid a $900 cash dividend.
10. Purchased land for $13,000 cash to use for its own facilities.
11. Paid $100 cash to bank as December interest expense on note payable.

REQUIRED

a. Report the effects for each of the separate transactions 1 through 11 using the financial statement effects template. Total all columns and prove that (1) assets equal liabilities plus equity at December 31, and (2) revenues less expenses equal net income for December.

b. Prepare an income statement for the month of December.

P2-58. Recording Transactions in Journal Entries and T-Accounts

LO6

Homework MBC

Use the information in Problem 2-57 to complete the following requirements.

REQUIRED

a. Prepare journal entries for each of the transactions 1 through 11.

b. Set up T-accounts for each of the accounts used in part *a* and post the journal entries to those T-accounts.

P2-59. Analyzing and Interpreting Balance Sheet Data and Interpreting Liquidity Measures

LO1, 7

Selected balance sheet amounts for **Apple Inc.**, a retail company, for four recent fiscal years follow:

Apple Inc. NYSE :: AAPL

($ millions)	Current Assets	Non-current Assets	Total Assets	Current Liabilities	Non-current Liabilities	Total Liabilities	Stockholders' Equity
2014	$ 68,531	$?	$231,839	$?	$ 56,844	$120,292	$111,547
2015	89,378	201,101	?	80,610	?	171,124	119,355
2016	106,869	214,817	?	?	114,431	193,437	?
2017	?	246,674	375,319	100,814	?	241,272	134,047

REQUIRED

a. Compute the missing balance sheet amounts for each of the four years shown.

b. What asset category would you expect to constitute the majority of Apple's current assets? Of its long-term assets?

c. Is the company conservatively financed; that is, is it financed by a greater proportion of equity than of debt?

d. Calculate the current ratio for 2014 and 2017.

e. Assume the industry average is 2.0 for the current ratio. Comment on Apple's current ratio relative to the industry.

P2-60. Analyzing Balance Sheet Numbers from Incomplete Data and Interpreting Liquidity Measures

LO1, 7

Selected balance sheet amounts for **Alibaba Group Holding Ltd**, a China-based online and mobile commerce company, for three recent fiscal years ending March 31 follow:

Alibaba Group Holding Ltd NYSE :: BABA

(millions of RMB)	Current Assets	Non-current Assets	Total Assets	Current Liabilities	Non-current Liabilities	Total Liabilities	Equity
2016	20,792	?	?	8,071	?	17,767	38,700
2017	?	47,114	73,630	?	12,919	26,542	47,088
2018	?	73,377	114,326	21,651	22,619	?	?

REQUIRED

a. Compute the missing balance sheet amounts for each of the three years shown.

b. What asset category do you expect to constitute the majority of the company's current assets?

c. Calculate Alibaba's current ratio for fiscal years 2016 and 2018.

d. Calculate net working capital for 2016 and 2018.

P2-61. Analyzing and Interpreting Income Statement Data

LO3

Selected income statement information for **Nike, Inc.**, a manufacturer of athletic footwear, for four recent fiscal years ending May 31 follows:

Nike, Inc. NYSE :: NKE

($ millions)	Revenues	Cost of Goods Sold	Gross Profit	Operating Expenses	Operating Income	Other Expenses	Net Income
2014	$27,799	$15,353	$?	$ 8,766	$3,680	$987	$?
2015	30,601	?	14,067	9,892	4,175	?	3,273
2016	?	17,405	14,971	10,469	4,502	742	?
2017	34,350	19,038	15,312	?	4,749	?	4,240

REQUIRED

a. Compute the missing amounts for each of the four years shown.

b. Compute the gross profit margin (gross profit/sales) for each of the four years and comment on its level and any trends that are evident.

c. What would you expect to be the major cost categories constituting its operating expenses?

LO1, 2, 3, 4 **P2-62. Analyzing Transactions Using the Financial Statement Effects Template and Preparing an Income Statement**

On June 1, 2019, a group of pilots in Melbourne, Australia, formed Outback Flights by issuing common stock for $50,000 cash. The group then leased several amphibious aircraft and docking facilities, equipping them to transport campers and hunters to outpost camps owned by various resorts in remote parts of Australia. The following transactions occurred during June 2019, and company accounts include the following: Cash, Accounts Receivable, Prepaid Insurance, Accounts Payable, Common Stock, Retained Earnings, Flight Services Revenue, Rent Expense, Entertainment Expense, Advertising Expense, Insurance Expense, Wages Expense, and Fuel Expense.

1. Issued common stock for $50,000 cash.
2. Paid $4,800 cash for June rent of aircraft, dockage, and dockside office.
3. Received $1,600 invoice for the cost of a reception to entertain resort owners in June.
4. Paid $900 cash for June advertising in various sport magazines.
5. Paid $1,800 cash for insurance premium for July.
6. Rendered flight services for various groups for $22,700 cash.
7. Billed client $2,900 for transporting personnel, and billed various firms for $13,000 in flight services.
8. Paid $1,500 cash to cover accounts payable.
9. Received $13,200 on account from clients in transaction 7.
10. Paid $16,000 cash to cover June wages.
11. Received $3,500 invoice for the cost of fuel used during June.
12. Declared and paid a $3,000 cash dividend.

REQUIRED

a. Report the effects for each of the separate transactions 1 through 12 using the financial statement effects template. Total all columns and prove that (1) assets equal liabilities plus equity at June 30, 2019, and (2) revenues less expenses equal net income for June.

b. Prepare an income statement for the month of June.

LO6 **P2-63. Recording Transactions in Journal Entries and T-Accounts**

Use the information in Problem 2-62 to complete the following requirements.

REQUIRED

a. Prepare journal entries for each of the transactions 1 through 12.

b. Set up T-accounts for each of the accounts used in part *a* and post the journal entries to those T-accounts.

LO3 

P2-64. Analyzing and Interpreting Income Statement Numbers from Incomplete Data

Starbucks Corporation
NASDAQ :: SBUX

Selected income statement information for **Starbucks Corporation**, a coffee-related restaurant chain, for four recent fiscal years follows.

($ millions)	Revenues	Cost of Sales	Gross Profit	Operating Expenses	Operating Income	Other Expenses	Net Income
2014	$?	$6,858.8	$ 9,589.0	$?	$3,081.1	$1,013.4	$?
2015	19,162.7	?	11,375.2	?	?	841.7	2,759.3
2016	21,315.9	8,511.1	?	8,632.9	4,171.9	?	2,818.9
2017	?	9,038.2	13,348.6	9,213.9	4,134.7	1,249.8	?

REQUIRED

a. Compute the missing amounts for each of the four years shown.

b. Compute the gross profit margin (gross profit/sales) for each of the four years and comment on its level and any trends that are evident.

c. What would you expect to be the major cost categories constituting its operating expenses?

LO3 **P2-65. Analyzing, Reconstructing, and Interpreting Income Statement Data**

Siemens AG
OTCMKTS :: SIEGY

Selected income statement information for **Siemens AG**, a global technology company, for four fiscal years follows:

(€ millions)	Revenues	Cost of Goods Sold	Gross Profit	Operating Expenses	Operating Income	Other Expense	Net Income
2014	€71,227	€50,869	€ ?	€ ?	€6,607	€ ?	€5,507
2015	75,636	?	21,847	15,805	?	?	7,380
2016	?	55,826	23,819	16,500	7,319	1,735	?
2017	83,049	58,021	?	17,337	?	1,512	6,179

REQUIRED

a. Compute the missing amounts for each of the four years shown.

b. Compute the gross profit margin (gross profit/sales) for each of the four years and comment on its level and any trends that are evident.

c. What would we expect to be the major cost categories constituting Siemens' operating expenses?

P2-66. Preparing the Income Statement, Statement of Stockholders' Equity, and the Balance Sheet **LO1, 3, 5**

The records of Geyer, Inc., show the following information after all transactions are recorded for 2018.

Notes payable.	$ 4,000	Supplies	$ 6,100
Service fees earned	67,600	Cash	14,800
Supplies expense.	9,700	Advertising expense.	1,700
Insurance expense.	1,500	Salaries expense	30,000
Miscellaneous expense	200	Rent expense.	7,500
Common stock (beg. year).	4,000	Retained earnings (beg. year)	6,200
Accounts payable.	1,800		

Geyer, Inc., raised $1,400 cash through the issuance of additional common stock during this year and it declared and paid a $13,500 cash dividend near year-end.

REQUIRED

a. Prepare its income statement for 2018.

b. Prepare its statement of stockholders' equity for 2018.

c. Prepare its balance sheet at December 31, 2018.

P2-67. Analyzing Transactions Using the Financial Statement Effects Template and Preparing Financial Statements **LO1, 2, 3, 4, 5** Homework MBC

Schrand Aerobics, Inc., rents studio space (including a sound system) and specializes in offering aerobics classes. On January 1, 2019, its beginning account balances are as follows: Cash, $5,000; Accounts Receivable, $5,200; Equipment, $0; Notes Payable, $2,500; Accounts Payable, $1,000; Common Stock, $5,500; Retained Earnings, $1,200; Services Revenue, $0; Rent Expense, $0; Advertising Expense, $0; Wages Expense, $0; Utilities Expense, $0; Interest Expense, $0. The following transactions occurred during January.

1. Paid $600 cash toward accounts payable.
2. Paid $3,600 cash for January rent.
3. Billed clients $11,500 for January classes.
4. Received $500 invoice from supplier for T-shirts given to January class members as an advertising promotion.
5. Collected $10,000 cash from clients previously billed for services rendered.
6. Paid $2,400 cash for employee wages.
7. Received $680 invoice for January utilities expense.
8. Paid $20 cash to bank as January interest on notes payable.
9. Declared and paid $900 cash dividend to stockholders.
10. Paid $4,000 cash on January 31 to purchase sound equipment to replace the rental system.

REQUIRED

a. Using the financial statement effects template, enter January 1 beginning amounts in the appropriate columns of the first row. (*Hint:* Beginning balances for columns can include amounts from more than one account.)

b. Report the effects for each of the separate transactions 1 through 10 in the financial statement effects template set up in part *a*. Total all columns and prove that (1) assets equal liabilities plus equity at January 31, and (2) revenues less expenses equal net income for January.

c. Prepare its income statement for January 2019.

d. Prepare its statement of stockholders' equity for January 2019.

e. Prepare its balance sheet at January 31, 2019.

LO6 Homework MBC

P2-68. Recording Transactions in Journal Entries and T-Accounts

Use the information in Problem 2-67 to complete the following requirements.

REQUIRED

a. Prepare journal entries for each of the transactions 1 through 10.

b. Set up T-accounts, including beginning balances, for each of the accounts used in part *a*. Post the journal entries to those T-accounts.

LO1, 2, 3, 4, 5

P2-69. Analyzing Transactions Using the Financial Statement Effects Template and Preparing Financial Statements

Kross, Inc., provides appraisals and feasibility studies. On January 1, 2019, its beginning account balances are as follows: Cash, $6,700; Accounts Receivable, $14,800; Notes Payable, $2,500; Accounts Payable, $600; Retained Earnings, $12,400; and Common Stock, $6,000. The following transactions occurred during January, and company accounts include the following: Cash, Accounts Receivable, Vehicles, Accounts Payable, Notes Payable, Services Revenue, Rent Expense, Interest Expense, Salary Expense, Utilities Expense, Common Stock, and Retained Earnings.

1. Paid $950 cash for January rent.
2. Received $8,800 cash on customers' accounts.
3. Paid $500 cash toward accounts payable.
4. Received $1,600 cash for services performed for customers.
5. Borrowed $5,000 cash from bank and signed note payable for that amount.
6. Billed the city $6,200 for services performed, and billed other credit customers for $1,900 in services.
7. Paid $4,000 cash for salary of assistant.
8. Received $410 invoice for January utilities expense.
9. Declared and paid a $6,000 cash dividend.
10. Paid $9,800 cash to acquire a vehicle (on January 31) for business use.
11. Paid $50 cash to bank for January interest on notes payable.

REQUIRED

a. Using the financial statement effects template, enter January 1 beginning amounts in the appropriate columns of the first row. (*Hint:* Beginning balances for columns can include amounts from more than one account.)

b. Report the effects for each of the separate transactions 1 through 11 in the financial statement effects template set up in part *a*. Total all columns and prove that (1) assets equal liabilities plus equity at January 31, and (2) revenues less expenses equal net income for January.

c. Prepare its income statement for January 2019.

d. Prepare its statement of stockholders' equity for January 2019.

e. Prepare its balance sheet at January 31, 2019.

LO6

P2-70. Recording Transactions in Journal Entries and T-Accounts

Use the information in Problem 2-69 to complete the following requirements.

REQUIRED

a. Prepare journal entries for each of the transactions 1 through 11.

b. Set up T-accounts, including beginning balances, for each of the accounts used in part *a*. Post the journal entries to those T-accounts.

CASES AND PROJECTS

LO1, 3, 4, 5

C2-71. Constructing Financial Statements from Cash Data

Sarah Penney operates the Wildlife Picture Gallery, selling original art and signed prints received on consignment (rather than purchased) from recognized wildlife artists throughout the country.

The firm receives a 30% commission on all art sold and remits 70% of the sales price to the artists. All art is sold on a strictly cash basis.

Sarah began the business on March 1, 2019. The business received a $10,000 loan from a relative of Sarah to help her get started; it took on a note payable agreeing to pay the loan back in one year. No interest is being charged on the loan, but the relative does want to receive a set of financial statements each month. On April 1, 2019, Sarah asks for your help in preparing the statements for the first month.

Sarah has carefully kept the firm's checking account up to date and provides you with the following complete listing of the cash receipts and cash disbursements for March 2019.

Cash Receipts	
Original investment by Sarah Penney	$ 6,500
Loan from relative	10,000
Sales of art	95,000
Total cash receipts	111,500
Cash Disbursements	
Payments to artists for sales made	54,000
Payment of March rent for gallery space	900
Payment of March wages to staff	4,900
Payment of airfare for personal vacation of Sarah (vacation will be in April)	500
Total cash disbursements	60,300
Cash balance, March 31, 2019	$ 51,200

Sarah also gives you the following documents she has received:

1. A $350 invoice for March utilities; payment is due by April 15, 2019.
2. A $1,700 invoice from Careful Express for the shipping of artwork sold in March; payment is due by April 10, 2019.
3. Sarah signed a one-year lease for the gallery space; as an incentive to sign the lease, the landlord reduced the first month's rent by 25%; the monthly rent starting in April is $1,200.

In your discussions with Sarah, she tells you that she has been so busy that she is behind in sending artists their share of the sales proceeds. She plans to catch up within the next week.

REQUIRED

From the above information, prepare the following financial statements for Wildlife Picture Gallery: (*a*) income statement for the month of March 2019; (*b*) statement of stockholders' equity for the month of March 2019; and (*c*) balance sheet as of March 31, 2019.

C2-72. Financial Records and Ethical Behavior LO3

Andrea Frame and her supervisor are sent on an out-of-town assignment by their employer. At the supervisor's suggestion, they stay at the Spartan Inn (across the street from the Luxury Inn). After three days of work, they settle their lodging bills and leave. On the return trip, the supervisor gives Andrea what appears to be a copy of a receipt from the Luxury Inn for three nights of lodging. Actually, the supervisor indicates that he prepared the Luxury Inn receipt on his office computer and plans to complete his expense reimbursement request using the higher lodging costs from the Luxury Inn.

REQUIRED

What are the ethical considerations that Andrea faces when she prepares her expense reimbursement request?

SOLUTIONS TO REVIEW PROBLEMS

Mid-Chapter Review 1

SOLUTION

1. A	2. C	3. B	4. E	5. B	6. E	7. X	8. B	9. E	10. B
11. X	12. A	13. B	14. C	15. A	16. D	17. A	18. A	19. E	20. C

Mid-Chapter Review 2

SOLUTION

Transaction	Balance Sheet									Income Statement				
	Cash Asset	+	Noncash Assets	=	Liabil-ities	+	Contrib. Capital	+	Earned Capital	Revenues	-	Expenses	=	Net Income
(a) Issue common stock for $20,000.	+20,000 Cash			=			+20,000 Common Stock				-		=	
(b) Purchase $8,000 of inventory on credit.			+8,000 Inventory	=	+8,000 Accounts Payable						-		=	
(c) Purchase equipment for $10,000 cash.	−10,000 Cash		+10,000 Equipment	=							-		=	
(d) Pay suppliers $3,000 cash.	−3,000 Cash			=	−3,000 Accounts Payable						-		=	
Totals	+7,000		+18,000	=	+5,000		+20,000							
	Assets			=	Liabilities	+	Equity							

Mid-Chapter Review 3

SOLUTION TO PART 1

SCHAEFER'S PHARMACY, INC.
Income Statement
For Year Ended December 31, 2018

Revenues		$45,000
Expenses		
Cost of goods sold	$20,000	
Wages expense	8,000	
Rent expense	5,000	
Utilities expense	2,000	
Other expenses	4,000	
Total expenses		39,000
Net income		$ 6,000

SOLUTION TO PART 2

SCHAEFER'S PHARMACY, INC.
Retained Earnings Reconciliation
For Year Ended December 31, 2018

Retained earnings, Dec. 31, 2017	$25,000
Add: Net income	6,000
Less: Dividends	(1,000)
Retained earnings, Dec. 31, 2018	$30,000

SOLUTION TO PART 3

SCHAEFER'S PHARMACY, INC.
Balance Sheet
December 31, 2018

Cash	$ 3,000	Accounts payable	$ 7,500
Accounts receivable	12,000		
Inventory	26,000		
Office equipment	32,250	Common stock	45,750
Land	10,000	Retained earnings	30,000
Total assets	$83,250	Total liabilities and equity	$83,250

Chapter-End Review

SOLUTION

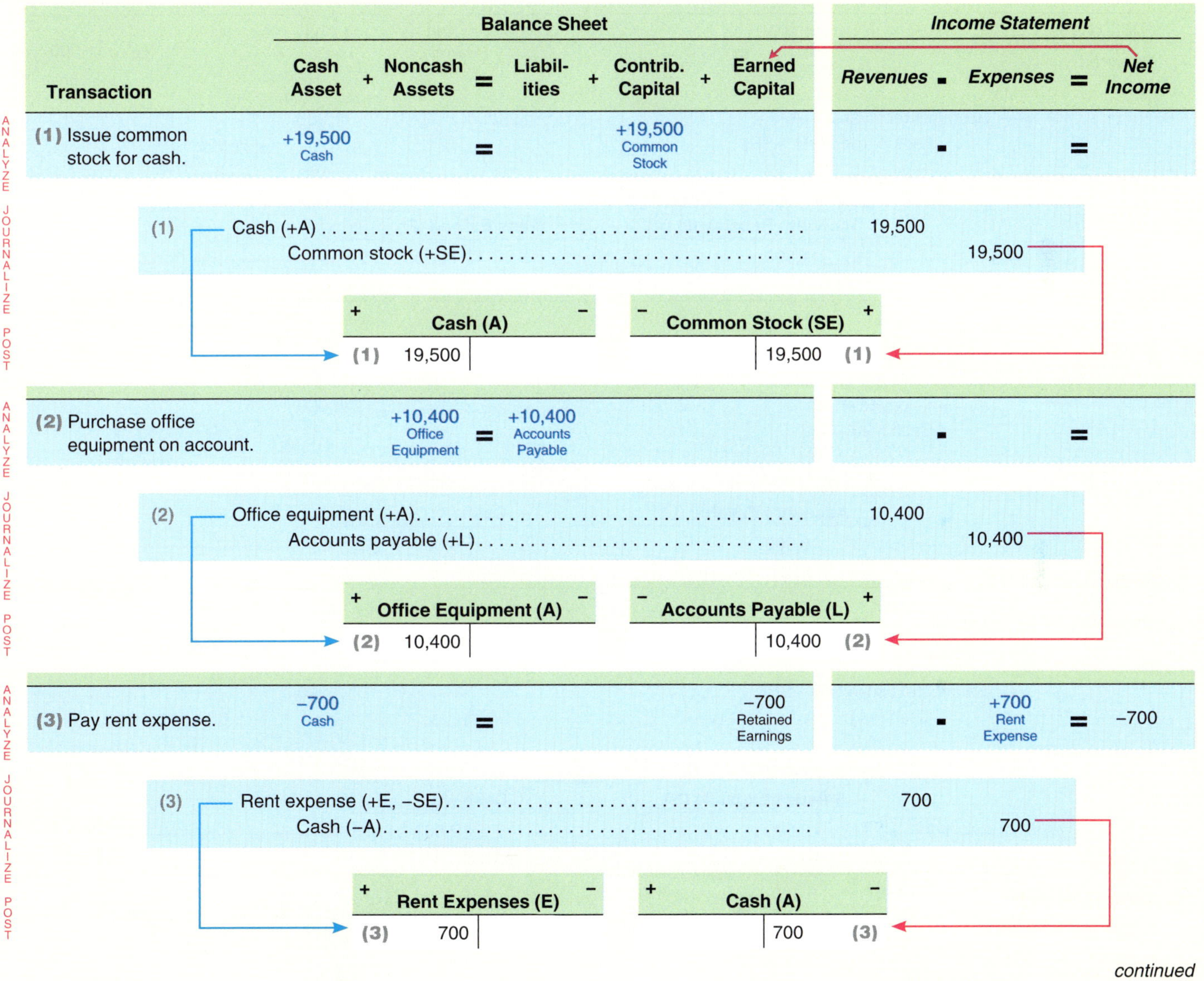

continued

continued from previous page

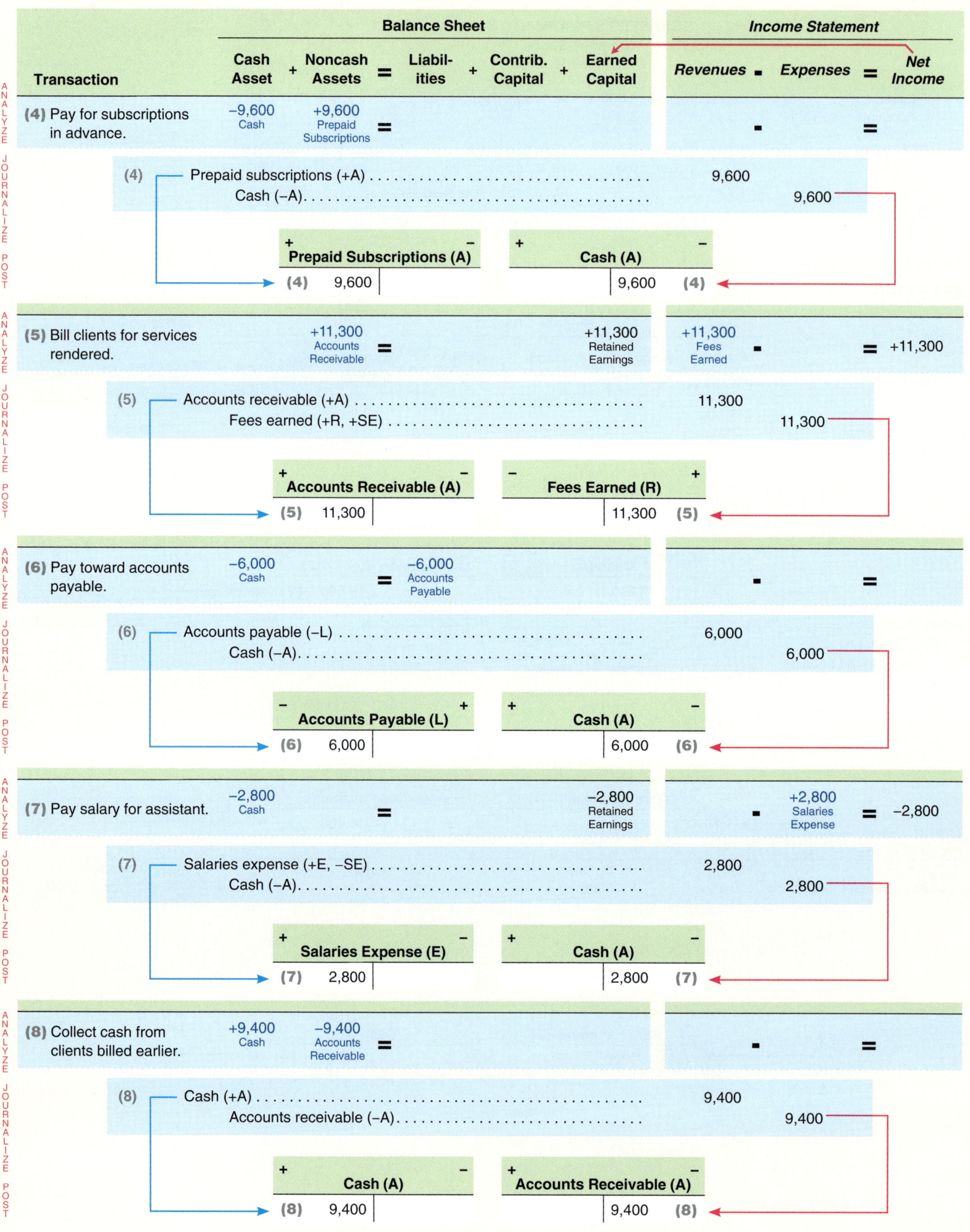

Transaction	Cash Asset	+	Noncash Assets	=	Liabil-ities	+	Contrib. Capital	+	Earned Capital	*Revenues*	−	*Expenses*	=	*Net Income*
	Balance Sheet									***Income Statement***				
ANALYZE **(4)** Pay for subscriptions in advance.	−9,600 Cash		+9,600 Prepaid Subscriptions	=							−		=	
ANALYZE **(5)** Bill clients for services rendered.			+11,300 Accounts Receivable	=					+11,300 Retained Earnings	+11,300 Fees Earned	−		=	+11,300
ANALYZE **(6)** Pay toward accounts payable.	−6,000 Cash			=	−6,000 Accounts Payable						−		=	
ANALYZE **(7)** Pay salary for assistant.	−2,800 Cash			=					−2,800 Retained Earnings		−	+2,800 Salaries Expense	=	−2,800
ANALYZE **(8)** Collect cash from clients billed earlier.	+9,400 Cash		−9,400 Accounts Receivable	=							−		=	

JOURNALIZE

(4) Prepaid subscriptions (+A) 9,600
  Cash (−A) 9,600

POST

+ Prepaid Subscriptions (A) −	
(4) 9,600	

+ Cash (A) −	
	9,600 (4)

JOURNALIZE

(5) Accounts receivable (+A) 11,300
  Fees earned (+R, +SE) 11,300

POST

+ Accounts Receivable (A) −	
(5) 11,300	

− Fees Earned (R) +	
	11,300 (5)

JOURNALIZE

(6) Accounts payable (−L) 6,000
  Cash (−A) 6,000

POST

− Accounts Payable (L) +	
(6) 6,000	

+ Cash (A) −	
	6,000 (6)

JOURNALIZE

(7) Salaries expense (+E, −SE) 2,800
  Cash (−A) 2,800

POST

+ Salaries Expense (E) −	
(7) 2,800	

+ Cash (A) −	
	2,800 (7)

JOURNALIZE

(8) Cash (+A) 9,400
  Accounts receivable (−A) 9,400

POST

+ Cash (A) −	
(8) 9,400	

+ Accounts Receivable (A) −	
	9,400 (8)

continued

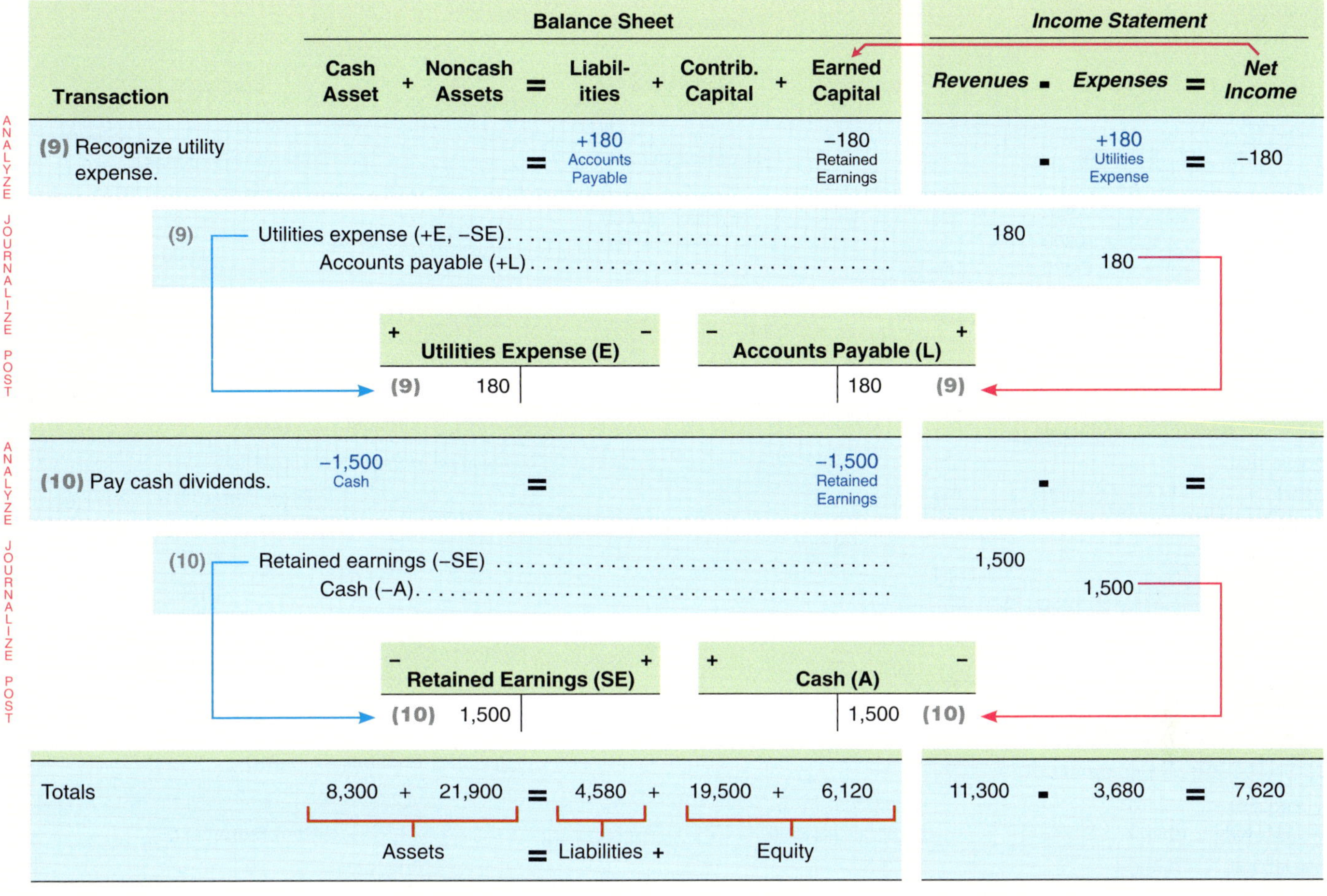

Balance Sheet
Income Statement
Transaction
Cash Asset + Noncash Assets = Liabil-ities + Contrib. Capital + Earned Capital
Revenues - Expenses = Net Income
ANALYZE
(9) Recognize utility expense.
= +180 Accounts Payable
−180 Retained Earnings
- +180 Utilities Expense = −180
JOURNALIZE
(9) Utilities expense (+E, −SE) 180
Accounts payable (+L) 180
POST
+ Utilities Expense (E) −
(9) 180
− Accounts Payable (L) +
180 (9)
ANALYZE
(10) Pay cash dividends.
−1,500 Cash
=
−1,500 Retained Earnings
- =
JOURNALIZE
(10) Retained earnings (−SE) 1,500
Cash (−A) 1,500
POST
− Retained Earnings (SE) +
(10) 1,500
+ Cash (A) −
1,500 (10)
Totals
8,300 + 21,900 = 4,580 + 19,500 + 6,120
11,300 - 3,680 = 7,620
Assets = Liabilities + Equity

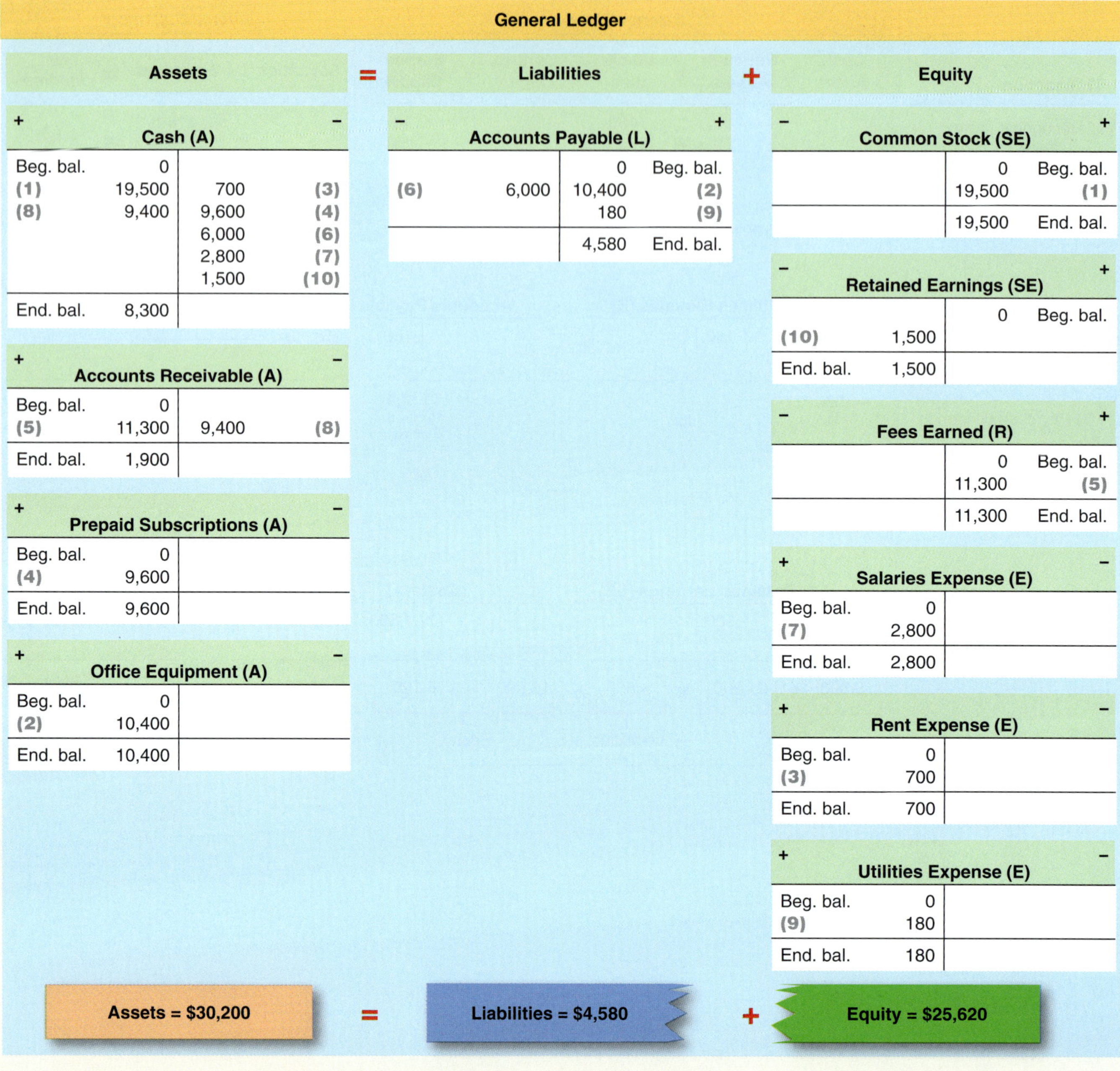

General Ledger

Assets = Liabilities + Equity

Assets

+	Cash (A)		−
Beg. bal.	0		
(1)	19,500	700	(3)
(8)	9,400	9,600	(4)
		6,000	(6)
		2,800	(7)
		1,500	(10)
End. bal.	8,300		

+	Accounts Receivable (A)		−
Beg. bal.	0		
(5)	11,300	9,400	(8)
End. bal.	1,900		

+	Prepaid Subscriptions (A)		−
Beg. bal.	0		
(4)	9,600		
End. bal.	9,600		

+	Office Equipment (A)		−
Beg. bal.	0		
(2)	10,400		
End. bal.	10,400		

Liabilities

−	Accounts Payable (L)		+
		0	Beg. bal.
(6)	6,000	10,400	(2)
		180	(9)
		4,580	End. bal.

Equity

−	Common Stock (SE)		+
		0	Beg. bal.
		19,500	(1)
		19,500	End. bal.

−	Retained Earnings (SE)		+
		0	Beg. bal.
(10)	1,500		
End. bal.	1,500		

−	Fees Earned (R)		+
		0	Beg. bal.
		11,300	(5)
		11,300	End. bal.

+	Salaries Expense (E)		−
Beg. bal.	0		
(7)	2,800		
End. bal.	2,800		

+	Rent Expense (E)		−
Beg. bal.	0		
(3)	700		
End. bal.	700		

+	Utilities Expense (E)		−
Beg. bal.	0		
(9)	180		
End. bal.	180		

Assets = $30,200 = Liabilities = $4,580 + Equity = $25,620

Adjusting Accounts for Financial Statements

LEARNING OBJECTIVES

1. Identify the major steps in the accounting cycle. (p. 102)
2. Review the process of journalizing and posting transactions. (p. 103)
3. Describe the adjusting process and illustrate adjusting entries. (p. 109)
4. Prepare financial statements from adjusted accounts. (p. 118)
5. Describe the process of closing temporary accounts. (p. 122)
6. Analyze changes in balance sheet accounts. (p. 125)

WALGREENS
www.walgreens.com

Walgreens Boots Alliance, Inc.'s strategy for growth has three principal components. Within its network of more than 12,000 stores worldwide, it strives to create a "Well Experience" for customers, by store design and layout, by employee training, and by digital applications. Their goal is to give the customer the "Three Ws"—What they want. Where they want it. When they want it. In fiscal year 2017, Walgreens reported an increase of 4.2% in U.S. retail pharmacy sales, but a 1% decrease in same-store sales.

Pharmacy sales represent almost two-thirds of Walgreens' revenue, and the aging U.S. population will cause this to grow. The 2014 acquisition of Alliance Boots GmbH and the 2017 acquisition of over 1,900 Rite-Aid stores create the world's "leading pharmacy-led health and well-being enterprise," and provide the company with a global platform for growth.

Because the financial statements should reflect the firm's underlying economic reality, Walgreens' management will need to "adjust" or "update" its financial statements to reflect the changes in its strategy and performance.

Accounting adjustments are a key part of creating the financial statements, and they are central to the difference between accrual and cash accounting. While cash accounting only records transactions that involve cash receipts and disbursements,

accrual accounting records revenues when they are earned (even if cash has not yet been received) and expenses as they are incurred (regardless of when the cash disbursement associated with that expense is made). The quality, or lack thereof, of the financial statements often hinges on the quality of those adjustments. Thus, understanding how and why accounting adjustments occur is fundamentally important to those who wish to analyze and interpret the financial statements.

This chapter describes the need for adjustments, how they are prepared, their financial statement effect, and the need for ethics and oversight in this process. We illustrate how financial statements are prepared from those adjusted accounts. Then, we end the chapter with the closing process for the financial statements. Such "closing of the books" enables firms to report their performance for the year and then "open the books" anew for the next period.

Sources: Walgreens Boots Alliance, Inc. 2017 10-K, *The Wall Street Journal, Bloomberg News.*

CHAPTER ORGANIZATION

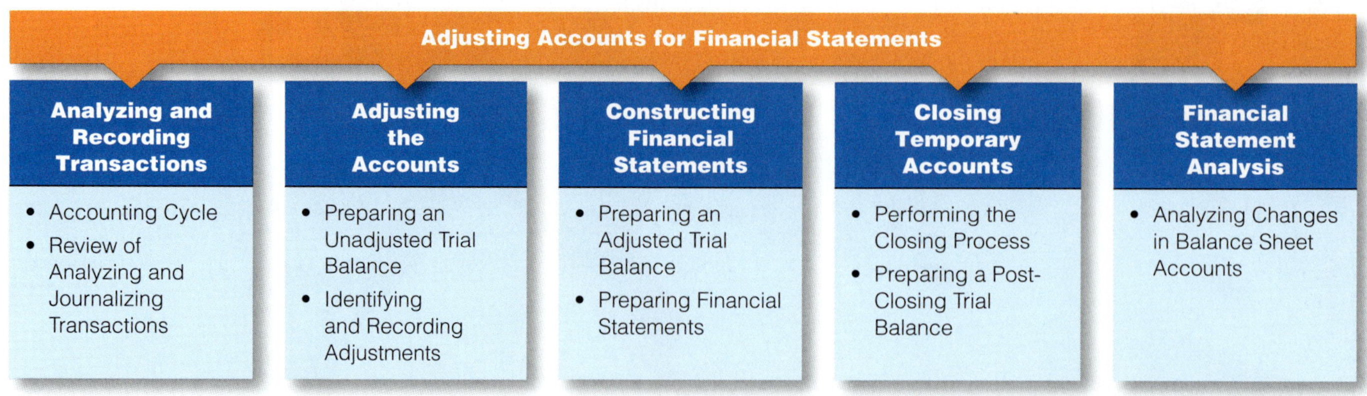

The double-entry accounting system introduced in Chapter 2 provides us with a framework for the analysis of business activities, and we use that framework to record transactions and create financial reports. This chapter describes more fully the procedures companies use to account for the operations of a business during a specific time period. All companies, regardless of size or complexity, perform accounting steps, known as the *accounting cycle*, to accumulate and report their financial information. An important step in the accounting cycle is the *adjusting* process that occurs at the end of every reporting period. This chapter focuses on the accounting cycle with emphasis on the adjusting process.

1 **LO1** Identify the major steps in the accounting cycle.

ACCOUNTING CYCLE

Companies engage in business activities. These activities are analyzed for their financial impact, and the results from that analysis are entered into the accounting information system. When management and others want to know where the company stands financially, and what its recent performance tells about future prospects, the financial data often require adjustment prior to financial statements being prepared. At the end of this adjustment process, the company *closes the books*. This closing process prepares accounts for the next accounting period.

The process described constitutes the major steps in the **accounting cycle**—a sequence of activities to accumulate and report financial statements. The steps are: analyze, record, adjust, report, and close. **Exhibit 3.1** shows the sequence of major steps in the accounting cycle.

EXHIBIT 3.1 Accounting Cycle—Abbreviated

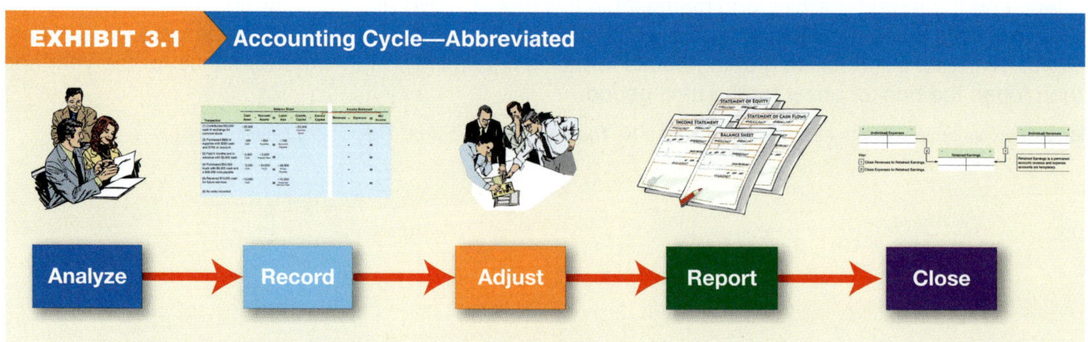

The steps in the accounting cycle do not occur with equal frequency. That is, companies analyze and record daily transactions throughout the accounting period, but they adjust and report only when management requires financial statements, often monthly or quarterly, but at least annually. Closing occurs once during the accounting cycle, at the period-end.

The annual (one-year) accounting period adopted by a company is known as its **fiscal year**. Companies with fiscal year-ends on December 31 are said to be on a **calendar year**. About 60% of U.S. companies are on a calendar-year basis. Many companies prefer to have their accounting year coincide with their "natural" year; that is, the fiscal year ends when business is slow. For example, **L Brands, Inc.**, a specialty retailer, ends its fiscal year on the Saturday nearest January 31. **Starbucks Corporation** ends its fiscal year on the Sunday nearest to September 30. The **Manchester United Ltd.**, a professional soccer team, ends its fiscal year on June 30, during its off-season.

ANALYZING AND RECORDING TRANSACTIONS

LO2 Review the process of journalizing and posting transactions.

2

The purpose of this section is to (1) review the analysis and recording of transactions as described in Chapter 2, and (2) to extend the Natural Beauty Supply example to illustrate the process of adjusting and closing accounts in the following sections. Natural Beauty Supply's fiscal year-end is December 31.

Review of Accounting Procedures

The **chart of accounts** for Natural Beauty Supply is in **Exhibit 3.2**, and lists the titles and numbers of all accounts found in its general ledger. The account titles are grouped into the five major sections of the general ledger (assets, liabilities, equity, revenues, and expenses). We saw in Chapter 2 that the recording process involves analyzing, journalizing, and posting. The **general journal**, or *book of original entry*, is a tabular record where business activities are captured in debits and credits and recorded in chronological order before they are posted to the general ledger. The word *journalize* means to record a transaction in a **journal**. Each transaction entered in the journal must be stated in terms of equal dollar amounts of debits and credits—the double-entry system at work. The account titles cited must correspond to those in the general ledger (per the chart of accounts).

EXHIBIT 3.2 Chart of Accounts for Natural Beauty Supply

Assets	**Equity**
110 Cash	310 Common Stock
120 Accounts Receivable	320 Retained Earnings
130 Other Receivables	
140 Inventory	**Revenues and Income**
150 Prepaid Insurance	410 Sales Revenue
160 Security Deposit	420 Interest Income
170 Fixtures and Equipment	
175 Accumulated Depreciation—Fixtures and Equipment	**Expenses**
	510 Cost of Goods Sold
	520 Wages Expense
Liabilities	530 Rent Expense
210 Accounts Payable	540 Advertising Expense
220 Interest Payable	550 Depreciation Expense—Fixtures and Equipment
230 Wages Payable	560 Insurance Expense
240 Taxes Payable	570 Interest Expense
250 Gift Card Liability	580 Tax Expense
260 Notes Payable	

After transactions are journalized, the debits and credits in each journal entry are transferred to their related general ledger accounts. This transcribing process is called posting to the general ledger, or simply **posting**. Journalizing and posting occur simultaneously when recordkeeping is automated.

Review of Recording Transactions

In Chapter 2, we recorded the November activities of Natural Beauty Supply (NBS) and created the end-of-November financial statements. As NBS continues its activities into the next month, the end-of-November balance sheet provides the starting point for December. **Exhibit 3.3** provides a summary of Natural Beauty Supply's December 2018 transactions.

EXHIBIT 3.3 Transactions for Natural Beauty Supply for December 2018

Event	Date	Description
(17)	Dec. 1	NBS signed a three-year note to borrow $11,000 cash from a financial institution. NBS will pay interest on the first business day of every month (starting in January) at the rate of 12% per year or 1% per month. The $11,000 principal is due at the end of three years.
(18)	Dec. 1	NBS purchased and installed improved fixtures and equipment for $18,000 cash.
(19)	Dec. 10	NBS paid $700 to advertise in the local newspaper for December.
(20)	Dec. 20	NBS paid $3,300 cash to its suppliers in partial payment for the delivery of inventory in November.
(21)	Dec. —	During the month of December, NBS sold products costing $5,000 to retail customers for $8,500 cash.
(22)	Dec. —	During the month of December, sales to wholesale customers totaled $4,500 for merchandise that had cost $3,000. Instead of paying cash, wholesale customers are required to pay for the merchandise within ten business days.
(23)	Dec. —	$1,200 of gift cards were sold during the month of December. Each gift card entitles the recipient to a one-hour consultation on the use of NBS's products.
(24)	Dec. —	NBS employed salespersons who were paid $1,625 in cash in December.
(25)	Dec. —	During the month of December, NBS received $3,200 in cash from wholesale customers for products that had been delivered earlier.
(26)	Dec. 28	NBS purchased and received $4,000 of inventory on account.
(27)	Dec. 31	NBS paid $1,500 to the landlord for December rent.
(28)	Dec. 31	NBS paid $50 cash dividend to its shareholders.

Most of these transactions are similar to those that we analyzed in Chapter 2. Each of the transactions involves an exchange of some kind. Suppliers provide inventory and employees provide labor services in exchange for cash or the promise of future cash payments. Customers receive products in exchange for cash or a promise to pay cash in the future. For each of these items, we analyze, journalize, and post as shown in Chapter 2.

NBS has the opportunity to secure long-term financing from a financial institution, and signs a note that must be paid back at the end of three years. Cash increases, and a noncurrent liability increases. Interest payments are made at the start of every month, beginning on January 2, 2019, but no entry is made for interest until time passes and an interest obligation is created.

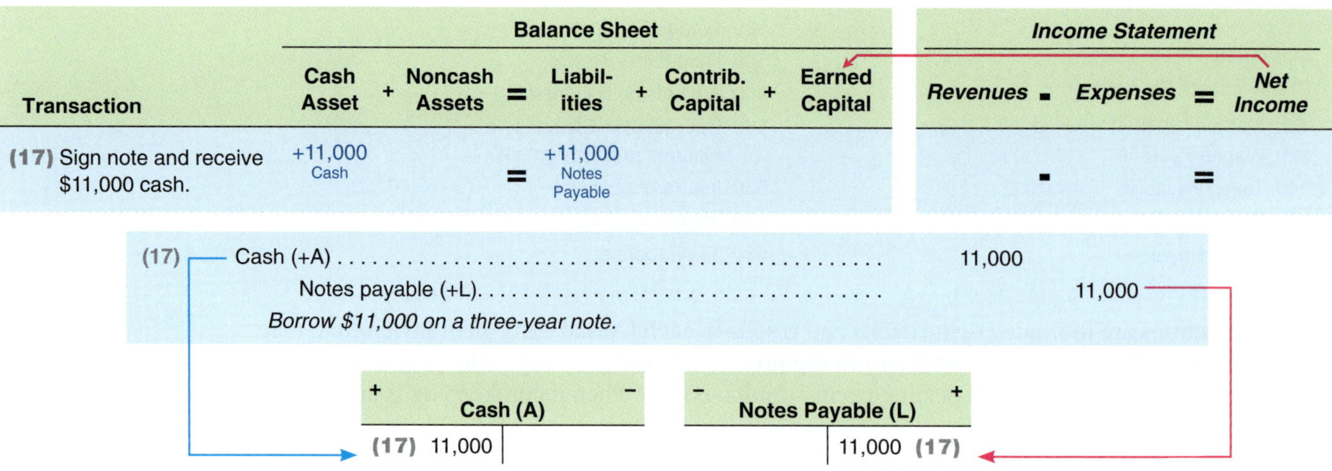

NBS pays $18,000 cash to purchase improved fixtures and equipment for its store location. One asset (cash) decreases, while a noncurrent asset (fixtures and equipment) is increased.

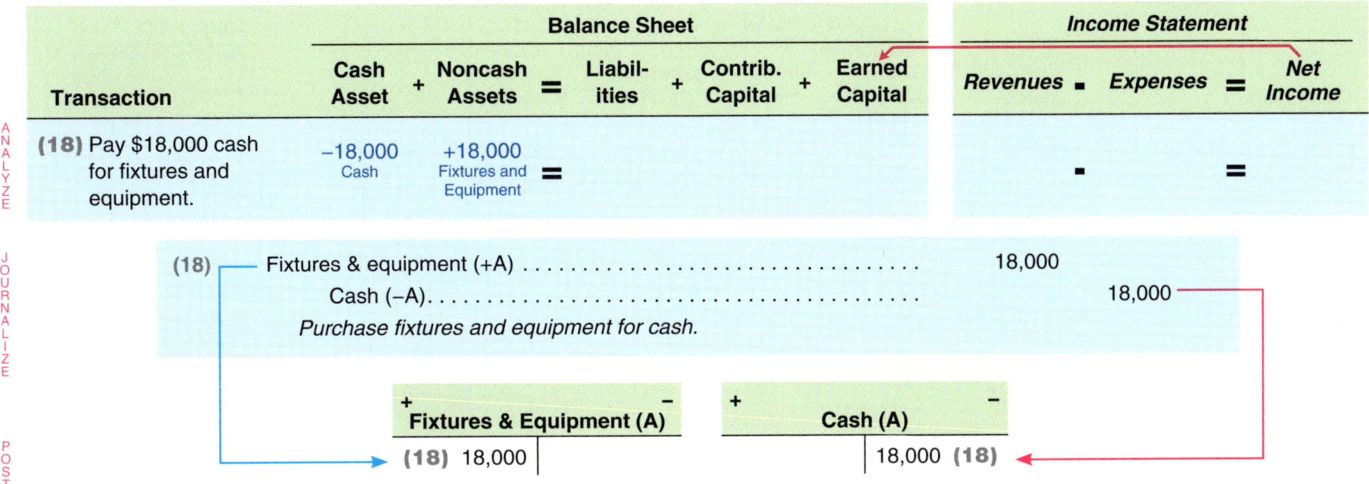

Transactions (19) and (20) are similar to ones that we saw in Chapter 2. The expenditure for advertising results in an expense that decreases net income and ultimately, retained earnings. The payment to suppliers fulfills (in part) an obligation that appeared in the November 30 balance sheet.

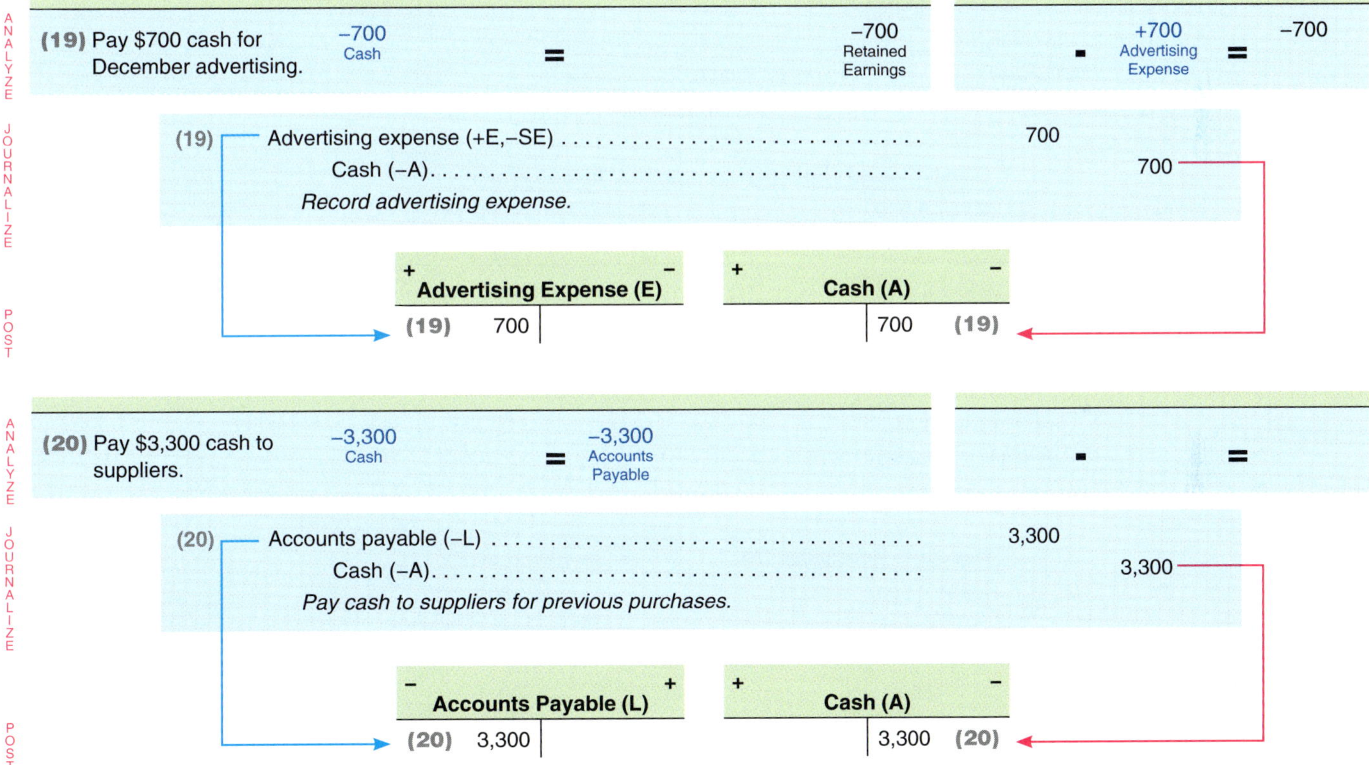

Sales to customers in (21), (22), and (23) are also similar to transactions in Chapter 2, and they are accounted for in similar fashion. Revenue is recognized when products are delivered to customers, rather than when cash is received. When cash is received after delivery, an accounts receivable asset is recorded; when cash is received before delivery, a performance obligation liability is recorded. In this case, NBS uses the account title "Gift Card Liability."[1] Cost of goods sold expense is recognized when the associated revenue is recognized.

[1] The Gift Card Liability represents NBS's obligation to deliver services to customers when the gift cards are redeemed. Companies sometimes use the terms "deferred revenue" or "unearned revenue" to refer to these liabilities. We use the preferred terms "performance obligation," "contract liability," or a more descriptive account title such as "Gift Card Liability" wherever possible.

Balance Sheet
Income Statement
Transaction
Cash Asset + Noncash Assets = Liabil-ities + Contrib. Capital + Earned Capital
Revenues - Expenses = Net Income
ANALYZE
(21a) Sell $8,500 of products for cash.
+8,500 Cash
=
+8,500 Retained Earnings
+8,500 Sales Revenue
-
=
+8,500
JOURNALIZE
(21a) Cash (+A) 8,500
Sales revenue (+R,+SE) 8,500
Sell products for cash.
POST
+ Cash (A) −
(21a) 8,500
− Sales Revenue (R) +
8,500 (21a)
ANALYZE
(21b) Record $5,000 for the cost of merchandise sold in transaction 21a.
−5,000 Inventory
=
−5,000 Retained Earnings
-
+5,000 Cost of Goods Sold
=
−5,000
JOURNALIZE
(21b) Cost of goods sold (+E,−SE) 5,000
Inventory (−A) 5,000
Record cost of merchandise sold as expense.
POST
+ Cost of Goods Sold (E) −
(21b) 5,000
+ Inventory (A) −
5,000 (21b)
ANALYZE
(22a) Sell $4,500 of products on account.
+4,500 Accounts Receivable
=
+4,500 Retained Earnings
+4,500 Sales Revenue
-
=
+4,500
JOURNALIZE
(22a) Accounts receivable (+A) 4,500
Sales revenue (+R,+SE) 4,500
Sell products on account.
POST
+ Accounts Receivable (A) −
(22a) 4,500
− Sales Revenue (R) +
4,500 (22a)
ANALYZE
(22b) Record $3,000 for the cost of merchandise sold in transaction 22a.
−3,000 Inventory
=
−3,000 Retained Earnings
-
+3,000 Cost of Goods Sold
=
−3,000
JOURNALIZE
(22b) Cost of goods sold (+E,−SE) 3,000
Inventory (−A) 3,000
Record cost of merchandise sold as expense.
POST
+ Cost of Goods Sold (E) −
(22b) 3,000
+ Inventory (A) −
3,000 (22b)

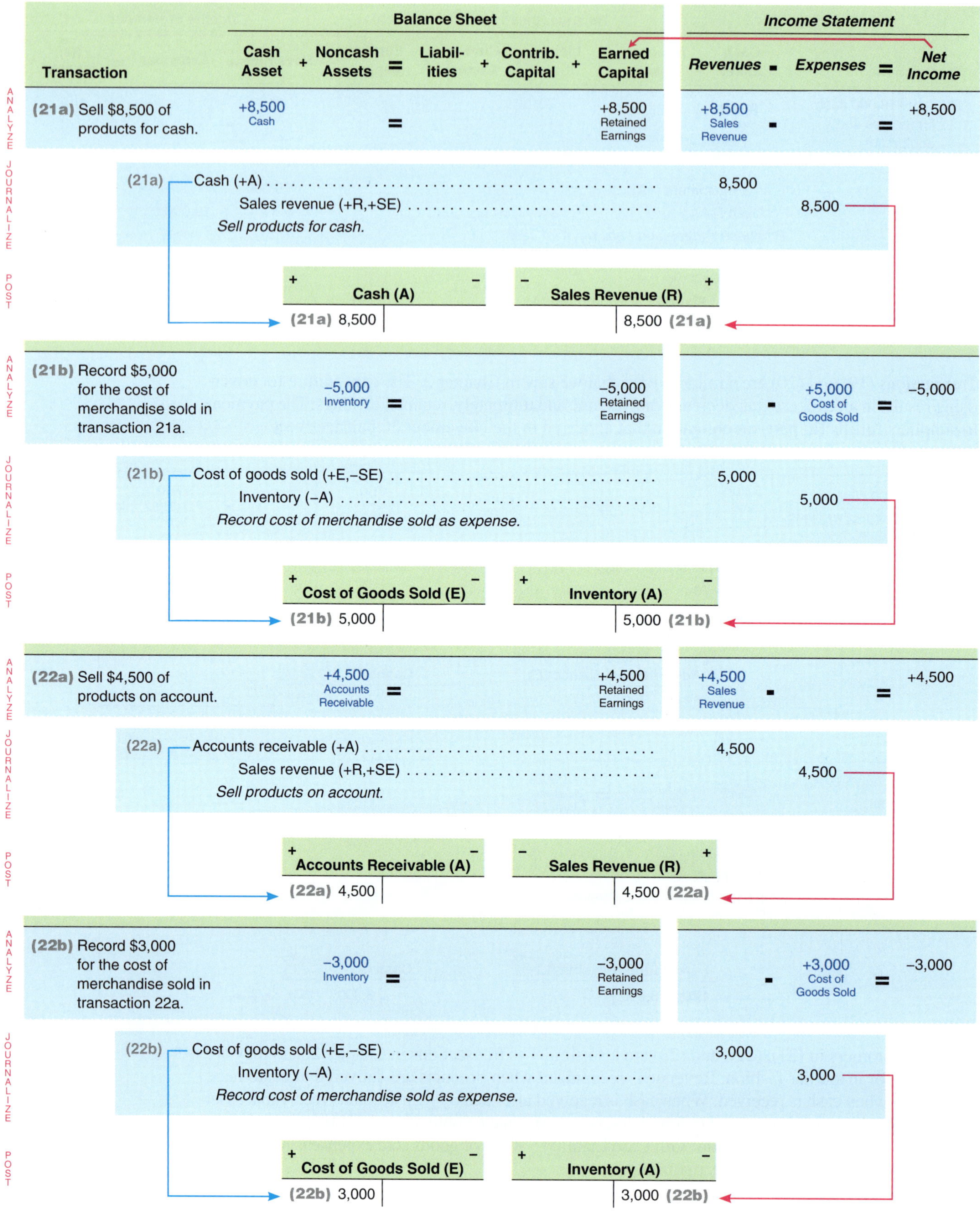

continued

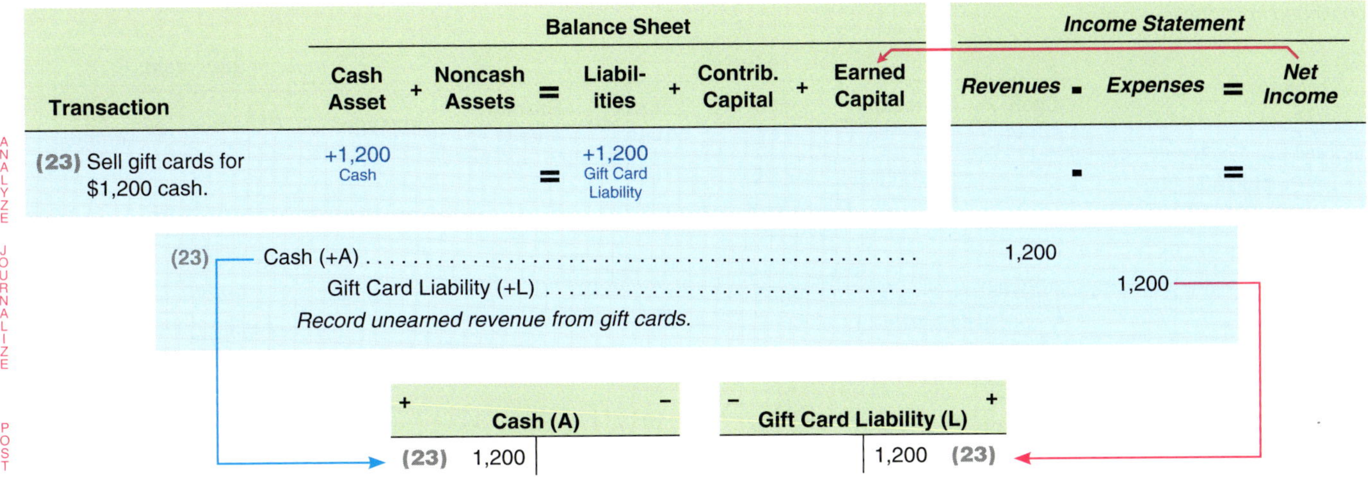

The final five transactions in December also are similar to transactions that NBS had in November. Payment of wages to the employee is reflected in a wage expense. Cash received from wholesale (credit) customers does not cause revenue; rather the increase in cash is balanced by a decrease in accounts receivable. Purchase of inventory on account does not create an expense—the cost of the inventory is held in the inventory asset account until it is purchased by a customer. Payments to the landlord are balanced by a rent expense in the income statement. The cash dividend to shareholders decreases an asset (cash) and shareholders' equity (retained earnings), but does not affect the income statement.

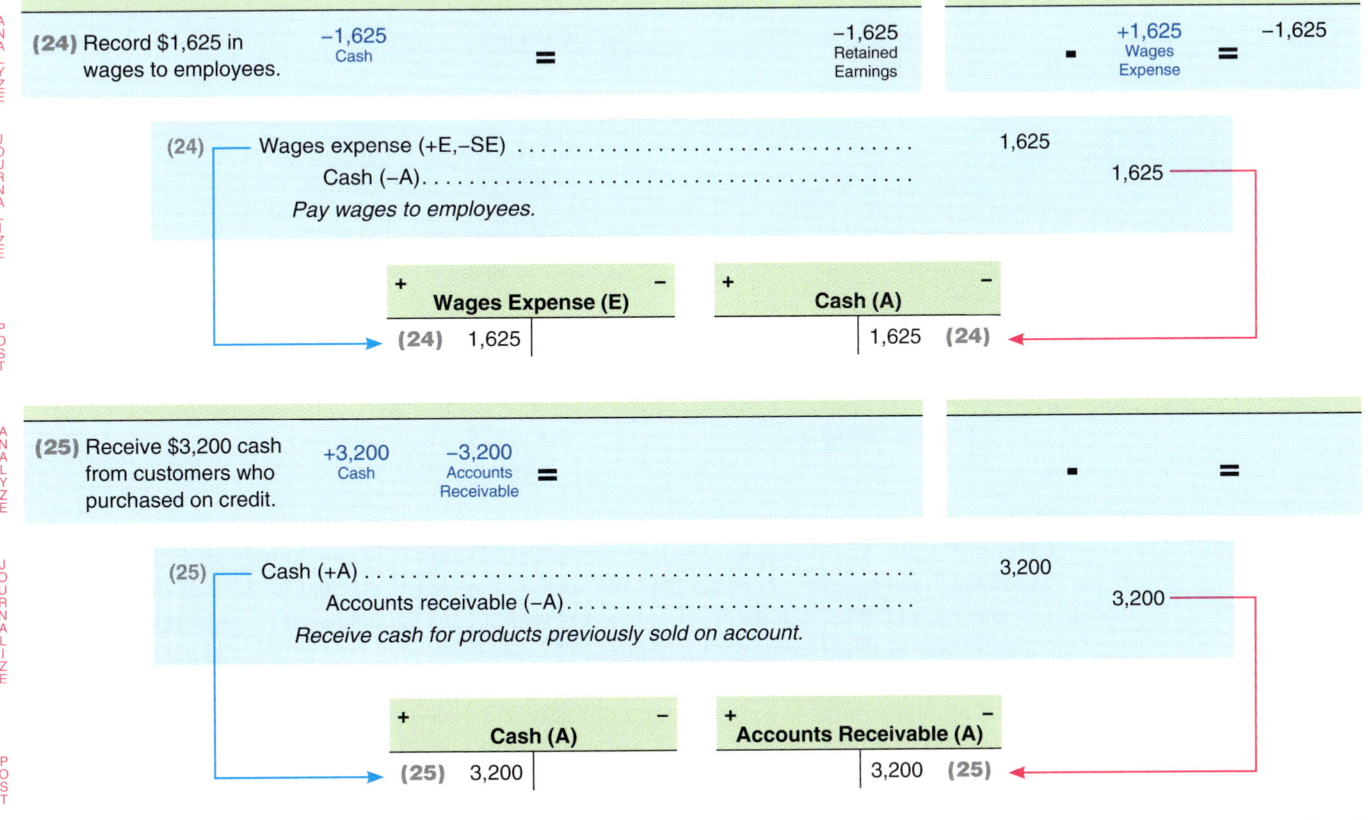

continued

continued from previous page

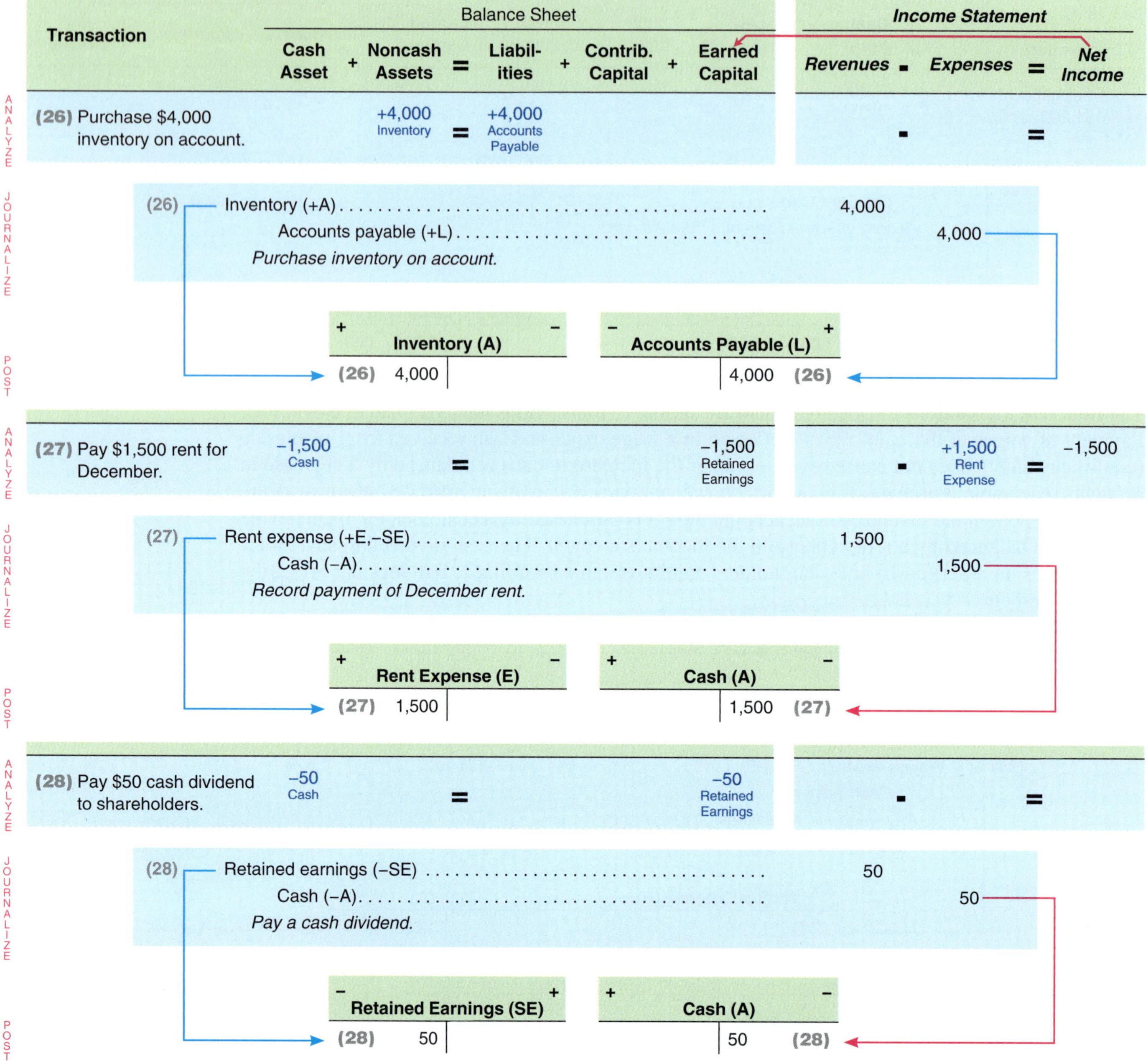

Exhibit 3.4 presents the general ledger accounts of Natural Beauty Supply in T-account form for December. Each balance sheet account has an opening balance equal to the end-of-November balance, and each income statement account starts with a zero balance so it records only the events of the current period. The December transactions (17–28) have been posted. We can trace each of the postings from the transactions above to these ledger accounts.

But the amounts in these accounts are not ready to be assembled into financial reports. There are revenues and expenses and changes in assets and liabilities that occur with the passage of time.[2] Accounting for these items is essential for us to determine how well a company has performed in an accounting period and to assess its financial standing.

[2] Natural Beauty Supply's November activities in Chapter 2 were carefully chosen so we could produce financial statements without adjusting entries. But, as **Exhibit 3.1** depicts, the adjusting process is an essential part of the accounting cycle.

EXHIBIT 3.4 General Ledger for Natural Beauty Supply before Adjustments

General Ledger

Assets = Liabilities + Equity

Assets

Cash (A) (+ / −)

Beg. bal.	8,100		
(17)	11,000	18,000	(18)
(21a)	8,500	700	(19)
(23)	1,200	3,300	(20)
(25)	3,200	1,625	(24)
		1,500	(27)
		50	(28)
Unadj. bal.	6,825		

Accounts Receivable (A) (+ / −)

Beg. bal.	950		
(22a)	4,500	3,200	(25)
Unadj. bal.	2,250		

Inventory (A) (+ / −)

Beg. bal.	11,300		
(26)	4,000	5,000	(21b)
		3,000	(22b)
Unadj. bal.	7,300		

Prepaid Insurance (A) (+ / −)

Beg. bal.	1,680		
Unadj. bal.	1,680		

Security Deposit (A) (+ / −)

Beg. bal.	2,000		
Unadj. bal.	2,000		

Fixtures and Equipment (A) (+ / −)

Beg. bal.	0		
(18)	18,000		
Unadj. bal.	18,000		

Liabilities

Accounts Payable (L) (− / +)

		3,700	Beg. bal.
(20)	3,300	4,000	(26)
		4,400	Unadj. bal.

Gift Card Liability (L) (− / +)

		300	Beg. bal.
		1,200	(23)
		1,500	Unadj. bal.

Notes Payable (L) (− / +)

		0	Beg. bal.
		11,000	(17)
		11,000	Unadj. bal.

Equity

Common Stock (SE) (− / +)

		20,000	Beg. bal.
		20,000	Unadj. bal.

Retained Earnings (SE) (− / +)

		30	Beg. bal.
(28)	50		
Unadj. bal.	20		

Sales Revenue (R) (− / +)

		0	Beg. bal.
		8,500	(21a)
		4,500	(22a)
		13,000	Unadj. bal.

Cost of Goods Sold (E) (+ / −)

Beg. bal.	0		
(21b)	5,000		
(22b)	3,000		
Unadj. bal.	8,000		

Wages Expense (E) (+ / −)

Beg. bal.	0		
(24)	1,625		
Unadj. bal.	1,625		

Rent Expense (E) (+ / −)

Beg. bal.	0		
(27)	1,500		
Unadj. bal.	1,500		

Advertising Expense (E) (+ / −)

Beg. bal.	0		
(19)	700		
Unadj. bal.	700		

Assets = \$38,055 = **Liabilities = \$16,900** + **Equity = \$21,155**

LO3 Describe the adjusting process and illustrate adjusting entries.

ADJUSTING THE ACCOUNTS

It is important that accounts in financial statements be properly reported. For many accounts, the balances shown in the general ledger after all transactions are posted are not the proper balances for financial statements. So, when it is time to prepare financial statements, management must review account balances and make proper adjustments to these balances. The adjustments required are based on accrual accounting and generally accepted accounting principles. This section focuses on this adjustment process.

Preparing an Unadjusted Trial Balance

The T-accounts in **Exhibit 3.4** show balances for each account after recording all transactions. This set of balances is called an **unadjusted trial balance** because it shows account balances before any adjustments are made. The purpose of an unadjusted trial balance is to be sure the general ledger is in balance before management adjusts the accounts. Showing all general ledger account balances in one place also makes it easier to review accounts and determine which account balances require adjusting. Natural Beauty Supply's unadjusted trial balance at December 31 is shown in **Exhibit 3.5**.

FYI Even if the unadjusted trial balance shows an equal amount of debits and credits, this does not mean that the general ledger is correct. Journal entries could have been omitted or falsified, or the accounts used or the amounts involved may have been wrong. Thus, the equality of debits and credits is a necessary, but not a sufficient, condition for the financial statements to be correct.

EXHIBIT 3.5 Unadjusted Trial Balance

NATURAL BEAUTY SUPPLY
Unadjusted Trial Balance
December 31, 2018

	Debit	Credit
Cash	$ 6,825	
Accounts receivable	2,250	
Inventory	7,300	
Prepaid insurance	1,680	
Security deposit	2,000	
Fixtures & equipment	18,000	
Accounts payable		$ 4,400
Gift card liability		1,500
Notes payable		11,000
Common stock		20,000
Retained earnings	20	
Sales revenue		13,000
Cost of goods sold	8,000	
Wages expense	1,625	
Rent expense	1,500	
Advertising expense	700	
Totals	$49,900	$49,900

Types of Adjustments

Accrual adjustments are caused by a variety of accounting practices. There are some revenues and expenses that arise with the passage of time, rather than in a transaction. There are asset and liability values that change over time or that require estimation based on recent events. All of these require adjustments before proper financial statements can be produced.

Adjusting entries have two common characteristics. First, they occur at the end of a reporting period, just before the construction of financial statements. Second, they (almost) never involve cash. Changes in cash require a transaction, and adjusting entries are not transactions.

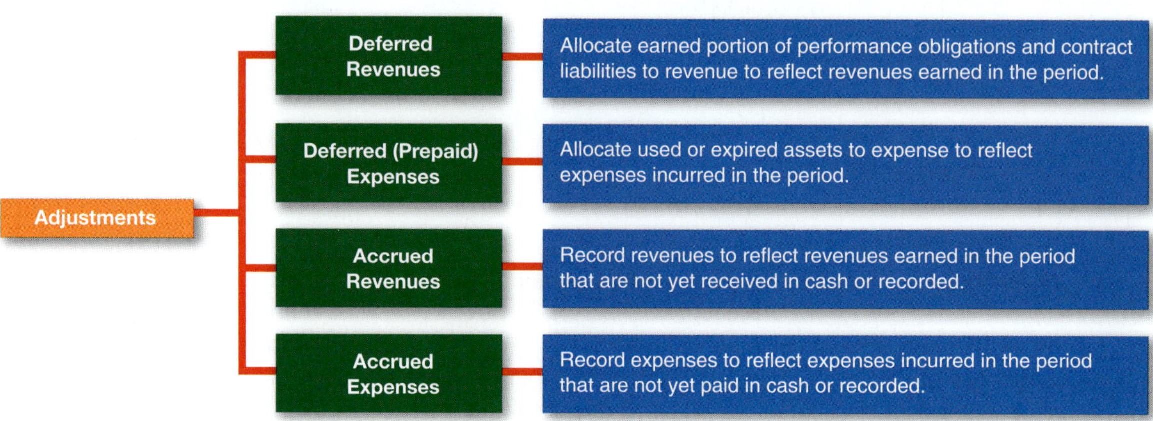

Through the course of this book, we will encounter quite a few required adjusting entries, but we will start with four general types of adjustments made at the end of an accounting period.

Journal entries made to reflect these adjustments are known as **adjusting entries**. Each adjusting entry usually affects a balance sheet account (an asset or liability account) and an income statement account (an expense or revenue account). The first two types of adjustments—allocating assets to expense and allocating unearned revenues to revenue—are often referred to as **deferrals**. The distinguishing characteristic of a deferral is that the adjustment deals with an amount previously recorded in a balance sheet account; the adjusting entry decreases the balance sheet account and increases an income statement account. The last two types of adjustments—accruing expenses and accruing revenues—are often referred to as **accruals**. The unique characteristic of an accrual is that the adjustment deals with an amount not previously recorded in any account; this type of adjusting entry increases both a balance sheet account and an income statement account. Both accruals and deferrals allow revenue to be recognized when it is earned and the expenses of the period to reflect asset decreases and liability increases from generating revenues or supporting that period's operations. Let's consider each of these adjustments in more detail.

Type 1: Deferred Revenue—Allocating Performance Obligation Liabilities to Revenue Companies often receive fees for products or services before those products or services are rendered. Such transactions are recorded by debiting Cash and crediting a performance obligation liability account for the **deferred revenue**. This account reflects the obligation for performing future services or delivering a product in the future. As services are performed or the product delivered, revenue is earned. At period-end, an adjusting entry records the revenue that was earned in the current accounting period and the liability amount that was reduced.

FYI Chapter 2 explained that revenue recognition is key to determining net income under accrual accounting, which recognizes revenues when services are performed or when goods are sold and recognizes expenses in the period that they help to generate the recorded revenues.

DEFERRED REVENUE During November and December, Natural Beauty Supply sold gift cards that entitled the recipient to a one-hour consultation with a salesperson on the use of natural and organic health and beauty products. When the gift cards were purchased, NBS recognized a gift card liability that reflected the obligation to provide these services. During the month of December, gift cards totaling $900 were redeemed. On December 31, Natural Beauty Supply made the adjustment (a) in the following template, journal entry, and T-accounts to recognize the (partial) fulfillment of the obligation and to recognize the $900 of revenue to which it is now entitled. The $900 increase in sales revenue is reflected in net income and carried over to retained earnings.

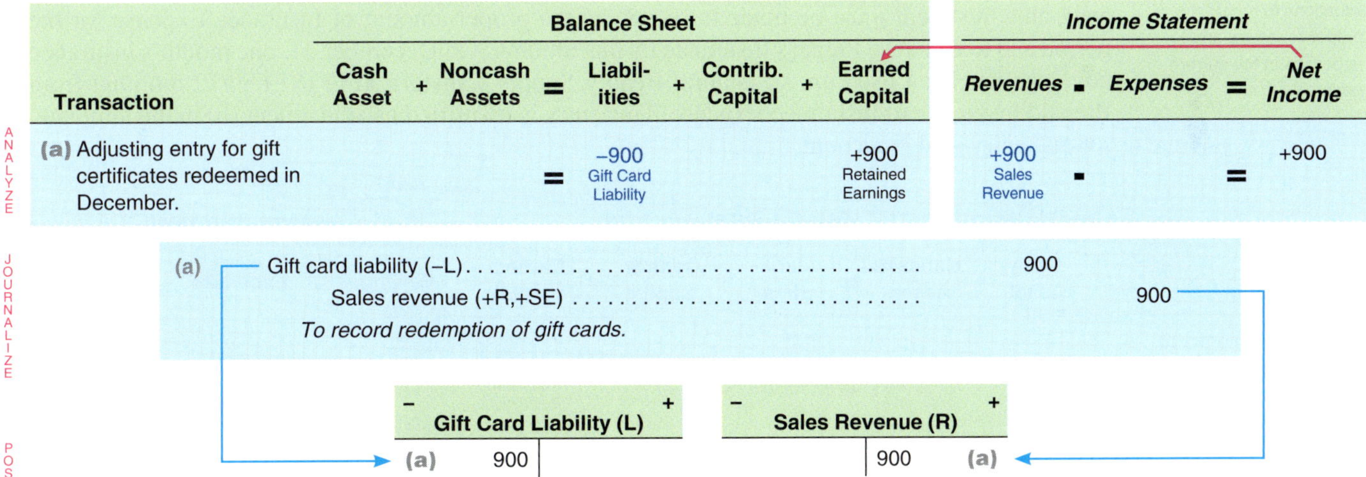

	Balance Sheet									Income Statement				
Transaction	Cash Asset	+	Noncash Assets	=	Liabilities	+	Contrib. Capital	+	Earned Capital	Revenues	−	Expenses	=	Net Income
ANALYZE (a) Adjusting entry for gift certificates redeemed in December.				=	−900 Gift Card Liability				+900 Retained Earnings	+900 Sales Revenue	−		=	+900

JOURNALIZE

(a) Gift card liability (−L) 900
Sales revenue (+R,+SE) 900
To record redemption of gift cards.

POST

− Gift Card Liability (L) +	
(a) 900	

− Sales Revenue (R) +	
	900 (a)

After this entry (a) is posted, the Gift Card Liability account has a balance of $600 for the remaining gift certificates outstanding, and the Sales Revenue account reflects the $900 earned in December.

In this case, the cost of the salesperson's time has already been recognized as an expense. If Natural Beauty Supply's gift cards had been redeemable for products, then we would have recognized a Cost of Goods Sold expense for the items purchased with the redeemed certificates.

Other examples of revenues received in advance include rental payments received in advance by real estate management companies, insurance premiums received in advance by insurance companies, subscription revenues received in advance by magazine and newspaper publishers, and membership fees received in advance by health clubs. In each case, a performance obligation liability account is set up when the advance payment is received. Later, an adjusting entry is made to reflect the revenues earned from the services provided or products delivered during the period.

YOU MAKE THE CALL

You are the Chief Accountant REI requires customers of its travel-vacation business to make an initial deposit equal to $400 when the trip is reserved and to make full payment two months before departure. REI's refunding policy is to return the entire deposit if the customer informs REI of the trip's cancellation three or more months in advance of the trip. REI will refund all but $400 of the deposit if the customer cancels between 60 and 90 days prior to the trip or 50% of the deposit if a customer cancels between 30 and 60 days prior to the trip. There is no refund if notification occurs within 30 days of the trip. REI's cancellation rate is very low. How should you account for deposits, and when should revenue be recorded? [Answers on page 128]

Type 2: Prepaid Expenses—Allocating Assets to Expenses Many cash outlays benefit several accounting periods. Examples are purchases of buildings, equipment, and supplies; prepayments of rent and advertising; and payments of insurance premiums covering several periods. These outlays are added to (debited to) an asset account when the expenditure occurs. Then at the end of each accounting period, the estimated portion of the outlay that has expired in that period or has benefited that period is transferred to an expense account.

We can usually see when adjustments of this type are needed by inspecting the unadjusted trial balance for costs that benefit several periods. Looking at the December 31 trial balance of Natural Beauty Supply (**Exhibit 3.5**), for example, adjustments are required to record the costs of prepaid insurance and the fixtures and equipment for the month of December.

FYI Many transactions reflected in ledger accounts affect net income of more than one period. Likewise, other events that are not yet recorded in accounts affect the current period's income. The adjusting process identifies these situations to record the proper revenues and expenses in the current period.

PREPAID INSURANCE On November 30, Natural Beauty Supply paid one year's insurance premium in advance and debited the $1,680 payment to Prepaid Insurance, an asset account. As each day passes and the insurance coverage is being used, insurance expense is being incurred, and the Prepaid Insurance asset is decreasing. It is not necessary to record insurance expense on a daily basis because financial statements are not prepared daily. At the end of an accounting period, however, an adjustment must be made to recognize the proper amount of Insurance Expense for the period and to decrease Prepaid Insurance by that amount. On December 31, one month's insurance coverage has been used up, so Natural Beauty Supply transfers $140 ($1,680/12 months) from Prepaid Insurance to Insurance Expense. This entry is identified as adjustment (b) in the template, journal entry, and T-accounts.

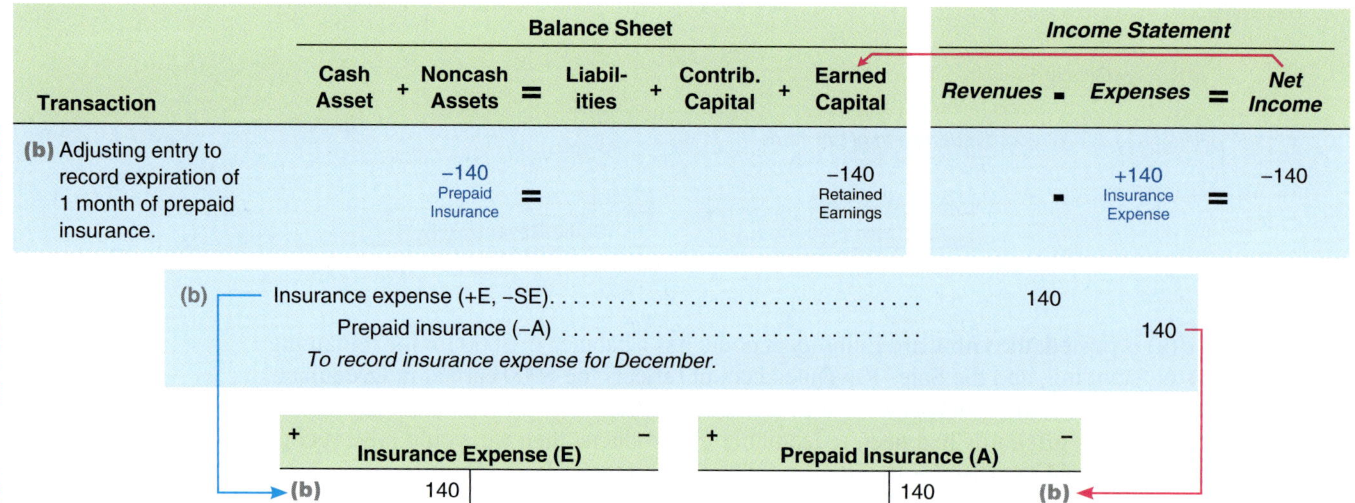

Transaction	Cash Asset	+	Noncash Assets	=	Liabilities	+	Contrib. Capital	+	Earned Capital	Revenues	−	Expenses	=	Net Income
(b) Adjusting entry to record expiration of 1 month of prepaid insurance.			−140 Prepaid Insurance	=					−140 Retained Earnings		−	+140 Insurance Expense	=	−140

(Balance Sheet: Cash Asset through Earned Capital; Income Statement: Revenues through Net Income)

ANALYZE

		Dr.	Cr.
(b)	Insurance expense (+E, −SE)	140	
	Prepaid insurance (−A)		140
	To record insurance expense for December.		

JOURNALIZE

+ Insurance Expense (E) −	
(b) 140	

+ Prepaid Insurance (A) −	
	140 (b)

POST

The posting of this adjusting entry creates the proper Insurance Expense of $140 for December in the Insurance Expense ledger account and reduces the Prepaid Insurance balance to the (eleven-month) amount that is prepaid as of December 31, which is $1,540.

Examples of other prepaid expenses for which similar adjustments are made include prepaid rent and prepaid advertising. When rent payments are made in advance, the amount is added to (debited to) a Prepaid Rent asset. At the end of an accounting period, an adjusting entry is made to record the portion of occupancy or usage that expired during the period. Rent Expense is debited (increased) and Prepaid Rent is credited (decreased). Similarly, when advertising services are purchased in advance, the payment is debited to Prepaid Advertising. At the end of an accounting period, an adjustment is needed to recognize the cost of any of the prepaid advertising used during the period. The adjusting entry debits (increases) Advertising Expense and credits (decreases) Prepaid Advertising.

DEPRECIATION The process of allocating the costs of equipment, vehicles, and buildings to the periods benefiting from their use is called **depreciation**. Each accounting period in which such assets are used must reflect a portion of their cost as expense because these assets helped generate revenue or support operations for those periods. This periodic expense is known as *depreciation expense*. Periodic depreciation expense is an estimate. The procedure we use here estimates the annual amount of depreciation expense by dividing the asset cost by its estimated useful life. (We assume that the entire asset cost is depreciated—so-called zero salvage value; later in the book we consider salvage values other than zero.) This method is called **straight-line depreciation** and is used by the great majority of companies in their financial reports.

FYI Contra accounts are used to provide more information to users of financial statements. For example, Accumulated Depreciation is a contra asset reported in the balance sheet, which enables users to estimate asset age. For Natural Beauty Supply, the December 31 balance sheet reveals that its Fixtures and Equipment is nearly new as its accumulated depreciation is only $375, which is 1/48th of the $18,000 original cost.

Expenses are recorded when business activities reduce net assets. But when we record depreciation expense, the asset amount is not reduced directly. Instead, the reduction is recorded in a **contra asset** account (labeled XA in the journal entries and T-accounts) called *Accumulated Depreciation*. **Contra accounts** are so named because they are used to record reductions in or offsets against a related account. The Accumulated Depreciation account normally has a credit balance and appears in the balance sheet as a deduction from the related asset amount. Use of the *contra asset* Accumulated Depreciation allows the original cost of the asset to be reported in the balance sheet, followed (and reduced) by the accumulated depreciation. Let's consider an example.

The fixtures and equipment purchased by Natural Beauty Supply for $18,000 are expected to last for four years. Straight-line depreciation recorded on the equipment is $4,500 per year ($18,000/4 years), or $375 per month ($18,000/48 months). At December 31, Natural Beauty Supply makes adjustment (c), as shown in the following template, journal entry, and T-accounts.

The introduction of contra assets requires a new column in the FSET for these accounts.[3] Increases in a contra asset decrease the net balance of the company's long-term assets. The new column is preceded by a minus sign to indicate that increases in contra assets create a decrease in the asset side of the accounting equation.

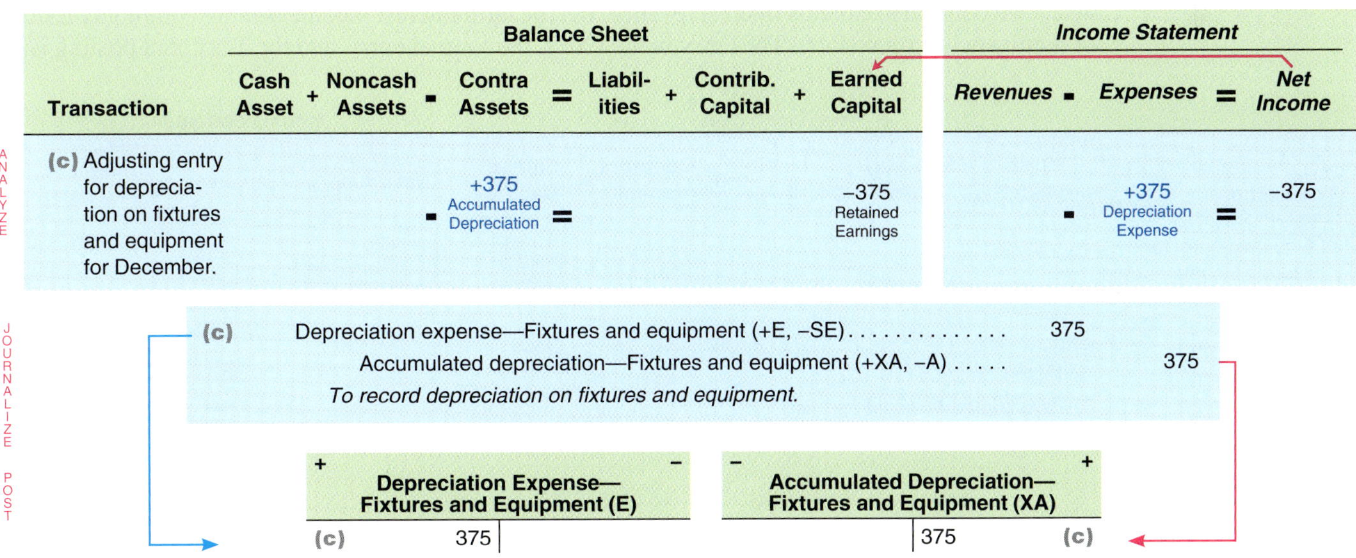

	Balance Sheet							Income Statement		
Transaction	Cash Asset	+ Noncash Assets	− Contra Assets	= Liabilities	+ Contrib. Capital	+ Earned Capital		Revenues	− Expenses	= Net Income
ANALYZE (c) Adjusting entry for depreciation on fixtures and equipment for December.			− +375 Accumulated Depreciation	=		−375 Retained Earnings			− +375 Depreciation Expense	= −375

JOURNALIZE

(c)	Depreciation expense—Fixtures and equipment (+E, −SE)	375	
	Accumulated depreciation—Fixtures and equipment (+XA, −A)		375
	To record depreciation on fixtures and equipment.		

POST

+ Depreciation Expense—Fixtures and Equipment (E) −		− Accumulated Depreciation—Fixtures and Equipment (XA) +	
(c) 375			375 (c)

[3] Our practice is to include a separate FSET column where contra assets are required, but not to do so all the time. As we progress through the topics in this text, we will also see examples of contra liability accounts and contra equity accounts.

When this entry is posted, it properly reflects the cost of using this asset during December, and the $375 depreciation expense appears in the December income statement. On the balance sheet, the accumulated depreciation is an offset to the asset amount. The resulting balance (cost less accumulated depreciation), which is the asset's **book value**, represents the unexpired asset cost to be allocated as an expense in future periods. For example, the December 31, 2018, balance sheet reports the equipment with a book value of $17,625, as follows.

FYI An increase in the contra asset account Accumulated Depreciation reduces the book value of the asset.

Fixtures and equipment	$18,000
Less: Accumulated depreciation	375
Fixtures and equipment, net	$17,625 (book value)

In each subsequent month, $375 is recognized as depreciation expense, and the Accumulated Depreciation contra asset is increased by the same amount (from $375 to $750 to $1,125 and so on). As a result, the book value of the fixtures and equipment is decreased by $375 each month. In Chapter 8, we will see the same principles applied to certain intangible assets.

Type 3: Accrued Revenues Revenue should be recognized when the company has transferred goods or services to customers, and in an amount that reflects the amount to which the company expects to be entitled from the transfer. Yet, a company often provides services or earns income during a period that is neither paid for by clients or customers nor billed before the end of the period. Such values should be included in the firm's current period income statement, reflecting the company's fulfillment of its agreement with the customer. To properly account for such situations, end-of-period adjusting entries are made to reflect any revenues or income earned, but not yet billed or received. Such accumulated revenue is often called **accrued revenue** or **accrued income**.

ACCRUED SALES REVENUE/INCOME At the end of December, Natural Beauty Supply learns that its bank has decided to provide interest on checking accounts for small businesses like NBS. Each month, NBS earns interest income based on the average balance in its checking account. The interest is paid into NBS's checking account on the fifth business day of the following month. Based on its average daily balance, NBS earned $30 in interest during December.

In this instance, Natural Beauty Supply does not receive the interest payment until January. Nevertheless, the company earned interest during the month of December. Therefore, it should recognize an interest receivable (or "other receivables") asset and interest income in the income statement. (We could also call this interest revenue, but the term interest income is more commonly used for nonfinancial companies.) The entry in the FSET, the journal entry, and the T-account posting is:

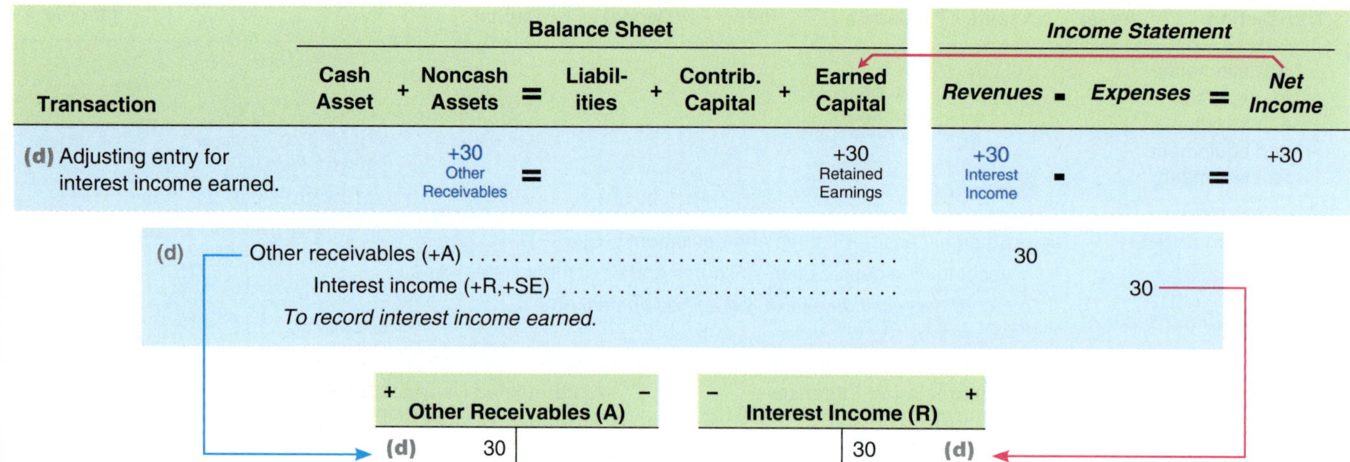

Revenue accruals also occur for landlords who receive rent payments after they are earned. In these cases, revenue has been earned over time as the customer receives and consumes the benefits of the services provided on a continuous basis. We look into these issues more closely in Chapter 6.

Type 4: Accrued Expenses Companies often incur expenses before paying for them. Wages, interest, utilities, and taxes are examples of expenses that are incurred before cash payment is made. Usually the payments are made at regular intervals of time, such as weekly, monthly, quarterly, or annually. If the accounting period ends on a date that does not coincide with a scheduled cash payment date, an adjusting entry is required to reflect the expense incurred since the last cash payment. Such an expense is referred to as an **accrued expense**. Natural Beauty Supply has three such required adjustments for December 31; one for wages, one for interest, and one for income tax.

ACCRUED WAGES Natural Beauty Supply employees are paid on a weekly basis. Recall that wages of $1,625 were paid during December in transaction 24. However, as of December 31, the company's employees have earned wages of $480 that will be paid in January. Wages expense of $480 must be recorded in the income statement for December because there is now an obligation to compensate employees, who helped generate revenues for December.

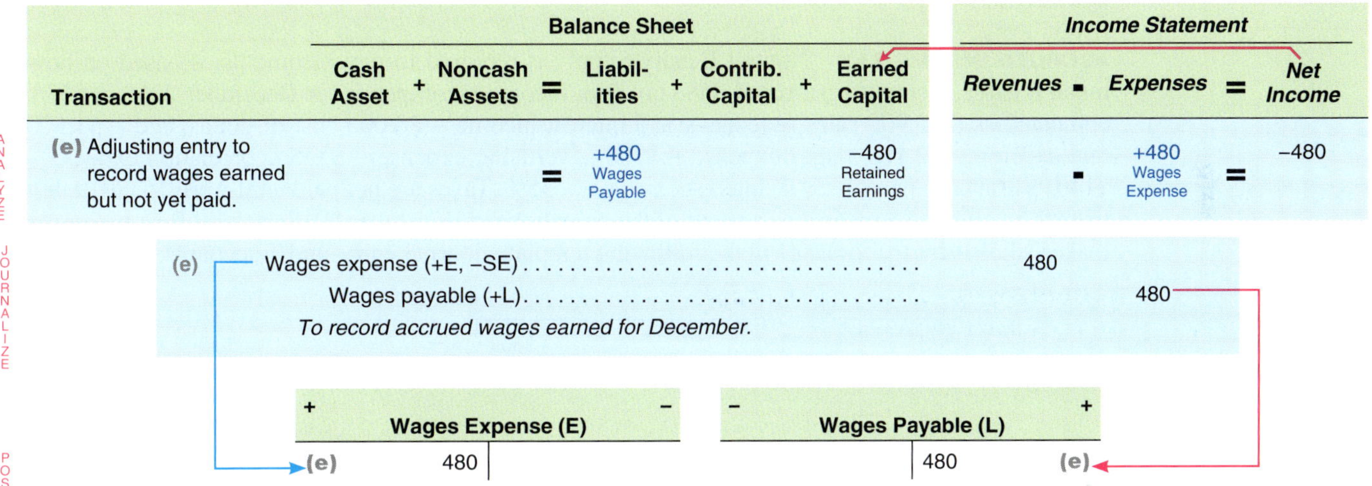

	Balance Sheet									Income Statement				
Transaction	Cash Asset	+	Noncash Assets	=	Liabil-ities	+	Contrib. Capital	+	Earned Capital	Revenues	−	Expenses	=	Net Income
(e) Adjusting entry to record wages earned but not yet paid.				=	+480 Wages Payable				−480 Retained Earnings		−	+480 Wages Expense	=	−480

		Dr.	Cr.
(e)	Wages expense (+E, −SE)	480	
	Wages payable (+L).		480
	To record accrued wages earned for December.		

+ Wages Expense (E) −		− Wages Payable (L) +	
(e) 480			480 (e)

This adjustment enables the firm to reflect as December expense the cost of all wages *incurred* during the month rather than just the wages *paid*. In addition, the balance sheet shows the liability for unpaid wages at the end of the period.

When the employees are paid in January, the following entry is made.

		Dr.	Cr.
Jan.	Wages payable (−L)	480	
	Cash (−A).		480

This entry eliminates the liability recorded in Wages Payable at the end of December and reduces Cash for the wages paid.

ACCRUED INTEREST On December 1, 2018, Natural Beauty Supply signed a three-year note payable for $11,000. This note has a 12% annual interest rate and requires monthly (interest-only) payments (1% per month), payable on the first business day of the following month. (The interest payment for the month of December is due on January 2.) The $11,000 principal on the note is due at the end of three years. An adjusting entry is required at December 31, 2018, to record interest expense for December and to recognize a liability. December's interest is $110 [$11,000 × (12%/12 months)], and at December 31, NBS makes adjustment (f) in the following template, journal entry, and T-accounts.

ANALYZE

Transaction	Balance Sheet: Cash Asset	+	Noncash Assets	=	Liabilities	+	Contrib. Capital	+	Earned Capital	Income Statement: Revenues	−	Expenses	=	Net Income
(f) Adjusting entry to record interest owed but not yet paid.				=	+110 Interest Payable				−110 Retained Earnings		−	+110 Interest Expense	=	−110

JOURNALIZE

		Dr.	Cr.
(f)	Interest expense (+E, −SE)	110	
	Interest payable (+L)		110
	To record December interest on note payable.		

POST

+ Interest Expense (E) −	
(f) 110	

− Interest Payable (L) +	
	110 (f)

When these entries are posted to the general ledger, the accounts show the correct interest expense for December and the interest liability for one month's interest on the note that has accrued by December 31.

ACCRUED INCOME TAX Natural Beauty Supply is required to pay income taxes based on how much it earns. Using an estimated 35% tax rate, income tax expense for December 2018 is $350, computed as ($13,900 sales revenue + $30 interest income − $8,000 cost of goods sold − $1,500 rent expense − $2,105 wages expense − $700 advertising expense − $375 depreciation expense − $140 insurance expense − $110 interest expense) × 35%. Taxes are not paid until April 15, 2019, but there is an obligation created as a result of the operations in December 2018. Natural Beauty Supply makes adjustment (g) for taxes in the following template, journal entry, and T-accounts.

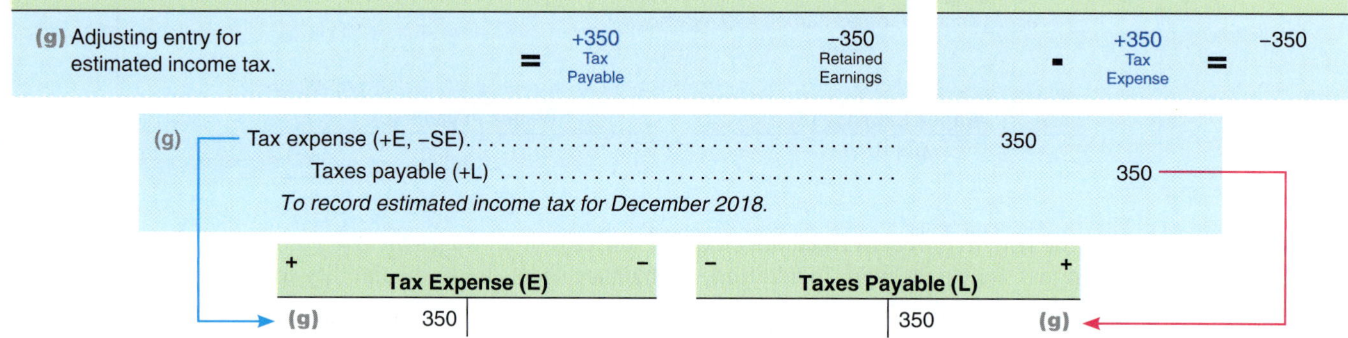

Exhibit 3.6 summarizes the four types of accounting adjustments, the usual journal entries required for each, and their financial impacts on the balance sheet and income statements.

EXHIBIT 3.6 Summary of Accounting Adjustments

Accounting Adjustment	Examples	Adjusting Entry	Financial Effects if *Not* Adjusted: Balance Sheet	Income Statement
Deferrals:				
Deferred revenues	Delivery on advances from clients, gift cards, and subscribers	Dr. Liability Cr. Revenue	Liability overstated Equity understated	Revenue understated
Prepaid expenses	Expiration of prepaid rent, insurance, and advertising; depreciation of buildings and equipment	Dr. Expense Cr. Asset (or Contra asset)	Asset overstated Equity overstated	Expense understated
Accruals:				
Accrued revenues	Earned but not received service, sales, and interest revenues	Dr. Asset Cr. Revenue	Asset understated Equity understated	Revenue understated
Accrued expenses	Incurred but unpaid wages, interest, and tax expenses	Dr. Expense Cr. Liability	Liabilty understated Equity overstated	Expense understated

Ethics and Adjusting Entries

When companies engage in transactions, there is some evidence of the exchange. Cash increases or decreases; asset and liability levels change. Adjusting entries are much more dependent on estimation processes. What was the value of service provided to customers? What obligations have arisen in the past period without a transaction? What is their value? What is the expected useful life of our depreciable assets?

The usefulness of financial performance measures such as net income depends on these questions being answered to the best of management's ability. However, there often are pressures not to provide the most accurate information. For instance, an estimate might convey information about management's strategy that could be used by competitors. Or, the financial community may have set expectations for performance that management cannot meet by executing its current business plan. In these circumstances, managers are sometimes pressured to use the discretion inherent in the reporting process to meet analysts' expectations or to disguise a planned course of action.

The financial reporting environment described in Chapter 1 imposes significant controls on financial reporting, because that reporting process is important to the health of the economy. Managers who do not report accurately and completely are potentially subject to severe penalties. Moreover, adjusting entry estimates have a "self-correcting" character. Underestimating expenses today means greater expenses tomorrow; overestimating revenues today means lower revenues tomorrow.

MID-CHAPTER REVIEW

The following transactions relate to Lundholm Transport Company.

a. The Supplies and Parts balance on September 30, 2019, the company's accounting year-end, reveals $100,000 available. This amount reflects its beginning-year balance and all purchases for the year. A physical inventory indicates that much of this balance has been used in service operations, leaving supplies valued at $9,000 remaining at year-end September 30, 2019.

b. A $5,000 bill for September and October rent on the warehouse was received on September 29, but has not yet been paid or recorded.

c. A building holding its offices was purchased for $400,000 five years ago. The building's life was estimated at eight years. Assume the entire asset cost is depreciated over its useful life. No depreciation has been recorded for this fiscal year.

d. An executive was hired on September 15 with a $120,000 annual salary. Payment and work are to start on October 15. No entry has yet been made to record this event.

e. A services contract is signed with the local university on September 1. Lundholm Transport Company received $1,200 cash on September 1 as a retainer for the months of September and October, but it has not yet been recorded. Lundholm Transport Company retains the money whether the university requires its services or not.

f. Employees are paid on the first day of the month following the month in which work is performed. Wages earned in September, but not yet paid or recorded as of September 30, amount to $25,000.

Lundholm Transport's ledger includes the following ledger accounts and unadjusted normal balances at September 30: Cash $80,000; Accounts Receivable $95,000; Supplies and Parts $100,000; Building $400,000; Accumulated Depreciation—Building $200,000; Land $257,500; Accounts Payable $20,000; Wages Payable $0; Contract Liability $0; Common Stock $80,000; Retained Earnings $380,000; Services Revenue $720,000; Rent Expense $27,500; Depreciation Expense $0; Wages Expense $440,000; Supplies and Parts Expense $0.

Required

1. For each of the six items described above, enter their effects in the financial statement effects template.
2. For each of the six items described above, enter their effects in journal entry form.
3. Set up T-accounts for all ledger accounts and enter the beginning unadjusted balance, the adjustments from part 2, and the adjusted ending balance.

The solution to this review problem can be found on pages 147–149.

CONSTRUCTING FINANCIAL STATEMENTS FROM ADJUSTED ACCOUNTS

4

LO4 Prepare financial statements from adjusted accounts.

This section explains the preparation of financial statements from the adjusted financial accounts.

Preparing an Adjusted Trial Balance

After adjustments are recorded and posted, the company prepares an adjusted trial balance. The **adjusted trial balance** lists all the general ledger account balances after adjustments. Much of the content for company financial statements is taken from an adjusted trial balance. **Exhibit 3.7** shows the general ledger accounts for Natural Beauty Supply after adjustments, in T-account form.

The adjusted trial balance at December 31 for Natural Beauty Supply is prepared from its general ledger accounts and is in the right-hand two columns of **Exhibit 3.8**. We show the unadjusted balances along with the adjustments to highlight the adjustment process.

Preparing Financial Statements

A company prepares its financial statements from the adjusted trial balance (and sometimes other supporting information). The set of financial statements consists of (and is prepared in the order of) the income statement, statement of stockholders' equity, balance sheet, and statement of cash flows. The following diagram summarizes this process.

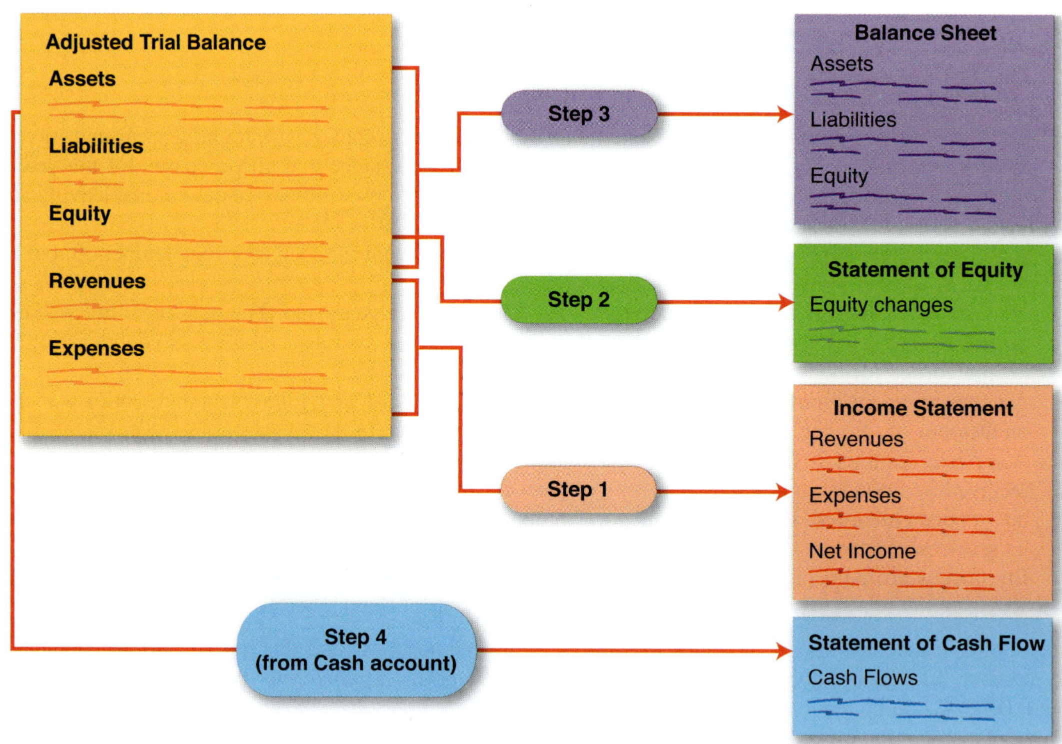

Income Statement The income statement reports a company's revenues and expenses. Natural Beauty Supply's adjusted trial balance contains two revenue/income accounts and eight expense accounts. The revenues and expenses are reported in Natural Beauty Supply's income statement for December as shown in **Exhibit 3.9**. Its net income for December is $650.

EXHIBIT 3.7 General Ledger for Natural Beauty Supply after Adjustments

General Ledger

Assets = Liabilities + Equity

Assets

+	Cash (A)		−
Beg. bal.	8,100		
(17)	11,000	18,000	(18)
(21a)	8,500	700	(19)
(23)	1,200	3,300	(20)
(25)	3,200	1,625	(24)
		1,500	(27)
		50	(28)
Adj. bal.	6,825		

+	Accounts Receivable (A)		−
Beg. bal.	950		
(22a)	4,500	3,200	(25)
Adj. bal.	2,250		

+	Other Receivables (A)		−
Beg. bal.	0		
(d)	30		
Adj. bal.	30		

+	Inventory (A)		−
Beg. bal.	11,300		
(26)	4,000	5,000	(21b)
		3,000	(22b)
Adj. bal.	7,300		

+	Prepaid Insurance (A)		−
Beg. bal.	1,680		
		140	**(b)**
Adj. bal.	1,540		

+	Security Deposit (A)		−
Beg. bal.	2,000		
Adj. bal.	2,000		

+	Fixtures and Equipment (A)		−
Beg. bal.	0		
(18)	18,000		
Adj. bal.	18,000		

−	Accumulated Depreciation—Fixtures and Equipment (XA)		+
		0	Beg. bal.
		375	**(c)**
		375	Adj. bal.

Liabilities

−	Accounts Payable (L)		+
		3,700	Beg. bal.
(20)	3,300	4,000	(26)
		4,400	Adj. bal.

−	Interest Payable (L)		+
		0	Beg. bal.
		110	**(f)**
		110	Adj. bal.

−	Wages Payable (L)		+
		0	Beg. bal.
		480	**(e)**
		480	Adj. bal.

−	Taxes Payable (L)		+
		0	Beg. bal.
		350	**(g)**
		350	Adj. bal.

−	Gift Card Liability (L)		+
		300	Beg. bal.
(a)	900	1,200	(23)
		600	Adj. bal.

−	Notes Payable (L)		+
		0	Beg. bal.
		11,000	(17)
		11,000	Adj. bal.

Equity

−	Common Stock (SE)		+
		20,000	Beg. bal.
		20,000	Adj. bal.

−	Retained Earnings (SE)		+
		30	Beg. bal.
(28)	50		
Adj. bal.	20		

−	Sales Revenue (R)		+
		0	Beg. bal.
		8,500	(21a)
		4,500	(22a)
		900	**(a)**
		13,900	Adj. bal.

−	Interest Income (R)		+
		0	Beg. bal.
		30	**(d)**
		30	Adj. bal.

+	Cost of Goods Sold (E)		−
Beg. bal.	0		
(21b)	5,000		
(22b)	3,000		
Adj. bal.	8,000		

+	Wages Expense (E)		−
Beg. bal.	0		
(24)	1,625		
(e)	480		
Adj. bal.	2,105		

+	Rent Expense (E)		−
Beg. bal.	0		
(27)	1,500		
Adj. bal.	1,500		

+	Advertising Expense (E)		−
Beg. bal.	0		
(19)	700		
Adj. bal.	700		

+	Depreciation Expense—Fixtures and Equipment (E)		−
Beg. bal.	0		
(c)	375		
Adj. bal.	375		

+	Insurance Expense (E)		−
Beg. bal.	0		
(b)	140		
Adj. bal.	140		

+	Interest Expense (E)		−
Beg. bal.	0		
(f)	110		
Adj. bal.	110		

+	Tax Expense (E)		−
Beg. bal.	0		
(g)	350		
Adj. bal.	350		

Assets = $37,570 = **Liabilities = $16,940** + **Equity = $20,630**

EXHIBIT 3.8 Unadjusted and Adjusted Trial Balances

NATURAL BEAUTY SUPPLY, INC.
Trial Balance
December 31, 2018

	Unadjusted Trial Balance		Adjustments				Adjusted Trial Balance	
	Debit	Credit	Debit		Credit		Debit	Credit
Cash	$ 6,825						$ 6,825	
Accounts receivable	2,250						2,250	
Other receivables			(d)	$ 30			30	
Inventory	7,300						7,300	
Prepaid insurance	1,680				(b)	$ 140	1,540	
Security deposit	2,000						2,000	
Fixtures and equipment	18,000						18,000	
Accumulated depreciation					(c)	375		$ 375
Accounts payable		$ 4,400						4,400
Interest payable					(f)	110		110
Wages payable					(e)	480		480
Taxes payable					(g)	350		350
Gift card liability		1,500	(a)	900				600
Notes payable		11,000						11,000
Common stock		20,000						20,000
Retained earnings	20						20	
Sales revenue		13,000			(a)	900		13,900
Interest income					(d)	30		30
Cost of goods sold	8,000						8,000	
Wages expense	1,625		(e)	480			2,105	
Rent expense	1,500						1,500	
Advertising expense	700						700	
Depreciation expense			(c)	375			375	
Insurance expense			(b)	140			140	
Interest expense			(f)	110			110	
Tax expense			(g)	350			350	
Totals	$49,900	$49,900		$2,385		$2,385	$51,245	$51,245

EXHIBIT 3.9 Income Statement

NATURAL BEAUTY SUPPLY, INC.
Income Statement
For Month Ended December 31, 2018

Sales revenue	$13,900
Cost of goods sold	8,000
Gross profit	5,900
Wages expense	2,105
Rent expense	1,500
Advertising expense	700
Depreciation expense	375
Insurance expense	140
Operating income	1,080
Interest income	30
Interest expense	(110)
Income before tax expense	1,000
Tax expense	350
Net income	$ 650

Statement of Stockholders' Equity The statement of stockholders' equity reports the events causing the major equity components to change during the accounting period. **Exhibit 3.10** shows Natural Beauty Supply's statement of stockholders' equity for December. A review of its common stock account in the general ledger provides some of the information for this statement; namely, its balance at the beginning of the period and stock issuances during the period. The net income (or net loss) amount comes from the income statement. Dividends during the period are reflected in the retained earnings balance from the adjusted trial balance.

EXHIBIT 3.10 Statement of Stockholders' Equity

NATURAL BEAUTY SUPPLY, INC.
Statement of Stockholders' Equity
For Month Ended December 31, 2018

	Contributed Capital	Earned Capital	Total Equity
Balance, November 30, 2015	$20,000	$ 30	$20,030
Net income	—	650	650
Common stock issued	—	—	—
Cash dividends	—	(50)	(50)
Balances, December 31, 2015	$20,000	$630	$20,630

FYI Financial statements are most commonly prepared for annual and quarterly accounting periods. A request for a bank loan is an example of a situation that can lead to financial statement preparation for a non-accounting period.

Balance Sheet The balance sheet reports a company's assets, liabilities, and equity. The assets and liabilities for Natural Beauty Supply's balance sheet at December 31, 2018, shown in **Exhibit 3.11**, come from the adjusted trial balance in **Exhibit 3.8**. The amounts reported for Common Stock and Retained Earnings in the balance sheet are taken from the statement of stockholders' equity for December (**Exhibit 3.10**).

EXHIBIT 3.11 Balance Sheet

NATURAL BEAUTY SUPPLY, INC.
Balance Sheet
December 31, 2018

Assets			**Liabilities**	
Cash		$ 6,825	Accounts payable	$ 4,400
Accounts receivable		2,250	Interest payable	110
Other receivables		30	Wages payable	480
Inventory		7,300	Taxes payable	350
Prepaid insurance		1,540	Gift card liability	600
Security deposit		2,000	Current liabilities	5,940
Current assets		19,945	Notes payable	11,000
Fixtures and equipment	$18,000		Total liabilities	16,940
Less: Accumulated depreciation	375		**Equity**	
Fixtures and equipment, net		17,625	Common stock	20,000
			Retained earnings	630
Total assets		$37,570	Total liabilities and equity	$37,570

Statement of Cash Flows The statement of cash flows is formatted to report cash inflows and outflows by the three primary business activities:

- *Cash flows from operating activities* Cash flows from the company's transactions and events that relate to its primary operations.
- *Cash flows from investing activities* Cash flows from acquisitions and divestitures of investments and long-term assets.
- *Cash flows from financing activities* Cash flows from issuances of and payments toward equity, borrowings, and long-term liabilities.

The net cash flows from these three sections yield the change in cash for the period.

In analyzing the statement of cash flows, we should not necessarily conclude that the company is better off if cash increases and worse off if cash decreases. It is not the cash change that is most important, but the reasons for the change. For example, what are the sources of the cash inflows?

FYI The income statement, statement of stockholders' equity, and statement of cash flows report on periods of time. These statements illustrate the accounting period concept—the concept that useful statements can be prepared for arbitrary time periods within a company's life span. The purpose of adjusting entries is to obtain useful statements for specific time periods.

Are these sources mainly from operating activities? To what uses have cash inflows been put? Such questions (and their answers) are key to properly using the statement of cash flows. In Chapter 4, we examine the statement of cash flows more closely and answer these questions. The procedures for preparing a statement of cash flows are discussed in the next chapter. For completeness, we present Natural Beauty Supply's statement of cash flows for December in **Exhibit 3.12**.

EXHIBIT 3.12 Statement of Cash Flows

NATURAL BEAUTY SUPPLY, INC.
Statement of Cash Flows
For Month Ended December 31, 2018

Cash Flows from Operating Activities	
Cash received from customers	$12,900
Cash paid for inventory	(3,300)
Cash paid for wages	(1,625)
Cash paid for rent	(1,500)
Cash paid for advertising	(700)
Net cash provided by operating activities	5,775
Cash Flows from Investing Activities	
Cash paid for fixtures and equipment	(18,000)
Net cash used for investing activities	(18,000)
Cash Flows from Financing Activities	
Cash received from loans	11,000
Cash paid for dividends	(50)
Net cash provided by financing activities	10,950
Net change in cash	(1,275)
Cash balance, November 30, 2018	8,100
Cash balance, December 31, 2018	$ 6,825

5

LO5 Describe the process of closing temporary accounts.

CLOSING TEMPORARY ACCOUNTS

The chart of accounts contains two different types of accounts. Income statement accounts (revenues, expenses, etc.) are used to measure the net assets generated and used in a specific accounting period. As such, their end-of-period balances are reported in the income statement for that period. We use those balances to construct the statements of stockholders' equity and cash flows. But then these account balances have served their purpose, and we must get them ready to do the same thing for the following accounting period. Specifically, we must set their balances to zero so they can accumulate the revenues and expenses for that following period. For this reason, income statement accounts are called **temporary accounts**. Their end-of-period values do not carry over to the next reporting period.

In contrast, balance sheet account balances do carry over to the next reporting period. For example, the end-of-period balance in accounts receivable is the beginning-of-period balance for the next period. Therefore, balance sheet accounts are referred to as **permanent accounts**.

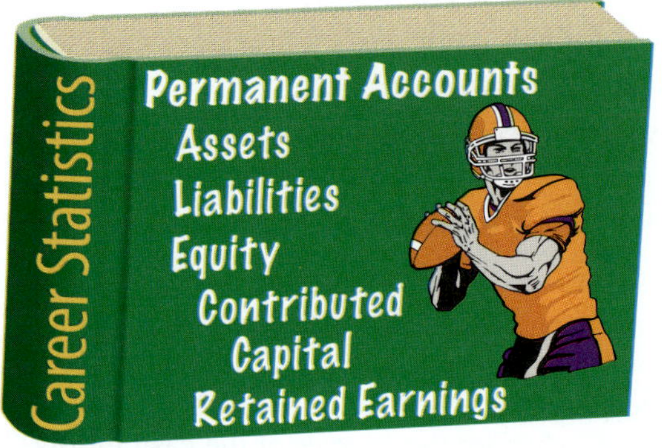

The **closing process** takes the end-of-period balances in the temporary accounts and moves them to a permanent account—the Retained Earnings account. A temporary account is *closed* when an entry is made that changes its balance to zero. The entry is equal in amount to the account's balance but is opposite to the balance as a debit or credit. An account that is closed is said to be closed *to* the account that receives the offsetting debit or credit. Thus, a closing entry simply transfers the balance of one account to another account. When closing entries bring temporary account balances to zero, the temporary accounts are then ready to accumulate data for the next accounting period.

Closing Process

The Retained Earnings account can be used to close the temporary revenue and expense accounts.[4] The entries to close temporary accounts are:

1. **Close revenue accounts**. Debit each revenue account for an amount equal to its balance, and credit Retained Earnings for the total of revenues.
2. **Close expense accounts**. Credit each expense account for an amount equal to its balance, and debit Retained Earnings for the total of expenses.

After these temporary accounts are closed, the difference equals the period's net income (if revenues exceed expenses) or net loss (if expenses exceed revenues) and that difference is now included in Retained Earnings. The closing process is graphically portrayed as follows.

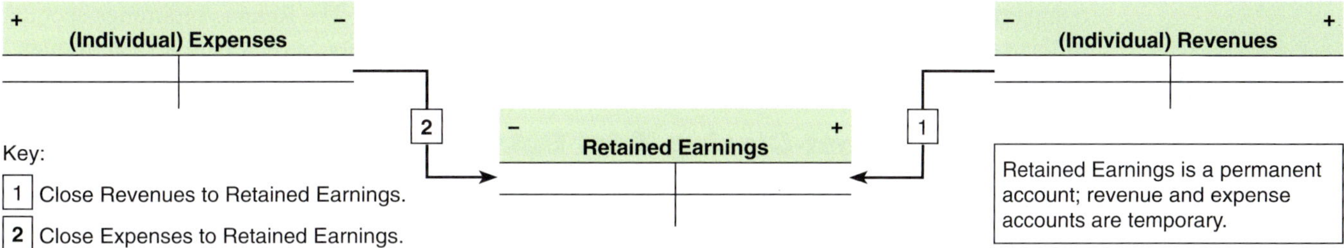

Closing Steps Illustrated

Exhibit 3.13 illustrates the entries for closing revenues and expenses for Natural Beauty Supply. The effects of these entries in T-accounts are shown after the journal entries. (We do not show the financial statement effects template for closing entries because the template automatically closes revenues and expenses to the Retained Earnings account as they occur—see earlier transactions for examples.)

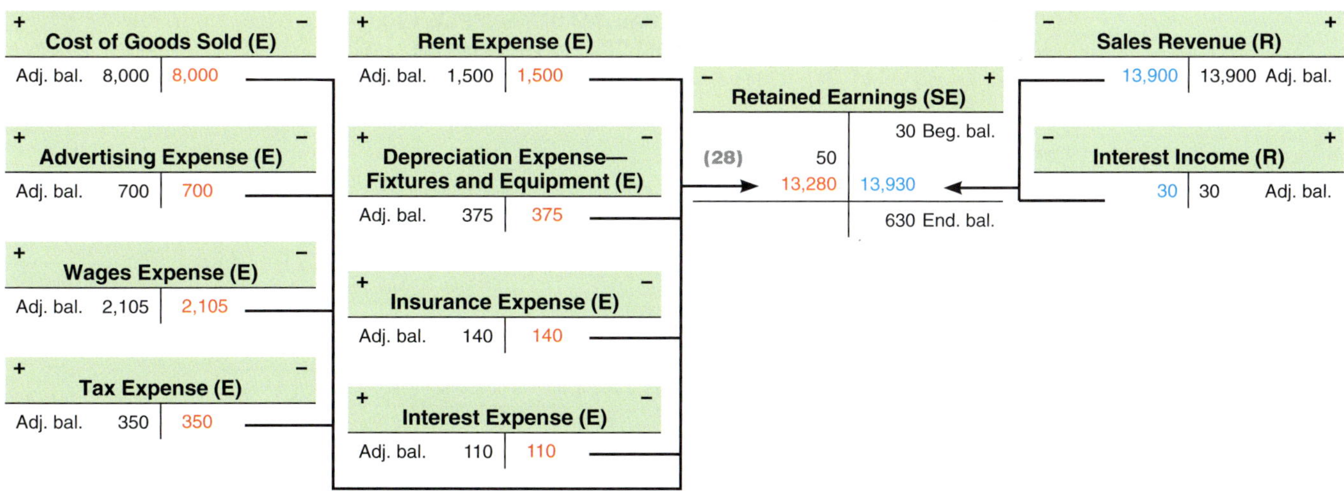

[4] *All* revenue and expense accounts are temporary accounts, so all revenue and expense accounts are closed to retained earnings at the end of the reporting period. In addition, companies often use a temporary account entitled Dividends Declared to record the amount of shareholder dividends declared during a reporting period. This account would accumulate a debit balance (because it reduces equity), and is closed to retained earnings at the end of the reporting period.

EXHIBIT 3.13 Closing Revenues and Expenses*

1	Dec. 31	Sales revenue (−R)	13,900	
		Interest income (−R)	30	
		Retained earnings (+SE)		13,930
2	Dec. 31	Retained earnings (−SE)	13,280	
		Cost of goods sold (−E)		8,000
		Wages expense (−E)		2,105
		Rent expense (−E)		1,500
		Advertising expense (−E)		700
		Depreciation expense (−E)		375
		Insurance expense (−E)		140
		Interest expense (−E)		110
		Tax expense (−E)		350

* The two entries in this exhibit can be combined into a single entry where the credit (debit) to retained earnings would be net income (loss).

After these two steps, the net adjustment to the Retained Earnings account is a credit equal to the company's net income of $650, computed as $13,930 less $13,280. The Retained Earnings account in this case is increased by $650. We also recall that Natural Beauty Supply paid a cash dividend of $50 (transaction 28), which reduces retained earnings and results in the ending balance of $630.

Preparing a Post-Closing Trial Balance

After closing entries are recorded and posted to the general ledger, all temporary accounts have zero balances. At this point, a **post-closing trial balance** is prepared. A balancing of this trial balance is evidence that an equality of debits and credits has been maintained in the general ledger throughout the adjusting and closing process and that the general ledger is in balance to start the next accounting period. Only balance sheet accounts appear in a post-closing trial balance because all income statement accounts have balances of zero. The post-closing trial balance for Natural Beauty Supply is shown in **Exhibit 3.14**.

EXHIBIT 3.14 Post-Closing Trial Balance

NATURAL BEAUTY SUPPLY, INC.
Post-Closing Trial Balance
December 31, 2018

	Debit	Credit
Cash	$ 6,825	
Accounts receivable	2,250	
Other receivables	30	
Inventory	7,300	
Prepaid insurance	1,540	
Security deposit	2,000	
Fixtures and equipment	18,000	
Accumulated depreciation		$ 375
Accounts payable		4,400
Interest payable		110
Wages payable		480
Taxes payable		350
Gift card liability		600
Notes payable		11,000
Common stock		20,000
Retained earnings		630
Totals	$37,945	$37,945

Subsequent Events

There is usually a few weeks' delay between the end of the fiscal reporting period and the issuing of the financial reports for that period. What happens if a significant event occurs (e.g., a fire at a production facility, an acquisition, etc.) during that interim? Should the previous period's financial statements be changed to reflect the event?

If the event doesn't provide information about the company's condition on the balance sheet date, then the answer is no. So, neither the fire nor the acquisition would be reported in the previous period's financial statements. Such events should be disclosed in a footnote, if they are material.

SUMMARIZING THE ACCOUNTING CYCLE

The sequence of accounting procedures known as the accounting cycle occurs each fiscal year (period) and represents a systematic process for accumulating and reporting financial data of a company. **Exhibit 3.15** expands on **Exhibit 3.1** to include descriptions of the five major steps in the accounting cycle.

EXHIBIT 3.15 Accounting Cycle

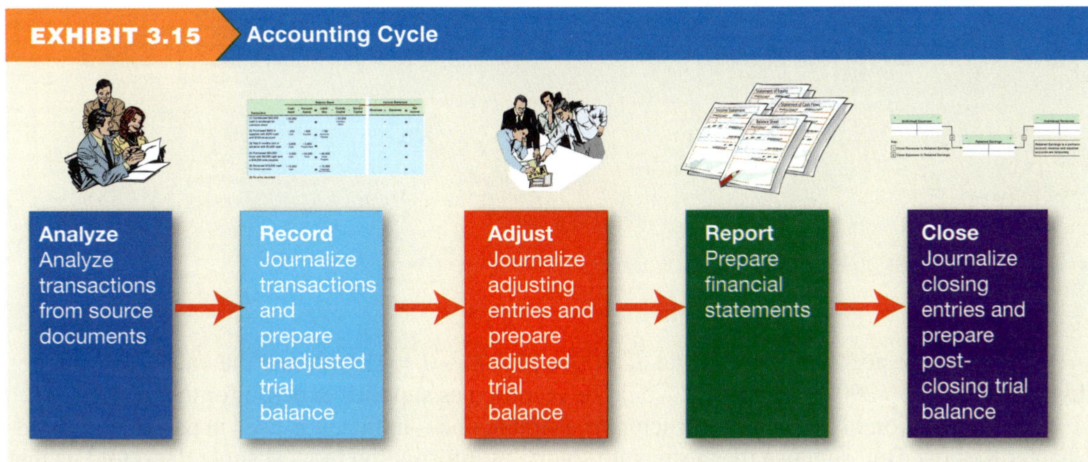

FINANCIAL STATEMENT ANALYSIS

Using Information on Levels and Flows

LO6 Analyze changes in balance sheet accounts.

6

A careful reader of financial statements must differentiate between those things that depict *levels* and those that depict *flows* or *changes*. The balance sheet portrays levels of resources and claims on those resources at a point in time, and the income statement portrays changes in those levels over a period of time. Knowing how the levels and flows relate to each other can be a very useful tool for analysis.

For instance, suppose that a service business has an inventory of office supplies. On July 1, an inventory count determined that the business has $2,400 of supplies inventory on hand. During the third calendar quarter, there were deliveries of office supplies with a cost of $5,700. And, at the end of the third quarter—on September 30—an inventory count finds $1,900 of supplies on hand. What amount of supplies expense should be recognized for the quarter?

Finding the answer to this question is easier if we recall the transactions that can affect the supplies inventory account, and that these transactions (changes) must lead from the beginning inventory level to the ending inventory level. At present, we know of two such transactions: the purchase of supplies inventory and the usage of supplies inventory.

(a)	Supplies inventory (+A)	5,700	
	Cash (−A) or Accounts payable (+L)		5,700
	Purchase supplies inventory.		
(b)	Supplies expense (+E, −SE)	?	
	Supplies inventory (−A)		?
	Record expense for supplies used.		

The supplies inventory T-account must look like the following:

+	Supplies Inventory (A)		–
Beg. bal.	2,400		
(a)	5,700	?	(b)
End. bal.	1,900		

An FSET version of this analysis would look like the following, with the only noncash account being supplies inventory, and assuming that the inventory purchase was made with cash.

	Balance Sheet					Income Statement		
Transaction	Cash Asset +	Supplies Inventory =	Liabil-ities +	Contrib. Capital +	Earned Capital	*Revenues* –	*Expenses* =	*Net Income*
Beginning balance		$2,400						
(a) Purchase office supplies	–5,700	+5,700						
(b) Office supplies taken for use in client service activities		–?			–? Retained Earnings		+? Supplies Expense	–?
Ending balance		$1,900						

Balancing the account requires that \$2,400 + \$5,700 – ? = \$1,900, and the value that satisfies this condition is \$6,200. That amount would be recorded as supplies expense for the quarter.

This application of the account structure is a simple one—in fact, it is used in part *a* of the Mid-Chapter Review. But, suppose that a separate source of information (e.g., scanner data) told us that \$5,900 in supplies had been taken from inventory for client service activities. When put into the FSET/T-account analysis above, this new fact would imply an additional \$300 in supplies had been removed for reasons such as breakage, obsolescence, or pilferage.

As we progress through the topics in future chapters, we will find that accounting reports do not always provide the information that is most useful for assessment of a company's current performance or standing. In those cases, we can often use T-accounts and journal entries or the FSET to analyze levels and changes and to develop the numbers that do a better job of answering important questions.

CHAPTER-END REVIEW

Assume that Atwell Laboratories, Inc., operates with an accounting fiscal year ending June 30. The company's accounts are adjusted annually and closed on that date. Its unadjusted trial balance as of June 30, 2019, is as follows.

ATWELL LABORATORIES, INC.
Unadjusted Trial Balance
June 30, 2019

	Debit	Credit
Cash	$ 1,000	
Accounts receivable	9,200	
Prepaid insurance	6,000	
Supplies	31,300	
Equipment	270,000	
Accumulated depreciation—equipment		$ 60,000
Accounts payable		3,100
Contract liability		4,000
Fees revenue		150,000
Wages expense	58,000	
Rent expense	22,000	
Common stock		120,400
Retained earnings		60,000
Totals	$397,500	$397,500

Additional Information

1. Atwell acquired a two-year insurance policy on January 1, 2019. The policy covers fire and casualty; Atwell had no coverage prior to January 1, 2019.
2. An inventory of supplies was taken on June 30 and the amount available was $6,300.
3. All equipment was purchased on July 1, 2016, for $270,000. The equipment's life is estimated at 9 years. Assume the entire asset cost is depreciated over its useful life.
4. Atwell received a $4,000 cash payment on April 1, 2019, from Beave Clinic for diagnostic work to be provided uniformly over the next 4 months, beginning April 1, 2019. The amount was credited to Contract Liability. The service was provided per the agreement.
5. Unpaid and unrecorded wages at June 30, 2019, were $600.
6. Atwell rents facilities for $2,000 per month. Atwell has not yet made or recorded the payment for June 2019.

In addition to the unadjusted accounts listed above, Atwell's ledger includes the following accounts, all with zero balances: Insurance Expense; Depreciation Expense; Supplies Expense; Wages Payable; and Rent Payable.

Required

1. Show the impact of the necessary adjusting entries using the FSET.
2. Show the impact of the necessary adjusting entries using journal entries.
3. Prepare T-accounts with the unadjusted balances as beginning balances and enter the adjusting entries from part 2. Prepare Atwell's June 30, 2019, adjusted trial balance by entering the adjusting journal entries into the T-accounts.
4. Prepare Atwell's closing journal entries and post them to the T-accounts (key the entries).
5. Prepare the company's June 30, 2019, balance sheet and its income statement and statement of stockholders equity for the year ended June 30, 2019.

The solution to this review problem can be found on pages 150–155.

SUMMARY

LO1 **Identify the major steps in the accounting cycle.** **(p. 102)**

- The major steps in the accounting cycle are
  a. Analyze *b.* Record *c.* Adjust *d.* Report *e.* Close

LO2 **Review the process of journalizing and posting transactions.** **(p. 103)**

- Transactions are initially recorded in a journal; the entries are in chronological order, and the journal shows the total effect of each transaction or adjustment.
- Posting is the transfer of information from a journal to the general ledger accounts.

LO3 **Describe the adjusting process and illustrate adjusting entries.** **(p. 109)**

- Adjusting entries achieve the proper recognition of revenues and the proper matching of expenses with those revenues; adjustments are summarized as follows.

Adjustment	Adjusting Entry
Adjusting prepaid (deferred) expenses	Increase expense Decrease asset
Adjusting unearned (deferred) revenues	Decrease liability Increase revenue
Accruing expenses	Increase expense Increase liability
Accruing revenues	Increase asset Increase revenue

LO4 **Prepare financial statements from adjusted accounts.** **(p. 118)**

- An income statement, statement of stockholders' equity, balance sheet, and statement of cash flows are prepared from an adjusted trial balance and other information.

LO5 **Describe the process of closing temporary accounts.** **(p. 122)**

- *Closing the books* means closing (yielding zero balances) revenues and expenses—that is, all temporary accounts. Revenue and expense account balances are transferred (closed) to the Retained Earnings account.

LO6 **Analyze changes in balance sheet accounts.** **(p. 125)**

- The combination of balance sheet levels and income statement flows allows a financial statement reader to infer the effects of transactions and adjustments that are not disclosed directly.

GUIDANCE ANSWERS . . . YOU MAKE THE CALL

You are the Chief Accountant Deposits represent a liability and should be included in REI's current liabilities at the time the cash or check is received. The account that would be used may have several names, including advances, trip deposits, contract liabilities, and/or performance obligations. Revenue should not be recognized until goods are transferred or services are provided to the customer. In this instance, REI should not recognize revenues until the trip has been completed. It is not unusual for events to occur that result in a refund of some portion or even all of the traveler's total payment. In the present case involving a low cancellation rate, waiting until the trip is over is not only conservative reporting, but is likely more efficient bookkeeping as well.

KEY TERMS

Accounting cycle (p. 102)
Accruals (p. 111)
Accrued expense (p. 115)
Accrued income (p. 114)
Accrued revenue (p. 114)
Adjusted trial balance (p. 118)
Adjusting entries (p. 111)
Book value (p. 114)
Calendar year (p. 102)
Chart of accounts (p. 103)
Close expense accounts (p. 123)
Close revenue accounts (p. 123)
Closing process (p. 123)
Contra accounts (p. 113)
Contra asset (p. 113)
Deferrals (p. 111)
Deferred revenue (p. 111)
Depreciation (p. 113)
Fiscal year (p. 102)
General journal (p. 103)
Journal (p. 103)
Permanent accounts (p. 122)
Post-closing trial balance (p. 124)
Posting (p. 103)
Straight-line depreciation (p. 113)
Temporary accounts (p. 122)
Unadjusted trial balance (p. 110)

Assignments with the logo in the margin are available in myBusinessCourse. See the Preface of the book for details.

MULTIPLE CHOICE

Multiple Choice Answers
1. b 2. a 3. b 4. c 5. c

1. An end-of-period journal entry made to reflect accrual accounting is called
a. a posted journal entry.
b. an adjusting journal entry.
c. an erroneous journal entry.
d. a compound journal entry.

2. Posting refers to the process whereby journal entry information is transferred from
a. journal to general ledger accounts.
b. general ledger accounts to a journal.
c. source documents to a journal.
d. a journal to source documents.

3. Which of the following is an example of an adjusting entry?
a. Recording the purchase of supplies on account
b. Recording depreciation expense on a truck
c. Recording cash received from customers for services rendered
d. Recording the cash payment of wages to employees

4. A piece of equipment was placed in service on January 1, 2017. The cost of the equipment was $20,000, and it is expected to have no value at the end of its eight-year life. Using straight-line depreciation, what amounts will be seen for depreciation expense and accumulated depreciation for fiscal (and calendar) year 2019?

	Fiscal Year 2019 Depreciation Expense	Fiscal Year-End 2019 Accumulated Depreciation
a.	$2,500	$ 2,000
b.	–0–	$20,000
c.	$2,500	$ 7,500
d.	$7,500	$ 7,500

5. When a customer places an order, Custom Cakes requires a deposit equal to the full purchase price. However, Custom Cakes does not recognize revenue until the completed cake is delivered. During the month of November, Custom Cakes received $24,000 in customer deposits. The balance in its customer deposits liability was $4,000 at the beginning of November and $6,000 at the end of November. How much revenue did Custom Cakes recognize during the month of November?
a. $26,000
b. $24,000
c. $22,000
d. $4,000

QUESTIONS

Q3-1. What are the five major steps in the accounting cycle? List them in their proper order.

Q3-2. What does the term *fiscal year* mean?

Q3-3. What are three examples of source documents that underlie business transactions?

Q3-4. What is the nature and purpose of a general journal?

Q3-5. Explain the process of posting.

Q3-6. What is an adjusting journal entry?

Q3-7. What is a chart of accounts? Give an example of a coding system for identifying different types of accounts.

Q3-8. Why is the adjusting step of the accounting cycle necessary?

Q3-9. What four different types of adjustments are frequently necessary at the close of an accounting period? Give examples of each type.

Q3-10. On January 1, Prepaid Insurance was debited with the cost of a two-year premium, $1,872. What adjusting entry should be made on January 31 before financial statements are prepared for the month?

Q3-11. What is a contra account? What contra account is used in reporting the book value of a depreciable asset?

Q3-12. A building was acquired on January 1, 2011, at a cost of $4,000,000, and its depreciation is calculated using the straight-line method. At the end of 2015, the accumulated depreciation contra asset for the building is $800,000. What will be the balance in the building's accumulated depreciation contra asset at the end of 2022? What is the building's book value at that date?

Q3-13. The publisher of *International View*, a monthly magazine, received two-year subscriptions totaling $9,720 on January 1. (a) What entry should be made to record the receipt of the $9,720? (b) What entry should be made at the end of January before financial statements are prepared for the month?

Q3-14. Globe Travel Agency pays an employee $475 in wages each Friday for the five-day workweek ending on that day. The last Friday of January falls on January 27. What adjusting entry should be made on January 31, the fiscal year-end?

Q3-15. The Bayou Company earns interest amounting to $360 per month on its investments. The company receives the interest every six months, on December 31 and June 30. Monthly financial statements are prepared. What adjusting entry should be made on January 31?

Q3-16. Which groups of accounts are closed at the end of the accounting year?

Q3-17. What are the two major steps in the closing process?

Q3-18. What is the purpose of a post-closing trial balance? Which of the following accounts should *not* appear in the post-closing trial balance: Cash; Unearned Revenue; Prepaid Rent; Depreciation Expense; Utilities Payable; Supplies Expense; and Retained Earnings?

Q3-19. Dehning Corporation is an international manufacturer of films and industrial identification products. Included among its prepaid expenses is an account titled Prepaid Catalog Costs; in recent years, this account's size has ranged between $2,500,000 and $4,000,000. The company states that catalog costs are initially capitalized and then written off over the estimated useful lives of the publications (generally eight months). Identify and briefly discuss the accounting principles that support Dehning Corporation's handling of its catalog costs.

Q3-20. At the beginning of January, the first month of the accounting year, the supplies account had a debit balance of $825. During January, purchases of $260 worth of supplies were debited to the account. Although only $630 of supplies were still available at the end of January, the necessary adjusting entry was omitted. How will the omission affect (a) the income statement for January, and (b) the balance sheet prepared at January 31?

MINI EXERCISES

LO2 Homework MBC

M3-21. Journalizing Transactions in Template, Journal Entry Form, and T-Accounts
Creative Designs, a firm providing art services for advertisers, began business on June 1, 2019. The following transactions occurred during the month of June.

June 1 Anne Clem invested $12,000 cash to begin the business in exchange for common stock.
2 Paid $950 cash for June rent.

June 3 Purchased $6,400 of office equipment on account.
6 Purchased $3,800 of art materials and other supplies; paid $1,800 cash with the remainder due within 30 days.
11 Billed clients $4,700 for services rendered.
17 Collected $3,250 cash from clients on their accounts.
19 Paid $3,000 cash toward the account for office equipment suppliers (see June 3).
25 Paid $900 cash for dividends.
30 Paid $350 cash for June utilities.
30 Paid $2,500 cash for June salaries.

REQUIRED

a. Record the above transactions for June using the financial statement effects template.

b. The following accounts in its general ledger are needed to record the transactions for June: Cash; Accounts Receivable; Supplies; Office Equipment; Accounts Payable; Common Stock; Retained Earnings; Service Fees Earned; Rent Expense; Utilities Expense; and Salaries Expense. Record the above transactions for June in journal entry form.

c. Set up T-accounts for each of the ledger accounts and post the entries to them (key the numbers in T-accounts by date).

M3-22. Journalizing Transactions in Template, Journal Entry Form, and T-Accounts **LO2**

Minute Maid, a firm providing housecleaning services, began business on April 1, 2019. The following transactions occurred during the month of April.

April 1 A. Falcon invested $9,000 cash to begin the business in exchange for common stock.
2 Paid $2,850 cash for six months' lease on van for the business.
3 Borrowed $10,000 cash from bank and signed note payable agreeing to repay it in 1 year plus 10% interest.
3 Purchased $5,500 of cleaning equipment; paid $2,500 cash with the remainder due within 30 days.
4 Paid $4,300 cash for cleaning supplies.
7 Paid $350 cash for advertisements to run in newspaper during April.
21 Billed customers $3,500 for services performed.
23 Paid $3,000 cash on account to cleaning equipment suppliers (see April 3).
28 Collected $2,300 cash from customers on their accounts.
29 Paid $1,000 cash for dividends.
30 Paid $1,750 cash for April wages.
30 Paid $995 cash to service station for gasoline used during April.

REQUIRED

a. Record the above transactions for April using the financial statement effects template.

b. The following accounts in its general ledger are needed to record the transactions for April: Cash; Accounts Receivable; Supplies; Prepaid Van Lease; Equipment; Accounts Payable; Notes Payable; Common Stock; Retained Earnings; Cleaning Fees Earned; Van Fuel Expense; Advertising Expense; and Wages Expense. Record the above transactions for April in journal entry form.

c. Set up T-accounts for each of the ledger accounts and post the entries to them (key the numbers in T-accounts by date).

M3-23. Journalizing Transactions and Adjusting Accounts **LO2, 3**

Deluxe Building Services offers custodial services on both a contract basis and an hourly basis. On January 1, 2019, Deluxe collected $20,100 in advance on a six-month contract for work to be performed evenly during the next six months. Assume that Deluxe closes its books and issues financial reports on a monthly basis.

a. Prepare the entry on January 1 to record the receipt of $20,100 cash for contract work (1) using the financial statements effect template and (2) in journal entry form.

b. Prepare the adjusting entry to be made on January 31, 2019, for the contract work done during January (1) using the financial statements effect template and (2) in journal entry form.

c. At January 31, a total of 30 hours of hourly rate custodial work was unbilled. The billing rate is $19 per hour. Prepare the adjusting entry needed on January 31, 2019, (1) using the financial statements effect template and (2) in journal entry form. (The firm uses the account Fees Receivable to reflect amounts due but not yet billed.)

LO3, 6

M3-24. Adjusting Accounts

Selected accounts of Ideal Properties, a real estate management firm, are shown below as of January 31, 2019, before any adjusting entries have been made.

Unadjusted Account Balances	Debits	Credits
Prepaid insurance	$6,660	
Supplies inventory	1,930	
Office equipment	5,952	
Unearned rent liability		$ 5,250
Salaries expense	3,100	
Rent revenue		15,000

Monthly financial statements are prepared. Using the following information, record the adjusting entries necessary on January 31 (a) using the financial statements effect template and (b) in journal entry form.

1. Prepaid Insurance represents a three-year premium paid on January 1, 2019.
2. Supplies of $850 were still available on January 31.
3. Office equipment—purchased on January 1, 2019—is expected to last eight years.
4. On January 1, 2019, Ideal Properties collected six months' rent in advance from a tenant renting space for $875 per month.
5. Accrued employee salaries of $490 have not been recorded as of January 31.

LO2, 3, 6

El Puerto de Liverpool
OTCMKTS :: ELPQF

M3-25. Inferring Transactions from Financial Statements

El Puerto de Liverpool (Liverpool) is a large retailer in Mexico. The following accounts are selected from its annual report for the fiscal year ended December 31, 2017. For the fiscal year ended December 31, 2017, Liverpool purchased merchandise inventory costing 78,023,979 thousand Mexican pesos. Assume that all purchases were made on account. The following T-accounts reflect information contained in the company's 2017 and 2016 (restated), balance sheets in thousands of Mexican pesos.

+ Inventories (A)	–
12/31/2016 Bal. 13,849,931	
12/31/2017 Bal. 18,486,423	

– Suppliers (Accounts Payable)	+
	15,210,743 12/31/2016 Bal.
	22,535,802 12/31/2017 Bal.

a. Prepare the entry, using the financial statement effects template and in journal entry form, to record Liverpool's purchases for the 2017 fiscal year.

b. What amount did Liverpool pay in cash to its suppliers for the fiscal year ended December 31, 2017? Explain. Assume that Suppliers (Accounts payable) is affected only by transactions related to inventory.

c. Prepare the entry, using the financial statement effects template and in journal entry form, to record cost of goods sold for the year ended December 31, 2017.

LO4

M3-26. Preparing a Statement of Stockholders' Equity

On December 31, 2017, the credit balances of the Common Stock and Retained Earnings accounts were $30,000 and $18,000, respectively, for Architect Services Company. Its stock issuances for 2018 totaled $6,000, and it paid $9,700 cash toward dividends in 2018. For the year ended December 31, 2018, the company had net income of $29,900. Prepare a 2018 statement of stockholders' equity for Architect Services.

LO5

M3-27. Applying Closing Procedures

Assume you are in the process of closing procedures for Echo Corporation. You have already closed all revenue and expense accounts to the Retained Earnings account. The total debits to Retained Earnings equal $308,800 and total credits to Retained Earnings equal $347,400. The Retained Earnings account had a credit balance of $99,000 at the start of this current year. What is the post-closing ending balance of Retained Earnings at the end of this current year?

LO5

M3-28. Preparing Closing Entries Using Journal Entries and T-Accounts

The adjusted trial balance at December 31, 2018, for Smith Company includes the following selected accounts.

Adjusted Account Balances	Debit	Credit
Commissions revenue		$84,900
Wages expense	$36,000	
Insurance expense	1,900	
Utilities expense	8,200	
Depreciation expense	9,800	
Retained earnings		72,100

a. Prepare entries to close these accounts in journal entry form.

b. Set up T-accounts for each of these ledger accounts, enter the balances above, and post the closing entries to them. After these entries are posted, what is the post-closing balance of the Retained Earnings account?

M3-29. Inferring Transactions from Financial Statements

LO2, 3, 6

Amazon.com Inc.
NASDAQ :: AMZN

Amazon.com Inc. is one of the world's leading e-commerce companies, with almost $120 billion in revenues for the fiscal year ended December 31, 2017. For the year ended December 31, 2017, Amazon's cost of goods sold was $111,934 million. Assume that all purchases were made on account. The following T-accounts reflect information contained in the company's 2017 and 2016 balance sheets (in millions).

+ Inventories		−
12/31/2016 Bal.	$11,461	
12/31/2017 Bal.	$16,047	

− Accounts Payable	+	
	$25,309	12/31/2016 Bal.
	$34,616	12/31/2017 Bal.

a. Prepare the entry, using the financial statement effects template and in journal entry form, to record cost of goods sold for the year ended December 31, 2017.

b. Prepare the entry, using the financial statement effects template and in journal entry form, to record Amazon's inventory purchases for the year ended December 31, 2017. (Assume all purchases are made on account.)

c. What amount did Amazon pay in cash to its suppliers for the year ended December 31, 2017?

M3-30. Preparing Entries Across Two Periods

LO2, 3, 5

Hatcher Company closes its accounts on December 31 each year. On December 31, 2018, Hatcher accrued $600 of interest income that was earned on an investment but not yet received or recorded (the investment will pay interest of $900 cash on January 31, 2019). On January 31, 2019, the company received the $900 cash as interest on the investment. Prepare journal entries to:

a. Accrue the interest earned on December 31, 2018;

b. Close the Interest Income account on December 31, 2018 (the account has a year-end balance of $2,400 after adjustments); and

c. Record the cash receipt of interest on January 31, 2019.

EXERCISES

E3-31. Journalizing and Posting Closing Entries

LO5

Homework MBC

The adjusted trial balance as of December 31, 2018, for Brooks Consulting Company contains the following selected accounts.

Adjusted Account Balances	Debit	Credit
Service fees earned		€80,300
Rent expense	€20,800	
Salaries expense	45,700	
Supplies expense	5,600	
Depreciation expense	10,200	
Retained earnings		67,000

a. Prepare entries to close these accounts in journal entry form.

b. Set up T-accounts for each of the ledger accounts, enter the balances above, and post the closing entries to them. After these entries are posted, what is the post-closing balance of the Retained Earnings account?

LO3

Hartford Financial Services Group
NYSE :: HIG

E3-32. Preparing and Journalizing Adjusting Entries

For each of the following separate situations, prepare the necessary adjustments (a) using the financial statement effects template, and (b) in journal entry form.

1. Unrecorded depreciation on equipment is $610.
2. On the date for preparing financial statements, an estimated utilities expense of $390 has been incurred, but no utility bill has yet been received or paid.
3. On the first day of the current period, rent for four periods was paid and recorded as a $2,800 debit to Prepaid Rent and a $2,800 credit to Cash.
4. Nine months ago, the **Hartford Financial Services Group** sold a one-year policy to a customer and recorded the receipt of the premium by debiting Cash for $624 and crediting Contract Liabilities for $624. No adjusting entries have been prepared during the nine-month period. Hartford's annual financial statements are now being prepared.
5. At the end of the period, employee wages of $965 have been incurred but not yet paid or recorded.
6. At the end of the period, $300 of interest income has been earned but not yet received or recorded.

LO2, 3, 5

E3-33. Preparing Adjusting and Closing Entries Across Two Periods

Norton Company closes its accounts on December 31 each year. The company works a five-day work week and pays its employees every two weeks. On December 31, 2018, Norton accrued $4,700 of salaries payable. On January 7, 2019, the company paid salaries of $12,000 cash to employees. Prepare journal entries to:

a. Accrue the salaries payable on December 31;
b. Close the Salaries Expense account on December 31 (the account has a year-end balance of $250,000 after adjustments); and
c. Record the salary payment on January 7.

LO3, 6

E3-34. Analyzing Accounts Using Adjusted Data

Selected T-account balances for Fields Company are shown below as of January 31, 2019; adjusting entries have already been posted. The firm uses a calendar-year accounting period but prepares *monthly* adjustments.

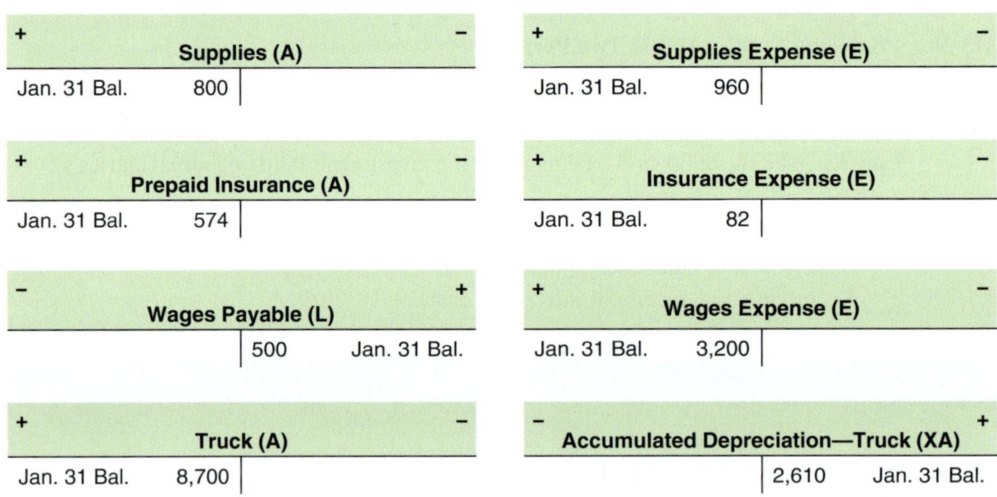

+ Supplies (A) −	
Jan. 31 Bal. 800	

+ Supplies Expense (E) −	
Jan. 31 Bal. 960	

+ Prepaid Insurance (A) −	
Jan. 31 Bal. 574	

+ Insurance Expense (E) −	
Jan. 31 Bal. 82	

− Wages Payable (L) +	
	500 Jan. 31 Bal.

+ Wages Expense (E) −	
Jan. 31 Bal. 3,200	

+ Truck (A) −	
Jan. 31 Bal. 8,700	

− Accumulated Depreciation—Truck (XA) +	
	2,610 Jan. 31 Bal.

a. If the amount in Supplies Expense represents the January 31 adjustment for the supplies used in January, and $620 worth of supplies were purchased during January, what was the January 1 beginning balance of Supplies?
b. The amount in the Insurance Expense account represents the adjustment made at January 31 for January insurance expense. If the original insurance premium was for one year, what was the amount of the premium and on what date did the insurance policy start?
c. If we assume that no beginning balance existed in wages payable or wages expense on January 1, how much cash was paid as wages during January?
d. If the truck has a useful life of five years, what is the monthly amount of depreciation expense and how many months has Fields owned the truck?

E3-35. Preparing Adjusting Entries

Jake Thomas began Thomas Refinishing Service on July 1, 2019. Selected accounts are shown below as of July 31, before any adjusting entries have been made.

Unadjusted Account Balances	Debit	Credit
Prepaid rent	$5,700	
Prepaid advertising	630	
Supplies inventory	3,000	
Performance obligation liability		$ 600
Refinishing fees revenue		2,500

Using the following information, prepare the adjusting entries necessary on July 31 (a) using the financial statement effects template and (b) in journal entry form. (c) Set up T-accounts for each of the ledger accounts, enter the balances above, and post the adjusting entries to them.

1. On July 1, the firm paid one year's advance rent of $5,700 in cash.
2. On July 1, $630 cash was paid to the local newspaper for an advertisement to run daily for the months of July, August, and September.
3. Supplies still available at July 31 total $1,100.
4. At July 31, refinishing services of $800 have been performed but not yet recorded or billed to customers. The firm uses the account Fees Receivable to reflect amounts due but not yet billed.
5. A customer paid $600 in advance for a refinishing project. At July 31, the project is one-half complete.

E3-36. Inferring Transactions from Financial Statements

LO2, 3, 6

Abercrombie & Fitch Co.
NYSE :: ANF

Abercrombie & Fitch Co. (ANF) is a specialty retailer of casual apparel. The following information is taken from ANF's fiscal 10-K report for the fiscal year 2017, which ended February 3, 2018. (All amounts in $ thousands.)

Selected Balance Sheet Data	February 3, 2018	January 28, 2017
Inventory	$424,393	$399,795
Accrued compensation	65,045	37,235

a. ANF reported Cost of Goods Sold of $1,408,848 (thousand) for its fiscal year 2017. What was the cost that ANF incurred to acquire inventory for its fiscal year 2017?

b. Assume that ANF reported Compensation Expense of $650,000 (thousand) for its fiscal year 2017. What amount of compensation was paid to its employees for fiscal year 2017?

c. Where would you expect ANF to report its balance of Accrued Compensation?

E3-37. Preparing Closing Procedures

LO5

The adjusted trial balance of Parker Corporation, prepared December 31, 2018, contains the following selected accounts.

Adjusted Account Balances	Debit	Credit
Service fees revenue		$92,500
Interest income		2,200
Salaries expense	$41,800	
Advertising expense	4,300	
Depreciation expense	8,700	
Income tax expense	9,900	
Retained earnings		42,700

a. Prepare entries to close these accounts in journal entry form.

b. Set up T-accounts for each of the ledger accounts, enter the balances above, and post the closing entries to them. After these entries are posted, what is the post-closing balance of the Retained Earnings account?

E3-38. Inferring Transactions from Financial Statements

LO2, 3, 6

Ethan Allen Interiors Inc.
NYSE :: ETH

Ethan Allen Interiors Inc., a leading manufacturer and retailer of home furnishings and accessories, sells products through an exclusive network of approximately 300 design centers. All of Ethan Allen's products are sold by special order. Customers generally place a deposit equal to 25%

to 50% of the purchase price when ordering. Orders take 4 to 12 weeks to be delivered. Selected fiscal-year information from the company's balance sheets is as follows ($ thousands):

Selected Balance Sheet Data	2017	2016
Inventories	$149,483	$162,323
Customer deposits	62,960	60,958

a. In fiscal 2017, Ethan Allen reported total sales revenue of $763,385 (thousand). Assume that the company collected customer deposits equal to $200,000 (thousand) over the year. Prepare entries, using the financial statement effects template and in journal entry form, to record customer deposits and its sales revenue for fiscal year 2017.

b. Ethan Allen's cost of goods sold for 2017 was $343,662 (thousand). Prepare the adjusting entry, using the financial statement effects template and in journal entry form, that it made to record inventory acquisitions.

c. Where would you expect Ethan Allen to report its Customer Deposits?

LO4, 5 Homework MBC

E3-39. Preparing Financial Statements and Closing Procedures

Solomon Corporation's adjusted trial balance for the year ending December 31, 2018, is:

SOLOMON CORPORATION Adjusted Trial Balance December 31, 2018	Debit	Credit
Cash	$ 4,000	
Accounts receivable	6,500	
Equipment	78,000	
Accumulated depreciation		$ 14,000
Notes payable		10,000
Common stock		43,000
Retained earnings		12,600
Service fees revenue		71,000
Rent expense	18,000	
Salaries expense	37,100	
Depreciation expense	7,000	
Totals	$150,600	$150,600

a. Prepare its income statement and statement of stockholders' equity for the current year, and its balance sheet for the current year-end. Cash dividends were $8,000 and there were no stock issuances or repurchases.

b. Prepare entries to close its temporary accounts in journal entry form.

c. Set up T-accounts for each of the ledger accounts, enter the balances above, and post the closing entries to them. After these entries are posted, what is the post-closing balance of the Retained Earnings account?

PROBLEMS

LO2, 3, 6

P3-40. Journalizing and Posting Transactions, and Preparing a Trial Balance and Adjustments

B. Lougee opened Lougee Roofing Service on April 1, 2019. Transactions for April are as follows:

Apr. 1 Lougee contributed $11,500 cash to the business in exchange for common stock.
1 Paid $2,880 cash for two-year premium toward liability insurance effective immediately.
2 Paid $6,100 cash for the purchase of a used truck.
2 Purchased $3,100 of ladders and other equipment; paid $1,000 cash, with the balance due in 30 days.
5 Purchased $1,200 of supplies on account.
5 Received an advance of $1,800 cash from a customer for roof repairs to be done during April and May.
12 Billed customers $5,500 for roofing services performed.

Apr 18 Collected $4,900 cash from customers on their accounts.
29 Paid $675 cash for truck fuel used in April.
30 Paid $100 cash for April newspaper advertising.
30 Paid $2,500 cash for assistants' wages.
30 Billed customers $4,000 for roofing services performed.

REQUIRED

a. Set up a general ledger in T-account form for the following accounts: Cash; Accounts Receivable; Supplies; Prepaid Insurance; Trucks; Accumulated Depreciation—Trucks; Equipment; Accumulated Depreciation—Equipment; Accounts Payable; Contract Liability; Common Stock; Roofing Fees Revenue; Fuel Expense; Advertising Expense; Wages Expense; Insurance Expense; Supplies Expense; Depreciation Expense—Trucks; and Depreciation Expense—Equipment.

b. Record these transactions for April (1) using the financial statement effects template and (2) in journal entry form. (3) Post these entries to their T-accounts (key numbers in T-accounts by date).

c. Prepare an unadjusted trial balance as of April 30, 2019.

d. Supplies still available on April 30 amount to $400; and depreciation for April was $125 on the truck and $35 on equipment; and one-fourth of the roofing fees received in advance was earned by April 30. Prepare entries to adjust the books for Insurance Expense, Supplies Expense, Depreciation Expense—Trucks, Depreciation Expense—Equipment, and Roofing Fees Revenue (1) using the financial statement effects template and (2) in journal entry form. (3) Post adjusting entries to their T-accounts.

P3-41. Preparing an Unadjusted Trial Balance and Adjustments

LO2, 3

Homework MBC

SnapShot Company, a commercial photography studio, has just completed its first full year of operations on December 31, 2018. General ledger account balances *before* year-end adjustments follow; no adjusting entries have been made to the accounts at any time during the year. Assume that all balances are normal.

Cash	$ 2,150	Accounts payable	$ 1,910
Accounts receivable	3,800	Performance obligations	2,600
Prepaid rent	12,600	Common stock	24,000
Prepaid insurance	2,970	Photography fee revenue	34,480
Supplies	4,250	Wages expense	11,000
Equipment	22,800	Utilities expense	3,420

An analysis of the firm's records discloses the following.

1. Photography services of $925 have been rendered, but customers have not yet paid or been billed. The firm uses the account Fees Receivable to reflect amounts due but not yet billed.
2. Equipment, purchased January 1, 2018, has an estimated life of 10 years.
3. Utilities expense for December is estimated to be $400, but the bill will not arrive or be paid until January of next year.
4. The balance in Prepaid Rent represents the amount paid on January 1, 2018, for a 2-year lease on the studio.
5. In November, customers paid $2,600 cash in advance for photos to be taken for the holiday season. When received, these fees were credited to Performance Obligations. By December 31, all of these fees are earned.
6. A 3-year insurance premium paid on January 1, 2018, was debited to Prepaid Insurance.
7. Supplies available at December 31 are $1,520.
8. At December 31, wages expense of $375 has been incurred but not paid or recorded.

REQUIRED

a. Prove that debits equal credits for SnapShot's unadjusted account balances by preparing its unadjusted trial balance at December 31, 2018.

b. Prepare its adjusting entries using the financial statement effects template.

c. Prepare its adjusting entries in journal entry form.

d. Set up T-accounts, enter the balances above, and post the adjusting entries to them.

P3-42. Preparing Adjusting Entries, Financial Statements, and Closing Entries

LO2, 3, 4, 5, 6

Murdock Carpet Cleaners ended its first month of operations on June 30, 2019. Monthly financial statements will be prepared. The unadjusted account balances are as follows.

MURDOCK CARPET CLEANERS
Unadjusted Trial Balance
June 30, 2019

	Debit	Credit
Cash	$ 1,180	
Accounts receivable	450	
Prepaid rent	3,100	
Supplies	2,520	
Equipment	4,440	
Accounts payable		$ 760
Common stock		2,000
Retained earnings		5,300
Service fees revenue		4,650
Wages expense	1,020	
	$12,710	$12,710

The following information is available.

1. The balance in Prepaid Rent was the amount paid on June 1 for the first four months' rent.
2. Supplies available at June 30 were $820.
3. Equipment, purchased June 1, has an estimated life of five years.
4. Unpaid and unrecorded employee wages at June 30 were $210.
5. Utility services used during June were estimated at $300. A bill is expected early in July.
6. Fees earned for services performed but not yet billed on June 30 were $380. The company uses the account Accounts Receivable to reflect amounts due but not yet billed.

REQUIRED

a. Prepare its adjusting entries at June 30, 2019, using the financial statement effects template.
b. Prepare its adjusting entries at June 30, 2019, in journal entry form.
c. Set up T-accounts, enter the balances above, and post the adjusting entries to them.
d. Prepare its income statement for June and its balance sheet at June 30, 2019.
e. Prepare entries to close its temporary accounts in journal entry form and post the closing entries to the T-accounts.

LO3 **P3-43. Preparing Adjusting Entries**

The following information relates to the December 31 adjustments for Kwik Print Company. The firm's fiscal year ends on December 31.

1. Weekly employee salaries for a five-day week total $1,800, payable on Fridays. December 31 of the current year is a Tuesday.
2. Kwik Print has $20,000 of notes payable outstanding at December 31. Interest of $200 has accrued on these notes by December 31, but will not be paid until the notes mature next year.
3. During December, Kwik Print provided $900 of printing services to clients who will be billed on January 2. The firm uses the account Fees Receivable to reflect amounts due but not yet billed.
4. Starting December 1, all maintenance work on Kwik Print's equipment is handled by Richardson Repair Company under an agreement whereby Kwik Print pays a fixed monthly charge of $400. Kwik Print paid six months' service charge in advance on December 1, debiting Prepaid Maintenance for $2,400.
5. The firm paid $900 cash on December 15 for a series of radio commercials to run during December and January. One-third of the commercials have aired by December 31. The $900 payment was debited to Prepaid Advertising.
6. Starting December 16, Kwik Print rented 400 square feet of storage space from a neighboring business. The monthly rent of $0.80 per square foot is due in advance on the first of each month. Nothing was paid in December, however, because the neighbor agreed to add the rent for the one-half of December to the January 1 payment.
7. Kwik Print invested $5,000 cash in securities on December 1 and earned interest of $38 on these securities by December 31. No interest payment will be received until January, and the end-of-December market value of the securities remains at $5,000.
8. Annual depreciation on the firm's equipment is $2,175. No depreciation has been recorded during the year.

REQUIRED

Prepare its adjusting entries required at December 31:

a. using the financial statement effects template, and

b. in journal entry form.

P3-44. Preparing Financial Statements and Closing Entries **LO4, 5**

The following adjusted trial balance is for Trueman Consulting Inc. at December 31, 2018. The company had no stock issuances or repurchases during 2018.

	Debit	Credit
Cash	$ 2,700	
Accounts receivable	3,270	
Supplies	3,060	
Prepaid insurance	1,500	
Equipment	6,400	
Accumulated depreciation—equipment		$ 1,080
Accounts payable		845
Long-term notes payable		7,000
Common stock		1,000
Retained earnings		3,305
Service fees revenue		58,400
Rent expense	12,000	
Salaries expense	33,400	
Supplies expense	4,700	
Insurance expense	3,250	
Depreciation expense—equipment	720	
Interest expense	630	
	$71,630	$71,630

REQUIRED

a. Prepare its income statement and statement of stockholders' equity for 2018 and its balance sheet at December 31, 2018.

b. Prepare entries to close its accounts in journal entry form.

P3-45. Preparing Closing Entries **LO5**

The following adjusted trial balance is for Wilson Company at December 31, 2018.

	Debit	Credit
Cash	$ 8,500	
Accounts receivable	8,000	
Prepaid insurance	3,600	
Equipment	72,000	
Accumulated depreciation		$ 12,000
Accounts payable		600
Common stock		25,000
Retained earnings		19,100
Service fees revenue		97,200
Miscellaneous income		4,200
Salaries expense	42,800	
Rent expense	13,400	
Insurance expense	1,800	
Depreciation expense	8,000	
Income tax expense	8,800	
Income tax payable		8,800
	$166,900	$166,900

REQUIRED

a. Prepare closing entries in journal entry form.

b. After the firm's closing entries are posted, what is the post-closing balance for the Retained Earnings account?

c. Prepare its post-closing trial balance.

LO2, 3 **P3-46. Preparing Entries Across Two Periods**
The following selected accounts appear in Shaw Company's unadjusted trial balance at December 31, 2018, the end of its fiscal year (all accounts have normal balances).

Prepaid advertising.	$ 1,200	Performance obligations.	$ 5,400
Wages expense	43,800	Service fees revenue	87,000
Prepaid insurance.	3,420	Rental income.	4,900

REQUIRED

a. Prepare its adjusting entries at December 31, 2018, (1) using the financial statement effects template, and (2) in journal entry form using the following additional information.
1. Prepaid advertising at December 31 is $800.
2. Unpaid and unrecorded wages earned by employees in December are $1,300.
3. Prepaid insurance at December 31 is $2,280.
4. Performance obligations represent service fees collected in advance of when the services are provided to customers. Performance obligations at December 31 are $3,000.
5. Rent revenue of $1,000 owed by a tenant is not recorded at December 31.

b. Prepare entries on January 4, 2019, using the financial statement effects template and in journal entry form, to record (1) payment of $2,400 cash in wages, which includes the $1,300 accrued at December 31 and (2) cash receipt of the $1,000 rent revenue owed from the tenant.

LO2, 3 **P3-47. Journalizing and Posting Transactions, and Preparing a Trial Balance and Adjustments**
Market-Probe, a market research firm, had the following transactions in June 2019, its first month of operations.

June 1 B. May invested $24,000 cash in the firm in exchange for common stock.
1 The firm purchased the following: office equipment, $11,040; office supplies, $2,840. Terms are $4,400 cash with the remainder due in 60 days. (Make a compound entry requiring two credits.)
2 Paid $875 cash for June rent owed to the landlord.
2 Contracted for three months' advertising in a local newspaper at $310 per month and paid for the advertising in advance.
2 Signed a six-month contract with a customer to provide research consulting services at a rate of $3,200 per month. Received two months' fees in advance. Work on the contract started immediately.
10 Billed various customers $5,800 for services rendered.
12 Paid $3,600 cash for two weeks' salaries (5-day week) to employees.
15 Paid $1,240 cash to employee for travel expenses to conference.
18 Paid $520 cash to post office for bulk mailing of research questionnaire (postage expense).
26 Paid $3,600 cash for two weeks' salaries to employees.
28 Billed various customers $5,200 for services rendered.
30 Collected $7,800 cash from customers on their accounts.
30 Paid $1,500 cash for dividends.

REQUIRED

a. Set up a general ledger in T-account form for the following accounts: Cash; Accounts Receivable; Office Supplies; Prepaid Advertising; Office Equipment; Accumulated Depreciation—Office Equipment; Accounts Payable; Salaries Payable; Contract Liabilities; Common Stock; Retained Earnings; Service Fees Revenue; Salaries Expense; Advertising Expense; Supplies Expense; Rent Expense; Travel Expense; Depreciation Expense—Office Equipment; and Postage Expense.

b. Record these transactions (1) using the financial statement effects template, and (2) in journal entry form. (3) Post these entries to their T-accounts (key numbers in T-accounts by date).

c. Prepare an unadjusted trial balance at June 30, 2019.

d. Prepare adjusting entries (1) using the financial statement effects template and (2) in journal entry form, that reflect the following information at June 30, 2019:

- Office supplies available, $1,530
- Accrued employee salaries, $725
- Estimated life of office equipment is 8 years

Adjusting entries must also be prepared for advertising and service fees per information in the June transactions. (3) Post all adjusting entries to their T-accounts.

P3-48. Preparing an Unadjusted Trial Balance and Adjusting Entries LO3

DeliverAll, a mailing service, has just completed its first full year of operations on December 31, 2018. Its general ledger account balances *before* year-end adjustments follow; no adjusting entries have been made to the accounts at any time during the year. Assume that all balances are normal.

Cash	$ 2,300	Accounts payable	$ 2,700
Accounts receivable	5,120	Common stock	9,530
Prepaid advertising	1,680	Mailing fees earned	86,000
Supplies	6,270	Wages expense	38,800
Equipment	42,240	Rent expense	6,300
Notes payable	7,500	Utilities expense	3,020

An analysis of the firm's records reveals the following.

1. The balance in Prepaid Advertising represents the amount paid for newspaper advertising for one year. The agreement, which calls for the same amount of space and cost each month, covers the period from February 1, 2018, to January 31, 2019. DeliverAll did not advertise during its first month of operations.
2. Equipment, purchased January 1, has an estimated life of eight years.
3. Utilities expense does not include expense for December, estimated at $325. The bill will not arrive until January 2019.
4. At year-end, employees have earned an additional $1,200 in wages that will not be paid or recorded until January.
5. Supplies available at year-end amount to $1,520.
6. At year-end, unpaid interest of $450 has accrued on the notes payable.
7. The firm's lease calls for rent of $525 per month payable on the first of each month, plus an amount equal to 1/2% of annual mailing fees earned. The rental percentage is payable within 15 days after the end of the year.

REQUIRED

a. Prove that debits equal credits for its unadjusted account balances by preparing its unadjusted trial balance at December 31, 2018.

b. Prepare its adjusting entries: (1) using the financial statement effects template, and (2) in journal entry form.

c. Set up T-accounts, enter the balances above, and post the adjusting entries to them.

P3-49. Preparing Adjusting Entries LO2, 3, 4, 5, 6

Wheel Place Company began operations on March 1, 2019, to provide automotive wheel alignment and balancing services. On March 31, 2019, the unadjusted balances of the firm's accounts are as follows.

WHEEL PLACE COMPANY
Unadjusted Trial Balance
March 31, 2019

	Debit	Credit
Cash	$ 1,900	
Accounts receivable	3,820	
Prepaid rent	4,770	
Supplies	3,700	
Equipment	36,180	
Accounts payable		$ 2,510
Service contract liability		1,000
Common stock		38,400
Service revenue		12,360
Wages expense	3,900	
Totals	$54,270	$54,270

The following information is available.

1. The balance in Prepaid Rent was the amount paid on March 1 to cover the first 6 months' rent.
2. Supplies available on March 31 amount to $1,720.
3. Equipment has an estimated life of nine years and a zero salvage value.
4. Unpaid and unrecorded wages at March 31 were $560.

5. Utility services used during March were estimated at $390; a bill is expected early in April.
6. The balance in Service Contract Liability was the amount received on March 1 from a car dealer to cover alignment and balancing services on cars sold by the dealer in March and April. The Wheel Place agreed to provide the services at a fixed fee of $500 each month.

REQUIRED

a. Prepare its adjusting entries at March 31, 2019, (1) using the financial statement effects template, and (2) in journal entry form.

b. Set up T-accounts, enter the balances above, and post the adjusting entries to them.

c. Prepare its income statement for March and its balance sheet at March 31, 2019.

d. Prepare entries to close its temporary accounts in journal entry form and post the closing entries to the T-accounts.

LO4, 5 **P3-50. Preparing Financial Statements and Closing Entries**

Trails, Inc., publishes magazines for skiers and hikers. The company's adjusted trial balance for the year ending December 31, 2018, is:

TRAILS, INC.
Adjusted Trial Balance
December 31, 2018

	Debit	Credit
Cash	$ 3,400	
Accounts receivable	8,600	
Supplies	4,200	
Prepaid insurance	930	
Office equipment	66,000	
Accumulated depreciation		$ 11,000
Accounts payable		2,100
Subscription liabilities		10,000
Salaries payable		3,500
Common stock		25,000
Retained earnings		23,220
Subscription revenue		168,300
Advertising revenue		49,700
Salaries expense	100,230	
Printing and mailing expense	85,600	
Rent expense	8,800	
Supplies expense	6,100	
Insurance expense	1,860	
Depreciation expense	5,500	
Income tax expense	1,600	
Totals	$292,820	$292,820

REQUIRED

a. Prepare its income statement and statement of stockholders' equity for 2018, and its balance sheet at December 31, 2018. There were no cash dividends and no stock issuances or repurchases during the year.

b. Prepare entries to close its accounts in journal entry form.

LO5 Homework MBC **P3-51. Preparing Closing Entries**

The following adjusted trial balance is for Mayflower Moving Service at December 31, 2018.

MAYFLOWER MOVING SERVICE Adjusted Trial Balance December 31, 2018	Debit	Credit
Cash	$ 3,800	
Accounts receivable	5,250	
Supplies	2,300	
Prepaid advertising	3,000	
Trucks	28,300	
Accumulated depreciation—trucks		$ 10,000
Equipment	7,600	
Accumulated depreciation—equipment		2,100
Accounts payable		1,200
Service contract liabilities		2,700
Common stock		5,000
Retained earnings		15,550
Service fees revenue		72,500
Wages expense	29,800	
Rent expense	10,200	
Insurance expense	2,900	
Supplies expense	5,100	
Advertising expense	6,000	
Depreciation expense—trucks	4,000	
Depreciation expense—equipment	800	
Totals	$109,050	$109,050

REQUIRED

a. Prepare closing entries in journal entry form.

b. After its closing entries are posted, what is the post-closing balance for the Retained Earnings account?

c. Prepare Mayflower's post-closing trial balance.

P3-52. Preparing Entries Across Two Periods **LO2, 3, 6** Homework MBC

The following selected accounts appear in Zimmerman Company's unadjusted trial balance at December 31, 2018, the end of its fiscal year (all accounts have normal balances).

Prepaid maintenance	$2,700	Commission revenue	$84,000
Supplies	8,400	Rent expense	10,800
Performance obligations	8,500		

Additional information is as follows.

1. On September 1, 2018, the company entered into a prepaid equipment maintenance contract. Zimmerman Company paid $2,700 to cover maintenance service for 6 months, beginning September 1, 2018. The $2,700 payment was debited to Prepaid Maintenance.
2. Supplies available on December 31 are $3,200.
3. Performance obligations at December 31 are $4,000.
4. Commission revenue earned but not yet billed at December 31 are $2,800. (*Hint:* Debit Commissions Receivable.)
5. Zimmerman Company's lease calls for rent of $900 per month payable on the first of each month, plus an annual amount equal to 1% of annual commission revenue. This additional rent is payable on January 10 of the following year. (*Hint:* Use the adjusted amount of commission revenue in computing the additional rent.)

REQUIRED

a. Prepare Zimmerman Company's adjusting entries at December 31, 2018, using the financial statement effects template.

b. Prepare entries on January 10, 2019, using the financial statement effects template to record (1) the billing of $4,600 in commissions earned (which includes the $2,800 of commissions earned but not billed at December 31) and (2) the cash payment of the additional rent owed for 2018. (*Hint for part (1)*: Zimmerman Company has two receivable accounts—Commissions Receivable is used for amounts earned, but not yet billed, and Accounts Receivable for amounts that are earned and billed to the customer.)

c. Prepare the adjusting entries from part *a* and the transactions in part *b* in journal entry form.

LO2, 3, 4, 5, 6

P3-53. Preparing Adjusting Entries, Financial Statements, and Closing Entries

Fischer Card Shop is a small retail shop. Fischer's balance sheet at year-end 2018 is as follows. The following information details transactions and adjustments that occurred during 2019.

1. Sales total $145,850 in 2019; all sales were cash sales.
2. Inventory purchases total $76,200 in 2019; at December 31, 2019, inventory totals $14,500. Assume all purchases were made on account.
3. Accounts payable totals $4,100 at December 31, 2019.
4. Annual store rent of $24,000 was paid on March 1, 2019, covering the next 12 months. The balance in prepaid rent at December 31, 2018, was the balance remaining from the advance rent payment in 2018.
5. Wages are paid every other week on Friday; during 2019, Fischer paid $12,500 cash for wages. At December 31, 2019, Fischer owed employees unpaid and unrecorded wages of $350.
6. Depreciation on equipment totals $1,700 in 2019.

FISCHER CARD SHOP
Balance Sheet
December 31, 2018

Cash		$ 8,500	Accounts payable	$ 5,200
Inventories		12,000	Wages payable	100
Prepaid rent		3,800	Total current liabilities	5,300
Total current assets		24,300	Total equity (includes retained earnings)	23,500
Equipment	$7,500		Total liabilities and equity	$28,800
Less accumulated depreciation	3,000			
Equipment, net		4,500		
Total assets		$28,800		

REQUIRED

a. Prepare any necessary transaction entries for 2019 and adjusting entries at December 31, 2019, using the financial statement effects template.

b. Prepare any necessary transaction entries for 2019 and adjusting entries at December 31, 2019, in journal entry form.

c. Set up T-accounts, enter the balances above, and post the transactions and adjusting entries to them.

d. Prepare its income statement for 2019, and its balance sheet at December 31, 2019.

e. Prepare entries to close its temporary accounts in journal entry form and post the closing entries to the T-accounts.

LO2, 3, 4, 5, 6

P3-54. Applying the Entire Accounting Cycle

Rhoades Tax Services began business on December 1, 2018. Its December transactions are as follows.

Dec. 1 Rhoades invested $20,000 in the business in exchange for common stock.
2 Paid $1,200 cash for December rent to Bomba Realty.
2 Purchased $1,080 of supplies on account.
3 Purchased $9,500 of office equipment; paying $4,700 cash with the balance due in 30 days.
8 Paid $1,080 cash on account for supplies purchased December 2.
14 Paid $900 cash for assistant's wages for 2 weeks' work.
20 Performed consulting services for $3,000 cash.
28 Paid $900 cash for assistant's wages for 2 weeks' work.
30 Billed clients $7,200 for December consulting services.
31 Paid $1,800 cash for dividends.

Additional information:

1. Supplies available at December 31 are $710.
2. Accrued wages payable at December 31 are $270.
3. Depreciation for December is $120.
4. Rhoades has spent 30 hours on an involved tax fraud case during December. When completed in January, his work will be billed at $75 per hour. (The account Fees Receivable is used to reflect amounts earned but not yet billed.)

REQUIRED

a. Record these transactions and any necessary adjusting entries using the financial statement effects template.

b. Set up a general ledger in T-account form for the following accounts: Cash; Fees Receivable; Supplies; Office Equipment; Accumulated Depreciation—Office Equipment; Accounts Payable; Wages Payable; Common Stock; Retained Earnings; Consulting Revenue; Supplies Expense; Wages Expense; Rent Expense; and Depreciation Expense.

c. Record the above transactions in journal entry form and post these entries to their T-accounts (key numbers in T-accounts by date).

d. Prepare an unadjusted trial balance at December 31, 2018.

e. Journalize the adjusting entries at December 31 in journal entry form, drawing on the information above. Then post adjusting entries to their T-accounts and prepare an adjusted trial balance at December 31, 2018.

f. Prepare a December 2018 income statement and statement of stockholders' equity, and a December 31, 2018, balance sheet.

g. Record its closing entries in journal entry form. Post these entries to their T-accounts.

h. Prepare a post-closing trial balance at December 31, 2018.

CASES AND PROJECTS

C3-55. Preparing Adjusting Entries, Financial Statements, and Closing Entries **LO2, 3, 4, 5, 6**

Seaside Surf Shop began operations on July 1, 2019, with an initial investment of $50,000. During the initial 3 months of operations, the following cash transactions were recorded in the firm's checking account.

Cash receipts		Cash payments	
Initial investment by owner	$ 50,000	Rent	$ 24,000
Collected from customers	81,000	Fixtures and equipment	25,000
Borrowed from bank 7/1/2019	10,000	Merchandise inventory	62,000
Total cash receipts	$141,000	Salaries	6,000
		Other expenses	13,000
		Total cash payments	$130,000

Additional information

1. Most sales were for cash; however, the store accepted a limited amount of credit sales; at September 30, 2019, customers owed the store $9,000.
2. Rent was paid on July 1 for six months.
3. Salaries of $3,000 per month are paid on the 1st of each month for salaries earned in the month prior.
4. Inventories are purchased for cash; at September 30, 2019, inventory worth $21,000 was available.
5. Fixtures and equipment were expected to last five years with zero salvage value.
6. The bank charges 12% annual interest (1% per month) on its bank loan.

REQUIRED

a. Prepare any necessary adjusting entries at September 30, 2019, (1) using the financial statement effects template, and (2) in journal entry form.

b. Set up T-accounts and post the adjusting entries to them.

c. Prepare its initial three-month income statement for 2019 and its balance sheet at September 30, 2019. (Ignore taxes.)

d. Analyze the statements from part *c* and assess the company's performance over its initial three months.

C3-56. Analyzing Transactions, Impacts on Financial Ratios, and Loan Covenants **LO2, 3, 6**

Wyland Consulting, a firm started three years ago by Reyna Wyland, offers consulting services for material handling and plant layout. Its balance sheet at the close of 2018 is as follows.

WYLAND CONSULTING Balance Sheet December 31, 2018				
Assets			**Liabilities**	
Cash		$ 3,400	Notes payable	$30,000
Accounts receivable		22,875	Accounts payable	4,200
Supplies		13,200	Contract liabilities	11,300
Prepaid insurance		4,500	Wages payable	400
Equipment	$68,500		Total liabilities	45,900
Less: accumulated depreciation	23,975	44,525	**Equity**	
			Common stock	8,000
			Retained earnings	34,600
Total assets		$88,500	Total liabilities and equity	$88,500

Earlier in the year Wyland obtained a bank loan of $30,000 cash for the firm. One of the provisions of the loan is that the year-end debt-to-equity ratio (ratio of total liabilities to total equity) cannot exceed 1.0. Based on the above balance sheet, the ratio at the end of 2018 is 1.08. Wyland is concerned about being in violation of the loan agreement and requests assistance in reviewing the situation. Wyland believes that she might have overlooked some items at year-end. Discussions with Wyland reveal the following.

1. On January 1, 2018, the firm paid a $4,500 insurance premium for 2 years of coverage; the amount in Prepaid Insurance has not yet been adjusted.
2. Depreciation on the equipment should be 10% of cost per year; the company inadvertently recorded 15% for 2018.
3. Interest on the bank loan has been paid through the end of 2018.
4. The firm concluded a major consulting engagement in December, doing a plant layout analysis for a new factory. The $6,000 fee has not been billed or recorded in the accounts.
5. On December 1, 2018, the firm received an $11,300 advance payment from Croy Corporation for consulting services to be rendered over a 2-month period. This payment was credited to the Contract Liabilities account. One-half of this fee was earned by December 31, 2018.
6. Supplies costing $4,800 were available on December 31; the company has made no entry in the accounts.

REQUIRED

a. What portion of the company is financed by debt versus equity (called the debt-to-equity ratio and defined in Chapter 1) at December 31, 2018?

b. Is the firm in violation of its loan agreement? Prepare computations to support the correct total liabilities and total equity figures at December 31, 2018.

LO2, 3 **C3-57. Ethics, Accounting Adjustments, and Auditors**

It is the end of the accounting year for Juliet Javetz, controller of a medium-sized, publicly held corporation specializing in toxic waste cleanup. Within the corporation, only Javetz and the president know that the firm has been negotiating for several months to land a large contract for waste cleanup in Western Europe. The president has hired another firm with excellent contacts in Western Europe to help with negotiations. The outside firm will charge an hourly fee plus expenses, but has agreed not to submit a bill until the negotiations are in their final stages (expected to occur in another 3 to 4 months). Even if the contract falls through, the outside firm is entitled to receive payment for its services. Based upon her discussion with a member of the outside firm, Javetz knows that its charge for services provided to date will be $150,000. This is a material amount for the company.

Javetz knows that the president wants negotiations to remain as secret as possible so that competitors will not learn of the contract the company is pursuing in Europe. In fact, the president recently stated to her, "Now is not the time to reveal our actions in Western Europe to other staff members, our auditors, or the readers of our financial statements; securing this contract is crucial to our future growth." No entry has been made in the accounting records for the cost of contract negotiations. Javetz now faces an uncomfortable situation. The company's outside auditor has just asked her if she knows of any year-end adjustments that have not yet been recorded.

REQUIRED

a. What are the ethical considerations that Javetz faces in answering the auditor's question?

b. How should Javetz respond to the auditor's question?

C3-58. Inferring Adjusting Entries from Financial Statements **LO2, 3, 4, 6**

Lady G's Fashions, a specialty retailer of women's apparel, markets its products through retail stores and catalogs. Selected information from its 2019 and 2018 balance sheets is as follows.

Selected Balance Sheet Data ($ thousands)	2018	2019
Prepaid catalog expenses (asset)	$3,894	$4,306
Advertising credits receivable	21	534
Gift certificate liability	6,108	7,053

The following excerpts are from Lady G's Fashions accompanying footnotes:

- Catalog costs in the direct segment are considered direct response advertising and as such are capitalized as incurred and amortized over the expected sales life of each catalog, which is generally a period not exceeding six months.
- The Company periodically enters into arrangements with certain national magazine publishers whereby the Company includes magazine subscription cards in its catalog mailings in exchange for advertising credits or discounts on advertising.

REQUIRED

a. Assume that Lady G's Fashions spent $62,550 to design, print, and mail catalogs in 2019. Also assume that it received advertising credits of $849. Prepare the entry, using the financial statement effects template and in journal entry form, that Lady G's Fashions would have recorded when these costs were incurred.

b. Prepare the adjusting entry, using the financial statement effects template and in journal entry form, that would be necessary to record its amortization of prepaid catalog costs.

c. How do advertising credits expire? Prepare the adjusting entry, using both the financial statement effects template and in journal entry form, that Lady G's Fashions would record to reflect the change in advertising credits.

d. Assume that Lady G's Fashions sold gift certificates valued at $19,175 in 2019. Prepare the entry, using the financial statement effects template and in journal entry form, that Lady G's Fashions would make to record these sales. Next, prepare the entry, using the financial statement effects template and in journal entry form, that it makes to record merchandise sales to customers who pay with gift certificates.

SOLUTIONS TO REVIEW PROBLEMS

Mid-Chapter Review

SOLUTION TO PARTS 1 AND 2

a.

Transaction	Balance Sheet											Income Statement				
	Cash Asset	+	Noncash Assets	−	Contra Assets	=	Liabil-ities	+	Contrib. Capital	+	Earned Capital	Revenues	−	Expenses	=	Net Income
(a) Adjusting entry to record supplies and parts used.			−91,000 Supplies and Parts	−		=					−91,000 Retained Earnings		−	+91,000 Supplies and Parts Expenses	=	−91,000

(a)	Supplies and parts expense (+E, −SE)	91,000	
	Supplies and parts (−A)		91,000

b.

Transaction	Cash Asset	+ Noncash Assets	− Contra Assets	= Liabilities	+ Contrib. Capital	+ Earned Capital	Revenues	− Expenses	= Net Income
(b) Adjusting entry to record rent expense accrued but not yet paid.				+2,500 Accounts Payable		−2,500 Retained Earnings		+2,500 Rent Expense	−2,500

(Balance Sheet: Cash Asset through Earned Capital; Income Statement: Revenues through Net Income)

		Debit	Credit
(b)	Rent expense (+E, −SE)	2,500	
	Accounts payable (+L)		2,500

The $2,500 expense for October is not recorded because it is not yet incurred as of September 30.

c.

Transaction	Cash Asset	+ Noncash Assets	− Contra Assets	= Liabilities	+ Contrib. Capital	+ Earned Capital	Revenues	− Expenses	= Net Income
(c) Adjusting entry to record depreciation on building.			+50,000 Accumulated Depreciation—Building			−50,000 Retained Earnings		+50,000 Depreciation Expense	−50,000

		Debit	Credit
(c)	Depreciation expense (+E, −SE)	50,000	
	Accumulated depreciation—Building (+XA, −A)		50,000

d. No entry required; the executive has not yet begun work, and thus, no expense is incurred.

e.

Transaction	Cash Asset	+ Noncash Assets	− Contra Assets	= Liabilities	+ Contrib. Capital	+ Earned Capital	Revenues	− Expenses	= Net Income
(e) Adjusting entry to record cash advance, of which a part is earned.	+1,200 Cash			+600 Contract Liability		+600 Retained Earnings	+600 Services Revenue		+600

		Debit	Credit
(e)	Cash (+A)	1,200	
	Contract liability (+L)		600
	Services revenue (+R, +SE)		600

f.

Transaction	Cash Asset	+ Noncash Assets	− Contra Assets	= Liabilities	+ Contrib. Capital	+ Earned Capital	Revenues	− Expenses	= Net Income
(f) Adjusting entry to record wages earned but not yet paid.				+25,000 Wages Payable		−25,000 Retained Earnings		+25,000 Wages Expense	−25,000

		Debit	Credit
(f)	Wages expense (+E, −SE)	25,000	
	Wages payable (+L)		25,000

SOLUTION TO PART 3

Chapter-End Review

SOLUTION TO PARTS 1 AND 2

Transaction	Cash Asset	+	Noncash Assets	−	Contra Assets	=	Liabil-ities	+	Contrib. Capital	+	Earned Capital	Revenues	−	Expenses	=	Net Income
(1) Adjustment to record insurance expense.			−1,500 Prepaid Insurance	−		=					−1,500 Retained Earnings		−	+1,500 Insurance Expense	=	−1,500
(2) Adjustment to record supplies expense.			−25,000 Supplies	−		=					−25,000 Retained Earnings		−	+25,000 Supplies Expense	=	−25,000
(3) Adjustment to record depreciation expense.				−	+30,000 Accumulated Depreciation —Equipment	=					−30,000 Retained Earnings		−	+30,000 Depreciation Expense	=	−30,000
(4) Adjustment to record fees revenue.				−		=	−3,000 Contract Liability				+3,000 Retained Earnings	+3,000 Fees Revenue	−		=	+3,000
(5) Adjustment to record wages expense.				−		=	+600 Wages Payable				−600 Retained Earnings		−	+600 Wages Expense	=	−600

		Debit	Credit
(1)	Insurance expense (+E, −SE).	1,500	
	Prepaid insurance (−A)		1,500
	Record insurance expired $6,000 × (6 months/24 months).		
(2)	Supplies expense (+E, −SE).	25,000	
	Supplies (−A)		25,000
	Record supplies used ($31,300 – $6,300).		
(3)	Depreciation expense (+E, −SE)	30,000	
	Accumulated depreciation—Equipment (+XA, −A)		30,000
	Record depreciation [($270,000 – $0) ÷ 9 years].		
(4)	Contract liability (−L).	3,000	
	Fees revenue (+R, +SE)		3,000
	Record fees earned.		
(5)	Wages expense (+E, −SE)	600	
	Wages payable (+L).		600
	Record employee wages incurred.		

	Balance Sheet												Income Statement				
Transaction	Cash Asset	+	Noncash Assets	-	Contra Assets	=	Liabil-ities	+	Contrib. Capital	+	Earned Capital		Revenues	-	Expenses	=	Net Income
(6) Adjustment to record rent expense.				-		=	+2,000 Rent Payable				−2,000 Retained Earnings			-	+2,000 Rent Expense	=	−2,000

(6)	Rent expense (+E, −SE)	2,000	
	Rent payable (+L)		2,000
	Record rent owed.		

SOLUTION TO PART 3

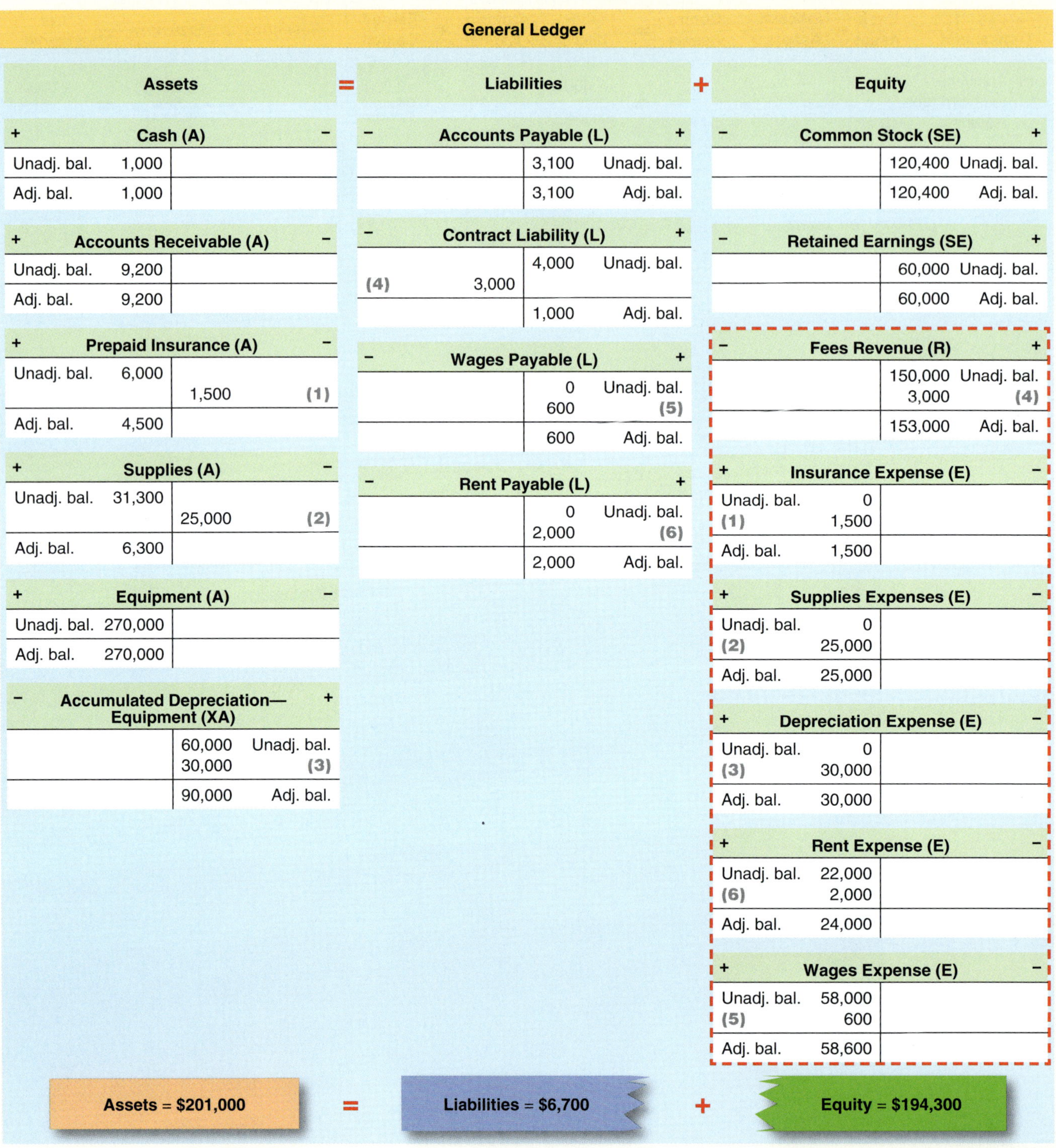

ATWELL LABORATORIES, INC.
Adjusted Trial Balance
June 30, 2019

	Debits	Credits
Cash	$ 1,000	
Accounts receivable	9,200	
Prepaid insurance	4,500	
Supplies	6,300	
Equipment	270,000	
Accumulated depreciation—equipment		$ 90,000
Accounts payable		3,100
Rent payable		2,000
Wages payable		600
Contract liability		1,000
Fees revenue		153,000
Wages expense	58,600	
Rent expense	24,000	
Insurance expense	1,500	
Supplies expense	25,000	
Depreciation expense	30,000	
Common stock		120,400
Retained earnings		60,000
Totals	$430,100	$430,100

SOLUTION TO PART 4

		Debit	Credit
a.	Retained earnings (–SE)	139,100	
	Insurance expense (–E)		1,500
	Supplies expense (–E)		25,000
	Depreciation expense (–E)		30,000
	Rent expense (–E)		24,000
	Wages expense (–E)		58,600

		Debit	Credit
b.	Fees revenue (–R)	153,000	
	Retained earnings (+SE)		153,000

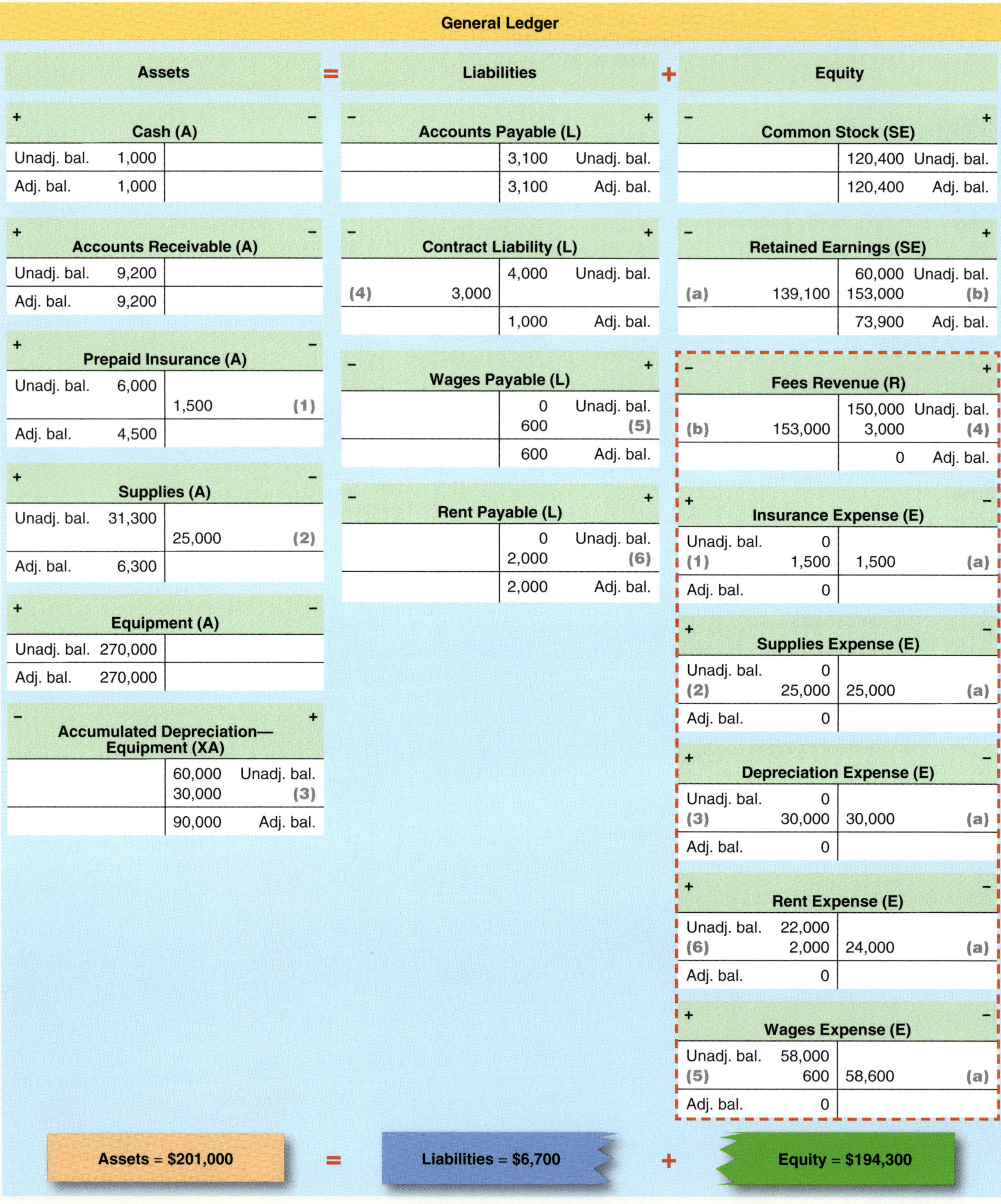

General Ledger

Assets = Liabilities + Equity

Assets

+	Cash (A)		−
Unadj. bal.	1,000		
Adj. bal.	1,000		

+	Accounts Receivable (A)		−
Unadj. bal.	9,200		
Adj. bal.	9,200		

+	Prepaid Insurance (A)		−
Unadj. bal.	6,000		
		1,500	(1)
Adj. bal.	4,500		

+	Supplies (A)		−
Unadj. bal.	31,300		
		25,000	(2)
Adj. bal.	6,300		

+	Equipment (A)		−
Unadj. bal.	270,000		
Adj. bal.	270,000		

−	Accumulated Depreciation—Equipment (XA)		+
		60,000	Unadj. bal.
		30,000	(3)
		90,000	Adj. bal.

Liabilities

−	Accounts Payable (L)		+
		3,100	Unadj. bal.
		3,100	Adj. bal.

−	Contract Liability (L)		+
		4,000	Unadj. bal.
(4)	3,000		
		1,000	Adj. bal.

−	Wages Payable (L)		+
		0	Unadj. bal.
		600	(5)
		600	Adj. bal.

−	Rent Payable (L)		+
		0	Unadj. bal.
		2,000	(6)
		2,000	Adj. bal.

Equity

−	Common Stock (SE)		+
		120,400	Unadj. bal.
		120,400	Adj. bal.

−	Retained Earnings (SE)		+
		60,000	Unadj. bal.
(a)	139,100	153,000	(b)
		73,900	Adj. bal.

−	Fees Revenue (R)		+
		150,000	Unadj. bal.
(b)	153,000	3,000	(4)
		0	Adj. bal.

+	Insurance Expense (E)		−
Unadj. bal.	0		
(1)	1,500	1,500	(a)
Adj. bal.	0		

+	Supplies Expense (E)		−
Unadj. bal.	0		
(2)	25,000	25,000	(a)
Adj. bal.	0		

+	Depreciation Expense (E)		−
Unadj. bal.	0		
(3)	30,000	30,000	(a)
Adj. bal.	0		

+	Rent Expense (E)		−
Unadj. bal.	22,000		
(6)	2,000	24,000	(a)
Adj. bal.	0		

+	Wages Expense (E)		−
Unadj. bal.	58,000		
(5)	600	58,600	(a)
Adj. bal.	0		

Assets = $201,000 = Liabilities = $6,700 + Equity = $194,300

SOLUTION TO PART 5

ATWELL LABORATORIES, INC.
Balance Sheet
June 30, 2019

Assets			Liabilities	
Cash		$ 1,000	Accounts payable	$ 3,100
Accounts receivable		9,200	Contract liability	1,000
Prepaid insurance		4,500	Wages payable	600
Supplies		6,300	Rent payable	2,000
Total current assets		21,000	Total current liabilities	6,700
Equipment, original cost	$270,000			
Less accumulated depreciation	90,000	180,000	**Equity**	
			Common stock	120,400
			Retained earnings	73,900
Total assets		$201,000	Totals liabilities and equity	$201,000

ATWELL LABORATORIES, INC.
Income Statement
For Year Ended June 30, 2019

Fees revenue		$153,000
Expenses		
Insurance expense	$ 1,500	
Supplies expense	25,000	
Depreciation expense	30,000	
Rent expense	24,000	
Wages expense	58,600	
Total expense		139,100
Net income		$ 13,900

ATWELL LABORATORIES, INC.
Statement of Stockholders' Equity
For Year Ended June 30, 2019

	Common Stock	Retained Earnings	Total
Balance at June 30, 2018	$120,400	$60,000	$180,400
Net Income	—	13,900	13,900
Balance at June 30, 2019	$120,400	$73,900	$194,300

Atwell's statement of stockholders' equity is much simpler than the usual statement because we have focused on the adjustment and closing process. In doing so, we did not consider additional activities in which corporations commonly engage, such as paying dividends, issuing stock, and repurchasing stock. (Requirements did not ask for a statement of cash flows. The next chapter is devoted to the statement of cash flows.)

Reporting and Analyzing Cash Flows

LEARNING OBJECTIVES

1. Explain the purpose of the statement of cash flows and classify cash transactions by type of business activity: operating, investing, or financing. (p. 158)
2. Construct the operating activities section of the statement of cash flows using the direct method. (p. 162)
3. Reconcile cash flows from operations to net income and use the indirect method to compute operating cash flows. (p. 171)
4. Construct the investing and financing activities sections of the statement of cash flows. (p. 174)
5. Compute and interpret ratios that reflect a company's liquidity and solvency using information reported in the statement of cash flows. (p. 182)
6. Appendix 4A: Use a spreadsheet to construct the statement of cash flows. (p. 186)

CVS HEALTH CORPORATION
www.cvshealth.com

Like **Walgreens Boots Alliance**, **CVS Health** started small, with a single store in Lowell, Massachusetts in 1963, where CVS stood for Consumer Value Stores. The company soon grew in number of stores and expanded beyond health and beauty products to include pharmaceuticals. CVS made frequent use of acquisitions to increase the number of stores and the geographic reach of the company. In its 2017 annual report, CVS Health reports that it had more than 9,800 retail locations and almost a quarter of a million colleagues working at the company.

CVS Health operates at the intersection of two industries—retail and healthcare. In retail, almost all companies are affected by the rapid growth of online retailers and the decline in "bricks and mortar" businesses. And, the political pressure on healthcare costs affects an assortment of parties besides the ultimate consumer—pharmacies, insurance companies, pharmacy benefit managers and pharmaceutical companies. Over time, CVS Health has expanded beyond its pharmacies into pharmacy benefit management to streamline costs, to provide better service to customers and to maintain market competitiveness. At the time this chapter is being written, CVS Health has expanded its scope further by reaching a definitive merger agreement to acquire an insurance company, **Aetna, Inc.** The Aetna acquisition will further expand CVS Health's role in the pharmacy market, giving it an opportunity to improve operations and customer service. In addition, analysts suggest the merger provides some protection against online retail companies who might enter the pharmacy market.

However, that acquisition comes at a cost. Aetna shareholders will receive $145 in cash and 0.8378 CVS Health shares for each Aetna share. To complete the merger, CVS Health estimates that it will be necessary to borrow approximately $45.0 billion, in addition to taking on Aetna's debt of approximately $8.3 billion. This additional debt

is about twice as large as CVS Health's current long-term debt. CVS Health will also issue an additional 280 million common shares, which will increase annual dividends by approximately $560 million after the merger.

How does a company with a cash balance of less than $2 billion spend almost $69 billion to make an acquisition? To accomplish its objectives, CVS Health must generate positive cash flow from *operating activities*, and its operating activities produced cash flows of $8 million in the fiscal year ended December 31, 2017. The company's operations are the engine that produces cash that can be used to grow the business and to provide a return to shareholders.

As we will discover in this chapter, a business must make sure that its cash inflows are adequate to fund new investments, meet obligations to creditors as they come due, and pay dividends to shareholders. Even a profitable company can fail if it does not have a healthy cash flow. We will also discover why it is important to look at the cash flow statement along with the income statement and balance sheet when trying to assess the financial health of a company.

Sources: CVS Health Corporation, Form 10-K 2017; www.cvshealth.com/about/company-history; "CVS Health: Surviving Amazon," Stone Fox Capital *Seeking Alpha* June 25, 2018; "Why CVS Would Want to Buy Aetna," Carolyn Johnson, *The Washington Post* October 26, 2017.

CHAPTER ORGANIZATION

Reporting and Analyzing Cash Flows

Purpose of the Statement of Cash Flows	Framework for the Statement of Cash Flows	Preparing the Statement of Cash Flows	Analysis of Cash Flows
• What Do We Mean by Cash? • What Does a Statement of Cash Flows Look Like?	• Operating Activities • Investing Activities • Financing Activities • Usefulness of Classifications	• Cash Flows from Operating Activities • Cash Flows from Investing and Financing Activities • Additional Detail in the Statement of Cash Flows • Preparing the Statement of Cash Flows Using a Spreadsheet (Appendix 4A)	• Operating Cash Flow to Current Liabilities • Operating Cash Flow to Capital Expenditures • Free Cash Flow

PURPOSE OF THE STATEMENT OF CASH FLOWS

1

LO1 Explain the purpose of the statement of cash flows and classify cash transactions by type of business activity: operating, investing, or financing.

In addition to the balance sheet and the income statement, corporations are required to report a statement of cash flows. The **statement of cash flows** tells us how a company generated cash (cash inflows) and how it used cash (cash outflows). The statement of cash flows complements the income statement and the balance sheet by providing information that neither the income statement nor the balance sheet can provide. For instance, slower collection of receivables doesn't affect income, but it does reduce the amount of cash coming into the company.

Understanding the statement of cash flows helps us understand trends in a firm's **liquidity** (ability to pay near-term liabilities and take advantage of investment opportunities), and it helps us assess a firm's **solvency** (ability to pay long-term liabilities). With information about how cash was generated or used, creditors and investors are better able to assess a firm's ability to settle its liabilities and pay dividends to shareholders. A firm's need for outside financing is also better evaluated when using cash flow data. Over time, the statement of cash flows permits users to observe and assess management's investing and financing policies. For example, a business that is not generating enough cash flow internally, i.e., from operations, must get cash from borrowing, issuing shares, or selling off its assets.

The statement of cash flows also provides information about a firm's ability to generate sufficient amounts of cash to respond to unanticipated needs and opportunities. Information about past cash flows, particularly cash flows from operations, helps in assessing a company's financial flexibility. An evaluation of a firm's ability to survive an unexpected drop in demand, for example, should include a review of its past cash flows from operations. The larger these cash flows, the greater is the firm's ability to withstand adverse changes in economic conditions.

So, whether we are a potential investor, loan officer, future employee, supplier, or customer, we greatly benefit from an understanding of the cash inflows and outflows of a company.

What Do We Mean by "CASH"?

FYI A cash equivalent is a short-term, highly liquid investment that is easily converted to cash and is close enough to maturity that its market value is not sensitive to interest rate changes.

The statement of cash flows explains the change in a firm's cash *and* cash equivalents. **Cash equivalents** are short-term, highly liquid investments that are (1) easily convertible into a known cash amount and (2) close enough to maturity that their market value is not sensitive to interest rate changes (generally, investments with remaining maturities of three months or less). Treasury bills, commercial paper (short-term notes issued by corporations), and money market funds are typical examples of cash equivalents.

When preparing a statement of cash flows, the cash and cash equivalents are added together and treated as a single sum. The addition is done because the purchase and sale of investments in cash equivalents are considered to be part of a firm's overall management of cash rather than a source or use of cash. As statement users evaluate and project cash flows, for example, it should not matter whether the cash is readily available in a cash register or safe, deposited in a bank account, or invested in cash equivalents. Consequently, transfers back and forth between a firm's cash on hand, its bank accounts, and its investments in cash equivalents, are not treated as cash inflows and cash outflows in its statement of cash flows. When discussing the statement of cash flows, managers generally use the word *cash* rather than the phrase *cash and cash equivalents.* We will follow the same practice.

What Does a Statement of Cash Flows Look Like?

Exhibit 4.1 reproduces CVS Health Corporation's cash flow statement for the fiscal year ended on December 31, 2017. During this fiscal year, CVS Health generated $8,007 million in cash from its operations.

Investing activities used $2,932 million in cash, and financing activities used another $6,751 million of cash. Over the entire year, the company's cash balance decreased by $1,675 million and ended the year at $1,696 million on December 31, 2017.

EXHIBIT 4.1 CVS Health Corporation Cash Flow Statement

CVS HEALTH CORPORATION Consolidated Statement of Cash Flows For the Fiscal Year Ended December 31, 2017 In millions	2017
Cash flows from operating activities	
Cash receipts from customers	$176,594
Cash paid for inventory and prescriptions dispensed by retail network pharmacies	(149,279)
Cash paid to other suppliers and employees	(15,348)
Interest received	21
Interest paid	(1,072)
Income taxes paid	(2,909)
Net cash provided by operating activities	8,007
Cash flows from investing activities	
Purchases of property and equipment	(1,918)
Proceeds from sale-leaseback transactions	265
Proceeds from sale of property and equipment and other assets	33
Acquisitions (net of cash acquired) and other investments	(1,287)
Purchase of available-for-sale investments	(86)
Maturities of available-for-sale investments	61
Net cash used in investing activities	(2,932)
Cash flows from financing activities	
Decrease in short-term debt	(598)
Dividends paid	(2,049)
Proceeds from exercise of stock options	329
Payments for taxes related to net share settlement of equity awards	(71)
Repurchase of common stock	(4,361)
Other	(1)
Net cash used in financing activities	(6,751)
Effect of exchange rate changes on cash and cash equivalents	1
Net decrease in cash and cash equivalents	(1,675)
Cash and cash equivalents at the beginning of the period	3,371
Cash and cash equivalents at the end of the period	**$ 1,696**

FRAMEWORK FOR THE STATEMENT OF CASH FLOWS

The statement of cash flows classifies cash receipts and payments into one of three categories: operating activities, investing activities, or financing activities. Classifying cash flows into these categories identifies the effects on cash of each of the major activities of a firm. The combined effects on cash of all three categories explain the net change in cash for the period. The period's net change in cash is then reconciled with the beginning and ending amounts of cash.

Operating Activities

FYI Cash flows from operating activities (cash flows from operations) refer to cash inflows and outflows directly related to the firm's primary day-to-day business activities.

A company's income statement mainly reflects the transactions and events that constitute its operating activities. The cash effects of these operating transactions and events determine the net cash flow from operating activities. The usual focus of a firm's **operating activities** is on selling goods or rendering services, but the activities are defined broadly enough to include any cash receipts or payments that are not classified as investing or financing activities. For example, CVS Health Corporation reports cash received from customers and for interest. The company paid cash to suppliers (of pharmaceuticals and other items) and employees and tax authorities and to lenders for interest. The following are examples of cash inflows and outflows relating to operating activities.

Cash Inflows

1. Cash receipts from customers for sales made or services rendered (or in anticipation of future deliveries of goods or services).
2. Cash receipts of interest and dividends.[1]
3. Other cash receipts that are not related to investing or financing activities, such as rentals, lawsuit settlements, and refunds received from suppliers.

Cash Outflows

1. Cash payments to employees or suppliers.
2. Cash payments to purchase inventories.
3. Cash payments of interest to creditors.[1]
4. Cash payments of taxes to government.
5. Other cash payments that are not related to investing or financing activities, such as contributions to charity and lawsuit settlements.

Investing Activities

FYI Cash flows from investing activities are cash inflows and outflows related to acquiring or selling productive assets and the investments in securities of other entities.

A firm's transactions involving (1) the acquisition and disposal of property, plant, and equipment (PPE) assets and intangible assets, (2) the purchase and sale of government securities and securities of other companies, including stocks, bonds, and other securities that are not classified as cash equivalents, and (3) the lending and subsequent collection of money constitute the basic components of its **investing activities**. The related cash receipts and payments appear in the investing activities section of the statement of cash flows and, if material in amount, inflows and outflows should be reported separately (not as a net amount). Examples of these cash flows follow:

Cash Inflows

1. Cash receipts from sales of property, plant, and equipment (PPE) assets and intangible assets.
2. Cash receipts from sales of investments in government securities and securities of other companies (including divestitures).
3. Cash receipts from repayments of loans by borrowers.

Cash Outflows

1. Cash payments to purchase property, plant, and equipment (PPE) assets and intangible assets.
2. Cash payments to purchase government securities and securities of other companies (including acquisitions).
3. Cash payments made to lend money to borrowers.

Financing Activities

FYI Cash flows from financing activities are cash inflows and outflows related to external sources of financing (owners and nonowners).

A firm engages in **financing activities** when it receives cash from shareholders, returns cash to shareholders, borrows from creditors, and repays amounts borrowed. Cash flows related to these

[1] Many financial statement readers believe that interest and dividends received should be considered cash inflows from investing activities and that interest payments should be considered cash outflows from financing activities. In fact, when the reporting standard was passed by the Financial Accounting Standards Board, three of the seven members dissented from the standard for this reason (among others). The majority based their decision on "the view that, in general, cash flows from operating activities should reflect the cash effects of transactions and other events that enter into the determination of net income." (Statement of Financial Accounting Standards No. 95, paragraph 88.)

transactions are reported in the financing activities section of the statement of cash flows and again, inflows and outflows should be reported separately (not as a net amount) if material. Examples of these cash flows follow:

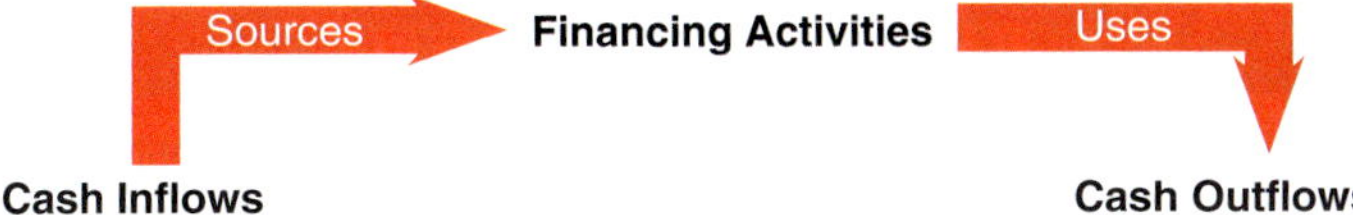

Cash Inflows

1. Cash receipts from issuances of common stock and preferred stock and from sales of treasury stock.
2. Cash receipts from issuances of bonds payable, mortgage notes payable, and other notes payable.

Cash Outflows

1. Cash payments to acquire treasury stock.
2. Cash payments of dividends.
3. Cash payments to settle outstanding bonds payable, mortgage notes payable, and other notes payable.

Paying cash to settle such obligations as accounts payable, wages payable, interest payable, and income tax payable are operating activities, not financing activities because they are related to the daily operations of the company such as buying and selling inventory. Also, cash received as interest and dividends and cash paid as interest (not dividends) are classified as cash flows from operating activities. However, cash paid to shareholders as dividends is classified as cash flows from financing activities.

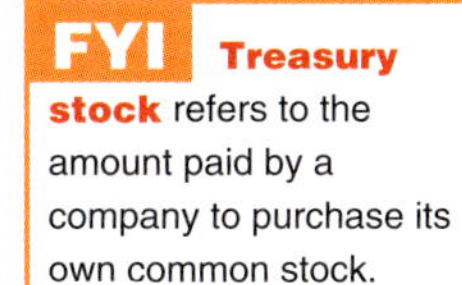

A GLOBAL PERSPECTIVE

Under U.S. accounting principles, payments for interest expense and receipts for interest and dividend income are considered part of cash from operations. International Financial Reporting Standards allow companies to report interest payments as part of either operating activities or financing activities and to report interest and dividend receipts as part of either operating activities or investing activities.

Usefulness of Classifications

The classification of cash flows into three categories of activities helps financial statement users interpret cash flow data. To illustrate, assume that Faultless, Inc., Peerless Co., and Dauntless Ltd. each reports a $100,000 cash increase during the current year. Information from their current-year statements of cash flows is summarized in **Exhibit 4.2**.

EXHIBIT 4.2 Summary Information for Three Competitors

	Faultless	Peerless	Dauntless
Net cash provided by operating activities	$100,000	$ 0	$ 0
Cash flows from investing activities			
Sale of property, plant, and equipment	0	100,000	0
Cash flows from financing activities			
Issuance of notes payable	0	0	100,000
Net increase in cash	$100,000	$100,000	$100,000

One of the keys to evaluating a company's worth is estimating its future cash flows based on the information available. Companies that can generate a stream of future cash flows are worth more than a company with a single cash flow. In **Exhibit 4.2**, each company's net cash increase was the same, but the source of the increase varied by company. This variation affects the analysis of the cash flow data, particularly for potential creditors who must evaluate the likelihood of obtaining repayment in the future for any funds loaned to the company. Based only on these cash flow data, a potential creditor would feel more comfortable lending money to Faultless than to either Peerless or Dauntless. This choice is because Faultless's cash increase came from its operating activities, and operations tend to be continuing. Both Peerless and Dauntless could only break even on their cash flows from operations. Also, Peerless's cash increase came from the sale of property, plant, and equipment (PPE) assets—a source of cash that is not likely to recur regularly.

Dauntless's cash increase came entirely from borrowed funds. This means Dauntless faces additional cash burdens in the future when the interest and principal payments on the note payable become due.

BUSINESS INSIGHT

Objectivity of Cash Usefulness of financial statements is enhanced when the underlying data are objective and verifiable. Measuring cash and the changes in cash are among the most objective measurements that accountants make. Thus, the statement of cash flows is arguably the most objective financial statement. This characteristic of the statement of cash flows is welcomed by those investors and creditors interested in evaluating the quality of a firm's income.

MID-CHAPTER REVIEW 1

Assume **CVS Health Corporation** executed the following transactions during 2017. Indicate whether the transaction creates a cash inflow (In) or outflow (Out). Next, determine how each item should be classified in the statement of cash flows: an operating activity (O), an investing activity (I), or a financing activity (F). For example: $50,000 cash received for the sale of snack foods. Answer: In/O

1. ____ $250,000 cash paid to purchase a warehouse
2. ____ $120,000 cash paid for interest on a loan
3. ____ $850,000 cash paid to employees as wages
4. ____ $20,000,000 cash raised through the issuance of stock
5. ____ $450,000 cash paid to the government for taxes
6. ____ $350,000 cash received as part of a settlement of a legal case
7. ____ $630,000 cash received from the sale of long-term securities
8. ____ $75,000 cash received from the sale of used office equipment
9. ____ $500,000 cash dividend paid to shareholders
10. ____ $90,000 cash received as interest earned on a government bond

The solution to this review problem can be found on page 214.

PREPARING THE STATEMENT OF CASH FLOWS—OPERATING ACTIVITIES

2 **LO2** Construct the operating activities section of the statement of cash flows using the direct method.

In Chapter 3's **Exhibit 3.12**, we presented a statement of cash flows for Natural Beauty Supply (hereafter, NBS) for the month of December 2018. This statement is reproduced in **Exhibit 4.3**. The statement details how NBS's cash balance decreases by $1,275 in December, from $8,100 to $6,825. The statement was prepared by examining all of the cash transactions that occurred during the month, and then grouping them according to the type of activity each represents—operating, investing, or financing—as illustrated in the cash T-account below. Transaction (17) was the loan, so that goes in the financing activity section, transaction (18) was the purchase of fixtures and equipment and belongs in the investing activity section, and so on.

	+	Cash (A)		–
	Beg. bal.	8,100		
Operating activities	(21)	8,500	700	(19)
	(23)	1,200	3,300	(20)
	(25)	3,200	1,625	(24)
			1,500	(27)
Investing activities			18,000	(18)
Financing activities	(17)	11,000	50	(28)
	End. bal.	6,825		

This approach to preparing the statement of cash flows is straightforward and doesn't require any additional bookkeeping steps, other than those introduced in Chapters 2 and 3.

EXHIBIT 4.3 NBS Statement of Cash Flows (Direct Method)

NATURAL BEAUTY SUPPLY, INC.
Statement of Cash Flows
For the Month Ended December 31, 2018

Cash Flows from Operating Activities		
Cash received from customers (entries 21, 23, 25)	$12,900	
Cash paid for inventory (entry 20)	(3,300)	
Cash paid for wages (entry 24)	(1,625)	
Cash paid for rent (entry 27)	(1,500)	
Cash paid for advertising (entry 19)	(700)	
Net cash provided by operating activities		$ 5,775
Cash Flows from Investing Activities		
Cash paid for fixtures and equipment (entry 18)	(18,000)	
Net cash used for investing activities		(18,000)
Cash Flows from Financing Activities		
Cash received from loans (entry 17)	11,000	
Cash paid for dividends (entry 28)	(50)	
Net cash provided by financing activities		10,950
Net change in cash		(1,275)
Cash balance, November 30, 2018		8,100
Cash balance, December 31, 2018		$ 6,825

However, for many companies, the number and variety of cash transactions that occur each period are so large that such an approach is often impractical. A company with revenues and assets and liabilities in the billions of dollars, like CVS Health for example, has thousands of cash transactions each day. It has accounts with several different banks in numerous locations, and regularly transfers cash from one account to another or back and forth between cash accounts and cash equivalents, as needed. For such a company, simply listing the cash transactions is not practical.

An alternative to this approach of compiling a list of cash flows is to reconcile the information in the income statement and balance sheet to prepare the cash flow statement. The statement of cash flows complements the balance sheet and the income statement. The balance sheet details the financial position of the company at a given point in time. Comparing two balance sheets prepared at the beginning and at the end of a period reveals changes that transpired during the accounting period. These changes are explained by the income statement and the statement of cash flows. Both the income statement and the cash flow statement summarize the events and transactions of the business during the accounting period, and as such, provide complementary descriptions of a company's activities. While the cash flow statement provides information that is not explicitly found in either of the other two statements, it must articulate with the balance sheet and income statement to present a complete picture of company activities.

One of the characteristics of the accounting system is that when an entry changes Net Income without a change in Cash, then it must change another account on the balance sheet. And, when an operating cash flow occurs without a change in Net Income, then there must be a change in some other balance sheet account. Therefore, we can start with information from the income statement and then use the balance sheet (and some additional information) to prepare the statement of cash flows. **Exhibit 4.4** presents the income statement and comparative balance sheets for NBS. We will use the data from these financial statements to prepare NBS's reconciliation of Net Income to Cash from Operating Activities.

EXHIBIT 4.4 NBS Income Statement and Comparative Balance Sheet

NATURAL BEAUTY SUPPLY Income Statement For the Month Ended December 31, 2018		
Sales revenue		$13,900
Cost of goods sold		8,000
Gross profit		5,900
Operating expenses:		
Rent	$1,500	
Wages	2,105	
Advertising	700	
Depreciation	375	
Insurance	140	
Total operating expenses		4,820
Operating income		1,080
Interest income		30
Interest expense		(110)
Income before taxes		1,000
Income tax expense		350
Net income		$ 650

NATURAL BEAUTY SUPPLY Comparative Balance Sheets	12/31/18	11/30/18
Assets:		
Cash	$ 6,825	$ 8,100
Interest receivable	30	
Accounts receivable	2,250	950
Inventory	7,300	11,300
Prepaid insurance	1,540	1,680
Security deposit	2,000	2,000
Fixtures and equipment	18,000	
Accumulated depreciation	(375)	
Total assets	$37,570	$24,030
Liabilities:		
Accounts payable	$ 4,400	$ 3,700
Unearned revenue	600	300
Wages payable	480	
Interest payable	110	
Income taxes payable	350	
Notes payable	11,000	
Stockholders' equity:		
Common stock	20,000	20,000
Retained earnings	630	30
Total liabilities and equity	$37,570	$24,030

Converting Revenues and Expenses to Cash Flows from Operating Activities

We know from Chapter 3 that net income consists of revenues and expenses. We also know that these are often not cash transactions. For example, sales on account will be considered revenue but are not cash inflows until collected. Depreciation is an expense, but is not a current-period cash outflow (the cash outflow presumably occurred when the underlying asset was acquired). We can compute cash flow from operating activities by making adjustments to the revenues and expenses presented in the income statement. The adjustment amounts represent differences between revenues, expenses, gains, and losses recorded under accrual accounting and the related operating cash inflows and outflows. The adjustments are added to or subtracted from net income, depending on whether the related cash flow is more or less than the accrual amount.

Convert Sales Revenues to Cash Received from Customers To illustrate this adjustment procedure for revenues and cash receipts from customers, consider the Chapter 3 transactions and adjusting entry that occurred for NBS in December 2018:

(21) Dec. 20 During the month of December, NBS sold products costing $5,000 to retail customers for $8,500 cash.

(22) Dec. During the month of December, sales to wholesale customers totaled $4,500 for merchandise that had cost $3,000. Instead of paying cash, wholesale customers are required to pay for the merchandise within ten working days.

(23) Dec. $1,200 of gift certificates were sold during the month of December. Each gift certificate entitles the recipient to a one-hour consultation on the use of NBS's products.

(25) Dec. During the month of December, NBS received $3,200 in cash from wholesale customers for products that had been delivered earlier.

(a) Dec. 31 Gift certificates worth $900 were redeemed during the month.

We enter the revenue and cash receipts implications of each of these into the Financial Statement Effects Template (FSET) on the following page. Whenever there is a difference between the revenue recognized and the cash received, that difference affects an operating asset (accounts receivable) or an operating liability (unearned revenue). For instance, in transaction (22a), NBS recognizes credit sales revenue. That is, revenue increases, but cash does not, and the accounting equation is kept by increasing accounts receivable, an operating asset. When NBS received cash in advance of revenue recognition, as in transaction (23), the balancing entry is in unearned revenue, an operating liability. We will find that when an operating transaction affects cash or income—but not both—the operating assets and operating liabilities serve as a temporary buffer between the two.

The total of each of these columns is given in the last row, and because each individual entry is balanced, the totals are balanced.

	Balance Sheet										Income Statement				
Transaction	Cash Asset	+	Noncash Assets	=	Liabil-ities	+	Contrib. Capital	+	Earned Capital		Revenues	−	Expenses	=	Net Income
(21a) Sell $8,500 of products for cash.	+8,500 Cash			=					+8,500 Retained Earnings		+8,500 Sales Revenue	−		=	+8,500
(22a) Sell $4,500 of products on account.			+4,500 Accounts Receivable	=					+4,500 Retained Earnings		+4,500 Sales Revenue	−		=	+4,500
(23) Sell gift certificates for $1,200 cash.	+1,200 Cash			=	+1,200 Unearned Revenue							−		=	
(25) Receive $3,200 cash from customers who purchased on credit.	+3,200 Cash		−3,200 Accounts Receivable	=								−		=	
(a) Adjusting entry for gift certificates redeemed in December.				=	−900 Unearned Revenue				+900 Retained Earnings		+900 Sales Revenue	−		=	+900
Total changes	+12,900 Cash	+	+1,300 Accounts Receivable	=	+300 Unearned Revenue	+	0	+	+13,900 Retained Earnings		+13,900 Sales Revenue	−	0	=	+13,900

We can see that December's revenue was $13,900, and NBS collected $12,900 from customers during the month. Accounts receivable increased by $1,300 over the month, and unearned revenue increased by $300. The FSET maintains the accounting equation at every entry, so we know that the equality will hold for the totals in the last row.

Cash flow (receipts)	+	**Change in accounts receivable**	=	**Change in unearned revenue**	+	**Net income (Sales revenue)**
$12,900	+	**$1,300**	=	**$300**	+	**$13,900**

And this relationship can be rewritten as the following:

Cash flow	=	**Net income**	−	**Change in accounts receivable**	+	**Change in unearned revenue**
$12,900	=	**$13,900**	−	**$1,300**	+	**$300**

So, when we start with net income and then subtract the change in accounts receivable and add the change in unearned revenue, we convert the revenues in net income into the cash receipts from customers needed for cash from operations.

Convert Cost of Goods Sold to Cash Paid for Merchandise Purchased As a second illustration, let's examine the December 2018 transactions involving NBS's inventory and its suppliers (**Exhibit 3.3** in Chapter 3).

(20) Dec. 20 NBS paid $3,300 cash to its suppliers in partial payment for the delivery of inventory in November.

(21) Dec. During the month of December, NBS sold products costing $5,000 to retail customers for $8,500 cash.

(22) Dec. During the month of December, sales to wholesale customers totaled $4,500 for merchandise that had cost $3,000. Instead of paying cash, wholesale customers are required to pay for the merchandise within ten working days.

(26) Dec. 28 NBS purchased and received $4,000 of inventory on account.

When a company like NBS purchases inventory for future sale, we know that the purchase will be followed by two events in the normal course of business. One event is that NBS will have to pay the supplier in cash according to the terms of the purchase, resulting in a cash outflow. The other event is the sale of that inventory to a customer of NBS, resulting in a cost of goods sold expense on the income statement. But these two events do not necessarily occur at the same point in time. As we enter these events into the FSET, we see that the differences between cash payments for inventory and cost of goods sold expense are buffered by inventory, an operating asset, and accounts payable, an operating liability.

	Balance Sheet										*Income Statement*				
Transaction	Cash Asset	+	Noncash Assets	=	Liabil-ities	+	Contrib. Capital	+	Earned Capital		*Revenues*	−	*Expenses*	=	*Net Income*
(20) Pay $3,300 cash to suppliers.	−3,300 Cash			=	−3,300 Accounts Payable							−		=	
(21b) Record $5,000 for the cost of merchandise sold in transaction 21a.			−5,000 Inventory	=					−5,000 Retained Earnings			−	+5,000 Cost of Goods Sold	=	−5,000
(22b) Record $3,000 for the cost of merchandise sold in transaction 22a.			−3,000 Inventory	=					−3,000 Retained Earnings			−	+3,000 Cost of Goods Sold	=	−3,000
(26) Purchase $4,000 inventory on account.			+4,000 Inventory	=	+4,000 Accounts Payable							−		=	
Total changes	−3,300 Cash	+	−4,000 Inventory	=	+700 Accounts Payable	+	0	+	−8,000 Retained Earnings		0	−	+8,000 Cost of Goods Sold	=	−8,000

Again, the FSET keeps the accounting equation with every entry, so we know that the total changes in the last row must also conform to the accounting equation.

Cash flow (payments)	+	Change in inventory	=	Change in accounts payable	+	Net income (COGS expense)
−$3,300	+	**−$4,000**	=	**$700**	+	**−$8,000**

And this relationship can be written as the following:

Cash flow	=	Net income	−	Change in inventory	+	Change in accounts payable
−$3,300	=	**−$8,000**	−	**(−$4,000)**	+	**$700**

The change in inventory is negative for NBS during December 2018, so when we subtract the change in inventory above, we must subtract a negative number, making a positive adjustment. (That is, −(−$4,000) = +$4,000.) And, when we subtract the change in inventory from net income and add the change in accounts payable to net income, we convert the (minus) cost of goods sold expense to the (minus) payments to suppliers we need for the cash from operations.

Stepping back to look at the big picture, we begin to see a pattern. The cash flow effect of an item is equal to its income statement effect, minus the change in any associated operating asset(s) plus the change in any associated operating liability(ies). That pattern can be confirmed as we look at the remaining necessary adjustments.

Convert Wages Expense to Cash Paid to Employees To determine the adjustment needed for transactions involving employees, we look at the two entries from Chapter 3 related to the wages earned and paid during the month of December 2018.

Transaction	Cash Asset	+	Noncash Assets	=	Liabil-ities	+	Contrib. Capital	+	Earned Capital	Revenues	−	Expenses	=	Net Income
	Balance Sheet									Income Statement				
(24) Record $1,625 in wages to employees.	−1,625 Cash			=					−1,625 Retained Earnings		−	+1,625 Wages Expense	=	−1,625
(e) Adjusting entry to record wages earned but not yet paid.				=	+480 Wages Payable				−480 Retained Earnings		−	+480 Wages Expense	=	−480
Total changes	−1,625 Cash	+	0	=	+480 Wages Payable	+	0	+	−2,105 Retained Earnings	0	−	+2,105 Wages Expense	=	−2,105

Using the same approach as above, the FSET tells us the following about the totals:

$$\text{Cash flow (payments)} = \text{Change in wages payable} + \text{Net income (wage expense)},$$

which can be rewritten as

$$\begin{array}{ccccc} \textbf{Cash flow} & = & \textbf{Net income} & + & \textbf{Change in wages payable} \\ -\$1{,}625 & = & -\$2{,}105 & + & \$480 \end{array}$$

NBS recorded more wage expense than it paid to its employees, and that additional expense goes into an operating liability, wages payable. If wages payable had decreased over the period, it would imply that NBS had paid more to its employees than they had earned during the period (perhaps because they were owed compensation from a prior period).

Convert Rent Expense to Cash Paid for Rent and Advertising Expense to Cash Paid for Advertising The December 2018 entries for rent and advertising are presented in the FSET below.

Transaction	Cash Asset	+	Noncash Assets	=	Liabil-ities	+	Contrib. Capital	+	Earned Capital	Revenues	−	Expenses	=	Net Income
(19) Pay $700 cash for December advertising.	−700 Cash			=					−700 Retained Earnings		−	+700 Advertising Expense	=	−700
(27) Pay $1,500 rent for December.	−1,500 Cash			=					−1,500 Retained Earnings		−	+1,500 Rent Expense	=	−1,500
Total changes	−2,200 Cash	+	0	=	0	+	0	+	−2,200 Retained Earnings	0	−	+2,200 Advertising and Rent Expense	=	−2,200

For these items, the amount paid is exactly equal to the amount recorded as expense, so no adjustment is necessary. The amounts included for advertising and rent in the determination of net income are exactly what we want in the cash from operations. If NBS had paid rent in advance or promised to pay later for its advertising, then operating assets and/or liabilities would have been created, and an adjustment would have been necessary (as we see in the case immediately following).

Other Adjustments There are five more items in NBS' income statement that require adjustment to arrive at the amount of cash from operations for the month of December. Four of these items are insurance expense, interest income, interest expense, and income tax expense. These items involved only adjusting entries during the month of December, so there were no cash flows involved, and we present the adjustments in an abbreviated fashion below.

Transaction	Cash Asset	+	Noncash Assets	=	Liabil-ities	+	Contrib. Capital	+	Earned Capital	Revenues	−	Expenses	=	Net Income
(b) Adjusting entry to record expiration of 1 month of prepaid insurance.			−140 Prepaid insurance	=					−140 Retained Earnings		−	+140 Insurance Expense	=	−140
Total changes	0 Cash	+	−140 Prepaid Insurance	=	0	+	0	+	−140 Retained Earnings	0	−	+140 Insurance Expense	=	−140

Cash flow + Change in prepaid insurance = Net income, or

Cash flow = Net income − Change in prepaid insurance, or
\$0 (zero) = −\$140 − (−\$140)

Transaction	Cash Asset	+	Noncash Assets	=	Liabil-ities	+	Contrib. Capital	+	Earned Capital	Revenues	−	Expenses	=	Net Income
(d) Adjusting entry for interest income earned.			+30 Other Receivables	=					+30 Retained Earnings	+30 Interest Income	−		=	+30
Total changes	0 Cash	+	+30 Other Receivables	=	0	+	0	+	+30 Retained Earnings	+30 Interest Income	−	0	=	+30

Cash flow + Change in other receivables = Net income, or

Cash flow = Net income − Change in other receivables, or
\$0 (zero) = \$30 − \$30

Transaction	Cash Asset	+	Noncash Assets	=	Liabil-ities	+	Contrib. Capital	+	Earned Capital	Revenues	−	Expenses	=	Net Income
(f) Adjusting entry to record interest owed but not yet paid.				=	+110 Interest Payable				−110 Retained Earnings		−	+110 Interest Expense	=	−110
Total changes	0 Cash	+	0	=	+110 Interest Payable	+	0	+	−110 Retained Earnings	0	−	+110 Interest Expense	=	−110

Cash flow = Change in interest payable + Net income, or

Cash flow = Net income + Change in interest payable, or
\$0 (zero) = −\$110 + \$110

Transaction	Cash Asset	+	Noncash Assets	=	Liabil-ities	+	Contrib. Capital	+	Earned Capital	Revenues	−	Expenses	=	Net Income
(g) Adjusting entry for estimated income tax.				=	+350 Tax Payable				−350 Retained Earnings		−	+350 Tax Expense	=	−350
Total changes	0 Cash	+	0	=	+350 Tax Payable	+	0	+	−350 Retained Earnings	0	−	+350 Tax Expense	=	−350

Cash flow = Change in tax payable + Net income, or

Cash flow = Net income + Change in tax payable, or
\$0 (zero) = −\$350 + \$350

Each of the above four items involved only an adjusting entry (i.e., an entry at the end of the fiscal period). Adjusting entries rarely involve cash, so the adjustment simply cancels out the item in the income statement. We will see more examples in later chapters (e.g., write-downs of physical or intangible assets, restructuring charges, etc.).

Eliminate Depreciation Expense and Other Noncash Operating Expenses

NBS recorded an adjusting entry for depreciation at the end of December 2018 for \$375. That entry into the FSET was the following.

	Balance Sheet									Income Statement				
Transaction	Cash Asset	+	Noncash Assets	=	Liabil-ities	+	Contrib. Capital	+	Earned Capital	Revenues	−	Expenses	=	Net Income
(c) Adjusting entry for depreciation on fixtures and equipment for December.					+375 Accumulated Depreciation	=			−375 Retained Earnings		−	+375 Depreciation Expense	=	−375
Total changes	0	+	0	−	+375 Accumulated Depreciation	=	0	+	−375 Retained Earnings	0	−	+375 Depreciation Expense	=	−375

We can see that this entry reduced net income by $375, but it had no effect on cash. When we look at the total impact of this entry on the FSET (in the last row), its effect can be written in the following way.

$$\textbf{Cash flow} - \textbf{Change in accumulated depreciation (for depreciation expense)} = \textbf{Net income,}$$

or

$$\textbf{Cash flow} = \textbf{Net income} + \textbf{Depreciation expense}$$
$$\$0\ (\text{zero}) = -\$375 + \$375$$

So, NBS's net income of $650 for December includes a depreciation expense of $375 that did not involve any cash outflow. When we add back depreciation expense (and similar items like amortization expense), we move the net income number one step closer to cash from operations.

Would increasing depreciation expense increase the cash flows from operations? That question is more complex than it initially appears. In Chapter 8, we will find that companies use different depreciation methods for tax reporting and financial reporting, and in Chapter 10 we will see how differences between tax and financial reporting are reconciled. Increasing the tax depreciation expense reduces taxable income and the amount of tax that has to be paid. Increasing depreciation expense in financial reports to shareholders has no effect on the amount of taxes paid and, therefore, no effect on the amount of cash generated.

A General Rule . . . with a Note of Caution The relationships illustrated in the above examples suggest a general rule that we can use to prepare the cash flow statement:

> The difference between a revenue or an expense reported in the income statement and a related cash receipt or expenditure reported in the statement of cash flows will be reflected in the balance sheet as a change in one or more balance sheet accounts.

More specifically, all the above reconciliation adjustments for NBS can be summarized in a pattern:

$$\textbf{Net income} + \textbf{Adjustments} = \textbf{Cash from operations}$$

Or, more particularly

$$\textbf{Net income} + \textbf{Depreciation expense} - \textbf{Change in operating assets} + \textbf{Change in operating liabilities} = \textbf{Cash from operations}$$

By "operating assets," we mean receivables, inventories, prepaid expenses and similar assets. "Operating liabilities" refers to accounts and wages payable, accrued expenses, unearned revenues, taxes payable, interest payable and similar items. Investing assets (like investment securities and property, plant, and equipment) and financing liabilities (like notes payable and long-term debt) would not be included in these adjustments.

Exhibit 4.5 summarizes the basic adjustments needed to convert the revenues, expenses, gains and losses presented in the income statement to cash receipts and payments presented in the statement of cash flows from operating activities. (The adjustments for nonoperating gains and losses will be discussed shortly.)

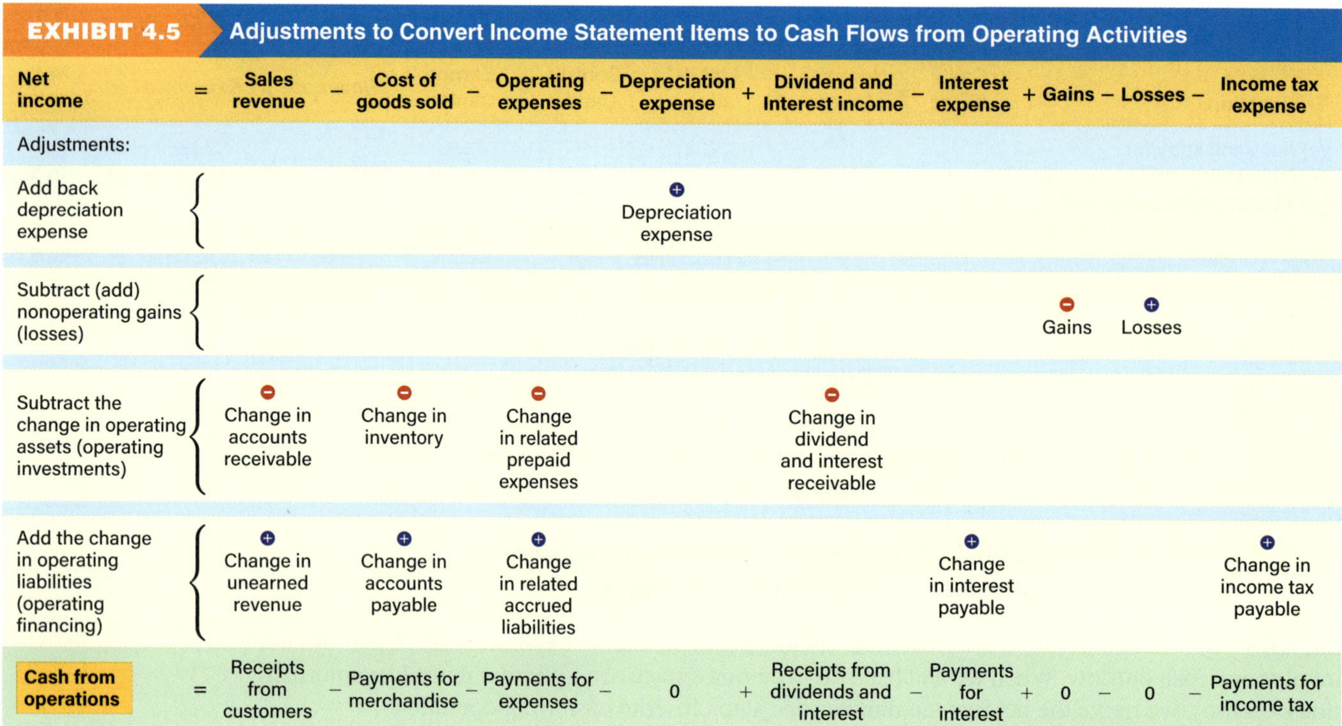

EXHIBIT 4.5 Adjustments to Convert Income Statement Items to Cash Flows from Operating Activities

Net income	=	**Sales revenue**	−	**Cost of goods sold**	−	**Operating expenses**	−	**Depreciation expense**	+	**Dividend and Interest income**	−	**Interest expense**	+	**Gains**	−	**Losses**	−	**Income tax expense**
Adjustments:																		
Add back depreciation expense								⊕ Depreciation expense										
Subtract (add) nonoperating gains (losses)														⊖ Gains		⊕ Losses		
Subtract the change in operating assets (operating investments)		⊖ Change in accounts receivable		⊖ Change in inventory		⊖ Change in related prepaid expenses				⊖ Change in dividend and interest receivable								
Add the change in operating liabilities (operating financing)		⊕ Change in unearned revenue		⊕ Change in accounts payable		⊕ Change in related accrued liabilities						⊕ Change in interest payable						⊕ Change in income tax payable
Cash from operations	=	Receipts from customers	−	Payments for merchandise	−	Payments for expenses	−	0	+	Receipts from dividends and interest	−	Payments for interest	+	0	−	0	−	Payments for income tax

We have now applied the adjustments to convert each accrual revenue and expense to the corresponding operating cash flow. We use these individual cash inflows and outflows to prepare the operating activities section of the statement of cash flows. The adjustments to convert revenues and expenses to operating cash flows are summarized in **Exhibit 4.6**, and this information can be used to produce NBS's cash from operating activities by using the information in the income statement and balance sheet.

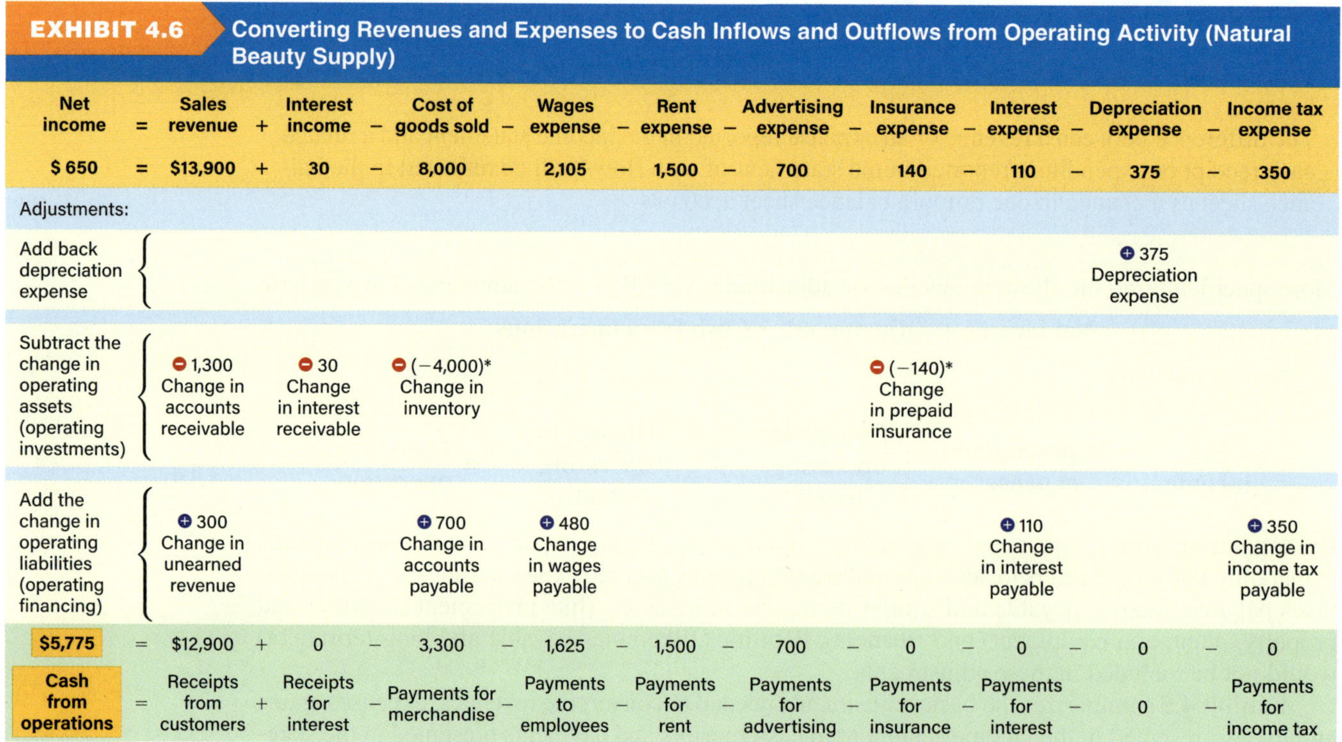

EXHIBIT 4.6 Converting Revenues and Expenses to Cash Inflows and Outflows from Operating Activity (Natural Beauty Supply)

Net income	=	**Sales revenue**	+	**Interest income**	−	**Cost of goods sold**	−	**Wages expense**	−	**Rent expense**	−	**Advertising expense**	−	**Insurance expense**	−	**Interest expense**	−	**Depreciation expense**	−	**Income tax expense**
$ 650	=	**$13,900**	+	**30**	−	**8,000**	−	**2,105**	−	**1,500**	−	**700**	−	**140**	−	**110**	−	**375**	−	**350**
Adjustments:																				
Add back depreciation expense																		⊕ 375 Depreciation expense		
Subtract the change in operating assets (operating investments)		⊖ 1,300 Change in accounts receivable		⊖ 30 Change in interest receivable		⊖ (−4,000)* Change in inventory								⊖ (−140)* Change in prepaid insurance						
Add the change in operating liabilities (operating financing)		⊕ 300 Change in unearned revenue				⊕ 700 Change in accounts payable		⊕ 480 Change in wages payable								⊕ 110 Change in interest payable				⊕ 350 Change in income tax payable
$5,775	=	$12,900	+	0	−	3,300	−	1,625	−	1,500	−	700	−	0	−	0	−	0	−	0
Cash from operations	=	Receipts from customers	+	Receipts for interest	−	Payments for merchandise	−	Payments to employees	−	Payments for rent	−	Payments for advertising	−	Payments for insurance	−	Payments for interest	−	0	−	Payments for income tax

* When the change in an operating asset is negative, subtracting that negative amount results in a positive adjustment.

Like all general rules, this one provides useful insights, but it also has limitations. As we learn more and more about business activities and the accounting for them, we find the need for refinements of this general rule. For instance, in Chapter 12, we will see that operating assets and liabilities can increase from acquisitions (an investing activity) as well as from operations. But for the time-being, the general rule is a useful way to approach the calculation and interpretation of operating cash flow.

MID-CHAPTER REVIEW 2

The income statement and comparative balance sheets for Mug Shots, Inc., (a photography studio) are presented below. Use the information in these financial statements and the frameworks in **Exhibits 4.5** and **4.6** to compute Mug Shots' cash flow from operating activities using the direct method.

MUG SHOTS, INC.
Income Statement
For Month Ended December 31, 2018

Revenue		
Sales revenue		$31,000
Expenses		
Cost of goods sold	$16,700	
Wages expense	4,700	
Interest expense	300	
Advertising expense	1,800	
Rent expense	1,500	
Depreciation expense	700	
Total expenses		25,700
Income before taxes		5,300
Income tax expense		1,855
Net income		$ 3,445

MUG SHOTS, INC.
Comparative Balance Sheets

	12/31/18	11/30/18
Assets		
Cash	$10,700	$ 5,000
Accounts receivable	2,500	
Inventory	32,300	24,000
Prepaid rent	7,500	9,000
Equipment	30,000	18,000
Accumulated depreciation	(700)	
Total assets	$82,300	$56,000
Liabilities		
Accounts payable	$25,000	$24,000
Interest payable	300	
Wages payable	2,200	
Income tax payable	1,855	
Unearned revenue	500	
Notes payable	30,000	12,000
Equity		
Common stock	20,000	20,000
Retained earnings	2,445	
Total liabilities and equity	$82,300	$56,000

The solution to this review problem can be found on page 214.

Reconciling Net Income and Cash Flow from Operating Activities

LO3 Reconcile cash flows from operations to net income and use the indirect method to compute operating cash flows.

3

We now have two metrics to consider when examining the operations of a company over a period of time—net income and cash from operations. For December 2018, NBS reported net income of $650 and cash from operations of $5,775. For its fiscal year ended December 31, 2017, CVS Health Corporation reported net income of $6,623 million and cash from operations of $8,007 million. While both net income and cash from operations measure aspects of operations over the same time period, they can sometimes be very far apart, as seen in the following table.

	2017 ($ millions)	
	Net Income	Cash from Operations
Delta Air Lines, Inc.	$ 3,577	$ 5,149
Southwest Airlines Co.	3,488	3,929
American Airlines Group, Inc.	1,919	4,744
Target Corporation	2,934	6,923
Walmart, Inc.	9,862	28,337
Amazon.com, Inc.	3,033	18,434
Alphabet Inc.	12,662	37,091
Facebook, Inc.	15,934	24,216
Tesla, Inc.	(1,727)	(61)
Bayerische Motoren Werke AG	8,620	5,909
Ford Motor Company	7,602	18,096
Toyota Motor Corporation	16,433	30,640
Carmax, Inc.	664	(81)
AutoNation, Inc.	435	540

It would be natural for a financial statement reader to want to understand the source(s) of the differences between net income and cash from operations. So, companies that present their statement of cash flows like CVS Health Corporation must also present a reconciliation of net income to cash from operations. The reconciliation for CVS Health's fiscal year ending December 31, 2017, is in **Exhibit 4.7**.

EXHIBIT 4.7 CVS Health Corporation Income to Operating Cash Flows Reconciliation

CVS HEALTH CORPORATION
CONSOLIDATED STATEMENT OF CASH FLOWS
For the Fiscal Year Ended December 31, 2017
RECONCILIATION OF NET INCOME TO NET CASH PROVIDED BY OPERATING ACTIVITIES

In millions	2017
Net income	**$6,623**
Adjustments required to reconcile net income to net cash provided by operating activities	
Depreciation and amortization	2,479
Goodwill impairments	181
Losses on settlements of defined benefit pension plans	187
Stock-based compensation	234
Deferred income taxes	(1,334)
Other noncash items	53
Change in operating assets and liabilities, net of effects from acquisitions:	
Accounts receivable, net	(941)
Inventories	(514)
Other current assets	(341)
Other assets	3
Accounts payable and claims and discounts payable	1,710
Accrued expenses	(371)
Other long-term liabilities	38
Net cash provided by operating activities	$8,007

This reconciliation leads to exactly the same number that was presented in the operating section of **Exhibit 4.1**, but in a very different format. How is it produced? It is constructed using exactly the same adjustment process depicted in **Exhibits 4.5** and **4.6**.

CVS Health's reconciliation contains a couple of entries that we did not see for Natural Beauty Supply. A company's income statement may contain gains and losses related to nonoperating activities. Examples include gains and losses from the sale of plant assets and gains and losses from the retirement of bonds payable. Because these gains and losses are not related to operating activities, **Exhibit 4.5** shows that we omit them as we convert income statement items to various cash flows from operating activities. The cash flows relating to these gains and losses are reported in the investing activities or financing activities sections of the statement of cash flows. NBS had no nonoperating gains or losses in December, but we will see an example of this type of adjustment in a later section.

Another adjustment involves stock-based compensation. Corporations often use their common stock to reward employees and to provide incentives for future performance. The value of such grants must be recognized in the income statement as an expense, but it is an expense that does not involve cash. Therefore, the amount expensed—$234 million for CVS Health in 2017—is added back in reconciling net income to cash from operations.

CVS Health also makes a $1,334 million adjustment for deferred income taxes and an adjustment of $187 million for the settlement of a pension plan. Deferred income taxes occur when companies use different accounting methods for tax and financial reporting and are beyond our scope for the moment. It will be covered later in Chapter 10, along with an examination of the accounting for pensions.

Cash Flow from Operating Activities Using the Indirect Method

Two alternative formats may be used to report the net cash flow from operating activities: the direct method and the indirect method. *Both methods report the same amount of net cash flow from operating activities.* Net cash flows from investing and financing activities are prepared in the same manner under both the indirect and direct methods; only the format for cash flows from operating activities differs.

For Natural Beauty Supply, we computed cash flow from operating activities using the direct method. The **direct method** presents the components of cash flow from operating activities as a list of gross cash receipts and gross cash payments. This format is illustrated in **Exhibit 4.3** and by CVS Health Corporation's statement in **Exhibit 4.1**.

The direct method is logical and relatively easy to follow. In practice, however, nearly all statements of cash flows are presented using what is called the **indirect method**. Under this method, the reconciliation of net income to operating cash flow (e.g., **Exhibit 4.7**) is used for the presentation of cash flow from operations. The cash flow from operations section begins with net income and applies a series of adjustments to net income to convert it to net cash flow from operating activities. However, the adjustments to net income are not cash flows themselves, so the indirect method does not report any detail concerning individual operating cash inflows and outflows. In fact, there are no cash flows in the indirect method operating section of the cash flow statement, except the subtotal—cash flow from operations. The **Apple Inc.** statement of cash flows on page 206 is an example.

While accounting standard-setters prefer the direct method presentation, it is not very popular with reporting companies. In the U.S., surveys have found that fewer than 5% of companies use the direct method presentation. The indirect method is popular because (1) it is easier and less expensive to prepare than the direct method and (2) companies that use the direct method are required to present a supplemental disclosure showing the reconciliation of net income to cash from operations (thus, essentially requiring the company to report both methods for cash from operations). International standard-setters also have stated a preference for the direct method, and its use is more frequent than in the U.S. But the indirect method of presenting cash flow from operations is used by a significant majority of companies.

The procedure for presenting indirect method cash flows from operations uses the same approach that we applied above to convert income statement items to operating cash flows. In fact, the indirect method can be viewed as a "short-cut" calculation of the process shown in **Exhibit 4.5**. That is:

Net income ± Adjustments = Cash flow from operating activities

In **Exhibit 4.5**, revenue and expense components of the income statement are presented in the orange row that totals to net income. The yellow rows list the adjustments, and cash receipts and payments are listed in the green row at the bottom. The total of the green row is cash flow from operating activities. The indirect method skips the listing of individual revenues and expenses and starts with net income. After adjustments, we have total cash flow from operating activities, but not individual receipts and payments.

Cash flow from December's operating activities for NBS is presented using the indirect method in **Exhibit 4.8**. The calculation begins with the December net income of $650 and ends with cash flow from operating activities, $5,775. The total cash flow from operating activities is the same amount as was computed in **Exhibit 4.6** using the direct method. If we compare **Exhibit 4.6** and **Exhibit 4.8**, we see that the two exhibits are very similar. The only difference is that all of the

FYI Managers can boost declining sales by lengthening credit periods or by lowering credit standards. The resulting increase in accounts receivable can cause net income to outpace operating cash flow. Consequently, many view a large receivables increase as a warning sign.

revenues and expenses are listed in the orange row at the top of **Exhibit 4.6**, while **Exhibit 4.8** lists only the total—net income. Similarly, the green row at the bottom of **Exhibit 4.6** lists all of the cash inflows and outflows, while the bottom line of **Exhibit 4.8** lists only the net cash flow from operating activities. In both exhibits, the center rows list the adjustments.

EXHIBIT 4.8 NBS Cash Flow from Operating Activities—Indirect Method

Net income		$ 650
Adjustments:		
Add back depreciation expense	375	
Subtract:		
Change in accounts receivable	1,300	
Change in interest receivable	30	
Change in inventory	(4,000)*	
Change in prepaid insurance	(140)*	
Add:		
Change in unearned revenue	300	
Change in accounts payable	700	
Change in wages payable	480	
Change in interest payable	110	
Change in income tax payable	350	
Total adjustments	5,125	
Cash flow from operating activities		$5,775

* When the change in an operating asset is negative, subtracting that negative amount results in a positive adjustment.

MID-CHAPTER REVIEW 3

Refer to the financial statements for Mug Shots, Inc. presented in Mid-Chapter Review 2. Compute cash flows from operating activities for Mug Shots, Inc. using the indirect method.

The solution to this review problem can be found on page 214.

PREPARING THE STATEMENT OF CASH FLOWS—INVESTING AND FINANCING ACTIVITIES

4 **LO4** Construct the investing and financing activities sections of the statement of cash flows.

The remaining sections of the statement of cash flows focus on investing and financing activities. Investing activities are concerned with transactions affecting noncurrent (and some current) noncash assets. Financing activities are concerned with raising capital from owners and creditors. The presentation of the cash effects of investing and financing transactions is not affected by the method of presentation (direct or indirect) of cash flows from operating activities.

Accounting standard-setters (both in the United States and International) require that financing and investing items be presented in the statement of cash flows using gross amounts instead of net amounts. In **Exhibit 4.1**, CVS Health reports that it spent $1,918 million in cash to acquire property, plant, and equipment in 2017, and it received $33 million in cash from the sale of property and equipment and other assets. It would not be acceptable to show the net amount—an outflow of $1,885 million—as a single item unless one of the components is consistently immaterial.

Cash Flows from Investing Activities

Investing activities cause changes in noncash asset accounts. Usually the accounts affected (other than cash) are noncurrent operating asset accounts such as property, plant, and equipment assets and investing assets like marketable securities and long-term financial investments. Cash paid for acquisitions of other companies would be included as well. To determine the cash flows from investing activities, *we analyze changes in all noncash asset accounts not used in computing net cash flow from operating activities.* Our objective is to identify any investing cash flows related to these changes.

Purchases of noncash assets cause cash outflow. Conversely, a sale of a noncash asset results in cash inflow. This relationship is highlighted in the following decision guide:

Cash flows increase due to:	Cash flows decrease due to:
Sales of assets	Purchases of assets

NBS had only one investing transaction during December—the purchase of fixtures and equipment for $18,000. Any change in the Fixtures and Equipment account in the balance sheet is usually the result of one or both of the following transactions: (1) buying assets, or (2) selling assets.[2] Buying and selling nonoperating assets are classified as investing transactions. NBS's journal entry to record the purchase of fixtures and equipment for cash is as follows:

(18)	Fixtures and equipment (+A)	18,000	
	Cash (−A)		18,000

The resulting $18,000 cash outflow is listed in the statement of cash flows under cash flow used for investing activities.

Cash Flows from Financing Activities

Financing activities cause changes in financial liabilities and stockholders' equity accounts. Financial liabilities include current liability items like seasonal bank borrowing and the current portion of long-term debt due within the next year, plus noncurrent items like long-term debt issues and longer term borrowing from financial institutions. Cash receipts from the issuance of these liabilities and cash payments to settle outstanding principal balances are considered cash flows from financing activities. Stockholders' equity accounts include contributed capital (common stock, additional paid-in-capital, and treasury stock) and retained earnings. Transactions with shareholders are always considered part of a company's financing activities. This relationship is highlighted in the following decision guide:

Cash flows increase due to:	Cash flows decrease due to:
Taking on a financial liability or issuing shares	Repaying principal on a financial liability or paying dividends to shareholders or making share repurchases

NBS had two financing transactions during December. It borrowed $11,000 on a three-year note, resulting in an increase in cash, and it paid $50 in cash dividends to shareholders. The journal entry to record the $11,000 note is illustrated as:

(17)	Cash (+A)	11,000	
	Notes payable (+L)		11,000

The resulting $11,000 cash inflow is listed in the statement of cash flows under cash flow from financing activities.

The journal entry to record dividends is illustrated as follows:

(28)	Retained earnings (−SE)	50	
	Cash (−A)		50

This dividend payment is a financing cash outflow and would be deducted from cash flow from financing activities.

When using the indirect method for the cash flow from operating activities, we should remember that there are some balance sheet accounts that will be affected by more than one type of activity.

[2] The Accumulated Depreciation—Fixtures and Equipment contra-asset account is affected by depreciation expense and selling assets.

For instance, the balance in retained earnings will be affected by net income (which is going to appear in the operations section) and shareholder dividends (which will appear in the financing section).

The statement of cash flows lists cash flows from operating activities first (using either the direct or the indirect method), followed by cash flows from investing activities, then cash flows from financing activities. Once all three categories of cash flows have been listed, we total the three amounts to arrive at net cash flow for the period. The final step is to reconcile the cash balance from the beginning of the period to the ending balance. The completed statement of cash flows for NBS using the indirect method for operating cash flows is presented in **Exhibit 4.9**. We see from this statement that operating activities produced a cash inflow of $5,775, while investing activities resulted in a cash outflow of $18,000, and financing activities resulted in a cash inflow of $10,950. The sum of these three amounts ($5,775 – $18,000 + $10,950) equals the change in cash for December of –$1,275 ($6,825 – $8,100).

YOU MAKE THE CALL

You are the Chief Accountant In its annual report for fiscal year 2017, **Sears Holdings Corp.** reported that its actions to secure adequate levels of liquidity included "Sales of properties and investments for proceeds of $1.1 billion." How would these proceeds be reflected in the company's cash flow statement? [Answer on page 190.]

FYI The net cash inflow or outflow for the period is the same amount as the increase or decrease in cash and cash equivalents for the period from the balance sheet.

EXHIBIT 4.9 NBS Statement of Cash Flows—Indirect Method

NATURAL BEAUTY SUPPLY
Statement of Cash Flows
For the Month Ended December 31, 2018

Operating activities:		
Net income	$ 650	
Adjustments:		
Add back Depreciation expense	375	
Subtract:		
Change in accounts receivable	1,300	
Change in interest receivable	30	
Change in inventory	(4,000)*	
Change in prepaid insurance	(140)*	
Add:		
Change in unearned revenue	300	
Change in accounts payable	700	
Change in wages payable	480	
Change in interest payable	110	
Change in income tax payable	350	
Total adjustments	5,125	
Cash flow from operating activities		$5,775
Investing activities:		
Purchase of fixtures and equipment	(18,000)	
Cash flow used for investing activities		(18,000)
Financing activities:		
Bank note	11,000	
Dividends paid	(50)	
Cash flow from financing activities		10,950
Net decrease in cash		(1,275)
Cash, November 30, 2018		8,100
Cash, December 31, 2018		$ 6,825

* When the change in an operating asset is negative, subtracting that negative amount results in a positive adjustment.

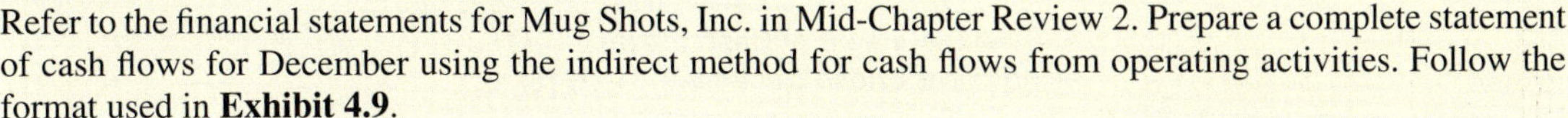

MID-CHAPTER REVIEW 4

Refer to the financial statements for Mug Shots, Inc. in Mid-Chapter Review 2. Prepare a complete statement of cash flows for December using the indirect method for cash flows from operating activities. Follow the format used in **Exhibit 4.9**.

The solution to this review problem can be found on page 215.

ADDITIONAL DETAIL IN THE STATEMENT OF CASH FLOWS

There are two additional types of transactions that we must explore to understand the statement of cash flows. The first of these is the sale of investing assets like equipment or an investment security. The transaction itself isn't very complicated, but the use of the indirect method for operating cash flows makes it seem so. And, companies often engage in investing and financing activities that do not involve cash (e.g., acquiring another company through an exchange of stock). This section explores the accounting for these two types of transactions and their effect on the statement of cash flows.

Case Illustration Natural Beauty Supply did not have any disposals of assets or repayments of debt in December 2018, so there is no adjustment to make in this case. However, let's consider the financial statements of One World Café, a coffee shop that is located next door to NBS. The income statement and comparative balance sheet for One World Café are presented in **Exhibit 4.10**. The cash flow statement is presented in **Exhibit 4.11**.

EXHIBIT 4.10 One World Café Income Statement and Comparative Balance Sheets

ONE WORLD CAFÉ, INC.
Income Statement
For Year Ended December 31, 2018

Revenue		
Sales revenue		$390,000
Expenses		
Cost of goods sold	$227,000	
Wages expense	82,000	
Advertising expense	9,800	
Depreciation expense	17,000	
Interest expense	200	
Loss on sale of plant assets	2,000	
Total expenses		338,000
Income before taxes		52,000
Income tax expense		17,000
Net income		$ 35,000

ONE WORLD CAFÉ, INC.
Comparative Balance Sheets
At December 31

	2018	2017
Assets		
Cash	$ 8,000	$ 12,000
Accounts receivable	22,000	28,000
Inventory	94,000	66,000
Prepaid advertising	12,000	9,000
Plant assets, at cost	208,000	170,000
Less accumulated depreciation	(72,000)	(61,000)
Total assets	$272,000	$224,000
Liabilities		
Accounts payable	$ 27,000	$ 14,000
Wages payable	6,000	2,500
Income tax payable	3,000	4,500
Notes payable	5,000	—
Equity		
Common stock	134,000	125,000
Retained earnings	97,000	78,000
Total liabilities and equity	$272,000	$224,000

EXHIBIT 4.11 Cash Flow Statement for One World Café

ONE WORLD CAFÉ, INC.
Statement of Cash Flows
For Year Ended December 31, 2018

Cash flows from operating activities		
Net income	$35,000	
Add (deduct) items to convert net income to cash basis		
Add back depreciation	17,000	
Add back loss on sale of plant assets	2,000	
Subtract change in:		
Accounts receivable	(6,000)*	
Inventory	28,000	
Prepaid advertising	3,000	
Add change in:		
Accounts payable	13,000	
Wages payable	3,500	
Income tax payable	(1,500)	
Net cash provided by operating activities		$44,000
Cash flows from investing activities		
Purchase of plant assets	(45,000)	
Proceeds from sale of plant assets	4,000	
Net cash used for investing activities		(41,000)
Cash flows from financing activities		
Issuance of common stock	9,000	
Payment of dividends	(16,000)	
Net cash flows used for financing activities		(7,000)
Net cash decrease		(4,000)
Cash at beginning of year		12,000
Cash at end of year		$ 8,000

* When the change in an operating asset is negative, subtracting that negative amount results in a positive adjustment.

For One World Café, creation of the statement of cash flows requires information that cannot be discerned from the income statement and balance sheet. (After all, the statement of cash flows is *supposed* to provide additional information!) In particular, the following events occurred during the year.

- Plant assets were purchased for cash.
- Obsolete plant assets, with original cost of $12,000 and accumulated depreciation of $6,000, were sold for $4,000 cash, resulting in a $2,000 loss.
- Additional common stock was issued for cash.
- Cash dividends of $16,000 were declared and paid during the year.
- One World Café acquired $5,000 of plant assets by issuing notes payable.

Reviewing One World Café's comparative balance sheet, we see that plant assets at cost increased from $170,000 to $208,000, an increase of $38,000. In addition, the accumulated depreciation contra-asset increased by $11,000 from $61,000 to $72,000. However, these are *net* increases, and we need information on the individual components of the increases. Consequently, we need to determine the gross amounts to ensure the statement of cash flows we create properly presents the gross amounts in the investing activities section.

In addition to the changes in plant assets and accumulated depreciation, notes payable increased by $5,000 in 2018. The best way to fully understand what happened to cause the changes in balance sheet accounts during the year, and the impact of these changes on cash flows, is to "work backwards" to reconstruct the investing and financing transactions using journal entries and T-accounts, especially the plant assets and accumulated depreciation accounts.

Gains and Losses on Investing and Financing Activities

The focus of the income statement is on the revenues and expenses that are generated by a company's transactions with customers, suppliers, employees, and other operating activities. But the income statement also contains gains and losses that result from investing or financing transactions. Gains and losses from the sale of investments, property, plant, and equipment, or intangible assets result from investing activities, not operating activities. A gain or loss from the retirement of bonds payable is an example of a financing gain or loss. When these transactions occur, the income statement does not show a revenue and an expense, but rather shows only the net amount as a gain or loss.

The full cash flow effect from these types of events is reported in the investing or financing sections of the statement of cash flows. To illustrate, we record the sale of Old World Café's obsolete plant assets at a loss with the following journal entry:

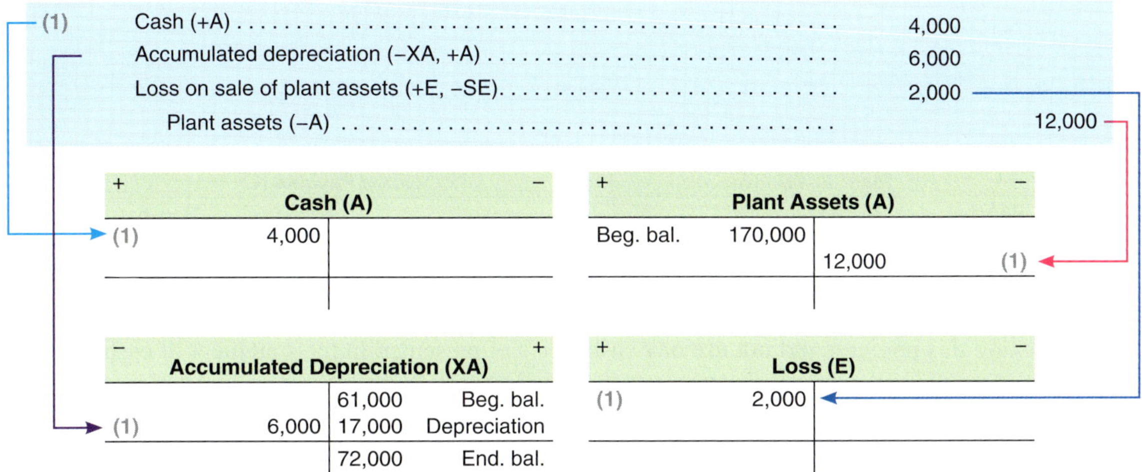

The $4,000 of cash received from this sale should be listed as a cash inflow under cash flows from investing activities, and it can be seen in **Exhibit 4.11**. The $4,000 cash flow is equal to the $6,000 net book value of the plant assets that were sold ($12,000 – $6,000) less the $2,000 loss on the sale.

If we were using the direct method to report the cash flows from operating activities, we wouldn't need to take any additional steps. But an indirect method operating cash flows starts with net income, and Old World Café's net income includes a $2,000 loss from this investing transaction (**Exhibit 4.10**). So, when we add back the investing loss to net income (or subtract an investing gain), we remove the effect of this investing transaction from the determination of cash flows from operating activities. It's one more step in the adjustments that are needed to reconcile net income to the cash flows from operating activities.

In Chapter 9, we will find that companies can experience financing gains (losses) from the early retirement of their debt. These gains and losses appear in the income statement, but they result from financing activities. In an indirect method statement of cash flows, the financing gains (losses) must be subtracted from (added to) net income to determine cash flows from operating activities.

We also see that the accumulated depreciation account started with a credit balance of $61,000, and the obsolete asset sale reduced this by $6,000 to $55,000. But the balance sheet in **Exhibit 4.10** tells us that the ending (credit) balance is $72,000. The difference is due to $17,000 depreciation expense for the year.

YOU MAKE THE CALL

You are the Securities Analyst You are analyzing a company's statement of cash flows. The company extends credit to customers that purchase its products. You see that the company has sold some of its accounts receivable to another company, receiving cash in return. As a result, the sale of receivables is reported as an asset sale, which reduces receivables and yields a gain or loss on sale. This action increases the company's operating cash flows. How should you interpret these items in the cash flow statement? [Answer on p. 190.]

Noncash Investing and Financing Activities

In addition to reporting how cash changed from one balance sheet to the next, cash flow reporting is intended to present summary information about a firm's investing and financing activities. Many of these activities affect cash and are therefore already included in the investing and financing sections of the statement of cash flows. Some significant investing and financing events, however, do not affect current cash flows. Examples of **noncash investing and financing activities** are the issuance of stocks, bonds, or leases in exchange for property, plant, and equipment (PPE) assets or intangible assets; the exchange of long-term assets for other long-term assets; and the conversion of long-term debt into common stock.

To illustrate the effect of noncash transactions on the preparation of the cash flow statement, consider One World Café's purchase of $5,000 of plant assets that was financed with notes payable. The journal entry to record the purchase is as follows:

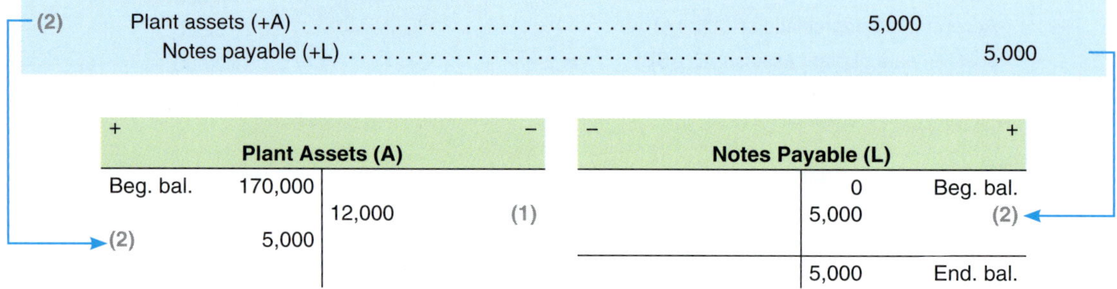

Because this purchase did not use any cash, it is not presented in the statement of cash flows. Only those capital expenditures that use cash are listed as cash flows from investing activities. That is, cash flows from investing activities should reflect the actual amount of cash spent to purchase plant assets or investment assets.

Noncash investing and financing transactions generally do affect *future* cash flows. Issuing notes payable to acquire equipment, for example, requires future cash payments for interest and principal on the notes, and should produce future operating cash flows from the equipment. Alternatively, converting bonds payable into common stock eliminates future cash payments related to the bonds, but may carry the expectation of future cash dividends. Knowledge of these types of events, therefore, is helpful to users of cash flow data who wish to assess a firm's future cash flows.

Information on noncash investing and financing transactions is disclosed in a schedule that is separate from the statement of cash flows. The separate schedule is reported either immediately below the statement of cash flows or among the notes to the financial statements.

Solving for Purchases of Plant Assets The remaining entry affecting plant assets is the purchase of plant assets for cash. The amount of plant assets purchased can be determined by solving for the missing amount in the Plant Assets T-account:

+	Plant Assets (A)		−
Beg. bal.	170,000		
		12,000	(1)
(2)	5,000		
(3)	X		
End. bal.	208,000		

Balancing the account requires that we solve for the unknown amount:

$$\$170{,}000 + \$5{,}000 + X - \$12{,}000 = \$208{,}000$$
$$X = \$45{,}000$$

Thus, plant assets costing $45,000 were purchased for cash. This amount is listed as a cash outflow under cash flows for investing activities.

Examining the cash flow statement for One World Café in **Exhibit 4.11**, we see that two cash flows are listed under investing activities: (1) a $45,000 cash outflow for the purchase of plant assets, and (2) a $4,000 cash inflow from the sale of plant assets. The purchase of plant assets costing $5,000 by issuing notes payable is not listed; nor is the increase in notes payable listed under financing activities.

Appendix 4A at the end of this chapter introduces a spreadsheet approach that can be used to prepare the statement of cash flows. The appendix uses the One World Café financial statements as the illustration.

MID-CHAPTER REVIEW 5

The balance sheet of Jack's Snacks, Inc. reports the following amounts:

	End-of-year	Beginning-of-year
Property, plant & equipment at cost	$670,000	$600,000
Accumulated depreciation	(150,000)	(140,000)
Property, plant & equipment, net	$520,000	$460,000

Additional information:

During the year, Jack's Snacks disposed of a used piece of equipment. The original cost of the equipment was $80,000 and, at the time of disposal, the accumulated depreciation on the equipment was $60,000. The purchaser of the used piece of equipment paid in cash, and Jack's Snacks reported a gain of $35,000 on the disposal.

All acquisitions of new property, plant, and equipment were paid for in cash.

Questions:

1. How much cash did Jack's Snacks receive from the used equipment disposal?
2. How much cash did Jack's Snacks spend to acquire new property, plant, and equipment during the year?
3. How much depreciation expense did Jack's Snacks record during the year?

The solution to this review problem can be found on pages 215–216.

The Effects of Foreign Currencies on the Cash Flow Statement

Multinational companies often engage in transactions that involve currencies other than U.S. dollars and may hold assets that were acquired with foreign currencies or liabilities that must be repaid in foreign currencies. Also, part of a company's cash balance may be held in a currency other than dollars. If the company prepares its financial statements in U.S. dollars, these foreign currency amounts must be converted, or *translated*, into dollars before preparing the financial statements. The process of translating transactions based in many currencies into one common currency for financial statement presentation is beyond the scope of an introductory text. However, foreign exchange rates fluctuate and these fluctuations can have an effect on the cash flow statement.

The statement of cash flows explains the change in the cash balance during the fiscal year, but part of this change may be due to changes in the dollar value of foreign currencies. This amount is typically small and it is not a cash flow, but it is included in the cash flow statement so that we can accurately reconcile the beginning balance in cash to the ending balance. The statement of cash flows for Nike, Inc. was summarized in Chapter 1 in **Exhibit 1.10** and is repeated here for illustration. A similar adjustment by CVS Health can be found toward the bottom of **Exhibit 4.1**.

NIKE Statement of Cash Flows For the Year Ended May 31, 2018 ($ millions)	
Operating cash flows	$4,955
Investing cash flows	276
Financing cash flows	(4,835)
Effect of exchange rate changes	45
Net decrease in cash and cash equivalents	441
Cash and equivalents, beginning of year	3,808
Cash and equivalents, end of year	$4,249

Supplemental Disclosures

When the indirect method is used in the statement of cash flows, three separate supplemental disclosures are required: (1) two specific operating cash outflows—cash paid for interest and cash paid for income taxes, (2) a schedule or description of all noncash investing and financing transactions, and (3) the firm's policy for determining which highly liquid, short-term investments are treated as cash equivalents. If the direct method is used, a reconciliation of net income to cash flows from operating activities is also required. A firm's policy regarding cash equivalents is placed in the financial statement notes. The other disclosures are reported either in the notes or at the bottom of the statement of cash flows.

One World Café Case Illustration One World Café incurred $200 of interest expense, which was paid in cash. It also reported income tax expense of $17,000 and reported a decrease in income taxes payable of $1,500 ($4,500 – $3,000). Thus, One World Café paid $18,500 ($17,000 + $1,500) in income taxes during 2018. It also had the noncash investment in plant assets costing $5,000, which was financed with notes payable. One World Café would provide the following disclosure:

Supplemental cash flow information	
Cash payments for interest	$ 200
Cash payments for income taxes	18,500
Noncash transaction—investment in plant assets financed with notes payable	5,000

LO5 Compute and interpret ratios that reflect a company's liquidity and solvency using information reported in the statement of cash flows.

5

ANALYZING FINANCIAL STATEMENTS

Cash is a special resource for companies because of its flexibility. At short notice, it can be used to fulfill obligations and to take advantage of investment opportunities. When companies run short of cash, their suppliers may be reluctant to deliver and lenders may be able to take over control of decision making. In Chapter 2, we introduced the current ratio, which compares the level of current assets to the level of current liabilities at a point in time. But the statement of cash flows gives us the opportunity to compare a company's ongoing cash generating activities to its obligations and to its investment opportunities.

Interpreting Indirect Method Cash from Operations

We want to interpret the cash flows from operations presented using the indirect method.

When companies use the indirect method to present their cash flows from operating activities, it is difficult to interpret the numbers presented to adjust net income to cash from operating activities. For instance, in **Exhibit 4.11**, One World Café reports $6,000 for the change in accounts receivable. Does that mean that the company received cash payments of $6,000 from its customers? It does not! Every item in the reconciliation has to be interpreted relative to the net income at the top. Net income includes revenue of $390,000, and the adjustment addition of

$6,000 means that One World Café received payments of $390,000 + $6,000 = $396,000 from its customers.

The $3,500 adjustment for wages payable does not mean that One World Café received payments of $3,500 from its employees. Rather, the company paid its employees $3,500 less than it recognized as wage expense in determining net income. The adjustment for income tax payable was $(1,500), but that doesn't mean that One World Café's tax payments totaled $1,500 for the year. Rather, the $35,000 net income already reflects a charge for tax expense of $17,000, so the adjustment means that One World's payments for income tax totaled $17,000 + $1,500 = $18,500. Depreciation expense is added back not because it increases cash, but because it is an expense that doesn't require a cash outflow.

How should we interpret the changes in operating assets and liabilities? These assets and liabilities are a function of both the scale of the business and the practices of the business. If we're selling to 10% more customers this year, then we would expect an increase in receivables of about 10% over the previous year. If the increase is substantially more than that amount, then there must have been some other change as well. Perhaps increasing sales required that we give more favorable payment terms and customers are taking longer to pay. Such a development could cause an investor to question the "quality" of the company's earnings. If sales are constant and accounts payable are increasing, that may imply that the company is taking longer to pay its suppliers. That change would appear as a positive adjustment in the indirect method cash from operations, but it may indicate an unfavorable development for the company.

The indirect method may also alert us to gains and losses from nonoperating transactions. These gains and losses are often in "other income" in the income statement, and therefore it's easy for a financial statement reader to miss them. The fact that gains must be subtracted and losses must be added back in the indirect cash from operations gives them a prominence that they don't have in the income statement.

Analysis Objective

We are trying to gauge CVS Health Corporations' generation of cash from its operating activities relative to its average short-term obligations found in the balance sheet.

Analysis Tool Operating Cash Flow to Current Liabilities (OCFCL)

$$\textbf{Operating cash flow to current liabilities} = \frac{\textbf{Operating cash flow}}{\textbf{Average current liabilities}}$$

Applying the Operating Cash Flow to Current Liabilities Ratio to CVS Health Corporation

$$\textbf{2015:} \frac{\$8,539}{\$21,098} = 0.40 \text{ or } 40\%$$

$$\textbf{2016:} \frac{\$10,141}{\$24,710} = 0.41 \text{ or } 41\%$$

$$\textbf{2017:} \frac{\$8,007}{\$28,449} = 0.28 \text{ or } 28\%$$

Guidance CVS Health Corporation's OCFCL is lower than the retail industry average. CVS Health's business is relatively low-margin, which means that it requires a large flow of resources to generate profits and cash from operations, and that large volume of activity results in high levels of current liabilities relative to the cash generated. The OCFCL ratio complements the current ratio and quick ratio introduced in Chapter 2. CVS Health's current ratio is 1.02, also lower than average for the retail industry, and its quick ratio of 0.49 is right at the industry average.

CVS Health Corporation in Context

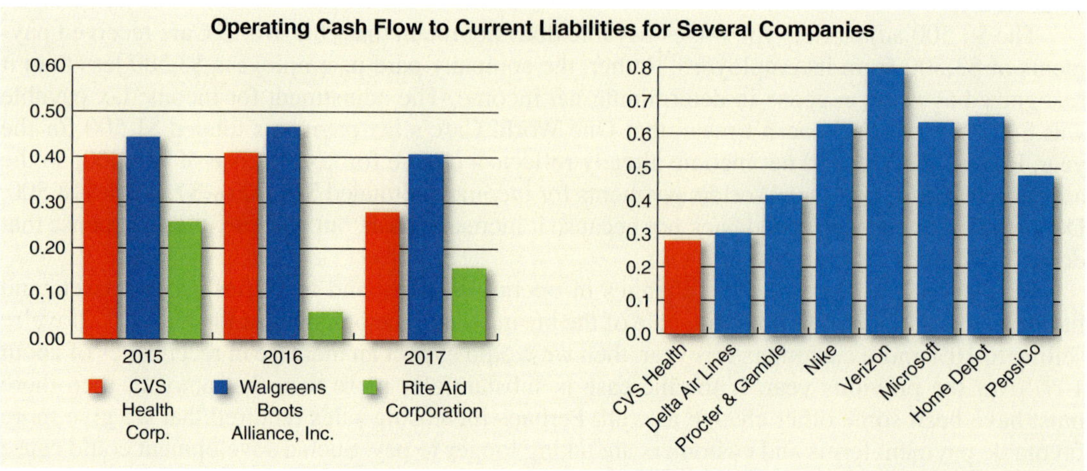

Takeaways Over the past three years, CVS Health's OCFCL ratio compares reasonably favorably to the two competitors that are included in the graph on the left. Both Walgreens Boots' and Rite Aid's ratios are below the industry average, with Walgreen Boots showing a more stable ratio. Rite Aid is consistently below both of the other companies. The 2017 drop in CVS Health's OCFCL ratio is due to a 20% drop in cash from operations and a current liability increase caused by an impending long-term loan repayment. The comparison of focus companies' OCFCLs in the right-hand graph show a range from 0.305 for Delta Air Lines to a high of over 0.799 for Verizon. CVS Health is lower than any of these companies.

Other Considerations There are some transactions that change both the numerator and the denominator, like using cash to pay current operating liabilities. Such a transaction would decrease both the numerator and the denominator, and these changes have an indeterminate effect on the ratio. Paying $100 to a creditor decreases operating cash flow and ending current liabilities by $100, with the average current liabilities decreasing by $50. If the OCFCL is below 2.0 prior to the transaction, it will be even lower after the transaction. If the OCFCL is greater than 2.0 prior to the transaction, it will be even higher after the transaction. Delaying a payment to the creditor would have the opposite effect.

It is also important to take a look at the components of current liabilities. Sometimes there is a large portion of long-term debt that comes due and increases current liabilities for one year. Or, in the case of Delta Air Lines, more than 25% of their current liabilities represent unearned revenue from customers who have purchased tickets in advance of travel (like the gift certificates at NBS). For this liability, Delta doesn't have to pay someone; they just need to keep flying.

Analysis Objective

We wish to determine CVS Health's ability to fund the capital expenditures needed to maintain and grow its operations and to make acquisitions.

Does CVS Health generate enough cash from its operations to make its capital investments? If it does not, then the company will have to finance those investments by selling other investments, by borrowing (resulting in future interest costs), by getting cash from shareholders, or by reducing cash balances. If it generates more cash than needed for capital expenditures, then the additional cash can be used to grow the business (e.g., by acquisition) or to distribute cash to investors. Two measures may be used in making this assessment. The first of these measures, operating cash flow to capital expenditures, is a ratio that facilitates comparisons with other companies. The second, free cash flow,[3] is a monetary amount that reflects the funds available for investing in new ventures, buying back stock, paying down debt, or returning funds to stockholders in the form of dividends. The concept is also used in mergers and acquisitions to indicate cash that would be available to the acquirer for investment.

[3] Free cash flow can be defined in several ways, but it always includes a measure of the cash resources generated by the company's current operations minus a measure of the cash required to sustain those operations. One of the simpler, more common definitions is presented here.

Analysis Tools Operating Cash Flow to Capital Expenditures (OCFCX)

$$\textbf{Operating cash flow to capital expenditures} = \frac{\textbf{Operating cash flow}}{\textbf{Annual capital expenditures}}$$

Free Cash Flow (FCF)

Free cash flow = Operating cash flow − Net capital expenditures

Applying the Operating Cash Flow to Capital Expenditures Ratio and Free Cash Flow to CVS Health Corporation

	OCFCX	FCF
2015:	$\frac{\$8{,}539}{\$2{,}367} = 3.61$ or 361%	\$8,529 − \$2,332 = \$6,197
2016:	$\frac{\$10{,}141}{\$2{,}224} = 4.56$ or 456%	\$10,141 − \$2,187 = \$7,954
2017:	$\frac{\$8{,}007}{\$1{,}818} = 4.40$ or 440%	\$8,007 − \$1,885 = \$6,122

Guidance Operating cash flows to capital expenditures ratios that exceed 1.0 (or free cash flows that are positive) mean that the company can make its capital investments without obtaining additional financing or reducing its cash balances. The excess cash could be used to reduce borrowing, make acquisitions, or it could be returned to shareholders. CVS Health Corporation's ratios are quite steady across these years, and the company has used this stability to return an average of $6.5 billion per year to shareholders in the form of dividends and share repurchases. However, the planned merger with Aetna will require an amount of cash that far exceeds the free cash flow generated by its current operations, necessitating new borrowing and the use of common stock to fund part of the purchase price.

CVS Health Corporation in Context

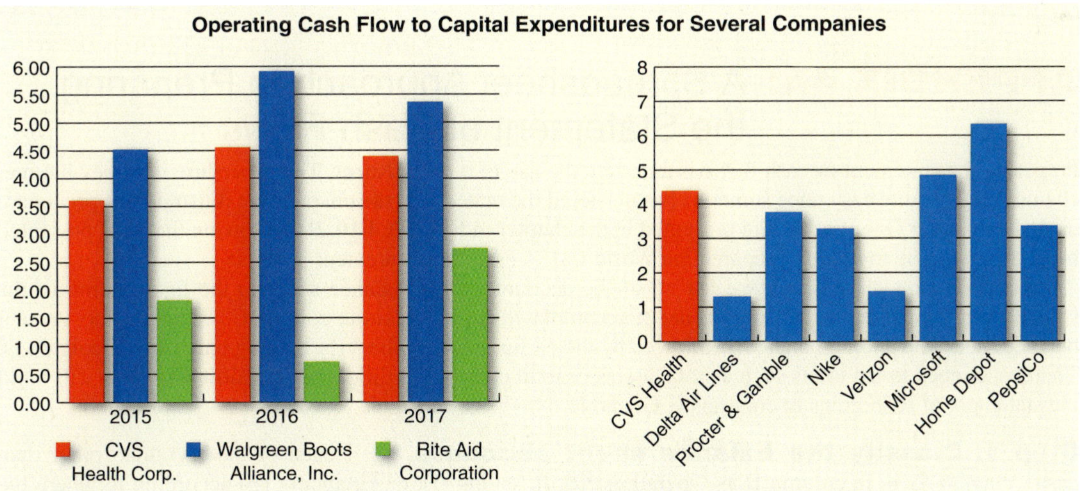

Takeaways OCFCX remained relatively steady over the last three years for CVS Health, and its OCFCX is slightly lower than Walgreens Boots and higher than Rite Aid. Like CVS Health, Walgreens Boots and Rite Aid have used the additional cash flow to acquire other businesses, pay dividends and repay long-term debt. But CVS Health's proposed merger with Aetna would require it to issue "approximately $45.0 billion of new debt." We can see that CVS Health's OCFCX is in the middle of the focus companies' levels. These companies can use the cash in excess of capital expenditures to make acquisitions or to return cash to shareholders in the form of dividends or common stock repurchases.

Other Considerations Measurement of cash flows is regarded as more objective than measures of income and less dependent on management judgments and estimates. But it may be subject to "lumpy" behavior from management's decisions, particularly for smaller companies. Capital expenditures may differ significantly from year to year if management takes on large, but infrequent, projects. A series of high values of OCFCX followed by a low value might mean deterioration in cash generating performance, but it might also mean that management has been accumulating cash in anticipation of a major project.

RESEARCH INSIGHT

Is the Cash Flow Statement Useful? Some analysts rely on cash flow forecasts to value common stock. Research shows that both net income and operating cash flows are correlated with stock prices, but that stock prices are more highly correlated with net income than with cash flows. So, do we need both statements? Evidence suggests that by using *both* net income and cash flow information, we can improve our forecasts of *future* cash flows. Also, net income and cash flow together are more highly correlated with stock prices than either net income or cash flow alone. This result suggests that, for purposes of stock valuation, information from the cash flow statement complements information from the income statement.

CHAPTER-END REVIEW

Refer to One World Café's statement of cash flows and comparative balance sheets from **Exhibits 4.10** and **4.11** to complete the following.

Required

1. Calculate the operating cash flow to current liabilities (OCFCL) ratio for One World Café and interpret your findings. Assume that the notes payable are due within the year and are a current liability.
2. Calculate One World Café's operating cash flow to capital expenditures (OCFCX) ratio. What observations can you make about your findings?
3. Calculate the free cash flow (FCF) for One World Café.

The solution to this review problem can be found on page 216.

APPENDIX 4A: A Spreadsheet Approach to Preparing the Statement of Cash Flows

6

LO6 Use a spreadsheet to construct the statement of cash flows.

Preparing the statement of cash flows is aided by the use of a spreadsheet. The procedure is somewhat mechanical and is quite easy once someone has mastered the material in the chapter. We illustrate this procedure using the data for One World Café presented in the chapter in **Exhibit 4.10**. By following the steps presented below, we are able to readily prepare One World Café's cash flow statement for 2018.

To set up the spreadsheet, we list all of the accounts in the balance sheet in the first column of the spreadsheet. We list depreciable assets net of accumulated depreciation. In column C, we list the most recent balance sheet (the ending balances) followed by the earlier balance sheet (beginning balances) in column D. There is no need to list totals such as total assets or total current liabilities. See **Exhibit 4A.1**. We will build the statement of cash flows in columns F, G, and H.

Step 1: Classify the balance sheet accounts. For each of the accounts (other than cash), classify them in column B as Operating (O), Investing (I), or Financing (F) according to where the effect of changes in that account will appear in the statement of cash flows. There are two accounts that have a double classification. Changes in the plant assets, net account can be caused by depreciation expense (which will appear in the indirect method cash from operations) and by investing activities, so we label it as (O, I). Changes in the retained earnings account are caused by net income (which appears in the indirect method cash from operations) and dividends, so we label it as (O, F).

For those rows labeled I or F, insert two rows below: one for increases in the account and one for decreases in the account because we must report increases and decreases separately. For plant assets, net, insert three rows below: one for depreciation expense, one for plant asset acquisitions, and one for plant asset sales. For retained earnings, insert two rows below: one for net income and one for dividends.

EXHIBIT 4A.1 Cash Flow Spreadsheet for One World Café

	A	B	C	D	E	F	G	H	I	J
1		O, I or				Effect of change on cash flow			No effect	Total
2		F?	2018	2017	Change	Operating	Investing	Financing	on cash	F,G,H,I
3	**Assets**									
4	Cash.		8,000	12,000	(4,000)					
5										
6	Accounts receivable	O	22,000	28,000	(6,000)	6,000				6,000
7	Inventory.	O	94,000	66,000	28,000	(28,000)				(28,000)
8	Prepaid advertising.	O	12,000	9,000	3,000	(3,000)				(3,000)
9	Plant assets, net.	O,I	136,000	109,000	27,000					
10	Depreciation expense					17,000				
11	Plant assets purchased.						(45,000)		(5,000)	(27,000)
12	Plant assets sold.					2,000	4,000			
13										
14	**Liabilities**									
15	Accounts payable	O	27,000	14,000	13,000	13,000				13,000
16	Wages payable.	O	6,000	2,500	3,500	3,500				3,500
17	Income tax payable	O	3,000	4,500	(1,500)	(1,500)				(1,500)
18	Notes payable.	F	5,000	—	5,000					
19	New borrowing								5,000	5,000
20	Borrowing repayments									
21										
22	**Shareholders' Equity**									
23	Common stock	F	134,000	125,000	9,000					
24	New issue of common stock. . . .							9,000		9,000
25	Repurchase of common stock . .									
26	Retained earnings	O,F	97,000	78,000	19,000					
27	Net income					35,000				19,000
28	Dividends							(16,000)		
29										
30	**Totals**.					44,000	(41,000)	(7,000)	—	(4,000)

Step 2: Compute the changes in the balance sheet accounts. Subtract the beginning balances in each account from the ending balances and record these in column E. We highlight the change in the cash balance, because this is the amount that we are trying to explain. At this point it is useful to verify that the change in cash is equal to the changes in liabilities plus the changes in stockholders' equity minus the changes in noncash assets:

$$\Delta \text{ Cash} = \Delta \text{ Liabilities} + \Delta \text{ Stockholders' Equity} - \Delta \text{ Noncash Assets}$$

In effect, we're going to use changes on the right-hand side of this equation to explain the changes in cash on the left-hand side.

Step 3: Handle the accounts that have single classifications. For those accounts that are operating-only assets (accounts receivable, inventory, prepaid expenses, etc.), we enter in column F the *negative* of the value in column E. The $28,000 increase in inventories in column E results in $(28,000) for the operating cash flows in column F. Changes in assets have the opposite effect on cash. Increases in assets have a negative effect on cash, while decreases in assets lead to positive adjustments to cash.

For those accounts that are operating only liabilities (accounts payable, wages payable, taxes payable, etc.), we enter in column F the value in column E. The $13,000 increase in accounts payable produces a $13,000 entry in column F.

For those accounts that are financing only (notes payable, common stock), we enter in column H the cash effect(s) of the change in column E. For example, we must be aware that the common stock account could have changed due to both issuing stock for cash and repurchasing stock for cash. For One World Café, there was only a $9,000 inflow due to a new stock issue in column H. (We will deal with the notes payable changes in the next step.)

One World Café has no assets that are investing only, but for such accounts (marketable securities, investments, etc.), we would again make entries for increases and decreases separately. And, since these are assets, the change in the balance sheet has the opposite sign of the entry in the cash flow columns. For instance, if One World Café had invested $10,000 in a financial security, its investments asset would increase, and we would put an entry of $(10,000) in column G.

Step 4: Enter the effect of investing/financing transactions that do not involve cash. We know from the information provided about One World Café that it arranged the purchase of $5,000 of plant assets by signing a note payable for the same amount. This transaction affected an investing asset and a financing liability at the same time, and we put the effects into column I. $5,000 is put in the new borrowing row (19), and $(5,000) is put in the plant assets purchased row (11). This transaction will not appear in the cash flow statement in columns F, G, and H, but it does explain some of the changes in the company's assets and liabilities.

Step 5: Analyze the change in retained earnings. Some accounts require special attention because the change in the account balance involves two types of cash flow effects. For example, the change in retained earnings is actually two changes—net income, which is related to operations, and dividends, which is a financing cash outflow.

One World Café's retained earnings increased by $19,000. It reported net income of $35,000, which is listed as an operating item (because we're using the indirect method), and paid dividends of $16,000, a cash outflow listed under financing activities. For clarity, it is helpful to list each of these changes on a separate line. Thus, we have inserted two lines into the spreadsheet immediately below retained earnings—the first for net income and the second for dividends. The $35,000 inflow and the $16,000 outflow net to $19,000.

Step 6: Analyze the change in plant assets. A change in depreciable assets is actually the result of both operating and investing items. The change in plant assets can be explained by looking at the individual transactions that caused the change. As was the case with retained earnings, it is helpful to list each of these transactions in a separate row in the spreadsheet. Thus, we have inserted three rows into the spreadsheet immediately below the change in plant assets. First, we recall that One World Café reported depreciation expense of $17,000, which reduced its plant assets, net. This is listed in the first row under plant assets as a positive adjustment to cash flow from operations because cash flow effects on the asset side have the opposite sign.

In the next row, we list purchases of plant assets. One World Café purchased plant assets for $45,000 in cash, which is listed under investing as a cash outflow in column F. There was also the $5,000 purchase of plant assets that was financed with notes payable. This transaction did not affect cash so it's in column I.

In the third row below plant assets, we list the sale of plant assets. One World Café sold plant assets for $4,000 cash, recognizing a loss of $2,000. The loss is listed in the operations column (as a positive adjustment to operating cash flow) and the proceeds from the sale are listed under investing as a cash inflow in column F.

When all of the balance sheet changes have been analyzed, the change for each account should add up to the sum of the effect on operating, investing, and financing cash flows, plus the amount in the "no effect" column. That is, for each change listed in the spreadsheet in column E, we can add columns F, G, H, and I to get the change in the balance sheet account in column J. For retained earnings: $35,000 – $16,000 = $19,000. For assets, the total will be the *negative* of the change. Adding up entries for plant assets: $17,000 – $45,000 – $5,000 + $2,000 + $4,000 = –$27,000, which is minus the amount in column E, row 9.

Step 7: Total the columns. We add up the effects listed in columns F, G, H, and I to get the cash flow subtotals. One World Café had cash flow from operations of $44,000, investing cash flows of –$41,000 and financing cash flows of –$7,000. The total for the "no effect" column (column I) should be $0, because the entries in this column had no effect on cash flow. Finally, we add up these totals to make sure that the cash flow effects equal the change in cash: $44,000 – $41,000 – $7,000 – $0 = –$4,000. If the totals do not add up to the change in cash, then there must be an error in analyzing one or more of the balance sheet changes. For example, if we had forgotten to subtract dividends, then the cash flow effects in columns F, G, and H would not add up to the change in retained earnings listed in column E. Likewise, if we had mistakenly omitted the sale of plant assets, then the change in plant assets would not add up correctly. Totaling the columns and rows is a check to verify that our analysis is complete and correct.

Step 8: Prepare the cash flow statement. Starting with operating cash flows (column F), we list each of the items in the statement of cash flows. We start with net income, and then add depreciation and the loss on the sale of plant assets, then we list the remaining adjustments, starting with the change in accounts receivable and working down the column. Next, we do the same for the items listed in the investing (column G) and financing (column H) sections of the cash flow statement. The resulting statement is identical to the statement presented in **Exhibit 4.11**.

APPENDIX 4A REVIEW

The comparative balance sheets and income statement for Rocky Road Bicycles, Inc., are as follows.

ROCKY ROAD BICYCLES, INC. Comparative Balance Sheets At December 31	2018	2017
Assets		
Cash	$ 106,000	$ 96,000
Accounts receivable	156,000	224,000
Inventory	752,000	528,000
Prepaid rent	68,000	72,000
Plant assets	1,692,000	1,360,000
Less accumulated depreciation	(562,000)	(488,000)
Total assets	$2,212,000	$1,792,000
Liabilities		
Accounts payable	$ 216,000	$ 112,000
Wages payable	18,000	20,000
Income tax payable	44,000	36,000
Equity		
Common stock	1,142,000	1,000,000
Retained earnings	792,000	624,000
Total liabilities and equity	$2,212,000	$1,792,000

Additional Information:

- Rocky Road reported net income of $326,000 in 2018.
- Depreciation expense was $122,000 in 2018.
- Rocky Road sold plant assets during 2018. The plant assets originally cost $88,000, with accumulated depreciation of $48,000, and were sold for a gain of $16,000.
- Rocky Road declared and paid a $158,000 cash dividend in 2018.

REQUIRED

Use a spreadsheet to create a statement of cash flows for Rocky Road Bicycles, Inc.

The solution to this review problem can be found on page 217.

SUMMARY

Explain the purpose of the statement of cash flows and classify cash transactions by type of business activity: operating, investing, or financing. (p. 158) **LO1**

- The statement of cash flows summarizes information about the flow of cash into and out of the business.
- Operating cash flow includes any cash transactions related to selling goods or rendering services, as well as interest payments and receipts, tax payments, and any transaction not specifically classified as investing or financing.
- Investing cash flow includes acquiring and disposing of plant assets, buying and selling securities, including securities of other companies, and lending and subsequently collecting funds from a borrower.
- Financing cash flow includes all cash received or paid to shareholders, including stock issued or repurchased and dividends paid. In addition, it includes amounts borrowed and repaid to creditors.

Construct the operating activities section of the statement of cash flows using the direct method. (p. 162) **LO2**

- The direct method presents net cash flow from operating activities by showing the major categories of operating cash receipts and payments.
- The operating cash receipts and payments are usually determined by converting the accrual revenues and expenses to corresponding cash amounts.

LO3 **Reconcile cash flows from operations to net income and use the indirect method to compute operating cash flows. (p. 171)**

- Because operating cash flow differs from net income, a reconciliation of these two amounts helps financial statement users understand the sources of this difference.
- The indirect method reconciles net income and operating cash flows by making adjustments for noncash revenues and expenses and changes in balance sheet accounts related to operations.

LO4 **Construct the investing and financing activities sections of the statement of cash flows. (p. 174)**

- Cash investment outlays are captured in the investing section along with any cash receipts from asset disposals. Because cash receipts include any gain on sale (or reflect any loss), the gain (loss) must be subtracted from (added to) net income in the operating section to avoid double-counting.
- Cash obtained from the issuance of securities or borrowings, and any repayments of debt, are disclosed in the financing section. Cash dividends are also included in this section. Interest payments are included in the operating section of the statement.
- Some events, for example assets donated to the firm, provide resources to the business that are important but which do not involve cash outlays. These events are disclosed separately, along with the statement of cash flows, as supplementary disclosures or in the notes.

LO5 **Compute and interpret ratios that reflect a company's liquidity and solvency using information reported in the statement of cash flows. (p. 182)**

- Interpreting indirect method cash from operations requires reference to those items that comprise net income. Each adjustment is intended to modify an income statement item to bring it to cash from operations.
- Two ratios of importance that are based on cash flows include:
  - Operating cash flow to current liabilities—a measure of the adequacy of current operations to cover current liability payments.
  - Operating cash flow to capital expenditures—a reflection of a company's ability to replace or expand its activities based on the level of current operations.
- Free cash flow is defined as: Cash flow from operations − Net capital expenditures.
- Free cash flow is a measure of a company's ability to apply its resources to new endeavors.

LO6 **Appendix 4A: Use a spreadsheet to construct the statement of cash flows. (p. 186)**

- A spreadsheet helps to prepare the statement of cash flows by classifying the effect of each change in the balance sheet as operating, investing, financing, or not affecting cash.
- The spreadsheet approach relies on the key relationship:

  Cash = Liabilities + Stockholders' equity − Noncash assets

GUIDANCE ANSWERS . . . YOU MAKE THE CALL

You are the Chief Accountant The transaction's effect will appear in the investing section of the cash flow statement in the amount of a positive $1.1 billion.

You are the Securities Analyst A company's operating activities are the "engine" that produces the cash flows that allow the investment necessary for growth and the funds that may be returned to the sources of capital. Accounting standards say that cash flows from operating activities include cash receipts from sales of goods or services, *including receipts from collection or sale of accounts.* So, receipts from the sale of accounts receivable should be included in cash from operations, along with ordinary cash receipts from customers. However, an analyst should consider the circumstances of the sale of receivables. Is such a sale part of the company's regular practices, enabling it to cut its borrowing or increase its growth? Or, if the sale is a new transaction, does it indicate that the company is having difficulty collecting from its customers or experiencing unusual expenditures or financing problems? Companies will almost always sell receivables at a discount—how much is it giving up to have access to the cash today? Many analysts argue that operating cash flows do not increase as a result of such transactions and that analysts should adjust the statement of cash flows to classify the sale of receivables as a financing activity.

KEY RATIOS

$$\text{Operating cash flow to current liabilities} = \frac{\text{Operating cash flow}}{\text{Average current liabilities}}$$

$$\text{Operating cash flow to capital expenditures} = \frac{\text{Operating cash flow}}{\text{Annual capital expenditures}}$$

Free cash flow = Operating cash flow – Net capital expenditures

KEY TERMS

Cash equivalents (p. 158)
Direct method (p. 173)
Financing activities (p. 160)
Indirect method (p. 173)
Investing activities (p. 160)
Liquidity (p. 158)
Noncash investing and financing activities (p. 180)
Operating activities (p. 160)
Solvency (p. 158)
Statement of cash flows (p. 158)
Treasury stock (p. 161)

Assignments with the MBC logo in the margin are available in myBusinessCourse. See the Preface of the book for details.

MULTIPLE CHOICE

Multiple Choice Answers
1. a 2. c 3. d 4. c 5. c

1. Which of the following is not disclosed in a statement of cash flows?
   a. A transfer of cash to a cash equivalent investment
   b. The amount of cash at year-end
   c. Cash outflows from investing activities during the period
   d. Cash inflows from financing activities during the period

2. Which of the following events appears in the cash flows from investing activities section of the statement of cash flows?
   a. Cash received from customers
   b. Cash received from issuance of common stock
   c. Cash purchase of equipment
   d. Cash payment of dividends

3. Which of the following events appears in the cash flows from financing activities section of the statement of cash flows?
   a. Cash purchase of equipment
   b. Cash purchase of bonds issued by another company
   c. Cash received as repayment for funds loaned
   d. Cash purchase of treasury stock

4. Tyler Company has a net income of $49,000 and the following related items:

Depreciation expense	$ 5,000
Accounts receivable increase	2,000
Inventory decrease	10,000
Accounts payable decrease	4,000

Using the indirect method, what is Tyler's net cash flow from operations?
   a. $42,000
   b. $46,000
   c. $58,000
   d. $38,000

5. Refer to information in Mid-Chapter Review 2. Assume that notes payable are not due within the coming year and are classified as a noncurrent liability. The operating cash flow to current liabilities ratio for Mug Shots, Inc., in December is
   a. 6.4%.
   b. 2.9%.
   c. 2.6%.
   d. impossible to determine from the data provided.

Superscript A denotes assignments based on Appendix 4A.

QUESTIONS

Q4-1. What is the definition of *cash equivalents*? Give three examples of cash equivalents.

Q4-2. Why are cash equivalents included with cash in a statement of cash flows?

Q4-3. What are the three major types of activities classified on a statement of cash flows? Give an example of a cash inflow and a cash outflow in each classification.

Q4-4. In which of the three activity categories of a statement of cash flows would each of the following items appear? Indicate for each item whether it represents a cash inflow or a cash outflow:
   a. Cash purchase of equipment.
   b. Cash collection on loans.
   c. Cash dividends paid.
   d. Cash dividends received.
   e. Cash proceeds from issuing stock.
   f. Cash receipts from customers.
   g. Cash interest paid.
   h. Cash interest received.

Q4-5. Traverse Company acquired a $3,000,000 building by issuing $3,000,000 worth of bonds payable. In terms of cash flow reporting, what type of transaction is this? What special disclosure requirements apply to a transaction of this type?

Q4-6. Why are noncash investing and financing transactions disclosed as supplemental information to a statement of cash flows?

Q4-7. Why is a statement of cash flows a useful financial statement?

Q4-8. What is the difference between the direct method and the indirect method of presenting net cash flow from operating activities?

Q4-9. In determining net cash flow from operating activities using the indirect method, why must we add depreciation back to net income? Give an example of another item that is added back to net income under the indirect method.

Q4-10. Vista Company sold for $98,000 cash land originally costing $70,000. The company recorded a gain on the sale of $28,000. How is this event reported in a statement of cash flows using the indirect method?

Q4-11. A firm uses the indirect method. Using the following information, what is its net cash flow from operating activities?

Net income	$88,000
Accounts receivable decrease	13,000
Inventory increase	9,000
Accounts payable decrease	3,500
Income tax payable increase	1,500
Depreciation expense	6,000

Q4-12. What separate disclosures are required for a company that reports a statement of cash flows using the indirect method?

Q4-13. If a business had a net loss for the year, under what circumstances would the statement of cash flows show a positive net cash flow from operating activities?

Q4-14. A firm is converting its accrual revenues to corresponding cash amounts using the direct method. Sales on the income statement are $925,000. Beginning and ending accounts receivable on the balance sheet are $58,000 and $44,000, respectively. What is the amount of cash received from customers?

Q4-15. A firm reports $86,000 wages expense in its income statement. If beginning and ending wages payable are $3,900 and $2,800, respectively, what is the amount of cash paid to employees?

Q4-16. A firm reports $43,000 advertising expense in its income statement. If beginning and ending prepaid advertising are $6,000 and $7,600, respectively, what is the amount of cash paid for advertising?

Q4-17. Rusk Company sold equipment for $5,100 cash that had cost $35,000 and had $29,000 of accumulated depreciation. How is this event reported in a statement of cash flows using the direct method?

Q4-18. What separate disclosures are required for a company that reports a statement of cash flows using the direct method?

Q4-19. How is the operating cash flow to current liabilities ratio calculated? Explain its use.

Q4-20. How is the operating cash flow to capital expenditures ratio calculated? Explain its use.

MINI EXERCISES

M4-21. Identifying the Impact of Account Changes on Cash Flow from Operating Activities (Indirect Method)

LO1, 3, 4

Target
NYSE :: TGT

The following account information was presented as adjustments to net income in a recent statement of cash flows for Target Corporation. Determine whether each item would be a positive adjustment or a negative adjustment to net income in determining cash from operations. ($ millions).

a. Operating activities increased accounts payable by $1,307.
b. Operating activities increased inventories by $348.
c. Early extinguishment of debt resulted in a loss of $123.
d. Depreciation and amortization expense was $2,445.
e. Operating activities increased other assets by $168.

M4-22. Classifying Cash Flows

LO1

For each of the items below, indicate whether the cash flow relates to an operating activity, an investing activity, or a financing activity.

a. Cash receipts from customers for services rendered.
b. Sale of long-term investments for cash.
c. Acquisition of plant assets for cash.
d. Payment of income taxes.
e. Bonds payable issued for cash.
f. Payment of cash dividends declared in previous year.
g. Purchase of short-term investments (not cash equivalents) for cash.

M4-23. Classifying Cash Flow Statement Components

LO1, 3

General Mills, Inc.
NYSE :: GIS

The following table presents selected items from a recent cash flow statement of General Mills, Inc. For each item, determine whether the amount would be disclosed in the cash flow statement under operating activities, investing activities, or financing activities. (General Mills uses the indirect method of reporting cash flows from operating activities.)

GENERAL MILLS, INC. Selected Items from Its Cash Flow Statement	
1	Payment of long-term debt
2	Change in receivables
3	Depreciation and amortization
4	Change in prepaid expenses
5	Dividends paid
6	Stock-based compensation
7	Cash received from sales of assets and businesses
8	Net earnings
9	Change in accounts payable
10	Proceeds from common stock issued
11	Purchases of land, buildings, and equipment

LO1, 4

M4-24. Classifying Cash Flows

For each of the items below, indicate whether it is (1) a cash flow from an operating activity, (2) a cash flow from an investing activity, (3) a cash flow from a financing activity, (4) a noncash investing and financing activity, or (5) none of the above.

a. Paid cash to retire bonds payable at a loss.
b. Received cash as settlement of a lawsuit.
c. Acquired a patent in exchange for common stock.
d. Received advance payments from customers on orders for custom-made goods.
e. Gave large cash contribution to local university.
f. Invested cash in 60-day commercial paper (a cash equivalent).

LO2, 3

M4-25. Reconciling Net Income and Cash Flow from Operations Using FSET

For fiscal year 2018, Beyer GmbH had the following summary information available concerning its operating activities. The company had no investing or financing activities this year.

1.	Sales of merchandise to customers on credit	€507,400
2.	Sales of merchandise to customers for cash	91,500
3.	Cost of merchandise sold on credit	320,100
4.	Cost of merchandise sold for cash	63,400
5.	Purchases of merchandise from suppliers on credit	351,600
6.	Purchases of merchandise from suppliers for cash	47,700
7.	Collections from customers on accounts receivable	483,400
8.	Cash payments to suppliers on accounts payable	340,200
9.	Operating expenses (all paid in cash)	172,300

REQUIRED

a. Enter the items above into the Financial Statement Effects Template. Under noncash assets, use two separate columns for accounts receivable and inventories. Calculate the totals for each column.
b. What was the company's net income for the year? What was the cash flow from operating activities? (Use the direct method.)
c. Indicate the direction and amounts by which each of the following accounts changed during the year.
   1. Accounts receivable
   2. Merchandise inventory
   3. Accounts payable
d. Using your results above, prepare the operating activities section of the statement of cash flows using the indirect format.

LO3

M4-26. Calculating Net Cash Flow from Operating Activities (Indirect Method)

The following information was obtained from Galena Company's comparative balance sheets. Assume that Galena Company's 2018 income statement showed depreciation expense of $8,000, a gain on sale of investments of $9,000, and net income of $45,000. Calculate the net cash flow from operating activities using the indirect method.

	Dec. 31, 2018	Dec. 31, 2017
Cash	$ 19,000	$ 9,000
Accounts receivable	44,000	35,000
Inventory	55,000	49,000
Prepaid rent	6,000	8,000
Long-term investments	21,000	34,000
Plant assets	150,000	106,000
Accumulated depreciation	40,000	32,000
Accounts payable	24,000	20,000
Income tax payable	4,000	6,000
Common stock	121,000	92,000
Retained earnings	106,000	91,000

LO2, 3

M4-27. Reconciling Net Income and Cash Flow from Operations Using FSET

For fiscal year 2018, Riffe Enterprises had the following summary information available concerning its operating activities. The company had no investing or financing activities this year.

1.	Sales of services to customers on credit	$769,200
2.	Sales of services to customers for cash	46,200
3.	Employee compensation earned	526,700
4.	Cash payment in advance to landlord for offices	149,100
5.	Cash paid to employees for compensation	521,600
6.	Rental expense for offices used over the year	117,900
7.	Collections from customers on accounts receivable	724,100
8.	Operating expenses (all paid in cash)	122,800
9.	Depreciation expense	23,000

REQUIRED

a. Enter the items above into the Financial Statement Effects Template. Under noncash assets, use three separate columns for accounts receivable and prepaid rent and the accumulated depreciation contra-asset. Calculate the totals for each column.

b. What was the company's net income for the year? What was the cash flow from operating activities? (Use the direct method.)

c. Indicate the direction and amounts by which each of the following accounts changed during the year.

1. Accounts receivable
2. Prepaid rent
3. Accumulated depreciation
4. Wages payable

d. Using your results above, prepare the operating activities section of the statement of cash flows using the indirect format.

M4-28. Calculating Net Cash Flow from Operating Activities (Indirect Method) **LO3**

Weber Company had a $21,000 net loss from operations for 2018. Depreciation expense for 2018 was $8,600 and a 2018 cash dividend of $6,000 was declared and paid. Balances of the current asset and current liability accounts at the beginning and end of 2018 follow. Did Weber Company's 2018 operating activities provide or use cash? Use the indirect method to determine your answer.

	Ending	Beginning
Cash	$ 3,500	$ 7,000
Accounts receivable	16,000	25,000
Inventory	50,000	53,000
Prepaid expenses	6,000	9,000
Accounts payable	12,000	8,000
Accrued liabilities	5,000	7,600

M4-29. Classifying Cash Flow Statement Components and Determining Their Effects **LO1, 3**

Nordstrom, Inc.
NYSE :: JWN

The following table presents selected items from a recent cash flow statement of **Nordstrom, Inc.**

a. For each item, determine whether the amount would be disclosed in the cash flow statement under operating activities, investing activities, or financing activities. (Nordstrom uses the indirect method of reporting.)

b. For each item, determine whether it will appear as a positive or negative in determining the net increase in cash and cash equivalents.

NORDSTROM, INC. Consolidated Statement of Cash Flows—Selected Items	
1	Decrease in accounts receivable
2	Capital expenditures
3	Proceeds from long-term borrowings
4	Increase in deferred income tax net liability
5	Principal payments on long-term borrowings
6	Increase in merchandise inventories
7	Increase in prepaid expenses and other assets
8	Proceeds from issuances under stock compensation plans
9	Increase in accounts payable
10	Net earnings
11	Payments for repurchase of common stock
12	Increase in accrued salaries, wages, and related benefits
13	Cash dividends paid
14	Depreciation and amortization expenses

LO2 **M4-30. Calculating Operating Cash Flows (Direct Method)**

Calculate the cash flow for each of the following cases.

a. Cash paid for rent:

Rent expense	$60,000
Prepaid rent, beginning year	10,000
Prepaid rent, end of year	8,000

b. Cash received as interest:

Interest income	$16,000
Interest receivable, beginning year	3,000
Interest receivable, end of year	3,700

c. Cash paid for merchandise purchased:

Cost of goods sold	$98,000
Inventory, beginning year	19,000
Inventory, end of year	22,000
Accounts payable, beginning year	11,000
Accounts payable, end of year	7,000

LO2 **M4-31. Calculating Operating Cash Flows (Direct Method)**

Chakravarthy Company's current year income statement reports the following:

Sales	$825,000
Cost of goods sold	550,000
Gross profit	$275,000

Chakravarthy's comparative balance sheets show the following (accounts payable relate to merchandise purchases):

	End of Year	Beginning of Year
Accounts receivable	$ 71,000	$60,000
Inventory	109,000	96,000
Accounts payable	31,000	37,000

Compute Chakravarthy's current-year cash received from customers and cash paid for merchandise purchased.

EXERCISES

E4-32. Comparing Firms Using Ratio Analysis LO5

Consider the following 2017 data for several pharmaceutical firms ($ millions). (None of the firms reported the proceeds from disposals of property, plant, and equipment.)

	Average current liabilities	Cash from operations	Expenditures on PPE
Merck & Co., Inc..	$17,909	$6,447	$1,888
Pfizer Inc..	30,771	16,470	1,956
Abbott Laboratories	7,786	5,570	1,135
Johnson & Johnson	28,412	21,056	3,279

Merck & Co. NYSE :: MRK
Pfizer Inc. NYSE :: PFE
Abbott Laboratories NYSE :: ABT
Johnson & Johnson NYSE :: JNJ

a. Compute the operating cash flow to current liabilities (OCFCL) ratio for each firm.
b. Compute the free cash flow for each firm.
c. Comment on the results of your computations.

E4-33. Comparing Firms Using Ratio Analysis LO5

Consider the following data for several firms from 2017 ($ millions):

	Average current liabilities	Cash from operations	Expenditures on PPE	Proceeds from the sale of PPE
Wal-Mart Stores, Inc.	$72,725	$28,337	$10,051	$378
The Coca-Cola Company	26,863	6,995	1,675	104
Exxon Mobil Corporation	52,705	30,066	15,402	3,103

Wal-Mart NYSE :: WMT
The Coca-Cola Company NYSE :: KO
Exxon Mobil Corp. NYSE :: XOM

a. Compute the operating cash flow to current liabilities (OCFCL) ratio for each firm.
b. Compute the free cash flow for each firm.
c. Comment on the results of your computations.

E4-34. Preparing a Statement of Cash Flows (Direct Method) LO2

Use the following information about the 2018 cash flows of Mason Corporation to prepare a statement of cash flows under the direct method. Refer to **Exhibit 4.3** for the appropriate format.

Cash balance, end of 2018	$ 12,000
Cash paid to employees and suppliers	148,000
Cash received from sale of land	40,000
Cash paid to acquire treasury stock	10,000
Cash balance, beginning of 2018	16,000
Cash received as interest	6,000
Cash paid as income taxes	11,000
Cash paid to purchase equipment	89,000
Cash received from customers	194,000
Cash received from issuing bonds payable	30,000
Cash paid as dividends	16,000

E4-35. Calculating Net Cash Flow from Operating Activities (Indirect Method) LO3, 5

Lincoln Company owns no plant assets and reported the following income statement for the current year:

Sales		$750,000
Cost of goods sold	$470,000	
Wages expense	110,000	
Rent expense	42,000	
Insurance expense	15,000	637,000
Net income		$113,000

Additional balance sheet information about the company follows:

	End of Year	Beginning of Year
Accounts receivable	$54,000	$49,000
Inventory	60,000	66,000
Prepaid insurance	8,000	7,000
Accounts payable	22,000	18,000
Wages payable	9,000	11,000

Use the information to

a. calculate the net cash flow from operating activities under the indirect method.

b. compute its operating cash flow to current liabilities (OCFCL) ratio. (Assume current liabilities consist of accounts payable and wages payable.)

LO4

E4-36. Accounting Sleuth: Reconstructing Entries

Meubles Fischer SA had the following balances for its property, plant, and equipment accounts (in thousands of euros):

	September 30, 2017	September 30, 2018
Property, plant, and equipment at cost	€1,000	€1,200
Accumulated depreciation	(350)	(390)
Property, plant, and equipment, net	€ 650	€ 810

During fiscal year 2018, Meubles Fischer acquired €100 thousand in property by signing a mortgage, plus another €300 thousand in equipment for cash. The company also received €100 thousand in cash from the sale of used equipment, and its income statement reveals a €20 thousand gain from this transaction.

a. What was the original cost of the used equipment that Meubles Fischer SA sold during fiscal year 2018?

b. How much depreciation had been accumulated on the used equipment at the time it was sold?

c. How much depreciation expense did Meubles Fischer SA recognize in its fiscal year 2018 income statement?

LO4

E4-37. Accounting Sleuth: Reconstructing Entries

Kasznik Ltd. had the following balances for its property, plant, and equipment accounts (in millions of pounds):

	December 31, 2017	December 31, 2018
Property, plant, and equipment at cost	£175	£183
Accumulated depreciation	(78)	(83)
Property, plant, and equipment, net	£ 97	£100

During 2018, Kasznik Ltd. paid £28 million in cash to acquire property and equipment, and this amount represents all the acquisitions of property, plant, and equipment for the period. The company's income statement reveals depreciation expense of £17 million and a £5 million loss from the disposal of used equipment.

a. What was the original cost of the used equipment that Kasznik Ltd. sold during 2018?

b. How much depreciation had been accumulated on the used equipment at the time it was sold?

c. How much cash did Kasznik Ltd. receive from its disposal of used equipment?

LO2, 4

E4-38. Reconciling Changes in Balance Sheet Accounts

The following table presents selected items from the 2017 and 2016 balance sheets and 2017 income statement of **Walgreens Boots Alliance, Inc.**

Walgreens Boots Alliance, Inc.
NYSE :: WBA

WALGREENS BOOTS ALLIANCE, INC. ($ millions)				
Selected Balance Sheet Data			Selected Income Statement Data	
	2017	2016		2017
Inventories	$ 8,899	$ 8,956	Cost of merchandise sold	$89,052
Property and equipment, less accumulated depreciation	13,642	14,335	Depreciation expense	1,545
Trade accounts payable	12,484	11,000	Net earnings	4,078
Retained earnings	30,137	27,684		

a. Compute the cash paid for merchandise inventories in 2017. Assume that trade accounts payable is only for merchandise purchases.

b. Compute the net cost of property acquired in 2017.

c. Compute the cash dividends paid in 2017.

E4-39. Analyzing Investing and Financing Cash Flows

LO4

During 2018, Paxon Corporation's long-term investments account (at cost) increased $15,000, which was the net result of purchasing stocks costing $80,000 and selling stocks costing $65,000 at a $6,000 loss. Also, its bonds payable account decreased $10,000, the net result of issuing $130,000 of bonds and retiring bonds with a book value of $140,000 at a $9,000 gain. What items and amounts appear in the (a) cash flows from investing activities and (b) cash flows from financing activities sections of its 2018 statement of cash flows?

E4-40. Reconciling Changes in Balance Sheet Accounts

LO4

Golden Enterprises, Inc.
NASDAQ :: GLDC

The following table presents selected items from the 2016 and 2015 balance sheets and 2016 income statement of Golden Enterprises, Inc.

GOLDEN ENTERPRISES, INC.				
Selected Balance Sheet Data			Selected Income Statement Data	
	2016	2015		2016
Property and equipment, cost	$98,190,992	$97,369,003	Depreciation expense	$3,876,111
Accumulated depreciation	76,156,389	72,880,525	Gain on sale of property and equipment	56,446
Retained earnings	20,738,143	19,049,500	Net income	3,184,803

Golden Enterprises reported expenditures for property and equipment of $1,182,854 in 2016. In addition, the company acquired property and equipment valued at $239,382 in a noncash transaction in 2016.

a. What was the original cost of the property and equipment that Golden Enterprises sold during 2016? What was the accumulated depreciation on that property and equipment at the time of sale?

b. Compute the cash proceeds from the sale of property and equipment in 2016.

c. Prepare the journal entry to describe the sale of property and equipment.

d. Determine the cash dividends paid in 2016.

E4-41. Calculating Operating Cash Flows (Direct Method)

LO2

Calculate the cash flow for each of the following cases.

a. Cash paid for advertising:

Advertising expense	$62,000
Prepaid advertising, beginning of year	11,000
Prepaid advertising, end of year	15,000

b. Cash paid for income taxes:

Income tax expense	$29,000
Income tax payable, beginning of year	7,100
Income tax payable, end of year	4,900

c. Cash paid for merchandise purchased:

Cost of goods sold	$180,000
Inventory, beginning of year	30,000
Inventory, end of year	25,000
Accounts payable, beginning of year	10,000
Accounts payable, end of year	12,000

LO3, 4

E4-42. Preparing a Statement of Cash Flows (Indirect Method)
The following financial statements were issued by Hoskins Corporation for the fiscal year ended December 31, 2018. All amounts are in millions of U.S. dollars.

Balance Sheets		December 31, 2017		December 31, 2018
Assets				
Cash		$ 300		$ 550
Accounts receivable		600		1,500
Inventory		400		500
Prepaid expenses		400		150
Current assets		1,700		2,700
Property, plant, and equipment at cost	6,200		6,100	
Less accumulated depreciation	(2,100)		(1,750)	
Property, plant, and equipment, net		4,100		4,350
Total assets		$5,800		$7,050
Liabilities and Shareholders' Equity				
Accounts payable		$ 400		$ 800
Income tax payable		200		100
Short-term debt		1,200		2,700
Current liabilities		1,800		3,600
Long-term debt		1,000		0
Total liabilities		2,800		3,600
Contributed capital		800		800
Retained earnings		2,200		2,650
Total shareholders' equity		3,000		3,450
Total liabilities and shareholders' equity		$5,800		$7,050

Income Statement	Fiscal year 2018
Sales revenues	$6,500
Cost of goods sold	3,400
Gross profit	3,100
Selling, general and administrative expenses	1,450
Depreciation expense	350
Operating income	1,300
Interest expense	350
Income before income tax expense	950
Income tax expense	250
Net income	$ 700

Additional information:

1. During fiscal year 2018, Hoskins Corporation acquired new equipment for $1,200 in cash. In addition, the company disposed of used equipment that had original cost of $1,300 and accumulated depreciation of $700, receiving $600 in cash from the buyer.

2. During fiscal year 2018, Hoskins Corporation arranged short-term bank financing and borrowed $1,500, using a portion of the cash to repay all of its outstanding long-term debt.
3. During fiscal year 2018, Hoskins Corporation engaged in no transactions involving its common stock, though it did declare and pay in cash a common stock dividend of $250.

REQUIRED

Prepare a statement of cash flows (all three sections) for Hoskins Corporation's fiscal year 2018, using the indirect method for the cash from operations section.

E4-43. Analyzing Operating Cash Flows (Direct Method) **LO2, 5**

Refer to the information in Exercise 4-35. Calculate the net cash flow from operating activities using the direct method. Show a related cash flow for each revenue and expense. Also, compute its operating cash flow to current liabilities (OCFCL) ratio. (Assume current liabilities consist of accounts payable and wages payable.)

E4-44. Interpreting Cash Flow from Operating Activities **LO2, 3**

Homework MBC

Carter Company's income statement and cash flow from operating activities (indirect method) are provided as follows ($ thousands):

Income statement	
Revenue	$400
Cost of goods sold	215
Gross profit	185
Operating expenses	110
Operating income	75
Interest expense	25
Income before taxes	50
Income tax expense	15
Net income	$ 35

Cash flow from operating activities	
Net income	$35
Plus depreciation expense	70
Operating asset adjustments	
Less increase in accounts receivable	(25)
Less increase in inventories	(50)
Less increase in prepaid rent	(5)
Plus increase in accounts payable	65
Plus increase in income tax payable	5
Cash flow from operating activities	$95

a. For each of the four statements below, determine whether the statement is true or false.

b. If the statement is false, provide the (underlined) dollar amount that would make it true.

1. Carter collected $375 from customers in the current period.
2. Carter paid $0 interest in the current period.
3. Carter paid $20 in income taxes in the current period.
4. If Carter increased the depreciation expense (for financial reporting to shareholders) by $50, it would increase its cash from operations by $50.

PROBLEMS

P4-45. Reconciling and Computing Operating Cash Flows from Net Income **LO3**

Petroni Company reports the following selected results for its calendar year 2018.

Net income	$135,000
Depreciation expense	25,000
Gain on sale of assets	5,000
Accounts receivable increase	10,000
Accounts payable increase	6,000
Prepaid expenses decrease	3,000
Wages payable decrease	4,000

REQUIRED

Prepare the operating section only of Petroni Company's statement of cash flows for 2018 under the indirect method of reporting.

LO3, 4, 5 **P4-46. Preparing a Statement of Cash Flows (Indirect Method)**
Wolff Company's income statement and comparative balance sheets follow.

WOLFF COMPANY Income Statement For Year Ended December 31, 2018		
Sales		$635,000
Cost of goods sold	$430,000	
Wages expense	86,000	
Insurance expense	8,000	
Depreciation expense	17,000	
Interest expense	9,000	
Income tax expense	29,000	579,000
Net income		$ 56,000

WOLFF COMPANY Balance Sheets	Dec. 31, 2018	Dec. 31, 2017
Assets		
Cash	$ 11,000	$ 5,000
Accounts receivable	41,000	32,000
Inventory	90,000	60,000
Prepaid insurance	5,000	7,000
Plant assets	250,000	195,000
Accumulated depreciation	(68,000)	(51,000)
Total assets	$329,000	$248,000
Liabilities and Stockholders' Equity		
Accounts payable	$ 7,000	$ 10,000
Wages payable	9,000	6,000
Income tax payable	7,000	8,000
Bonds payable	130,000	75,000
Common stock	90,000	90,000
Retained earnings	86,000	59,000
Total liabilities and equity	$329,000	$248,000

Cash dividends of $29,000 were declared and paid during 2018. Also in 2018, plant assets were purchased for cash, and bonds payable were issued for cash. Bond interest is paid semiannually on June 30 and December 31. Accounts payable relate to merchandise purchases.

REQUIRED

a. Compute the change in cash that occurred during 2018.
b. Prepare a 2018 statement of cash flows using the indirect method.
c. Compute and interpret Wolff's
   (1) operating cash flow to current liabilities ratio, and
   (2) operating cash flow to capital expenditures ratio.

LO2 **P4-47. Computing Cash Flow from Operating Activities (Direct Method)**
Refer to the income statement and comparative balance sheets for Wolff Company presented in P4-46.

REQUIRED

a. Compute Wolff Company's cash flow from operating activities using the direct method. Use the format illustrated in **Exhibit 4.5** in the chapter.
b. What can we learn from the direct method that may not be readily apparent when reviewing a cash flow statement prepared using the indirect method?

P4-48. Preparing a Statement of Cash Flows (Indirect Method) **LO3, 4, 5**

Arctic Company's income statement and comparative balance sheets follow.

ARCTIC COMPANY Income Statement For Year Ended December 31, 2018		
Sales		$728,000
Cost of goods sold	$534,000	
Wages expense	190,000	
Advertising expense	31,000	
Depreciation expense	22,000	
Interest expense	18,000	
Gain on sale of land	(25,000)	770,000
Net loss		$ (42,000)

ARCTIC COMPANY Balance Sheets	Dec. 31, 2018	Dec. 31, 2017
Assets		
Cash	$ 49,000	$ 28,000
Accounts receivable	42,000	50,000
Inventory	107,000	113,000
Prepaid advertising	10,000	13,000
Plant assets	360,000	222,000
Accumulated depreciation	(78,000)	(56,000)
Total assets	$490,000	$370,000
Liabilities and Stockholders' Equity		
Accounts payable	$ 17,000	$ 31,000
Interest payable	6,000	—
Bonds payable	200,000	—
Common stock	245,000	245,000
Retained earnings	52,000	94,000
Treasury stock	(30,000)	—
Total liabilities and equity	$490,000	$370,000

During 2018, Arctic sold land for $70,000 cash that had originally cost $45,000. Arctic also purchased equipment for cash, acquired treasury stock for cash, and issued bonds payable for cash in 2018. Accounts payable relate to merchandise purchases.

REQUIRED

a. Compute the change in cash that occurred during 2018.

b. Prepare a 2018 statement of cash flows using the indirect method.

c. Compute and interpret Arctic's
   (1) operating cash flow to current liabilities ratio, and
   (2) operating cash flow to capital expenditures ratio.

P4-49. Computing Cash Flow from Operating Activities (Direct Method) **LO2**

Refer to the income statement and comparative balance sheets for Arctic Company presented in P4-48.

REQUIRED

a. Compute Arctic Company's cash flow from operating activities using the direct method. Use the format illustrated in **Exhibit 4.5** in the chapter.

b. What can we learn from the direct method that may not be readily apparent when reviewing a cash flow statement prepared using the indirect method?

LO3, 4, 5 **P4-50. Preparing a Statement of Cash Flows (Indirect Method)**

Dair Company's income statement and comparative balance sheets follow.

DAIR COMPANY
Income Statement
For Year Ended December 31, 2018

Sales		$700,000
Cost of goods sold	$440,000	
Wages and other operating expenses	95,000	
Depreciation expense	22,000	
Amortization expense	7,000	
Interest expense	10,000	
Income tax expense	36,000	
Loss on bond retirement	5,000	615,000
Net income		$ 85,000

DAIR COMPANY
Balance Sheets

	Dec. 31, 2018	Dec. 31, 2017
Assets		
Cash	$ 27,000	$ 18,000
Accounts receivable	53,000	48,000
Inventory	103,000	109,000
Prepaid expenses	12,000	10,000
Plant assets	360,000	336,000
Accumulated depreciation	(87,000)	(84,000)
Intangible assets	43,000	50,000
Total assets	$511,000	$487,000
Liabilities and Shareholders' Equity		
Accounts payable	$ 32,000	$ 26,000
Interest payable	4,000	7,000
Income tax payable	6,000	8,000
Bonds payable	60,000	120,000
Common stock	252,000	228,000
Retained earnings	157,000	98,000
Total liabilities and equity	$511,000	$487,000

During 2018, the company sold for $17,000 cash old equipment that had cost $36,000 and had $19,000 accumulated depreciation. Also in 2018, new equipment worth $60,000 was acquired in exchange for $60,000 of bonds payable, and bonds payable of $120,000 were retired for cash at a loss. A $26,000 cash dividend was declared and paid in 2018. Any stock issuances were for cash.

REQUIRED

a. Compute the change in cash that occurred in 2018.

b. Prepare a 2018 statement of cash flows using the indirect method.

c. Prepare separate schedules showing
(1) cash paid for interest and for income taxes and
(2) noncash investing and financing transactions.

d. Compute its
(1) operating cash flow to current liabilities ratio,
(2) operating cash flow to capital expenditures ratio, and
(3) free cash flow.

LO2, 3, 4 **CVS Health Corp.** NYSE :: CVS

P4-51. Interpreting the Statement of Cash Flows

For this question, refer to the information in **Exhibits 4.1** and **4.7**.

a. Based on the information presented in its statement of cash flows, what amount of revenues should CVS Health report in its 2017 income statement?

b. CVS Health reported retained earnings of $38,983 at the end of 2016. What amount of retained earnings did the company report in its 2017 balance sheet?

c. Why is "stock-based compensation" listed under "Adjustments necessary to reconcile net income to net cash provided by operating activities"?

d. Why does CVS Health list the "effect of exchange rate changes on cash and cash equivalents" in its statement of cash flows? What does this amount represent?

e. Using three bullet points, explain what CVS Health did with the $8 billion in cash that was provided by operating activities is 2017.

P4-52. Preparing a Statement of Cash Flows (Indirect Method) LO3, 4, 5

Rainbow Company's income statement and comparative balance sheets follow.

RAINBOW COMPANY Income Statement For Year Ended December 31, 2018		
Sales		$750,000
Dividend income		15,000
Total revenue		765,000
Cost of goods sold	$440,000	
Wages and other operating expenses	130,000	
Depreciation expense	39,000	
Patent amortization expense	7,000	
Interest expense	13,000	
Income tax expense	44,000	
Loss on sale of equipment	5,000	
Gain on sale of investments	(3,000)	675,000
Net income		$ 90,000

RAINBOW COMPANY Balance Sheets	Dec. 31, 2018	Dec. 31, 2017
Assets		
Cash and cash equivalents	$ 19,000	$ 25,000
Accounts receivable	40,000	30,000
Inventory	103,000	77,000
Prepaid expenses	10,000	6,000
Long-term investments	—	57,000
Land	190,000	100,000
Buildings	445,000	350,000
Accumulated depreciation—buildings	(91,000)	(75,000)
Equipment	179,000	225,000
Accumulated depreciation—equipment	(42,000)	(46,000)
Patents	50,000	32,000
Total assets	$903,000	$781,000
Liabilities and Stockholders' Equity		
Accounts payable	$ 20,000	$ 16,000
Interest payable	6,000	5,000
Income tax payable	8,000	10,000
Bonds payable	155,000	125,000
Preferred stock ($100 par value)	100,000	75,000
Common stock ($5 par value)	379,000	364,000
Paid-in capital in excess of par value—common	133,000	124,000
Retained earnings	102,000	62,000
Total liabilities and equity	$903,000	$781,000

During 2018, the following transactions and events occurred:

1. Sold long-term investments costing $57,000 for $60,000 cash.
2. Purchased land for cash.
3. Capitalized an expenditure made to improve the building.

4. Sold equipment for $14,000 cash that originally cost $46,000 and had $27,000 accumulated depreciation.
5. Issued bonds payable at face value for cash.
6. Acquired a patent with a fair value of $25,000 by issuing 250 shares of preferred stock at par value.
7. Declared and paid a $50,000 cash dividend.
8. Issued 3,000 shares of common stock for cash at $8 per share.
9. Recorded depreciation of $16,000 on buildings and $23,000 on equipment.

REQUIRED

a. Compute the change in cash and cash equivalents that occurred during 2018.
b. Prepare a 2018 statement of cash flows using the indirect method.
c. Prepare separate schedules showing (1) cash paid for interest and for income taxes and (2) noncash investing and financing transactions.
d. Compute its (1) operating cash flow to current liabilities ratio, (2) operating cash flow to capital expenditures ratio, and (3) free cash flow.

LO2, 3, 4 Homework MBC

P4-53. Preparing a Statement of Cash Flows (Direct Method)
Refer to the data for Rainbow Company in Problem 4-52.

REQUIRED

a. Compute the change in cash that occurred in 2018.
b. Prepare a 2018 statement of cash flows using the direct method. Use one cash outflow for "cash paid for wages and other operating expenses." Accounts payable relate to inventory purchases only.
c. Prepare separate schedules showing (1) a reconciliation of net income to net cash flow from operating activities and (2) noncash investing and financing transactions.

LO3, 4 Apple Inc. NASDAQ :: AAPL

P4-54. Interpreting Cash Flow Information
The 2017 cash flow statement for Apple Inc. is presented below (all $ amounts in millions):

APPLE INC.
Consolidated Statement of Cash Flows
Year Ended September 30, 2017

Cash and cash equivalents, beginning of the year	$ 20,484
Operating activities	
Net income	48,351
Adjustments to reconcile net income to cash generated by operating activities:	10,157
Depreciation, and amortization	4,840
Share-based compensation expense	5,966
Deferred income tax expense	(166)
Changes in operating assets and liabilities:	
Accounts receivable, net	(2,093)
Inventories	(2,723)
Vendor nontrade receivables	(4,254)
Other current and noncurrent assets	(5,318)
Accounts payable	9,618
Deferred revenue	(626)
Other current and noncurrent liabilities	(154)
Cash generated by operating activities	63,598
Investing activities	
Purchases of marketable securities	(159,486)
Proceeds from maturities of marketable securities	31,775
Proceeds from sales of marketable securities	94,564
Payments made in connection with business acquisitions, net	(329)
Payments for acquisition of property, plant and equipment	(12,451)
Payments for acquisitions of intangible assets	(344)
Payments for strategic investments, net	(395)
Other	220
Cash used in investing activities	(46,446)

continued

Financing activities	
Proceeds from issuance of common stock	555
Excess tax benefits from equity awards	627
Payments for taxes related to net share settlement of equity awards	(1,874)
Payments for dividends and dividend equivalents	(12,769)
Repurchases of common stock	(32,900)
Proceeds from issuance of term debt, net	28,662
Repayments of term debt	(3,500)
Change in commercial paper, net	3,852
Cash used in financing activities	(17,347)
Increase (decrease) in cash and cash equivalents	(195)
Cash and cash equivalents, end of the year	$ 20,289
Supplemental cash flow disclosure:	
Cash paid for income taxes, net	$ 11,591
Cash paid for interest	$ 2,092

REQUIRED

a. Did Apple's accounts receivable go up or down in 2017? Apple reported net sales of $229,234 in its fiscal 2017 income statement. What amount of cash did Apple collect from customers during the year? (Ignore the Vendor nontrade receivables account, which relates to Apple's suppliers.)

b. Apple's cost of goods sold was $141,048 million in 2017. Assuming that accounts payable applies only to the purchase of inventory, what amount did Apple pay to purchase inventory in 2017?

c. At September 30, 2017, Apple reported a balance of $33.8 billion in property, plant, and equipment, net of accumulated depreciation, and its footnotes revealed that depreciation expense on property, plant, and equipment was $8.2 billion for fiscal 2017. What was the balance in property, plant, and equipment, net of accumulated depreciation at the end of fiscal 2016?

d. Apple lists stock-based compensation as a positive amount—$4,840 million—under cash flow from operating activities. Why is this amount listed here? Explain how this amount increases cash flow from operating activities.

P4-55.[A] Preparing the Statement of Cash Flows Using a Spreadsheet

LO3, 4, 5, 6
Golden Enterprises, Inc.
NASDAQ :: GLDC

The table below provides the balance sheets for Golden Enterprises, Inc. for the fiscal years ended June 3, 2016, and May 29, 2015.

	Year Ended	
Consolidated Balance Sheets	**June 3, 2016**	**May 29, 2015**
Assets		
Cash and cash equivalents	$ 1,993,854	$ 1,159,449
Receivables, net	10,666,986	11,085,689
Inventories	5,735,110	5,242,197
Prepaid expenses	1,275,918	1,350,201
Income tax receivable	22,473	476,154
Total current assets	19,694,341	19,313,690
Property, plant, and equipment at cost	98,190,992	97,369,003
Accumulated depreciation	76,156,389	72,880,525
Property, plant, and equipment, net	22,034,603	24,488,478
Cash surrender value of life insurance	438,429	630,259
Other	917,533	973,195
Total assets	$43,084,906	$45,405,622

continued

continued from previous page

	June 3, 2016	May 29, 2015
Liabilities & stockholders' equity		
Liabilities		
Checks outstanding in excess of bank balances	$ —	$ 1,068,745
Accounts payable	4,235,488	4,049,333
Current portion of long-term debt	837,225	799,204
Line of credit outstanding	—	2,823,477
Other accrued expenses	5,158,236	5,021,286
Salary continuation plan	114,958	106,148
Total current liabilities	10,345,907	13,868,193
Note payable to bank, noncurrent	5,351,057	6,213,513
Capital lease obligation	208,412	—
Salary continuation plan	920,440	921,882
Deferred income taxes, net	2,632,762	2,717,360
Total liabilities	19,458,578	23,720,948
Stockholders' equity		
Common stock at par	9,219,195	9,219,195
Additional paid-in capital	6,805,984	6,552,973
Retained earnings	20,738,143	19,049,500
Treasury shares, at cost (2,537,036 shares in 2016 and 2015)	(13,136,994)	(13,136,994)
Total stockholders' equity	23,626,328	21,684,674
Total liabilities and stockholders' equity	$43,084,906	$45,405,622

Additional information:

1. Net income for the year ended June 3, 2016, was $3,184,803.
2. Depreciation expense for the year ended June 3, 2016, was $3,876,111.
3. Accounts for other assets, for the life insurance asset, and for salary continuation liabilities (both current and noncurrent) should be classified as operating.
4. Checks outstanding in excess of bank balances should be treated as an operating liability.
5. During the year ended June 3, 2016, Golden Enterprises sold used property, plant, and equipment, receiving $56,446 in cash and recognizing a gain of $56,446.
6. For the year ended June 3, 2016, debt proceeds (encompassing the liabilities for current portion of long-term debt, line of credit outstanding, and note payable to bank, noncurrent) were zero and debt repayments were $3,647,912.
7. During the fiscal year ending June 3, 2016, Golden Enterprises acquired a long-term asset in a noncash transaction. At the time of the transaction, the asset and the liability were both valued at $239,382. The asset is included under property, plant, and equipment in the balance sheet, and it is being depreciated. The associated financial liability is included on the balance sheet under the "capital lease obligation" liability. During the year ending June 3, 2016, Golden Enterprises repaid $30,970 of principal on this obligation.
8. During the year ended June 2, 2016, Golden Enterprises recognized an expense of $253,011 for stock-based compensation. The expense increased additional paid-in capital by the same amount.

REQUIRED

a. Set up a spreadsheet to analyze the changes in Golden Enterprises' comparative balance sheets. Use the format illustrated in **Exhibit 4A.1**.

b. Prepare a statement of cash flows (including operations, investing and financing) for Golden Enterprises for the year ended June 3, 2016, using the indirect method for the operating section.

c. Using information in the statement of cash flows prepared in part b, compute (1) the operating cash flow to current liabilities ratio and (2) the operating cash flow to capital expenditures ratio.

LO3, 4, 5 **P4-56. Managing Cash Flows**

Amazin, Inc. is a specialty online wholesaler that has just completed initial financing and acquired the physical facilities to support its operations. The management team is optimistic about the company's growth opportunities as they begin operations, but they also recognize that there are significant risks for any young company's survival. The current financial condition is shown in the following balance sheet.

Balance Sheet (in $ thousands)	
Assets	
Cash	$ 400
Accounts receivable	—
Property, plant, and equipment at cost	600
Total assets	$1,000
Liabilities and shareholders' equity	
Accounts payable	—
Contributed capital	$1,000
Retained earnings	—
Total liabilities and shareholders' equity	$1,000

Amazin's management team has "benchmark" financial projections for the first quarter of operation. Revenue is forecasted to be $1,000 in Q1. Cost of goods sold will be 40% of revenue, depreciation will be $75 for the quarter, and selling, general and administrative expenses (SG&A) will be 30% of revenue. This benchmark case is based on the assumption that customers will pay for purchases in the subsequent quarter, and Amazin, Inc. will be able to delay the payments to suppliers for the same length of time.

Amazin's growth plans will require capital expenditures of $150 in Q1 and subsequent quarters. The dynamic nature of the company's operations means that these physical assets have a useful life of only eight quarters. The family and friends who funded the start-up are expecting dividends equal to 20% of profits. (Taxes may be ignored.)

REQUIRED

a. Produce projected income statement, statement of cash flows, and ending balance sheet for Q1.

b. One team member suggests a more aggressive approach to growth. By increasing SG&A from 30% of revenue to 33%, revenue would increase from $1,000 to $1,200. What would be the effect of such a change on Amazin's income statement? On its cash flows and financial position?

c. One team member notes that suppliers are not going to be pleased to wait a quarter to be paid. Relative to the benchmark plan, he forecasts that cost of goods sold expense would be lower by 10% if suppliers were paid promptly. What would be the effect of such a change on Amazin's income statement? On its cash flows and financial position?

CASES AND PROJECTS

C4-57. Analyzing a Projected Statement of Cash Flows and Loan Covenants **LO3, 4**

The president and CFO of Lambert Co. will be meeting with their bankers next week to discuss the short-term financing needs of the company for the next six months. Lambert's controller has provided a projected income statement for the next six-month period, and a current balance sheet along with a projected balance sheet for the end of that six-month period. These statements are presented below ($ millions).

LAMBERT CO. Projected Six-Month Income Statement	
Revenues	$400
Cost of goods sold	200
Gross profit	200
Selling and administrative expense	50
Depreciation expense	120
Income before income taxes	30
Income taxes	12
Net income	$ 18

LAMBERT CO. Current and Projected Six-Month Balance Sheets	Current	6-month projected
Cash	$ 50	$???
Accounts receivable	180	220
Inventory	200	180
Total current assets	430	???
Property, plant & equipment, cost	400	500
Less accumulated depreciation	(150)	(220)
Property, plant & equipment, net	250	280
Total assets	$680	???
Accounts payable	$150	$180
Income taxes payable	20	10
Short-term borrowing	50	???
Long-term debt	200	180
Total liabilities	420	???
Common stock at par	100	125
Retained earnings	160	148
Total liabilities and shareholders' equity	$680	???

Additional Information (already reflected in the projected income statement and balance sheet):

- Lambert's current long-term debt includes $100 that is due within the next six months. During the next six months, the company plans to take advantage of lower interest rates by issuing new long-term debt that will provide $80 in cash proceeds.
- During the next six months, the company plans to dispose of equipment with an original cost of $125 and accumulated depreciation of $50. An appraisal by an equipment broker indicates that Lambert should be able to get $75 in cash for the equipment. In addition, Lambert plans to acquire new equipment at a cost of $225.
- A small issue of common stock for cash ($25) and a cash dividend to shareholders ($30) are planned in the next six months.
- Lambert's outstanding long-term debt imposes a restrictive loan covenant on the company that requires Lambert to maintain a debt-to-equity ratio below 1.75.

REQUIRED

The CFO says, "I would like a clear estimate of the amount of short-term borrowing that we will need six months from now. I want you to prepare a forecasted statement of cash flows that we can take to the meeting next week."

Prepare the required statement of cash flows, using the indirect method to compute cash flow from operating activities. The forecasted statement should include the needed amount of short-term borrowing and should be consistent with the projected balance sheet and income statement, as well as the loan covenant restriction.

LO1, 3, 4 **C4-58. Reconstructing Journal Entries and T-Accounts from Completed Financial Statements** Lundholm Company's comparative balance sheets, income statement, and statement of cash flows for July are presented below:

LUNDHOLM COMPANY
Comparative Balance Sheets

	July 1	July 31
Cash	$ 600	$ 1,184
Accounts receivable	6,500	6,800
Inventory	2,400	1,800
Prepaid rent	—	400
Current assets	9,500	10,184
Fixtures and equipment at cost	1,900	2,620
Accumulated depreciation	(800)	(880)
Plant and equipment, net	1,100	1,740
Total assets	$10,600	$11,924
Accounts payable	$ 3,000	$ 3,100
Salaries and wages payable	100	70
Taxes payable	—	374
Bank loan payable	1,600	—
Current liabilities	4,700	3,544
Long-term loan	—	2,000
Common stock	4,600	4,600
Retained earnings	1,300	1,780
Total liabilities and shareholders' equity	$10,600	$11,924

LUNDHOLM COMPANY
Income Statement
Month Ended July 31

Revenue		$3,800
Operating expenses:		
Cost of goods sold	$1,800	
Salaries and wages	700	
Rent	200	
Depreciation	150	
Total operating expenses		2,850
Operating income		950
Interest expense		16
Income before taxes		934
Income taxes		374
Net income		$ 560

LUNDHOLM COMPANY Statement of Cash Flows Month Ended July 31	
Operating activities:	
Net income	$ 560
Adjustments:	
Depreciation	150
Increase in accounts receivable	(300)
Decrease in inventory	600
Increase in prepaid rent	(400)
Increase in accounts payable	100
Decrease in salaries and wages payable	(30)
Increase in taxes payable	374
Total adjustments	494
Cash flow from operating activities	1,054
Investing activities:	
Proceeds from disposal of fixtures and equipment	10
Purchases of fixtures and equipment	(800)
Cash flow used for investing activities	(790)
Financing activities:	
Loan repayment	(1,600)
Proceeds from new loan	2,000
Dividends paid to shareholders	(80)
Cash flow from financing activities	320
Net increase in cash	584
Cash balance, July 1	600
Cash balance, July 31	$1,184

REQUIRED

a. Set up T-accounts and enter beginning and ending balances for each account in Lundholm Company's balance sheet.

b. Provide a set of *summary journal entries* for July that would produce the financial statements presented above. For simplicity, you may assume that all of Lundholm Company's sales are made on account and that all of its purchases are made on account. One such entry is provided as an example.

(1)	Accounts receivable (+A)	3,800	
	Sales revenue (+R, +SE)		3,800

c. Post the journal entries from part *b* to T-accounts and verify ending balances.

C4-59. Interpreting the Statement of Cash Flows

LO1, 2, 3, 4, 5
Daimler AG
ETR :: DAI

The statement of cash flows for Daimler AG follows:

DAIMLER AG Consolidated Statement of Cash Flows Year Ended December 31, 2017 (€ millions)	
Profit before income taxes	€14,301
Depreciation and amortization/impairments	5,676
Other noncash expense and income	(1,507)
Gains (−)/losses (+) on disposals of assets	(453)
Change in operating assets and liabilities	
Inventories	(1,455)
Trade receivables	(1,592)
Trade payables	1,288
Receivables from financial services	(11,145)
Vehicles on operating leases	(3,681)
Other operating assets and liabilities	(48)
Dividends received from equity-method investments	843
Income taxes paid	(3,879)
Cash used for/provided by operating activities	(1,652)
Additions to property, plant, and equipment	(6,744)
Additions to intangible assets	(3,414)
Proceeds from disposals of property, plant, and equipment and intangible assets	812
Acquisition of Athlon Car Lease International B.V.	41
Investments in shareholdings	(1,146)
Proceeds from disposals of shareholdings	418
Acquisition of marketable debt securities	(6,729)
Proceeds from sales of marketable debt securities	7,266
Other	(22)
Cash used for investing activities	(9,518)
Change in short-term financing liabilities	751
Additions to long-term financing liabilities	63,116
Repayment of long-term financing liabilities	(47,073)
Dividend paid to shareholders of Daimler AG	(3,477)
Dividends paid to noncontrolling interests	(250)
Proceeds from issuance of share capital	114
Acquisition of treasury shares	(42)
Acquisition of noncontrolling interests in subsidiaries	(10)
Cash provided by financing activities	13,129
Effect of foreign exchange rate changes on cash and cash equivalents	(868)
Net increase in cash and cash equivalents	1,091
Cash and cash equivalents at the beginning of the period	10,981
Cash and cash equivalents at the end of the period	€12,072

REQUIRED

a. Daimler begins its cash flow statement with before-tax income of €14,301 million, then adds €5,676 million for depreciation and amortization. Why is Daimler adding depreciation and amortization to net income in this computation?

b. Why does Daimler subtract €453 million of gains on disposals of assets in its indirect method cash flows from operating activities? If these gains are all created by disposals of property, plant, and equipment and intangible assets, what was the book value of the assets Daimler disposed of during fiscal year 2017?

c. Daimler shows a negative €1,455 million for inventories in the statement of cash flows. Does this mean that Daimler paid €1,455 million for inventories in 2017? Explain.

d. Compute Daimler's free cash flow for 2017. How did the company finance its investing activities?

e. Daimler reports a net cash outflow from operating activities of €1,652 million, despite reporting pre-tax income of €14,301 million. What principal activities account for this difference? Does this raise concerns about the health of Daimler AG?

f. Why does Daimler list the "effect of foreign exchange rate changes on cash and cash equivalents" in its statement of cash flows? What does this amount represent?

SOLUTIONS TO REVIEW PROBLEMS

Mid-Chapter Review 1

SOLUTION

1. Out/I; 2. Out/O; 3. Out/O; 4. In/F; 5. Out/O; 6. In/O; 7. In/I; 8. In/I; 9. Out/F; 10. In/O

Mid-Chapter Review 2

SOLUTION

MUG SHOTS, INC.
Computation of Cash Flow from Operating Activities
For Month Ended December 31, 2018

	Net income $3,445	= Sales revenue $31,000	− Cost of goods sold 16,700	− Wage expenses 4,700	− Interest expense 300	− Advertising expense 1,800	− Rent expense 1,500	− Depreciation expense 700	− Income tax expense 1,855
Adjustments:									
Add back depreciation expense								+ 700 Depreciation expense	
Subtract (add) nonoperating gains (losses)									
Subtract the change in operating assets (operating investments).		− 2,500 Change in accounts receivable	− 8,300 Change in inventory				− (−1,500) Change in prepaid rent		
Add the change in operating liabilities (operating financing)		+ 500 Change in unearned revenue	+ 1,000 Change in accounts payable	+ 2,200 Change in wages payable	+ 300 Change in interest payable				+ 1,855 Change in income tax payable
	$700 Cash from operations	= $29,000 Receipts from customers	− 24,000 Payments for merchandise	− 2,500 Payments for wages	− 0 Payments for interest	− 1,800 Payments for advertising	− 0 Payments for rent	− 0	− 0 Payments for income tax

Mid-Chapter Review 3

SOLUTION

MUG SHOTS, INC.
Cash Flow from Operating Activities—Indirect Method

Net income		$3,445
Adjustments:		
Add back depreciation expense	$ 700	
Subtract changes in:		
Accounts receivable	(2,500)	
Inventory	(8,300)	
Prepaid rent.	1,500	
Add changes in:		
Unearned revenue.	500	
Accounts payable	1,000	
Wages payable	2,200	
Interest payable.	300	
Income tax payable	1,855	
Total adjustments		(2,745)
Cash flow from operating activities		$ 700

Mid-Chapter Review 4

SOLUTION

MUG SHOTS, INC. Statement of Cash Flows For Month Ended December 31, 2018		
Cash flow from operating activities		
Net income	$ 3,445	
Add back depreciation	700	
Subtract changes in:		
Accounts receivable	(2,500)	
Inventory	(8,300)	
Prepaid rent	1,500	
Add changes in:		
Accounts payable	1,000	
Unearned revenue	500	
Income tax payable	1,855	
Wages payable	2,200	
Interest payable	300	
Net cash provided by operating activities		$700
Cash flow from investing activities		
Purchase of equipment	(12,000)	
Net cash used by investing activities		(12,000)
Cash flow from financing activities		
Bank loan	18,000	
Payment of dividend	(1,000)	
Net cash provided by financing activities		17,000
		5,700
Cash, beginning of period		5,000
Cash, end of period		$10,700

Mid-Chapter Review 5

SOLUTION

There are three entries that affected the balance sheet accounts of Property, Plant, and Equipment at cost and Accumulated Depreciation. We know some of the amounts involved, but not all. Let P be the proceeds on the sale of used equipment, let A be the cash spent to acquire new property, plant, and equipment, and let D be the year's depreciation expense. Here are the entries:

1. Disposal:

DR Cash (+A)	P	
DR Accumulated depreciation (−XA, +A)	60,000	
CR Property, plant, and equipment at cost (−A)		80,000
CR Gain on equipment disposal (+R, +SE)		35,000

The value of P must be $55,000, because Jack's Snacks reported a gain of $35,000 on selling an asset with book value of $20,000 (= $80,000 − $60,000).

2. Acquisition:

DR Property, plant, and equipment at cost (+A)	A	
CR Cash (−A)		A

We can determine the cost of acquired assets by looking at the T-account for Property, Plant, and Equipment at Cost.

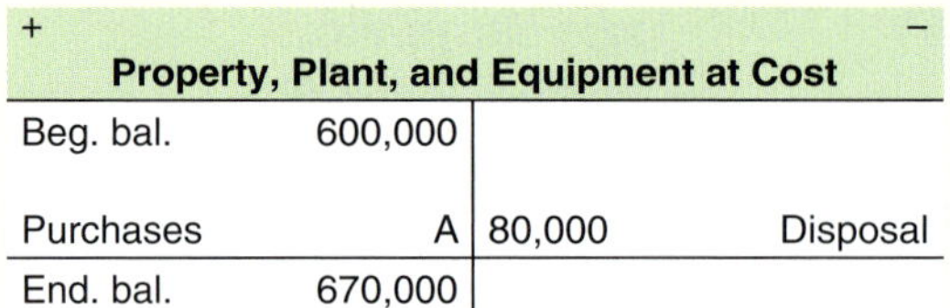

+	Property, Plant, and Equipment at Cost		−
Beg. bal.	600,000		
Purchases	A	80,000	Disposal
End. bal.	670,000		

The value of A, i.e., the amount spent on acquiring PPE, must have been $150,000.

3. Depreciation expense:

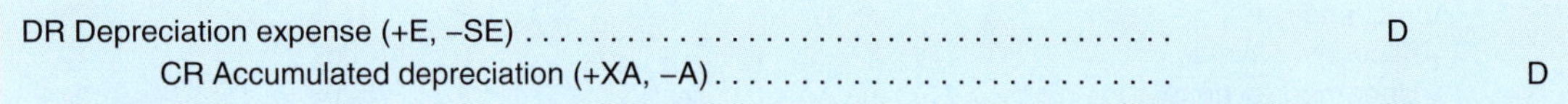

DR Depreciation expense (+E, −SE)	D	
CR Accumulated depreciation (+XA, −A)		D

We can determine the depreciation expense by looking at the T-account for the Accumulated Depreciation contra-asset.

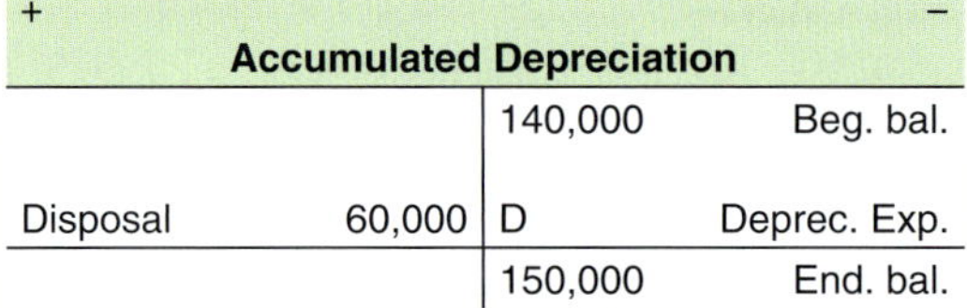

+	Accumulated Depreciation		−
		140,000	Beg. bal.
Disposal	60,000	D	Deprec. Exp.
		150,000	End. bal.

The depreciation expense for the year, D, must have been $70,000, because the contra-asset increased by $10,000 even though the disposal decreased it by $60,000.

Chapter-End Review

SOLUTION

1. We assume that One World Café's notes payable are classified as current liabilities. If so, current liabilities are $41,000 ($27,000 + $6,000 + $3,000 + $5,000) in 2018 and $21,000 ($14,000 + $2,500 + $4,500) in 2017.

   $44,000 / [($41,000 + $21,000)/2] = 1.42

   One World Café is generating cash flows from operations in excess of its current liabilities. Assuming that this continues, it should have no difficulty meeting its obligations.

2. $44,000 / $45,000 = 0.98

   One World Café spent a little more on plant capacity than it generated through operations. However, for a small business, capital expenditures are often irregular. Thus, this ratio is not alarmingly low.

3. $44,000 – ($45,000 – $4,000) = $3,000.

Appendix 4A Review

SOLUTION

Cash Flow Spreadsheet for Rocky Road Bicycles, Inc.

	A	B	C	D	E	F	G	H	I	J
1						Effect of change on cash flow				
2		O, I, or F?	2018	2017	Change	Operating	Investing	Financing	No effect on cash	Total F, G, H, I
3	**Assets**									
4	Cash		106,000	96,000	10,000					
5										
6	Accounts receivable	O	156,000	224,000	(68,000)	68,000				68,000
7	Inventory	O	752,000	528,000	224,000	(224,000)				(224,000)
8	Prepaid rent	O	68,000	72,000	(4,000)	4,000				4,000
9	Plant assets, net	O, I	1,130,000	872,000	258,000					
10	Depreciation expense					122,000				
10	Plant assets purchased						(420,000)			(258,000)
12	Plant assets sold					(16,000)	56,000			
13										
14	**Liabilities**									
15	Accounts payable	O	216,000	112,000	104,000	104,000				104,000
16	Wages payable	O	18,000	20,000	(2,000)	(2,000)				(2,000)
17	Income tax payable	O	44,000	36,000	8,000	8,000				8,000
18	Notes payable	F								
19	New borrowing									—
20	Borrowing repayments									
21										
22	**Shareholders' Equity**									
23	Common stock	F	1,142,000	1,000,000	142,000					
24	New issue of common stock							142,000		142,000
25	Repurchase of common stock									
26	Retained earnings	O, F	792,000	624,000	168,000					
27	Net income					326,000				168,000
28	Dividends							(158,000)		
29										
30	Totals					390,000	(364,000)	(16,000)	—	10,000

$390,000 – $364,000 – $16,000 = $10,000.

ROCKY ROAD BICYCLES, INC.
Statement of Cash Flows
For Year Ended December 31, 2018

Cash flows from operating activities		
Net income	$326,000	
Add (deduct) items to convert net income to cash basis		
Depreciation	122,000	
Gain on sale of plant assets	(16,000)	
Accounts receivable	68,000	
Inventory	(224,000)	
Prepaid rent	4,000	
Accounts payable	104,000	
Wages payable	(2,000)	
Income tax payable	8,000	
Net cash provided by operating activities		$390,000
Cash flows from investing activities		
Purchase of plant assets	(420,000)	
Proceeds from sale of plant assets	56,000	
Net cash used for investing activities		(364,000)
Cash flows from financing activities		
Issuance of common stock	142,000	
Payment of dividends	(158,000)	
Net cash used for financing activities		(16,000)
Net cash increase		10,000
Cash at beginning of year		96,000
Cash at end of year		$106,000

Analyzing and Interpreting Financial Statements

LEARNING OBJECTIVES

1. Prepare and analyze common-size financial statements. (p. 221)
2. Compute and interpret measures of return on investment, including return on equity (ROE), return on assets (ROA), and return on financial leverage (ROFL). (p. 225)
3. Disaggregate ROA into profitability (profit margin) and efficiency (asset turnover) components. (p. 228)
4. Compute and interpret measures of liquidity and solvency. (p. 233)
5. Appendix 5A: Measure and analyze the effect of operating activities on ROE. (p. 241)
6. Appendix 5B: Prepare financial statement forecasts. (p. 243)

PEPSICO
www.pepsico.com

PepsiCo Chief Executive Officer Ramon Laguarta faces a variety of challenges as he takes his new position. The company operates in very competitive markets for beverages (**The Coca-Cola Company**) and for snack foods (**Kellogg Company**, **Nestlé S. A.**, **Snyder's-Lance, Inc**). Consumer tastes change constantly, and various governmental entities are enacting measures to reduce consumption of the industry's products. Global trade uncertainties also confront PepsiCo, which generates almost 40% of its revenues outside the United States. PepsiCo has developed a portfolio of products that span "Fun for you" items like Pepsi and Fritos, "Better for you" products like Pepsi Zero Sugar and Stacy's Pita Chips, and "Good for you" items like Naked Juice and Sabra hummus. While the latter two categories accounted for 38% of PepsiCo's revenue in 2016, they generated 50% of the company's revenue in 2017. To continue this evolution, PepsiCo invested more than $700 million in 2017 on research and development to meet consumer demands for lower sugar and fat content and to reduce the company's impact on the environment.

The operational side of PepsiCo's business also presents challenges and opportunities. PepsiCo is well-known for its retail and foodservice partner relationships, but the disruption of the retail industry affects this distribution channel. The fast-changing digital landscape provides opportunities for increased efficiency by using "big data" to make sure customers will find their favorite PepsiCo product.

As is the case in most companies, PepsiCo's management employs a number of financial measures to assess the performance and financial condition of its operating units. These measures include ratios related to profitability and asset utilization as well as return on investment. Investors, creditors, and financial analysts use similar measures to evaluate company performance, assess credit risk, and estimate share value.

This chapter focuses on the analysis of information reported in the financial statements. We discuss a variety of measures that provide insights into a company's performance to answer questions such as: Is it managed efficiently and profitably?

Does it use assets efficiently? Is the performance achieved with an optimal amount of debt? We pay especially close attention to measures of return. In Chapter 1, we introduced one such return metric, namely return on equity (ROE). In this chapter, we review ROE and add another return metric—return on assets (ROA).

ROE and ROA differ by the use of debt financing, or financial leverage. Companies can increase ROE by borrowing money and using these funds to finance investment in operating assets. However, debt financing can increase company risk and, if not used judiciously, can have a detrimental effect on ROE and even lead to financial distress. In the latter part of this chapter, we examine metrics that measure liquidity and solvency that allow us to assess that risk.

PepsiCo tackled its sluggish beverage sales by launching a major "rebranding" program for all of its beverage product lines, including Pepsi, Gatorade, Tropicana, SoBe Lifewater, Sierra Mist, and others. Rebranding requires creating new product logos, new packaging, new slogans and, most importantly, new advertising campaigns. PepsiCo's most recent efforts include the 2018 agreement to acquire SodaStream International, Ltd. and investments in marketing to maintain its brand equity and ability to charge premium prices, while identifying productivity enhancements that reduced costs by $1 billion in 2017. It is too soon to tell whether these efforts will produce the growth that investors desire. Ultimately, we will be able to assess the success of these initiatives by looking at specific measures of PepsiCo's performance. In doing so, we seek the answer to the root question: Can the company achieve a high return on investment and, if so, is that return sustainable?

Sources: PepsiCo annual report 2017; PepsiCo press release August 2018; *Wall Street Journal*, October 3, 2018

CHAPTER ORGANIZATION

Analyzing and Interpreting Financial Statements

Common-Size Statements	Return on Investment	Liquidity and Solvency	Appendices
• Vertical Analysis • Horizontal Analysis	• Return on Equity • Return on Assets • Return on Financial Leverage • Disaggregating ROA into Profit Margin and Asset Turnover	• Short-term Liquidity: Current Ratio and Quick Ratio • Long-term Solvency: Debt-to-Equity and Times Interest Earned • Limitations of Ratio Analysis	• Analyzing Core Operating Activities • Preparing Financial Statement Forecasts

INTRODUCTION

Companies prepare financial statements to be used. These statements are used by investors who rely on financial statement information to assess investment risk, forecast income and dividends, and estimate value. They are used by creditors to assess credit risk and monitor outstanding loans for compliance with debt covenants. And, as the PepsiCo example illustrates, they are used by management to evaluate the performance of operating units. **Financial statement analysis** identifies relationships between numbers within the financial statements and trends in these relationships from one period to the next. The goal is to help users such as investors, creditors, and managers interpret the information presented in the financial statements.

Financial statement analysis is all about making comparisons. Accounting information is difficult to interpret when the numbers are viewed in isolation. For example, a company that reports net income of $7 million may have had a good year or a bad year. However, if we know that total sales were $100 million, assets total $90 million, and that the previous year's net income was $6 million, we have a better idea about how well the company performed. If we go a step further and compare these numbers to those of a competing company or to an industry average, we begin to make an assessment about the relative quality of management, the prospects for future growth, overall company risk, and the potential to earn sustainable returns.

Assessing the Business Environment

Financial statement analysis cannot be undertaken in a vacuum. A meaningful interpretation of financial information requires an understanding of the business, its operations, and the environment in which it operates. That is, before we begin crunching the numbers, we must consider the broader business context in which the company operates. This approach requires starting with the Management's Discussion and Analysis section of the financial reports and asking questions about the company and its business environment, including:

- *Life cycle*—At what stage in its life is this company? Is it a start-up, experiencing the growing pains that often result from rapid growth? Is it a mature company, reaping the benefits of its competitive advantages? Is it in decline?
- *Outputs*—What products does it sell? Are its products new, established, or dated? Do its products have substitutes? Are its products protected by patents? How complicated are its products to produce?
- *Customers*—Who are its customers? How often do customers purchase the company's products? What demographic trends are likely to have an effect on future sales?
- *Competition*—Who are the company's competitors? How is it positioned in the market relative to its competition? Is it easy for new competitors to enter the market for its products? Are its products differentiated from competitors' products? Does it have any cost advantages over its competitors?
- *Inputs*—Who are the company's suppliers? Are there multiple supply sources? Does the company depend on one (or a few) key supply sources creating the potential for high input costs?

- *Labor*—Who are the company's managers? How effective are they? Is the company unionized? Does it depend on a skilled or educated workforce?
- *Technology*—What technology does the company employ to produce its products? Does the company outsource production? What transport systems does the company rely on to deliver its products?
- *Capital*—To what extent does the company rely on public markets to raise needed capital? Has it recently gone public? Does it have expansion plans that require large sums of cash to carry out? Is it planning to acquire another company? Is it in danger of defaulting on its debt?
- *Political*—How does the company interact with the communities, states, and countries in which it operates? What government regulations affect the company's operations? Are any proposed regulations likely to have a significant impact on the company?

These are just a few of the questions that we should ask before we begin analyzing a company's financial statements. Ultimately, the answers will help us place our numerical analysis in the proper context, so that we can effectively interpret the accounting numbers.

In this chapter, we introduce the tools that are used to analyze and interpret financial statements. These tools include common-size financial statements that are used in vertical and horizontal analysis and ratios that measure return on investment and help to assess liquidity and solvency.

VERTICAL AND HORIZONTAL ANALYSIS

LO1 Prepare and analyze common-size financial statements.

1

Companies come in all sizes, a fact that presents difficulties when making comparisons between firms and over time. **Vertical analysis** is a method that attempts to overcome this obstacle by restating financial statement information in ratio (or percentage) form. Specifically, it is common to express components of the income statement as a percent of net sales, and balance sheet items as a percent of total assets. This restatement is often referred to as **common-size financial statements** and it facilitates comparisons across companies of different sizes as well as comparisons of accounts within a set of financial statements.

Exhibit 5.1 presents PepsiCo's summarized comparative balance sheets for 2017 and 2016. Next to the comparative balance sheets are common-size balance sheets for the same two years. Vertical analysis helps us interpret the composition of the balance sheet. For example, as of the end of 2017, 38.9% of PepsiCo's assets were current assets and 21.6% were property, plant, and equipment. Intangible assets made up a greater share of the company's total assets. In addition, 86.2% of PepsiCo's total assets were financed with liabilities—up from 84.8% in 2016 (and 68.5% in 2013). Long-term debt obligations were 42.3% of total assets in 2017, but as recently as 2009, long-term liabilities were 18.6% of total assets. This significant change in liabilities is due largely to the acquisition of Pepsi Bottling Group, Inc. (PBG) and PepsiAmericas, Inc. (PAS) in February 2010, but can also be attributed to the historically low interest rates of the recent past. Financial statement analysts should be aware of changes in a company's organization that produce significant changes in financial statement relationships. It is not uncommon for companies to use lower-cost debt financing to finance expansion, especially if low stock prices discourage management from issuing common stock. However, increasing debt levels are a concern if profits and cash flows are not growing fast enough to cover the rising interest and principal payments.

In **Exhibit 5.2**, we present PepsiCo's summarized comparative income statements for 2017 and 2016, along with common-size income statements for the same years. Vertical analysis reveals that cost of sales is 45.3% of net revenue, up from 44.9% in 2016. The company's "productivity initiatives" resulted in a decreased percentage for selling, general and administrative expenses that left operating profit slightly higher as a percentage of revenue compared to the year before—16.5% versus 15.6%. A decrease in selling, general and administrative expenses could be due to lower marketing and advertising costs, supply chain or distribution improvements, or decreased management costs. The most significant departure from the previous year is in the provision for income taxes (i.e., income tax expense). The passage of the Tax Cuts and Jobs Act (TCJA) in late 2017 resulted in a net increase in the income tax provision from 3.5% of revenue in 2016 to 7.4% of revenue in 2017. This effect is a one-time occurrence that is neither an indicator of the year's performance nor a predictor of tax expense for subsequent periods. Chapter 10 provides more information on the accounting for taxes.

EXHIBIT 5.1 PepsiCo Comparative Balance Sheets

PEPSICO, INC.
Balance Sheets and Common-Size Balance Sheets
December 30, 2017 and December 31, 2016

	As reported ($ millions)		As a percentage of Total Assets	
	2017	2016	2017	2016
Assets				
Current assets				
Cash and cash equivalents	$10,610	$ 9,158	13.3%	12.5%
Short-term investments	8,900	6,967	11.2%	9.5%
Accounts and notes receivable, net	7,024	6,694	8.8%	9.1%
Inventories	2,947	2,723	3.7%	3.7%
Prepaid expenses and other current assets	1,546	908	1.9%	1.2%
Total current assets	31,027	26,450	38.9%	36.0%
Property, plant, and equipment, net	17,240	16,591	21.6%	22.6%
Amortizable intangible assets, net	1,268	1,237	1.6%	1.7%
Goodwill	14,744	14,430	18.5%	19.6%
Other nonamortizable intangible assets	12,570	12,196	15.8%	16.6%
Investments in noncontrolled affiliates	2,042	1,950	2.6%	2.7%
Other assets	913	636	1.1%	0.9%
Total assets	$79,804	$73,490	100.0%	100.0%
Liabilities and equity				
Current liabilities				
Short-term debt obligations	$ 5,485	$ 6,892	6.9%	9.4%
Accounts payable and other current liabilities	15,017	14,243	18.8%	19.4%
Total current liabilities	20,502	21,135	25.7%	28.8%
Long-term debt obligations	33,796	30,053	42.3%	40.9%
Other liabilities	11,283	6,669	14.1%	9.1%
Deferrred income taxes	3,242	4,434	4.1%	6.0%
Total liabilities	68,823	62,291	86.2%	84.8%
Total equity	10,981	11,199	13.8%	15.2%
Total liabilities and equity	$79,804	$73,490	100.0%	100.0%

EXHIBIT 5.2 PepsiCo Comparative Income Statements

PEPSICO, INC.
Income Statements and Common-Size Income Statements
Fiscal years ended December 30, 2017 and December 31, 2016

	As reported ($ millions)		As a percentage of Net Revenue	
	2017	2016	2017	2016
Net revenue	$63,525	$62,799	100.0%	100.0%
Cost of sales	28,785	28,209	45.3%	44.9%
Gross profit	34,740	34,590	54.7%	55.1%
Selling, general and administrative expenses	24,231	24,805	38.1%	39.5%
Operating profit	10,509	9,785	16.5%	15.6%
Interest expense	(1,151)	(1,342)	(1.8)%	(2.1)%
Interest income and other	244	110	0.4%	0.2%
Income before income taxes	9,602	8,553	15.1%	13.6%
Provision for income taxes	4,694	2,174	7.4%	3.5%
Net income	$ 4,908	$ 6,379	7.7%	10.2%

Horizontal analysis examines changes in financial data across time. Comparing data across two or more consecutive periods is helpful in analyzing company performance and in predicting future performance. **Exhibit 5.3** presents a horizontal analysis of a few selected items from PepsiCo's income statement—revenue, operating income, and net income. The dollar amounts reported in each year from 2013 through 2017 are shown for each item along with a percentage change for each item. The amount of the change for a given year is computed by subtracting the amount for the prior year from the amount for the current year. The change is then divided by the reported amount for the prior year to get the percentage change. For example, PepsiCo's percentage change in net revenue was +1.2% in 2017, computed as follows:

$$+1.2\% = \frac{\$63{,}525 \text{ million} - \$62{,}799 \text{ million}}{\$62{,}799 \text{ million}}$$

Exhibit 5.3 highlights some important information in PepsiCo's income statement. The table shows that revenue increases have been quite small, reflecting a number of factors like the general move away from sugary carbonated drinks.[1] PepsiCo has improved its operating profit (operating income) over the past two years by better control of expenses. In addition, the company has reduced its interest expense and increased its non-operating income. Interpreting these numbers requires looking into factors that affect the company, but are beyond its control, e.g., fluctuations in raw material prices and international currencies.

EXHIBIT 5.3 Horizontal Analysis of Selected Income Statement Items

PEPSICO, INC.
Revenue, Operating Profit and Net Income
($ millions and percent changes)

	2017	2016	2015	2014	2013
Revenue	$63,525	$62,799	$63,056	$66,683	$66,415
	1.2%	−0.4%	−5.4%	0.4%	
Operating profit	$10,509	$ 9,785	$ 8,353	$ 9,581	$ 9,705
	7.4%	17.1%	−12.8%	−1.3%	
Net income	$ 4,908	$ 6,379	$ 5,501	$ 6,558	$ 6,787
	−23.1%	16.0%	−16.1%	−3.4%	

Horizontal analysis is useful in identifying unusual changes that might not be obvious when looking at the reported numbers alone. At the same time, it is important to look at both the percentage change and the reported dollar amount. If a reported amount is close to $0 in one year, the percentage change will likely be very large the following year, even if the amount reported in that year is small. Similarly, if reported earnings is negative one year and positive the next, the percentage change will be negative even though the earnings increased. Horizontal analysis that is based on a denominator that is negative or zero is not meaningful.

MID-CHAPTER REVIEW 1

Following are summarized 2017 and 2016 income statements and balance sheets for The Coca-Cola Company.

Required

Prepare common-size income statements and balance sheets for Coca-Cola. Comment on any noteworthy relationships that you observe.

continued

[1] One feature of PepsiCo's annual reporting practices is that its fiscal year is 52 weeks long in most years, but every five or six years, it is 53 weeks long. 2016 was a 53-week year, so the percentage increase in 2017's revenues is really a little better than +1.2%. (And, the percentage decrease in 2016's revenues is actually a little worse than −0.4%.)

continued from previous page

THE COCA-COLA COMPANY AND SUBSIDIARIES
Consolidated Statements of Income
($ millions)

Year ended December 31	2017	2016
Net operating revenues	$35,410	$41,863
Cost of goods sold	13,256	16,465
Gross profit	22,154	25,398
Selling, general and administrative expenses	12,496	15,262
Other operating charges	2,157	1,510
Operating income	7,501	8,626
Interest income	677	642
Interest expense	841	733
Equity income (loss)—net	1,071	835
Other income (loss)—net	(1,666)	(1,234)
Income from continuing operations before income taxes	6,742	8,136
Income taxes from continuing operations	5,560	1,586
Net income from continuing operations	1,182	6,550
Income from discontinued operations (net of income taxes of $47 and $0, respectively	101	—
Consolidated net income	$ 1,283	$ 6,550

THE COCA-COLA COMPANY AND SUBSIDIARIES
Consolidated Balance Sheets
($ millions)

December 31,	2017	2016
Assets		
Cash and cash equivalents	$ 6,006	$ 8,555
Short-term investments and marketable securities	14,669	13,646
Trade accounts receivable	3,667	3,856
Inventories	2,655	2,675
Prepaid expenses and other current assets	9,548	5,278
Total current assets	36,545	34,010
Equity method investments	20,856	16,260
Other investments	1,096	989
Property, plant, and equipment, net	8,203	10,635
Goodwill and other intangible assets	16,636	21,128
Other assets	4,560	4,248
Total assets	$87,896	$87,270
Liabilities and Equity		
Accounts payable and accrued expenses	$ 8,748	$ 9,490
Loans and notes payable	13,205	12,498
Current maturities of long-term debt	3,298	3,527
Accrued income taxes	410	307
Other current liabilities	1,533	710
Total current liabilities	27,194	26,532
Long-term debt	31,182	29,684
Other liabilities	8,021	4,081
Deferred income taxes	2,522	3,753
Total liabilities	68,919	64,050
Total equity	18,977	23,220
Total liabilities and equity	$87,896	$87,270

The solution to this review problem can be found on page 266.

RETURN ON INVESTMENT

LO2 Compute and interpret measures of return on investment, including return on equity (ROE), return on assets (ROA), and return on financial leverage (ROFL).

2

Common-size financial statements and percentage changes are useful, but there is a limit to what we can learn from this type of analysis. While vertical and horizontal analysis focuses on relationships within a particular financial statement, either the income statement or the balance sheet, many of the questions that we might ask about a company can be answered only by comparing amounts between statements. For example, return on investment measures are ratios that divide some measure of performance—typically reported in the income statement—by the average amount of investment as reported in the balance sheet.

In this section, we discuss three important return metrics—return on equity (ROE), return on assets (ROA), and return on financial leverage (ROFL). We also examine return on investment in detail by disaggregating ROA into performance drivers that capture profitability and efficiency.

Return on Equity (ROE)

Return on equity (ROE) is the primary summary measure of company performance and is defined as:

$$\text{ROE} = \frac{\text{Net income}}{\text{Average stockholders' equity}}$$

ROE relates net income to the average investment by shareholders as measured by total stockholders' equity from the balance sheet. The net income number in the numerator measures the performance of the firm for a specific period (typically a fiscal year). Therefore, in order to accurately capture the return for that period, we use the average level of stockholders' equity for the same period as the denominator. The average is computed by adding the beginning and ending stockholders' equity balances and then dividing by two.

FYI Whenever we compare an income statement amount with a balance sheet amount, the balance sheet amount should be the *average* balance for the period (beginning balance plus ending balance divided by 2) rather than the year-end balance.

PepsiCo's ROE was 44.26% in 2017. This return is computed as $4,908 million/[($10,981 million + $11,199 million)/2]. PepsiCo's ROE has been consistently high over the past 5 years, ranging from a low of 29.01% in 2013 to a high of 54.83% in 2016.

ROE is widely used by analysts, investors, and managers as a key overall measure of company performance. Billionaire investor Warren Buffett highlights ROE as part of his acquisition criteria: "businesses earning good returns on equity while employing little or no debt." Companies can use debt to increase their return on equity, but too much debt increases risk as the failure to make required debt payments is likely to yield many legal consequences, including bankruptcy. This is one reason why many analysts focus on returns generated by assets used in operations, rather than on returns produced by increasing the amount of debt financing. Next, we discuss each of these sources of return in more detail.

Return on Assets (ROA)

ROE measures the return on the investment made by the firm's stockholders. In contrast, **return on assets (ROA)** measures the return earned on each dollar that the firm invests in assets. By focusing on the asset side of the balance sheet, ROA captures the returns generated by the firm's operating and investing activities, without regard for how those activities are financed. ROA is defined as:

$$\text{Return on assets (ROA)} = \frac{\text{Earnings without interest expense (EWI)}}{\text{Average total assets}}$$

Average total assets is computed in much the same way that we calculated average stockholders' equity for ROE. We add the beginning and ending balances in total assets and then divide by two. The numerator in this ratio, **earnings without interest expense (EWI)**, is defined to be:

$$\textbf{Earnings without interest expense (EWI)} = \textbf{Net income} + [\textbf{Interest expense} \times (1 - \textbf{Statutory tax rate})]$$

EWI measures the income generated by the firm before taking into account any of its financing costs. Interest costs should be excluded from the ROA calculation so that return is measured without the effect of debt financing. Because interest expense is subtracted when net income is calculated, it must be added back to net income when we compute EWI. However, interest expense is tax deductible and, as such, it reduces the firm's tax obligation. That is, interest expense produces a tax *savings* for the firm. This tax savings is equal to the interest expense times the statutory tax rate. In order to eliminate the full effect of interest cost on EWI, we must add back the interest expense *net* of the resulting tax savings. To accomplish this, we multiply the interest expense by (1 – the statutory tax rate). This amount is then added to net income to get EWI. Thus, we can compute ROA as follows:

$$\textbf{Return on assets (ROA)} = \frac{\textbf{Net income} + [\textbf{Interest expense} \times (1 - \textbf{Statutory tax rate})]}{(\textbf{Beginning total assets} + \textbf{Ending total assets}) / 2}$$

ROA is an important measure of how well a company's management has utilized assets to earn a profit. If ROA is high, the firm can pay its interest costs to creditors and still have sufficient resources left over to distribute to stockholders as a dividend or to reinvest in the firm.

PepsiCo's ROA was 7.38% in 2017. PepsiCo's return is computed as follows:[2]

$$\text{ROA} = \frac{\$4{,}908 \text{ million} + [\$1{,}151 \text{ million} \times (1 - 0.35)]}{(\$79{,}804 \text{ million} + \$73{,}490 \text{ million})/2} = 7.38\%$$

PepsiCo's return on assets fluctuated from a high of 10.13% in 2016 to a low of 7.38% in 2017, although the 2017 figure is lowered by the one-time effects of the TCJA described earlier.

Return on Financial Leverage (ROFL)

The principal difference between ROE and ROA is the effect that liabilities (including debt financing) have on the return measure. ROA is calculated so that it is independent of financing costs, whereas ROE is computed net of the cost of debt financing. **Financial leverage** refers to the effect that liabilities (including debt financing) have on ROE. A firm's management can increase the return to shareholders (ROE) by effectively using financial leverage. On the other hand, too much financial leverage can be risky. To help gauge the effect that financial leverage has on a firm, the **return on financial leverage (ROFL)** is defined as:

$$\textbf{ROFL} = \textbf{ROE} - \textbf{ROA}$$

This return metric captures the amount of ROE that can be attributed to financial leverage. In the case of PepsiCo, the 2017 ROFL is 36.88% (44.26% – 7.38%). Over the past 5 years, financial leverage has had a significant impact on PepsiCo's ROE performance as illustrated in **Exhibit 5.4**. The height of each bar in the graph reflects PepsiCo's ROE for that year. Each bar is split into two components—ROA for the same year (the lower portion of each bar) and ROFL (the upper portion of each bar).

[2] The statutory federal tax rate for corporations has been 35% (per U.S. tax code) since the early 1990s. Beginning in 2018, the federal income tax rate for corporations has been reduced to 21%, with the transition producing many one-time tax expense effects as described above for PepsiCo. To make the mental math simpler, we will use income tax rate approximations of 35% in years prior to 2018 and 25% for years 2018 and thereafter. Most companies provide components of income tax expense as percentages in the income tax footnote that may be used for more detailed analysis.

EXHIBIT 5.4 Contribution of Financial Leverage to PepsiCo's ROE

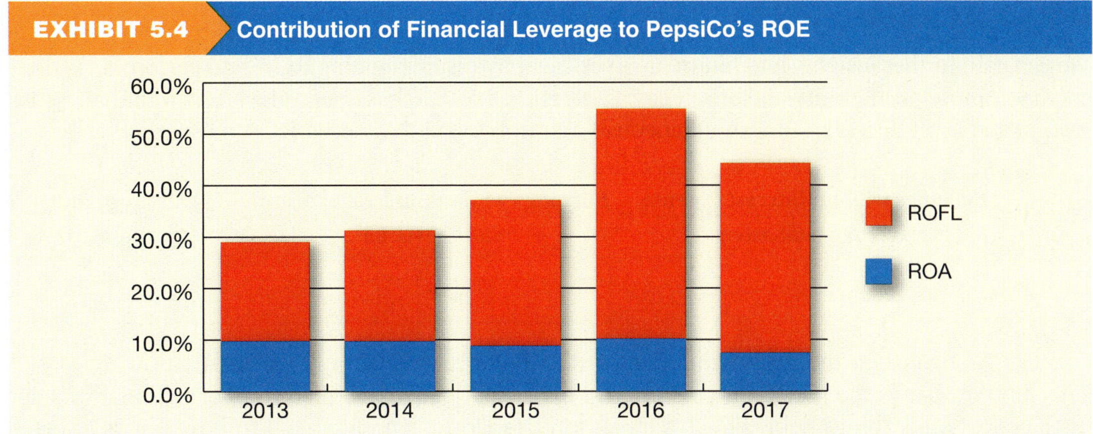

In **Exhibit 5.5**, we compare the ROE, ROA and ROFL of PepsiCo to that of several other companies featured in this text. As in **Exhibit 5.4**, the height of each bar represents the company's ROE for 2017. The lower portion of each bar is the company's ROA and the upper portion reflects the contribution of financial leverage (ROFL). The graph suggests that, with the exception of Verizon, PepsiCo's ROE is influenced to a greater extent by financial leverage than the other companies.

EXHIBIT 5.5 ROE, ROA and ROFL for PepsiCo and Comparison Companies[3]

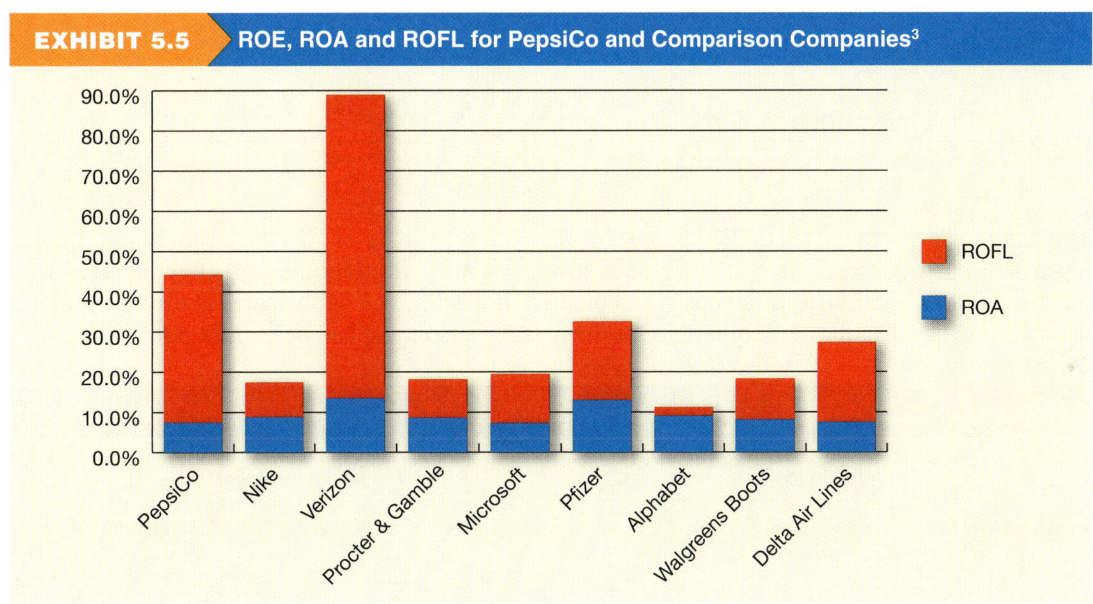

Later in this chapter, we examine the effects of financial leverage more closely and discuss several ratios that measure liquidity and solvency. These ratios help us to evaluate the risk associated with using financial leverage.

MID-CHAPTER REVIEW 2

Required

Refer to the financial statements for the **Coca-Cola Company** presented in Mid-Chapter Review 1 earlier in this chapter. Calculate Coca-Cola's ROE, ROA and ROFL for 2017. Assume a 35% income tax rate for this year.

The solution to this review problem can be found on page 267.

[3] Comparisons of profitability in 2017 are difficult due to the transition effects of the Tax Cuts and Jobs Act (TCJA) of 2017. As discussed earlier in the chapter, the TCJA increased PepsiCo's tax expense (and decreased net income) by about $2.5 billion. On the other hand, the TCJA decreased Verizon's tax expense by about $16.8 billion and increased its income by the same amount. A careful reader of financial statements should consider the components of income, rather than focusing just on the bottom line.

LO3 Disaggregate ROA into profitability (profit margin) and efficiency (asset turnover) components.

Disaggregating ROA

We can gain further insights into return on investment by disaggregating ROA into performance drivers that capture profitability and efficiency. ROA can be restated as the product of two ratios—profit margin and asset turnover—by simultaneously multiplying and dividing ROA by sales revenue:

$$\text{ROA} = \frac{\text{Earnings without interest expense}}{\text{Average total assets}} = \underbrace{\frac{\text{Earnings without interest expense}}{\text{Sales revenue}}}_{\text{Profit Margin}} \times \underbrace{\frac{\text{Sales revenue}}{\text{Average total assets}}}_{\text{Asset Turnover}}$$

The first ratio on the right-hand side of the above relationship is the **profit margin (PM)**. This ratio measures the profit, without interest expense, that is generated from each dollar of sales revenue. All other things being equal, a higher profit margin is preferable. Profit margin is affected by the level of gross profit that the company earns on its sales (sales revenue minus cost of goods sold), which depends on product prices and the cost of manufacturing or purchasing its product. It is also affected by operating expenses that are required to support sales of products or services. These include wages and salaries, marketing, research and development, as well as depreciation and other **capacity costs**. Finally, profit margin is affected by the level of competition, which affects product pricing, and by the company's operating strategy, which affects operating costs, especially discretionary costs such as advertising and research and development.

PepsiCo's profit margin ratio was 8.9% in 2017, computed as follows ($ millions):

$$\text{Profit margin (PM)} = \frac{\text{Earnings without interest expense (EWI)}}{\text{Sales revenue}} = \frac{\$4{,}908 + [\$1{,}151 \times (1 - 0.35)]}{\$63{,}525} = 8.90\%$$

This ratio indicates that each dollar of sales revenue produces 8.9¢ of after-tax profit before financing costs. PepsiCo's profit margin for 2017 is down somewhat from recent years. It reported a profit margin ratio of 11.55% in the previous year, but the 2017 decline can be attributed to the TCJA effects described earlier. The profit margin ratio for the past 5 years is graphed in **Exhibit 5.6**.

EXHIBIT 5.6 PepsiCo's Profit Margin and Asset Turnover Ratios, 2013–2017

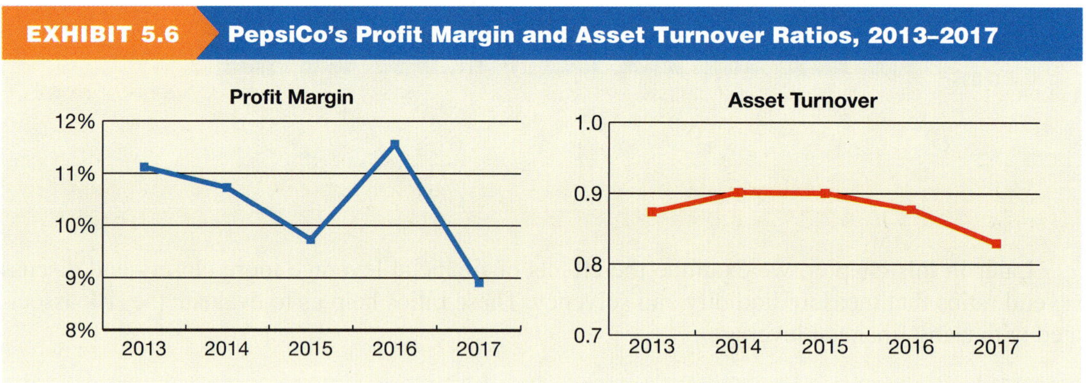

The **asset turnover (AT)** ratio reveals insights into a company's productivity and efficiency. This metric measures the level of sales generated by each dollar that a company invests in assets. A high asset turnover ratio suggests that assets are being used efficiently so, all other things being equal, a high asset turnover ratio is preferable. The ratio is affected by inventory management practices, credit policies, and most of all, the technology employed to produce a company's products or deliver its services.

The asset turnover ratio can be improved by increasing the level of sales for a given level of assets, or by efficiently managing assets. For many companies, efficiently managing working capital—primarily inventories and receivables—is the easiest way to limit investment in assets and increase turnover. On the other hand, it is usually more difficult to increase asset turnover by managing investment in long-term assets. Capital intensive companies, such as those in the telecommunications or energy production industries, tend to have lower asset turnover ratios (often less than 1.0) because the production technology employed by these firms requires a large investment in property, plant, and equipment. Retail companies, on the other hand, tend to have a relatively small investment in plant assets. As a result, they tend to have higher asset turnover ratios (sometimes over 3.0). Historically, these ratios have also been affected by leasing, the use of contract manufacturers and other methods of using assets that do not appear on the balance sheet. The new accounting procedures for leasing are discussed in Chapter 10. When they go into effect in 2019, leasing will no longer be a method for off-balance-sheet financing of assets.

PepsiCo's asset turnover ratio is computed as follows ($ millions):

$$\textbf{Asset turnover (AT)} = \frac{\textbf{Sales revenue}}{\textbf{Average total assets}} = \frac{\$63,525}{(\$79,804 + \$73,490)/2} = 0.829$$

The ratio indicates that each dollar of assets generates 82.9¢ in sales revenue each year. Over the past five years, PepsiCo's asset turnover has ranged from 0.901 in 2014 to 0.829 in 2017 as illustrated by the graphic in **Exhibit 5.6**. The 2017 decline in AT results from slow growth in sales revenue and an increase in current assets, which we will explore shortly.

YOU MAKE THE CALL

You are the Entrepreneur You are analyzing the performance of your start-up company. Your analysis of ROA reveals the following (industry benchmarks in parentheses): ROA is 16% (10%), PM is 18% (17%), and AT is 0.89 (0.59). What interpretations do you draw that are useful for managing your company? [Answer, page 251.]

Trade-Off Between Profit Margin and Asset Turnover

ROA is the product of profit margin and asset turnover. By decomposing ROA in this way, we can identify the source of PepsiCo's decline in ROA between 2016 and 2017:

	ROA	=	Profit Margin	×	Asset Turnover
2016:	10.13%	=	11.55%	×	0.877
2017:	7.38%	=	8.90%	×	0.829

Between 2016 and 2017, PepsiCo's profit margin declined from 11.55% to 8.90% while, at the same time, asset turnover declined from 0.877 to 0.829. As we saw back in the common-size income statement, the decline in return-on-assets and profit margin can be attributed to the transition effects of the TCJA at the end of 2017, which more than doubled tax expense in the income statement. If we calculate an ROA and PM based on pre-tax numbers, the ROA goes from 13.82% in 2016 to 14.02% in 2017, and the PM shows a similar increase. These improvements are due in part to PepsiCo's efforts to reduce costs, particularly in selling, general and administrative expenses, even though cost of sales expense increased by a small margin.

Basic economics tells us that any successful business must earn an acceptable return on investment if it wants to attract capital from investors and survive. Yet, there are an infinite number of combinations of asset turnover and profit margin that will yield a given ROA. The trade-off between profit margin and asset turnover is heavily influenced by a company's business model. A company can attempt to increase its ROA by targeting higher profit margins, or by increasing its asset turnover. To an extent, this trade-off is the result of strategic decisions made by management. However, to a greater extent, the relative mix of margin and turnover is dictated by the industry in which the company operates. As mentioned earlier, one determinant of a company's profit margin is its competitive environment, while asset turnover is heavily influenced by the production technology employed. For this reason, companies in the same industry tend to exhibit similar combinations of margin and turnover while comparisons between industries can exhibit much greater variation. That is, within a given industry, differences in the mix of profit margin and asset turnover often reflect the specific strategy employed by each individual firm, while variations between industries are caused by differences in the competitive environment and production technology of each industry.

This trade-off is illustrated in **Exhibit 5.7**. The solid curved line represents the average ROA for all companies over the period from 2015 to 2017. Each point along that curve represents a combination of asset turnover and profit margin that yields the average ROA. Industries that are plotted near the upper left side of the graph are those that achieve their ROA targets by maintaining a high asset turnover. These industries are often characterized by intense competition and low profit margins. On the other hand, industries in the lower right-hand portion of the graph have lower asset turnover ratios because they typically employ capital-intensive production technologies. At the same time, the competitive environment within these industries allows companies to achieve higher profit margins to offset the lower turnover ratios.

EXHIBIT 5.7 Profit Margin and Turnover Across Industries

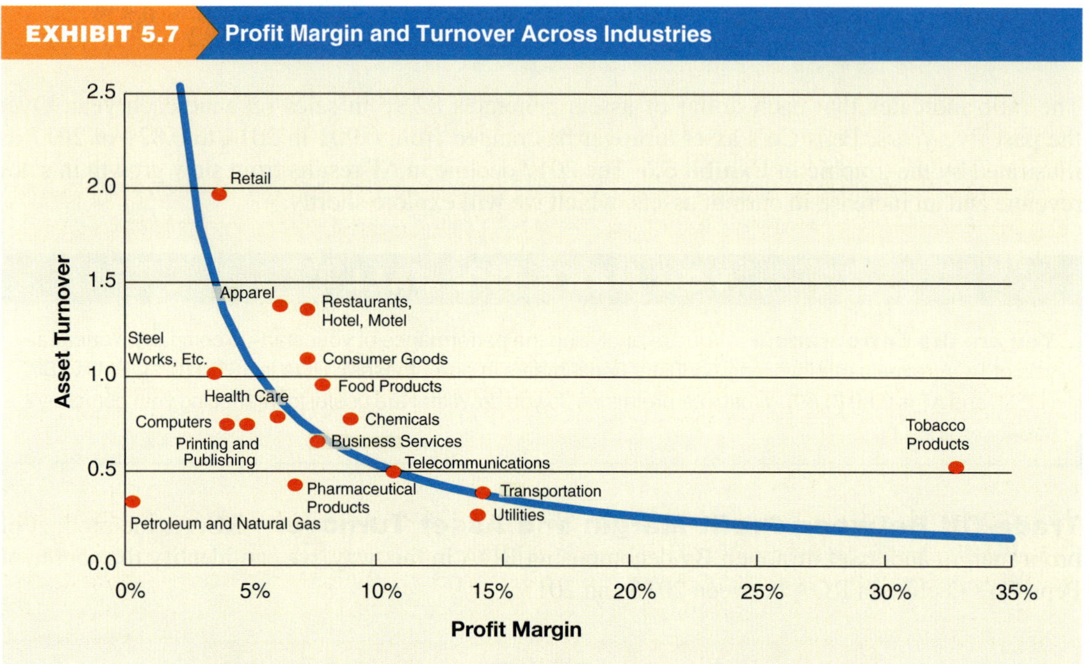

BUSINESS INSIGHT

The DuPont Model Disaggregation of return on equity (ROE) into three components—profitability, turnover, and financial leverage—was initially introduced by the **E.I. DuPont de Nemours and Company** to aid its managers in performance evaluation. DuPont realized that management's focus on profit alone was insufficient because profit can be increased simply by adding investments in low-yielding, but safe, assets. Further, DuPont wanted managers to think like investors and to manage their portfolio of activities using investment principles that allocate scarce investment capital to competing projects based on a goal of maximizing return on investment.

The basic DuPont model disaggregates ROE as the product of three ratios as follows:

$$\text{ROE} = \frac{\text{Net income}}{\text{Sales}} \times \frac{\text{Sales}}{\text{Average total assets}} \times \frac{\text{Average total assets}}{\text{Average stockholders' equity}}$$

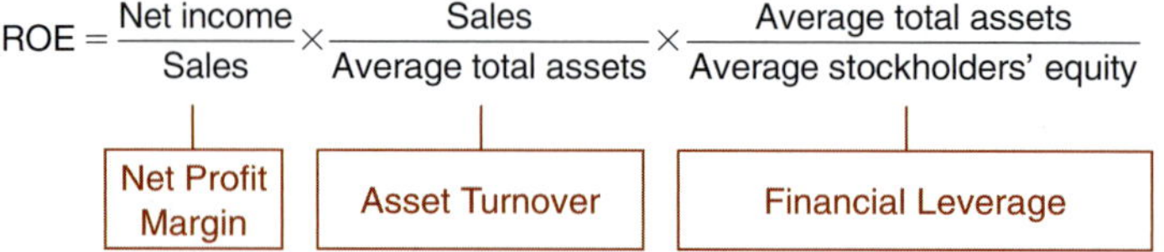

An important limitation of the DuPont model is that net profit margin is measured using net income in the numerator rather than earnings without interest expense (EWI). This means that this measure of profitability is affected by financial leverage—as financial leverage increases, interest expense increases and the net profit margin decreases. As a consequence, the model fails to adequately separate the effects of operating profitability on ROE from the effects of financial leverage. Despite this limitation, the DuPont model is widely used as a simple, straightforward way to disaggregate ROE.

Further Disaggregation of Profit Margin and Asset Turnover While disaggregation of ROA into profit margin and asset turnover yields useful insights into the factors driving company performance, analysts, investors, creditors, and managers often disaggregate these measures even further. The purpose of this analysis is to be more precise about the specific determinants of profitability and efficiency.

To disaggregate profit margin (PM), we examine gross profit on products sold and individual expense accounts that contribute to the total cost of operations. The key ratios include the gross profit margin and expense-to-sales ratios. **Gross profit margin (GPM)** is defined as:

$$\text{Gross profit margin (GPM)} = \frac{\text{Sales revenue} - \text{Cost of goods sold}}{\text{Sales revenue}}$$

PepsiCo's GPM is 54.7% ([$63,525 million – $28,785 million]/$63,525 million). That is, just over half (54.7%) of every sales dollar is gross profit while slightly less than half (45.3%) goes to cover the cost of products sold.

Gross profit margin measures the percentage of each sales dollar that is left over after product costs are subtracted. It is easily determined by looking at the common-size income statement. This ratio is discussed in more detail in Chapter 7.

An **expense-to-sales (ETS)** ratio measures the percentage of each sales dollar that goes to cover a specific expense item and is computed by dividing the expense by sales revenue. Expense items that might be examined with ETS ratios include selling, general and administrative (SG&A) expenses, advertising expense, or research and development (R&D) expense, among others. Which specific ETS ratio is appropriate depends on the company being analyzed. For instance, advertising expense is an important expense item for a consumer products company, such as PepsiCo, while R&D expense is important for an R&D intensive pharmaceutical company, such as **Pfizer**. Analysts study trends in ETS ratios over time in an effort to uncover clues that might explain changes in profit margin and make predictions about future profitability.

PepsiCo's SG&A ETS ratio is computed by dividing selling, general and administrative expenses by net revenue. The resulting ETS ratio is 38.1% ($24,231 million/$63,525 million). This ratio indicates that 38.1¢ of every sales dollar goes to pay marketing and administrative costs. This ETS ratio is relatively high because this expense item includes PepsiCo's advertising expenditures.

To disaggregate asset turnover (AT), we examine individual asset accounts and compare them to sales or cost of goods sold. We focus on three specific turnover ratios—accounts receivable turnover (ART), inventory turnover (INVT), and property, plant, and equipment turnover (PPET).

Accounts receivable turnover (ART) is defined as follows:

$$\text{Accounts receivable turnover (ART)} = \frac{\text{Sales revenue}}{\text{Average accounts receivable}}$$

ART measures how many times receivables have been turned (collected) during the period. More turns indicate that accounts receivable are being collected more quickly, while low turnover often indicates difficulty with a company's credit policies. PepsiCo's ART is 9.3 times ($63,525 million/[{$7,024 million + $6,694 million}/2]).

A variation on this measure is days-sales-outstanding = 365/ART = 39.25 for PepsiCo. It implies that—on average—PepsiCo waits just over 39 days to be paid by its customers. ART is discussed in Chapter 6.

Inventory turnover (INVT) is defined as:

$$\text{Inventory turnover (INVT)} = \frac{\text{Cost of goods sold}}{\text{Average inventory}}$$

INVT measures the number of times during a period that total inventory is turned (sold). A high INVT indicates that inventory is managed efficiently. Retail companies, such as **Walmart** and **Home Depot** focus a great deal of management attention on maintaining a high INVT ratio. PepsiCo's INVT is 10.2 times ($28,785 million/[{$2,947 million + $2,723 million}/2]).

A variation on this measure is days-inventory = 365/INVT = 35.78 for PepsiCo. It implies that—on average—PepsiCo's inventory stays in the company for almost 36 days before it's delivered to a customer and becomes cost of goods sold expense. This ratio is discussed further in Chapter 7.

Property, plant, and equipment turnover (PPET) measures the sales revenue produced for each dollar of investment in PP&E. It is computed as the ratio of sales to average PP&E assets:

$$\text{Property, plant, and equipment turnover (PPET)} = \frac{\text{Sales revenue}}{\text{Average PP \& E}}$$

PPET provides insights into asset utilization and how efficiently a company operates given its production technology. PepsiCo's PPET is 3.8 times ($63,525 million/[{$17,240 million + $16,591 million}/2]). This ratio is revisited in Chapter 8.

In the next section, we examine ratios that focus on liquidity and solvency. These ratios help us evaluate the risk associated with debt financing and weigh the costs and benefits of financial leverage. **Exhibit 5.8** presents a schematic summary of the disaggregation of ROE. It identifies the two primary components of ROE—ROA and ROFL—and highlights the disaggregation of ROA into profit margin and asset turnover, along with the drivers of these ratios. In addition, the link between ROFL and liquidity and solvency analysis is highlighted.

EXHIBIT 5.8 ROE Disaggregation

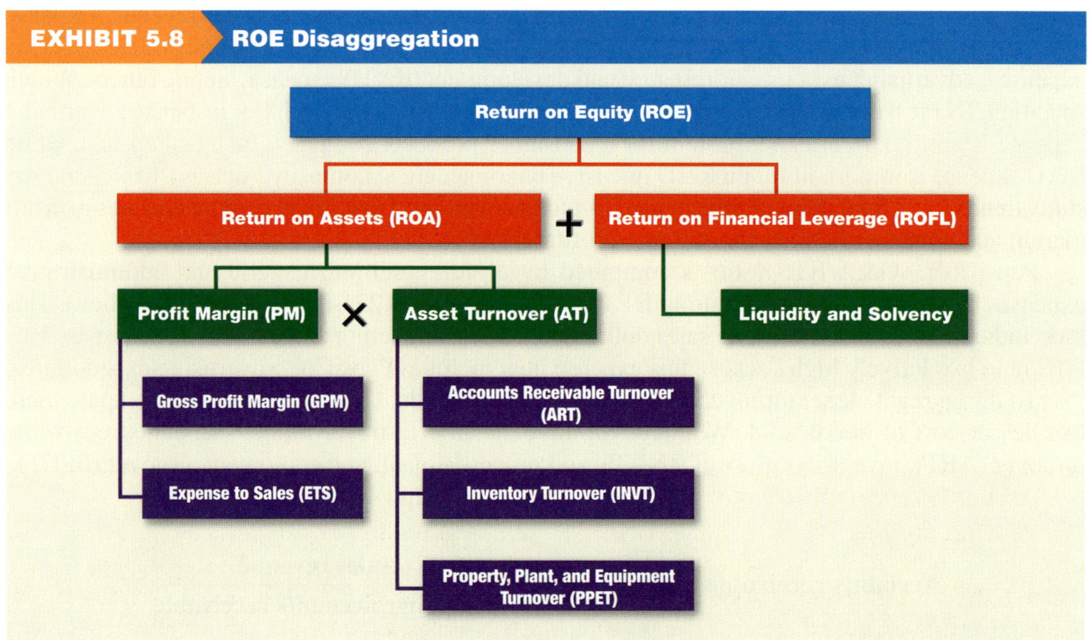

MID-CHAPTER REVIEW 3

Required

Refer to the financial statements for the Coca-Cola Company presented in Mid-Chapter Review 1 earlier in this chapter.

1. Calculate Coca-Cola's profit margin (PM) and asset turnover (AT) ratios for 2017.
2. Show that ROA = PM × AT using Coca-Cola's financial data.
3. Calculate Coca-Cola's gross profit margin (GPM), accounts receivable turnover (ART), inventory turnover (INVT), and property, plant, and equipment turnover (PPET) ratios for 2017.
4. Evaluate Coca-Cola's ratios in comparison to those of PepsiCo.

The solution to this review problem can be found on page 267.

LIQUIDITY AND SOLVENCY

LO4 Compute and interpret measures of liquidity and solvency.

4

Companies can use debt to increase financial leverage and boost ROE. The increase in ROE due to the use of debt is called *return on financial leverage (ROFL).* The primary advantage of debt financing is that it is typically less costly than equity financing for two reasons. For the borrower, interest payments to lenders are tax-deductible, so paying $1 in interest reduces pre-tax income by $1 and reduces tax payments by *t*, the marginal tax rate. If the tax rate were 25%, the effective cost of $1 in interest to $(1 – 0.25) = $0.75. In addition, lenders require a lower rate of return than shareholders because they are subject to less risk than shareholders. Interest payments have priority over share dividends. And, in the event a firm fails, creditors collect their investment first, while shareholders receive any residual.

Exhibit 5.9 illustrates a comparison between two companies—one (Company A) is financed with 100% equity and the other (Company B) is financed with 50% debt and 50% equity. Both companies have $1,000 in (average) assets and EWI of $100, producing an ROA of 10% ($100/$1,000). Because Company A does not use liability financing, average equity equals average total assets. Also, it reports no interest expense in its income statement so net income equals EWI. Therefore, for Company A, ROE = ROA, and its ROFL = 0%.

EXHIBIT 5.9 The Effect of Debt Financing on ROE (ROA > interest rate)

	Company A	Company B
Assets (average)	$1,000	$1,000
EWI	100	100
ROA (EWI/Assets)	10%	10%
Equity (average)	$1,000	$ 500
Debt	0	500
Interest expense (4% of debt)	0	20
Net income (EWI – interest)	100	80
ROE (Net income/equity)	10%	16%
ROFL (ROE – ROA)	0%	6%

In contrast, Company B has $500 of equity financing and $500 of debt financing. It reports interest expense of $20 ($500 × 4%) leaving net income of $80 ($100 – $20). Company B's ROE is 16% ($80/$500), which means that its ROFL is 6% (16% – 10%). Company B has made effective use of debt financing to increase its ROE. As long as a company's ROA is greater than its cost of debt, its ROFL will be positive.[4]

We might further ask: If a higher ROE is desirable, why don't companies use as much debt financing as possible? The answer is that there are risks associated with debt financing. As the amount of debt in a company's balance sheet increases, so does the burden of interest costs on income and debt payments on cash flows. In the best of times, financial leverage increases returns to stockholders (ROE). In contrast, when earnings are depressed, financial leverage has the effect of making a bad year even worse. In the worst case, too much debt can lead to financial distress and even bankruptcy.

To illustrate how debt financing can reduce shareholder returns, **Exhibit 5.10** compares Company A and Company B in a year when reported profits are lower than in the previous example. Both companies have $1,000 in (average) assets and both report EWI of $30, producing an ROA of 3% ($30/$1,000). Company A does not use liability financing, so its ROE = 3%, and its ROFL = 0%. Because Company B has $500 of equity and $500 of debt, it reports interest expense of $20 ($500 × 4%) leaving net income of $10 ($30 – $20). Company B's ROE is 2% ($10/$500), which means that its ROFL is –1% (2% – 3%). That is, for Company B, the use of financial leverage has a negative effect on ROE. As this example illustrates, whenever ROA is less than the interest rate on the debt, debt financing reduces the return to shareholders.

[4] The interest cost on debt is tax deductible. Therefore, the relevant cost of debt to use to compare to ROA is the after-tax interest rate.

EXHIBIT 5.10 The Effect of Debt Financing on ROE (ROA < interest rate)

	Company A	Company B
Assets (average)	$1,000	$1,000
EWI	30	30
ROA (EWI/Assets)	3%	3%
Equity (average)	$1,000	$ 500
Debt	0	500
Interest expense (4% of debt)	0	20
Net income (EWI − interest)	30	10
ROE (Net income/equity)	3%	2%
ROFL (ROE − ROA)	0%	−1%

As a general rule, shareholders benefit from increased use of debt financing provided that the assets financed with the debt earn a return that exceeds the cost of the debt. However, increasing levels of debt result in successively higher interest rates charged by creditors. At some point, the cost of debt exceeds the return on assets that a company can expect from the debt financing. Thereafter, further debt financing does not make economic sense. The market, in essence, places a limit on the amount that a company can borrow.

In addition, creditors usually require a company to execute a loan agreement that places various restrictions on its operating activities. These restrictions, called **covenants**, help safeguard debtholders in the face of increased risk. This occurs because debtholders do not have a voice on the board of directors like stockholders do. These debt covenants impose a "cost" on the company beyond that of the interest rate, and these covenants are more stringent as a company increases its reliance on debt financing.

The median ratio of total liabilities to stockholders' equity, which measures the relative use of debt versus equity in a company's capital structure, is just over 1.3 for large, publicly traded companies. This means that the typical company relies more on debt financing than on equity. However, the relative use of debt varies considerably across industries as illustrated in **Exhibit 5.11**.

EXHIBIT 5.11 Median Ratio of Liabilities to Equity for Selected Industries

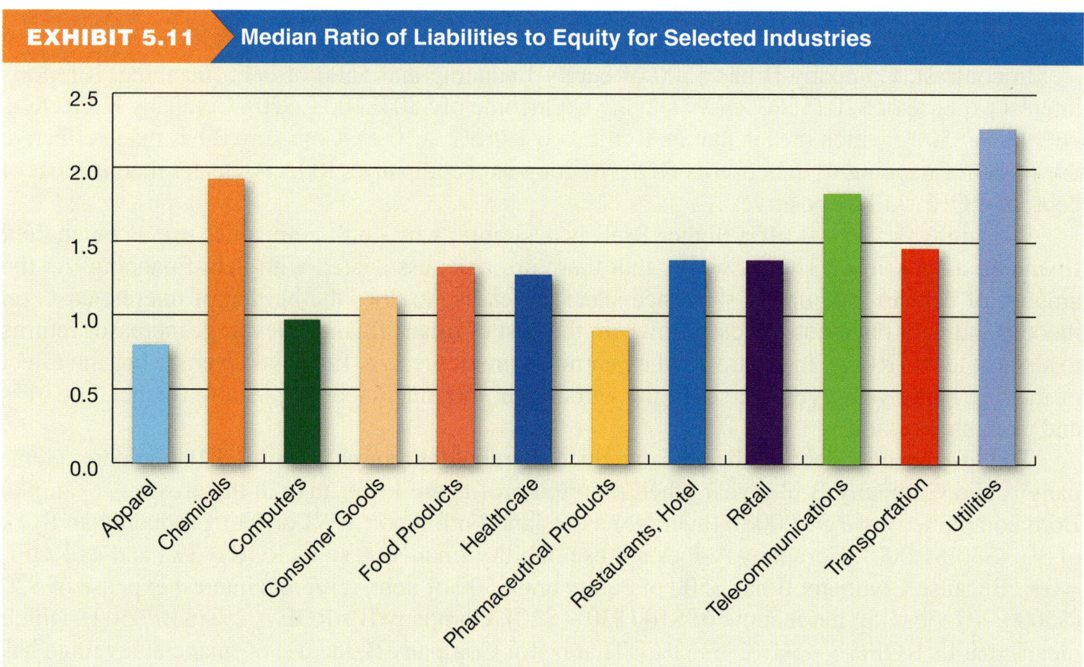

Companies in the utilities industry have relatively high proportions of debt. Because the utilities industry is regulated, profits and cash flows are relatively certain and stable and, as a result, utility companies can support a higher debt level. The chemicals and telecommunications industries also utilize a relatively high proportion of debt. These industries are not regulated, but their heavy investments in property, plant, and equipment require significant long-term debt. At the lower end of debt financing are pharmaceuticals and apparel companies. Historically, these industries have been characterized by relatively uncertain profits and cash flows. In addition, success in these industries depends heavily on intellectual property and human resources devoted to research and product development. These "assets" do not appear on the balance sheet and cannot be used as collateral when borrowing funds. Consequently, they use less debt in their capital structures.

To summarize, companies can effectively use debt to increase ROE. Although it reduces financing costs, debt increases **default risk**: the risk that the company will be unable to repay debt when it comes due. Because of this risk, analysts carefully examine a company's financial statements to determine if it is using debt financing effectively and judiciously.

The core of our analysis relating to debt is the examination of a company's ability to generate cash to *service* its debt (that is, to make required debt payments of both interest and principal). Analysts, investors, and creditors are primarily concerned about whether the company has sufficient cash available or, alternatively, whether it is able to generate the required cash in the future to cover its debt obligations. The analysis of available cash is called **liquidity analysis**. The analysis of the company's ability to generate sufficient cash in the future is called **solvency analysis** (so named because a bankrupt company is said to be "insolvent").

Liquidity Analysis

Liquidity refers to cash availability: how much cash a company has, and how much it can raise on short notice. The most common ratios used to assess the degree of liquidity are the current ratio and the quick ratio, which were first introduced in Chapter 2, as well as the operating cash flow to current liabilities ratio, which was introduced in Chapter 4. Each of these ratios links required near-term payments to cash available in the near term.

Current Ratio *Current assets* are those assets that a company expects to convert into cash within the next operating cycle, which is typically a year. *Current liabŠities* are those liabilities that come due within the next year. An excess of current assets over current liabilities (Current assets − Current liabilities), is known as *net working capital* or simply **working capital**. Positive working capital implies more expected cash inflows than cash outflows in the short run. The **current ratio** expresses working capital as a ratio and is computed as follows:

$$\textbf{Current ratio (CR)} = \frac{\textbf{Current assets}}{\textbf{Current liabilities}}$$

A current ratio greater than 1.0 implies positive working capital. Both working capital and the current ratio consider existing balance sheet data only and ignore cash inflows from future sales or other sources. The current ratio is more commonly used than working capital because ratios allow comparisons across companies of different sizes. Generally, companies prefer a higher current ratio; however, an excessively high current ratio indicates inefficient asset use. Furthermore, a current ratio less than 1.0 is not always problematic for at least two reasons:

1. A cash-and-carry company (like a grocery store) can have little or no receivables (and a low current ratio), but consistently large operating cash inflows ensure the company will be sufficiently liquid. A company can efficiently manage its working capital by minimizing receivables and inventories and maximizing payables. **The Kroger Company** and **Walmart**, for example, use their buying power to exact extended credit terms from suppliers. Consequently, because both companies are essentially cash-and-carry companies, their current ratios are less than 1.0 and both are sufficiently liquid.
2. A service company will typically report little or no inventories among its current assets. In addition, some service companies do not report significant accounts receivable. If short-term borrowings and accrued expenses exceed cash and temporary investments, a current ratio of less than 1.0 would result. **United Continental Holdings, Inc.** is an example of such a firm.

The aim of current-ratio analysis is to discern if a company is having, or is likely to have, difficulty meeting its short-term obligations. If a company cannot cover its short-term debts with cash provided by operations, it may need to liquidate current assets to meet its obligations. **PepsiCo**'s current ratio was 1.51 ($31,027 million/$20,502 million) at December 30, 2017. At the end of 2016, its current ratio was 1.25 ($26,450 million/$21,135 million).

Quick Ratio The **quick ratio** is a variant of the current ratio. It focuses on quick assets, which are those assets likely to be converted to cash within a relatively short period of time, usually less than 90 days. Specifically, quick assets include cash, short-term securities, and accounts receivable; they exclude inventories and prepaid assets. The quick ratio is defined as follows:

$$\text{Quick ratio (QR)} = \frac{\text{Cash} + \text{Short-term securities} + \text{Accounts receivable}}{\text{Current liabilities}}$$

The quick ratio reflects on a company's ability to meet its current liabilities without liquidating inventories that could require markdowns. It is a more stringent test of liquidity than the current ratio and may provide more insight into company liquidity in some cases.

At the end of 2017, PepsiCo's quick ratio was 1.29 ([$10,610 million + $8,900 million + $7,024 million]/$20,502 million), which was up from 1.08 in 2016 ([$9,158 million + $6,967 million + $6,694 million]/$21,135 million). **Exhibit 5.13** shows that the median food products company has a quick ratio well below 1.0, and even further below PepsiCo's value.

Operating Cash Flow to Current Liabilities The **operating cash flow to current liabilities (OCFCL)** ratio was introduced in Chapter 4 and is defined as follows:

$$\text{Operating cash flow to current liabilities (OCFCL)} = \frac{\text{Cash flow from operations}}{\text{Average current liabilities}}$$

Cash flow from operations is taken directly from the statement of cash flows. It represents the net amount of cash derived from operating activities during the year. Ultimately the ability of a company to pay its debts is determined by whether its operations can generate enough cash to cover debt payments. Thus, a higher OCFCL ratio is generally preferred by analysts.

PepsiCo reported an OCFCL ratio of 0.48 in 2017 ($9,994 million/[($20,502 million + $21,135 million)/2]). Its 2016 OCFCL ratio was 0.55 ($10,673 million/[($21,135 million + $17,578 million)/2]). PepsiCo's OCFCL ratio has decreased slightly over the past two years after a few years of improvement. The decrease in the OCFCL ratio is tempered by the increase in the CR and QR. In Chapter 4 we saw that reductions in inventory and receivables *increased* operating cash flows. As a consequence, the improvement may not be sustainable and continued improvement is certainly limited. **Exhibit 5.12** provides a plot of all three liquidity ratios over the past 5 years.

EXHIBIT 5.12 PepsiCo's Liquidity Ratios, 2010–2014

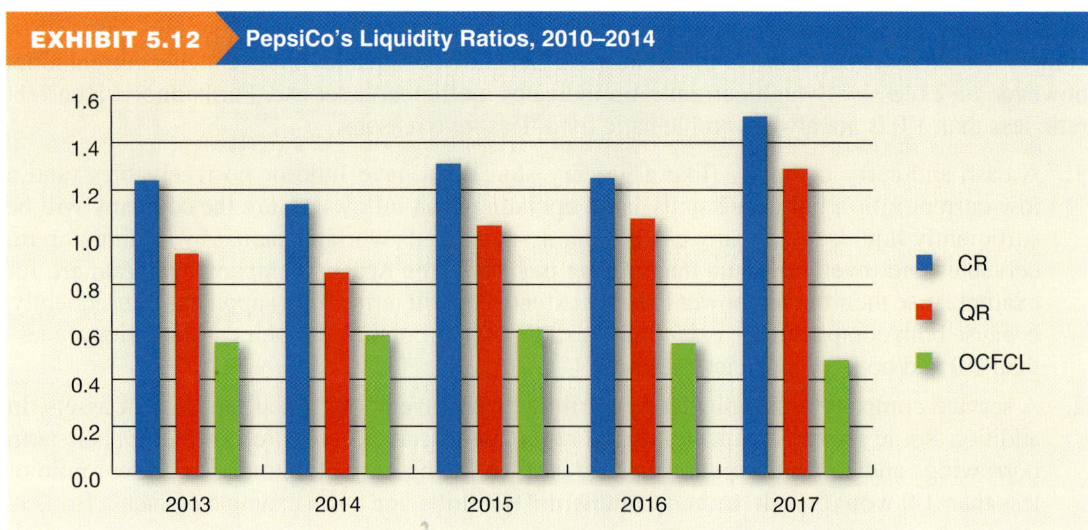

Cash Burn Rate The **cash burn rate (CBR)** is used when a company's free cash flow (cash from operations minus net investments in property, plant and equipment) is negative. Free cash flow can be negative in a variety of circumstances—for young companies working to become established (e.g., **Tesla**) or for established companies that have run into financial distress (e.g., **Sears**). For the first half of fiscal year 2018, **Blue Apron Holdings, Inc.** reported that its cash flows used in operations were $38.6 million, and its net investments in property and equipment were $9.0 million, making free cash flow a negative $47.6 million. There were 181 days in the first half of 2018, so Blue Apron's cash burn rate would be the following:

Cash burn rate = Free cash flow in the period ÷ number of days in the period
= −$47.6 million ÷ 181 days = −$263 thousand/day

In its efforts to attract and retain subscribers, Blue Apron is using cash at the rate of $263 thousand per day, or a little more than a million dollars every four days. This represents a significant improvement over the same period in 2017, when the free cash flow was a negative $162.4 million and cash burn rate was $897 thousand per day.

Naturally, the interpretation of the cash burn rate depends on the depth of the company's pockets. In its June 30, 2018 balance sheet, Blue Apron reports cash and cash equivalents of $180.8 million, so it would appear that the company can, if necessary, continue on its present course for quite a while. (We don't calculate PepsiCo's cash burn rate because its free cash flow is positive.)

Solvency Analysis

Solvency refers to a company's ability to meet its debt obligations, including both periodic interest payments and the repayment of the principal amount borrowed. Solvency is crucial because an insolvent company is a failed company. There are two general approaches to measuring solvency. The first approach uses balance sheet data and assesses the proportion of capital raised from creditors. The second approach uses income statement data and assesses the profit generated relative to debt payment obligations. We discuss each approach in turn.

Debt-to-Equity The **debt-to-equity ratio**, which was introduced in Chapter 1, is a useful tool for the first type of solvency analysis. It is defined as follows:

$$\textbf{Debt-to-equity ratio} = \frac{\textbf{Total liabilities}}{\textbf{Total stockholders' equity}}$$

This ratio conveys how reliant a company is on creditor financing (which are fixed claims) compared with equity financing (which are flexible or residual claims). A higher ratio indicates less solvency, and more risk. PepsiCo's debt-to-equity ratio is 6.27 for 2017 ($68,823 million/$10,981 million). In 2016, its ratio was 5.56 ($62,291 million/$11,199 million). Between 2013 and 2017, PepsiCo's debt-to-equity ratio has risen rather dramatically (as seen in the graph below). Like many large companies, PepsiCo has returned cash to shareholders in the form of dividends and share buybacks and increased debt to take advantage of unusually low interest rates. Over this period, liabilities have increased by 26%, and shareholders' equity has decreased by 55%. At some point, the increase in the debt-to-equity ratio may have an impact on PepsiCo's ability to borrow at favorable interest rates. PepsiCo's debt-to-equity ratio is well above the average of approximately 1.33 for other companies in the food industry.

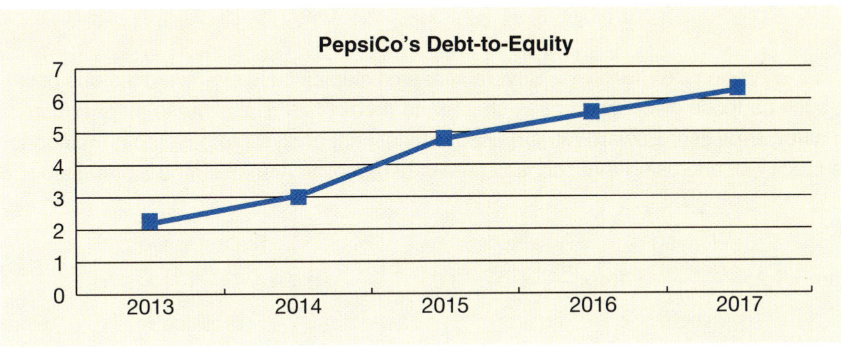

In practice, analysts use a variety of solvency measures that are similar to the debt-to-equity ratio. One variant of this ratio considers a company's *long-term* debt divided by equity. This approach assumes that current liabilities are repaid from current assets (so-called self-liquidating). Thus, it assumes that creditors and stockholders need only focus on the relative proportion of long-term capital.

Times Interest Earned The second type of solvency analysis compares profits to liabilities. This approach assesses how much operating profit is available to cover debt obligations. A common measure for this type of solvency analysis is the **times interest earned (TIE)** ratio (see Chapter 9) defined as follows:

$$\text{Times interest earned} = \frac{\text{Earnings before interest expense and taxes}}{\text{Interest expense}}$$

The times interest earned ratio reflects the operating income available to pay interest expense. The underlying assumption is that only interest needs to be paid because the principal will be refinanced. This ratio is sometimes abbreviated as EBIT/I. The numerator is similar to earnings without interest (EWI), but it is *pretax* instead of after tax.

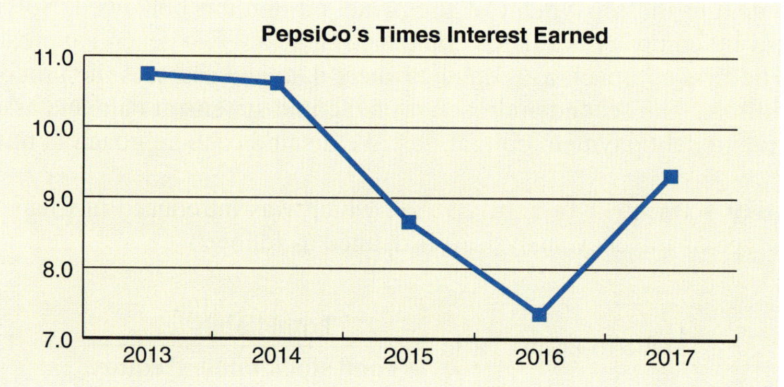

Management wants this ratio to be sufficiently high so that there is little risk of default. PepsiCo's TIE ratio was 9.34 times in 2017 ([$9,602 million + $1,151 million]/$1,151 million), which is up significantly from 7.37 times in 2016 ([$8,553 million + $1,342 million]/$1,342 million). Over the 5-year period between 2013 and 2017, PepsiCo's TIE ratio has ranged from a low of 7.37 in 2016 to a high of 10.76 in 2013. The current level of this ratio suggests that PepsiCo is more than capable of earning income that is sufficient to cover its financing costs.

There are many variations of solvency and liquidity analysis and the ratios used. The basic idea is to construct measures that reflect a company's credit risk exposure. There is not one "best" financial leverage ratio. Instead, as financial statement users, we want to use measures that capture the risk we are most concerned with. It is also important to compute the ratios ourselves to ensure we know what is included and excluded from each ratio.

RESEARCH INSIGHT

Using Ratios to Predict Bankruptcy Several research studies have examined the use of various financial ratios, such as those discussed in this chapter, to predict financial distress of large companies. In a pioneering study, Professor Edward Altman used discriminant analysis to develop a method for scoring a company's credit risk and using that score to predict bankruptcy. Altman's model produced a **Z-score** as follows:

$$\text{Z-score} = 1.2 \times \frac{\text{Working capital}}{\text{Total assets}} + 1.4 \times \frac{\text{Retained earnings}}{\text{Total assets}} + 3.3 \times \frac{\text{EBIT}}{\text{Total assets}} + 0.6 \times \frac{\text{Market value of equity}}{\text{Total liabilities}} + 0.99 \times \frac{\text{Sales}}{\text{Total assets}}$$

continued

continued from previous page

The first variable is a measure of liquidity. The second and third variables measure long-term and short-term profitability. The fourth variable captures a company's financial leverage and the last variable is asset turnover. A Z-score greater than 3.0 indicates a healthy company, while a Z-score below 1.8 suggests a high potential for near-term bankruptcy. The model was 95% accurate at predicting bankruptcy one year in advance and 72% accurate two years in advance. Today, credit scoring models like Altman's Z-score are used by nearly all financial institutions and many other businesses to evaluate credit risk. (Altman, E., "Financial Ratios, Discriminant Analysis and the Prediction of Corporate Bankruptcy," *Journal of Finance*, September, 1968.)

Limitations of Ratio Analysis

The quality of financial statement analysis depends on the quality of financial information. We ought not blindly analyze numbers; doing so can lead to faulty conclusions and suboptimal decisions. Instead, we need to acknowledge that current accounting rules (GAAP) have limitations, and be fully aware of the company's environment, its competitive pressures, and any structural and strategic changes. **Exhibit 5.13** shows how ratios can differ significantly across industries, so comparisons to companies with similar customers, technologies and competitive pressures will be most meaningful. Even within industries, there may be differences in strategy that create big differences in ratio values. There can be other factors that limit the usefulness of financial accounting information for ratio analysis.

EXHIBIT 5.13 Industry Ratios: Medians of Companies with Market Capitalization > $500 Million (2015–2017)

	ROE	ROA	ROFL	PM	GPM	AT	ART	INVT	PPET	DE	TIE	CR	QR	OCFCL
Apparel	13.6%	8.9%	5.6%	6.2%	48.0%	1.38	9.75	3.16	8.43	0.80	19.36	2.71	1.50	0.65
Business Services	11.4%	5.1%	4.9%	7.7%	53.1%	0.66	5.65	31.09	9.97	1.78	5.61	1.53	1.25	0.43
Chemicals	15.4%	6.9%	7.6%	9.0%	34.2%	0.78	6.37	4.44	2.48	1.92	5.51	2.08	1.22	0.58
Computers	6.2%	3.7%	1.9%	4.1%	48.0%	0.75	5.19	6.79	9.87	0.97	3.72	1.80	1.51	0.36
Consumer Goods	15.6%	8.0%	7.9%	7.3%	50.2%	1.10	7.59	4.50	6.65	1.12	12.04	1.69	0.92	0.48
Food Products	12.4%	6.7%	5.5%	7.9%	34.0%	0.96	12.79	5.97	4.52	1.33	6.35	1.71	0.82	0.69
Healthcare	8.0%	5.0%	2.8%	6.1%	28.7%	0.79	6.56	45.06	4.98	1.28	2.73	1.56	1.24	0.62
Petroleum	–3.7%	0.1%	–2.6%	0.3%	27.9%	0.34	5.88	14.21	0.46	1.07	–0.04	1.45	1.03	0.70
Pharmaceutical	6.0%	3.3%	1.6%	6.8%	69.6%	0.43	5.79	2.26	4.94	0.90	2.25	2.60	2.03	0.43
Printing & Publishing	8.2%	3.9%	3.4%	4.9%	52.6%	0.75	7.98	18.26	7.63	1.66	4.22	1.34	1.02	0.45
Restaurants, Hotel	13.1%	9.4%	6.2%	7.3%	27.4%	1.36	26.66	86.21	2.61	1.38	6.91	0.98	0.65	0.89
Retail	14.5%	7.2%	6.8%	3.8%	32.5%	1.97	45.70	5.26	7.23	1.38	7.49	1.47	0.50	0.48
Steel	5.8%	3.7%	1.4%	3.6%	18.7%	1.02	8.97	5.28	2.59	1.18	3.32	2.46	1.15	0.48
Telecommunications	6.0%	4.6%	1.9%	10.7%	53.4%	0.50	7.26	15.99	1.41	1.83	2.57	1.19	1.02	0.68
Tobacco	29.5%	20.3%	17.8%	32.8%	62.4%	0.53	60.29	2.92	9.10	1.58	11.60	1.01	0.46	0.52
Transportation	13.2%	6.9%	5.8%	14.2%	37.9%	0.39	11.48	28.86	0.51	1.46	4.55	1.01	0.82	0.80
Utilities	9.4%	4.1%	5.1%	14.0%	32.6%	0.27	7.69	11.71	0.36	2.27	3.47	0.74	0.44	0.67
Overall	10.2%	5.4%	4.2%	6.7%	37.2%	0.74	7.48	6.24	4.47	1.32	4.80	1.76	1.10	0.57

GAAP Limitations Several limitations in GAAP can distort financial ratios. Limitations include:

1. **Measurability**. Financial statements reflect what can be reliably measured. This results in nonrecognition of certain assets, often internally developed assets, the very assets that are most likely to confer a competitive advantage and create value. Examples are brand name, a superior management team, employee skills, and a reliable supply chain.
2. **Non-capitalized costs**. Related to the concept of measurability is the expensing of costs relating to "assets" that cannot be identified with enough precision to warrant capitalization. Examples are brand equity costs from advertising and other promotional activities, and research and development costs relating to future products.
3. **Historical costs**. Assets and liabilities are often recorded at original acquisition or issuance costs. Subsequent increases in value are not recorded until realized, and declines in value are recognized only if deemed permanent.

Thus, GAAP balance sheets omit important and valuable assets. Our analysis of ROE, including that of liquidity and solvency, must consider that assets can be underreported and that ratios can be distorted. We discuss many of these limitations in more detail in later chapters.

Company Changes Many companies regularly undertake mergers, acquire new companies, and divest subsidiaries. Such major operational changes can impair the comparability of company ratios across time. Companies also change strategies, such as product pricing, R&D, and financing. We must understand the effects of such changes on ratios and exercise caution when we compare ratios from one period to the next. Companies also behave differently at different points in their life cycles. For instance, growth companies possess a different profile than do mature companies. Seasonal effects also markedly impact analysis of financial statements at different times of the year. Thus, we must consider life cycle and cyclicality when we compare ratios across companies and over time.

Conglomerate Effects Few companies are pure-play; instead, most companies operate in several businesses or industries. Most publicly traded companies consist of a parent company and multiple subsidiaries, often pursuing different lines of business. PepsiCo reports financial information for six separate business segments. Most heavy equipment manufacturers, for example, have finance subsidiaries (**Ford Motor Credit Company** and **Caterpillar Financial Services Corporation** are subsidiaries of **Ford** and **Caterpillar** respectively). Financial statements of such conglomerates are consolidated and include the financial statements of the parent and its subsidiaries. Consequently, such consolidated statements are challenging to analyze. Typically, analysts break the financials apart into their component businesses and separately analyze each component. Fortunately, companies must report financial information (albeit limited) for major business segments in their 10-Ks.

Means to an End Ratios reduce, to a single number, the myriad complexities of a company's operations. No one number can accurately capture the qualitative aspect of a company. Ratios cannot hope to capture the innumerable transactions and events that occur each day between a company and various parties. Ratios cannot meaningfully convey a company's marketing and management philosophies, its human resource activities, its financing activities, its strategic initiatives, and its product management. In our analysis we must learn to look through the numbers and ratios to better understand the operational factors that drive financial results. Successful analysis seeks to gain insight into what a company is really about and what the future portends. Our overriding purpose in analysis is to understand the past and present to better predict the future. Computing and examining ratios is just one step in that process.

CHAPTER-END REVIEW

Refer to the income statements and balance sheets for the **Coca-Cola Company** presented in Mid-Chapter Review 1 earlier in this chapter.

Required

Compute the following liquidity and solvency ratios for Coca-Cola and interpret your results in comparison to those of PepsiCo.

1. Current ratio
2. Quick ratio
3. Debt-to-equity ratio
4. Times interest earned

The solution to this review problem can be found on pages 267-268.

APPENDIX 5A: Analyzing and Interpreting Core Operating Activities

eLectures MBC

LO5 Measure and analyze the effect of operating activities on ROE.

5

In Chapter 4, we analyzed cash flows by grouping them into three categories—operating, investing, and financing. Similarly, the income statement and balance sheet can be formatted to distinguish between operating and nonoperating (investing and financing) activities. In this appendix, we consider the effect of operating activities on the return on investment. The distinction between returns earned from operating activities and those generated by nonoperating activities is important. Operations provide the primary value drivers for stockholders. It is for this reason that many analysts argue that operating activities must be executed successfully if a company expects to remain profitable in the long run.

Operating activities refer to the core transactions and events of a company. They consist of those activities required to deliver a company's products and services to its customers. A company is engaged in operating activities when it conducts research and development, establishes supply chains, assembles administrative support, produces and markets its products, and follows up with after-sale customer service. Although nonoperating activities, namely investing and financing activities, are important and must be managed well, they are not the primary value drivers for investors and creditors.

Operating returns are measured by the **return on net operating assets (RNOA)**. This return metric is defined as follows:

$$\text{RNOA} = \frac{\textbf{Net operating profit after taxes (NOPAT)}}{\textbf{Average net operating assets (NOA)}}$$

In order to calculate this ratio, we must first classify the income statement and balance sheet accounts into operating and nonoperating components so that we can assess each separately. First, we will consider operating components of the income statement and the calculation of NOPAT. Then, we consider operating and nonoperating components of the balance sheet and the calculation of NOA.

Reporting Operating Activities in the Income Statement

The income statement reports operating activities through accounts such as sales revenue, cost of goods sold, selling, general and administrative (SG&A) expenses, depreciation, rent, insurance, wages, advertising, and R&D expenses. These activities create the most long-lasting effects on profitability and cash flows. Nonoperating items in the income statement include interest expense on borrowed funds and interest and dividend income on investments as well as gains and losses on those investments.

A commonly used measure of operating income is **net operating profit after taxes (NOPAT)**. NOPAT is calculated as:

$$\text{NOPAT} = \text{Net income} - [(\text{Nonoperating revenues} - \text{Nonoperating expenses}) \times (1 - \text{Marginal tax rate})]$$

NOPAT is an important measure of profitability. It is similar to net income except that NOPAT focuses exclusively on after-tax *operating* performance.

Computation of NOPAT requires that we separate nonoperating revenues and expenses from operating sources of income. Companies often report income from operations as a subtotal (before income taxes) within the income statement. These numbers should be interpreted with caution. Currently, there are no requirements within GAAP that specify which revenue and expense items should be included in operating income. As a consequence, some nonoperating items may be included (as part of SG&A expense, for example). PepsiCo has investments in affiliated companies that distribute its snack foods in certain parts of the world. PepsiCo's income from these investments is included in its SG&A expense in the income statement, but the amount is not disclosed. While this income might appear to be nonoperating, most analysts would argue that this amount should be included in the calculation of NOPAT for PepsiCo, because these distribution operations are part of the core operating activities of the business.

The tax rate used to compute NOPAT is the **marginal tax rate**. This rate is the effective tax rate on nonoperating revenues and expenses. That federal tax rate changed from 35% in 2017 and earlier to 21% in 2018 and later. As we have done throughout this chapter, we use the federal statutory tax rate of 35% to approximate the marginal tax rate in 2017 and earlier and 25% (rounded for simplicity) for 2018 and later periods.[5] PepsiCo's 2017 NOPAT can be computed using this tax rate:

[5] As we argued earlier in this chapter, the federal statutory tax rate is a reasonable approximation of the marginal tax rate in many instances, including our analysis of PepsiCo. However, some nonoperating sources of revenue and expense are not taxed at this rate. For example, most dividend income received from investments in the stock of other corporations is excluded from taxable income. A detailed analysis of marginal tax rates is beyond the scope of this text. Nevertheless, a thorough analysis of operating return would normally include a close examination of a company's income taxes.

$$\text{NOPAT} = \$4{,}908 \text{ million} - [(\$244 \text{ million} - \$1{,}151 \text{ million}) \times (1 - 0.35)] = \$5{,}497.6 \text{ million}$$

PepsiCo's NOPAT is greater than its net income of $4,908 million in 2017. The difference between net income and NOPAT is the interest expense on its debt and interest income on its investments.

Reporting Operating Activities in the Balance Sheet The balance sheet also reflects both operating and nonoperating activities. The asset side of the balance sheet reports resources devoted to operating activities in accounts such as cash, receivables, inventories, property, plant, and equipment, and intangible assets. Among liabilities, accounts payable, accrued expenses, and some long-term liabilities such as deferred compensation and pension benefits arise out of operating activities. In addition, accrued and deferred income taxes are generally considered operating liabilities.

Investments in securities of other companies are usually considered nonoperating. The exception is that some equity-type investments are related to operations. PepsiCo's investment in its snack foods distributors is an example of this type of investment. Equity investments are discussed further in Chapter 12. Among a company's liabilities, short-term and long-term debt accounts are classified as nonoperating. These include accounts such as notes payable, interest payable, current maturities of long-term debt, capital leases, and long-term debt.

PepsiCo reports short-term investments of $8,900 million in 2017 ($6,967 million in 2016), which are nonoperating. It also reports long-term investments in non-controlled affiliates of $2,042 million in 2017 ($1,950 million in 2016). These long-term investments are the aforementioned equity investments in companies distributing PepsiCo's snack foods, and most analysts would consider them to be part of operations. PepsiCo's footnotes show that its noncurrent Other assets account includes nonoperating assets of $346 million in 2017 ($338 million in 2016). Its nonoperating liabilities include short-term debt obligations of $5,485 million in 2017 ($6,892 million in 2016) and long-term debt obligations of $33,796 million in 2017 ($30,053 million in 2016).

By subtracting total operating liabilities from total operating assets, we get **net operating assets (NOA)**.[6] PepsiCo's NOA for 2017 and 2016 is calculated as follows ($ millions):

	2017	2016
Operating assets	$79,804 − $8,900 − $346 = $70,558	$73,490 − $6,967 − $338 = $66,185
Operating liabilities	$68,823 − $5,485 − $33,796 = $29,542	$62,291 − $6,892 − $30,053 = $25,346
NOA	$41,016	$40,839

Given NOPAT and NOA we can compute PepsiCo's RNOA as follows:

$$\text{RNOA} = \frac{\text{NOPAT}}{\text{Average NOA}} = \frac{\$5{,}497.6 \text{ million}}{(\$41{,}016 \text{ million} + \$40{,}839 \text{ million})/2} = 13.4\%$$

PepsiCo's ROE is 44.3% in 2017. Its RNOA is 13.4%, which represents 30% of the total return earned by stockholders.

Disaggregating RNOA

We gain further insights into operating returns by disaggregating RNOA into operating profit margin and asset turnover. RNOA can be presented as the product of net operating profit margin (NOPM) and net operating asset turnover (NOAT). We define **net operating profit margin (NOPM)** as the amount of operating profit produced as a percentage of each sales dollar. NOPM is similar to the profit margin (PM) ratio defined in the chapter, except that it excludes all nonoperating revenues and expenses from the calculation. PepsiCo's NOPM was 8.65% in 2017, computed as:

$$\text{NOPM} = \frac{\text{NOPAT}}{\text{Sales revenue}} = \frac{\$5{,}497.6 \text{ million}}{\$63{,}525 \text{ million}} = 8.65\%$$

The ratio indicates that each dollar of sales revenue generated 8.65¢ of after-tax operating profit. PepsiCo's NOPAT is very close to PepsiCo's EWI because the primary nonoperating item in the company's income statement is interest expense. Thus its NOPM is almost identical to its profit margin of 8.9%.

Net operating asset turnover (NOAT) is defined as the ratio of sales revenue to average net operating assets (NOA). NOAT captures the amount of sales revenue generated by each dollar of net investment in operating assets. PepsiCo's NOAT is 1.38 times, computed as:

[6] Total operating assets can be computed by subtracting nonoperating assets from total assets. Similarly, we can determine operating liabilities either by adding up the operating items or by subtracting the nonoperating items from total liabilities.

$$\text{NOAT} = \frac{\text{Sales revenue}}{\text{Average NOA}} = \frac{\$63,525\text{ million}}{(\$41,016\text{ million} + \$40,839\text{ million})/2} = 1.55$$

This ratio suggests that each dollar of investment in net operating assets generates $1.55 of sales revenue. This ratio is considerably higher than PepsiCo's asset turnover (AT) ratio of 0.829. This difference is caused by the difference between net operating assets (NOA) and total assets. NOAT is computed using average NOA in the denominator rather than average total assets. Thus, nonoperating assets are excluded, and operating assets are presented net of operating liabilities. The resulting denominator is, therefore, considerably smaller.

PepsiCo's RNOA is 13.4%. This return can be disaggregated into the product of NOPM and NOAT as follows:

RNOA = NOPM × NOAT

13.4% = 8.65% × 1.55

APPENDIX 5A REVIEW

Refer to the financial statements of the Coca-Cola Company presented in Mid-Chapter Review 1. Calculate Coca-Cola's return on net operating assets (RNOA) and then disaggregate RNOA into net operating profit margin (NOPM) and net operating asset turnover (NOAT). Assume an income tax rate of 35% for 2016 and 2017, and that equity method investments, other assets, and other liabilities are operating items.

The solution to this review problem can be found on page 268.

APPENDIX 5B: Financial Statement Forecasts

LO6 Prepare financial statement forecasts.

6

The ability to forecast future financial activities is an important aspect of many business decisions. We might, for example, wish to estimate the value of a company's common stock before purchasing its shares. Or, we might want to evaluate the creditworthiness of a prospective borrower. We might also be interested in comparing the financial impact of alternative business strategies or tactics. For each of these decision contexts, a forecast of future earnings and cash flows would be relevant to such an evaluation.

Financial statement forecasts are hypothetical statements prepared to reflect specific assumptions about the company and its transactions. These forecasts are prepared for future periods based on assumptions about the future activities of a business. By varying the assumptions, forecasts of statements allow us to ask "what if" questions about the future activities of the company, the answers to which provide the necessary inputs underlying most business decisions.

In this appendix, we present a common, yet simple method for preparing financial statement forecasts. This method proceeds in seven steps:

1. Forecast sales revenue.
2. Forecast operating expenses, such as cost of goods sold and SG&A expenses.
3. Forecast operating assets and liabilities, including accounts receivable, inventory, property, plant, and equipment, accounts payable, and prepaid and accrued expenses.
4. Forecast nonoperating assets, liabilities, contributed capital, revenues and expenses.
5. Forecast net income, dividends and retained earnings.
6. Forecast the amount of cash required to balance the balance sheet.
7. Prepare a cash flow statement based on the forecasted income statement and balance sheet.

Step 1. Forecast Sales Revenue

The sales forecast is the crucial first step in the preparation of financial statement forecasts because many of the accounts in the income statement and balance sheet depend on their relation to the sales forecast. The general method for forecasting sales is to assume a revenue growth rate and apply that rate to the current sales revenue amount:

Forecasted revenues = Current revenues × (1 + Revenue growth rate)

A good starting point for estimating the revenue growth rate is the historical rate of sales growth. This is obtained by using data from the horizontal analysis discussed earlier in the chapter. For example, over the past four years, PepsiCo has experienced an average sales decline of 1.1% per year. Once we have this historical rate as a starting point, we can then adjust the growth rate up or down based on other relevant information. For example, we might attempt to answer the following questions:

- How will future sales be affected by economic conditions? What will happen in the economy in the coming year? Do we expect economic growth or a recession? How will economic growth vary in various markets, such as the United States, Europe, Asia, and Latin America? How will foreign currency exchange rates come into play?
- What changes are expected from the company? Are there any new strategic initiatives planned? Is the company planning to open new stores, launch new products, new advertising campaigns, or new pricing tactics? Do we expect any acquisitions of other businesses?
- What changes in the competitive environment do we expect? Are new competitors entering the market? How will existing competitors respond to changes in the company's strategy? How will substitute products affect sales?

To answer each of the above questions, we rely on a variety of information sources, not the least of which is the management's discussion and analysis (MD&A) section of the company's 10-K report. We can also use publicly available information from competitors, suppliers, customers, industry organizations and government agencies to provide some insight into trends that can have an effect on future revenues. Our objective is to be able to adjust the historical growth rate up or down to reflect the insights we gain from reviewing this additional information. Revenue for 2017 increased by about 1% over 2016, but once the difference in fiscal years is taken into account (52 weeks in 2017 versus 53 weeks in 2016), the growth rate was 2%. Therefore, we forecast the 2018 revenue to be $64,796 million ($63,525 million × 1.02).

Step 2. Forecast Operating Expenses

Given our forecast of sales revenue, we then turn to forecasting operating expenses. We rely on the common-size income statement as a starting point to identify the relationship between operating expense items and sales revenue. That is, we use the expense-to-sales (ETS) ratio for each operating expense item to compute the forecasted expense:

$$\textbf{Forecasted operating expense} = \textbf{Forecasted revenues} \times \textbf{ETS ratio}$$

While historical ETS ratios provide a good place to start, we may want to adjust these ratios up or down based on observed trends or any additional information that we might have. For example, when we examined PepsiCo's common-size income statements, we learned that cost of goods sold increased to 45.3% of sales in 2017, up from 44.9% in 2016. Will this trend continue into 2018? What are the effects of developments in the sugar market or from tariffs on imported aluminum? What about PepsiCo's cost-cutting efforts over recent years? Or, do we anticipate that this expense item will revert to historical levels in relation to sales? As was the case with the sales forecast, there are numerous sources of information that are potentially useful for making adjustments to the historical relationships.

For the purpose of illustration, we assume that 2018 Cost of sales will increase to 46% of revenues ($29,806 million) and that Selling, general and administrative expenses will drop slightly to 38% of revenues in 2018 ($24,622 million).

Step 3. Forecast Operating Assets and Liabilities

The sales forecast can also be used to forecast operating assets and liabilities. The relationship between operating assets and revenues is based on asset turnover analysis. For example, when we compute accounts receivable turnover (ART), sales revenue is divided by average accounts receivable. When forecasting accounts receivable, we assume a relationship between sales revenue and year-end accounts receivable:

$$\textbf{Forecasted accounts receivable} = \frac{\textbf{Forecasted sales revenue} \times \textbf{Reported accounts receivable}}{\textbf{Reported sales revenue}}$$

PepsiCo reports accounts and notes receivable of $7,024 million in 2017, which is 11.06% of the reported sales revenue of $63,525 million. The forecasted accounts receivable for 2018 is, therefore, $7,166 million ($64,796 million × 11.06%).

The same procedure can be used to forecast other operating assets, such as inventories, prepaid expenses and property, plant, and equipment, as well as operating liabilities such as accounts payable and accrued expenses. Intangible assets, including Goodwill, arise when one company acquires another. Goodwill and some intangibles are not amortized after purchase (more in Chapter 12), but some do get amortized. Forecasting these values requires forecasts of PepsiCo's acquisitions in 2018. For this illustration, we assume no acquisitions in 2018, no impairments of nonamortizable intangibles, and the amortization of intangible assets in 2018 is $69 million, the same as in 2017.

Step 4. Forecast Nonoperating Assets, Liabilities, Revenues and Expenses

While operating expenses, assets, and liabilities tend to be related to sales revenue, this is typically not the case for nonoperating items. Instead, nonoperating revenues, such as interest and dividend income, tend to be related to investments, while nonoperating expense, namely interest expense, is related to debt financing. As a starting point, we forecast each of these items by assuming no change from the current amounts. For example, PepsiCo reported long-term debt of $33,796 million in 2017 along with short-term obligations of $5,485 million. We forecast the same level of debt financing in 2018. Likewise, interest expense should remain the same at $1,151 million.

There may be information in the notes or in the MD&A section of the 10-K report to suggest other assumptions. For example, the notes typically reveal the amount of long-term debt that will come due in each of the next five years. This information can be used to adjust the balance in short-term obligations, because current maturities of long-term debt would be included under this item. Nevertheless, an assumption of no change is a good place to start.

Step 5. Forecast Net Income, Dividends, and Retained Earnings

Once we have forecasts of sales revenue (from step 1), operating expenses (step 2), and nonoperating revenues and expenses (step 4), we can calculate pretax earnings, income tax expense, and net income. Income tax expense is forecasted by multiplying pretax income by the effective tax rate:

Forecasted income tax expense = Forecasted pretax income × Effective tax rate

The **effective tax rate** is the average tax rate applied to pretax earnings, and is computed by dividing reported income tax expense by reported pretax earnings. PepsiCo's effective tax rate was 48.9% in 2017 ($4,694 million/$9,602 million), but this is artificially high due to the transition effect of 2017's Tax Cuts and Jobs Act. And the TCJA reduced the corporate tax rate from 35% to 21% starting in 2018. Although this rate can be adjusted up or down based on additional information, we apply a 25% effective tax rate to compute 2018 forecasted income taxes. This assumption results in forecasted income taxes of $2,365 million ($9,461 million × 25%) and forecasted net income of $7,096 million ($9,461 million – $2,365 million). PepsiCo's forecasted 2018 income statement is presented in **Exhibit 5B.1** alongside its 2017 reported income statement.

EXHIBIT 5B.1 PepsiCo Income Statement Forecast

PEPSICO, INC.
2017 Income Statement and 2018 Income Statement Forecast

($ millions)	Forecast 2018	As reported 2017
Net revenue ($63,525 × 1.02)	$64,796	$63,525
Cost of sales ($64,796 × 0.46)	29,806	28,785
Selling, general & administrative expenses ($64,796 × 0.38)	24,622	24,231
Operating profit	10,368	10,509
Interest expense (no change)	(1,151)	(1,151)
Interest income (no change)	244	244
Income before income taxes	9,461	9,602
Provision for income taxes ($9,461 × 0.25)	2,365	4,694
Net income	$ 7,096	$ 4,908

Our forecast of dividends relies on the **dividend payout ratio**, defined as dividend payments divided by net income.

Forecasted dividends = Forecasted net income × Dividend payout ratio

PepsiCo paid cash dividends of $4,472 million in 2017, which is 91.1% of its net income of $4,908 million. But the TCJA effect makes this measure artificially high. The comparable numbers for 2016 and 2015 are 66.3% and 73.4%, respectively. Using a dividend payout ratio of 70%, we forecast 2018 dividends to be $4,967 million ($7,096 million × 70%).

Next, we can forecast retained earnings using the forecasts of net income and dividends:

$$\text{Forecasted retained earnings} = \text{Beginning retained earnings} + \text{Forecasted net income} - \text{Forecasted dividends}$$

Throughout this chapter, we have presented PepsiCo's stockholders' equity as a single amount, without separating retained earnings from contributed capital. Contributed capital increases when common stock is issued, and decreases when common stock is repurchased. PepsiCo has repurchased shares every year for the past eight years and every indication is that it will continue to repurchase shares in 2018. Stock repurchases, net of common stock issued, have averaged $2,862 million over the past three years. If we assume that this rate will continue in 2018, total stockholders' equity in 2018 will equal $10,248 computed as follows:

Forecasted stockholders' equity	=	Beginning stockholders' equity	+	Forecasted net income	−	Forecasted dividends	−	Forecasted stock repurchases
$10,248 million	=	**$10,981 million**	+	**$7,096 million**	−	**$4,967 million**	−	**$2,862 million**

Step 6. Forecast Cash

If the forecasts of all other components of the balance sheet are in place, we can then forecast the cash balance. This forecast is simply a "plug" amount that makes the balance sheet balance:

$$\text{Forecasted cash} = \text{Forecasted liabilities} + \text{Forecasted stockholders' equity} - \text{Forecasted noncash assets}$$

It is possible that the resulting forecast of cash will be negative or unreasonably small or large. If this occurs, we then revisit steps 4 and 5. If the cash forecast is negative or too low, we adjust our forecast of short-term debt and interest expense to reflect increased borrowing to cover cash needs. If the cash forecast is too large, we can assume that excess cash is invested in marketable securities and increase the amount of interest income. In either case, we then modify our forecast of income taxes, net income, dividends and retained earnings, before recalculating the cash forecast.

PepsiCo's 2018 balance sheet forecast is presented in **Exhibit 5B.2**, alongside the company's 2017 actual balance sheet. The cash balance is forecasted to decrease slightly, from $10,610 million in 2017 to $9,938 million in 2018.

EXHIBIT 5B.2 PepsiCo Balance Sheet Forecast

PEPSICO, INC.
2017 Balance Sheet and 2018 Balance Sheet Forecast

($ millions)	Forecast 2018	As reported 2017
Assets		
Cash and cash equivalents (plug to balance)	$ 9,938	$10,610
Short-term investments (no change)	8,900	8,900
Accounts and notes receivable, net ($64,796 × 11.06%)	7,166	7,024
Inventories ($64,796 × 4.64%)	3,007	2,947
Prepaid expenses and other current assets ($64,796 × 2.43%)	1,575	1,546
Total current assets	30,586	31,027
Property, plant and equipment, net ($64,796 × 27.14%)	17,586	17,240
Amortizable intangible assets, net ($1,268 – $69)	1,199	1,268
Goodwill (no change)	14,744	14,744
Other nonamortizable intangible assets (no change)	12,570	12,570
Investments in noncontrolled affiliates (no change)	2,042	2,042
Other assets ($64,796 × 1.44%)	933	913
Total assets	$79,660	$ 79,804
Liabilities and equity		
Short-term obligations (no change)	$ 5,485	$ 5,485
Accounts payable and other current liabilities ($64,796 × 23.64%)	15,318	15,017
Total current liabilities	20,803	20,502
Long-term debt obligations (no change)	33,796	33,796
Other liabilities ($64,796 × 17.76%)	11,508	11,283
Deferred income taxes ($64,796 × 5.10%)	3,305	3,242
Total liabilities	69,412	68,823
Total equity ($10,981 + $7,096 – $4,967 – $2,862)	10,248	10,981
Total liabilities and equity	$79,660	$79,804

Step 7. Prepare the Cash Flow Statement Forecast

Once we have a forecast of the income statement and balance sheet, we can prepare a forecast of the cash flow statement using the methods illustrated in Chapter 4. To do so, we need a forecast of depreciation expense (if that item is not explicitly listed as an operating expense in the income statement). The procedure for forecasting depreciation expense is the same as was used for other operating expenses—we simply use the depreciation ETS ratio.

PepsiCo reported depreciation and amortization expense of $2,369 million in 2017, which was 3.73% of sales revenue. Using this ETS ratio, we can forecast depreciation expense of $2,417 million in 2018 ($64,796 million × 3.73%). Using this forecast, along with other items forecasted earlier, we can prepare the cash flow statement, which is presented in **Exhibit 5B.3**.

Additional Considerations

Forecasts of financial statements are based on a set of assumptions about the future. Any decisions that are based on such statements are only as good as the quality of these assumptions. Therefore it is important that we appreciate the effect that each assumption has on the forecasted amounts. To this end, it is often helpful to use **sensitivity analysis** to examine the effect of alternative assumptions on the forecasted statements. For example, we might prepare three different forecasted income statements, one using our "most-likely" assumption for the sales forecast, and one each for the "best-case" and "worst-case" scenarios. In some situations, a change in the sales forecast can have a dramatic effect on net income and cash flows, particularly in the presence of large fixed costs. Sensitivity analysis helps to identify these effects before a decision is made so that costly mistakes can be avoided.

It is also important to remember that these statements are predictions about the future and, as such, are bound to be wrong. That is, we expect that there will be **forecast errors**—differences between the forecasted and the actual amounts. The goal of a good forecast is accuracy, which means that we want the forecast errors to be as small as possible. Generating forecasted statements using a computer is relatively easy and the efficiency and precision of spreadsheet software can provide a false sense of confidence in the numbers. Spreadsheets routinely calculate forecasted amounts to the "nth" decimal place whether or not such precision is justified. However, an amount forecasted to the nearest penny may not be useful if the forecast is off by millions of dollars. It is better to be imprecisely accurate than to be precisely inaccurate.

EXHIBIT 5B.3 PepsiCo Cash Flow Statement Forecast

PEPSICO, INC.
2018 Cash Flow Statement Forecast

($ millions)	2018 Forecast
Operations:	
Net income	$ 7,096
Adjustments:	
Depreciation and amortization ($64,796 × 3.73%)	2,417
Minus change in accounts and notes receivable	(142)
Minus change in inventories	(60)
Minus change in prepaid expenses and other current assets	(29)
Minus change in other assets	(20)
Plus change in accounts payable and other current liabilities	301
Plus change in other liabilities	225
Plus change in deferred income taxes	63
Cash flow from operations	9,851
Investing activities:	
Investment in property, plant and equipment [$2,417 + ($17,586 − $17,240) + ($1,199 − $1,268)]	(2,694)
Cash used for investing activities	(2,694)
Financing activities:	
Dividends paid	(4,967)
Share repurchases, net	(2,862)
Cash used for financing activities	(7,829)
Net decrease in cash ($9,851 − $2,694 − $7,829)	(672)
Cash and cash equivalents, 2017	10,610
Cash and cash equivalents, 2018	$ 9,938

APPENDIX 5B REVIEW

Refer to the income statements and balance sheets of the Coca-Cola Company presented in Mid-Chapter Review 1.

Required

Make the following assumptions:

- 2018 sales revenue increases 4% from 2017 to $36,826 million.
- Operating expenses increase in 2018 in proportion to sales revenue.
- Operating assets and liabilities increase based on their 2017 relation to sales revenue. Classify "Goodwill and other intangible assets," "Other assets," and "Other liabilities" as operating.
- Assume that nonoperating revenues, expenses, assets and liabilities do not change from 2017 to 2018 and there are no discontinued operations in 2018. Assume no change for equity income or equity method investments.
- Dividend payout is 60% of net income.
- Assume 25% income tax rate.

Prepare a forecast income statement and balance sheet for 2018.

The solution to this review problem can be found on page 268–269.

SUMMARY

LO1 Prepare and analyze common-size financial statements. (p. 221)

- Vertical analysis restates items in the income statement as a percentage of sales revenue and items in the balance sheet as a percentage of total assets.
- Horizontal analysis examines the percentage change from one year to the next for specific items in the income statement and balance sheet.

LO2 Compute and interpret measures of return on investment, including return on equity (ROE), return on assets (ROA), and return on financial leverage (ROFL). (p. 225)

- ROE is the primary measure of company performance. It captures the return earned by shareholder investment in the firm.
- ROA measures the return earned on the firm's investment in assets. It is not affected by the way those assets are financed.
- ROFL is the difference between ROE and ROA and measures the effect that financial leverage has on ROE.

LO3 Disaggregate ROA into profitability (profit margin) and efficiency (asset turnover) components. (p. 228)

- ROA can be disaggregated as the product of profit margin (PM) and asset turnover (AT).
- PM can be analyzed further by examining the gross profit margin and expense-to-sales ratios.
- AT can be analyzed further by examining accounts receivable turnover (ART), inventory turnover (INVT), and property, plant, and equipment turnover (PPET).
- The trade-off between PM and AT is determined by the company's strategy and its competitive environment.

LO4 Compute and interpret measures of liquidity and solvency. (p. 233)

- The current ratio (CR) and quick ratio (QR) measure short-term liquidity by comparing liquid assets to short-term obligations. The operating cash flow to current assets ratio (OCFCL) and the cash burn rate (CBR) relate a company's cash flows to its existing obligations and liquid resources.
- The debt-to-equity ratio (D/E) and times interest earned ratio (TIE) measure long-term solvency by comparing sources of financing and the level of earnings to the cost of debt (interest).

LO5 Appendix 5A: Measure and analyze the effect of operating activities on ROE. (p. 241)

- Net operating profit after taxes (NOPAT) measures the portion of income that results from a business' core operating activities.

- Return on net operating assets (RNOA), defined as NOPAT/average net operating assets, measures the return on a company's net investment in operating assets.

Appendix 5B: Prepare financial statement forecasts. (p. 243) **LO6**

- Financial statement forecasts are prepared for future periods based on assumptions about the future activities of the business.
- Financial statement forecasts can be used to evaluate the effects of alternative actions or assumptions on the financial statements.

KEY RATIOS

RETURN MEASURES

$$\text{Return on equity (ROE)} = \frac{\text{Net income}}{\text{Average stockholders' equity}}$$

$$\text{Earnings without interest expense (EWI)} = \text{Net income} + [\text{Interest expense} \times (1 - \text{Statutory tax rate})]$$

$$\text{Return on assets (ROA)} = \frac{\text{Earnings without interest expense (EWI)}}{\text{Average total assets}}$$

$$\text{Return on financial leverage (ROFL)} = \text{ROE} - \text{ROA}$$

PROFITABILITY RATIOS

$$\text{Profit margin (PM)} = \frac{\text{Earnings without interest expense (EWI)}}{\text{Sales revenue}}$$

$$\text{Gross profit margin (GPM)} = \frac{\text{Sales revenue} - \text{Cost of goods sold}}{\text{Sales revenue}}$$

$$\text{Expense-to-sales (ETS)} = \frac{\text{Individual expense items}}{\text{Sales revenue}}$$

TURNOVER RATIOS

$$\text{Asset turnover (AT)} = \frac{\text{Sales revenue}}{\text{Average total assets}}$$

$$\text{Accounts receivable turnover (ART)} = \frac{\text{Sales revenue}}{\text{Average accounts receivable}}$$

$$\text{Inventory turnover (INVT)} = \frac{\text{Cost of goods sold}}{\text{Average inventory}}$$

$$\text{Property, plant, and equipment turnover (PPET)} = \frac{\text{Sales revenue}}{\text{Average PP \& E}}$$

LIQUIDITY RATIOS

$$\text{Current ratio (CR)} = \frac{\text{Current assets}}{\text{Current liabilities}}$$

$$\text{Quick ratio (QR)} = \frac{\text{Cash} + \text{Short-term securities} + \text{Accounts receivable}}{\text{Current liabilities}}$$

$$\text{Operating cash flow to current liabilities (OCFCL)} = \frac{\text{Operating cash flow}}{\text{Average current liabilities}}$$

$$\text{Cash burn rate} = \frac{\text{Free cash flow in the period}}{\text{Number of days in the period}}$$

SOLVENCY RATIOS

$$\text{Times interest earned (TIE)} = \frac{\text{Earnings before interest expense and taxes (EBIT)}}{\text{Interest expense}}$$

$$\text{Debt-to-equity (DE)} = \frac{\text{Total liabilities}}{\text{Total stockholders' equity}}$$

KEY TERMS

Accounts receivable turnover (ART) (p. 231)
Asset turnover (AT) (p. 228)
Capacity costs (p. 228)
Cash burn rate (CBR) (p. 236)
Common-size financial statements (p. 221)
Covenants (p. 234)
Current ratio (p. 235)
Debt-to-equity ratio (p. 237)
Default risk (p. 235)
Dividend payout ratio (p. 245)
Earnings without interest expense (EWI) (p. 225)
Effective tax rate (p. 245)
Expense-to-sales (ETS) (p. 231)
Financial leverage (p. 226)
Financial statement analysis (p. 220)
Financial statement forecasts (p. 243)
Forecast error (p. 247)
Gross profit margin (GPM) (p. 231)
Horizontal analysis (p. 223)
Inventory turnover (INVT) (p. 231)
Liquidity (p. 235)
Liquidity analysis (p. 235)
Marginal tax rate (p. 241)
Net operating assets (NOA) (p. 242)
Net operating asset turnover (NOAT) (p. 242)
Net operating profit after taxes (NOPAT) (p. 241)
Net operating profit margin (NOPM) (p. 242)
Operating cash flow to current liabilities (OCFCL) (p. 236)
Profit margin (PM) (p. 228)
Property, plant, and equipment turnover (PPET) (p. 232)
Quick ratio (p. 236)
Return on assets (ROA) (p. 225)
Return on equity (ROE) (p. 225)
Return on financial leverage (ROFL) (p. 226)
Return on net operating assets (RNOA) (p. 241)
Sensitivity analysis (p. 247)
Solvency (p. 237)
Solvency analysis (p. 235)
Times interest earned (TIE) (p. 238)
Vertical analysis (p. 221)
Working capital (p. 235)

Assignments with the MBC logo in the margin are available in myBusinessCourse. See the Preface of the book for details.

MULTIPLE CHOICE

Multiple Choice Answers
1. c 2. b 3. b 4. b 5. b

1. Which of the following ratios would not be affected by an increase in cost of goods sold?
a. ROA
b. INVT
c. Quick ratio
d. PM

2. A company has the following values: PM = 0.07; EWI = $1,885; Average total assets = $37,400. AT equals
a. 0.05
b. 0.72
c. 0.36
d. AT is not determinable because its sales are not reported.

3. A company's current ratio is 2 and its quick ratio is 1. What can be said about the sum of the company's cash + short-term securities + accounts receivable?
a. The sum exceeds the current liabilities.
b. The sum is equal to the sum of the current liabilities.
c. The sum is equal to 1/2 of the total current liabilities.
d. None of the above is correct.

4. A company's interest expense is $500,000 and its net income is $14 million. If the company's effective tax rate is 30%, what is the company's times interest earned (TIE) ratio?

a. 90
b. 41
c. 32
d. 16

5. If a company's ROFL is negative, which of the following is *not* true?

a. ROA > ROE
b. The DE ratio is negative.
c. ROA < net interest rate
d. The company likely has a low TIE ratio.

GUIDANCE ANSWERS . . . YOU MAKE THE CALL

You are the Entrepreneur Your company is performing substantially better than its competitors. Namely, your ROA of 16% is markedly superior to competitors' ROA of 10%. However, ROA disaggregation shows that this is mainly attributed to your AT of 0.89 versus competitors' AT of 0.59. Your PM of 18% is essentially identical to competitors' PM of 17%. Accordingly, you will want to maintain your AT as further improvements are probably difficult to achieve. Importantly, you are likely to achieve the greatest benefit with efforts at improving your PM of 18%, which is only marginally better than the industry norm of 17%.

Superscript $^{A(B)}$ denotes assignments based on Appendix 5A (5B).

QUESTIONS

Q5-1. Explain in general terms the concept of return on investment. Why is this concept important in the analysis of financial performance?

Q5-2. (a) Explain how an increase in financial leverage can increase a company's ROE. (b) Given the potentially positive relation between financial leverage and ROE, why don't we see companies with 100% financial leverage (entirely nonowner financed)?

Q5-3. Gross profit margin [(Sales revenue − Cost of goods sold)/Sales revenue] is an important determinant of profit margin. Identify two factors that can cause gross profit margin to decline. Is a reduction in the gross profit margin always bad news? Explain.

Q5-4. Explain how a reduction in operating expenses as a percentage of sales can produce a short-term gain at the cost of long-term performance.

Q5-5. Describe the concept of asset turnover. What does the concept mean and why is it so important to understanding and interpreting financial performance?

Q5-6. Explain what it means when a company's ROE exceeds its ROA.

Q5-7. What are common-size financial statements? What role do they play in financial statement analysis?

Q5-8. How does a firm go about increasing its AT ratio? What strategies are likely to be most effective?

Q5-9.^{A} What is meant by the term "net" in net operating assets (NOA)?

Q5-10. Why is it important to disaggregate ROA into profit margin (PM) and asset turnover (AT)?

Q5-11. What insights do we gain from the graphical relation between profit margin and asset turnover?

Q5-12. Explain the concept of liquidity and why it is crucial to company survival.

Q5-13. Identify at least two factors that limit the usefulness of ratio analysis.

MINI EXERCISES

M5-14. Return on Investment, DuPont Analysis and Financial Leverage **LO2, 3**

The following table presents selected 2019 financial information for Sunder Company.

SUNDER COMPANY Selected 2019 Financial Data	
Balance Sheet:	
Average total assets	$1,000,000
Average total liabilities	500,000
Average stockholders' equity	500,000
Income statement:	
Sales revenue	$1,000,000
Earnings before interest (net of tax)	20,000
Interest expense (net of tax)	15,000
Net income	5,000

a. Compute Sunder's ROE, ROA and ROFL for 2019.

b. Use the DuPont analysis described in the Business Insight on page 230 to disaggregate ROE.

c. How did the use of financial leverage affect Sunder's ROE in 2019? Explain.

LO1

Target Corporation
NYSE :: TGT

M5-15. Common-Size Balance Sheets

Following is the balance sheet for **Target Corporation**. Prepare Target's common-size balance sheets as of February 3, 2018 and January 28, 2017.

($ millions)	February 3, 2018	January 28, 2017
Assets		
Cash and cash equivalents	$ 2,643	$ 2,512
Inventory	8,657	8,309
Other current assets	1,264	1,169
Total current assets	12,564	11,990
Property and equipment, net	25,018	24,658
Other noncurrent assets	1,417	783
Total assets	$38,999	$37,431
Liabilities and shareholders' investment		
Accounts payable	$ 8,677	$ 7,252
Accrued and other current liabilities	4,254	3,737
Current portion of long-term debt and other borrowings	270	1,718
Total current liabilities	13,201	12,707
Long-term debt and other borrowings	11,317	11,031
Deferred income taxes	713	861
Other noncurrent liabilities	2,059	1,879
Total noncurrent liabilities	14,089	13,771
Total shareholders' investment	11,709	10,953
Total liabilities and shareholders' investment	$38,999	$37,431

LO1

Homework MBC

Target Corporation
NYSE :: TGT

M5-16. Common-Size Income Statements

Following is the income statement for **Target Corporation**. Prepare Target's common-size income statement for the fiscal year ended February 3, 2018.

($ millions)	Fiscal year ended February 3, 2018
Sales	$71,879
Cost of sales	51,125
Selling, general and administrative expenses	14,248
Depreciation and amortization	2,194
Earnings from continuing operations before interest expense and income taxes	4,312
Net interest expense	666
Earnings from continuing operations before income taxes	3,646
Provision for income taxes	718
Net earnings from continuing operations	2,928
Discontinued operations, net of tax	6
Net earnings	$ 2,934

M5-17. Compute ROA, Profit Margin, and Asset Turnover

LO2, 3

Target Corporation
NYSE :: TGT

Refer to the financial information for **Target Corporation**, presented in M5-15 and M5-16.

a. Compute its return on assets (ROA) for the fiscal year ending February 3, 2018. Compute two ROA measures, one using net earnings from continuing operations and one using net earnings. Assume an income tax rate of 25%.

b. Disaggregate ROA into profit margin (PM) and asset turnover (AT). Confirm that ROA = PM × AT.

M5-18. Analysis and Interpretation of Liquidity and Solvency

LO4

Target Corporation
NYSE :: TGT

Refer to the financial information of **Target Corporation** in M5-15 and M5-16 to answer the following.

a. Compute Target's current ratio and quick ratio for February 2018 and January 2017. Comment on any observed trends.

b. Compute Target's times interest earned for the year ended February 3, 2018, and its debt-to-equity ratios for February 2018 and January 2017. Comment on any trends observed.

c. Summarize your findings in a conclusion about the company's liquidity and solvency. Do you have any concerns about Target's ability to meet its debt obligations?

M5-19. Common-Size Balance Sheets

LO1

3M Company
NYSE :: MMM

Following is the balance sheet for **3M Company**. Prepare common-size balance sheets for 2017 and 2016.

3M COMPANY AND SUBSIDIARIES		
December 31 ($ millions)	**2017**	**2016**
Assets		
Cash, cash equivalents and marketable securities	$ 4,129	$ 2,678
Accounts receivable—net of allowances of $103 and $88	4,911	4,392
Total inventories	4,034	3,385
Prepaids	937	821
Other current assets	266	450
Total current assets	14,277	11,726
Property, plant and equipment—net	8,866	8,516
Goodwill	10,513	9,166
Intangible assets—net	2,936	2,320
Other assets	1,395	1,178
Total assets	$37,987	$32,906
Liabilities and Shareholders' Equity		
Current liabilities		
Short-term borrowings and current portion of long-term debt	$ 1,853	$ 972
Accounts payable	1,945	1,798
Accrued payroll	870	678
Accrued income taxes	310	299
Other current liabilities	2,709	2,472
Total current liabilities	7,687	6,219
Long-term debt	12,096	10,678
Pension and postretirement benefits	3,620	4,018
Other liabilities	2,962	1,648
Total liabilities	$26,365	$22,563
Total equity	$11,622	$10,343
Total liabilities and equity	$37,987	$32,906

M5-20. Common-Size Income Statements

LO1

3M Company
NYSE :: MMM

Following is the income statement for **3M Company**. Prepare common-size income statements for 2017 and 2016.

3M COMPANY AND SUBSIDIARIES Year ended December 31 ($ millions)	2017	2016
Net sales	$31,657	$30,109
Operating expenses		
Cost of sales	16,001	15,040
Selling, general and administrative expenses	6,572	6,222
Research, development and related expenses	1,850	1,735
Gain on sale of businesses	(586)	(111)
Total operating expenses	23,837	22,886
Operating income	7,820	7,223
Interest expense	322	199
Interest income	(50)	(29)
Income before income taxes	7,548	7,053
Provision for income taxes	2,679	1,995
Net income including noncontrolling interest	$ 4,869	$ 5,058

LO2, 3 MBC

3M Company
NYSE :: MMM

M5-21. Compute ROA, Profit Margin, and Asset Turnover

Refer to the balance sheet and income statement information for **3M Company**, presented in M5-19 and M5-20.

a. Compute 3M's 2017 return on assets (ROA). Use 35% as the effective tax rate.

b. Disaggregate ROA into profit margin (PM) and asset turnover (AT). Confirm that ROA = PM × AT.

LO2, 3

Urban Outfitters, Inc.
NASDAQ :: URBN
TJX Companies
NYSE :: TJX

M5-22. Compute ROA, Profit Margin and Asset Turnover for Competitors

Selected balance sheet and income statement information from **Urban Outfitters, Inc.** and **TJX Companies**, clothing retailers in the high-end and value-priced segments, respectively, follows.

Company ($ millions)	2017 Sales	2017 Earnings Without Interest Expense (EWI)	2017 Total Assets	2016 Total Assets
Urban Outfitters	$ 3,616	$ 108	$ 1,953	$ 1,903
TJX Companies	35,865	2,653	14,058	12,884

a. Compute the 2017 return on assets (ROA) for both companies.

b. Disaggregate ROA into profit margin (PM) and asset turnover (AT) for each company. Confirm that ROA = PM × AT.

c. Discuss differences observed with respect to PM and AT and interpret these differences in light of each company's business model.

LO4 MBC

Verizon Communications, Inc.
NYSE :: VZ

M5-23. Compute and Interpret Liquidity and Solvency Ratios

Selected balance sheet and income statement information from **Verizon Communications, Inc.**, follows.

($ millions)	2017	2016
Current assets	$ 29,913	$ 26,395
Current liabilities	33,037	30,340
Total liabilities	212,456	220,148
Equity	43,096	22,524
Earnings before interest and taxes	25,327	25,362
Interest expense	4,733	4,376
Net cash flow from operating activities	25,305	22,810

a. Compute the current ratio for each year and discuss any change in liquidity. How does Verizon's current ratio compare to the median for the telecommunications industry in **Exhibit 5.13**? What additional information about the numbers used to calculate this ratio might be useful in helping us assess liquidity? Explain.

b. Compute times interest earned, the debt-to-equity, and the operating cash flow to current liabilities ratios for each year and discuss any trends for each. (In 2015, current liabilities totaled $35,052 million.) Compare Verizon's ratios to those that are typical for its industry (refer to **Exhibit 5.13**). Do you have any concerns about the extent of Verizon's financial leverage and the company's ability to meet interest obligations? Explain.

c. Verizon's capital expenditures are expected to remain high as it seeks to respond to competitive pressures to upgrade the quality of its communication infrastructure. Assess Verizon's liquidity and solvency in light of this strategic direction.

M5-24. Computing Turnover Ratios for Companies in Different Industries

LO3

Selected data from recent financial statements of **The Procter & Gamble Company**, **CVS Health Corporation**, and **Valero Energy Corporation** are presented below:

The Procter & Gamble Company NYSE :: PG
CVS Health Corporation NYSE :: CVS
Valero Energy Corporation NYSE :: VLO

($ millions)	Procter & Gamble	CVS Health	Valero Energy
Sales	$66,832	$184,765	$88,407
Cost of sales	33,449	156,208	81,926
Average receivables	4,640	12,673	6,296
Average inventories	4,681	15,028	6,047
Average PP&E	20,247	10,234	26,976
Average total assets	66,119	94,797	48,166

a. Compute the asset turnover (AT) ratio for each company.

b. Compute the accounts receivable turnover (ART), inventory turnover (INVT), and PP&E turnover (PPET) for each company.

c. Discuss any differences across these three companies in the turnover ratios computed in *a* and *b*.

EXERCISES

E5-25. Compute and Interpret ROA, Profit Margin, and Asset Turnover of Competitors

LO2, 3

Selected balance sheet and income statement information for **McDonald's Corporation** and **Yum! Brands, Inc.**, follows.

McDonald's Corporation NYSE :: MCD
Yum! Brands, Inc. NYSE :: YUM

($ millions)	Sales Revenue	Interest Expense	Net Income	Average Total Assets
McDonald's	$22,820	$921	$5,192	$32,414
Yum! Brands	5,878	440	1,340	5,382

a. Compute the return on assets (ROA) for each company. Use the 35% statutory tax rate that was in force for 2017.

b. Disaggregate ROA into profit margin (PM) and asset turnover (AT) for each company.

c. Discuss any differences in these ratios for each company. Your interpretation should reflect the distinct business strategies of each company.

E5-26. Compute ROA, ROE and ROFL and Interpret the Effects of Leverage

LO2

Basic income statement and balance sheet information is given below for six different cases. For each case, the assets are financed with a mix of non-interest-bearing liabilities, 10% interest-bearing liability and stockholders' equity. In all cases, the income tax rate is 40%.

Case	A	B	C	D	E	F
Average assets	1,000	1,000	1,000	1,000	1,000	1,000
Non-interest-bearing liabilities	0	0	0	0	200	200
Interest-bearing liabilities	0	250	500	500	0	300
Average shareholders' equity	1,000	750	500	500	800	500
Earnings before interest and taxes (EBIT)	120	120	120	80	100	80

a. For each case, calculate the return on equity (ROE), return on assets (ROA) and return on financial leverage (ROFL).

b. Consider cases A, B and C. How does increasing leverage affect the three ratios? Why does the ROE grow from case A to case C?

c. Consider cases C and D. When does leverage work in favor of shareholders? Does that hold for case E?

d. Case F has two types of liabilities. How does ROA compare to the rate on interest-bearing liabilities? Does leverage work in favor of the shareholders? Why?

LO2, 3 Homework MBC

CVS Health Corporation
NYSE :: CVS
Walgreens Boots Alliance, Inc.
NASDAQ :: WBA

E5-27. Compute, Disaggregate, and Interpret Competitors' Rates of Return
Selected balance sheet and income statement information for the drug retailers **CVS Health Corporation** and **Walgreens Boots Alliance** follows. Assume an incremental tax rate of 35%.

($ millions)	CVS Health	Walgreens Boots
Sales revenue—2017	$184,765	$118,214
Interest expense—2017	1,062	728
Net income—2017	6,623	4,101
Total assets—2017	95,131	66,009
Total assets—2016	94,462	72,688
Stockholders' equity—2017	37,695	28,274
Stockholders' equity—2016	36,834	30,281

a. Compute the 2017 return on assets (ROA) for each company.
b. Disaggregate ROA into profit margin (PM) and asset turnover (AT) for each company.
c. Compute the 2017 return on equity (ROE) and return on financial leverage (ROFL) for each company.
d. Discuss any differences in these ratios for each company. Identify the factor(s) that drives the differences in ROA observed from your analyses in parts *a* through *c*.

LO2, 3 Homework MBC

Intel Corporation
NASDAQ :: INTC

E5-28. Compute, Disaggregate, and Interpret ROE
Selected fiscal year balance sheet and income statement information for the computer chip maker, **Intel Corporation**, follows ($ millions).

Balance sheet information ($ millions)	2017	2016	2015
Total assets	$123,249	$113,327	$101,459
Total shareholders' equity	69,019	66,226	61,085
Income statement information ($ millions)	**2017**	**2016**	**2015**
Sales revenue	$ 2,761	$ 59,387	$ 55,355
Interest expense	637	725	345
Net income	9,601	10,316	11,420

a. Calculate Intel's return on equity (ROE) for fiscal years 2017 and 2016.
b. Calculate Intel's return on assets (ROA) and return on financial leverage (ROFL) for each year. Is financial leverage working to the advantage of Intel's shareholders? Use an incremental tax rate of 35%.
c. Use the DuPont formulation in the Business Insight on page 230 to analyze the variations in Intel's ROE over this period. How does this analysis differ from your answers to *a* and *b* above?

LO2, 3 Homework MBC

E5-29. Return on Investment, Financial Leverage, and DuPont Analysis
The following tables provide information from the recent annual reports of HD Rinker, AG.

Balance sheets (€ millions)	2019	2018	2017	2016
Total assets	€6,108	€6,451	€7,173	€6,972
Total liabilities	5,970	4,974	4,989	5,097
Total shareholders' equity	138	1,477	2,184	1,875

Income statements (€ millions) 52 weeks ended	2019	2018	2017
Sales revenue	€10,364	€9,613	€8,632
Earnings before interest and income taxes	1,473	1,459	887
Interest expense	246	208	237
Earnings before income taxes	1,227	1,251	650
Income tax expense	377	446	202
Net earnings	€ 850	€ 805	€ 448

a. Calculate HD Rinker's return on equity (ROE) for fiscal years 2019, 2018, and 2017.

b. Calculate HD Rinker's return on assets (ROA) and return on financial leverage (ROFL) for each year. Is financial leverage working to the advantage of HD Rinker's shareholders? Use an incremental tax rate of 25%

c. Use the DuPont formulation in the Business Insight on page 230 to analyze the variations in HD Rinker's ROE over this period. How does this analysis differ from your answers to *a* and *b* above?

E5-30. Compute, Disaggregate and Interpret ROE and ROA

LO2, 3

Homework MBC

Office Depot, Inc.
NASDAQ :: ODP

Selected balance sheet and income statement information from Office Depot, Inc., follows ($ millions).

Sales	Interest Expense	Net Income	Total Assets		Stockholders' Equity	
2017	2017	2017	2017	2016	2017	2016
$10,240	$62	$181	$6,323	$5,540	$2,120	$1,852

a. Compute the 2017 return on equity (ROE), return on assets (ROA), and return on financial leverage (ROFL). Use 35% as the incremental tax rate.

b. Disaggregate ROA into profit margin (PM) and asset turnover (AT).

c. What inferences do we draw from PM compared to AT? How do these ratios compare to industry medians?

E5-31. Compute, Disaggregate and Interpret ROE and ROA

LO2, 3

Homework MBC

Intuit Inc.
NASDAQ :: INTU

Selected balance sheet and income statement information from the software company, Intuit Inc., follows ($ millions).

Sales	Interest Expense	Net Income	Total Assets		Stockholders' Equity	
2017	2017	2017	2017	2016	2017	2016
$5,964	$20	$1,211	$5,178	$4,068	$2,354	$1,354

a. Compute the 2017 return on equity (ROE), return on assets (ROA), and return on financial leverage (ROFL). Use 35% as the incremental tax rate.

b. Disaggregate the ROA from part *a* into profit margin (PM) and asset turnover (AT).

c. What can we learn by comparing PM to AT? What explanation can we offer for the relation between ROE and ROA observed and for Intuit's use of financial leverage?

E5-32. Compute and Interpret Liquidity and Solvency Ratios

LO4

Homework MBC

Tesla, Inc.
NASDAQ :: TSLA

Selected balance sheet, income statement and cash flow statement information from Tesla, Inc. for 2017 and 2016 follows ($ thousands).

December 31	2017	2016
Cash and cash equivalents	$ 3,367,914	$ 3,393,216
Restricted cash	155,323	105,519
Net receivables	515,381	499,142
Inventory	2,263,537	2,067,454
Other current assets	268,365	194,465
Current assets	6,570,520	6,259,796
Current liabilities	7,674,670	5,827,005
Total liabilities	23,022,980	16,750,167
Stockholders' equity	5,632,392	5,913,909
Year ended December 31,	**2017**	
Loss before income taxes	$(2,209,032)	
Interest expense	471,259	
Cash flows from operating activities	(60,654)	
Capital expenditures	(3,414,814)	

a. Compute the current ratio and quick ratio for each year and discuss any trend in liquidity. Do you believe the company is sufficiently liquid? How should the balance in restricted cash affect your analysis?

b. Compute the debt-to-equity ratio for 2017 and 2016 and the times-interest-earned ratio for 2017. Discuss the trend in the debt-to-equity ratio.

c. Compute the cash burn rate for 2017. What questions are raised by this figure?

LO4

Siemens AG
OTCMKTS :: SIEGY

E5-33. Compute and Interpret Liquidity and Solvency Ratios
Selected balance sheet and income statement information from **Siemens, AG**, for 2015 through 2017 follows (€ millions).

	Total Current Assets	Total Current Liabilities	Cash Flow from Operations	Pretax Income	Interest Expense	Total Liabilities	Stockholders' Equity
2015	€51,442	€39,562	€6,612	€7,218	€ 818	€85,293	€34,474
2016	55,329	42,916	7,611	7,404	989	90,901	34,211
2017	58,429	43,394	7,176	8,306	1,051	89,277	43,089

a. Compute the current ratio for each year and discuss any trend in liquidity. Also compute the operating cash flow to current liabilities (OCFCL) ratio for each year. (In 2014, current liabilities totaled €36,598 million.) Do you believe the company is sufficiently liquid? Explain. What additional information about the accounting numbers comprising this ratio might be useful in helping you assess liquidity? Explain.

b. Compute times interest earned and the debt-to-equity ratio for each year and discuss any trends for each.

c. What is your overall assessment of the company's liquidity and solvency from the analyses in *a* and *b*? Explain.

LO2, 3

The Gap, Inc.
NYSE :: GPS

E5-34. Compute, Disaggregate and Interpret ROE and ROA
Income statements for **The Gap, Inc.**, follow, along with selected balance sheet information ($ millions).

THE GAP, INC.
Consolidated Statement of Earnings

Fiscal year ended	Feb. 3, 2018	Jan. 28, 2017
Net sales.	$15,855	$15,516
Cost of goods sold and occupancy expenses	9,789	9,876
Gross profit.	6,066	5,640
Operating expenses	4,587	4,449
Operating income.	1,479	1,191
Interest expense.	74	75
Interest income.	(19)	(8)
Income before income taxes	1,424	1,124
Income taxes	576	448
Net income	$ 848	$ 676

THE GAP, INC.
Selected Balance Sheet Data

	Feb. 3, 2018	Jan. 28, 2017
Merchandise inventories.	$1,997	$1,830
Total assets	7,989	7,610
Total stockholders' equity	3,144	2,904

a. Compute the return on equity (ROE), return on assets (ROA), and return on financial leverage (ROFL) for the fiscal year ended February 3, 2018. Assume an incremental tax rate of 35%.

b. Disaggregate ROA into profit margin (PM) and asset turnover (AT).

c. Compute the gross profit margin (GPM) and inventory turnover (INVT) ratios for the fiscal year ended February 3, 2018.

d. Assess the Gap's performance. What are the most important drivers of the Gap's success?

LO1, 6

E5-35.[B] Common-Size and Forecast Income Statements
Refer to the income statements for **The Gap, Inc.**, presented in E5-34.

a. Prepare common-size income statements for fiscal years 2017 (ending February 3, 2018) and 2016 (ending January 28, 2017).

The Gap, Inc.
NYSE :: GPS

b. Prepare an income statement forecast for the fiscal year 2018 (ending February 2, 2019), based on the following assumptions:
- Net sales total $16,300 million.
- Cost of goods sold and occupancy expenses are 62% of sales.
- Operating expenses total 29% of sales.
- Interest income and interest expense are unchanged from the 2017 amounts.
- The Gap's effective tax rate on income before taxes is 25% in 2018.

c. Given the Gap's business strategy, what are the factors that ultimately determine the accuracy of the income statement forecast prepared in *b*?

PROBLEMS

P5-36. Analysis and Interpretation of Return on Investment for Competitors

LO2, 3
Nike, Inc.
NYSE :: NKE
Adidas Group, AG
OTCMKTS :: ADDYY

Balance sheets and income statements for Nike, Inc., and Adidas Group follow. Refer to these financial statements to answer the requirements.

	NIKE, INC. Balance Sheets ($ millions) May 31,		ADIDAS GROUP, AG Balance Sheets (€ millions) December 31,	
	2018	2017	2017	2016
Assets				
Current assets:				
Cash and cash equivalents	$ 4,249	$ 3,808	€ 1,598	€ 1,510
Short-term investments	996	2,371	398	734
Accounts receivable, net	3,498	3,677	2,315	2,200
Inventories	5,261	5,055	3,693	3,764
Prepaid expenses and other current assets	1,130	1,150	641	678
Total current assets	15,134	16,061	8,645	8,886
Property, plant, and equipment, net	4,454	3,989	2,000	1,915
Goodwill and identifiable intangible assets, net	439	422	2,684	3,259
Deferred income taxes and other assets	2,509	2,787	1,193	1,116
Total assets	$22,536	$23,259	€14,522	€15,176
Liabilities and shareholders' equity				
Current liabilities:				
Short-term debt	$ 342	$ 331	€ 136	€ 636
Accounts payable	2,279	2,048	2,337	2,697
Accrued liabilities	3,269	3,011	2,921	2,596
Income taxes payable	150	84	424	402
Other current liabilities	—	—	473	434
Total current liabilities	6,040	5,474	6,291	6,765
Long-term debt	3,468	3,471	1,005	1,004
Other noncurrent liabilities	3,216	1,907	791	952
Total shareholders' equity	9,812	12,407	6,435	6,455
Total liabilities and shareholders' equity	$22,536	$23,259	€14,522	€15,176

	NIKE, INC. Income Sheets ($ millions) Year ended May 31,		ADIDAS GROUP, AG Income Sheets (€ millions) Year ended December 31,	
	2018	2017	2017	2016
Revenues	$36,397	$34,350	€21,218	€18,483
Cost of sales	20,441	19,038	10,514	9,383
Gross profit	15,956	15,312	10,703	9,100
Total selling and administrative expense	11,511	10,563	8,634	7,518
Operating profit	4,445	4,749	2,069	1,582
Interest expense (income), net	54	59	93	74
Other expense (income), net	66	(196)	(46)	(28)
Income before income taxes	4,325	4,886	2,022	1,536
Income tax expense	2,392	646	668	454
Net income from continuing operations	1,933	4,240	1,354	1,082
Loss from discontinued operations, net of tax	—	—	254	62
Net income	$ 1,933	$ 4,240	€ 1,100	€ 1,020

REQUIRED

a. Compute return on equity (ROE), return on assets (ROA), and return on financial leverage (ROFL) for Nike and Adidas in the most recent year. The corporate tax rate in Germany, where Adidas is headquartered, is about 30%. Assume a tax rate of 25% for Nike.

b. Disaggregate the ROA's computed into profit margin (PM) and asset turnover (AT) components. Which of these factors drives ROA for each company?

c. Compute the gross profit margin (GPM) and operating expense-to-sales ratios for each company. How do these companies' profitability measures compare?

d. Compute the accounts receivable turnover (ART), inventory turnover (INVT), and property, plant, and equipment turnover (PPET) for each company. How do these companies' turnover measures compare?

e. Nike's fiscal year ends on May 31, 2018, while Adidas's fiscal year ends on December 31, 2017 (a difference of seven months). How does this difference affect your analysis of ROE and ROA for these two companies?

f. Nike's financial statements are prepared in accordance with U.S. GAAP, while Adidas, a German company, follows IFRS rules. How does this difference in financial reporting standards affect your comparison of these companies' financial statements?

LO4
Nike, Inc.
NYSE :: NKE
Adidas Group, AG
OTCMKTS :: ADDYY

P5-37. Analysis and Interpretation of Liquidity and Solvency for Competitors
Refer to the financial statements of Nike and Adidas presented in P5-36.

REQUIRED

a. Compute each company's current ratio and quick ratio for each year. Comment on any changes that you observe.

b. Compute each company's times interest earned ratio and debt-to-equity ratio for each year. Comment on any observed changes.

c. Compare these two companies on the basis of liquidity and solvency. Do you have any concerns about either company's ability to meet its debt obligations?

LO2, 3
The Home Depot, Inc.
NYSE :: HD
Lowe's Companies, Inc.
NYSE :: LOW

P5-38. Analysis and Interpretation of Return on Investment for Competitors
Balance sheets and income statements for The Home Depot, Inc., and Lowe's Companies, Inc., follow. Refer to these financial statements to answer the requirements.

($ millions)	HOME DEPOT, INC. Balance Sheets 2017	2016	LOWE'S COMPANIES Balance Sheets 2017	2016
Assets				
Current assets:				
Cash and cash equivalents	$ 3,595	$ 2,538	$ 588	$ 558
Short-term investments	—	—	102	100
Receivables, net	1,952	2,029	—	—
Merchandise inventories	12,748	12,549	11,393	10,458
Other current assets	638	608	689	884
Total current assets	18,933	17,724	12,772	12,000
Net property and equipment	22,075	21,914	19,721	19,949
Goodwill	2,275	2,093	1,307	1,082
Long-term investments	—	—	408	366
Other assets	1,246	1,235	1,083	1,011
Total assets	$44,529	$42,966	$35,291	$34,408
Liabilities and shareholders' equity				
Current liabilities:				
Short-term debt and current maturities of long-term debt	$ 2,761	$ 1,252	$ 1,431	$ 1,305
Accounts payable	7,244	7,000	6,590	6,651
Accrued salaries and related expenses	1,640	1,484	747	790
Deferred revenue	1,805	1,669	1,378	1,253
Income taxes payable	54	25	—	—
Other current liabilities	2,690	2,703	1,950	1,975
Total current liabilities	16,194	14,133	12,096	11,974
Long-term debt, excluding current maturities	24,267	22,349	15,564	14,394
Deferred income taxes	440	296	—	—
Other long-term liabilities	2,174	1,855	1,758	1,606
Total liabilities	43,075	38,633	29,418	27,974
Total stockholders' equity	1,454	4,333	5,873	6,434
Total liabilities and shareholders' equity	$44,529	$42,966	$35,291	$34,408

($ millions)	HOME DEPOT, INC. Income Statements 2017	2016	LOWE'S COMPANIES Income Statements 2017	2016
Net sales	$100,904	$94,595	$68,619	$65,017
Cost of sales	66,548	62,282	45,210	42,553
Gross profit	34,356	32,313	23,409	22,464
Operating expenses:				
Selling, general and administrative	17,864	17,132	15,376	15,129
Depreciation and amortization	1,811	1,754	1,447	1,489
Operating income	14,681	13,427	6,586	5,846
Interest and other (income) expense:				
Interest and investment income	(74)	(36)	(16)	(12)
Interest expense	1,057	972	649	657
Loss on extinguishment of debt	0	0	464	—
Earnings before provision for income taxes	13,698	12,491	5,489	5,201
Provision for income taxes	5,068	4,534	2,042	2,108
Net earnings	$ 8,630	$ 7,957	$ 3,447	$ 3,093

REQUIRED

a. Compute return on equity (ROE), return on assets (ROA), and return on financial leverage (ROFL) for each company in fiscal year 2017. Assume a tax rate of 35% for these years.

b. Disaggregate the ROA's computed into profit margin (PM) and asset turnover (AT) components. Which of these factors drives ROA for each company?

c. Compute the gross profit margin (GPM) and operating expense-to-sales ratios for each company. How do these companies' profitability measures compare?

d. Compute the accounts receivable turnover (ART), inventory turnover (INVT), and property, plant, and equipment turnover (PPET) for each company. How do these companies' turnover measures compare?

e. Compare and evaluate these competitors' performance in 2017.

LO4
Home Depot, Inc.
NYSE :: HD
Lowe's Companies, Inc.
NYSE :: LOW

P5-39. Analysis and Interpretation of Liquidity and Solvency for Competitors

Refer to the financial statements of Home Depot and Lowe's presented in P5-38.

REQUIRED

a. Compute each company's current ratio and quick ratio for each year. Comment on any changes that you observe.

b. Compute each company's times interest earned ratio and debt-to-equity ratio for each year. Comment on any observed changes.

c. Compare these two companies on the basis of liquidity and solvency. Do you have any concerns about either company's ability to meet its debt obligations?

LO5
Home Depot, Inc.
NYSE :: HD
Lowe's Companies, Inc.
NYSE :: LOW

P5-40.[A] Analysis of the Effect of Operations on ROE

Refer to the financial statements of Home Depot and Lowe's presented in P5-38.

REQUIRED

a. Compute each company's net operating profit after taxes (NOPAT) for 2017 and net operating assets (NOA) for 2017 and 2016. Classify other assets and other liabilities (both current and noncurrent) as operating assets and liabilities in the balance sheet. Assume a 35% tax rate. *Hint:* Gains and losses on extinguishment of debt result from financing activities and are not part of operations.

b. Compute each company's return on net operating assets (RNOA) for 2017.

c. Compute the 2017 net operating profit margin (NOPM) and net operating asset turnover (NOAT) for each company.

d. Compare operating returns for these two companies. How does RNOA compare to ROA? What insights are gained by focusing on operating returns?

LO2, 3
United Parcel Service, Inc.
NYSE :: UPS

P5-41. Analysis and Interpretation of Profitability

Balance sheets and income statements for United Parcel Service, Inc., (UPS) follow. Refer to these financial statements to answer the following requirements.

UNITED PARCEL SERVICE, INC.
Income Statement

Years Ended December 31 ($ millions)	2017	2016	2015
Revenue	$65,872	$60,906	$58,363
Operating expenses:			
Compensation and benefits	34,588	34,770	31,028
Repairs and maintenance	1,600	1,538	1,400
Depreciation and amortization	2,282	2,224	2,084
Purchased transportation	10,989	9,129	8,043
Fuel	2,690	2,118	2,482
Other occupancy	1,155	1,037	1,022
Other expenses	5,039	4,623	4,636
Total operating expenses	58,343	55,439	50,695
Operating profit	7,529	5,467	7,668
Other income and (expense):			
Investment income and other	72	50	15
Interest expense	(453)	(381)	(341)
Total other income and (expense)	(381)	(331)	(326)
Income before income taxes	7,148	5,136	7,342
Income tax expense	2,238	1,705	2,498
Net income	$ 4,910	$ 3,431	$ 4,844

UNITED PARCEL SERVICE, INC.
Balance Sheet

December 31 ($ millions)	2017	2016	2015
Assets			
Current assets:			
Cash and cash equivalents	$ 3,320	$ 3,476	$ 2,730
Marketable securities	749	1,091	1,996
Accounts receivable, net	8,773	7,695	7,134
Other current assets	2,706	1,587	1,348
Total current assets	15,548	13,849	13,208
Property, plant and equipment, net	22,118	18,800	18,352
Goodwill	3,872	3,757	3,419
Intangible assets, net	1,964	1,758	1,549
Investments and restricted cash	483	476	473
Deferred income tax assets	265	591	255
Other noncurrent assets	1,153	1,146	1,055
Total assets	$45,403	$40,377	$38,311
Liabilities and shareholders' equity			
Current liabilities:			
Current maturities of long-term debt and commercial paper	$ 4,011	$ 3,681	$ 3,018
Accounts payable	3,872	3,042	2,587
Accrued wages and withholdings	2,521	2,317	2,253
Hedge margin liabilities	17	575	717
Self-insurance reserves	705	670	657
Accrued group welfare and retirement plan contributions	677	598	525
Other current liabilities	905	847	939
Total current liabilities	12,708	11,730	10,696
Long-term debt	20,278	12,394	11,316
Pension and postretirement benefit obligations	7,061	12,694	10,638
Deferred income tax liabilities	757	112	115
Self-insurance reserves	1,765	1,794	1,831
Other noncurrent liabilities	1,804	1,224	1,224
Total liabilities	44,373	39,948	35,820
Total shareowners' equity	1,030	429	2,491
Total liabilities and shareowners' equity	$45,403	$40,377	$38,311

REQUIRED

a. Compute ROA and disaggregate it into profit margin (PM) and asset turnover (AT) for 2017 and 2016. Comment on the drivers of the ROA. Assume a 35% tax rate for this period.

b. Compute any expense to sales (ETS) ratios that you think might help explain UPS's profitability.

c. Compute return on equity (ROE) for 2017 and 2016.

d. Comment on the difference between ROE and ROA. What does this relation suggest about UPS's use of debt?

P5-42. Analysis and Interpretation of Liquidity and Solvency

LO4
United Parcel Service
NYSE :: UPS

Refer to the financial information of **United Parcel Service** in P5-41 to answer the following requirements.

REQUIRED

a. Compute its current ratio and quick ratio for 2017 and 2016. Comment on any observed trends.

b. Compute its times interest earned and its debt-to-equity ratios for 2017 and 2016. Comment on any trends observed.

c. Summarize your findings in a conclusion about the company's liquidity and solvency. Do you have any concerns about its ability to meet its debt obligations?

P5-43.[A] Computing and Analyzing Operating Returns

LO5
United Parcel Service
NYSE :: UPS

Refer to the financial statements of **United Parcel Service** in P5-41 to answer the following requirements.

REQUIRED

a. Compute net operating profit after taxes (NOPAT) for 2017 and net operating assets (NOA) for 2017 and 2016. Assume a tax rate of 35%.

b. Compute the return on net operating assets (RNOA) for 2017. What percentage of UPS's ROE is generated by operations?

c. Decompose RNOA by computing net operating profit margin (NOPM) and net operating asset turnover (NOAT) for 2017.

d. What can be inferred about UPS from these ratios?

LO6
United Parcel Service
NYSE :: UPS

P5-44.[B] Preparing Financial Statement Forecasts

Refer to the financial statements of United Parcel Service in P5-41 to answer the following requirements. The following assumptions should be useful:

- UPS's sales forecast for 2018 is $70,000 million.
- Operating expenses and operating profits increase in proportion to sales.
- Investment income and interest expense are unchanged in 2018.
- Income taxes are 25% of pretax earnings.
- Marketable securities and noncurrent investments are unchanged in 2018; all other assets (except cash) increase in proportion to sales.
- Long-term debt and current maturities of long-term debt are unchanged in 2018; all other liabilities increase in proportion to sales.
- Dividends are 50% of net income. Income and dividends are the only changes to stockholders' equity in 2018.

REQUIRED

a. Prepare an income statement forecast for 2018.

b. Prepare a balance sheet forecast for 2018.

LO3
Homework MBC

Abbott Laboratories
NYSE :: ABT
Bristol-Myers Squibb Company
NYSE :: BMY
Johnson & Johnson
NYSE :: JNJ
GlaxoSmithKline plc (ADR)
NYSE :: GSK
Pfizer Inc.
NYSE :: PFE

P5-45. Comparing Profitability Ratios for Competitors

Selected income statement data for Abbott Laboratories, Bristol-Myers Squibb Company, Johnson & Johnson, GlaxoSmithKline plc, and Pfizer, Inc. is presented in the following table:

(millions)	Abbott Laboratories	Bristol-Myers Squibb	Johnson & Johnson	Glaxo Smith Kline plc	Pfizer
Sales revenue	$27,390	$19,258	$76,450	£30,186	$52,546
Cost of sales	12,337	6,066	25,354	10,342	11,240
SG&A expense	9,117	4,687	21,420	9,672	14,784
R&D expense	2,235	6,411	10,554	4,476	7,657
Interest expense	904	196	934	734	1,270
Net income	477	975	1,300	2,169	21,355

REQUIRED

a. Compute the profit margin (PM) and gross profit margin (GPM) ratios for each company. (As a British company, GlaxoSmithKline plc has a statutory tax rate of 19.25% in 2017. Assume a tax rate of 35% for the others.)

b. Compute the research and development (R&D) expense to sales ratio and the selling, general and administrative (SG&A) expense to sales ratio for each company.

c. Compare the relative profitability of these pharmaceutical companies.

LO3
Homework MBC

Best Buy Co., Inc.
NYSE :: BBY
The Kroger Co.
NYSE :: KR
Nordstrom, Inc.
NYSE :: JWN
Office Depot, Inc.
NASDAQ :: ODP
Walgreens Boots Alliance, Inc.
NASDAQ :: WBA

P5-46. Comparing Profitability and Turnover Ratios for Retail Companies

Selected financial statement data for Best Buy Co., Inc., The Kroger Co., Nordstrom, Inc., Office Depot, Inc., and Walgreens Boots Alliance, Inc. is presented in the following table:

($ millions)	Best Buy	Kroger	Nordstrom	Office Depot	Walgreens Boots
Sales revenue	$42,151.0	$122,662.0	$15,478.0	$10,240.0	$131,537.0
Cost of sales	32,275.0	95,662.0	9,890.0	7,779.0	100,745.0
Interest expense	75.0	601.0	168.0	62.0	622.0
Net income	1,000.0	1,889.0	437.0	181.0	5,031.0
Average receivables	1,198.0	1,643.0	172.0	809.0	6,550.5
Average inventories	5,036.5	6,547.0	1,961.5	1,186.0	9,232.0
Average PP&E	2,357.0	21,043.5	3,918.0	663.0	13,776.5
Average total assets	13,452.5	36,851.0	15,974.0	5,931.5	67,066.5

REQUIRED

a. Compute return on assets (ROA), profit margin (PM), and asset turnover (AT) for each company. Assume an income tax rate of 25%. Discuss the relative importance of PM and AT for each company.

b. Compute accounts receivable turnover (ART), inventory turnover (INVT) and property, plant, and equipment turnover (PPET) for each company. Discuss any difference that you observe.

c. Compute the gross profit margin (GPM) for each company. How does the GPM differ across companies? Does this difference seem to correlate with differences in ART or INVT? Explain.

CASES AND PROJECTS

C5-47. Management Application: Gross Profit and Strategic Management LO3

One way to increase overall profitability is to increase gross profit. This can be accomplished by raising prices and/or by reducing manufacturing costs.

REQUIRED

a. Will raising prices and/or reducing manufacturing costs unambiguously increase gross profit? Explain.

b. What strategy might you develop as a manager to (i) yield a price increase for your product, or (ii) reduce product manufacturing cost?

C5-48. Management Application: Asset Turnover and Strategic Management LO3

Increasing net operating asset turnover requires some combination of increasing sales and/or decreasing net operating assets. For the latter, many companies consider ways to reduce their investment in working capital (current assets less current liabilities). This can be accomplished by reducing the level of accounts receivable and inventories, or by increasing the level of accounts payable.

REQUIRED

a. Develop a list of suggested actions to achieve all three of these objectives as manager.

b. Examine the implications of each. That is, describe the marketing implications of reducing receivables and inventories, and the supplier implications of delaying payment. How can a company achieve working capital reduction without negatively impacting its performance?

C5-49. Ethics and Governance: Earnings Management LO2, 3, 4

Companies are aware that analysts focus on profitability in evaluating financial performance. Managers have historically utilized a number of methods to improve reported profitability that are cosmetic in nature and do not affect "real" operating performance. These are typically subsumed under the general heading of "earnings management." Justification for such actions typically includes the following arguments:

- Increasing stock price by managing earnings benefits shareholders; thus, no one is hurt by these actions.
- Earnings management is a temporary fix; such actions will be curtailed once "real" profitability improves, as managers expect.

REQUIRED

a. Identify the affected parties in any scheme to manage profits to prop up stock price.

b. Do the ends (of earnings management) justify the means? Explain.

c. To what extent are the objectives of managers different from those of shareholders?

d. What governance structure can you envision that might prohibit earnings management?

SOLUTIONS TO REVIEW PROBLEMS

Mid-Chapter Review 1

SOLUTION

THE COCA-COLA COMPANY AND SUBSIDIARIES
Consolidated Statements of Income
($ millions)

Year ended December 31	2017	2016
Net operating revenues	100.0%	100.0%
Cost of goods sold	37.4%	39.3%
Gross profit	62.6%	60.7%
Selling, general and administrative expenses	35.3%	36.5%
Other operating charges	6.1%	3.6%
Operating income	21.2%	20.6%
Interest income	1.9%	1.5%
Interest expense	2.4%	1.8%
Equity income (loss)—net	3.0%	2.0%
Other income (loss)—net	–4.7%	–2.9%
Income from continuing operations before income taxes	19.0%	19.4%
Income taxes from continuing operations	15.7%	3.8%
Net income from continuing operations	3.3%	15.6%
Income from discontinued operations (net of income taxes of $47 and $0, respectively)	0.3%	0.0%
Consolidated net income	3.6%	15.6%

THE COCA-COLA COMPANY AND SUBSIDIARIES
Common Size Balance Sheets

December 31,	2017	2016
Assets		
Cash and cash equivalents	6.8%	9.8%
Short-term investments and marketable securities	16.7%	15.6%
Trade accounts receivable	4.2%	4.4%
Inventories	3.0%	3.1%
Prepaid expenses and other current assets	10.9%	6.0%
Total current assets	41.6%	39.0%
Equity method investments	23.7%	18.6%
Other investments	1.2%	1.1%
Property, plant, and equipment, net	9.3%	12.2%
Goodwill and other intangible assets	18.9%	24.2%
Other assets	5.2%	4.9%
Total assets	100.0%	100.0%
Liabilities and equity		
Accounts payable and accrued expenses	10.0%	10.9%
Loans and notes payable	15.0%	14.3%
Current maturities of long-term debt	3.8%	4.0%
Accrued income taxes	0.5%	0.4%
Other current liabilities	1.7%	0.8%
Total current liabilities	30.9%	30.4%
Long-term debt	35.5%	34.0%
Other liabilities	9.1%	4.7%
Deferred income taxes	2.9%	4.3%
Total liabilities	78.4%	73.4%
Total equity	21.6%	26.6%
Total liabilities and equity	100.0%	100.0%

Mid-Chapter Review 2

SOLUTION ($ MILLIONS)

$$\text{ROE} = \frac{\$1{,}283}{(\$18{,}977 + \$23{,}220)/2} = 0.0608 \text{ or } 6.08\%$$

$$\text{ROA} = \frac{\$1{,}283 + [\$841 \times (1 - 0.35)]}{(\$87{,}896 + \$87{,}270)/2} = 0.0209 \text{ or } 2.09\%$$

$$\text{ROFL} = 0.0608 - 0.0209 = 0.0399 \text{ or } 3.99\%$$

Mid-Chapter Review 3

SOLUTION ($ MILLIONS)

$$\text{PM} = \frac{\$1{,}283 + [\$841 \times (1 - 0.35)]}{\$35{,}410} = 0.0517 \text{ or } 5.17\%$$

$$\text{AT} = \frac{\$35{,}410}{(\$87{,}896 + \$87{,}270)/2} = 0.4043 \text{ times}$$

$$0.0517\% \times 0.4043 = 0.0209$$

$$\text{GPM} = \frac{\$35{,}410 - \$13{,}256}{\$35{,}410} = 0.6256 \text{ or } 62.56\%$$

$$\text{ART} = \frac{\$35{,}410}{(\$3{,}667 + \$3{,}856)/2} = 9.4138 \text{ times}$$

$$\text{INVT} = \frac{\$13{,}256}{(\$2{,}655 + \$2{,}675)/2} = 4.9741 \text{ times}$$

$$\text{PPET} = \frac{\$35{,}410}{(\$8{,}203 + \$10{,}635)/2} = 3.7594 \text{ times}$$

PepsiCo and Coca-Cola have similar business models, and in normal years, both companies achieve high returns on the capital invested by their shareholders. In 2017, the one-time transition effects of the Tax Cuts and Jobs Act create significant differences in their ROEs. PepsiCo has a much higher ROE and a higher ROA. The significance of this tax effect can be seen in the common-size income statements of the two companies. Coca-Cola's Operating income is 21.2% of revenues, while PepsiCo's comparable number is 16.5%. But after taxes, Coca-Cola's net income from continuing operations is 3.3% of revenues, while PepsiCo's is 7.7%. In addition, a significant cause of the difference in ROE is due to the fact that PepsiCo has a much higher ROFL, caused by its higher use of liabilities as a source of financing. Coca-Cola has higher GPM, while PepsiCo achieves a higher turnover of total assets. Closer analysis of turnover ratios reveals that ART is similar, implying that they employ similar credit policies. PepsiCo's inventory turns over significantly more quickly than Coca-Cola's inventory, perhaps reflecting differences in their product mix (e.g., PepsiCo's snack foods). This difference plays a significant role in PepsiCo's superior asset turnover. The two companies' PPET ratios are essentially identical, so utilization of fixed assets is not a factor in PepsiCo's higher total asset turnover.

Chapter-End Review

SOLUTION ($ MILLIONS)

$$\text{Current ratio} = \frac{\$36{,}545}{\$27{,}194} = 1.344$$

$$\text{Quick ratio} = \frac{\$6{,}006 + \$14{,}669 + \$3{,}667}{\$27{,}194} = 0.895$$

$$\text{Debt-to-equity ratio} = \frac{\$68{,}919}{\$18{,}977} = 3.632$$

$$\text{Times interest earned} = \frac{\$6{,}742 + \$841}{\$841} = 9.017$$

PepsiCo is slightly more liquid than Coca-Cola as indicated by a higher current ratio (1.51 vs. 1.34) and a higher quick ratio (1.29 vs. 0.90). In addition, PepsiCo has a much higher debt-to-equity ratio than Coca-Cola (6.27 vs. 3.63) suggesting that PepsiCo is relying more on debt financing. This is consistent with the higher ROFL ratio computed in Mid-Chapter Review 2. Nevertheless, neither company has significant issues related to solvency. Both report reasonably high times-interest-earned ratios (9.34 for PepsiCo and 9.02 for Coca-Cola).

Appendix 5A Review

SOLUTION ($ MILLIONS)

Operating assets:
2017: $87,896 – $14,669 – $1,096 = $72,131
2016: $87,270 – $13,646 – $989 = $72,635

Operating liabilities:
2017: $68,919 – $13,205 – $3,298 – $31,182 = $21,234
2016: $64,050 – $12,498 – $3,527 – $29,684 = $18,341

Net operating assets (NOA):
2017: $72,131 – $21,234 = $50,897
2016: $72,635 – $18,341 = $54,294

$$\text{NOPAT} = \$1{,}283 - [(\$677 - \$841 - \$1{,}666) \times (1 - 0.35)] = \$2{,}472.50$$

$$\text{RNOA} = \frac{\$2{,}472.50}{(\$50{,}897 + \$54{,}294)/2} = 4.70\%$$

$$\text{NOPM} = \frac{\$2{,}472.50}{\$35{,}410} = 6.98\%$$

$$\text{NOAT} = \frac{\$35{,}410}{(\$50{,}897 + \$54{,}294)/2} = 0.673$$

Appendix 5B Review

SOLUTION ($ MILLIONS)

THE COCA-COLA COMPANY AND SUBSIDIARIES
Forecasted Statements of Income
($ millions)

Year ended December 31	2018
Net operating revenues	$36,826 (4% growth)
Cost of goods sold ($36,826 × 37.4%)	13,773
Gross profit	23,053
Selling, general and administrative expenses ($36,826 × 35.3%)	13,000
Other operating charges ($36,826 × 6.1%)	2,246
Operating income	7,807
Interest income	677
Interest expense	841
Equity income (loss)—net	1,071
Other income (loss)—net	(1,666)
Income from continuing operations before income taxes	7,048
Income taxes from continuing operations ($7,048 × 25.0%)	1,762
Consolidated net income	$ 5,286

THE COCA-COLA COMPANY AND SUBSIDIARIES
Forecasted Balance Sheet
($ millions)

December 31,	2018
Assets	
Cash and cash equivalents	$ 7,159
Short-term investments and marketable securities	14,669
Trade accounts receivable ($3,667 × 1.04)	3,814
Inventories ($2,655 × 1.04)	2,761
Prepaid expenses and other current assets ($9,548 × 1.04)	9,930
Total current assets	38,333
Equity method investments	20,856
Other investments	1,096
Property, plant and equipment, net ($8,203 × 1.04)	8,531
Goodwill and other intangible assets ($16,636 × 1.04)	17,301
Other assets ($4,560 × 1.04)	4,742
Total assets	$90,859
Liabilities and shareholders' equity	
Accounts payable and accrued expenses ($8,748 × 1.04)	$ 9,098
Loans and notes payable	13,205
Current maturities of long-term debt	3,298
Accrued income taxes ($410 × 1.04)	426
Other current liabilities ($1,533 × 1.04)	1,594
Total current liabilities	27,621
Long-term debt	31,182
Other liabilities ($8,021 × 1.04)	8,342
Deferred income taxes ($2,522 × 1.04)	2,623
Total liabilities	69,768
Total equity [$18,977 + $5,286 – (0.60 × $5,286)]	21,091
Total liabilities and equity	$90,859

Reporting and Analyzing Revenues, Receivables, and Operating Income

LEARNING OBJECTIVES

1. Describe and apply the criteria for determining when revenue is recognized. (p. 274)
2. Illustrate revenue and expense recognition when the transaction involves future deliverables and/or multiple elements. (p. 276)
3. Illustrate revenue and expense recognition for long-term projects. (p. 280)
4. Estimate and account for uncollectible accounts receivable. (p. 284)
5. Calculate return on net operating assets, net operating profit after taxes, return on net operating assets, net operating profit margin, accounts receivable turnover, and average collection period. (p. 291)
6. Discuss earnings management and explain how it affects analysis and interpretation of financial statements. (p. 296)
7. Appendix 6A: Describe and illustrate the reporting for nonrecurring items. (p. 298)

MICROSOFT CORPORATION

www.microsoft.com

Microsoft Corporation has adopted a broad mission—to provide technology that will "empower every person and every organization on the planet to achieve more." To accomplish that objective, the company provides a wide range of software, services, devices, and solutions. In its early years, Microsoft concentrated on software products—operating systems and productivity tools.

Microsoft's current products include operating systems, productivity applications, server and business solution applications, tools to manage servers and to develop software, and video games. The company's products also include personal computers, tablets, and gaming equipment.

But the technology industry is notable for quick, substantial changes, with formidable competition. Microsoft has expanded its offerings in cloud computing services that include software, platforms, content, and consulting. The company is the second-largest provider of cloud computing. This service area is where Microsoft is experiencing significant growth. From 2016 to 2018, revenue from products declined by 4%, while revenue from services increased by 93%.

Profitability is the primary measure by which financial statement users gauge a company's success in efficiently offering products and services that receive a favorable response from customers. In this chapter, we focus on how companies report operating income. Operating income is determined by decisions about how and when to recognize revenues and expenses. In addition, the income statement

also includes *nonrecurring* (or *transitory*) *items*, such as restructuring charges. Transitory items are often important events reflecting very large dollar amounts and are distinguished by the fact that they are unlikely to recur in subsequent years. Understanding how such nonrecurring items are reported is crucial to interpreting a company's profitability.

Microsoft's performance cannot be measured by profits alone. In order to control costs and improve operating profits, Microsoft has to effectively manage operating assets. For example, accounts receivable is an important operating asset at Microsoft—accounting for almost 20% of its operating assets. By extending credit to customers on favorable credit terms, Microsoft stimulates sales. However, extending credit exposes the company to collectibility risk—the risk that some customers will not pay the amounts owed. In addition, accounts receivable do not earn interest, and involve administrative costs associated with billing and collection. Hence, management of receivables is critical to financial success. This chapter describes the reporting of receivables. The reporting of other operating assets is covered in subsequent chapters.

Sources: Microsoft Corporation Annual Report 10-K 2018; Microsoft Earnings Release FY18 Q4.

CHAPTER ORGANIZATION

Reporting and Analyzing Revenues, Receivables, and Operating Income

Reporting Operating Income	Reporting Receivables	Analyzing Financial Statements	Further Considerations
• Revenue Recognition • Accounting for Transactions with Future Deliverables • Accounting for Long-term Projects	• Allowance for Uncollectible Accounts • Footnote Disclosures and Interpretations	• Net Operating Profit After Taxes • Return on Net Operating Assets • Net Operating Profit Margin • Accounts Receivable Turnover • Average Collection Period	• Earnings Management • Reporting Nonrecurring Items (Appendix A)

REPORTING OPERATING INCOME

The income statement is the primary source of information about recent company performance. This information is used to predict future performance for investment purposes and to assess the credit-worthiness of a company. The income statement is also used to evaluate the quality of management.

This section describes the information reported in the income statement and its analysis implications. The central questions that the income statement attempts to answer are:

- How profitable has the company been recently?
- How did it achieve that profitability?
- Will the current profitability level persist?

To answer these three profitability questions, it is not enough to focus on a company's net income. Rather, we must use the various classifications within the income statement to see how profits were achieved and what the future prospects look like. **Exhibit 6.1** provides a schematic of the primary income statement classifications.

EXHIBIT 6.1 Income Statement Classifications

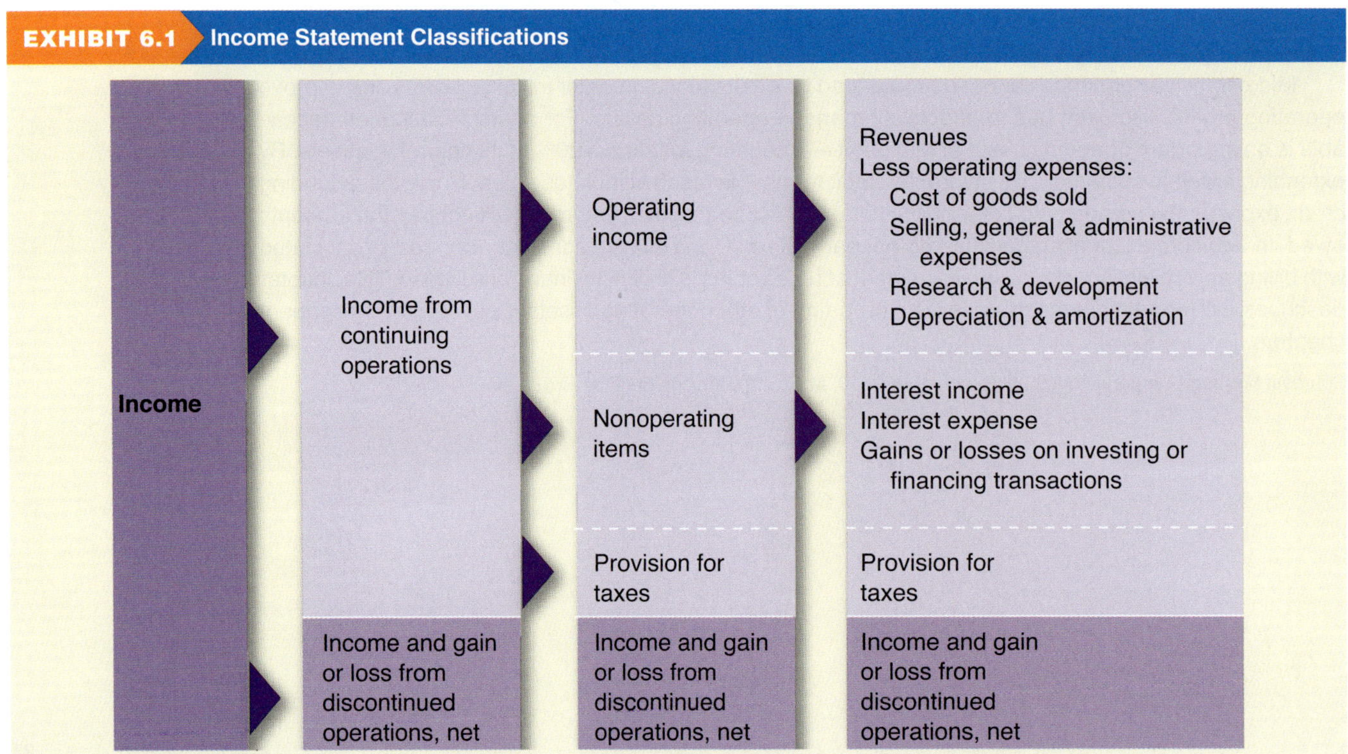

Operating activities refer to the primary transactions and events of a company. These include the purchase of goods from suppliers, the employment of personnel, the conversion of materials into finished products, the promotion and distribution of goods, the sale of goods and services to customers, and post-sale customer support. Operating activities are reported in the income statement under items such as sales, cost of goods sold, and selling, general, and administrative expenses (including research and development). They represent a company's primary activities, which must be executed successfully for a company to remain consistently profitable.

Nonoperating activities relate to the financial (borrowing) and securities investment activities of a company. These activities are typically reported in the income statement under items such as interest income and expenses, dividend revenues, and gains and losses on sales of securities. Distinguishing income components by operating versus nonoperating is an important part of effective financial statement analysis because operating activities drive company performance. It is of interest, for example, to know whether company profitability results from operating activities, or whether poorly performing operating activities are being masked by income from nonoperating activities.

FYI When analyzing a company's income statement, it is important to distinguish operating activities from nonoperating activities and recurring activities from nonrecurring activities.

All the line items in income from continuing operations are presented before taxes, with the final line item being provision for income taxes, or tax expense. Microsoft's 2018 provision for income taxes includes the one-time effect of the Tax Cuts and Jobs Act that was enacted at the end of calendar year 2017. The accounting for income taxes is discussed more fully in Chapter 10.

If the company has income or gain/loss items that qualify as discontinued operations, these will be presented after income from continuing operations for the current year and for other income statements presented. Discontinued operations are reported net of income tax expense or benefit. The appendix at the end of this chapter provides a more detailed description of nonrecurring items. Finally, many large corporations report something called **net income attributable to noncontrolling interests**. Such an amount arises when a company consolidates a subsidiary that it controls, but for which it holds less than 100% ownership. This topic is covered in later chapters.

Exhibit 6.2 presents the 2018, 2017, and 2016 income statements (sometimes called statements of operations) for Microsoft Corporation. Microsoft has no discontinued operations during this time period, so income from continuing operations is the same as net income. Like many companies, Microsoft presents operating income as a subtotal in its income statement. Microsoft's operating income is computed by subtracting its total operating expenses (including cost of sales, research and development, sales and marketing, general and administrative, amortization, and restructuring charges) from total sales revenues. Nonoperating income and expenses, such as

EXHIBIT 6.2 Distinguishing Operating and Nonoperating Sources of Income

MICROSOFT CORPORATION
Income Statements

(In millions, except per share amounts)	2018	2017	2016
Revenue:			
Product	**$ 64,497**	$63,811	$67,336
Service and other	**45,863**	32,760	23,818
Total revenue	**110,360**	96,571	91,154
Cost of revenue:			
Product	**15,420**	15,175	17,880
Service and other	**22,933**	19,086	14,900
Total cost of revenue	**38,353**	34,261	32,780
Gross margin	**72,007**	62,310	58,374
Research and development	**14,726**	13,037	11,988
Sales and marketing	**17,469**	15,461	14,635
General and administrative	**4,754**	4,481	4,563
Impairment and restructuring	**0**	306	1,110
Operating income	**35,058**	29,025	26,078
Other income (expense), net	**1,416**	876	(439)
Income before income taxes	**36,474**	29,901	25,639
Provision for income taxes	**19,903**	4,412	5,100
Net income	**$ 16,571**	$25,489	$20,539

interest income and expense, and other income and expense, are added to or deducted from the subtotal for operating income.

At this time, GAAP does not have specific rules for classifying revenue and expense items as either operating or nonoperating, so management must use judgment in reporting, and financial statement users must be careful to examine each revenue and expense item to determine if it is appropriately listed as part of operating income. Specifically, sales, cost of goods sold, and most selling, general, and administrative expenses are categorized as operating activities. Alternatively, investment-related income from dividends and interest is nonoperating, as is interest expense. Gains and losses on debt retirements and sales of investments are also nonoperating.[1]

While we think of Microsoft as a provider of software, hardware, and services, it had more than $120 billion (47% of its total assets) invested in financial instruments (mostly government and government-backed securities) at 2018 fiscal year-end. And these assets provided $2.2 billion in interest income for 2018. So, making predictions about Microsoft's profitability for 2019 would be improved by separating the results of its product and service operations from those of its investing activities. In addition, operating income is the normal focus of business unit managers in a company—financing activities and investments in financial instruments and tax administration are usually determined at the central corporate level.

1 **LO1** Describe and apply the criteria for determining when revenue is recognized.

Revenue Recognition

Revenue is one of the most important metrics of a company's operating success. The objective of almost all operating activities is to obtain a favorable response from customers, and revenue is a primary indicator of how customers view the company's product and service offerings. Companies can improve profits by reducing costs, but the effects of those improvements are limited unless revenues are increasing. Accordingly, growth in revenue is carefully monitored by management and by investors, as exemplified by the attention given to "same-store sales growth" in the retail industry.

Revenue recognition refers to the timing and amount of revenue reported by the company. The decision of when to recognize revenue depends on certain criteria. Determining whether the criteria for revenue recognition are met is often subjective and requires judgment. Therefore, financial statement readers should pay careful attention to companies' revenue recognition, particularly when companies face market pressures to meet income targets. Indeed, many SEC enforcement actions against companies for inaccurate and sometimes fraudulent financial reporting are for improper (usually premature) revenue recognition.

Sales transactions between companies and their customers generally consist of an exchange in which the company provides a product or a service and, in return, receives a payment (usually, but not necessarily, a payment in cash). For many companies, this is a simple process—the customer walks into the convenience store, selects a soft drink, pays the store clerk for the soft drink, and then consumes the soft drink on the way home. The convenience store's revenue is the amount paid by the customer for the soft drink as the customer walks out with it (minus any sales taxes collected on behalf of government entities).

But other company/customer arrangements can be quite complicated, with delivery of the product and/or service occurring over time and with payments not coinciding with delivery. Revenue is such a vital component of companies' financial results, accounting standard setters formulated a broad principle and a process that is applied to almost all situations. The core principle is the following.

> An entity should recognize revenue to depict the transfer of goods or services to customers in an amount that reflects the consideration to which the entity expects to be entitled in exchange for those goods and services.

---

[1] To further complicate matters, the classification of some items in the income statement as nonoperating is not consistent with their classification in the cash flow statement. Specifically, interest and dividend income and interest expense are classified as operating in the cash flow statement and nonoperating in most income statements. Of course, the distinction between operating and nonoperating items depends on the company's business. For Microsoft, interest income and expense would be classified as nonoperating, but for a financial institution (e.g., a bank), those same items would be considered part of their operations. Purchases and sales of production equipment would be considered nonoperating for Microsoft, but operating for a company in the business of buying and selling used equipment.

To accomplish this principle, companies follow a five-step process.

Step 1: Identify the contract with a customer.
Step 2: Identify the performance obligations in the contract.
Step 3: Determine the transaction price.
Step 4: Allocate the transaction price (if necessary).
Step 5: Recognize revenue when or as the entity satisfies a performance obligation.

The first step is to determine whether the transaction has commercial substance. The word "contract" is used here in a general sense—it may refer to a legal document, but can also reflect an oral agreement or be implied by the entity's (i.e., the seller's) customary business practices. The agreement must create enforceable rights and obligations for the parties.

The second step breaks the contract down into distinct "**performance obligations**" which the entity agrees to perform. Essentially, the entity must determine how many distinct goods and services it has agreed to provide to the customer. These are the "deliverables" for the entity, and the accounting standards require the performance obligations to be distinct from each other. That is, the customer can benefit from each performance obligation on its own or together with readily accessible resources. For instance, if the entity regularly sells the good or service separately, then it can be distinct. For instance, a manufacturer's product warranty is *not* a separate performance obligation if the warranty terms are set to assure the customer that the product will perform as promised. Ford Motor Company's base warranty comes with every vehicle and is not considered a separate performance obligation. On the other hand, a customer may purchase a ticket for travel on an airline, and that purchase would be comprised of transportation services on the scheduled flight *and* frequent flyer miles that can be used for travel in the future. Are the frequent flyer miles a separate performance obligation? The answer is yes, because airlines sell frequent flyer miles separately from travel services.[2] On the other hand, if there are multiple goods and/or services, but they require significant integration or coordination, then there is only one deliverable.

For the third step, the transaction price is the amount of consideration to which the entity expects to be entitled in exchange for transferring promised goods or services.[3] The accounting standard allows for "**variable consideration**," which may include (but is not limited to) price concessions, volume discounts, rebates, refunds, credits, incentives, performance bonuses, and royalties. Determining variable consideration can require significant estimation by the entity's management, and the standard has features that are intended to control undue optimism on the part of management. Consider the following from Raytheon's 10-K regarding revenue recognition.

> It is common for our long-term contracts to contain award fees, incentive fees, or other provisions that can either increase or decrease the transaction price. These variable amounts generally are awarded upon achievement of certain performance metrics, program milestones or cost targets and can be based upon customer discretion. We estimate variable considerable at the most likely amount to which we expect to be entitled.

If there are multiple performance obligations, then Step 4 requires that the transaction price from Step 3 be allocated to these individual performance obligations based on their stand-alone selling prices. This process is simple if stand-alone selling prices are readily available. But if such prices do not exist, then the company must estimate the stand-alone selling prices. For example, if the stand-alone selling prices of performance obligations A and B are $150 and $350 respectively, and the entity agrees to deliver them to the customer for a combined price of $400, then it should recognize $120 (= $400 × (150/(150 + 350))) when A is delivered and $280 = $400 × [350/(150 + 350)] when B is delivered.

Finally, Step 5 requires that the entity recognize revenue as it satisfies a performance obligation. A performance obligation is considered to be satisfied when the customer obtains control, i.e., when the customer obtains the ability to direct the use of and obtain substantially all of the remaining

---

[2] If the contract involves providing a series of distinct goods or services that are substantially the same, then the series is treated as a single performance obligation that is satisfied over time. For example, a company might agree to provide nightly cleaning services for an office. While one could treat each day's cleaning as a separate performance obligation, it was deemed easier to view the cleaning contract as a single performance obligation that is fulfilled over time.

[3] Amounts collected for third parties (e.g., sales taxes) are not included in the entity's revenue.

benefits of the asset/service that constitutes the performance obligation. In some cases, the customer obtains control over time, but if control does not transfer over time, then it is presumed to transfer at a point in time.

In many instances, the sole performance obligation is to deliver a product or service to the customer. Delivery doesn't refer only to transportation to the customer's location, but rather the transfer of title and the risks and rewards of ownership to the customer. Revenue recognition complications arise if there is uncertainty about collectability or when the sale is contingent on product performance, product approval or similar contingencies. In some industries, it is standard practice to allow customers to return the product within a specified period of time. When these uncertainties are substantial, companies may have to reconsider the first step in the revenue recognition process. That is, does the delivery have commercial substance?

But for many companies, returns and uncollectible accounts are either immaterial in amount or relatively easy to predict based on history of a large number of similar transactions. The expected returns are estimated and reduce the reported revenue from the sale.

As noted earlier, revenue is a key performance indicator for almost every company, and there exists a wide variety of practices used in formulating a sales contract between a company and its customers. Given that diversity, the process to determine when to recognize revenue and how much revenue to recognize requires substantial judgment on the part of management. Therefore, it's important for the financial statement reader to check the footnote disclosures describing a company's practices.

BUSINESS INSIGHT

Performance Obligations and Product Returns at The Gap, Inc. Following is an excerpt from **The Gap, Inc.**'s accounting policies as reported in its quarterly financial statements

> For online sales, ship-from-stores sales, and catalog sales the Company has elected to treat shipping and handling as fulfillment activities, and not a separate performance obligation. Accordingly, we recognize revenue for our single performance obligation related to online sales, ship-from-store sales, and catalog sales at the time control of the merchandise passes to the customer, which is generally at the time of shipment. We also record an allowance for estimated returns based on our historical return patterns and various other assumptions that management believes to be reasonable . . .

The Gap's policy regarding product returns is consistent with GAAP in that expected returns are estimated and deducted from sales at the time that the sale is recorded. This represents the amount to which the company "expects to be entitled" when it makes the sale. If returns cannot be estimated at that point in time, then GAAP would assess that there was not a contract with the customer, and no revenue would be recognized at that point.

The term "delivery" does not refer solely to transportation to the customer's location, but also the transfer of title and of the control of the item's benefits. In a **consignment** sale, a *consignor* delivers product to a *consignee*, but retains ownership until the consignee sells the product to the ultimate customer. As long as ownership remains with the consignor, a sale has not taken place. Only when the consignee sells the product should the consignor record the sale revenue. Also at that point, the consignee, who has been acting as an agent for the consignor, will recognize the commission earned (not the full purchase price paid by the ultimate customer).

2

LO2 Illustrate revenue and expense recognition when the transaction involves future deliverables and/or multiple elements.

Revenue Recognition Subsequent to Customer Purchase

There are many businesses in which customers purchase a product or a service prior to its delivery. For instance, a customer may pay for a year's subscription to a periodical. The publisher receives the cash at the start of the subscription, but it earns revenue as it fulfills its performance obligation to deliver the periodical to the subscriber. Or, a homeowner may pay for the upcoming year's casualty insurance, but the insurance company can only recognize revenue as it fulfills its performance obligation to provide insurance coverage over that year.

In settings where a company's customers pay for the product or service prior to its delivery, the company must recognize a **contract liability**. The term contract liability refers to an entity's obligation to transfer goods or services to a customer for which the entity has received consideration (or the amount is due) from the customer. Such contract liabilities are frequently labeled as **unearned revenue** or **deferred revenue**[4] or some other descriptive term. Then this liability is reduced, and revenue recognized, as the performance obligation is fulfilled.

Suppose that on January 1, a subscriber pays $36 for an annual subscription to a monthly magazine. At the time of payment, the publisher would make the following entry:

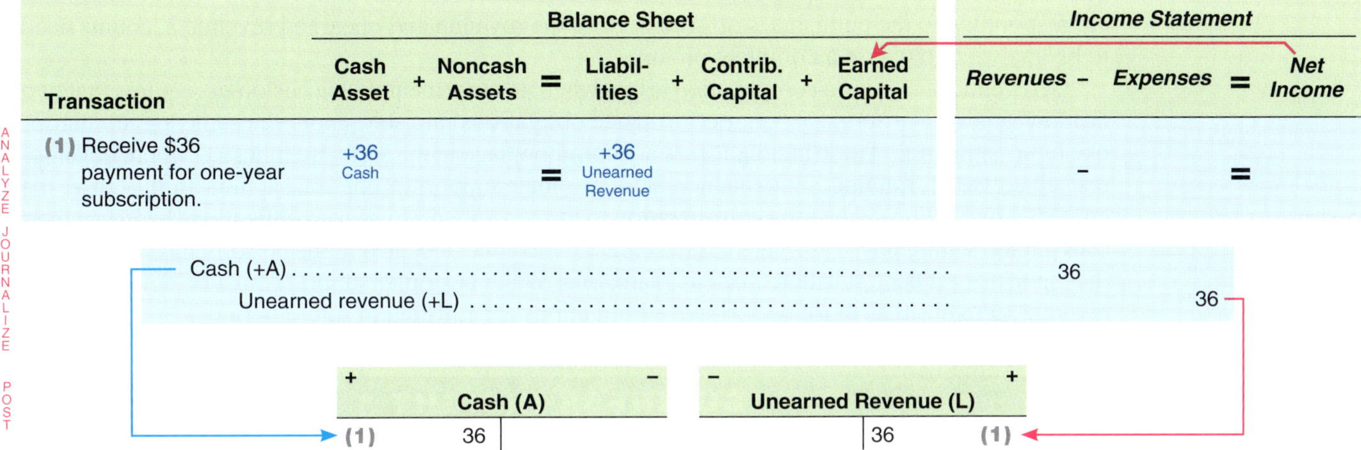

The unearned revenue liability represents the publisher's obligation—not to make a payment, but to provide the promised publication. Most liabilities reflect obligations to make a future payment, but unearned revenue is one of a handful of *contract liabilities* that represent an obligation for future performance.

On March 31, at the end of its first quarter, the publisher would recognize that three magazines had been delivered to the subscriber, and the publisher has earned three times the monthly revenue of $3, or $9. The entry to recognize this revenue is the following.

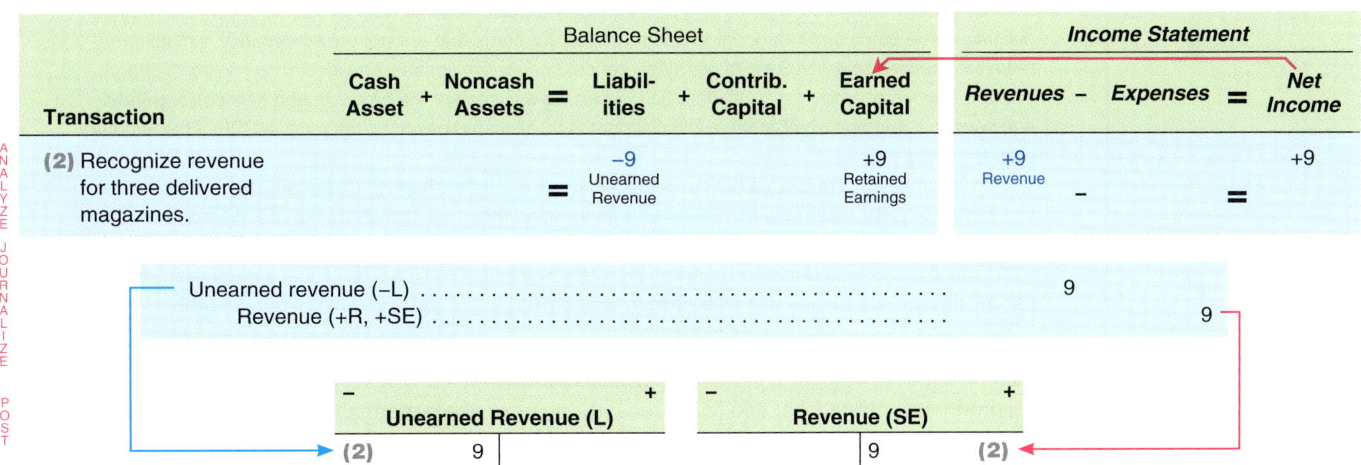

The same entries would be made until the subscription expired. In the March 31 balance sheet, the publisher would have an unearned revenue liability of $27, reflecting the remaining obligation for nine months of subscription delivery. And, the quarter's indirect method operating cash flows would include $9 in revenue (in net income) and the $27 increase in unearned revenue liability which, in total, reflect the $36 received from the customer.

---

[4] The term used for a contract liability may be particular to the company's business. For instance, **Delta Air Lines** shows an Air Traffic Liability of $6,360 million in its June 30, 2018 quarterly report, which represents customers' purchases of tickets in advance of their flights. **The Allstate Corporation** uses the term *Unearned Premiums*.

Unearned revenue is seen in a growing number of financial statements as companies increase the use of gift cards as well as their promises of future deliveries of products and service due to the changing nature of products and services in the economy and also in an effort to build a continuing relationship with their customers. From the point of view of a financial analyst, one implication of revenue deferral is that the change in revenue from one period to the next is not equal to the change in customer purchases over the same period. In the case of our publisher with one-year subscriptions, quarterly revenue is actually a composite of subscriber purchases over the current quarter plus the last three quarters and, therefore, not an ideal indicator of how current customers are responding to the publisher's offerings. Both the revenue and unearned revenue accounts need to be analyzed to obtain a complete picture.

A revenue recognition complication arises when an agreement with a customer requires that two or more products or services (i.e., performance obligations) are sold under the same agreement for one lump-sum price. These bundled sales are commonplace in the software industry, where developers sell software, training, maintenance, and customer support in one transaction. In this case, the company must allocate the total consideration to the separate performance obligations based on their stand-alone selling price (estimated, if necessary). Revenue allocated to the performance obligations that have not yet been fulfilled (such as maintenance and customer support) must be deferred, with revenue recognized as those performance obligations are fulfilled in future periods.

BUSINESS INSIGHT

Microsoft's Revenue Recognition Following is an excerpt from Microsoft Corporation's policies on revenue recognition as reported in footnotes to its recent annual report.

> Licenses for on-premises software provide the customer with a right to use the software as it exists when made available to the customer. Customers may purchase perpetual licenses or subscribe to licenses, which provide customers with the same functionality and differ mainly in the duration over which the customer benefits from the software. Revenue from distinct on-premises licenses is recognized upfront at the point in time when the software is made available to the customer. In cases where we allocate revenue to software updates, primarily because the updates are provided at no additional charge, revenue is recognized as the updates are provided, which is generally ratably over the estimated life of the related device or license . . . .
>
> Judgment is required to determine the SSP (Stand-alone Selling Price) for each distinct performance obligation. We use a single amount to estimate SSP for items that are not sold separately, including on-premises licenses sold with SA (Software Assurance) or software updates provided at no additional charge. We use a range of amounts to estimate SSP when we sell each of the products and services separately and need to determine whether there is a discount to be allocated based on the relative SSP of the various products and services.
>
> In instances where SSP is not directly observable, such as when we do not sell the product or service separately, we determine the SSP using information that may include market conditions and other observable inputs. We typically have more than one SSP for individual products and services due to the stratification of those products and services by customers and circumstances. In these instances, we may use information such as the size of the customer and geographic region in determining the SSP.

Microsoft emphasizes that judgment is required at many points in the revenue recognition process, from estimating the total selling price, to identifying distinct performance obligations, to allocating the total price to the performance obligations, and finally recognizing when the performance obligations are fulfilled.

To illustrate revenue recognition for a multiple performance obligation arrangement (or bundled sale), assume that Software Innovations, Inc., develops marketing software designed to track customer questions and comments on the Internet and through social media. The software license sells for $125,000 and includes user training for up to 12 individuals and customer support for three years. Software Innovations estimates that the software, if licensed without training or customer support, would sell for $120,000. In addition, it estimates that the value of the user training services, if sold separately, would be $18,000 and the customer support would sell for $12,000. Software Innovations would allocate the $125,000 sales price as illustrated in **Exhibit 6.3**.

EXHIBIT 6.3 Allocation of the Sales Price in a Multiple Performance Obligation Arrangement

Performance Obligation	Estimated value	Percent of total value		Bundle sales price		Sales price allocated to each performance obligation
Software license	$120,000	80%	×	$125,000	=	$100,000
Training	18,000	12	×	125,000	=	15,000
Customer support	12,000	8	×	125,000	=	10,000
Total	$150,000	100%				$125,000

The sale would be recorded as revenue for the portion that was allocated to software and as deferred (or unearned) revenue for that portion that was allocated to training and customer support:

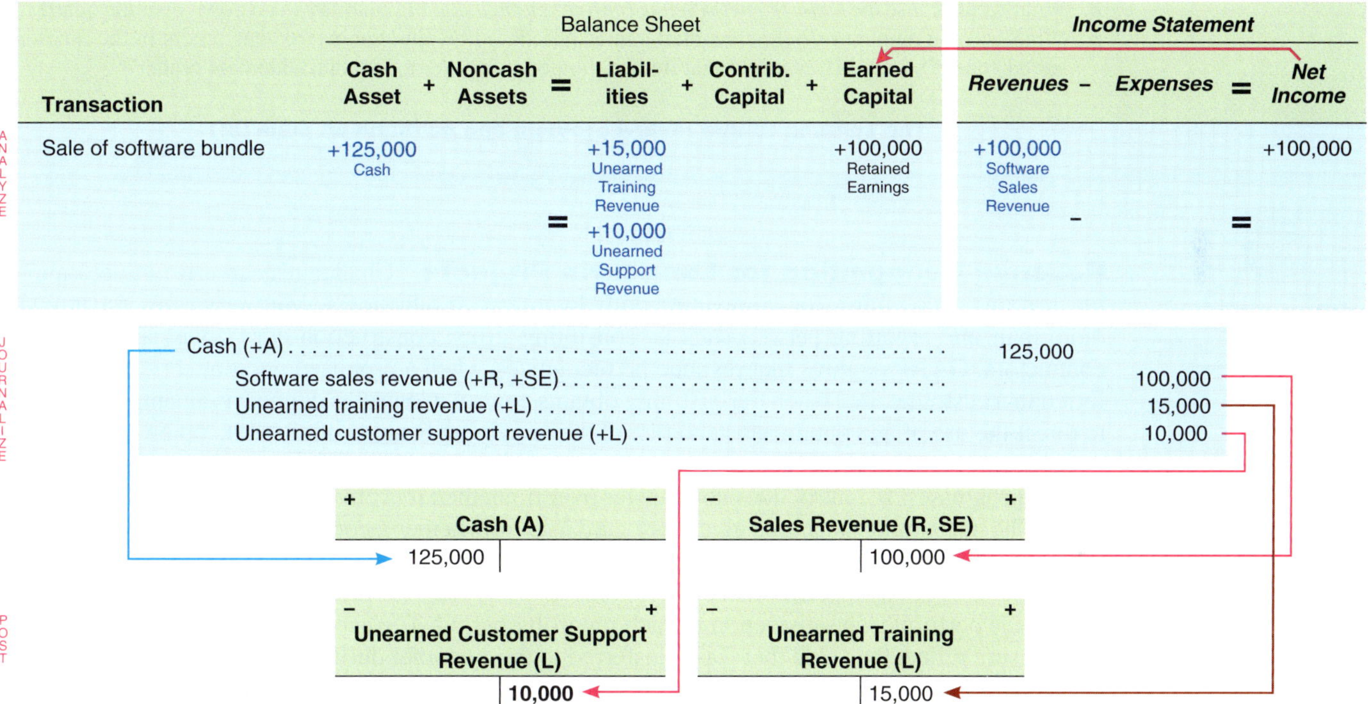

Transaction	Cash Asset	+ Noncash Assets	= Liabilities	+ Contrib. Capital	+ Earned Capital	Revenues	− Expenses	= Net Income
Sale of software bundle	+125,000 Cash		= +15,000 Unearned Training Revenue; +10,000 Unearned Support Revenue		+100,000 Retained Earnings	+100,000 Software Sales Revenue	−	= +100,000

	Debit	Credit
Cash (+A)	125,000	
Software sales revenue (+R, +SE)		100,000
Unearned training revenue (+L)		15,000
Unearned customer support revenue (+L)		10,000

The unearned training revenue would be recognized as training services are provided. Software Innovations might recognize 1/12 of the $15,000, or $1,250 for each individual trained. The unearned customer support revenue would be recognized over time ($10,000/3 = $3,333 each year).

MID-CHAPTER REVIEW 1

From the first quarter of fiscal 2019, Electronic Arts, Inc., described the following in its 10-Q:

> [F]or an individual sale of a game with both online and offline functionality, we typically have three distinct performance obligations; (1) the software license; (2) a right to receive future updates; and (3) online hosting. The software license performance obligation represents the game that is delivered digitally or via physical disc at the time of sale and typically provides access to offline core game content. The future update rights performance obligation includes updates on a when-and-if-available basis such as software patches or updates, and/or additional free content to be delivered in the future. The online hosting performance obligation consists of providing the customer with a hosted connection for online playability. Since we do not sell the performance obligations on a stand-alone basis, we consider market conditions and other observable inputs to estimate the stand-alone selling price

continued

continued from previous page

for each performance obligation. For games with services . . . , generally 75 percent of the sales price is allocated to the software license performance obligation and recognized at a point in time upon delivery (which is usually at or near the same time as the booking of the transaction), and the remaining 25 percent is allocated to the future update rights and the online hosting performance obligations and recognized ratably over . . . the period in which we offer to provide the future update rights and/or online hosting for the game and related extra content sold.

In its income statement for the quarter ended June 30, 2018, Electronic Arts reported *Total net revenue* of $1,137 million. At the beginning of that quarter, the company had a liability for *Deferred net revenue (online-enabled games)* of $949 million. At the end of the quarter, that liability was $602 million, a decrease of $347 million.

REQUIRED

a. What would cause the *Deferred net revenue (online-enabled gaming)* liability to go down over the quarter?

b. What was the amount of online-enabled games purchased by Electronic Arts' customers in the quarter ended June 30, 2018? How might that information be useful for a financial statement reader?

The solution to this review problem can be found on page 321.

3

LO3 Illustrate revenue and expense recognition for long-term projects.

Revenue Recognition for Long-term Projects Challenges can arise in determining revenue recognition for companies with long-term production/service processes (spanning more than one reporting period) such as consulting firms, construction companies, and defense contractors. GAAP requires that revenue be recognized when a promised good or service is transferred to a customer, i.e., when the customer obtains control. Control is defined as an entity's ability to direct the use of and obtain substantially all the remaining benefits of an asset. When a company engages in long-term projects, it must determine whether it will transfer control over time, as the project progresses. If control does not transfer over time, then it is presumed to transfer at a point in time. (The accounting standards give more guidance on whether a company's performance obligations are satisfied over time or at a point in time.)

When a company's performance obligations are satisfied over time, it must then choose a measure of the performance satisfaction in each reporting period. The accounting standards prefer that the measure reflect the value that was transferred to the customer during that period (contract milestones, surveys of performance). However, companies may use an input measure (costs incurred, hours worked, etc.) as long as that input measure reflects the value transferred to the customer.

Additional considerations are also important in the accounting for long-term projects. First, the company must make an assessment of the performance obligations in the contract with the customer. Are there separate performance obligations, or only one? A construction company may agree to construct a warehouse for a customer, and that project could include several facets—site preparation, utilities, foundation, structure, roofing, electrical, HVAC, and so on. Does the company have separate performance obligations for each of these, or just one—to deliver a functioning warehouse to the customer? This question can only be answered by careful consideration of the contract and the circumstances.

PERFORMANCE OBLIGATION SATISFIED OVER TIME To illustrate the revenue recognition when the performance obligation is satisfied over time, assume that Built-Rite Construction signs a $10 million contract to construct a building for a customer. Built-Rite estimates $7.5 million in construction costs, yielding an expected gross profit of $2.5 million. Based on its review of the contract, Built-Rite determines that the building construction is a single performance obligation satisfied over time. In addition, the construction costs incurred reflect the amount of value transferred to the customer during a reporting period, so the company can use the "cost-to-cost"[5] measure of performance.

[5] That is, the cost incurred compared to the estimated total cost. This approach is often referred to as "percentage-of-completion."

In the first year of construction, Built-Rite incurs $4.5 million in construction costs. The remaining $3.0 million are incurred during the second year. The amount of revenue and gross profit that Built-Rite would report each year (in millions) is illustrated in **Exhibit 6.4**.

EXHIBIT 6.4 Performance Obligation Satisfied over Time Based on Cost-to-Cost

Year	Measure of value transferred	Revenue recognized	Expense recognized	Gross profit
1	$4.5/$7.5 = 60%	$10.0 × 60% = $ 6.0	$4.5	$1.5
2	$3.0/$7.5 = 40%	$10.0 × 40% = 4.0	3.0	$1.0
Total	100%	$10.0	$7.5	$2.5

Using this method, Built-Rite would report $1.5 million in gross profit in the first year and $1.0 million in the second year. The timing of revenue and gross profit coincides with the transfer of value to the customer.

When a company's performance obligation is satisfied over time and cost is used to assess performance, it requires an estimate of the total cost to completion. This estimate is initially made at the start of the contract, usually used to bid the contract. However, estimates are inherently prone to error. If total completion costs are underestimated, the percentage of completion is overestimated (the denominator is too small) and too much revenue and gross profit are recognized in the early years of the project. Therefore the reliability of the reported performance depends on the quality of judgments made by the company's management.

PERFORMANCE OBLIGATION SATISFIED AT A POINT IN TIME In some circumstances, the company will determine that its performance obligation is not satisfied over time, but rather at a point in time. If Built-Rite Construction had determined that its performance obligation to construct the customer's building was not satisfied until delivery of the completed building to the customer, the revenue and gross profit would be reported as in **Exhibit 6.5**.

EXHIBIT 6.5 Performance Obligation Satisfied over Time versus at a Point in Time

Performance obligation satisfied over time			Performance obligation satisfied at a point in time		
	Year 1	Year 2		Year 1	Year 2
Revenues	$6.0	$4.0	Revenues	$0.0	$10.0
Expenses	4.5	3.0	Expenses	0.0	7.5
Gross profit.	$1.5	$1.0	Gross profit.	$0.0	$ 2.5

The total revenue and gross profit are the same under either method. The only difference is in the timing of the income statement reporting. Revenue and gross profit will show more variability when the performance obligation is satisfied at the end of the process.

TIMING DIFFERENCES BETWEEN REVENUES AND CASH RECEIPTS It is very likely that Built-Rite would have received some cash payments from the customer during the construction period, perhaps as advances or based on milestones in the construction process. However, the recognition of revenue is tied to the completion of performance obligations, which may differ from the measures used to determine progress payments. If a company receives payment prior to completion of the performance obligation, then it should recognize a **contract liability**, like deferred revenue or unearned revenue. If the project progress entitles the company to payment, it would also recognize an account receivable.

In addition, the company should recognize revenue in the amount to which it expects to be entitled for completing the performance obligation. So, if a contract includes an incentive payment for timely completion of the project, the company should recognize its estimate of the amount of incentive that it expects to receive, prior to the actual receipt of that payment at the end of the contract. This contract arrangement can result in the company recognizing revenue when it cannot yet send an invoice to the customer. That is, the company is not yet entitled to an unconditional right to future payment. When such revenue is credited, the account debited is referred to as a **contract asset** (sometimes referred to as unbilled receivables). A contract asset represents an amount that the company expects to receive from the customer for performance to date, but for which it is not yet entitled to payment.

As an example, suppose Built-Rite's contract with the customer allows it to bill the customer for half the project once 60% of the work was complete at the end of year 1. The entry made to reflect revenue recognized for year 1 would be the following (all amounts in $ millions):

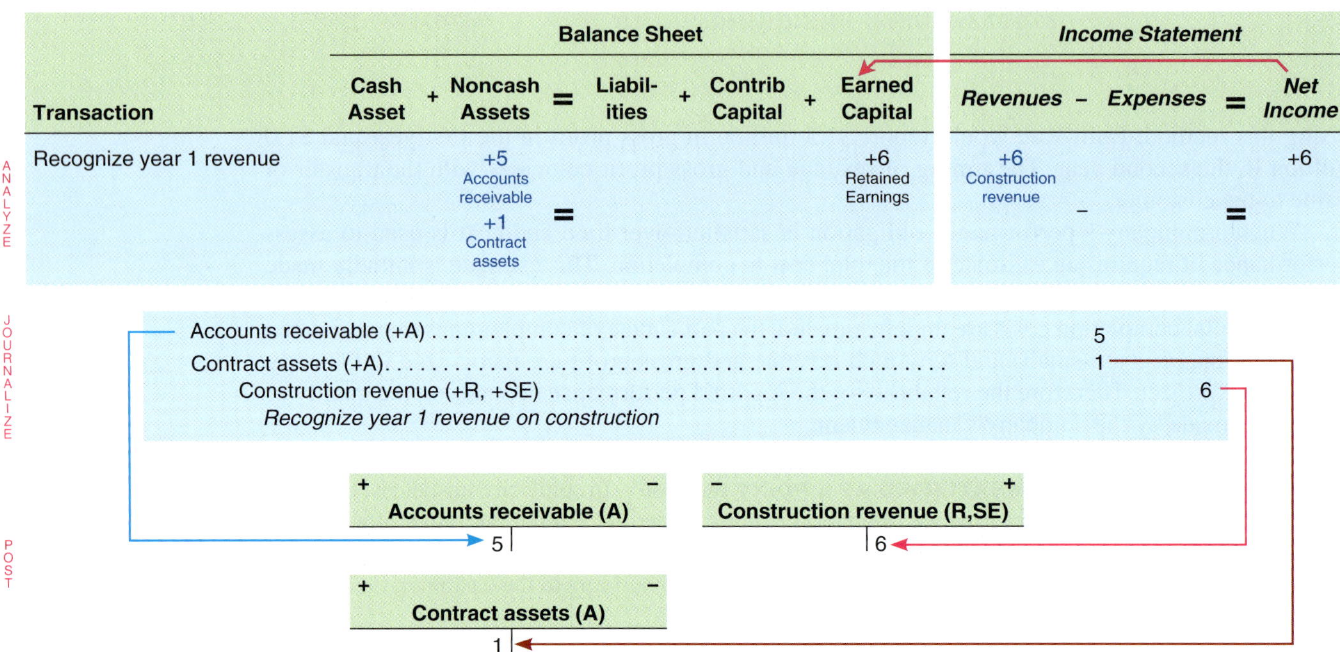

On completion of the project at the end of year 2, Built-Rite would recognize as revenue the 40% of the project completed. It would bill the customer for this amount *plus* the amount of revenue previously held as contract assets.

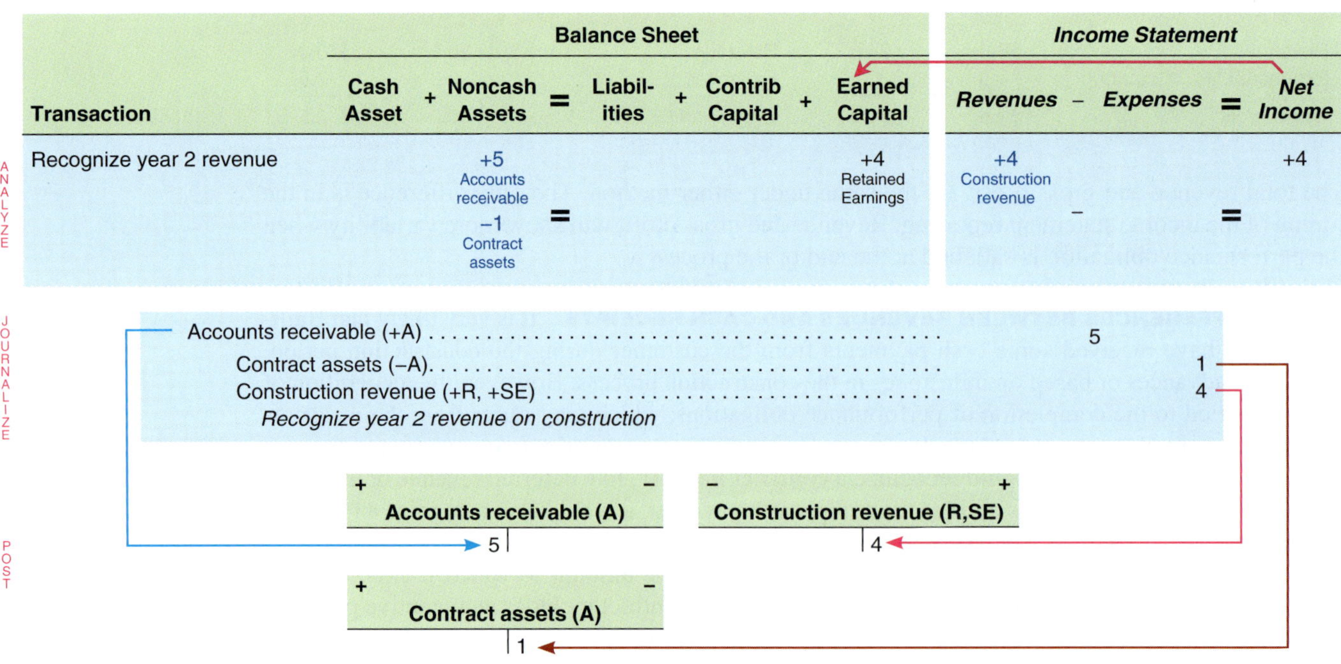

BUSINESS INSIGHT

Fluor Corporation engages in engineering and construction activities for its customers. The following excerpts from its second quarter 2018 10-Q are taken from its footnote on revenue recognition.

> "ASU 2014-09, 'Revenue from Contracts with Customers' outlines a single comprehensive model for entities to use in accounting for revenue arising from contracts with customers and supersedes most current revenue recognition guidance, including industry-specific guidance. ASU 2014-09 outlines a five-step process for revenue recognition that focuses on transfer of control, as opposed to transfer of risk and rewards, and also requires enhanced disclosures regarding the nature, amount, timing and uncertainty of revenues and cash flows from contracts with customers. Major provisions include determining which goods and services are distinct and represent separate performance obligations, how variable consideration (which may include change orders and claims) is recognized, whether revenue should be recognized at a point in time or over time and ensuring the time value of money is considered in the transaction price . . .
>
> "In the past . . . 'the company typically segmented revenue and margin recognition between the engineering and construction phases of its contracts.' Now, 'engineering and construction contracts are generally accounted for as a single unit of account (a single performance obligation), resulting in a more constant recognition of revenue and margin over the term of the contract . . .
>
> "The company recognizes engineering and construction contract revenue over time, as performance obligations are satisfied, due to the continuous transfer of control to the customer. Engineering and construction contracts are generally accounted for as a single unit of account (a single performance obligation) and are not segmented between types of services. The company recognizes revenue using the percentage-of-completion method, based primarily on contract cost incurred to date compared to total estimated contract cost. The percentage-of-completion method (an input method) is the most faithful depiction of the company's performance because it directly measures the value of the services transferred to the customer . . .
>
> "The nature of the company's contracts gives rise to several types of variable consideration, including claims and unpriced change orders; awards and incentive fees; and liquidated damages and penalties. The company recognizes revenue for variable consideration when it is probable that a significant reversal in the amount of cumulative revenue recognized will not occur . . . "

In its June 30, 2018 balance sheet, Fluor Corporation reports *Contract assets* of $1,587 million (17.5% of total assets) and *Contract liabilities* of $944 million (42.6% of total liabilities). The contract assets represent revenue that has been recognized but not yet billed to the customer. When Fluor bills a customer for an amount that exceeds the recognized revenue, the excess is reported as a contract liability.

MID-CHAPTER REVIEW 2

Haskins, Inc., has reached an agreement with a customer, Skaife Corporation, to deliver 200 units of a customized product. The standard billing price per unit is $1,000, and there are no discounts. At the time of the agreement on April 6, Skaife Corporation provides a $40,000 cash deposit to Haskins, Inc. Haskins agrees to deliver 120 units to Skaife Corporation on May 31 and at that time, Haskins can send an invoice for $50,000 to be paid by Skaife Corporation on June 15. The remaining 80 units are to be delivered on July 15, accompanied by an invoice for the remaining amount of the total $200,000 purchase price to be paid on July 31.

REQUIRED:

Assume that Haskins, Inc., has no uncertainties about its own ability to meet the terms of the contract or about Skaife Corporation's ability and willingness to pay. Provide the journal and FSET entries to record Haskins' revenue from the above events (leaving out the accounting for Haskins, Inc.'s costs).

The solution to this review problem can be found on pages 322–323.

REPORTING ACCOUNTS RECEIVABLE

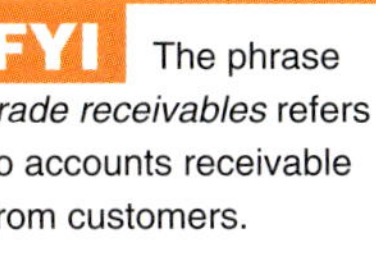

The phrase *trade receivables* refers to accounts receivable from customers.

Receivables are usually a major part of operating working capital. They must be carefully managed as they represent a substantial asset for most companies. GAAP requires companies to report revenues in the amount to which they expect to be entitled and receivables in the amount to which they have an unconditional right to payment. But the balance sheet value of receivables should be the amount they expect to collect, necessitating an estimation of uncollectible accounts. These estimates determine the amount of receivables reported on the balance sheet as well as revenues and expenses reported on the income statement. Accordingly, it is important that companies accurately assess uncollectible accounts and report them. It is also necessary that readers of financial reports understand management's accounting choices and the effects of those choices on reported balance sheets and income statements.

FYI Receivables are claims held against customers and others for money, goods, or services.

When companies sell to other companies, they usually do not expect cash upon delivery as is common with retail customers. Instead, they offer credit terms, and the resulting sales are called **credit sales** or *sales on account.*

Companies establish credit policies (to determine which customers receive credit) by weighing the expected losses from uncollectible accounts against the expected profits generated by offering credit. Sellers know that some buyers will be unable to pay their accounts when they become due. Buyers, for example, can suffer business downturns that are beyond their control and which limit their cash available to meet liabilities. They must, then, make choices concerning which of their liabilities to pay. Liabilities to the IRS, to banks, and to bondholders are usually paid, as those creditors have enforcement powers and can quickly seize assets and disrupt operations, leading to bankruptcy and eventual liquidation. Buyers also try to cover their payroll, as they cannot exist without employees. Then, if there is cash remaining, these customers will pay suppliers to ensure a continued flow of goods.

When a customer faces financial difficulties, suppliers are often the last creditors to receive payment and are often not paid in full. Consequently, there is risk in the collectibility of accounts receivable. This *collectibility risk* is crucial to analysis of accounts receivable.

Accounts receivable are reported on the balance sheet of the seller at **net realizable value**, which is the net amount that the seller expects to collect. Microsoft reports $26,481 million of accounts receivable in the current asset section of its 2018 balance sheet. Its receivables are reported net of allowances for doubtful accounts of $377 million. This means that the total amount owed to Microsoft by customers is $26,858 million ($26,481 million + $377 million), but the company *estimates* that $377 million of these receivables will be uncollectible. Thus, only the net amount that Microsoft expects to collect is reported on the balance sheet.

FYI Receivables are classified into three types: (1) current or noncurrent, (2) trade or nontrade, (3) accounts receivable or notes receivable. **Notes receivable** and **notes payable** are discussed in Chapter 9.

We might ask why the management of Microsoft would sell to companies from whom they do not expect to collect the amounts owed.[6] The answer is they would not *if* they knew beforehand who those companies were. That is, Microsoft probably cannot identify those companies that constitute the $377 million in uncollectible accounts as of its statement date. Yet, Microsoft knows from past experience that a certain portion of its receivables will prove uncollectible. GAAP requires a company to estimate the dollar amount of uncollectible accounts each time it issues its financial statements (even if it cannot identify specific accounts that are uncollectible), and to report its accounts receivable at the resulting *net realizable value* (total receivables less an **allowance for doubtful (uncollectible) accounts**).

4

LO4 Estimate and account for uncollectible accounts receivable.

Determining the Allowance for Uncollectible Accounts

The amount of expected uncollectible accounts is usually estimated based on an **aging analysis**. When aging the accounts, an analysis of receivables is performed as of the balance sheet date. Specifically, each customer's account balance is categorized by the number of days or months that the related invoices are outstanding. Based on prior experience, assessment of current economic conditions, or on other available statistics, uncollectible (bad debt) percentages are applied to each of these categorized amounts, with larger percentages applied to older accounts. The result of this analysis is a dollar amount for the allowance for uncollectible accounts (also called allowance for doubtful accounts) at the balance sheet date.

[6] GAAP requires that companies distinguish between amounts that they expected to receive that turned out to be uncollectible and amounts that represent an "implied price concession." For example, suppose a healthcare provider treats an uninsured patient, and the list price of the services is $10,000. But it is common for the healthcare company to accept, say, $1,500 from uninsured patients receiving such services. Should the healthcare company report revenue of $10,000 and $8,500 of bad debt expense? GAAP says that if there is an expectation that the healthcare company will accept the lower amount, then it should recognize $1,500 in revenue, not $10,000.

To illustrate, **Exhibit 6.6** shows an aging analysis for a seller that began operations this year and is owed $100,000 of accounts receivable at year-end. Those accounts listed as current consist of those outstanding that are still within their original credit period. Accounts listed as 1–60 days past due are those 1 to 60 days past their due date. This classification would include an account that is 45 days outstanding for a net 30-day invoice. This same logic applies to all aged categories.

EXHIBIT 6.6 Aging of Accounts Receivable

Age of Accounts Receivable	Receivable Balance	Estimated Percent Uncollectible	Accounts Estimated Uncollectible
Current	$ 50,000	2%	$1,000
1–60 days past due	30,000	3	900
61–90 days past due	15,000	4	600
Over 90 days past due	5,000	8	400
Total	$100,000		$2,900

The calculation illustrated in **Exhibit 6.6** also reflects the seller's experience with uncollectible accounts, which manifests itself in the uncollectible percentages for each aged category. For example, on average, 3% of buyers' accounts that are 1–60 days past due prove uncollectible for this seller. Hence, it estimates a potential loss of $900 for those $30,000 in receivables for that aged category.

Another means of estimating uncollectible accounts is to use the **percentage of sales**. To illustrate, if our seller reports sales of $100,000 and estimates the uncollectible accounts at 3% of sales, estimated uncollectible accounts would be $3,000. The percentage of sales approach focuses on the amount of potentially uncollectible accounts among current-period sales, whereas the aging analysis is based on the current balance in accounts receivable. Thus, these two methods nearly always result in different estimates of uncollectible accounts. While the percentage of sales method is arguably simpler, an aging analysis generally provides more accurate estimates.

Reporting the Allowance for Uncollectible Accounts

How does the accounting system record this estimate? The amount that appears in the balance sheet as accounts receivable represents a collection of individual accounts—one or more receivables for each customer. Because we need to keep track of exactly how much each customer owes us, we cannot simply subtract estimated uncollectibles from individual accounts receivable.

In Chapter 3, we introduced contra-asset accounts to record accumulated depreciation. A contra-asset account is directly associated with an asset account, but serves to offset the balance of the asset account. To record the estimated uncollectible accounts without disturbing the balance in accounts receivable, we use another contra-asset—the allowance for uncollectible accounts.

To illustrate, we use the data from **Exhibit 6.6**. The summary journal entry to reflect credit sales follows.

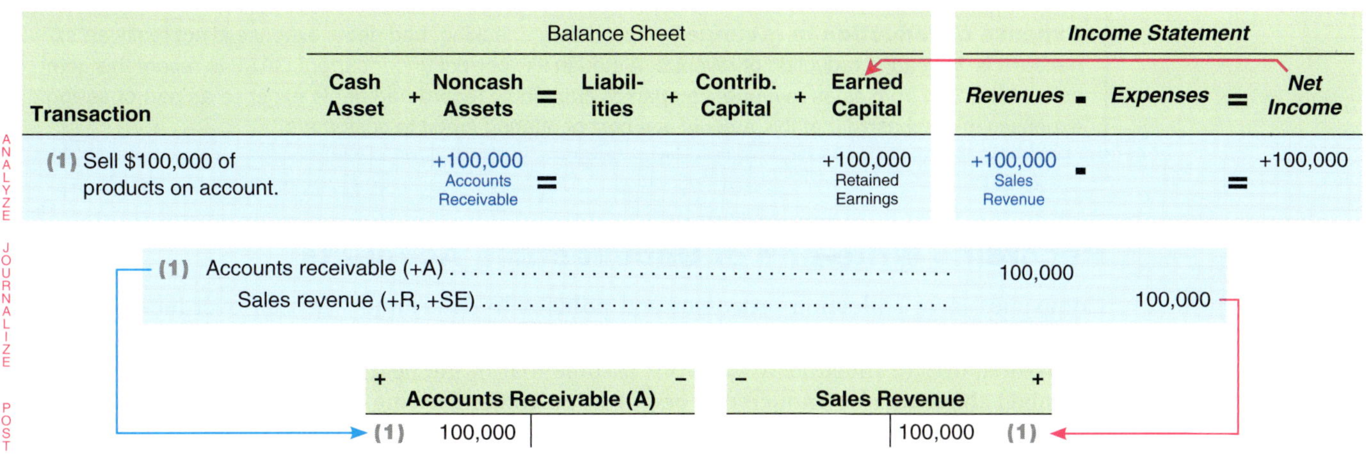

FYI The term *provision* is sometimes used as a substitute for expense; often when the reported expense is an estimate.

For an adjusting entry at year-end, uncollectible accounts are estimated and recorded as follows as **bad debts expense** (also called *provision for uncollectible or doubtful accounts*). The allowance for uncollectible accounts is a contra-asset account. It offsets (reduces) accounts receivable.

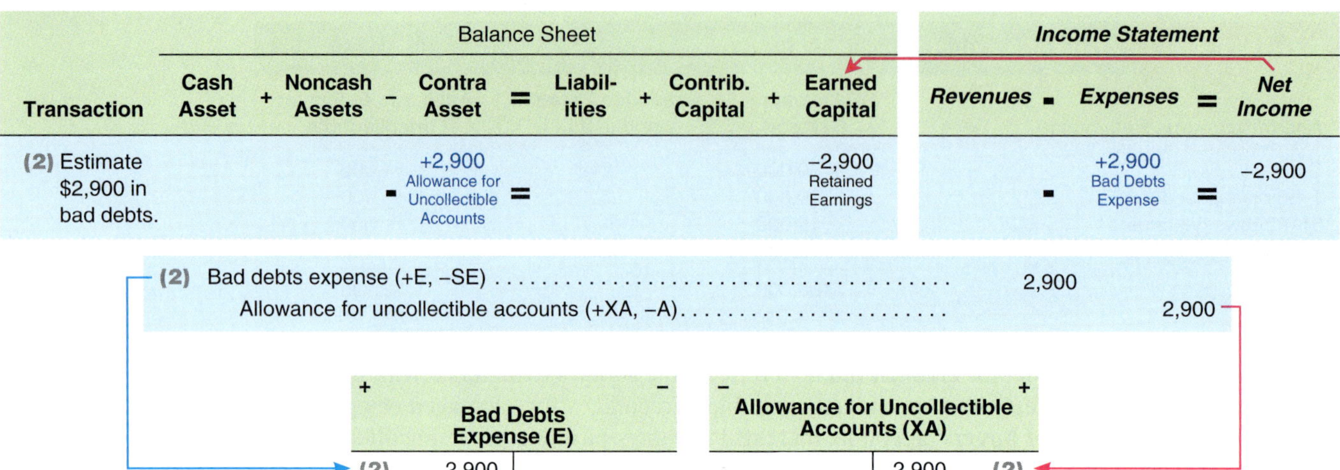

	Balance Sheet							Income Statement		
Transaction	Cash Asset	+ Noncash Assets	− Contra Asset	= Liabil-ities	+ Contrib. Capital	+ Earned Capital		Revenues	− Expenses	= Net Income
ANALYZE (2) Estimate $2,900 in bad debts.			+2,900 Allowance for Uncollectible Accounts			−2,900 Retained Earnings			+2,900 Bad Debts Expense	−2,900

JOURNALIZE

(2) Bad debts expense (+E, −SE)	2,900	
Allowance for uncollectible accounts (+XA, −A)		2,900

POST

+ Bad Debts Expense (E) −	
(2) 2,900	

− Allowance for Uncollectible Accounts (XA) +	
	2,900 (2)

This accounting treatment serves three purposes. First, the balance in accounts receivable is reported in the balance sheet net of estimated uncollectible accounts as follows:

Accounts receivable, net of $2,900 in allowances	$97,100

The $97,100 is the estimated net realizable value of the accounts receivable. Second, the original value of accounts receivable is preserved. The individual accounts that add up to the $100,000 in accounts receivable have not been altered. Third, bad debts expense of $2,900, which is part of the cost of offering credit to customers, is matched against the $100,000 sales generated on credit and reported in the income statement. Bad debts expense is usually included in SG&A expenses.

The allowance for uncollectible accounts is increased by bad debts expense (estimated provision for uncollectibles) and decreased when an account is written off. Because the allowance for uncollectible accounts is a contra-asset account, credit entries increase its balance. The greater the balance in the contra-asset account, the more the corresponding asset account is offset.

BUSINESS INSIGHT

Expense or reduction in revenue? Technically speaking, bad debts expense is not really an expense. It is, instead, a reduction of revenue. Although it is correct under current GAAP to record this item as a subtraction from sales revenue, companies commonly record bad debts expense as part of selling expenses to emphasize that this amount is a cost of offering credit to customers.

Recording Write-offs of Uncollectible Accounts

Companies have collection processes and policies to determine when an overdue receivable should be classified as uncollectible. When an individual account reaches that classification, it is written off. To illustrate a write-off, assume that in the next period (Year 2), the company described above receives notice that one of its customers, owing $500 at the time, has declared bankruptcy. The seller's attorneys believe that the legal costs necessary to collect the amount would exceed the $500 owed. The seller could then decide to write off the account with the following entry.

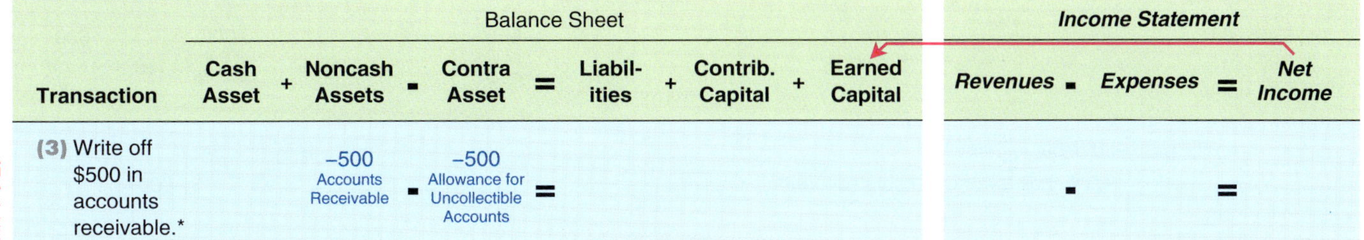

*There is no effect on accounts receivable, net of the allowance for uncollectible accounts. Consequently, there is no *net* effect on the balance sheet.

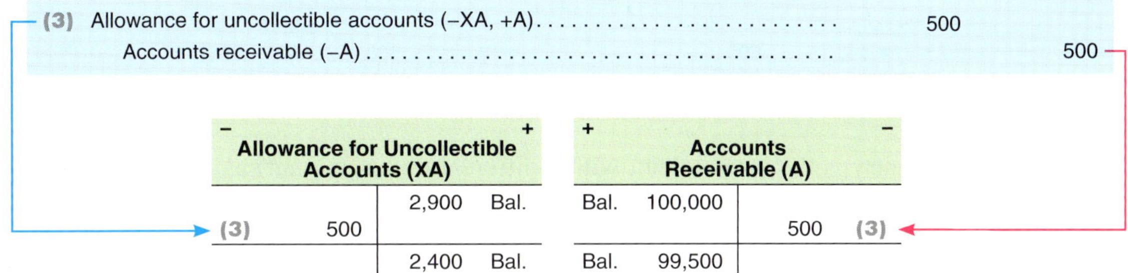

Exhibit 6.7 summarizes the effects of this write-off on the individual accounts.

EXHIBIT 6.7 Effects of an Accounts Receivable Write-Off

	Before Write-Off	Effects of Write-Off	After Write-Off
Accounts receivable	$100,000	$ (500)	$99,500
Less: Allowance for uncollectible accounts	2,900	500	2,400
Accounts receivable, net of allowance	$ 97,100		$97,100

The net amount of accounts receivable that is reported in the balance sheet after the write-off is the same amount that was reported before the write-off. This is always the case. The individual account receivable was reduced and the contra-asset was reduced by the same amount. Also, no entry was made to the income statement. The expense was estimated and recorded in the period when the credit sales were recorded.[7]

To complete the illustration, assume that management's aging of accounts at the end of Year 2 shows that the ending balance in the allowance account should be $3,000, so another $600 should be added to the allowance account at the end of Year 2. This $600 amount would reflect sales made in Year 2, as well as the seller's experience with collections during Year 2. The entry to record the Year 2 provision follows.

[7] Suppose a previously written off account is unexpectedly paid, often referred to as a *recovery*. If that occurs, the write-off entry (3) is reversed (reinstating the receivable and increasing the allowance), and the payment of this reinstated receivable is accounted for in the usual fashion.

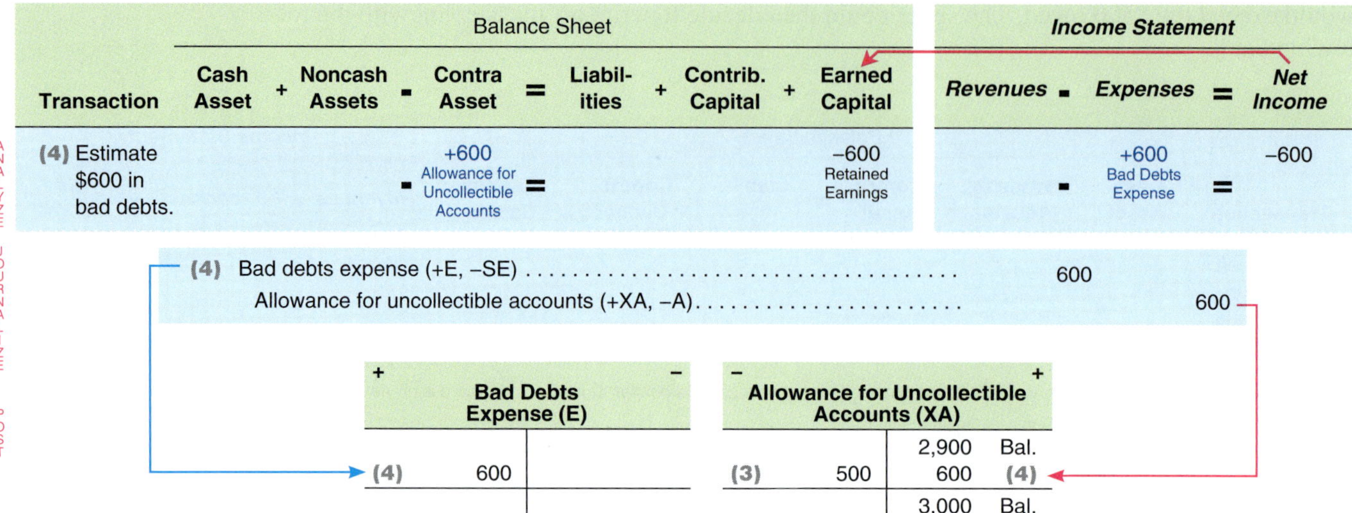

This entry is the same (albeit with a different dollar amount) as the entry made to record the estimate in Year 1. A reconciliation of allowance for uncollectible accounts for the two years follows.

	Year 1	Year 2
Allowance for uncollectible accounts, beginning balance	$ 0	$2,900
Add: provision for uncollectible accounts (bad debts expense estimate)	2,900	600
Subtract: write-offs of uncollectible accounts receivable	0	(500)
Allowance for uncollectible accounts, ending balance	$2,900	$3,000

To summarize, the *main balance sheet and income statement effects occur when the provision is made to the allowance for uncollectible accounts.* Accounts receivable (net) is reduced, and that reduction is reflected in the income statement as bad debts expense (usually part of selling, general, and administrative expenses). The net income reduction yields a corresponding equity reduction (via reduced retained earnings). Importantly, the main financial statement effects are at the point of *estimation*, not upon the event of *write-off.* In this way, the net accounts receivable reflects the most up-to-date judgments about future customer payments, and bad debts expense matches the current period's sales and incorporates any changes in management's assessment of the likelihood that customers will pay.

Footnote Disclosures and Interpretations

In its balance sheets, Microsoft reports current accounts receivable, net of allowance for doubtful accounts, of $26,481 million at June 30, 2018, and $22,431 million at June 30, 2017. In its MD&A (Management Discussion and Analysis), the company provides the following information.

> The allowance for doubtful accounts reflects our best estimate of probable losses inherent in the accounts receivable balance. We determine the allowance based on known trouble accounts, historical experience, and other currently available evidence.

continued

continued from previous page

Activity in the allowance for doubtful accounts was as follows:

(In millions)			
Year Ended June 30,	**2018**	**2017**	**2016**
Balance, beginning of period	$361	$409	$289
Charged to costs and other	134	58	175
Write-offs	(98)	(106)	(55)
Balance, end of period	$397	$361	$409

Allowance for doubtful accounts included in our consolidated balance sheets:

June 30,	**2018**	**2017**	**2016**
Accounts receivable, net allowance for doubtful accounts	$377	$345	$392
Other long-term assets	20	16	17
Total	$397	$361	$409

In Microsoft's 10-K report filed with the Securities and Exchange Commission, it discloses that its provision for doubtful accounts (bad debts expense) was $134 million, $58 million, and $175 million in fiscal years 2018, 2017, and 2016, respectively. Based on this information, we could construct a reconciliation of Microsoft's allowance for doubtful accounts (for both current and long-term receivables) as presented in **Exhibit 6.8**.

EXHIBIT 6.8 Reconciliation of Microsoft's Allowance for Doubtful Accounts

Allowance for Doubtful Accounts ($ millions)	
Balance at June 30, 2017	$361
Provision for doubtful accounts	134
Write-offs	(98)
Balance at June 30, 2018	$397

The footnotes may also disclose whether or not a company has *pledged* its accounts receivable as collateral for a short-term loan. If this is the case, a short-term loan is presented in the liabilities section of the balance sheet and a footnote explains the arrangement. As an alternative to borrowing, a company may *factor* (or sell) its accounts receivable to a bank or other financial institution. If the receivables have been factored, the bank or other financial institution accepts all responsibility for collection. Consequently, the receivables do not appear on the balance sheet of the selling company because they have been sold.

The reconciliation of Microsoft's allowance account provides insight into the level of its annual provision (bad debts expense) relative to its write-offs. In 2018, Microsoft wrote off $98 million in uncollectible accounts while recording a provision for doubtful accounts (bad debts expense) of $134 million. Because the provision exceeded the write-offs, the total allowance increased from $361 million in 2017 to $397 million in 2018.

Microsoft's bad debts expense (or provision) has been volatile in recent years, though the magnitude is small relative to the size of their accounts receivable. It reported a provision for bad debts of $175 million in 2016 and $58 million in 2017. The changes in bad debts expense, both in absolute amount and as a percentage of sales revenue, could be caused by a number of factors. For example, the creditworthiness of Microsoft's customers may have changed. These changes can be caused by changing economic conditions or changes in Microsoft's credit policies (including collection efforts).

The magnitude of Microsoft's uncollectible accounts relative to the company's overall size and profitability makes it an unlikely place for earnings management. But companies in other industries (banking, publishing, retail) often have receivables that require substantial adjustments for expected returns or uncollectible accounts. For instance, the publisher **John Wiley & Sons, Inc.**, reports accounts receivable of $212.4 million in its April 30, 2018, balance sheet, but this amount is net of an allowance for doubtful accounts of $10.1 million and an allowance for sales returns of $18.6 million. So, Wiley only expects to collect about 88% of the amounts it has billed customers. For such companies, modest changes in expectations of returns or collections can have a material effect on reported income. Wiley reports that a 1% change in the estimated return rate would decrease net income by $1.6 million.

Experience tells us that many companies have used the allowance for uncollectible accounts to shift income from one period into another. For instance, a company may overestimate its allowance in some years. Such an overestimation may have been unintentional, or it may have been an intentional attempt to manage earnings by building up a reserve (during good years) that can be drawn down in subsequent periods in order to increase reported income. Such a reserve is sometimes called a **cookie jar reserve**. Alternatively, a company may underestimate its provision in some years. This underestimation may be unintentional, or it may be an attempt to boost earnings to achieve some desired target. Looking at the patterns in the reconciliation of the allowance for uncollectible accounts may provide some indicators of this behavior.[8]

The MD&A section of a company's 10-K report often provides insights into changes in company policies, customers, or economic conditions to help explain changes in the allowance account. Further, the amount and timing of the uncollectible provision is largely controlled by management. Although external auditors assess the reasonableness of the allowance for uncollectible accounts, auditors do not possess the inside knowledge of management and are, therefore, at an information disadvantage, particularly if a dispute arises.

Some insight can be gained by comparing Microsoft's allowance to those of its competitors. **Exhibit 6.9** illustrates that Microsoft's allowance as a percentage of total receivables is in the middle of other technology companies, **Intel Corporation**, **Intuit Inc.**, and **Alphabet Inc.** These percentages decreased for all of these companies, perhaps reflecting the improving economic conditions of this time period.

EXHIBIT 6.9 Allowance for Doubtful Accounts as a Percentage of Gross Receivables

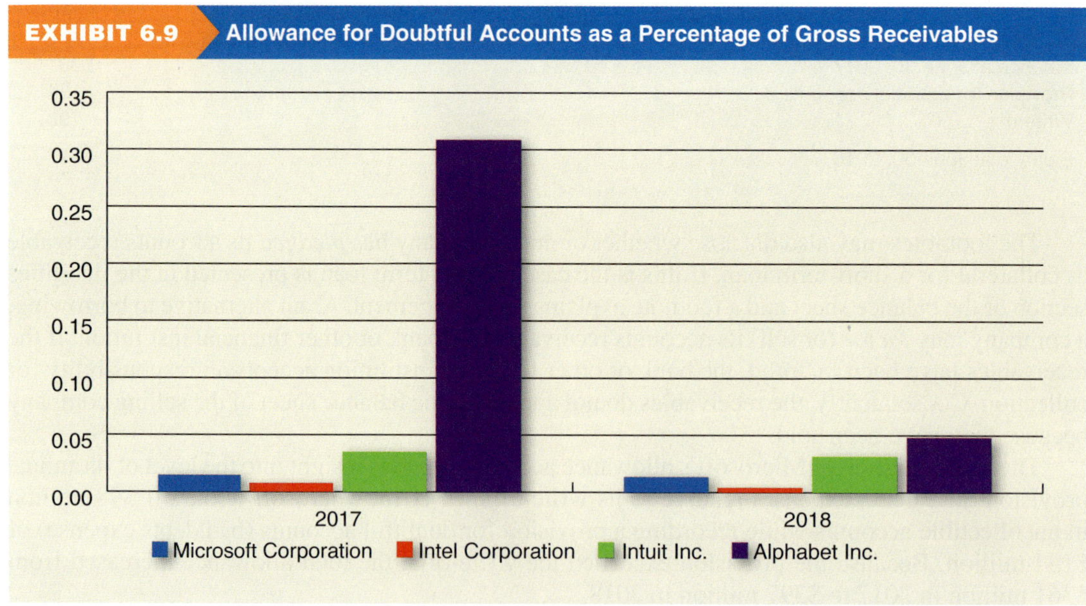

These companies do not have identical fiscal year-ends. Microsoft's fiscal year ends on June 30, Intel on the last Saturday in December, Intuit on July 31, and Alphabet on December 31. The comparisons in this exhibit (and in those following) are based on the most recent financial statements for each company.

Ultimately, a company makes two representations when reporting accounts receivable (net) in the current asset section of its balance sheet:

---

[8] See McNichols, Maureen and G. Peter Wilson, "Evidence of Earnings Management from the Provision for Bad Debts," *Journal of Accounting Research*, Supplement 1988.

1. It expects to collect the asset amount reported on the balance sheet (remember, accounts receivable are reported net of allowance for uncollectible accounts).
2. It expects to collect the asset amount within the next year (implied from its classification as a current asset).

From an analysis viewpoint, we scrutinize the adequacy of a company's provision for its uncollectible accounts. If the provision is inadequate, the cash ultimately collected will be less than what the company is reporting as net receivables.

The financial statement effects of uncollectible accounts are at the point of estimation, not at the time of a write-off. Nevertheless, it is important to remember that management sets the size of the allowance, albeit with auditor assurances.

MID-CHAPTER REVIEW 3

GuidedExamples MBC

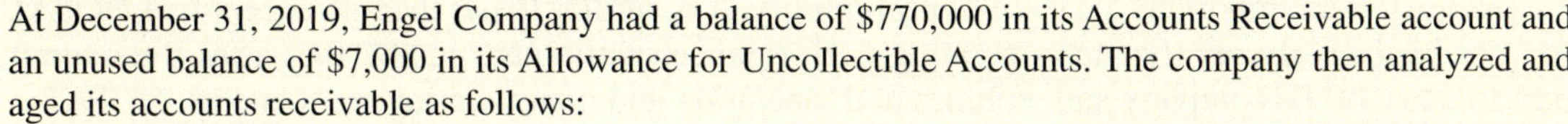

At December 31, 2019, Engel Company had a balance of $770,000 in its Accounts Receivable account and an unused balance of $7,000 in its Allowance for Uncollectible Accounts. The company then analyzed and aged its accounts receivable as follows:

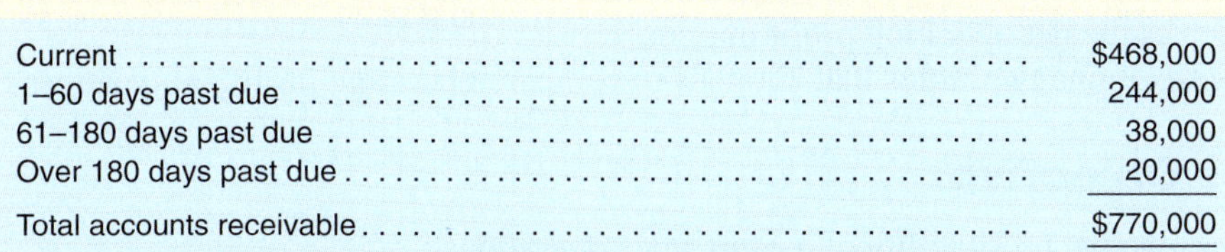

Current	$468,000
1–60 days past due	244,000
61–180 days past due	38,000
Over 180 days past due	20,000
Total accounts receivable	$770,000

In the past, the company experienced losses as follows: 1% of current balances, 5% of balances 1–60 days past due, 15% of balances 61–180 days past due, and 40% of balances over 180 days past due. The company bases its provision for credit losses on the aging analysis.

REQUIRED

1. What amount of uncollectible accounts (bad debts) expense will Engel report in its 2019 income statement?
2. Show how Accounts Receivable and the Allowance for Uncollectible Accounts appear in its December 31, 2019, balance sheet.
3. Assume that Engel's allowance for uncollectible accounts has maintained a historical average of 2% of gross accounts receivable. How do you interpret the level of the current allowance percentage?
4. Report the effects for each of the following summary transactions in the financial statement effects template, prepare journal entries, and then post the amounts to the appropriate T-accounts.
   a. Bad debts expense estimated at $23,580.
   b. Write off $5,000 in customer accounts.

The solution to this review problem can be found on pages 323–324.

ANALYZING FINANCIAL STATEMENTS

We began this chapter with a discussion of operating income and revenues and proceeded to examine receivables. We now introduce ratios that will aid in our analysis of income, revenue, and receivables. The first ratio is a measure of performance that relates the firm's operating achievements to the resources available. The next ratio, net operating profit margin, relates operating profit to sales. The last two ratios, accounts receivable turnover ratio and the average collection period, aid in the analysis of receivables. Before we discuss these ratios, we examine a commonly-used measure of operating profit first introduced in Chapter 5, net operating profit after taxes (NOPAT).

LO5 Calculate return on net operating assets, net operating profit after taxes, return on net operating assets, net operating profit margin, accounts receivable turnover, and average collection period.

5

Net Operating Profit After Taxes (NOPAT)

Net operating profit after taxes (NOPAT) is a widely used measure of operating profitability. NOPAT is calculated as follows:

NOPAT = Net income − [(Nonoperating revenues − Nonoperating expenses) × (1 − Statutory tax rate)]

As described in Appendix A of Chapter 5, we assume that the applicable statutory tax rate on nonoperating revenues and expenses is equal to 25%—a combination of the statutory federal tax rate of 21% and 4% for an estimated state income tax rate. To illustrate the calculation of NOPAT, refer to Microsoft's income statement presented in **Exhibit 6.2**. Microsoft reported net income of \$16,571 million in 2018. It also reported Other income (expense), net of \$1,416 million. Therefore, Microsoft's NOPAT for 2018 is \$15,509 million {\$16,571 million − [\$1,416 million × (1 − 0.25)]}. In 2017, Microsoft's NOPAT was \$24,832 million {\$25,489 million − [\$876 million × (1 − 0.25)]}, with the 2018 decline largely explained by tax law changes that are described in Chapter 10.

NOPAT is an important measure of profitability. It is similar to net income except that NOPAT focuses exclusively on after-tax operating performance, while net income measures the overall performance of the company and includes both operating and nonoperating components. NOPAT is used as a performance measure by management and analysts alike and it is also used in a number of ratios, such as the net operating profit margin.

Next, we examine two ratios that allow us to compare operating profitability across firms.

Analysis Objective

We want to gauge the profitability of a company's operations.

Analysis Tool Return on net operating assets (RNOA).

$$\textbf{Return on net operating assets (RNOA)} = \frac{\textbf{NOPAT}}{\textbf{Average net operating assets}}$$

Applying the Ratio to Microsoft

$$\textbf{2017:}\ \text{RNOA} = \frac{\$24{,}832}{\$36{,}490.5} = 0.681 \text{ or } 68.1\%$$

$$\textbf{2018:}\ \text{RNOA} = \frac{\$15{,}509}{\$48{,}331.5} = 0.321 \text{ or } 32.1\%$$

Microsoft's average total assets for fiscal 2018 total \$254,580 ([\$258,848 million + \$250,312 million]/2), but \$123,570 of this amount represents average investments in marketable securities. So, average operating assets are \$131,010 million. Microsoft also reports average operating liabilities of \$82,678.5 million. Subtracting this amount from average operating assets gives average net operating assets of \$48,331.5 million. The principal cause of the drop in RNOA is an increased reported income tax rate in 2018, which is discussed in Chapter 10.

BUSINESS INSIGHT

What constitutes "cash" and when is cash operating and when is it nonoperating? To compute RNOA in this book we make a simplifying assumption and consider marketable securities and other investments as nonoperating assets, but we consider cash to be an operating asset. This is a matter of judgment for the financial statement user when doing financial statement analysis. The categorization of investment securities as cash or as investments varies across firms. Some companies, such as Hewlett Packard Enterprise, classify a significant amount of investments as cash equivalents, and thus include the amount in the cash balance on the balance sheet. Other companies include investments in a separate line item on the balance sheet (either in current, long-term assets, or some in each).

Guidance **Return on net operating assets (RNOA)** is conceptually similar to return on assets (ROA) except that it excludes all nonoperating components of income and investment from the calculation. The resulting ratio is a measure of how well the company is performing relative to its core objective. A company can use investments in securities and financial leverage to report a satisfactory level of profit and return overall, even when its primary operating activities are not performing well. RNOA can reveal weaknesses in a company's operating strategy that are not readily apparent from overall measures such as return on equity and return on assets.

A variation on RNOA is the **return on capital employed**. This ratio examines the return on net operating assets *before* income taxes and is often used to measure performance of business units and division managers within a large organization. Operating managers generally do not have responsibility for income taxes or financing activities. (These functions are typically the responsibility of central management.) Consequently, return on capital employed excludes income taxes and focuses exclusively on the resources made available to the unit manager.

Microsoft does not provide enough information to calculate return on capital employed for individual business units, but we can do so for the company as a whole. From **Exhibit 6.2**, we see that 2018 pretax operating income is \$35,058 million. Average net operating assets for 2018, adjusted for income tax assets and liabilities, total \$52,888.5 million.[9] Thus, Microsoft's return on capital employed is 66.3% (\$35,058 million/\$52,888.5 million) for 2018.

Microsoft in Context

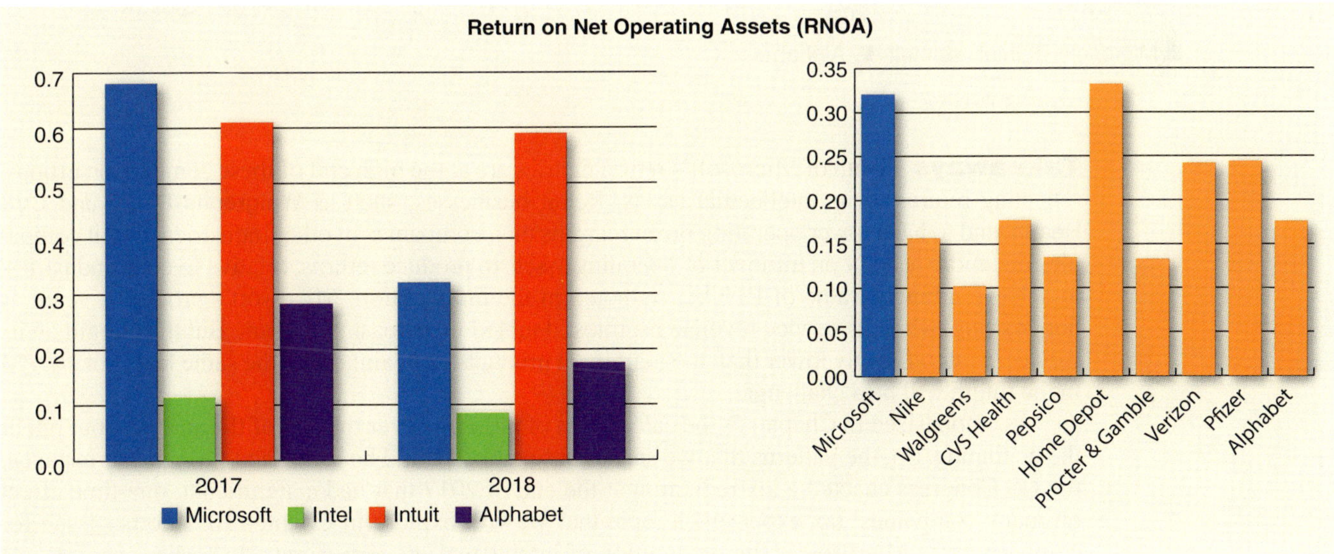

Analysis Tool Net operating profit margin (NOPM)

$$\textbf{Net operating profit margin (NOPM)} = \frac{\textbf{NOPAT}}{\textbf{Sales revenue}}$$

Applying the Ratio to Microsoft

$$\textbf{2017:}\ \text{NOPM} = \frac{\$24{,}832}{\$96{,}571} = 0.257 \text{ or } 25.7\%$$

$$\textbf{2018:}\ \text{NOPM} = \frac{\$15{,}509}{\$110{,}360} = 0.141 \text{ or } 14.1\%$$

[9] Because we use operating profit before taxes, accrued income taxes payable, and deferred income taxes (assets and liabilities) should be excluded when computing net operating assets for this ratio. Microsoft reported average deferred tax liabilities of \$3,137.5 million and income taxes payable of \$1,419.5 million. Thus, the average net operating assets used to calculate return on capital employed equals \$48,331.5 million + (\$3,137.5 million + \$1,419.5 million) = \$52,888.5 million.

Guidance Profit margins are commonly used to compare a company to its competitors and to evaluate the performance of business segments. **Net operating profit margin (NOPM)** is a useful summary measure that focuses on the overall operating profitability of the company relative to its sales revenue.

Microsoft in Context

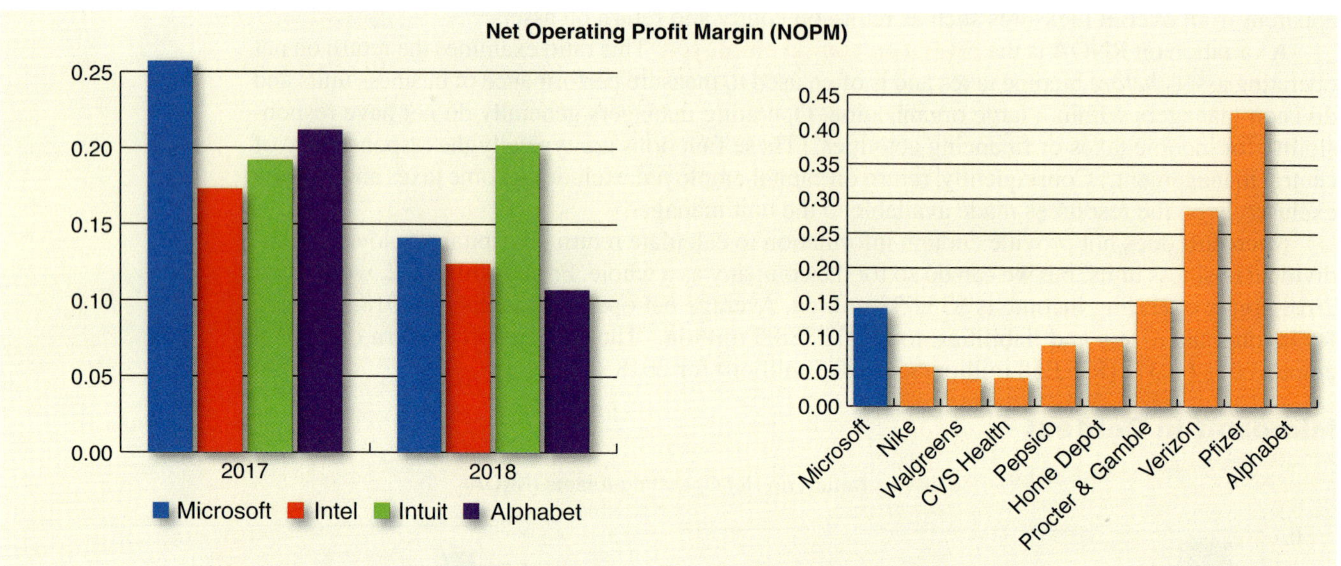

Takeaways Both of Microsoft's return metrics are at the high end of these comparison groups, reflecting returns to its intellectual assets. Retail businesses, such as **Walgreens Boots** and **CVS Health** tend to have lower operating profit margins than companies in other industries. Retail companies rely more heavily on turnover of operating assets to produce returns, relative to other industries, to achieve a higher value of RNOA. As noted in the introduction, Microsoft's product revenue is not growing, while its service revenue is almost doubled in the past two years. But the margin on its services is significantly lower than the margin on products, so maintaining the same levels of NOPM in the future will be a challenge.

As emphasized in Chapter 5, the calculation of ratios is never the end of the analysis, but rather the beginning. So, the patterns that we see in these ratios should be examined further. For instance, the US Congress enacted a tax reduction at the end of 2017 that had a significant, one-time effect on many companies' tax expense—a topic that we will explore in Chapter 10. Another issue for companies like Microsoft is the recognition of intellectual property assets. In earlier chapters, we explored the differing accounting rules for asset purchases and R&D activities. The former are recognized as assets on the balance sheet, while the latter are not—a factor that could influence the denominator in RNOA calculations.

Analysis Objective

We want to evaluate a company's management of its receivables.

Analysis Tool Accounts receivable turnover (ART) and average collection period (ACP)

$$\textbf{Accounts receivable turnover (ART)} = \frac{\textbf{Sales revenue}}{\textbf{Average accounts receivable}}$$

Applying the Accounts Receivable Turnover Ratio to Microsoft

$$\textbf{2017:}\ \text{ART} = \frac{\$96{,}571}{(\$22{,}431 + \$18{,}277)/2} = 4.74 \text{ times}$$

$$\textbf{2018:}\ \text{ART} = \frac{\$110{,}360}{(\$26{,}481 + \$22{,}431)/2} = 4.51 \text{ times}$$

Guidance **Accounts receivable turnover** measures the number of times each year that accounts receivable is converted into cash. A high turnover ratio suggests that receivables are well managed and that sales revenue quickly leads to cash collected from customers.

A companion measure to accounts receivable turnover is the **average collection period**, also called *days sales outstanding*, which is defined as:

$$\textbf{Average collection period (ACP)} = \frac{\textbf{Average accounts receivable}}{\textbf{Average daily sales}} = \frac{\textbf{365 days}}{\textbf{Accounts receivable turnover}}$$

Average daily sales equals sales during the period divided by the number of days in the period (for example, 365 for a year). The ACP ratio indicates how many days of sales revenue are invested in accounts receivable, or alternatively, how long, on average, it takes the company to collect cash after the sale. Microsoft's ACP is approximately 81 days (365/4.51), which indicates that the average dollar of sales is collected within 81 days of the sale.

Microsoft in Context

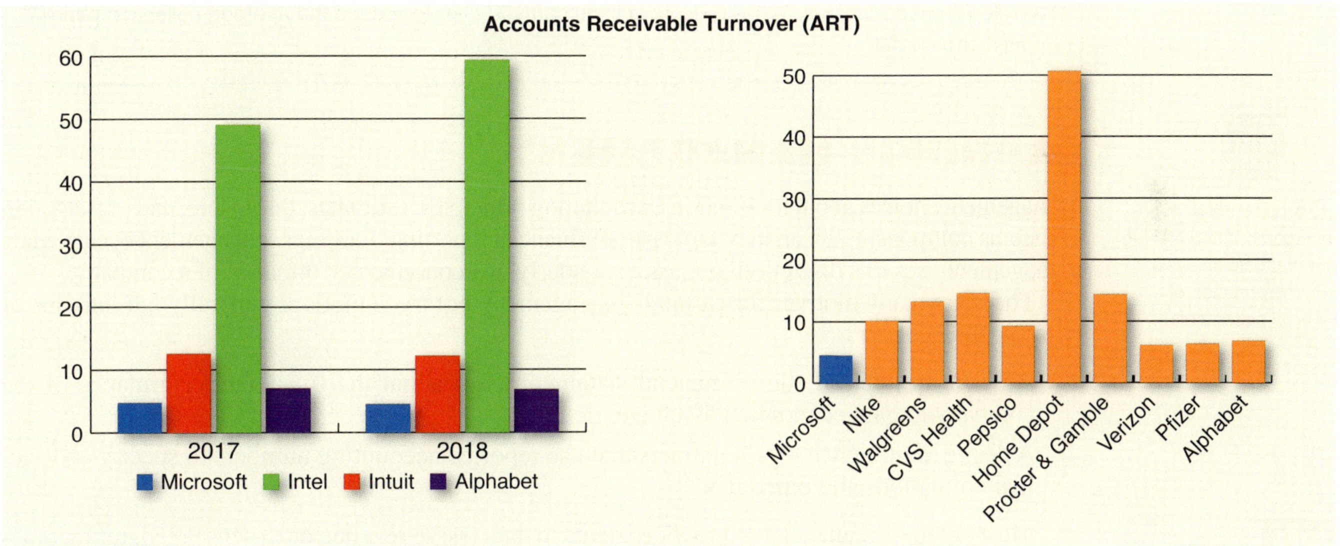

Takeaways The accounts receivable turnover and the average collection period yield valuable insights on at least two dimensions:

1. *Receivables quality.* A change in receivables turnover (and collection period) provides insight into accounts receivable quality. If turnover slows (collection period lengthens), the reason could be deterioration in collectibility of receivables. However, before reaching this conclusion, consider at least three alternative explanations:
   a. A seller can extend its credit terms. If the seller is attempting to enter new markets or take market share from competitors, it may extend credit terms to attract buyers.
   b. A seller can take on longer-paying customers. For example, facing increased competition, many computer and automobile companies began leasing their products, thus reducing the cash outlay for customers and stimulating sales. The change in mix away from cash

sales and toward leasing had the effect of reducing receivables turnover and increasing the collection period.

c. The seller can increase the allowance provision. Receivables turnover is often computed using net receivables (after the allowance for uncollectible accounts). Overestimating the provision reduces net receivables and increases turnover.

2. *Asset utilization.* Asset turnover is an important measure of financial performance, both by managers for internal performance goals, as well as by the market in evaluating companies. High performing companies must be both efficient (controlling margins and operating expenses) and productive (getting the most out of their asset base). An increase in receivables ties up cash as the receivables must be financed, and slower-turning receivables carry increased risk of loss. One of the first "low-hanging fruits" that companies pursue in efforts to improve asset utilization is efficiency in receivables collection.

Other Considerations Accounts receivable are sometimes used by companies to obtain financing. This is done in one of two ways: (1) the company can use accounts receivable as collateral for a short-term loan in a transaction called *securitizatÚn*, or (2) the company can sell its receivables, which is referred to as *factoring*. A thorough discussion of these transactions is beyond the scope of this text. Nonetheless, if a firm uses securitization or factoring of receivables to obtain short-term financing, the amount of accounts receivable listed on the balance sheet is altered which, in turn, affects the ART ratio.

YOU MAKE THE CALL

You are the Receivables Manager You are analyzing your receivables turnover report for the period, and you are concerned that the average collection period is lengthening, causing a drop in cash flow from operations. What specific actions can you take to reduce the average collection period? [Answers on page 302]

EARNINGS MANAGEMENT

LO6 Discuss earnings management and explain how it affects analysis and interpretation of financial statements.

Management choices about transactions, accounting principles, estimates, disclosure, and presentation of income components are an inevitable part of financial reporting. Earnings management occurs when management uses this discretion to mask the underlying economic performance of a company.

There are many motives for earnings management, but these motives generally fall into one of two categories:

1. A desire to mislead some financial statement users about the financial performance of the company to gain economic advantage, or
2. A desire to influence legal contracts that use reported accounting numbers to specify contractual obligations and outcomes.[10]

FYI Earnings management involves earnings quality and management ethics. For the latter, management must consider both legal and personal ethical standards of conduct.

Most earnings management practices relate to aggressive revenue or expense recognition practices. However, financial statement presentation can also be a concern. Below, we identify several examples of potentially misleading reporting.

- *Overly optimistic (or overly pessimistic) estimates.* The use of estimates in accrual accounting is extensive. For instance, revenue recognition requires estimates of things like future discounts and performance awards and the stand-alone value of individual performance obligations. Depreciation expense depends on estimates of useful life, and bad debts expense depends on estimates of future customer payments. Although changes in estimates may be warranted by changes in business conditions, they can have a significant effect on reported net income and,

[10] See Healy, Paul M., and James M. Wahlen, "A Review of Earnings Management Literature and Its Implications for Standard Setting," *Accounting Horizons*, December 1999, and Graham, John R., Campbell R. Harvey, and Shiva Rajgopal, "The Economic Implications of Corporate Financial Reporting," *Journal of Accounting & Economics,* December 2005.

thereby, may provide opportunities for managers to report income that is better (or worse) than it should be.

- *Channel stuffing.* **Channel stuffing** arises when a company uses its market power over customers or distributors to induce them to purchase more goods than necessary to meet their normal needs. Or, the seller may offer significant price reductions to encourage buyers to stock up on its products. Channel stuffing usually occurs immediately before the end of an accounting period and boosts the seller's revenue for that period (while increasing the buyer's inventory). The practice is not illegal and revenue may be recorded, as long as the transactions meet the necessary criteria for revenue recognition.
- *Strategic timing and disclosure of transactions and nonrecurring gains and losses.* Management has some discretion over the timing of transactions that can affect financial statements. If management has an asset (e.g., a tract of land) with book value less than market value, it can choose when to sell the asset to recognize a gain and maintain steady improvements in net income. This practice is known as **income smoothing**. In some cases, these smoothing effects are reported in combination with other items, making it more difficult to separate recurring amounts from nonrecurring amounts. Or, a company could take a **big bath** by recording a nonrecurring loss in a period of already depressed income. Concentrating bad news in a single period reduces the amount of bad news recognized in other periods. Given adequate disclosure, the astute reader of the financial statements will separate nonrecurring income items from persistent operating income, making these income management tactics transparent.
- *Mischaracterizing transactions as arm's-length.* Transfers of inventories or other assets to related entities typically are not recorded until later **arm's-length** sales occur. Sometimes sales are disguised as being sold to unrelated entities to inflate income when (1) the buyer is a related party to the seller, or (2) financing is provided or guaranteed by the seller, or (3) the buyer is a special-purpose entity that fails to meet independence requirements. This financial reporting practice is not consistent with GAAP and may be fraudulent.

FYI An arm's-length transaction is any transaction between two unrelated parties.

The consequence of earnings management is that the usefulness of the information presented in the income statement is compromised. **Quality of earnings** is a term that analysts often use to describe the extent to which reported income reflects the underlying economic performance of a company. Financial statement users must be careful to examine the quality of a company's earnings before using that information to evaluate performance or value its securities.[11]

YOU MAKE THE CALL

You are the Controller While evaluating the performance of your sales staff, you notice that one of the salespeople consistently meets his quarterly sales quotas but never surpasses his goals by very much. You also discover that his customers often return an unusually large amount of product at the beginning of each quarter. What might be happening here? How would you investigate for potential abuse? [Answer on page 302]

RESEARCH INSIGHT

Non-GAAP Income Nonrecurring items in income such as discontinued operations and restructuring charges make it difficult for investors to determine what portion of income is sustainable into the future. In its fourth-quarter earnings release, Microsoft Corporation provided non-GAAP income numbers for 2017 and 2018. Microsoft's GAAP numbers reported a restructuring charge of $306 million for 2017, and the non-GAAP adjustments removed this amount, making non-GAAP net income $243 million higher than GAAP net income. The 2018 adjustment was more substantial. The 2017 Tax Cuts and Jobs Act produced one-time accounting effects for companies like Microsoft. The one-time increase in tax expense was $13.7 billion for Microsoft, resulting in a decrease in net income of 35% from 2017 to 2018. But that item will not be present in Microsoft's 2019 financial results.

continued

[11] See Dechow, Patricia, Weili Ge, and Catherine Schrand, "Understanding Earnings Quality: A Review of the Proxies, Their Determinants, and Their Consequences," *Journal of Accounting and Economics*, December, 2010.

continued from previous page

Microsoft has used its non-GAAP adjustments to let financial statement readers see the one-time items affecting its current financial results, but that should not be present in future results. This disclosure should improve forecasts of results for future years.

The past decade has seen more companies reporting **non-GAAP** or **pro forma income**, which purportedly excludes the effects of nonrecurring or noncash items that companies feel are unimportant for valuation purposes. Research, however, provides no evidence that more exclusions via pro forma income lead to more predictable future cash flows. More important, investors appear to be misled by the exclusions at the time of the non-GAAP income release. Research also finds that companies issuing non-GAAP income are more likely to be young companies concentrated in technology and business services. Too often, these companies are characterized by below-average sales and income when they choose to report pro forma income. Evidence also shows that the pro forma income can exceed GAAP income by as much as 20%.

Critics of non-GAAP income argue that the items excluded by managers from GAAP income are inconsistent across companies and time. They contend that a major motive for pro forma income is to mislead stakeholders. Legendary investor Warren Buffett puts pro forma in context (Berkshire Hathaway, Annual Report): "When companies or investment professionals use terms such as 'EBITDA' and 'pro forma,' they want you to unthinkingly accept concepts that are dangerously flawed."

CHAPTER-END REVIEW

The following data were taken from the 2017 10-K reports of **Comcast Corporation** and **CCO Holdings LLC**:

($ millions)	Comcast Corp (Xfinity)	CCO Holdings (Spectrum)
Sales revenue	$ 84,526	$ 41,578
Net income	22,900	883
Nonoperating revenues	421	70
Nonoperating expenses	3,086	3,159
Accounts receivable, net (end-of-year)	8,546	1,611
Accounts receivable, net (beginning-of-year)	7,955	1,387
Operating assets (end-of-year)	180,018	145,693
Operating assets (beginning-of-year)	175,253	148,319
Operating liabilities (end-of-year)	51,587	10,357
Operating liabilities (beginning-of-year)	61,834	9,448

REQUIRED

1. Compute the following for each company:
   a. Net operating profit after taxes (NOPAT). Assume a 25% statutory tax rate.
   b. Return on net operating assets (RNOA).
   c. Net operating profit margin (NOPM).
   d. Accounts receivable turnover (ART).
   e. Average collection period (ACP).
2. Compare these two companies based on the ratios computed in (1). What inferences can you make about these competitors?

The solution to this review problem can be found on page 325.

7

LO7 Describe and illustrate the reporting for nonrecurring items.

APPENDIX 6A: Reporting Nonrecurring Items

In addition to categorizing income statement elements as either operating or nonoperating, it is also useful to separate **recurring** components of income from those sources that are **nonrecurring**. Isolating nonrecurring earnings components is useful for two reasons. First, to evaluate company performance or management quality, it is helpful to make comparisons of current performance with prior years and with other companies facing similar economic circumstances. It is easier to make these comparisons if we focus on recurring income components. Nonrecurring income components are likely to be specific to one company and one accounting period, making them irrelevant for comparative purposes. Second, estimation of company value involves forecasts of income and cash flows. Such forecasts are better when we can identify any nonrecurring effects in income and cash flows and then eliminate them from projections. Recurring earnings and cash flows are more **persistent** and, therefore, more useful in estimating company value.

Accounting standards attempt to distinguish some nonrecurring income components. Two of the most common nonrecurring items are:

- **Discontinued operations**—income related to business units that the company has discontinued and sold or plans to sell.
- **Restructuring charges**—expenses and losses related to significant reorganization of a company's operations.

Discontinued Operations

Discontinued operations refer to separately identifiable components of the company that management sells or intends to sell. Recent guidance for discontinued operations (ASU 2014-08) provides that only disposals representing a strategic shift in operations should be reported as discontinued operations. Examples include a disposal of a major geographical segment, a major line of business, or a major equity investment. The new guidance was issued because of concerns that too many disposals of small asset groups were being classified as discontinued operations.

The income or loss of the discontinued operations (net of tax), and the after-tax gain or loss on sale of the unit, are reported in the income statement below income from continuing operations. The segregation of discontinued operations means that its revenues and expenses are *not* reported with revenues and expenses from continuing operations.

To illustrate, assume that Chapman Company's income statement results were the following.

	Continuing Operations	Discontinued Operations	Total
Revenues	$10,000	$3,000	$13,000
Expenses	7,000	2,000	9,000
Pretax income	3,000	1,000	4,000
Tax expense (40%)	1,200	400	1,600
Net income	$ 1,800	$ 600	$ 2,400

The reported income statement would then appear with the separate disclosure for discontinued operations (shown in bold, separately net of any related taxes) as follows.

Revenues	$10,000
Expenses	7,000
Pretax income	3,000
Tax expense (40%)	1,200
Income from continuing operations	1,800
Income from discontinued operations, net of income taxes	**600**
Net income	$ 2,400

Revenues and expenses reflect the continuing operations only, and the (persistent) income from continuing operations is reported after deducting the related tax expense. Results from the (transitory) discontinued operations are collapsed into one line item and reported separately net of any related taxes. The same is true for any gain or loss from sale of the discontinued operation's net assets. The net income figure is unchanged by this presentation, but our ability to evaluate and interpret income information is greatly improved.

FYI Income, gains, and losses from discontinued operations are reported separately from other items to alert readers to their transitory nature.

Exit or Disposal Costs

Exit or disposal costs include but are not limited to **restructuring costs**. Exit and disposal costs typically include activities such as consolidating production facilities, reorganizing sales operations, outsourcing product lines, or discontinuing product lines within a business unit or that do not represent a strategic shift in operations. These costs should be separately disclosed if material, but if not material are not required to be shown as a separate line item on the income statement. Often these costs, such as restructuring costs, are material in nature and are shown as a separate line item or are detailed in the notes to the financial statements.

FYI Management's ability to reduce income using restructuring charges and later reverse some of that charge (creating subsequent period income) reduces earnings quality. U.S. GAAP requires disclosures that enable a financial statement reader to track the restructuring activities and to identify any reversals that occur.

These costs are considered transitory because many companies do not engage in restructuring activities every year. As such, these costs should be classified to a transitory category for analysis purposes even though the costs are included in income from continuing operations. Restructuring costs include, but are not limited to, the following types of costs:

1. Employee severance costs
2. Costs to consolidate and close facilities, including asset write-downs

The first of these, **employee severance costs**, represent accrued (estimated) costs for termination of employees as part of a restructuring program. The second part of restructuring costs consists of **asset write-downs**, also called *write-offs* or *charge-offs*. Restructuring activities usually involve closure or relocation of manufacturing or administrative facilities. This process can require the write-down of long-term assets (such as plant assets), and the write-down of inventories that are no longer salable at current carrying costs.

Microsoft reported no impairment or restructuring charges for 2018, but it did have them for the two previous fiscal years. Footnote 14 of the company's 2018 10-K had the following information:

2017 Restructuring

In June 2017, management approved a sales and marketing restructuring plan. In fiscal year 2017, we recorded employee severance expenses of $306 million primarily related to this sales and marketing restructuring plan. We do not expect to incur additional charges for this restructuring plan in subsequent years. The actions associated with this restructuring plan are expected to be completed by the end of fiscal year 2018.

Restructuring Summary

Restructuring charges associated with each of these plans were included in impairment, integration, and restructuring expenses on our consolidated income statements, and were reflected in Corporate and Other in our table of operating income (loss) by segment.

Changes in the restructuring liability were as follows:

(In millions)	Severance	Other[(a)]	Total
Balance, as of June 30, 2016	$470	$239	$709
Restructuring charges	306	0	306
Cash paid	(367)	(101)	(468)
Other	(36)	(79)	(115)
Balance, as of June 30, 2017	$373	$ 59	$432

At the end of fiscal year 2016, Microsoft had an outstanding liability for restructuring costs of $709 million. The balance represents the costs charged to income prior to June 30, 2016 and consists of employee severance and "other" (asset impairments and contract termination costs). During fiscal year 2017, Microsoft recognized $306 million in restructuring expenses (for the sales and marketing restructuring) and used $468 million in cash and $115 million in other resources to fulfill (in part) the obligations from 2017 and prior years. The remaining obligation of $432 million at the end of 2017 was fulfilled in 2018, leaving a balance of zero on June 30, 2018.

RESEARCH INSIGHT

Restructuring Costs and Managerial Incentives Research has investigated the circumstances and effects of restructuring costs. Some research finds that stock prices increase upon announcement of a restructuring as if the market appreciates the company's candor. Research also finds that many companies that reduce income through restructuring costs later reverse those costs, resulting in a substantial income boost for the period of reversal. These reversals often occur when their absence would have yielded an earnings decline. Whether or not the market responds favorably to trimming the fat or simply disregards such transitory items as uninformative, managers have incentives to exclude such income-decreasing items from operating income. These incentives are contractually-based, extending from debt covenants and restrictions to managerial bonuses.

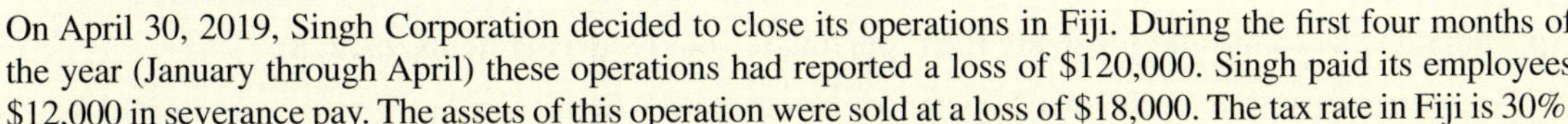

You are the Financial Analyst You are analyzing the financial statements of a company that has reported a large restructuring cost, involving both employee severance and asset write-downs, in its income statement. How do you interpret and treat this cost in your analysis of its current and future period profitability? [Answer on page 302]

APPENDIX 6A REVIEW

On April 30, 2019, Singh Corporation decided to close its operations in Fiji. During the first four months of the year (January through April) these operations had reported a loss of $120,000. Singh paid its employees $12,000 in severance pay. The assets of this operation were sold at a loss of $18,000. The tax rate in Fiji is 30%.

REQUIRED

a. If this closure is recorded as discontinued operations, how should it be presented in Singh's income statement?

b. If this closure is classified as a restructuring charge, how would it be presented in Singh's income statement?

c. What would determine whether this event should be reported as discontinued operations or a restructuring charge?

The solution to this review problem can be found on page 325.

SUMMARY

Describe and apply the criteria for determining when revenue is recognized. (p. 274) LO1

- Revenue is recognized as a company fulfills the performance obligations in its contract with a customer.

Illustrate revenue and expense recognition when the transaction involves future deliverables and/or multiple elements. (p. 276) LO2

- When customers pay prior to the delivery of all elements of the product (or service) package, a contract liability must be recognized.
- When a company recognizes a contract liability, its reported revenue for a period does not coincide with the purchases made by customers in that period.

Illustrate revenue and expense recognition for long-term projects. (p. 280) LO3

- When a company engages in long-term projects, it must determine whether it will transfer control over time, as the project progresses. If it does, then its performance obligation on the contract is fulfilled over time.
- When a company engages in long-term projects, it must determine whether it transfers control over time, as the project progresses. If it does not, then its performance obligation on the contract is fulfilled at a point in time.
- If the long-term project's performance obligations are satisfied over time, the revenue recognition should reflect the value transferred to the customer during the period.

Estimate and account for uncollectible accounts receivable. (p. 284) LO4

- Uncollectible accounts are usually estimated by aging the accounts receivable.
- Estimated uncollectible accounts are recorded as a contra-asset called allowance for uncollectible accounts.
- Write-offs of uncollectible accounts are deducted from accounts receivable and from the allowance account.

Calculate return on net operating assets, net operating profit after taxes, return on net operating assets, net operating profit margin, accounts receivable turnover, and average collection period. (p. 291) LO5

- Net operating profit after taxes (NOPAT) and the net operating profit margin (NOPM) are measures of the profitability of operating activities.

- Return on net operating assets (RNOA) measures after-tax operating performance relative to available net operating assets; similarly, return on capital employed is a pretax measure that is used to evaluate business unit performance.
- Accounts receivable turnover (ART) and average collection period (ACP) measure the ability of the company to convert receivables into cash through collection.

LO6 Discuss earnings management and explain how it affects analysis and interpretation of financial statements. (p. 296)

- Earnings management occurs when management uses its discretion to mask the underlying economic performance of a company.
- The consequence of earnings management is that the usefulness of the information presented in the income statement is compromised.

LO7 Appendix 6A: Describe and illustrate the reporting for nonrecurring items. (p. 298)

- Income or loss from discontinued operations is a transitory (nonrecurring) item that is reported net of income taxes after earnings from continuing operations.
- Restructuring charges include asset write-downs and employee severance costs. Even though these charges are typically reported among earnings from continuing operations, they are classified as transitory for analysis purposes.

GUIDANCE ANSWERS . . . YOU MAKE THE CALL

You are the Receivables Manager First, you must realize that the extension of credit is an important tool in the marketing of your products, often as important as advertising and promotion. Given that receivables are necessary, there are some methods we can use to speed their collection. (1) We can better screen the customers to whom we extend credit. (2) We can negotiate advance or progress payments from customers. (3) We can use bank letters of credit or other automatic drafting prcedures so that billings need not be sent. (4) We can make sure products are sent as ordered to reduce disputes. (5) We can improve administration of past due accounts to provide for more timely notices of delinquencies and better collection procedures.

You are the Controller The salesperson may be channel stuffing or recording sales without a confirmed sales order. The unusual amount of returns suggests that sales revenues are most likely being recognized prematurely. To investigate, you could examine specific sales orders from customers who returned goods early in the following quarter, or contact customers directly. Most companies delay bonuses until after an appropriate return period expires and only credit the sales staff with net sales.

You are the Financial Analyst There are two usual components to a restructuring charge: asset write-downs (such as inventories, property, plant, and goodwill) and severance costs. Write-downs occur when the cash flow generating ability of an asset declines, thus reducing its current market value below its book value reported on the balance sheet. Arguably, this decline in cash flow generating ability did not occur solely in the current year and, most likely, has developed over several periods. Delays in loss recognition, such as write-downs of assets, are not uncommon. Thus, prior period income is arguably not as high as reported, and the current period loss is not as great as is reported. Turning to severance costs, their recognition can be viewed as an investment decision by the company that is expected to increase future cash flows (through decreased wages). If this cost accrual is capitalized on the balance sheet, current period income is increased and future period income would bear the amortization of this "asset" to match against future cash flow benefits from severance. This implies that current period income is not as low as reported; however, this adjustment is not GAAP as such severance costs cannot be capitalized. Yet, we can make such an adjustment in our analysis.

KEY RATIOS

Net operating profit after taxes (NOPAT)

$$\text{NOPAT} = \text{Net income} - [(\text{Nonoperating revenues} - \text{Nonoperating expenses}) \times (1 - \text{Statutory tax rate})]$$

Return on net operating assets (RNOA)

$$\text{RNOA} = \frac{\text{NOPAT}}{\text{Average net operating assets}}$$

Accounts receivable turnover (ART)

$$\text{ART} = \frac{\text{Sales revenue}}{\text{Average accounts receivable}}$$

Net operating profit margin (NOPM)

$$\text{NOPM} = \frac{\text{Net operating profit after taxes (NOPAT)}}{\text{Sales revenue}}$$

Average collection period (ACP)

$$\text{ACP} = \frac{\text{Average accounts receivable}}{\text{Average daily sales}} = \frac{365}{\text{Accounts receivable turnover (ART)}}$$

$$\text{Return on capital employed} = \frac{\text{Income from operations before taxes}}{\text{Average net operating assets}}$$

KEY TERMS

Accounts receivable turnover (p. 295)
Aging analysis (p. 284)
Allowance for doubtful (uncollectible) accounts (p. 284)
Arm's-length (p. 297)
Asset write-downs (p. 300)
Average collection period (p. 295)
Bad debts expense (p. 286)
Big bath (p. 297)
Channel stuffing (p. 297)
Consignment (p. 276)
Contract asset (p. 282)
Contract liability (p. 276, 281)
Cookie jar reserve (p. 290)
Credit sales (p. 284)
Deferred revenue (p. 277)
Discontinued operations (p. 299)
Employee severance costs (p. 300)
Income smoothing (p. 297)
Net income attributable to noncontrolling interests (p. 273)
Net operating profit after taxes (NOPAT) (p. 292)
Net operating profit margin (NOPM) (p. 294)
Net realizable value (p. 284)
non-GAAP (p. 298)
Nonrecurring (p. 298)
Notes payable (p. 284)
Notes receivable (p. 284)
Percentage of sales (p. 285)
Performance obligations (p. 275)
Persistent (p. 299)
Pro forma income (p. 298)
Quality of earnings (p. 297)
Recurring (p. 298)
Restructuring charges (p. 299)
Restructuring costs (p. 299)
Return on capital employed (p. 293)
Return on net operating assets (RNOA) (p. 293)
Revenue recognition (p. 274)
Unearned revenue (p. 277)
Variable consideration (p. 275)

Assignments with the MBC logo in the margin are available in myBusinessCourse. See the Preface of the book for details.

MULTIPLE CHOICE

Multiple Choice Answers
1. c 2. b 3. d 4. d 5. a 6. d

1. Which of the following best describes the condition(s) that must be present for the recognition of revenue from a contract with a customer?
a. Cash payment must have been received from the customer.
b. All of the performance obligations must be fulfilled.
c. One of the contract's performance obligations must be fulfilled.
d. There must be no uncertainty about the amount to be received from the customer.

2. When multiple products or services are bundled and sold for one price, the revenue should be
a. recognized when the bundle of products or services is sold.
b. allocated among the distinct performance obligations and recognized as each of these is fulfilled.
c. deferred until all elements of the bundle are delivered to the customer.
d. recognized when the customer pays cash for the bundle of products or services.

3. A construction company engages in a contract to build a production facility for a customer. The construction company should recognize revenue as the construction progresses only:
a. if it receives advance cash payments from the customer.
b. if it retains title to the project until completion.
c. if there are no contingent payments (e.g., bonuses, penalties) in the contract with the customer.
d. if title to the project transfers to the customer as the project progresses.

4. When management selectively excludes some revenues, expenses, gains, and losses from earnings calculated using generally accepted accounting principles, it is an example of
   a. income smoothing.
   b. big bath accounting.
   c. cookie jar accounting.
   d. Non-GAAP reporting.

5. If bad debts expense is determined by estimating uncollectible accounts receivable, the entry to record the write-off of a specific uncollectible account would decrease
   a. allowance for uncollectible accounts.
   b. net income.
   c. net book value of accounts receivable.
   d. bad debts expense.

6. If management intentionally underestimates bad debts expense, then net income is
   a. overstated and assets are understated.
   b. understated and assets are overstated.
   c. understated and assets are understated.
   d. overstated and assets are overstated.

Superscript A denotes assignments based on Appendix 6A.

QUESTIONS

Abercrombie & Fitch
NYSE :: ANF

Q6-1. What is the process that guides firms in the recognition of revenue? What does each of the steps mean? How does this process work for a company like **Abercrombie & Fitch Co.**, a clothing retailer? How would it work for a construction company that builds offices under long-term contracts with developers?

Q6-2. Why are discontinued operations reported separately from continuing operations in the income statement?

Q6-3. Identify the two typical categories of restructuring costs and their effects on the balance sheet and the income statement.

Q6-4. Explain the concept of a *big bath* and why restructuring costs are often identified with this event.

Q6-5. Why might companies want to manage earnings? Describe some of the tactics that some companies use to manage earnings.

Q6-6. What is the concept of *non-GAAP income* or *pro forma income* and why has this income measure been criticized?

Q6-7. Why does GAAP allow management to make estimates of amounts that are included in financial statements? Does this improve the usefulness of financial statements? Explain.

Q6-8. How might earnings forecasts that are published by financial analysts encourage companies to manage earnings?

Q6-9. Explain how management can shift income from one period into another by its estimation of uncollectible accounts.

Q6-10. During an examination of Wallace Company's financial statements, you notice that the allowance for uncollectible accounts has decreased as a percentage of accounts receivable. What are the possible explanations for this change?

Q6-11. Under what circumstances would it be correct to say that a company would be better off with more uncollectible accounts?

Q6-12. Estimating the bad debts expense by aging accounts receivable generally results in smaller errors than the percentage of credit sales approach. Can you explain why?

MINI EXERCISES

LO3 Homework MBC

M6-13. Computing Revenues on Long-term Projects

Bartov Corporation agreed to build a warehouse for $2,500,000. Expected (and actual) costs for the warehouse follow: 2019, $400,000; 2020, $1,000,000; and 2021, $500,000. The company completed the warehouse in 2021. Compute revenues, expenses, and income for each year 2019 through 2021 assuming that Bartov's performance obligation for the warehouse is fulfilled over time and that the costs incurred provide a close approximation of the value conveyed to the customer.

M6-14. Assessing Revenue Recognition of Companies

LO1

The GAP Inc. NYSE :: GPS
Merck & Company Inc. NYSE :: MRK
CVS Health Corporation NYSE :: CVS
Walgreens Boots Alliance, Inc. NYSE :: WBA
Deere & Company NYSE :: DE
Bank of America Corporation NYSE :: BAC
Johnson Controls, INC. NYSE :: JCI

Identify and explain when each of the following companies should recognize revenue.

a. **The GAP Inc.**: The GAP is a retailer of clothing items for all ages.

b. **Merck & Company Inc.**: Merck engages in the development, manufacturing, and marketing of pharmaceutical products. It sells its drugs to retailers like **CVS Health Corporation** and **Walgreens Boots Alliance, Inc.**

c. **Deere & Company**: Deere manufactures heavy equipment. It sells equipment to a network of independent distributors, who in turn sell the equipment to customers. Deere provides financing and insurance services both to distributors and customers.

d. **Bank of America Corporation**: Bank of America is a banking institution. It lends money to individuals and corporations and invests excess funds in marketable securities.

e. **Johnson Controls Inc.**: Johnson Controls manufactures products for the U.S. government under long-term contracts.

M6-15. Estimating Revenue Recognition with Right of Return

LO1

The Unlimited Company offers an unconditional return policy for its retail clothing business. It normally expects 2% of sales at retail selling prices to be returned at some point prior to the expiration of the return period, and returned items cannot be resold. Assuming that it records total sales of $5 million for the current period, how much net revenue would it report for this period?

M6-16. Using Percentage-of-Completion and Completed Contract Methods

LO3

Halsey Building Company signed a contract to build an office building for $40,000,000. The scheduled construction costs follow.

Year	Cost
2019	$ 9,000,000
2020	15,000,000
2021	6,000,000
Total	$30,000,000

The building should be completed in 2021.

For each year, compute the revenue, expense, and gross profit reported for this construction project under each of the following assumptions:

a. Halsey's performance obligation to build the office building is fulfilled as construction proceeds, and the cost incurred is an accurate reflection of the value transferred to the customer.

b. Halsey's contract does not transfer ownership rights to the customer until the building is completed.

M6-17. Explaining Revenue Recognition and Bundled Sales

LO1, 2

A.J. Smith Electronics is a retail consumer electronics company that also sells extended warranty contracts for many of the products that it carries. The extended warranty provides coverage for three years beyond expiration of the manufacturer's warranty. In 2019, A.J. Smith sold extended warranties amounting to $1,700,000. The warranty coverage for all of these begins in 2020 and runs through 2022. The total expected cost of providing warranty services on these contracts is $500,000.

a. How should A.J. Smith recognize revenue on the extended warranty contracts? Assume that providing the warranty coverage is considered a single performance obligation that is fulfilled over time.

b. Estimate the revenue, expense, and gross profit reported from these contracts in the year(s) that the revenue is recognized.

c. In 2020, as a special promotion, A.J. Smith sold a digital camera (retail price $300), a digital photograph printer (retail price $125), and an extended warranty contract for each (total retail price $75) as a package for a special price of $399. The extended warranty covers the period from 2021 through 2023. The company sold 200 of these camera–printer packages. Compute the revenue that A.J. Smith should recognize in each year from 2020 through 2023.

M6-18. Reporting Uncollectible Accounts and Accounts Receivables

LO4

Mohan Company estimates its uncollectible accounts by aging its accounts receivable and applying percentages to various aged categories of accounts. Mohan computes a total of $2,100 in estimated losses as of December 31, 2019. Its Accounts Receivable has a balance of $98,000, and its allowance for Uncollectible Accounts has an unused balance of $500 before adjustment at December 31, 2019.

a. What is the amount of bad debts expense that Mohan will report in 2019?

b. Determine the net amount of accounts receivable reported in current assets at December 31, 2019.

c. Set up T-accounts for both Bad Debt Expense and for Allowance for Uncollectible Accounts. Enter any beginning balances and effects from the information above (including your results from parts *a* and *b*). Explain the numbers for each of your T-accounts.

LO4 **M6-19. Explaining the Allowance Method for Accounts Receivable**

At a recent board of directors meeting of Ascot, Inc., one of the directors expressed concern over the allowance for uncollectible accounts appearing in the company's balance sheet. "I don't understand this account," he said. "Why don't we just show accounts receivable at the amount owed to us and get rid of that allowance?" Respond to that director's question. Include in your response (a) an explanation of why the company has an allowance account, (b) what the balance sheet presentation of accounts receivable is intended to show, and (c) how the concept of expense recognition relates to the analysis and presentation of accounts receivable.

LO4, 5 Homework MBC

Ralph Lauren Corporation NYSE :: RL

M6-20. Analyzing the Allowance for Uncollectible Accounts

Following is the current asset section from the **Ralph Lauren Corporation** balance sheet:

($ millions)	March 31, 2018	April 1, 2017
ASSETS		
Current assets:		
Cash and cash equivalents	$1,304.6	$ 668.3
Short-term investments	699.4	684.7
Accounts receivable, net of allowances of $222.2 million and $214.4 million	421.4	450.2
Inventories	761.3	791.5
Income tax receivable	38.0	79.4
Prepaid expenses and other current assets	323.7	280.4
Total current assets	**$3,548.4**	**$2,954.5**

The 2018 allowance consists of $202.5 for returns and $19.7 for uncollectible accounts. The amounts for 2017 were $202.8 and $11.6

a. Compute the gross amount of accounts receivable for both 2018 and 2017. Compute the percentage of the allowance for uncollectible accounts relative to the gross amount of accounts receivable for each of these years.

b. How do you interpret the change in the percentage of the allowance for uncollectible accounts relative to total accounts receivable computed in part *a*?

c. Ralph Lauren reported net sales of $6,182.3 million in 2018. Compute its accounts receivable turnover and average collection period.

LO4 Homework MBC **M6-21. Analyzing Accounts Receivable Changes**

The comparative balance sheets of Sloan Company reveal that accounts receivable (before deducting allowances) increased by $15,000 in 2019. During the same time period, the allowance for uncollectible accounts increased by $2,100. If sales revenue was $120,000 in 2019 and bad debts expense was 2% of sales, how much cash was collected from customers during the year?

LO5  **M6-22. Evaluating Accounts Receivable Turnover for Competitors**

The Procter & Gamble Company and **Colgate-Palmolive Company** report the following sales and accounts receivable balances ($ millions):

The Procter & Gamble Company NYSE :: PG

Colgate-Palmolive Company NYSE :: CL

	Procter & Gamble			Colgate-Palmolive	
Fiscal year	Sales	Accounts Receivable	Fiscal year	Sales	Accounts Receivable
June 30, 2018	$66,832	$4,686	December 31, 2017	$15,454	$1,480
June 30, 2017	65,058	4,594	December 31, 2016	15,195	1,411

a. Compute accounts receivable turnover and average collection period for both companies.

b. Identify and discuss a potential explanation for the difference between these competitors' accounts receivable turnover.

M6-23. Analyzing Accounts Receivable Changes LO4

In 2019, Grant Corporation recorded credit sales of $3,200,000 and bad debts expense of $42,000. Write-offs of uncollectible accounts totaled $39,000 and one account, worth $12,000, that had been written off in an earlier year was collected in 2019.

a. Prepare journal entries to record each of these transactions.

b. If net accounts receivable increased by $220,000, how much cash was collected from credit customers during the year? Prepare a journal entry to record cash collections.

c. Set up T-accounts and post each of the transactions in parts *a* and *b* to them.

d. Record each of the above transactions in the financial statement effects template to show the effect of these entries on the balance sheet and income statement.

M6-24. Analyzing Unearned Revenue Changes LO2

Finn Publishing Corp. produces a monthly publication aimed at competitive swimmers, with articles profiling current stars of the sport, advice from coaches, and advertising by swimwear companies, training organizations, and others. The magazine is distributed through newsstands and bookstores, and by mail to subscribers. The most common subscription is for twelve months. When Finn Publishing receives payment of an annual subscription, it records an Unearned Revenue liability that is reduced by 1/12th each month as publications are provided.

The table below provides four years of revenues from the income statement and unearned revenue from the balance sheet. (All amounts in $ thousands.)

Fiscal year	Revenue	Unearned revenue liability (end of year)
2018	$48,000	$20,000
2019	55,000	24,000
2020	62,000	26,000
2021	62,000	25,000

a. Calculate the growth in revenue from 2018 to 2019, 2019 to 2020, and from 2020 to 2021.

b. Calculate the amount of customer purchases in 2019, 2020, and 2021. Customer purchases are defined as sales made at newsstands and bookstores, plus the amount paid for new or renewal subscriptions. Again, calculate the growth rates from 2019 to 2020 and from 2020 to 2021.

c. Explain the differences in growth rates between parts *a* and *b* above.

M6-25. Applying Revenue Recognition Criteria LO2

Commtech, Inc., designs and sells cellular phones. The company creates the technical specifications and the software for its products, though it outsources the production of the phones to an overseas contract manufacturer. Commtech has arrangements to sell its phones to the major wireless communications companies who, in turn, sell the phones to end customers packaged with calling plans.

The product life cycle for a phone model is about six months, and Commtech recognizes revenue at the time of delivery to the wireless communications company. The product team for the CD924 model has met to consider a possible modification to the phone. The software team has developed an improved global positioning application for a new phone model, and this application works in the CD924. It could be uploaded to existing phones through the wireless networks.

Marketing's analysis of focus groups and customer feedback is that further sales of the CD924 would be enhanced significantly if the new application were made available. The software engineers have demonstrated that the new GPS application can be successfully sent wirelessly to the CD924.

However, the finance manager points out that Commtech's financial statements have been based on the assumption that the company's phones do not involve multiple performance obligations, like upgrades. All revenue is recognized at the point of sale to the wireless communications companies. Like many communications hardware companies, Commtech has been under pressure to demonstrate its financial performance. Offering an upgrade to the CD924's navigation capabilities would probably be viewed as a significant deliverable in terms of customer value, and the finance manager says that "the accounting won't let us do it."

How should the product team proceed?

M6-26. Earnings Management and the Allowance for Doubtful Accounts LO6

Verdi Co. builds and sells PC computers to customers. The company sells most of its products for immediate payment but also extends credit to some customers. The industry is competitive and in the most recent year many competitors showed declines in revenue. However, Verdi Co. showed stable revenues. It is later revealed that Verdi Co. made sales and extended credit to customers previously deemed to have credit scores too low for the company to extend credit. The company did not disclose this practice in its financial statements or elsewhere.

a. Explain how this practice would have enabled Verdi Co. to show stable sales.

b. How should Verdi Co. have accounted for these additional sales and related receivables in its financial statements?

c. How would the actions by Verdi Co. in the current period affect financial statements in future periods if the customers cannot pay for the computers they purchased on credit?

EXERCISES

LO1, 2, 3

L Brands, Inc.
NYSE :: LB
Boeing Company
NYSE :: BA
Supervalu, Inc.
NYSE :: SVU
Wells Fargo & Company
NYSE :: WFC
Harley-Davidson, Inc.
NYSE :: HOG
Gannett Co., Inc.
NYSE::GCI

E6-27. Assessing Revenue Recognition Timing

Discuss and justify when each of the following businesses should recognize revenues:

a. A clothing retailer like **L Brands, Inc.**

b. A contractor like **The Boeing Company** that performs work under long-term government contracts.

c. An operator of grocery stores like **SUPERVALU, INC.**

d. A residential real estate developer who constructs only speculative houses and later sells these houses to buyers.

e. A banking institution like **Wells Fargo & Company** that lends money for home mortgages.

f. A manufacturer like **Harley-Davidson, Inc.**

g. A publisher of newspapers like **Gannett Co., Inc.**

LO1, 2, 3

E6-28. Contract Assets and Liabilities

Haskins, Inc. has reached an agreement with a customer, Skaife Corporation, to deliver 200 units of a customized product. The standard billing price per unit is $1,000, and there are no discounts, so Skaife Corporation will pay $200,000 in total. At the time of the agreement on April 6, Skaife Corporation provides a $40,000 cash deposit to Haskins, Inc. Haskins agrees to deliver 120 units to Skaife Corporation on May 31 and at that time, Haskins can send an invoice for $50,000 to be paid by Skaife Corporation on June 15. The remaining 80 units are to be delivered on July 15, accompanied by an invoice for the remaining amount of the total $200,000 purchase price to be paid on July 31.

REQUIRED

Assume that Haskins, Inc. has no uncertainties about its own ability to meet the terms of the contract or about Skaife Corporation's ability and willingness to pay. Provide the journal entries to record the above events (leaving out the accounting for Haskins, Inc.'s costs).

LO3 Homework MBC

General Electric Company
NYSE :: GE
Eversource Energy
NYSE :: ES

E6-29. Constructing and Assessing Income Statements Using Percentage of Completion

Assume that **General Electric Company** agreed in February 2019 to construct an electricity generating facility for **Eversource Energy**, a utility serving the Boston area. The contract price of $500 million is to be paid as follows: $200 million at the time of signing; $100 million on December 31, 2019; and $200 million at completion in May 2020. General Electric incurred the following costs in constructing the power plant: $100 million in 2019, and $300 million in 2020. The construction of the power generating facility is considered to be a single performance obligation.

a. Compute the amount of General Electric's revenue, expense, and income for both 2019 and 2020 assuming that its performance obligation is fulfilled over time and that the costs it incurs are reflective of the value conveyed to Eversource.

b. Compute the amount of GE's revenue, expense, and income for both 2019 and 2020 assuming that its performance obligation to construct the facility is fulfilled at a point in time (at the completion of construction).

c. What performance ratios would be affected by the different contract terms in parts (a) and (b)?

LO3 Homework MBC

E6-30. Distinct Performance Obligations

Floyd Corporation is a large engineering and construction company that designs and builds office buildings, apartment buildings, distribution warehouses and other structures for its customers. Projects usually begin with a design and engineering phase, followed by construction of the customer's facility. The design/engineering and construction activities take place in separate divisions of Floyd Corporation, and these two divisions bill separately for their work.

A typical three-year project might have the following pattern of work and billing (in $ millions).

	Design/Engineering		Construction		Total	
Year	Cost incurred	Billings to customer	Cost incurred	Billings to customer	Cost incurred	Billings to customer
1	7	10	0	0	7	10
2	2	3	15	12	17	15
3	1	2	10	18	11	20
Total	10	15	25	30	35	45

REQUIRED

a. Assume that Floyd Corporation determines that the work of the design/engineering division and the construction division are separate performance obligations, that these performance obligations are satisfied over time, and that cost incurred is reflective of the value transferred to the customer. For years 1, 2, and 3, determine the amount that Floyd Corporation will recognize in revenue and expense. What is the margin percentage reported in each year?

b. Assume that Floyd Corporation determines that the work of the design/engineering division and the construction division requires too much coordination to be considered separate performance obligations. The combined performance obligation is satisfied over time and cost incurred is reflective of the value transferred to the customer. For years 1, 2, and 3, determine the amount that Floyd Corporation will recognize in revenue and expense. What is the margin percentage reported in each year?

c. If this is a typical project, how does the performance obligation assessment affect the company's financial statements? For example, how is the debt-to-equity ratio (total liabilities ÷ total shareholders' equity) affected?

E6-31. Accounting for Contracts with Multiple Performance Obligations LO2

Amazon.com
NASDAQ :: AMZN

Amazon.com, Inc. provides the following description of its revenue recognition policies in its second quarter of 2018 10-Q report.

> ***Revenue***
> Revenue is measured based on the amount of consideration that we expect to receive, reduced by estimates for return allowances, promotional discounts, and rebates. Revenue also excludes any amounts collected on behalf of third parties, including sales and indirect taxes. In arrangements where we have multiple performance obligations, the transaction price is allocated to each performance obligation using the relative stand-alone selling price. We generally determine stand-alone selling prices based on the prices charged to customers or using expected cost plus a margin.
>
> A description of our principal revenue generating activities is as follows:
>
> *Retail sales*—We offer consumer products through our online and physical stores. Revenue is recognized when control of the goods is transferred to the customer, which generally occurs upon our delivery to the carrier or the customer.
>
> *Third-party seller services*—We offer programs that enable sellers to sell their products on our websites and their own branded websites, and fulfill orders through us. We are not the seller of record in these transactions. The commissions and any related fulfillment and shipping fees we earn from these arrangements are recognized as the services are rendered.
>
> *Subscription services*—Our subscription sales include fees associated with Amazon Prime memberships and access to content including audiobooks, ebooks, digital video, digital music, and other non-AWS subscription services. Prime memberships provide our customers with access to an evolving suite of benefits that represent a single stand-ready obligation. Subscriptions are paid for at the time of or in advance of delivering the services. Revenue from such arrangements is recognized over the subscription period.
>
> *AWS*—Our AWS sales arrangements include global sales of compute, storage, database, and other service offerings. Revenue is allocated to the services provided based on stand-alone selling prices and is recognized as the services are rendered. Sales commissions we pay in connection with contracts that exceed one year are capitalized and amortized over the contract term.
>
> *Other*—Other revenue primarily includes sales of advertising services and is recognized as the services are rendered.

a. What is an "arrangement with multiple performance obligations? How are revenues recognized in such arrangements?

b. Suppose that Amazon.com sells a Fire Tablet with a one-year membership in Amazon Prime. Assume that the device has a stand-alone selling price of $110, and a one-year Prime membership costs $120. Suppose the price charged for the combination is $200, and a customer buys the combination on July 1. What amount of revenue would Amazon recognize in the third calendar quarter (July through September)? How would the remaining revenues be recognized?

c. Record the July 1 transaction described in part b using the financial statement effects template and in journal entry form.

LO5 Homework MBC

LVMH
OTCMKTS::LVMUY

E6-32. Computing NOPAT, NOPM, and RNOA

LVMH Moët Hennessy Louis Vuitton SE (LVMH) is a French multinational luxury goods conglomerate headquartered in Paris. The following information is selected from their 2017 annual report.

(€ millions)	2017	2016
Revenue	42,636	37,600
Operating income	8,113	6,904
Net interest expense and other nonoperating charges	179	432
Net income	5,616	4,363
Operating assets	67,246	58,504
Operating liabilities	26,714	24,340

LVMH has an income tax rate of approximately 30%.

a. Compute LVMH's net operating profit after taxes (NOPAT) for 2017 and 2016.

b. Compute LVMH's net operating profit margin (NOPM) for each year.

c. Compute LVMH's return on net operating assets (RNOA) for 2017.

LO1, 6

E6-33. Applying Revenue Recognition Criteria

Simpyl Technologies, Inc., manufactures electronic equipment used to facilitate control of production processes and tracking of assets using RFID and other technologies. Since its initial public offering in 1996, the company has shown consistent growth in revenue and earnings, and the stock price has reflected that impressive performance.

Operating in a very competitive environment, Simpyl Technologies provides significant bonus incentives to its sales representatives. These representatives sell the company's products directly to end customers, to value-added resellers, and to distributers.

Consider the four situations below. In each case, determine whether Simpyl Technologies can recognize revenue at this time. Describe the reasons for your judgment.

a. When selling directly to the end customer, Simpyl Technologies requires a sales contract with authorized signatures from the customer company. At the end of Simpyl's fiscal year, sales representative A asks to book revenue from a customer. The customer's purchasing manager has confirmed the intention to complete the purchase, but the contract has only one of the two required signatures. The second person is traveling and will return to the office in a few days (but after the end of Simpyl's fiscal year). The inventory to fulfill the order is sitting in Simpyl's warehouse. Can Simpyl recognize revenue at this time?

b. Sales representative B has an approved contract to deliver units that must be customized to meet the customer's specifications. Just prior to the end of the fiscal year, the uncustomized units are shipped to an intermediate staging area where they will be reconfigured to meet the customer's requirements. Can Simpyl recognize revenue on the basic, uncustomized units at this time?

c. Sales representative C has finalized an order from a value-added reseller who regularly purchases significant volumes of Simpyl's products. The products have been delivered to the customer at the beginning of the fiscal year, and Simpyl Technologies has no further responsibilities for the items. However, the sales representative (with the regional sales manager) is still conducting negotiations with the value-added reseller as to the volume discounts that will be offered for the current year. Can Simpyl recognize revenue on the items delivered to the customer?

d. Sales representative D has finalized an order from a distributor, and the items have been delivered. However, an examination of the distributor's financial condition shows that it does not have the resources to pay Simpyl for the items it has purchased. It needs to sell those items, so the resulting proceeds can be used to pay Simpyl. Can Simpyl recognize revenue on the items delivered to the distributor?

LO4

E6-34. Reporting Uncollectible Accounts and Accounts Receivable

LaFond Company analyzes its accounts receivable at December 31, 2019, and arrives at the aged categories below along with the percentages that are estimated as uncollectible.

Age Group	Accounts Receivable	Estimated Loss %
Current (not past due)	$250,000	0.5%
1–30 days past due	90,000	1
31–60 days past due	20,000	2
61–120 days past due	11,000	5
121–180 days past due	6,000	10
Over 180 days past due	4,000	25
Total accounts receivable	$381,000	

At the beginning of the fourth quarter of 2019, there was a credit balance of $4,350 in the Allowance for Uncollectible Accounts. During the fourth quarter, LaFond Company wrote off $3,830 in receivables as uncollectible.

a. What amount of bad debts expense will LaFond report for 2019?

b. What is the balance of accounts receivable that it reports on its December 31, 2019, balance sheet?

c. Set up T-accounts for both Bad Debts Expense and for the Allowance for Uncollectible Accounts. Enter any unadjusted balances along with the dollar effects of the information described (including your results from parts *a* and *b*). Explain the numbers in each of the T-accounts.

d. Suppose LaFond wrote off $1,000 more in receivables in the quarter? Or, $1,000 less? How would that affect the bad debt expense for the fourth quarter? How does the aging of accounts deal with the inevitable differences between estimated cash collections and actual cash collections?

E6-35. Analysis of Accounts Receivable and Allowance for Doubtful Accounts

LO4, 5

Steelcase, Inc.
NYSE :: SCS

Steelcase, Inc. reported the following amounts in its 2018 and 2017 10-K reports (years ended February 23, 2018, and February 24, 2017).

($ millions)	2018	2017
From the income statement:		
Revenue	$3,055.5	$3,032.4
From the balance sheet:		
Accounts receivable, net	300.3	307.6
Customer deposits	28.2	15.9
From the disclosure on allowance for doubtful accounts:		
Balance at beginning of period	11.2	11.7
Additions (reductions) charged to income	2.5	4.5
Adjustments or deductions	(2.6)	(5.0)
Balance at end of period	11.1	11.2

a. Prepare the journal entry to record accounts receivable written off as uncollectible in 2018. Also prepare the entry to record the provision for doubtful accounts (bad debts expense) for 2018. What effect did these entries have on Steelcase's income for that year?

b. Calculate Steelcase's gross receivables for the years given, and then determine the allowance for doubtful accounts as a percentage of the gross receivables.

c. Calculate Steelcase's accounts receivable turnover for 2018. (Use Accounts receivable, net for the calculation.)

d. How much cash did Steelcase receive from customers in 2018?

E6-36. Analyzing and Reporting Receivable Transactions and Uncollectible Accounts (Using Percentage-of-Sales Method)

LO4

At the beginning of 2019, Penman Company had the following (normal) account balances in its financial records:

Accounts receivable	$122,000
Allowance for uncollectible accounts	7,900

During 2019, its credit sales were $1,173,000 and collections on credit sales were $1,150,000. The following additional transactions occurred during the year:

Feb. 17 Wrote off Nissim's account, $3,600.
May 28 Wrote off White's account, $2,400.

Dec. 15 Wrote off Ohlson's account, $900.

Dec. 31 Recorded the provision for uncollectible accounts at 0.8% of credit sales for the year. (*Hint*: The allowance account is increased by 0.8% of credit sales regardless of any prior write-offs.)

Compute and show how accounts receivable and the allowance for uncollectible accounts are reported in its December 31, 2019, balance sheet.

LO4 Homework MBC

E6-37. Estimating Bad Debts Expense and Reporting of Receivables

At December 31, 2019, Sunil Company had a balance of $375,000 in its accounts receivable and an unused balance of $4,200 in its allowance for uncollectible accounts. The company then aged its accounts as follows:

Current	$304,000
0–60 days past due	44,000
61–180 days past due	18,000
Over 180 days past due	9,000
Total accounts receivable	$375,000

The company has experienced losses as follows: 1% of current balances, 5% of balances 0–60 days past due, 15% of balances 61–180 days past due, and 40% of balances over 180 days past due. The company continues to base its provision for credit losses on this aging analysis and percentages.

a. What amount of bad debts expense does Sunil report on its 2019 income statement?

b. Show how accounts receivable and the allowance for uncollectible accounts are reported in its December 31, 2019, balance sheet.

c. Set up T-accounts for both Bad Debts Expense and for the Allowance for Uncollectible Accounts. Enter any unadjusted balances along with the dollar effects of the information described (including your results from parts *a* and *b*). Explain the numbers in each of the T-accounts.

LO4 Homework

E6-38. Estimating Uncollectible Accounts and Reporting Receivables over Multiple Periods

Barth Company, which has been in business for three years, makes all of its sales on credit and does not offer cash discounts. Its credit sales, customer collections, and write-offs of uncollectible accounts for its first three years follow:

Year	Sales	Collections	Accounts Written Off
2018	$751,000	$733,000	$5,300
2019	876,000	864,000	5,800
2020	972,000	938,000	6,500

a. Barth uses the allowance method of recognizing credit losses that provides for such losses at the rate of 1% of sales. (This means the allowance account is increased by 1% of credit sales regardless of any write-offs and unused balances.) What amounts for accounts receivable and the allowance for uncollectible accounts are reported on its balance sheet at the end of 2020? What total amount of bad debts expense appears on its income statement for each of the three years?

b. Comment on the appropriateness of the 1% rate used to provide for bad debts based on your results in part *a*. (*Hint*: T-accounts can help with this analysis.)

LO5, 7 Homework MBC

Hewlett-Packard
NYSE :: HPQ

E6-39.[A] Evaluating Business Segment Information

Hewlett-Packard Company reports that its "operations are organized into three segments for financial reporting purposes: Personal Systems, Printing and Corporate Investments" with the last segment encompassing HP Labs and incubation projects. The company provides the following information about these business segments:

($ millions)	2017	2016
Total net revenues		
Personal systems	$33,374	$29,987
Printing	18,801	18,260
Corporate investments	8	7

continued

continued from previous page

($ millions)	2017	2016
Earnings (loss) from continuing operations		
Personal systems	1,213	1,150
Printing	3,161	3,128
Corporate investments	(87)	(98)
Total assets		
Personal systems	12,156	10,686
Printing	10,548	9,959
Corporate investments	3	1

a. Calculate the 2017 return on capital employed for each segment. (Base the calculation on total assets instead of net operating assets in the denominator. HP does not disclose operating assets and liabilities by segment.)

b. Which segment is more profitable? Which is growing more quickly?

c. The Corporate Investments segment is dwarfed by the other two reporting segments. Why would HP's management want to keep Corporate Investments separate rather than combining it with one of the others?

E6-40. Analyzing Unearned Revenue Liabilities

LO1, 2

The Metropolitan Opera Association, Inc., was founded in 1883 and is widely regarded as one of the world's greatest opera companies. The Metropolitan's performances run from September to May, and the season may consist of more than two dozen different operas. Many of the opera's loyal subscribers purchase tickets for the upcoming season prior to the end of the opera's fiscal year-end at July 31. In its annual report, the Metropolitan recognizes a Deferred Revenue liability that is defined in their footnotes as follows. "Advance ticket sales, representing the receipt of payments for ticket sales for the next opera season, are reported as deferred revenue in the consolidated balance sheets." Ticket sales are recognized as box office revenue "on a specific performance basis."

Fiscal year ended July 31	Revenues (Box office and tours)	Deferred revenue
2017	$88,514	$42,649
2016	87,582	46,609
2015	90,952	47,801
2014	91,319	40,259

a. What revenue recognition principle(s) drive The Metropolitan Opera's deferral of advance ticket purchases?

b. Recreate the summary journal entries to recognize ticket sales revenue (box office and tours) for The Metropolitan Opera's fiscal year 2017 and advance sales for the fiscal year 2018 season. (Assume that advance ticket sales extend no further than the next year's opera season.)

c. The Metropolitan Opera's season changes every year. At the end of each fiscal year, management of the opera can observe the revenue generated by the season just concluded and also its subscribers' enthusiasm for the upcoming season. How might that information be used in managing the organization?

E6-41. Accounting for Membership Fees and Rewards Program

LO2

Homework MBC

BJ's Wholesale Club Holdings, Inc. provides the following description of its revenue recognition policies for membership fees and its reward program.

BJ's Wholesale Club Holdings, Inc.
NYSE::BJ

Performance Obligations
The Company identifies each distinct performance obligation to transfer goods (or bundle of goods) or services. The Company recognizes revenue when (or as) it satisfies a performance obligation by transferring control of the goods or services to the customer.

Merchandise sales—The Company recognizes sale of merchandise at clubs and gas stations at the point of sale when the customer takes possession of the goods and tenders payment.

BJ's Perks Rewards—The Company has a customer loyalty program called the BJ's Perks Rewards ® Program for which the Company offers points based on dollars spent by the customer. The Company also has a co-branded credit card program which provides members additional reward dollars for certain purchases. The Company's BJ's Perks Rewards ® members earn 2% cash back, up to a maximum of $500 per year, on all qualified purchases made at BJ's. The Company's My BJ's Perks Mastercard holders earn 3% or 5% cash back on all qualified purchases made at BJ's and 1% or 2% cash back on purchases made with the card outside of BJ's. Cash back is in the form of electronic awards issued in $20 increments that may be used online or in-club at the register and expire six months from the date issued.

Earned rewards may be redeemed on future purchases made at the Company. The Company recognizes revenue for earned rewards when customers redeem such rewards as part of a purchase at one of the Company's clubs or the Company's website. The Company accounts for these transactions as multiple element arrangements and allocates the transaction price to separate performance obligations using their relative fair values. The Company includes the fair value of reward dollars earned in deferred revenue at the time the reward dollars are earned.

Membership—The Company charges a membership fee to its customers. That fee allows customers to shop in the Company's clubs, shop on the Company's website, and purchase gas at the Company's gas stations for the duration of the membership, which is 12 months. Because the Company has the obligation to provide access to its clubs, website, and gas stations for the duration of the membership term, the Company recognizes membership fees on a straight-line basis over the life of the membership.

The following data were extracted from income statement, balance sheet, and footnotes of BJ's 10-Q report for the second quarter of 2018:

($ millions)	**Twenty-six weeks ended August 4, 2018**	
Net sales	$6,230.4	
Membership fee income	138.4	
Total revenues	6,368.8	
	August 4, 2018	**January 28, 2017**
Deferred revenue—membership fees	$ 129.9	$126.2

a. Explain BJ's accounting for membership fees.

b. Prepare journal entries to record (1) membership fees collected in cash in the first half of fiscal year 2018 and (2) membership fee revenue recognized over that period.

c. Explain BJ's accounting for its BJ's Perks Rewards program that provides 2% cash back, up to a maximum of $500 per year on qualified purchases made at BJ's.

PROBLEMS

LO5, 7 Homework MBC

DowDuPont Inc.
BYSE :: DWDP

P6-42.[A] Identifying Operating and Nonrecurring Income Components

The following information comes from recent **DowDuPont Inc.** income statements.

(In millions, except per share amounts) For the Years Ended December 31	**2017**	**2016**
Net sales	$62,484	$48,158
Cost of sales	50,414	37,640
Research and development expenses	2,110	1,584
Selling, general, and administrative expenses	4,021	2,956
Amortization of intangibles	1,013	544
Restructuring, goodwill impairment and asset-related charges—net	3,280	595
Integration and separation costs	1,101	349
Asbestos-related charge	—	1,113
Equity in earnings of nonconsolidated affiliates	764	442
Sundry income (expense)—net	966	1,452
Interest expense and amortization of debt discount	1,082	858
Income from continuing operations before income taxes	1,193	4,413
Provision (Credit for income taxes on continuing operations)	(476)	9
Income from continuing operations, net of tax	1,669	4,404
Loss from discontinued operations, net of tax	(77)	—
Net income	$ 1,592	$ 4,404

REQUIRED

a. Identify the components in its statement that you would consider operating.

b. Identify those components that you would consider nonrecurring.

c. Compute net operating profit after taxes (NOPAT) and net operating profit margin (NOPM) for each year. Use an income tax rate of 25%.

P6-43. Performance Obligation Fulfilled Over Time LO3 Homework MBC

Philbrick Company signed a three-year contract to develop custom sales training materials and provide training to the employees of Elliot Company. The contract price is $1,200 per employee and the number of employees to be trained is 400. Philbrick can send a bill to Elliot at the end of every training session. Once developed, the custom training materials will belong to Elliot Company, but Philbrick does not consider them to be a separate performance obligation.

The expected number to be trained in each year and the expected development and training costs follow.

	Number of employees	Development and training costs incurred
2019	125	$ 65,000
2020	200	80,000
2021	75	30,000
Total	400	$175,000

REQUIRED

a. For each year, compute the revenue, expense, and gross profit reported assuming revenue is recognized over time using . . .

1. the number of employees trained as a measure of the value provided to the customer.
2. the cost incurred as a measure of the value provided to the customer.

b. Assume that Philbrick's costs are $15,000 to develop the custom training materials at the beginning of the contract and then $400 for each employee trained. Which method do you believe is more appropriate in this situation? Explain.

P6-44. Incentives for Earnings Management LO6

Harris Corporation pays senior management an annual bonus from a bonus pool. The size of the bonus pool is determined as follows.

Reported net income	Bonus pool
Less than or equal to $10 million	$0
Greater than $10 million, but less than or equal to $20 million	10% of income in excess of $10 million
Greater than $20 million	$1 million

REQUIRED

a. Assume that senior management expects current earnings to be $21 million and next year's earnings to be $18 million. What incentive does management of Harris Corporation have for managing earnings?

b. Assume that senior management expects current earnings to be $17 million and next year's earnings to be $24 million. What incentive does management of Harris Corporation have for managing earnings?

c. Assume that senior management expects current earnings to be $9.5 million and next year's earnings to be $12 million. What incentive does management of Harris Corporation have for managing earnings?

d. How might the bonus plan be structured to minimize the incentives for earnings management?

P6-45. Interpreting Accounts Receivable and Uncollectible Accounts LO4, 5 Mattel, Inc. NASDAQ::MAT

Mattel, Inc. designs, manufactures, and markets a broad variety of toy products worldwide which are sold to its customers and directly to consumers. The company's brands include American Girl, Fisher-Price, Hot Wheels, and Barbie. The following information is taken from the company's 10-K annual report for its fiscal year ending December 31, 2017.

($ thousands)	2017	2016	2015
Accounts receivable	$1,153,988	$1,136,593	$1,169,469
Allowance for doubtful accounts	25,378	21,376	24,370
Accounts receivable, net	1,128,610	1,115,217	1,145,099

Activity in the allowance for doubtful accounts for the past three fiscal years is as follows:

($ thousands)	2017	2016	2015
Balance at beginning of year	$21,376	$24,370	$26,283
Charged to income	17,568	9,165	5,813
Deductions[a]	13,566	12,159	7,726
Allowance at end of year	25,378	21,376	24,370

[a] Includes write-offs, recoveries of previous write-offs, and currency translation adjustments.

Mattel's revenues were $4,881,951 thousand and $5,456,650 thousand for fiscal years 2017 and 2016, respectively.

REQUIRED

a. What amount did Mattel report as accounts receivable, net in its January 31, 2017, balance sheet?

b. Prepare journal entries to record bad debts expense and write-offs of uncollectible accounts in fiscal 2017. (Assume that Deductions did not include recoveries or foreign currency adjustments.) Post these entries to T-accounts. Now suppose Mattel experienced a $350 thousand recovery of a previously written-off receivable. How should the company record this recovery?

c. Compute the ratio of allowance for doubtful accounts to gross accounts receivable for fiscal 2016 and 2017.

d. Compute Mattel's accounts receivable turnover and average collection period for 2017 and 2016.

e. What might be the cause of the changes that you observe in parts c and d?

LO4 The GAP, Inc. NYSE :: GPS

P6-46. Accounting for Product Returns

In its income statement for the first quarter of fiscal year 2018, The Gap, Inc., reported net sales of $3,783 million and cost of goods sold and occupancy expenses of $2,356 million, resulting in a gross profit of $1,427 million. In its footnotes, The Gap reports that "We also record an allowance for estimated returns based on our historical return patterns and various other assumptions that management believes to be reasonable, which are presented on a gross basis on our Condensed Consolidated Balance Sheet."

When The Gap accounts for estimated sales returns, it makes two entries. First, it reduces sales revenue by the returns' expected sales price and recognizes a sales return allowance as a liability for the same amount. Then, The Gap reduces cost of goods sold by the returns' expected cost and recognizes a right of return merchandise asset for that same amount.

At the end of the first quarter of fiscal year 2018, The Gap reported a sales return allowance liability of $93 million and a right of return merchandise asset of $38 million.

REQUIRED

a. What was the estimated gross profit margin on the items The Gap expected to be returned following the first quarter of fiscal year 2018? How does that compare with the gross profit margin reported in the income statement for the first quarter of fiscal year 2018? What might account for the difference?

b. Suppose The Gap sells 100 units of an item for $50 each, and its gross profit on each unit is $20. Further, suppose The Gap expects that 10 of the units will be returned. What entries will be made to record the sale of 100 units (for cash) and the expected returns? What entry is made when ten customers subsequently return the items and receive a cash refund? Assume that the units are undamaged and can be sold to other customers.

LO2 Homework MBC Take-Two Interactive Software, Inc. NASDAQ :: TTWO

P6-47. Analyzing Unearned Revenue Changes

Take-Two Interactive Software, Inc. (TTWO) is a developer, marketer, publisher, and distributor of video game software and content to be played on a variety of platforms. There is an increasing demand for the ability to play these games in an online environment, and TTWO has developed this capability in many of its products. In addition, TTWO maintains servers (or arranges for servers) for the online activities of its customers.

TTWO considers that its products have multiple performance obligations. The first performance obligation is to provide software to the customer that enables the customer to play the game offline or online. That performance obligation is fulfilled at the point at which the software is provided to the customer. In addition, TTWO's customers benefit from "online functionality that is dependent on our online support services and/or additional free content updates." This second performance obligation is fulfilled over time, and the estimated time period for which an average user plays the software product is judged to be a faithful depiction of the fulfillment of this performance obligation.

At the beginning of the first quarter of fiscal year 2018, TTWO had a deferred net revenue liability of $566,141 thousand. When that quarter ended on June 30, 2018, the deferred net revenue liability was $466,429 thousand. Revenue for the quarter was $387,982 thousand.

REQUIRED

a. What would cause the *deferred net revenue* liability to go down over the quarter?

b. What was the amount of online-enabled games purchased by TTWO's customers in the first quarter ended June 30, 2018? Were the purchases greater or less than the revenue recognized in the income statement? How might that information be useful for a financial statement reader?

CASES AND PROJECTS

C6-48. Revenue Recognition and Refunds
From the first quarter 2018 10-Q of **Groupon, Inc.**:

LO1, 2, 6
Groupon, Inc.
NASDAQ :: GRPN

Groupon operates online local commerce marketplaces throughout the world that connect merchants to consumers by offering goods and services, generally at a discount. Consumers access those marketplaces through our websites, primarily localized groupon.com sites in many countries, and our mobile applications. Traditionally, local merchants have tried to reach consumers and generate sales through a variety of methods, including online advertising, paid telephone directories, direct mail, newspaper, radio, television and other promotions. By bringing the brick and mortar world of local commerce onto the Internet, Groupon is helping local merchants to attract customers and sell goods and services. We provide consumers with savings and help them discover what to do, eat, see, buy and where to travel.

The same filing provides the following information about the company's revenue recognition policies.

10. REVENUE RECOGNITION

Product and service revenue are generated from sales transactions through the Company's online marketplaces in three primary categories: Local, Goods and Travel.

Product revenue is earned from direct sales of merchandise inventory to customers and includes any related shipping fees. Service revenue primarily represents the net commissions earned by the Company from selling goods and services provided by third-party merchants. Those marketplace transactions generally involve the online delivery of a voucher that can be redeemed by the purchaser with the third-party merchant for goods or services (or for discounts on goods or services). To a lesser extent, service revenue also includes commissions earned when customers make purchases with retailers using digital coupons accessed through the Company's websites and mobile applications. Additionally, in the United States the Company has recently been developing and testing voucherless offerings that are linked to customer credit cards. Customers claim those voucherless merchant offerings through the Company's online marketplaces and earn cash back on their credit card statements when they transact with the related merchants, who pay the Company commissions for such transactions.

In connection with most of our product and service revenue transactions, we collect cash from credit card payment processors shortly after a sale occurs. For transactions in which the Company earns commissions when customers make purchases with retailers using digital coupons accessed through its websites and mobile applications, the Company generally collects payment from affiliate networks on terms ranging from 30 to 150 days.

For merchant agreements with redemption payment terms, the merchant is not paid its share of the sale price for a voucher sold through one of the Company's online marketplaces until the customer redeems the related voucher. If the customer does not redeem a voucher with such merchant payment terms, the Company retains all of the gross billings for that voucher, rather than retaining only its net commission.

[T]he Company estimates the variable consideration from vouchers that will not ultimately be redeemed and recognizes that amount as revenue at the time of sale, rather than when the Company's legal obligation expires. The Company estimates variable consideration from unredeemed vouchers using its historical voucher redemption experience.

REQUIRED

a. Assume that Groupon sells an Invicta Chronograph Watch in its Product marketplace. The price of the watch is $80, and the watch cost Groupon $40. Using journal entries, illustrate how Groupon would record the sale of the watch.

b. Assume that Groupon sells a restaurant voucher in its Local marketplace. The consumer pays $80, and Groupon will pay the restaurant $40 after the consumer has redeemed the voucher at the restaurant. The consumer has 60 days to redeem the voucher. Using journal entries, illustrate how Groupon would record the sale of the voucher. Assume that the consumer will redeem the voucher with certainty.

c. Refer to the facts presented in part *b* above. Assume that Groupon estimates that 10% of the Groupon customers will not redeem the voucher within the 60-day period. How does this change the entry in part *b*?

LO1, 2, 6
Dell Inc.
NASDAQ :: DELL

C6-49. Interpreting Revenue Recognition Policies and Earnings Management

A *Wall Street Journal* article dated October 31, 2007, reported that an internal investigation at **Dell Inc.** had uncovered evidence of earnings management. The article states:

> An internal investigation found that senior executives and other employees manipulated the company's financial statements to give the appearance of hitting quarterly performance goals.
>
> One of the biggest problems uncovered in the investigation was the way Dell recognized revenue on software products it sells. Dell, a large reseller of other companies' software products, said it historically recognized revenue from software licenses at the time that the products were sold. . . . Based on its internal review, it should have deferred more revenue from software sales.
>
> Another issue was product warranties. In some cases, Dell said it improperly recognized revenue associated with [extended] warranties over a shorter period of time than the duration of the contract.

The income statements from Dell's 2007 10-K report are presented below, along with the footnote outlining Dell's revenue recognition policies:

	Fiscal Year Ended		
	February 2, 2007	February 3, 2006 As Restated	January 28, 2005 As Restated
Net revenue	$57,420	$55,788	$49,121
Cost of net revenue	47,904	45,897	40,103
Gross margin	9,516	9,891	9,018
Operating expenses:			
Selling, general, and administrative	5,948	5,051	4,352
Research, development, and engineering	498	458	460
Total operating expenses	6,446	5,509	4,812
Operating income	3,070	4,382	4,206
Investment and other income, net	275	226	197
Income before income taxes	3,345	4,608	4,403
Income tax provision	762	1,006	1,385
Net income	$ 2,583	$ 3,602	$ 3,018

Revenue Recognition Net revenue includes sales of hardware, software and peripherals, and services (including extended service contracts and professional services). These products and services are sold either separately or as part of a multiple-element arrangement. Dell allocates revenue from multiple-element arrangements to the elements based on the relative fair value of each element, which is generally based on the relative sales price of each element when sold separately. The allocation of fair value for a multiple-element arrangement involving software is based on vendor specific objective evidence ("VSOE"), or in the absence of VSOE for delivered elements, the residual method. Under the residual method, Dell allocates revenue to software licenses at the inception of the license term when VSOE for all undelivered elements, such as Post Contract Customer Support ("PCS"), exists and all other revenue recognition criteria have been satisfied. In the absence of VSOE for undelivered elements, revenue is deferred and subsequently recognized over the term of the arrangement. For sales of extended warranties with a separate contract price, Dell defers revenue equal to the separately stated price. Revenue associated with undelivered elements is deferred and recorded when delivery occurs. Product revenue is recognized, net of an allowance for estimated returns, when both title and risk of loss transfer to the customer, provided that no significant obligations remain. Revenue from extended warranty and service contracts, for which Dell is obligated to perform, is recorded as deferred revenue and subsequently recognized over the term of the contract or when the service is completed. Revenue from sales of third-party extended warranty and service contracts or software PCS, for which Dell is not obligated to perform, and for which Dell does not meet the criteria for gross revenue recognition under EITF 99-19 is recognized on a net basis. All other revenue is recognized on a gross basis.

REQUIRED

a. Explain how Dell accounts for sales of other companies' software products. What are the potential risks of abuse of these accounting policies as a means to manage earnings?

b. Explain how Dell accounts for sales of extended warranty contracts. How did Dell employees manipulate these policies to manage earnings?

c. Discuss the incentives that exist to manage earnings to "give the appearance of hitting quarterly performance goals." How can a company such as Dell prevent earnings management in circumstances such as this?

C6-50. Accounting for Doubtful Accounts and Returns

LO2, 4, 5
John Wiley and Sons, Inc.
NYSE :: JW

John Wiley and Sons, Inc. publishes books, periodicals, software, and other digital content. Its April 30, 2018, balance sheet reported the following amounts for accounts receivable ($ thousands):

April 30,	2018	2017
Accounts receivable, net	$212,377	$188,679

Wiley's income statement provided the following detail of operating income ($ thousands):

Year ended April 30	2018	2017
Revenue	$1,796,103	$1,718,530
Cost of Expenses		
Cost of sales	485,220	460,756
Operating and administrative expenses	994,552	988,597
Restructuring and related charges	28,566	13,355
Amortization of intangibles	48,230	49,669
Operating income	$ 239,535	$ 206,153

Wiley normally charges operating and administrative expenses for estimated doubtful accounts. The company provided the following supplemental information concerning doubtful accounts and returns in its footnotes ($ thousands):

	Balance at Beginning of Period	Charged to Expenses and Other	Deductions from Reserves	Balance at End of Period
Year ended April 30, 2018				
Allowance for sales returns	$24,300	$(3,486)	$ 2,186	$18,628
Allowance for doubtful accounts	7,186	5,439	2,518	10,107
Year ended April 30, 2017				
Allowance for sales returns	19,861	53,482	49,043	24,300
Allowance for doubtful accounts	7,254	2,913	2,981	7,186

Net sales return reserves are reflected in the following accounts of the Consolidated Statements of Financial Position—increase (decrease):

April 30,	2018	2017
Accounts receivable	$(28,302)	$(34,769)
Inventories	4,626	4,727
Royalties payable	(5,048)	(5,741)
Decrease in net assets	$(18,628)	$(24,300)

REQUIRED

a. Prepare journal entries to record bad debts expense and accounts receivable write-offs for 2017 and 2018. Post to the Allowance for doubtful accounts T-account.

b. Compute the allowance for doubtful accounts as a percentage of accounts receivable. What might account for the change from 2017 to 2018?

c. Wiley has also established an allowance for returns. How do returns differ from doubtful accounts? Under what circumstances might this difference affect the accounting for returns?

d. Calculate the accounts receivable turnover ratio and average collection period for 2018 using net accounts receivable.

LO7
3M Company
NYSE: MMM

C6-51.[A] Interpreting Restructuring Charges

The following is from the most recent 10-K report of **3M Company** for the year ended December 31, 2017.

3M COMPANY AND SUBSIDIARIES Consolidated Statement of Income (Millions, except per share amounts)	2017
Net sales	$31,657
Operating expenses	
Costs of sales	16,001
Selling, general and administrative expenses	6,572
Research, development and related expenses	1,850
Gain on sale of businesses	(586)
Total operating expenses	23,837
Operating income	7,820
Other expense (income), net	272
Income before income taxes	7,548
Provision for income taxes	2,679
Net income including noncontrolling interest	$ 4,869

In its footnotes, 3M provided the following information about the gain on sale of businesses in the income statement.

Gain on Sale of Businesses:

In 2017, 3M sold the assets of its safety prescription eyewear business, completed the related sale or transfer of control, as applicable, of its identity management business, sold its tolling and automated license/number plate recognition and electronic monitoring businesses, and sold the assets of its electrical marking/labeling business. On a combined basis, these divestitures resulted in a gain on the sale of businesses of $586 million.

In addition, 3M provided information about restructuring charges for fiscal year 2017:

2017 Restructuring Actions:

During the second quarter of 2017, management approved and committed to undertake certain restructuring actions primarily focused on portfolio and footprint optimization. These actions affected approximately 1,300 positions worldwide and resulted in a second quarter 2017 pre-tax charge of $99 million. Remaining activities related to restructuring are expected to be completed by the end of 2018.

Restructuring charges are summarized by business segment as follows:

(Millions)	Second Quarter 2017 Employee-Related
Industrial	$39
Safety and graphics	9
Health care	2
Electronics and energy	7
Consumer	36
Corporate and unallocated	6
Total expense	$99

The preceding restructuring charges were recorded in the income statement as follows:

(Millions)	Second Quarter 2017
Cost of sales	$86
Selling, general and administrative expenses	5
Research, development and related expenses	8
Total	$99

Restructuring actions, including cash and non-cash impacts, follow:

(Millions)	Employee-Related
Expense incurred in the second quarter of 2017	$99
Cash payments	(8)
Adjustments	(3)
Accrued restructuring action balances as of December 31, 2017	$88

REQUIRED

a. Describe where on the income statement the above described restructuring charges and gain on sale of businesses are included.

b. Describe how an analyst of the company should treat these items when making financial statement projections.

c. What incentives might management have to either overstate or understate the above described restructuring charges? Describe how future financial statements would be affected if the costs were overstated or understated when these charges were recorded in 2017.

SOLUTIONS TO REVIEW PROBLEMS

Mid-Chapter Review 1

SOLUTION

(All dollar amounts are in millions.)

a. The *Deferred net revenue* liability increases when Electronic Arts sells a game, and it decreases when the company recognizes revenue from providing post-sale services to customers. So a decrease means that the amount sold was less than the amount recognized.

b. Electronic Arts' sales to customers equals its *Total net revenue* plus the change in the *Deferred net revenue* liability, or $1,137 + (–$347) = $790. So, a significant part of the company's revenue could be attributed to sales in past quarters. Some of that pattern could be due to seasonality of purchases or to the timing of new game introductions, and it would have the effect of smoothing out the revenue stream. A financial statement reader should recognize that the reported revenues are a weighted average of customer purchases made in the current period and in prior periods. Changes in the deferred revenue liability can be a useful indicator of the revenue in future income statements.

Mid-Chapter Review 2

SOLUTION

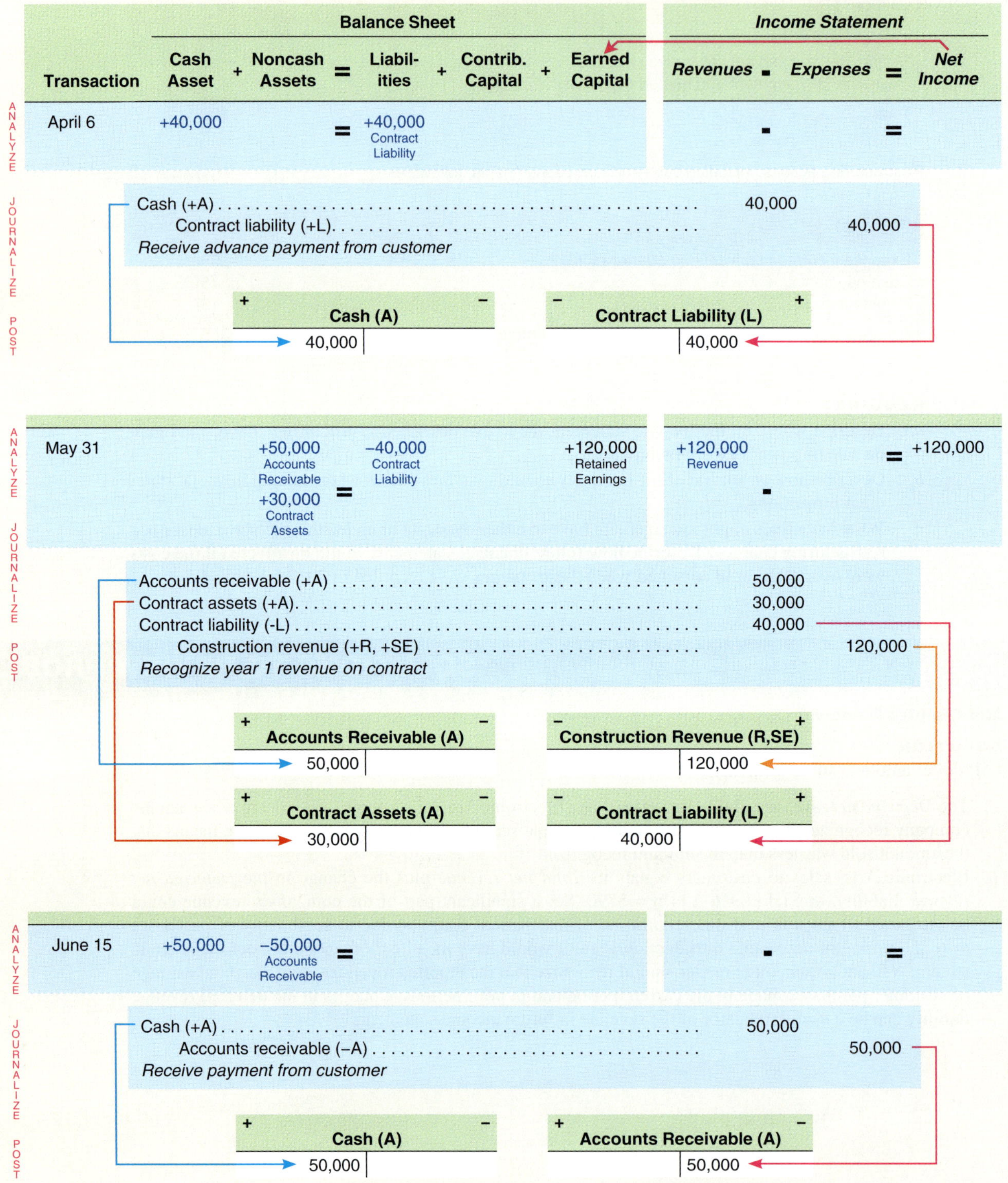

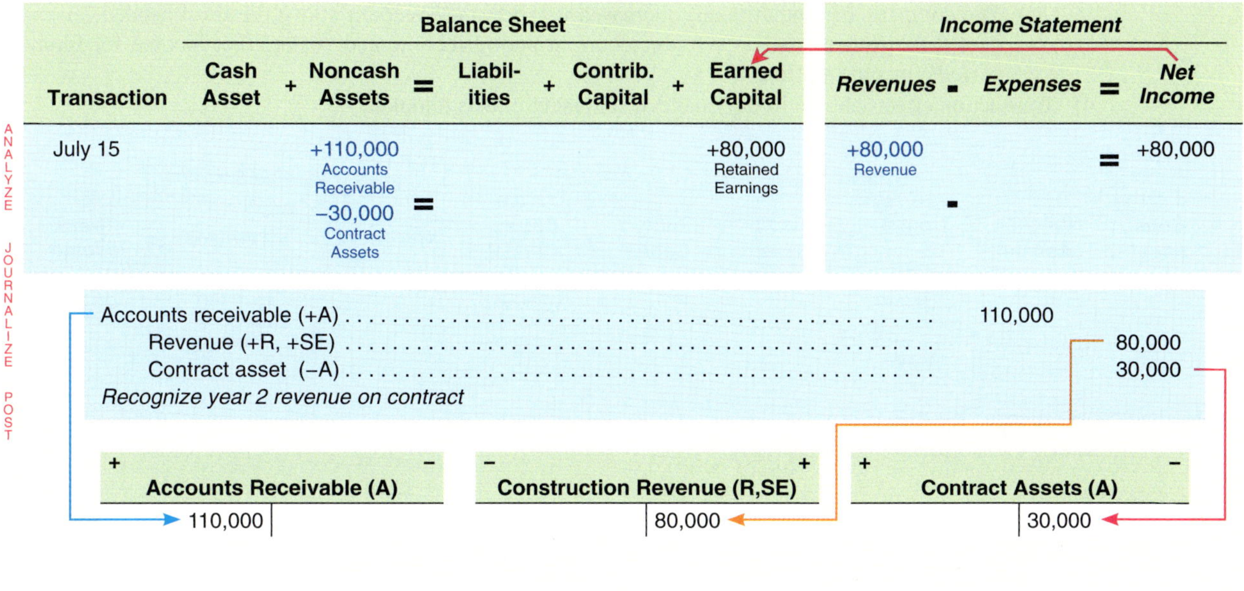

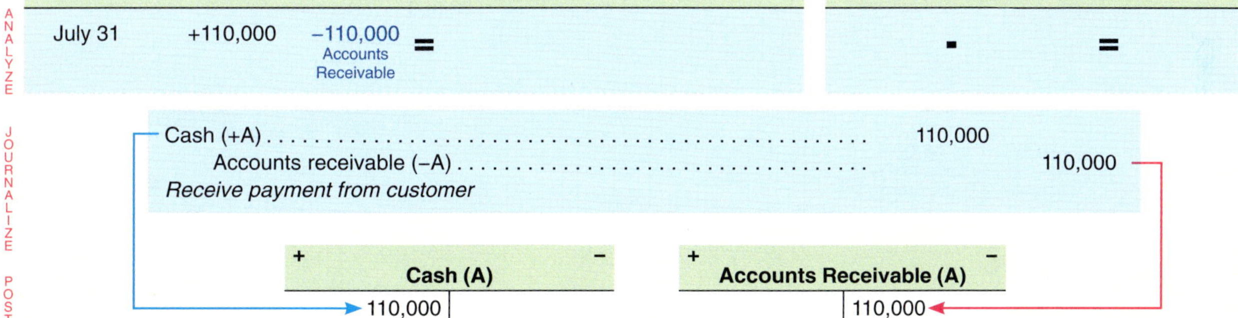

Mid-Chapter Review 3

SOLUTION

1. As of December 31, 2019,

Current	$468,000	×	1%	=	$ 4,680
1–60 days past due	244,000	×	5%	=	12,200
61–180 days past due	38,000	×	15%	=	5,700
Over 180 days past due	20,000	×	40%	=	8,000
Amount required					$30,580
Unused allowance balance					7,000
Provision					$23,580 2019 bad debts expense

2. Current assets section of balance sheet.

Accounts receivable, net of $30,580 in allowances	$739,420

3. Engel Company has markedly increased the percentage of the allowance for uncollectible accounts to gross accounts receivable—from the historical 2% to the current 4% ($30,580/$770,000). There are at least two possible interpretations:

   a. The quality of Engel Company's receivables has declined. Possible causes include the following: (1) sales can stagnate and the company can feel compelled to sell to lower-quality accounts to maintain sales volume; (2) it may have introduced new products for which average credit losses are higher; and (3) its administration of accounts receivable can become lax.

b. The company has intentionally increased its allowance account above the level needed for expected future losses so as to reduce current period income and "bank" that income for future periods (income shifting).

4. Transaction effects shown in the financial statement effects template.

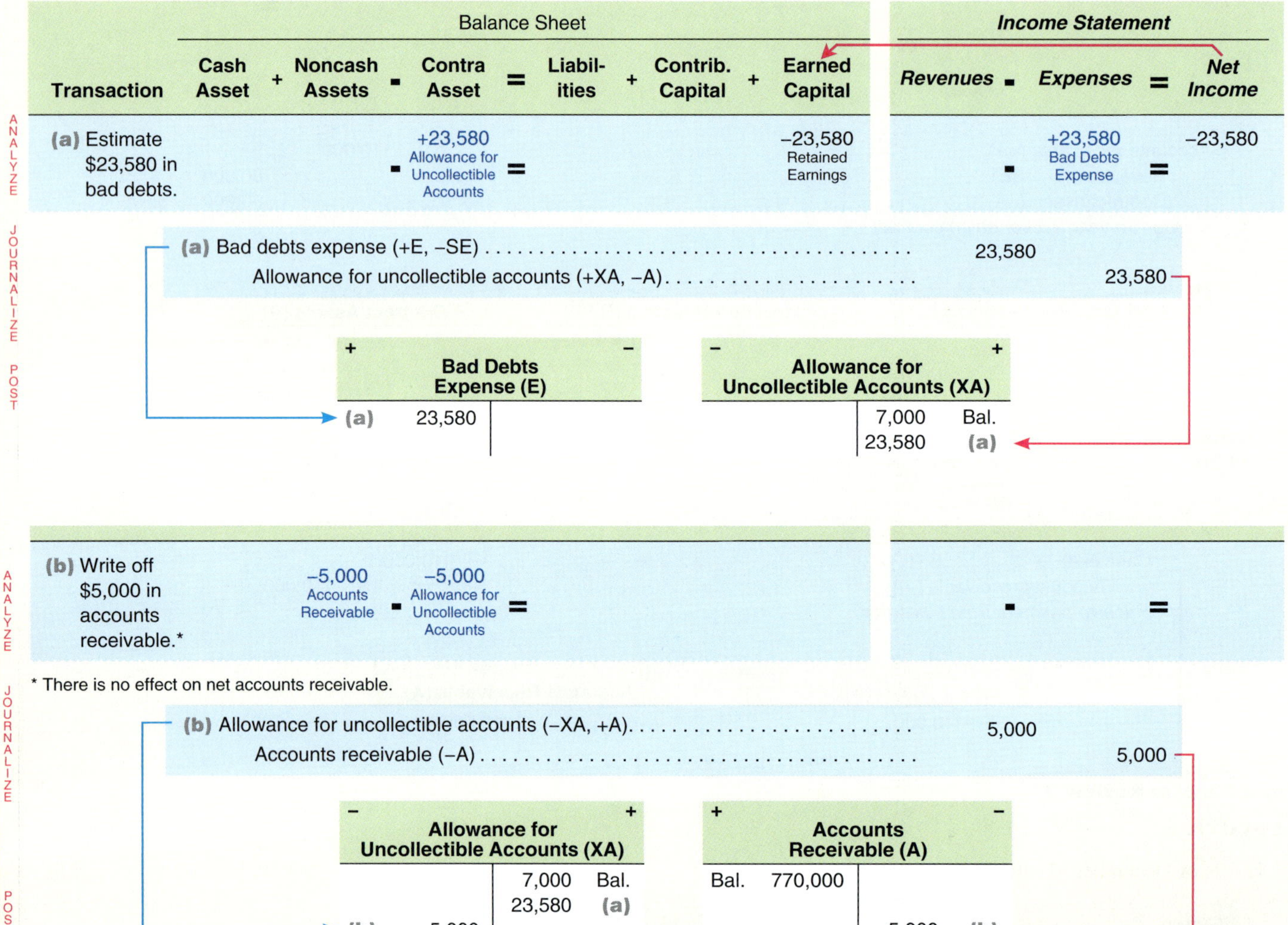

Chapter-End Review

SOLUTION

1.

($ millions)	Comcast (Xfinity)	CCO Holdings (Spectrum)
NOPAT	$22,900 – [($421 – $3,086) × (1 – 0.25)] = $24,898.75	$883 – [($70 – $3,159) × (1 – 0.25)] = $3,199.75
Average net operating assets	[($180,018 – $51,587) + ($175,253 – $61,834)]/2 = $120,925.00	[($145,693 – $10,357) + ($148,319 – $9,448)]/2 = $137,103.50
Return on net operating assets	$24,898.75/$120,925.00 = 0.206	$3,199.75/$137,103.50 = 0.023
Net operating profit margin	$24,898.75/$84,526.00 = 0.295	$3,199.75/$41,578.00 = 0.077
Accounts receivable turnover	$84,526.00/[($8,546 + $7,955)/2] = 10.245	$41,578.00/[(1,611 + $1,387)/2] = 27.7
Average collection period	365/10.245 = 35.6 days	365/27.7 = 13.2 days

2. These two companies present very different pictures in their ratios. Comcast has much higher NOPAT, lower operating assets, and higher operating liabilities. As a result, Comcast has much higher return measures (RNOA and NOPM). A significant part of this difference is due to a one-time tax benefit for Comcast—instead of having its usual $5 billion tax expense, it recorded a $7.6 billion tax *benefit* from the Tax Cut and Jobs Act at the end of 2017. Another big contrast is in operating liabilities—Comcast's operating liabilities are 29% of operating assets, while CCO's ratio is 7%. It appears that Comcast is getting a leverage effect with its operating liabilities.

Appendix 6A Review

SOLUTION

a. A loss from discontinued operations of $105,000 would be reported below income from continuing operations. The loss is net of tax and is calculated as follows:
$105,000 = ($120,000 + $12,000 + $18,000) × (1 – 30%).

b. A restructuring charge of $30,000 ($12,000 + $18,000) would be reported as part of operating income. The loss is before taxes. The tax effect of the restructuring charge would be included in the provision for income taxes (income tax expense).

c. Singh could report this loss as discontinued operations only if the closure represented a separate business unit within the company and the closure represents a strategic shift in operations. Otherwise, it must be reported as a restructuring charge.

Reporting and Analyzing Inventory

LEARNING OBJECTIVES

1. Interpret disclosures of information concerning operating expenses, including manufacturing and retail inventory costs. (p. 328)
2. Account for inventory and cost of goods sold using different costing methods. (p. 332)
3. Apply the lower of cost or net realizable value rule to value inventory. (p. 337)
4. Evaluate how inventory costing affects management decisions and outsiders' interpretations of financial statements. (p. 341)
5. Define and interpret gross profit margin and inventory turnover ratios. Use inventory footnote information to make appropriate adjustments to ratios. (p. 345)
6. Appendix 7A: Analyze LIFO liquidations and the impact they have on the financial statements. (p. 351)

HOME DEPOT
www.HomeDepot.com

The Home Depot, Inc. is the world's largest home improvement retailer and the second largest specialty retailer in the United States. At January 28, 2018, the company operated 2,284 retail stores worldwide, and reported sales of just over $100 billion. This performance represents the eighth year of increasing revenues.

Management of The Home Depot has focused in recent years on "improving the performance of our existing stores,"[1] with less emphasis on expansion. Indeed, their stated strategic framework consists of three key initiatives—1) customer service, 2) product authority, and 3) disciplined capital allocation, productivity, and efficiency. The Home Depot's net operating profit margin (net operating profit divided by sales revenue) has increased significantly between 2012 and 2017, reflecting a combination of management's attention to costs and an improving economy. The company has performed very well in recent years.

A key element of Home Depot's operating strategy is inventory management. Inventory represents one of the largest assets on Home Depot's balance sheet. A

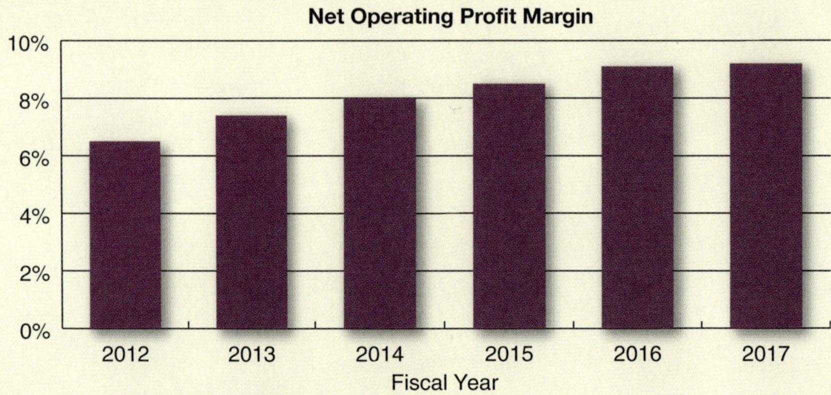

[1] Home Depot CEO Frank Blake in an interview with Rachel Tobin Blake published in *The Atlantic Journal-Constitution*, February 1, 2009.

typical Home Depot store carries 30,000 to 40,000 products during the year, ranging from garden supplies to hardware and lumber to household appliances. These stores are stocked through a sophisticated logistics program designed to ensure product availability for customers and low supply chain costs. The fiscal 2017 annual report states that the company "continued to focus on optimizing our supply chain network and improving our inventory, transportation and distribution productivity." As of January 28, 2018, the company operated over 90 distribution centers. The company also utilizes its retail stores as a network of locations for customers who shop online. Online sales have increased from 2.4% of total revenue in fiscal 2012 to 6.7% in 2017.

In this chapter, we examine the reporting of inventory and cost of goods sold. For most retail and manufacturing businesses, cost of goods sold and the related inventory management costs represent the largest source of expenses in the income statement. Carrying large stocks of inventory is costly for any business. The more that a business can minimize the amount of resources tied up in merchandise or materials, while still meeting customer demand, the more profitable it will be. Moreover, excessive inventory balances can indicate poor inventory management, obsolete products, and weakening sales. We explore accounting methods designed to measure inventory costs and determine cost of goods sold. We also look at measures that help us assess the effectiveness of inventory management practices for companies such as The Home Depot.

Sources: *Fortune*, May 2012; The Home Depot, Inc. 2010-2014 10-K reports; The Home Depot does not end its fiscal year on December 31, but rather on the Sunday closest to January 31. So, "Fiscal Year 2014" actually ended on February 1, 2015. One interesting aspect of this practice is that most of The Home Depot's fiscal years have 52 weeks, but periodically a fiscal year will have 53 weeks. (Fiscal Year 2012 was the most recent year of this event.)

CHAPTER ORGANIZATION

Reporting and Analyzing Inventory

Reporting Operating Expenses	Inventory Costing Methods	Financial Statement Effects and Disclosure	Analyzing Financial Statements
• Expense Recognition • Recording and Reporting Inventory Costs • Manufacturing Inventory	• FIFO • LIFO • Average Cost • Lower of Cost or NRV	• Footnote Disclosures • Income Statement Effects • Balance Sheet Effects • Cash Flow Effects	• Gross Profit Analysis • Inventory Turnover • LIFO Liquidation (Appendix 7A)

REPORTING OPERATING EXPENSES

1 **LO1** Interpret disclosures of information concerning operating expenses, including manufacturing and retail inventory costs.

In Chapter 6, we introduced the concept of operating income and discussed issues surrounding revenue recognition and how best to measure and report a company's performance. But the amount of revenue from customers must be interpreted relative to the resources that were required to achieve it. Operating expenses include the costs of acquiring the products (and services) that customers purchase, plus the costs of selling efforts, administrative functions, and any other activities that support the operations of the company. Careful examination of these costs allows financial statement users to judge management's performance, to identify emerging problems, and to make predictions of future performance. For instance, we may address the following questions.

- Are the company's costs of providing products and services increasing or decreasing?
- Is the company able to maintain its margins in the face of changes in costs or competition?
- Does management's ability to judge customer tastes and preferences allow it to avoid overstocks of unpopular inventory and the resulting price discounts that reduce margins?

In this chapter, we begin our examination of operating expenses by studying inventory and cost of goods sold. The reporting of inventory and cost of goods sold is important for three reasons. First, cost of goods sold is often the largest single expense in a company's income statement, and inventory may be one of the largest assets in the balance sheet. Consequently, information about inventory and cost of goods sold is critical for interpreting the financial statements. Second, in order to effectively manage operations and resources, management needs accurate and timely information about inventory quantities and costs. Finally, alternative methods of accounting for inventory and cost of goods sold can distort interpretations of margins and turnovers unless the information in the financial statement footnotes is used.

Expense Recognition Principles

In addition to determining when to recognize revenues to properly measure and report a company's performance, we must also determine when to recognize expenses. In general, expenses are recognized when assets are diminished (or liabilities increased) as a result of earning revenue or supporting operations, even if there is no immediate decrease in cash. Expense recognition can be generally divided into the following three approaches.

- **Direct association**. Any cost that can be *directly* associated with a specific source of revenue should be recognized as an expense at the same time that the related revenue is recognized. For a merchandising company (a retailer or a wholesaler), an example of direct association is recognizing cost of goods sold and sales revenue when the product is delivered to the customer. The cost of acquiring the inventory is recorded in the inventory asset account where it remains until the item is sold. At that point, the inventory cost is removed from the inventory asset and transferred to expenses. The future costs of any obligations arising from current revenues should also be estimated and recognized as liabilities and matched as expenses against those revenues. An example of such an expense is expected warranty costs, a topic covered in Chapter 9.

  For a manufacturing company, the accounting system distinguishes between *product costs* and *period costs*. Product costs are incurred to benefit the company's manufacturing activities and include raw materials, production workers and supervisors, depreciation on equipment and facilities, utilities, and so on. Even though some of these costs cannot be directly associated with a unit of production, the accounting system accumulates product costs and assigns them to inventory assets until the unit is sold. All costs not classified as product costs are considered period costs.

- **Immediate recognition.** Many period costs are necessary for generating revenues and income but cannot be directly associated with specific revenues. Some costs can be associated with all of the revenues of an accounting period, but not with any specific sales transaction that occurred during that period. Examples include most administrative and marketing costs. These costs are recognized as expenses in the period when the costs are incurred. Other expense items, such as research and development (R&D) expense, are recognized immediately because of U.S. GAAP requirements.
- **Systematic allocation.** Costs that benefit more than one accounting period and cannot be associated with specific revenues or assigned to a specific period must be allocated across all of the periods benefited. The most common example is depreciation expense. When an asset is purchased, it is capitalized (recorded in an asset account). The asset cost is then converted into an expense over the duration of its useful life according to a depreciation formula or schedule established by management. Depreciation of long-term assets is discussed in Chapter 8.

Inventory and cost of goods sold expense are important for product companies—manufacturers, wholesalers, and retailers. But before turning to an examination of these accounts at The Home Depot, we should recognize that cost of sales expense is also a critical performance component for many service companies, particularly those who engage in projects for their clients and customers. For fiscal 2017, the consulting firm **Accenture PLC** reports revenues of $36.8 billion and cost of services of $23.8 billion; the professional staffing company **Kelly Services, Inc.** reported net service revenues of $5.4 billion and direct costs of services of $4.4 billion; and **Alphabet, Inc.** reported revenue of $110.9 billion and cost of sales of $45.6 billion. While these companies report no inventory, the relationship of revenues to costs of revenues remains important.

Reporting Inventory Costs in the Financial Statements

To help frame our discussion of inventory, **Exhibits 7.1** and **7.2** present information from the current asset section of the balance sheet and the continuing operations section of the income statement for The Home Depot. We highlight merchandise inventories in the balance sheet as well as cost of goods sold in the income statement.

When inventory is purchased or produced, it is capitalized and carried on the balance sheet as an asset until it is sold, at which time its cost is transferred from the balance sheet to the income statement as an expense (cost of goods sold). Cost of goods sold (COGS) is then subtracted from sales revenue to yield **gross profit**:

Gross profit = Sales revenue − Cost of goods sold

The manner in which inventory costs are transferred from the balance sheet to the income statement affects both the level of inventories reported on the balance sheet and the amount of gross profit (and net income) reported on the income statement.

EXHIBIT 7.1 Balance Sheets (Current Assets Only)

THE HOME DEPOT, INC.
Consolidated Balance Sheets

($ millions)	January 28, 2018	January 29, 2017
Assets		
Current assets:		
Cash and cash equivalents	$ 3,595	$ 2,538
Receivables, net	1,952	2,029
Merchandise inventories	12,748	12,549
Other current assets	638	608
Total current assets	$18,933	$17,724

EXHIBIT 7.2 Income Statement (Continuing Operations Only)

THE HOME DEPOT, INC.
Consolidated Statement of Earnings

($ millions)	Fiscal year 2017
Net sales	$100,904
Cost of sales	66,548
Gross profit	34,356
Total operating expenses	19,675
Operating income	14,681
Interest and other, net	983
Earnings before provision for income taxes	13,698
Provision for income taxes	5,068
Net earnings	$ 8,630

Recording Inventory Costs in the Financial Statements

To illustrate the inventory purchasing and selling cycle, assume that a start-up company purchases 800 units of merchandise inventory at a cost of $4 cash per unit. We account for this transaction as follows:

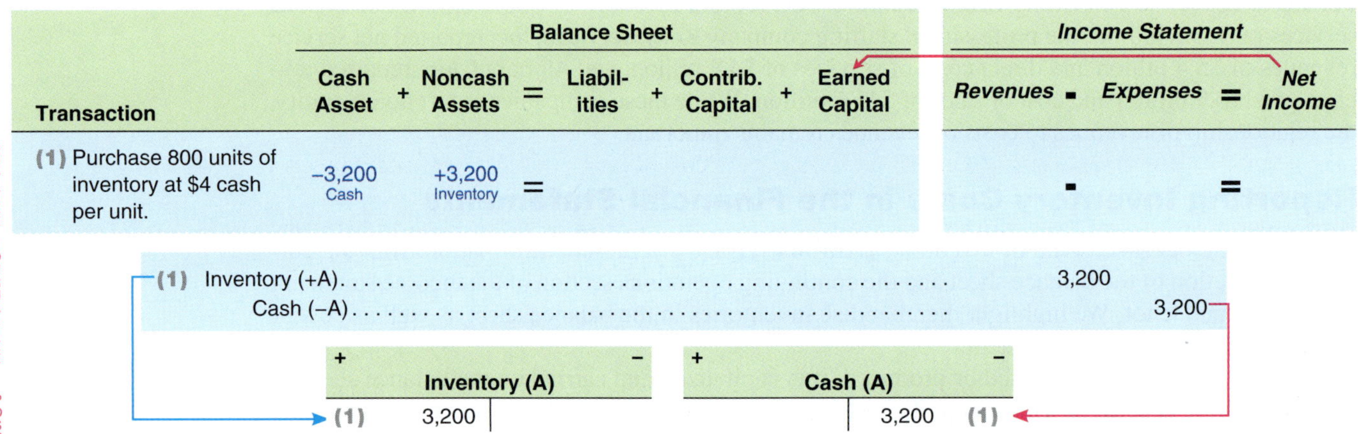

Next, assume this company sells 500 of those units for $7 cash per unit. The two following entries are required to record (a) the sales revenue and (b) the expense for the cost of the inventory sold.

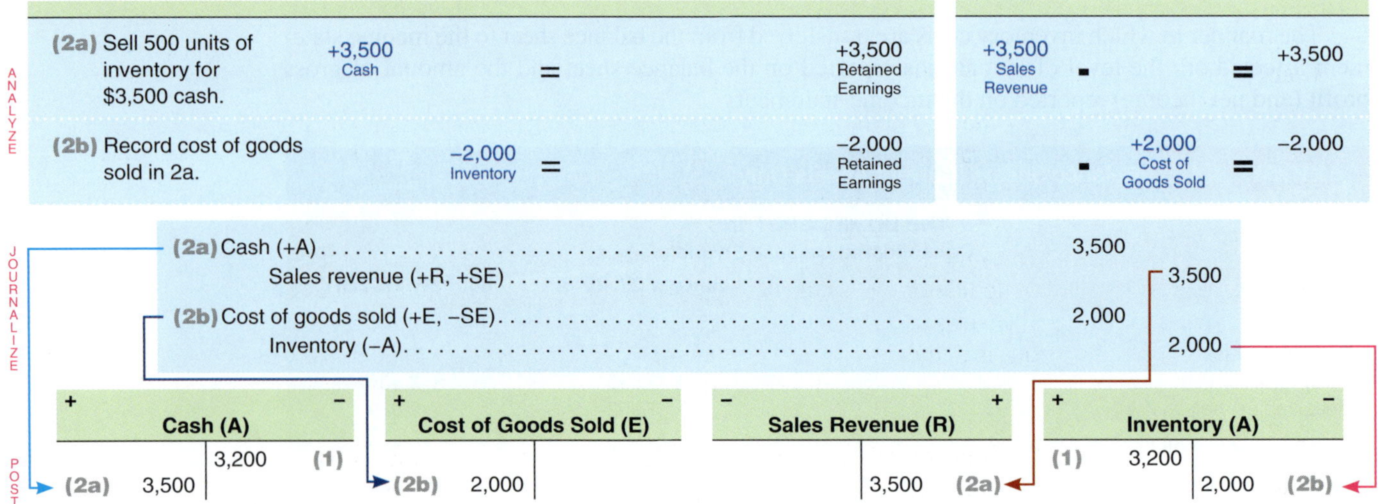

The gross profit from this sale is $1,500 ($3,500 – $2,000). Also, $1,200 worth of merchandise remains in inventory (300 units × $4 per unit).

Inventory and the Cost of Acquisition

In general, a company should recognize all inventories to which it holds legal title, and that inventory should be recognized at the cost of acquiring the inventory. On occasion, that means that the company will recognize items in inventory that are not on its premises. For instance, if a company purchases inventory from a supplier on an "FOB shipping point" basis, meaning that the purchasing company receives title to the goods as soon as they are shipped by the supplier, the purchasing company should recognize the inventory as soon as it receives notice that the goods have been shipped. A similar situation occurs when a company ships its own products to a customer, but has not yet fulfilled the requirements for recognizing revenue on the shipment. In this case, the cost of the products remains in the selling company's inventory account until revenue (and cost of goods sold) can be recognized.

FYI The term **FOB** ("free on board") **shipping point** means that title passes to the purchaser as soon as it is shipped by the seller. **FOB destination** means that the seller retains title until the item arrives at the purchaser's location.

It is also possible for a company to have physical possession of inventory items, but not to have legal title. Target Corporation, for example, reports the following in a recent 10-K.

> We routinely enter into arrangements with certain vendors whereby we do not purchase or pay for merchandise until the merchandise is ultimately sold to a guest. Activity under this program is included in sales and cost of sales in the Consolidated Statements of Operations, but the merchandise received under the program is not included in inventory in our Consolidated Statements of Financial Position because of the virtually simultaneous purchase and sale of this inventory.

Inventory is reported in the balance sheet at its cost, including any cost to acquire, transport, and prepare goods for sale. In some cases, determining the cost of inventory requires accounting for various incentives that suppliers offer to purchase more or to pay promptly. If a company qualifies for a supplier's volume discount or rebate, it should immediately recognize the effective reduction in the cost of inventory and cost of goods sold. Or, if the company purchases inventory on credit, suppliers often grant **cash discounts** to buyers if payment is made within a specified time period. Cash discounts are usually established as part of the credit terms and stated as a percentage of the purchase price. For example, credit terms of 1/10, n/30 (one-ten, net-thirty) indicate that a 1% cash discount is allowed if the payment is made within 10 days. If the cash discount is not taken, the full purchase price is due in 30 days. Cash discounts are discussed in greater detail in Chapter 9.

Inventory Reporting by Manufacturing Firms

Retail and wholesale businesses purchase merchandise for resale to customers. In contrast, a manufacturing firm produces the goods it sells. Its inventory reporting is designed to reflect this difference in the nature of its operations.

FYI Only one inventory account appears in the financial statements of a merchandiser. A manufacturer normally has three inventory accounts: Raw Materials, Work-in-Process, and Finished Goods.

Manufacturing firms typically report three categories of inventory account:

- **Raw materials inventory**—the cost of parts and materials purchased from suppliers for use in the production process. When raw materials are used in the production process, the cost of the materials used is transferred from raw materials inventory into the work-in-process inventory account.
- **Work-in-process inventory**—the cost of the inventory of partially completed goods. Work-in-process (abbreviated WIP) includes the materials used in the production of the product as well as labor cost and overhead cost. (Methods by which labor and overhead costs are assigned to products in the WIP account is a *managerial accounting* topic.) When the production process is completed, the **cost of goods produced** is transferred from WIP into the finished goods inventory account.
- **Finished goods inventory**—the cost of the stock of completed product ready for delivery to customers. When finished goods are sold, cost of goods sold is debited and finished goods inventory is credited, much the same as in a retail business.

EXHIBIT 7.3 Components of Inventory for Pfizer, Inc.

	Dec. 31, 2017
Inventories ($ millions):	
Finished goods	$2,883
Work in process	3,908
Raw materials and supplies	788
Total	$7,578

A complete illustration of the accounting process for a manufacturing business is beyond the scope of this text. However, it is useful to understand how these inventory accounts are presented in the financial statements of manufacturing firms. In some cases, each of the three categories of inventory is presented in the balance sheet. Usually, however, the balance sheet only presents the combined total of the three accounts, leaving the detail to be presented in the footnotes. Pfizer, Inc. reported inventory of $7,578 million in its balance sheet dated December 31, 2017. **Exhibit 7.3** details the components of Pfizer's inventory balance as presented in its 10-K report. It shows that work in process inventory represented the largest portion of the total inventory balance. **Exhibit 7.3** is representative of the footnote disclosure provided by many manufacturing companies.

BUSINESS INSIGHT

If a manufacturing company has an unexpected buildup of inventory, the interpretation depends on the type of inventory. A larger-than-normal buildup of finished goods would imply that the company was having difficulty getting customers to purchase its products. However, if the buildup is in work-in-process inventory, it might imply a problem with manufacturing processes, particularly if accompanied by a decrease in finished goods inventory.

2 **LO2** Account for inventory and cost of goods sold using different costing methods.

INVENTORY COSTING METHODS

The computation of cost of goods sold is important and is shown in **Exhibit 7.4**.

EXHIBIT 7.4 Cost of Goods Sold Computation

	Beginning inventory value (prior period ending balance sheet)
+	Cost of inventory purchases and/or production
	Cost of goods available for sale
−	Ending inventory value (current period balance sheet)
	Cost of goods sold (current income statement)

The cost of inventory available at the beginning of a period is a carryover from the ending inventory balance of the prior period. The costs of current period purchases of inventory (or costs of newly manufactured inventories) are added to the costs of beginning inventory on the balance sheet, yielding the total cost of goods (inventory) available for sale. Then, the total cost of goods available either ends up in cost of goods sold for the period (reported on the income statement) or is carried forward as inventory to start the next period (reported on the ending balance sheet). This cost flow is schematically shown in **Exhibit 7.5**.

Understanding the flow of inventory costs is important. If the beginning inventory plus all inventory purchased or manufactured during the period is sold, then COGS is equal to the cost of the goods available for sale. However, when inventory remains at the end of a period, companies must identify the cost of those inventories that have been sold and the cost of those inventories that remain.

EXHIBIT 7.5 Inventory Cost Flows to Financial Statements

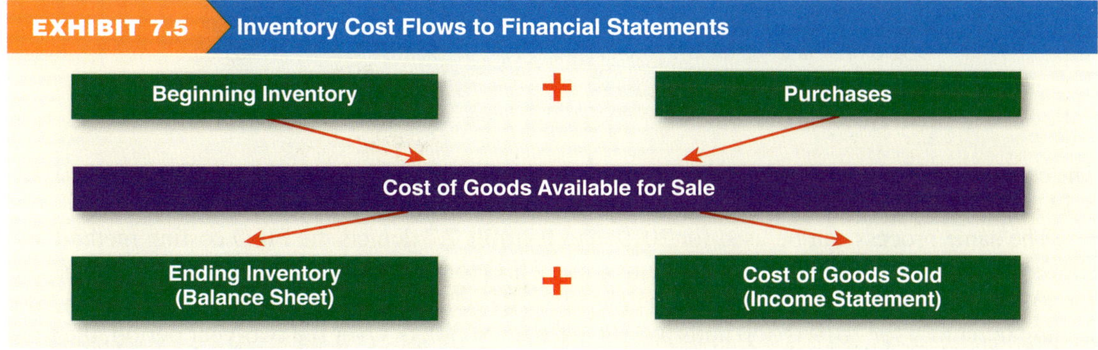

Most companies will organize the physical flow of their inventories to keep the cost of inventory management low, while minimizing the likelihood of spoilage or obsolescence. However, the accounting for inventory and cost of goods sold does not have to follow the physical flow of the units of inventory, so companies may report using a **cost flow assumption** that does not conform to the actual movement of product through the firm. (For instance, many grocery chains use last-in, first-out to account for inventory costs, but that doesn't mean that they put the newest produce out to sell while keeping the older produce back in the storeroom.)

Illustration To illustrate the possible cost flow assumptions that companies can adopt, assume that **Exhibit 7.6** reflects the inventory records of Butler Company.

EXHIBIT 7.6 Summary Inventory Records for Butler Company

		Number of Units	Cost per Unit	Total Cost	Number of Units	Price per Unit	Total Revenue
January 1, 2018	Beginning inventory . . .	500	$100	$ 50,000			
2018	Inventory purchased. . .	200	170	34,000			
	Inventory sold.				450	$250	$112,500
2019	Inventory purchased. . .	600	180	108,000			
	Inventory sold.				500	255	127,500

Butler Company began the period with inventory consisting of 500 units it purchased at a total cost of $50,000 ($100 each). During the two-year period, the company purchased an additional 200 units costing $34,000 and 600 units costing $108,000. The total cost of goods available for sale for this two-year period equals $192,000.

Tracking the number of units available for sale each year and in inventory at the end of each year is simple. However, the changing cost per unit makes it more complicated to determine the cost of goods sold and the ending inventory. The relationships depicted in **Exhibit 7.5** can hold in multiple ways, depending on the cost flow assumption chosen. Three inventory costing methods are acceptable under U.S. GAAP (though only two are permitted under IFRS, as we discuss later).[2]

First-In, First-Out (FIFO)

The **first-in, first-out (FIFO)** inventory costing method transfers costs from inventory in the order that they were initially recorded. That is, FIFO assumes that the first costs recorded in inventory (first-in) are the first costs transferred from inventory (first-out) to cost of goods sold. Conversely, the costs of the last units purchased are the costs that remain in inventory at year-end. Applying FIFO to the data in **Exhibit 7.6** means that the costs relating to the 450 units sold are all taken from its *beginning* inventory, which consists of 500 units. The company's 2018 cost of goods sold and gross profit, using FIFO, is computed as follows:

FYI First-in, first-out (FIFO) assumes that goods are used in the order in which they are purchased; the inventory remaining represents the most recent purchases.

[2] Of the firms in the Standard and Poor's 500 Index as of December 31, 2017, 12.95% have a LIFO reserve reported on Compustat (database of annual reports). A few additional firms may be on LIFO but have a zero reserve.

Sales	$112,500
COGS (450 @ $100 each)	45,000
Gross profit	$ 67,500

The cost remaining in inventory and reported on its 2018 year-end balance sheet is $39,000 ($50,000 + $34,000 – $45,000; also computed 50 × $100 + 200 × $170).

The same process can be used for 2019, and **Exhibit 7.7** depicts the FIFO costing method and shows the resulting financial statement items using FIFO for 2018 and 2019. FIFO cost of goods sold for 2019 is 50 units at $100 each plus 200 units at $170 each plus 250 units at $180 each, or $84,000. Ending inventory for 2019 is 350 units at $180 each, or $63,000. Over the two-year period, the total cost of goods available for sale of $192,000 is either recognized as cost of goods sold ($45,000 + $84,000 = $129,000) or remains in ending inventory ($63,000).

EXHIBIT 7.7 Butler Company using FIFO Inventory Costing

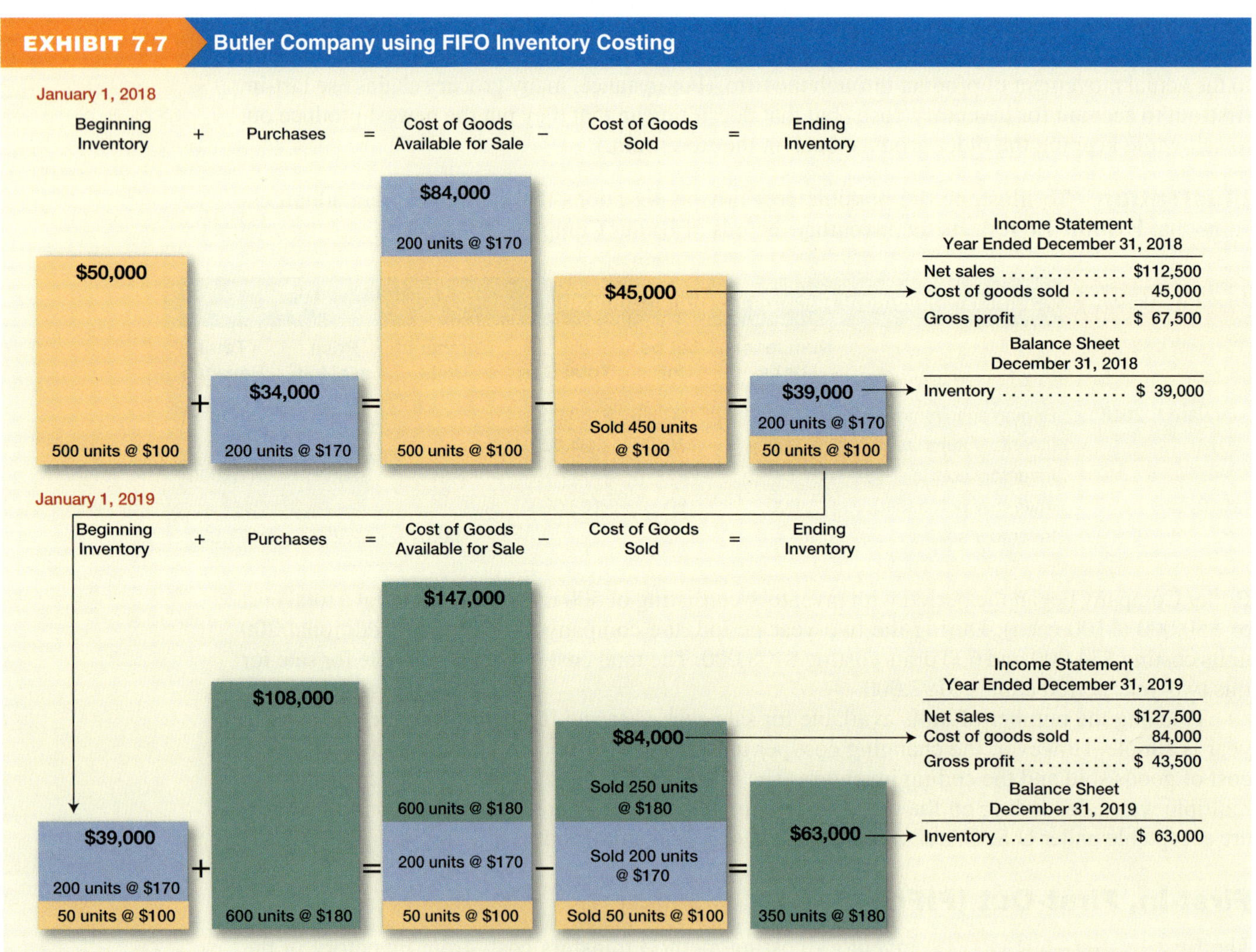

Last-In, First-Out (LIFO)

FYI Last-in, first-out (LIFO) matches the cost of the last goods purchased against revenue.

The **last-in, first-out (LIFO)** inventory costing method transfers to cost of goods sold the most recent costs that were recorded in inventory. That is, we assume that the most recent costs recorded in inventory (last-in) are the first costs transferred from inventory (first-out). Conversely, the costs of the first units purchased are the costs that remain in inventory at year-end. Butler Company's 2018 cost of goods sold and gross profit, using LIFO, are computed as follows:

Sales.	$112,500
COGS: (200 @ $170 each = $34,000)	
(250 @ $100 each = $25,000).	59,000
Gross profit.	$ 53,500

The cost remaining in inventory and reported on its 2018 balance sheet is $25,000 ($50,000 + $34,000 – $59,000; also computed 250 × $100).

The same process can be used for 2019, and **Exhibit 7.8** depicts the LIFO costing method and shows the resulting financial statement values using LIFO for both years. LIFO cost of goods sold for 2019 is 500 units at $180 each, or $90,000. Ending inventory is 250 units at $100 each plus 100 units at $180 each, or $43,000. Again, the two-year total cost of goods available for sale of $192,000 is either recognized as cost of goods sold ($59,000 + $90,000 = $149,000) or remains in inventory ($43,000).

EXHIBIT 7.8 Butler Company using LIFO Inventory Costing

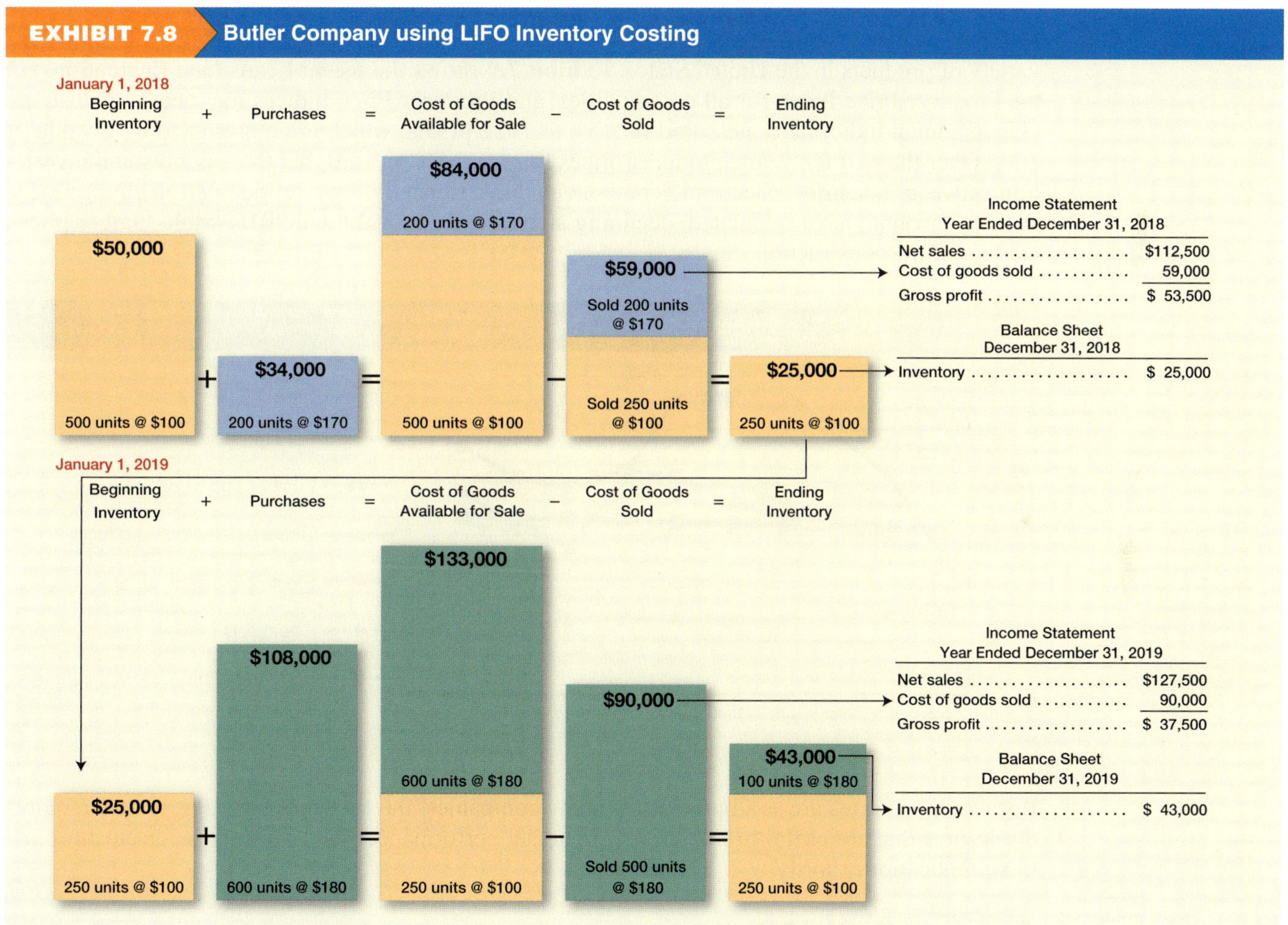

The exhibit shows that **LIFO layers** of inventories added in each year are kept separately. So, the ending inventory in 2019 consists of a pre-2018 layer of 250 units at $100 each plus a 2019 layer of 100 units at $180 each. When unit sales exceed purchases (as we discuss in the appendix), the first costs carried to cost of goods sold are those purchased in the current year, followed by the most recent layer of LIFO inventory and working down to the oldest layers. So, the 2018 beginning inventory value of $100 per unit remains in LIFO inventory as long as there are 250 units remaining at the end of the year. One aspect of this flow assumption is that reported LIFO inventory values can be significantly lower than the current cost of acquiring the same inventory.

LIFO inventory costing is always applied on a periodic, annual basis. This means that Butler's cost of goods sold and ending inventory for 2019 do not depend on the timing of the sales and purchases within the year. Inventory levels might be drawn down below 250 units *during* the year, but the 250 unit LIFO layer at $100 each remains in ending inventory as long as inventory is built up to 250 units by the *end* of the year.

Inventory Costing and Price Changes

There are several important aspects of inventory costing that are illustrated by the Butler Company example. First, both LIFO and FIFO are historical cost methods, though they allocate the costs of inventory differently. All costs are accounted for, but in different ways.

Second, the differences between LIFO and FIFO arise when the costs of inventory change over time. In general, LIFO puts more recent costs into cost of goods sold expense, so LIFO cost of goods sold is higher than FIFO cost of goods sold (and gross profit correspondingly lower) when the costs of inventory are rising over time. This phenomenon can be seen in years 2018 and 2019 for Butler Company. If the costs of inventory are falling, then FIFO cost of goods sold exceeds LIFO cost of goods sold.

One place where we can observe the cost trends of acquiring inventory is in the U.S. Bureau of Labor Statistics' Producer Price Indices. These indices track the costs of producing a wide variety of products in the United States. **Exhibit 7.9** shows the recent trends (and fluctuations) in the Producer Price Index for all commodities, and Producer Price Indices for specific industries. (These annual indices are measured relative to 1982 prices, which are represented by a value of 100.) Over the past ten years, producer prices have trended upward, but there is substantial variation between industries. Electronic components have trended down, refined petroleum products, such as gasoline, have fluctuated, declining significantly in 2014 and 2015, while lumber prices tend to follow construction trends.

EXHIBIT 7.9 Recent Producer Price History

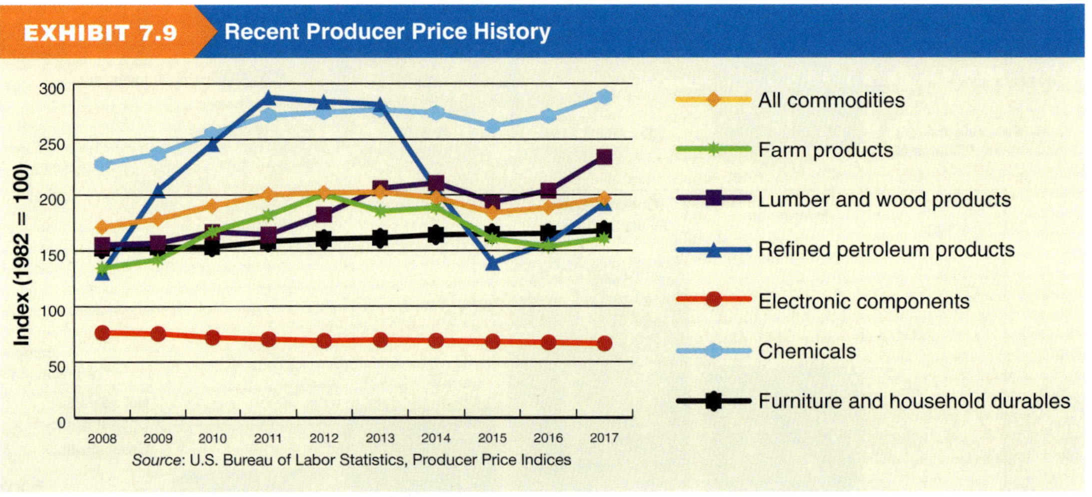

Source: U.S. Bureau of Labor Statistics, Producer Price Indices

Because inventories are so important for many companies, the financial reporting system requires disclosures that are useful in interpreting financial performance. We turn to those disclosures and their implications shortly.

Average Cost (AC)

FYI Average cost values inventory on the basis of the average cost of all similar goods available during the period.

The **average cost (AC)** method computes the 2018 cost of goods sold as an average of the cost to purchase all of the inventories that were available for sale during the period as follows:

Sales.	$112,500
COGS (450 @ $120 [{$50,000 + $34,000}/700 units] each)	54,000
Gross profit.	$ 58,500

The average cost of $120 per unit is determined from the total cost of goods available for sale divided by the number of units available for sale ($84,000/700 units). The cost remaining in inventory and reported on its 2018 balance sheet is $30,000 ($84,000 – $54,000; also computed 250 × $120).

When average cost is applied to the future years, the beginning inventory balance's average cost is again averaged with the inventory acquisitions made during the year. This new average is used to assign costs to that year's ending inventory and cost of goods sold. For the Butler Company, the average cost is $120 for 2018 and $162.35 (rounded) for 2019. The average cost for 2019 is the opening inventory balance plus the period's purchases ($30,000 + $108,000) divided by the total number of units available for sale (250 + 600). So, 2019 cost of goods sold is 500 units at $162.35 each, and ending inventory is 350 units at that same average cost. **Exhibit 7.10** depicts the average cost method and shows the resulting financial statement values using average cost for both years.

EXHIBIT 7.10 Butler Company using Average Cost Inventory Costing

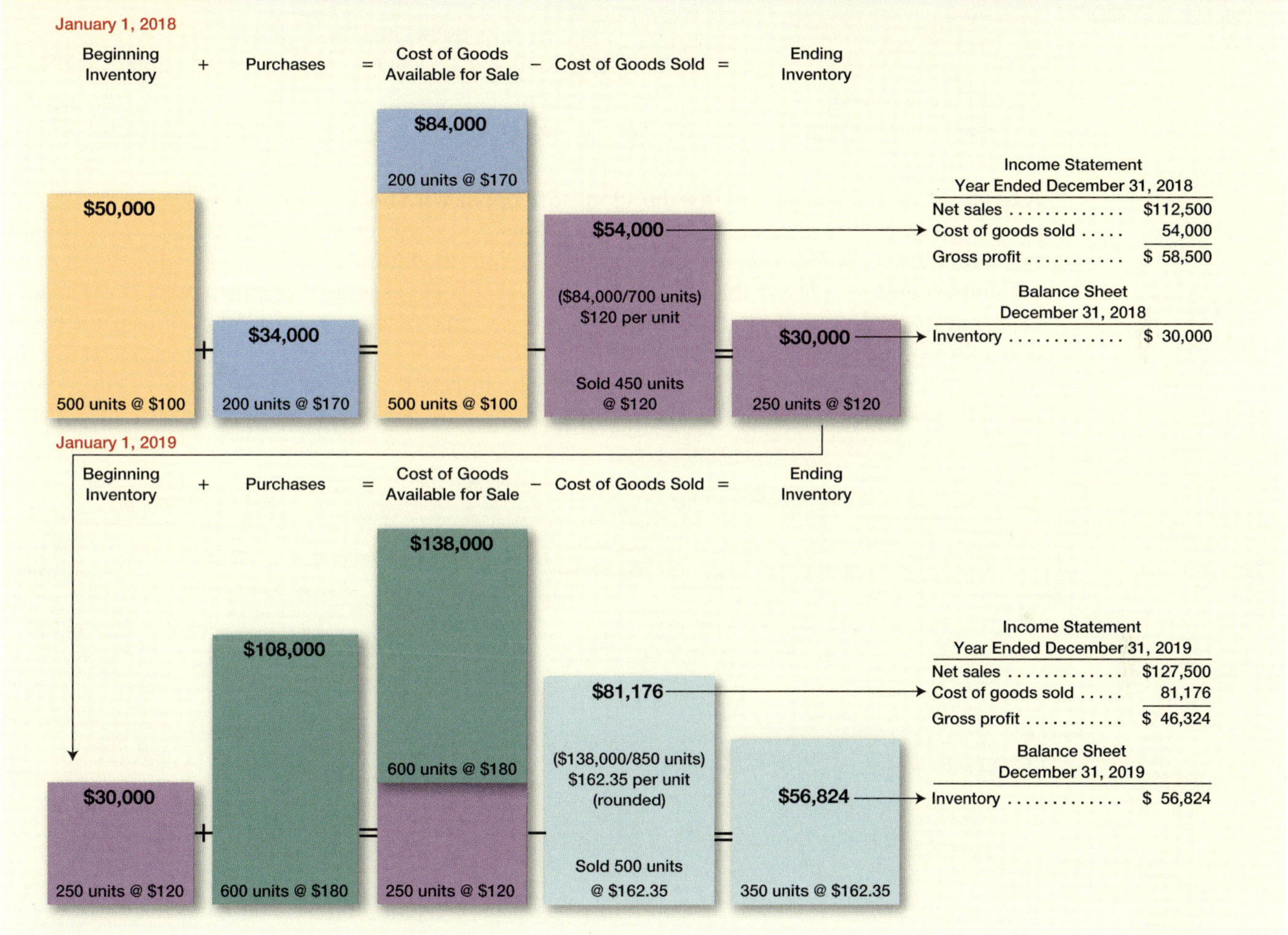

January 1, 2018

Beginning Inventory + Purchases = Cost of Goods Available for Sale − Cost of Goods Sold = Ending Inventory

$50,000
500 units @ $100

+ $34,000
200 units @ $170

= $84,000
200 units @ $170
500 units @ $100

− $54,000
($84,000/700 units)
$120 per unit
Sold 450 units @ $120

= $30,000
250 units @ $120

Income Statement Year Ended December 31, 2018	
Net sales	$112,500
Cost of goods sold	54,000
Gross profit	$ 58,500

Balance Sheet December 31, 2018	
Inventory	$ 30,000

January 1, 2019

Beginning Inventory + Purchases = Cost of Goods Available for Sale − Cost of Goods Sold = Ending Inventory

$30,000
250 units @ $120

+ $108,000
600 units @ $180

= $138,000
600 units @ $180
250 units @ $120

− $81,176
($138,000/850 units)
$162.35 per unit (rounded)
Sold 500 units @ $162.35

= $56,824
350 units @ $162.35

Income Statement Year Ended December 31, 2019	
Net sales	$127,500
Cost of goods sold	81,176
Gross profit	$ 46,324

Balance Sheet December 31, 2019	
Inventory	$ 56,824

Lower of Cost or Net Realizable Value

LO3 Apply the lower of cost or net realizable value rule to value inventory.

3

Companies are required to write down the carrying amount of inventories on the balance sheet, *if* the reported cost (using FIFO, for example) exceeds the net realizable value. This process is called reporting inventories at the **lower of cost or net realizable value (LCNRV)**. Should the net realizable value be less than reported cost, the inventories must be written down from cost to net realizable value, resulting in the following financial statement effects.

- Inventory book value is written down to current net realizable value, reducing total assets.
- Inventory write-down is reflected as an expense (part of cost of goods sold) on the income statement, reducing current period gross profit, income, and equity.

The most common occurrence of inventory write-downs is in connection with restructuring activities. These write-downs are either included in cost of goods sold or on a separate line in the income statement.

FYI If inventory declines in value below its original cost, for whatever reason, the inventory is written down to reflect this loss.

The write-down of inventories can potentially shift income from one period to another. If, for example, inventories were written down below current replacement cost (too conservative), future gross profit would be increased as lower future costs would be reflected in cost of goods sold. GAAP anticipates this possibility by requiring that inventories not be written down below a floor that is equal to net realizable value less a normal markup. Although this does allow some discretion (and the ability to manage income), the net realizable value and markup values must be confirmed by the company's auditors.

FYI Standards require the consistent application of costing methods from one period to another.

Illustration To illustrate the lower of cost or net realizable value rule, assume Home Depot has the following items in its current period ending inventory:

Item	Quantity	Cost per Unit	Net Realizable Value	LCNRV per Unit	Total LCNRV
Spools of copper wire	250	$10	$15	$10	250 × $10 = $2,500
Sheets of wood paneling	500	$ 8	$ 6	$ 6	500 × $ 6 = $3,000

A write-down is not necessary for the spools of copper wire because the net realizable value ($15 per unit) is higher than the acquisition cost ($10 per unit). However, the 500 sheets of wood paneling should be recorded in the current period's ending inventory at the net realizable value of $6 per unit because it is lower than the acquisition cost of $8 per unit. When the net realizable value of inventory declines below its acquisition cost, we must record a write-down. Before the write-down, inventory is recorded at cost of $6,500. With the write-down of $1,000, inventory after the write-down is recorded at LCNRV of $5,500. The effects of this write-down and corresponding journal entries follow:

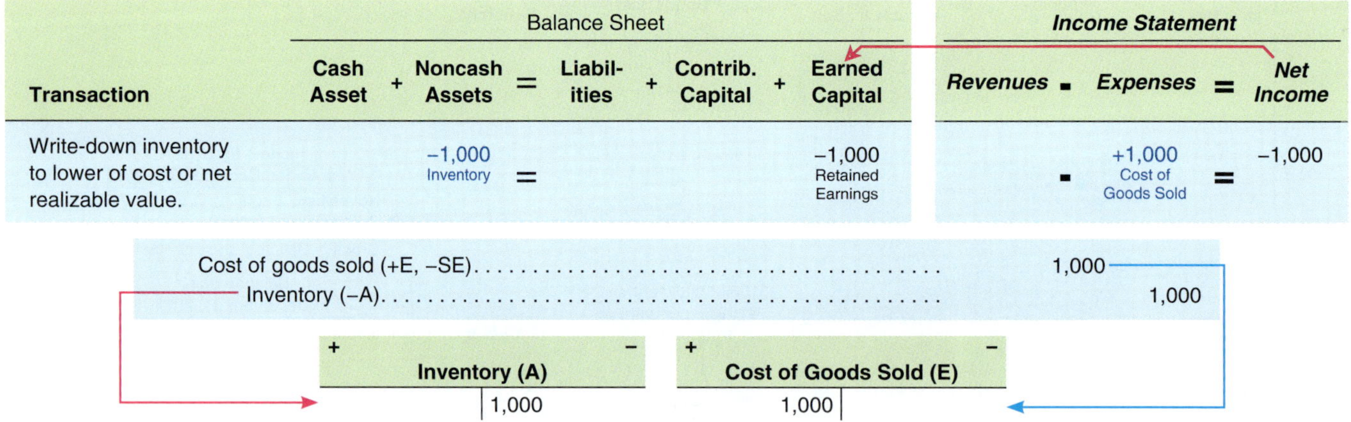

A GLOBAL PERSPECTIVE

Under U.S. GAAP, inventory that has been written down cannot be revalued later at higher levels even if the net realizable value of that inventory increases. IFRS, on the other hand, does allow companies to reverse the write-down of the inventory up to the acquisition cost if market values warrant. The revaluation results in a debit to Inventory and a credit to Cost of Goods Sold. The option to revalue inventory after a write-down differs across countries.

MID-CHAPTER REVIEW

PART 1

At the beginning of the current period, Hutton Company holds 1,000 units of its only product with a per-unit cost of $18. A summary of purchases during the current period follows:

	Units	Unit Cost	Cost
Beginning Inventory	1,000	$18.00	$18,000
Purchases: #1	1,800	18.25	32,850
#2	800	18.50	14,800
#3	1,200	19.00	22,800
Goods available for sale	4,800		$88,450

During the current period, Hutton sells 2,800 units.

Required

1. Assume that Hutton uses the first-in, first-out (FIFO) method. Compute the cost of goods sold for the current period and the ending inventory balance.
2. Assume that Hutton uses the last-in, first-out (LIFO) method. Compute the cost of goods sold for the current period and the ending inventory balance.
3. Assume that Hutton uses the average cost (AC) method. Compute the cost of goods sold for the current period and the ending inventory balance.
4. As manager, which one of these three inventory costing methods would you choose:
   a. To reflect what is probably the physical flow of goods? Explain.
   b. To minimize income taxes for the period? Explain.
5. Assume that Hutton utilizes the LIFO method and instead of purchasing lot #3, the company allows its inventory level to decline and delays purchasing lot #3 until the next period. Compute cost of goods sold under this scenario and discuss the effect of end-of-year purchases under LIFO.
6. Record the effects of each of the following summary transactions *a* and *b* in the financial statement effects template, prepare journal entries, set up T-accounts for each of the accounts used, and post the journal entries to those T-accounts.
   a. Purchased inventory for $70,450 cash.
   b. Sold $50,850 of inventory for $85,000 cash.

PART 2

Venner Company had the following inventory at December 31, 2019.

	Quantity	Unit Price Cost	NRV
Fans			
Model X1	300	$18	$19
Model X2	250	22	24
Model X3	400	29	26
Heaters			
Model B7	500	24	28
Model B8	290	35	32
Model B9	100	41	38

Required

1. Determine ending inventory by applying the lower of cost or NRV rule to
   a. Each item of inventory.
   b. Each major category of inventory.
   c. Total inventory.
2. Which of the LCNRV procedures from requirement 1 results in the lowest net income for 2019? Explain.

The solution to this review problem can be found on pages 366–369.

FINANCIAL STATEMENT EFFECTS AND DISCLOSURE

FYI Standards require financial statement disclosure of (1) the composition of the inventory (in the balance sheet or a separate schedule in the notes), (2) significant or unusual inventory financing arrangements, and (3) inventory costing methods employed (which can differ for different types of inventory).

The notes to the financial statements describe, at least in general terms, the inventory accounting method used by a company. To illustrate, The Home Depot reports $12,748 million in merchandise inventory on its January 28, 2018, balance sheet as a current asset. The following note was taken from that 10-K report:

> The majority of our merchandise inventories are stated at the lower of cost (first-in, first-out) or market, as determined by the retail inventory method. As the inventory retail value is adjusted regularly to reflect market conditions, the inventory valued using the retail method approximates the lower of cost or market. Certain subsidiaries, including retail operations in Canada and Mexico, and distribution centers, record merchandise inventories at the lower of cost or market, as determined by a cost method. These merchandise inventories represent approximately 30% of the total merchandise inventories balance. We evaluate the inventory valued using a cost method at the end of each quarter to ensure that it is carried at the lower of cost or net realizable value. The valuation allowance for merchandise inventories valued under a cost method was not material to our consolidated financial statements at the end of fiscal 2017 or 2016.
>
> Independent physical inventory counts or cycle counts are taken on a regular basis in each store and distribution center to ensure that amounts reflected in merchandise inventories are properly stated. Shrink (or in the case of excess inventory, "swell") is the difference between the recorded amount of inventory and the physical inventory. We calculate shrink based on actual inventory losses occurring as a result of physical inventory counts during each fiscal period and estimated inventory losses occurring between physical inventory counts. The estimate for shrink occurring in the interim period between physical inventory counts is calculated on a store-specific basis based on recent shrink results and current trends in the business.

This note includes several items that would be of interest to financial statement users:

1. The Home Depot uses the FIFO method to determine the cost of most of its inventory suggesting several methods are likely to be in use.
2. Inventory is reported at the lower of cost or net realizable value, and the amount of write-down (the valuation allowance) was not material at the financial statement date.
3. The company periodically takes a physical count of inventory to identify "shrink." Shrink refers to the loss of inventory due to theft, breakage or damage, spoilage (for perishable goods), or other losses, as well as inaccurate records.

When businesses adjust inventory balances for shrink, the loss is debited to cost of goods sold. Hence, cost of goods sold expense on the income statement includes the actual cost of products sold during the period plus the loss due to shrink as well as losses resulting from lower of cost or market adjustments and discounts lost.

Another illustration of inventory disclosure is taken from the notes of **Kaiser Aluminum Corporation**. Kaiser reports an inventory of $207.9 million on its December 31, 2017, balance sheet. The following note was taken from its 2017 10-K report ($ millions):

> *Inventories.* Inventories are stated at the lower of cost or market value. On March 31, 2016, we recorded a lower of cost or market inventory write-down of $4.9 million, as a result of a decrease in our net realizable value of inventory. The net realizable value reflected commitments as of that date from customers to purchase our inventory at prices that exceeded the Midwest Transaction Price ("Midwest Price"), which reflects the primary aluminum supply/demand dynamics in North America, reduced by an approximate normal profit margin. There were no additional lower of cost or market inventory adjustments since the quarter ended March 31, 2016.
>
> Finished products, work-in-process and raw material inventories are stated on the last-in, first-out ("LIFO") basis. At December 31, 2017, the current cost of our inventory exceeded its stated LIFO value by $24.3 million. The stated LIFO value of our inventory represented its net realizable value (less a normal profit margin) and exceeded the current cost of our inventory by $8.5 million at December 31, 2016. Other inventories are stated on the first-in, first-out basis and consist of operating supplies, which are materials and supplies to be consumed during the production process. Inventory costs consist of material, labor and manufacturing overhead, including depreciation.

There are several interesting items disclosed in Kaiser's note:

1. Kaiser uses LIFO to report the cost of its raw materials, work in process, and finished goods inventory, but uses average cost for supplies and other. Neither U.S. GAAP nor tax authorities such as the IRS require the use of a single inventory costing method. That is, companies are allowed to, and frequently do, use different inventory costing methods for different categories of inventory. In addition, multinational companies may use one costing method in the United States and a different method for foreign inventory stocks.
2. Kaiser reports inventory values at the lower of cost or market, where "market" is defined as the net realizable value. The current cost of its inventory (which is approximately equal to the FIFO value) differs from the LIFO cost. In 2017, the current cost was $24.3 million higher than the LIFO cost, while in 2016, the current cost was $8.5 million lower than LIFO. Companies using LIFO are required to report the difference between the LIFO cost and current value—determined either as market value or replacement cost or as the FIFO cost. The difference between the ending inventory's FIFO cost (or current cost) and its LIFO cost is called the **LIFO reserve**.

Why do companies disclose such details on inventory, and why is so much attention paid to inventory in financial statement analysis? First, the magnitude of a company's investment in inventory is often large—affecting both balance sheets and income statements. Second, risks of inventory losses are often high, as they are tied to technical obsolescence and consumer tastes. Third, it can provide insight into future performance—both good and bad. Fourth, high inventory levels result in substantial costs for the company, such as:

- Financing costs to purchase inventories (when not purchased on credit)
- Storage costs of inventories (such as warehousing and related facilities)
- Handling costs of inventories (including wages)
- Insurance costs of inventories

Consequently, companies seek to keep inventories at levels that balance these costs against the cost of insufficient inventory (stock-out and resulting lost sales and delays in production, as machines and employees sit idle awaiting inventories to process).

Next, we turn our focus on the effects of the different inventory costing assumptions on the financial statements.

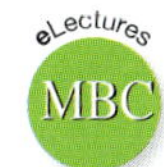

Financial Statement Effects of Inventory Costing

LO4 Evaluate how inventory costing affects management decisions and outsiders' interpretations of financial statements.

The three inventory costing methods described a few pages earlier yield differing levels of gross profit for our illustrative example, as shown in **Exhibit 7.11**.

We emphasize that, even though the various methods produce different financial statements, the underlying events are the same. That is, different accounting methods can make similar situations seem more different than they really are.

LIFO Reserve **Exhibit 7.11** demonstrates one of the income statement/balance sheet links that proves useful in analyzing financial statements. In the beginning inventory for 2018, LIFO and FIFO start from the same point—500 units at $100 each. But during 2018, FIFO would record cost of goods sold that is $14,000 less than LIFO ($45,000 versus $59,000). During 2018, LIFO put $14,000 more into cost of goods sold than FIFO did, but that also means that LIFO put $14,000 less into ending inventory. We can see that the LIFO reserve has grown from zero to $14,000, the same amount. This relationship continues in 2019: the LIFO reserve increased by $6,000 (from $14,000 to $20,000), and the LIFO cost of goods sold was $6,000 greater than the FIFO cost of goods sold ($90,000 versus $84,000). The LIFO reserve equals the ending inventory's FIFO cost less LIFO cost, but it is also the *cumulative* difference between LIFO and FIFO cost of goods sold. The *change* in the LIFO reserve is the difference between LIFO and FIFO cost of goods sold for the current period.

FYI If ending inventory is misstated, then (1) the inventory, retained earnings, working capital, and current ratio in the balance sheet are misstated, and (2) the cost of goods sold and net income in the income statement are misstated.

So, if Butler Company chose to report using LIFO, we could estimate what the company's FIFO cost of goods sold would have been by seeing how the LIFO reserve changed.

FIFO cost of goods sold = LIFO cost of goods sold − Change in the LIFO reserve

4

EXHIBIT 7.11 Financial Statement Effects of Inventory Costing Methods for Butler Company

		FIFO	LIFO	Average Cost
January 1, 2018	**Balance Sheet**			
	Beginning inventory	$ 50,000	$ 50,000	$ 50,000
	LIFO Reserve	—	—	—
Year Ended 2018	**Income Statement**			
	Revenue	$112,500	$112,500	$112,500
	Cost of goods sold:			
	Beginning inventory	50,000	50,000	50,000
	Add: Purchases	34,000	34,000	34,000
	Goods available for sale	84,000	84,000	84,000
	Subtract: Ending inventory	39,000	25,000	30,000
	Cost of goods sold	45,000	59,000	54,000
	Gross profit	67,500	53,500	58,500
	Selling, general and administrative expenses (assumed number)	10,000	10,000	10,000
	Income before income taxes	57,500	43,500	48,500
	Income tax expense (25%)	14,375	10,875	12,125
	Net income	$ 43,125	$ 32,625	$ 36,375
December 31, 2018	**Balance Sheet**			
	Ending inventory	$ 39,000	$ 25,000	$ 30,000
	LIFO Reserve	—	$ 14,000	—
Year Ended 2019	**Income Statement**			
	Revenue	$127,500	$127,500	$127,500
	Cost of goods sold:			
	Beginning inventory	39,000	25,000	30,000
	Add: Purchases	108,000	108,000	108,000
	Goods available for sale	147,000	133,000	138,000
	Subtract: Ending inventory	63,000	43,000	56,824
	Cost of goods sold	84,000	90,000	81,176
	Gross profit	43,500	37,500	46,324
	Selling, general and administrative expenses (assumed number)	10,000	10,000	10,000
	Income before income taxes	33,500	27,500	36,324
	Income tax expense (25%)	8,375	6,875	9,081
	Net income	$ 25,125	$ 20,625	$ 27,243
December 31, 2019	**Balance Sheet**			
	Ending inventory	63,000	43,000	56,824
	LIFO Reserve	—	20,000	—

That relationship proves useful if we want to compare Butler Company's gross profit to that of another company using FIFO. A changes in the LIFO reserve also provides some information about how a company's inventory costs changed over the period.

Income Statement Effects The income differences between inventory accounting methods are a function of two factors. First is the speed and direction of inventory cost changes. For Butler Company, inventory costs have increased from $100 per unit to $180 per unit in a two-year period. If costs increased more slowly, the difference between LIFO and FIFO would decrease. And, if costs decreased, the differences would reverse: FIFO cost of goods sold would be greater than LIFO cost of goods sold.

The second factor determining the differences is the length of time inventory is held by the company. If Butler Company were able to operate with zero inventory (or at least begin and end the reporting period with zero inventory), the three inventory accounting methods would yield exactly the same cost of goods sold. On the other hand, if inventory must be held for a long period, the differences would increase.

Effects of Changing Costs When the cost of a company's products is changing, management usually makes corresponding changes in the prices it charges for those products. If costs are declining, competitive pressures are likely to push down the prices customers are willing to pay. If costs are increasing, the company will try to increase prices to recover at least some of the greater cost. When costs fluctuate (for example, for a commodity), management may act to cause its prices to fluctuate in an effort to maintain its target profit margin.[3]

If costs and prices are rising, then FIFO reports a higher gross margin, because the costs of older, lower-cost inventory are being matched against current selling prices. For tax purposes, the company would prefer to use LIFO because it would decrease gross profit and decrease taxable income. If Butler Company were subject to a 25% income tax rate, the use of LIFO rather than FIFO reduces taxes by $3,500 in 2018 ($14,375 – $10,875 in **Exhibit 7.11**, or 25% of the $14,000 difference in 2018 cost of goods sold) and by $1,500 in 2019 ($8,375 – $6,875 in **Exhibit 7.11**, or 25% of the $6,000 difference in 2019 cost of goods sold). In total over the two years, using LIFO (rather than FIFO) would reduce Butler's tax bill by $5,000 (which equals 25% of the $20,000 LIFO reserve at the end of 2019).

In the United States, LIFO is a popular tax method for accounting for inventories that have an upward trend in costs. But, the Internal Revenue Service has imposed a LIFO conformity requirement. If Butler Company is using LIFO for tax reporting, it must use LIFO for reporting to its shareholders. For inventories with a decreasing trend in costs, FIFO reduces the amount of taxes paid. FIFO is allowed by the Internal Revenue Service, but there is no corresponding conformity requirement for firms that use FIFO.

FYI When a company adopts LIFO in its tax filings, the company is required to use LIFO for reporting to its shareholders (in its 10-K). This requirement is known as the LIFO conformity rule.

Balance Sheet Effects The ending inventory using LIFO for our illustration is less than that reported using FIFO. In prolonged periods of rising costs, using LIFO yields ending inventories that are markedly lower than FIFO. As a result, balance sheets using LIFO do not accurately represent the cost that a company would incur to replace its current investment in inventories.

Kaiser, for example, reported that the current value of its inventory was $24.3 million higher than the LIFO cost at the end of 2017. That is, the amount presented in its balance sheet was understated (relative to current value) by more than $24 million. For purposes of analysis, the value of the LIFO reserve can be viewed as an **unrealized holding gain**—a gain resulting from holding inventory as prices are rising. That is, there is a holding gain due to rising inventory costs that has not been recorded in the financial statements. This gain is not recognized until the inventory is sold. In its December 31, 2017, balance sheet, Kaiser reported current assets of $656.6 million and current liabilities of $173.1 million, for a current ratio of $656.6 ÷ $173.1, or about 3.79. However, Kaiser's inventory is not reported at an up-to-date amount, while the accounts payable would reflect the current prices owed to suppliers. Therefore, an improved measure of the current ratio would be [$656.6 + $24.3] ÷ $173.1, or about 3.93.

In contrast, by assigning the most recently purchased inventory items to ending inventory, FIFO costing tends to approximate current value in the balance sheet. Hence, companies using FIFO tend not to have large unrealized inventory holding gains. However, if prices fall, companies using FIFO are more likely to adjust inventory values to the lower of cost or net realizable value.

FYI Some companies highlight this in their disclosures. For example, another company that uses LIFO, Chevron Corporation, mentions the current ratio effect in the notes to their statements saying "The current ratio was adversely affected by the fact that Chevron's inventories are valued on a last-in, first-out basis."

Cash Flow Effects The increased gross profit using FIFO results in higher pretax income and, consequently, higher taxes payable (assuming FIFO is also used for tax reporting). Conversely, the use of LIFO in an inflationary environment results in a lower tax liability.

Use of LIFO has reduced the dollar amount of Kaiser inventories by $24.3 million, resulting in a cumulative increase in cost of goods sold and a cumulative decrease in gross profit and pretax profit of that same amount.[4] The decrease in cumulative pretax profits has lowered Kaiser's tax bill over the life of the company by roughly $6.075 million ($24.3 million × 25% assumed corporate tax rate), which has increased Kaiser's cumulative operating cash flow by that same amount. The increased cash flow from tax savings is often cited as a compelling reason for management to adopt LIFO.

[3] LIFO has a reporting advantage when inventory costs fluctuate, in that it matches current period costs against current period revenues. For a company that holds one quarter's worth of inventory, FIFO matches the costs from three months ago against current period revenues. Such a "mismatch" might make it difficult for management to convey its success in maintaining its current profit margin.

[4] Cost of Goods Sold = Beginning Inventories + Purchases – Ending Inventories. Thus, as ending inventories decrease, cost of goods sold increases.

Adjusting the Balance Sheet to FIFO For analysis purposes, we can use the LIFO reserve to adjust the balance sheet and income statement to achieve comparability between companies that utilize different inventory costing methods. For example, if we wanted to compare Kaiser with another company using FIFO, we add the LIFO reserve to its LIFO inventory. As explained above, this $24.3 million increase in 2017 inventories increases its cumulative pretax profits by $24.3 million and taxes by $6.075 million. Thus, the balance sheet adjustments involve increasing inventories by $24.3 million, tax liabilities by $6.075 million, and retained earnings by the remaining after-tax amount of $18.225 million (computed as $24.3 million – $6.075 million).

A GLOBAL PERSPECTIVE

One of the important differences in inventory accounting between U.S. GAAP and IFRS is that the latter does not allow the use of last-in, first-out (LIFO) accounting. Only FIFO and Average Cost are allowed for companies reporting under IFRS.

An analyst comparing a U.S. GAAP company to an IFRS company would need to keep an eye on these inventory differences and, when necessary, do the conversions described in the preceding paragraphs. While FIFO firms are not required to disclose what they would have looked like under LIFO, LIFO firms must disclose enough information to do a rough approximation of what they would have looked like under FIFO—making for an improved comparison with an IFRS company.

The fact that IFRS does not allow LIFO—combined with the U.S. Internal Revenue Service's conformity requirement—creates a dilemma if the United States were to adopt IFRS. For instance, if Kaiser were to have adopted IFRS for fiscal year 2017, reporting FIFO inventory and cost of goods sold in subsequent financial reports, the IRS would consider that Kaiser had given up its LIFO election and would require payment of the $6.075 million in taxes that had been deferred by the use of LIFO. This concern often appears in companies' comment letters to the Securities and Exchange Commission on the proposed move to IFRS in the United States.

It is also worth noting that when comparing companies in the same industry, accounting choices can differ. For example, GM and Ford use LIFO while Honda, a Japanese firm, uses FIFO.

Adjusting the Income Statement to FIFO To adjust the income statement from LIFO to FIFO, we use the *change* in the LIFO reserve. For Kaiser, the LIFO reserve changed from $8.5 million in 2016 to $24.3 million in 2017, an increase of $15.8 million. To adjust the income statement to FIFO, we subtract $15.8 million from the cost of goods sold (reported using LIFO) and add the same amount to gross profit and pretax income. To estimate net income, we need to adjust for income taxes. Assuming a corporate tax rate of 25%, the use of LIFO provides Kaiser with tax savings of $3.95 million ($15.8 million × 25%). Thus, 2017 net income using FIFO would be higher by $11.85 million ($15.8 million – $3.95 million).

RESEARCH INSIGHT

LIFO and Stock Prices The value-relevance of inventory disclosures depends at least partly on whether investors rely more on the income statement or the balance sheet to assess future cash flows. Under LIFO, cost of goods sold reflects current costs, whereas FIFO ending inventory reflects current costs. This implies that LIFO enhances the usefulness of the income statement to the detriment of the balance sheet. This trade-off partly motivates the required LIFO reserve disclosure (the adjustment necessary to restate LIFO ending inventory and cost of good sold to FIFO).

Research suggests that LIFO-based income statements better reflect stock prices than do pro forma FIFO income statements that are constructed using the LIFO reserve. Research also shows a negative relation between stock prices and LIFO reserve—meaning that higher magnitudes of LIFO reserve are associated with lower stock prices. This is consistent with the LIFO reserve being viewed as an inflation indicator (for either current or future inventory costs) detrimental to company value.

ANALYZING FINANCIAL STATEMENTS

Analysis Objective

LO5 Define and interpret gross profit margin and inventory turnover ratios. Use inventory footnote information to make appropriate adjustments to ratios.

We are trying to determine whether Home Depot's sales provide sufficient revenues to cover its operation costs, primarily selling and administrative expenses, after allowing for the costs of manufacturing.

Analysis Tool Gross Profit Margin (GPM) Ratio

$$\textbf{Gross profit margin} = \frac{\textbf{Sales revenue} - \textbf{Cost of goods sold}}{\textbf{Sales revenue}}$$

Applying the Gross Profit Margin Ratio to Home Depot

$$2015: \frac{(\$88,519 - \$58,254)}{\$88,519} = 0.342 \text{ or } 34.2\%$$

$$2016: \frac{(\$94,595 - \$62,282)}{\$94,595} = 0.342 \text{ or } 34.2\%$$

$$2017: \frac{(\$100,904 - \$66,548)}{\$100,904} = 0.340 \text{ or } 34.0\%$$

Guidance The gross profit margin is commonly used instead of the dollar amount of gross profit as it allows for comparisons across companies and over time. A decline in GPM is usually cause for concern because it indicates that the company has less ability to pass on to customers increased costs in its products. Because companies try to charge the highest price the market will bear, a decline in GPM is often the result of market forces beyond the company's control. Some possible reasons for a GPM decline are:

- Product line is stale. Perhaps it is out of fashion and the company must resort to markdowns to reduce overstocked inventories. Or, perhaps the product lines have lost their technological edge, yielding reduced demand.
- A change in product mix resulting from a change in buyers' behavior (more generic brands, more necessities, fewer big-ticket items).
- New competitors enter the market. Perhaps substitute products or new technologies are now available from competitors, yielding increased pressure to reduce selling prices.
- General decline in economic activity. Perhaps an economic downturn reduces product demand. The weak housing market during the latter half of the decade likely affected the gross profits of home improvement companies.
- Inventory is overstocked. Perhaps the company overproduced goods and finds itself in an overstock position. This can require reduced selling prices to move inventory.

Takeaways The Home Depot's sales revenue has increased from fiscal year 2015 to fiscal year 2017. It would appear that the company is maintaining its gross profit margin. However, to properly evaluate gross profit margin, it is useful to make comparisons with other companies in the same industry. **Exhibit 7.12** graphically compares The Home Depot's gross profit margin with that of its largest (but smaller) competitor, **Lowe's Companies, Inc.**

As the bar graph illustrates, The Home Depot and Lowe's have reported nearly identical, and very stable, gross profit margins in the last three years. In addition, in 2017 The Home Depot's sales revenue increased by 6.7%, while Lowe's revenues increased by 5.5%.

To gain further insights, **Exhibit 7.13** compares the gross profit margin of The Home Depot with that of several other retailers: **Target Corporation**, a national chain of retail variety stores; **Staples, Inc.**, a retail office supply store; and **Whole Foods Market Inc.**, a retail specialty grocery store chain. The graph illustrates that in 2015 and 2016, the highest gross profit margin belongs to Whole Foods, the specialty grocery store, while in 2017, Home Depot earned that distinction. For all three years, the lowest was that of Staples. Also, while the percentages fluctuate slightly from year to year, the *relative* level of gross profit percentage remains the same over time, reflecting the fact that the industry or type of business is a major determinant of gross profit margin.

EXHIBIT 7.12 Gross Profit Margin Comparison

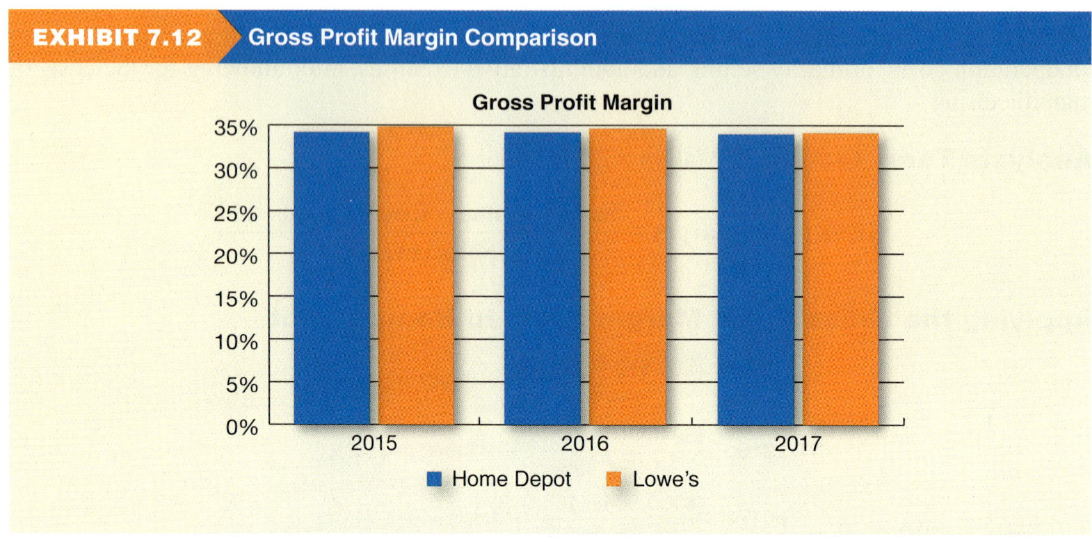

EXHIBIT 7.13 Comparison of Gross Profit Margins among Retailers

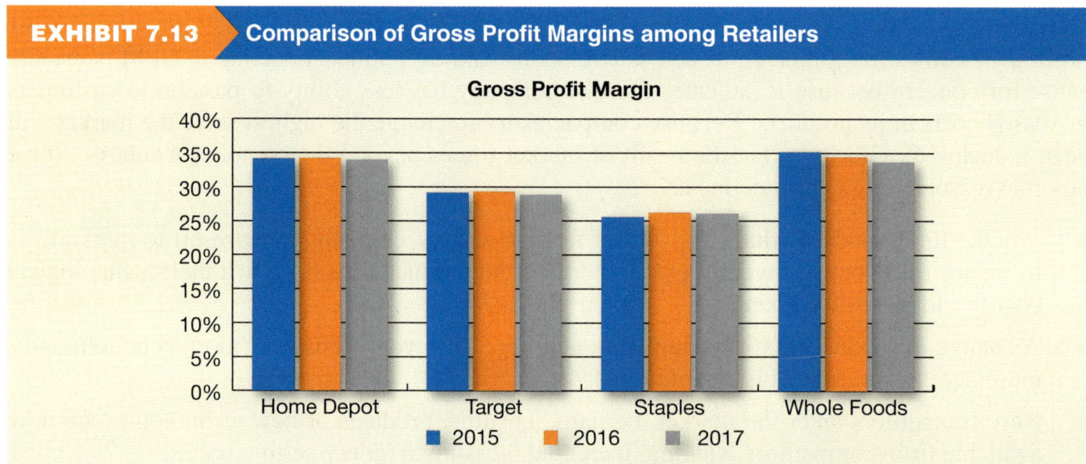

Because of competitive pressures, companies rarely have the opportunity to affect gross margin with price increases. (Of course, an astute choice of product offerings is likely to reduce pricing discounts and improve the gross profit margin.) Most improvements in gross margin that we witness are the result of better management of supply chains, production processes, or distribution networks. Similarly, a decline in gross profit margin suggests problems or inefficiencies in these processes. Companies that succeed typically do so because of better performance on basic business processes. This is one of The Home Depot's primary objectives.

Comparison of gross profit margins across selected focus companies:

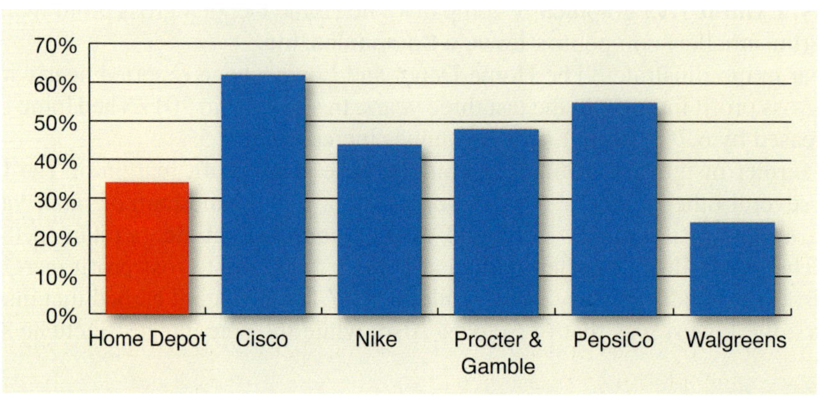

Analysis Objective

We wish to determine how quickly inventory passes through the production process and results in sales.

Analysis Tool Inventory Turnover (INVT) Ratio

$$\text{Inventory turnover} = \frac{\text{Cost of goods sold}}{\text{Average inventory}}$$

Applying Inventory Turnover Ratio to Home Depot

2015:	$58,254/[($11,809 + $11,079)/2] = 5.1 Times per year
2016:	$62,282/[($12,549 + $11,809)/2] = 5.1 Times per year
2017:	$66,548/[($12,748 + $12,549)/2] = 5.3 Times per year

Home Depot in Context

EXHIBIT 7.14 Inventory Turnover Comparison

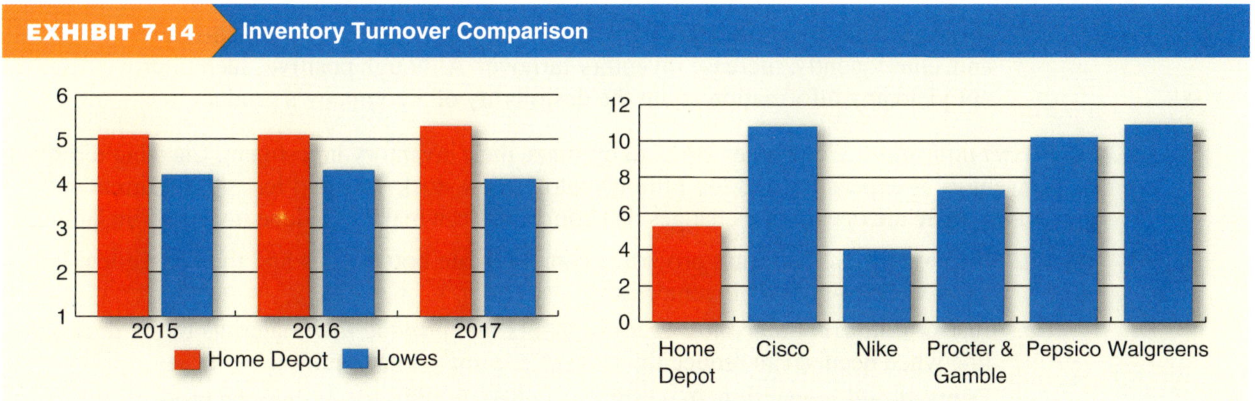

Cost of goods sold is in the numerator because inventory is reported at cost. The denominator is the average of beginning inventory and ending inventory to recognize growth (or decline) in the company's investment in inventory over the period. Inventory turnover indicates how many times inventory turns (is sold) during a period. More turns indicate that inventory is being sold more quickly.

Analysis Tool Average inventory days outstanding (AIDO), also called *days inventory outstanding*:

$$\text{Average inventory days outstanding} = \frac{\text{Average inventory}}{\text{Average daily cost of goods sold}}$$

Applying Average Inventory Days Outstanding Ratio to Home Depot

2015:	[($11,809 + $11,079)/2]/($58,254/365) = 72 Days
2016:	[($12,549 + $11,809)/2]/($62,282/365) = 71 Days
2014:	[($12,748 + $12,549)/2]/($66,548/365) = 69 Days

Home Depot in Context

The average daily cost of goods sold equals cost of goods sold divided by the number of days in the period (for our example, 365 for a year).

Average inventory days outstanding indicates how long, on average, inventories are on the shelves or in production before being sold. For example, if a retailer's annual cost of goods sold is $1,200 and average inventories are $300, inventories are turning four times and are on the shelves 91.25 days [$300/($1,200/365)] on average. This performance might be an acceptable turnover for the retail fashion industry where it needs to sell out its inventories each retail selling season, but it would not be acceptable for the grocery industry.

Guidance Analysis of inventory turnover is important for at least two reasons:

1. *Inventory quality*. Inventory turnover can be compared with those of prior periods and competitors. Higher turnover is viewed favorably, implying that products are salable, preferably without undue discounting of selling prices, or that production processes are functioning smoothly. Conversely, lower turnover implies that inventory is on the shelves for a longer period of time, perhaps from excessive purchases or production, missed fashion trends or technological advances, increased competition, and so forth. Our conclusions about higher or lower turnover must consider alternative explanations including:
   - *a.* Company product mix can change to higher-margin, slower-turning inventories or vice-versa. This change can occur from business acquisitions and the resulting consolidated inventories.
   - *b.* A company can change its promotion policies. Increased, effective advertising is likely to increase inventory turnover. Advertising expense is in SG&A, not COGS. Therefore, the cost is in operating expenses, but the benefit is in gross profit and turnover. If the promotion campaign is successful, the positive effects in margin and turnover should offset the promotion cost in SG&A.
   - *c.* A company can realize improvements in manufacturing efficiency and lower investments in direct materials and work-in-process inventories. Such improvements reduce inventory and, consequently, increase inventory turnover. Although positive, such improvements do not yield any information about the desirability of a company's product line.

2. *Asset utilization.* Companies strive to optimize their inventory investment. Carrying too much inventory is expensive, and too little inventory risks stock-outs and lost sales (current and future). There are operational changes that companies can make to reduce inventory including:
   - *a.* Improved manufacturing processes can eliminate bottlenecks and the consequent build-up of work-in-process inventories.
   - *b.* Just-in-time (JIT) deliveries from suppliers that provide raw materials to the production line when needed can reduce the level of raw materials required.
   - *c.* Demand-pull production, in which raw materials are released into the production process when final goods are demanded by customers instead of producing for estimated demand, can reduce inventory levels. **Dell Inc.** was founded on a business model that produced for actual, rather than estimated, demand; many of its computers are manufactured after the customer order is received.

   Reducing inventories reduces inventory carrying costs, thus improving profitability and increasing cash flow (asset reduction is reflected as a cash inflow adjustment in the statement of cash flows). However, if inventories get too low, production can be interrupted and sales lost.

There is normal tension between the sales side of a company that argues for depth and breadth of inventory and the finance side that monitors inventory carrying costs and seeks to maximize cash flow. Companies, therefore, seek to *optimize* inventory investment, not *minimize* it.

RESEARCH INSIGHT

In a recent *Wall Street Journal* article, it was reported that in 2013, companies reported deficiencies in their procedures to account for inventory and cost of sales, i.e., internal control weaknesses, so numerous that the category ranked number two in areas with such deficiencies.[5] Recent academic research suggests these deficiencies are important. According to a study of companies over 2004–2009, the evidence is consistent with firms that have inventory-related material weaknesses having systematically lower inventory turnover ratios and being more likely to report inventory impairments relative to firms with effective internal control. In addition, the study shows that firms that fix their internal control weaknesses show improvements in inventory turnover rates.[6]

[5] "More Accounting Deficiencies Linked to Inventory," *Wall Street Journal* August 26, 2014.

[6] See Feng, Mei, Chan Li, Sarah E. McVay, and Hollis Skaife, "Does Ineffective Internal Control over Financial Reporting affect a Firm's Operations? Evidence from Firms' Inventory Management." The Accounting Review, March 2015.

Takeaways **Exhibit 7.14** compares inventory turnover for The Home Depot with that of its chief rival, Lowe's. Home Depot's inventory turnover and AIDO improved over the period 2015–2017. Lowe's inventory turnover increased and then decreased, but increases in inventories probably helped it to maintain revenues and gross profit in the changing economic climate.

It is also instructive to compare the home improvement retail industry, represented by The Home Depot, with other retailers as illustrated in **Exhibit 7.15**.

EXHIBIT 7.15 Inventory Turnover for Various Retail Companies

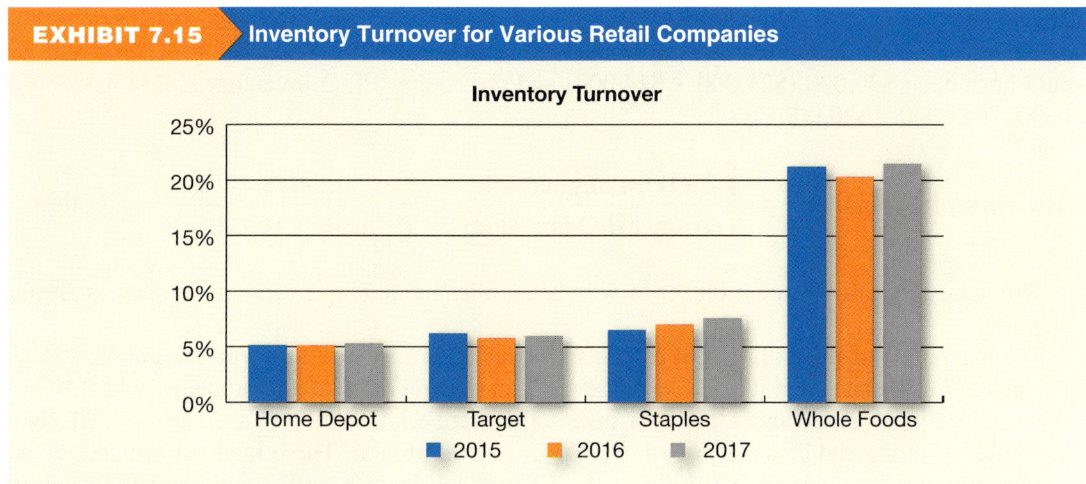

In the retail grocery industry, high inventory turnover is a necessity given that a significant portion of a grocer's inventory is perishable. Whole Foods' high turnover is typical of what we might expect from retail grocers. The Home Depot's turnover is lower than any of the comparison companies. Target's turnover is lower than that of Staples, the consumer office products retailer, despite the fact that part of Target's sales is food related. The small portion of food product sales as a percentage of total sales explains why Target's turnover is not comparable to that of Whole Foods.

YOU MAKE THE CALL

You are the Plant Manager You are analyzing your inventory turnover report for the month and are concerned that the average inventory days outstanding is lengthening. What actions can you take to reduce average inventory days outstanding? [Answer on page 354]

Adjusting Turnover Ratios For a company using the last-in, first-out (LIFO) inventory method, it is advisable to make an adjustment before calculating the inventory turnover ratio. LIFO is most commonly used when management has experienced a trend of rising inventory costs. As a result, LIFO puts higher (newer) costs into cost of goods sold and leaves lower (older) costs in inventory. This creates a potential mismatch between the numerator and denominator of the inventory turnover ratio.

For instance, consider Butler Company's 2019 financial information in **Exhibit 7.11**. Measured in physical terms, Butler started 2019 with 250 units, sold 500 units during 2019, and ended 2019 with 350 units. So, the physical inventory turnover would be

$$\textbf{Physical inventory turnover} = \frac{\textbf{Units sold}}{\textbf{Average units held}} = \frac{500}{(250+350)/2} = 1.67 \text{ times}$$

However, the 2019 inventory turnover calculated using the LIFO reported numbers does not agree with the physical inventory turnover.

$$\textbf{LIFO inventory turnover} = \frac{\textbf{Cost of goods sold}}{\textbf{Average inventory}} = \frac{\$90,000}{(\$25,000+\$43,000)/2} = 2.65 \text{ times}$$

Why is the LIFO inventory turnover higher? The distortion occurs because the LIFO cost of goods sold is 500 units valued at $180 each, while the beginning inventory is 250 units valued at $100 each and the ending inventory is 250 units valued at $100 each plus 100 units valued at $180 each. The difference between 1.67 and 2.65 comes about because LIFO causes the value per unit to be higher in the numerator than in the denominator.

A quick fix would be to use the LIFO reserve information to put the beginning and ending inventory values on a more up-to-date basis. LIFO puts the newer costs in cost of goods sold, while FIFO puts the newer costs in inventory. If Butler were using LIFO, we could use the reported inventory balances and the LIFO reserve information to determine that the beginning FIFO inventory would have been $39,000 ($25,000 + $14,000) and the ending FIFO inventory would have been $63,000 ($43,000 + $20,000).

$$\textbf{Adjusted inventory turnover} = \frac{\textbf{LIFO cost of good sold}}{\textbf{Average FIFO inventory}} = \frac{\$90{,}000}{(\$39{,}000 + \$63{,}000)/2} = 1.76 \text{ times}$$

This adjusted ratio is much closer to what's actually happening to the inventories at Butler Company.

The magnitude of this adjustment can be significant. For instance, **Chevron Corporation** in its 2017 annual report states that its 2017 expense for "Purchased crude oil and products" was $75,765 million. Chevron's balance sheet totals for inventories were $5,419 million at the end of 2016 and $5,585 million at the end of 2017, for an average of $5,502 million. These numbers would give an inventory turnover ratio of $75,765 million ÷ $5,502 million, or 13.8 times, implying that inventory is held less than 27 days on average.

However, we know that the LIFO inventory balances are out of date. Chevron's LIFO reserve disclosure says that the replacement cost of inventories was higher than the reported amounts by $2,942 million at the end of 2016 and $3,937 million at the end of 2017, making the replacement cost of inventories equal to $8,361 million at the end of 2016 and $9,522 million at the end of 2017. The adjusted inventory turnover ratio would be $75,765/[($8,361 + $9,522)/2] = 8.5, implying that inventory is held about 43 days.

Following a similar line of analysis, it would be possible to construct a FIFO inventory turnover for Chevron, which could be useful in making comparisons to another company that uses IFRS in its financial reports.

CHAPTER-END REVIEW

Publix Super Markets Inc. reports inventory and cost of goods sold using the last-in, first-out (LIFO) costing method for a "significant portion" of U.S. inventory. The table below presents financial information from its 2015, 2016, and 2017 10-K reports.

($ millions)	2017	2016	2015
Revenue	$34,837	$34,274	$32,619
Cost of goods sold	25,130	24,734	23,460
Gross profit	$ 9,707	$ 9,540	$ 9,159
Balance Sheet:			
Inventory	$ 1,877	$ 1,722	$ 1,741
Notes to financial statements			
LIFO reserve	$ 465	$ 442	$ 447

REQUIRED

1. Compute the gross profit margin for each year, 2015 through 2017, and the inventory turnover ratio for 2016 and 2017.
2. What amount for cost of goods sold and gross profit would Publix report in 2016 and 2017 if FIFO were used to assign costs to inventory and cost of goods sold? (Assume that FIFO cost is equal to the current value of Publix's inventory.)
3. Recalculate Publix's inventory turnover ratio for 2016 and 2017 assuming that FIFO had been used to value inventory.

The solution to this review problem can be found on page 369.

APPENDIX 7A: LIFO Liquidation

LO6 Analyze LIFO liquidations and the impact they have on the financial statements.

When companies use LIFO inventory costing, the most recent costs of purchasing inventory are transferred to cost of goods sold, while older costs remain in ending inventory. Each time inventory is purchased at a different price, a new *layer* (also called a **LIFO layer**) is added to the inventory balance. As long as a year's purchases equal or exceed the quantity sold, older cost layers remain in inventory—sometimes for several years. On the other hand, when the quantity sold exceeds the quantity purchased, inventory costs from these older cost layers are transferred to cost of goods sold. This situation is called **LIFO liquidation**. Because these older costs are usually much lower than current replacement costs, LIFO liquidation normally yields a boost to current gross profit as these older costs are matched against current revenues.

To illustrate the effects of LIFO liquidation, we return to the example of Butler Company in **Exhibit 7.6** and add an additional year. At the end of 2019, Butler has 350 units in inventory, 250 at $100 each and 100 at $180 each. Suppose that during 2020, the company purchases 500 units at $190 and sells 650 units at $250. At the end of 2020, Butler will have only 200 units remaining in inventory and, under LIFO, those units will be assigned a cost of $100 each. The determination of cost of goods sold and ending inventory for 2020 can be seen in **Exhibit 7A.1**.

EXHIBIT 7A.1 Calculation of 2020 LIFO Inventory and Cost of Goods Sold

Beginning Inventory	250 units at $100 each plus 100 units at $180 each	$ 43,000
Purchases.	500 units at $190 each	95,000
Cost of goods available for sale		138,000
Ending inventory.	200 units at $100 each	20,000
Cost of goods sold	500 units at $190 each plus 100 units at $180 each plus 50 units at $100 each	$118,000

Exhibit 7A.2 portrays graphically that the inventory reduction in 2020 eliminated the LIFO layer added in 2019 and reduced the original LIFO layer from the start of 2018.

EXHIBIT 7A.2 Butler Company LIFO Inventory Flows

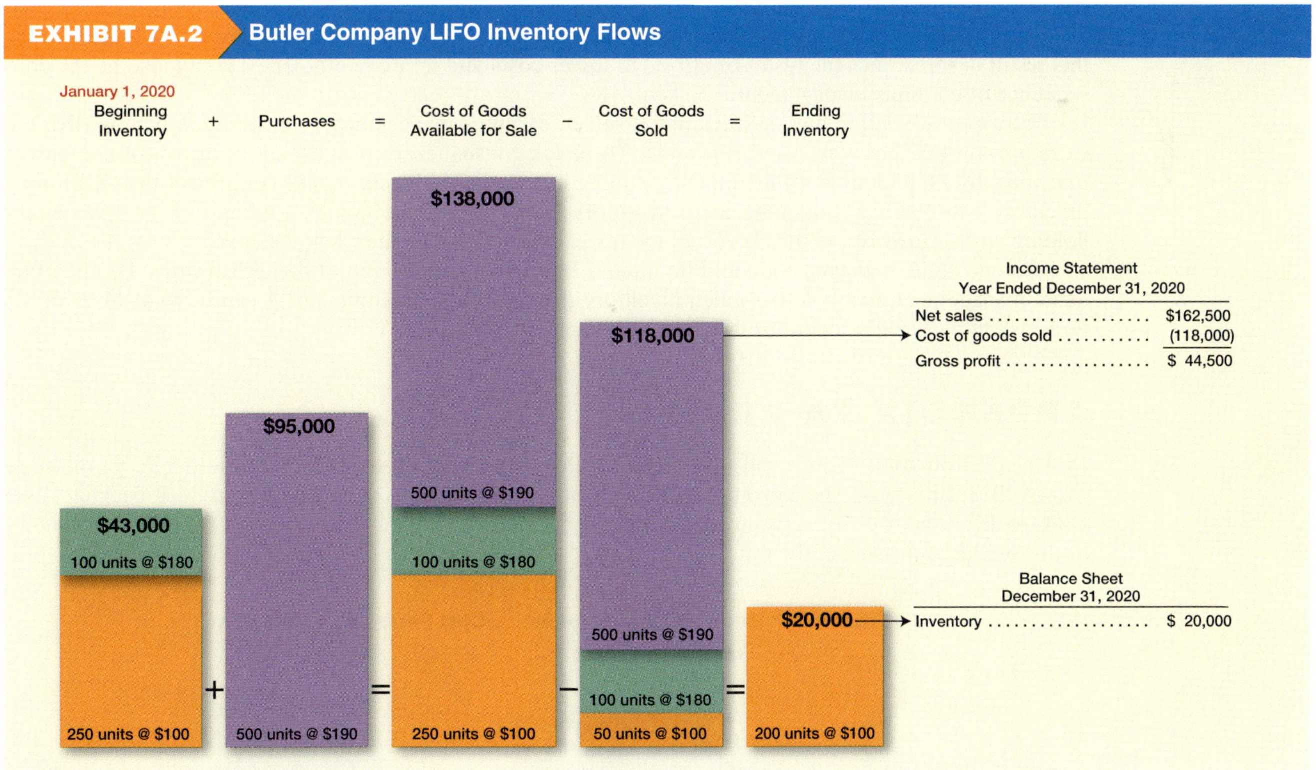

What would have happened if Butler had purchased 650 units at $190 in 2020? The ending inventory would have been identical to the beginning inventory. And, the cost of goods sold would have been $123,500 (650 units at $190 each), $5,500 higher than the $118,000 cost of goods sold in **Exhibit 7A.1**. This difference can be attributed to the differences between the current unit cost of inventory ($190) and the old unit costs ($180 and $100) that had been in inventory but are now in cost of goods sold.

Thus, Butler's cost of goods sold has been *reduced* by $5,500 due to the LIFO liquidation, and its gross profit and income before tax have been *increased* by the same amount. If Butler's tax rate were 25%, the net income would be increased by $4,125. This **LIFO liquidation gain** must be disclosed in the company's footnotes.

The effect of LIFO liquidation is evident in the following footnote information from Notes A and G to **Alcoa Inc.**'s 2014 annual report.

Notes A and G: Inventories

Inventory Valuation. Inventories are carried at the lower of cost or market, with cost for a substantial portion of U.S. and Canadian inventories determined under the last-in, first-out (LIFO) method. The cost of other inventories is principally determined under the average-cost method.

Note G: (dollars in millions) At December 31, 2014 and 2013, the total amount of inventories valued on a LIFO basis was $1,514 and $1,169, respectively. If valued on an average-cost basis, total inventories would have been $767 and $691 higher at December 31, 2014 and 2013, respectively. During 2013 and 2012, reductions in LIFO inventory quantities caused partial liquidations of the lower cost LIFO inventory base. These liquidations resulted in the recognition of income of $26 ($17 after-tax) in 2013 and $1 ($1 after-tax) in 2012.

Alcoa reports that reductions in inventory quantities led to the sale (at current selling prices) of products that carried costs from prior years that were less than current costs. As a result of these inventory reductions, pretax income increased by $26 million in 2013 and by $1 million in 2012.

Analysis Implications

LIFO liquidation boosts gross profit when older, lower costs are matched against revenues based on current sales prices. This increase in gross profit is transitory. Once an old LIFO layer is liquidated, it can only be replaced at current prices. The transitory boost in gross profit temporarily distorts the gross profit margin (GPM) ratio.

It is important that we ask why the LIFO liquidation happened. Involuntary LIFO liquidations result from circumstances beyond the company's control, such as disruptions in supply due to a natural disaster. Voluntary LIFO liquidations are the result of a management decision to reduce inventory levels. While this result is sometimes the result of efforts to lower costs and improve efficiency, it can also be the consequence of earnings management.

If a voluntary LIFO liquidation is the result of earnings management, we should remember that the extra gross profit that is reported is taxable. These tax consequences provide an incentive for companies to *avoid* LIFO liquidations by maintaining ending inventories at levels equal to or greater than beginning inventory quantities. Maintaining these inventory levels can be inefficient, leading to higher inventory holding costs. However, in the short run, the tax savings can be greater than the costs.

On one hand, management could liquidate LIFO inventories to report higher earnings. On the other hand, management may hold too much inventory to avoid paying extra taxes. A careful evaluation of future cash flows usually identifies the preferred course of action.

APPENDIX 7A REVIEW

Dickhaut Corporation imports and sells a product that is produced in the Dominican Republic. In the summer of 2018, a hurricane disrupted production and affected Dickhaut's supply of this product. Dickhaut uses LIFO to determine the cost of its inventory and cost of goods sold. On January 1, 2018, Dickhaut's inventory of this product consisted of the following:

Year Purchased	Quantity (units)	Cost Per Unit	Total Cost
2016	2,000	$20	$ 40,000
2017	3,000	30	90,000
Total	5,000		$130,000

Through mid-December, purchases were limited to 7,000 units, because the cost had increased to $70 per unit. Dickhaut sold 11,500 units during 2018 at a price of $65 per unit, which significantly depleted its inventory. However, the cost was expected to drop to $55 per unit by early January 2019.

continued

continued from previous page

Required

a. Assume that Dickhaut makes no further purchases during 2018. Compute its gross profit for 2018.

b. Assume that Dickhaut purchases 4,500 units for $70 per unit before the end of December 2018, so that it maintains its balance of inventory at 5,000 units. Compute its gross profit for 2018.

c. How should Dickhaut disclose the LIFO liquidation if it chooses not to make a year-end purchase?

d. If Dickhaut's corporate tax rate is 25%, should it make a year-end purchase? If so, how many units should the company purchase before December 31, 2018? Assume that the management of Dickhaut believes it is efficient (in the long run) to carry 5,000 units in inventory.

The solution to this review problem can be found on pages 369–370.

SUMMARY

Interpret disclosures of information concerning operating expenses, including manufacturing and retail inventory costs. (p. 328) **LO1**

- Inventory is reported in the balance sheet at its cost, including any cost to acquire, transport and prepare goods for sale.
- Manufacturing inventory consists of raw materials, work in process and finished goods. The cost of manufacturing inventory includes the cost of materials and labor used to produce goods, as well as overhead cost.

Account for inventory and cost of goods sold using different costing methods. (p. 332) **LO2**

- FIFO places the cost of the most recent purchases in ending inventory and older costs in the cost of goods sold.
- LIFO places the cost of the most recent purchases in cost of goods sold and older costs in inventory.
- The average cost method computes an average unit cost, which is used to value inventories *and* cost of goods sold.

Apply the lower of cost or net realizable value rule to value inventory. (p. 337) **LO3**

- If the net realizable value of inventory falls below its cost, the inventory is written down to net realizable value, thereby reducing total assets.
- The loss is added to cost of goods sold and reported in the income statement (unless it is large enough to warrant separate disclosure).

Evaluate how inventory costing affects management decisions and outsiders' interpretations of financial statements. (p. 341) **LO4**

- When inventory costs are rising, LIFO costing reports higher cost of goods sold and lower income than either FIFO or average costing.
- If LIFO is used for tax reporting, it must be used for financial reporting.
- LIFO distorts the inventory turnover ratio because inventories are often severely undervalued (relative to current cost of goods sold). Management can boost earnings by liquidating these undervalued inventories.
- International Financial Reporting Standards (IFRS) allows FIFO and average costing methods. LIFO is not permitted.

Define and interpret gross profit margin and inventory turnover ratios. Use inventory footnote information to make appropriate adjustments to ratios. (p. 345) **LO5**

- Gross profit margin (GPM)—a measure of profitability that focuses on the amount of revenue in excess of cost of goods sold as a percentage of revenue
- Gross profit margin is defined as Gross profit/Sales revenue.
- Inventory turnover (INVT)—a measure of the frequency at which the average balance in inventory is sold each year
- Inventory turnover is defined as Cost of goods sold/Average inventory.
- These ratios provide insight into how efficiently the company is managing inventory.
- Footnote disclosures enable a financial statement reader to determine the up-to-date costs of LIFO inventories, to estimate what cost of goods sold would have been under FIFO, and to compute an inventory turnover ratio that is not subject to the distortions noted in LO4.

LO6 **Appendix 7A: Analyze LIFO liquidations and the impact they have on the financial statements. (p. 351)**

- LIFO liquidation is the result of selling and not replenishing inventory stocks purchased in previous accounting periods.
- When inventory costs are increasing, LIFO liquidation results in higher net income as the unrealized holding gains from LIFO are realized.
- Companies that use LIFO have an incentive to hold inventories to avoid LIFO *liquidation* and the resulting higher income taxes.

GUIDANCE ANSWERS . . . YOU MAKE THE CALL

You are the Plant Manager Companies need inventories to avoid lost sales opportunities; however, there are several ways to minimize inventory needs. (1) We can reduce product costs by improving product design to eliminate costly features not valued by customers. (2) We can use more cost-efficient suppliers, possibly including production in lower wage-rate parts of the world. (3) We can reduce raw material inventories with just-in-time delivery from suppliers. (4) We can eliminate bottlenecks in the production process that increase work-in-process inventories. (5) We can manufacture for orders rather than for estimates of demand to reduce finished goods inventories. (6) We can improve warehousing and distribution to reduce duplicate inventories. (7) We can monitor product sales and adjust product mix as demand changes to reduce finished goods inventories.

KEY RATIOS

Gross profit (GP)

$$\text{GP} = \text{Sales revenue} - \text{Cost of goods sold}$$

Gross profit margin (GPM)

$$\text{Gross profit margin} = \frac{\text{Sales revenue} - \text{Cost of goods sold}}{\text{Sales revenue}}$$

Inventory turnover (INVT)

$$\text{INVT} = \frac{\text{Cost of goods sold}}{\text{Average inventory}}$$

Average inventory days outstanding (AIDO)

$$\text{AIDO} = \frac{\text{Average inventory}}{\text{Average daily cost of goods sold}}$$

KEY TERMS

Average cost (AC) (p. 336)
Cash discounts (p. 331)
Cost flow assumption (p. 333)
Cost of goods produced (p. 331)
Direct association (p. 328)
Finished goods inventory (p. 331)
First-in, first-out (FIFO) (p. 333)
FOB destination (p. 331)
FOB shipping point (p. 331)
Gross profit (p. 329)
Immediate recognition (p. 329)
Last-in, first-out (LIFO) (p. 334)
LIFO layer (p. 351)
LIFO layers (p. 335)
LIFO liquidation (p. 351)
LIFO liquidation gain (p. 352)
LIFO reserve (p. 341)
Lower of cost or net realizable value (LCNRV) (p. 337)
Raw materials inventory (p. 331)
Systematic allocation (p. 329)
Unrealized holding gain (p. 343)
Work-in-process inventory (p. 331)

Assignments with the MBC logo in the margin are available in myBusinessCourse. See the Preface of the book for details.

MULTIPLE CHOICE

1. Which of the following is not normally reported as part of total manufacturing inventory cost?
   a. work-in-process
   b. finished goods
   c. property, plant, and equipment
   d. raw materials

2. When the current year's ending inventory amount is overstated, then the
   a. current year's cost of goods sold is overstated.
   b. current year's total assets are understated.
   c. current year's net income is overstated.
   d. next year's income is overstated.

3. In a period of rising prices, the inventory cost allocation method that tends to result in the lowest reported net income is
   a. LIFO.
   b. FIFO.
   c. average cost.
   d. specific identification.

4. Assume that Beyer Corporation has the following initial balance and subsequent purchase of inventory:

Beginning inventory, 2020	2,000 units @ $50 each	$100,000
Inventory purchased in 2020	5,000 units @ $75 each	$375,000
Cost of goods available for sale in 2020	7,000 units	$475,000

During 2020, Beyer Corporation sold 6,000 units. Which of the following is not true?
   a. FIFO cost of goods sold would be $400,000.
   b. FIFO ending inventory would be $75,000.
   c. LIFO cost of goods sold would be $425,000.
   d. LIFO ending inventory would be $75,000.

5. Sletten Industries uses the last-in, first-out (LIFO) method of accounting for the inventories of its single product. For fiscal year 2020, the company reported sales revenue of $200 million and cost of goods sold of $135 million. The following table was reported in the financial statement footnotes.

($ millions)	January 1, 2020	December 31, 2020
Inventory value at LIFO	$25	$28
LIFO Reserve	14	22
Inventory value at FIFO	$39	$50

If Sletten Industries had used FIFO to account for its inventory, its 2020 gross profit would be
   a. $87 million.
   b. $73 million.
   c. $57 million.
   d. $65 million.

Multiple Choice Answers
1. c 2. c 3. a 4. d 5. b

Superscript [A] denotes assignments based on Appendix 7A.

QUESTIONS

Q7-1. Under what circumstances is it justified to include transportation costs in the value of the inventory purchased?

Q7-2. Why do relatively stable inventory costs reduce the importance of management's choice of an inventory costing method?

Q7-3. What is one explanation for increased gross profit during periods of rising inventory costs when FIFO is used?

Q7-4. If inventory costs are rising, which inventory costing method—first-in, first-out; last-in, first-out; or average cost—yields the (a) lowest ending inventory? (b) lowest net income? (c) largest ending inventory? (d) largest net income? (e) greatest cash flow assuming that method is used for tax purposes?

Q7-5. Even though it does not reflect their physical flow of goods, why might companies adopt last-in, first-out inventory costing in periods when costs are consistently rising?

Kaiser Aluminum Corporation
NASDAQ :: KALU

Q7-6. In a recent annual report, Kaiser Aluminum Corporation made the following statement in reference to its inventories: "The Company recorded pretax charges of approximately $19.4 million because of a reduction in the carrying values of its inventories caused principally by prevailing lower prices for alumina, primary aluminum, and fabricated products." What basic accounting principle caused Kaiser Aluminum to record this $19.4 million pretax charge? Briefly describe the rationale for this principle.

Q7-7. Under what conditions would each of the inventory costing methods discussed in the chapter produce the same results?

Q7-8. What is inventory "shrink?" How does a company determine the amount of inventory shrink that may have occurred?

Q7-9. What is a LIFO reserve? How is the LIFO reserve related to unrealized holding gains?

Q7-10. Analysts claim that it is more difficult to forecast net income for a company that uses LIFO. Why might this be true?

Q7-11.[A] LIFO liquidation may be involuntary—that is beyond the control of management. Suggest two situations that might lead to involuntary LIFO liquidation.

Q7-12.[A] LIFO liquidation is often discretionary. What motives might management have to liquidate LIFO inventory?

MINI EXERCISES

LO1

M7-13. Recording an Inventory Purchase

Shields Company has purchased inventories incurring the following costs: (a) the invoice amount of $500, (b) shipping charges of $30, (c) interest of $10 on the $500 borrowed to finance the purchase, and (d) $5 for the cost of moving the inventory to the company's warehouse.

REQUIRED

Determine the cost to be assigned to the inventory and record the purchase using "T" accounts.

LO1

M7-14. Recording Inventory Costs

Schrand Inc., a merchandiser, is requesting help in determining what costs ought to be considered as costs when incurred or treated as inventory costs, which are expensed as COGS. The costs include: sales persons wages, utilities such as heat and light in the store, the floor supervisor's salary, the cost of merchandise to be sold, costs of packaging and shipping to buyers.

REQUIRED

Determine the items above that should be included in inventory.

LO1

M7-15. Determining Cost of Goods Sold for a Manufacturing Company

Ybarra Products began operations in 2020. During its first year, the company purchased raw materials costing $84,000 and used $63,000 of those materials in the production of its products. The company's manufacturing operations also incurred labor costs of $58,000 and overhead costs of $28,000. At year end 2020, Ybarra had $19,000 of partially completed product in work-in-process inventory and $35,000 in finished goods inventory. What was Ybarra Company's cost of goods sold in 2020?

M7-16. Calculating Gross Profit Margin LO5

Johnson & Johnson reported the following revenue and cost of goods sold information in its 10-K report for 2017, 2016, and 2015.

Johnson & Johnson
NYSE :: JNJ

($ millions)	2017	2016	2015
Sales to customers	$76,450	$71,890	$70,074
Cost of products sold	25,354	21,685	21,536

Compute Johnson & Johnson's gross profit margin for each year.

M7-17. Calculating Effect of Inventory Errors LO1

For each of the following scenarios, determine the effect of the error on income in the current period and in the subsequent period. To answer these questions, rely on the inventory equation:

Beginning inventory + Purchases − Cost of goods sold = Ending inventory

a. Porter Company received a shipment of merchandise costing $32,000 near the end of the fiscal year. The shipment was mistakenly recorded at a cost of $23,000.

b. Chiu, Inc., purchased merchandise costing $16,000. When the shipment was received, it was determined that the merchandise was damaged in shipment. The goods were returned to the supplier, but the accounting department was not notified and the invoice was paid.

c. After taking a physical count of its inventory, Murray Corporation determined that it had "shrink" of $12,500, and the books were adjusted accordingly. However, inventory costing $5,000 was never counted.

M7-18. Calculating LIFO, FIFO, Income and Cash Flows LO2, 4

An acquaintance has proposed the following business plan to you. A local company requires a consistent quantity of a commodity and is looking for a reliable supplier. You could become that reliable supplier.

The cost of the commodity is expected to rise steadily over the foreseeable future, but the company is willing to pay more than the price that is current at the time. All you would need to do is make an investment, purchase the inventory and then deliver inventory to the company over the following year. One complication is that the commodity is available for purchase only seasonally, so at the end of every year you would need to purchase the supply for the following year. The customer pays promptly on delivery.

An initial cash investment of $62,000 would be used to purchase $50,000 of inventory in December 2019. The remaining cash would be held for liquidity needs. In the following year, you would deliver this inventory to the customer. Inventory costs are expected to increase by $10,000 per year, and the customer agrees to pay $15,000 more than the current cost of inventory. So, during 2020, you would deliver inventory that originally cost $50,000, receive payment of $75,000 and pay $60,000 to purchase inventory for the current year. This pattern would continue in future years, but with annually increasing costs of inventory and corresponding increases in the price charged the customer.

If you accept this proposal, your objective would be to receive $9,000 in dividends (about a 15% return on the $62,000 investment) at the end of each year. Assume your business would have an income tax rate of 40%.

a. Construct a projected balance sheet as of the end of December 2019.

b. Construct financial forecasts of income statements, cash flows (direct method) and balance sheets for the next three years (through 2022). Assume that your business would operate in a tax jurisdiction that requires the use of FIFO for inventory. Would this opportunity meet your financial objective?

c. Suppose that your business would operate in a tax jurisdiction that allowed the use of LIFO for inventory. Would this opportunity meet your financial objective? Why?

M7-19. Computing Cost of Goods Sold and Ending Inventory Under FIFO, LIFO, and Average Cost LO2

Assume that Gode Company reports the following initial balance and subsequent purchase of inventory:

Beginning inventory, 2020	1,000 units @ $100 each	$100,000
Inventory purchased in 2020	2,000 units @ $150 each	300,000
Cost of goods available for sale in 2020..........	3,000 units	$400,000

Assume that 1,700 units are sold during 2020. Compute the cost of goods sold for 2020 and the balance reported as ending inventory on its 2020 balance sheet under the following inventory costing methods:

a. FIFO

b. LIFO

c. Average cost

LO2

M7-20. Inferring Purchases Using Cost of Goods Sold and Inventory Balances

Geiger Corporation, a retail company, reported inventories of $1,320,000 in 2019 and $1,460,000 in 2020. The 2020 income statement reported cost of goods sold of $6,980,000.

a. Compute the amount of inventory purchased during 2020.

b. Prepare journal entries to record (1) purchases, and (2) cost of goods sold.

c. Post the journal entries in part *b* to their respective T-accounts.

d. Record each of the transactions in part *b* in the financial statement effects template to show the effect of these entries on the balance sheet and income statement.

LO2

M7-21. Computing Cost of Goods Sold and Ending Inventory

Bartov Corporation reports the following beginning inventory and purchases for 2020:

Beginning inventory, 2020	400 units @ $10 each	$ 4,000
Inventory purchased in 2020	700 units @ $12 each	8,400
Cost of goods available for sale in 2020..........	1,100 units	$12,400

Bartov sells 600 of these units in 2020. Compute its cost of goods sold for 2020 and the ending inventory reported on its 2020 balance sheet under each of the following inventory costing methods:

a. FIFO

b. LIFO

c. Average cost

LO5

Wal-Mart Stores, Inc.
NYSE :: WMT
Target Corporation
NYSE :: TGT

M7-22. Computing and Evaluating Inventory Turnover

Wal-Mart Stores, Inc., and Target Corporation reported the following in their financial reports:

($ billions)	Wal-Mart			Target		
Fiscal Year	Sales	COGS	Inventory	Sales	COGS	Inventory
2017	$496	$373	$43.8	$71.9	$51.1	$8.66
2016	481	361	43.0	69.5	49.1	8.31
2015	479	361	44.5	73.8	52.2	8.60

a. Compute the 2017 and 2016 inventory turnovers for each of these two retailers.

b. Discuss any changes that are evident in inventory turnover across years and companies from part *a*.

c. Describe ways in which a retailer can improve its inventory turnover. Are there ways to increase inventory turnover that are not beneficial to the company's long-term interests?

LO2

M7-23. Inferring Purchases Using Cost of Goods Sold and Inventory Balances

Penno Company reported ending inventories of $23,560,000 in 2020 and $25,790,000 in 2019. Cost of goods sold totaled $142,790,000 in 2020.

a. Prepare the journal entry to record cost of goods sold.

b. Set up a T-account for inventory and post the cost of goods sold entry from part *a* to this account.

c. Using the T-account from *b*, determine the amount of inventory that was purchased in 2020. Prepare a journal entry to record those purchases.

d. Using the financial statement effects template, show the effects of the entries in parts *a* and *c* on the balance sheet and income statement.

M7-24. Determining Lower of Cost or Net Realizable Value (NRV) LO3

The following data refer to Froning Company's ending inventory.

Item Code	Quantity	Unit Cost	Unit NRV
LXC	60	$45	$48
KWT	210	38	34
MOR	300	22	20
NES	100	27	32

Determine the ending inventory amount by applying the lower of cost or net realizable value rule to (*a*) each item of inventory and (*b*) the total inventory.

EXERCISES

E7-25. Analyzing Inventory and Margin in a Seasonal Business LO5

West Marine, Inc.
NASDAQ :: WMAR

West Marine, Inc., opened its first boating supply store in 1975. Since that time, the company has grown to be one of the largest boating supply companies in the world, with fiscal year 2014 revenues in excess of $675 million. The accompanying table provides financial information for two recent years. West Marine's fiscal year is closely aligned with the calendar year. All amounts are in millions.

Time Period	Net Revenues	Cost of Goods Sold	Ending Inventory
Fiscal year 2014	—	—	$214
First quarter 2015	$127	$100	257
Second quarter 2015	253	162	258
Third quarter 2015	194	138	237
Fourth quarter 2015	130	102	223
Fiscal year 2015	705	503	223
First quarter 2016	130	98	269
Second quarter 2016	252	162	254
Third quarter 2016	192	137	232
Fourth quarter 2016	130	101	212
Fiscal year 2016	703	497	212

a. Using the fiscal year (annual) information for 2015 and 2016, calculate the gross profit margin and the inventory turnover ratio.

b. West Marine is in a seasonal business, in which the sales total for the second and third quarters is substantially higher than the sales total for the first and fourth quarters. Calculate the company's gross profit margin by quarter. What do you learn from the seasonal pattern in the gross profit margin?

c. What is the seasonal pattern in inventory balances? What effect does West Marine's choice of fiscal year-end have on the inventory turnover ratio calculated in *a*?

d. Recalculate West Marine's inventory turnover ratios for 2015 and 2016 using a weighted average of the company's inventory investment over the year.

E7-26.[A] Applying and Analyzing Inventory Costing Methods LO2, 4, 6

At the beginning of the current period, Chen carried 1,000 units of its product with a unit cost of $20. A summary of purchases during the current period follows:

	Units	Unit Cost	Cost
Beginning Inventory	1,000	$20	$20,000
Purchases: #1	1,800	22	39,600
#2	800	26	20,800
#3	1,200	29	34,800

During the current period, Chen sold 2,800 units.

a. Assume that Chen uses the first-in, first-out method. Compute its cost of goods sold for the current period and the ending inventory balance.

b. Assume that Chen uses the last-in, first-out method. Compute its cost of goods sold for the current period and the ending inventory balance.

c. Assume that Chen uses the average cost method. Compute its cost of goods sold for the current period and the ending inventory balance.

d. Which of these three inventory costing methods would you choose to:
1. Reflect what is probably the physical flow of goods? Explain.
2. Minimize income taxes for the period? Explain.
3. Report the largest amount of income for the period? Explain.

LO2 **E7-27. Computing Cost of Sales and Ending Inventory**

Stocken Company has the following financial records for the current period:

	Units	Unit Cost
Beginning inventory	100	$46
Purchases: #1	650	42
#2	550	38
#3	200	36

Ending inventory at the end of this period is 350 units. Compute the ending inventory and the cost of goods sold for the current period using (*a*) first-in, first-out, (*b*) average cost, and (*c*) last-in, first-out.

LO3 **E7-28. Determining Lower of Cost or Net Realizable Value (NRV)**

Homework MBC

Crane Company had the following inventory at December 31, 2017.

		Unit Price	
	Quantity	Cost	NRV
Desks			
Model 9001	70	$190	$210
Model 9002	45	280	268
Model 9003	20	350	360
Cabinets			
Model 7001	120	60	64
Model 7002	80	95	88
Model 7003	50	130	126

a. Determine the ending inventory amount by applying the lower of cost or net realizable value rule to
1. Each item of inventory.
2. Each major category of inventory.
3. Total inventory.

b. Which of the LCNRV procedures from requirement *a* results in the lowest net income for 2017? Explain.

LO2, 4, 6 **E7-29.[A] Analyzing Inventory Footnote Disclosure**

General Motors
NYSE :: GM

General Motors Corporation reported the following information in its 10-K report:

Inventories at December 31 ($ millions)	2008	2007
Productive material, work in process, and supplies	$ 4,849	$ 6,267
Finished product, service parts, etc.	9,426	10,095
Total inventories at FIFO	14,275	16,362
Less LIFO allowance	(1,233)	(1,423)
Total automotive and other inventories, less allowances	$13,042	$14,939

The company reports its inventory using the LIFO costing method during 2007 and 2008.

a. At what dollar amount are inventories reported on its 2008 balance sheet?

b. At what dollar amount would inventories have been reported in 2008 if FIFO inventory costing had been used?

c. What cumulative effect has the use of LIFO had, as of year-end 2008, on GM's pretax income, compared to the pretax income that would have been reported using the FIFO costing method?

d. Assuming a 35% income tax rate, what is the cumulative effect on GM's tax liability as of year-end 2008?

e. In July 2009, GM changed its inventory accounting to FIFO costs. Why do you suppose GM made that choice?

E7-30.[A] Analyzing of Inventory and Footnote Disclosure

LO2, 4, 6

Deere & Company
NYSE :: DE

The inventory footnote from Deere & Company's 2013 10-K follows ($ millions).

15. INVENTORIES

A majority of inventory owned by Deere & Company and its US equipment subsidiaries are valued at cost, on the "last-in, first-out" (LIFO) basis. Remaining inventories are generally valued at the lower of cost, on the "first-in, first-out" (FIFO) basis, or net realizable value. The value of gross inventories on the LIFO basis at October 28, 2018 and October 29, 2017 represented 54 percent and 61 percent, respectively, of worldwide gross inventories at FIFO value. If all inventories had been valued on a FIFO basis, estimated inventories by major classification at October 28, 2018 and October 29, 2017 in millions of dollars would have been as follows:

	2018	2017
Raw materials and supplies	$2,233	$1,688
Work-in-process	776	495
Finished goods and parts	4,777	3,182
Total FIFO value	7,786	5,365
Less adjustment to LIFO value	(1,637)	(1,461)
Inventories	$6,149	$3,904

We note that not all of Deere's inventories are reported using the same inventory costing method (companies can use different inventory costing methods for different inventory pools).

a. At what dollar amount are Deere's inventories reported on its 2018 balance sheet?

b. At what dollar amount would inventories have been reported on Deere's 2018 balance sheet had it used FIFO inventory costing?

c. What *cumulative* effect has the use of LIFO inventory costing had, as of year-end 2018, on its pretax income compared with the pretax income it would have reported had it used FIFO inventory costing? Explain.

d. Assuming a 25% income tax rate, by what *cumulative* dollar amount has Deere's tax liability been affected by use of LIFO inventory costing as of year-end 2018? Has the use of LIFO inventory costing increased or decreased its cumulative tax liability?

e. What effect has the use of LIFO inventory costing had on Deere's pretax income and tax liability for 2018 (assume a 25% income tax rate)?

f. Deere's 2016 annual report has similar disclosures but also states: "The pretax favorable income effects from the liquidation of LIFO inventory during 2016 and 2015 were approximately $4 million and $22 million, respectively." Explain what happened in 2015 and 2016 with respect to Deere's inventory and why there were favorable income effects.

E7-31. Analyzing Inventories Using LIFO Inventory Footnote

LO2, 4, 5

Whole Foods
NASDAQ :: WFMI

The footnote below is from the 2017 10-K report of Whole Foods Market, Inc., a Texas-based retail grocery chain.

Inventories

The Company values inventories at the lower of cost or market. Cost was determined using the dollar value retail last-in, first-out ("LIFO") method for approximately 92.9% and 91.8% of inventories in fiscal years 2017 and 2016, respectively. Under the LIFO method, the cost assigned to items sold is based on the cost of the most recent items purchased. As a result, the costs of the first items purchased remain in inventory and are used to value ending inventory. The excess of estimated current costs over LIFO carrying value, or LIFO reserve, was approximately $47 million and $42 million at September 24, 2017 and September 25, 2016, respectively. Costs for remaining inventories are determined by the first-in, first-out method. Cost before the LIFO adjustment is principally determined using the item cost method, which is calculated by counting each item in inventory, assigning costs to each of these items based on the actual purchase cost (net of vendor allowances) of each item and recording the actual cost of items sold.

Whole Foods operates the world's largest chain of natural and organic food stores. In 2017, Whole Foods reported sales revenue of $16,030 million and cost of goods sold of $10,633 million. The following information was extracted from the company's 2017 and 2016 balance sheets:

($ millions)	2017	2016
Merchandise inventories	$471	$517

a. Calculate the amount of inventories purchased by Whole Foods in 2017.

b. What amount of gross profit would Whole Foods have reported if the FIFO method had been used to value all inventories?

c. Calculate the gross profit margin (GPM) as reported and assuming that the FIFO method had been used to value all inventories.

LO5

Tiffany & Co.
NYSE :: TIF
Best Buy
NYSE :: BBY
RH, Inc.
NYSE :: RH

E7-32. Calculating Gross Profit Margin and Inventory Turnover

The following table presents sales revenue, cost of goods sold, and inventory amounts for three specialty retailers, Tiffany & Co., Best Buy, and RH.

($ millions)	2017	2016
Tiffany & Co.		
Revenues	$ 4,170	$ 4,002
Cost of goods sold	1,565	1,512
Inventory	2,254	2,158
Best Buy		
Revenues	$42,151	$39,403
Cost of goods sold	32,275	29,963
Inventory	5,209	4,864
RH		
Revenues	$ 2,440	$ 2,135
Cost of goods sold	1,591	1,455
Inventory	527	752

a. Compute the gross profit margin (GPM) for each of these companies for 2017 and 2016.

b. Compute the inventory turnover ratio and the average inventory days outstanding for 2017 for each company.

c. What factors might determine the differences among these three companies' ratios?

PROBLEMS

LO2, 4, 5

Caterpillar, Inc.
NYSE :: CAT
Komatsu Ltd. (ADR)
OTC :: KMTUY

P7-33. Analyzing Inventory and Its Footnote Disclosure

Caterpillar Inc. and Komatsu Ltd. are international manufacturers of industrial and construction equipment. Caterpillar's headquarters is in the United States, while Komatsu's headquarters is in Japan. The following information comes from their recent financial statements.

Caterpillar—fiscal year ending December 31, 2017 ($ millions)	
Cost of goods sold	$31,049
Beginning inventory	8,614
Ending inventory	10,018
Komatsu—fiscal year ending March 31, 2018 (¥ millions)	
Cost of goods sold	¥1,765,832
Beginning inventory	533,897
Ending inventory	730,288

In its footnotes, Caterpillar also provides the following information (assume no LIFO liquidation):

Inventories

Inventories are stated at the lower of cost or market. Cost is principally determined using the last-in, first-out (LIFO) method. The value of inventories on the LIFO basis represented about 65 percent of total inventories at December 31, 2017, and about 60 percent at December 31, 2016. If the FIFO (first-in, first-out) method had been in use, inventories would have been $1,934 million and $2,139 million higher than reported at December 31, 2017 and 2016, respectively.

REQUIRED

a. Calculate the inventory turnover and average inventory days outstanding ratios for Caterpillar and Komatsu using the information reported in their financial statements. Describe some operational reasons that companies might have differing inventory ratios, even if they are in the same industry.

b. Did the cost of Caterpillar's acquiring (i.e., producing) products go up or down in 2017?

c. Assuming a 25% income tax rate, by what cumulative dollar amount has Caterpillar's tax liability been affected by use of LIFO inventory costing as of fiscal year-end 2017? Has the use of LIFO inventory costing increased or decreased its cumulative tax liability?

d. What effect has the use of LIFO inventory costing had on Caterpillar's pretax income and tax liability for fiscal year 2017? (Assume a 25% tax rate.)

e. In its footnotes, Komatsu reports that it "determines cost of work in process and finished products using the specific identification method based on actual costs accumulated under a job-order cost system. The cost of finished parts is determined principally using the first-in, first-out method." What effect does this footnote have on your interpretation in question *a* above? Use the information available to make a more appropriate comparison of the two companies' inventory turnover.

P7-34. Analyzing Inventory Disclosure Comparing LIFO and FIFO **LO2, 4, 5**

Kroger
NYSE :: KR

The current asset section of the 2017 and 2016 fiscal year end balance sheets of The Kroger Co. are presented in the accompanying table:

($ millions)	February 3, 2018	January 28, 2017
Current assets		
Cash and temporary cash investments	$ 347	$ 322
Deposits in-transit	1,161	910
Receivables	1,637	1,649
FIFO inventory	7,781	7,852
LIFO reserve	(1,248)	(1,291)
Assets held for sale	604	—
Prepaid and other current assets	835	898
Total current assets	$11,117	$10,340

In addition, Kroger provides the following footnote describing its inventory accounting policy (assume the following is their complete disclosure):

Inventories are stated at the lower of cost (principally on a LIFO basis) or market. In total, approximately 93% of inventories in 2017 and 89% of inventories in 2016 were valued using the LIFO method. Cost for the balance of the inventories, including substantially all fuel inventories, was determined using the FIFO method. Replacement cost was higher than the carrying amount by $1,248 million at February 3, 2018 and $1,291 million at January 28, 2017. We follow the Link-Chain, Dollar-Value LIFO method for purposes of calculating our LIFO charge or credit.

REQUIRED

a. At what dollar amount does Kroger report its inventory in its February 3, 2018, balance sheet?

b. What is the cumulative effect (through February 3, 2018) of the use of LIFO on Kroger's pretax earnings?

c. Assuming a 25% tax rate, what is the cumulative (through February 3, 2018) tax effect of the use of LIFO to determine inventory costs?

d. Kroger reported net earnings of $1,907 million in its fiscal year 2017 income statement. Assuming a 25% tax rate, what amount of net earnings would Kroger report if the company used the FIFO inventory costing method?

e. Kroger reported merchandise costs (cost of goods sold) of $95,662 million in fiscal year 2017. Compute its inventory turnover for the year.

f. How would the inventory turnover ratio differ if the FIFO costing method had been used?

LO5 Homework MBC

Samsung Electronics Co. Ltd.
KRX :: 005930
Hewlett-Packard Company
NYSE :: HPQ
Apple Inc.
NASDAQ :: AAPL

P7-35. Calculating Gross Profit and Inventory Turnover

The following table presents sales revenue, cost of goods sold, and inventory amounts for three computer/electronics companies, Samsung Electronics Co., Hewlett-Packard Company, and Apple Inc.

($ millions)	Fiscal year ending		
Samsung Electronics Co. Ltd. (S. Korean won)	Dec. 31, 2017	Dec. 31, 2016	Dec. 31, 2015
Revenues	239,575,376	201,866,745	200,653,482
Cost of goods sold	129,290,661	120,277,715	123,482,118
Inventory	24,983,355	18,353,503	18,811,794
Hewlett-Packard Company (US dollar)	Oct. 31, 2018	Oct. 31, 2017	Oct. 31, 2016
Revenues (products only)	58,472	52,056	48,238
Cost of goods sold	47,803	42,478	39,240
Inventory	6,062	5,786	4,484
Apple Inc. (US dollar)	Sep. 30, 2018	Sep. 30, 2017	Sep. 30, 2016
Revenues	265,395	229,234	215,639
Cost of goods sold	163,756	141,048	131,376
Inventory	3,956	4,855	2,132

REQUIRED

a. Compute the gross profit margin (GPM) for each of these companies for all three fiscal years.

b. Compute the inventory turnover ratio and the average inventory days outstanding for each company for the last two fiscal years. (All three firms use FIFO inventory costing.)

c. What factors might determine the differences among these three companies' ratios?

LO2, 4, 6

Seneca Foods Corporation
NASDAQ :: SENEA

P7-36.[A] Analyzing and Interpreting Inventories and Its Related Ratios and Disclosures

The current asset section from Seneca Foods Corporation, a low-cost producer and distributor of quality fruits and vegetables, March 31, 2018 annual report follows:

($ thousands)	March 31, 2018	March 31, 2017
Current Assets		
Cash and cash equivalents	$ 15,102	$ 11,992
Accounts receivable, net	78,796	72,080
Inventories	680,828	628,935
Refundable income taxes	1,142	2,471
Other current assets	2,144	3,671
Total current assets	$778,012	$719,149

Seneca reports the following related to its gross profit:

	Fiscal Years	
($ thousands)	2018	2017
Net sales	$1,314,765	$1,262,198
Cost of sales	1,240,178	1,150,194
Gross profit	$ 74,587	$ 112,004

Seneca further reports the following footnote:

11. Inventories

Effective December 30, 2007 (beginning of 4th quarter of Fiscal Year 2008), the Company changed its inventory valuation method from the lower of cost, determined under the FIFO method, or market to the lower of cost, determined under the LIFO method, or market. In the high inflation environment that the Company was experiencing, the Company believed that the LIFO inventory method was preferable over the FIFO method because it better compares the cost of current production to current revenue. The effect of LIFO was to reduce net earnings by $11.2 million in 2018, increase net earnings by $6.6 million in 2017 and increase net earnings by $18.0 million in 2016, compared to what would have been reported using the FIFO inventory method. There were no LIFO liquidations during the three-year period ending March 31, 2018. The excess of FIFO cost of inventory over the LIFO cost of inventory was $158.8 million in 2018 and $143.8 million in 2017.

In prior financial statements, Seneca has stated that it "manages the Company for cash, not reported earnings" and that the "decision to switch to LIFO has turned out to be a very prudent one of the last five years."

a. Compute the ratio of inventories to total current assets for 2018. As recently as 2014, this ratio was 77%. Is the change observed for the ratio a positive development for a company such as Seneca? Explain.

b. Compute inventory turnover for both 2018 and 2017 (2016 ending inventories were $609,481). Interpret and explain the change in inventory turnover as positive or negative for the company.

c. What inventory costing method does Seneca use? What effect has the use of this method (relative to FIFO or LIFO) had on its reported income for 2018 and 2017? Was the result an increase or decrease? Explain.

d. Seneca claims that it manages its company for cash flow. Does its inventory reporting help the Company to do so? How much in taxes has Seneca saved, assuming a 25% tax rate, by the inventory approach it adopted?

CASES AND PROJECTS

C7-37.[A] Analyzing Effects of LIFO on Inventory Turnover Ratios LO2, 4, 5, 6

Exxon Mobil Corp. NYSE :: XOM
BP, p.l.c. NYSE :: BP

The current assets of Exxon Mobil Corporation follow:

($ millions)	2017	2016
Current assets		
Cash and cash equivalents	$ 3,177	$ 3,657
Notes and accounts receivable, less estimated doubtful amounts	25,597	21,394
Inventories:		
Crude oil, products and merchandise	12,871	10,877
Materials and supplies	4,121	4,203
Other current assets	1,368	1,285
Total current assets	$47,134	$41,416

In addition, the following note was provided in its 2017 10-K report:

Inventories. Crude oil, products and merchandise inventories are carried at the lower of current market value or cost (generally determined under the last-in, first-out method—LIFO). Inventory costs include expenditures and other charges (including depreciation) directly and indirectly incurred in bringing the inventory to its existing condition and location. Selling expenses and general and administrative expenses are reported as period costs and excluded from inventory cost. Inventories of materials and supplies are valued at cost or less.

In 2017, 2016 and 2015, net income included losses of $10 million, $295 million and $186 million, respectively, attributable to the combined effects of LIFO inventory accumulations and drawdowns. The aggregate replacement cost of inventories was estimated to exceed their LIFO carrying values by $10.8 billion and $8.1 billion at December 31, 2017, and 2016, respectively.

REQUIRED

a. Exxon Mobil reported pretax earnings of $18,674 million in 2017. What amount of pretax earnings would have been reported by the company if inventory had been reported using the FIFO costing method?

b. Exxon Mobil reported cost of goods sold of $128,217 million in 2017. Compute its inventory turnover ratio for 2017 using total inventories.

c. BP, p.l.c. (BP) reports its financial information using IFRS. For fiscal year 2017, BP reported cost of goods sold of $179,716 million, beginning inventory of $17,655 million and ending inventory of $19,011 million. Compute BP's inventory turnover ratio for fiscal year 2017.

d. Compare your answers in parts *b* and *c*. BP can't use LIFO to report under IFRS, so revise your calculations in such a way as to find out which company has faster inventory turnover.

e. What is meant by the statement that "2017 net income included losses of $10 million attributable to the combined effects of LIFO inventory accumulations and draw-downs"?

LO2, 4
Virco Manufacturing Corp.
NASDAQ :: VIRC

C7-38. Analyzing Effects of Change from LIFO to FIFO Inventory Costing
Virco Manufacturing Corp. provided the following note in its annual report for the year ended January 31, 2011:

> On January 31, 2011, the Company elected to change its costing method for the material component of raw materials, work in process, and finished goods inventory to the lower of cost or market using the first-in first-out ("FIFO") method, from the lower of cost or market using the last-in first out ("LIFO") method. The labor and overhead components of inventory have historically been valued on a FIFO basis. The Company believes that the FIFO method for the material component of inventory is preferable as it conforms the inventory costing methods for all components of inventory into a single costing method and better reflects current acquisition costs of those inventories on our consolidated balance sheets. Additionally, presentation of inventory at FIFO aligns the financial reporting with the Company's borrowing base under its line of credit (see Note 3 for further discussion of the line of credit). Further, this change will promote greater comparability with companies that have adopted International Financial Reporting Standards, which does not recognize LIFO as an acceptable accounting method. In accordance with FASB ASC Topic 250, "Accounting Changes and Error Corrections," all prior periods presented have been adjusted to apply the new accounting method retrospectively. In addition, as an indirect effect of the change in our inventory costing method from LIFO to FIFO, the Company recorded additional inventory lower of cost or market expenses and changes in deferred tax assets and income tax expense. The retroactive effect of the change in our inventory costing method...increased the February 1, 2008, opening retained earnings balance by $4.1 million, and increased our inventory and retained earnings balances by $8.5 million and $5.4 million as of January 31, 2009, by $6.9 million and $4.3 million as of January 31, 2010, and by $7.6 million and $4.7 million as of January 31, 2011, respectively.

REQUIRED

a. What do the stated changes in inventory in each year represent (e.g., the $7.6 million in 2011)? Equity? What is the difference between the two?

b. What were Virco's stated reasons for the change to FIFO?

c. In the Annual Report for the year ended January 2010, Virco states the following: "Inventories are stated at the lower of cost or market. Cost is determined using the last-in, first-out ("LIFO") method of valuation for the material content of inventories and the first-in, first-out ("FIFO") method for labor and overhead. The Company uses LIFO as it results in a better matching of costs and revenues." What are some possible motivations behind why Virco changed to the FIFO method of accounting beyond those listed by management?

SOLUTIONS TO REVIEW PROBLEMS

Mid-Chapter Review Part 1

SOLUTION

Preliminary computation: Units in ending inventory = 4,800 available – 2,800 sold = 2,000

1. First-in, first-out (FIFO)

Cost of goods sold computation:	Units		Cost		Total
	1,000	@	$18.00	=	$18,000
	1,800	@	$18.25	=	32,850
	2,800				**$50,850**
Cost of goods available for sale		$88,450			
Less: Cost of goods sold		50,850			
Ending inventory ($22,800 + $14,800)		**$37,600**			

2. Last-in, first-out (LIFO)

Cost of goods sold computation:	**Units**		**Cost**		**Total**
	1,200	@	$19.00	=	$22,800
	800	@	$18.50	=	14,800
	800	@	$18.25	=	14,600
	2,800				**$52,200**
Cost of goods available for sale	$88,450				
Less: Cost of goods sold	52,200				
Ending inventory [$18,000 + (1,000 × $18.25)]	**$36,250**				

3. Average cost (AC)

Average unit cost	= $88,450/4,800	= $18.427
Cost of goods sold	= 2,800 × $18.427	= $51,596
Ending inventory	= 2,000 × $18.427	= $36,854

4. *a.* FIFO in most circumstances reflects physical flow. For example, FIFO would apply to the physical flow of perishables and to situations where the earlier items acquired are moved out first because of risk of deterioration or obsolescence.
   b. LIFO results in the lowest ending inventory amount during periods of rising costs, which in turn yields the lowest net income and the lowest income taxes.
5. Last-in, first-out with LIFO liquidation

Cost of goods sold computation:	**Units**		**Cost**		**Total**
	800	@	$18.50	=	$14,800
	1,800	@	$18.25	=	32,850
	200	@	$18.00	=	3,600
	2,800				**$51,250**
Cost of goods available for sale	$65,650				
Less: Cost of goods sold	51,250				
Ending inventory (800 × $18)	**$14,400**				

The company's LIFO gross profit has increased by $950 ($52,200 – $51,250). This increase is from LIFO liquidation, which is the reduction of inventory quantities that results in matching older (lower) cost layers against current selling prices. The company has, in effect, dipped into lower-cost layers to boost current period profit—all from a simple delay of inventory purchases.

6. Transaction effects shown in the financial statement effects template, journal entries, and T-accounts.

	Balance Sheet									**Income Statement**				
Transaction	**Cash Asset**	+	**Noncash Assets**	=	**Liabil-ities**	+	**Contrib. Capital**	+	**Earned Capital**	***Revenues***	−	***Expenses***	=	***Net Income***
(1) Purchase $70,450 of inventory.	−70,450 Cash		+70,450 Inventory	=							−		=	

ANALYZE JOURNALIZE POST

(1) Inventory (+A)	70,450	
Cash (−A)		70,450

+	**Inventory (A)**	−
(1) 70,450		

+	**Cash (A)**	−
		70,450 (1)

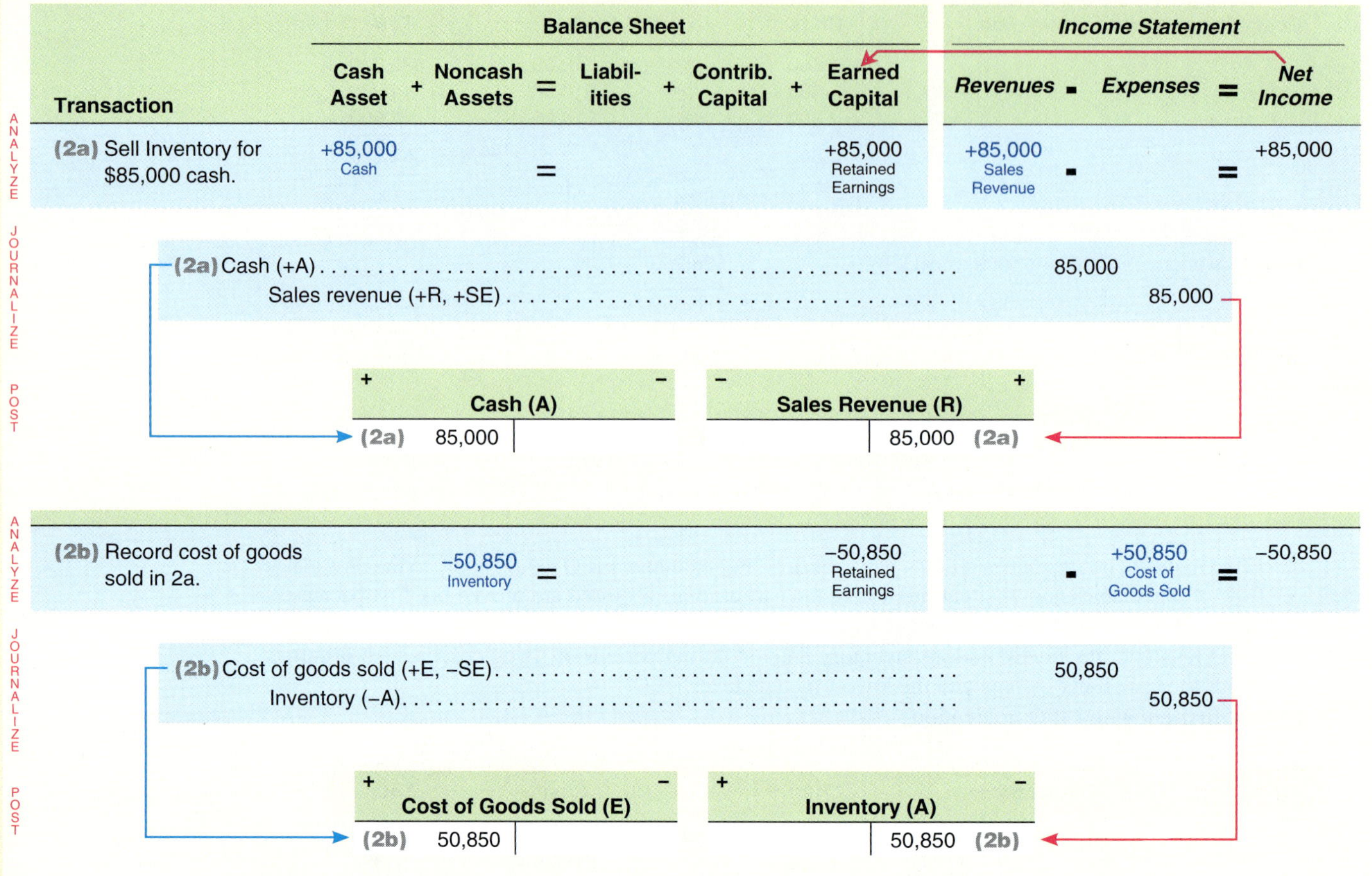

Mid-Chapter Review Part 2

SOLUTION

1.

Item	Quantity	Cost	NRV	Inventory Amounts: Cost	NRV	LCNRV (by Item)
Fans						
Model X1	300	$18	$19	$ 5,400	$ 5,700	$ 5,400
Model X2	250	22	24	5,500	6,000	5,500
Model X3	400	29	26	11,600	10,400	10,400
Totals				$22,500	$22,100	$21,300
Heaters						
Model B7	500	24	28	$12,000	$14,000	$12,000
Model B8	290	35	32	10,150	9,280	9,280
Model B9	100	41	38	4,100	3,800	3,800
Totals				26,250	27,080	25,080
Totals				$48,750	$49,180	$46,380

a. As shown in this schedule, applying the lower of cost or NRV rule to each item of the inventory results in an ending inventory amount of $46,380.

b. Applying the lower of cost or NRV rule to each major category of the inventory results in an ending inventory amount of $48,350, calculated as follows:

Fans	$22,100
Heaters.	26,250
	$48,350

c. As shown in this schedule, applying the lower of cost or NRV rule to the total inventory results in an ending inventory amount of $48,750.

2. The LCM procedure that results in the lowest ending inventory amount also results in the lowest net income for the year (the lower the ending inventory amount, the higher the cost of goods sold). Applying the lower of cost or NRV rule to each item of the inventory results in the lowest net income for the year.

Chapter-End Review

SOLUTION

1. The gross profit margin and inventory turnover are calculated as follows:

Gross profit margin:		
2015:	$9,159/$32,619 =	0.281 (or 28.1%)
2016:	$9,540/$34,274 =	0.278 (or 27.8%)
2017:	$9,707/$34,837 =	0.279 (or 27.9%)
Inventory turnover:		
2016:	$24,734/[($1,741 + $1,722)/2] =	14.3 times
2017:	$25,130/[($1,722 + $1,877)/2] =	14.0 times

2. Cost of goods sold and gross profit must be adjusted by the change in the LIFO reserve to convert to FIFO.

Cost of goods sold		
2016:	$24,734 – ($442 – $447) =	$24,739
2017:	$25,130 – ($465 – $442) =	$25,107
Gross profit		
2016:	$9,540 + ($442 – $447) =	$ 9,535
2017:	$9,707 + ($465 – $442) =	$ 9,730

The use of LIFO resulted in a higher cost of goods sold and a lower gross profit in 2016, but a lower cost of goods sold and a higher gross profit in 2018.

3. Restated inventory turnover calculations:

2016:	$24,739/[($2,164 + $2,188)/2] =	11.4 times
2017:	$25,107/[($2,342 + $2,164)/2] =	11.1 times

Because inventory values are higher and cost of goods sold is lower in 2017 and slightly higher in 2016 under FIFO, the inventory turnover ratio is lower when FIFO numbers are used.

Appendix 7A Review

SOLUTION

a.

Sales revenue	
(11,500 × $65).	$747,500
Cost of goods sold	
(7,000 × $70) + (3,000 × $30) + (1,500 × $20) . . .	610,000
Gross profit.	$137,500

b.

Sales revenue	
(11,500 × $65).	$747,500
Cost of goods sold	
(11,500 × $70).	805,000
Gross profit.	$ (57,500)

c. Dickhaut should report in its footnotes that gross profit was increased by $195,000 [$137,500 – $(57,500)] due to LIFO liquidation. It's worth noting that Dickhaut could report any gross profit between $(57,500) and $137,500 by adjusting its end-of-year purchases.

d. The replenishment decision should depend on the cash flows from each alternative over the planning period (until the point where inventory could be replenished next year at $55). The following table looks at three alternatives—no year-end purchase, a year-end purchase of 4,500 units, and a year-end purchase of 1,500 units. The second alternative would retain all the LIFO layers that were in the beginning inventory, while the third alternative would retain only the 2016 layer at $20 per unit. For this last alternative, cost of goods sold would be $685,000 (8,500 units at $70 each plus 3,000 units at $30 each).

As the table shows, the third alternative is preferred to the second, but the first alternative is preferred over the other two. (Of course, this analysis is based on the assumption that 5,000 units will be held in inventory for the entire planning horizon. If Dickhaut anticipates future inventory reductions, e.g., due to product changes, end-of-year purchases would only defer the payment of taxes and their relative benefits would decrease.)

	No purchase		Purchase 4,500 units		Purchase 1,500 units	
	Income	**Cash Flows**	**Income**	**Cash Flows**	**Income**	**Cash Flows**
Revenue	$747,500	$747,500	$747,500	$747,500	$747,500	$747,500
COGS	610,000		805,000		685,000	
Gross profit	137,500		(57,500)		62,500	
Tax (25%)	(34,375)	(34,375)	14,375	14,375	(15,625)	(15,625)
Year-end purchases				(315,000)		(105,000)
2020 purchases		(247,500)				(165,000)
Total cash flows		$465,625		$446,875		$461,875

Reporting and Analyzing Long-Term Operating Assets

LEARNING OBJECTIVES

1. Describe and distinguish between tangible and intangible assets. (p. 374)
2. Determine which costs to capitalize and report as assets and which costs to expense. (p. 375)
3. Apply different depreciation methods to allocate the cost of assets over time. (p. 377)
4. Determine the effects of asset sales and impairments on financial statements. (p. 381)
5. Describe the accounting and reporting for intangible assets. (p. 388)
6. Analyze the effects of tangible and intangible assets on key performance measures. (p. 393)

PROCTER & GAMBLE
www.pg.com

The Procter & Gamble Company (P&G) has successfully reinvented itself . . . again. Founded in 1837 by William Procter and James Gamble, P&G is the largest consumer products company in the world today. P&G markets its products in more than 180 countries and its annual sales now are in excess of $66 billion, which far exceeds competitors such as **Colgate-Palmolive Company** and **Kimberly-Clark Corporation**. P&G has focused on its higher-margin products such as those in beauty care. P&G's advertising budget is approximately 11% of sales, which is slightly larger than Colgate's and more than twice as large as Kimberly-Clark's.

P&G's financial performance has been impressive. Its return on equity (ROE) in 2018 was 18%. Although more financially leveraged than the average publicly traded company, there is little need for concern because P&G generates almost $15 billion in operating cash flow, which is more than sufficient to cover its $529 million in interest payments. P&G also paid $7 billion in dividends and repurchased more than $7 billion of its own shares in 2018. (Stock repurchases are covered more fully in Chapter 11.)

P&G has made divesting underperforming brands a strategic goal. For example, P&G recently sold off its pet care business to Mars, Inc. and Spectrum Brands Holdings, Inc. In addition, P&G agreed to divest its Duracell batteries business to Berkshire Hathaway, Inc. and has entered into deals to exit Vicks VapoStream, Camay and Zest bar soap brands, and several skin care and fragrance brands.

P&G's remaining product stable consists of numerous well-recognized household brands. Surveys in the business press show that the company is widely admired. A partial listing follows by business segment, including some "Billion Dollar Brands" in each segment:

- **Baby and Family Care**—Bounty, Charmin, Pampers
- **Beauty**— CoverGirl, Head & Shoulders, Olay, Pantene, Wella
- **Fabric and Home Care**—Ace, Febreze, Cascade, Cheer, Dawn, Downy, Gain, Tide
- **Grooming**—Braun, Gillette, Mach3
- **Health Care**—Always, Crest, Oral-B

However, substantial risks exist. In the fiscal 2018 annual report, management states that "Our business model relies on continued growth and success of existing brands and products, as well as the creation of new innovative products. The markets and industry segments in which we offer our products are highly competitive. . . Our growth strategy is to provide meaningful and noticeable superiority in all elements of our consumer proposition." External risks also exist. For example, in recent years commodity costs have risen rapidly and significantly, and cautious consumers have made it difficult for P&G to increase prices and maintain margins. Around 60% of the company's business is generated outside North America. Currency exchange rate fluctuations and trade policies can have a disruptive effect on distribution channels and sales growth.

In this chapter, we explore the reporting and analysis of long-term operating assets. In order to maintain growth in sales, income, and cash flows, capital-intensive companies like P&G must be diligent in managing long-term operating assets. As is the case with P&G, many companies have made large investments in innovation and brand value. These investments are not always reflected adequately in the balance sheet. Management's choices and GAAP rules concerning the reporting of long-term operating assets can have a marked impact on the analysis and interpretation of financial statements.

Sources: *Procter & Gamble* 2018 Annual Report and 10-K.

CHAPTER ORGANIZATION

Reporting and Analyzing Long-Term Operating Assets

Property, Plant, and Equipment	Analyzing Financial Statements	Intangible Assets
• Determining Costs to Capitalize • Depreciation Methods • Changes in Accounting Estimates • Asset Sales and Impairments • Footnote Disclosures	• PPE Turnover • Percent Depreciated Ratio • Cash Flow Effects	• Research and Development Costs • Patents, Copyrights, Trademarks, and Franchise Rights • Amortization and Impairment • Goodwill • Footnote Disclosures • Analysis Implications

1

LO1 Describe and distinguish between tangible and intangible assets.

INTRODUCTION

Investments in long-term operating assets often represent the largest component of a company's balance sheet. Effectively managing long-term operating assets is crucial, because these investments affect company performance for several years and are frequently irreversible. To evaluate how well a company is managing operating assets, we need to understand how they are measured and reported.

This chapter describes the accounting, reporting, and analysis of long-term operating assets including tangible and intangible assets. **Tangible assets** are assets that have physical substance. They are frequently included in the balance sheet as *property, plant, and equipment*, and include land, buildings, machinery, fixtures, and equipment. **Intangible assets**, such as trademarks and patents, do not have physical substance, but provide the owner with specific rights and privileges.

Long-term operating assets have two common characteristics. First, unlike inventory, these assets are not acquired for resale. Instead, they are necessary to produce and deliver the products and services that generate revenues for the company. Second, these assets help produce revenues for multiple accounting periods. Consequently, accountants focus considerable attention on how they are reported in the balance sheet and how these costs are transferred over time to the income statement as expenses.

To illustrate the size and importance of long-term operating assets, the asset section (only) of P&G's balance sheet is reproduced in **Exhibit 8.1**. We can see as of June 30, 2018, the end of P&G's fiscal year, P&G's net investment in property, plant, and equipment totaled approximately $20.6 billion and its intangible assets represent a $69.1 billion investment. Together, these two categories of assets make up over three-fourths of P&G's total assets.

This chapter is divided into two main sections. The first section focuses on accounting for tangible property, plant, and equipment and the related depreciation expense that is reported each period in the income statement. The second section examines the measurement and reporting of intangible assets.

PROPERTY, PLANT, AND EQUIPMENT (PPE)

For many companies, the largest category of operating assets is long-term property, plant, and equipment (PPE) assets. The size and duration of this asset category raises several important questions, including:

- Which costs should be **capitalized** on the balance sheet as assets? Which should be expensed?
- How should capitalized costs be allocated to the accounting periods that benefited from the asset?
- How should asset sales or significant changes in assets' fair values be reported?

This section explains the accounting, reporting, and analysis of PPE assets and related items.

EXHIBIT 8.1 Procter & Gamble Balance Sheet (assets only)

	June 30	
($ millions)	2018	2017
Assets		
Current assets		
Cash and cash equivalents	$2,569	5,569
Available-for-sale investment securities	9,281	9,568
Accounts receivable	4,686	4,594
Inventories		
Materials and supplies	1,335	1,308
Work in process	588	529
Finished goods	2,815	2,787
Total inventories	4,738	4,624
Prepaid expenses and other current assets	2,046	2,139
Total current assets	23,320	26,494
Property, plant, and equipment		
Buildings	7,188	6,943
Machinery and equipment	30,595	29,505
Land	841	765
Construction in progress	3,223	2,935
	41,847	40,148
Accumulated depreciation	(21,247)	(20,255)
Net property, plant, and equipment	20,600	19,893
Goodwill	45,175	44,699
Trademarks and other intangible assets, net	23,902	24,187
Other noncurrent assets	5,313	5,133
Total assets	$118,310	$120,406

Determining Costs to Capitalize

LO2 Determine which costs to capitalize and report as assets and which costs to expense. 2

When a company acquires an asset, it must first decide which portion of the cost should be included among the expenses of the current period and which costs should be capitalized as part of the asset and reported in the balance sheet. Outlays to acquire PPE are called **capital expenditures**. Expenditures that are recorded as an asset must possess each of the following two characteristics:

1. The asset is owned or controlled by the company.
2. The asset is expected to provide future benefits.

All normal costs incurred to acquire an asset and prepare it for its intended use should be capitalized and reported in the balance sheet. These costs would include the purchase price of the asset plus any of the following: installation costs, taxes, shipping costs, legal fees, and setup or calibration costs. If owning an asset carries legal obligations at the end of the asset's life (for example, to remove the asset or to perform environmental remediation), the current cost of those obligations should be included in the asset's cost and recognized as a liability at the time the asset is acquired. This cost will be included in the subsequent depreciation of the asset.

Determining the specific costs that should be capitalized requires judgment. There are two important considerations to address when deciding which costs to capitalize. First, companies can only capitalize costs that are *directly linked* to future benefits. Incidental costs or costs that would be incurred regardless of whether the asset is purchased should not be capitalized. Second, the costs capitalized as an asset can be no greater than the expected future benefits to be derived from use of the asset. This requirement means that if a company reports a $200 asset, we can reasonably expect that it will derive at least $200 in expected future cash inflows from the use and ultimate disposition of the asset.

Sometimes, companies construct assets for their own use rather than purchasing a similar asset from another company. In this case, all of the costs incurred to construct the asset—including materials, labor, and a reasonable amount of overhead—should be included in the cost that is capitalized. In addition, in many cases, a portion of the interest expense incurred during the construction period should also be capitalized as part of the asset's cost. This interest is called **capitalized interest**. Capitalizing some of a company's interest cost as part of the cost of a self-constructed asset reduces interest expense in the current period and increases depreciation expense in future periods when the asset is placed in service.

Once an asset is placed in service, additional costs are often incurred to maintain and improve the asset. Routine repairs and maintenance costs are necessary to realize the full potential benefits of ownership of the asset and should be treated as expenses of the period in which the maintenance is performed. However, if the cost can be considered an *improvement or betterment* of the asset, the cost should be capitalized. An improvement or betterment is an outlay that either enhances the usefulness of the asset or extends the asset's useful life beyond the original expectation.

YOU MAKE THE CALL

You are the Company Accountant Your company has just purchased a plot of land as a building site for an office building. After the purchase, you discover that the building site was once the site of an oil well. Before construction can commence, your company must spend $40,000 to properly cap the oil well and prepare the site to meet current environmental standards. How should you account for the $40,000 cleanup cost? [Answers on page 395]

Depreciation

FYI Depreciation is a systematic allocation of asset cost over the useful life—not a measure of the change in fair value.

Once an asset has been recorded in the balance sheet, the cost must be transferred over time from the balance sheet to the income statement and reported as an expense. The nature of long-term operating assets is that they benefit more than one period. As a consequence, it is impossible to match a specific portion of the cost *directly* to the revenues of a particular period. Accounting principles require that this expense be recognized as equitably as possible over the asset's useful economic life. Therefore, we rely on a *systematic allocation* to assign a portion of the asset's cost to each period benefited. This systematic allocation of cost is called **depreciation**.

The concept of systematic allocation of an asset's cost is important. When depreciation expense is recorded, the reported value of the asset (also called the *book value* or *carrying value*) is reduced. Naturally, it is tempting to infer that the fair value of the asset is lower as a result. However, this reported value does not reflect the fair value of the asset. The fair value of the asset may decline by more or less than the amount of depreciation expense, and can even increase in some periods. Depreciation expense should only be interpreted as an assignment of costs to an accounting period and not a measure of the decline in fair value of the asset.

The amount of cost that is allocated to a given period is recorded as depreciation expense in the income statement with a balancing entry in **accumulated depreciation** in the balance sheet. Accumulated depreciation is a contra-asset account (denoted "XA" in the journal entry). Like all contra-asset accounts, it offsets the balance in the corresponding asset account. To illustrate, assume that Dehning Company purchases a heavy-duty delivery truck for $100,000 and decides to record $18,000 of depreciation expense in the first year of operation. The following entries would be recorded with a cash outflow reflected in the investing section of the statement of cash flows.

The asset would be presented in the balance sheet at period-end at its net book value.

Truck, at cost	$100,000	
Less accumulated depreciation	18,000	
Truck, net	$ 82,000	(Book Value)

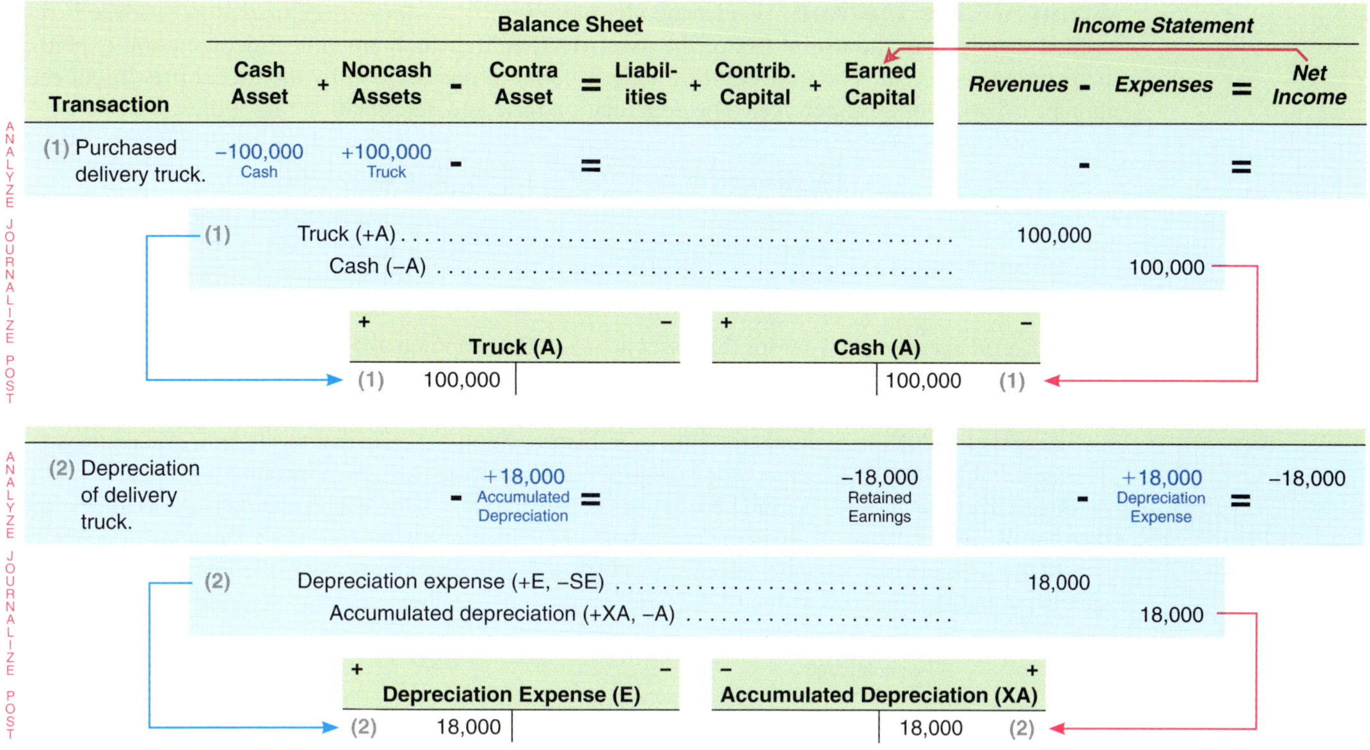

By presenting the information using a contra-asset account, the original acquisition cost of the asset is preserved in the asset account. The net book value of the asset reflects the acquisition cost less the balance in the accumulated depreciation account. The balance in the accumulated depreciation account is the sum of the depreciation expense that has been recorded to date. In **Exhibit 8.1**, Procter & Gamble reports that the original cost of its property, plant, and equipment is $41,847 million and the depreciation accumulated as of June 30, 2018 is $21,247 million. The result is a net book value of $20,600 million.

Depreciation Methods

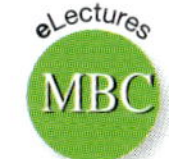

LO3 Apply different depreciation methods to allocate the cost of assets over time.

3

Two estimates are required to compute the amount of depreciation expense to record each period.

1. **Useful life**. The useful life is the period of time over which the asset is expected to provide economic benefits to the company. The useful life is not the same as the physical life of the asset. An asset may or may not provide economic benefits to the company for its entire physical life. This useful life should not exceed the period of time that the company intends to use the asset. For example, if a company has a policy of replacing automobiles every two years, the useful life should be set at no longer than two years, even if the automobiles physically last three years or more.
2. **Residual (or salvage) value**. The residual value is the expected realizable value of the asset at the end of its useful life. This value may be the disposal or scrap value, or it may be an estimated resale value for a used asset.

These factors must be estimated when the asset is acquired. The **depreciation base**, also called the *nonrecoverable cost*, is the portion of the cost that is depreciated. The depreciation base is the capitalized cost of the asset less the estimated residual value. This amount is allocated over the useful life of the asset according to the *depreciation method* that the company has selected.

To illustrate alternative depreciation methods, we return to the example presented earlier. Assume that Dehning Company purchases a delivery truck for $100,000. The company expects the truck to last five years and estimates a residual value of $10,000. The depreciation base is $90,000 ($100,000 – $10,000). We illustrate the three most common depreciation methods:

1. Straight-line method
2. Double-declining-balance method
3. Units-of-production method

Straight-Line Method Under the **straight-line (SL) method**, depreciation expense is recorded evenly over the useful life of the asset. That is, the same amount of depreciation expense is recorded each year. The **depreciation rate** is equal to one divided by the useful life. In our example, 1/5 = 0.2 or 20% per year. The depreciation base and depreciation rate follow.

Depreciation Base	Depreciation Rate
Cost – Salvage value = $100,000 – $10,000 = $90,000	1/Estimated useful life = 1/5 years = 20%

Depreciation expense per year for this asset is $18,000, computed as $90,000 × 20%. For the asset's first full year of usage, $18,000 of depreciation expense is reported in the income statement. At the end of that first year the asset is reported on the balance sheet as shown earlier in the chapter.

Accumulated depreciation is the sum of all depreciation expense that has been recorded to date. The asset **book value (BV)**, or *net book value* or *carrying value,* is cost less accumulated depreciation. Although the word "value" is used here, it does not refer to fair value. Depreciation is a cost allocation concept (transfer of costs from the balance sheet to the income statement), not a valuation concept.

In the second year of usage, another $18,000 of depreciation expense is recorded in the income statement and the net book value of the asset on the balance sheet is shown as follows:

Truck, at cost	$100,000
Less accumulated depreciation	36,000
Truck, net	$ 64,000

Accumulated depreciation now includes the sum of the first and second years' depreciation ($36,000), and the net book value of the asset is now reduced to $64,000. After the fifth year, a total of $90,000 of accumulated depreciation will be recorded, yielding a net book value for the truck of $10,000, its estimated salvage value.

Double-Declining-Balance Method GAAP allows companies to use **accelerated depreciation** methods. Accelerated depreciation methods record more depreciation expense in the early years of an asset's useful life and less expense in the later years. The total depreciation expense recorded *over the entire useful life* of the asset is the same as with straight-line depreciation. The only difference is in the amount of depreciation recorded for *any given year.*

The **double-declining-balance (DDB) method** is an accelerated depreciation method that computes the depreciation rate as twice the straight-line rate. This double rate is then multiplied by the net book value of the asset, which declines each period as accumulated depreciation increases. For Dehning Company, the depreciation base and the depreciation rate are computed as follows:

Depreciation Base	Depreciation Rate
Net Book Value = Cost – Accumulated Depreciation	2 × SL rate = 2 × 20% = 40%

FYI When calculating DDB depreciation, the depreciation rate is multiplied by the book value; residual value is not subtracted from book value.

The depreciation expense for the first year of usage for this asset is $40,000, computed as $100,000 × 40%. At the end of the first full year, $40,000 of depreciation expense is reported on the income statement (compared with $18,000 under the SL method), and the asset is reported on the balance sheet as follows:

Truck, at cost	$100,000
Less accumulated depreciation	40,000
Truck, net	$ 60,000

In the second year, $24,000 ($60,000 × 40%) of depreciation expense is reported in the income statement and the net book value of the asset on the balance sheet is shown as follows:

Truck, at cost	$100,000
Less accumulated depreciation	64,000
Truck, net	$ 36,000

The double-declining-balance method continues to record depreciation expense in this manner until the salvage amount is reached, at which point the depreciation process is discontinued. This leaves a net book value equal to the salvage value as with the straight-line method. The DDB depreciation schedule for the life of this asset is illustrated in **Exhibit 8.2**.

EXHIBIT 8.2 Double-Declining-Balance Depreciation Schedule

Year	Book Value at Beginning of Year	Depreciation Expense	Book Value at End of Year
1	$100,000	100,000 × 40% = $40,000	$60,000
2	60,000	60,000 × 40% = 24,000	36,000
3	36,000	36,000 × 40% = 14,400	21,600
4	21,600	21,600 × 40% = 8,640	12,960
5	12,960	12,960 − 10,000 = 2,960*	10,000

*The depreciation expense in the fifth year is not calculated as 40% × $12,960 because the resulting depreciation would reduce the net book value below the $10,000 residual value. Instead, the residual value ($10,000) is subtracted from the remaining book value ($12,960), resulting in depreciation expense of $2,960.

Exhibit 8.3 compares the depreciation expense and net book value for both the SL and DDB methods. During the first two years, the DDB method yields higher depreciation expense in comparison with the SL method. Beginning in the third year, this pattern reverses and the SL method produces higher depreciation expense. Over the asset's life, the same $90,000 in total depreciation expense is recorded, leaving a residual value of $10,000 on the balance sheet under both methods.

EXHIBIT 8.3 Comparison of Straight-Line and Double-Declining-Balance Depreciation

	Straight-Line		Double-Declining-Balance	
Year	Depreciation Expense	Book Value at End of Year	Depreciation Expense	Book Value at End of Year
1	$18,000	$82,000	$40,000	$60,000
2	18,000	64,000	24,000	36,000
3	18,000	46,000	14,400	21,600
4	18,000	28,000	8,640	12,960
5	18,000	10,000	2,960	10,000
	$90,000		$90,000	

All depreciation methods yield the same salvage value

Total depreciation over asset life is identical for all methods

Units-of-Production Method Under the **units-of-production method**, the useful life of the asset is defined in terms of the number of units of service provided by the asset. For instance, this could be the number of units produced, the number of hours that a machine is operated, or, as with Dehning Company's delivery truck, the number of miles driven. To illustrate, assume that Dehning Company estimates that the delivery truck will provide 150,000 miles of service before it is sold for its residual value of $10,000. The depreciation rate is expressed in terms of a cost per mile driven, computed as follows:

$$\frac{\$100,000 - \$10,000}{150,000 \text{ miles}} = \$0.60 \text{ per mile}$$

If the delivery truck is driven 35,000 miles in year 1, the depreciation expense for that year would be $21,000 (35,000 × $0.60). This method produces an amount of depreciation that varies from year to year as the use of the asset varies.

The units-of-production method is used by companies with natural resources such as oil reserves, mineral deposits, or timberlands. These assets are often referred to as **wasting assets**, because the asset is consumed as it is used. The acquisition cost of a natural resource, plus any costs incurred to prepare the asset for its intended use, should be capitalized and reported among PPE assets in the balance sheet.

When the natural resource is used or extracted, inventory is created. The cost of the resource is transferred from the long-term asset account into inventory and, once the inventory is sold, to the income statement as cost of goods sold. The process of transferring costs from the resource account into inventory is called **depletion**.

Depletion is very much like depreciation of tangible operating assets, except that the amount of depletion recorded each period should reflect the amount of the resource that was actually extracted or used up during that period. As a result, depletion is usually calculated using the units-of-production method. The depletion rate is calculated as follows:

$$\textbf{Depletion rate per unit consumed} = \frac{\textbf{Acquisition cost} - \textbf{Residual value}}{\textbf{Estimated quantity of resource available}}$$

The calculation requires an estimate of the quantity of the resource available, which usually requires the assistance of experts, such as geologists or engineers, who are trained to make these determinations.

Depreciation for Tax Purposes Most companies use the straight-line method for financial reporting purposes and an accelerated depreciation method for tax returns.[1] Governments allow accelerated depreciation, in part, to provide incentives for taxpayers to invest. As a result of the differing depreciation methods used for financial accounting and tax purposes, lower depreciation expense (and higher income) is reported for financial accounting purposes early in the life of an asset relative to tax purposes. Even though this difference reverses in later years, companies prefer to defer the tax payments so that the cash savings can be invested to produce earnings. Further, even with the reversal in the later years of an asset's life, if total depreciable assets are growing at a fast enough rate, the additional first-year depreciation on newly acquired assets more than offsets the lower depreciation expense on older assets, yielding a continuing deferral of taxable income and taxes paid. There are other differences between financial reporting and tax reporting that create issues in determining a company's tax expense. In Chapter 10, we explore these differences further and examine deferred tax liabilities and deferred tax assets.

Changes in Accounting Estimates

The estimates required in the depreciation process are made when the asset is acquired. When necessary, companies can, and do, change these estimates during the useful lives of assets. When either the useful life or residual value estimates change, the change is applied prospectively. That is, companies use the new estimates from the date of the change going forward and do not restate the financial statements of prior periods.

To illustrate, assume that, after three years of straight-line depreciation, Dehning Company decided to extend the useful life of its truck from 5 years to 6 years. From **Exhibit 8.3**, the book value of the delivery truck at the end of the third year is $46,000. The change in estimated useful life would not require a formal accounting entry. Instead, depreciation expense would be recalculated for the remaining three years of the truck's useful life:

$$\frac{\$46,000 - \$10,000}{3 \text{ years}} = \$12,000 \text{ per year}$$

Thus, beginning in year four, depreciation expense of $12,000 (instead of $18,000) would be recorded each year.

[1] The IRS mandates the use of MACRS (Modified Accelerated Cost Recovery System) for tax purposes. This method fixes the useful life for various classes of assets, assumes no salvage value, and generally produces depreciation amounts consistent with the double-rate, double-declining-balance method. When a declining balance method is used with zero salvage, the depreciation schedule must switch after the midpoint of the asset's life to straight-line depreciation of the remaining balance over the remaining life.

Asset Sales and Impairments

This section discusses gains and losses from asset sales and computation and disclosure of asset impairments.

LO4 Determine the effects of asset sales and impairments on financial statements.

4

Gains and Losses on Asset Sales The gain or loss on the sale (disposition) of a long-term asset is computed as follows:

Gain or loss on asset sale = Proceeds from sale − Book value of asset sold

The book (carrying) value of an asset is its acquisition cost less accumulated depreciation. When an asset is sold, its acquisition cost and related accumulated depreciation are removed from the balance sheet and any gain or loss is reported in income from continuing operations. To illustrate such a transaction, assume that Dehning Company decided to sell the delivery truck after four years of straight-line depreciation. From **Exhibit 8.3**, we know that the book value of the truck is $28,000 ($100,000 – $72,000). If the truck is sold for $30,000, the entry to record the sale follows.

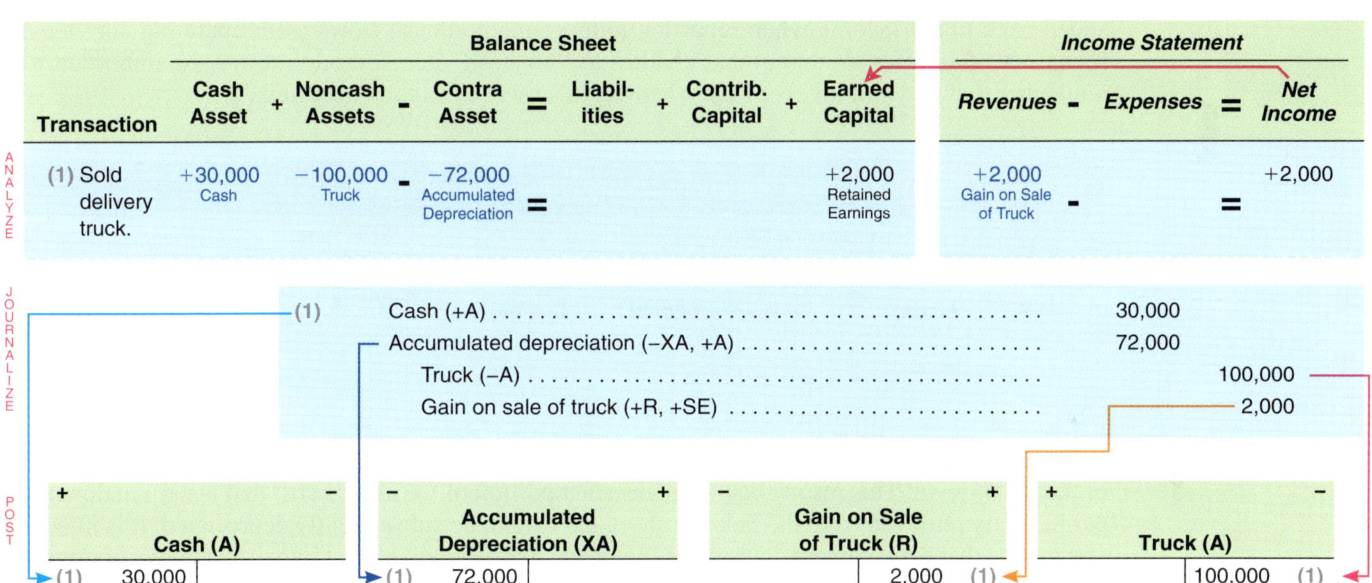

Transaction	Cash Asset	+	Noncash Assets	−	Contra Asset	=	Liabil-ities	+	Contrib. Capital	+	Earned Capital	Revenues	−	Expenses	=	Net Income
(1) Sold delivery truck.	+30,000 Cash		−100,000 Truck	−	−72,000 Accumulated Depreciation	=					+2,000 Retained Earnings	+2,000 Gain on Sale of Truck	−		=	+2,000

		Dr.	Cr.
(1)	Cash (+A)	30,000	
	Accumulated depreciation (−XA, +A)	72,000	
	Truck (−A)		100,000
	Gain on sale of truck (+R, +SE)		2,000

Cash (A)		Accumulated Depreciation (XA)		Gain on Sale of Truck (R)		Truck (A)	
+	−	−	+	−	+	+	−
(1) 30,000		(1) 72,000			2,000 (1)		100,000 (1)

Gains and losses on asset sales can be large, and analysts must be aware of these nonrecurring operating income components. Further, if the gains are deemed immaterial, companies often include such gains and losses in general line items of the income statement—often as a component of selling, general and administrative expenses. As described in Chapter 4, the $30,000 increase in cash is an investing cash inflow in the statement of cash flows, and the $2,000 gain would be subtracted from net income in an indirect-method statement of cash flows from operating activities.

Asset Impairments Property, plant, and equipment assets are reported at their net book values (original cost less accumulated depreciation). This is the case even if fair values of these assets increase subsequent to acquisition. As a result, there can be unrecognized gains hidden in the balance sheet.

However, if fair values of PPE assets subsequently decrease—and it can be determined that the asset value is permanently impaired—then companies must recognize losses on those assets. **Impairment** of PPE assets is determined by comparing the sum of *expected* future (undiscounted) cash flows from the asset with its net book value. If these expected cash flows are greater than net book value, no impairment is deemed to exist. However, if the sum of expected cash flows is less than net book value, the asset is deemed impaired and it is written down to its current fair value (generally, the discounted present value of those expected cash flows). **Exhibit 8.4** depicts this impairment analysis.

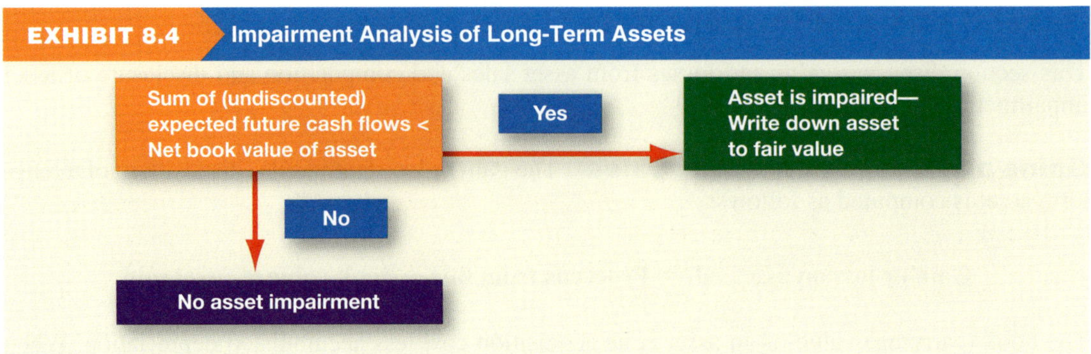

When a company records an impairment charge, assets are reduced by the amount of the write-down and the loss is recognized in the income statement, which reduces current period income. These effects are illustrated in **Exhibit 8.5**. Impairment charges are often included as part of **restructuring costs** along with future costs of workforce reductions. The entry in **Exhibit 8.5** reduces net income, but does not affect current cash flows, so the impairment charges would be added back to net income when reporting indirect-method cash flows from operating activities. Managers often refer to impairment charges as "noncash" items, though it may be important to remember that they did involve cash when the asset was originally acquired.

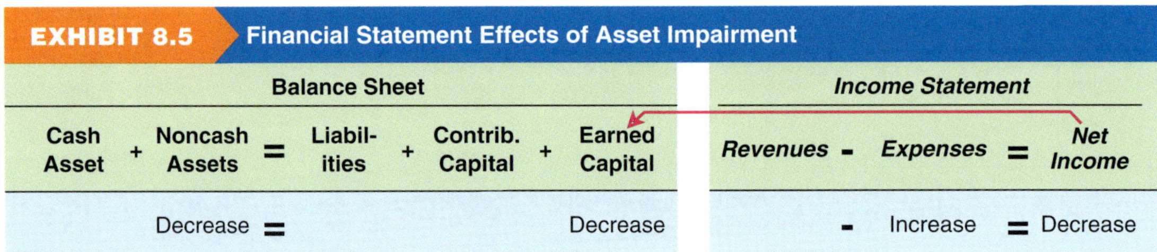

EXHIBIT 8.5 Financial Statement Effects of Asset Impairment

Balance Sheet										Income Statement				
Cash Asset	+	Noncash Assets	=	Liabil-ities	+	Contrib. Capital	+	Earned Capital		*Revenues*	-	*Expenses*	=	*Net Income*
		Decrease	=					Decrease			-	Increase	=	Decrease

Once a depreciable asset is written down, future depreciation charges are reduced by the amount of the write-down. This result occurs because that portion of the asset's cost that is written down is permanently removed from the balance sheet and cannot be subsequently depreciated. It is important to note that management determines if and when to recognize asset impairments. Write-downs of long-term assets are often recognized in connection with a restructuring program.

Analysis of asset write-downs presents two potential challenges:

1. *Insufficient write-down*. Assets sometimes are impaired to a larger degree than is recognized. This situation can arise if management is overly optimistic about future prospects or is reluctant to recognize the full loss in income. Underestimation of an impairment causes current income to be overstated and income in future years to be lower relative to income that would have been reported had the impairment been correctly recorded.
2. *Aggressive write-down*. This *big bath* scenario can arise if income is currently and severely depressed by recognizing a larger impairment charge than the actual costs. Management's view is that the market will not penalize the firm for an extra write-off, and that doing so purges the balance sheet of costs that would otherwise reduce future years' income. This leads to income being overstated for several years after the write-down.

Neither of these cases is condoned under GAAP. Yet, because management is estimating future cash flows for the impairment test and such estimates are difficult to verify, it has some degree of latitude over the timing and amount of the write-off and can use that discretion to manage reported income.

Footnote Disclosure

Procter & Gamble provides the following information in footnote 1 of its 2018 Annual Report to describe its accounting for PPE assets.

Property, plant, and equipment

Property, plant, and equipment is recorded at cost reduced by accumulated depreciation. Depreciation expense is recognized over the assets' estimated useful lives using the straight-line method.

Machinery and equipment includes office furniture and fixtures (15-year life), computer equipment and capitalized software (3- to 5-year lives) and manufacturing equipment (3- to 20-year lives). Buildings are depreciated over an estimated useful life of 40 years. Estimated useful lives are periodically reviewed and, where appropriate, changes are made prospectively. Where certain events or changes in operating conditions occur, asset lives may be adjusted and an impairment assessment may be performed on the recoverability of the carrying amounts.

The note details P&G's depreciation method (straight-line) and the estimated useful lives of various classes of PPE assets. Later in the notes, the company reports "asset-related costs" included in its restructuring charges for the year ended June 30, 2018. The company describes these costs as follows:

Asset-related costs

Asset-related costs consist of both asset write-downs and accelerated depreciation. Asset write-downs relate to the establishment of a new fair value basis for assets held-for-sale or disposal. These assets were written down to the lower of their current carrying basis or amounts expected to be realized upon disposal, less minor disposal costs. Charges for accelerated depreciation relate to long-lived assets that will be taken out of service prior to the end of their normal service period. These assets related primarily to manufacturing consolidations and technology standardization. The asset-related charges will not have a significant impact on future depreciation charges.

A GLOBAL PERSPECTIVE

International Financial Reporting Standards (IFRS) are very similar to U.S. GAAP in the recognition of asset values when acquired and in the depreciation methods allowed. However, IFRS requires that companies recognize depreciation separately on the significant components of an asset. So, a U.S. company that acquires a building might recognize a single asset and depreciate it over the expected useful life of the building. An IFRS company would be required to recognize a bundle of assets like the structure, the roof, the elevators, the HVAC system, etc. Each of these components would be depreciated separately over its expected useful life, generally producing a more accelerated depreciation expense.

One implication of this difference is that subsequent expenditures might be dealt with differently. The U.S. company that replaces the HVAC system after its expected fifteen-year life would classify the expenditure as a maintenance expense. But the IFRS company would have fully depreciated the original HVAC system, and the new system would be treated as a capital expenditure, creating a new asset.

International Financial Reporting Standards for changes in long-term operating asset values have significant differences from U.S. GAAP. IFRS allows companies to report their property, plant, and equipment on a revalued basis. That is, companies may choose to conduct regular appraisals of their property, plant, and equipment and to adjust their balance sheet amounts to those appraised values. Depreciation expense is also adjusted for changes in values. While this option is allowed under IFRS, it appears that the vast majority of companies use historical cost to account for property, plant, and equipment. (IFRS also has provisions for companies operating in hyperinflationary environments.)

For IFRS companies using historical cost, impairment is a single-step process in which an asset's book value is compared to the larger of its value in use (present value of future cash flows) and its net selling price (fair value less cost to sell). If the book value is higher, an impairment is reported. Unlike U.S. GAAP, if an impairment is subsequently recovered, an IFRS company may increase the asset's value to what it would have been without the prior impairment.

RESEARCH INSIGHT

Recent research provides evidence that while IFRS provides a free choice between fair value and historical cost for non-financial assets, most companies using IFRS commit to historical cost accounting for plant and equipment. The evidence is consistent with market demands leading managers to utilize historical cost when the reliability of fair value is lower and when costs of estimating fair value are higher.[2]

ANALYZING FINANCIAL STATEMENTS

Most companies produce their financial performance with their long-term operating assets like property, plant, and equipment and with their intellectual property. Effective use of these assets represents one of the key components of success for companies. In addition, these assets are acquired with the anticipation that they will provide benefits for an extended period of time. They are often expensive relative to their annual benefit, and most of these assets require replenishment on an ongoing basis.

Analysis Objective

We are trying to gauge the effectiveness of Procter & Gamble's use of its physical productive assets.

Analysis Tool PPE Turnover (PPET)

$$\text{PPE Turnover (PPET)} = \frac{\text{Sales revenue}}{\text{Average PPE, net}}$$

Applying the PPE Turnover Ratio to Procter & Gamble

$$\textbf{2016:}\ \frac{\$65{,}299}{\$19{,}520} = 3.35$$

$$\textbf{2017:}\ \frac{\$65{,}058}{\$19{,}639} = 3.31$$

$$\textbf{2018:}\ \frac{\$66{,}832}{\$20{,}247} = 3.30$$

Guidance Property, plant, and equipment turnovers vary greatly by industry and are affected by companies' manufacturing strategies, so it is difficult to give specific guidance. In general, a higher ratio is preferred, as it is one significant component of the company's return on assets.

Procter & Gamble in Context

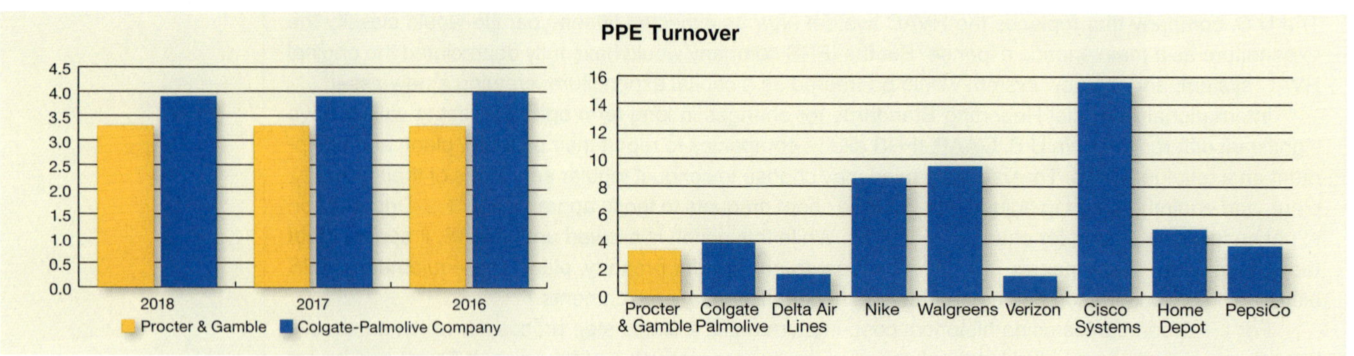

These companies do not have identical fiscal year-ends. Procter & Gamble's year end is June 30, 2018. For the other companies we used financial statements ending as follows: Colgate-Palmolive, Delta, Verizon Communications, and PepsiCo—all December 2018; Nike—May 2018; Walgreens—August 2014; Cisco—July 2018; Home Depot—February 2019.

[2] See Christensen, Hans B., and Valeri V. Nikolaev, "Does fair value accounting for non-financial assets pass the market test?" *Review of Accounting Studies*, September 2013.

Takeaways P&G's fiscal 2018 and 2017 PPET decreased slightly from the value in 2016. Companies prefer that PPET be higher rather than lower, because it implies a lower level of capital investment is required to achieve a given level of sales revenue. P&G's PPET is lower than Colgate-Palmolive, though it is higher than some others in its industry. We can also see that PPET differs considerably by industry—capital-intensive businesses with long-lived assets like Delta Air Lines and Verizon Communications have a low ratio.

Other Considerations Besides effectiveness of asset usage, PPET depends on a number of factors that affect the denominator and that should be taken into account in interpreting the numbers. First, it reflects the company's manufacturing strategy; a company that outsources its production will have a very high PPET, like Nike. Or, a company that has assets that are more fully depreciated will also report a high PPET. In Chapter 12, we discuss how ratios mixing income statement and balance sheet information can be affected by acquisitions of other companies.

Analysis Objective

We are trying to gauge the age of P&G's long-term tangible operating assets relative to their expected useful lives.

Analysis Tool Percent Depreciated

$$\textbf{Percent depreciated} = \frac{\textbf{Accumulated depreciation}}{\textbf{Cost of depreciable assets}}$$

Applying the Percent Depreciated Ratio to Procter & Gamble Accumulated depreciation can be seen in the balance sheet or footnotes. The original cost of depreciable assets can be found in the same places. (See **Exhibit 8.1** for P&G's presentation.) Two types of property, plant, and equipment are not depreciated. Land is one type, and the other is construction in progress. Land is not depreciated because it has an indefinite life, and construction in progress is not depreciated until the constructed asset is placed in service. For P&G, the $41,847 million original cost of property, plant, and equipment includes $841 million for land and $3,223 for construction in progress, which must be removed from the denominator.

$$\textbf{2016:} \quad \frac{\$20{,}481}{\$36{,}391} = 56.3\%$$

$$\textbf{2017:} \quad \frac{\$20{,}255}{\$36{,}448} = 55.6\%$$

$$\textbf{2018:} \quad \frac{\$21{,}247}{\$37{,}783} = 56.2\%$$

Guidance Percent depreciated depends on a company's age and on the occurrence of disruptive technological shifts in products and production methods. A new company will have a lower ratio, as will a company that has just made substantial investments in new productive facilities. A high ratio could mean that a company's productive resources are nearing the end of their useful lives and that substantial investments will be required in the near future.[3]

[3] Some companies do not provide complete disclosure for this computation. For example, Cisco Systems combines land and buildings in one line item and thus, an external reader of the statements cannot subtract the book value of land from the denominator to compute the percent depreciated accurately.

Procter & Gamble in Context

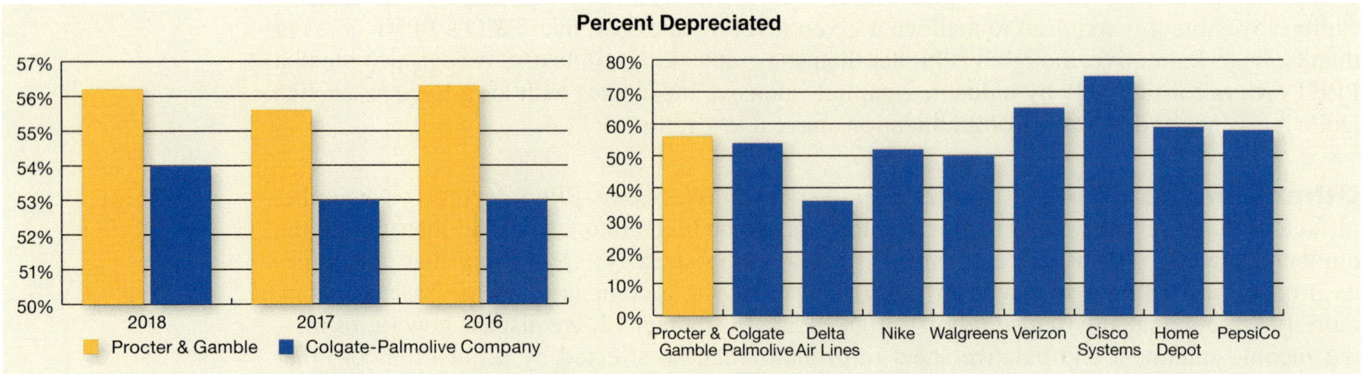

Takeaways Both Procter & Gamble and Colgate-Palmolive are mature companies experiencing long-term steady growth. They acquire assets on a continuing basis and, as a result, they have some assets that are brand-new and others that are reaching the end of their productive lives. The net result is that the percent depreciated ratio is approximately 53% to 56% for both companies.

Other Considerations Companies' percent depreciated ratio may differ because they are using different depreciation methods (straight-line or accelerated) or because they have chosen different useful lives for their assets. For instance, one airline depreciates its aircraft over twenty-five years to zero salvage value, while another depreciates its aircraft over fifteen years to ten percent salvage. A percent depreciated ratio of 50% for the first company would mean its average aircraft is 12.5 years old, while the same 50% ratio would imply aircraft that was 8.3 years old for the second company. As a result, it is always advisable to check companies' footnotes to make sure that the ratios are interpreted correctly.

BUSINESS INSIGHT

Federal authorities arrested **WorldCom, Inc.**'s CEO, Bernie Ebbers, and chief financial officer, Scott Sullivan, in August 2002 for allegedly conspiring to alter the telecommunications giant's financial statements to meet analyst expectations. They were accused of *cooking the books* so the company would not show a loss for 2001 and subsequent quarters.

Specifically, WorldCom incurred large costs in anticipation of an increase in Internet-related business that did not materialize. The executives shifted these costs to the balance sheet and recorded them as PPE, thereby inflating current profitability. By capitalizing these costs (moving them from the income statement to the balance sheet), WorldCom was able to disguise these costs as an asset to be allocated as future costs. Contrary to WorldCom's usual practices and prevailing accounting principles, no support existed for capitalization.

Although the WorldCom case also involved alleged fraud, an astute analyst would have suspected something was amiss from analysis of WorldCom's property, plant, and equipment turnover (Sales/Average property, plant, and equipment) as shown below. The decline in turnover reveals that its assets constituted an ever-increasing percent of total sales during 1995 to 2002, by quarter. This finding does not, in itself, imply fraud. It does, however, raise serious questions that should have been answered by WorldCom executives in meetings with analysts.

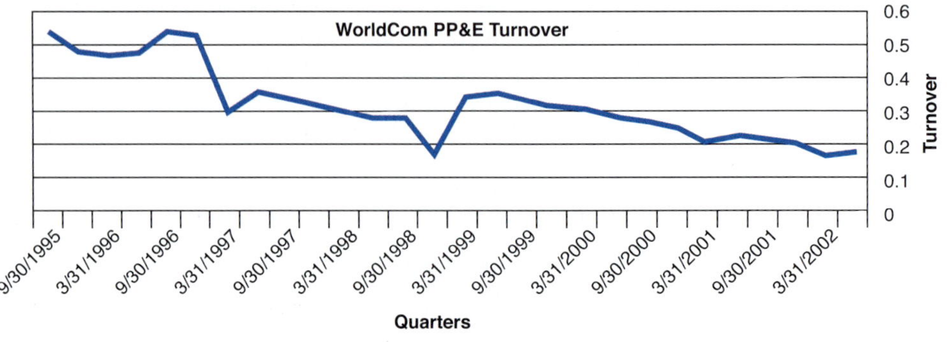

Cash Flow Effects

When cash is involved in the acquisition of plant or equipment, the cash amount is reported as a use of cash in the investment section of the statement of cash flows as discussed in Chapter 4. Any cash received from asset sales is reported as a source of cash. The investing section of Procter & Gamble's 2018 annual report is shown below.

($ millions)	2018
Investing activities	
Capital expenditures	$(3,717)
Proceeds from asset sales	269
Acquisitions, net of cash acquired	(109)
Purchases of short-term investments	(3,909)
Proceeds from sale and maturity of short-term investments	3,928
Change in other investments	27
Total investing activities	$(3,511)

In 2018, P&G paid cash of $3,717 million to acquire plant assets and received cash of $269 million on the disposal of plant and equipment. Losses (gains) on these disposal transactions would be added (subtracted) as adjustments in the operating section. Acquisitions of other companies cost $109 million in 2018.

For the Dehning Company delivery truck sale described earlier in this chapter, the investing section of the cash flow statement would show $30,000 of cash proceeds. The gain on the sale would be subtracted from net income in the operating section. No receivable was involved in the sale.

YOU MAKE THE CALL

You are the Division Manager You are the division manager for a main operating division of your company. You are concerned that a declining PPE turnover is adversely affecting your division's profitability. What specific actions can you take to increase PPE turnover? [Answers on page 395]

MID-CHAPTER REVIEW

GuidedExamples MBC

On January 2, Lev Company purchases equipment for use in fabrication of a part for one of its key products. The equipment costs $95,000, and its estimated useful life is five years, after which it is expected to be sold for $10,000.

REQUIRED

1. Compute depreciation expense for each year of the equipment's useful life for each of the following depreciation methods:
   a. Straight-line
   b. Double-declining-balance
2. Assume that Lev Company uses the straight-line depreciation method. Show the effects of these entries on the balance sheet and the income statement using the financial statement effects template. Prepare journal entries to record the initial purchase of the equipment on January 2 and the year-end depreciation adjustment on December 31, and post the journal entries to T-accounts.
3. Show how the equipment is reported on Lev's balance sheet at the end of the third year assuming straight-line depreciation.
4. Assume that this is the only depreciable asset the company owns and that it uses straight-line depreciation. Using the depreciation expense computed in 1*a* and the balance sheet presentation from *3*, estimate the percent depreciated for this asset at the end of the third year.

The solution to this review problem can be found on pages 407–408.

5

LO5 Describe the accounting and reporting for intangible assets.

INTANGIBLE ASSETS

Intangible assets are assets that lack physical substance but provide future benefits to the owner in the form of specific property rights or legal rights. For many companies, these assets have become an important source of competitive advantage and company value.

For financial accounting purposes, intangible assets are classified as either *separately transferable* or *not separately transferable. Separately transferable* intangible assets generally fall into one of two categories. The first category is assets that are the product of contractual or other legal rights. These intangibles include patents, trademarks, copyrights, franchises, license agreements, broadcast rights, mineral rights, and noncompetition agreements. The second category of separately transferable intangible assets includes benefits that are not contractually or legally defined, but can be separated from the company and sold, transferred, or exchanged. Examples include customer lists, unpatented technology, formulas, processes, and databases. There are also intangible assets that are not separately transferable, primarily goodwill. Procter & Gamble reports its intangible assets on its 2018 balance sheet in just two categories ($ in millions): Goodwill $45,175; Trademarks and Other Intangible Assets $23,902. The majority of these assets resulted from the acquisition of **The Gillette Company**.

The issues involved in reporting intangible assets are conceptually similar to those of accounting for property, plant, and equipment. We must first decide which costs to capitalize and then we need to determine how and when those costs will be transferred to the income statement. However, intangible assets often pose a particularly difficult problem for accountants. This problem arises because the benefits provided by these assets are often uncertain and difficult to quantify. In addition, the useful life of an intangible asset is often impossible to estimate with confidence.

As was the case with property, plant, and equipment, intangible assets are either purchased from another individual or company or internally developed. Like PPE assets, the cost of purchased intangible assets is capitalized. Unlike PPE assets, though, we generally do not capitalize the cost of internally developed intangible assets. Research and development (R&D) costs, and the patents and technologies that are created as a result of R&D, serve as useful examples.

Research and Development Costs

R&D activities are a major expenditure for most companies, especially for those in technology and pharmaceutical industries where R&D expenses can exceed 10% of revenues. These expenses include employment costs for R&D personnel, R&D-related contract services, and R&D plant asset costs.

Companies invest millions of dollars in R&D because they expect that the future benefits resulting from these activities will eventually exceed the costs. Successful R&D activities create new products that can be sold and new technologies that can be utilized to create and sustain a competitive advantage. Unfortunately, only a fraction of R&D projects reach commercial production, and it is difficult to predict which projects will be successful. Moreover, it is often difficult to predict when the benefits will be realized, even if the project is successful.

Because of the uncertainty surrounding the benefits of R&D, accounting for R&D activities follows a uniform method—*immediate recognition as an expense*. This approach applies to all R&D costs incurred prior to the start of commercial production, including the salaries and wages of personnel engaged in R&D activities, the cost of materials and supplies, and the equipment and facilities used in the project. Should any of the R&D activities prove successful, the benefits should result in higher net income in future periods. Costs incurred internally to develop new software products do not satisfy the capitalization requirement of providing expected future profits until the technological feasibility of the product is established. Therefore, until the feasibility requirement can be met, these costs are expensed.

If equipment and facilities are purchased for a specific R&D project, and have no other use, their cost is expensed immediately even though their useful life would typically extend beyond the current period. The expensing of R&D equipment and facilities is in stark contrast to the capitalization-and-depreciation of non-R&D plant assets. The expensing of R&D plant assets is mandated unless those assets have alternative future uses (in other R&D projects or otherwise). For example, a general research facility housing multi-use lab equipment should be capitalized and depreciated like any other depreciable asset. However, project-directed research buildings and equipment with no alternate uses must be expensed.

BUSINESS INSIGHT

R&D Costs at Cisco Systems Cisco spends between $6 billion and $6.5 billion annually for R&D compared with its revenues of around $45–$50 billion, or about 12%–14%. This level reflects a high percent of revenues devoted to R&D in comparison with nontechnology companies, but typifies companies that compete in the high-tech arena. Following is the R&D-expense-to-sales ratio (also called *R&D Intensity*) for Cisco and some related companies.

	2018	2017	2016
Cisco Systems, Inc.	12.8%	12.6%	12.8%
Juniper Networks, Inc.	21.6%	19.5%	20.3%
Hewlett-Packard Company (HP, Inc.)	2.4%	2.3%	2.5%

RESEARCH INSIGHT

Research has provided evidence consistent with managers reducing R&D spending when trying to meet certain earnings targets or other earnings goals. Part of this is due to the accounting—research and development costs are expensed immediately reducing reported earnings in the current period. Thus, although the research and development spending should provide better future performance, it harms current performance leading "myopic" managers to cut back.[4] Recent research also suggests that some firms do not disclose research spending even when it appears that they must have such costs. One theory is that these firms do not want to disclose their research and development spending in order to hide the extent of their costs from their competitors.[5]

Patents

Successful research and development activity often leads a company to obtain a **patent** for its discoveries. A patent is an exclusive right to produce a product or use a technology. Patents are granted to protect the inventor of the new product or technology by preventing other companies from copying the innovation. The fair value of a patent depends on the commercial success of the product or technology. For example, a patent on the formula for a new drug to treat diabetes could be worth billions of dollars.

If a patent is purchased from the inventor, the purchase price is capitalized and reported in the balance sheet as an intangible asset. On the other hand, if the patent is developed internally, only the legal costs and registration fees are capitalized. The R&D cost to develop the new product or technology is expensed as incurred. This accounting illustrates the marked difference between purchased and internally created intangible assets.

Copyrights

A copyright is an exclusive right granted by the government to an individual author, composer, play writer, or similar individual for the life of the creator plus 70 years. Corporations can also obtain a copyright for varying periods set by law. Copyrights, like patents, can be acquired. The acquisition cost would be capitalized and amortized over the expected remaining economic life.

Trademarks

A **trademark** is a registered name, logo, package design, image, jingle, or slogan that is associated with a product. Many trademarks are easily recognizable, such as the **Nike** "swoosh," the shape of a **Coca-Cola** bottle, **McDonald's** golden arches, and the musical tones played in computer advertisements featuring **Intel** computer chips. Companies spend millions of dollars developing and protecting trademarks and their value is enhanced by advertising programs that increase their recognition.

---

[4] See Bushee, Brian, "The Influence of Institutional Investors on Myopic R&D Investment Behavior." *Accounting Review*, 1998; Graham, John R., Cam Harvey and Shiva Rajgopal, "The Economic Implications of Corporate Financial Reporting." *Journal of Accounting and Economics*, 2005; and Sloan, Richard and P. Dechow. "Executive Incentives and the Horizon Problem: An Empirical Investigation," *Journal of Accounting and Economics*, 1991, for examples of research on this topic.

[5] See Koh, P.S., and D. M. Reeb. "Missing R&D," *Journal of Accounting and Economics*, Forthcoming.

If a trademark is purchased from another company, the purchase price is capitalized. However, the cost of internally developed trademarks is expensed as incurred. Likewise, all advertising costs are expensed immediately, even if the value of a trademark is enhanced by the advertisement. For these reasons, many trademarks are not presented in the balance sheet.

BUSINESS INSIGHT

Trademarks and Patents at P&G Procter & Gamble has acquired many of the products it currently markets to consumers. Others were developed internally. The following paragraph from the Management Discussion and Analysis section of P&G's 2018 annual report emphasizes the importance of these intangible assets to the company.

> (Our) trademarks are important to the overall marketing and branding of our products. . . . In part, our success can be attributed to the existence and continued protection of these trademarks, patents, and licenses.

Franchise Rights

A **franchise** is a contractual agreement that gives a company the right to operate a particular business in an area for a particular period of time. For example, a franchise may give the owner the right to operate a number of fast-food restaurants in a particular geographic region for twenty years. *Operating rights* and *licenses* are similar to franchise rights, except that they are typically granted by government agencies. Most franchise rights are purchased and, as a result, the purchase price should be capitalized and presented as an intangible asset in the balance sheet.

Amortization and Impairment of Identifiable Intangible Assets

When intangible assets are acquired and capitalized, a determination must be made as to whether the asset has a **definite life**. Examples of intangible assets with definite lives include patents and franchise rights. An intangible asset with a definite life must be *amortized* over the expected useful life of the asset. **Amortization** is the systematic allocation of the cost of an intangible asset to the periods benefited, similar to depreciation of tangible assets.

Amortization expense is generally recorded using the straight-line method. The expense is included in the income statement as a component of operating income, and is often included among selling, general and administrative expenses. The cost of the intangible asset is presented in the balance sheet net of accumulated amortization.

Amortization To illustrate, assume that Landsman Company spent $100,000 in early 2019 to purchase a patent. The entry to record the capitalization of this cost follows.

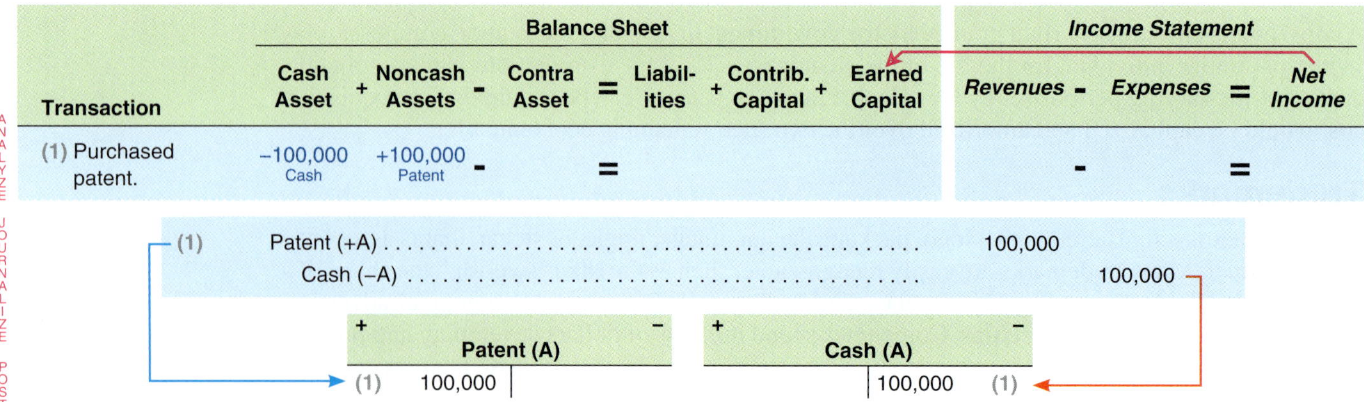

Transaction	Cash Asset	+ Noncash Assets	− Contra Asset	= Liabilities	+ Contrib. Capital	+ Earned Capital	Revenues	− Expenses	= Net Income
(1) Purchased patent.	−100,000 Cash	+100,000 Patent	−	=				−	=

		Dr.	Cr.
(1)	Patent (+A)	100,000	
	Cash (−A)		100,000

Patent (A) +	−
(1) 100,000	

Cash (A) +	−
	100,000 (1)

Although the patent had a remaining legal life of 12 years, Landsman estimated that the useful life of the patent was 5 years. Thus the intangible asset has a definite life. The entry to record the annual amortization expense at the end of 2019 follows.

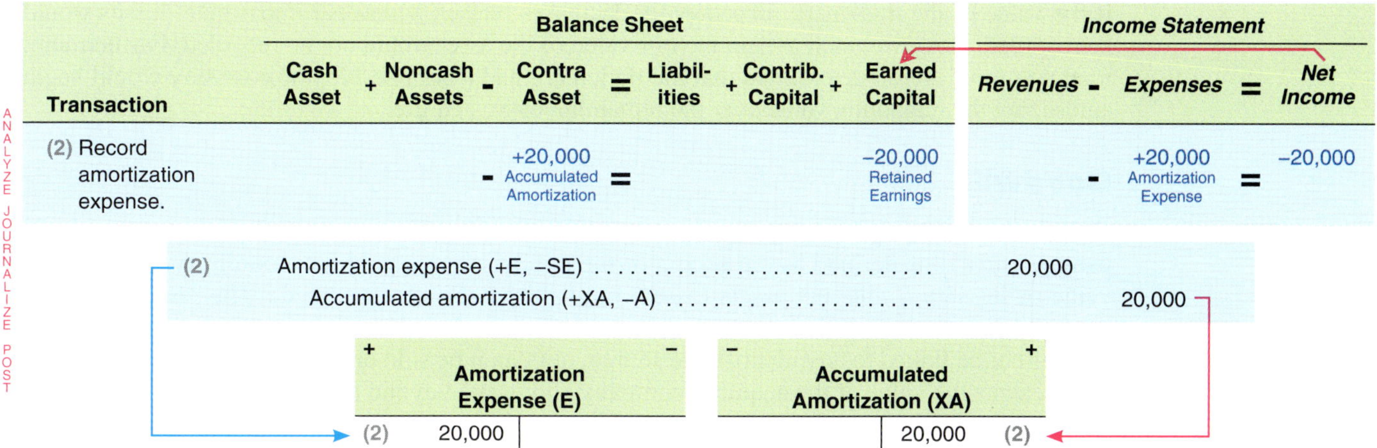

Impairment Some transferable intangible assets, such as some trademarks, have indefinite lives. For these assets, the expected useful life extends far enough into the future that it is impossible for management to estimate a useful life. An intangible asset with an indefinite life should not be amortized until the useful life of the asset can be specified. That is, no expense is recorded until management can reasonably estimate the useful life of the asset.

Although intangible assets with indefinite lives are not subject to amortization, they must be tested annually to determine if their value has been impaired. The impairment test for intangibles is slightly different from the impairment test used to evaluate PPE assets. The intangible asset is impaired if the book value of the asset exceeds its fair value and the write-down is equal to the difference between the book value and the fair value.

To illustrate, assume that Norell Company purchased a trademark in 2017 for $240,000 and determined that the intangible asset had an indefinite life. The entry to record the purchase of the trademark follows.

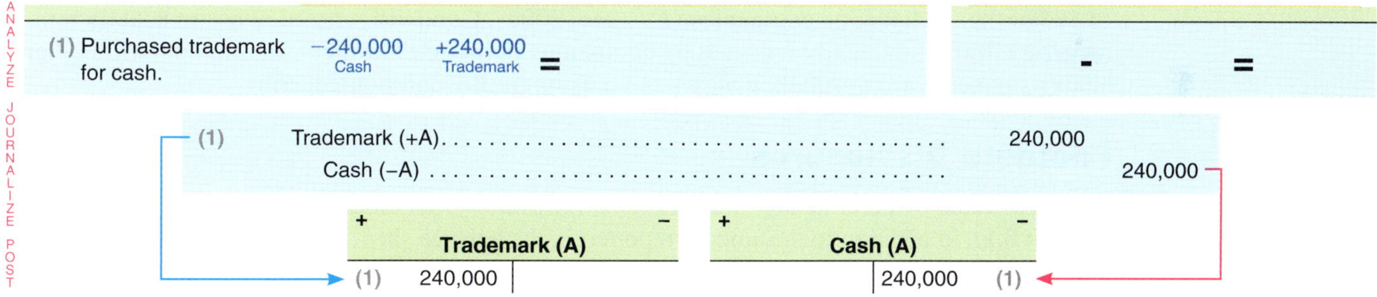

In 2020, changes in regulations caused Norell to conclude that the value of the trademark had been impaired. They estimated the current fair value was $100,000, resulting in a loss of $140,000 ($240,000 – $100,000). The entry to record the impairment of the trademark would be as follows.

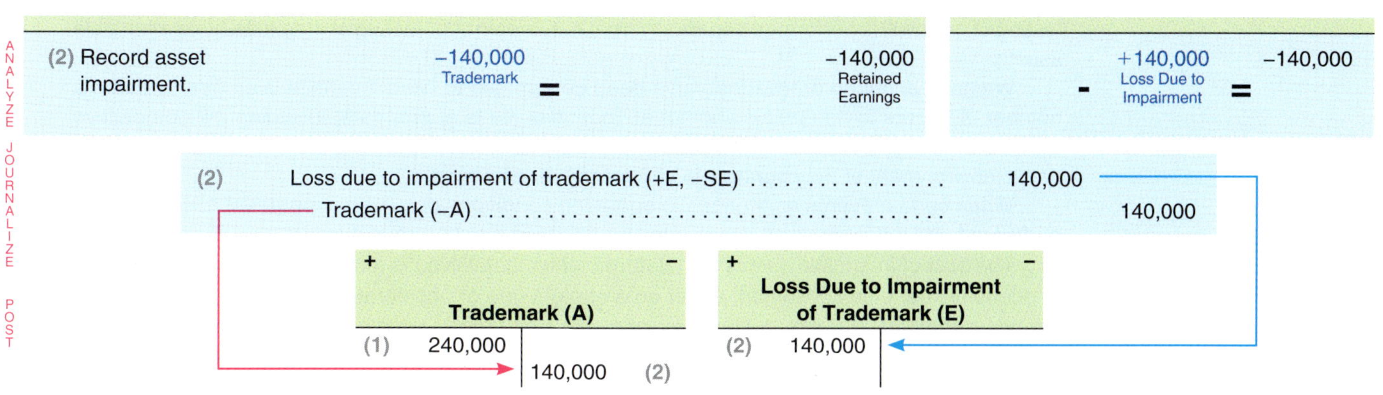

If the value of the trademark subsequently decreases further, additional impairment losses would be recorded. However, increases in the fair value of the asset would not be recorded. Furthermore, if, at any time, Norell determined that the trademark had a definite life, the company would begin amortizing the remaining value over the remaining estimated life.

Goodwill

Goodwill is an intangible asset that is recorded only when one company acquires another company. **Goodwill** is defined as the excess of the purchase price paid for a company over the fair value of its *identifiable* net assets (assets minus the liabilities assumed). The identifiable net assets include any *identifiable intangible assets* acquired in the purchase. Therefore, goodwill can neither be linked to any identifiable source, nor can it be sold or separated from the company. It represents the value of the acquired company above and beyond the specific identifiable assets listed on the balance sheet.

By definition, goodwill has an indefinite life. Once it is recorded in the balance sheet, it is not amortized. Instead, it is subject to an annual impairment test. Goodwill is impaired when the fair value of the acquired business (more specifically, any testable reporting unit) is less than the recorded book value. If this occurs, goodwill is written down to an imputed value. The goodwill write-down (also called a goodwill write-off) results in the immediate transfer of some or all of a company's goodwill book value from the balance sheet to the income statement as an expense. The book value of goodwill is immediately reduced and a corresponding expense is reported in the income statement. Like the impairment write-down of tangible assets, the write-down of goodwill is a discretionary expense whose amount and timing are largely determined by management (with auditor acceptance).

It is commonplace to see goodwill impairment write-downs related to unsuccessful acquisitions, particularly those from the acquisition boom of the late 1990s and the recession of 2008–2009. Goodwill write-downs usually represent material amounts. For example, **Time Warner Inc.** wrote off $54 billion of goodwill in the second quarter of 2002, which arose from the $106 billion merger of AOL and Time-Warner. This write-off exceeded the *total revenues* of 483 of the Fortune 500 companies (*Fortune*, 2002). Goodwill write-downs are usually nonrecurring, but are typically reported by companies in income from continuing operations. For analysis purpose we normally classify them as operating and nonrecurring.

Footnote Disclosures

The book value of P&G intangible assets is almost 60% of its total asset value in 2018 (refer to **Exhibit 8.1**). In addition to the amount reported in the balance sheet, P&G provides the following in footnotes 1 and 2 that more fully describes its intangible asset accounting.

Note 1: Summary of Significant Accounting Policies—
Goodwill and Other Intangible Assets

Goodwill and indefinite-lived intangible assets are not amortized, but are evaluated for impairment annually or more often if indicators of a potential impairment are present. Our annual impairment testing of goodwill is performed separately from our impairment testing of indefinite-lived intangible assets.

We have acquired brands that have been determined to have indefinite lives. We evaluate a number of factors to determine whether an indefinite life is appropriate, including the competitive environment, market share, brand history, product life cycles, operating plans and the macroeconomic environment of the countries in which the brands are sold.

When certain events or changes in operating conditions occur, an impairment assessment is performed and indefinite-lived assets may be adjusted to a determinable life.

The cost of intangible assets with determinable useful lives is amortized to reflect the pattern of economic benefits consumed, either on a straight-line or accelerated basis over the estimated periods benefited. Patents, technology and other intangible assets with contractual terms are generally amortized over their respective legal or contractual lives. Customer relationships, brands and other non-contractual intangible assets with determinable lives are amortized over periods

continued

continued from previous page

generally ranging from 5 to 30 years. When certain events or changes in operating conditions occur, an impairment assessment is performed and remaining lives of intangible assets with determinable lives may be adjusted.

Procter & Gamble's largest intangible is goodwill ($45.2 billion). The acquisition of Gillette in 2006 resulted in the recognition of $35.3 billion of goodwill, some of which remains as part of goodwill currently on the balance sheet. P&G paid $53.4 billion for Gillette upon acquisition in 2006, and at the time allocated $29.7 billion to other intangibles.

Note 2: Goodwill and Intangible Assets
Identifiable intangible assets were comprised of:

	2018		2017	
	Gross Carrying Amount	**Accumulated Depreciation**	**Gross Carrying Amount**	**Accumulated Depreciation**
Intangible assets with determinable lives				
Brands	$3,146	$(2,046)	$3,094	$(1,898)
Patents and technology	2,617	(2,350)	2,617	(2,261)
Customer relationships	1,372	(616)	1,377	(564)
Other	241	(144)	239	(132)
Total	7,376	(5,156)	7,327	(4,855)
Brands with indefinite lives	21,682	—	21,715	—
Total	$29,058	$(5,156)	$29,042	$(4,855)

There are two observations that we can make from the above disclosures. First, P&G has purchased a significant amount of intangible assets by acquiring other companies. We can infer this from the large amount of goodwill assets reported in the balance sheet. Second, most of P&G's identifiable intangible assets are trademarks and most have indefinite lives. Hence, we might expect that the amount of amortization expense in any given year would be small, as indicated by the total in the above table. However, goodwill impairment write-offs could be substantial in any given year.

Analysis Implications

LO6 Analyze the effects of tangible and intangible assets on key performance measures.

6

Because internally generated intangible assets are not capitalized, an important component of a company's assets is potentially hidden from users of the financial statements. Moreover, differential treatment of purchased and internally created assets makes it difficult to compare companies. If one company generates its patents and trademarks internally, while another company purchases these intangibles, their balance sheets can differ dramatically, even if the two companies are otherwise very similar.

These hidden intangible assets can distort our analysis of the financial statements. For example, when a company expenses R&D costs, especially R&D equipment and facilities that can potentially benefit more than one period, both the income statement and balance sheet are distorted. Net income, assets, and stockholders' equity are all understated.

The income statement effects may be small if a company regularly purchases R&D assets and the amount of purchases is relatively constant from year to year. Specifically, after the average useful life is reached, say in 5 to 10 years, the expensing of current-year purchases will be approximately the same as the depreciation that would have been reported had the assets been capitalized. Thus, the income statement effect is mitigated. However, the recorded assets and equity are still understated. This accounting produces an upward bias in asset turnover ratios and ROE.

Finally, the statement of cash flows is also affected by the manner in which a company acquires its intellectual assets. A company that generates its patents and trademarks internally recognizes the expenditures as part of cash flow from operating activities. However, a company that purchases its patents and trademarks from an independent party or through acquisitions recognizes the expenditures as part of cash flow from investing activities.

A GLOBAL PERSPECTIVE

Under International Financial Reporting Standards, development costs can be capitalized as intangible assets when specific criteria are met. For instance, the company must be able to demonstrate that it has the ability and the intention to complete the development process and to produce an intangible asset that will generate future benefits through use or sale.

Here is an example from GlaxoSmithKline plc's footnotes:

> **Research and development**
> Research and development expenditure is charged to the income statement in the period in which it is incurred. Development expenditure is capitalised when the criteria for recognising an asset are met, usually when a regulatory filing has been made in a major market and approval is considered highly probable. Property, plant, and equipment used for research and development is capitalised and depreciated in accordance with the Group's policy.

Under IFRS, similar to under U.S. GAAP, goodwill must be periodically evaluated for impairment. The overall concepts are very similar between IFRS and GAAP but the details differ. For example, under IFRS companies are required to compare the recoverable amount (defined as the higher of the fair value or value-in-use) of a cash-generating unit to the carrying value of that unit to determine an impairment loss. Just as under U.S. GAAP, once impaired, goodwill cannot be revalued upward. Although, note that this is different from the treatment of PPE under IFRS, as discussed earlier in the chapter.

CHAPTER-END REVIEW

In 2018, Bowen Company's R&D department developed a new production process that significantly reduced the time and cost required to manufacture its product. R&D costs were $120,000. The process was patented on July 1, 2018. Legal costs and fees to acquire the patent totalled $12,500. Bowen estimated the useful life of the patent at 10 years.

On July 1, 2020, Bowen sold the nonexclusive right to use the new process to Kennedy Company for $90,000. Because Bowen retained the patent, the agreement allows Kennedy to use, but not sell, the new technology for a period of 5 years. Both Bowen Company and Kennedy Company have December 31 fiscal years.

On July 1, 2022, another competitor obtained a patent on a new process that made Bowen's patent obsolete.

Required

1. How should Bowen Company account for the R&D costs and legal costs incurred to obtain the patent? Show the effects of these entries using the financial statement effects template, prepare the appropriate journal entries necessary to account for the costs incurred in 2018, and post the entries to T-accounts.
2. What amount of amortization expense would Bowen record each year? Show the effects of these transactions using the financial statement effects template, prepare a journal entry to record amortization expense on December 31, 2018, and post the entries to T-accounts.
3. How would Kennedy Company record the acquisition of the rights to use the new technology? Show the effects of this transaction using the financial statement effects template, prepare a journal entry to record the purchase of the technology rights, and post the entry to T-accounts.
4. What effect would the new patent registered by the other competitor have on Bowen Company? On Kennedy Company? Show the effects of this transaction using the financial statement effects template, prepare a journal entry to record the impairment loss for Kennedy Company, and post the entry to T-accounts.

The solution to this review problem can be found on pages 408–410.

SUMMARY

LO1 Describe and distinguish between tangible and intangible assets. **(p. 374)**

- Tangible assets, including land, buildings, machinery, and equipment are assets with physical substance and are usually classified as property, plant, and equipment.
- Intangible assets are long-term assets lacking in physical substance, such as patents, trademarks, franchise rights and goodwill.

Determine which costs to capitalize and report as assets and which costs to expense. (p. 375) **LO2**

- All costs incurred to acquire an asset and prepare it for its intended use should be capitalized and reported in the balance sheet.
- The cost of self-constructed assets should include all costs incurred during construction, including the interest cost of financing the construction.

Apply different depreciation methods to allocate the cost of assets over time. (p. 377) **LO3**

- Depreciation methods generally fall into three categories:
  (1) Straight-line depreciation
  (2) Accelerated depreciation, such as the double-declining-balance method
  (3) Units-of-production method

Determine the effects of asset sales and impairments on financial statements. (p. 381) **LO4**

- The sale of a long-term asset will result in a gain or loss if the proceeds from the sale are greater than or less than the book value of the asset.
- If the expected benefits (undiscounted cash flows) derived from an asset fall below its book value, the asset is impaired and should be written down to fair value.

Describe the accounting and reporting for intangible assets. (p. 388) **LO5**

- For the most part, internally generated intangible assets are not recognized in the balance sheet.
- Intangible assets purchased from other companies are capitalized and presented separately in the balance sheet.
- Intangible assets with definite lives are amortized using the straight-line method.
- Intangible assets with indefinite lives are not amortized.

Analyze the effects of tangible and intangible assets on key performance measures. (p. 393) **LO6**

- PPE turnover and long-term asset turnover ratios provide insights into the capital intensity of a company and how efficiently the company is utilizing these investments.
- The ratio of accumulated depreciation divided by the cost of depreciable assets measures the percent depreciated.

GUIDANCE ANSWERS . . . YOU MAKE THE CALL

You are the Company Accountant Any cost that is necessary in order to bring an asset into service should be capitalized as a part of the cost of the asset. In this case, your company cannot build an office building on this property until the oil well is properly capped. Therefore, the $40,000 cost of capping the oil well should be capitalized as part of the cost of the land.

You are the Division Manager To increase PPE turnover one must either increase sales or reduce PPE assets. The first step is to identify unproductive or inefficiently utilized assets. Unnecessary assets can be sold, and some processes can be outsourced. Also, by reducing down time, effective maintenance practices will increase asset productivity.

KEY RATIOS

$$\text{PPE Turnover (PPET)} = \frac{\text{Sales revenue}}{\text{Average PPE, net}} \qquad \text{Percent depreciated} = \frac{\text{Accumulated depreciation}}{\text{Cost of depreciable assets}}$$

KEY TERMS

Accelerated depreciation (p. 378)
Accumulated depreciation (p. 376)
Amortization (p. 390)
Book value (BV) (p. 378)
Capital expenditures (p. 375)
Capitalized (p. 374)
Capitalized interest (p. 376)
Definite life (p. 390)
Depletion (p. 380)
Depreciation (p. 376)
Depreciation base (p. 377)
Depreciation rate (p. 378)

Double-declining-balance (DDB) method (p. 378)
Franchise (p. 390)
Goodwill (p. 392)
Impairment (p. 381)
Intangible assets (p. 374)
Patent (p. 389)
Residual (or salvage) value (p. 377)
Restructuring costs (p. 382)
Straight-line (SL) method (p. 378)
Tangible assets (p. 374)
Trademark (p. 389)
Units-of-production method (p. 379)
Useful life (p. 377)
Wasting assets (p. 380)

Assignments with the MBC logo in the margin are available in myBusinessCourse. See the Preface of the book for details.

MULTIPLE CHOICE

Multiple Choice Answers
1. a 2. b 3. c 4. d 5. c 6. b

1. Burgstahler Corporation bought a lot to construct a new corporate office building. An older building on the lot was razed immediately so that the office building could be constructed. The cost of razing the older building should be
a. recorded as part of the cost of the land.
b. written off as a loss in the year of purchase.
c. written off as an extraordinary item in the year of purchase.
d. recorded as part of the cost of the new building.

2. The purpose of recording periodic depreciation of long-term PPE assets is to
a. report declining asset values on the balance sheet.
b. allocate asset costs over the periods benefited by use of the assets.
c. account for costs to reflect the change in general price levels.
d. set aside funds to replace assets when their economic usefulness expires.

3. When the estimate of an asset's useful life is changed,
a. depreciation expense for all past periods must be recalculated.
b. there is no change in the amount of depreciation expense recorded for future years.
c. only depreciation expense for current and future years is affected.
d. only depreciation expense in the current year is affected.

4. If the sale of a depreciable asset results in a loss, the proceeds from the sale were
a. less than current fair value.
b. greater than cost.
c. greater than book value.
d. less than book value.

5. Which of the following principles best describes the current method of accounting for research and development costs?
a. Revenue recognition method
b. Systematic and rational allocation
c. Immediate recognition as an expense
d. Income tax minimization

6. Goodwill should be recorded in the balance sheet as an intangible asset only when
a. it is sold to another company.
b. it is acquired through the purchase of another business.
c. a company reports above-normal earnings for five or more consecutive years.
d. it can be established that a definite benefit or advantage has resulted from some item such as an excellent reputation for service.

QUESTIONS

Q8-1. How should companies account for costs, such as maintenance or improvements, which are incurred after an asset is acquired?

Q8-2. What is the effect of capitalized interest on the income statement in the period that an asset is constructed? What is the effect in future periods?

Q8-3. Why is the recognition of depreciation expense necessary for proper expense recognition?

Q8-4. Why do companies use accelerated depreciation for income tax purposes, when the total depreciation taken over the asset's useful life is identical to straight-line depreciation?

Q8-5. How should a company treat a change in an asset's estimated useful life or residual value? Which period(s)—past, present, or future—is affected by this change?

Q8-6. What factors determine the gain or loss from the sale of a long-term operating asset?

Q8-7. When is a PPE asset considered to be impaired? How is the impairment loss determined?

Q8-8. What is the proper accounting treatment for research and development costs? Why are R&D costs not capitalized under GAAP?

Q8-9. Why are some intangible assets amortized while others are not? What is meant by an intangible asset with an "indefinite life"?

Q8-10. Under what circumstances should a company report goodwill in its balance sheet? What is the effect of goodwill on the income statement?

MINI EXERCISES

M8-11. Determining Whether to Capitalize or Expense LO2

For each of the following items, indicate whether the cost should be capitalized or expensed immediately:

a. Paid $1,200 for routine maintenance of machinery
b. Paid $5,400 to rent equipment for two years
c. Paid $2,000 to equip the production line with new instruments that measure quality
d. Paid $20,000 to repair the roof on the building
e. Paid $1,600 to refurbish a machine, thereby extending its useful life
f. Purchased a patent for $5,000

M8-12. Computing Depreciation Under Straight-Line and Double-Declining-Balance LO3

A delivery van costing $18,000 is expected to have a $1,500 salvage value at the end of its useful life of 5 years. Assume that the truck was purchased on January 1, 2019. Compute the depreciation expense for 2020 (its second year) under each of the following depreciation methods:

a. Straight-line
b. Double-declining-balance

M8-13. Computing Depreciation Under Alternative Methods LO3

Equipment costing $130,000 is expected to have a residual value of $10,000 at the end of its six-year useful life. The equipment is metered so that the number of units processed is counted. The equipment is designed to process 1,000,000 units in its lifetime. In 2019 and 2020, the equipment processed 180,000 units and 140,000 units respectively. Calculate the depreciation expense for 2019 and 2020 using each of the following methods:

a. Straight-line
b. Double-declining-balance
c. Units of production

M8-14. Recording the Sale of PPE Assets LO4

As part of a renovation of its showroom, O'Keefe Auto Dealership sold furniture and fixtures that were eight years old for $3,500 in cash. The assets had been purchased for $40,000 and had been depreciated using the straight-line method with no residual value and a useful life of ten years.

a. Prepare a journal entry to record this transaction.
b. Show how the sale of the furniture and fixtures affects the balance sheet and income statement using the financial statement effects template.

M8-15. Recording the Sale of PPE Assets LO4

Gaver Company sold machinery that had originally cost $75,000 for $25,000 in cash. The machinery was three years old and had been depreciated using the double-declining-balance method assuming a five-year useful life and a residual value of $5,000.

a. Prepare a journal entry to record this sale.
b. Using the financial statement effects template, show how the sale of the machinery affects the balance sheet and income statement.

LO3

M8-16. Computing Depreciation Under Straight-Line and Double-Declining-Balance for Partial Years

A machine costing $145,800 is purchased on May 1, 2019. The machine is expected to be obsolete after three years (36 months) and, thereafter, no longer useful to the company. The estimated salvage value is $5,400. Compute depreciation expense for both 2019 and 2020 under each of the following depreciation methods:

a. Straight-line
b. Double-declining-balance

LO1, 2, 5
Siemens AG
NYSE :: SI

M8-17. Accounting for Research and Development Under IFRS

The following information on **Siemens AG**'s treatment of research and development is extracted from its 2018 financial statements. Siemens AG is an integrated technology company with activities in the fields of industry, energy and healthcare. The company is incorporated under the laws of Germany and reports using International Financial Reporting Standards (IFRS).

Research and development costs—Costs of research activities are expensed as incurred. Costs of development activities are capitalized when the recognition criteria in IAS 38 are met. Capitalized development costs are stated at cost less accumulated amortization and impairment losses with an amortization period of generally three to ten years.

a. How does the reporting under IFRS differ from reporting under U.S. GAAP for research and development?
b. At year-end September 30, 2018 Siemens had a gross carrying amount of Other Intangible Assets of 19.9 billion Euros and accumulated amortization and impairment related to those assets of 9.8 billion Euros. Should the amounts capitalized be tested annually for impairment?

LO3

M8-18. Computing Double-Declining-Balance Depreciation

DeFond Company purchased equipment for $50,000. For each of the following sets of assumptions, prepare a depreciation schedule (all years) for this equipment assuming that DeFond uses the double-declining-balance depreciation method.

Useful life	Residual value
a. Four years	$8,000
b. Five years	$3,000
c. Ten years	$1,000

LO3

M8-19. Computing and Recording Depletion Expense

The Nelson Oil Company estimated that the oil reserve that it acquired in 2019 would produce 4 million barrels of oil. The company extracted 300,000 barrels the first year, 500,000 barrels in 2020, and 600,000 barrels in 2021. Nelson paid $32,000,000 for the oil reserve.

a. Compute the depletion expense for each year—2019, 2020, and 2021.
b. Prepare the journal entries to record (i) the acquisition of the oil reserve, and (ii) the depletion for 2019.
c. Open T-accounts and post the entries from part *b* in the accounts.

LO6

Texas Instruments Incorporated
NYSE :: TXN
Intel Corporation
NASDAQ :: INTC

M8-20. Computing and Comparing PPE Turnover for Two Companies

Texas Instruments Incorporated and **Intel Corporation** report the following information:

	Texas Instruments		Intel Corp	
($ millions)	Sales	PPE, net	Sales	PPE, net
2018	$15,784	$3,183	$70,848	$48,976
2017	14,961	2,664	62,761	41,109

a. Compute the 2018 PPE turnover for both companies. Comment on any difference you observe.
b. Discuss ways in which high-tech manufacturing companies like these can increase their PPE turnover.

M8-21. Assessing Research and Development Expenses

LO5, 6

Abbott Laboratories
NYSE :: ABT

Abbott Laboratories reports the following income statement (in partial form):

Year Ended December 31 ($ millions)	2018
Net sales	$30,578
Cost of products sold	12,706
Amortization of intangible assets	2,178
Research and development*	2,300
Selling, general and administrative	9,744
Total operating cost and expenses	26,928
Operating earnings	$ 3,650

* including acquired in-process and collaborations R&D

a. Compute the percent of net sales that Abbott Laboratories spends on research and development (R&D). How would you assess the appropriateness of its R&D expense level?

b. Using the financial statement effects template, describe how the accounting for R&D expenditures affects Abbott Laboratories' balance sheet and income statement.

EXERCISES

E8-22. Recording Asset Acquisition, Depreciation, and Disposal

LO2, 3, 4

On January 2, 2019, Verdi Company acquired a machine for $85,000. In addition to the purchase price, Verdi spent $2,000 for shipping and installation, and $2,500 to calibrate the machine prior to use. The company estimates that the machine has a useful life of five years and residual value of $7,000.

a. Prepare journal entries to record the acquisition costs.

b. Calculate the annual depreciation expense using straight-line depreciation and prepare a journal entry to record depreciation expense for 2019.

c. On December 31, 2022, Verdi sold the machine to another company for $12,000. Prepare the necessary journal entry to record the sale.

E8-23. Computing Straight-Line and Double-Declining-Balance Depreciation

LO3

On January 2, Haskins Company purchases a laser cutting machine for use in fabrication of a part for one of its key products. The machine cost $80,000, and its estimated useful life is five years, after which the expected salvage value is $5,000. Compute depreciation expense for each year of the machine's useful life under each of the following depreciation methods:

a. Straight-line

b. Double-declining-balance

E8-24. Computing Depreciation, Asset Book Value, and Gain or Loss on Asset Sale

LO3, 4

Sloan Company uses its own executive charter plane that originally cost $800,000. It has recorded straight-line depreciation on the plane for six full years, with an $80,000 expected salvage value at the end of its estimated 10-year useful life. Sloan disposes of the plane at the end of the sixth year.

a. At the disposal date, what is the (1) accumulated depreciation and (2) net book value of the plane?

b. Prepare a journal entry to record the disposal of the plane assuming that the sales price is

1. Cash equal to the book value of the plane.
2. $195,000 cash.
3. $600,000 cash.

E8-25. Computing Straight-Line and Double-Declining-Balance Depreciation

LO3

On January 2, 2019, Dechow Company purchases a machine to help manufacture a part for one of its key products. The machine cost $218,700 and is estimated to have a useful life of six years, with an expected salvage value of $23,400.

Compute each year's depreciation expense for 2019 and 2020 for each of the following depreciation methods.

a. Straight-line

b. Double-declining-balance

LO3, 4 

E8-26. Computing Depreciation, Asset Book Value, and Gain or Loss on Asset Sale

Palepu Company owns and operates a delivery van that originally cost $27,200. Straight-line depreciation on the van has been recorded for three years, with a $2,000 expected salvage value at the end of its estimated six-year useful life. Depreciation was last recorded at the end of the third year, at which time Palepu disposes of this van.

a. Compute the net book value of the van on the sale date.

b. Compute the gain or loss on sale of the van if its sales price is for:
1. Cash equal to book value of van.
2. $15,000 cash.
3. $12,000 cash.

LO3 

E8-27. Computing Depreciation and Accounting for a Change of Estimate

Lambert Company acquired machinery costing $110,000 on January 2, 2019. At that time, Lambert estimated that the useful life of the equipment was 6 years and that the residual value would be $15,000 at the end of its useful life. Compute depreciation expense for this asset for 2019, 2020, and 2021 using the

a. straight-line method.

b. double-declining-balance method.

c. Assume that on January 2, 2021, Lambert revised its estimate of the useful life to 7 years and changed its estimate of the residual value to $10,000. What effect would this have on depreciation expense in 2021 for each of the above depreciation methods?

LO3 

E8-28. Computing Depreciation and Accounting for a Change of Estimate

In January 2019, Rankine Company paid $8,500,000 for land and a building. An appraisal estimated that the land had a fair value of $2,500,000 and the building was worth $6,000,000. Rankine estimated that the useful life of the building was 30 years, with no residual value.

a. Calculate annual depreciation expense using the straight-line method.

b. Calculate depreciation for 2019 and 2020 using the double-declining-balance method.

c. Assume that in 2021, Rankine changed its estimate of the useful life of the building to 25 years. If the company is using the double-declining-balance method of depreciation, what amount of depreciation expense would Rankine record in 2021?

LO6 

Deere & Company
NYSE :: DE

E8-29. Estimating the Percent Depreciated

The property and equipment footnote from the Deere & Company balance sheet follows ($ millions):

PROPERTY AND DEPRECIATION

A summary of property and equipment at October 28, 2018, in millions of dollars follows:

	2018
Land	$ 283
Buildings and building equipment	3,848
Machinery and equipment	5,570
Dies, patterns, tools, etc.	1,564
All other	1,032
Construction in progress	619
Total at cost	12,916
Less accumulated depreciation	7,095
Property and equipment—net	$ 5,821

During 2018, the company reported $754 million of depreciation expense.

Estimate the percent depreciated of Deere's depreciable assets. How do you interpret this figure?

LO6 

3M Company
NYSE :: MMM

E8-30. Computing and Evaluating Receivables, Inventory, and PPE Turnovers

3M Company reports the following financial statement amounts in its 10-K report:

($ millions)	Sales	Cost of Sales	Receivables	Inventories	PPE, net
2018	$32,765	$16,682	$5,020	$4,366	$8,738
2017	31,657	16,055	4,911	4,034	8,866
2016	30,109	15,118	4,392	3,385	8,516

a. Compute the receivables, inventory, and PPE turnover ratios for both 2018 and 2017. (Receivables turnover and inventory turnover are discussed in Chapters 6 and 7, respectively.)

b. What changes are evident in the turnover rates of 3M for these years? Discuss ways in which a company such as 3M can improve its turnover within each of these three areas.

E8-31. Identifying and Accounting for Intangible Assets

LO1, 5

On the first day of 2019, Holthausen Company acquired the assets of Leftwich Company including several intangible assets. These include a patent on Leftwich's primary product, a device called a plentiscope. Leftwich carried the patent on its books for $1,500, but Holthausen believes that the fair value is $200,000. The patent expires in seven years, but competitors can be expected to develop competing patents within three years. Holthausen believes that, with expected technological improvements, the product is marketable for at least 20 years.

The registration of the trademark for the Leftwich name is scheduled to expire in 15 years. However, the Leftwich brand name, which Holthausen believes is worth $500,000, could be applied to related products for many years beyond that.

As part of the acquisition, Leftwich's principal researcher left the company. As part of the acquisition, he signed a five-year noncompetition agreement that prevents him from developing competing products. Holthausen paid the scientist $300,000 to sign the agreement.

a. What amount should be capitalized for each of the identifiable intangible assets?

b. What amount of amortization expense should Holthausen record in 2019 for each asset?

E8-32. Computing and Recording Depletion Expense

LO3

In 2019, Eldenburg Mining Company purchased land for $7,200,000 that had a natural resource reserve estimated to be 500,000 tons. Development and road construction costs on the land were $420,000, and a building was constructed at a cost of $50,000. When the natural resources are completely extracted, the land has an estimated residual value of $1,200,000. In addition, the cost to restore the property to comply with environmental regulations is estimated to be $800,000. Production in 2019 and 2020 was 60,000 tons and 85,000 tons, respectively.

a. Compute the depletion charge for 2019 and 2020.

b. Prepare a journal entry to record each year's depletion expense as determined in part *a*.

E8-33. Computing and Interpreting Percent Depreciated and PPE Turnover

LO6

The following footnote is from Note 8 to the 2018 10-K of **Tesla, Inc.**:

Tesla, Inc.:
NASDAQ :: ADGF

Note 8—Property, Plant and Equipment

Our property, plant and equipment, net, consisted of the following (in thousands):

	2018	2017
Machinery, equipment, vehicles and office furniture	$ 6,328,966	$ 4,251,711
Tooling	1,397,514	1,255,952
Leasehold improvements	960,971	789,751
Land and buildings	4,047,006	2,517,247
Computer equipment, hardware and software	487,421	395,067
Construction in progress	807,297	2,541,588
	14,029,175	11,751,316
Less: Accumulated depreciation	(2,699,098)	(1,723,794)
Total	$11,330,077	$10,027,522

The summary of significant accounting policies included the following description of Tesla's depreciation policies:

Property, plant and equipment, including leasehold improvements, are recognized at cost less accumulated depreciation. Depreciation is generally computed using the straight-line method over the estimated useful lives of the respective assets, as follows:

Machinery, equipment, vehicles and office furniture	2 to 12 years
Building and building improvements	15 to 30 years
Computer equipment and software	3 to 10 years

Depreciation for tooling is computed using the units-of-production method whereby capitalized costs are amortized over the total estimated productive life of the respective assets. As of December 31, 2018, the estimated productive life for Model S and Model X tooling was 325,000 vehicles based on our current estimates of production. As of December 31, 2018, the estimated productive life for Model 3 tooling was 1,000,000 vehicles based on our current estimates of production.

1. Tesla's revenue totaled $21,461,268 ($ thousands) in 2018. Compute its PPE turnover for the year.
2. Compute the percent depreciated ratio for 2018.
3. Comment on these ratios. What effect does Tesla's depreciation policies have on these ratios?

LO5 **E8-34. Evaluating R&D Expenditures of Companies**

Callaway Golf Co. NYSE :: ELY
Apple, Inc. NASDAQ :: AAPL
Samsung Electronics Co., Ltd KS :: 005930
Intel Corporation NASDAQ :: INTC
Microsoft Corporation NASDAQ :: MSFT
Baxter International, Inc. NYSE :: BAX
Pfizer, Inc. NYSE :: PFE
Merck & Co., Inc NYSE :: MRK
Monsanto Co. NYSE :: MON
Syngenta AG NYSE :: SYT
Deere & Co. NYSE :: DE

R&D intensity is measured by the ratio of research and development expense to sales revenue. The following table compares the R&D intensity for various companies.

Company	R&D Intensity
Callaway Golf Co.	3.28%
Samsung Electronics Co., Ltd (Korea)	7.65%
Apple, Inc.	5.36%
Intel Corporation	19.11%
Microsoft Corporation	13.34%
Baxter International, Inc.	5.84%
Pfizer, Inc.	14.92%
Merck & Co., Inc.	23.06%
Monsanto Co.	10.98%
Syngenta AG (Switzerland)	9.61%
Deere & Company	4.97%

a. Comment on the differences among these companies. To what extent are the differences related to industry affiliation?

b. What other factors (besides industry affiliation) might determine a company's R&D intensity?

LO4 Homework MBC **E8-35. Computing and Assessing Plant Asset Impairment**

Zeibart Company purchases equipment for $225,000 on July 1, 2016, with an estimated useful life of 10 years and expected salvage value of $25,000. Straight-line depreciation is used. On July 1, 2020, economic factors cause the fair value of the equipment to decline to $90,000. On this date, Zeibart examines the equipment for impairment and estimates $125,000 in future cash inflows related to use of this equipment.

a. Is the equipment impaired at July 1, 2020? Explain.

b. If the equipment is impaired on July 1, 2020, compute the impairment loss and prepare a journal entry to record the loss.

c. What amount of depreciation expense would Zeibart record for the 12 months from July 1, 2020 through June 30, 2021? Prepare a journal entry to record this depreciation expense. (*Hint:* Assume no change in salvage value.)

d. Using the financial statement effects template, show how the entries in parts *b* and *c* affect Zeibart Company's balance sheet and income statement.

PROBLEMS

LO4 Homework MBC **P8-36. Computing and Recording Proceeds from the Sale of PPE**

Hilton Worldwide Holdings Inc. NASDAQ :: HLT

The following information was provided in the 2018 10-K of Hilton Worldwide Holdings, Inc.

Note 7: Property and Equipment ($ millions)

	2018	2017
Property and equipment, gross	$848	$803
Accumulated depreciation	(481)	(450)
Property and equipment, net	367	353

Note 7 also revealed that depreciation expense on property and equipment totaled $54 million in 2018. The cash flow statement reported that expenditures for property and equipment totaled $72 million in 2018 and that there was no gain or loss on the sale of property and equipment during the year.

REQUIRED

Using the information provided, prepare a journal entry to record the sale of property and equipment in 2018. Explain how a gain or loss on the sale would have changed the journal entry you recorded.

P8-37. Analyzing and Assessing Research and Development Expenses

LO5

Agilent Technologies, Inc. NYSE :: A
Hewlett-Packard Company NYSE :: HPQ

Aglent Technologies, Inc., the high-tech spin-off from **Hewlett-Packard Company**, reports the following operating profit for 2018 in its 10-K ($ millions):

Net revenue	
Products	$3,746
Services and other	1,168
Total net revenue	4,914
Costs and expenses	
Cost of products	1,588
Cost of services and other	639
Total costs	2,227
Research and development	385
Selling, general and administrative	1,374
Total costs and expenses	3,986
Income from operations	$ 928

REQUIRED

a. What percentage of its total net revenue is Agilent spending on research and development?

b. How are its balance sheet and income statement affected by the accounting for R&D costs?

c. In 2003, Agilent's spending on R&D was $1,051 million—17.4% of its total net revenue. What are some possible ways that the company might have reduced its R&D intensity from 2003 to 2018? What are some of the possible implications for the company?

P8-38. Analyzing PPE Accounts and Recording PPE Transactions, Including Discontinued Operations

LO4

Target Corporation NYSE :: TGT

The 2018 and 2017 income statements and balance sheets (asset section only) for **Target Corporation** follow, along with its footnote describing Target's accounting for property and equipment. Target's cash flow statement for fiscal 2018 reported capital expenditures of $3,516 million and disposal proceeds for property and equipment of $85 million. No gain or loss was reported on property and equipment disposals. In addition, Target acquired property and equipment through non-cash acquisitions not reported on the statement of cash flows.

Consolidated Statements of Operations ($ millions)	2018	2017
Sales	$74,433	$71,786
Other revenue	923	928
Total revenues	75,356	72,714
Cost of sales	53,299	51,125
Selling, general and administrative expenses	15,723	15,140
Depreciation and amortization	2,224	2,225
Operating income	4,110	4,224
Net interest expense	461	653
Other (income) expense	(27)	(59)
Earnings from continuing operations before income taxes	3,676	3,630
Provision for income taxes	746	722
Net earnings from continuing operations	2,930	2,908
Discontinued operations, net of tax	7	6
Net (loss)/earnings	$ 2,937	$ 2,914

Consolidated Statements of Financial Position (Asset Section Only) ($ millions)	February 2, 2019	February 3, 2018
Assets		
Cash and cash equivalents	$ 1,556	$ 2,643
Inventory	9,497	8,597
Other current assets	1,466	1,300
Total current assets	12,519	12,540
Property and equipment		
Land	6,064	6,095
Buildings and improvements	29,240	28,131
Fixtures and equipment	5,912	5,623
Computer hardware and software	2,544	2,645
Construction-in-progress	460	440
Accumulated depreciation	(18,687)	(18,398)
Property and equipment, net	25,533	24,536
Other noncurrent assets	3,238	3,227
Total assets	$41,290	$40,303

11. Property and Equipment

Property and equipment is depreciated using the straight-line method over estimated useful lives or lease terms if shorter. We amortize leasehold improvements purchased after the beginning of the initial lease term over the shorter of the assets' useful lives or a term that includes the original lease term, plus any renewals that are reasonably assured at the date the leasehold improvements are acquired. Depreciation expense for 2018, 2017 and 2016 was $2,460 million, $2,462 million, and $2,305 million, respectively, including depreciation expense included in Cost of Sales. For income tax purposes, accelerated depreciation methods are generally used. Repair and maintenance costs are expensed as incurred. Facility pre-opening costs, including supplies and payroll, are expensed as incurred.

We review long-lived assets for impairment when events or changes in circumstances—such as a decision to relocate or close a store or distribution center, make significant software changes or discontinue projects—indicate that the asset's carrying value may not be recoverable. We recognized impairment losses of $92 million, $91 million, and $43 million during 2018, 2017, and 2016, respectively. . . . Impairments are recorded in SG&A Expenses on the Consolidated Statements of Operations.

REQUIRED

a. Prepare journal entries to record the following for 2018:
   i. Depreciation expense
   ii. Capital expenditures
   iii. Disposal of property, plant, and equipment
   iv. Impairments and write-downs (Assume that impairments and write-downs reduce the property and equipment account, rather than increasing accumulated depreciation.)

b. Estimate the amount of property and equipment that was acquired, if any, through non-cash transactions.

LO4 Williams-Sonoma NYSE :: WSM

P8-39. Reporting PPE Transactions and Asset Impairment

Note B from the fiscal 2010 10-K report of **Williams-Sonoma, Inc.**, (February 3, 2019) follows. Its cash flow statement reported that the company made capital expenditures of $190,102,000 during fiscal 2018, impaired assets of $9,639,000 and recorded depreciation expense of $182,533,000, excluding amortization of intangibles. In addition, the company reported a loss on the disposal of property and equipment of $570,000.

Note B: Property and Equipment

Property and equipment consists of the following:

($ thousands)	Feb. 3, 2019	Jan. 28, 2018
Leasehold improvements	$ 950,259	$ 950,024
Fixtures and equipment	836,400	800,003
Capitalized software	733,941	621,730
Land and buildings	175,181	173,457
Corporate systems projects in progress	39,416	65,283
Construction in progress	7,205	8,615
Total	2,742,402	2,619,112
Accumulated depreciation and amortization	(1,812,767)	(1,686,829)
Property and equipment—net	$ 929,635	$ 932,283

We review the carrying value of all long-lived assets for impairment, primarily at a store level, whenever events or changes in circumstances indicate that the carrying value of an asset may not be recoverable. We review for impairment all stores for which current or projected cash flows from operations are not sufficient to recover the carrying value of the assets. Impairment results when the carrying value of the assets exceeds the estimated undiscounted future cash flows over the remaining useful life. Our estimate of undiscounted future cash flows over the store lease term is based upon our experience, historical operations of the stores and estimates of future store profitability and economic conditions. The future estimates of store profitability and economic conditions require estimating such factors as sales growth, gross margin, employment rates, lease escalations, inflation on operating expenses and the overall economics of the retail industry, and are therefore subject to variability and difficult to predict. If a long-lived asset is found to be impaired, the amount recognized for impairment is equal to the difference between the net carrying value and the asset's fair value.

REQUIRED

Prepare journal entries to record the following for fiscal 2018:

a. Depreciation expense
b. Capital expenditures
c. Impairment of property and equipment (Assume that impairments and write-downs reduce the property and equipment account, rather than increasing accumulated depreciation.)
d. Disposal of property and equipment

CASES AND PROJECTS

C8-40. Interpreting and Reporting Property, Plant, and Equipment (PPE) Expenditures

LO4, 6
General Mills, Inc.
NYSE :: GIS

General Mills, Inc. is a global consumer foods company. The firm manufactures and sells a wide range of branded products and is a major supplier to the foodservice and baking industries. The company's core product areas are ready-to-eat cereal, super-premium ice cream, convenient meal solutions, and healthy snacking. The following data are taken from the company's 2018 annual report.
From the balance sheet:

($ millions)	May 27, 2018	May 28, 2017
Land, buildings, and equipment:		
Land	$ 77.7	$ 79.8
Buildings	2,396.3	2,249.2
Buildings under capital lease	0.3	0.3
Equipment	6,236.6	6,095.9
Equipment under capital lease	5.8	3.0
Capitalized software	593.6	545.4
Construction in progress	692.9	553.0
Total land, buildings, and equipment	10,003.2	9,526.6
Less accumulated depreciation	(5,956.0)	(5,838.9)
Total	$ 4,047.2	$3,687.7

From the income statement ($ millions):

	2018	2017
Net sales	$15,740.4	$15,619.8

REQUIRED

a. Compute the PPE turnover for 2018. Assuming an average PPE turnover of 4.0 for the company's closest competitors, does General Mills appear to be capital intensive?
b. Calculate the percentage depreciated of General Mills' depreciable assets at the end of fiscal year 2018. What implications might the result suggest for the company's future cash flows?
c. General Mills reports depreciation expense of approximately $589 million in 2018. Estimate the average useful life of its depreciable assets by dividing average depreciable assets by depreciation expense.
d. During 2018, General Mills purchased $622.7 million of land, buildings and equipment for cash. Create the necessary journal entries to reflect the asset purchases and the year's depreciation charge.

LO6 **C8-41. Managing Operating Assets to Improve Performance. A Management Application**
Return on a company's net operating assets is commonly used to evaluate financial performance. One way to increase performance is to focus on operating assets.

REQUIRED

Indicate how this might be done in relation to the following asset categories. Indicate also any potential problems a given action might create.

a. Receivables
b. Inventories
c. Property, plant, and equipment
d. Intangibles

LO4, 5, 6
Take-Two Interactive Software, Inc.
NASDAQ :: TTWO
Electronic Arts, Inc.
NASDAQ :: EA

C8-42. Determining the Effects of Capitalizing Versus Expensing Software Development Costs
The following information is taken from the March 31, 2018 annual report of **Take-Two Interactive Software, Inc.**, a maker and distributor of video games. All amounts are in thousands of U.S. dollars.

Income Statement Information:	2018
Net sales	$1,792,892
Cost of goods sold	898,311
Operating expenses	759,004
Income (loss) from operations	$ 135,577

Information from the Management Discussion, Balance Sheet and Note 8:

Software Development Costs and Licenses

Capitalized software development costs include direct costs incurred for internally developed titles and payments made to third-party software developers under development agreements. We capitalize internal software development costs (including stock-based compensation, specifically identifiable employee payroll expense and incentive compensation costs related to the completion and release of titles), third-party production and other content costs, subsequent to establishing technological feasibility of a software title. Technological feasibility of a product includes the completion of both technical design documentation and game design documentation. Significant management judgments and estimates are utilized in the assessment of when technological feasibility is established. For products where proven technology exists, this may occur early in the development cycle. Technological feasibility is evaluated on a product by product basis. Amortization of capitalized software development costs and licenses commences when a product is released and is recorded on a title-by-title basis in cost of goods sold. For capitalized software development costs, amortization is calculated using (1) the proportion of current year revenues to the total revenues expected to be recorded over the life of the title or (2) the straight-line method over the remaining estimated useful life of the title, whichever is greater. For capitalized licenses, amortization is calculated as a ratio of (1) current period revenues to the total revenues expected to be recorded over the remaining life of the title or (2) the contractual royalty rate based on actual net product sales as defined in the licensing agreement, whichever is greater. We evaluate the future recoverability of capitalized software development costs and licenses on a quarterly basis. Recoverability is primarily assessed based on the actual title's performance. For products that are scheduled to be released in the future, recoverability is evaluated based on the expected performance of the specific products to which the cost or license relates. We utilize a number of criteria in evaluating expected product performance, including: historical performance of comparable products developed with comparable technology; market performance of comparable titles; orders for the product prior to its release; general market conditions; and, past performance of the franchise. When we determine that the value of the title is unlikely to be recovered by product sales, capitalized costs are charged to cost of goods sold in the period in which such determination is made.

Capitalized Software Development Costs and Licenses	2018
Beginning balance	$423,631
Additions	326,909
Amortization and write-downs	(77,887)
Ending balance	$672,653

Assume an income tax rate of 25% where necessary.

REQUIRED

You wish to compare the performance of Take-Two with one of its competitors, **Electronic Arts, Inc.** However, Electronic Arts does not capitalize any significant amounts of its software development costs. Estimate Take-Two's 2018 Income from operations if it did not capitalize any software development costs. *Briefly* explain your adjustment(s).

C8-43. Analyzing Impairment Charges

LO4
DreamWorks Animation SKG Inc.
NASDAQ :: DWA

In the last quarter of 2014, **DreamWorks Animation SKG Inc.** recorded a loss. Part of this loss was due to impairment charges. In its annual report the company stated:

We are required to amortize capitalized production costs over the expected revenue streams as we recognize revenue from the associated films or other projects. The amount of production costs that will be amortized each quarter depends on, among other things, how much future revenue we expect to receive from each project. Unamortized production costs are evaluated for impairment each reporting period on a project-by-project basis. If estimated remaining revenue is not sufficient to recover the unamortized production costs, the unamortized production costs will be written down to fair value. In any given quarter, if we lower our previous forecast with respect to total anticipated revenue from any individual feature film or other project, we may be required to accelerate amortization or record impairment charges with respect to the unamortized costs, even if we have previously recorded impairment charges for such film or other project. For instance, in the quarter ended December 31, 2013, we incurred a write-down of $13.5 million for our film *Turbo* and in the year ended December 31, 2014, we incurred write-downs of $66.5 million for our film *Mr. Peabody and Sherman* and $30.3 million for our film *The Penguins of Madagascar*. Such impairment charges adversely impacted our business, operating results and financial condition.

REQUIRED

a. DreamWorks reported an $86.2 million pre-tax loss for the year 2014. What would pre-tax income or loss have been without the above described impairment charges?

b. DreamWorks is in the film production/media industry. From the paragraph above, describe how companies in this industry account for their film production costs—when incurred and over time.

c. Show the journal entry for 2014 to record the impairment charges related to *Mr. Peabody and Sherman* and *The Penguins of Madagascar*.

SOLUTIONS TO REVIEW PROBLEMS

Mid-Chapter Review

SOLUTION

1*a*. Straight-line Depreciation expense = ($95,000 – $10,000)/5 years = $17,000 per year

1*b*. Double-declining-balance (twice straight-line rate = 2 × (1/5) = 40%)

Year	Book Value × Rate	Depreciation Expense
1	$95,000 × 0.40 =	$38,000
2	($95,000 – $38,000) × 0.40 =	22,800
3	($95,000 – $60,800) × 0.40 =	13,680
4	($95,000 – $74,480) × 0.40 =	8,208
5	($95,000 – $82,688) × 0.40 =	2,312*

*The formula value of $4,925 is not reported because it would depreciate the asset below residual value. Only the $2,312 needed to reach residual value is depreciated.

2.

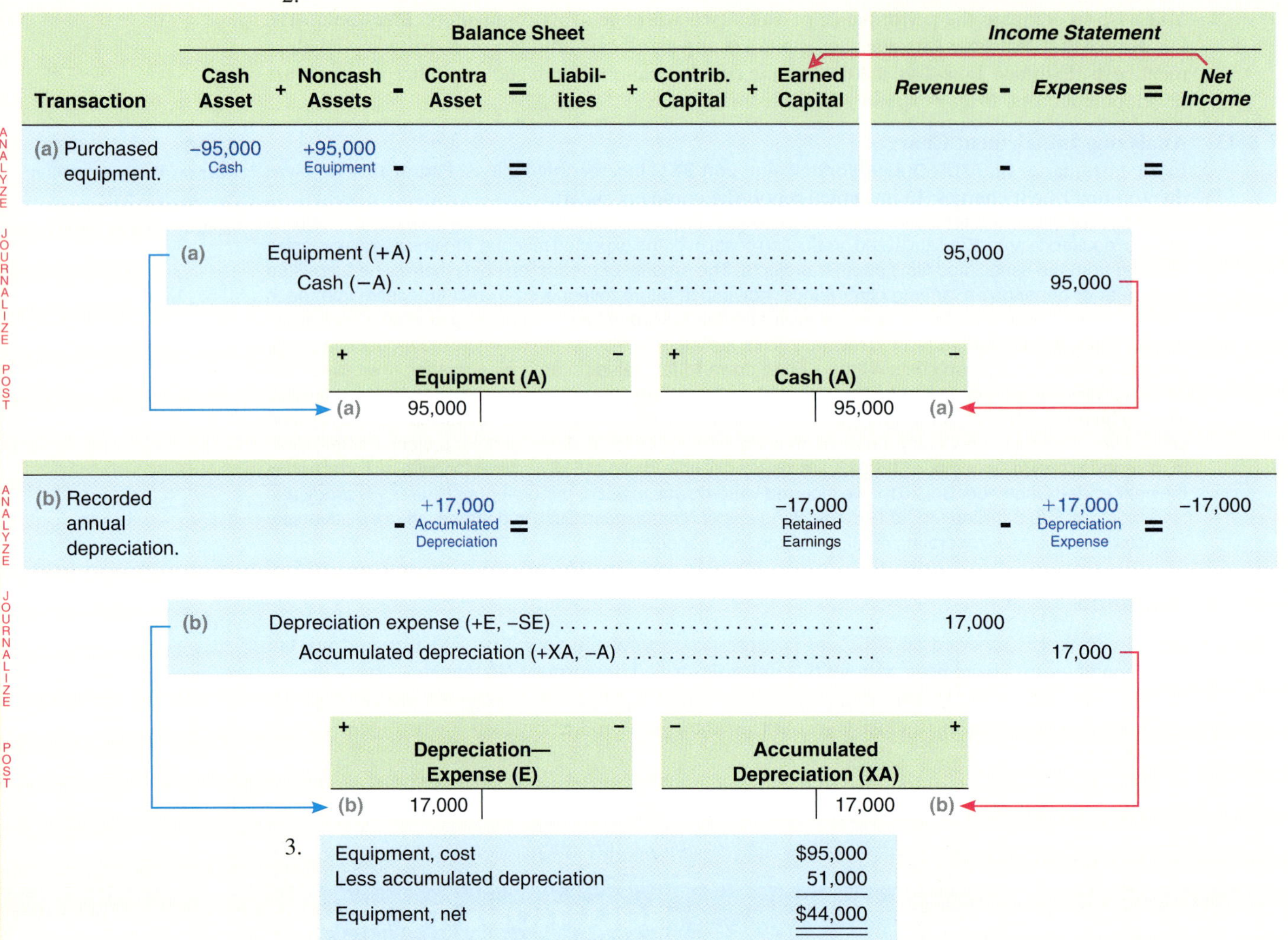

3.

Equipment, cost	$95,000
Less accumulated depreciation	51,000
Equipment, net	$44,000

Equipment is reported on Lev's balance sheet at its net book value of $44,000.

4. The percent depreciated is computed as: Accumulated Depreciation/Depreciable Asset Cost = $51,000/$95,000 = 53.7%. The equipment is more than one-half depreciated at the end of the third year. Still, this estimate is useful in that we know that the company's asset is over one-half depreciated and is likely to require replacement in about 2 years (less than one-half of its useful life of 5 years). This replacement will become a cash outflow or financing need when it arises and should be considered in our projections of future cash flows.

Chapter-End Review

SOLUTION

1. Bowen Company would expense the $120,000 in R&D costs in 2018. The $12,500 in legal fees to obtain the patent would be capitalized. As a result, the book value of the patent would be $12,500 on July 1, 2018. The entries to record these costs would be:

ANALYZE

Transaction	Balance Sheet: Cash Asset	+ Noncash Assets	− Contra Asset	= Liabilities	+ Contrib. Capital	+ Earned Capital	Income Statement: Revenues	− Expenses	= Net Income
(a) Record R&D costs as R&D expense.	−120,000 Cash					−120,000 Retained Earnings		+120,000 R&D Expense	−120,000

JOURNALIZE

		Debit	Credit
(a)	R&D expense (+E, −SE)	120,000	
	Cash (−A)		120,000

POST

+ Research & Development Expense (E) −		+ Cash (A) −	
(a) 120,000			120,000 (a)

ANALYZE

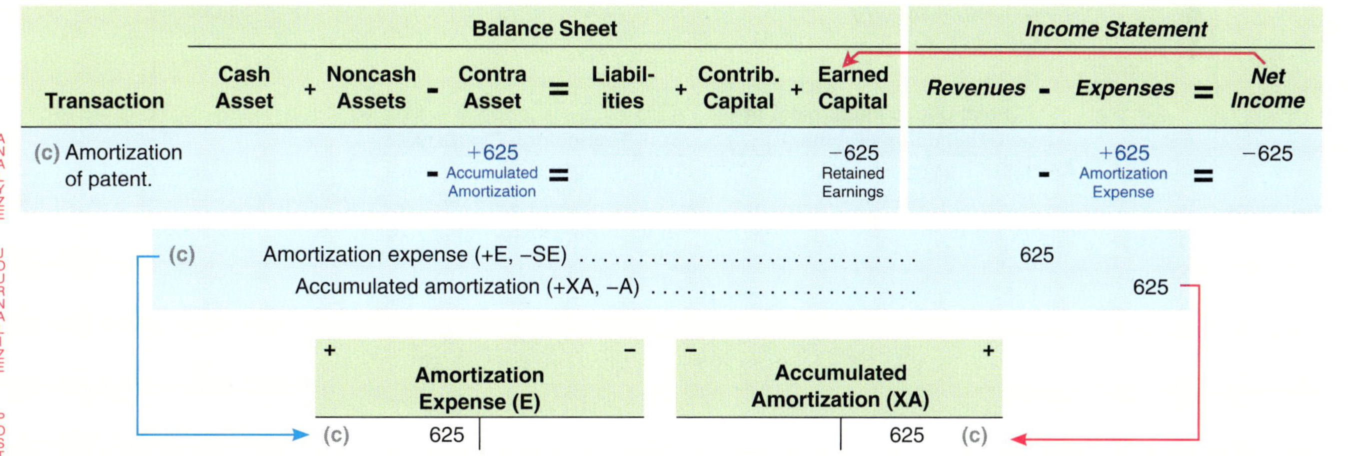

Transaction	Cash Asset	+ Noncash Assets	− Contra Asset	= Liabilities	+ Contrib. Capital	+ Earned Capital	Revenues	− Expenses	= Net Income
(b) Record acquisition of patent.	−12,500 Cash	+12,500 Patent							

JOURNALIZE

		Debit	Credit
(b)	Patent (+A)	12,500	
	Cash (−A)		12,500

POST

+ Patent (A) −		+ Cash (A) −	
(b) 12,500			120,000 (a)
			12,500 (b)

2. Each year, beginning on July 1, 2018, Bowen would record amortization expense of $1,250 ($12,500/10). For 2018, six months of amortization expense, or $625, would be recorded ($1,250/2). The journal entry would be:

ANALYZE

Transaction	Balance Sheet: Cash Asset	+ Noncash Assets	− Contra Asset	= Liabilities	+ Contrib. Capital	+ Earned Capital	Income Statement: Revenues	− Expenses	= Net Income
(c) Amortization of patent.			+625 Accumulated Amortization			−625 Retained Earnings		+625 Amortization Expense	−625

JOURNALIZE

		Debit	Credit
(c)	Amortization expense (+E, −SE)	625	
	Accumulated amortization (+XA, −A)		625

POST

+ Amortization Expense (E) −		− Accumulated Amortization (XA) +	
(c) 625			625 (c)

3. Because Kennedy purchased the right to use the technology, the purchase price can be capitalized as an intangible asset and amortized over the five-year length of the agreement. Kennedy would record amortization expense of $18,000 ($90,000/5) each year, beginning July 1, 2020. (Bowen would recognize the $90,000 as revenue.) The journal entry that Kennedy Company would need to record the acquisition of the technology rights would be as follows:

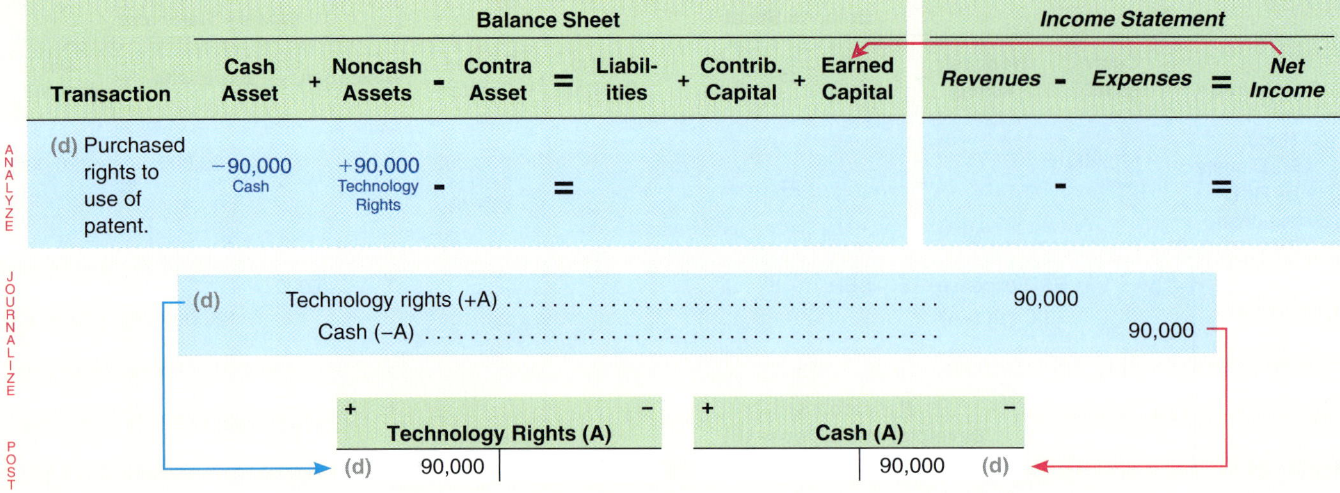

Transaction	Cash Asset	+	Noncash Assets	-	Contra Asset	=	Liabilities	+	Contrib. Capital	+	Earned Capital	Revenues	-	Expenses	=	Net Income
(d) Purchased rights to use of patent.	−90,000 Cash		+90,000 Technology Rights	-		=							-		=	

(d) Technology rights (+A) 90,000
Cash (−A) 90,000

+ Technology Rights (A) −	
(d) 90,000	

+ Cash (A) −	
	90,000 (d)

4. Given that the patent is obsolete, both Bowen Company and Kennedy Company would record impairment losses. Bowen would write off the unamortized balance in the patent account, resulting in a loss of $7,500 [$12,500 − ($1,250 × 4)]. Kennedy Company would write off the remaining value of the technology agreement, recording an impairment loss of $54,000 [$90,000 − ($18,000 × 2)]. Kennedy's journal entry would be:

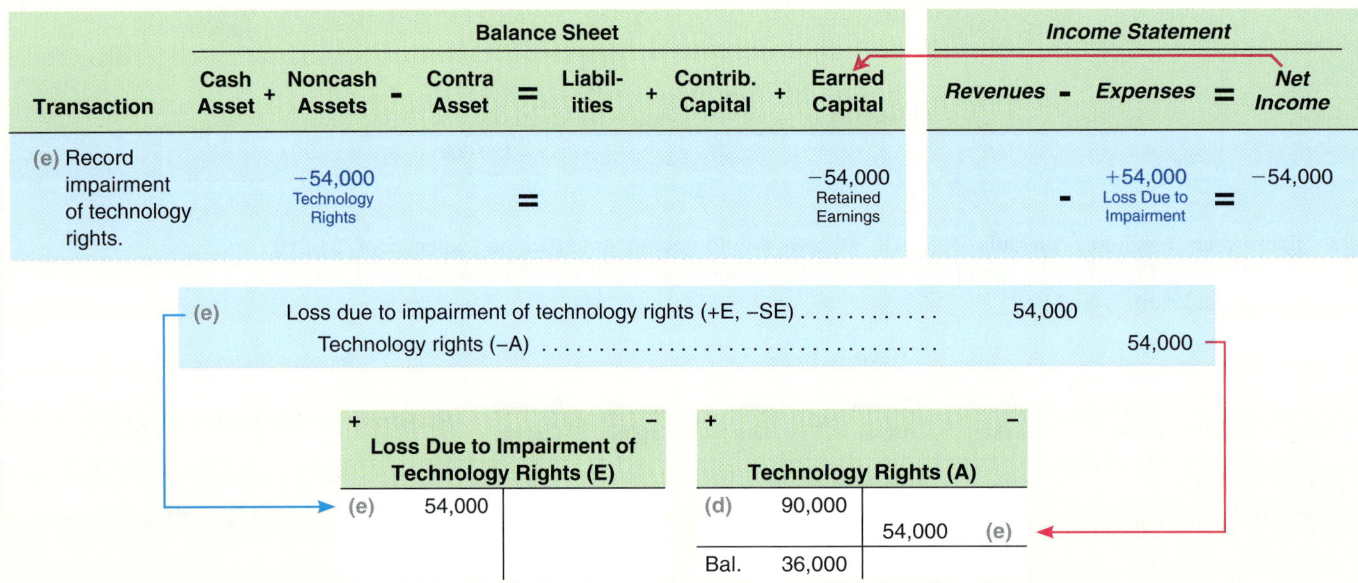

Transaction	Cash Asset	+	Noncash Assets	-	Contra Asset	=	Liabilities	+	Contrib. Capital	+	Earned Capital	Revenues	-	Expenses	=	Net Income
(e) Record impairment of technology rights.			−54,000 Technology Rights			=					−54,000 Retained Earnings		-	+54,000 Loss Due to Impairment	=	−54,000

(e) Loss due to impairment of technology rights (+E, −SE) 54,000
Technology rights (−A) 54,000

+ Loss Due to Impairment of Technology Rights (E) −	
(e) 54,000	

+ Technology Rights (A) −	
(d) 90,000	
	54,000 (e)
Bal. 36,000	

Reporting and Analyzing Liabilities

LEARNING OBJECTIVES

1. Identify and account for current operating liabilities. (p. 415)
2. Describe and account for current nonoperating (financial) liabilities. (p. 422)
3. Explain and illustrate the pricing of long-term nonoperating liabilities. (p. 427)
4. Analyze and account for financial statement effects of long-term nonoperating liabilities. (p. 430)
5. Explain how solvency ratios and debt ratings are determined and how they impact the cost of debt. (p. 438)

VERIZON
www.verizon.com

In 2000, **Bell Atlantic Corporation** merged with **GTE** to form **Verizon Communications**. After its 2006 acquisition of **MCI Communications Corp.** and subsequent acquisition of **Alltel Corporation** in 2008, the corporation became the world's largest provider of communications services. Verizon acquired AOL in 2015 and Yahoo! in 2017.

Verizon's industry is constantly changing and extremely competitive. Hans Vestberg, who became the CEO in 2018, faces the challenging task of fending off a host of competitors including **AT&T**, **Comcast**, **Sprint**, and others.

In recent years Verizon has embarked upon a strategic transformation as advances in technology have changed the ways that people communicate in their personal and professional lives. During 2017, the company focused on leveraging their network leadership and retaining and growing their customer base while balancing profitability and driving monetization of their networks and solutions. This strategy requires significant capital investment to acquire wireless spectrum, put the spectrum into service, expand the fiber optic network that supports wireless and wireline service, maintain networks, and develop and maintain database capacity. The company has been a leading developer in fifth generation (5G) wireless technologies. This investment program requires a significant amount of cash at a time when the company is faced with more than $117 billion in oustanding debt (a total liability balance of $212.5 billion) and $22 billion in employee benefit obligations. Fortunately, Verizon's operating cash flow remains strong at $25.3 billion in 2017.

Previous chapters focused on the reporting of operating assets, including receivables, inventories, property, plant, and equipment, and intangible assets, along

with the related expenses. We now turn our attention to the other side of the balance sheet. Chapter 9 examines how we value liabilities and how debt financing along with the subsequent payment of interest and principal affect the financial statements. We also discuss the required disclosures that enable us to effectively analyze a company's ability to make its liability payments as they mature. Chapter 10 focuses on the reporting for specific types of liabilities, and Chapter 11 examines the reporting of stockholders' equity.

As Verizon faces increased competition from other telecom companies, cable, and Internet providers, it must continue to innovate in order to maintain its position as the industry leader. This objective will require large investments in technology and infrastructure, only part of which will come from its operating cash flow. The company faces other substantial risks as well, including (1) the threat of cyberattacks, (2) changes in regulation in their industry, (3) technological disruptions, and (4) their significant debt burden and possibility of rising interest rates. To be successful, Vestberg will need to manage Verizon's debt burden and efficiently allocate cash resources between strategic investments and debt payments.

Sources: *The Wall Street Journal* 5/2011; *Verizon* 2018 10-K.

CHAPTER ORGANIZATION

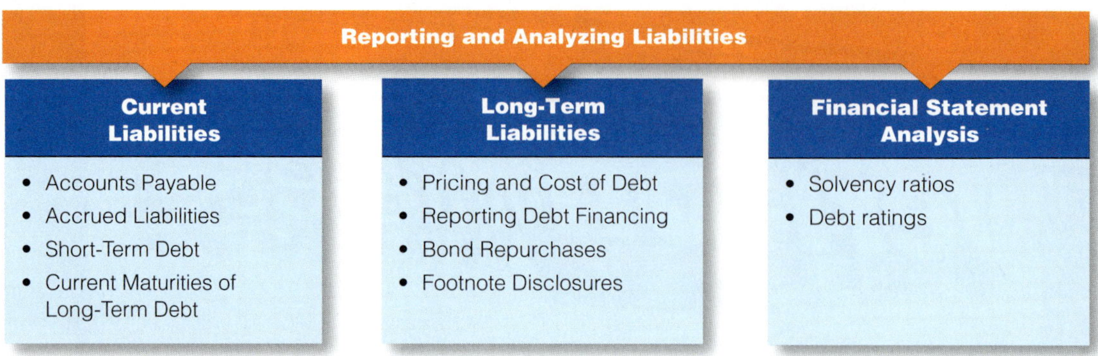

INTRODUCTION

Just as asset disclosures provide us with information on where a company invests its funds, the disclosures concerning liabilities and equity inform us as to how those assets are financed. To be successful, a company must not only invest funds wisely, but must also be astute in the manner in which it finances those investments.

Companies hope to finance their assets at the lowest possible cost. The cost of financing assets with liabilities is the interest charged by the lender. While many liabilities bear explicit interest rates, many other liabilities (such as accounts payable and accrued liabilities) are non-interest-bearing. This fact does not mean that these liabilities are cost-free. For example, while a supplier may appear to offer interest-free credit terms, the cost of that credit is implicitly included in the price it charges for the goods or services it sells.

Verizon's liabilities and equity, as taken from its 2017 10-K report, are presented in **Exhibit 9.1**. Just as assets are classified as either current or noncurrent, so are liabilities presented in the balance sheet as either current or noncurrent.

Current liabilities, as the name implies, are short-term in nature, generally requiring payment within the coming year. As a result, they are not a suitable source of funding for long-term assets that generate cash flows over several years. Instead, companies often finance long-term assets with long-term liabilities that require payments over several years, so that the cash outflows required by the financing source match the cash inflows produced by the assets to which they relate.

EXHIBIT 9.1 Verizon Communications' Liabilities and Equity

At December 31 ($ millions)	2017	2016
Current liabilities		
Debt maturing within one year	$ 3,453	$ 2,645
Accounts payable and accrued liabilities	21,232	19,593
Other	8,352	8,102
Total current liabilities	33,037	30,340
Long-term debt	113,642	105,433
Employee benefit obligations	22,112	26,166
Deferred income taxes	31,232	45,964
Other liabilities	12,433	12,245
Total liabilities	212,456	220,148
Total equity	44,687	24,032
Total liabilities and equity	$257,143	$244,180

When a company acquires assets, and finances them with liabilities, its **financial leverage** increases. Because the magnitude of required liability payments increases with the level of liability financing, those larger payments increase the chance of default should a downturn in business occur. Increasing levels of liabilities make the company riskier to creditors who, consequently, demand a higher return on the financing they provide to the company. The assessment of default risk is part of liquidity and solvency analysis.

This chapter, along with Chapter 10, focuses on liabilities that are reported on the balance sheet and the corresponding interest costs reported in the income statement. All such liabilities represent probable, nondiscretionary, future obligations that are the result of events that have already occurred. Chapter 10 also addresses *off-balance sheet financing*, which encompasses future obligations that are reported in the notes, but not on the face of the balance sheet. An understanding of both on-balance-sheet and off-balance-sheet financing is central to evaluating a company's financial condition and assessing its risk of default.

CURRENT LIABILITIES

Liabilities are separated on the balance sheet into current and noncurrent (long-term). We first focus our attention on current liabilities, which are obligations that must be met (paid) within one year. Most current liabilities such as those related to utilities, wages, insurance, rent, and taxes, generate a corresponding impact on operating expenses.

Verizon reports three categories of current liabilities: (1) debt maturing within one year, which includes short-term borrowings as well as long-term obligations that are scheduled for payment in the upcoming year, (2) accounts payable and accrued liabilities, and (3) other current liabilities, which consist mainly of customer deposits, dividends declared but not yet paid, and miscellaneous short-term obligations too small to list separately.

It is helpful to separate current liabilities into operating and nonoperating components. These two components primarily consist of:

1. Current operating liabilities
   - **Accounts payable** Obligations to others for amounts owed on purchases of goods and services. These are usually non-interest-bearing.
   - **Accrued liabilities** Obligations for expenses incurred that have not been paid as of the end of the current period. These include, for example, accruals for employee wages earned but yet unpaid, accruals for taxes (usually quarterly) on payroll and current-period profits, and accruals for other liabilities such as rent, utilities, interest, and insurance. Accruals are made to properly reflect the liabilities owed as of the statement date and the expenses incurred in the period. Each one is journalized by a debit to an expense account (an increase in the expense) and a credit to a related liability (an increase in the liability).
   - **Deferred performance liabilities** Obligations that will be satisfied, not by paying cash, but instead, by providing products or services to customers. Examples of deferred performance liabilities include customer deposits, other types of contract liabilities (ASC 606) such as the unconditional right to receive payment from a customer, unearned gift card revenues for retail companies, and liabilities for frequent flier programs offered by airlines.
2. Current nonoperating liabilities
   - **Short-term interest-bearing debt** Short-term bank borrowings and notes expected to mature in whole or in part during the upcoming year.
   - **Current maturities of long-term debt** Long-term borrowings that are scheduled to mature in whole or in part during the upcoming year.

The remainder of this section describes current liabilities.

Accounts Payable

LO1 Identify and account for current operating liabilities.

1

Accounts payable, which are part of current operating liabilities, arise from the purchase of goods and services from others on credit. Verizon reports $21,232 million in accounts payable and accrued liabilities as of December 31, 2017. Its accounts payable represent $7,063 million, or 33%, of this total amount.

Accounts payable are a non-interest-bearing source of financing. Increased payables reduce the amount of net working capital, because these payables are deducted from current assets in the computation of net working capital. Also, increased payables improve operating cash flow (because inventories were purchased without using cash). An increase in accounts payable also increases profitability because it causes a reduction in the level of interest-bearing debt that is required to finance operating assets. ROE increases when companies make use of this low-cost financing source. However, management must be careful to avoid excessive "**leaning on the trade**" because short-term income and cash flow gains can result in long-term costs such as damaged supply channels.[1]

When a company purchases goods or services on credit, suppliers often grant **cash discounts** to buyers if payment is made within a specified time period. Cash discounts are usually established as part of the credit terms and stated as a percentage of the purchase price. For example, credit terms of 1/10, n/30 (one-ten, net-thirty) indicate that a 1% cash discount is allowed if the payment is made within 10 days. If the cash discount is not taken, the full purchase price is due in 30 days.

Net-of-Discount Method To illustrate a cash discount, assume that a company purchases 1,000 units of merchandise at \$4 per unit on terms of 1/10, n/30. The total purchase price is 1,000 × \$4 = \$4,000. However, if payment is made within 10 days, the net purchase price would then be \$3,960 (\$4,000 – \$40). While this difference seems like a small amount, consider the cost of not taking the discount. If the discount is missed, the buyer is afforded an extra 20 days to pay for the merchandise, for which it pays a penalty of \$40, or \$2 per day. Two dollars per day is the equivalent of \$730 per year which, in turn, is equivalent to paying interest at an annual rate of 18.4% (\$730/\$3,960).

When cash discounts are offered, the inventory purchase should be recorded at its cost using the **net-of-discount method**. When the net-of-discount method is used, inventory is capitalized at the net cost, assuming that the discount will be taken by the buyer. Continuing with our example, the following entry would be recorded by the buyer at the time of purchase:

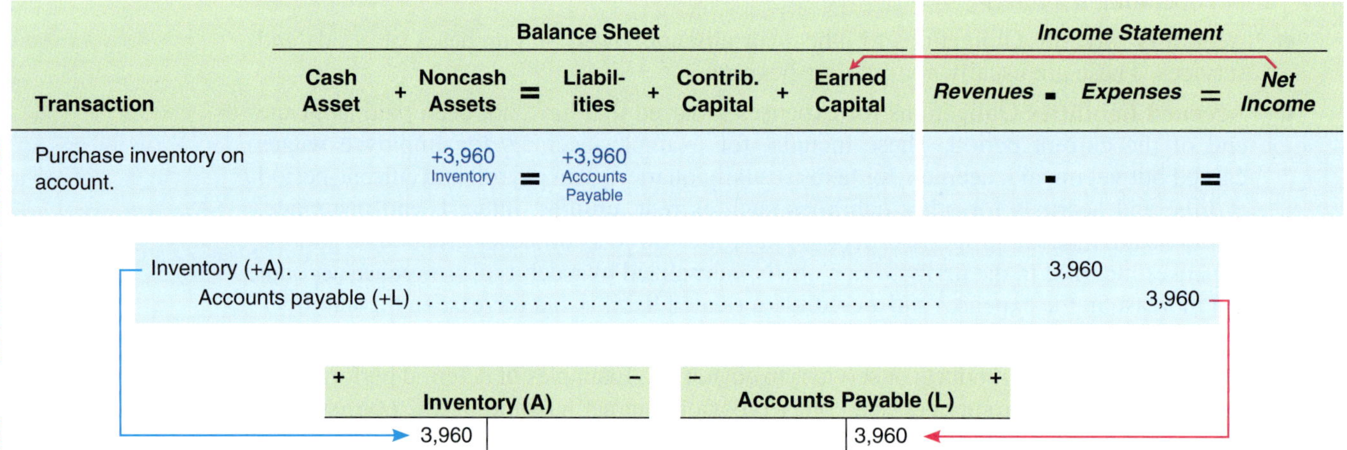

Transaction	Cash Asset	+	Noncash Assets	=	Liabilities	+	Contrib. Capital	+	Earned Capital	Revenues	−	Expenses	=	Net Income
Purchase inventory on account.			+3,960 Inventory	=	+3,960 Accounts Payable						−		=	

Journal entry	Dr.	Cr.
Inventory (+A)	3,960	
Accounts payable (+L)		3,960

+ Inventory (A) −	− Accounts Payable (L) +
3,960	3,960

When payment is made within the 10-day discount period, accounts payable is debited and cash is credited:

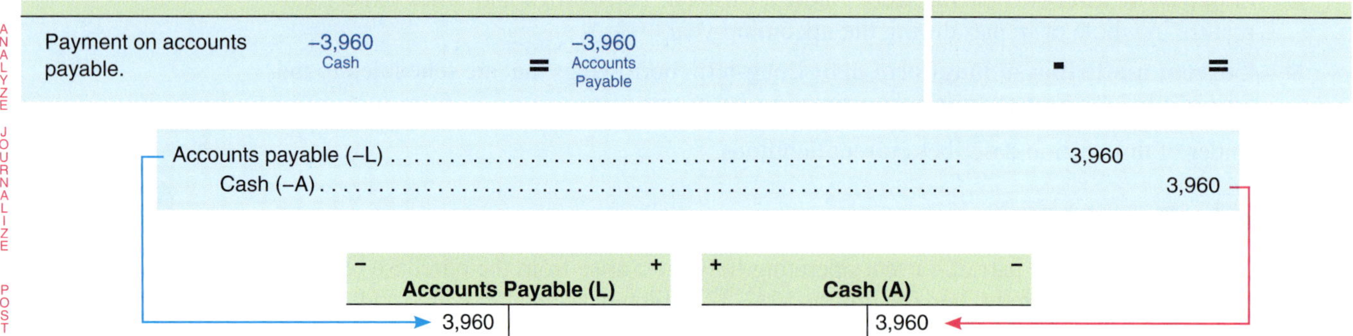

Transaction	Cash Asset	+	Noncash Assets	=	Liabilities	+	Contrib. Capital	+	Earned Capital	Revenues	−	Expenses	=	Net Income
Payment on accounts payable.	−3,960 Cash			=	−3,960 Accounts Payable						−		=	

Journal entry	Dr.	Cr.
Accounts payable (−L)	3,960	
Cash (−A)		3,960

− Accounts Payable (L) +	+ Cash (A) −
3,960	3,960

However, when a discount is missed, the lost discount must be recorded. For example, if full payment is made after the 10-day discount period, the payment is recorded as follows:

[1] One must be careful, because excessive delays in the payment of payables can result in suppliers charging a higher price for their goods or, ultimately, refusing to sell to certain buyers. This situation is a hidden "financing" cost that, even though it is not interest, is a real cost.

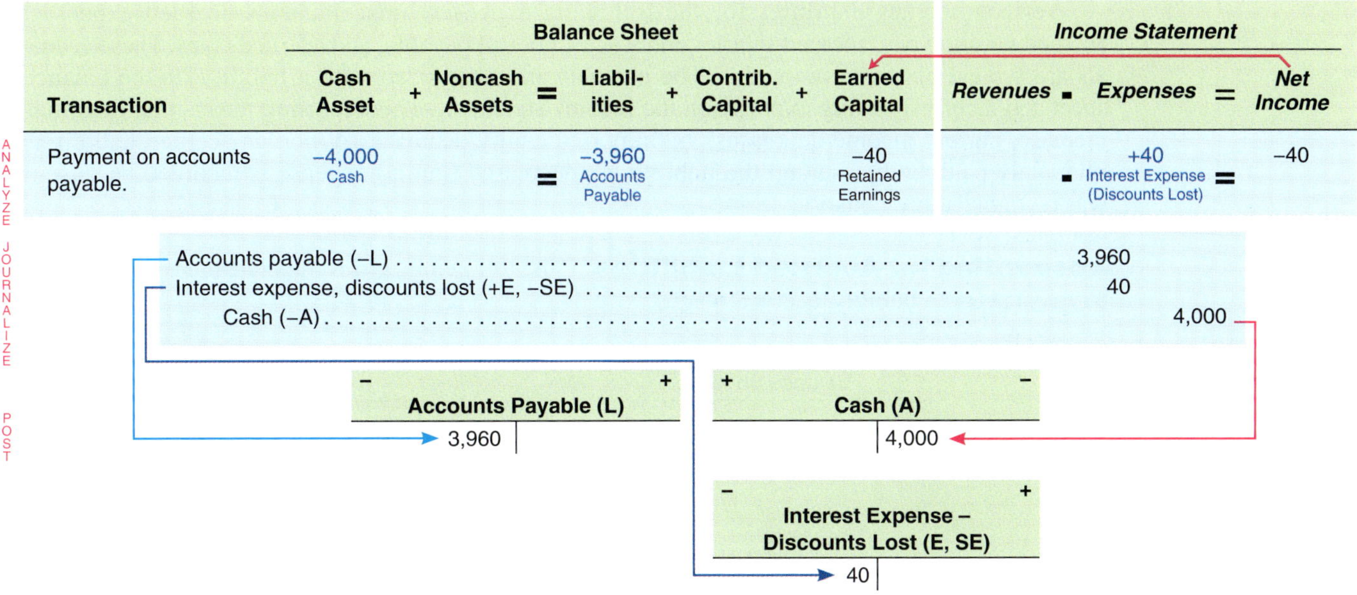

The missed discount is an expense in the period when the discount is lost. This serves two purposes. First, discounts lost are not capitalized as part of inventory and are not added to cost of goods sold. Instead, the lost discounts are treated like a finance charge and recorded as an expense of the period when the discount is missed. Second, the net-of-discount method highlights late payments by explicitly keeping a record of lost discounts. Given the high cost of missed cash discounts, most businesses would likely want to minimize the amount of discounts lost. Thus, keeping a record of discounts lost is useful when it comes to managing cash and accounts payable.

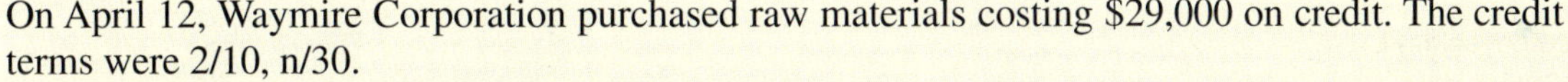

MID-CHAPTER REVIEW 1

On April 12, Waymire Corporation purchased raw materials costing $29,000 on credit. The credit terms were 2/10, n/30.

a. If Waymire paid for the materials on April 19, how much would it pay?
b. Compute the cost of a lost discount as an annual percentage interest rate.

The solution to this review problem can be found on page 458.

Accrued Liabilities

Accrued liabilities are identified at the end of an accounting period to reflect liabilities and expenses that have been incurred during the period but are not yet paid.[2] **Verizon** reports details of its $21,232 million accounts payable and accrued liabilities, including its $7,063 accounts payable, in footnote 14 to its 2017 10-K report:

December 31 ($ millions)	2017	2016
Accounts payable	$ 7,063	$ 7,084
Accrued expenses	6,756	5,717
Accrued vacation pay, salaries, and wages	4,521	3,813
Interest payable	1,409	1,463
Taxes payable	1,483	1,516
Total	$21,232	$19,593

[2] Accruals can also be made for recognition of revenue and a corresponding receivable. An example of this situation would be revenue recognition on a long-term contract that has reached a particular milestone, or for interest earned but not received on an investment in bonds that is still outstanding at period-end.

Verizon accrues liabilities for the following expenses: miscellaneous accrued expenses, accrued vacation pay, accrued salaries and wages, interest payable, and accrued taxes. These accruals are typical of most companies. The accruals are recognized with a liability on the balance sheet and a corresponding expense on the income statement. This reporting means that liabilities increase, current income decreases, and reported equity decreases. When an accrued liability is ultimately paid, both cash and the liability are decreased (but no expense is recorded because it was recognized previously).

Accounting for Accrued Liabilities The following entries illustrate the accounting for a typical accrued liability, accrued wages:

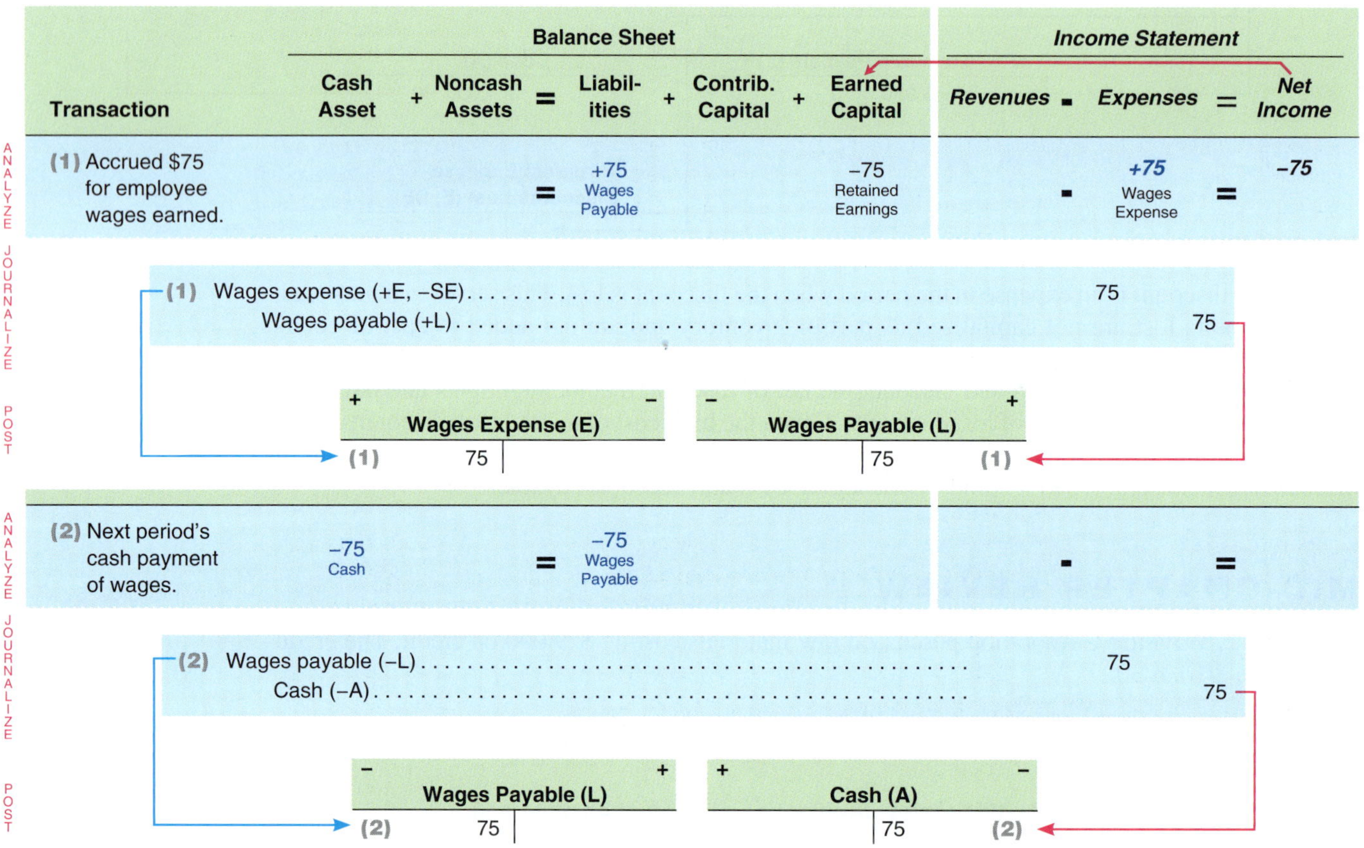

The following financial statement effects result from this accrual of employee wages:

- Employees have worked during a period and have not yet been paid. The effect of this accrual is to increase wages payable on the balance sheet and to recognize wages expense on the income statement. Failure to recognize this liability and associated expense would understate liabilities on the balance sheet and overstate income.
- Employees are paid in the following period, resulting in a cash decrease and a reduction in wages payable. This payment does not result in expense because the expense was recognized in the prior period when incurred.

Contingent Liabilities The accrued wages illustration relates to events that are fairly certain. We know, for example, when wages are incurred but not paid. Other examples of such accruals are rental costs, insurance premiums due but not yet paid, and taxes owed.

Some accrued liabilities, however, are less certain than others. Consider a company facing a lawsuit. Should it record the possible liability and related expense? The answer depends on the likelihood of occurrence and the ability to estimate the obligation. Specifically, if the obligation is *probable* **and** the amount *estimable,* then a company will recognize this obligation, called a **contingent liability**, with a corresponding charge to income. If an obligation is only *reasonably possible,* regardless of the company's ability to estimate the amount, the contingent liability is not reported on the balance sheet and is merely disclosed in the footnotes (we discuss further below). All other contingent liabilities that are less than reasonably possible are not accrued—disclosure in a note is permitted but not required.

A GLOBAL PERSPECTIVE

Reporting Contingent Liabilities U.S. GAAP and IFRS are similar with respect to reporting accrued liabilities. The one exception is contingencies. IFRS uses the term *provisions* to refer to contingent liabilities that are accrued and reported on the balance sheet while an obligation that is disclosed in the notes is labeled *contingent liability.* Both GAAP and IFRS require accrual of the "best estimate" of the liability. However, if the best estimate of the future payments required to settle the obligation is a range of values, IFRS requires that the midpoint of the range be used as the estimated value of the contingent liability or provision. In the same situation, U.S. GAAP requires that the low end of the range be used, with disclosure of the maximum.

Warranties The new revenue recognition standard discussed in Chapter 6 has implications for the accounting for warranty obligations. When a company delivers a product with a warranty, is the warranty simply assurance that the product will function as intended, or should it be considered a separate performance obligation? If it is considered a separate performance obligation, then the company would allocate the purchase price between the product and the warranty and recognize an unearned revenue liability at the time of purchase. However, if the warranty is not a separate performance obligation (e.g., it cannot be purchased separately from the product and is intended as assurance that the product will perform as expected), none of the purchase price is allocated to the warranty, and a liability accrual for the warranty obligation must be made at the time of purchase, as mentioned in Chapter 6.

The expected cost of the warranty commitment usually is reasonably estimated at the time of sale based on past experience. GAAP requires manufacturers to record the expected cost of warranties as a liability, and to record the related expected warranty expense in the income statement to match against the sales revenue reported for that period.

To illustrate, the effects of an accrual of a $1,000 warranty liability are:

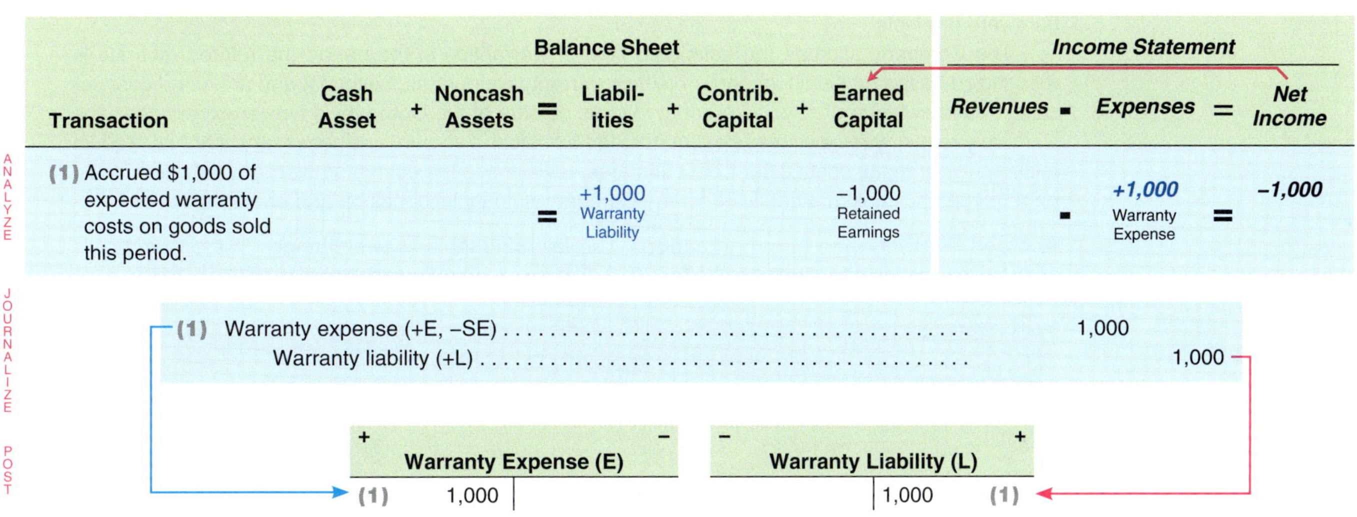

	Balance Sheet												Income Statement				
Transaction	Cash Asset	+	Noncash Assets	=	Liabil-ities	+	Contrib. Capital	+	Earned Capital				Revenues	-	Expenses	=	Net Income
(2) Next period's costs (sent $950 in replacement products) to cover failures under warranty.			−950 Inventory	=	−950 Warranty Liability									-		=	

ANALYZE

JOURNALIZE

	Dr.	Cr.
(2) Warranty liability (−L)	950	
Inventory (−A)		950

POST

− Warranty Liability (L) +		+ Inventory (A) −	
(2) 950		950	(2)

Reporting of warranty liabilities has the same effect on financial statements as does the accrual of wages expense in the previous section. That is, a liability is recorded on the balance sheet and an expense is reported in the income statement, reducing income by the warranty accrual. When the defective product is later replaced (or repaired), the liability is reduced together with the cost of the inventory (or other assets) spent to satisfy the claim. (Only a portion of the products estimated to fail does so in the current period; we expect other product failures in future periods. Using methods similar to the aging of accounts in Chapter 6, management monitors this estimate and adjusts it if failure is higher or lower than expected.) As in the accrual of wages, the expense is reported when it is incurred and the liability is estimated at that time, not when payments are made.

Apple Inc. reports $3,692 million of warranty liability in its 2018 balance sheet. The footnotes reveal the following additional information:

Several notes are combined below: Accrued Warranty and Indemification, Warranty, and Warranty Costs The Company offers a limited parts and labor warranty on its hardware products. The basic warranty period is typically one year from the date of purchase by the original end user. The Company also offers a 90-day limited warranty on the service parts used to repair the Company's hardware products. In certain jurisdictions, local law requires that manufacturers guarantee their products for a period prescribed by statute, typically at least two years. In addition, where available, consumers may purchase APP or AC+, which extends service coverage on many of the Company's hardware products.

The Company accrues the estimated cost of warranties in the period the related revenue is recognized based on historical and projected warranty claim rates, historical and projected cost per claim and knowledge of specific product failures outside of the Company's typical experience. The Company regularly reviews these estimates and adjusts the amounts as necessary. If actual product failure rates or repair costs differ from estimates, revisions to the estimated warranty liabilities would be required and could materially affect the Company's financial condition and operating results.

Accrued Warranty and Indemnification The following table shows changes in the Company's accrued warranties and related costs for 2018, 2017 and 2016 (in millions):

	2018	2017	2016
Beginning accrued warranty and related costs	$3,834	$3,702	$4,780
Cost of warranty claims	(4,115)	(4,322)	(4,663)
Accruals for product warranty	3,973	4,454	3,585
Ending accrued warranty and related costs	$3,692	$3,834	$3,702

In 2018, Apple incurred $4,115 million in cost to replace or repair defective products during the year, reducing the liability by this amount. This cost can be in the form of cash paid to customers or to employees as wages, and in the form of parts used for repairs. The company accrued an additional $3,973 million in new warranty liabilities in 2018. It is important to realize that only the increase in the liability resulting from additional accruals affects the income statement, reducing income through the additional warranty expense. Warranty payments reduce the warranty liability but have no impact on the income statement.

U.S. GAAP requires that the warranty liability reflect the estimated amount of cost that the company expects to incur as a result of warranty claims. This amount is often difficult to estimate and is prone to error. There is also the possibility that a company might intentionally underestimate its warranty liability to report higher current income, or overestimate it so as to depress current income and create an additional liability on the balance sheet that can be used to absorb future warranty costs without the need to record additional expense. Doing so would shift income from the current period to one or more future periods. Warranty liabilities should be compared with sales levels. Any deviations from the historical relation of the warranty liability to sales may indicate a change in product quality or, alternatively, it may reveal earnings management.

All accrued liabilities result in a liability on the balance sheet and an expense on the income statement. Management has some latitude in determining the amount and timing for accruals. This latitude can lead to misreporting of income and liabilities (unintentional or otherwise). For example, if accruals are underestimated, then liabilities are underestimated, income is overestimated, and retained earnings are overestimated. In subsequent periods when an understated accrued liability is reversed (it is recognized in the account), reported income is lower than it should be; this is because prior period income was higher than it should have been. (The reverse holds for overestimated accruals.) The over- and under-reporting of accruals, therefore, results in the shifting of income from one period into another.

Experience tells us that some accrued liabilities are more prone to misstatement than others. Estimated accruals that are linked with restructuring programs, including severance accruals and accruals for asset write-downs, are often overstated, as are estimated environmental liabilities. Companies sometimes overestimate these "one-time" accruals, resulting in early recognition of expenses (as "nonrecurring items") and a corresponding reduction in current period income. This choice, in turn, boosts income in future years when management decides that the accrual can be reversed because it was initially too large. This may suggest that management is conservative and wants to avoid understating liabilities. It can also reflect a desire by management to show earnings growth in the future by shifting current income to future periods. Accrued liabilities set up to smooth income over future periods are called "**cookie jar reserves**." The terms "clearing the decks" and "taking a big bath" have also been applied to such accounting practices.

YOU MAKE THE CALL

You are the Analyst DowDuPont Inc. disclosed the following in their 2017 10-K:

Environmental Matters

At December 31, 2017, the Company had accrued obligations of $1,311 million for probable environmental remediation and restoration costs, including $219 million for the remediation of Superfund sites.

What conditions needed to be met before these liabilities could be reported?

The company then stated that "considerable uncertainty exists with respect to environmental remediation and costs, and under adverse changes in circumstances, it is reasonably possible that the ultimate cost with respect to these particular matters could range up to two and a half times above that amount."

How does this uncertainty affect the company's balance sheet? [Answers on page 444]

Other Current Liabilities

Verizon provides more detailed disclosure for the line item on the balance sheet labeled "other" under current liabilities. Here is the table they provide:

Other Current Liabilities	2017	2016
Advance billings and customer deposits	$3,084	$2,914
Dividends payable	2,429	2,375
Other	2,839	2,813
Total	$8,352	$8,102

Advance billings and customer deposits represent contract liabilities (under ASC 606). Either customers have prepaid for work (i.e., another term for this is deferred revenue) or the unconditional right to payment has occurred according to the contract terms. If the customer has prepaid, cash is increased (debited) and the liability is increased (credited). If the unconditional right to payment has occurred but no payment has been made, then the company increases a receivable (debits a receivable) and increases the liability (credits the liability).

Dividends payable is a liability for dividends that have been declared but not yet paid. There is a liability for the dividends to be paid in this case, but recall dividends are never expensed. The other side of the entry is a decrease to equity (a debit to equity).

NYSE :: TTC

MID-CHAPTER REVIEW 2

The **Toro Company** reported warranty liabilities of $74,155,000 in its October 31, 2017, balance sheet. On its October 31, 2018, balance sheet, it reported a liability of $76,214,000. It recognized $47,721,000 in net warranty expenses during fiscal year 2018, ending October 31, 2018. What amount of cost did Toro incur to cover warranty claims in 2018? How would the fulfillment of these claims be recorded?

The solution to this review problem can be found on pages 458–459.

2

LO2 Describe and account for current nonoperating (financial) liabilities.

Current Nonoperating (Financial) Liabilities

Current nonoperating (financial) liabilities include short-term bank loans, the accrual of interest on those loans, and the current maturities of long-term debt. Companies generally try to structure their financing so that debt service requirements (payments) of those financing obligations coincide with the cash inflows from the assets financed. This strategy means that current assets are usually financed with current liabilities, and that long-term assets are financed with long-term liability (and equity) sources.

The use of short-term financing is particularly important for companies that have seasonal sales. To illustrate, a seasonal company's investment in current assets tends to fluctuate during the year as depicted in the graphic below:

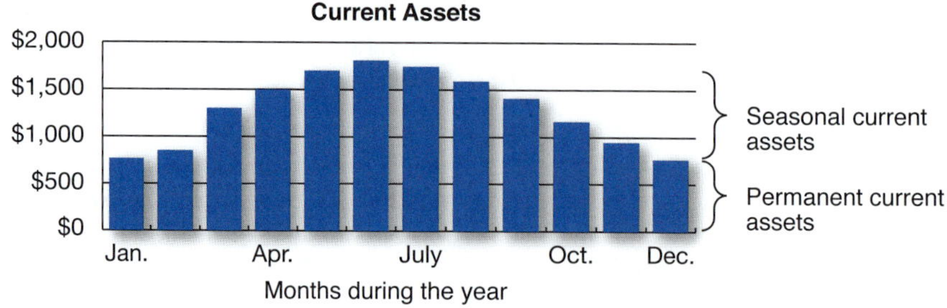

This particular company does most of its selling in the summer months. More inventory is purchased and manufactured in the early spring than at any other time of the year. Sales of the company's manufactured goods are also greater during the summer months, giving rise to accounts receivable that are higher than normal during the summer and fall. The peak working capital level is reached at the height of the selling season and is lowest when the business slows in the off-season. There is a permanent level of working capital required for this business (about $750), and a seasonal component (maximum of about $1,000). Businesses differ in their working capital requirements, but many have permanent and seasonal components.

If a company's working capital needs fluctuate from one season to the next, then the financing needs of the company are also seasonal. Some assets can be financed with short-term operating liabilities. For example, seasonal increases in inventory balances are typically financed with increased levels of accounts payable. However, operating liabilities are unlikely to meet all of the financing needs of a company. Additional financing is provided by short-term interest-bearing debt.

This section focuses on short-term nonoperating liabilities. These include short-term debt and interest as well as current maturities of long-term liabilities.

Short-Term Interest-Bearing Debt Seasonal swings in working capital are often financed with a bank line of credit (short-term debt). In this case the bank provides a commitment to lend up to a given level with the understanding that the amounts borrowed are repaid in full sometime during the year. An interest-bearing note is evidence of such borrowing.

When these short-term funds are borrowed, the cash received is reported on the balance sheet together with an increase in liabilities (notes payable). The note is reported as a current liability because the expectation is that it will be paid within a year. This borrowing transaction has no effect on income or equity, but there will be a financing cash inflow on the statement of cash flows. The borrower incurs (and the lender earns) interest on the note as time passes. U.S. GAAP requires the borrower to accrue the interest liability and the related interest expense each time financial statements are issued.

To illustrate, assume that Verizon borrows $1,000 cash from 1st Bank on January 1. The note bears interest at a 12% annual (3% quarterly) rate, and the interest is payable on the first of each subsequent quarter (April 1, July 1, October 1, January 1). Assuming that Verizon issues calendar-quarter financial statements, this borrowing results in the following financial statement effects for the period January 1 through April 1:

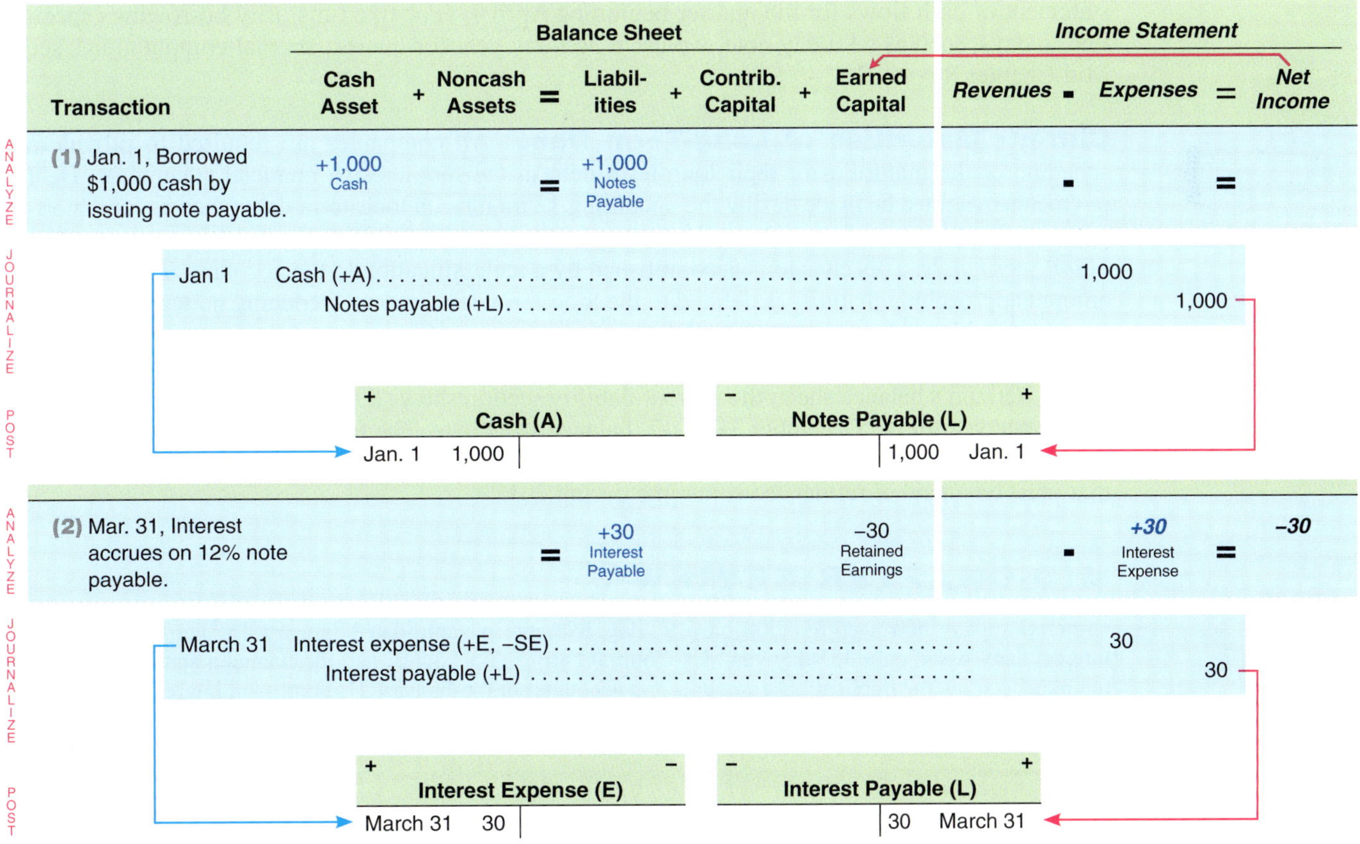

continued

	Balance Sheet										Income Statement				
Transaction	Cash Asset	+	Noncash Assets	=	Liabil-ities	+	Contrib. Capital	+	Earned Capital		Revenues	−	Expenses	=	Net Income
(3) Apr.1, Cash paid to cover interest due.	−30 Cash			=	−30 Interest Payable							−		=	

ANALYZE

JOURNALIZE

April 1	Interest payable (−L)	30	
	Cash (−A)		30

POST

− Interest Payable (L) +	
April 1 30	

+ Cash (A) −	
	30 April 1

The January 1 borrowing is reflected by an increase in cash and in notes payable. On March 31, this company issues its quarterly financial statements. Although interest is not paid until April 1, the company has incurred three months' interest obligation as of March 31. Failure to recognize this liability and the expense incurred would not fairly present the financial condition of the company. Accordingly, the quarterly accrued interest is computed as follows:

Interest Expense	=	Principal	×	Annual Rate	×	Portion of Year Outstanding
$30	=	$1,000	×	12%	×	3/12

The subsequent interest payment on April 1 is reflected in the financial statements as a reduction of cash and a reduction of the interest payable liability accrued on March 31. There is no expense reported on April 1, because it was recorded the previous day (March 31) when the financial statements were prepared; however, the payment of interest would be an operating cash outflow in the statement of cash flows for the quarter beginning April 1. (For fixed-maturity borrowings specified in days, such as a 90-day note, we use a 365-day year for interest accrual computations; see Mid-Chapter Review 3.)

Current Maturities of Long-Term Debt All companies are required to provide a schedule of the maturities of their long-term debt in the footnotes to financial statements. Debt payments that must be made during the upcoming 12 months on long-term debt (such as for a mortgage) or the maturity of a bond or note are reported as current liabilities called *current maturities of long-term debt.* This change is accomplished by a reclassification in the accounts. The principal amount approaching maturity is debited to the long-term debt account (reducing noncurrent liabilities by that amount) and credited to the current maturities of long-term debt account (increasing current liabilities by that amount).

In Verizon's balance sheet, the current liability section shows $3,453 million in debt maturing within one year of the December 31, 2017, balance sheet date. The footnotes reveal that $150 million of this amount represents short-term debt, and the remaining $3,303 million is long-term debt that must be repaid or refinanced sometime during 2018.

MID-CHAPTER REVIEW 3

Gigler Company borrowed $10,000 on a 90-day, 6% note payable dated January 15. The bank accrues interest daily based on a 365-day year. Use journal entries, T-accounts, and the financial statement effects template to show the implications (amounts and accounts) of the January 31 month-end interest accrual.

The solution to this review problem can be found on pages 459–460.

LONG-TERM LIABILITIES

Companies generally try to fund long-term investments in assets with long-term financing. Long-term financing consists of long-term liabilities and stockholders' equity. The remainder of this chapter focuses on long-term debt liabilities. Other long-term liabilities are discussed in Chapter 10 and stockholders' equity is the focus of Chapter 11.

Installment Loans

Companies can borrow small amounts of long-term debt from banks, insurance companies, or other financial institutions. These liabilities are often designed as installment loans and may be secured by specific assets called **collateral**. Installment loans are loans that require a fixed periodic payment for a fixed duration of time. For example, assume that a company decides to finance an office building with a 15-year mortgage requiring 180 equal monthly payments (180 payments = 15 years × 12 months). The fixed payment on an installment loan includes a portion of the principal (i.e., the amount borrowed) plus any interest that has accrued on the loan.

To illustrate the accounting for installment loans, assume that Shevlin Company borrowed \$40,000 from 1st Bank on July 1, 2018. The terms of the loan require that Shevlin repay the loan in 12 equal quarterly payments over a three-year period and require 8% interest per year. The quarterly payment is \$3,782 and can be calculated using the Table A3 (page 659) present value factor for 12 periods (3 years × 4 quarters) and 2% interest (8% per year ÷ 4 quarters) as follows:

$$\text{Present Value} = \text{Payment} \times \text{Present Value Factor}$$

$$\frac{\text{Present Value}}{\text{Present Value Factor}} = \text{Payment}$$

$$\frac{\$40,000}{10.57534} = \$3,782$$

Using a financial calculator, we can compute the payment by letting N be the number of quarters and setting I/Yr equal to the interest rate per quarter. The payment can then be calculated as follows: N = 12; I/Yr = 2; PV = 40,000; FV = 0:

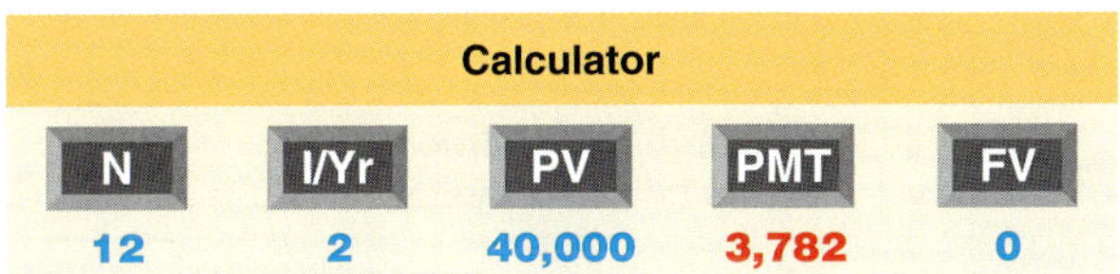

When Shevlin Company agrees to the loan terms, it receives the loan amount, \$40,000 in cash, and incurs a \$40,000 liability (installment loan payable). The loan is recorded on July 1 as follows:

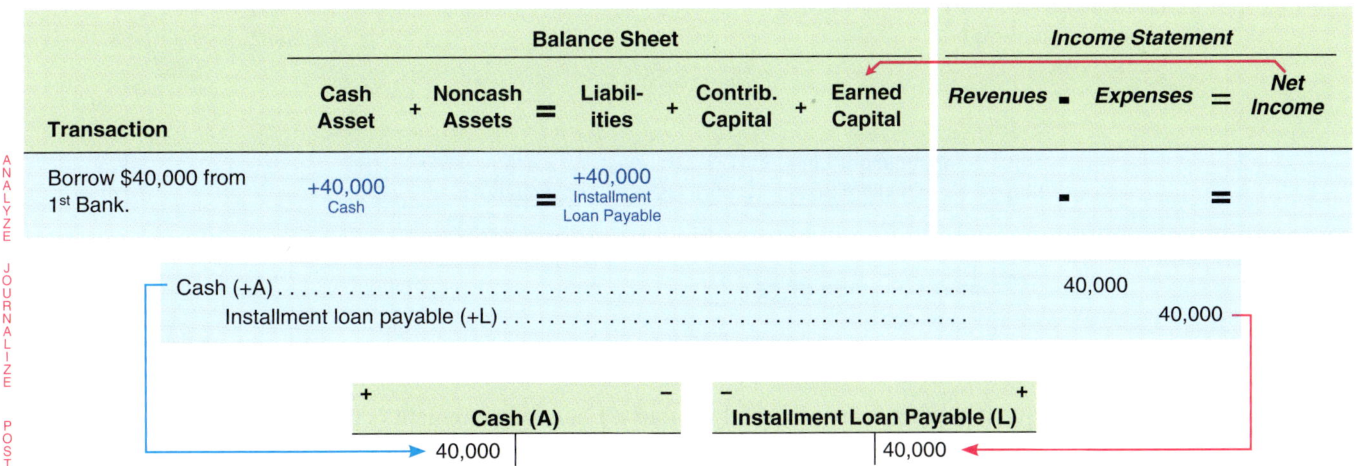

On October 1, 2018, the first payment of \$3,782 is due. The payment includes both interest for the three months from July 1 through September 30, and some portion of the original loan amount (the **principal**). The division of the payment between interest and principal is best illustrated using a **loan amortization table**, like the one in **Exhibit 9.2**. (Pages 644–654 in Appendix A demonstrate the use of Excel to calculate the required payment and the amortization table.)

Each payment includes interest and principal. The first loan payment, due on October 1, 2018, is summarized in the second row of the table. Column [B] is the quarterly loan payment. Column [C] is the interest expense, computed by multiplying column [A] by the interest rate (2 percent per quarter). Column [D] is the principal portion of the payment, which is the cash payment (column [B]) less the interest (column [C]). The remaining balance on the loan is in column [E], which is equal to the beginning balance in column [A] less the principal payment from column [D]. The loan balance decreases with each payment until the loan is paid off on July 1, 2021.

EXHIBIT 9.2 Loan Amortization Table

Date	[A] Beginning Balance	[B] Cash Payment	[C] ([A] × interest %) Interest	[D] ([B] – [C]) Principal	[E] ([A] – [D]) Balance
07/01/18					40,000
10/01/18	40,000	3,782	800	2,982	37,018
01/01/19	37,018	3,782	740	3,042	33,976
04/01/19	33,976	3,782	679	3,103	30,873
07/01/19	30,873	3,782	617	3,165	27,708
10/01/19	27,708	3,782	554	3,228	24,480
01/01/20	24,480	3,782	489	3,293	21,187
04/01/20	21,187	3,782	423	3,359	17,828
07/01/20	17,828	3,782	356	3,426	14,402
10/01/20	14,402	3,782	288	3,494	10,908
01/01/21	10,908	3,782	218	3,564	7,344
04/01/21	7,344	3,782	146	3,636	3,708
07/01/21	3,708	3,782	74	3,708	0

The first payment is recorded as follows:

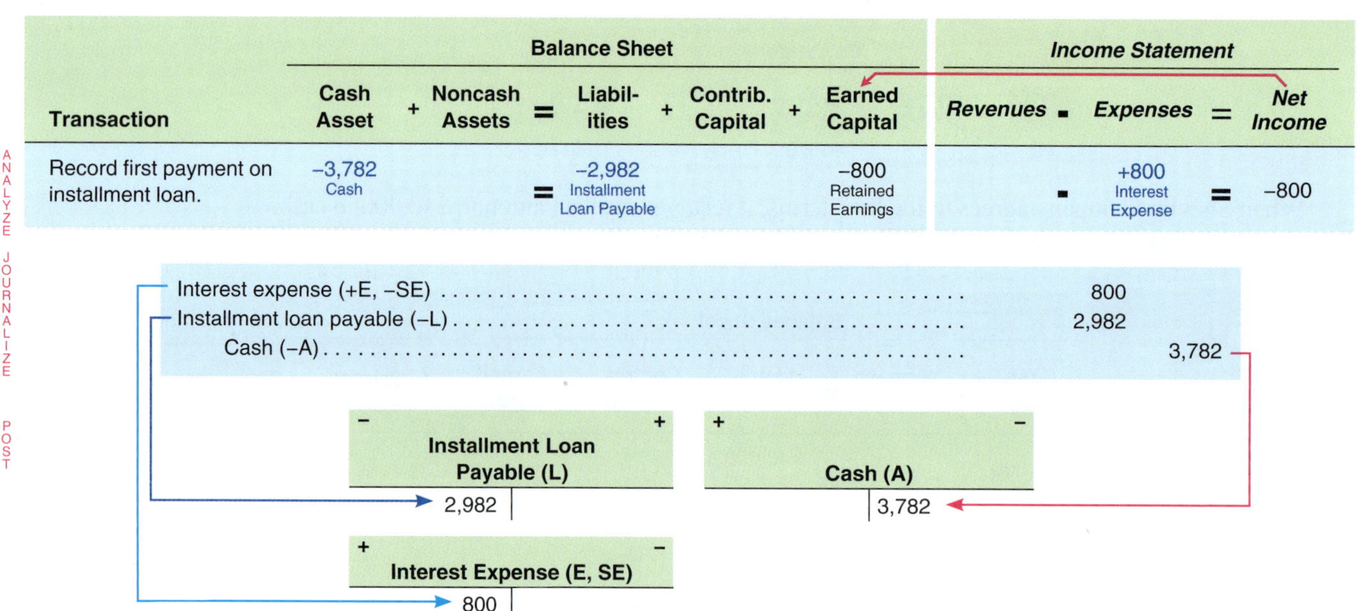

Subsequent payments are recorded similarly. Each loan payment is the same amount, quarter after quarter. And each period's interest expense is equal to the beginning loan balance times the periodic interest rate. Any difference between the payment and the interest expense affects the loan balance. In **Exhibit 9.2**, each payment contains some portion of interest expense and some portion of principal repayment, and the amounts change over time. As principal is repaid, the loan balance decreases, reducing the subsequent periods' interest expense and increasing the subsequent periods' principal repayment.

Bonds

Sometimes the amount or duration of financing required by a company is greater than the amount that a bank or insurance company can provide. Companies can borrow larger amounts of money by issuing bonds (or notes) in the capital markets. Bonds and notes are debt securities issued by companies and traded in the bond markets. When a company issues bonds, it is borrowing money. The investors who buy the bonds are lending money to the issuing company. That is, the bondholders are the company's creditors. Because the bond markets provide companies with access to large amounts of capital, bonds represent a very common, cost-effective source of long-term debt financing.

Bonds and notes are structured like any other borrowing. The borrower receives cash and agrees to pay it back with interest. Generally, the entire **face amount** (principal) of the bond or note is repaid at maturity and interest payments are made (usually semiannually) in the interim.

Companies wishing to raise funds in the bond market normally work with an underwriter (e.g., **Goldman Sachs**) to set the terms of the bond issue. The underwriter sells individual bonds (usually in $1,000 denominations) from this general bond issue to its retail clients, corporations, and professional portfolio managers (e.g., **The Vanguard Group**), and it receives a fee for underwriting the bond issue.

Once issued, the bonds can be traded in the secondary market between investors just like stocks. Market prices of bonds fluctuate daily despite the fact that the company's obligation for payment of principal and interest remains fixed throughout the life of the bond. This occurs because of fluctuations in the general level of interest rates and changes in the financial condition of the borrowing company.

The following sections analyze and interpret the reporting for bonds. We first examine the mechanics of bond pricing. In a subsequent section, we address the accounting for and reporting of bonds.

Pricing of Bonds

LO3 Explain and illustrate the pricing of long-term nonoperating liabilities.

3

Two different interest rates are crucial for understanding how a bond is priced.

- **Coupon (contract** or **stated) rate** The coupon rate of interest is stated in the bond contract. It is used to compute the dollar amount of (semiannual) interest payments that are paid to bondholders during the life of the bond issue.
- **Market (yield) rate** The market rate is the interest rate that investors expect to earn on the investment for this debt security. This rate is used to price the bond issue.

The coupon (contract) rate is used to compute interest payments and the market (yield) rate is used to price the bond. The coupon rate and the market rate are nearly always different. The coupon rate is fixed prior to issuance of the bond and remains so throughout its life (unless the interest rate "floats" with market rates). Market rates of interest, on the other hand, fluctuate continually with the supply and demand for bonds in the marketplace, general macroeconomic conditions, and the financial condition of borrowers.

The bond price equals the **present value** of the expected cash flows to the bondholder. Specifically, bondholders normally expect to receive two different cash flows:

1. **Periodic interest payments** (usually semiannual) during the bond's life. These cash flows are typically in the form of equal payments at periodic intervals, called an **annuity**.
2. **Single payment** of the face (principal) amount of the bond at maturity.

The bond price equals the present value of the periodic interest payments plus the present value of the principal payment at maturity. We next illustrate the issuance of bonds at three different prices: at par, at a discount, and at a premium.

Bonds Issued at Par When a bond is issued at par, its coupon rate is identical to the market rate. Under this condition, a $1,000 bond sells for $1,000 in the market. To illustrate bond pricing, assume that investors wish to value a bond issue with a face amount of $100,000, a 6% annual coupon rate with interest payable semiannually (3% semiannual rate), and a maturity of 4 years.[3]

[3] Semiannual interest payments are typical for bonds. With semiannual interest payments, the issuer pays bondholders two interest payments per year. The semiannual interest rate is the annual rate divided by two.

Investors purchasing this issue receive the following cash flows:

	Number of Payments	Dollars per Payment	Total Cash Flows
Semiannual interest payments	4 years × 2 = 8	$100,000 × 3% = $ 3,000	$ 24,000
Principal payment at maturity	1	$100,000	100,000
			$124,000

Specifically, the bond agreement dictates that the borrower makes 8 semiannual payments of $3,000 each, computed as $100,000 × (6%/2), plus the $100,000 face amount at maturity, for a total of $124,000 in cash flows. Each $1,000 bond in this bond issue provides the bondholder with an annuity of 8 payments of $30 and a principal payment of $1,000 at maturity. For an individual bond, the cash flows total $1,240 (= $30 × 8 + $1,000).

When pricing bonds, the number of periods used for computing the present value is the number of interest (coupon) payments required by the bond. In this case, there are 8 semiannual interest payments required, so we use 8 six-month periods to value the bond. The market interest rate (yield) is 6% per year, which is 3% per six-month period.

The bond price is the present value of the interest annuity plus the present value of the principal payment. Assuming that investors desire a 6% annual market rate (yield), the bond sells for exactly $100,000, which is computed as follows:

	Payment	Present Value Factor[a]	Present Value
Interest	$ 3,000	7.01969[b]	$ 21,059
Principal	$100,000	0.78941[c]	78,941
			$100,000

[a] Mechanics of using tables to compute present values are explained in Appendix A at the end of the text. Present value factors are taken from tables provided in Appendix A.

[b] Present value of ordinary annuity for 8 periods discounted at 3% per period.

[c] Present value of single payment in 8 periods, hence discounted at 3% per period.

Because the bond contract pays investors a 6% annual rate when investors demand a 6% market rate, investors purchase these bonds at the **par (face) value** of $1,000 per bond, or $100,000 in total.[4] Using a financial calculator, we can compute the bond value as follows: N = 8; I/Yr = 3; PMT = 3,000; FV = 100,000:

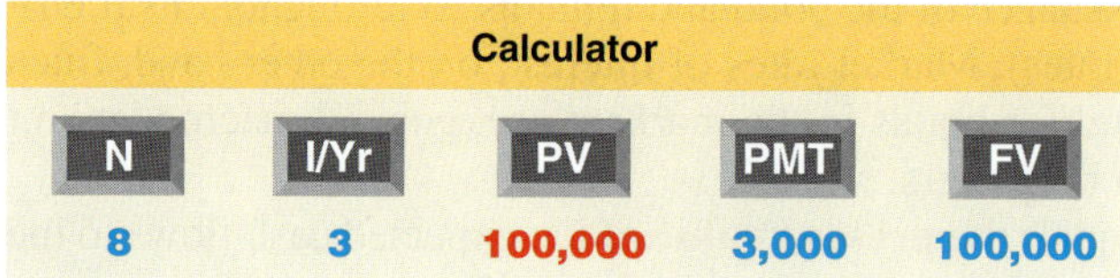

Bonds Issued at a Discount As a second illustration, assume that market conditions are such that investors demand an 8% annual yield (4% semiannual) for the 6% coupon bond, while all other details remain the same. The bond now sells for $93,267, computed as follows:

	Payment	Present Value Factor	Present Value
Interest	$ 3,000	6.73274[a]	$20,198
Principal	$100,000	0.73069[b]	73,069
			$93,267

[a] Present value of ordinary annuity for 8 periods discounted at 4% per period.

[b] Present value of single payment in 8 periods, hence discounted at 4% per period.

[4] If we purchase a bond after the semiannual interest date, we must pay accrued interest in addition to the purchase price. This interest is returned to us in the regular interest payment. (This procedure makes the bookkeeping easier for the issuer/underwriter.)

Using a financial calculator, the bond is priced as follows: N = 8; I/Yr = 4; PMT = 3,000; FV = 100,000:

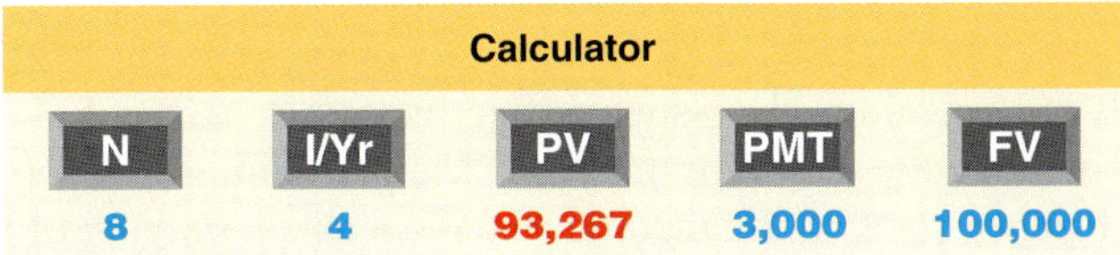

The market price of the bond issue is, therefore, $93,267. The price of each bond in the bond issue is $932.67 (= $93,267/100).

Because the bond carries a coupon rate *lower* than that which investors demand, the bond is less desirable and sells at a **discount**. In general, bonds sell at a discount whenever the coupon rate is less than the market rate.[5]

Bonds Issued at a Premium As a third illustration, assume that investors in the bond market demand a 4% annual yield (2% semiannual) for the 6% coupon bonds, while all other details remain the same. The bond issue now sells for $107,325, computed as follows:

	Payment	Present Value Factor	Present Value
Interest	$ 3,000	7.32548[a]	$ 21,976
Principal	$100,000	0.85349[b]	85,349
			$107,325

[a] Present value of ordinary annuity for 8 periods discounted at 2% per period.

[b] Present value of single payment in 8 periods, hence discounted at 2% per period.

Using a financial calculator, the bond is priced as follows: N = 8; I/Yr = 2; PMT = 3,000; FV = 100,000:

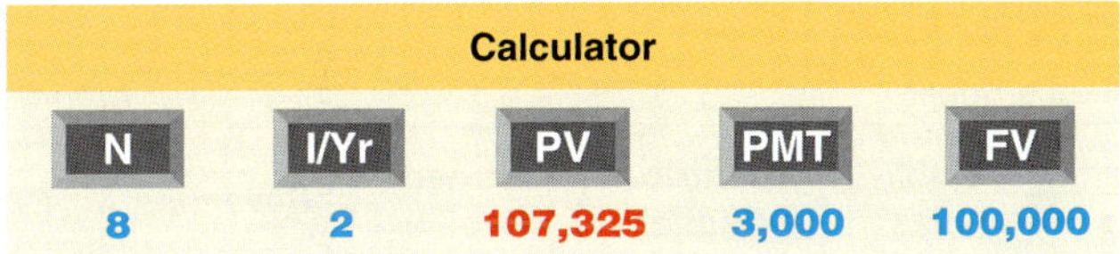

The market price of the bond issue is, therefore, $107,325. The price of each bond in the bond issue is $1,073.25 (= $107,325/100).

Because the bond carries a coupon rate higher than that which investors demand, the bond is more desirable and sells at a **premium**. In general, bonds sell at a premium whenever the coupon rate is greater than the market rate. **Exhibit 9.3** summarizes this relation for bond pricing.

EXHIBIT 9.3 Coupon Rate, Market Rate, and Bond Pricing

Coupon rate > market rate	→	Bond sells at a **premium** (above face amount)
Coupon rate = market rate	→	Bond sells at **par** (at face amount)
Coupon rate < market rate	→	Bond sells at a **discount** (below face amount)

Effective Cost of Debt

When a bond sells for par, the cost to the issuing company is the cash interest paid. In our first illustration where the bond is issued at par, the *effective cost* of the bond is the 6% interest paid by the issuer.

When a bond sells at a discount, the issuer's effective cost consists of two parts: (1) the cash interest paid and (2) the discount incurred. The discount, which is the difference between par and the lower issue price, is a cost that must eventually be reflected in the issuer's income statement as an

[5] Bond prices are often stated in percent form. For example, a bond sold at par is said to be sold at 100 (that is, 100% of its face value, par). The bond sold at $932.67 is said to be sold at 93.267 (93.267% of par, computed as $932.67/$1,000).

expense. This fact means that the effective cost of a discount bond is greater than if the bond had sold at par. A discount is a cost and, like any other cost, must eventually be transferred from the balance sheet to the income statement as an expense. In the previous section's discount example, the economic substance is that the bond issuer has not borrowed $100,000 at 6%, but rather $93,267 at 8%.

When a bond sells at a premium, the issuer's effective cost consists of (1) the cash interest paid and (2) a cost reduction due to the premium received. The premium is a benefit that must eventually find its way from the balance sheet to the income statement as a *reduction* of interest expense. As a result of the premium, the effective cost of a premium bond is less than if the bond had sold at par. Effectively, the bond issuer has borrowed $107,325 at 4% in the premium example above.

Bonds are priced to yield the return (market rate) demanded by investors in the bond market, which results in the effective interest rate of a bond *always* equaling the yield (market) rate, regardless of the coupon (stated) rate of the bond. Bond prices are set by the market so as to always yield the rate required by investors based on the terms and qualities of the bond. Companies cannot influence the effective cost of debt by raising or lowering the coupon rate. We discuss the factors affecting the market yield later in the chapter.

The effective cost of debt is ultimately reflected in the amount reported in the issuer's income statement as interest expense. This amount can be, and usually is, different from the cash interest paid. The two are the same only for a bond issued at par. The next section discusses how management reports bonds on the balance sheet and interest expense on the income statement.

4

LO4 Analyze and account for financial statement effects of long-term nonoperating liabilities.

Reporting of Bond Financing

This section identifies and describes the financial statement effects of bond transactions.

Bonds Issued at Par When a bond sells at par, the issuing company receives the cash proceeds and accepts an obligation to make payments per the bond contract. Specifically, cash is increased and a liability (bonds payable) is increased by the same amount. Using the facts from our earlier illustration, the issuance of bonds at par has the following financial statement effects (there is no revenue or expense at the date the bond is issued):

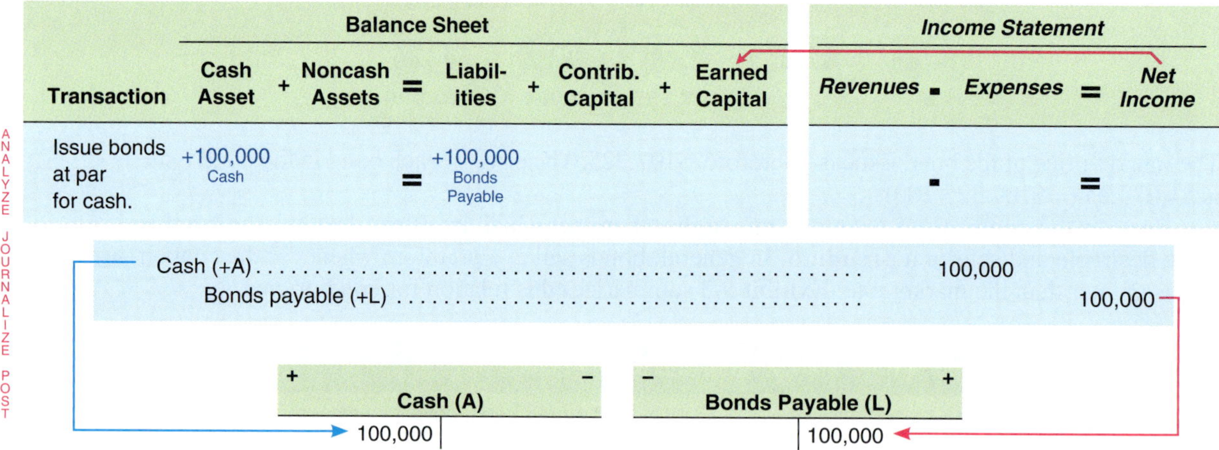

ANALYZE

	Balance Sheet									Income Statement				
Transaction	Cash Asset	+	Noncash Assets	=	Liabilities	+	Contrib. Capital	+	Earned Capital	Revenues	−	Expenses	=	Net Income
Issue bonds at par for cash.	+100,000 Cash			=	+100,000 Bonds Payable						−		=	

JOURNALIZE

	Debit	Credit
Cash (+A)	100,000	
Bonds payable (+L)		100,000

POST

+ Cash (A) −	
100,000	

− Bonds Payable (L) +	
	100,000

Bonds Issued at a Discount For the discount bond case, cash is increased by the proceeds from the sale of the bonds, and the liability increases by the same amount. However, the net liability consisting of the two components shown below (including a bond discount contra liability) is reported on the balance sheet.

FYI "Bonds Payable, Net" is a common title reflecting the face value of the bond less the unamortized discount.

Bonds payable, face	$100,000
Less bond discount	(6,733)
Bonds payable, net	$ 93,267

Using the facts above from our bond discount illustration, the financial statement effects follow:

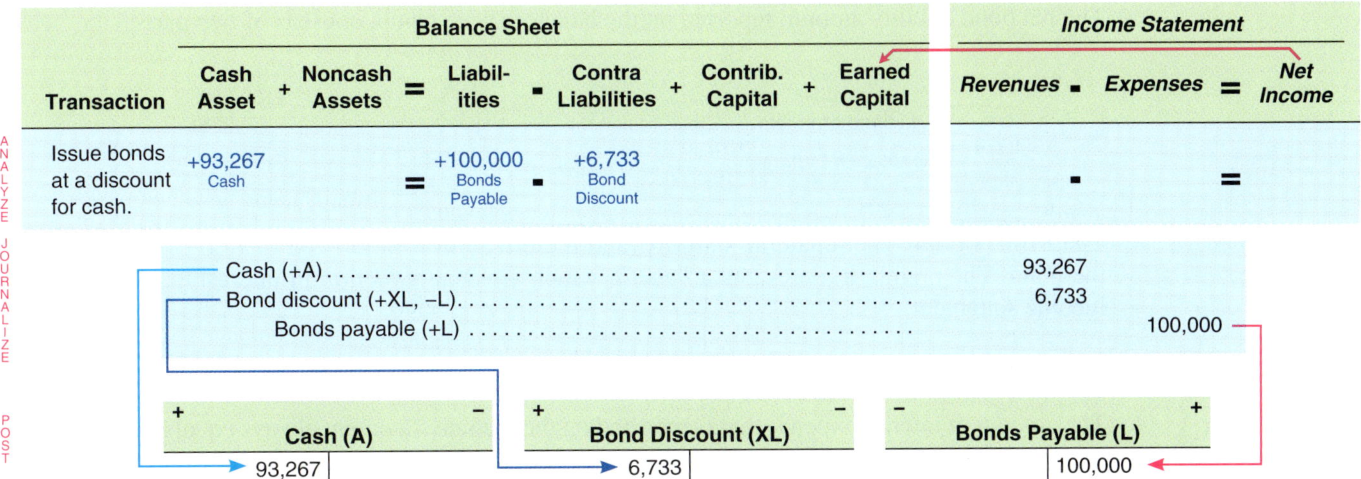

Bonds are reported on the balance sheet net of any discount (or plus any premium). When the bond matures, however, the company is obligated to repay $100,000. Accordingly, at maturity, the bond liability must read $100,000, the amount that is owed. Therefore, between the bond issuance and its maturity, the discount must decline to zero. This reduction of the discount over the life of the bond is called **amortization**. This amortization causes the effective interest expense to be greater than the periodic cash interest payments based on the coupon rate.

BUSINESS INSIGHT

Zeros and Strips Zero coupon bonds and notes, called *zeros*, do not carry an explicit coupon rate. However, the pricing of these bonds and notes is done in the same manner as those with coupon rates—the exception is the absence of an interest annuity. This omission means that the price is the present value of just the principal payment at maturity; hence the bond is sold at a *deep discount*. For example, consider a 4-year, $100,000 zero coupon bond, priced to yield a market rate of 6% that compounds semi-annually. The only payment would be the return of principal 4 years away. We already know that the present value of this single payment is $78,941. This "zero" would initially sell for $78,941 resulting in a substantial discount of $21,059.

Bonds Issued at a Premium When a bond is sold at a premium, the cash proceeds and net bond liability are recorded at the amount of the proceeds received (not the face amount of the bond). Again, using the facts above from our premium bond illustration, the financial statement effects are:

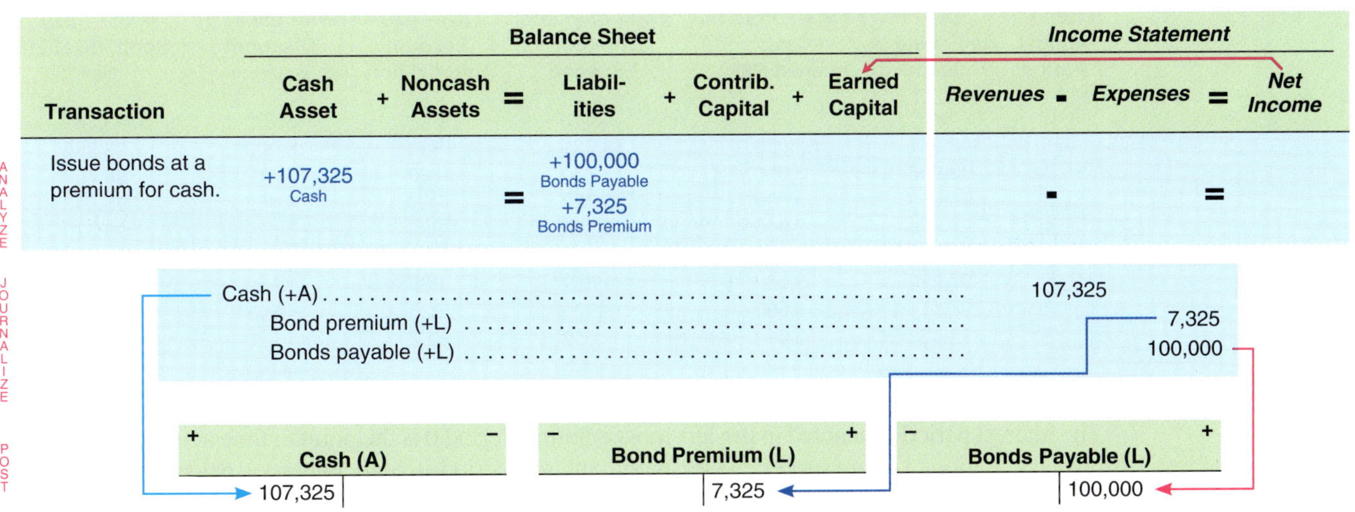

The net bond liability amount reported on the balance sheet, again, consists of two parts:

Bonds payable, face	$100,000
Add bond premium	7,325
Bonds payable, net	$107,325

The $100,000 must be repaid at maturity, and the premium is amortized to zero over the life of the bond. The premium represents a *benefit,* which yields a *reduction* in interest expense on the income statement.

Effects of Discount and Premium Amortization

The amount of interest expense that is reported on the income statement always equals the loan balance at the beginning of the period (bonds payable, net of discount or premium) times the market interest rate at the time of issue. For bonds issued at par, interest expense equals the cash interest payment. However, for bonds issued at a discount or premium, interest expense reported on the income statement equals interest paid adjusted for the amortization of the discount or premium:

	Cash interest paid			Cash interest paid
+	Amortization of discount	or	−	Amortization of premium
	Interest expense			Interest expense

Specifically, periodic amortization of a discount is added to the cash interest paid to get interest expense for a discount bond. Amortization of the discount reflects the additional cost the issuer incurs from issuance of the bonds at a discount and its recognition, via amortization, as an increase to interest expense. For a premium bond, the premium is a benefit the issuer receives at issuance. Amortization of the premium reduces interest expense over the debt term. Consequently, interest expense on the income statement represents the *effective cost* of debt (the *nominal cost* of debt is the cash interest paid). This is true whether the bonds are issued at par, at a discount, or at a premium.

Companies amortize discounts and premiums using the effective interest method. To illustrate, recall the assumptions of the discount bond above—face amount of $100,000, a 6% annual coupon rate payable semiannually (3% semiannual rate), a maturity of 4 years, and a market (yield) rate of 8% annual (4% semiannual). These facts resulted in a bond issue price of $932.67 per bond or $93,267 for the entire bond issue. **Exhibit 9.4** illustrates a bond discount amortization table for this bond.

EXHIBIT 9.4 Bond Discount Amortization Table

Semi-Annual Period	[A] Beginning Balance	[B] *(Face × coupon%)* Cash Interest Paid	[C] *([A] × market%)* Interest Expense	[D] *([C] − [B])* Discount Amortization	[E] *(Prior bal − [D])* Discount Balance	[F] *(Face − [E])* Bond Payable Net
0					$6,733	$ 93,267
1	$93,267	$3,000	$3,731	$731	6,002	93,998
2	93,998	3,000	3,760	760	5,242	94,758
3	94,758	3,000	3,790	790	4,452	95,548
4	95,548	3,000	3,822	822	3,630	96,370
5	96,370	3,000	3,855	855	2,775	97,225
6	97,225	3,000	3,889	889	1,886	98,114
7	98,114	3,000	3,925	925	962*	99,038
8	99,038	3,000	3,962	962	0	100,000

* rounding

The interest period is denoted in the left-most column. Period 0 is the point in time at which the bond is issued. Periods 1–8 are successive six-month interest periods (recall, interest is paid semiannually). Column [B] is cash interest paid, which is a constant $3,000 per period (face amount × coupon rate). Column [C] is interest expense, which is reported in the income statement. This column is computed as the carrying amount of the bond at the beginning of the period (column [A]) multiplied by the 4%

semiannual yield rate used to compute the bond issue price. Column [D] is discount amortization, which is the difference between interest expense and cash interest paid. Column [E] is the discount balance, which is the previous balance of the discount less the discount amortization in column [D]. Column [F] is the net bond payable, which is the $100,000 face amount less the unamortized discount from column [E]. Column [A] is the value from the previous period's column [F].

The amortization process continues until period 8, at which time the discount balance is $0 and the net bond payable is $100,000 (the maturity value). An amortization table reveals the financial statement effects of the bond for its duration. Specifically, we see the cash effects in column [B], the income statement effects in column [C], and the balance sheet effects in columns [D], [E], and [F].

To record the interest payment at the end of period 1, we use the values in row 1 of the amortization table. The resulting entry is recorded as follows:

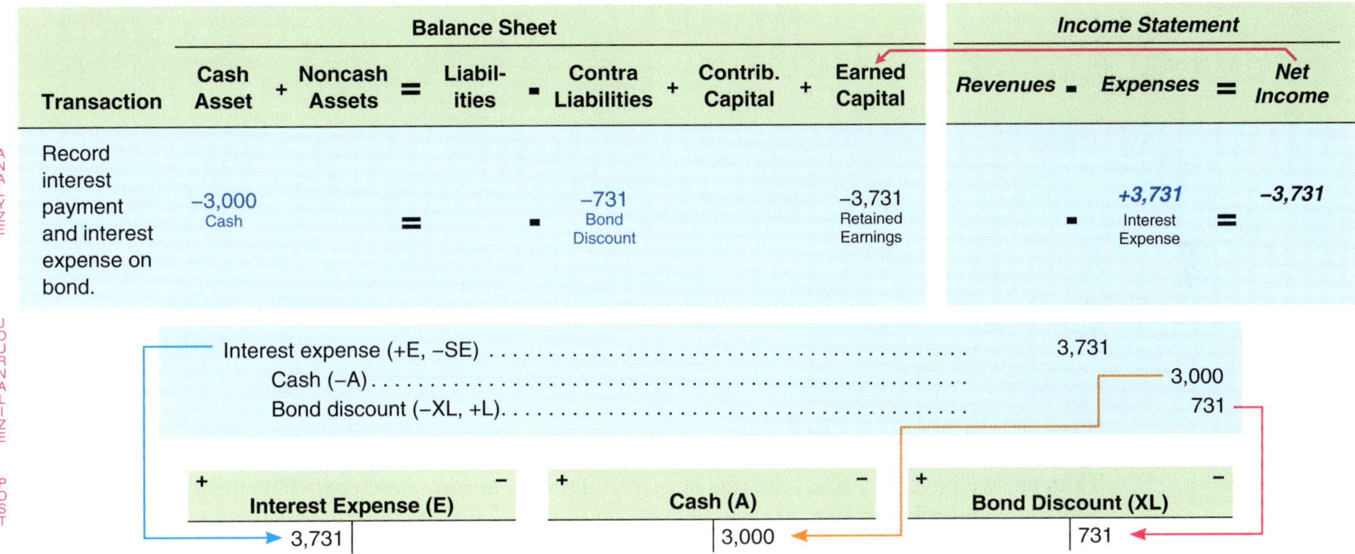

To illustrate amortization of a premium bond, we use the assumptions of the premium bond above—$100,000 face value, a 6% annual coupon rate payable semiannually (3% semiannual rate), a maturity of 4 years, and a 4% annual market (yield) rate (2% semiannual). These parameters resulted in a bond issue price of $1,073.25 per bond or $107,325 for the entire bond issue. **Exhibit 9.5** shows the bond premium amortization table for this bond.

EXHIBIT 9.5 Bond Premium Amortization Table

Semi-Annual Period	[A] Beginning Balance	[B] *(Face × coupon%)* Cash Interest Paid	[C] *([A] × market%)* Interest Expense	[D] *([B] − [C])* Premium Amortization	[E] *(Prior bal − [D])* Premium Balance	[F] *(Face + [E])* Bond Payable Net
0					$7,325	$107,325
1	$107,325	$3,000	$2,147	$853	6,472	106,472
2	106,472	3,000	2,129	871	5,601	105,601
3	105,601	3,000	2,112	888	4,713	104,713
4	104,713	3,000	2,094	906	3,807	103,807
5	103,807	3,000	2,076	924	2,883	102,883
6	102,883	3,000	2,058	942	1,941	101,941
7	101,941	3,000	2,039	961	980	100,980
8	100,980	3,000	2,020	980	0	100,000

Interest expense is computed using the same process that we used for discount bonds. The difference is that the yield rate is 4% (2% semiannual) in the premium case. Cash interest paid follows from the bond contract (face amount × coupon rate), and the other columns' computations reflect the premium amortization. After period 8, the premium is fully amortized (equals zero) and the net bond payable balance is $100,000, the amount owed at maturity. The book value of bonds issued at a discount starts below the face value and, over time, increases. The book value of bonds issued at a premium starts above the bonds' face value and, over time, decreases. At maturity, the book value of both types of bonds equals the face value that must be paid to the bondholders. Again, an amortization table reveals the financial statement effects of the bond—the cash effects in column [B], the income statement effects in column [C], and the balance sheet effects in columns [D], [E], and [F].

To record the interest payment at the end of period 1, we, again, use the values in row 1 of the amortization table. The resulting entry is recorded as follows:

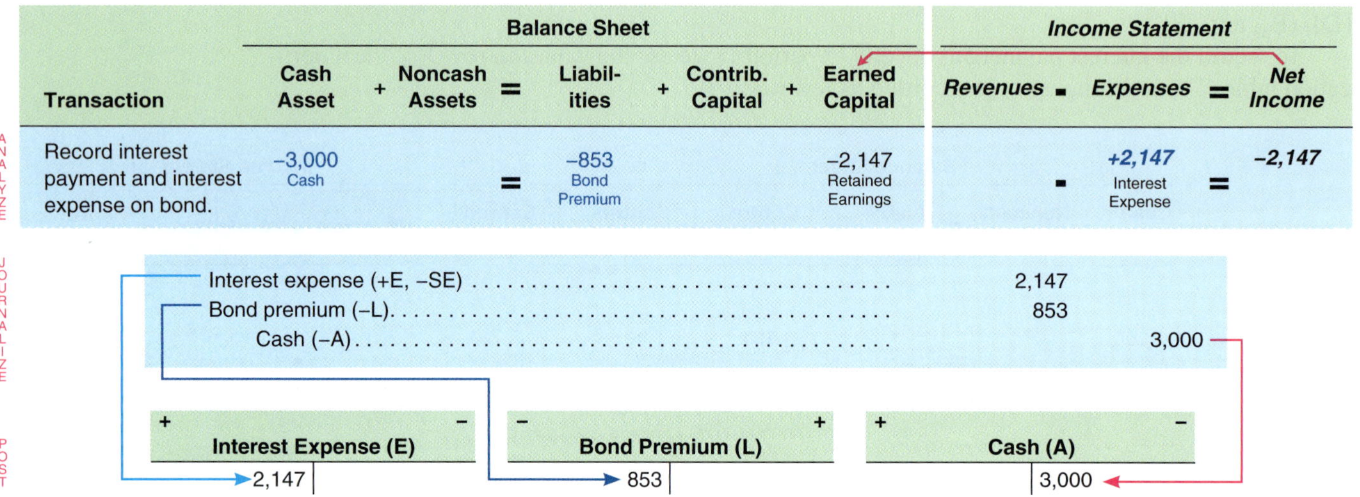

The Fair Value Option

Thus far, we have described the reporting of liabilities at *historical cost*. This means that all financial statement relationships are established on the date that the liability is created and do not subsequently change. For example, the interest rate used to value a bond is the market rate of interest on the date that the bond is issued and the reported value of the bond is the face value plus the unamortized premium or minus the unamortized discount. Yet, once issued, bonds can be traded in secondary markets. Market interest rates fluctuate and, as a consequence, the market value of a bond is likely to change after the bond is issued.

As an alternative to historical cost, a company may elect to report some or all of its financial liabilities at *fair value*. Moreover, a company may choose to report some of its liabilities at historical cost and others at fair value. It must make this choice at the inception of the liability (e.g., at the time that a bond is issued) and cannot subsequently switch between fair value and historical cost for that liability. If a company elects to report a liability at fair value in its balance sheet, then any changes in fair value are reported as a gain or loss in its income statement. If a liability is to be reported at historical cost, then its fair value is disclosed in the notes.

To illustrate how we report a liability at fair value, we refer to our example of a 4-year, 6% bond issued at a discount to yield 8%. The issue price of this bond is $93,267 and we assume that the bond is issued on June 30, 2018. Six months later, on December 31, the issuing company pays the first of eight coupon payments of $3,000. From **Exhibit 9.4**, we know that after this coupon payment, the bond payable, net of the discount, is equal to $93,998. Now assume that the market value of the bond has increased to $96,943. (This price increase is consistent with a market interest rate that has decreased to 7%.) The bond would now be reported on the balance sheet at a value of $96,943:

Bonds payable	$100,000
Less, unamortized discount	6,002
Bond payable, net (historical cost)	$ 93,998
Plus, fair value adjustment	2,945
Bond payable, net (fair value)	$ 96,943

The increase in the bond's fair value must be added to an account that adjusts the bond payable liability. The balancing entry is included as a loss in the income statement, and ends up in retained earnings. The fair value adjustment would be recorded as follows:

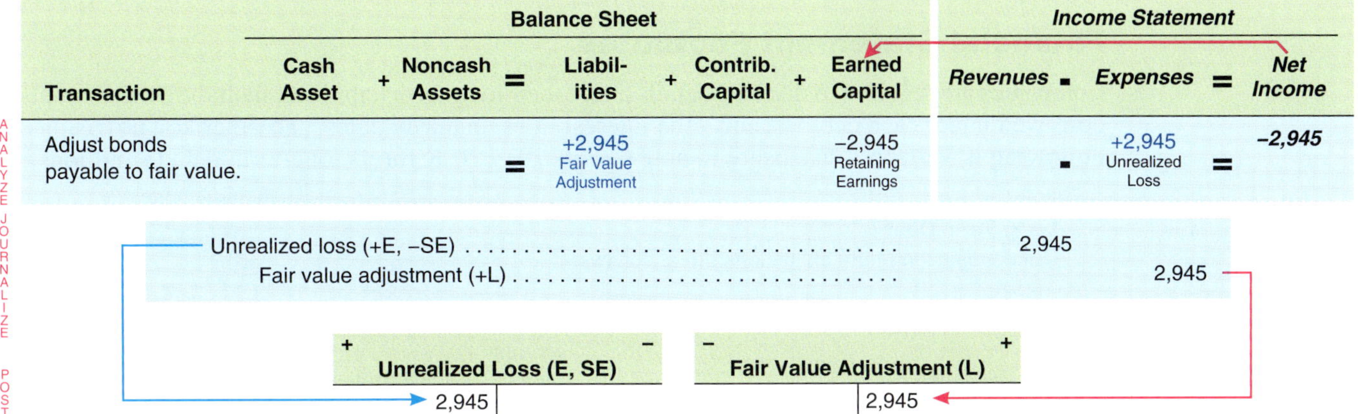

	Balance Sheet									Income Statement				
Transaction	Cash Asset	+	Noncash Assets	=	Liabil-ities	+	Contrib. Capital	+	Earned Capital	Revenues	−	Expenses	=	Net Income
Adjust bonds payable to fair value.				=	+2,945 Fair Value Adjustment				−2,945 Retaining Earnings		−	+2,945 Unrealized Loss	=	−2,945

Unrealized loss (+E, −SE)	2,945	
Fair value adjustment (+L)		2,945

+ Unrealized Loss (E, SE) −		− Fair Value Adjustment (L) +	
2,945			2,945

The fair value computation does not affect the calculation of interest expense or the amortization of the bond discount in this or any subsequent period. The unrealized loss does have an effect on the income statement. For this illustration, the total effect on income for 2018 is $6,676, which is computed as:

Coupon payment, July 1—December 31	$3,000
Amortization of the bond discount	731
Interest expense	$3,731
Unrealized loss	2,945
Total effect (decrease) on earnings	$6,676

If the fair value of this bond decreases (e.g., because interest rates increase), the fair value adjustment account would be debited and an unrealized gain would be credited and reported in the income statement.[6] We discuss the fair value option further in Chapter 12.

Effects of Bond Repurchase

Companies can and sometimes do repurchase (also called *redeem*) their bonds prior to maturity. The bond indenture (contract agreement) often includes a **call provision** giving the company the right to repurchase its bond by paying a small premium above face value. Alternatively, the company can repurchase bonds in the open market. When a company uses historical cost to account for its bonds, a bond repurchase usually results in a gain or loss, and is computed as follows:

Gain or loss on bond repurchase = Book value of the bond − Repurchase payment

The *book (carrying) value of the bond* is the net amount reported on the balance sheet. If the issuer pays more to retire the bonds than the amount carried on its balance sheet, a loss is reported on its income statement, usually called *loss on bond retirement.* The issuer reports a *gain on bond retirement* if the repurchase price is less than the book value of the bond.

GAAP dictates that any gains or losses on bond repurchases be reported as part of ordinary income unless they meet the criteria for treatment as part of discontinued operations. Relatively few debt retirements meet these criteria and, hence, most gains and losses on bond repurchases are reported as part of income from continuing operations.

[6] In ASU 2016-01 (effective for years starting after December 15, 2017), FASB included a requirement that companies separately report in comprehensive income (rather than in net income), the portion of the total change in the fair value of a liability resulting from a change in the instrument-specific credit risk when the entity has elected to value the instrument using the fair-value option. For example, if the entity's own credit quality deteriorates, the company does not report this reduction of the fair value of the liability as income on their income statement, but rather as an item in other comprehensive income.

The question arises as to how gains and losses on the redemption of bonds should affect our analysis of a company's profitability. Because bonds and notes payable represent nonoperating items, activities including the refunding of bonds and any gain or loss resulting from such activity should be omitted from our computation of net operating profit.

Financial Statement Footnotes

Companies are required to disclose details about their long-term liabilities, including the amounts borrowed under each debt issuance, the interest rates, maturity dates, and other key provisions. Following is Verizon's disclosure in note 6 to its 2017 10-K for its long-term debt ($ millions):

Long-Term Debt

Outstanding long-term obligations are as follows:

			(dollars in millions)	
At December 31	Interest Rates %	Maturities	2017	2016
Verizon—notes payable and other	1.38—3.96	2018—2047	$ 31,370	$ 28,491
	4.09—5.51	2020—2055	67,906	53,909
	5.82—6.90	2026—2054	5,835	11,295
	7.35—8.95	2029—2039	1,106	1,860
	Floating	2018—2025	6,684	9,750
Verizon—Alltel assumed notes	6.80—7.88	2029—2032	234	525
Telephone subsidiaries—debentures	5.13—6.50	2028—2033	226	319
	7.38—7.88	2022—2032	341	561
	8.00—8.75	2022—2031	229	328
Other subsidiaries—notes payable debentures and other	6.70—8.75	2018—2028	748	1,102
Verizon Wireless and other subsidiaries—asset-backed debt	1.42—2.65	2021—2022	6,293	2,485
	Floating	2021 - 2022	2,620	2,520
Capital lease obligations (average rate of 3.6% and 3.5% in 2017 and 2016, respectively)			1,020	950
Unamortized discount, net of premium			(7,133)	(5,716)
Unamortized debt issuance costs			(534)	(469)
Total long-term debt, including current maturities			116,945	107,910
Less long-term debt maturing within one year			3,303	2,477
Total long-term debt			$113,642	$105,433

Verizon reports a book value for long-term debt of $116,945 million at year-end 2017. Of this amount, $3,303 million matures in the next year, hence its classification as a current liability (current maturities of long-term debt) and the remainder matures after 2018. Verizon also reports $7,133 million in unamortized discount (net of unamortized premium) on this debt.

In addition to amounts, rates, and due dates on its long-term debt, Verizon also reports aggregate maturities for the 5 years subsequent to its balance sheet date:

Maturities of Long-Term Debt

Maturities of long-term debt outstanding at December 31, 2017, are as follows ($ millions):

2018	$ 3,308
2019	6,306
2020	6,587
2021	6,403
2022	9,520
Thereafter	85,355

This reporting reveals that Verizon is required to make principal payments of $32,124 million between 2018 and 2022, and $85,355 million thereafter. Such maturities are important as a company must meet its required payments, negotiate a rescheduling of the indebtedness, or refinance the debt to avoid default. The latter (default) usually has severe consequences as debt holders have legal remedies available to them, which can result in bankruptcy of the company.

Verizon's disclosure on the fair value of its total debt follows:

The fair value of our debt is determined using various methods, including quoted prices for identical terms and maturities . . . as well as quoted prices for similar terms and maturities in inactive markets and future cash flows discounted at current rates. . . The fair value of our short-term and long-term debt, excluding capital leases, was as follows ($ millions):

	2017		2016	
At December 31,	**Carrying Amount**	**Fair Value**	**Carrying Amount**	**Fair Value**
Short-term and long-term debt, excluding capital leases	$116,075	$128,658	$107,128	$117,584

As of December 31, 2017, indebtedness with a book value of $116,075 million had a fair value of $128,658 million, resulting in an unrecognized liability (and loss if the debt is redeemed) of $12,583 million (due mainly to a decline in interest rates subsequent to bond issuance). The justification for not recognizing unrealized gains and losses on the balance sheet and income statement is that such amounts can reverse with future fluctuations in interest rates. Further, because only the face amount of debt is repaid at maturity, unrealized gains and losses that arise during intervening years are not necessarily relevant. (This same logic is used to justify the nonrecognition of gains and losses on held-to-maturity investments in debt securities, a topic covered in Chapter 12.) At this time, Verizon, like most U.S. companies, has elected to report liabilities at historical cost in the financial statements and disclose fair values in the footnotes.

Sensitivity Analysis

As part of the disclosure, many companies including Verizon also disclose the sensitivity of their estimate of fair value to changes in underlying factors or assumptions. This allows readers to see the effects of changes in assumptions.

The table that follows summarizes the fair values of our long-term debt, including current maturities, and interest rate swap derivatives as of December 31, 2017 and 2016. The table also provides a sensitivity analysis of the estimated fair values of these financial instruments assuming 100-basis-point upward and downward shifts in the yield curve. Our sensitivity analysis does not include the fair values of our commercial paper and bank loans, if any, because they are not significantly affected by changes in market interest rates.

(dollars in millions) Long-term debt and related derivatives	**Fair Value**	**Fair Value assuming + 100 basis point shift**	**Fair Value assuming – 100 basis point shift**
At December 31, 2017	$128,867	$119,235	$140,216
At December 31, 2016	117,580	109,029	128,007

Interest and the Statement of Cash Flows

GAAP requires that interest payments (and receipts) be included in cash flows from operating activities. For companies using the indirect method for operating cash flows, net income already includes interest expense. Because interest expense does not equal interest payments, the reconciliation of net income to cash flows from operating activities should include an adjustment for any amortization of bond discounts or premiums.

However, interest income and interest expense are typically related to nonoperating assets (investments in securities) and nonoperating liabilities (interest-bearing bonds and notes), respectively. As such, they should be omitted from all computations of net operating profit (as in Appendix A to Chapter 5) and also separated from other cash flows when analyzing a company's operations, even though it sometimes requires some digging in the financial statements to determine their magnitudes.

Disclosure of Commitments and Contingencies

All significant contractual commitments must be disclosed in the notes to the financial statements. We discuss this further in Chapter 10.

As discussed above, for contingent liabilities that have a likelihood of occurrence that is probable and the cost that can be estimated, the amount of the liability is recognized on the balance sheet and expensed on the income statement. However, if the liability is only reasonably possible (i.e., less likely than probable), then the liability is disclosed in the notes to the financial statements. If the liability is even less likely to occur than "reasonably possible," then disclosure is permitted but not required.

Many companies are required to include a line item labeled "Commitments and Contingent Liabilities" or some variant of this on the face of the balance sheet.[7] This line item does not have associated amounts on the balance sheet.

The following is Verizon's liability section of the balance sheet, including this line item:

Liabilities and Equity	2017	2016
Current liabilities		
Debt maturing within one year	$ 3,453	$ 2,645
Accounts payable and accrued liabilities	21,232	19,593
Other	8,352	8,102
Total current liabilities	33,037	30,340
Long-term debt	113,642	105,433
Employee benefit obligations	22,112	26,166
Deferred income taxes	31,232	45,964
Other liabilities	12,433	12,245
Total long-term liabilities	179,419	189,808
Commitments and Contingencies (Note 15)		

Note 15 in Verizon's footnotes is one page long and discusses various accruals as well as potential litigation and environmental losses, some of which have been accrued (i.e., those that are probable and estimable) and some have not. The note also discusses various contractual commitments and guarantees (we discuss in Chapter 10).[8]

ANALYZING FINANCIAL STATEMENTS

5

LO5 Explain how solvency ratios and debt ratings are determined and how they impact the cost of debt.

A major concern of managers and analysts is the solvency of the corporation. In this chapter we revisit two ratios discussed in previous chapters, both of which are designed to measure a firm's solvency. The first ratio is the debt-to-equity ratio (D/E), first introduced in Chapter 1. It measures the extent to which a company relies on debt financing, also known as financial leverage. The second ratio is times interest earned (TIE), which measures the ability of current operations to cover interest costs.

---

[7] Recent SEC guidance (S-X 5-02 (25)) requires that commercial and industrial companies that are SEC registrants include this line item. The SEC requires this caption to appear on the balance sheet whenever a footnote bears such a title. If no such footnote exists or the only disclosed items are immaterial items, then the caption need not appear on the balance sheet.

[8] On the balance sheet after "Commitments and contingencies" is what is known as a mezzanine section of the balance sheet (meaning in between the liabilities section and equity section of the balance sheet). This section contains certain types of redeemable preferred stocks, redeemable noncontrolling interests, and some types of convertible notes. These are debt-equity hybrid securities, meaning they have some characteristics of debt and some characteristics of equity. A detailed discussion of each of these securities is outside the scope of this text. For most ratio analysis in this introductory-level textbook, we include all the securities in the mezzanine section as either debt or equity for the sake of simplicity. Analysts or other financial statement users might go into more detail and view some of these securities as debt and some of the securities as equity in their analyses. We note that IFRS does not have a mezzanine section of the balance sheet.

Analysis Objective

We want to gauge the ability of a company to satisfy its long-term debt obligations and remain solvent.

Analysis Tool Debt-to-Equity Ratio

$$\textbf{Debt-to-equity ratio (D/E)} = \frac{\textbf{Total liabilities}}{\textbf{Total stockholders' equity}}$$

Applying the Ratio to Verizon

$$\textbf{2015:}\ \frac{\$226{,}333}{\$17{,}842} = 12.69 \text{ or } 1{,}269\%$$

$$\textbf{2016:}\ \frac{\$220{,}148}{\$24{,}032} = 9.16 \text{ or } 916\%$$

$$\textbf{2017:}\ \frac{\$212{,}456}{\$44{,}687} = 4.75 \text{ or } 475\%$$

Guidance A debt-to-equity ratio equal to 1.0 implies that the company is relying on debt and equity financing in equal amounts. As a company's reliance on debt increases and the company's long-term solvency becomes more of a concern, this ratio increases. A debt-to-equity ratio of about 1.3 is about average, though **Exhibit 5.13** (in Chapter 5) shows that the ratio varies by industry.

Verizon in Context

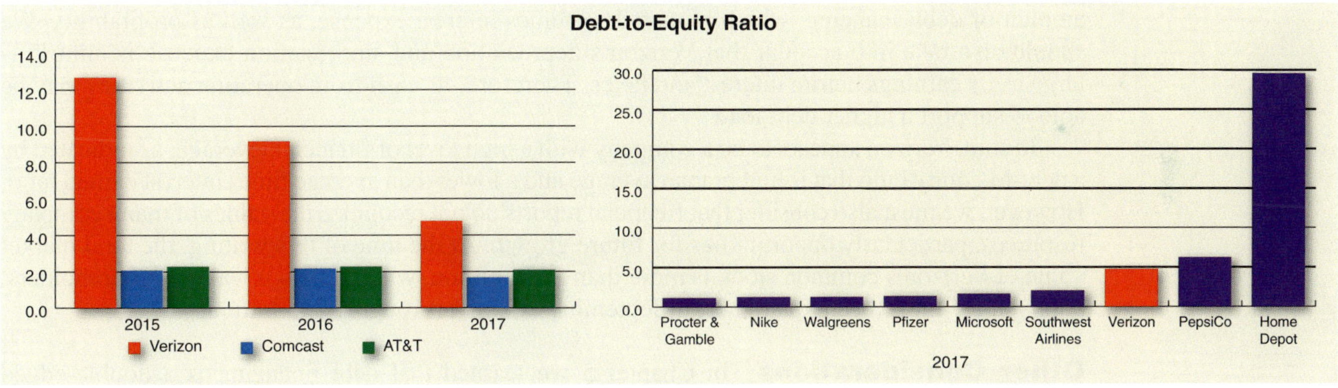

Analysis Tool Times Interest Earned

$$\textbf{Times interest earned (TIE)} = \frac{\textbf{Earnings before interest and taxes}}{\textbf{Interest expense}}$$

Applying the Ratio to Verizon

$$\textbf{2015:}\ \frac{\$33{,}160}{\$4{,}920} = 6.7 \text{ times}$$

$$\textbf{2016:}\ \frac{\$25{,}362}{\$4{,}376} = 5.8 \text{ times}$$

$$\textbf{2017:}\ \frac{\$25{,}327}{\$4{,}733} = 5.4 \text{ times}$$

Guidance When a company relies on debt financing, it assumes the burden of paying the interest on the debt. The times interest earned ratio measures the burden of interest costs by comparing earnings before interest and taxes (EBIT) to annual interest expense. A high TIE ratio indicates that a company is able to meet its interest costs without adversely affecting profitability.

Verizon in Context

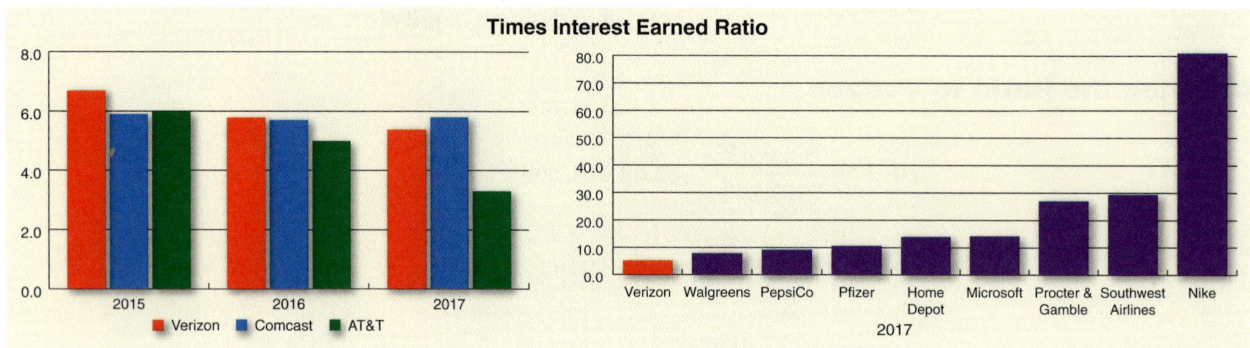

Takeaways Before 2014, Verizon's debt-to-equity ratio was lower than either Comcast or AT&T, two of its competitors. In 2014, Verizon engaged in a transaction to buy out the 45% equity interest of its wireless partner (Vodafone Group Plc) that had the effect of reducing its cash and reducing its shareholders equity by a substantial amount. Verizon's debt to equity increased significantly in 2014; the ratio has been in steady decline over the last three years but is not yet to the pre-2014 levels. Its times interest earned ratio is lower than the other featured companies in this text, but the ratio for Verizon is quite similar to that of its close competitors. Indeed, in 2016 and 2017, AT&Ts ratio is lower than Verizon's. The size of this ratio is driven by two factors—the amount of debt financing, which in turn determines interest expense, as well as profitability. We should also take into account that Verizon's depreciation and amortization expense is almost as large as its earnings before interest and taxes. Therefore, its cash from operating activities may be able to support a higher debt load.

In sum, Verizon appears to be a company with a high level of financial leverage, as indicated by a debt-to-equity ratio that is higher than average and a lower than average times interest earned ratio. However, we must also consider that financial reports do not recognize the values of many company resources, particularly opportunities for future growth. At the time of this writing, the total market value of Verizon's common stock is more than $236 billion, while the book value of shareholders' equity at the most recent quarter-end (September 2018) was roughly $55 billion.

Other Considerations In Chapter 5 we learned that debt financing is a double-edged sword. When used effectively, financial leverage increases return on equity because debt financing is generally less costly than equity financing. However, debt carries with it the risk of **default**, which is the risk that the company will be unable to pay its obligations when they come due (insolvency). To provide some protection against default risk, creditors usually require a company to execute a loan agreement that places restrictions on the company's activities. These restrictions, called covenants, impose indirect costs on a firm beyond the explicit cost of interest, and these indirect costs tend to increase as a company increases its reliance on debt financing. When a company's solvency ratios are close to the limits specified by its covenants, management is more likely to pass up profitable investment opportunities or engage in counterproductive earnings management activities to avoid violating these restrictions.

Walgreens Boots Alliance, Inc. has several revolving credit facilities with aggregate borrowing capacity of over $5 billion as of its year-end, August 31, 2018. In its footnotes, Walgreens reports:

> Each of the Company's credit facilities described above contain a covenant to maintain, as of the last day of each fiscal quarter, a ratio of consolidated debt to total capitalization not to exceed 0.60:1.00. The credit facilities contain various other customary covenants. As of August 31, 2018, the Company was in compliance with all such applicable covenants. . . .

continued

continued from previous page

> If we breach any of these restrictions or covenants and do not obtain a waiver from the lenders, then, subject to applicable cure periods, our outstanding indebtedness could be declared immediately due and payable. This could have a material adverse effect on our business operations and financial condition.

In prior years, the company has also mentioned other covenant restrictions more specifically, such as maintaining a minimum net worth and limitations on the sale of assets and purchases of investment. There are several variations on the ratios that we have discussed and there is no single ratio that can be described as the best measure of company solvency. As with all ratios, solvency measures can be distorted by uncertain, inappropriate, or inaccurate data. It is always helpful to analyze the footnotes to better understand the components of debt financing, their interest rates, when major payments are due, and what, if any, restrictive covenants exist. There is no substitute for diligence.

Debt Ratings and the Cost of Debt

Earlier in the chapter we learned that the effective cost of debt to the issuing company is the market (yield) rate of interest used to price the bond, regardless of the bond coupon rate. The rate of interest that a company must pay on its debt is a function of the maturity of that debt and the creditworthiness of the issuing company.

RESEARCH INSIGHT

Accounting Conservatism and Cost of Debt Research indicates that companies applying more conservative accounting methods incur a lower cost of debt. Research also suggests that while accounting conservatism can lead to lower-quality accounting income (because such income does not fully reflect economic reality), creditors are more confident in the numbers and view them as more credible. Evidence also implies that companies can lower the required return demanded by creditors (the risk premium) by issuing high-quality financial reports that include enhanced footnote disclosures and detailed supplemental reports.

A company's debt rating, also referred to as credit quality and creditworthiness, is related to default risk. Companies seeking to obtain bond financing from the capital markets normally first seek a rating on their proposed debt issuance from one of several rating agencies such as **Standard & Poor's**, **Moody's Investors Service**, or **Fitch**. The aim of rating agencies is to rate debt so that its default risk is more accurately determined and priced by the market. Such debt issuances carry debt ratings from one or more of the three large rating agencies as shown in **Exhibit 9.6**. This exhibit includes the general description attached to the debt for each rating class—for example, AAA is assigned to debt of prime maximum safety (maximum creditworthiness). Bonds with credit ratings below investment grade (below Baa or BBB) are referred to as "high yield" bonds or, more pejoratively, "junk bonds," which may not be purchased by many professionally managed portfolios.[9]

EXHIBIT 9.6 Corporate Debt Ratings and Descriptions

Moody's	S&P	Fitch	Description
Aaa	AAA	AAA	Prime Maximum Safety
Aa	AA	AA	High Grade, High Quality
A	A	A	Upper-Medium Grade
Baa	BBB	BBB	Lower-Medium Grade
Ba	BB	BB	Non-Investment Grade
B	B	B	Speculative
Caa	CCC	CCC	Substantial Risk
Ca	CC	CC	Extremely Speculative
C	C	C	Exceptionally High Risk
	D		Default

[9] Standard & Poor's and Fitch modify their ratings to more detail with the addition of a plus (+) or minus (−) sign (e.g., BBB+, BBB, BBB−). Similarly, Moody's uses numerical modifiers within ratings (e.g., Aa1, Aa2, Aa3).

YOU MAKE THE CALL

You are the Vice President of Finance Your company is currently rated BB by credit rating agencies. You are considering possible financial and other restructurings of the company to increase your credit rating. What types of restructurings might you consider? What benefits will your company receive from those restructurings? What costs will your company incur to implement such restructurings? [Answers on page 444]

Walgreens provides detailed disclosures about its ratings in the notes to their financial statements. Their note is as follows:

Credit ratings
As of October 10, 2018, the credit ratings of Walgreens Boots Alliance were:

Rating Agency	Long-Term Debt Rating	Commercial Paper Rating	Outlook
Fitch	BBB	F2	Stable
Moody's	Baa2	P-2	Stable
Standard & Poor's	BBB	A-2	Stable

In assessing the Company's credit strength, each rating agency considers various factors including the Company's business model, capital structure, financial policies and financial performance. There can be no assurance that any particular rating will be assigned or maintained. The Company's credit ratings impact its borrowing costs, access to capital markets and operating lease costs. The rating agency ratings are not recommendations to buy, sell or hold the Company's debt securities or commercial paper. Each rating may be subject to revision or withdrawal at any time by the assigning rating agency and should be evaluated independently of any other rating.

It is these ratings that, in conjunction with the maturity of its bonds, establish the market interest rate and consequent selling price. There are a number of considerations that affect the rating of a bond. **Standard & Poor's** lists the following factors among its credit rating criteria:

Business Risk
- Industry characteristics
- Competitive position (e.g., marketing, technology, efficiency, regulation)
- Management

Financial Risk
- Financial characteristics
- Financial policy
- Profitability
- Capital structure
- Cash flow protection
- Financial flexibility

Rating agencies use a number of accounting ratios to help establish creditworthiness, including measures of liquidity, solvency, and profitability. These ratios are variants of the ratios we describe in Chapter 5 and in this chapter, especially those used to assess solvency.

There are other relevant factors in setting debt ratings, including the following:

- **Collateral** Companies can provide security for debt in the form of mortgages on assets. To the extent debt is secured, the debt holder is in a preferred position vis-à-vis other creditors.
- **Covenants** Debt agreements (indentures) can contain restrictions on the issuing company to protect debt holders. Examples are restrictions on excessive dividend payment, on other company acquisitions, on further borrowing, and on maintaining minimum levels for key liquidity and solvency ratios. These covenants provide debt holders some means of control over the issuer's operations because, unlike equity investors, they do not have voting rights.
- **Options** Debt obligations involve contracts between the borrowing company and debt holders. Options are sometimes written into debt contracts. Examples are options to convert debt

into stock (so that debt holders have a stake in value creation) and options allowing the issuing company to repurchase its debt before maturity (usually at a premium).

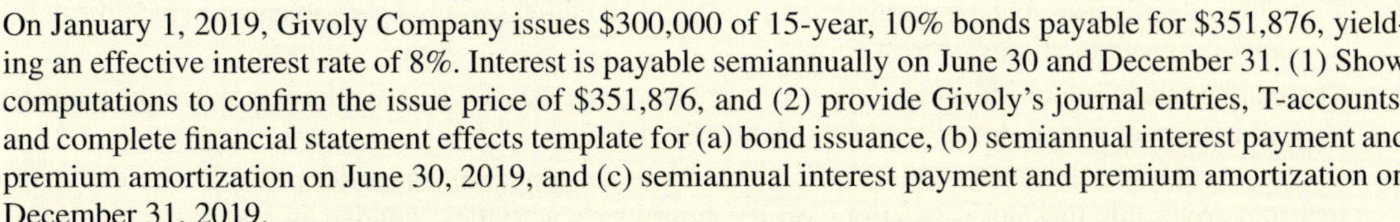

CHAPTER-END REVIEW

On January 1, 2019, Givoly Company issues $300,000 of 15-year, 10% bonds payable for $351,876, yielding an effective interest rate of 8%. Interest is payable semiannually on June 30 and December 31. (1) Show computations to confirm the issue price of $351,876, and (2) provide Givoly's journal entries, T-accounts, and complete financial statement effects template for (a) bond issuance, (b) semiannual interest payment and premium amortization on June 30, 2019, and (c) semiannual interest payment and premium amortization on December 31, 2019.

The solution to this review problem can be found on pages 458-459.

SUMMARY

Identify and account for current operating liabilities. (p. 415) **LO1**

- Current liabilities are short-term and generally non-interest-bearing; accordingly, firms try to maximize the financing of their assets using these sources of funds.
- ROE increases when firms make use of accounts payable increases to finance operating assets; a firm must avoid excessive "leaning on the trade" for short-term gains that can damage long-term supplier relationships.
- When cash discounts are offered by creditors, companies use the net of discount method to report accounts payable information.
- Accrued liabilities reflect amounts that have been recognized as expenses in the current (or a prior) period, but not yet paid.
- While all accruals result in a liability on the balance sheet and an expense on the income statement, management has latitude in determining (in some cases, estimating) their amount and timing; this discretion offers the opportunity for managing earnings.

Describe and account for current nonoperating (financial) liabilities. (p. 422) **LO2**

- Management will generally try to assure that the debt service on financial (nonoperating) liabilities coincides with the cash flows from the assets financed.
- When large amounts of financing are required for, say, plant and equipment, firms find that bonds, notes, and other forms of long-term financing provide a cost-efficient means of raising capital.

Explain and illustrate the pricing of long-term nonoperating liabilities. (p. 427) **LO3**

- The coupon rate indicated on a bond contract determines the periodic interest payment. The required return on any bond called the market (yield or effective) rate is determined by market conditions and rarely equals the coupon (contract) rate. The market rate is used to price the bond and determines the effective cost of the debt to the issuer.
- If the market rate is below the coupon rate, the bond will sell at a premium to its face value, assuring that the owner of the bond earns only the market rate of interest. If the market rate exceeds the coupon rate, the bond will sell at a discount so that the bond is issued at less than its face value.

Analyze and account for financial statement effects of long-term nonoperating liabilities. (p. 430) **LO4**

- A discount for a bond selling below its face value represents additional interest expense over time to the issuer because the issuer received less than face value upon issuance, but must pay the holder the face value at the bond's maturity; this discount represents additional interest beyond the coupon payment to the holder. The premium on a bond selling above its face value lowers the interest cost to the issuer.
- Companies may choose to report liabilities at fair value; if the fair value option is elected, changes in fair value are reported as gains and losses in the income statement.[10]

[10] Unless the change in fair value results from a change in instrument-specific credit risk. If it is caused by instrument-specific credit risk (i.e., a change in fair value because of a change in the credit quality of the issuer), that portion of the change in fair value is reported in other comprehensive income.

- Gains and losses on bonds repurchased must be reported in operating income, unless they are part of discontinued operations. Such transactions do not represent operating activities, and gains/losses should be removed when determining cash from operations with the indirect method.

LO5 **Explain how solvency ratios and debt ratings are determined and how they impact the cost of debt. (p. 438)**

- Two debt-related ratios that are particularly useful in evaluating a company's solvency include the debt-to-equity ratio and the times interest earned ratio.
- The market rate of interest to a firm reflects the creditworthiness of the particular issuer. Credit agencies play an important role in this process by issuing debt ratings.
- Borrowing is typically secured by collateral that places the lender in a superior position to other creditors and covenants that put restrictions on the borrower's activities; bonds can also contain options including those for conversion or repurchase.

GUIDANCE ANSWERS . . . YOU MAKE THE CALL

You are the Analyst Accrued liabilities must be probable and estimable before they can be reported in the balance sheet. If DowDuPont's environmental costs turn out to be higher than management estimates, it may be understating its liabilities (and overstating equity). As an analyst, if you suspect that DowDuPont's estimate is too low, you should add an additional estimated liability to the company's balance sheet amounts to conduct analysis.

You are the Vice President of Finance The types of restructurings you might consider are those yielding a strengthening of the financial ratios typically used to assess liquidity and solvency by the rating agencies. Such restructurings include inventory reduction to generate cash, the reallocation of cash outflows from investing activities (PPE or intangible assets) to debt reduction, and reducing the cash outflows for repurchases of the company's stock (treasury stock). These actions increase liquidity or reduce financial leverage and, thus, should yield an improved debt rating. An improved debt rating gives the company access to more debt holders, as the current debt rating is below investment grade and is not a suitable investment for many professionally managed portfolios. An improved debt rating also yields a lower interest rate on debt. Offsetting these benefits are costs such as the following: (1) potential loss of sales from inventory stock-outs; (2) potential future cash flow reductions and loss of market power from reduced investing in PPE and intangibles; and (3) possible reductions in share price if shareholders were expecting more cash to be returned in the form of dividends and stock buybacks. All cost and benefits must be assessed before you pursue any restructurings.

KEY RATIOS

$$\text{Debt-to-equity (D / E)} = \frac{\text{Total liabilities}}{\text{Total stockholders' equity}} \qquad \text{Times interest earned (TIE)} = \frac{\text{Earnings before interest and taxes}}{\text{Interest}}$$

KEY TERMS

Accounts payable (p. 415)
Accrued liabilities (p. 415)
Amortization (p. 431)
Annuity (p. 427)
Call provision (p. 435)
Cash discounts (p. 416)
Collateral (p. 425, 442)
Contingent liability (p. 419)
Cookie jar reserves (p. 421)
Coupon (contract or stated) rate (p. 427)
Covenants (p. 442)
Current maturities of long-term debt (p. 415)
Default (p. 440)
Deferred performance liabilities (p. 415)
Discount (p. 429)
Face amount (p. 427)
Financial leverage (p. 414)
Leaning on the trade (p. 416)
Loan amortization table (p. 425)
Market (yield) rate (p. 427)
Net-of-discount method (p. 416)
Options (p. 442)
Par (face) value (p. 428)
Periodic interest payments (p. 427)
Premium (p. 429)
Present value (p. 427)
Principal (p. 425)
Short-term interest-bearing debt (p. 415)
Single payment (p. 427)

Assignments with the MBC logo in the margin are available in  BusinessCourse.
See the Preface of the book for details.

MULTIPLE CHOICE

1. Which of the following statements is correct? A decrease in accrued wages liability:
   a. decreases cash flows from operations.
   b. decreases working capital.
   c. increases net income.
   d. increases net nonoperating (financial) assets.

2. On April 1, 2019, a firm borrows $12,000 at an annual interest rate of 10% with payments required semiannually on September 30 and March 31. How much interest payable and how much interest expense should appear on the firm's annual report at the end of the firm's fiscal year, December 31, 2019?
   a. $900 payable and $300 expense.
   b. $300 payable and $900 expense.
   c. $600 payable and $600 expense.
   d. $900 payable and $600 expense.

3. A firm issues $30,000,000 of 10-year bonds and receives $29.5 million in cash. Which of the following statements is correct?
   a. The bonds do not have a coupon rate because they are zeros.
   b. The market rate exceeds the coupon rate.
   c. The contract rate exceeds the market rate.
   d. The bonds were issued at par.

4. A firm issues $5 million of 10-year, 6% notes with interest paid semiannually. At issuance the firm received $5,817,565 cash reflecting a 4% yield. What is the amount of premium written off against interest expense in the first year the notes are outstanding?
   a. $48,318
   b. $24,527
   c. $67,971
   d. $33,649

5. On May 1, 2019, Wild, Inc., makes an early repayment of long-term debt due to mature on June 1, 2021. Which of the following ratios for the year 2019 is (are) decreased by this repayment?
   a. Current Ratio
   b. Quick Ratio
   c. Times Interest Earned
   d. Debt-to-Equity

Multiple Choice Answers
1. a 2. b 3. b
4. c 5. a, b, and d

QUESTIONS

Q9-1. What does the term *current liabilities* mean? What assets are usually used to settle current liabilities?

Q9-2. What is the justification for using the net-of-discount method to record inventory purchases when cash discounts are offered?

Q9-3. What is an accrual? How do accruals impact the balance sheet and the income statement?

Q9-4. What is the difference between a bond coupon rate and its market interest rate (yield)?

Q9-5. How does issuing a bond at a premium or discount affect the bond's *effective* interest rate vis-à-vis the coupon (stated) rate?

Q9-6. Why do companies report a gain or loss on the repurchase of their bonds (assuming the repurchase price is different from bond book value)?

Q9-7. How do debt ratings affect the cost of borrowing for a company?

Q9-8. How would you interpret a company's reported gain or loss on the repurchase of its bonds?

Q9-9. What do the following terms mean? (a) bonds payable, (b) call provision, (c) face value, (d) coupon, (e) bond discount, (f) bond premium, and (g) amortization of bond premium or discount.

Q9-10. What are the advantages and disadvantages of issuing bonds rather than common stock?

Q9-11. A $3,000,000 issue of 10-year, 9% bonds was sold at 98 plus accrued interest three months after the bonds were dated. What net amount of cash is received?

Q9-12. How does issuing bonds at a premium or discount "adjust the contract rate to the applicable market rate of interest"?

Q9-13. Regardless of whether premium or discount is involved, what generalization can be made about the change in the book value of bonds payable during the period in which they are outstanding?

Q9-14. If the effective interest amortization method is used for bonds payable, how does the periodic interest expense change over the life of the bonds when they are issued (a) at a discount and (b) at a premium?

Q9-15. How should premium and discount on bonds payable be presented in the balance sheet?

Q9-16. On April 30, 2019, one year before maturity, Weber Company retired $200,000 of 9% bonds payable at 101. The book value of the bonds on April 30 was $197,600. Bond interest was last paid on April 30, 2019. What is the gain or loss on the retirement of the bonds?

Q9-17. Brownlee Company borrowed money by issuing a 20-year mortgage note payable. The note will be repaid in equal monthly installments. The interest expense component of each payment decreases with each payment. Why?

MINI EXERCISES

LO1

M9-18. Recording Cash Discounts

On November 15, 2018, Shields Company purchased inventory costing $6,200 on credit. The credit terms were 2/10, n/30.

a. Assume that Shields Company paid the invoice on November 23, 2018. Prepare journal entries to record the purchase of this inventory and the cash payment to the supplier using the net-of-discount method.

b. Set up the necessary T-accounts and post the journal entries from question *a* to the accounts.

c. Compute the cost of a lost discount as an annual percentage rate.

LO1

M9-19. Recording Cash Discounts

Schrand Corporation purchases materials from a supplier that offers credit terms of 2/15, n/60. It purchased $12,500 of merchandise inventory from that supplier on January 20, 2019.

a. Assume that Schrand Corporation paid the invoice on February 15, 2019. Prepare journal entries to record the purchase of this inventory and the cash payment to the supplier using the net-of-discount method.

b. Set up the necessary T-accounts and post the journal entries from question *a* to the accounts.

c. Compute the cost of a lost discount as an annual percentage rate.

LO2

M9-20. Analyzing and Computing Financial Statement Effects of Loan Interest

Huddart Company gave a creditor a 90-day, 8% note payable for $7,200 on December 16.

a. Prepare the journal entry to record the year-end December 31st accounting adjustment Huddart must make. (Round to the nearest dollar.)

b. Post the journal entries from part *a* to their respective T-accounts.

c. Record the transaction from part *a* in the financial statement effects template.

	Balance Sheet									Income Statement				
Transaction	Cash Asset	+	Noncash Assets	=	Liabil-ities	+	Contrib. Capital	+	Earned Capital	Revenues	−	Expenses	=	Net Income

LO1, 2

M9-21. Analyzing and Determining the Amount of a Liability

For each of the following situations, indicate the liability amount, if any, which is reported on the balance sheet of Hirst, Inc., at December 31, 2018.

a. Hirst owes $110,000 at year-end 2018 for its inventory purchases.

b. Hirst agreed to purchase a $28,000 drill press in January 2019.

c. During November and December of 2018, Hirst sold products to a firm with a 90-day warranty against product failure. Estimated 2019 costs of honoring this warranty are $2,200.

d. Hirst provides a profit-sharing bonus for its executives equal to 5% of its reported pretax annual income. The estimated pretax income for 2018 is $600,000. Bonuses are not paid until January of the following year.

M9-22. Interpreting Relations Between Bond Price, Coupon, Yield, and Rating

LO3, 5 — Microsoft Corporation NASDAQ :: MSFT

In January 2017, **Microsoft Corporation** issued $17 billion of bonds in seven parts, with maturities ranging from 2020 to 2057. The bond issue was rated Aaa by Moody's. Two of the bond offerings are described below.

Amount: $4 billion; Maturity: February 6, 2027; Coupon: 3.3%; Price: 99.31; Yield: 3.383%.
Amount: $2 billion; Maturity: February 6, 2057; Coupon: 4.5%; Price: 99.49; Yield: 4.528%.

a. Discuss the relation between the coupon rate, issuance price, and yield for the 2027 issue.
b. Compare the yields on the two bond issues. Why are the yields different when the bond ratings are the same?

M9-23. Determining Gain or Loss on Bond Redemption

LO4

On January 1, 2019, two years before maturity, Easton Company retires $400,000 of its 8.5% bonds payable at the current market price of 102 (102% of the bond face amount, or $400,000 × 1.02 = $408,000). The bond book value on January 1, 2019, is $397,000 reflecting an unamortized discount of $3,000. Bond interest is presently fully paid and recorded up to the date of retirement. What is the gain or loss on retirement of these bonds?

M9-24. Interpreting Bond Footnote

LO4 — Pfizer, Inc. NYSE :: PFE

In its 2017 balance sheet, **Pfizer, Inc.**, reports a value of $3,546 million as current portion of long-term debt. In addition, Pfizer reports the following maturity schedule for its remaining $32,783 million in long-term debt outstanding:

($ millions)	2019	2020	2021	2022	After 2022
Maturities	$4,848	$1,528	$3,550	$1,199	$21,658

a. Why does the table not include 2018? How much long-term debt is due in 2018?
b. What implications does the payment schedule have for your evaluation of Pfizer's liquidity and solvency?

M9-25. Classifying Debt Accounts into the Balance Sheet or Income Statement

LO1 — Homework MBC

Indicate the proper financial statement classification (balance sheet or income statement) for each of the following accounts:

a. Gain on Bond Retirement
b. Discount on Bonds Payable
c. Mortgage Notes Payable
d. Bonds Payable
e. Bond Interest Expense
f. Bond Interest Payable (due next period)
g. Premium on Bonds Payable
h. Loss on Bond Retirement

M9-26. Interpreting Bond Footnote Disclosures

LO4 — Cencosud SA NYSE :: CNCO

Cencosud SA is a leading Latin American retailer, with approximately US$4.12 billion in short- and long-term debt outstanding as of December 31, 2017. In its 20-F filing with the Securities and Exchange Commission, Cencosud reports the following:

Our loan agreements and outstanding bonds contain a number of covenants requiring us to comply with certain financial ratios and other tests. The most restrictive financial covenants under these loan agreements and bonds require us to maintain:

- a ratio of consolidated Net Financial Debt to consolidated net worth not exceeding 1.2 to 1;
- a ratio of consolidated Net Financial Debt to EBITDA (as defined in the relevant credit agreements) for the most recent four consecutive fiscal quarters for such period of less than 5.25 to 1;
- unencumbered assets in an amount equal to at least 120% of the outstanding principal amount of total liabilities;
- minimum consolidated assets of at least UF 50.5 million[11]; and
- minimum consolidated net worth of at least UF 28.0 million.

As of the date of this annual report, we are in compliance with all of our loan and debt instruments.

a. Why do creditors impose restrictive covenants on borrowers?
b. How might restrictive covenants such as these affect management decisions?
c. What implications do these restrictions have on an analysis of the company and its solvency?

[11] "UF" refers to *Unidades de Fomento*. The UF is an inflation-indexed Chilean monetary unit with a value in Chilean pesos that is adjusted daily to reflect changes in the official Consumer Price Index ("CPI").

LO4 

M9-27. Analyzing Financial Statement Effects of Bond Redemption

Holthausen Corporation issued $400,000 of 11%, 20-year bonds at 108 on January 1, 2013. Interest is payable semiannually on June 30 and December 31. Through January 1, 2019, Holthausen amortized $4,191 of the bond premium. On January 1, 2019, Holthausen retires the bonds at 103.

a. Prepare journal entries to record the issue and retirement of these bonds.
b. Post the journal entries from part *a* to their respective T-accounts.
c. Record each of the transactions from part *a* in the financial statement effects template.

LO4 

M9-28. Analyzing Financial Statement Effects of Bond Redemption

Dechow, Inc., issued $250,000 of 8%, 15-year bonds at 96 on July 1, 2012. Interest is payable semiannually on December 31 and June 30. Through June 30, 2019, Dechow amortized $3,186 of the bond discount. On July 1, 2019, Dechow retired the bonds at 101.

a. Prepare journal entries to record the issue and retirement of these bonds. (Assume the June interest expense has already been recorded.)
b. Post the journal entries from part *a* to their respective T-accounts.
c. Record each of the transactions from part *a* in the financial statement effects template.

LO4 

M9-29. Analyzing and Computing Accrued Interest on Notes

Compute any interest accrued for each of the following notes payable owed by Penman, Inc., as of December 31, 2018 (use a 365-day year):

Lender	Issuance Date	Principal	Interest Rate (%)	Term
Nissim	11/21/18	$18,000	10%	120 days
Klein	12/13/18	14,000	9	90 days
Bildersee	12/19/18	16,000	12	60 days

LO5
General Mills, Inc.
NYSE :: GIS

M9-30. Debt Ratings and Capital Structure

General Mills, Inc., reports the following information in cash flow statement for the year ended May 27, 2018:

Cash Flows from Financing Activities ($ millions)	Year ended May 27, 2018
Change in notes payable	$ 327.7
Issuance of long-term debt	6,550.0
Payment of long-term debt	(600.1)
Proceeds from common stock issued on exercised options	99.3
Proceeds from common stock issued	969.9
Purchases of common stock for treasury	(601.6)
Dividends paid	(1,139.7)
Dividends to noncontrolling interests and other, net	(159.8)
Net cash used by financing activities	$5,445.5

a. General Mills reported net income of $2,163.0 million in the year ended May 2018. What effect did these financing cash flows have on General Mills solvency measures for the year? Explain.
b. Would the changes in financing tend to lower or increase the firm's debt rating? (Currently General Mills' long-term debt is rated at upper medium grade.)

LO3 

M9-31. Computing Bond Issue Price

Bushman, Inc., issues $500,000 of 9% bonds that pay interest semiannually and mature in 10 years. Compute the bond issue price assuming that the bonds' market rate is:

a. 8% per year compounded semiannually.
b. 10% per year compounded semiannually.

LO3 

M9-32. Computing Issue Price for Zero-Coupon Bonds

Baiman, Inc., issues $500,000 of zero-coupon bonds that mature in 10 years. Compute the bond issue price assuming that the bonds' market rate is:

a. 8% per year compounded semiannually.
b. 10% per year compounded semiannually.
c. If prior to the debt issue at 10%, the firm had total assets of $3 million and total equity of $1 million, what would be the effect of the new borrowing on the financial leverage of the firm?

M9-33. Financial Statement Effects of Accounts Payable Transactions LO1

Petroni Company engages in the following sequence of transactions every month:

1. Purchases $300 of inventory on credit.
2. Sells $300 of inventory for $420 on credit.
3. Pays other operating expenses of $110 in cash.
4. Collects $420 in cash from customers.
5. Pays supplier of inventory $300.

a. Create a monthly income statement and statement of operating cash flow (direct method) for four consecutive months.

b. The CFO is disappointed with the cash flows from the business. They do not provide the support for investment and growth that she wants. She proposes delaying supplier payments by a month. That is, each month's inventory purchase will be paid for in the following month. How would this change the monthly income statements and operating cash flows in part *a*? Would it provide the steady flow of cash that the CFO is looking for? Why?

M9-34. Computing Bond Issue Price and Preparing an Amortization Table in Excel LO3, 4

On December 31, 2018, Kaplan, Inc., issues $500,000 of 9% bonds that pay interest semiannually and mature in 10 years (December 31, 2028).

a. Using the Excel PV worksheet function, compute the issue price assuming that the bonds' market rate is 8% per year compounded semiannually. (Refer to Appendix A for illustration.)

b. Prepare an amortization table in Excel to demonstrate the amortization of the book (carrying) value to the $500,000 maturity value at the end of the 20th semiannual period. (Refer to Appendix A for illustration.)

M9-35. Classifying Bond-Related Accounts LO3, 4

Indicate the proper financial statement classification for each of the following accounts:

Gain on Bond Retirement (material amount)
Discount on Bonds Payable
Mortgage Notes Payable
Bonds Payable
Bond Interest Expense
Bond Interest Payable
Premium on Bonds Payable

M9-36. Recording and Assessing the Effects of Installment Loans LO3, 4

On December 31, 2018, Thomas, Inc., borrowed $700,000 on a 12%, 15-year mortgage note payable. The note is to be repaid in equal semiannual installments of $50,854 (payable on June 30 and December 31).

a. Prepare journal entries to record (1) the issuance of the mortgage note payable, (2) the payment of the first installment on June 30, 2019, and (3) the payment of the second installment on December 31, 2019. Round amounts to the nearest dollar.

b. Post the journal entries from part *a* to their respective T-accounts.

c. Record each of the transactions from part *a* in the financial statement effects template.

M9-37. Determining Bond Prices LO3

Lunar, Inc., plans to issue $900,000 of 10% bonds that will pay interest semiannually and mature in 5 years. Assume that the effective interest rate is 12% per year compounded semiannually. Compute the selling price of the bonds. Use Tables A.2 and A.3 in Appendix A near the end of the book.

EXERCISES

E9-38. Analyzing and Computing Accrued Warranty Liability and Expense LO1

Waymire Company sells a motor that carries a 60-day unconditional warranty against product failure. Waymire estimates that between the sale and lapse of the product warranty, 2% of the 69,000 units sold this period will require repair at an average cost of $50 per unit. The warranty liability for this product had a beginning-of-period balance of $30,000, and $27,000 has already been spent on warranty repairs and replacements during the period.

a. How much warranty expense must Waymire report in its income statement and what amount of warranty liability must it report on its balance sheet for this year?

b. What analysis issues do we need to consider with respect to the amount of reported warranty liability?

c. What solvency ratios are increased if warranty liabilities rise?

LO1 **E9-39. Analyzing Contingencies and Assessing Liabilities**

The following independent situations represent various types of liabilities. Analyze each situation and indicate which of the following is the proper accounting treatment for each company: (1) record in accounts, (2) disclose in a financial statement footnote, or (3) neither record nor disclose.

a. A stockholder has filed a lawsuit against Clinch Corporation. Clinch's attorneys have reviewed the facts of the case. Their review revealed that similar lawsuits have never resulted in a cash award and it is highly unlikely that this lawsuit will either.

b. Foster Company signed a 60-day, 10% note when it purchased (and received) items from another company.

c. The Department of Environment Protection notifies Shevlin Company that a state where it has a plant is filing a lawsuit for groundwater pollution against Shevlin and another company that has a plant adjacent to Shevlin's plant. Test results have not identified the exact source of the pollution. Shevlin's manufacturing process often produces by-products that can pollute groundwater.

d. Sloan Company manufactured and sold products to a retailer that sold the products to consumers. The Sloan Company warranty offers replacement of the product if it is found to be defective within 90 days of the sale to the consumer. Historically, 1.2% of the products are returned for replacement.

LO1 **E9-40. Analyzing and Computing Accrued Wages Liability and Expense**

Demski Company pays its employees on the 1st and 15th of each month. It is March 31 and Demski is preparing financial statements for this quarter. Its employees have earned $25,000 since the 15th of this month and have not yet been paid. How will Demski's balance sheet and income statement change to reflect the accrual of wages that must be made at March 31? What balance sheet and income statement accounts would be incorrectly reported if Demski failed to make this accrual (for each account indicate whether it would be overstated or understated)?

LO3, 4 **E9-41. Analyzing and Reporting Financial Statement Effects of Bond Transactions**

On January 1, 2019, Hutton Corp. issued $300,000 of 15-year, 11% bonds payable for $377,814, yielding an effective interest rate of 8%. Interest is payable semiannually on June 30 and December 31.

a. Show computations to confirm the issue price of $377,814.

b. Prepare journal entries to record the bond issuance, semiannual interest payment, and premium amortization on June 30, 2019, and semiannual interest payment and premium amortization on December 31, 2019. Use the effective interest rate method.

c. Post the journal entries from part *b* to their respective T-accounts.

d. Record each of the transactions from part *b* in the financial statement effects template.

LO3 **E9-42. Computing the Bond Issue Price**

D'Souza, Inc., issues $900,000 of 11% bonds that pay interest semiannually and mature in seven years. Assume that the market interest (yield) rate is 12% per year compounded semiannually. Compute the bond issue price.

LO1 **E9-43. Interpreting Warranty Liability Disclosures**

Siemens AG
OTCMKTS :: SIEGY

The following disclosures were provided by **Siemens AG** in its 2018 annual report:

Product-related expenses

Provisions for estimated costs related to product warranties are recorded in line item Cost of sales at the time the related sale is recognized.

continued

continued from previous page

Note 23 Provisions

(in millions of €)	Provision for Warranties Year ended September 30 2018	2017
Beginning balance	€4,632*	€4,249
Additions	1,786	1,820
Usage	(993)	(1,160)
Reversals	(928)	(972)
Translation differences and other	78	694
Ending balance	€4,575	€4,631

* Beginning balance adjusted in the 2018 annual report.

a. The Provision that Siemens reports is an estimated warranty liability. What would constitute "additions" to the provision in 2018? Prepare a journal entry to record this addition.

b. What constitutes "usage" of the provision? Besides the provision, what other accounts are likely to be affected by usage? Prepare a journal entry to record usage of €993 million in 2018.

c. "Reversals" are corrections of previous estimates of warranty obligations. Why would it be useful to report reversals separately from additions?

d. Siemens reported sales revenue of €83,044 million in 2018 and €82,863 in 2017. Calculate the ratio of warranty expense to sales for each year.

E9-44. Reporting Financial Statement Effects of Bond Transactions LO3, 4

Lundholm, Inc., which reports financial statements each December 31, is authorized to issue $500,000 of 9%, 15-year bonds dated May 1, 2018, with interest payments on October 31 and April 30. Assume the bonds are issued at par on May 1, 2018.

a. Prepare journal entries to record the bond issuance, payment of the first semiannual period's interest, and retirement of $300,000 of the bonds at 101 on November 1, 2019.

b. Post the journal entries from part *a* to their respective T-accounts.

c. Record each of the transactions from part *a* in the financial statement effects template.

E9-45. Reporting Financial Statement Effects of Bond Transactions

On January 1, 2019, McKeown, Inc., issued $250,000 of 8%, 9-year bonds for $220,776, yielding a market (yield) rate of 10%. Semiannual interest is payable on June 30 and December 31 of each year.

a. Show computations to confirm the bond issue price.

b. Prepare journal entries to record the bond issuance, semiannual interest payment, and discount amortization on June 30, 2019, and semiannual interest payment and discount amortization on December 31, 2019. Use the effective interest rate.

c. Post the journal entries from part *b* to their respective T-accounts.

d. Record each of the transactions from part *b* in the financial statement effects template.

E9-46. Reporting Financial Statement Effects of Bond Transactions

On January 1, 2019, Shields, Inc., issued $800,000 of 9%, 20-year bonds for $879,172, yielding a market (yield) rate of 8%. Semiannual interest is payable on June 30 and December 31 of each year.

a. Show computations to confirm the bond issue price.

b. Prepare journal entries to record the bond issuance, semiannual interest payment, and premium amortization on June 30, 2019, and semiannual interest payment and premium amortization on December 31, 2019. Use the effective interest rate method.

c. Post the journal entries from part *b* to their respective T-accounts.

d. Record each of the transactions from part *b* in the financial statement effects template.

E9-47. Analyzing Bond Pricing, Interest Rates, and Financial Statement Effect of a Bond Issue LO3, 4

Deere & Company
NYSE :: DE

Following is a price quote for $200 million of 6.55% coupon bonds issued by Deere & Company that mature in October 2028:

Ratings/Industry	Issue/Call Information	Coupon/Maturity	Price/YTM
A2/A	Deere & Company.	6.550	123.962
Industrial.	Non Callable, NYBE, DE . . .	10-01-2028	4.178

This quote indicates that, on this day, Deere's bonds have a market price of 123.962 (123.962% of face value), resulting in a yield of 4.178%.

a. Assuming that these bonds were originally issued at or close to par value, what does the above market price reveal about the direction that interest rates have changed since Deere issued its bonds? (Assume that Deere's debt rating has remained the same.)

b. Does the change in interest rates since the issuance of these bonds affect the amount of interest expense that Deere is reporting in its income statement? Explain.

c. If Deere were to repurchase its bonds at the above market price of 123.962, how would the repurchase affect its current income? Assume that the bonds were issued at face value (100).

d. Assuming that the bonds remain outstanding until their maturity, at what market price will the bonds sell on their due date of October 1, 2028?

LO3, 4

E9-48. Analyzing and Reporting Financial Statement Effects of Bond Transactions

On January 1, 2019, Trueman Corp. issued $600,000 of 20-year, 11% bonds for $554,860, yielding a market (yield) rate of 12%. Interest is payable semiannually on June 30 and December 31.

a. Confirm the bond issue price.

b. Prepare journal entries to record the bond issuance, semiannual interest payment, and discount amortization on June 30, 2019, and semiannual interest payment and discount amortization on December 31, 2019. Use the effective interest rate method.

c. Post the journal entries from part *b* to their respective T-accounts.

d. Trueman elected to report these bonds in its financial statements at fair value. On December 31, 2019, these bonds were listed in the bond market at a price of 101 (or 101% of par value). What entry is required to adjust the reported value of these bonds to fair value?

e. Prepare a table summarizing the effect of these bonds on earnings for 2019.

LO2, 4

E9-49. Reporting and Interpreting Bond Disclosures

The adjusted trial balance for the Hass Corporation at the end of 2018 contains the following accounts:

$ 25,000	Bond Interest Payable
600,000	9% Bonds Payable due 2020
500,000	10% Bonds Payable due 2019
19,000	Discount on 9% Bonds Payable
2,000	Premium on 8% Bonds Payable
170,500	Zero-Coupon Bonds Payable due 2021
100,000	8% Bonds Payable due 2023

Prepare the long-term liabilities section of the balance sheet. Indicate the proper balance sheet classification for accounts listed above that do not belong in the long-term liabilities section.

LO3, 4

E9-50. Recording and Assessing the Effects of Installment Loans

On December 31, Dehning, Inc., borrowed $500,000 on an 8%, 10-year mortgage note payable. The note is to be repaid in equal quarterly installments of $18,278 (beginning March 31).

a. Prepare journal entries to reflect (1) the issuance of the mortgage note payable, (2) the payment of the first installment on March 31, and (3) the payment of the second installment on June 30. Round amounts to the nearest dollar.

b. Post the journal entries from part *a* to their respective T-accounts.

c. Record each of the transactions from part *a* in the financial statement effects template.

PROBLEMS

LO1

Hewlett-Packard Enterprise Company
NYSE :: HPQ
Cisco Systems, Inc.
NASDAQ :: CSCO

P9-51. Interpreting Warranty Liability Disclosures

The following information was extracted from the 10-K reports for the years ended in 2018 for Hewlett-Packard Enterprise and Cisco Systems, Inc.

($ millions)	Hewlett-Packard Enterprise Company 2018	2017	Cisco Systems, Inc. 2018	2017
Revenue from product sales	$19,504	$17,597	$36,709	$35,705
Warranty expense	265	292	582	691
Accrued warranty liability	430	475	359	407

REQUIRED

a. Compute the amount of warranty costs incurred in 2018 for each company. (That is, what amount was spent for warranty repairs and settlements in 2018? Assume no other adjustments to the account are made.)

b. Compare these two companies on the basis of the ratio of warranty expense to sales. What factors might explain any difference that you observe?

P9-52. Recording and Assessing the Effects of Bond Financing (with Accrued Interest) LO3, 4

Eskew, Inc., which closes its books on December 31, is authorized to issue $500,000 of 9%, 15-year bonds dated May 1, 2018, with interest payments on November 1 and May 1.

REQUIRED

Assuming that the bonds were sold at 100 plus accrued interest on October 1, 2018, prepare the necessary journal entries for items *a–f* below.

a. The bond issuance.

b. Payment of the first semiannual period's interest on November 1, 2018.

c. Accrual of bond interest expense at December 31, 2018.

d. The adjustment to fair value on December 31, 2018, assuming that Eskew, Inc., elected to use the fair value option. On that date, the bond traded at a price of 99 (99% of par value) in the bond market. (Assume that the change in fair value results from a change in market interest rates rather than a change in instrument-specific credit risk.)

e. Payment of the semiannual interest on May 1, 2019. (The firm does not make reversing entries.)

f. Retirement of $300,000 of the bonds at 101 on May 1, 2023 (immediately after the interest payment on that date). Assume that the fair value adjustment account for the entire issue has a debit balance of $15,000 as of that date. *Hint:* Sixty percent of the outstanding bonds were retired in this transaction.

g. Suppose fair value adjustments of bond values were not posted to net income, but rather to other comprehensive income. How would Eskew, Inc.'s December 31, 2018, financial statements change?

P9-53. Interpreting Debt Footnotes on Interest Rates and Expense LO3, 4 CVS Health Corp. NYSE :: CVS

CVS Health Corp. discloses the following footnote in its 10-K relating to its debt:

Following is a summary of the Company's borrowings as reported in note 5 to the firm's 10-K.

In millions	2017	2016
Commercial paper	$ 1,276	$ 1,874
1.9% senior notes due 2018	2,250	2,250
2.25% senior notes due 2018	1,250	1,250
2.25% senior notes due 2019	850	850
2.8% senior notes due 2020	2,750	2,750
2.125% senior notes due 2021	1,750	1,750
4.125% senior notes due 2021	550	550
2.75% senior notes due 2022	1,250	1,250
3.5% senior notes due 2022	1,500	1,500
4.75% senior notes due 2022	399	399
4% senior notes due 2023	1,250	1,250
3.375% senior notes due 2024	650	650
5% senior notes due 2024	299	299
3.875% senior notes due 2025	2,828	2,828
2.875% senior notes due 2026	1,750	1,750
6.25% senior notes due 2027	372	372
3.25% senior exchange debentures due 2035	1	1
4.875% senior notes due 2035	652	652
6.125% senior notes due 2039	477	477

continued

continued from previous page

In millions	2017	2016
5.75% senior notes due 2041	133	133
5.3% senior notes due 2043	750	750
5.125% senior notes due 2045	3,500	3,500
Capital lease obligations	670	648
Other	43	23
Total debt principal	27,170	27,726
Debt premiums	28	33
Debt discounts and deferred financing costs	(196)	(228)
	27,002	27,531
Less:		
Short-term debt (commercial paper)	(1,276)	(1,874)
Current portion of long-term debt	(3,545)	(42)
Long-term debt	$22,181	$25,615

CVS also discloses that its interest expense was $1.04 billion in 2017, after deducting capitalized interest of $8 million. It paid interest of $1.07 billion.

REQUIRED

a. What was the average interest rate on CVS debt in 2018?

b. Does your computation in part *a* seem reasonable given the disclosure relating to specific bond issues? Explain.

c. Why can the amount of interest paid be different from the amount of interest expense recorded in the income statement?

LO3, 4 **P9-54. Recording and Assessing the Effects of Bond Financing (with Accrued Interest)**
Petroni, Inc., which closes its books on December 31, is authorized to issue $800,000 of 9%, 20-year bonds dated March 1, 2019, with interest payments on September 1 and March 1.

REQUIRED

Assuming that the bonds were sold at 100 plus accrued interest on July 1, 2019, prepare the necessary journal entries, post the journal entries to their respective T-accounts, and record each transaction in the financial statement effects template.

a. The bond issuance.

b. Payment of the semiannual interest on September 1, 2019.

c. Accrual of bond interest expense at December 31, 2019.

d. Payment of the semiannual interest on March 1, 2020. (The firm does not make reversing entries.)

e. Retirement of $200,000 of the bonds at 101 on March 1, 2020 (immediately after the interest payment on that date).

LO3, 4 **P9-55. Preparing an Amortization Schedule and Recording the Effects of Bonds**
On December 31, 2018, Kasznik, Inc., issued $720,000 of 11%, 10-year bonds for $678,708, yielding an effective interest rate of 12%. Semiannual interest is payable on June 30 and December 31 each year. The firm uses the effective interest method to amortize the discount.

REQUIRED

a. Prepare an amortization schedule showing the necessary information for the first two interest periods. Round amounts to the nearest dollar.

b. Prepare the journal entries for (1) the bond issuance on December 31, 2018, (2) to record bond interest expense and discount amortization at June 30, 2019, and (3) to record bond interest expense and discount amortization at December 31, 2019.

c. Post the journal entries from part *b* to their respective T-accounts.

d. Record each of the transactions from part *b* in the financial statement effects template.

P9-56. Preparing an Amortization Schedule and Recording the Effects of Bonds LO3, 4

On April 30, 2019, Cheng, Inc., issued $250,000 of 6%, 15-year bonds for $206,770, yielding an effective interest rate of 8%. Semiannual interest is payable on October 31 and April 30 each year. The firm uses the effective interest method to amortize the discount.

REQUIRED

a. Prepare an amortization schedule showing the necessary information for the first two interest periods. Round amounts to the nearest dollar.

b. Prepare the journal entries (1) for the bond issuance on April 30, 2019, (2) to record the bond interest payment and discount amortization at October 31, 2019, (3) the adjusting entry to record bond interest expense and discount amortization at December 31, 2019, the close of the firm's accounting year, and (4) to record the bond interest payment and discount amortization at April 30, 2020.

c. Post the journal entries from part *b* to their respective T-accounts.

d. Record each of the transactions from part *b* in the financial statement effects template.

P9-57. Recording and Assessing the Effects of Installment Loans: Semiannual Installments LO3, 4

Homework MBC

On December 31, 2018, Wasley Corporation borrowed $500,000 on a 10%, 10-year mortgage note payable. The note is to be repaid with equal semiannual installments, beginning June 30, 2019.

REQUIRED

a. Compute the amount of the semiannual installment payment. Use the appropriate table (in Appendix A near the end of the book) or a financial calculator, and round amount to the nearest dollar.

b. Prepare the journal entry (1) to record Wasley's borrowing of funds on December 31, 2018, (2) to record Wasley's installment payment on June 30, 2019, and (3) to record Wasley's installment payment on December 31, 2019. (Round amounts to the nearest dollar.)

c. Post the journal entries from part *b* to their respective T-accounts.

d. Record each of the transactions from part *b* in the financial statement effects template.

P9-58. Recording and Assessing the Effects of Installment Loans: Quarterly Installments LO3, 4

On December 31, 2018, Watts Corporation borrowed $950,000 on an 8%, 5-year mortgage note payable. The note is to be repaid with equal quarterly installments, beginning March 31, 2019.

REQUIRED

a. Compute the amount of the quarterly installment payment. Use the appropriate table (in Appendix A near the end of the book) or a financial calculator, and round amount to the nearest dollar.

b. Prepare the journal entries (1) to record the borrowing of funds by Watts Corporation on December 31, 2018, (2) to record the installment payment by Watts Corporation on March 31, 2019, and (3) to record the installment payment by Watts Corporation on June 30, 2019.

c. Post the journal entries from part *b* to their respective T-accounts.

d. Record each of the transactions from part *b* in the financial statement effects template.

P9-59. Contingent Liabilities LO1

BP, PLC
NYSE :: BP

BP operates off-shore oil drilling platforms including rigs in the Gulf of Mexico. In April 2010, explosions and a fire on the Deepwater Horizon rig led to the death of 11 crew members and a 200-million-gallon oil spill in the Gulf of Mexico. BP's 2010 annual report included the following description of its contingent liabilities (provision) related to this accident:

> In estimating the amount of the provision, BP has determined a range of possible outcomes for Individual and Business Claims, and State and Local Claims.... BP has concluded that a reasonable range of possible outcomes for the amount of the provision at December 31, 2010, is $6 billion to $13 billion. BP believes that the provision recorded at December 31, 2010, of $9.2 billion represents a reliable best estimate from within this range of possible outcomes.

REQUIRED

a. BP prepares its financial statements in accordance with IFRS. How did BP report the $9.2 billion estimate in its 2010 financial statements?

b. How would the accounting for this provision differ if BP prepared its financial statements in accordance with U.S. GAAP?

CASES AND PROJECTS

LO3, 4, 5
Comcast
NASDAQ :: CMCSA

C9-60. Interpreting Debt Disclosures

Comcast Corporation's 2017 income statement and partial balance sheet (liabilities and equity, only) are presented below. In addition, footnote 10 pertaining to Comcast's long-term debt obligations is provided. All $ amounts are presented in millions.

Summarized Consolidated Statement of Income Year ended December 31 (in millions)	2017	2016
Revenue	$84,526	$80,403
Costs and expenses:		
Programming and production	25,384	24,463
Other operating and administrative	25,013	23,416
Advertising, marketing and promotion	6,317	6,107
Depreciation	7,914	7,464
Amortization	2,353	2,094
Other operating gains	(442)	0
	66,539	63,544
Operating income	17,987	16,859
Other income (expense)		
Interest expense	(3,086)	(2,942)
Other	421	436
	(2,665)	(2,506)
Income before income taxes	15,322	14,353
Income tax benefit (expense)	7,578	(5,308)
Net income	$22,900	$ 9,045

Summarized Consolidated Balance Sheet (Liabilities and Equity only) December 31 (in millions)	2017	2016
Current liabilities:		
Accounts payable and accrued expenses related to trade creditors	$ 6,926	$ 6,915
Accrued participations and residuals	1,683	1,726
Deferred revenue	1,552	1,132
Accrued expenses and other current liabilities	6,266	6,282
Current portion of long-term debt	5,134	5,480
Total current liabilities	21,561	21,535
Long-term debt, less current portion	59,422	55,566
Deferred income taxes	24,256	34,854
Other noncurrent liabilities	10,904	10,925
Commitments and contingencies (Note 16)		
Redeemable noncontrolling interests and subsidary preferred stock	1,357	1,446
Total liabilities	117,500	124,326
Total equity	69,449	56,174
Total liabilities and equity	$186,949	$180,500

Note 10: Long-Term Debt **Long-Term Debt Outstanding December 31 (in millions)**	**Weighted-Average Interest Rate as of December 31, 2017**	**2017**	**2016**
Commercial paper	1.84%	$ 903	$ 2,781
Term loans[a]	0.82%	3,880	3,262
Senior notes with maturities of 5 years or less	4.18%	15,680	13,850
Senior notes with maturities between 5 and 10 years	3.31%	13,277	12,049
Senior notes with maturities greater than 10 years[b]	4.74%	31,838	28,587
Other, including capital lease obligations	—%	921	842
Debt issuance costs, premiums, discounts and fair value adjustments[c]	—%	(1,943)	(325)
Total debt	4.04%[d]	64,556	61,046
Less: Current portion		5,134	5,480
Long-term debt		$59,422	$55,566

[a] The December 31, 2017 and 2016, amounts primarily consist of ¥435 billion and ¥382 billion, respectively, of Universal Studios Japan term loans translated using the exchange rates as of these dates. In May 2017, Universal Studios Japan entered into ¥450 billion of new term loans with a final maturity of March 2022. We used the proceeds from these borrowings to repay in full Universal Studios Japan's existing yen-denominated term loans and a portion of amounts outstanding under our commercial paper program.

[b] The December 31, 2017 and 2016, amounts include £625 million of 5.50% notes due 2029, which translated to $845 million and $771 million, respectively, using the exchange rates as of these dates.

[c] The December 31, 2017, amount includes the difference between the principal amount of the new senior notes and the carrying amount of the exchanged senior notes at the time of the senior notes exchange. See below under the heading "Senior Notes Exchange" for additional information on this transaction.

[d] Includes the effects of our derivative financial instruments.

As of December 31, 2017 and 2016, our debt had an estimated fair value of $71.7 billion and $66.3 billion, respectively. The estimated fair value of our publicly traded debt was primarily based on Level 1 inputs that use quoted market values for the debt. The estimated fair value of debt for which there are no quoted market prices was based on Level 2 inputs that use interest rates available to us for debt with similar terms and remaining maturities. See Note 19 for additional information on our cross-guarantee structure.

Debt Maturities December 31 (in millions)	
2018	$ 5,127
2019	2,367
2020	3,688
2021	3,884
2022	5,879
Thereafter	45,554

REQUIRED

a. Comcast provided cash flow information revealing that the company paid interest equal to $2,820 million in 2017. Explain why this amount is different from the amount of interest expense reported in its 2017 income statement.

b. Comcast reports its debt using historical cost. What would be the impact on the financial statements if the company elected to report all of its debt at fair value? (Assume no changes to fair values due to changes in instrument-specific credit risk.) Be specific.

c. The financial ratios specified in Comcast's loan agreements include the solvency measures described in this chapter. Calculate Comcast's debt-to-equity ratio and times interest earned for 2017. Explain why creditors might include these ratios in the restrictive covenants of loan agreements.

d. Violation of debt covenants can be a serious event that can impose substantial costs on a company. What actions might management take to avoid violating debt covenants if the company's ratios are near the covenant limits?

e. Explain what type of dislosures are likely present in Note 16—"Commitment and Contingencies," which is repressented as a line item on the balance sheet with no amounts.

LO3, 4, 5 **C9-61. Assessing Debt Financing, Company Interests, and Managerial Ethics**

Foster Corporation is in the third quarter of the current year, and projections are that net income will be down about $600,000 from the previous year. Foster's return on assets is also projected to decline from its usual 15% to approximately 13%. If earnings do decline, this year will be the second consecutive year of decline. Foster's president is quite concerned about these projections (and his job) and has called a meeting of the firm's officers for next week to consider ways to "turn things around—and fast."

Margot Barth, treasurer of Foster Corporation, has received a memorandum from her assistant, Lorie McNichols. Barth had asked McNichols if she had any suggestions as to how Foster might improve its earnings performance for the current year. McNichols' memo reads as follows:

> As you know, we have $3,000,000 of 4%, 20-year bonds payable outstanding. We issued these bonds 10 years ago at face value, so they have 10 years left to maturity. When they mature, we would probably replace them with other bonds. The economy is expecting a period of greater inflation, and interest rates have increased to about 8%. My proposal is to replace these bonds right now. More specifically, I propose:
>
> 1. Immediately issue $3,000,000 of 20-year, 8% bonds payable. These bonds will be issued at face value.
> 2. Use the proceeds from the new bonds to buy back and retire our outstanding 4% bonds. Because of the current high rates of interest, these bonds are trading in the market at about $2,200,000.
> 3. The benefits to Foster are that (a) the retirement of the old bonds will generate an $800,000 gain for the income statement and (b) there will be an extra $800,000 of cash available for other uses.

Barth is intrigued by the possibility of generating an $800,000 gain for the income statement. However, she is not sure this proposal is in the best long-run interests of the firm and its stockholders.

REQUIRED

a. How is the $800,000 gain calculated from the retirement of the old bonds? Where would this gain be reported in Foster's income statement?

b. Why might this proposal not be in the best long-run interests of the firm and its stockholders?

c. What possible ethical conflict is present in this proposal?

SOLUTIONS TO REVIEW PROBLEMS

Mid-Chapter Review 1

SOLUTION

a. The discount would be $580 ($29,000 × 0.02). Thus, Waymire would pay $28,420 ($29,000 – $580).

b. The cost of the lost discount is $29 per day ($580/20) or $10,585 per year (simple interest). The implicit financing cost of the lost discount is 37.24% ($10,585/$28,420).

Mid-Chapter Review 2

SOLUTION

Toro Company incurred $45,662 thousand in warranty claims in 2018 ($000):

$74,155 + $47,721 – warranty claims = $76,214. Warranty claims = $45,662.

This cost would be recorded as follows:

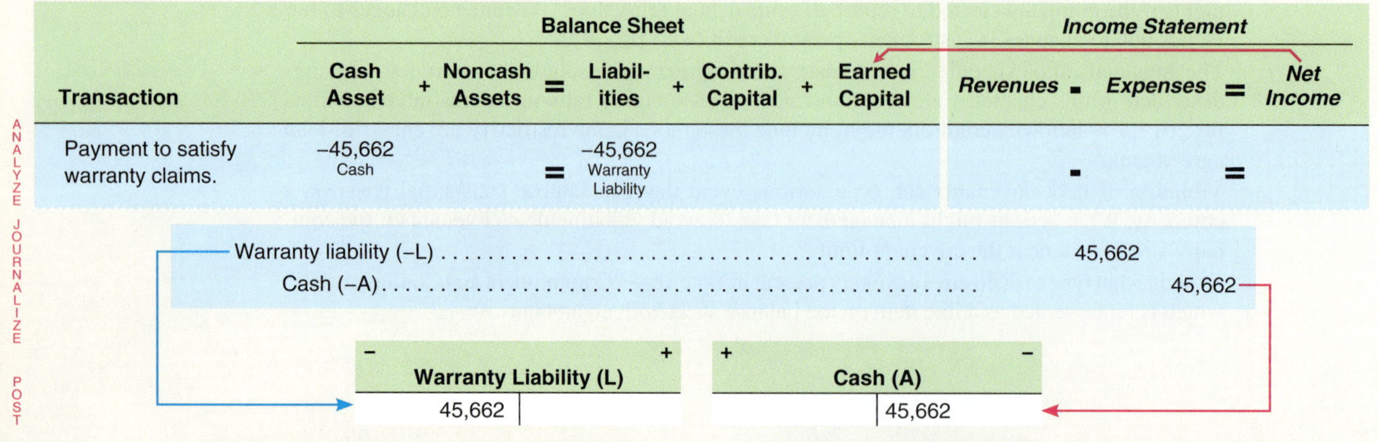

Transaction	Cash Asset	+ Noncash Assets	= Liabilities	+ Contrib. Capital	+ Earned Capital	Revenues	– Expenses	= Net Income
Payment to satisfy warranty claims.	–45,662 Cash		= –45,662 Warranty Liability				–	=

	Dr.	Cr.
Warranty liability (–L)	45,662	
Cash (–A)		45,662

Warranty Liability (L) (– / +): debit 45,662

Cash (A) (+ / –): credit 45,662

The credit entry to cash assumes that cash was paid to satisfy the warranty claims. Toro could also have credited wages payable, or parts inventory as needed.

Mid-Chapter Review 3

SOLUTION

The related journal entry to recognize the accrual of interest is:

ANALYZE

Transaction	Cash Asset	+	Noncash Assets	=	Liabil-ities	+	Contrib. Capital	+	Earned Capital	Revenues	−	Expenses	=	Net Income
Accrued $26 of interest as of January 31*.				=	+26 Interest Payable				−26 Retained Earnings		−	+26 Interest Expense	=	−26

JOURNALIZE

Interest expense (+E, −SE)	26	
Interest payable (+L)		26

POST

+ Interest Expense (E) −	− Interest Payable (L) +
26	26

*Accrued interest for a 16-day period at January 31 = $10,000 × 0.06 × 16/365 = $26.

Chapter-End Review

SOLUTION

1. Issue price for $300,000, 15-year, 10% semiannual bonds discounted at 8%:

Present value of principal payment ($300,000 × 0.30832)	$ 92,496
Present value of semiannual interest payments ($15,000 × 17.29203)	259,380
Issue price of bonds	$351,876

2.

ANALYZE

Transaction	Cash Asset	+	Noncash Assets	=	Liabil-ities	+	Contrib. Capital	+	Earned Capital	Revenues	−	Expenses	=	Net Income
(a) Jan. 1 Issuance.	+351,876 Cash			=	+300,000 Bonds Payable +51,876 Bonds Premium						−		=	

JOURNALIZE

(a) Jan. 1	Cash (+A)	351,876	
	Bonds premium (+L)		51,876
	Bonds payable (+L)		300,000

POST

+ Cash (A) −	− Bonds Premium (L) +	− Bonds Payable (L) +
Jan. 1 351,876	51,876 Jan. 1	300,000 Jan.1

continued

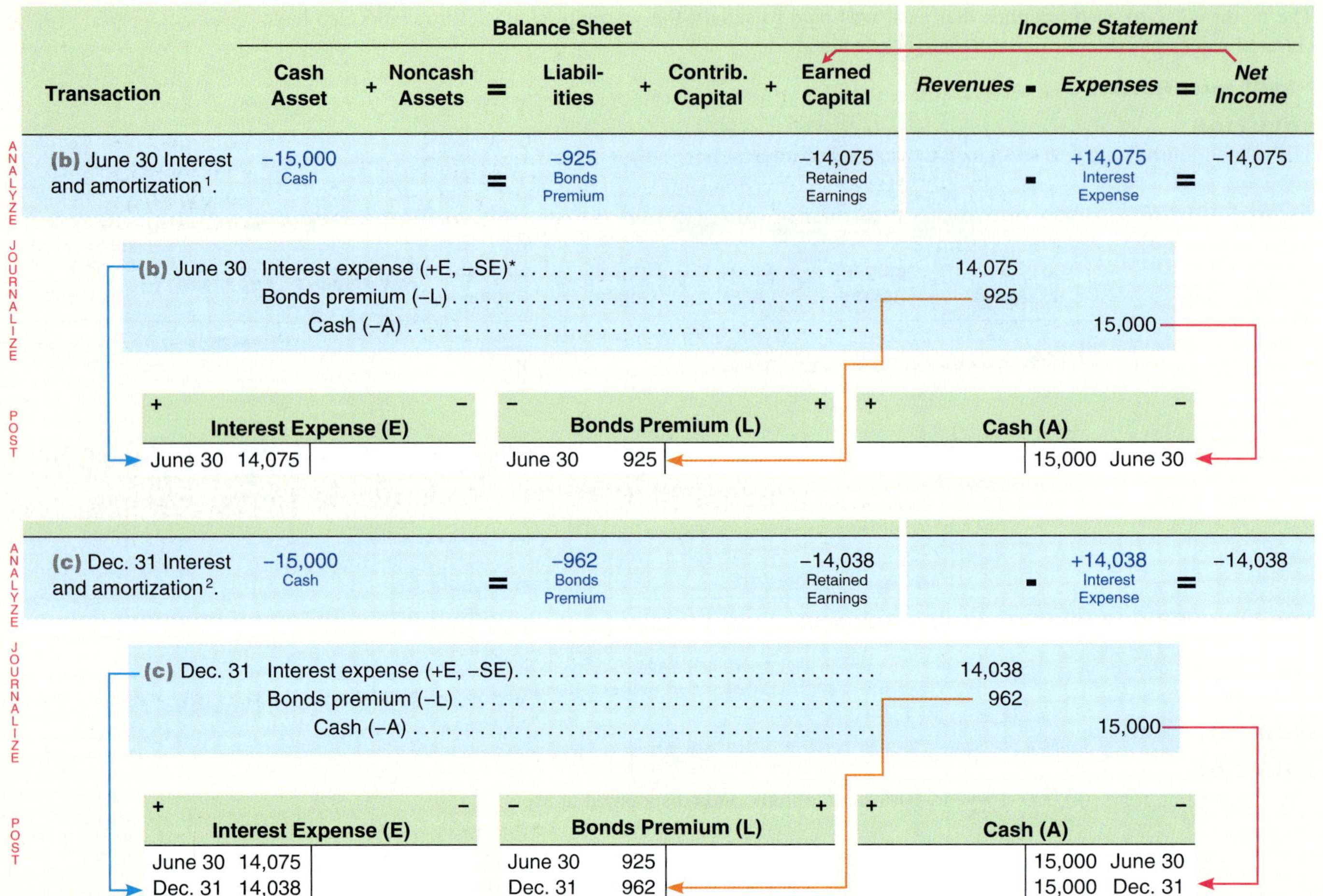

[1] $300,000 × 0.10 × 6/12 = $15,000 cash payment; 0.04 × $351,876 = $14,075 interest expense; the difference is the bond premium amortization, a reduction of the net bond carrying amount.

[2] 0.04 × ($351,876 − $925) = $14,038 interest expense. The difference between this amount and the $15,000 cash payment is the premium amortization, a reduction of the net bond carrying amount.

Reporting and Analyzing Leases, Pensions, Income Taxes, and Commitments and Contingencies

LEARNING OBJECTIVES

1. Define off-balance-sheet financing and explain its effects on financial analysis. (p. 464)
2. Account for leases using the operating lease method and the finance lease method. Compare and analyze the two methods. (p. 465)
3. Explain and interpret the reporting for pension plans. (p. 477)
4. Analyze and interpret pension footnote disclosures. (p. 480)
5. Describe and interpret accounting for income taxes. (p. 486)
6. Describe disclosures regarding future commitments and contingencies. Analyze financial statements after converting off-balance-sheet items to be considered on balance sheet. (p. 498)

DELTA AIR LINES
www.delta.com

Delta Air Lines confronts competing demands for its available cash flow as a result of a heavy debt load that includes borrowed money, aircraft leases, and pension and other post-employment obligations. The magnitude of obligations arising from aircraft leases often surprises those outside the industry. Many airlines historically have not owned all the planes that they fly. The airlines often lease a significant portion of their planes from commercial leasing companies rather than own the planes themselves.

Historically, in many cases, neither the leased planes (the assets) nor the lease obligations (the liabilities) would be on Delta's balance sheet. However, the accounting standards recently changed to reflect these assets and liabilities on companies' balance sheets. Thus, while many lease oblgations were previously "off-balance sheet," starting in 2019 (for most companies) the amounts are on the balance sheet. We explain this change in accounting standards and evaluate the effects of the change in this chapter.

Pensions and deferred income taxes are major liabilities (and/or assets) reported in many firms' financial statements, including Delta Air Lines. The U.S. enacted substantial tax reform in 2017. In this chapter we discuss and illustrate how this changed the reporting of income tax expense and the related tax assets and liabilities.

In summary, we will explore the reporting of leases, pensions, income taxes, and commitments and contingencies, along with the various assumptions that underlie the reported figures. We also examine the impact that these items have on reported earnings and cash flows, and how they affect the company's financial position and performance. Understanding this information is essential if we are to assess the future potential of Delta Air Lines and other companies.

CHAPTER ORGANIZATION

Reporting and Analyzing Leases, Pensions, and Income Taxes

Leases	Pensions	Income Taxes
• Lessee Reporting of Operating and Finance Leases • Footnote Disclosures • Analyzing Financial Statements Including the Comparability of Financial Statements	• Reporting of Defined Benefit Pension Plans • Footnote Disclosures • Other Postretirement Benefits	• Reporting Tax Expense • Book-Tax Differences • Footnote Disclosures • Computation and Analysis

1

LO1 Define off-balance-sheet financing and explain its effects on financial analysis.

INTRODUCTION

Investors, creditors, and other users of financial statements assess the composition of a company's balance sheet and its relation to the income statement. Chapter 6 introduced the concept of earnings quality to refer to the extent to which reported income reflects the underlying economic performance of a company. Similarly, the quality of the balance sheet refers to the extent to which the assets and liabilities of a company are reported in a manner that accurately reflects its economic resources and obligations. For example, in previous chapters, we highlighted the reporting of LIFO inventories and noncapitalized intangible assets to illustrate how some assets can be undervalued or even excluded from the balance sheet.

Financial managers are keenly aware of the importance that financial markets place on the quality of balance sheets. This importance creates pressure on companies to *window dress* their financial statements in order to report their financial condition and performance in the best possible light. One means of improving the perceived financial condition of the company is by keeping debt off the balance sheet. **Off-balance-sheet financing** refers to financial obligations of a company that are not reported as liabilities in the balance sheet.

Off-balance-sheet financing reduces the amount of debt reported on the balance sheet, thereby lowering the company's financial leverage ratios. Additionally, many off-balance-sheet financing techniques (e.g., contract manufacturing) remove assets from the balance sheet, along with the liabilities, without reducing revenues or markedly affecting net income. Such techniques cause operation ratios, such as return on assets (ROA), to appear stronger than they are. Interestingly, the accounting standards have moved many of the "off-balance-sheet" items onto the balance sheet (e.g., parts of pensions, special-purpose entities, and now operating leases). However, there are still some off-balance-sheet items such as contractual obligations that do not meet the FASB definition of a liability. One example is the set of endorsement contract obligations a company such as Nike has when it endorses high-profile athletes. We discuss these in this chapter as well as an analytical procedure for external financial statement users to employ to estimate "as if" balance sheets that include estimates of the off-balance-sheet items.

The first part of this chapter focuses on three common financial obligations (along with any related assets) that companies report in their financial statements—leases, pensions, and income taxes. We also discuss other commitments and contingencies at the end of the chapter.

Delta Air Lines' (abbreviated) balance sheet is presented in **Exhibit 10.1**. The amounts reported on Delta's balance sheet related to leases, pensions, taxes, and commitments and contingencies are highlighted. Delta reports a deferred asset related to income taxes; we discuss what this means later in the chapter.

EXHIBIT 10.1 Delta Air Lines Balance Sheets (excerpts)

DELTA AIR LINES, INC.
Consolidated Balance Sheets (excerpts)

(in millions, except share data)	December 31, 2018	2017
ASSETS		
Current Assets:		
Total current assets	$ 6,340	$ 7,804
Noncurrent Assets:		
Property and equipment, net	28,335	26,563
Operating lease right-of-use assets	5,994	—
Goodwill	9,781	9,794
Identifiable intangibles, net	4,830	4,847
Cash restricted for airport construction	1,136	—
Deferred income taxes, net	242	1,354
Other noncurrent assets	3,608	3,309
Total noncurrent assets	53,926	45,867
Total assets	$60,266	$53,671
LIABILITIES AND STOCKHOLDERS' EQUITY		
Current Liabilities:		
Current maturities of long-term debt and finance leases	$ 1,518	$ 2,242
Current maturities of operating leases	955	—
Air traffic liability	4,661	4,364
Accounts payable	2,976	3,634
Accrued salaries and related benefits	3,287	3,022
Loyalty program deferred revenue	2,989	2,762
Fuel card obligation	1,075	1,067
Other accrued liabilities	1,117	1,868
Total current liabilities	18,578	18,959
Noncurrent Liabilities:		
Long-term debt and finance leases	8,253	6,592
Pension, postretirement and related benefits	9,163	9,810
Loyalty program deferred revenue	3,652	3,559
Noncurrent operating leases	5,801	—
Other noncurrent liabilities	1,132	2,221
Total noncurrent liabilities	28,001	22,182
Commitments and Contingencies		
Stockholders' Equity:		
Total stockholders' equity	13,687	12,530
Total liabilities and stockholders' equity	$60,266	$53,671

LEASES

LO2 Account for leases using the operating lease method and the finance lease method. Compare and analyze the two methods.

A lease is a contract between the owner of an asset (the **lessor**) and the party desiring to use that asset (the **lessee**). Because this is a private contract between two willing parties, it is governed only by applicable commercial law, and can include whatever provisions are negotiated between the parties. The lessor and lessee can be any legal form of organization, including private individuals, corporations, partnerships, and joint ventures.

2

Leases generally contain the following terms:

- The lessor allows the lessee the unrestricted right to use the asset during the lease term.
- The lessee agrees to make periodic payments to the lessor and to maintain the asset.
- The legal title to the asset remains with the lessor. At the end of the lease, either the lessor takes physical possession of the asset, or the lessee purchases the asset from the lessor at a price specified in the lease contract.

From the lessor's standpoint, lease payments are set at an amount that yields an acceptable return on investment, commensurate with the credit standing of the lessee. The lessor, thus, obtains a quality investment, and the lessee gains use of the asset.

From the lessee's perspective, the lease serves as a financing vehicle, similar to an intermediate-term secured bank loan. However, there are several advantages to leasing over bank financing:

- Leases often require less equity investment than bank financing. That is, banks often only lend a portion of the asset's cost and require the borrower to make up the difference from its available cash.
- Leases often require payments to be made at the beginning of the period (e.g., the first of the month). However, because leases are contracts between two parties, their terms can be structured in any way to meet their respective needs. For example, a lease can allow variable payments to match seasonal cash inflows of the lessee, or have graduated payments for companies in their start-up phase.
- If the lessee requires the use of the asset for only a part of its useful life, leasing avoids the need to sell a used asset.
- Because the lessor retains ownership of the asset, leases provide the lessor with tax benefits such as accelerated depreciation deductions. This fact can lead to lower payments for lessees.

Lessee Reporting of Leases

FASB's new Topic 842, *Leases* (hereafter, the new lease standard) is effective for fiscal years and interim periods beginning after December 15, 2018. The new standard requires lessees to recognize a **right-of-use asset** and a lease liability for all leases (with the exception of short-term leases) at the commencement date and recognize expenses on their income statements related to the leases. This is a substantial change from prior accounting where leases classified as operating leases under the prior accounting standards were "off-balance" sheet—meaning there was no lease asset or lease liability on the balance sheet. Many leases were structured to achieve operating lease classification and, thus, off-balance-sheet financing.

Estimates by the International Accounting Standards Board were that, worldwide, public firms had more than $3 trillion in off-balance-sheet leases before the new standards took effect.[1] Just a quick look at Delta's balance sheet in **Exhibit 10.1** indicates that capitalized operating lease assets are 11% of assets (excluding operating lease assets) and the operating lease liabilities are roughly 17% of liabilities (excluding operating lease liabilities). The new accounting standard will significantly change the balance sheets of lessees.

There are two classifications of leases for lessees: operating leases and finance leases. The main distinction between the categories is that some leases are considered equivalent to a sale/purchase (finance lease), whereas others are not (operating lease). The new standard requires lessees to record a right-of-use asset and lease liability for *all* leases (with an exception for leases of less than 12 months). However, the income statement treatment is not the same across the two classifications of leases under U.S. GAAP; we discuss the differences below. There are different lease classifications for the lessor. In this text, we focus primarily on the accounting from the lessee's perspective.[2]

[1] IFRS Fact Sheet—IFRS 16 Leases

[2] There are classifications of leases for lessors as well: sales-type leases, direct financing leases, and operating leases. The accounting for leases for lessors is essentially unchanged.

An overall summary of lease classification and accounting treatment for lessees is as follows:

Lessee			
	Finance Lease		
Classification Rule	**Accounting**		
	Balance Sheet	**Income Statement**	**Cash Flows**
Meets at least one of the five lease classification criteria.	Recognize a right-of-use asset and test for impairment. Recognize a lease liability.	Recognize amortization expense on the right-of-use asset (typically straight line over lease term or useful life). Recognize interest expense on the lease liability using the effective interest method.	Interest is operating cash flow; principal is financing.
	Operating Lease		
Classification Rule	**Accounting**		
	Balance Sheet	**Income Statement**	**Cash Flows**
Meets none of the five lease classification criteria.	Recognize a right-of-use asset and test for impairment. Recognize a lease liability.	Recognize lease expense on a straight-line basis as a single line item.	Lease payment is operating cash flow.

Note that finance leases require a recording of interest expense and amortization, conceptually consistent with how capital leases were accounted for under legacy lease standards. The operating leases are expensed on a straight-line basis (rather than high interest costs early in the term of the lease), which is consistent with how operating leases were accounted for under legacy lease standards. Thus, the significant change is on the balance sheet with the capitalization of the asset and the recording of the liability for operating leases.

The new lease accounting standard is aligned in concept with the new revenue recognition standard that we discussed in Chapter 6. Specifically, the parties need to identify the contract and the consideration. Whether a lease exists is to be determined on the date the contract is signed or authorized (the inception of the lease). The company must determine if the contract is a lease or includes a lease. Next, the consideration for the lease must be determined. Lease payments can consist of five amounts: fixed payments, variable payments, a purchase option, a lease termination penalty, and residual value guarantee. Lease payments are critical because these are the basis for determining the classification of the lease and the amount of the lease liability.

Classification Rules The classification rules are intended to classify leases based on the extent of control of the asset that is passed to the lessee in the contract. If control has passed (the lease meets one of the criteria), the lease is a finance lease. The lease is to be classified (and measurement of the right-of-use asset and lease liability measured) on the lease commencement date (when the asset is available for use). FASB uses five criteria to classify leases; if a lease meets *at least one* of the criteria, it is classified as a finance lease (lessee) and a sales-type lease (lessor).[3] The five criteria, briefly, are as follows:

1. *Ownership transfer*: the lease transfers ownership of the underlying asset to the lessee by the end of the lease term.
2. *Purchase option*: the lease grants the lessee an option to purchase the underlying asset that the lessee is reasonably expected to exercise.
3. *Lease term length*: the lease term is for the major part of the remaining economic life of the underlying asset.
4. *Present value of lease payments*: the present value of the lease payments (and any residual value guaranteed by the lessee that is not already reflected in the lease payments) equals or exceeds substantially all of the fair value of the underlying asset.
5. *Alternative use*: the underlying asset is expected to have no alternative use to the lessor at the end of the lease term.

[3] Though, the lessor and lease make the determination independently.

To illustrate the accounting for the two classifications of leases, we use the following example. Gillette Electronics agrees to lease retail store space in a shopping center. The lease is a 5-year lease with annual payments of $10,000 due at each year-end. (Many leases require payments up front; we generally use end-of-year annual payments in this textbook for simplicity.) Using a 7% interest rate, the present value of the five annual future lease payments equals $41,002, computed as $10,000 × 4.10020 (Appendix A, Table A.3). Using a calculator, the present value of the annual lease payments is computed as follows:[4]

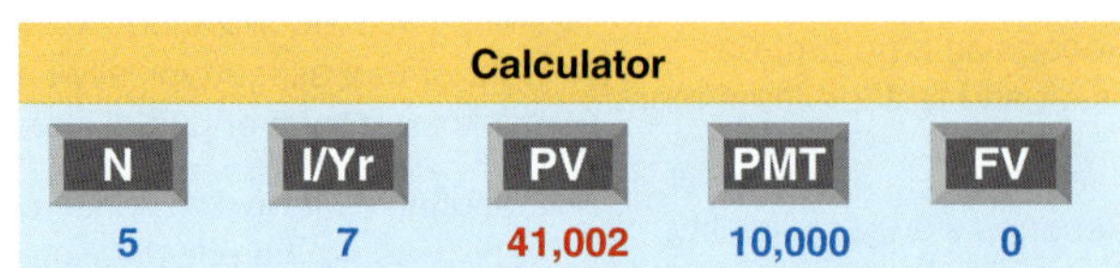

Finance Lease When the lease is a finance lease, the lessee records a lease liability equal to the present value of the remaining lease payments discounted using the rate implicit in the lease (or if that rate is not available, the lessee's incremental borrowing rate). The lease is recorded on the lease commencement date. In our example, the liability is recorded for $41,002 as follows:

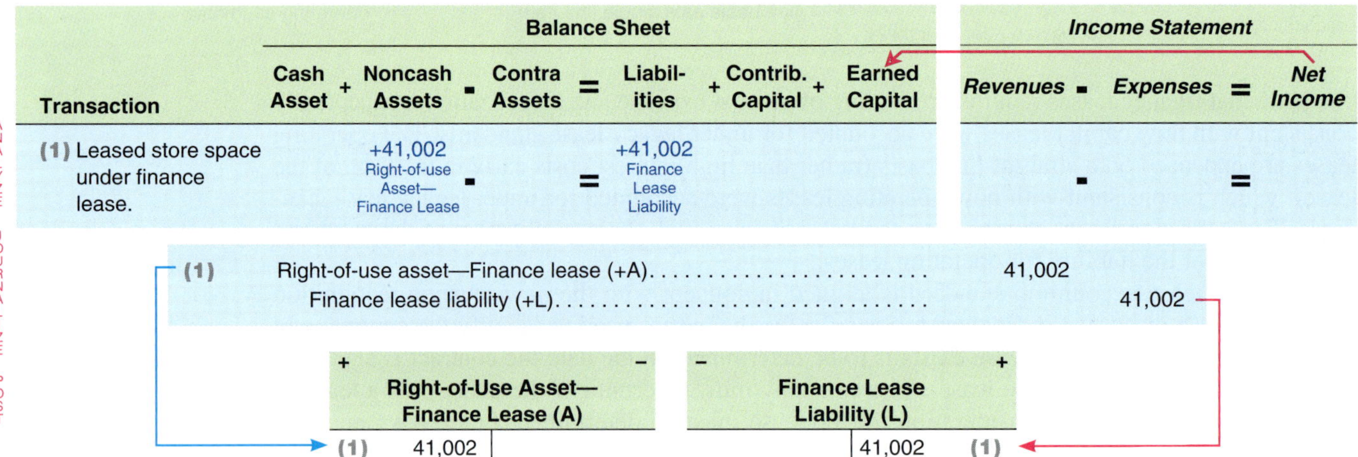

The asset is reported among long-term (PPE) assets in the balance sheet and the liability is reported both in current and long-term debt.

At the end of the first year, two entries are required, one to account for the asset and the other to account for the lease payment. The right-of-use asset must be amortized, similar to how purchased long-term assets must be depreciated. The entry to amortize Gillette's leased asset (assuming straight-line amortization, a useful life of 5 years, and zero residual value [$41,002/5 = $8,200]) is:[5]

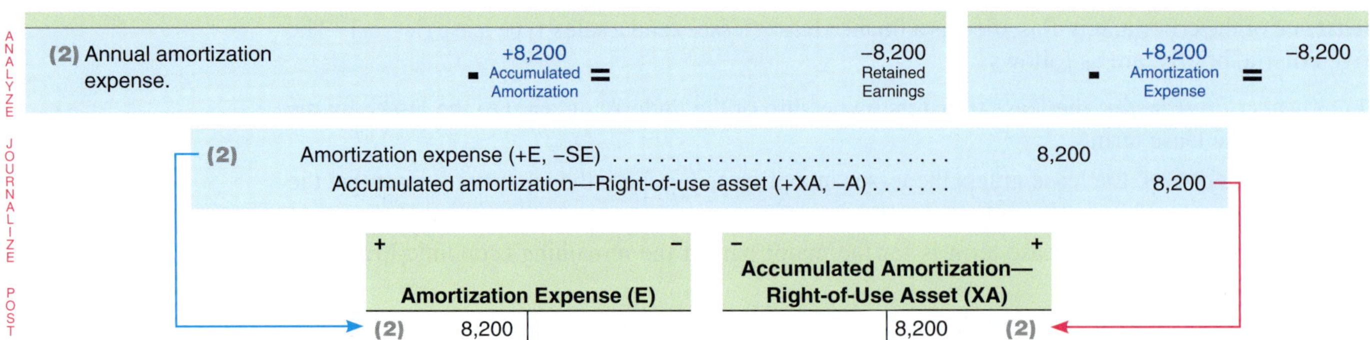

[4] The result produced by the financial calculator is actually −41,002. The present value will always have the opposite sign from the payment. So, if the payment is positive, the present value will be negative. **Appendix A** illustrates the use of a financial calculator to compute present values. In this calculation, it is important to set the payments per year (period) to 1 and make sure that the payments are set to occur at the end of each period.

[5] Companies can choose whether to create an accumulated amortization account (contra-asset) or to simply reduce (credit) the right-of-use asset directly.

The financial statement effects and related entry to record the annual lease payment are:

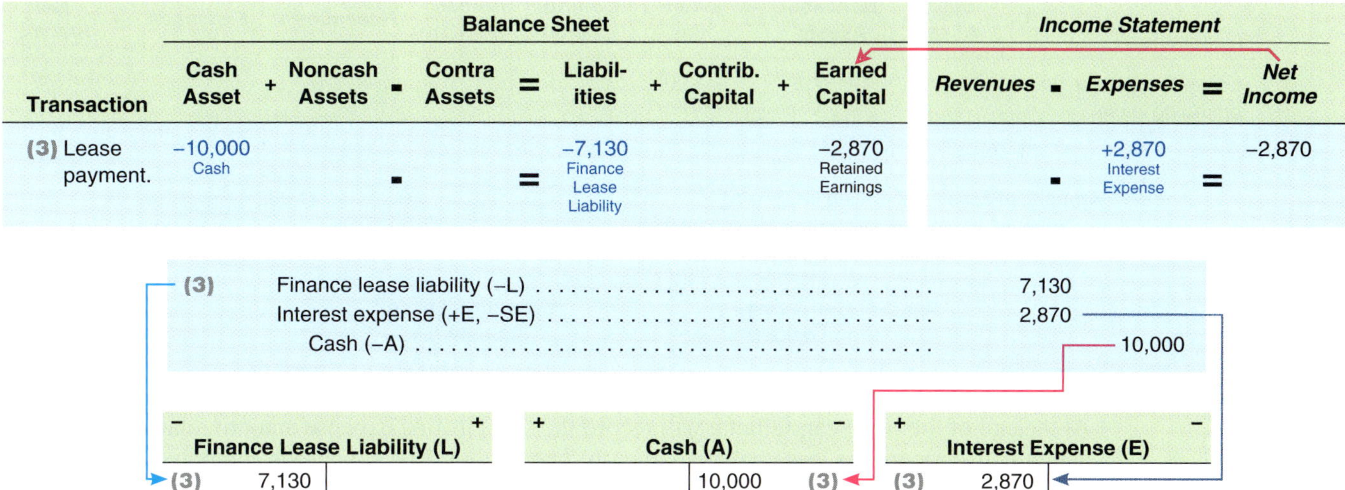

The $10,000 cash payment is split between interest expense and principal repayment. The $2,870 interest expense is computed by multiplying the unpaid balance in the lease liability by the interest rate ($41,002 × 7%). The $7,130 debit to lease liability (principal repayment) is the difference between the lease payment and interest expense ($10,000 − $2,870). The year-end balance in the lease liability account is $33,872, calculated as ($41,002 − $7,130).

Exhibit 10.2 presents the amortization table for Gillette's lease liability under the finance lease method. The amortization of finance leases is identical to the amortization of installment loans introduced in Chapter 9.

EXHIBIT 10.2 Amortization Table for a Finance Lease Liability

A	B	C	D	E	F
Year	Beginning-Year Lease Liability	Interest Expense (B × 7%)	Payment	Principal Repayment (D − C)	Ending-Year Lease Liability (B − E)
1	$41,002	$2,870	$10,000	$7,130	$33,872
2	33,872	2,371	10,000	7,629	26,243
3	26,243	1,837	10,000	8,163	18,080
4	18,080	1,266	10,000	8,734	9,346
5	9,346	654	10,000	9,346	0

Operating Lease When the lease is an operating lease, the initial measurement of the right-of-use asset and liability is measured at the same time and in the same manner as we just discussed for finance leases. Gillette will need to prepare an amortization schedule as shown in **Exhibit 10.2** for the operating lease liability. Even though control has not passed to the lessee, the lessee still has a right-of-use asset and an obligation to make lease payments. The difference in accounting occurs subsequent to the initial measurement. Unlike a finance lease, for operating leases an equal amount of expense is recorded each period on the income statement, using the straight-line method for expense recognition.

To illustrate, let's assume the Gillette Electronics lease from our example above is classified as an operating lease. Again, initial measurement is the same as above and the initial entry is as follows:

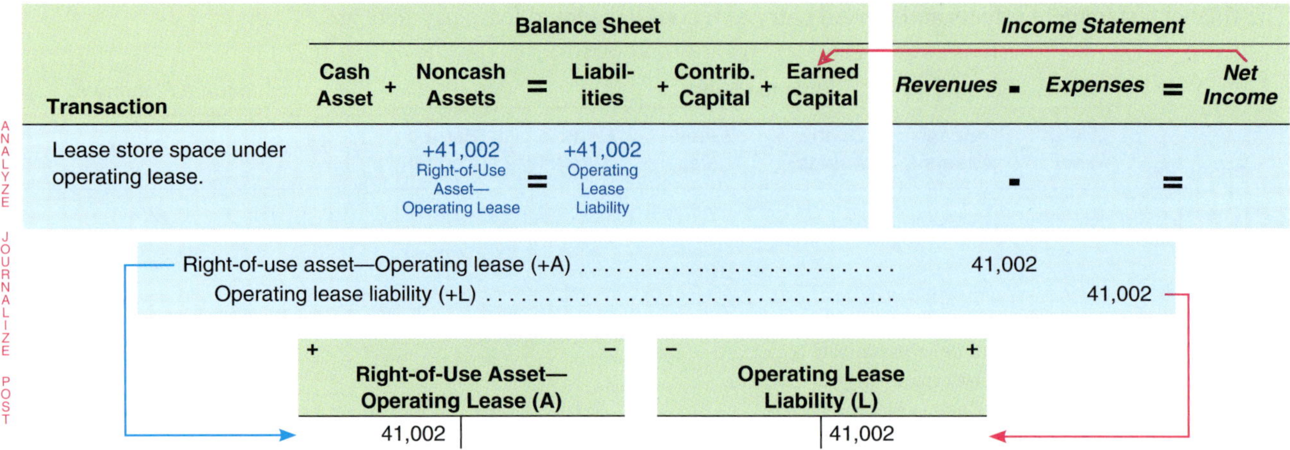

At the end of the first year, Gillette will record the straight-line expense amount related to the lease and will also record the lease payment in cash. The straight-line expense is computed by taking the total cost of the lease divided by the total number of lease payments. The total cost of the lease in our example is straightforward because this is a simple lease.[6] The total cost of the lease is \$50,000 and if we divide by the 5-year term, we obtain \$10,000 as the annual straight-line expense amount. As stated above, Gillette still needs to prepare the amortization schedule for the liability. Though no interest expense line item is recorded for the operating lease liability, Gillette needs to compute the "interest" on the lease liability. Gillette also needs to compute the amortization of the right-of-use asset. The amortization is computed as the straight-line expense amount less the computed "interest" amount (though again no actual amortization expense line item is recorded). The entries to record the payment of the lease payment as well as the recording of the straight-line expense are as follows:

Recording of the lease payment:

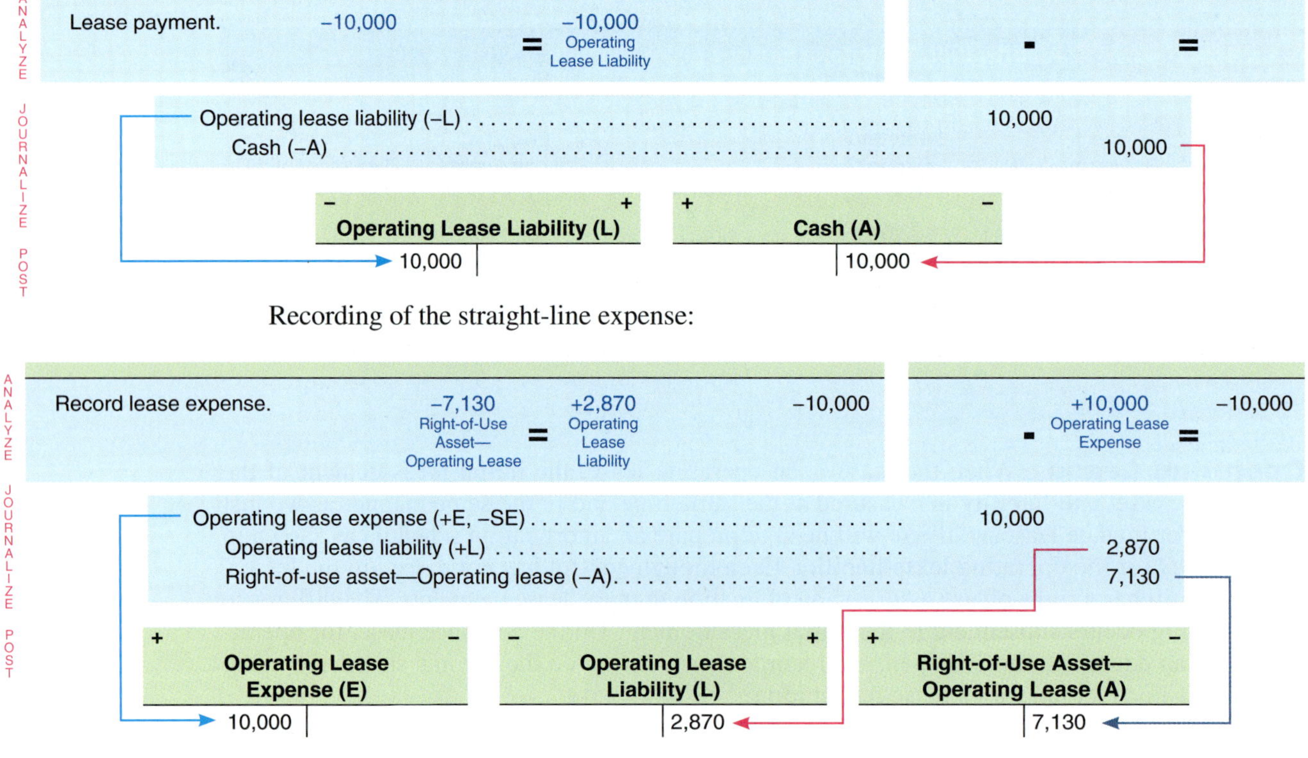

[6] For example the lease could include prepayments, escalation provisions, other required or optional payments, lessee initial direct costs, lease incentives, or other items. In more complicated leases such as these, the amortization of the operating lease asset in subsequent entries can only be computed as a "plug" number equal to the straight-line expense amount less the "interest" expense for the reporting period. In other words, at commencement of the lease, the right-of-use asset value will not always equal the liability value when the lease terms are more complicated. In such cases, the "amortization" of the right-of-use asset will not equal the principal reduction of the liability.

This will continue on each year, following the amortization schedule above, to reduce the asset value on the lessee's books to zero and the liability on the lessee's books to zero. In every year of the lease, the same amount of expense will be recorded, in this case, \$10,000.

In year 5 of this lease for Gillette, the entries would be as follows:

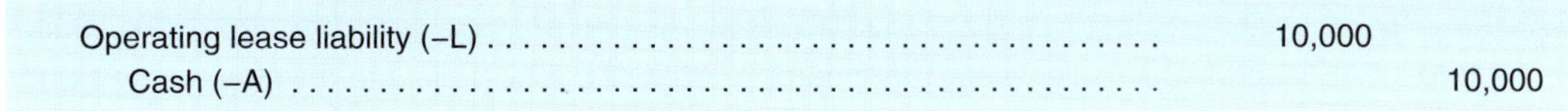

The entry for the straight-line-expense amount is:

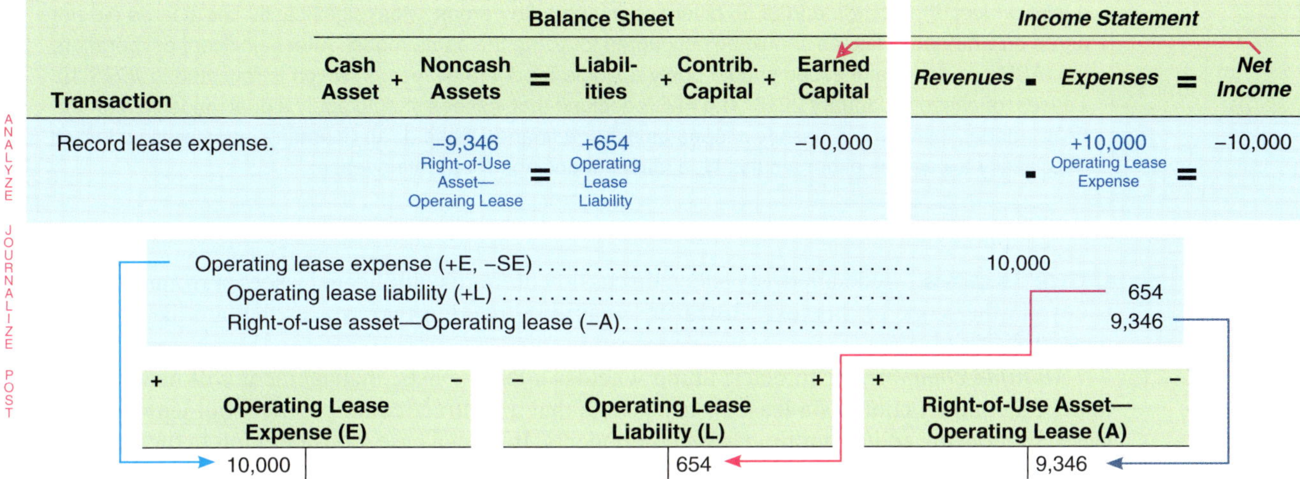

Thus, at the end of the lease term, the liability will be zero (\$41,002 – \$10,000 + \$2,870 – \$10,000 + \$2,371 – \$10,000 + \$1,837 – \$10,000 + 1,266 – \$10,000 + \$654). The asset also will have a zero balance (\$41,002 – \$7,130 – \$7,629 – \$8,163 – \$8,734 – \$9,346).

Comparison of Operating and Finance Lease Treatment The accounting for operating leases might seem odd in some ways to readers. Gillette is required to compute an "interest" cost using the amortization of the liability table to adjust the lease liability account and to compute the "amortization" of the right-of-use asset to adjust the right-of-use asset account. But there is no interest expense or amortization expense ever recorded—only one straight-line Lease Expense. The goal (in the end, anyway) of the standard was to achieve (retain) straight-line expensing for these leases: the related expenses are not greater in the earlier part of the lease as they are with finance lease treatment. For example, even in our simple lease illustration above, the total expense in the first year for Gillette if the lease was a finance lease was \$11,070 (amortization of the right-of-use asset is \$8,200 and interest expense is \$2,870). However, with the operating lease classification, the first year expense amount is \$10,000. Note also that the balance of the asset on the balance sheet differs—the balance of the asset declines faster for the finance lease than the operating lease (i.e., amortization is faster for the finance lease). A full comparison is below:

EXHIBIT 10.3 Comparison of Expenses and Right-of-Use Asset Balance

	Finance Lease Method				Operating Lease Method	
Year	Interest Expense	Amortization Expense	Total Expense	Right-of-Use Asset Balance End of Year	Lease Expense	Right-of-Use Asset Balance End of Year
1	\$2,870	\$ 8,200	\$11,070	\$32,802	\$10,000	\$33,872
2	2,371	8,200	10,571	24,602	10,000	26,243
3	1,837	8,200	10,037	16,401	10,000	18,080
4	1,266	8,201	9,467	8,200	10,000	9,346
5	654	8,201	8,855	0	10,000	0
Total . . .	\$8,998	\$41,002	\$50,000		\$50,000	

Exhibit 10.3 shows how the finance lease method reports a higher total expense (amortization plus interest) in the early years of the lease and a lower total expense in the later years. Total expense over the 5-year life of the lease is the same under both methods.

A GLOBAL PERSPECTIVE

In 2008, the FASB and IASB (collectively, the "boards") initiated a joint project to develop a new standard to account for leases. Although many of the perceived problems with the previous leasing guidance related to a lessee's accounting for operating leases, the boards thought it beneficial to reflect on lease accounting holistically, and to consider lease accounting while concurrently developing a proposal on revenue recognition (ASC 606, Revenue from Contracts with Customers). Although the project began as a joint project, the boards ended up diverging in some key areas. Most significantly, the boards did not agree on whether all leases should be accounted for using the same model. After significant deliberation, the IASB decided that lessees should apply a single model to all leases, which is reflected in *IFRS 16, Leases*, released in January 2016. The FASB decided that lessees should apply a dual model. Under the FASB model, lessees will classify a lease as either a finance lease or an operating lease, while a lessor will classify a lease as either a sales-type, direct financing, or operating lease.

Other Issues A detailed, expanded discussion of more complicated issues surrounding leases is beyond the scope of this text. However, we briefly mention two aspects that are likely to be of interest.

Multiple components: In determining whether a lease exists, management will need to determine if a contract contains a lease. It is possible that a contract could contain both lease and nonlease components and/or multiple lease components. In such a case, consideration in the contract is allocated to the separate components based on relative standalone selling prices.

As a disclosure example of such issues, the following excerpt is from Delta's 2018 10-K:

> In addition, we have regional aircraft leases that are embedded within our capacity purchase agreements and included in the right-of-use ("ROU") asset and lease liability. We allocated the consideration in each capacity purchase agreement to the lease and nonlease components based on their relative standalone value. Lease components of these agreements consist of 172 aircraft as of December 31, 2018 and nonlease components primarily consist of flight operations, in-flight and maintenance services. We determined our best estimate of the standalone value of the individual components by considering observable information including rates paid by our wholly owned subsidiary, Endeavor Air, Inc., and rates published by independent valuation firms.

Impairment: Lessees need to determine if the leased asset (finance or operating) is impaired. If a lessee records an impairment charge on a right-of-use asset associated with a finance lease, it should revise the amortization expense by calculating a new straight-line amortization based on the revised asset value.

If the lease is an operating lease and the right-of-use asset requires an impairment, once impaired, lease expense will no longer be recognized on a straight-line basis. A lessee should continue to amortize the lease liability using the same effective interest method as before the impairment charge. The right-of-use asset, however, should be subsequently amortized on a straight-line basis.

As can be seen in **Exhibit 10.3** the unamortized value of a right-of-use asset resulting from an operating lease is typically greater than it would have been had the lease been classified as a finance lease. Because of this higher value, a right-of-use asset arising from an operating lease may have a higher risk of impairment.

BUSINESS INSIGHT

A recent *Wall Street Journal* article discusses an interesting consequence of the new accounting lease standard. The new standard requires companies to collect and disclose lease data to a much greater extent than had been the case previously. While this was a large task for many companies, it provided a more detailed look into their lease spending than they had performed before enabling management to implement cost cutting and achieve greater efficiency. The article provides several examples:

> Tyson Foods Inc. spent about three years analyzing and digitizing its leases to get the comprehensive view of the portfolio required under the new rules. As a result, the Springdale, Ark., meat producer expects to reduce roughly $450 million in lease obligations it has for transportation and material handling equipment and real estate. "The improved visibility gives us a lot better management of our overall lease portfolio," said Brian Martfeld, the company's senior director for controls and automation. CVS Health Corp. spent about $2.5 billion on operating leases in 2017, according to a company spokesman. As it wrangled more than 10,000 lease agreements, the Woonsocket, R.I.-based health-care company found some areas it could trim. "We are considering curtailing the leasing of certain low-dollar equipment in the future," a company spokesman said. "Laptop and desktop computers would be two common examples."

Because many of these leases are long term it may take time to realize the savings.

Source: *Wall Street Journal*, January 22, 2019, "CFOs Uncover Surprise Savings as They Implement New Lease-Accounting Rules"

Footnote Disclosures of Leases

Delta has adopted the new lease standard, although few other companies have as of the time of this writing. Thus, until all companies have adopted the new standard, analysts and other financial statement users will have to adjust the financial statement numbers of those that have not adopted the new standard to make meaningful comparisons and to evaluate those companies' off-balance-sheet debt appropriately.

Delta's balance sheet as shown in **Exhibit 10.1** reflects the operating right-of-use assets as well as both current and long-term liabilities for their operating leases. In the notes to their 2018 financial statements Delta discloses the following (excerpted and reordered to some extent):

> We lease property and equipment under finance and operating leases. For leases with terms greater than 12 months, we record the related asset and obligation at the present value of lease payments over the term. Many of our leases include rental escalation clauses, renewal options and/or termination options that are factored into our determination of lease payments when appropriate. We do not separate lease and nonlease components of contracts, except for regional aircraft and information technology ("IT") assets as discussed below. . . . Including aircraft operated by our regional carriers, we lease 376 aircraft, of which 50 are under finance leases and 326 are operating leases. Our aircraft leases generally have long durations with remaining terms of one month to 13 years. Aircraft finance leases continue to be reported on our balance sheet, while operating leases were added to the balance sheet in 2018 with the adoption of the new standard.
>
> When available, we use the rate implicit in the lease to discount lease payments to present value; however, most of our leases do not provide a readily determinable implicit rate. Therefore, we must estimate our incremental borrowing rate to discount the lease payments based on information available at lease commencement.
>
> As of December 31, 2018 we have additional leases that have not yet commenced of $189 million. These leases will commence between 2019 and 2020 with lease terms of 1 year to 17 years.
>
> ***Lease Position as of December 31, 2018***
>
> The table below presents the lease-related assets and liabilities recorded on the balance sheet.

continued

continued from previous page

(in millions)	Classification on the Balance Sheet	December 31, 2018
Assets		
Operating lease assets	Operating lease right-of-use assets	$5,994
Finance lease assets	Property and equipment, net	490
Total lease assets		$6,484
Liabilities		
Current		
Operating	Current maturities of operating leases	$ 955
Finance	Current maturities of long-term debt and finance leases	109
Noncurrent		
Operating	Noncurrent operating leases	5,801
Finance	Long-term debt and finance leases	294
Total lease liabilities		$7,159
Weighted-average remaining lease term		
Operating leases		12 years
Finance leases		7 years
Weighted-average discount rate		
Operating leases[(1)]		3.69%
Finance leases		5.23%

[(1)] Upon adoption of the new lease standard, discount rates used for existing leases were established at January 1, 2018.

Lease Costs

The table below presents certain information related to the lease costs for finance and operating leases during 2018.

(in millions)	Year Ended December 31, 2018
Finance lease cost	
Amortization of leased assets	$ 100
Interest of lease liabilities	22
Operating lease cost	994
Short-term lease cost	458
Variable lease cost	1,427
Total lease cost	$3,001

Other Information

The table below presents supplemental cash flow information related to leases during 2018.

(in millions)	Year Ended December 31, 2018
Cash paid for amounts included in the measurement of lease liabilities	
Operating cash flows for operating leases	$1,271
Operating cash flows for finance leases	22
Financing cash flows for finance leases	108

Analysis of Delta's ratios, such as a return on assets or a debt-to-equity ratio, using reported balance sheet numbers for Delta, will not be straightforward in the year the new lease standard is adopted. Delta adopted the new lease standard in 2018 and Delta used a method of adoption where prior year numbers were not restated. Thus, in 2017 operating leases are not shown as having assets and liabilities on the balance sheet and in 2018 they are. To correctly compare year-over-year numbers, analysts and other financial statement users need to adjust the 2017 financial statements.

Let's look at Delta's balance sheet to illustrate the issue. Delta's total debt-to-equity ratio computed using reported numbers for 2018 is 3.4 or 340% ($46,579/$13,687). The same ratio in 2017 was 3.28 or 328% ($41,141/$12,530).

To make a better comparison, and consistently treat operating leases as liabilities, the analyst needs to adjust the 2017 balance sheet. One way to estimate the "as if" operating-leases-were-capitalized balance sheet for 2017 is to estimate the present value of the lease payments using the disclosures Delta provides in their 2017 10-K.

Operating Leases

(in millions)	Total
2018	$ 1,735
2019	1,589
2020	1,430
2021	1,156
2022	1,036
Thereafter	9,290
Total minimum lease payments	$16,236

An estimate of the "as if" amount can be computed as follows:

1. Estimate a discount rate. One reasonable proxy is the interest rate Delta discloses for 2018, 3.69%.
2. Estimate the future payments and the number of years those payments will be made. One limitation of the above disclosure is the first five years show the annual payment but the remaining payments are lumped in a column "thereafter." An estimate of the number of years for the amount in the "thereafter" column can be computed by dividing the amount ($9,290) by the previous year's payment ($1,036). In this case, this estimate yields almost almost nine years. To estimate using full years, divide the amount in the "thereafter" column by nine and arrive at an estimate of the payment amount for each of the next nine years. In this case, $1,032 million ($9,290/9).
3. Find the present value of the future payments. The present value of the stream of payments listed above, at 3.69% over the 14 years, is roughly $12,791 million. This can be computed using one of several methods, for example, 1) the present value tables in Appendix A to find the present value of each payment or 2) Excel's NPV function.
4. Next the analyst would need to estimate an asset value. In this case, one approximation would be the relative asset-to-liability value in the reported numbers for 2018. Delta added an operating lease asset that is roughly 89% of the lease liability [$5,994/($955 + $5,801)]. Thus, multiply the estimated 2017 liability by 89%, to arrive at an estimate of the "as if" operating lease asset value for 2017. $12,791 million × 89% = $11,384 million.
5. Assume the difference between the asset and liability reduces equity. In this case, a reduction of $1,407 million.

Armed with these estimates we can estimate an "as-if" balance sheet for 2017 that is more comparable to the 2018 balance sheet as reported.

	2017 Reported Values	"As-if" Lease Adjustments	"As-if" 2017 Balance Sheet
Assets	$53,671	$11,384	$65,055
Liabilities	41,141	12,791	53,932
Equity	12,530	(1,407)	11,123

The debt-to-equity ratio using the adjusted balance sheet numbers is 4.85 or 485%. While recognizing that these are estimates, it is fairly clear that in this case while the reported numbers would lead one to believe that the debt-to-equity ratio has increased from 2017 to 2018, it has likely decreased economically based on these estimates. One possible explanation is that Delta took some actions with respect to its leases once the amounts were required to be reported on the balance sheet.

Indeed, the undiscounted cash flows for future operating lease payments reported in 2017 were $16,236 million while in 2018 Delta's disclosures state that the undiscounted future cash flows for operating leases as of the end of 2018 were much lower, at $8,537 million.

Eventually, all presented years for all companies will be governed by the new lease standard. As a result, analysts and other financial statement users will no longer need to perform these adjustments (unless comparing over a number of years that includes some periods before the new standard is in effect).

Leases and the Cash Flow Statement A lease results in an increase to long-term operating assets and an increase in liabilities. However, in many cases, there is no effect on cash flows at the inception of the lease—see entry (1) on page 468. As a consequence, the initial inception of the lease should be reported as a material noncash transaction and not presented in the cash flow statement under either investing or financing cash flows. Subsequently, the amortization of the leased asset for a finance lease is added (in an indirect method cash flow statement) to cash flow from operations (an expense that does not require a cash outlay) and the principal portion of the lease payment is treated as debt repayment under cash flows from financing activities.

YOU MAKE THE CALL

You are the CEO While implementing the new lease accounting standard, your CFO gathers more information on your lease contracts than your company has ever had before. What are some decisions and potential outcomes that this information might lead to? [Answer on page 502]

MID-CHAPTER REVIEW 1

PART A

Assume that The Gap Inc. leased a vacant retail space with the intention of opening another store. The lease calls for annual lease payments of $32,000, due at the end of each of the next ten years. Assume the appropriate discount rate is 7%.

1. If the lease is treated as a finance lease, what journal entry(ies) would Gap make to record the commencement of the lease agreement?
2. How would Gap record amortization expense and the first lease payment at the end of the first year of the lease?
3. If this lease is accounted for as an operating lease, what entry(ies) would be necessary during the first year?

PART B

Following is part of the leasing footnote disclosure from note 12 in The Gap Inc.'s 2018 10-K report (for the year ended February 2, 2019).

> We expect the adoption of ASC 842 will result in the recording of a right-of-use asset and an operating lease liability of approximately $5.8 billion and $6.6 billion, respectively, as of February 3, 2019. . . . We do not expect that the adoption of ASC 842 will result in a material impact to our Consolidated Statements of Cash Flows and we are currently assessing the impact to our Consolidated Statements of Income. The implementation of the new standard will also result in changes to our accounting systems and related internal controls over financial reporting.

1. Describe where and how, if at all, the amounts discussed above will be recognized on Gap's balance sheet after the new lease standard is adopted.
2. Gap states that it cannot yet estimate income statement effects. What effects, for example, on the debt-to-equity ratio, are likely (what should an analyst consider)? For specific numbers, refer to The Gap's Annual Report (or just answer conceptually).

The solution to this review problem can be found on pages 523–526.

PENSIONS

LO3 Explain and interpret the reporting for pension plans.

Companies frequently offer retirement or pension plans as a benefit for their employees. There are two general types of pension plans:

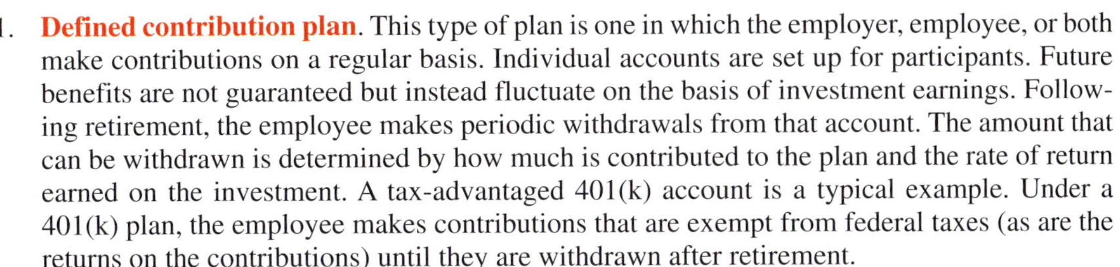

1. **Defined contribution plan**. This type of plan is one in which the employer, employee, or both make contributions on a regular basis. Individual accounts are set up for participants. Future benefits are not guaranteed but instead fluctuate on the basis of investment earnings. Following retirement, the employee makes periodic withdrawals from that account. The amount that can be withdrawn is determined by how much is contributed to the plan and the rate of return earned on the investment. A tax-advantaged 401(k) account is a typical example. Under a 401(k) plan, the employee makes contributions that are exempt from federal taxes (as are the returns on the contributions) until they are withdrawn after retirement.

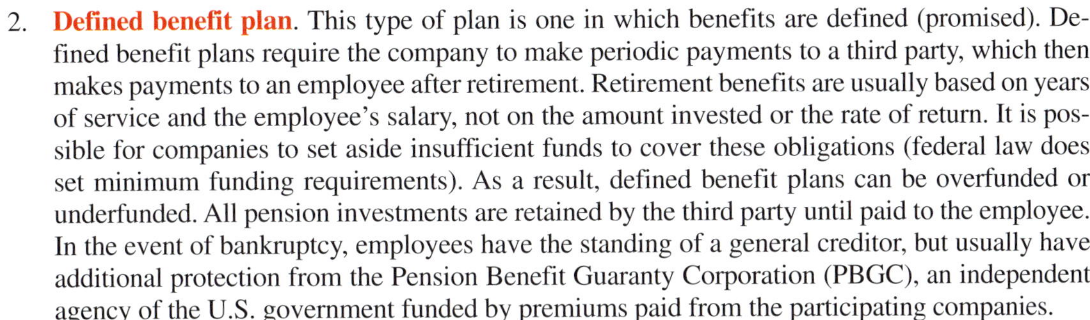

2. **Defined benefit plan**. This type of plan is one in which benefits are defined (promised). Defined benefit plans require the company to make periodic payments to a third party, which then makes payments to an employee after retirement. Retirement benefits are usually based on years of service and the employee's salary, not on the amount invested or the rate of return. It is possible for companies to set aside insufficient funds to cover these obligations (federal law does set minimum funding requirements). As a result, defined benefit plans can be overfunded or underfunded. All pension investments are retained by the third party until paid to the employee. In the event of bankruptcy, employees have the standing of a general creditor, but usually have additional protection from the Pension Benefit Guaranty Corporation (PBGC), an independent agency of the U.S. government funded by premiums paid from the participating companies.

For a defined contribution plan, the company contribution is recorded as an expense in the income statement when the cash is paid or the liability accrued. A defined benefit plan is more complex. Although the company contributes cash or securities to the pension investment account, the pension obligation is not satisfied until the employee receives pension benefits, which may be many years into the future. This section focuses on how a defined benefit plan is reported in the financial statements, and how we assess company performance and financial condition when such a plan exists.

We note that the use of defined benefit plans has declined significantly. Many companies are instead establishing defined contribution plans for employees. For example, as of 2015 IRS data (Form 5500 summary data from the Department of Labor website, so including private companies) reveal that there are 648,000 defined contribution plans covering 97.6 million active employees compared with 45,000 defined benefit plans covering 37.3 million active employees. Many companies, such as Delta, disclose that their defined benefit pension plans are "closed to new entrants and frozen for future benefit accruals." Despite this decline in the use or contribution to defined benefit plans, such plans still constitute a significant liability for many companies.

Balance Sheet Effects of Defined Benefit Pension Plans

Pension plan assets are primarily investments in stocks and bonds (mostly of other companies, but it is not uncommon for companies to invest pension funds in their own stock). Pension liabilities (called the **projected benefit obligation** or **PBO**) are the company's obligations to pay current and former employees. The difference between the fair value of the pension plan assets and the projected benefit obligation is called the **funded status** of the pension plan. If the PBO exceeds the pension plan assets, the pension is **underfunded**. Conversely, if pension plan assets exceed the PBO, the pension plan is **overfunded**. Under current U.S. GAAP, companies are required to record only the funded status on their balance sheets (that is, the *net* amount, not the pension plan assets and PBO separately), either as an asset if the plan is overfunded, or as a liability if it is underfunded.

Pension plan assets consist of stocks and bonds whose value changes each period in three ways. First, the value of the investments increases or decreases as a result of interest, dividends, and gains or losses on the stocks and bonds held. Second, the pension plan assets increase when the company contributes additional cash or stock to the investment account. Third, the pension plan assets decrease by the amount of benefits paid to retirees during the period. These three changes in the pension plan assets are articulated below.

	Pension Plan Assets
	Pension plan assets, beginning balance
+	Actual returns on investments (interest, dividends, gains and losses)
+	Company contributions to pension plan
−	Benefits paid to retirees
=	Pension plan assets, ending balance

The pension liability, or PBO (projected benefit obligation), is computed as the present value of the expected future benefit payments to employees. The future payments depend on the number of years the employee is expected to work (years of service) and the employee's salary level at retirement. Consequently, companies must estimate future wage increases, as well as the number of employees expected to reach retirement age (or the vesting requirement) with the company. In addition, in order to compute the present value of benefit payments, the company has to estimate how long the plan participants are likely to receive pension benefits following retirement (that is, how long the employee—and often surviving spouse—will live). Once the future retiree pool is determined and the expected future payments under the plan are estimated, the expected payments are then discounted to arrive at the present value of the pension obligation. This is the PBO. A reconciliation of the PBO from beginning balance to year-end balance follows.

	Projected Benefit Obligation
	Projected benefit obligation, beginning balance
+	Service cost
+	Interest cost
+/−	Actuarial losses (gains)
−	Benefits paid to retirees
=	Projected benefit obligation, ending balance

As this reconciliation shows, the balance in the PBO changes during the period for four reasons.

- First, as employees continue to work for the company, their pension benefits increase. The annual **service cost** represents the additional (future) pension benefits earned by employees during the current year.
- Second, **interest cost** accrues on the outstanding pension liability, just as it would with any other long-term liability (see the accounting for bond liabilities in Chapter 9). Because there are no scheduled interest payments on the PBO, the interest cost accrues each year; that is, interest is added to the existing liability.
- Third, the PBO can increase (or decrease) due to **actuarial losses (and gains)**, which arise when companies make changes in their pension plans or make *changes in actuarial assumptions* (including assumptions that are used to estimate the PBO, such as the rate of wage inflation, termination and mortality rates, and the discount rate used to compute the present value of future obligations). For example, if a company increases the discount rate used to compute the present value of future pension plan payments from, say, 8% to 9%, the present value of future benefit payments declines (just like bond prices) and the company records a gain. Conversely, if the discount rate is reduced to 7%, the present value of the PBO increases and a loss is recorded. Other assumptions used to estimate the pension liability (such as the expected wage inflation rate or the expected life span of current and former employees) can create similar actuarial losses or gains.
- Fourth, pension benefit payments to retirees reduce the PBO (that portion of the liability is now paid).

Finally, the net pension liability (or asset) that is reported in a company's balance sheet, then, is computed as follows.

Net Pension Asset (or Liability)	
	Pension plan assets (at fair value)
–	Projected benefit obligation (PBO)
	Funded status

If the funded status is positive (assets exceed liabilities), the overfunded pension plan is reported on the balance sheet as an asset, typically called prepaid pension cost. If the funded status is negative (liabilities exceed assets), it is reported as a liability.[7] During the early 2000s, long-term interest rates declined drastically and many companies lowered their discount rate for computing the present value of future pension payments. Lower discount rates meant higher PBO values. This period also witnessed two bear markets—the "dot com crash" in 2000–2001 and the financial crisis of 2008–2010—and pension plan assets declined in value. The combined effect of the increase in PBO and the decrease in asset values caused many pension funds to become severely underfunded. They have not fully recovered. Willis Towers Watson, a compensation consulting firm, analyzed the 389 Fortune 1000 corporations that sponsor a defined benefit plan and found that aggregate funding was 83% of the projected liability. Delta Air Lines reported an underfunded pension obligation of $6.4 billion in 2018. This amount was equal to 10.5 percent of its total assets. (Note that as of the end of 2014 Delta's underfunded obligation was $12.5 billion.) Many companies with a defined benefit plan report that their plans are underfunded. The underfunded liability as a percent of total assets for Delta and several other companies is reported in the graphic below.[8]

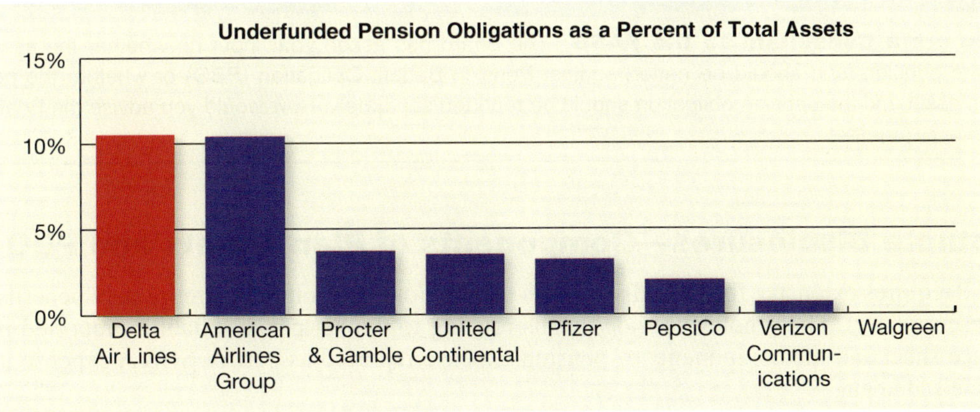

Income Statement Effects of Defined Benefit Pension Plans

In a defined benefit plan, pension expense is not determined by the company's contribution to the pension fund. Instead, net pension expense is computed as follows.

Net Pension Expense	
	Service cost
+	Interest cost
–	*Expected* return on pension plan assets
±	Amortization of deferred amounts
	Net pension expense

The net pension expense is rarely reported separately on the income statement.

[7] Companies that have a defined benefit plan typically maintain many pension plans. Some are overfunded and others are underfunded. Current U.S. GAAP requires companies to group all of the overfunded and underfunded plans together, and to present a net asset for the overfunded plans and a net liability for the underfunded plans.

[8] Southwest Airlines does not offer a defined benefit plan, but does offer a defined contribution plan.

As shown above, the net pension expense has four components. The previous section about the PBO described the first two components: service costs and interest costs. The third component of pension expense relates to the return on pension plan assets, which *reduces* total pension expense. To compute this component, companies use the long-term *expected* rate of return on the pension plan assets, rather than the *actual* return, and multiply that expected rate by the balance in the pension plan assets account. Use of the expected return rather than actual return is an important distinction. Company CEOs and CFOs dislike income variability because they believe that stockholders react negatively to it, so company executives intensely (and successfully) lobbied the FASB to use the more stable expected long-term investment return, rather than the actual return, in computing pension expense. Thus, the pension plan assets' expected return is subtracted to compute net pension expense.

Any difference between the expected and the actual return is accumulated, together with other deferred amounts, off-balance-sheet and reported in the footnotes. Other deferred amounts include changes in PBO resulting from changes in estimates used to compute the PBO and from amendments to the pension plans made by the company. However, if the deferred amounts exceed certain limits, the excess is recognized on-balance-sheet with a corresponding amount recognized as amortization in the income statement.[9] This amortization is the fourth component of pension expense and can be either a positive or negative amount depending on the sign of the difference between expected and actual return on plan assets.

YOU MAKE THE CALL

You are a Consultant to the FASB The Board has asked your input on whether the assets in the pension fund should be netted against Pension Benefit Obligation (PBO) or whether the pension asset and the pension obligation should be reported separately. How would you advise the Board? [Answer on page 502]

4

LO4 Analyze and interpret pension footnote disclosures.

Footnote Disclosures—Components of Plan Assets and PBO

GAAP requires extensive footnote disclosures for pensions (and other postretirement benefits that we discuss later). These notes provide details relating to the net pension liability reported in the balance sheet and the components of pension expense reported as part of SG&A expense in the income statement.

Delta Air Lines indicates in footnote 10 to its 2018 10-K that the funded status of its pension plan is $(6,350) million on December 31, 2018. This means Delta's plan is underfunded. Following are the disclosures Delta makes in its pension footnote.

NOTE 10—EMPLOYEE BENEFIT PLANS

We sponsor defined benefit and defined contribution pension plans, healthcare plans and disability and survivorship plans for eligible employees and retirees and their eligible family members. . . . [our] defined benefit pension plans are closed to new entrants and frozen for future benefit accruals. The Pension Protection Act of 2006 allows commercial airlines to elect alternative funding rules ("Alternative Funding Rules") for defined benefit plans that are frozen. We elected the Alternative Funding Rules under which the unfunded liability for a frozen defined benefit plan may be amortized over a fixed 17-year period and is calculated using an 8.85% discount rate. We have no minimum funding requirements in 2019, but we plan to voluntarily contribute approximately $500 million to these plans.

continued

[9] To avoid amortization, the deferred amounts must be less than 10% of the PBO or pension investments, whichever is less. The excess, if any, is amortized until no further excess remains. When the excess is eliminated (by investment returns or company contributions, for example), the amortization ceases.

continued from previous page

Benefit Obligations, Fair Value of Plan Assets and Funded Status ($ millions):	2018	2017
Benefit obligation at beginning of period	$21,696	$20,859
Service cost	—	—
Interest cost	781	853
Actuarial loss (gain)	(1,560)	1,068
Benefits paid, including lump sums and annuities	(1,093)	(1,075)
Participant contributions	—	—
Settlements	(15)	(9)
Benefit obligation at end of period	$19,809	$21,696
Fair value of plan assets at beginning of period	$14,744	$10,301
Actual gain (loss) on plan assets	(700)	1,966
Employer contributions	523	3,561
Participant contributions	—	—
Benefits paid, including lump sums and annuities	(1,093)	(1,075)
Settlements	(15)	(9)
Fair value of plan assets at end of period	13,459	14,744
Funded status at end of period	$(6,350)	$(6,952)

Delta's PBO began 2018 with a balance of $21,696 million. It increased by the accrual of $781 million in interest cost. During the year, Delta also realized an actuarial gain of $1,560 million, which decreased the pension liability. The PBO decreased as a result of $1,093 million in benefits paid to retirees and $15 million in settlements, leaving a balance of $19,809 million at year-end.

Pension plan assets began the year with a fair value of $14,744 million, which decreased by $700 million from investment returns (losses) and increased by $523 million from company contributions. The company drew down its investments to make pension payments of $1,093 million to retirees, and made $15 million in settlements leaving the pension plan assets with a year-end balance of $13,459 million. The funded status of Delta's pension plan at year-end is $(6,350) million ($19,809 million − $13,459 million). The negative balance indicates that its pension plan is underfunded. The PBO and pension plan assets account cannot be separated into operating and nonoperating components; thus, most analysts treat the entire funded status as an operating item (either asset or liability).

Footnote Disclosures—Components of Pension Expense

Delta Air Lines incurred $660 million of pension expense in 2018. Details of this expense are found in its pension footnote. Delta reported $926 million in pension cost related to defined contribution plans. In addition, Delta reported its expense (benefit) related to its defined benefit plans as follows ($ millions):

	2018	2017
Service cost	$ —	$ —
Interest cost	781	853
Expected return on assets	(1,318)	(1,143)
Recognized net actuarial loss	267	262
Settlements	4	3
Net periodic cost for defined benefit plans	$ (266)	$ (25)

Most analysts have long considered the service cost portion of pension expense to be an operating expense, similar to salaries and other benefits. In contrast, the other components were considered nonoperating. A recent update to the accounting standards (ASU 2017-07) requires companies to report the service cost component in the same line item as compensation. Meanwhile the other components of net (benefit) cost are required to be presented outside of income from operations. We note that Delta states that service cost is recorded in salaries (an operating expense) in the income statement and the other components are in miscellaneous non-operating expense. Because Delta's defined benefit pension plan is closed and further accrual of benefits is frozen, it reported no service cost in 2018 and the entire $(266) million of defined benefit pension benefit would likely be treated as nonoperating for analysis purposes. The costs related to the defined contribution plan are considered operating expenses.

RESEARCH INSIGHT

Valuation of Pension Footnote Disclosures The FASB requires footnote disclosure of the major components of pension cost presumably because it is useful for investors. Pension-related research has examined whether investors assign different valuation multiples to the components of pension cost when assessing company market value. Research finds that the market does, indeed, attach different interpretation to pension components, reflecting differences in information about recurring vs. nonrecurring expenses.

Interest cost is the product of the PBO and the discount rate. This discount rate is set by the company. The expected dollar return on pension assets is the product of the pension plan asset balance and the expected long-run rate of return on the investment portfolio. This rate is also set by the company. Further, the PBO is affected by the expected rate of wage inflation, termination, and mortality rates, all of which are estimated by the company.

U.S. GAAP requires disclosure of several rates used by the company in its estimation of PBO and the related pension expense. Delta Air Lines discloses the following table in its pension footnote:

	2018	2017
Weighted-average assumptions for the years ended December 31		
Discount rate—benefit obligation	4.33%	3.69%
Discount rate—pension cost (benefit)	3.69%	4.14%
Expected long-term rate of return on plan assets	8.97%	8.96%

During 2018, Delta increased its assumed discount rate used to compute the present value of the PBO. Delta decreased the discount rate used to compute the interest cost component of pension benefit. The expected rate of return on plan assets remained nearly constant.

Changes in these assumptions have the following general effects on pension expense and, thus, profitability. This table summarizes the effects of increases in the various rates used to compute the pension cost. Decreases have the exact opposite effects of increases. In the computation of the PBO, the higher the discount, the lower the obligation.

Estimate Change	Probable Effect on Pension Expense	Reason for Effect
Discount rate increase	Increases	If the PBO is discounted at a higher rate, the PBO liability will be smaller. This will increase the actuarial gain which may have to be amortized into pension cost (benefit) over time (along with other items). If the rate used to compute the interest cost increases, then the PBO is multiplied by a higher interest rate, resulting in increased interest cost component of the pension expense. Often, the interest cost effect dominates.
Investment return increase	Decreases	The dollar amount of expected return on plan assets is the product of the plan assets balance and the expected long-term rate of return. Increasing the return increases the expected return on plan assets, thus reducing pension expense.
Wage inflation increase	Increases	The expected rate of wage inflation affects future wage levels that determine expected pension payments. An increase, thus, increases PBO, which increases both the service and interest cost components of pension expense.

In the case of Delta Air Lines, for example, net actuarial gains decreased their end-of-year benefit obligation due to the increase in discount rate used to compute the PBO. In addition, the rate used to compute interest cost decreased. Delta recorded a higher expected return on plan assets (the expected rate was nearly constant but the base must have changed). Delta recorded a similar amount of recognized net actuarial loss (which is really an amortization of a deferred amount) in 2018 compared to 2017. Thus, the net cost in 2018 is lower (really, in this case the net benefit is greater). It is often the case that companies reduce the expected investment returns with a lag, but increase them without a lag, to favorably impact profitability. We must be aware of the impact of these changes in assumptions in our evaluation of company profitability.

BUSINESS INSIGHT

Pension Buyout at GM General Motors' pension obligation was at one time the largest of any company in the world. In 2011, its defined benefit plans were underfunded by $25.4 billion. Because pension fund assets are invested in securities, the underfunded balance can increase if the stock market falls. Analysts argued that the size, risk, and long duration of these obligations depressed GM's credit rating and its stock price.

In an effort to remove some of the projected obligations from its balance sheet, GM offered to buy out the pensions of 42,000 retirees in 2012. The pensions of an additional 76,000 retirees were transferred to Prudential Financial who will make the annuity payments to the retirees. Although the buyout required an immediate cash payment, the move removed approximately $26 billion of pension obligations from GM's 2012 balance sheet, thus improving solvency ratios. In addition, the reduced obligation means that future income statements will reflect lower pension expense due to reduced interest costs. GM's 2018 financial statement shows that the defined benefit pension plans are still underfunded by $11.5 billion. Note that this is a considerable improvement from 2014 when the plans were underfunded by $24.1 billion. The related pension expense included in the income statement for 2018 was a benefit of $1,530 million.

Footnote Disclosures and Future Cash Flows

The net periodic defined benefit pension cost for Delta in 2018 is a *benefit* of $266 million; this is very different than the $523 million in cash that Delta contributed to its defined benefit plans. In addition, Delta paid $926 million into its defined contribution plans. Thus, its total pension expense for 2018 was $660 million ($(266) million + $926 million) and its cash contributions totaled $1,449 million ($523 million + $926 million).

Companies use their pension plan assets to pay pension benefits to retirees. When markets are booming, as was true during the 1990s, pension plan assets can grow rapidly. However, when markets reverse, as in the bear market of the early 2000s and in 2008–2009, the value of pension plan assets can decline. The company's annual pension plan contribution is an investment decision influenced, in part, by market conditions and minimum required contributions specified by law.[10] Companies' cash contributions come from borrowed funds or operating cash flows.

RESEARCH INSIGHT

Why Do Companies Offer Pensions? Research examines why companies choose to offer pension benefits. It finds that deferred compensation plans and pensions help align the long-term interests of owners and employees. Research also examines the composition of pension investments. It finds that a large portion of pension fund assets are invested in fixed-income securities, which are of lower risk than other investment securities. This implies that pension assets are less risky than nonpension assets. However, in severe economic downturns, some corporations curtail their pension plan contributions in order to protect cash flow.

Delta Air Lines paid $1,093 million in pension benefits to retirees in 2018, yet it contributed only $523 million to pension assets that year. The remaining amount was paid out of available funds

[10] The Pension Protection Act of 2006 tightens funding requirements so employers make greater cash contributions to pension funds, closes loopholes that allow companies with underfunded plans to skip cash pension payments, prohibits employers and union leaders from promising extra benefits if pension plans are markedly underfunded, and strengthens disclosure rules to give workers and retirees more information about the status of their pension plan.

in the investment account. Cash contributions to the pension plan assets are the relevant amounts for an analysis of projected cash flows. Benefits paid in relation to the pension liability balance can provide a clue about the need for *future* cash contributions. Companies are required to disclose the expected benefit payments for five years after the statement date and the remaining obligations thereafter. Following is Delta's benefit disclosure statement:

The following table summarizes the benefit payments that are scheduled to be paid in the years ending December 31 ($ millions):

	Pension Benefits
2019	$1,187
2020	1,197
2021	1,218
2022	1,238
2023	1,252
2024–2028	6,380

Delta's unfunded pension amount declined by roughly $602 million from 2017 to 2018. The company contributed $523 million but the plan assets had an actual return of amounting to a loss of $700 million. The reason for the decline in the net unfunded balance in its pension plan is from decreases in the pension liability essentially because of the actuarial gains that resulted from an assumed increase in discount rates.

BUSINESS INSIGHT

How Pensions Confound Income Analysis Overfunded pension plans and boom markets can inflate income. Specifically, when the stock market is booming, pension investments realize large gains that flow to income (via reduced pension expense). Although pension plan assets do not belong to shareholders (as they are the legal entitlement of current and future retirees), the gains and losses from those plan assets are reported in income. The following graph plots the funded status of General Electric Company's pension plan together with pension expense (revenue) that GE reported from 2000 to 2018.

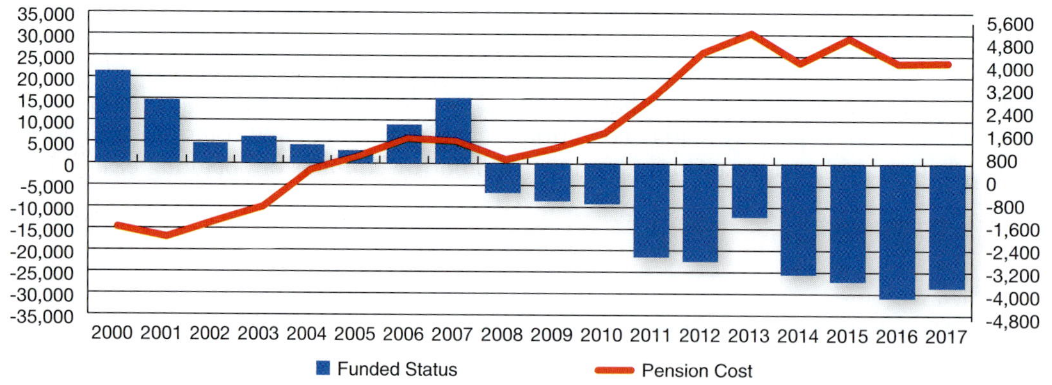

GE's funded status was consistently positive (indicating an overfunded plan) until 2008. The degree of overfunding peaked in 1999 at the height of the stock market, and began to decline during the bear market of the early 2000s. GE reported pension *revenue* (not expense) during this period. In 2001, GE's reported pension *revenue* was $2,095 million (10.6% of its pretax income). Because of the plan's overfunded status, the expected return and amortization of deferred gains components of pension expense amounted to $5,288 million, far in excess of the service and interest costs of $3,193 million. Since 2004, GE has recorded pension expense (rather than revenue) as the pension plan's overfunding and expected long-term rates of return declined, and in 2008 the funded status turned negative. In 2017, GE reported an unfunded liability of $28.7 billion and a pension expense of roughly $4 billion.

One application of the pension footnote is to assess the likelihood that the company will be required to increase its cash contributions to the pension plan. This estimate is made by examining the funded status of the pension plan and the projected payments to retirees. For severely underfunded plans, the projected payments to retirees will not be covered by existing pension assets and current negative investment returns. When this occurs, the company will need to divert operating cash flow from other prospective projects to cover its pension plan. Alternatively, if operating cash flows will not be sufficient, it will likely need to borrow to fund those payments. This decision can be especially troublesome as the debt service payments include interest, thus, effectively increasing the cost of the pension contribution.

Other Post-Employment Benefits

In addition to pension benefits, many companies provide health care and insurance benefits to retired employees. These benefits are referred to as **other post-employment benefits (OPEB)**. These benefits present reporting challenges similar to pension accounting. However, companies most often provide these benefits on a "pay-as-you-go" basis and it is rare for companies to make contributions in advance for OPEB. As a result, this liability, known as the **accumulated post-employment benefit obligation (APBO)**, is largely, if not totally, unfunded. GAAP requires that the unfunded APBO liability be reported in the balance sheet and the annual service costs and interest costs be accrued as expenses each year. This requirement is controversial for two reasons. First, future health care costs are especially difficult to estimate, so the value of the resulting APBO (the present value of the future benefits) is fraught with error. Second, these benefits are provided at the discretion of the employer and can be altered or terminated at any time. Consequently, employers argue that without a legal obligation to pay these benefits, the liability should not be reported in the balance sheet.

Other post-employment benefits can produce large liabilities. For example, Delta Air Lines reports an underfunded health care obligation of $2,588 million and a related expense of $103 million in 2018. Our analysis of cash flows related to pension obligations can be extended to other post-employment benefit obligations. For example, in addition to its pension payments, Delta also discloses that it is obligated to make health care payments to retirees totaling $2,917 million over the next 10 years. Our analysis of projected cash flows must consider this potential cash outflow.

RESEARCH INSIGHT

Valuation of Nonpension Post-Employment Benefits The FASB requires employers to accrue the costs of all nonpension post-employment benefits; known as *accumulated post-employment benefit obligation* (APBO). These benefits consist primarily of health care and insurance. This requirement is controversial due to concerns about the reliability of the liability estimate. Research finds that the APBO (alone) is associated with company value. However, when other pension-related variables are included in the research, the APBO liability is no longer useful in explaining company value. Research concludes that the pension-related variables do a better job at conveying value-relevant information than the APBO number alone, which implies that the APBO number is less reliable.

A GLOBAL PERSPECTIVE

Pension Fund Status IFRS and U.S. GAAP require companies to report the funded status of their defined benefit pension plans on the balance sheet. IFRS, however, calculates pension expense differently. First, unlike U.S. GAAP, IFRS requires that the expected return on pension assets must be the same rate as the discount rate used to value the PBO. In addition, IFRS recognizes the cost of plan amendments in the income statement immediately, rather than amortizing those costs over the service life of employees. There are also other differences that make direct comparison across IFRS and U.S. GAAP firms difficult.

MID-CHAPTER REVIEW 2

The following pension data is taken from footnote 8 of United Continental Holdings, Inc., 10-K report.

($ millions)	2018
Change in Benefit Obligation	
Projected benefit obligation at beginning of year	$ 5,852
Service cost	228
Interest cost	217
Actuarial loss (gain)	(601)
Gross benefits paid and settlements	(292)
Other	(8)
Projected benefit obligation at end of year	$ 5,396
Change in Plan Assets	
Fair value of plan assets at beginning of year	$ 3,932
Actual return on plan assets	(215)
Employer contributions	413
Gross benefits paid and settlements	(292)
Other	(11)
Fair value of plan assets at end of year	$ 3,827
Funded status—Net amount recognized	$(1,569)

Following is United Continental's footnote for its pension cost as reported in its income statement.

Components of Net Periodic Benefit Cost	Defined Benefit Pension 2018
Service cost	$228
Interest cost	217
Expected return on plan assets	(292)
Amortization and other	131
Net periodic benefit cost	$284

Required

1. In general, what factors impact a company's pension benefit obligation during a period?
2. In general, what factors impact a company's pension plan investments during a period?
3. What amount is reported on the balance sheet relating to the United Continental pension plan?
4. How does the expected return on plan assets affect pension cost?
5. How does United Continental's expected return on plan assets compare with its actual return (in $s) for 2018?
6. How much net pension cost is reflected in United Continental's 2018 income statement?
7. Assess United Continental's ability to meet payment obligations to retirees.

The solution to this review problem can be found on page 526.

5

LO5 Describe and interpret accounting for income taxes.

ACCOUNTING FOR INCOME TAXES

Companies maintain two sets of books, one for reporting to their shareholders and creditors and one to report to tax authorities. This is not unethical or illegal. In fact, it is often required. Companies with publicly traded securities compute and report financial accounting income under the rules (e.g., GAAP or IFRS) provided by the financial accounting standards setters (e.g., FASB in the United States). As we have discussed, this income computation is done on the accrual basis, and it is meant to provide information about firm performance to outside stakeholders, such as investors and creditors.[11] Companies must also compute taxable income and report the amount on their tax return(s) filed

[11] All companies have to report to tax authorities but many privately held companies do not have to comply with GAAP.

with the tax authorities in the jurisdictions in which they are required to file (e.g., the Internal Revenue Service and state tax authorities in the United States). Taxable income is determined under the rules promulgated by the government of the taxing jurisdiction (e.g., the Internal Revenue Code in the United States). Tax authorities have different objectives from financial accounting standard setters. The tax rules are set in order to raise money to fund government activities, to encourage or discourage certain behaviors, and (hopefully) based on some sense of fairness and equity. In contrast, financial accounting income is meant to provide information about firm performance to investors, creditors, and other stakeholders so that these parties can make informed decisions about such things as investments and loans. The rules and objectives are very different for the two income measures, and as a result, the two resulting income numbers for a company can be very different.

Our objective here is to learn how to determine a corporation's income tax expense that is reported on the income statement for financial accounting purposes. Financial accounting uses accrual accounting; thus, income tax expense is determined using accrual accounting just like all other expenses. As a result, income tax expense on the income statement is not the cash taxes paid for the reporting period. Instead, it is the accrual-based expense measure, meaning it is the total income tax expense related to the financial accounting income reported in the period regardless of whether those income taxes are actually paid in the current period or not. Furthermore, because it is accrual-based, there will be resulting assets and liabilities that need to be accounted for on the balance sheet. These include what are called deferred tax assets and deferred tax liabilities.

The U.S. recently enacted tax reform through legislation known as the Tax Cuts and Jobs Act (TCJA). We provide an overview of the provisions of this legislation where it is relevant for our discussion. One of the key features of the legislation was a reduction in the top statutory corporate income tax rate from 35% to 21%. As mentioned previously early on in the textbook, we employ a 25% rate for our calculations (mainly for ease of mental math but also because raising the rate is already being discussed!).

Book-Tax Differences

There are two general types of differences between taxable income and financial accounting (book) income, also known as book-tax differences: permanent differences and temporary differences.

A permanent difference is an item of income or expense that is accounted for differently for book and tax purposes in the current year and never reverses in a future year. A simple example of a permanent difference is interest income on municipal bonds. Municipal bond interest income is included in financial accounting income. However, municipal bond interest is tax exempt at the federal level, meaning it is not included in taxable income. Thus, if a company has municipal bond interest income, its financial accounting income will be higher than its taxable income by the amount of municipal bond interest. This difference will not reverse in the future because the municipal bond interest is never included in taxable income. The accounting for income tax with respect to a permanent difference is straightforward; no deferred tax assets or liabilities are created. Income tax expense is lower (in this case) in the current year as a result of the (explicit) income taxes saved by investing in municipal bonds.

A temporary difference is an item of income or expense that is different between book and taxable income in the current year, but will reverse in a future year such that the same amount is included in taxable income and book income over time. Temporary differences are:

1. created by using accrual accounting for book, and cash accounting for tax, and/or
2. created by using different rules for determining the accrual amount for book than for tax.

FYI We use the term book income to refer to income before income taxes, as reported in financial statements. Taxable income refers to income reported in the income tax return.

A common example of a temporary difference is depreciation. For financial accounting purposes companies often use straight-line depreciation as discussed in Chapter 8. For U.S. tax purposes, however, companies use an accelerated method of depreciation (the Modified Accelerated Cost Recovery System (MACRS)). Thus, early in an asset's life, tax depreciation will be greater than book depreciation. However, over the life of the asset the same amount of depreciation will be recorded for book and tax (assuming zero salvage value). This is a temporary difference because tax depreciation is higher earlier on but will be equal to or less than book depreciation in later years in the asset's life. In other words, the book-tax difference will reverse. The computation of the income tax expense is more difficult in this case. We need to account for the taxes due on taxable income (the cash taxes) *and* an accrual of taxes that are known to be due in a future period when the depreciation difference reverses. In other words, total income tax expense is the tax expense related to financial accounting income for the period regardless of whether the taxes are actually paid this year. The accrual for the portion not yet paid creates a **deferred tax liability**—the book-tax difference in this period will lead to higher taxable income relative to book income in the future. This higher relative taxable income means higher cash taxes to be paid in the future—that is, a liability. Furthermore, as part of the TCJA, businesses are now allowed to 'fully expense' certain asset purchases (generally with useful lives of 20 years or less) in the first year the asset is put into service. This means that for tax purposes the taxpayer can deduct the entire cost of the qualifying asset as depreciation in the first year. In such cases, the difference between financial accounting treatment and tax treatment is extreme. This full expensing provision is optional to the taxpayer and is currently in the law for assets purchased between December 2017 and December 31, 2022 (the extra (bonus) depreciation phases down for assets purchased after that and will be zero at the start of 2027). For our purposes, we first provide an example using accelerated depreciation for tax purposes and then modify the example to illustrate what happens when the asset is fully deducted for tax purposes in the first year. The concepts are the same, but the illustration is useful nonetheless.

FYI Income tax expense is also titled **provision for income tax**.

Example Assume Clark Corporation is in its first year of business. It purchases a piece of equipment that costs $200,000 with a useful life of 4 years and no net salvage value. The firm uses straight-line depreciation for financial reporting purposes and accelerated depreciation under MACRS for tax purposes (we will use double declining balance depreciation as an approximation for our example). Comparing the depreciation schedules reveals the following information:

	Tax Reporting	Financial Reporting		
Year	DDB Depreciation	Straight-Line Depreciation	Tax vs. Book Difference	Cumulative Tax-Book Difference
1	$100,000	$50,000	$50,000	$50,000
2	50,000	50,000	0	50,000
3	25,000	50,000	(25,000)	25,000
4	25,000	50,000	(25,000)	0

Assume the corporate statutory tax rate is 25%, we expect the tax rate to stay at 25% for the entire 4 years, and that depreciation is the only book-tax difference for the Clark Corporation. The deferred tax liability at the end of each year is the cumulative book-tax difference times the tax rate. The tax rate to be used is the enacted tax rate expected to be in effect when the book-tax difference reverses. The deferred tax expense each period is the current year book-tax difference (which is the change in the cumulative book-tax difference) times the tax rate. The deferred tax liability at the end of each year and the deferred tax expense for each year for Clark Corporation would be:

Year	Cumulative Tax-Book Difference	Tax Rate	Deferred Tax Liability, End of Year	Deferred Tax Expense
1	$50,000	25%	$12,500	$12,500
2	50,000	25%	12,500	0
3	25,000	25%	6,250	(6,250)
4	0	25%	0	(6,250)

Now assume for illustration that financial accounting earnings each year before depreciation and taxes are $325,000 and there are no other book-tax differences. The yearly calculation of financial reporting and taxable income along with the income tax expense is as follows:

	Tax Reporting			
Year	1	2	3	4
Earnings before depreciation	$325,000	$325,000	$325,000	$325,000
Depreciation deduction.	(100,000)	(50,000)	(25,000)	(25,000)
Taxable income	225,000	275,000	300,000	300,000
Tax due on the tax return (@ 25%)	56,250	68,750	75,000	75,000

Year	Financial Accounting Reporting 1	2	3	4
Earnings before depreciation	$325,000	$325,000	$325,000	$325,000
Depreciation expense	(50,000)	(50,000)	(50,000)	(50,000)
Earnings before tax	275,000	275,000	275,000	275,000
Tax expense	68,750	68,750	68,750	68,750

The entry to record income tax expense in Year 1 follows using the financial statement effects template and journal entry form (We show the entries as if the company is paying in cash at the time the entry is recorded. If the company pays in cash at a later time, a short-term liability account, income tax payable, would be credited in the entries below.):

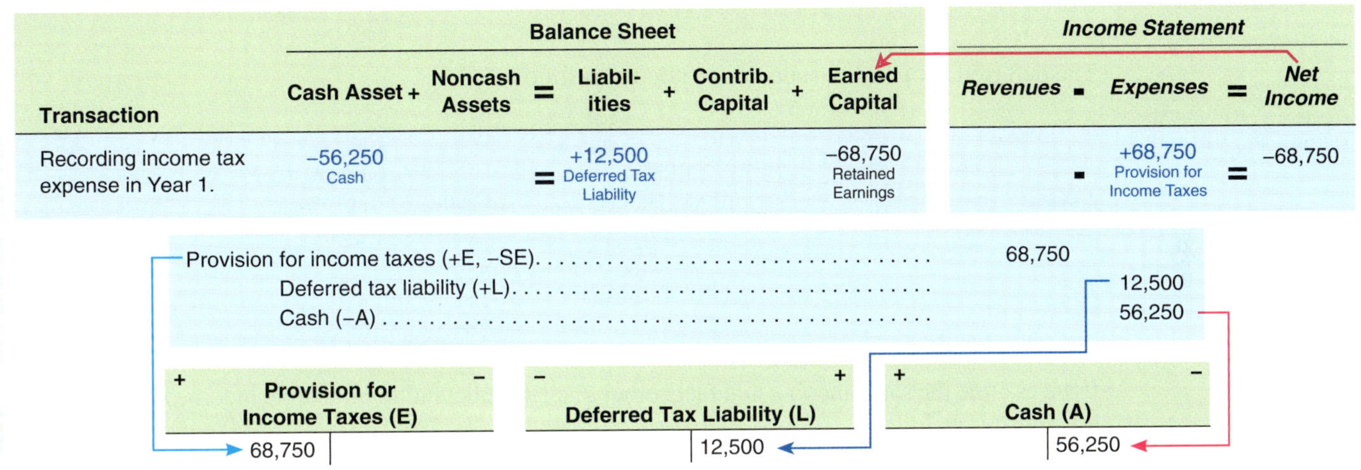

In Year 4, Clark Corporation records its income tax expense. The entry is recorded as follows:

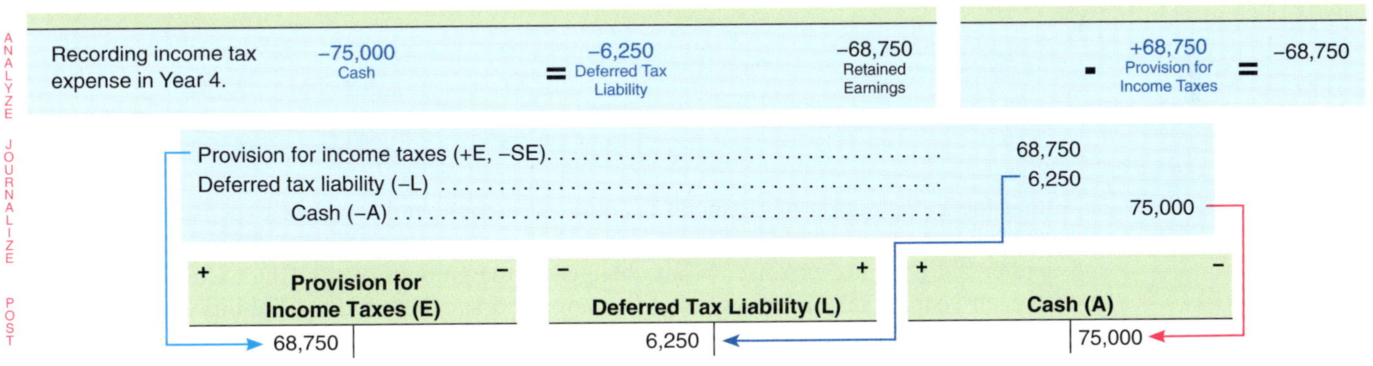

The analysis highlights several facts:

1. Over the 4 years, tax payments to the IRS total $275,000 = $56,250 + $68,750 + $75,000 + $75,000. Total tax expense on the books for the 4 years also equals $275,000 = 4 × $68,750.
2. The timing of the tax payments differs from the tax expense recognized on the books.
3. The deferred tax liability created in the first year is reduced to zero in the 4th year when the useful life of the asset is over.
4. The cash flow takes place consistent with the tax code. The accounting expense amount is an accrual-basis measure.
5. In year 1, the corporation's provision for income tax consists of current income tax expense of $56,250 and deferred income tax expense of $12,500 for the total income tax expense of $68,750. In year 4, the corporation has current income tax expense of $75,000 and deferred income tax expense of $(6,250) for a total income tax expense of $68,750. The total income

tax expense is shown on the income statement and the more detailed breakout into current and deferred expense is disclosed in the notes to the financial statements.

What would occur if Clark Corporation deducted the full cost of the asset for tax purposes under the new rules in the TCJA?

Now we would have the following comparative depreciation schedules:

	Tax Reporting	Financial Accounting Reporting		
Year	Full Deduction	Straight-Line Depreciation	Tax vs. Book Difference	Cumulative Tax-Book Difference
1	$200,000	$50,000	$150,000	$150,000
2	0	50,000	(50,000)	100,000
3	0	50,000	(50,000)	50,000
4	0	50,000	(50,000)	0

The deferred tax liability schedule would be as follows:

Year	Cumulative Tax-Book Difference	Tax Rate	Deferred Tax Liability, End of Year	Deferred Tax Expense
1	$150,000	25%	$37,500	$37,500
2	100,000	25%	25,000	(12,500)
3	50,000	25%	12,500	(12,500)
4	0	25%	0	(12,500)

If we assume the same income and facts otherwise, the calculation of taxable income and tax on the tax return is as follows:

	Tax Reporting			
Year	1	2	3	4
Earnings before depreciation	$325,000	$325,000	$325,000	$325,000
Depreciation deduction.	(200,000)	0	0	0
Taxable income	125,000	325,000	325,000	325,000
Tax due on the tax return (@ 25%)	31,250	81,250	81,250	81,250

Note that the computation of financial accounting income and total tax expense for financial accounting is exactly the same as it was before! Financial accounting depreciation did not change and neither did total tax expense. What changed is the amount of tax Clark Corporation pays in cash each year versus the amount that is recognized as a deferred tax liability (or reversal of deferred tax liability).

For example, in year 1, the journal entry would be as follows:

Provision for income taxes (+E, −SE).	68,750	
Deferred tax liability (+L).		37,500
Cash (−A)		31,250

Notice that Clark Corporation saves a significant amount of cash taxes in year one between the two different tax treatments of the assets – the tax savings are $25,000 ($56,250 – $31,250; can also compute as additional depreciation deduction of $100,000 multiplied by the tax rate of 25%). However, for financial accounting purposes the deferred tax liability and deferred tax expense must increase because the company needs to account for all the taxes on the reported financial accounting income of $275,000, and that has not changed. Thus, the new tax law saves Clark Corporation cash taxes early in the asset's life and saves Clark Corporation money overall in terms of the time value of money (note that Clark Corporation's total cash taxes over the life of the asset did not change).

However, these savings are not reflected on GAAP financial statements because GAAP financial statements are accrual based and do not take the time value of money into account when accounting for income taxes.

RESEARCH INSIGHT

As tax reform was debated over the last decade in the U.S., this issue about the tax versus financial accounting treatment entered into the conversation. The question is whether publicly traded companies, whose financial statements (not tax returns) are the focus of the capital markets, would respond to the tax incentives provided by the immediate expensing of assets. Research suggests that publicly traded companies will respond less than private companies, and maybe less than policymakers would otherwise estimate, because the benefits of the accelerated depreciation, even full expensing, are not reflected on financial statements. One of the authors of this text testified about these issues to both the U.S. House Ways and Means Committee and the Senate Finance Committee. Actual evidence on how companies respond to the TCJA will be forthcoming over time once data are available. However, testing the effects of immediate deducting of asset purchases for tax purposes will be more difficult than it may seem because of confounding factors.

There are also transactions that generate the necessity to record a **deferred tax asset**. For example, bad debts, warranty expense, and many other accrued expenses usually require an associated deferred tax asset to be recorded. For financial accounting purposes, bad debt expense and warranty expense are expensed using management estimates before the receivable actually goes bad and before the warranty costs are actually paid. Again, this is because financial accounting is done on the accrual method and expenses that are associated with the revenue recorded generally are estimated and accrued before they are paid in cash. This is the conservative nature of financial reporting. For tax purposes, these expenses cannot be estimated but instead are deductible generally only when paid. This difference in timing between tax reporting and financial accounting leads to temporary differences where the tax deduction is later in time than the financial accounting expense (opposite of what we just illustrated for depreciation). Because in this case a tax deduction will occur in the future due to a transaction or event in the current period, the company has a deferred tax asset (future benefit) that needs to be recorded.

Temporary book-tax differences also occur with items of revenue. Take, for example, unearned revenue we described in Chapter 6. If a company receives cash in advance of being able to recognize revenue, the company will record unearned revenue (a liability) until the revenue can be recognized. For tax purposes, however, the cash received is generally recorded as income in the period it is received. Thus, there is often a book-tax difference. In this case, the revenue is recorded for tax in an earlier period than for financial accounting, meaning that in some future year(s), taxable income will be less than financial accounting income when the revenue is recognized according to the GAAP rules. That means the company has a deferred tax asset to record in the year the cash is received in the amount of the book-tax difference for revenue times the applicable tax rate.

As a brief example, let's say that the corporation Josie's Jewelry, Inc., makes sales of $100,000 in the current period and estimates and records a bad debt expense of $5,000. This is an expense for financial reporting purposes but there is no deduction allowed for tax purposes in the current period. The tax deduction is not allowed until the receivable actually goes bad (i.e., is deemed to be uncollectible). Using a tax rate of 25%, Josie's Jewelry would report an increase in a deferred tax asset in the current period of $1,250 ($5,000 × 25%) and a corresponding deferred tax benefit (i.e., a negative deferred tax expense) on the income statement. When the receivable is deemed uncollectible and written off in a future period and the deduction is taken for tax purposes, the corporation will reverse the deferred tax asset to zero (assuming the full $5,000 is the amount that eventually is deducted for tax purposes) and record a $1,250 deferred tax expense. Notice that in this future period, the deduction is taken for tax purposes so the actual tax paid is lower, and thus, current tax expense is lower by $1,250. Thus, the net effect on income in the future period is zero (deferred tax expense is higher by $1,250 and current tax expense is lower by $1,250 netting to a zero total effect). This is correct because the tax benefit was accrued (recognized) in the first period when the revenue was earned, bad debt expense was recorded, and deferred tax asset was established.

BUSINESS INSIGHT

As part of the TCJA, the United States changed the manner in which the foreign earnings of U.S. businesses are taxed. Previously, the U.S. had a regime that was a worldwide tax system, with deferral. This meant that the U.S. taxed the worldwide earnings of U.S. companies but the U.S. taxation of certain foreign earnings (i.e., foreign operating earnings of a subsidiary of a U.S. company) was deferred until repatriation to the U.S. When the earnings were repatriated back to the U.S. (e.g., as a dividend to the parent company), then U.S. taxes were due (net of a foreign tax credit). This led to many negative economic consequences, such as U.S. multinational enterprises having an estimated $2 trillion in foreign earnings "locked out" of the U.S. In addition, it led to varied financial accounting outcomes because companies could accrue the U.S. taxes for financial accounting or not accrue the U.S. taxes because of an exception to deferred tax accounting (based on management's plans for the use of the foreign earnings).

The TCJA fundamentally changed the U.S. international tax system. The U.S. now has what some are calling a modified territorial tax system (and some are calling it a sort of worldwide minimum tax system). At a very high level, the new system exempts foreign earnings of U.S. multinationals from U.S. taxation unless the earnings are "high return" earnings in "low tax" jurisdictions, in which case the U.S. will tax those earnings currently (albeit at a lower rate). The system includes other base erosion protections that require companies to compute a type of alternative tax after disallowing certain payments to foreign parties that are considered "base eroding." Much of this is far beyond an introductory accounting textbook; however, one feature that affected financial statements for many of multinational companies in 2017 was a mandatory deemed repatriation tax on the accumulated foreign earnings of the company as of the time the TCJA was passed (roughly). As part of the transition to the modified territorial system from the worldwide system, the U.S. required a tax payment on the accumulated earnings at a rate of 15.5% if the earnings were held in cash or cash equivalents, or a rate of 8% if the earnings were in noncash assets. (This tax is sometimes referred to as the transition tax.) This was a mandatory tax but could be paid over installments that stretch eight years. For financial accounting, the standard setters required companies to accrue the tax expense for this tax in the fiscal year containing December 2017, with no discounting for the time value of money, consistent with the rest of the accounting for income taxes.

Because of the variation in the accounting prior to the TCJA, there was some marked variation in terms of the effects of this mandatory tax for financial accounting. If a company had already accrued significant U.S. taxes on its unremitted foreign earnings, the accounting charge for the repatriation tax might not have been very large. Apple, Inc., for example, had substantial unremitted foreign earnings, but had accrued U.S. tax on a portion of these earnings. The accrued U.S. tax, recorded as a deferred tax liability before the TCJA, was $36.4 billion. Apple reports that it owed a deemed repatriation tax of $37.3 billion. Thus, there was very little of the mandatory repatriation tax that needed to have additional U.S. tax expense recorded for financial accounting. On the other hand, Cisco reported that it had $76 billion of unremitted earnings on which it owed a mandatory repatriation tax of $8.1 billion. Cisco did not have any deferred tax liability recorded (meaning no U.S. tax was previously accrued on those earnings). Thus, Cisco had to record all of the $8.1 billion as additional tax expense in their year ended July 28, 2018. The company's effective tax rate for the year was 99.2%!

Net Operating Losses Another book-tax difference is a net operating loss carryover. For tax purposes, corporations can carry over operating losses to future years.[12] Financial accounting does not have such a rule; if a corporation has a loss for financial reporting, the loss is recorded and the corporation starts the next year with a clean slate and measures income for that next year only. Thus, the net operating loss carryover is a temporary book-tax difference. Because the loss carry over represents future deductions for tax purposes, the company has and must record an increase to deferred tax assets and a deferred tax benefit (i.e., negative deferred tax expense) in the amount of the loss carryover times the tax rate (the enacted tax rate expected to be in effect when the loss carryover will be used to offset taxes). Thus, even though the corporation is not getting the cash benefits of the deduction yet, the accounting rules require the company to accrue the benefit to the current period.

[12] Prior to the TCJA, corporations could carry net operating losses back two years for tax purposes and forward for 20 years. The TCJA changed the rules. Now corporations cannot carry losses (starting with losses generated in 2018) back in time, but can only carry them forward. The TCJA also changes the carryforward period to be indefinite. However, another change in the TCJA is that tax loss carryforwards can only be used to offset 80% of taxable income in the future period. In essence, the concept of allowing loss carryovers for tax purposes approximates an averaging of income over time so companies with volatile income are not required to pay high taxes in years with high income and then get no relief in years with losses.

Valuation Allowance After a corporation computes its income tax expense and records its deferred tax assets and liabilities, the corporation has yet another step to complete. The corporation must evaluate the realizability of the deferred tax assets. This means that management must estimate whether the company will have sufficient future taxable income to offset the future deductions represented by the deferred tax assets. If management does not think the company will have enough future taxable income to be able to use all the deferred tax assets, then a contra-asset must be established against the deferred tax assets. Thus, the deferred tax assets on the balance sheet will not be overstated. As an analogy, recall that when a company has accounts receivables, it must evaluate the collectability of those receivables and establish an allowance for doubtful accounts to ensure the accounts receivable asset is not overstated. Similarly, if a corporation has deferred tax assets that management does not expect to be able to use to offset future taxable income, then the company must record a **valuation allowance**. When the contra-asset is recorded, deferred tax expense is increased, which decreases accounting income (and if a valuation allowance is reduced, deferred tax expense is reduced, increasing income). A more detailed discussion is beyond the scope of this text, but net operating losses and associated valuation allowances have been an important part of many companies', including Delta's, accounting for income taxes as we will see below.

Unrecognized Tax Benefit (Uncertain Tax Positions) Another step in accounting for income taxes is the computation of what is known as an unrecognized tax benefit. Essentially, corporations must estimate what amount tax authorities might assess in additional tax during future audits by the tax authorities (e.g., the IRS). In other words, this is a contingent liability—the corporation might owe more tax if the tax authority disagrees with the tax positions the company has taken on past tax returns. U.S. GAAP requires companies to record additional tax expense for this amount as well as an additional liability. The liability is included in total liabilities on the balance sheet (it is not an off-balance-sheet amount) but is not a separate line item. Details about the account are in the notes to the financial statements.

An example of disclosure about this amount is from Apple, Inc.'s most recent 10-K.

Apple, Inc.
Uncertain Tax Positions
The aggregate changes in the balance of gross unrecognized tax benefits, which excludes interest and penalties, for 2018, 2017 and 2016, is as follows (in millions):

	2018	2017	2016
Beginning balances	$8,407	$7,724	$6,900
Increases related to tax positions taken during a prior year	2,431	333	1,121
Decreases related to tax positions taken during a prior year	(2,212)	(952)	(257)
Increases related to tax positions taken during the current year	1,824	1,880	1,578
Decreases related to settlements with taxing authorities	(756)	(539)	(1,618)
Decreases related to expiration of statute of limitations	—	(39)	—
Ending balances	$9,694	$8,407	$7,724

Revaluation of Deferred Tax Assets and Liabilities due to a Tax Rate Change

As we have mentioned, deferred tax assets and liabilities are measured using the enacted corporate statutory tax rate expected to be in effect when the deferred tax asset or liability reverses. In addition, as we have also mentioned, the TCJA lowered the U.S. corporate statutory tax rate to 21% from a top rate of 35%. When this occurred, companies had to revalue their deferred tax assets and liabilities on their financial statements. For financial accounting, the rules require that the revaluation occur in the period the tax law is enacted not when it is effective (again, because the rate used to value the deferred tax assets and liabilities is the enacted rate expected to be in effect when the items reverse, not the rate applicable to the current period). Thus, if the company had net deferred tax liabilities, the company would reduce the value of the liability on the balance sheet and record a reduction to deferred tax expense. As a result, accounting income increases (because tax expense is lower). To illustrate a simple case, the Koehler Company had net deferred tax liabilities (meaning deferred tax liabilities in excess of deferred tax assets) of $1 million at the end of 2017 valued at the pre-TCJA tax rate of 35%. The simplest way to think about the tax rate change is that there was a 40% reduction in the tax rate. Thus, Koehler Company is required to devalue its deferred tax liabilities by 40%.[13] In 2017, the company would record the following entry to revalue the deferred tax liabilities at 21% and show the reduction to deferred tax expense:

Deferred tax liability (L)	400,000	
Deferred tax benefit (−E, +SE)		400,000

The balance sheet equation would be as follows:

Transaction	Cash Asset +	Noncash Assets	=	Liabilities +	Contrib. Capital +	Earned Capital	Revenues −	Expenses =	Net Income
	Balance Sheet						Income Statement		
Revalue deferred tax liabilities for a tax rate change			=	(400,000) Deferred Tax Liability		400,000 Retained Earnings	−	(400,000) Provision for Income Taxes =	400,000

Conversely, if the company had net deferred tax assets, the company would revalue those assets at the lower rate and increase deferred tax expense. This would result in a higher expense and a "hit" to (a decrease in) accounting earnings.

CVS, one of our focus companies in the text, is a relatively simple company (with little to no foreign operations). Thus, their discussion of this issue is illustrative for our purposes.

The following is a portion of the tax footnote in CVS's 2017 10-K:

> On December 22, 2017, the President signed into law the Tax Cuts and Jobs Act (the "TCJA"). Among numerous changes to existing tax laws, the TCJA permanently reduces the federal corporate income tax rate from 35% to 21% effective on January 1, 2018. The effects on deferred tax balances of changes in tax rates are required to be taken into consideration in the period in which the changes are enacted, regardless of when they are effective. As the result of the reduction of the corporate income tax rate under the TCJA, the Company estimated the revaluation of its net deferred tax liabilities and recorded a provisional income tax benefit of approximately $1.5 billion for year ended December 31, 2017. The Company has not completed all of its processes to determine the TCJA's final impact. The final impact may differ from this provisional amount due to, among other things, changes in interpretations and assumptions the Company has made thus far and the issuance of additional regulatory or other guidance. The accounting is expected to be completed by the time the 2017 federal corporate income tax return is filed in 2018.

Income Tax Disclosures

Delta Air Lines reported income before income taxes of $5,151 million in 2018. Delta reported an income tax expense of $1,216 million in 2018. In 2017, Delta reported income before income taxes of $5,500 million and income tax expense of $2,295 million.

To fully understand how income tax expense is determined, we refer to the footnotes. Note 12 to Delta's 2018 10-K report contains the table shown in **Exhibit 10.4**.

EXHIBIT 10.4 Delta Air Lines Income Tax Expense

Year Ended December 31 ($ millions)	2018	2017
Current income tax (provision) benefit	$ 148	$ (53)
Deferred tax (provision) benefit net of valuation allowance	(1,364)	(2,242)
Income tax (provision) benefit	$(1,216)	$(2,295)

[13] More specifically, the deferred tax liability is $1,000,000 and was computed using a 35% tax rate. Thus, the cumulative book-tax difference was $2,857,143 ($1,000,000/.35). To find the new deferred tax liability, multiple the cumulative book-tax difference by 21%. This yields, $600,000 for the new deferred tax liability balance. To get to this balance, the deferred tax liability needs to be reduced by $400,000.

The income tax expense or benefit reported in the income statement consists of two primary components:

Current tax expense—this can be thought of for our purposes as the amount that has been paid or is payable to tax authorities in the current period (it also usually contains the income effects of some tax accruals that are beyond the scope of this text).

Deferred tax expense—this is the effect on tax expense due to changes in deferred tax liabilities and assets. It is the result of temporary differences between the reported income statement and the tax return.

Based on the table shown in **Exhibit 10.4**, Delta reported a tax benefit of $148 million for current taxes. This tax benefit potentially suggests that Delta reported a loss on its tax return in 2018 and potentially expects tax refunds. However, such a benefit could also result from other tax accruals (beyond the scope of this text) being recorded in current tax expense, changes in which would cause current tax expense to be negative (i.e., a benefit). It also reported a net deferred tax expense of $1,364 million.

Companies must also disclose the components of deferred tax assets and liabilities. The components of Delta's deferred tax assets and liabilities are presented in **Exhibit 10.5**.

EXHIBIT 10.5 Components of Delta Air Lines' Deferred Income Tax Assets and Liabilities

Deferred Taxes

Deferred income taxes reflect the net tax effect of temporary differences between the carrying amounts of assets and liabilities for financial reporting and income tax purposes. The following table shows significant components of our deferred tax assets and liabilities:

December 31 ($ millions)	2018	2017
Deferred Tax Assets:		
Net operating loss carryforwards	$ 674	$1,297
Pension, postretirement and other benefits	2,435	2,544
Alternative minimum tax credit carryforward	189	379
Deferred revenue	1,620	1,416
Operating lease liabilities	1,579	—
Other	357	728
Valuation allowance	(13)	(15)
Total deferred tax assets	$6,841	$6,349
Deferred Tax Liabilities:		
Depreciation	$4,185	$3,847
Operating lease right-of-use assets	1,388	—
Intangible assets	1,052	1,043
Other	137	105
Total deferred tax liabilities	$6,762	$4,995
Deferred tax assets, net	$ 79	$1,354

Delta's deferred tax assets and deferred tax liabiities are nearly equal in 2018; in 2017 Delta's deferred tax assets were greater than their deferred tax liabilities. Notice that Delta has a large deferred tax liability for depreciation. We would expect this for a capital-intensive company like an airline. Notice also that Delta has a large deferred tax asset for pensions and other postretirement benefits. As we discussed earlier in the chapter, Delta has a large unfunded pension liability. The company has to record the liability and a pension expense for financial accounting on the accrual basis but does not get a tax deduction until funds are contributed to the plan. Thus, larger expenses have been recorded for book relative to the deductions taken for tax. In the future, this will reverse (assuming Delta eventually funds its pension) and the deductions for tax will be greater than the expenses for book. Thus, Delta has a deferred tax asset (again, the total income tax expense is the accrual-basis expense related to financial accounting income, not cash taxes paid). Finally, note that Delta has a deferred tax asset related to net operating loss carryforwards. In prior years, the loss carryforwards were much larger. For example, in 2013 the deferred tax asset related to net operating losses was over $6 billion. As recent as 2011 and 2012, Delta established a large valuation allowance against its deferred tax assets indicating that management did not think the company would have enough future taxable income to be able to offset the net operating loss carryovers. However, starting in 2012 and to a large degree in 2013, Delta decreased the valuation allowance (by $8 billion in 2013) indicating that management thinks that taxable income will be high enough in the future to use all the tax loss carryforwards. In the 2014 10-K, management states that "During 2014 we continued our trend of sustained profitability, recording pre-tax profit of $1.1 billion for the year. After considering all available positive and negative evidence, we released additional valuation allowance related to net operating losses . . . " As Delta reduces the valuation allowance, more of the deferred tax assets related to the net operating loss carryovers are recognized on the balance sheet. Analysts sometimes consider management's assessment and changes in valuation allowances an indicator of future prospects for the company. In addition, one has to consider large increases to net income from changes in the valuation allowance (like Delta had in 2013) and understand that such large changes will not happen every year; the income from the valuation allowance release is nonrecurring. As we can see, by the end of 2018 the loss carryovers are much smaller (and now only valued at a 21% tax rate) and management assesses very little in the way of a valuation allowance against their deferred tax assets. Delta's performance and prospects have improved. Finally, notice that Delta added new deferred tax assets and deferred tax liabilities related to the new lease accounting standard we discussed earlier in the chapter.

In terms of where deferred tax assets and liabilities are reflected on the balance sheet, under the current accounting standards all are recorded in the noncurrent section of the balance sheet. A net amount (asset or liability) is shown.

Companies also report in the footnotes a reconciliation of differences between the statutory U.S. tax rate (currently 21%) and the tax expense reported in the income statement. The **effective tax rate** is determined by dividing the provision for income taxes (tax expense) by the income before income taxes. Delta's effective tax rate for 2018 was 23.6% ($1,216 million/$5,151 million). Delta's rate reconciliation lists the principal reasons for the difference between the effective tax rate and the U.S. federal statutory income tax rate:

	Year Ended December 31,		
	2018	**2017**	**2016**
U.S. federal statutory income tax rate	21.0%	35.0%	35.0%
State taxes, net of federal benefit	2.5	1.8	1.8
Foreign tax rate differential	0.1	(2.2)	(2.1)
Tax Cuts and Jobs Act adjustment	(0.5)	7.2	—
Other	0.5	—	(0.7)
Effective income tax rate	23.6%	41.8%	34.0%

Effective tax rates can vary considerably from one company to another due to permanent differences, tax credits, and other factors. A comparison of the effective tax rate for several companies is presented in **Exhibit 10.6**. The leftmost graph shows companies' 2018 ETR split by current and deferred portions of the tax expense. The rightmost graph compares ETRs for companies in 2018 and 2017.

EXHIBIT 10.6 Comparison of Effective Tax Rates

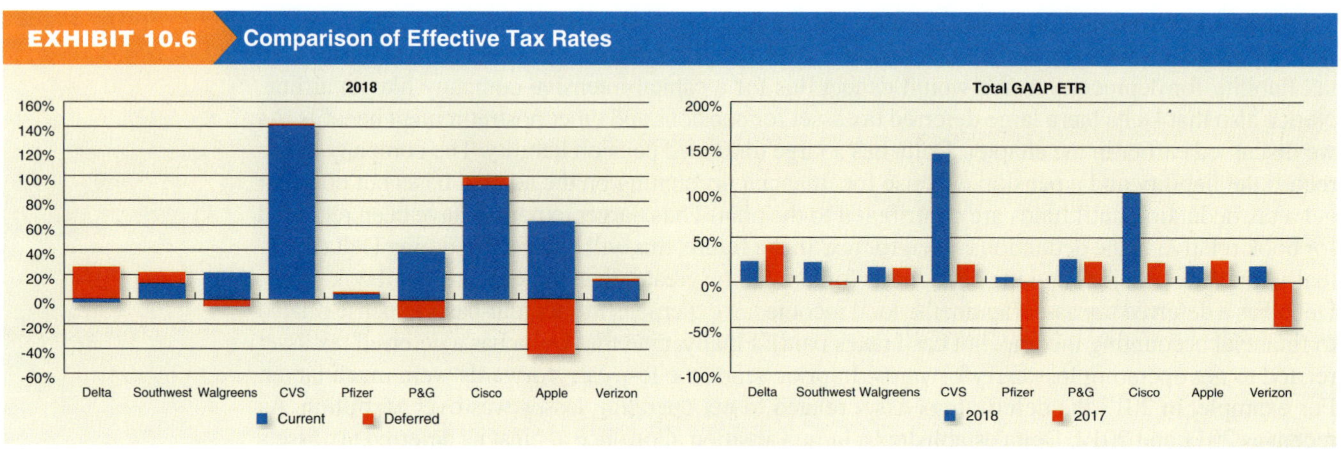

The highest effective rates in 2018 were reported by CVS and Cisco. In this instance, an examination of their disclosures reveal that CVS reported a large writedown of goodwill for financial accounting purposes. This amount is not deductible for tax purposes leading to a high tax expense and a relatively low book income which increases CVS's ETR significantly. Something different occurred at Cisco. As mentioned in the Business Insight above, Cisco had large amounts of foreign earnings on which no U.S. tax had been accrued. Cisco's ETRs in this figure are for their year ended in July of 2018, which includes the effects of the TCJA. Cisco accrued a large mandatory deemed repatriation tax (transition tax) which increased their ETR for this year significantly. Verizon and Pfizer both had large values of deferred tax liabilities when the TCJA was passed. Thus, these deferred tax liabilities needed to be revalued to 21% during 2017, when the TCJA passed, and thus the companies recorded a large deferred tax benefit in that year lowering their reported ETRs. As these data show, effective tax rates can swing wildly year-to-year (especially when there is tax reform!).

Deferred Taxes in the Cash Flow Statement

Income taxes, including deferred income taxes, are reported in the operating section of the cash flow statement. When the cash flow statement is prepared using the direct method, deferred income taxes are excluded from taxes paid in cash. When the indirect (or reconciliation) method is used, the deferred portion of the income tax expense must be added back to net income as an expense not requiring the use of cash. The amount of income taxes paid in cash is then reported at the bottom of the cash flow statement or in the footnotes.

Computation and Analysis of Taxes

An analysis of deferred taxes can yield useful insights. An increase in deferred tax liabilities indicates that a company is reporting higher profits in its income statement than in its tax return. The difference between reported corporate profits and taxable income increased substantially in the late 1990s, just prior to the stock market decline.

Although an increase in deferred tax liabilities can be the result of legitimate differences between financial reporting standards and tax rules, we must be aware of the possibility that such differences can also be caused by tax avoidance or by earnings management, improper revenue recognition, or other questionable accounting practices. More advanced courses cover the accounting for income taxes in more depth.

RESEARCH INSIGHT

Recent research has studied the accounting for income tax. Several papers have examined whether the overall difference between a company's taxable income and its financial accounting income contains any information about earnings quality. The idea is that if managers use accruals to manage financial accounting earnings upward, taxable income would not likely be similarly managed because there are fewer accruals for tax purposes (e.g., allowance for doubtful accounts, warranty reserves, etc.). The evidence is generally consistent with this hypothesis.[14]

MID-CHAPTER REVIEW 3

The following footnote is from the 2019 annual report of Adler Corporation.

Note 9: Income Taxes
The provision for income taxes includes the following

($ thousands)	2019
Current provision	
Domestic	$1,342
Foreign	146

continued

[14] See the following studies: 1) Phillips, John, Mort Pincus, and Sonja Rego, "Earnings Management: New Evidence Based on Deferred Tax Expense." *The Accounting Review*, 1999, 2) Lev, Baruch and Doron Nissim, "Taxable Income, Future Earnings, and Equity Values," *The Accounting Review*, October 2004, and 3) Hanlon, Michelle, "The Persistence and Pricing of Earnings, Accruals, and Cash Flows When Firms Have Large Book-Tax Differences," *The Accounting Review*, January 2005.

continued from previous page

	2019
Deferred provision (credit)	
Domestic	960
Foreign	(58)
Total	$2,390

Required

1. (a) What is the amount of income tax expense reported on its income statement? (b) How much of the income tax expense is payable in cash? (c) Assuming that the deferred tax liability increased, identify an example that could account for such a change.
2. Prepare the entry, using both the financial statement effects template and in journal entry form, to record its income tax expense for 2019. Post journal entries to the appropriate T-accounts.

The solution to this review problem can be found on page 526.

6

LO6 Describe disclosures regarding future commitments and contingencies. Analyze financial statements after converting off-balance-sheet items to be considered on balance sheet.

COMMITMENTS AND CONTENGENCIES AND OTHER DISCLOSURES

FASB and SEC guidance also require entities to provide additional detail and disclosure about various commitments and contingencies. Often companies will list a line item on the balance sheet "Commitments and Contingencies" with no corresponding amount. **Exhibit 10.1** shows that Delta includes such a line item on their balance sheet.

In the notes to the financial statements, Delta provides detailed disclosure about such items as 1) future aircraft purchase commitments, including a schedule of future payments, 2) contract carrier agreements, 3) legal contingencies (e.g., lawsuits regarding employment practices, environmental issues, and antitrust matters), 4) a discussion of indemnification clauses, and 5) the number of union workers Delta employs.

Generally, many of the items in such disclosures are not on the balance sheet as liabilities (though some are); thus financial statement users need to evaluate how to treat such items.

Nike, Inc., includes the line item "commitments and contingencies" on their balance sheet and discloses the details in a note to their financial statements. Nike also includes a broader disclosure about contractual obligations and off-balance-sheet commitments in the Management Discussion and Analysis section of their annual 10-K. The disclosure in their May 31, 2018, annual report is as follows:

Off-Balance-Sheet Arrangements

In connection with various contracts and agreements, we routinely provide indemnification relating to the enforceability of intellectual property rights, coverage for legal issues that arise and other items where we are acting as the guarantor. Currently, we have several such agreements in place. Based on our historical experience and the estimated probability of future loss, we have determined that the fair value of such indemnification is not material to our financial position or results of operations.

Contractual Obligations

Our significant long-term contractual obligations as of May 31, 2018, and significant endorsement contracts, including related marketing commitments, entered into through the date of this report are as follows:

continued

continued from previous page

Description of Commitment (in millions)	Cash Payments Due During the Year Ended May 31,						
	2019	2020	2021	2022	2023	Thereafter	Total
Operating leases	$ 589	$ 523	$ 472	$ 412	$ 361	$ 1,608	$ 3,965
Capital leases and other financing obligations	44	37	40	38	36	229	424
Long-term debt	115	115	112	109	609	4,713	5,773
Endorsement contracts	1,391	1,306	1,158	1,266	942	4,438	10,501
Product purchase obligations	4,566	—	—	—	—	—	4,566
Other purchase obligations	1,437	512	281	92	70	254	2,646
Transition tax related to the Tax Act	94	94	94	94	94	702	1,172
TOTAL	$8,236	$2,587	$2,157	$2,011	$2,112	$11,944	$29,047

The endorsement contracts have included contracts with well-known athletes such as Serena Williams, LeBron James, Maria Sharapova, Roger Federer, Tiger Woods, and of course, Michael Jordan. The athletes sign long-term, multimillion dollar contracts to use and promote Nike shoes, apparel, and accessories. These long-term endorsement contracts are just one of Nike's off-balance-sheet obligations.

In the table above, long-term debt and the transition tax related to the Tax Act (discussed previously) are included in the balance sheet. Operating leases will soon be included in the balance sheet once Nike adopts the new lease standard. The endorsement contracts, one of the largest items, are not included on the balance sheet as liabilities. If an analyst desires to estimate the associated "as if" liability with such contracts, the following approach could be used (similar to how financial statement users estimated the off-balance-sheet liability associated with operating leases).

1. Estimate a discount rate. One reasonable proxy is the interest rate on Nike's debt, which is roughly 3% per their debt footnote.
2. Estimate the future payments and the number of years those payments will be made. One limitation of the above disclosure is that the first five years show the annual payment but the remaining payments are lumped in a column "thereafter." An estimate of the number of years for the amount in the "thereafter" column can be computed by dividing the amount ($4,438) by the previous year's payment ($942). In this case, this estimate yields almost 5 years. To estimate using full years, divide the amount in the "thereafter" column by five and arrive at an estimate of the payment amount for each of the next five years. In this case, $888 million ($4,438/5).
3. Find the present value of the future payments. The present value of the payments listed above, at 3% over the 10 years, is roughly $9.09 billion. This can be computed using one of several methods; for example, 1) the present value tables in Appendix A to find the present value of each payment or 2) Excel's NPV function.

This yields a rough approximation of the "as if" liability related to these payments. In this case, the off-balance-sheet liability is 71% of total recorded liabilities from Nike's balance sheet! However, the associated asset value, if any, for this off-balance-sheet item—the value of advertising through endorsements—is very hard to estimate.

ANALYZING FINANCIAL STATEMENTS

Analysis Objective

We want to assess the effect of financial obligations, including off-balance-sheet commitments, on financial solvency and liquidity.

Analysis Tool Fixed Commitments Ratio

$$\text{Fixed commitments ratio} = \frac{\text{Operating cash flow before fixed commitments}}{\text{Fixed commitments}}$$

Applying the Fixed Commitments Ratio to Delta Air Lines Some fixed commitments, such as operating lease payments and purchase commitments, are cash outflows that are classified as operating activities in the cash flow statement. Others (for example, payments due on long-term debt) are classified as financing cash flows and some can be classified as investing (for example, commitments to purchase plant assets). Delta reports total fixed commitments of $8,954 million in its 10-K report. Of these, $1,550 million is for noninterest payments on long-term debt and finance leases (financing) and $3,290 million is for aircraft purchase commitments (investing). Subtracting these amounts leaves the amount of fixed commitments that are part of operating cash flows ($8,954 million – $1,550 million – $3,290 million = $4,114 million). To compute the **fixed commitments ratio**, we start with operating cash flows, add back the fixed commitments that are classified as operating and then divide by the total amount of fixed commitments.

$$\textbf{2016:}\ 1.36 = \frac{\$7{,}205 + \$5{,}892}{\$9{,}632}$$

$$\textbf{2017:}\ 0.93 = \frac{\$5{,}148 + \$4{,}794}{\$10{,}644}$$

$$\textbf{2018:}\ 1.24 = \frac{\$7{,}014 + \$4{,}114}{\$8{,}954}$$

Guidance A fixed commitments ratio less than 1.0 indicates that a company is generating insufficient cash flows from operations to meet its contractual obligations. Some commitments may be met by selling assets, or by raising additional financing. For example, when long-term debt comes due, it can be refinanced with new debt if the company is otherwise in sound financial health.

Delta Air Lines in Context

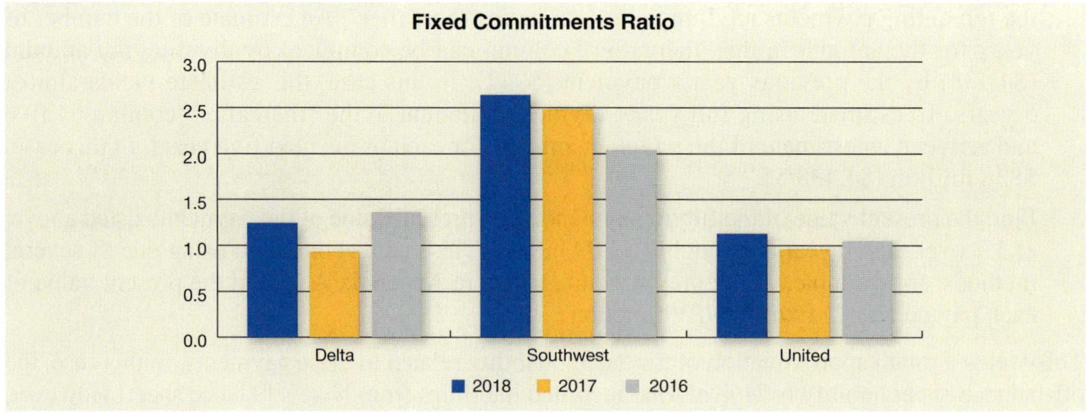

Takeaways In our set of companies above for 2018, the ratio ranges from 1.12 for United Continental to 2.61 for Southwest Airlines. Historically, airlines have had relatively low ratios due to large amounts of operating leases, pension commitments, and other obligations. Southwest has always been an exception and now that Delta has improved its performance and cash flows, their ratio is over 1.0 in two out of the three years we present. The key takeaway is that off-balance-sheet obligations can have a significant impact on our analysis and understanding of a company's solvency and liquidity.

Other Considerations The fixed commitments ratio is but one measure of financial solvency and liquidity. It should be used in conjunction with other ratios, such as the debt-to-equity ratio and the current ratio in an effort to gauge the ability of the firm to meet its financial obligations.

SUMMARY

Define off-balance-sheet financing and explain its effects on financial analysis. (p. 464) **LO1**

- Off-balance-sheet financing refers to financial obligations of the company that are not recognized as liabilities in the balance sheet. Recognizing these obligations often requires recognizing off-balance-sheet assets.
- Off-balance-sheet financing improves financial leverage ratios and the corresponding unrecognized assets improve performance measures.

Account for leases using the operating lease method and the finance lease method. Compare and analyze the two methods. (p. 465) **LO2**

- For both a finance lease and an operating lease, a right-of-use asset and a lease liability are recorded by the lessee. The amount of the liability is the present value of the future lease payments. The amount recognized for the right-of-use asset is equal to the amount of the liability adjusted for items such as lease prepayments, lease incentives, and initial direct costs.
- For finance leases, the income statement reports interest expense related to the liability and amortization expense related to the right-of-use asset.
- For operating leases, a straight-line lease expense is recognized on the income statement. The straight-line lease expense is measured by taking the total cost of the lease divided by the total number of lease periods. The amortization of the right-of-use asset (reduction in book value on the balance sheet) is determined by subtracting the interest on the lease liability from the straight-line-expense amount. Thus, while the expense is straight-line, a loan amortization table like that used for finance leases is used to determine the reduction in book value of the asset and reduction in liability as payments are made.
- Right-of-use book value declines more quickly with the finance lease method.
- An asset leased using a finance lease will have higher related expenses early in the asset's life relative to an asset leased using an operating lease.
- For companies that utilize operating leases, in order to compare financial statements before and after the new lease standard, an analyst or other financial statement user needs to compute the present value of the future lease payments and treat this present value as an "as-if" liability. In addition, an estimate of the asset would need to be determined.

Explain and interpret the reporting for pension plans. (p. 477) **LO3**

- Pension and other postretirement obligations represent a large obligation for many companies.
- The projected benefit obligation is the present value of the estimated future benefits that a company expects to pay retired employees.
- The net liability that a company reports on the balance sheet is the projected benefit obligation offset by the plan assets.

Analyze and interpret pension footnote disclosures. (p. 480) **LO4**

- Pension footnotes provide detailed information about changes in pension obligations, changes in plan assets, and the determinants of pension expense.
- Pension footnotes provide information allowing us to interpret pension expenses and cash flows.

Describe and interpret accounting for income taxes. (p. 486) **LO5**

- While income tax expense is reported below income from operations, it is an operating expense. The initial item in an indirect cash flow statement is net income, which reflects the deduction of the tax expense.
- Income tax expense is determined as the sum of the tax computed due to the government and the net change in deferred assets and liabilities.
- Deferred taxes occur because of differences between U.S. GAAP reporting and the tax due based on the rules of the tax authority. The former are based on accrual accounting while the latter are often based on a hybrid accrual and cash-based accounting system.
- Deferred tax assets and liabilities are valued at the enacted tax rate expected to be in effect when the temporary differences between financial accounting and tax bases reverse.

Describe disclosures regarding future commitments and contingencies. Analyze financial statements after converting off-balance-sheet items to be considered on balance sheet. (p. 498) **LO6**

- Disclosure of future commitments and contingent payments is required,
- Some of these items will be recognized on the balance sheet and some are off-balance-sheet. If the item is off-balance-sheet but an analyst or creditor desires to analyze the company's financials as if the item were treated as a liability, the present value of the future payments should be computed and included in liabilities for analysis purposes.

GUIDANCE ANSWERS . . . YOU MAKE THE CALL

You are the CEO Normally we think that managers inside the firm have full information about firm activities and performance. However, they likely do not have perfect information. Gathering a new level of data regarding lease contracts and terms may lead corporations to consolidate leases, negotiate better lease terms, and/or potentially reduce the quantity of assets leased. You, as the CEO, may even decide to invest in machine learning software or textual analysis software to gather more data and help your company be more efficient and cost-effective in setting lease contracts.

You are a Consultant to the FASB Normally accountants do not favor offsetting liabilities against the related assets as is currently the reporting practice required under GAAP. However, because the pension fund is a separate legal entity, there is a problem with reporting the pension plan assets among the firm's assets. A company does not have unilateral control over a pension trust. It can put assets into the trust but can not easily get them out of the trust. For this reason, the pension assets do not meet the criteria we normally require for recognition. Thus, reporting a net amount (PBO - pension assets) seems the best course of action.

KEY RATIOS

$$\text{Fixed commitments ratio} = \frac{\text{Operating cash flow before fixed commitments}}{\text{Fixed commitments}}$$

$$\text{Effective tax rate} = \frac{\text{Provision for income taxes}}{\text{Income before income taxes}}$$

KEY TERMS

Accumulated post-employment benefit obligation (APBO) (p. 485)
Actuarial losses and gains (p. 478)
Deferred tax asset (p. 491)
Deferred tax liability (p. 488)
Defined benefit plan (p. 477)
Defined contribution plan (p. 477)
Effective tax rate (p. 496)
Fixed commitments ratio (p. 500)
Funded status (p. 477)
Interest cost (p. 478)
Lessee (p. 465)
Lessor (p. 465)
Off-balance-sheet financing (p. 464)
Other post-employment benefits (OPEB) (p. 485)
Overfunded (p. 477)
Pension plan assets (p. 477)
Projected benefit obligation (PBO) (p. 477)
Provision for income tax (p. 488)
Right-of-use asset (p. 466)
Service cost (p. 478)
Underfunded (p. 477)
Valuation allowance (p. 493)

Assignments with the MBC logo in the margin are available in myBusinessCourse. See the Preface of the book for details.

MULTIPLE CHOICE

1. U.S. GAAP requires that certain leases be accounted for as *finance leases*. The reason for this treatment is that this type of lease
a. is essentially viewed as a sale/purchase.
b. is an example of form over substance.
c. provides the use of the leased asset to the lessee for a limited period of time.
d. is an example of off-balance-sheet financing.

2. For a lease that is accounted for as an operating lease by the lessee, the rent expense should be
a. allocated and recorded as interest expense and depreciation expense.
b. allocated and recorded as a reduction in the liability for leased assets and interest expense.
c. recorded as rent expense with no other entries recorded.
d. recorded as a straight-line lease expense with associated entries to record the cash payment, reduce the liability, and amortize the right-of-use asset on the balance sheet.

3. The balance sheet liability for a finance lease would be reduced each period by the
   a. lease payment.
   b. lease payment plus the amortization of the related asset.
   c. lease payment less the amortization of the related asset.
   d. lease payment less the periodic interest expense.

4. Which of the following statements characterizes defined benefit pension plans?
   a. The employer's obligation is satisfied by making the necessary periodic contribution.
   b. Retirement benefits are based on the plan's benefit formula.
   c. Retirement benefits depend on how well pension fund assets have been managed.
   d. Contributions are made in equal amounts by employer and employees.

5. When the value of pension plan assets is greater than the projected benefit obligation,
   a. the difference is added to pension expense.
   b. the difference is reported as deferred pension cost.
   c. the difference is reported as a contra equity adjustment.
   d. the pension plan is overfunded.

6. Which of the following is *not* a component of net pension expense?
   a. Interest cost
   b. Expected return on plan assets
   c. Benefits paid to retirees
   d. Amortization of actuarial gains or losses

7. Deferred tax assets and liabilities should be reported using
   a. the tax rate in effect in the current period.
   b. the tax rates management thinks will be passed in the next year.
   c. the enacted tax rate that will be in effect when the temporary differences reverse.
   d. the enacted tax rate that was in effect when the temporary difference was created.

Multiple Choice Answers
1. a 2. d 3. d 4. b 5. d 6. c 7. c

QUESTIONS

Q10-1. Under the new lease accounting standard (Topic 842), what are the financial reporting differences between an operating lease and a finance lease? Explain.

Q10-2. For comparative purposes, when the old lease standard was in effect, were footnote disclosures sufficient to overcome nonrecognition on the balance sheet of assets and related liabilities for operating leases? Explain.

Q10-3. Is the expense of a lease over its entire life the same whether it is a finance or an operating lease? Explain.

Q10-4. What are the economic and accounting differences between a defined contribution plan and a defined benefit plan?

Q10-5. Under what circumstances will a company report a net pension asset? A net pension liability?

Q10-6. What are the components of pension expense that is reported in the income statement?

Q10-7. What effect does the use of expected returns on pension investments and the deferral of unexpected gains and losses on those investments have on income?

Q10-8. How is the initial valuation determined for lease liability and the right-of-use asset for both an operating lease and a finance lease?

Q10-9. Over what time period should the cost of providing retirement benefits to employees be expensed?

Q10-10. What is the conceptual reason why income tax expense on the income statement is not equal to cash taxes paid?

Q10-11. Under what circumstances would a tax payment be made that also requires the recording of a deferred tax asset or liability?

Q10-12 Explain what an unrecognized tax benefit is and where it is recorded on the balance sheet.

MINI EXERCISES

LO2 **M10-13. Accounting for Leases**

On January 3, 2020, Hanna Corporation signed a lease on a machine for its manufacturing operation and the lease commences on the same date. The lease requires Hanna to make six annual lease payments of $12,000 with the first payment due December 31, 2020. Hanna could have financed the machine by borrowing the purchase price at an interest rate of 7%.

a. Prepare the journal entries that Hanna Corporation would make on January 3 and December 31, 2020, to record this lease assuming
   i. the lease is reported as an operating lease.
   ii. the lease is reported as a finance lease.

b. Post the journal entries of part *a* to the appropriate T-accounts.

c. Show how the entries posted in part *b* would affect the financial statements using the financial statement effects template.

d. Explain how the financial statement effects differ between the two treatments.

LO2 **M10-14. Accounting for Leases**

On July 1, 2020, Shroff Company leased a warehouse building under a 10-year lease agreement. The lease requires quarterly lease payments of $4,500. The first lease payment is due on September 30, 2020. The lease was reported as a finance lease using an 8% annual interest rate.

a. Prepare the journal entry to record the commencement of the lease on July 1, 2020.

b. Prepare the journal entries that would be necessary on September 30 and December 31, 2020.

c. Post the entries from parts *a* and *b* in their appropriate T-accounts.

d. Prepare a financial statement effects template to show the effects of the entries from parts *a* and *b* on the balance sheet and income statement.

LO2 **M10-15. Accounting for Operating and Finance Leases**

On January 1, 2020, Weber, Inc., entered into two lease contracts. The first lease contract was a six-year lease for computer equipment with $15,000 annual lease payments due at the end of each year. Weber took possession of the equipment on January 1, 2020. The second lease contract was a six-month lease, beginning January 1, 2020, for warehouse storage space with $1,000 monthly lease payments due the first of each month. Weber made the first month's payment on January 1, 2020. The present value of the lease payments under the first contract is $74,520. The present value of the lease payments under the second contract is $5,853.

REQUIRED

a. Assume that the first lease contract is a finance lease. Prepare the appropriate journal entry for this lease on January 1, 2020.

b. Assume the second lease contract is an operating lease. Prepare the proper journal entry for this lease on January 1, 2020.

LO2 **M10-16 Accounting for Operating Leases**

On January 1, 2020, Samuels, Inc., purchased a building for $2 million to be leased. The building is expected to have a 45-year life with no salvage value. The building was leased immediately by Verdi Corp. (a calendar year-end company) for $130,000 a year payable December 31 of each year. The lease term is five years. The rate of interest implicit in the lease is 7%. The lease is classified as an operating lease.

a. Prepare an amortization schedule of the lease liability.

b. Prepare an amortization schedule for the right-of-use asset.

c. Prepare the entries for Verdi Corp for the years 2020 and 2021.

LO2 **M10-17. Accounting for Operating Leases**

Redo Mini-Exercise M10-16 but now assume the payments are made on January 1 of each year (including the first year January 1, 2020).

LO3 **M10-18. Accounting for Pension Benefits**

Bartov Corporation has a defined contribution pension plan for its employees. Each year, Bartov contributes to the plan an amount equal to 4% of the employee payroll for the year. Bartov's 2019 payroll was $400,000. Bartov also provides a life insurance benefit that pays a $50,000 death benefit to the beneficiaries of retired employees. At the end of 2019, Bartov estimates that its liability under the life insurance program is $625,000. Bartov has assets with a fair value of $175,000 in a trust fund that are available to meet the death benefit payments.

REQUIRED

a. Prepare the journal entry at December 31, 2019, to record Bartov's 2019 defined contribution to a pension trustee who will manage the pension funds for the firm's employees.

b. What amount of liability for death benefit payments must Bartov report in its December 31, 2019, balance sheet? Explain.

M10-19. Analyzing and Interpreting Pension Disclosures—Expenses and Returns

LO3, 4
Exxon Mobil Corporation
NYSE :: XOM

Exxon Mobil Corporation discloses the following information in its pension footnote in its 10-K report:

(In millions)	2017
Service cost	$1,380
Interest cost	1,570
Expected return on plan assets	(1,775)
Amortization of actuarial loss (gain)	914
Amortization of prior service cost	52
Net pension enhancement and curtailment/settlement cost	628
Net periodic pension benefit cost	$2,769

a. How much pension expense does Exxon Mobil Corporation report in its 2017 income statement?

b. What effect does its "expected return on plan assets" have on its reported pension expense? Explain.

c. Explain use of the word *expected* as it relates to results of pension plan investments.

M10-20. Analyzing and Interpreting Pension Disclosures—Expenses and Returns

LO3, 4
YUM! Brands
NYSE :: YUM

YUM! Brands, Inc., discloses the following pension footnote in its 10-K report:

	Pension Benefits	
(In millions)	2017	2016
Service cost	$10	$17
Interest cost	41	54
Amortization of prior service cost	6	6
Expected return on plan assets	(45)	(65)
Amortization of net loss	5	6
Net periodic benefit cost	$17	$18

a. How much pension expense does Yum report in its 2017 income statement?

b. What effect does its "expected return on plan assets" have on its reported pension expense? Explain.

c. Explain use of the word *expected* as it relates to results of pension plan investments.

M10-21. Analyzing and Interpreting Retirement Benefit Footnote

LO3, 4
Abercrombie & Fitch
NYSE :: ANF

Abercrombie & Fitch Co. discloses the following footnote relating to its retirement plans in its 2017 10-K report:

16. SAVINGS AND RETIREMENT PLANS: The Company maintains the Abercrombie & Fitch Co. Savings & Retirement Plan, a qualified plan. All U.S. associates are eligible to participate in this plan if they are at least 21 years of age. In addition, the Company maintains the Abercrombie & Fitch Co. Nonqualified Savings and Supplemental Retirement, composed of two sub-plans (Plan I and Plan II). Plan I contains contributions made through December 31, 2004, while Plan II contains contributions made on and after January 1, 2005. Participation in these plans is based on service and compensation. The Company's contributions to these plans are based on a percentage of associates' eligible annual compensation. The cost of the Company's contributions to these plans was $14.4 million, $11.1 million and $15.4 million for Fiscal 2017, Fiscal 2016 and Fiscal 2015, respectively.

a. Does Abercrombie have a defined contribution or defined benefit pension plan? Explain.

b. How does Abercrombie account for its contributions to its retirement plan?

c. How is Abercrombie's obligation to its retirement plan reported on its balance sheet?

LO1

Nike
NYSE :: NKE

M10-22. Analyzing and Interpreting Footnote on Contract Manufacturers

Nike, Inc., reports the following information relating to its manufacturing activities in the footnotes to its 2018 10-K report:

> We are supplied by 124 footwear factories located in 13 countries. The largest single footwear factory accounted for approximately 9% of total fiscal 2018 NIKE Brand footwear production. Virtually all of our footwear is manufactured outside of the United States by independent contract manufacturers which often operate multiple factories. For fiscal 2018, contract factories in Vietnam, China and Indonesia manufactured approximately 47%, 26% and 21% of total NIKE Brand footwear, respectively. We also have manufacturing agreements with independent contract manufacturers in Argentina, India, Brazil, Mexico and Italy to manufacture footwear for sale primarily within those countries. For fiscal 2018, five footwear contract manufacturers each accounted for greater than 10% of footwear production and in the aggregate accounted for approximately 69% of NIKE Brand footwear production.

a. What effect does the use of contract manufacturers have on Nike's balance sheet?

b. Nike executes purchase contracts with its contract manufacturers to purchase their output. How are executory contracts reported under GAAP? Does your answer suggest a possible motivation for the use of contract manufacturing?

LO5

M10-23. Computing and Reporting Deferred Income Taxes

Fisk, Inc., purchased $600,000 of construction equipment on January 1, 2019. The equipment is being depreciated on a straight-line basis over six years with no expected salvage value. MACRS depreciation is being used on the firm's tax returns. At December 31, 2021, the equipment's book value is $300,000 and its tax basis is $173,000 (this is Fisk's only temporary difference). Over the next three years, straight-line depreciation will exceed MACRS depreciation by $31,000 in 2022, $31,000 in 2023, and $65,000 in 2024. Assume that the income tax rate in effect for all years is 25%.

a. What amount of deferred tax liability should appear in Fisk's December 31, 2021, balance sheet?

b. What amount of deferred tax liability should appear in Fisk's December 31, 2022, balance sheet?

c. What amount of deferred tax liability should appear in Fisk's December 31, 2023, balance sheet?

d. Where should the deferred tax liability accounts be classified in Fisk's balance sheets?

EXERCISES

LO2

E10-24. Account for and Compare Leases Using Finance and Operating Lease Methods

Core Co. leased a piece of manufacturing equipment from E-So Co. with the following terms:

Annual lease payment:	$1,100,000
Term of lease:	5 years
Interest rate:	4.0%
Lease commences on January 1, 2020	
Payments are made on December 31 of each year in the lease term	

a. Compute the value of the right-of-use asset and the lease liability on the date the lease commences.

b. Prepare a lease liability amortization schedule and right-of-use asset amortization schedule for the lessee.

c. Record the journal entries for Core Co. for January 1, 2020–December 31, 2021, if the lease is classified as a finance lease.

d. Record the journal entries for Core Co. for January 1, 2020–December 31, 2021, if the lease is classified as an operating lease.

e. Explain the differences in the operating lease and finance lease treatments for the financial accounting statements including showing the right-of-use asset value over the term of the lease.

LO3, 4

Target
NYSE :: TGT

E10-25. Analyzing and Interpreting Pension Plan Benefit Footnote

Target Corporation provides the following footnote relating to its retirement plans in its 2017 10-K report:

> **Defined Contribution Plans** Team members who meet eligibility requirements can participate in a defined contribution 401(k) plan by investing up to 80 percent of their eligible earnings, as limited by statute or regulation. We match 100 percent of each team member's contribution up to 5 percent of eligible earnings.

Company match contributions are made to funds designated by the participant, none of which are based on Target common stock. Benefits expense related to these matching contributions was $219 million, $197 million, and $224 million in 2017, 2016, and 2015, respectively.

a. Does Target have a defined contribution or defined benefit pension plan? Explain.
b. How would Target account for its contributions to its retirement plan?
c. How is Target's obligation to its retirement plan reported on its balance sheet?
d. Do you see any problems for employees in Target's plan?

E10-26. Analyzing Lease Disclosures Regarding the Adoption of the New Lease Standard and Analyzing Across Companies **LO2**

JetBlue Airways Corporation
NASDAQ :: JBLUE
Delta Air Lines, Inc.
NYSE :: DEL

JetBlue's balance sheet and discussion of the new lease standard is as follows in their 2018 10-K:

(in millions)	2018	2017
Total assets	$10,426	$9,781
Total liabilities	5,815	5,049
Total equity	4,611	4,732

In February 2016, the FASB issued ASU 2016-02, *Leases (Topic 842)* of the Codification, which requires lessees to recognize leases on the balance sheet and disclose key information about leasing arrangements. . . . Under the new standard, a lessee will recognize liabilities on the balance sheet, initially measured at the present value of the lease payments, and right-of-use (ROU) assets representing its right to use the underlying asset for the lease term. . . .

For JetBlue, we believe the most significant impact of the new standard relates to the recognition of new assets and liabilities on our balance sheet for operating leases related to our aircraft, engines, airport terminal space, airport hangars, office space, and other facilities and equipment. Upon adoption, we expect to recognize additional lease assets and lease liabilities ranging from $1.0 billion to $1.4 billion.

1. If JetBlue records $1.2 billion of the operating leases as both an asset and a liability on January 1, 2019, how much will their debt-to-equity ratio from December 31, 2018, change (assume no other changes for JetBlue)?
2. If an analyst wants to compare Delta, who adopted in the fourth quarter of 2018, to JetBlue, who is adopting in 2019, what would the analyst need to consider and do?

E10-27. Analyzing and Interpreting Lease Footnote Disclosures Prior to and Upon Conversion to the New Lease Standard **LO1, 2**

Verizon
NYSE :: VZ

Verizon Communications Inc. provides the following balance sheet (excerpted and abbreviated) and discussion and disclosure of leases:

Verizon Communications Inc. and Subsidiaries
2018 Annual Report
Consolidated Balance Sheet information (in millions)

	2018	2017
Total assets	$248,829	$257,143
Total liabilities	210,119	212,456
Total equity	54,710	44,687

Notes to the Financial Statements
Leases

At December 31,	2018	2017
Capital leases	**$1,756**	$1,463
Less accumulated amortization	**(998)**	(692)
Total	**$ 758**	$ 771

The aggregate minimum rental commitments under noncancelable leases for the periods shown at December 31, 2018, are as follows:

	(dollars in millions)	
Years	Capital Leases	Operating Leases
2019	$ 343	$ 4,043
2020	245	3,678
2021	148	3,272
2022	100	2,871
2023	52	2,522
Thereafter	115	10,207
Total minimum rental commitments	$1,003	$26,593
Less interest and executory costs	$ (98)	
Present value of minimum lease payments	905	
Less current installments	(316)	
Long-term obligation at December 31, 2018	$ 589	

The company also discloses the following in the summary of significant accounting policies:

In February 2016, the FASB issued this standard update to increase transparency and improve comparability by requiring entities to recognize assets and liabilities on the balance sheet for all leases, with certain exceptions. In addition, through improved disclosure requirements, the standard update will enable users of financial statements to further understand the amount, timing, and uncertainty of cash flows arising from leases. . . . Upon adoption of this standard, there will be a significant impact in our consolidated balance sheet as we expect to recognize a right-of-use asset and liability related to substantially all operating lease arrangements, which we currently estimate will range between $21.0 billion and $23.0 billion. Verizon's current operating lease portfolio included in this range is primarily comprised of network equipment including towers, distributed antenna systems, and small cells, real estate, connectivity mediums including dark fiber, and equipment leases.

a. As of the end of 2018, what amount of assets are included on the balance sheet with respect to leases? What amount of liabilities?

b. What amount does Verizon state they need to add to the balance sheet as a right-of-use asset for operating leases and a lease liability for operating leases?

c. If Verizon would have adopted the new lease standard on December 31, 2018, and had determined that the right-of-use lease asset for operating leases and the liability amount were both $22 billion, how would the company's debt-to-equity ratio change? Assume no other changes on the balance sheet. (Note that they would not necessarily be the same amount; we are just assuming the same amount for simplicity.)

d. What do you predict will happen to ratios such as return-on-assets using reported numbers for both before and after the new standard is adopted?

LO6 **E10-28. Analyzing Commitments and Contingencies**

Under Armour, Inc., provides the following disclosure in the notes to its 2018 financial statements:

Under Armour, Inc.
NYSE :: UA

7. Commitments and Contingencies
(excerpts only)

Sports Marketing and Other Commitments
Within the normal course of business, the Company enters into contractual commitments in order to promote the Company's brand and products. These commitments include sponsorship agreements with teams and athletes on the collegiate and professional levels, official supplier agreements, athletic event sponsorships and other marketing commitments. The following is a schedule of the Company's future minimum payments under its sponsorship and other marketing agreements as of December 31, 2018, as well as significant sponsorship and other marketing agreements entered into during the period after December 31, 2018 through the date of this report:

(In thousands)	
2019	$126,221
2020	106,782
2021	101,543
2022	98,353
2023	91,337
2024 and thereafter	210,634
Total future minimum sponsorship and other payments	$734,869

The amounts listed above are the minimum compensation obligations and guaranteed royalty fees required to be paid under the Company's sponsorship and other marketing agreements. The amounts listed above do not include additional performance incentives and product supply obligations provided under certain agreements.

Data Incident

In early 2018, an unauthorized third party acquired data associated with the Company's Connected Fitness users' accounts for the Company's MyFitnessPal application and website. A consumer class action lawsuit has been filed against the Company in connection with this incident, and the Company has received inquiries regarding the incident from certain government regulators and agencies. The Company does not currently consider these matters to be material and believes its insurance coverage will provide coverage should any significant expense arise.

a. The above amounts of promised contractual payments to sponsored athletes are not reported on the financial statements. How might financial analysts think about these payments?

b. Compute an estimate of the present value of these payments, using Under Armour's interest rate on its debt, roughly 3%. (Note: For 2024 and thereafter, compute the number of payments to the nearest whole number.)

c. Does Under Armour record a liability associated with the litigation in response to the data incident? Why or why not?

E10-29. Analyzing Commitments and Contingencies LO6

Apple Inc. provides the following disclosure in the notes to its 2018 financial statements:

Apple Inc.
NYSE :: AAPL

Other Off-Balance-Sheet Commitments

Unconditional Purchase Obligations

The Company has entered into certain off-balance-sheet arrangements which require the future purchase of goods or services ("unconditional purchase obligations"). The Company's unconditional purchase obligations primarily consist of payments for supplier arrangements, internet and telecommunication services and intellectual property licenses. Future payments under noncancelable unconditional purchase obligations having a remaining term in excess of one year as of September 29, 2018, are as follows (in millions):

2019	$2,447
2020	3,202
2021	1,749
2022	1,596
2023	268
Thereafter	66
Total	$9,328

Contingencies

The Company is subject to various legal proceedings and claims that have arisen in the ordinary course of business and that have not been fully adjudicated . . . The outcome of litigation is inherently uncertain. If one or more legal matters were resolved against the Company in a reporting period for amounts in excess of management's expectations, the Company's financial condition and operating results for that reporting period could be materially adversely affected. In the opinion of management, there was not at least a reasonable possibility the Company may have incurred a material loss, or a material loss in excess of a recorded accrual, with respect to loss contingencies for asserted legal and other claims, except for the following matters:

Qualcomm

On January 20, 2017, the Company filed a lawsuit against Qualcomm Incorporated and affiliated parties ("Qualcomm") in the U.S. District Court for the Southern District of California seeking, among other things, to enjoin Qualcomm from requiring the Company to pay royalties at the rate demanded by Qualcomm. As the Company does not believe the demanded royalty it has historically paid contract manufacturers for each applicable device is fair, reasonable and non-discriminatory, and believes it to be invalid and/or overstated in other respects as well, no Qualcomm-related royalty payments have been remitted by the Company to its contract manufacturers since the beginning of the second quarter of 2017. The Company believes it will prevail on the merits of the case and has accrued its best estimate for the ultimate resolution of this matter.

1. Apple discloses that its rate of interest on 5-year debt securities is roughly 2.5%. Compute the present value of the future payments related to their off-balance-sheet purchase obligations. (Note: Assume that the "Thereafter" amount on the table is all paid in 2024.)
2. What would an analyst consider this to be—an asset, a liability, or equity?
3. Has Apple recorded a liability with respect to the litigation and contract with Qualcomm? What amount is recorded, if any?

YUM! Brands
NYSE :: YUM

E10-30. Analyzing and Interpreting Pension Footnote—Funded and Reported Amounts
YUM! Brands, Inc., reports the following pension footnote in its 10-K report.

December 27 (in millions)	Pension Benefits 2017
Change in benefit obligation:	
Projected benefit obligation at beginning of year	$ 993
Service cost	10
Interest cost	41
Plan amendments	2
Curtailments	(2)
Special termination benefits	2
Benefits paid	(76)
Settlement payments	(73)
Actuarial (gain) loss	115
Administrative expense	(5)
Projected benefit obligation at end of year	$1,007
Change in plan assets:	
Fair value of plan assets at beginning of year	$ 837
Actual return on plan assets	129
Employer contributions	52
Settlement payments	(73)
Benefits paid	(76)
Administrative expenses	(5)
Fair value of plan assets at end of year	$ 864
Funded status—end of year	$ (143)

a. Describe what is meant by *service cost* and *interest cost.*
b. What is the source of funds to make payments to retirees?
c. Show the computation of the 2017 funded status for Yum.
d. What net pension amount is reported on its 2017 balance sheet?

Verizon
NYSE :: VZ

E10-31. Analyzing and Interpreting Pension Footnote—Funded and Reported Amounts
Verizon Communications Inc. reports the following pension data in its 2017 10-K report.

At December 31 ($ millions)	Pension 2017
Change in Benefit Obligations:	
Beginning of year	$21,112
Service cost	280
Interest cost	683
Actuarial loss (gain), net	1,377
Benefits paid and settlements	(1,932)
Curtailment and termination benefits	11
End of year	$21,531
Change in Plan Assets:	
Beginning of year	$14,663
Actual return on plan assets	2,342
Company contributions	4,141
Benefits paid and settlements	(1,932)
Divestiture	(39)
End of year	$19,175
Funded Status:	
End of year	$ (2,356)

a. Describe what is meant by *service cost* and *interest cost.*
b. What is the source of funds to make payments to retirees?
c. Show the computation of Verizon's 2017 funded status.
d. What net pension amount is reported on its 2017 balance sheet?

E10-32. Computing and Reporting Deferred Income Taxes

LO5

Early in January 2019, Oler, Inc., purchased equipment costing $16,000. The equipment had a 2-year useful life and was depreciated in the amount of $8,000 in 2019 and 2020. Oler deducted the entire $16,000 on its tax return in 2019. This difference was the only one between its tax return and its financial statements. Oler's income before depreciation expense and income taxes was $236,000 in 2019 and $245,000 in 2020. The tax rate in each year was 25%.

REQUIRED

a. What amount of deferred tax liability should Oler report in 2019 and 2020?

b. Prepare the journal entries to record income taxes for 2019 and 2020.

c. Repeat requirement *b* if in 2019 the U.S. enacts a permanent tax rate change to be effective in 2020; the rate will increase to 35%.

E10-33. Calculating and Reporting Deferred Income Taxes

LO5

Bens' Corporation paid $12,000 on December 31, 2019, for equipment with a three-year useful life. The equipment will be depreciated in the amount of $4,000 each year. Bens' took the entire $12,000 as an expense in its tax return in 2019. Assume this is the only timing difference between the firm's books and its tax return. Bens' tax rate is 25%.

REQUIRED

a. What amount of deferred tax liability should appear in Bens' 12/31/2019 balance sheet?

b. Where in the balance sheet should the deferred tax liability appear?

c. What amount of deferred tax liability should appear in Bens' 12/31/2020 balance sheet?

E10-34. Recording Income Tax Expense

LO5

Homework MBC

Nike
NYSE :: NKE

Nike, Inc., reports the following tax information in the notes to its 2018 financial report.

Income before income taxes is as follows:

Year Ended May 31 (In millions)	2018	2017	2016
Income before income taxes:			
United States	$ 744	$1,240	$ 956
Foreign	3,581	3,646	3,667
	$4,325	$4,886	$4,623

The provision for income taxes is as follows:

Year Ended May 31 (In millions)	2018	2017	2016
Current:			
United States			
Federal	$1,167	$398	$304
State	45	82	71
Foreign	533	439	568
	1,745	919	943
Deferred:			
United States			
Federal	595	(279)	(57)
State	25	(9)	(16)
Foreign	27	15	(7)
	647	(273)	(80)
	$2,392	$646	$863

Nike also states the following:

The effective tax rate for the year ended May 31, 2018 was higher than the effective tax rate for the year ended May 31, 2017 primarily due to the enactment of the Tax Act, which included provisional expense of $1,875 million for the one-time transition tax on the deemed repatriation of undistributed foreign earnings, and $158 million due to the remeasurement of deferred tax assets and liabilities.

a. Record Nike's provision for income taxes for 2018 using the financial statement effects template.

b. Record Nike's provision for income taxes for 2018 using journal entries.
c. Explain how the provision for income taxes affects Nike's financial statements.
d. Calculate and compare Nike's effective tax rate for 2018, 2017, and 2016.

LO5 **E10-35. Recording Income Tax Expense**

Boeing
NYSE :: BA

The Boeing Company reports the following tax information in its 2018 financial report.

Year Ended December 31,	2018	2017	2016
Current tax expense:			
U.S. federal	$1,873	$1,276	$1,193
Non-U.S.	169	149	133
U.S. state	97	23	15
	2,139	1,448	1,341
Deferred tax expense			
U.S. federal	(996)	204	(544)
Non-U.S.	(4)	3	(4)
U.S. state	5	(6)	(44)
	(995)	201	(592)
Total income tax expense	$1,144	$1,649	$ 749

a. Record Boeing's provision for income taxes for 2018 using the financial statement effects template.
b. Record Boeing's provision for income taxes for 2018 using journal entries.
c. Explain how the provision for income affects Boeing's financial statements.

PROBLEMS

LO2 **P10-36. Analyzing and Interpreting Leases**

United Continental Holdings, Inc.
NASDAQ :: UAL

United Continental Holdings, Inc., did not adopt the new lease standard in 2018 but provides the following disclosure its 2018 10-K report ($ millions).

Consolidated Balance Sheets as of December 31,	As Reported		New Lease Standard Adjustments		As Adjusted	
	2018	2017	2018	2017	2018	2017
Operating property and equipment:						
Other property and equipment (owned)	$ 7,919	$ 6,946	$(1,041)	$(922)	$ 6,878	$ 6,024
Less-accumulated depreciation and amortization (owned)	(12,760)	(11,159)	140	92	(12,620)	(11,067)
Flight equipment (finance leases)[(a)]	1,029	1,151	(37)	(211)	992	940
Less-accumulated amortization	(654)	(777)	8	169	(646)	(608)
Operating lease assets						
Flight equipment	—	—	2,380	3,102	2,380	3,102
Other property and equipment	—	—	2,882	2,975	2,882	2,975
Current liabilities:						
Current maturities of finance leases[(a)]	149	128	(26)	(50)	123	78
Current maturities of operating leases	—	—	719	949	719	949
Other	619	576	(66)	(58)	553	518
Long-term obligations under finance leases[(a)]	1,134	996	(910)	(766)	224	230
Long-term obligations under operating leases	—	—	5,276	5,789	5,276	5,789

[(a)] Finance leases, under the New Lease Standard, are the equivalent of capital leases under Topic 840.

The adoption of the New Lease Standard primarily resulted in the recording of assets and obligations of our operating leases on our consolidated balance sheets. Certain amounts recorded for prepaid and accrued rent associated with historical operating leases were reclassified to the newly captioned Operating lease assets in the consolidated balance sheets. Also, certain leases designated under Topic 840 as owned assets and capitalized finance leases will not be considered assets under the New Lease Standard and will be removed from the consolidated balance sheets, along with the related capital lease liability.

a. What is the amount United discloses that it would have capitalized for operating leases as right-of-use lease assets for the year ended December 31, 2018?

b. What is the amount of additional liability United discloses that it would have recorded for operating leases had United adopted the new lease standard in 2018?

c. What is the amount of asset under the new lease standard for finance leases? For the lease liability related to finance leases?

d. Why do you think the amount of operating leases is so much greater than finance leases?

e. United reported total assets of $44,792 million, total liabilities of $34,797 million, and total shareholders' equity of $9,995 million. Net income for the year was reported as $2,129 for the year and is essentially unchanged as a result of the new lease standard. Compute the reported return-on-assets and debt-to-equity ratios. Compute the ratios adjusted for the new lease standard, only taking into account the changes for operating leases (ignore all other changes).

P10-37. Analyzing Lease Disclosures

LO2
American Airlines Group, Inc.
NASDAQ :: AAL

American Airlines Group, Inc., provides the following disclosures in the notes to their 2018 financial statements (excerpted for brevity):

Note 1: Basis of Presentation and Summary of Significant Accounting Policies

ASU 2016-02: Leases (Topic 842) (the New Lease Standard)

The New Lease Standard requires lessees to recognize a lease liability and a right-of-use (ROU) asset on the balance sheet for operating leases. Accounting for finance leases is substantially unchanged. The New Lease Standard is effective for fiscal years beginning after December 15, 2018, including interim periods within those fiscal years. Early adoption is permitted.

In the fourth quarter of 2018, we elected to early adopt the New Lease Standard as of January 1, 2018 using a modified retrospective transition, with the cumulative-effect adjustment to the opening balance of retained earnings as of the effective date (the effective date method). Under the effective date method, financial results reported in periods prior to 2018 are unchanged. ...

The adoption of the New Lease Standard had a significant impact on our consolidated balance sheet due to the recognition of approximately $10 billion of lease liabilities with corresponding right-of-use assets for operating leases.

6. Leases

We lease certain aircraft and engines, including aircraft under capacity purchase agreements. As of December 31, 2018, we had 660 leased aircraft, with remaining terms ranging from less than one year to 12 years.

Supplemental balance sheet information related to leases was as follows (in millions, except lease term and discount rate):

	December 31, 2018
Operating leases:	
Operating lease ROU assets	$9,151
Current operating lease liabilities	$1,654
Noncurrent operating lease liabilities	7,902
Total operating lease liabilities	$9,556
Finance leases:	
Property and equipment, at cost	$ 936
Accumulated amortization	(391)
Property and equipment, net	$ 545
Current obligations of finance leases	$ 81
Finance leases, net of current obligations	613
Total finance lease liabilities	$ 694

The components of lease expense were as follows (in millions):

	Year Ended December 31, 2018
Operating lease cost	$1,907
Finance lease cost:	
Amortization of assets.	78
Interest on lease liabilities.	48
Variable lease cost.	2,353
Total net lease cost.	$4,386

a. What is the right-of-use asset for operating leases as of the end of 2018?

b. What is the net asset recorded for finance leases?

c. What is the lease liability balance for operating leases as of the end of 2018? What does this amount represent?

d. What is the amount of amortization expense recorded in 2018 for finance leases? For operating leases?

e. What is the amount of interest expense recorded in 2018 for finance leases? For operating leases?

f. Using the $10 billion round figure that American cites, show the journal entry that American would have recorded to account for operating leases under the new standard on the date of adoption.

LO6
Cisco Systems, Inc.
NASDAQ :: CSCO

P10-38. Analyze Commitment and Contingency Disclosures

Cisco Systems, Inc., reports the following in the Commitments and Contingencies note to their 10-K for the year ended July 2018.

Purchase Commitments with Contract Manufacturers and Suppliers

We purchase components from a variety of suppliers and use several contract manufacturers to provide manufacturing services for our products. During the normal course of business, in order to manage manufacturing lead times and help ensure adequate component supply, we enter into agreements with contract manufacturers and suppliers that either allow them to procure inventory based upon criteria as defined by us or establish the parameters defining our requirements. A significant portion of our reported purchase commitments arising from these agreements consists of firm, noncancelable, and unconditional commitments. Certain of these purchase commitments with contract manufacturers and suppliers relate to arrangements to secure long-term pricing for certain product components for multi-year periods. In certain instances, these agreements allow us the option to cancel, reschedule, and adjust our requirements based on our business needs prior to firm orders being placed.

The following table summarizes our purchase commitments with contract manufacturers and suppliers (in millions):

Commitments by Period	July 28, 2018	July 29, 2017
Less than 1 year.	$5,407	$4,620
1 to 3 years.	710	20
3 to 5 years.	360	—
Total	$6,477	$4,640

We record a liability for firm, noncancelable, and unconditional purchase commitments for quantities in excess of our future demand forecasts consistent with the valuation of our excess and obsolete inventory. As of July 28, 2018 and July 29, 2017, the liability for these purchase commitments was $159 million and $162 million, respectively, and was included in other current liabilities.

a. What effect does the use of contract manufacturers have on Cisco's balance sheet?

b. Assuming an interest rate of 4% and payments due in 2 years ($710 million) and 4 years ($360 million), what is the present value of these commitments as of July 2018?

c. What amount does Cisco state that it has accrued as of July 2018?

LO3, 4

P10-39. Analyzing and Interpreting Pension Disclosures

Hoopes Corporation's December 31, 2019, 10-K report has the following disclosures related to its retirement plans.

The following table provides a reconciliation of the changes in the pension plans' benefit obligations and fair value of assets over the two-year period ended December 31, 2019, and a statement of the funded status as of December 31, 2019 and 2018 (in millions):

	Pension Plans	
(in millions)	**2019**	**2018**
Changes in Projected Benefit Obligation ("PBO")		
PBO at beginning of year	$14,484	$11,050
Service cost	521	417
Interest cost	900	823
Actuarial (gain) loss	1,875	2,607
Benefits paid	(468)	(391)
Other	60	(22)
PBO at end of year	$17,372	$14,484
Change in Plan Assets		
Fair value of plan assets at beginning of year	$13,295	$10,812
Actual return on plan assets	2,425	1,994
Company contributions	557	900
Benefits paid	(468)	(391)
Other	32	(20)
Fair value of plan assets at end of year	$15,841	$13,295

Net periodic benefit cost for the three years ended December 31 were as follows (in millions):

	Pension Plans		
(in millions)	**2019**	**2018**	**2017**
Service cost	$ 521	$417	$ 499
Interest cost	900	823	798
Expected return on plan assets	(1,062)	(955)	(1,059)
Recognized actuarial (gains) losses and other	184	23	(61)
Net periodic benefit cost	$ 543	$308	$ 177

Weighted-average actuarial assumptions for our primary U.S. pension plans, which represent substantially all of our PBO, are as follows:

	Pension Plans		
(in millions)	**2019**	**2018**	**2017**
Discount rate used to determine benefit obligation	5.76%	6.37%	7.68%
Rate of increase in future compensation levels used to determine benefit obligation	4.58	4.63	4.42
Expected long-term rate of return on assets	8.00	8.00	8.50

REQUIRED

a. How much pension expense (revenue) does Hoopes report in its 2019 income statement?

b. Hoopes reports a $1,062 million expected return on plan assets as an offset to 2019 pension expense. Approximately, how is this amount computed? What is the actual gain or loss realized on its 2019 plan assets? What is the purpose of using this estimated amount instead of the actual gain or loss?

c. What factors affected its 2019 pension liability? What factors affected its 2019 plan assets?

d. What does the term *funded status* mean? What is the funded status of the 2019 Hoopes retirement plans? What amount of asset or liability does Hoopes report on its 2019 balance sheet relating to its retirement plans?

e. Hoopes decreased its discount rate from 6.37% to 5.76% in 2019. What effect(s) does this have on its balance sheet and its income statement?

f. Hoopes changed its estimate of expected annual wage increases used to determine its defined benefit obligation in 2019. What effect(s) does this change have on its financial statements? In general, how does such a change affect income?

LO3, 4
Johnson and Johnson
NYSE :: JNJ

P10-40. Analyzing and Interpreting Pension Footnote—Funded and Reported Amounts
JoÚson and JoÚson reports the following pension footnote as part of its 2017 10-K report.

(in millions)	Pension Benefits 2017
Change in Benefit Obligation:	
Projected benefit obligation—beginning of year	$28,116
Service cost	1,080
Interest cost	927
Plan participant contributions	60
Amendments	(7)
Actuarial (gains) losses	2,996
Divestitures and acquisitions	201
Curtailments, settlements and restructuring	(35)
Benefits paid from plan	(1,050)
Effect of exchange rates	933
Projected benefit obligation—end of year	$33,221
Change in Plan Assets:	
Plan assets at fair value—beginning of year	$23,633
Actual return on plan assets	4,274
Company contributions	664
Plan participant contributions	60
Settlements	(32)
Divestitures and acquisitions	173
Benefits paid from plan assets	(1,050)
Effect of exchange rates	682
Plan assets at fair value—end of year	$28,404
Funded status—end of year	$ (4,817)

a. Describe what is meant by *service cost* and *interest cost*.
b. What is the actual return on pension investments in 2017?
c. Provide an example under which an “actuarial loss,” such as the $2,996 million loss that Johnson and Johnson reports in 2017, might arise.
d. What is the source of funds to make payments to retirees?
e. How much cash did Johnson and Johnson contribute to its pension plans in 2017?
f. How much cash did the company pay to retirees in 2017?
g. Show the computation of its 2017 funded status.
h. What net pension amount is reported on its 2017 balance sheet?

LO5
Deere & Company
NYSE :: DE

P10-41. Interpreting the Income Tax Expense Footnote
Deere & Company reports the following tax information in its fiscal 2018 financial report.

The provision for income taxes by taxing jurisdiction and by significant component consisted of the following in millions of dollars:

	2018	2017	2016
Current:			
U.S.:			
Federal	$ (268)	$360	$ 51
State	123	48	26
Foreign	392	463	340
Total current	247	871	417

continued

continued from previous page

	2018	2017	2016
Deferred:			
U.S.:			
Federal	1,233	59	297
State	(40)	7	11
Foreign	287	34	(25)
Total deferred	1,480	100	283
Provision for income taxes	$1,727	$971	$700
Earnings before taxes on the income statement	$4,070.7	$3,153.8	$2,224.0

REQUIRED

a. What amount of tax expense is reported in Deere's 2018 income statement? In 2017? In 2016? How much of each year's income tax expense is current tax expense and how much is deferred tax expense?

b. Compute Deere's effective tax rate for each year.

c. Assume that Deere's deferred tax in 2018 is due to deferred tax liabilities. Provide one possible example that would be consistent with this situation.

P10-42. Calculating and Reporting Income Tax Expense **LO5** Homework MBC

Lynch Company began operations in 2019. The company reported $24,000 of depreciation expense on its income statement in 2019 and $26,000 in 2020. On its tax returns, Lynch deducted $32,000 for depreciation in 2019 and $37,000 in 2020. The 2020 tax return shows a tax obligation (liability) of $12,000 based on a 25% tax rate.

REQUIRED

a. Determine the temporary difference between the book value of depreciable assets and the tax basis of these assets at the end of 2019 and 2020.

b. Calculate the deferred tax liability for each year.

c. Calculate the income tax expense for 2020.

d. Prepare a journal entry to record income tax expense and post the entry to the appropriate T-accounts for 2020.

P10-43. Calculating and Reporting Income Tax Expense **LO5**

Carter Inc. began operations in 2019. The company reported $130,000 of depreciation expense on its 2019 income statement and $128,000 in 2020. Carter Inc. deducted $140,000 for depreciation on its tax return in 2019 and $122,000 in 2020. The company reports a tax obligation of $45,150 for 2020 based on a tax rate of 25%.

REQUIRED

a. Determine the temporary difference between the book value of depreciable assets and the tax basis of these assets at the end of 2019 and 2020.

b. Calculate the deferred tax liability at the end of each year.

c. Calculate the income tax expense for 2020.

d. Prepare a journal entry to record income tax for 2020 and post the entry to the appropriate T-accounts.

P10-44. Computing and Reporting Deferred Income Taxes **LO5** **Macy's, Inc.** NASDAQ :: M

Macy's, Inc., reported the following in its 2017 annual report:

On December 22, 2017, H.R. 1 was enacted into law. This new tax legislation, among other things, reduced the U.S. federal corporate tax rate from 35% to 21% effective January 1, 2018.

In applying the impacts of the new tax legislation to its 2017 income tax provision, the Company remeasured its deferred tax assets and liabilities based on the rates at which they are expected to reverse in the future, which is generally a 21% federal tax rate and its related impact on the state tax rates. The resulting impact was the recognition of an income tax benefit of $571 million in the fourth quarter of 2017. In addition, applying the new U.S. federal corporate tax rate of 21% on January 1, 2018, resulted in a federal income tax statutory rate of 33.7% in 2017. Combining the impacts on the Company's current income tax provision and the remeasurement of its deferred tax balances, the Company's effective income tax rate was a benefit of 1.9% in 2017.

The tax effects of temporary differences that give rise to significant portions of the deferred tax assets and deferred tax liabilities are as follows:

(millions)	Feb. 3, 2018	Jan. 28, 2017
Deferred tax assets		
Postemployment and postretirement benefits	$ 188	$ 405
Accrued liabilities accounted for on a cash basis for tax purposes	218	379
Long-term debt	25	63
Unrecognized state tax benefits and accrued interest	39	76
State operating loss and credit carryforwards	101	79
Other	165	347
Valuation allowance	(65)	(36)
Total deferred tax assets	671	1,313
Deferred tax liabilities		
Excess of book basis over tax basis of property and equipment	(923)	(1,381)
Merchandise inventories	(389)	(604)
Intangible assets	(276)	(380)
Other	(205)	(391)
Total deferred tax liabilities	(1,793)	(2,756)
Net deferred tax liability	$(1,122)	$(1,443)

a. What was the amount of income tax expense or benefit that Macy's reported related to revaluing deferred tax assets and liabilities to the new, lower tax rate?

b. Explain why Macy's reported an income tax *benefit* when it revalued its deferred income tax liabilities and deferred income tax assets to the new, lower tax rate.

CASES AND PROJECTS

LO3, 4
DowDuPont Inc.
NYSE :: DWDP

C10-45. Analyzing and Interpreting Pension Disclosures

DowDuPont Inc. provides the following footnote disclosures in its 10-K report relating to its pension plans.

	Defined Benefit Pension Plans	
(in millions)	2018	2017
Service cost	$ 651	$ 555
Interest cost	1,638	1,130
Expected return on plan assets	(2,846)	(1,955)
Amortization of prior service cost	(24)	(25)
Amortization of unrecognized loss (gain)	649	638
Curtailment/settlement/other	(10)	683
Net periodic cost	$ 58	$ 1,026
Change in Project Benefit Obligation:		
Benefit obligation at beginning of year	$57,401	$30,280
Merger impact	—	26,036
Service cost	651	555
Interest cost	1,638	1,130
Plan participants' contributions	29	20
Actuarial changes in assumptions and experience	(2,832)	1,781
Benefits paid	(3,223)	(2,170)
Plan amendments	34	14
Acquisitions/divestitures/other	(57)	72
Effect of foreign exchange rates	(627)	875
Termination benefits/curtailment cost/settlements	—	(1,192)
Benefit obligation at end of year	$53,014	$57,401

continued

continued from previous page

	2018	2017
Change in Plan Assets:		
Fair value of plan assets at beginning of year	$43,685	$21,208
Merger impact	—	20,395
Actual return on plan assets	(1,524)	3,049
Employer contributions	2,964	1,744
Plan participants' contributions	29	20
Benefits paid	(3,223)	(2,170)
Acquisition/divestiture/other	(7)	14
Effect of foreign exchange rates	(462)	613
Settlements	—	(1,188)
Fair value of plan assets at end of year	$41,462	$43,685

	Benefit Obligations at December 31	
Weighted Average Assumptions for All Pension Plans	**2018**	**2017**
Discount rate	3.80%	3.26%
Interest crediting rate for applicable benefits	3.72%	3.61%
Rate of compensation increase	3.42%	3.95%
Expected return on plan assets	—	—

REQUIRED

a. How much pension expense (revenue) does DowDuPont report in its 2018 income statement?

b. DowDuPont reports a $2,846 million expected return on plan assets as an offset to 2018 pension expense. Estimate the rate of return DowDuPont expected to earn on its plan assets in 2018.

c. What factors affected its 2018 pension liability? What factors affected its 2018 plan assets?

d. What does the term *funded status* mean? What is the funded status of the 2018 DowDuPont retirement plans at the end of 2018? What amount of asset or liability should DowDuPont report on its 2018 balance sheet relating to its retirement plans?

e. DowDuPont changed its discount rate from 3.26% to 3.80% in 2018. What effect(s) does this change have on its balance sheet and its income statement?

f. Suppose DowDuPont increased its estimate of expected returns on plan assets in 2019. What effect(s) would this increase have on its income statement? Explain.

g. DowDuPont provides us with its weighted-average discount rate. The company operates 441 manufacturing facilities and has roughly 98,000 employees all over the world. Would you expect that the discount rate differed in the United States from the average rate outside the United States? Explain. What would you expect for future compensation levels?

C10-46. Interpreting Finance and Operating Leases

LO1, 2
Target Corporation
NYSE: TGT

Target Corporation disclosed the following in the notes to their 2018 10-K. (Note that Target adopted the new lease standard using a method of adoption that restates prior years to be presented as if the new standard were adopted in the prior years.)

Leases

We adopted ASU No. 2016-02—*Leases (Topic 842)*, as amended, as of February 4, 2018, using the modified retrospective approach. The modified retrospective approach provides a method for recording existing leases at adoption and in comparative periods that approximates the results of a full retrospective approach. In addition, we elected the package of practical expedients permitted under the transition guidance within the new standard, which among other things, allowed us to carry forward the historical lease classification. We also elected the practical expedient related to land easements, allowing us to carry forward our accounting treatment for land easements on existing agreements.

Adoption of the new standard resulted in the recording of additional net lease assets and lease liabilities of approximately $1.3 billion and $1.4 billion respectively, as of February 4, 2018. The difference between the additional lease assets and lease liabilities, net of the deferred tax impact, was recorded as an adjustment to retained earnings. The standard did not materially impact our consolidated net earnings and had no impact on cash flows.

Leases (millions)	Classification	Feb. 2, 2019	Feb. 3, 2018
Assets			
Operating	Operating lease assets.	$1,965	$1,884
Finance	Buildings and improvements, net of accumulated depreciation[(a)]. . . .	872	836
Total leased assets.		$2,837	$2,720
Liabilities			
Current			
Operating	Accrued and other current liabilities	$ 166	$ 148
Finance	Current portion of long-term debt and other borrowings.	53	80
Noncurrent			
Operating	Noncurrent operating lease liabilities	2,004	1,924
Finance	Long-term debt and other borrowings	968	885
Total lease liabilities		$3,191	$3,037

Note: As most of our leases do not provide an implicit rate, we use our incremental borrowing rate based on the information available at commencement date in determining the present value of lease payments. We use the incremental borrowing rate on January 31, 2016, for operating leases that commenced prior to that date.

[(a)] Finance lease assets are recorded net of accumulated amortization of $371 million and $317 million as of February 2, 2019 and February 3, 2018, respectively.

Lease Cost (millions)	Classification	2018	2017	2016
Operating lease cost[(a)]	SG&A expenses	$251	$221	$199
Finance lease cost				
Amortization of leased assets	Depreciation and amortization[(b)]. . . .	65	63	87
Interest on lease liabilities	Net interest expense.	42	42	36
Sublease income[(c)]	Other revenue.	(11)	(9)	(7)
Net lease cost.		$347	$317	$315

[(a)] Includes short-term leases and variable lease costs, which are immaterial.

[(b)] Supply chain-related amounts are included in Cost of Sales.

[(c)] Sublease income excludes rental income from owned properties of $47 million for 2018, 2017, and 2016, which is included in Other Revenue.

Maturity of Lease Liabilities (millions)	Operating Leases[(a)]	Finance Leases[(b)]	Total
2019	$ 245	$ 98	$ 343
2020	238	98	336
2021	232	98	330
2022	226	99	325
2023	217	94	311
After 2023.	1,746	974	2,720
Total lease payments	$2,904	$1,461	$4,365
Less: Interest	734	440	
Present value of lease liabilities	$2,170	$1,021	

[(a)] Operating lease payments include $778 million related to options to extend lease terms that are reasonably certain of being exercised and exclude $341 million of legally binding minimum lease payments for leases signed but not yet commenced.

[(b)] Finance lease payments include $127 million related to options to extend lease terms that are reasonably certain of being exercised and exclude $193 million of legally binding minimum lease payments for leases signed but not yet commenced.

a. What is the right-of-use asset for operating leases as of the end of fiscal 2018?

b. What is the net asset recorded for finance leases at the end of fiscal 2018?

c. What is the lease liability balance for operating leases as of the end of fiscal 2018? What does this amount represent?

d. What is the amount of amortization expense recorded in 2018 for finance leases?

e. What is the amount of interest expense recorded in 2018 for finance leases?

f. What is recorded on the income statement for operating leases?

g. Assume the lease payment for 2018 for finance leases is $125 million. Record the entries for 2018 (year ended February 2, 2019) for finance leases.

h. Discuss the implications of the different line items on the income statement for expensing lease costs for both types of leases that Target discloses.

i. Target has reported total assets for 2018 (year ended February 2, 2019) of $41,290, total liabilities of $29,993, and equity of $11,297. Explain the effect on debt-to-equity from having the operating leases "on-balance sheet."

C10-47. Interpreting Income Tax Footnotes

LO5
Williams-Sonoma
NYSE :: WSM

The following information is taken from **Williams-Sonoma, Inc.**'s 10-K.

Note D: Income Taxes

The components of earnings before income taxes, by tax jurisdiction, are as follows:

	Fiscal Year Ended		
(in thousands)	**2017**	**2016**	**2015**
United States	$379,000	$425,517	$462,701
Foreign	73,439	46,394	25,306
Total earnings before income taxes	$452,439	$471,911	$488,007

The provision for income taxes consists of the following:

	Fiscal Year Ended		
(in thousands)	**2017**	**2016**	**2015**
Current			
Federal	$ 97,202	$125,760	$156,812
State	19,552	26,197	22,969
Foreign	12,759	7,453	5,594
Total current	129,513	159,410	185,375
Deferred			
Federal	62,893	8,307	(6,093)
State	460	(807)	1,258
Foreign	28	(386)	(2,601)
Total deferred	63,381	7,114	(7,436)
Total provision	$192,894	$166,524	$177,939

Deferred Tax Assets (Liabilities), in thousands	**Jan. 28, 2018**	**Jan. 29, 2017**
Customer deposits	$ 23,601	$ 64,776
Merchandise inventories	23,314	32,003
Deferred rent	18,387	24,182
Compensation	14,127	16,781
Accrued liabilities	13,626	23,994
Stock-based compensation	9,024	17,437
Federal and state net operating loss	6,026	2,797
Exective deferred compensation	5,886	7,060
State taxes	5,099	7,107
Deferred lease incentive	(24,854)	(36,715)
Depreciation	(17,361)	(22,477)
Prepaid catalog expenses	(5,386)	(8,726)
Other	(3,116)	8,014
Valuation allowance	(1,067)	(995)
Total deferred income tax assets, net	$ 67,306	$135,238

We have historically elected not to provide for U.S. income taxes with respect to the undistributed earnings of our foreign subsidiaries as we intended to utilize those earnings in our foreign operations for an indefinite period of time. As a result of the Tax Act, we are deemed to have remitted all of the post-1986 accumulated earnings of our foreign subsidiaries to the U.S. as of December 31, 2017 as part of the transition tax. . . . In light of the Tax Act, we continue to evaluate our permanent reinvestment assertion and expect our evaluation of the impact to be completed within the one-year measurement period under SAB 118. . . .

Our U.S. federal statutory rate for fiscal 2017 was a blended rate of 33.9%, and our rate will be 21% for future fiscal years. Based on information available as of January 28, 2018, we recorded a net tax expense of $13,200,000 for the transition tax and $28,300,000 for the remeasurement of our deferred tax assets.

REQUIRED

a. What amount of income tax expense did Williams-Sonoma report for the year ended January 28, 2018?

b. Calculate Williams-Sonoma's effective tax rate for each year reported. In addition, calculate the rate of U.S. federal taxes on U.S. income in the fiscal year ended January 28, 2018.

c. Williams-Sonoma reported income taxes payable of $56,783 thousand in its January 28, 2018, balance sheet, and $23,245 thousand at January 29, 2017. What amount of income taxes did it pay in cash during the fiscal year ended January 28, 2018?[15]

d. Prepare a journal entry to record income tax expense for the fiscal year ended January 28, 2018.

e. The company reported a net book value of property, plant, and equipment of $932,283 thousand on January 28, 2018. Given a tax rate of 21% (assume they are all in the U.S.), what is an estimate of the tax basis of these assets on that date?

f. The company reported prepaid catalog expense of $58,693 thousand as a current asset in its January 28, 2018, balance sheet. The company provided the following explanation of this asset in the footnotes to its 10-K:

Advertising and Prepaid Catalog Expenses
Advertising expenses consist of media and production costs related to catalog mailings, e-commerce advertising and other direct marketing activities. All advertising costs are expensed as incurred, or upon the release of the initial advertisement, with the exception of prepaid catalog expenses. Prepaid catalog expenses consist primarily of third party incremental direct costs, including creative design, paper, printing, postage and mailing costs for all of our direct response catalogs. Such costs are capitalized as prepaid catalog expenses and are amortized over their expected period of future benefit. . . . Each catalog is generally fully amortized over a six to nine month period, with the majority of the amortization occurring within the first four to five months.

Explain how this expense results in a temporary difference between tax and financial reporting.

g. What does Williams-Sonoma say they have accrued for the TCJA Transition Tax? How did this amount affect income tax expense?

h. Williams-Sonoma has a valuation allowance listed in its schedule of deferred tax assets and liabilities. Briefly and in general explain what a valuation allowance is and how it affects deferred taxes and reported income.

i. Williams-Sonoma states that the company recorded a $28.3 million additional tax expense for the remeasurement of deferred tax assets. Explain what this is and why the company had to record this expense.

LO5 **C10-48. Interpreting Income Tax Disclosures**

Alphabet Inc.
NASDAQ :: GOOG

Alphabet Inc. reported the following in note 14 to its 2018 10-K report:

Note 14. Income Taxes
Income from continuing operations before income taxes included income from domestic operations of $12.0 billion, $10.7 billion, and $15.8 billion for the years ended December 31, 2016, 2017, and 2018, respectively, and income from foreign operations of $12.1 billion, $16.5 billion, and $19.1 billion for the years ended December 31, 2016, 2017, and 2018, respectively.

The provision for income taxes consists of the following (in millions):

[15] For this problem, assume a simple case. The complicating factors that would change the answer are beyond the scope of this text. For those readers aware of these complicating factors, assume there are no acquisitions of other companies during the year and that Williams-Sonoma has no unrecognized tax benefits.

	Year Ended December 31,		
	2016	2017	2018
Current:			
Federal and state	$3,826	$12,608	$2,153
Foreign	966	1,746	1,251
Total	4,792	14,354	3,404
Deferred:			
Federal and state	(70)	220	907
Foreign	(50)	(43)	(134)
Total	(120)	177	773
Provision for income taxes	$4,672	$14,531	$4,177

One-time transition tax

The Tax Act required us to pay U.S. income taxes on accumulated foreign subsidiary earnings not previously subject to U.S. income tax at a rate of 15.5% to the extent of foreign cash and certain other net current assets and 8% on the remaining earnings. We recorded a provisional amount for our one-time transitional tax liability and income tax expense of $10.2 billion as of December 31, 2017.

REQUIRED

a. Compute Alphabet's effective tax rate for each year presented. Also, compute Alphabet's domestic tax rate (federal plus state) and its foreign tax rate on income from foreign operations.

b. How much did Alphabet record for the one-time transition tax related to the TCJA. How does this affect the income statement? The balance sheet?

SOLUTIONS TO REVIEW PROBLEMS

Mid-Chapter Review 1

SOLUTION TO PART A

The present value of the lease payments is $224,755, computed as $32,000 × 7.02358 (from Appendix A, Table A-3) or computed using a financial calculator or Excel. At the commencement of the finance lease, The Gap would record a Right-of-Use Asset for the finance lease and a Finance Lease Liability.

The amortization table for the loan is as follows:

Amortization Table for a Lease Liability*

A	B	C	D	E	F
Year	Beginning of Year Lease Liability	Interest Expense (B x 7%)	Payment	Principal Payment (D – C)	Ending-year Lease Liability (B – E)
1	$224,755	15,733	32,000	16,267	208,488
2	208,488	14,594	32,000	17,406	191,082
3	191,082	13,376	32,000	18,624	172,458
4	172,458	12,072	32,000	19,928	152,530
5	152,530	10,677	32,000	21,323	131,207
6	131,207	9,184	32,000	22,816	108,391
7	108,391	7,587	32,000	24,413	83,978
8	83,978	5,878	32,000	26,122	57,856
9	57,856	4,050	32,000	27,950	29,906
10	29,906	2,093	32,000	29,907	0

* Small differences due to rounding

1. Entry for finance lease treatment—commencement of lease.

ANALYZE

Transaction	Cash Asset	+ Noncash Assets	− Contra Assets	= Liabil-ities	+ Contrib. Capital	+ Earned Capital	Revenues	− Expenses	= Net Income
	Balance Sheet						***Income Statement***		
Lease store space using finance-type lease.		+224,755 Right-of-Use Asset—Finance Lease		= +224,755 Finance Lease Liability				−	=

JOURNALIZE

(1) Right-of-use asset—Finance lease (+A)	224,755	
Finance lease liability (+L)		224,755

POST

+ Right-of-Use Asset—Finance Lease (A) −	
(1) 224,755	

− Finance Lease Liability (L) +	
	224,755 (1)

2. At the end of the first year, Gap would record amortization expense of $22,476 ($224,755/10), interest expense of $15,733 ($224,755 × .07; and see table above), and the lease payment.

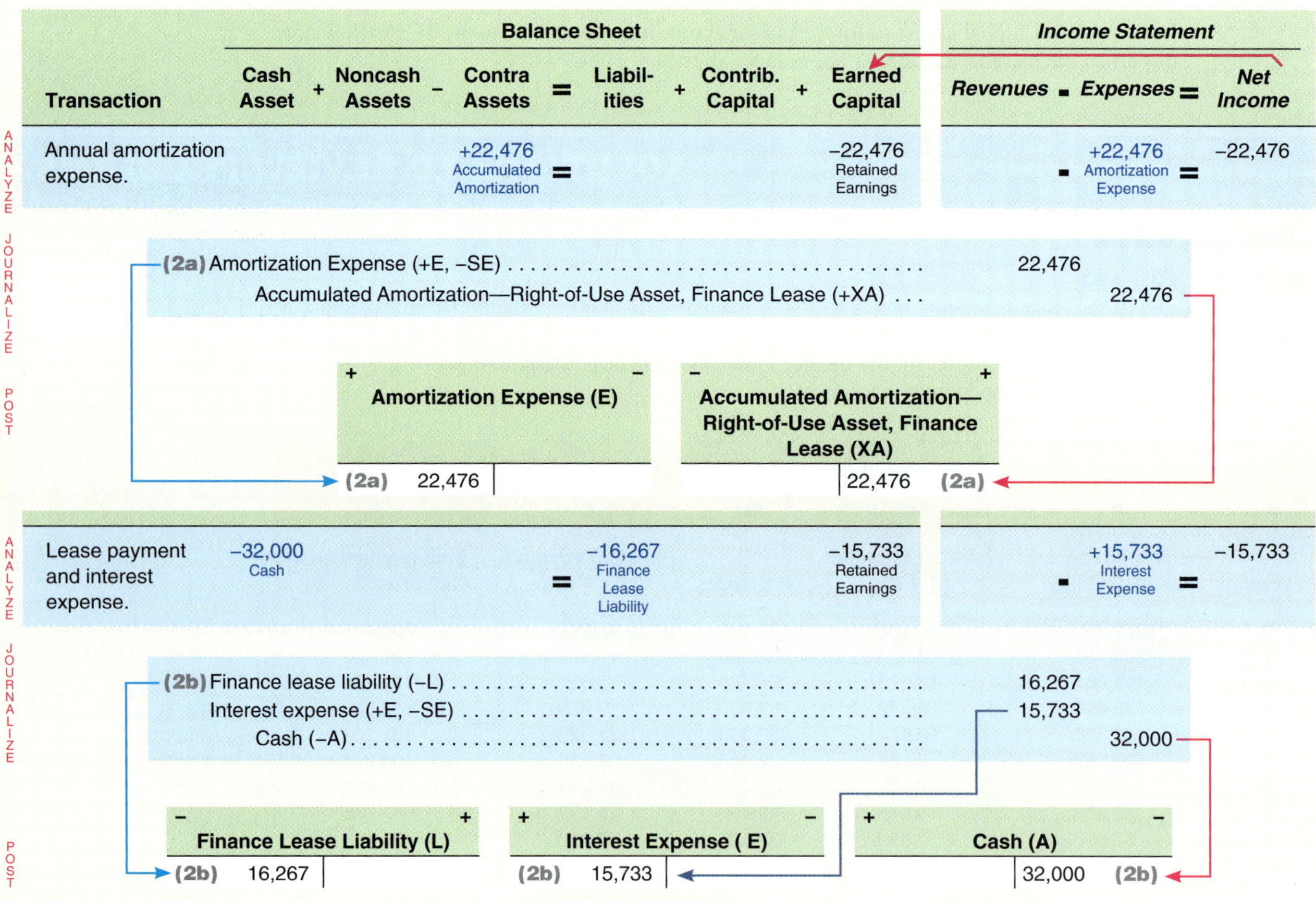

ANALYZE

Transaction	Cash Asset	+ Noncash Assets	− Contra Assets	= Liabil-ities	+ Contrib. Capital	+ Earned Capital	Revenues	− Expenses	= Net Income
	Balance Sheet						***Income Statement***		
Annual amortization expense.			+22,476 Accumulated Amortization	=		−22,476 Retained Earnings		− +22,476 Amortization Expense	= −22,476

JOURNALIZE

(2a) Amortization Expense (+E, −SE)	22,476	
Accumulated Amortization—Right-of-Use Asset, Finance Lease (+XA)		22,476

POST

+ Amortization Expense (E) −	
(2a) 22,476	

− Accumulated Amortization—Right-of-Use Asset, Finance Lease (XA) +	
	22,476 (2a)

ANALYZE

Transaction	Cash Asset	+ Noncash Assets	− Contra Assets	= Liabil-ities	+ Contrib. Capital	+ Earned Capital	Revenues	− Expenses	= Net Income
Lease payment and interest expense.	−32,000 Cash			= −16,267 Finance Lease Liability		−15,733 Retained Earnings		− +15,733 Interest Expense	= −15,733

JOURNALIZE

(2b) Finance lease liability (−L)	16,267	
Interest expense (+E, −SE)	15,733	
Cash (−A)		32,000

POST

− Finance Lease Liability (L) +	
(2b) 16,267	

+ Interest Expense (E) −	
(2b) 15,733	

+ Cash (A) −	
	32,000 (2b)

3. If the lease were an operating lease, the entries would be as follows:

(3a) To record lease asset and liability at commencement of lease.

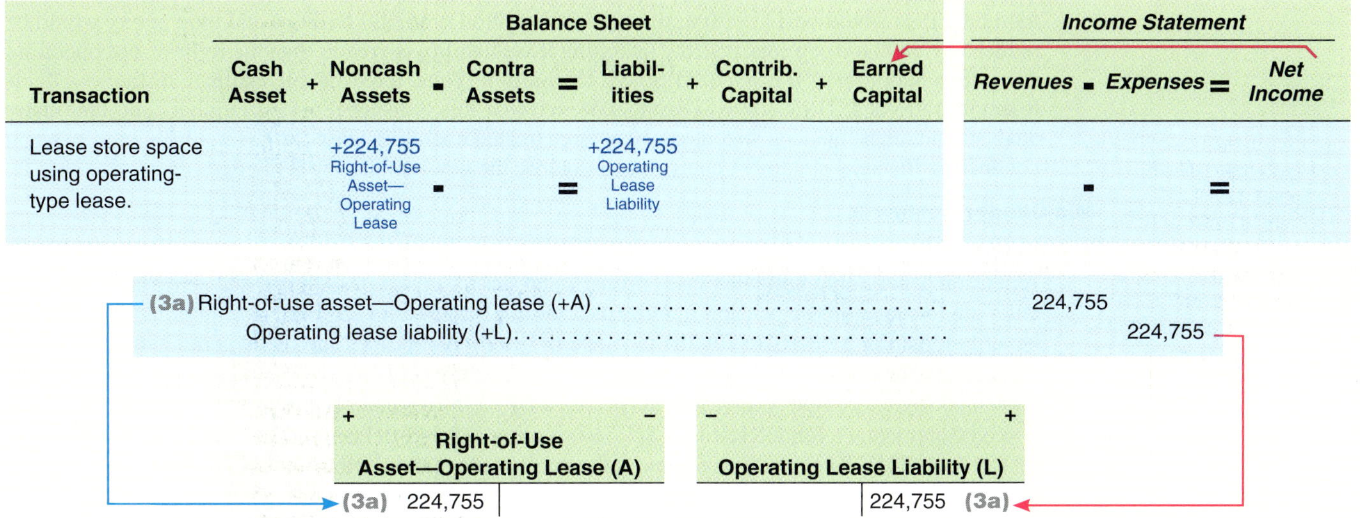

Transaction	Cash Asset	+	Noncash Assets	−	Contra Assets	=	Liabilities	+	Contrib. Capital	+	Earned Capital	Revenues	−	Expenses	=	Net Income
Lease store space using operating-type lease.			+224,755 Right-of-Use Asset—Operating Lease	−		=	+224,755 Operating Lease Liability						−		=	

(3b) At the end of the year the lease payment is recorded, as well as the straight line lease expense and effects on the balance sheet.

Lease payment

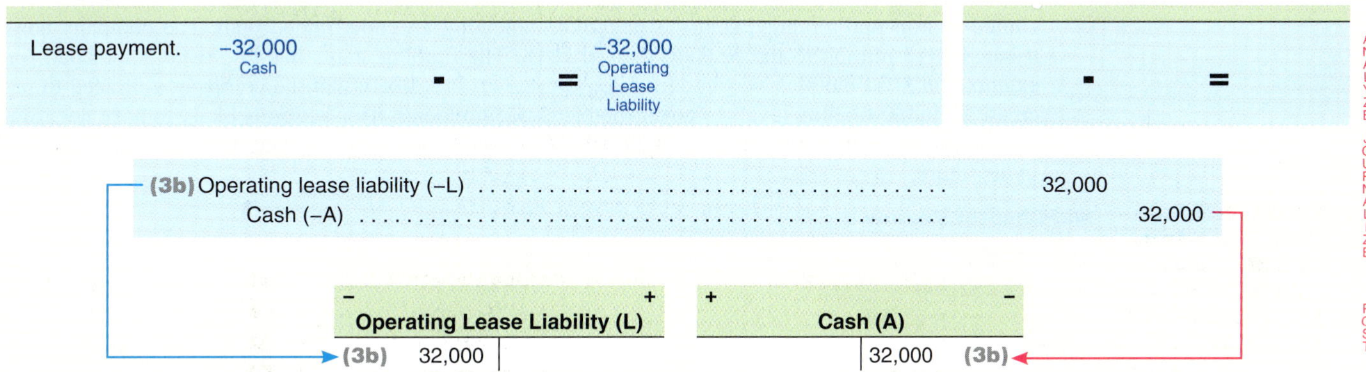

Transaction	Cash Asset	+	Noncash Assets	−	Contra Assets	=	Liabilities	+	Contrib. Capital	+	Earned Capital	Revenues	−	Expenses	=	Net Income
Lease payment.	−32,000 Cash			−		=	−32,000 Operating Lease Liability						−		=	

(3c) At the end of the year, the straight-line lease expense is recorded and the balance sheet items are adjusted.

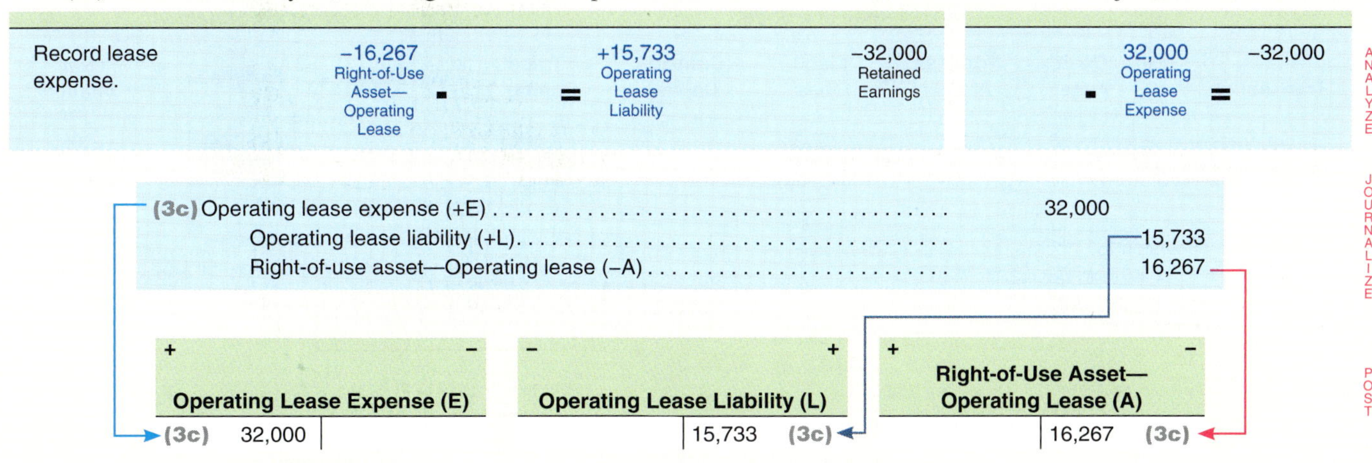

Transaction	Cash Asset	+	Noncash Assets	−	Contra Assets	=	Liabilities	+	Contrib. Capital	+	Earned Capital	Revenues	−	Expenses	=	Net Income
Record lease expense.			−16,267 Right-of-Use Asset—Operating Lease	−		=	+15,733 Operating Lease Liability				−32,000 Retained Earnings		−	32,000 Operating Lease Expense	=	−32,000

SOLUTION TO PART B

1. When **The Gap** adopts the new standard, the company will record a Right-of-use operating lease asset on the balance sheet for $5.8 billion in long-term assets. The company will also record $6.6 billion as a

lease liability. The portion due within the next year will be shown as a current liability and the remainder will be in long-term liabilities.

2. **The Gap**'s debt-to-equity ratio as currently reported is 1.26 or 126%. If the new standard were adopted total liabilities would be $11,096 million ($4,496 million + $6,600 million) and total equity would be reduced by $800 million (because the operating lease liability is greater than the right-of-use operating asset upon adoption of the standard) to $2,753 million. Thus, a reasonable estimate of the new debt-to-equity ratio is 4.03 or 403%. Recall, however, that this is using reported numbers and that many analysts and other financial statement users often treated operating leases as generating a liability when conducting financial statement analysis even before the new standard was in effect.

Mid-Chaper Review 2

SOLUTION

1. A pension benefit obligation increases primarily by service cost, interest cost, and actuarial losses. The latter are increases in the pension liability as a result of changes in actuarial assumptions. The pension benefit obligation is decreased by the payment of benefits to retirees and by actuarial gains.
2. Pension investments increase through positive investment returns for the period and by cash contributions made by the company. Investments decrease by payments made to retirees and investment losses.
3. United Continental's funded status is $(1,569) million ($5,396 million PBO – $3,827 million pension assets) as of 2018. The negative amount indicates that the plan is underfunded. Therefore, this amount is reported as a liability on the company's balance sheet.
4. Expected return on plan assets acts as an offset to service cost and interest cost in computing the net pension cost. As the expected return increases (decreases), net pension cost decreases (increases).
5. United Continental's expected return of $292 million exceeded its actual return, which was a loss of $215 million in 2018.
6. United Continental reports net pension expense of $284 million in 2018.
7. United Continental's funded status is negative, indicating an underfunded plan. The company contributed $413 million to the pension plan in 2018. The funding status has improved somewhat, for example, in 2014 the plan was underfunded by $2,241. It is likely that the company will need to increase its future funding levels to cover the plan's requirements. This action is likely to have negative consequences for its ability to fund other operating needs, and could damage its competitive position in the future.

Mid-Chapter Review 3

SOLUTION

1. *a.* $2,390.
   b. $1,488 = $1,342 + $146 is currently payable or has already been paid in 2019.
   c. The most obvious example would be depreciation allowed in 2019 by the tax code exceeded that calculated by the straight-line method.

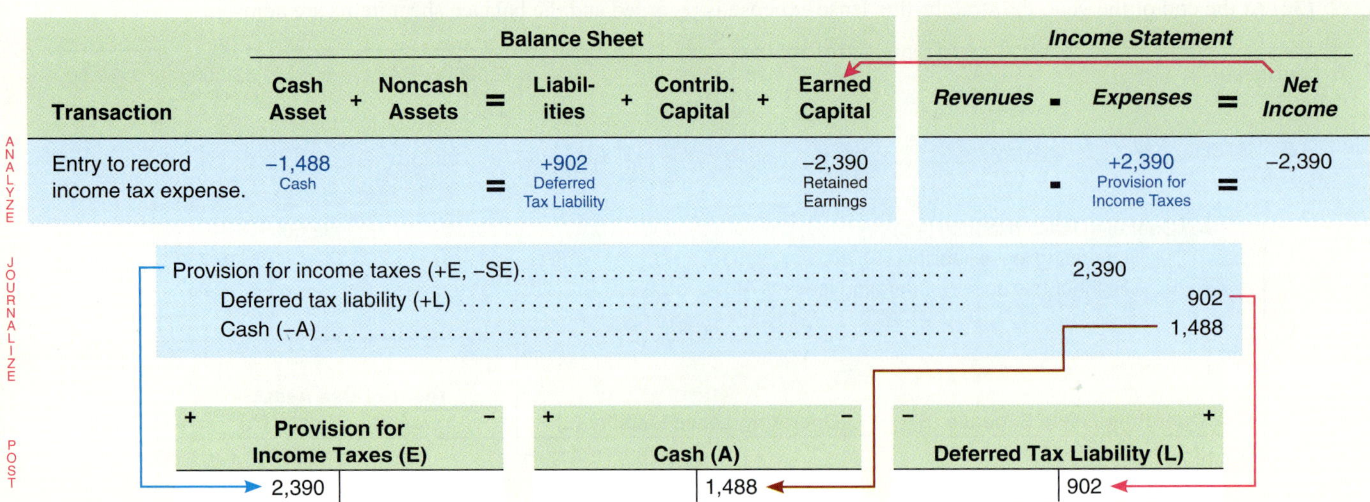

11

Reporting and Analyzing Stockholders' Equity

LEARNING OBJECTIVES

1. Describe business financing through stock issuances. (p. 530)
2. Explain and account for the issuance and repurchase of stock. (p. 533)
3. Describe how operations increase the equity of a business. (p. 538)
4. Explain and account for dividends and stock splits. (p. 538)
5. Define and illustrate comprehensive income. (p. 543)
6. Describe and illustrate the basic and diluted earnings per share computations. (p. 546)
7. Appendix 11A: Analyze the accounting for convertible securities, stock rights, stock options, and restricted stock. (p. 549)

PFIZER
www.pfizer.com

Pfizer Inc. is a research-based, global pharmaceutical company that discovers, develops, manufactures, and markets prescription medicines. Pfizer's 2017 revenues were almost $53 billion. Pfizer discloses revenue details for two categories of drugs: Pfizer Innovative Health ($31 billion) and Pfizer Essential Health ($21 billion). Prevnar led the company with almost 11% of the sales revenue, Lyrica's revenues were 8.6% of total revenues, and Ibrance revenues were roughly 6% of the company's total revenues.

Revenues at pharmaceutical firms are substantially dependent on patent protection following the research and development to discover and produce the drug. As patent protections expire, revenues fall. To counter expiring patents, Pfizer must either acquire companies with innovative drug pipelines (in-process research and development), enter into collaborations to develop drugs with other companies, or develop new drugs in-house.To discover new drugs, Pfizer spends sizeable amounts each year on research and development: $7.9 billion in 2016 and $7.7 billion in 2017.

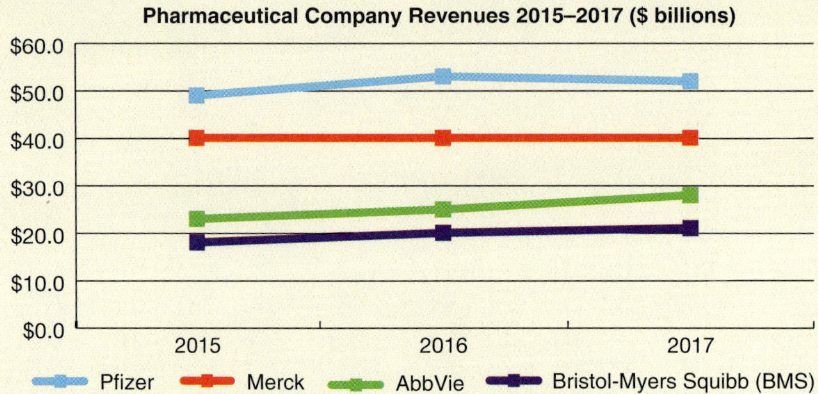

Pfizer faces increased competition from its major rivals, **Merck & Co., Inc.**, **AbbVie Inc.**, and **Bristol-Myers Squibb**, and also from generic manufacturers. On January 22, 2019, Wall Street analysts downgraded Pfizer and Merck on what they called a "patent cliff" in the coming years as well as competition. In addition, over time, Pfizer

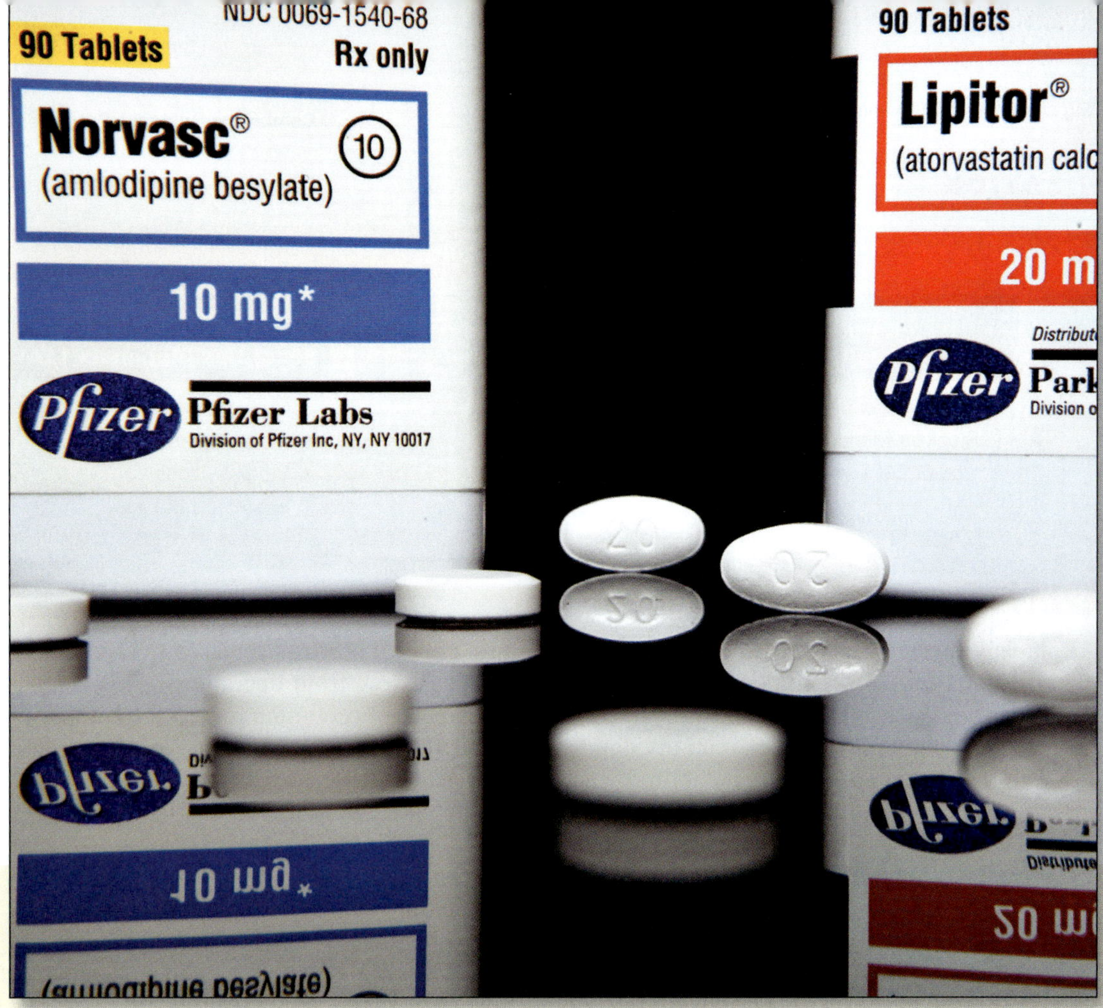

has disclosed that many regulatory actions affect their business. For example, Pfizer reported that the Patient Protection and Affordable Care Act of 2010 cost the company almost $1 billion in 2014 and in their 2017 annual report stated that their industry may be looked at to raise revenues for the U.S. government, for example, the "Bipartisan Budget Act of 2018, which increased the discount we pay in the Medicare Part D coverage gap from 50% to 70%, which will modestly reduce our future Medicare Part D revenues."

One critical component of Pfizer's recent strategy has been to spread its high overhead costs across a broader sales base and to rationalize its production and sales activities. In 2000, Pfizer merged with **Warner-Lambert Company**, and in 2003 it acquired **Pharmacia**. The merger with Warner-Lambert and acquisition of Pharmacia made Pfizer the largest pharmaceutical company in the world. Since 2003, Pfizer has continued to acquire other companies, including **Esperion Therapeutics, Inc.** (2004), **Vicuron Pharmaceuticals, Inc.** (2005), **BioRexis Pharmaceuticals Corporation** (2007), **Coley Pharmaceutical Group** (2008), **Wyeth** (2009), and **King Pharmaceuticals, Inc.** in 2011. In 2014, Pfizer made an unsuccessful $119 billion bid to acquire **AstraZeneca plc**. In 2015, Pfizer acquired Hospira for $17 billion and tried to invert out of the U.S. by acquiring **Allergan plc**, but the deal was terminated due to the U.S. government's efforts to block inversion transactions. In 2016, Pfizer acquired **Medivation** for $14 billion. In 2018, Pfizer and **GlaxoSmithKline** announced a joint venture to create a consumer healthcare company (Pfizer will have a 32% equity stake). At times Pfizer decides to divest part of its business (some of which was acquired in the acquisitions) to focus on its core strengths. For example, in 2018 Pfizer announced it would end its internal neuroscience discovery efforts, in 2017 Pfizer sold its global infusion systems net assets, in 2013, Pfizer divested its animal health business, and in 2012 Pfizer divested its nutrition business.

Pfizer must balance the capital needs of its acquisition strategy and its heavy commitment to research and development with the expectations of shareholders. From 2015 to 2017, the company reported $47 billion of net cash flow from operating activities, but it also paid $38 billion in cash to shareholders in the form of dividends and share repurchases. Other transactions involving shareholders' equity included share-based compensation for employees and conversions of one form of shareholders' equity to another.

This chapter describes the reporting and analysis of equity transactions, including sales and repurchases of stock, dividends, comprehensive income, and convertible securities.

Sources: CNBC.com "Pfizer, Merck drop after Wall Street downgrades on 'patent cliff' and competition" January 23, 2019; *The Wall Street Journal* (January 27, 2009; May 21, 2009; April 21, 2015), *New York Times* (January 27, 2009; May 27, 2014), *Business Week* (April and June, 2009), *Fortune* (August, 2009), and Pfizer 2014 10-K Report.

CHAPTER ORGANIZATION

Reporting and Analyzing Stockholders' Equity			
Contributed Capital	**Earned Capital**	**Earnings per Share**	**Potentially Dilutive Securities (Appendix 11A)**
• Classes of Stock • Accounting for Stock	• Cash Dividends • Stock Dividends and Splits • Comprehensive Income	• Basic EPS • Diluted EPS	• Convertible Securities • Stock Rights • Stock Options • Restricted Stock

1

LO1 Describe business financing through stock issuances.

INTRODUCTION

A company finances its assets from one of three sources: either it borrows funds from creditors, it obtains funds from shareholders, or it reinvests excess cash flow from operations. This chapter describes the issues relating to stockholders' equity, including the accounting for stock transactions (issues and repurchases of stock, and dividends), the accounting for stock options, the accounting for restricted stock, and the computation of earnings per share. Finally, we discuss the accounting for convertible securities, an increasingly prevalent financing vehicle.

When a company issues stock to the investing public, it records the receipt of cash (or other assets) and an increase in contributed capital, a part of stockholders' equity, representing investment in the company by shareholders. The increases in cash and equity equal the issue price of the stock on the issue date multiplied by the number of shares sold.

Contributed capital is accounted for at *historical cost*. Consequently, fluctuations in the market price of the issuer's stock subsequent to the initial public offering do not directly affect the financial statements of the issuing company. These fluctuations are the result of transactions between outside parties not involving the issuer. When and if stock is repurchased and subsequently resold, the issuer's contributed capital decreases (increases) by the current purchase (sales) price of the shares.

FYI Corporations never record gains or losses on the purchase or sale of stock or the payment of dividends.

There is an important difference between accounting for stockholders' equity and accounting for transactions involving assets and liabilities: *there is never any gain or loss reported on the purchase and sale of stock or the payment of dividends.* Instead, these "gains and losses" are reflected as increases and decreases in the contributed capital component of the issuing company's stockholders' equity.

This chapter focuses on the two broad categories of shareholder investment: contributed capital and earned capital. **Exhibit 11.1** provides an illustration of this breakdown using Pfizer's stockholders' equity as of December 31, 2017.

EXHIBIT 11.1 Stockholders' Equity from Pfizer's Balance Sheet

	Shareholders' Equity (millions except preferred stock issued and per common share data)	Dec. 31, 2017
Contributed capital	Preferred stock, no par value, at stated value; 27 shares authorized; issued: 2017—524; 2016—597	$ 21
	Common stock, $0.05 par value; 12,000 shares authorized; issued: 2017—9,275; 2016—9,230	464
	Additional paid-in capital	84,278
	Treasury stock, shares at cost: 2017—3,296; 2016—3,160	(89,425)
Earned capital	Retained earnings	85,291
	Accumulated other comprehensive loss	(9,321)
	Total Pfizer Inc. shareholders' equity	71,308
	Equity attributable to noncontrolling interests	348
	Total equity	$71,656

Pfizer, like other companies, has two broad categories of stockholders' equity:

1. **Contributed capital** This section reports the proceeds received by the issuing company from original stock issuances. Contributed capital often includes common stock, preferred

stock, and additional paid-in capital. Netted against these capital accounts is treasury stock, the amounts paid to repurchase shares of the issuer's stock from its investors less the proceeds from the resale of such shares. Collectively, these accounts are generically referred to as contributed capital (or *paid-in capital*).

2. **Earned capital** This section consists of (a) retained earnings (or accumulated deficit, if negative), which represent the cumulative income and losses of the company less any dividends to shareholders, and (b) accumulated other comprehensive income (AOCI), which includes changes to equity that are not included in income and are, therefore, not reflected in retained earnings. For Pfizer, AOCI includes foreign currency translation adjustments, changes in market values of derivatives, unrecognized gains and losses on available-for-sale securities, and pension adjustments.

Before turning to a discussion of contributed capital and earned capital, we note one other item in **Exhibit 11.1**—Equity attributable to **noncontrolling interests**. This amount results from the practice of consolidating subsidiaries that are controlled, but not wholly owned, and it represents neither capital contributed to Pfizer nor capital earned by Pfizer's shareholders. Chapter 12 provides a brief introduction to this topic.

CONTRIBUTED CAPITAL

We begin our discussion with contributed capital. Contributed capital represents the cumulative cash inflow that the company has received from the sale of various classes of stock, less the net cash that it has paid out to repurchase its stock from the market.

Pfizer's contributed capital consists of preferred and common stock, additional paid-in capital, less costs of treasury stock (repurchased shares).

Classes of Stock

There are two general classes of stock: preferred and common. The difference between the two lies in the respective legal rights conferred upon each class.

Common Stock Shares of **common stock** represent the primary ownership unit in a corporation. Common stockholders have voting rights which allow them to participate in the governance of the corporation. The total number of common shares is usually presented on the face of the balance sheet. There are three numbers of shares to be aware of:

- The number of **shares authorized** represents the upper limit on the number of shares that the corporation can issue. This number is established in the *articles of incorporation* and can only be increased by an affirmative shareholder vote.
- The number of **shares issued** is the actual number of shares that have been sold to stockholders by the corporation.
- The number of **shares outstanding** is the number of issued shares less the number of shares repurchased as treasury stock.

Pfizer's common stock is described as follows in its 2017 balance sheet (shares in millions):

Common stock, $0.05 par value; 12,000 shares authorized; issued: 2017—9,275

The Pfizer common stock has the following important characteristics:

- Pfizer common stock has a par value of $0.05 per share. The **par value** is an arbitrary amount set by company organizers at the time of formation. Generally, par value has no substance from a financial reporting or statement analysis perspective (there are some legal implications, which are usually minor). Its main impact is in specifying the allocation of proceeds from stock issuances between the two contributed capital accounts on the balance sheet: common stock and additional paid-in capital.

- Pfizer has authorized the issuance of 12,000 million shares. As of December 31, 2017, 9,275 million shares are issued yielding a total par value of $464 million = $0.05 × 9,275 million shares. When shares are first issued, the number of shares outstanding equals those issued. Any shares subsequently repurchased are subtracted from issued shares to derive outstanding shares.

Some corporations issue multiple classes of stock, with differential voting rights. For instance, **Alphabet Inc.** has Class A common stock with one vote per share, Class B common stock with ten votes per share, and Class C capital stock with no voting rights at all. All shares participate equally in dividends, but this structure has allowed the original management team to raise capital while retaining significant voting rights.

Preferred Stock **Preferred stock** generally has some preference, or priority, with respect to common stock but does not have voting rights. Two typical preferences are:

1. **Dividend preference** Preferred shareholders receive dividends on their shares before common shareholders do. If dividends are not paid in a given year, those dividends are normally forgone. However, some preferred stock contracts include a *cumulative provision* stipulating that any forgone dividends must first be paid to preferred shareholders, together with the current year's dividends, before any dividends are paid to common shareholders.
2. **Liquidation preference** If a company fails, its assets are sold (liquidated) and the proceeds are paid to the creditors and shareholders, in that order. Shareholders, therefore, have a greater risk of loss than do creditors. Among shareholders, the preferred shareholders receive payment in full before any proceeds are paid to common shareholders. This liquidation preference makes preferred shares less risky than common shares. Any liquidation payment to preferred shares is normally at its par value, although it is sometimes specified in excess of par, called a **liquidating value**.

The preferred stock of Pfizer is described in Note 12 to its 2017 10-K:

> The Series A convertible perpetual preferred stock is held by an employee stock ownership plan (Preferred ESOP) Trust and provides dividends at the rate of 6.25%, which are accumulated and paid quarterly. The per-share stated value is $40,300 and the preferred stock ranks senior to our common stock as to dividends and liquidation rights. Each share is convertible, at the holder's option, into 2,574.87 shares of our common stock with equal voting rights. The conversion option is indexed to our common stock and requires share settlement, and, therefore, is reported at the fair value at the date of issuance. We may redeem the preferred stock at any time or upon termination of the Preferred ESOP, at our option, in cash, in shares of common stock, or a combination of both at a price of $40,300 per share.

Following are several important features of the Pfizer preferred stock:

- There are 27 million preferred shares authorized, of which 524 shares are issued as of December 31, 2017. The articles of incorporation set the number of shares authorized for issuance. Once that limit is reached, shareholders must approve any increase in authorized shares.
- Pfizer preferred stock has a preference with respect to dividends and liquidation; meaning that preferred shareholders are paid before common shareholders.
- Pfizer preferred stock pays a dividend of 6.25% of its par (stated) value of $40,300. This feature means that each preferred share is entitled to annual dividends of $2,518.75 ($40,300 × 6.25%), payable quarterly.
- Pfizer preferred stock is convertible into common stock at the option of the holder and at a predetermined exchange rate. A preferred share is convertible, at the holder's option, into 2,574.87 common shares.
- Pfizer can redeem (repurchase) its preferred stock at any time in cash, common stock, or both.

Pfizer's cumulative preferred shares carry a dividend yield of 6.25%. This dividend yield compares favorably with the $1.28 per share (3.9% yield on a $32.59 average share price) paid to its common shareholders. Generally, preferred stock can be an attractive investment for shareholders seeking higher dividend yields, especially when tax laws wholly or partially exempt such dividends from taxation.

There are additional features sometimes seen in preferred stock agreements:[1]

1. **Call feature** The call feature provides the issuer with the right, but not the obligation, to repurchase the preferred shares at a specified price (also called redeemable preferred stock). This price can vary according to a specified time. A decline in the market rate of interest is one event that can lead to the firm exercising the call provision. While of value to the issuer of the preferred stock, the call provision makes the issue less attractive to potential investors. The result is a lower offering price per share.
2. **Conversion feature** The yield on preferred stock, especially when coupled with a cumulative feature, is similar to the interest rate on a bond or note. Further limited protection is offered because preferred shareholders receive the par value at liquidation like debtholders receive face value. The fixed yield and liquidation value for the preferred stock limit the upside potential return of preferred shareholders. This constraint can be overcome by inclusion of a *conversion feature* that allows preferred stockholders to convert their shares into common shares at their option at a predetermined conversion ratio. Some preferred contracts give the company an option to force conversion.

   The conversion feature causes the shares to be more attractive to potential investors because the preferred stockholders now have the opportunity to share in the fruits of a successful company with the common stockholders. Indeed, the market price of preferred stock tends to reflect the added value of the conversion feature.
3. **Participation feature** Preferred shares sometimes carry a *participation feature* that allows preferred shareholders to share ratably with common stockholders in dividends. The dividend preference over common shares can be a benefit when dividend payments are meager, but a fixed dividend yield limits upside potential if the company performs exceptionally well. This limitation can be overcome with a participation feature.

A GLOBAL PERSPECTIVE

Under IFRS, convertible debt securities are termed compound financial instruments because the conversion feature has a value even if it is not legally detachable for sale. IFRS splits the convertible bonds' value into the separate debt and equity values for reporting purposes. GAAP splits the value only in certain circumstances. Another difference is that GAAP has a mezzanine section of the balance sheet between equity and liabilities where securities with both equity and debt features are recorded. IFRS does not allow a mezzanine section of the balance sheet.

Accounting for Stock Transactions

LO2 Explain and account for the issuance and repurchase of stock.

2

We cover the accounting for stock transactions in this section, including the accounting for stock issuances and for stock repurchases.

Stock Issuance Stock issuances, whether common or preferred, yield an increase in both assets and stockholders' equity. Companies use stock issuances to obtain cash and other assets for use in their business.

[1] Preferred shares, in general, are somewhat debt-like. For example, preferred shares have a higher and more certain rate of dividends, approaching something more like interest. In addition, they have preference over common stockholders in the event of bankruptcy. More features can be added to the preferred shares that make them even more debt-like. In some cases, the classification for accounting changes accordingly. For example, if entities have mandatorily redeemable preferred stock that do not contain a conversion option, these securities are to be included as liabilities on the balance sheet, not in equity and not in the mezzanine section of the balance sheet (i.e., the section between the liabilities section and the equity section in the balance sheet). Entities are required to present contingently redeemable preferred stock—meaning redeemable upon the occurrence of an event outside the control of the issuer—and preferred stock that is redeemable at the option of the holder in the mezzanine section of the balance sheet (i.e., the section between the liabilities section and the equity section). The purpose of this classification is to convey to the reader that such a security may not permanently be part of equity and could result in a demand for cash or other assets of the entity in the future. These are the accounting rules, but as discussed elsewhere in the text, analysts and other financial statement users may treat these securities differently than FASB (and may treat some of the securities as debt and some as equity) when conducting ratio-analysis or other evaluations of company performance. Also, we note that IFRS does not allow a mezzanine section of the balance sheet.

Stock issuances increase assets (cash) by the number of shares sold multiplied by the issuance price of the stock on the issue date. Equity increases by the same amount, which is reflected in contributed capital accounts. Specifically, assuming the issuance of common stock, the common stock account increases by the number of shares sold multiplied by its par value and the additional paid-in capital account is increased for the remainder of the purchase price.[2]

BUSINESS INSIGHT

Alibaba's IPO In September of 2014, **Alibaba Group** offered its shares to the general public for the first time. The first public sale of common stock by a corporation is called an initial public offering, or IPO for short. After the IPO, any offering of stock to the public is called a seasoned equity offering.

At the time, Alibaba's IPO was the largest in history, raising approximately $25 billion. The common stock had a par value of $0.000025, but was offered to the public for $68 per share. Within a couple of months after the stock opened for trade on the New York Stock Exchange, the price increased to almost $120 per share, but then began to fall. By the company's fiscal year end in March 2015, Alibaba's shares were trading for just over $83 per share, about 20% greater than their original offer price and almost 50 times their earnings per share.

To illustrate, assume that Davis Company issues 10,000 shares of $1 par value common stock at a market price of $43 cash per share. The financial statement effects and entries for this stock issuance follow.

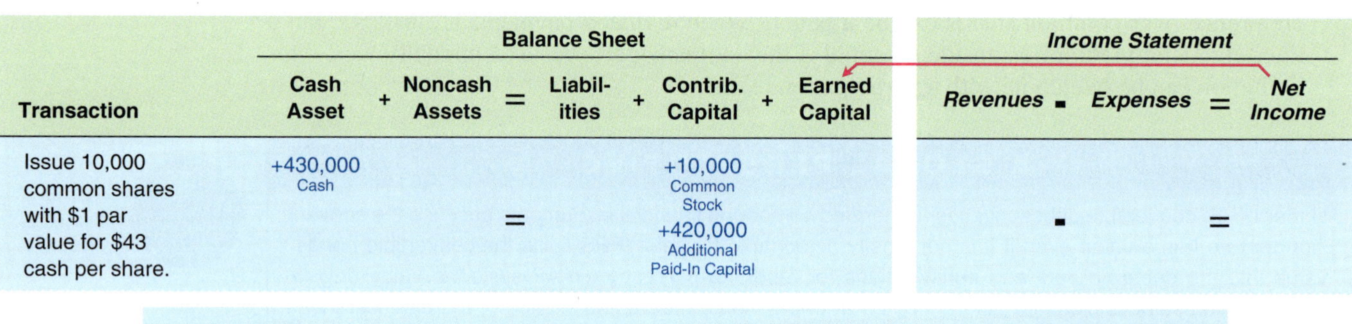

	Balance Sheet									Income Statement				
Transaction	Cash Asset	+	Noncash Assets	=	Liabil-ities	+	Contrib. Capital	+	Earned Capital	Revenues	−	Expenses	=	Net Income
ANALYZE: Issue 10,000 common shares with $1 par value for $43 cash per share.	+430,000 Cash			=			+10,000 Common Stock +420,000 Additional Paid-In Capital				−		=	

JOURNALIZE

Cash (+A)	430,000	
Common stock (+SE)		10,000
Additional paid-in capital (+SE)		420,000

POST

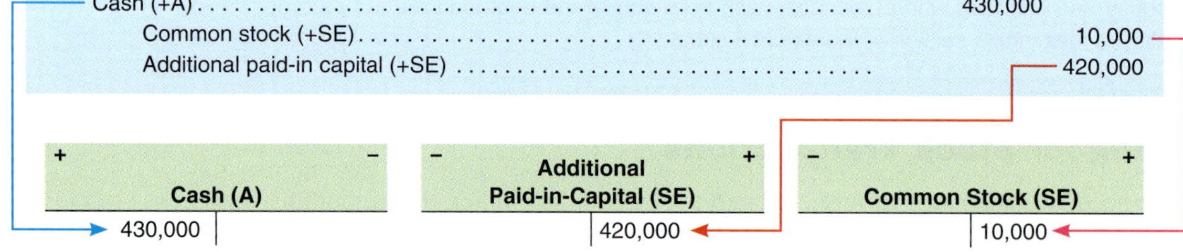

FYI Stock issuance affects the balance sheet, the statement of cash flows, and the statement of stockholders' equity. There is no revenue or gain from stock issuance reported in the income statement.

Specifically, the following financial statement effects of the stock issuance are:

1. Cash increases by $430,000 (10,000 shares × $43 per share) and is reported as a cash inflow from financing activities on the statement of cash flows.
2. Common stock increases by the $10,000 par value of shares sold (10,000 shares × $1 par value).[3]
3. Additional paid-in capital increases by the $420,000 difference between the issue price and par value ($430,000 – $10,000).

[2] Companies who offer their shares for sale to the general public are called *public corporations*. In a *private company*, ownership is limited to a smaller number of investors and the stock is not available to the general public. The distinction between public and private corporations should not be confused with media references to the public sector and the private sector. The *public sector* refers to government entities. Virtually all business entities, including public corporations, are considered part of the *private sector*.

[3] Common stock can also be issued as "no par" or as "no par with a stated value." For no par stock, the common stock account is increased by the entire proceeds of the sale and no amount is assigned to additional paid-in capital. For no par stock with a stated value, the stated value is treated just like par value; that is, common stock is increased by the number of shares multiplied by the stated value, and the remainder is assigned to the additional paid-in capital account.

Once shares are issued, they are freely traded in the market among investors. The proceeds of those sales and any gains and losses on those sales do not affect the issuing company and are not recorded in its accounting records. Further, fluctuations in the issuing company's stock price subsequent to issuance do not directly affect its financial statements. Hence, the equity section of the balance sheet cannot be used to determine the current market value of the company. The market value (or market capitalization) is given by the product of the number of common shares outstanding times the current per-share market price of the stock.

Pfizer's outstanding common shares, repeated from **Exhibit 11.1** are (in millions):

Common stock, $0.05 par value; 12,000 shares authorized; issued: 2017—9,275	$ 464
Additional paid-in capital	84,278

Pfizer's common stock, in the amount of $464 million, equals the number of shares issued multiplied by the common stock's par value: 9,275 million × $0.05 = $464 million.[4] The balance of the proceeds from stock issuances is included in the additional paid-in capital account. Total proceeds from stock issuances are $84,742 ($464 + $84,278) million, or $9.14 per share ($84,742/9,275 million shares).

RESEARCH INSIGHT

Stock Issuance and Stock Returns Seasoned equity offerings are issuances of common stock by firms that already have outstanding shares. On average, stock price declines when a company announces that it will issue additional shares of common stock. Investors infer that issuing common stock rather than debt is an indication that management believes the stock is overvalued in the market, making it a more attractive form of financing. In addition, research has found that companies engage in earnings management around seasoned equity offerings, using both accrual estimates (e.g., underestimating bad debt expense or warranty expense) and real transactions (e.g., cutting R&D or accelerating sales). As a result, both earnings and stock returns decline in subsequent periods.

Stock Repurchase Pfizer provides the following description of its stock repurchase program in notes to its 10-K report.

> We purchase our common stock through privately negotiated transactions or in open market purchases as circumstances and prices warrant. Purchased shares under each of the share-purchase plans, which are authorized by our Board of Directors, are available for general corporate purposes. ... In December 2015, the Board of Directors authorized a new $11 billion share repurchase program (the December 2015 Stock Purchase Plan) to be utilized over time, and share repurchases commenced thereunder in the first quarter of 2017. In December 2017, the Board of Directors authorized a new $10 billion share repurchase program to be utilized over time. This new program is in addition to the $6.4 billion remaining under the December 2015 Stock Purchase Plan as of December 31, 2017. . . .
>
> On February 2, 2017, we entered into an accelerated share repurchase agreement with Citibank to repurchase $5 billion of our common stock. Pursuant to the terms of the agreement, on February 6, 2017, we paid $5 billion to Citibank and received an initial delivery of approximately 126 million shares of our common stock from Citibank at a price of $31.73 per share, which represented, based on the closing price of our common stock on the NYSE on February 2, 2017, approximately 80% of the notional amount of the accelerated share repurchase agreement. On May 16, 2017, the accelerated share repurchase agreement with Citibank was completed, which, per the terms of the agreement, resulted in Citibank owing us a certain number of shares of Pfizer common stock. Pursuant to the agreement's settlement terms, we received an additional 24 million shares of our common stock from Citibank on May 19, 2017. The average price paid for all of the shares delivered under the accelerated share repurchase agreement was $33.31 per share. The common stock received is included in Treasury Stock. This agreement was entered into pursuant to our previously announced share repurchase authorization.

continued

[4] The number of shares issued and the par value of those shares are both rounded to the nearest million.

continued from previous page

The following table provides the number of shares of our common stock purchased and the cost of purchases under our publicly announced share repurchase plans, including our accelerated share repurchase agreements:

(SHARES IN MILLIONS, DOLLARS IN BILLIONS)	2017[(a)]	2016[(b)]	2015[(c)]
Shares of common stock purchased	150	154	182
Cost of purchase	$5.0	$5.0	$6.2

At December 31, 2017, our remaining share-purchase authorization was approximately $16.4 billion.

Pfizer has initiated multiple stock buyback programs over time. One reason a company will repurchase shares is if it feels that the market undervalues them. Management reasons that the repurchase sends a positive signal to the market about the company's financial condition that favorably affects its share price. Recent research provides evidence that share prices generally increase following the announcement of a share repurchase program. Any gain on resale is *never* reflected in the income statement. Instead, the excess of the resale price over the repurchase price is added to additional paid-in capital. GAAP prohibits companies from reporting gains via stock transactions with their own shareholders.

Another reason shares are repurchased is to offset the dilutive effects of an employee stock option program. When employees are compensated with equity-based pay, the number of shares outstanding will increase over time as the shares are given to employees. These additional shares reduce earnings per share and are, therefore, viewed as *dilutive.* In response, many companies repurchase an equivalent number of shares in a desire to keep outstanding shares constant. Corporations also buy back their own shares in order to concentrate ownership to avoid an unwelcome takeover action. Repurchased shares do not participate in dividends or in shareholder votes.

A GLOBAL PERSPECTIVE

The accounting for share repurchases under IFRS is similar to GAAP. IFRS allows the repurchase also to be recorded as a decrease to the common equity, additional paid-in capital, and retained earnings or some combination.

A stock repurchase has the opposite financial statement effects from a stock issuance. That is, cash is reduced by the price of the shares repurchased (number of shares repurchased multiplied by the purchase price per share) and stockholders' equity is reduced by the same amount. The reduction in equity is achieved by increasing a contra equity account called **treasury stock**. *A contra equity account is a negative equity account with a debit balance,* which reduces stockholders' equity. Thus, when a contra equity account increases, total equity decreases.

Any subsequent reissuance of treasury stock does not yield a gain or loss. Instead, the difference between the proceeds received and the repurchase price of the treasury stock is reflected as an increase or decrease to additional paid-in capital.[5]

To illustrate, assume that 3,000 common shares of Davis Company stock previously issued for $43 are later repurchased for $40. The financial statement effects and entries for this stock repurchase follow.

[5] Repurchased shares do not have to be held in treasury, but could be retired by the company.

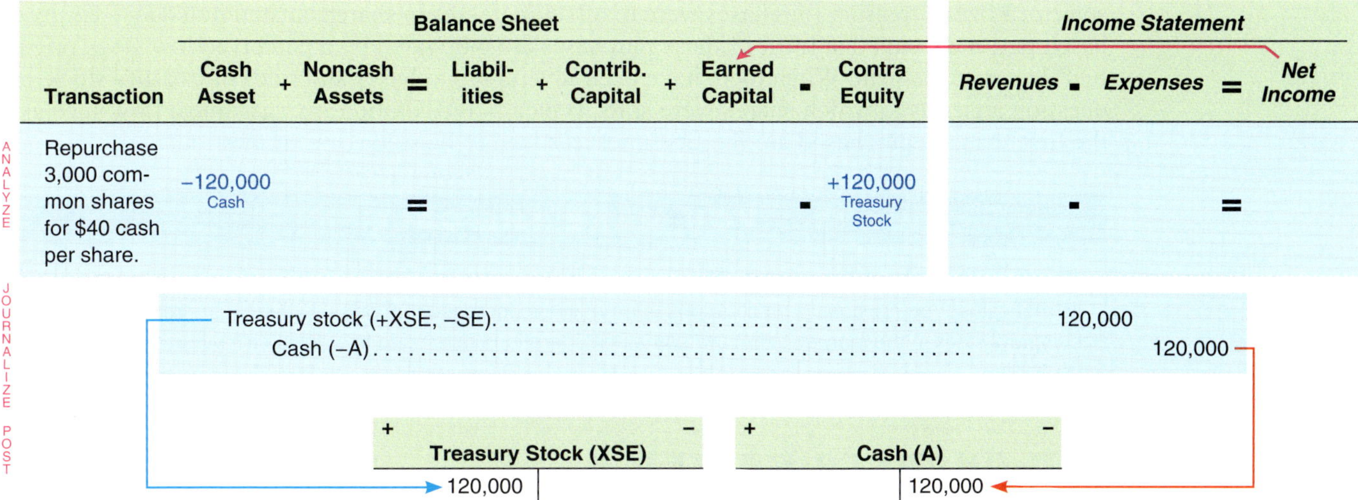

Assets (cash) and equity both decrease. Treasury stock (a contra equity account) increases by $120,000, which reduces stockholders' equity by that same amount.

Assume that these 3,000 shares are then subsequently resold for $42 cash per share. The financial statement effects and entries for this treasury stock sale follow.

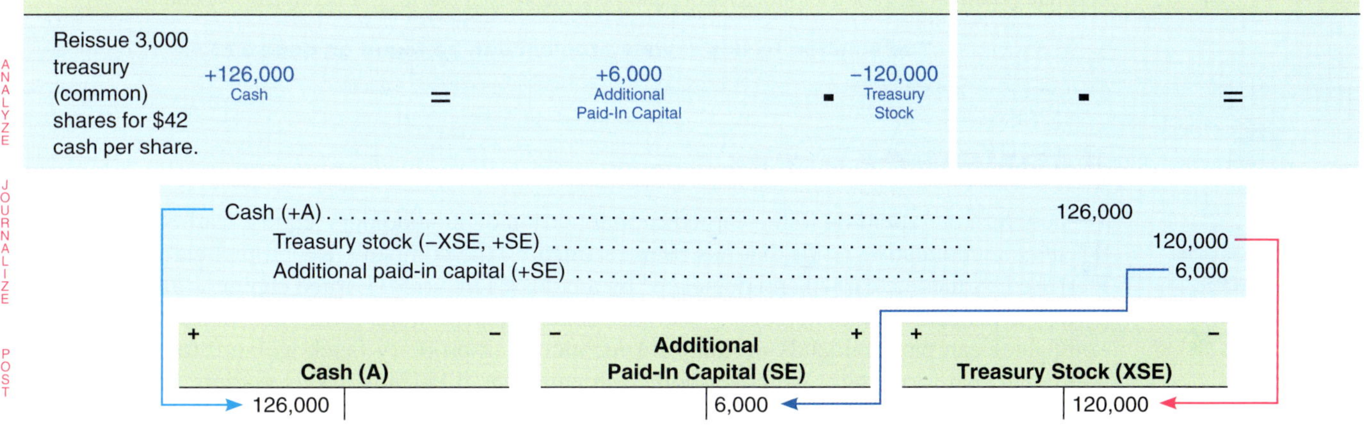

Cash assets increase by $126,000 (3,000 shares × $42 per share), the treasury stock account is reduced by the $120,000 cost of the treasury shares issued, and the $6,000 excess (3,000 shares × $2 per share) is reported as an increase in additional paid-in capital.[6] Again, there is no effect on the income statement—companies are prohibited from reporting gains and losses from repurchases and reissuances of their own stock.

The treasury stock section of Pfizer's 2017 balance sheet is reproduced below.

At December 31 (millions)	2017
Treasury stock, shares at cost: 2017—3,296	$(89,425)

Pfizer has repurchased a cumulative total of 3,296 million shares of its common stock for $89,425 million, an average repurchase price of $27.13 per share. This compares with total contributed capital of $84,763 million ($21 million + $464 million + $84,278 million). Although

[6] If the reissue price is below the repurchase price, then additional paid-in capital is reduced until it reaches a zero balance, after which retained earnings is reduced.

some of Pfizer's treasury purchases were to offset increases in shares outstanding due to equity-based pay, it appears that most of these purchases are motivated by a perceived low stock price by Pfizer management. When there have been several repurchases and sales of treasury stock, a question arises as to which shares were sold. Typically the solution is to assume a flow such as the first shares repurchased are the first ones assumed to be sold (first-in, first-out).

YOU MAKE THE CALL

You are the Chief Financial Officer You believe that your company's stock price is lower than its real value. You are considering various alternatives to increase that price, including the repurchase of company stock in the market. What are some considerations relating to this decision? [Answer on page 556]

MID-CHAPTER REVIEW 1

Plesko Corporation reported the following transactions relating to its stock accounts in 2018.

Jan.	15	Issued 10,000 shares of $5 par value common stock at $17 cash per share.
Mar.	31	Purchased 2,000 shares of its own common stock at $15 cash per share.
June	25	Reissued 1,000 shares of its treasury stock at $20 cash per share.

Show the financial impact of each transaction using the financial statement effects template, provide the appropriate journal entry for each transaction, and post the journal entries to the related T-accounts.

The solution to this review problem can be found on page 576.

3 **LO3** Describe how operations increase the equity of a business.

EARNED CAPITAL

We now turn our attention to the earned capital portion of stockholders' equity. Earned capital represents the cumulative profit that has been retained by the company. Recall that earned capital is increased by income earned and decreased by any losses incurred. Earned capital is also decreased by dividends paid to shareholders. Not all dividends are paid in the form of cash, however. In fact, companies can pay dividends in many forms, including property (such as land, for example) or additional shares of stock. We cover both cash and stock dividends in this section. Earned capital also includes the positive or negative effects of accumulated other comprehensive income (AOCI). The earned capital of Pfizer is highlighted in the following graphic:

Shareholders' Equity (millions except preferred stock issued and per common share data)	Dec. 31, 2017
Preferred stock, no par value, at stated value; 27 shares authorized; issued: 2017—524; 2016—597	$ 21
Common stock, $0.05 par value; 12,000 shares authorized; issued: 2017—9,275; 2016—9,230	464
Additional paid-in capital	84,278
Treasury stock, shares at cost: 2017—3,296; 2016—3,160	(89,425)
Retained earnings	85,291
Accumulated other comprehensive loss	(9,321)
Total Pfizer Inc. shareholders' equity	71,308
Equity attributable to noncontrolling interests	348
Total equity	$71,656

4 **LO4** Explain and account for dividends and stock splits.

Cash Dividends

Many companies, but not all, pay dividends. Their reasons for dividend payments are varied. Most dividends are paid in cash on a quarterly basis. The following is a description of Pfizer's dividend policy from its 2017 10-K.

> **Dividends on Common Stock**
> We paid dividends on our common stock of $7.7 billion in 2017, $7.3 billion in 2016 and $6.9 billion in 2015. In December 2017, our Board of Directors declared a first-quarter 2018 dividend of $0.34 per share, payable on March 1, 2018, to shareholders of record at the close of business on February 2, 2018. The first-quarter 2018 cash dividend will be our 317th consecutive quarterly dividend.
>
> Our current and projected dividends provide a return to shareholders while maintaining sufficient capital to invest in growing our businesses and to seek to increase shareholder value. Our dividends are not restricted by debt covenants. While the dividend level remains a decision of Pfizer's Board of Directors and will continue to be evaluated in the context of future business performance, we currently believe that we can support future annual dividend increases, barring significant unforeseen events.

Outsiders closely monitor dividend payments. It is generally perceived that the level of dividend payments is related to the expected long-term core income. Accordingly, dividend increases are usually accompanied by stock price increases, and companies rarely reduce their dividends unless absolutely necessary. Dividend reductions are, therefore, met with substantial stock-price declines.

BUSINESS INSIGHT

General Electric (GE) was one of the biggest dividend payers in the U.S. However, in 2017, the company cut its dividend in half, from 24 cents/share to 12 cents per share, in an effort to save cash—about $4 billion per year. GE's dividend cut was one of the largest in the history of the S&P 500 and the biggest since the great recession era (2009). Even after this dividend cut, it was projected that about 85% of the company's free cash flow would go toward dividends, which illuminates the change in the company and its business over time. The stock price fell around 7% on the day the dividend cut was announced and almost 6% the next day (though other negative news was simultaneously announced so not all of the price drop was likely due to the dividend news). In December of 2018, the company slashed the dividend further to only 1 cent per share.

Financial Effects of Cash Dividends Cash dividends reduce both cash and retained earnings by the amount of the cash dividends paid. To illustrate, Pfizer paid $7.7 billion in 2017 cash dividends on its common and preferred shares. The financial statement effects of this cash dividend payment are reflected as a reduction in assets (cash) and a reduction in retained earnings as follows.

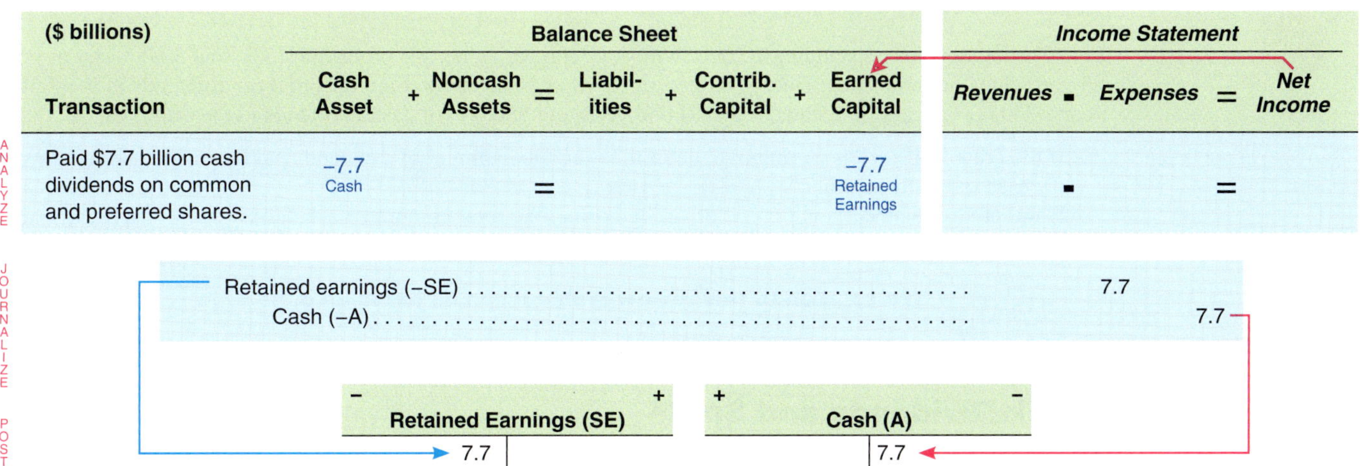

($ billions)	Balance Sheet									Income Statement				
Transaction	Cash Asset	+	Noncash Assets	=	Liabil-ities	+	Contrib. Capital	+	Earned Capital	Revenues	-	Expenses	=	Net Income
ANALYZE: Paid $7.7 billion cash dividends on common and preferred shares.	−7.7 Cash			=					−7.7 Retained Earnings		-		=	

JOURNALIZE

	Dr.	Cr.
Retained earnings (−SE)	7.7	
Cash (−A)		7.7

POST

− Retained Earnings (SE) +	
7.7	

+ Cash (A) −	
	7.7

Dividend payments have no effect on profitability. They are a direct reduction to retained earnings (and cash) and bypass the income statement.

BUSINESS INSIGHT

While many technology companies appear to have ample financial resources to pay dividends, the tax strategies previously employed to avoid U.S. taxes as described in Chapter 10 made it costly to use those resources. For instance, **Apple Inc.** reported end-of-fiscal year 2014 cash and financial investments of \$155 billion, 67% of the company's total assets. However, \$137 billion of this amount was held by Apple's foreign subsidiaries and had not yet been subject to U.S. taxation. If Apple repatriated some portion of these resources to pay dividends to its shareholders, it would have to pay approximately one-third of the amount to U.S. tax authorities. As a result, Apple borrowed a total of \$35 billion in fiscal years 2013 and 2014, at least in part to return cash to shareholders in the form of dividends and repurchases of common stock. This continued through 2017. In late 2017, the U.S. passed tax reform, which many expected to lead companies to repatriate foreign earnings and increase their returns to shareholders. As of the time of this writing, this activity has occurred, but not as much as some expected.

Preferred stock dividends have priority over those for common shares, including unpaid prior years' preferred dividends (dividends in arrears) when preferred stock is cumulative. To illustrate, assume that Hanna Company has 15,000 shares of \$50 par value, 8% preferred stock outstanding, and 50,000 shares of \$5 par value common stock outstanding. During its first three years in business, assume that Hanna declares \$20,000 dividends in the first year, \$260,000 of dividends in the second year, and \$60,000 of dividends in the third year. If the preferred stock is cumulative, the total amount of dividends paid to each class of stock in each of the three years would be:

	Preferred Stock	Common Stock
Year 1		
Current-year dividend (\$15,000 × \$50 × 8%; but only \$20,000 is paid, leaving \$40,000 in arrears)	\$20,000	
Balance to common		\$ 0
Year 2		
Arrearage from Year 1 [(\$15,000 × \$50 × 8%) − \$20,000]	40,000	
Current-year dividend (\$15,000 × \$50 × 8%)	60,000	
Balance to common [\$260,000 − (\$40,000 + \$60,000)]		160,000
Year 3		
Current-year dividend (\$15,000 × \$50 × 8%)	60,000	
Balance to common		0

MID-CHAPTER REVIEW 2

Finn Corporation has outstanding 10,000 shares of \$100 par value, 5% preferred stock, and 50,000 shares of \$5 par value common stock. During its first three years in business, Finn declared no dividends in the first year, \$300,000 of cash dividends in the second year, and \$80,000 of cash dividends in the third year.

a. If the preferred stock is cumulative, determine the total amount of dividends paid to each class of stock for each of the three years.

b. If the preferred stock is not cumulative, determine the total amount of dividends paid to each class of stock for each of the three years.

The solution to this review problem can be found on page 577.

Stock Dividends and Splits

Dividends need not be paid in cash. Many companies pay **stock dividends**, that is dividends in the form of additional shares of stock. Companies can also distribute additional shares to their stockholders with a stock split. We cover both of these distributions in this section.

Stock Dividends When dividends are paid in the form of the company's stock, retained earnings are reduced and contributed capital is increased. However, the amount by which retained earnings are reduced depends on the proportion of the outstanding shares distributed to the total outstanding shares on the issue date. **Exhibit 11.2** illustrates two possibilities depending on whether a stock dividend is classified as either a small stock dividend or a large stock dividend. When the additional number of shares issued as a stock dividend is so great that it is likely to have a negative impact on the market price per share of the stock, the dividend must be treated as a large stock dividend. Dividends of less than 20%–25% of the outstanding shares are considered to be small stock dividends, while dividends of more than 20%–25% are classified as large stock dividends.[7]

EXHIBIT 11.2 Analysis of Stock Dividend Effects

Percentage of Outstanding Shares Distributed	Retained Earnings	Contributed Capital
Less than 20%–25% *(small stock dividend)*	Reduce by **market value** of shares distributed	Common stock increased by par value of shares distributed; additional paid-in capital increased for the balance
More than 20%–25% *(large stock dividend)*	Reduce by **par value** of shares distributed	Common stock increased by par value of shares distributed

For *small stock dividends,* retained earnings are reduced by the *market* value of the shares distributed (dividend shares × market price per share) and contributed capital is increased by the same amount. For the contributed capital increase, the common stock is increased by the par value of the shares distributed and the remainder [dividend shares × (market value per share – par value per share)] increases additional paid-in capital. For *large stock dividends,* retained earnings are reduced by the *par* value of the shares distributed (dividend shares × par value per share), and common stock is increased by the same amount (no change to additional paid-in capital). A large stock dividend is referred to as a stock split effected in the form of a dividend in the financial statements.

To illustrate the financial statement effects of dividends, assume that a company has 1 million shares of $5 par common stock outstanding. It then declares a small stock dividend of 15% of the outstanding shares (1,000,000 shares × 15% = 150,000 shares) when the market price of the stock is $30 per share. This small stock dividend has the following financial statement effects:

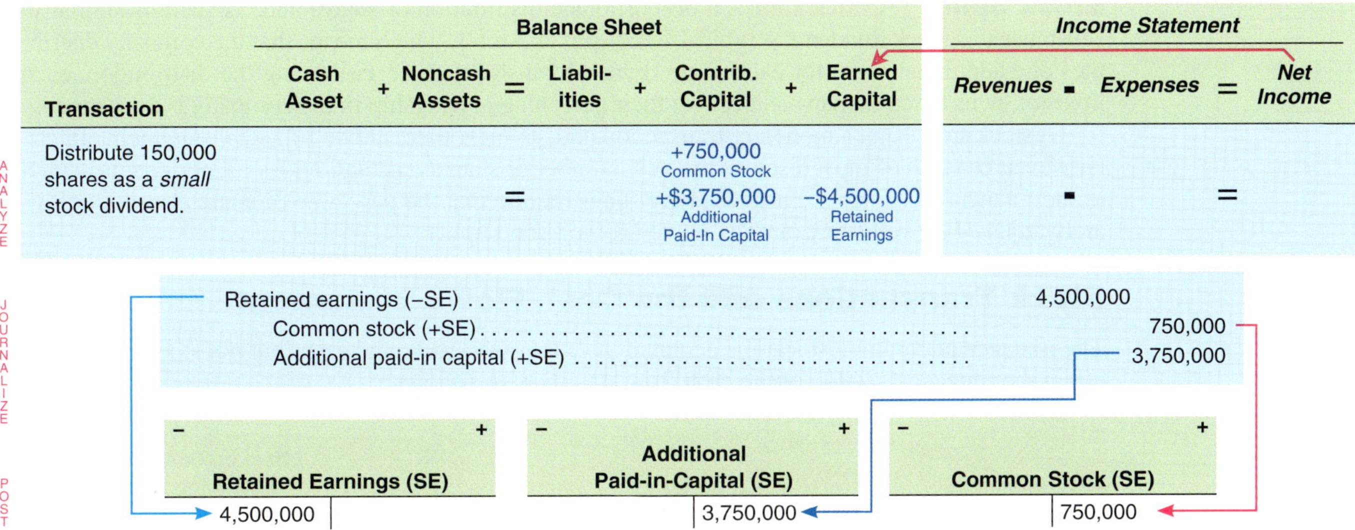

Retained earnings are reduced by $4,500,000, which equals the market value of the small stock dividend (150,000 shares × $30 market price per share). The increase in contributed capital is treated as

[7] Standard setters did not want a "bright-line" test and allow facts and circumstances to dictate the treatment between 20% and 25%. The determining factor is the effect on price. For example, if a 25% stock dividend does not affect the stock price, it would be treated as a small stock dividend. Likewise, if a 20% stock dividend does affect price, it would be treated as a large stock dividend for accounting purposes.

follows: common stock is increased by the par value of $750,000 (150,000 shares × $5 par value), and the remainder of $3,750,000 increases additional paid-in capital. Similar to cash dividend payments, the stock dividends, whether large or small, never impact income. But unlike cash dividends, stock dividends do not affect the cash flows from financing activities.

Next, assume instead that a company declares a large stock dividend of 70% of the 1 million outstanding common ($5 par) shares when the market price of the stock is $30 per share. This large stock dividend has the following financial statement effects and related entries:

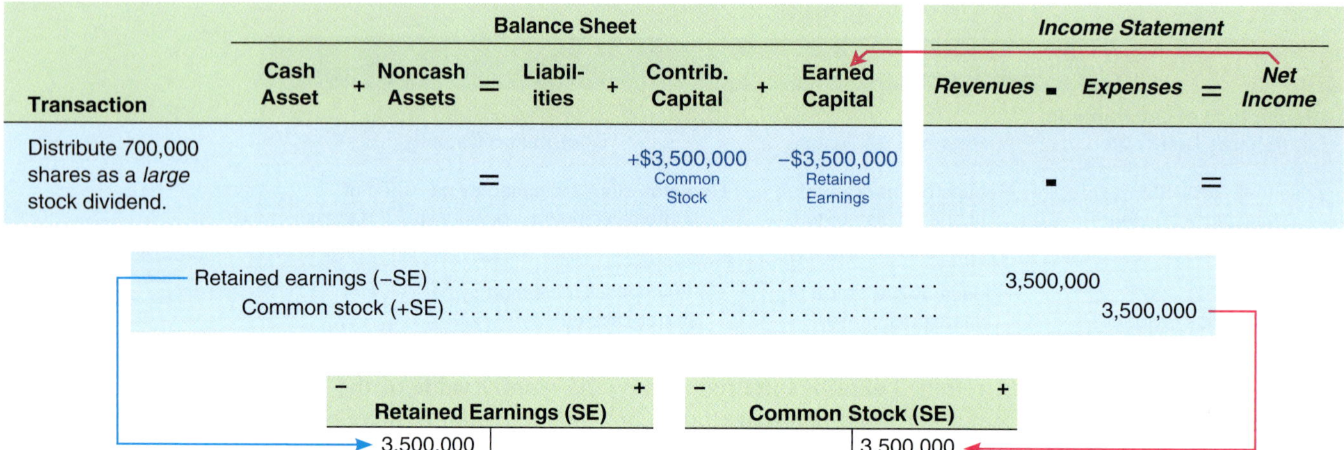

Retained earnings are reduced by $3,500,000, which equals the par value of the large stock dividend (700,000 shares × $5 par value per share). Common stock is increased by the par value of $3,500,000. There is no effect on additional paid-in capital because the dividend is reported at par value.

For both large and small stock dividends, companies are required to show comparable shares outstanding for all prior periods for which earnings per share (EPS) is reported in the statements. The reasoning is that a stock dividend has no effect on the ownership percentage of each common stockholder. As such, to show a dilution in reported EPS would erroneously suggest a decline in profitability when it is simply due to an increase in shares outstanding.

Stock Splits A **stock split** is a proportionate distribution of shares and, as such, is similar in substance to a stock dividend. A typical stock split is 2-for-1, which means that the company distributes one additional share for each share owned by a shareholder. Following the distribution, each investor owns twice as many shares, yet their percentage ownership in the company is unchanged.

A stock split is not a monetary transaction and, as such, there are no financial statement effects. However, companies must disclose the new number of shares outstanding for all periods presented in the financial statements. Further, many states require that the par value of shares be proportionately adjusted as well (for example, halved for a 2-for-1 split).

Stock Transactions and the Cash Flows Statement

The issuance of common stock, the acquisition of treasury stock, and cash (but not stock) dividends affect the financing section of the cash flow statement as follows:

Transaction	Effect on Cash Flow from Financing Activities
Issuance of Common Stock	Increase
Acquisition of Treasury Stock	Decrease
Sale of Treasury Stock	Increase
Cash Dividends Paid	Decrease

Stock splits and stock dividends do not influence the cash flows statement and are often used when cash is short but the continuation of a dividend is considered necessary.

MID-CHAPTER REVIEW 3

The stockholders' equity of Zhang Corporation at December 31, 2018, follows.

5% preferred stock, $100 par value, 10,000 shares authorized; 4,000 shares issued and outstanding . . .	$ 400,000
Common stock, $5 par value, 200,000 shares authorized; 50,000 shares issued and outstanding	250,000
Paid-in capital in excess of par value—Preferred stock	40,000
Paid-in capital in excess of par value—Common stock	300,000
Retained earnings	656,000
Total stockholders' equity	$1,646,000

The following transactions occurred during 2019. Show the financial impact of each transaction using the financial statement effects template, provide the appropriate journal entry for each transaction, and post the journal entries to the related T-accounts.

Apr. 1 Declared and issued a 100% stock dividend on all outstanding shares of common stock when the market value of the stock was $11 per share.

Dec. 7 Declared and issued a 3% stock dividend on all outstanding shares of common stock when the market value of the stock was $7 per share.

Dec. 31 Declared and paid a cash dividend of $1.20 per share on all outstanding common shares.

The solution to this review problem can be found on pages 577–578.

Comprehensive Income

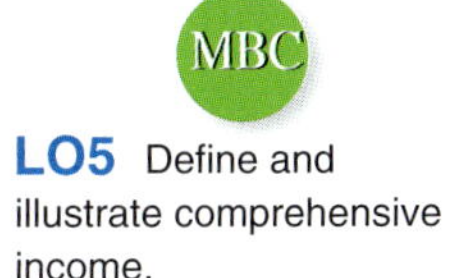

LO5 Define and illustrate comprehensive income.

5

Comprehensive income is a more inclusive notion of company performance than net income. It includes all recognized changes in equity that occur during a period except those resulting from contributions by and distributions to owners.

Specifically, comprehensive income includes net income *plus* additional gains and losses not included in the income statement. These additional gains and losses are called *other comprehensive income* and include, for example, foreign currency adjustments, unrealized gains or losses on available-for-sale debt securities, unrealized gains and losses on some derivatives, and adjustments to pension and other benefit plans. Comprehensive income includes the effects on a company of some economic events that are often outside of management's control. Accordingly, some observers assert that net income is a measure of management's performance, while comprehensive income is a measure of company performance.

Comprehensive income can be reported by firms in one of two ways. The first reporting method is to present a statement of comprehensive income that combines net income and other comprehensive income in one statement. Such a statement begins much like any income statement, with revenues, cost of goods sold, operating expenses and so forth. However, in the statement of comprehensive income, net income is a subtotal, followed by the gains and losses that are classified as other comprehensive income. The second reporting approach presents other comprehensive income in a separate statement immediately following the income statement. Pfizer follows the second reporting approach. Its statement of comprehensive income is presented in **Exhibit 11.3**.

EXHIBIT 11.3 Pfizer's 2017 Abridged Consolidated Statement of Comprehensive Income ($ millions)

Net income before allocation to noncontrolling interests		$21,355
Other comprehensive income:		
Foreign currency translation adjustments, net	1,278	
Unrealized holding gains/(losses) and reclassification adjustments on derivative financial instruments, net	(530)	
Unrealized holding gains/(losses) and reclassification adjustments on available-for-sale securities, net	574	
Benefit plans: actuarial gains/(losses) and reclassification adjustments, net	348	
Benefit plans: prior service (cost)/credit and reclassification adjustments, net	(203)	
Tax (benefit) provision on other comprehensive income/(loss)	262	
Total other comprehensive income/(loss)		1,730
Comprehensive income before allocation to noncontrolling interests		23,085
Less: Comprehensive income attributable to noncontrolling interests		62
Comprehensive income attributable to Pfizer Inc.		$23,023

* Does not add due to rounding.

Unlike net income, other comprehensive income is not closed to retained earnings at the end of each accounting period. Instead, other comprehensive income is closed to a separate earned capital account called **accumulated other comprehensive income** (abbreviated AOCI).

In its 2017 balance sheet, Pfizer reports accumulated other comprehensive income of $(9,321), compared to $(11,036) in 2016. The $1,715 increase from 2016 to 2017 is (almost) equal to the $(1,730) other comprehensive income for 2017 that Pfizer reported in its statement of comprehensive income (**Exhibit 11.3**). (The $15 million "slippage" is due to noncontrolling interests' share of other comprehensive income items.)

A GLOBAL PERSPECTIVE

As with U.S. GAAP, companies reporting under IFRS have a choice of presenting a single statement including components of profit and loss and other comprehensive income or presenting two statements—one for profit and loss (the income statement) and one that begins with profit or loss and then provides other comprehensive income components.

Summary of Stockholders' Equity

A summary of transactions that affect stockholders' equity is included in the statement of stockholders' equity. This statement reports a reconciliation of the beginning and ending balances of important stockholders' equity accounts. Pfizer's statement of stockholders' equity is shown in **Exhibit 11.4**. Pfizer's statement of shareholders' equity reveals the following key transactions for 2017:

- Total comprehensive income increased shareholders' equity by $23,023 million (net income of $21,308 million less other comprehensive income of $1,715 million).
- Dividends to preferred and common shareholders decreased stockholders' equity by $7,790 million ($1 million + $7,789 million).
- Employee share-based compensation increased equity by $1,536 million.
- Common stock repurchases decreased equity by $5,000 million.
- Conversion of preferred stock into common stock and redemptions decreased the preferred stock account, for a net decrease in stockholders' equity of $5 million.

EXHIBIT 11.4 Pfizer's Stockholders' Equity (December 31, 2017)

(Millions, Except Preferred Shares)	Preferred Stock		Common Stock		Additional Paid-In Capital	Treasury Stock		Retained Earnings	Accum. Other Comp. Loss	Share-holders Equity	Non-controlling Interests	Total Equity
	Shares	Stated Value	Shares	Par Value		Shares	Cost					
Balance December 31, 2016	597	$24	9,230	$461	$82,685	(3,160)	$(84,364)	$71,774	$(11,036)	$59,544	$296	$59,840
Net income								21,308		21,308	47	21,355
Other comprehensive income/(loss), net of tax									1,715	1,715	14	1,730
Cash dividends declared:												
Common stock								(7,789)		(7,789)		(7,789)
Preferred stock								(1)		(1)		(1)
Noncontrolling interests											(9)	(9)
Share-based payment transactions			45	2	1,597	15	(63)			1,536		1,536
Purchases of common stock						(150)	(5,000)			(5,000)		(5,000)
Preferred stock conversions and redemptions	(73)	(3)			(3)		1			(5)		(5)
Other								0		0		0
Balance December 31, 2017	524	$21	9,275	$464	$84,278	(3,296)	$(89,425)	$85,291	$(9,321)	$71,308	$348	$71,656

*Amounts may be off by $1 due to rounding.

ANALYZING FINANCIAL STATEMENTS

Analysis Objective

We want to measure the return on investment by common shareholders.

Before getting to the specifics of the performance ratio, we must address a complexity introduced when a company (like Pfizer) has a subsidiary that is not 100% owned. Suppose Company

A owns 85% of the common stock of Company B. The remaining 15% of B's shareholders are called a "noncontrolling interest." Company A would be required to incorporate the assets, liabilities, revenues, and expenses of Company B in its reports. As a result, Company A's reported net income would include all the income from both A and B. But then there is an adjustment in which 15% of B's income is subtracted (as "net income attributable to noncontrolling interests"), and the resulting number is "net income attributable to common shareholders." We use this information to develop the following measure of profit that can be attributed to common shareholders of the reporting company.

Net income available for common shareholders =
Net income − Net income attributable to noncontrolling interests − Preferred dividends

A similar adjustment is required on the balance sheet, where total equity consists of "equity attributable to noncontrolling interests" plus "common shareholders' equity" (as can be seen in **Exhibit 11.4**).

Analysis Tool Return on Common Equity (ROCE)

$$\textbf{Return on Common Equity (ROCE)} = \frac{\textbf{Net income available for common shareholders}}{\textbf{Average common shareholders' equity}}$$

Applying the Ratio to Pfizer

$$\text{2016 ROCE} = \frac{\$7{,}246 - \$31 - \$2}{[(\$59{,}840 - \$296 - \$24) + (\$64{,}998 - \$278 - \$26)]/2} = 0.116, \text{ or } 11.6\%$$

$$\text{2017 ROCE} = \frac{\$21{,}355 - \$47 - \$1}{[(\$71{,}656 - \$348 - \$21) + (\$59{,}840 - \$296 - \$24)]/2} = 0.326, \text{ or } 32.6\%$$

Guidance ROCE is similar to ROE except that when we compute ROCE, we remove the effect of noncontrolling interests and preferred stock from both the numerator and denominator.

Pfizer in Context

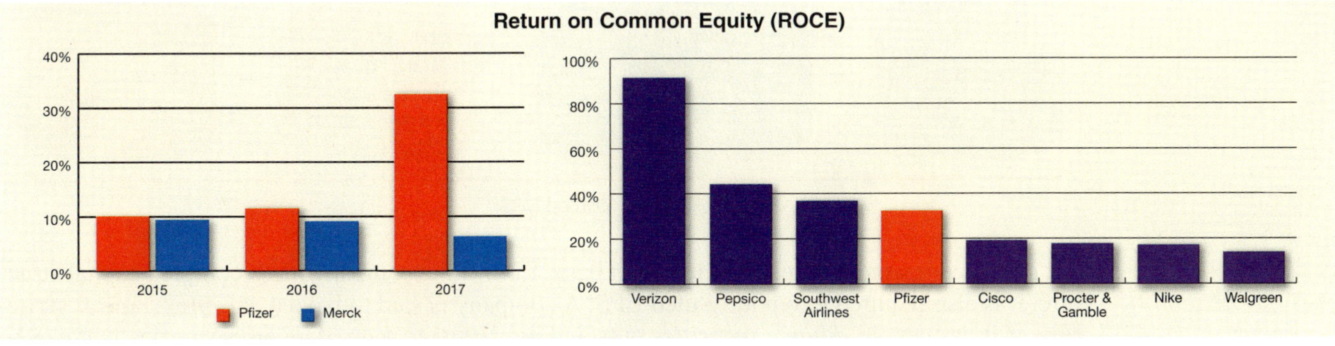

Takeaways Neither Pfizer's nor Merck's ROCE has been stable for the past few years (e.g., in 2014, Merck's was over 20%). Such volatility can occur from changes in equity, perhaps due to large share repurchases in a year which decreases equity, or large changes in income, either from operations or one-time items such as gains (losses) on sales of discontinued operations. Pfizer's 2017 ROCE is roughly in the middle, relative to many of the other focus companies in this textbook.

Many companies have little or no preferred stock or noncontrolling interests. So the difference between return on common equity (ROCE) and return on equity (ROE) will be immaterial for these firms. When preferred stock is present, ROCE is a more accurate measure of return to common shareholders.

Other Considerations In Chapter 5, we learned that ROE can be decomposed into two components: return on assets and return on financial leverage. Differences between firms may reflect a difference in performance, or a difference in the reliance on debt financing. A similar division can be done with ROCE with the caveat that ROCE essentially treats preferred stock as debt rather than equity.

One final point: the financial press sometimes refers to a measure called **book value per share**. This amount is the net book value of the company that is available to common shareholders, defined as: stockholders' equity less preferred stock less equity attributable to noncontrolling interest divided by the number of common shares outstanding (issued common shares less treasury shares). Pfizer's 2017 book value per share is computed as: ($71,657 million – $21 million – $348 million)/(9,275 million shares – 3,295 million shares) = $11.92 book value per common share.

MID-CHAPTER REVIEW 4

The stockholders' equity of Sloan Corporation at December 31, 2018, follows.

Common stock, $5 par value, 400,000 shares authorized; 160,000 shares issued and outstanding . . .	$800,000
Paid-in capital in excess of par value . . .	920,000
Retained earnings . . .	513,000

During 2019, the following transactions occurred:

June 28	Declared and issued a 10% common stock dividend when the market value is $11 per share.
Dec. 5	Declared and paid a cash dividend of $1.25 per share.
Dec. 31	Updated retained earnings for net income of $412,000.

Compute the year-ending balance of retained earnings for 2019.

The solution to this review problem can be found on page 578.

EARNINGS PER SHARE

6

LO6 Describe and illustrate the basic and diluted earnings per share computations.

The income statement reports at least one, and potentially two, earnings per share (EPS) numbers: basic and diluted. The difference between the two measures is illustrated as follows:

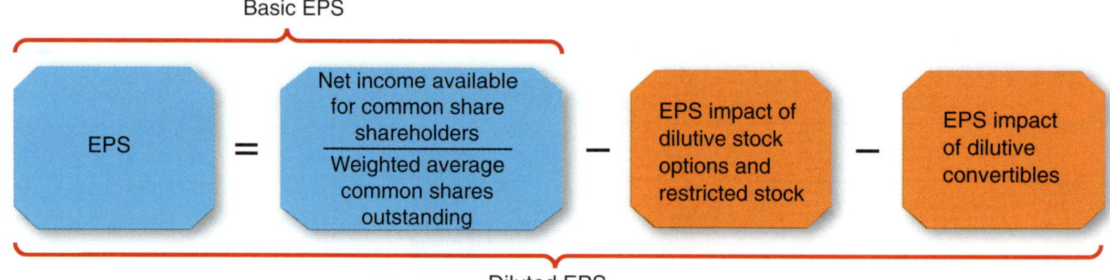

All public companies are required to report basic EPS. If the company has a complex capital structure, it is also required to report diluted EPS. A company is said to have a **complex capital structure** if it has certain *dilutive securities* outstanding. **Dilutive securities** are securities that can be converted into shares of common stock and would therefore reduce (or dilute) the earnings per share upon conversion. A few of the more prominent types of potentially dilutive securities are:

- Equity-based pay, including stock options and restricted stock
- Convertible debt
- Convertible preferred stock

The Appendix at the end of this chapter details the accounting for these securities. A company with none of these dilutive securities outstanding is said to have a **simple capital structure**.

Basic EPS (BEPS) is computed as earnings available for common shareholders (net income less net income attributable to noncontrolling interests and preferred dividends) divided by the weighted average number of common shares outstanding for the year. (The number of shares is "weighted" by the amount of time each share was outstanding during the year.) The subtraction of net income attributable to noncontrolling interests and preferred stock dividends yields the income per common share available for dividend payments to common shareholders. The preferred dividends are subtracted because this portion of net income does not accrue to the common stockholders.

Computation of **Diluted EPS (DEPS)** reflects the added shares that would have been issued if all "in the money" stock options, unvested restricted stock, and other convertible securities had been exercised at the beginning of the year. When DEPS is calculated, the corporation needs to consider the maximum potential reduction (dilution) of its BEPS that could occur if the conversion of these securities took place. To do so means that any of these securities that do not reduce BEPS upon conversion are not to be considered converted. The result (DEPS) must be a figure that is lower than BEPS. The actual calculation can be quite complex. This does not detract from the importance of the DEPS value. The diluted earnings per share figure is favored by analysts as a better indicator of performance compared to basic earnings per share. Because reported DEPS never exceeds reported BEPS, the calculation is considered conservative.

Computation and Analysis of EPS

The computation of basic EPS is relatively straightforward, particularly when the firm neither issues nor buys any of its shares during the year. The formula is:

$$\text{Basic EPS (BEPS)} = \frac{\text{Net income available for common shareholders}}{\text{Weighted average number of common shares outstanding}}$$

To illustrate this calculation, assume that United Bridge Corporation reported net income of \$200,000 in 2018 and paid \$24,000 in preferred dividends. At the beginning of the year, the company had 44,000 shares of common stock outstanding. On June 30 (exactly the midpoint of the year) United Bridge purchased 8,000 shares of stock as treasury stock. Thus, the number of shares outstanding for the first six months of 2018 was 44,000 and, for the second half of the year, the company had 36,000 shares outstanding. The weighted average number of shares outstanding was, therefore, 40,000 [(44,000 + 36,000)/2]. Basic EPS would be calculated as follows:

$$\text{Basic EPS} = \frac{\$200{,}000 - \$24{,}000}{40{,}000 \text{ shares}} = \$4.40 \text{ per share}$$

The computation of diluted EPS is more complex in that it requires adjusting the basic EPS calculation for the effect of dilutive securities. This will typically require adjusting both the numerator and denominator of the calculation.

$$\text{Diluted earnings per share (DEPS)} = \frac{\text{Net income available for common shareholders + Add-backs}}{\text{Weighted average number of common shares + Shares of convertible securities and stock options assumed to be converted}}$$

To illustrate, assume that United Bridge Corporation's preferred stock is convertible into 8,000 shares of common stock. To calculate diluted EPS, we must assume that the convertible preferred shares were converted at the beginning of the year. If this had occurred, two things would have been different for United Bridge. First, the weighted average number of shares outstanding would be higher by 8,000 shares. Second, the company would not have paid preferred dividends of \$24,000. The resulting calculation would be:

$$\text{Diluted EPS} = \frac{\$200{,}000}{48{,}000 \text{ shares}} = \$4.17 \text{ per share}$$

A full description of the procedures for calculating diluted EPS is beyond the scope of this text.[8] However, as the calculation above illustrates, diluted EPS adjusts basic EPS for the effect of dilutive securities. Reported DEPS must be no larger than BEPS to reflect its conservative message.

Pfizer reports both basic and diluted EPS. The table below, drawn from Pfizer's 2017 consolidated income statement, presents its basic and diluted EPS figures.

Year Ended December 31	2017	2016
Earnings per common share—basic		
Income from continuing operations attributable to Pfizer Inc. common shareholders	$3.57	$1.18
Discontinued operations—net of tax	—	—
Net income attributable to Pfizer Inc. common shareholders	$3.57	$1.18
Earnings per common share—diluted		
Income from continuing operations attributable to Pfizer Inc. common shareholders	$3.52	$1.17
Discontinued operations—net of tax	—	—
Net income attributable to Pfizer Inc. common shareholders	$3.52	$1.17
Weighted average shares—basic (millions)	5,970	6,089
Weighted average shares—diluted (millions)	6,058	6,159

Several observations should be made regarding Pfizer's EPS disclosures:

1. Pfizer reports basic EPS of $3.57 in 2017 and $1.18 in 2016. Diluted EPS is $0.05 lower and $0.01 lower in 2017 and 2016, respectively. The difference between basic and diluted EPS is caused by the effect of dilutive securities. Specifically, Pfizer has outstanding stock options and convertible preferred stock. Most publicly traded companies have at least one type of dilutive security outstanding. However, the dilutive effect of these securities on Pfizer's EPS is small.
2. The income statement further separates these EPS figures into EPS from continuing operations and EPS from discontinued operations. Income from discontinued operations in 2017 and 2016 was too small to affect the EPS computations. However, the effects of discontinued operations were large in 2013, accounting for almost half of basic EPS. GAAP requires separate reporting of the effects of nonrecurring items on EPS, including discontinued operations (see Chapter 6).
3. Pfizer used weighted average shares outstanding of 5,970 million shares to calculate basic EPS. This number is not the same as the number of shares outstanding in its December 31, 2017, balance sheet. Nor is it the simple average of the beginning and ending numbers of shares outstanding. The precise number of shares used in the EPS calculations requires knowing exactly when common stock and treasury stock transactions occurred during the year so that the weighted average number of shares outstanding can be calculated. Such detailed information is seldom available in a company's 10-K report.

EPS figures are sometimes used as a method of comparing operating results for companies of different sizes under the assumption that the number of shares outstanding is proportional to the income level (that is, a company twice the size of another will report double the income and will have double the common shares outstanding, leaving EPS approximately equal for the two companies). This assumption is erroneous. Management controls the number of common shares outstanding. Different companies also have different philosophies regarding share issuance and repurchase. For example, consider that most companies report annual EPS of less than $5, while **Berkshire Hathaway Inc.** reported EPS of $27,326 for 2017! The large amount occurs because Berkshire Hathaway has so few common shares outstanding, not necessarily because it has stellar profits.

Most analysts prefer to concentrate their attention on diluted EPS versus basic EPS as the more important measure, but the value of the EPS number is influenced by a number of factors including the number of common shares outstanding. For this reason, comparisons are more useful over time than across firms, but a careful reader should differentiate between EPS growth that comes from increases in the numerator and EPS growth that comes from decreases in the denominator. For these reasons, EPS may be of limited use in evaluating a firm's operational performance.

[8] Also, some more complicated securities, including securities in the mezzanine section of the balance sheet, may lead to required adjustments to the numerator of basic EPS at times, and to both the numerator and denominator of diluted EPS. These are beyond the scope of this text.

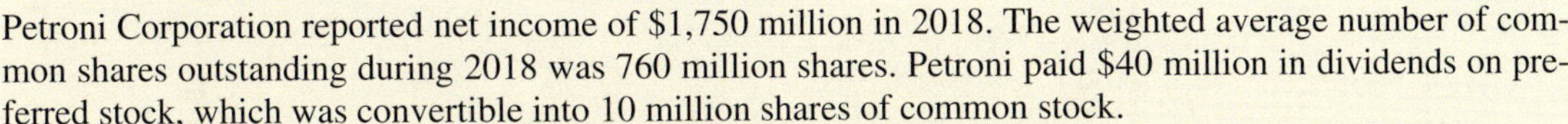

BUSINESS INSIGHT

It is possible that reported earnings declines but Basic EPS increases. Indeed, of all the public firms that filed with the SEC in the years 2015–2017, this occurred almost 800 times. Notably, Signet Jewelers had a decline in earnings of almost 5% and an increase in Basic EPS of 8%. A similar relation held for IBM in the years 2012–2014. Often this is due to reductions in the number of shares due to share repurchases.

CHAPTER-END REVIEW

Petroni Corporation reported net income of $1,750 million in 2018. The weighted average number of common shares outstanding during 2018 was 760 million shares. Petroni paid $40 million in dividends on preferred stock, which was convertible into 10 million shares of common stock.

1. Calculate Petroni's basic earnings per share for 2018.
2. Calculate Petroni's diluted earnings per share for 2018.
3. What EPS numbers should Petroni report on its 2018 income statement?

The solution to this review problem can be found on page 578.

APPENDIX 11A: Dilutive Securities: Accounting for convertible securities, stock options, and restricted stock

Convertible Securities

LO7 Analyze the accounting for convertible securities, stock rights, stock options, and restricted stock.

7

Convertible securities are debt and equity securities that provide the holder with an option to convert those securities into other securities. Convertible debentures, for example, are debt securities that give the holder the option to convert the debt into common stock at a predetermined conversion price. Preferred stock can also contain a conversion privilege.

To illustrate, assume 5,000 shares of preferred stock were issued at a stated value of $100 per share, with each share convertible into 12 shares of $5 par value common stock. The appropriate journal entry would be:

Cash (+A)	500,000	
Preferred stock (stated value) (+SE)		500,000

Now assume that 2,000 shares are converted to (2,000 × 12) = 24,000 shares of common stock. The appropriate journal entry is:

Preferred stock (stated value) (−SE)	200,000	
Common stock (par $5) (+SE)		10,000
Additional paid-in capital (+SE)		190,000

Conversion privileges offer an additional benefit to the holder of a security. That is, debtholders and preferred stockholders carry senior positions as claimants in bankruptcy, and carry a fixed-interest or dividend yield. With a conversion privilege, they can enjoy the residual benefits of common shareholders should the company perform well.

A conversion option is valuable and yields a higher price for the securities than they would otherwise command. However, conversion privileges impose a cost on common shareholders. That is, the higher market price received for convertible securities is offset by the cost imposed on the subordinate (common) securities. Conversion of these securities into common shares dilutes the ownership percentage of existing holders of the firm's common stock.

Accounting for the issuance of a convertible security is straightforward: the conversion option is *not* valued on the balance sheet unless it is detachable from the security (and, thus, separately saleable). Instead, the convertible preferred stock or convertible debt is recorded just like preferred stock or debt that does not have a conversion feature.

When securities are converted, the book value of the converted security is removed from the balance sheet and a corresponding increase is made to contributed capital. To illustrate the most commonly used method, assume that a company has convertible bonds with a face value of $1,000 and an unamortized premium of $100. Its holders convert them into 20 shares of $10 par value common stock. The financial statement effects and related entries of this conversion would be:

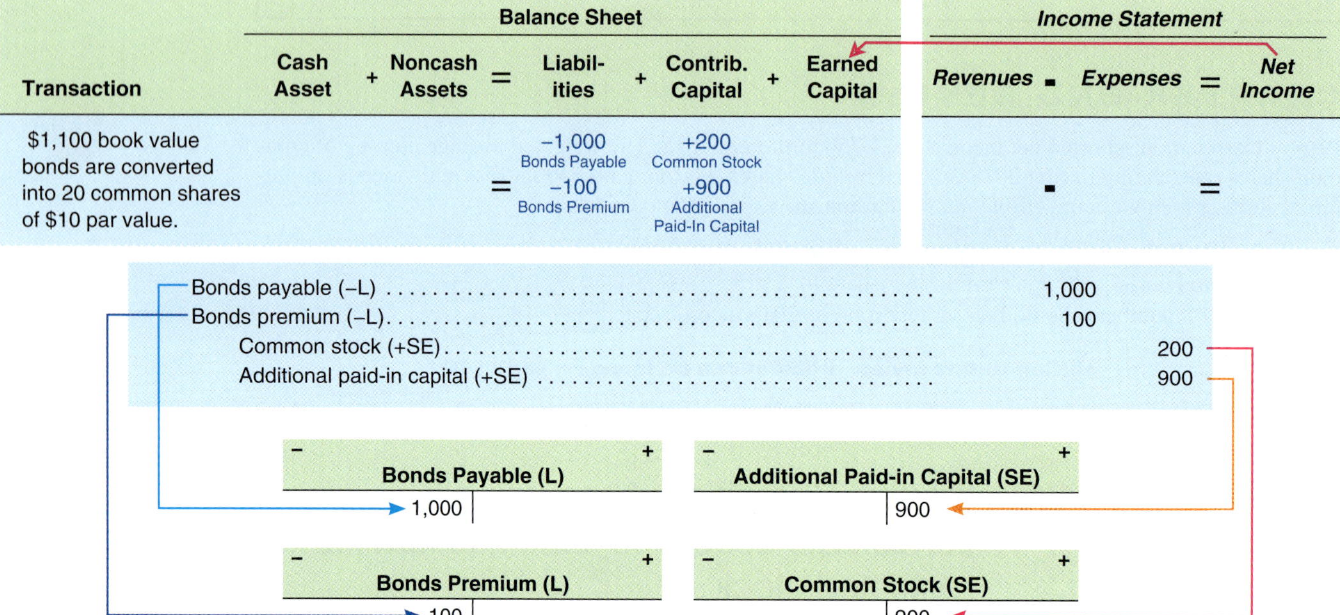

	Balance Sheet									Income Statement				
Transaction	Cash Asset	+	Noncash Assets	=	Liabil-ities	+	Contrib. Capital	+	Earned Capital	Revenues	−	Expenses	=	Net Income
$1,100 book value bonds are converted into 20 common shares of $10 par value.				=	−1,000 Bonds Payable −100 Bonds Premium		+200 Common Stock +900 Additional Paid-In Capital				−		=	

Bonds payable (−L)	1,000	
Bonds premium (−L)	100	
Common stock (+SE)		200
Additional paid-in capital (+SE)		900

− Bonds Payable (L) +	
	1,000

− Additional Paid-in Capital (SE) +	
	900

− Bonds Premium (L) +	
	100

− Common Stock (SE) +	
	200

The key financial statement effects of this transaction are:

- The bond's face value ($1,000) and unamortized premium ($100) of the bonds are removed from the balance sheet.
- Common stock increases by the par value of the shares issued (20 shares × $10 par = $200) and additional paid-in capital increases for the balance ($900).
- There is no effect on income from this conversion unless an interest accrual is required.

One final note: the potentially dilutive effect of convertible securities is taken into account in the computation of diluted earnings per share (DEPS). Specifically, the diluted EPS computation assumes conversion at the beginning of the year (or when the security is issued if during the year). The earnings available to common shares in the numerator are increased by any forgone after-tax interest expense or preferred dividends, and the additional shares to be issued in the conversion increase the shares outstanding in the denominator.

Stock Rights

Corporations often issue **stock rights** that give the holder an option to acquire a specified number of shares of capital stock under prescribed conditions and within a stated period. The evidence of stock rights is a certificate called a **stock warrant**. Stock rights are issued for several reasons that include the following:

- To compensate outside parties (such as underwriters, promoters, board members, and other professionals) for services provided to the company;
- As a preemptive right that gives existing stockholders the first chance to buy additional shares when the corporation decides to raise additional equity capital through share issuances;
- To enhance the marketability of other securities issued by the company (an example is issuing rights to purchase common stock with convertible bonds).

Stock rights or warrants specify the:

- Number of rights represented by the warrant
- Option price per share (which can be zero)
- Number of rights needed to obtain a share of the stock
- Expiration date of the rights
- Instructions for the exercise of rights

Accounting for stock rights is complex. The goals of this discussion are to understand the essence of stock rights issued to current stockholders.

Stock rights issued to current stockholders have three important dates: (1) Announcement date of the rights offering; (2) Issuance date of the rights; and (3) Expiration date of the rights. Between the announcement date and the issuance date, the price of the stock will reflect the value of the rights. After the issuance date, the shares and the rights trade separately. Shareholders can exercise their rights, sell their stock, or allow the rights to lapse.

To illustrate, assume on December 10, 2018, a company announces the issue of rights to purchase one additional share of its $5 par value common stock for every 10 shares currently held on January 1, 2019. The exercise price per share is $20 and the rights expire September 1, 2019. Assume further that 7,000 of the rights are exercised.

- No recognition is required at the announcement date and at the issuance date.
- The first entry is made when the first stock right is exercised. We give only the summary entry that would be appropriate after September 1, 2019.

Sept 1: To record the issuance of 7,000 shares of common stock on exercise of stock rights:
The financial statement effects and related entries would be (amounts in millions):

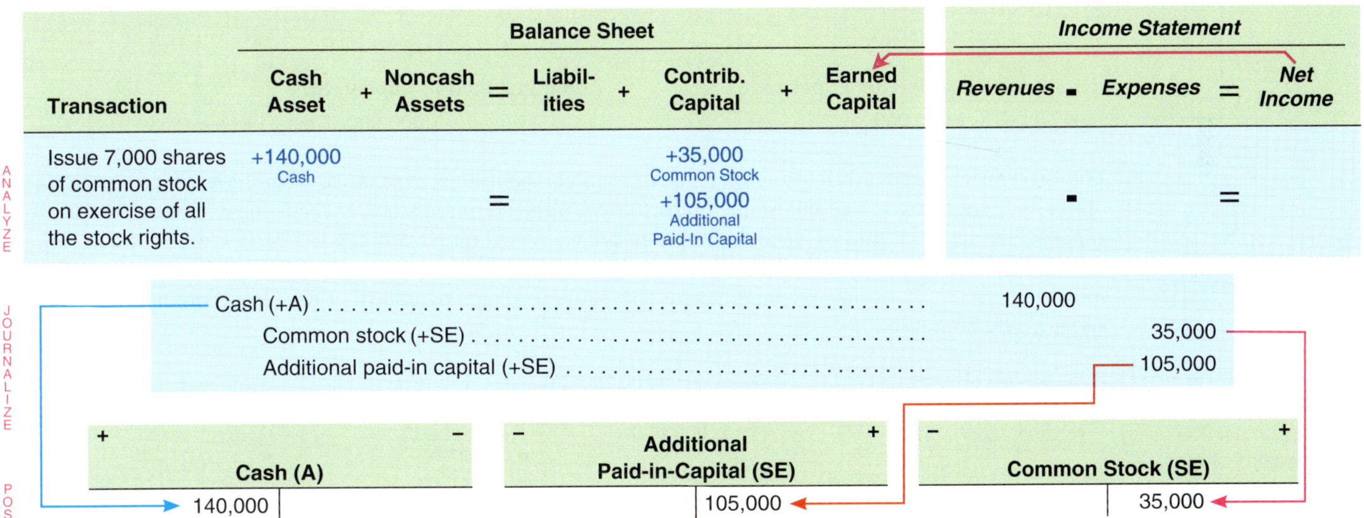

Employee Stock Options

Accounting for stock options has been a contentious issue for a number of years. Accounting standard setters, on the one hand, argue that the options to purchase a corporation's stock at a discount (or even without a discount) are valuable. They point to the willingness of senior management and others to accept stock options instead of cash in payment for services rendered as evidence of their value. Thus, the FASB concluded that the fair value of each stock option award must be recognized as an expense on the firm's income statement.

However, senior managements of start-up firms typically argue that it is necessary in the face of cash shortages to compensate those providing service at least partly using stock options. If these option grants are treated as an expense, it will cause their firms to appear less profitable, thereby stifling investment and business growth. Those arguing against recognizing an expense also point to the difficulties in obtaining precise values for these options.

These difficulties are real, but methods of valuing options do exist that provide reasonable estimates of option values. The FASB decided that such awards are expenses and the expense must be reported at the fair value of the option grant. For example, in Note 13 to its 10-K report, Pfizer reports the fair value of stock option grants to be $5.6 million (1.4 million options granted × $4.01 per option).

Stock option grants normally require a vesting period. The **vesting period** is a period of time during which the employee is not allowed to exercise the stock option. For example, a stock option may expire in 5 years and vest over a period of 3 years. Such an option would be exercisable in the fourth or fifth year of its life. Rather than recognizing the entire option value as compensation expense at the time that the option grant is awarded, GAAP requires that the fair value of the option be recorded ratably over the vesting period.

To illustrate stock option accounting, suppose that on January 1, 2018, a company grants options to purchase 200,000 shares to senior management as part of its performance bonus plan. The options are granted with an exercise price of $30 (the current price), and can be exercised after vesting in 2 years. The firm uses an accepted valuation method (not discussed here) to obtain a fair value of $10 per option. The accounting and financial statement effects and related entries for 2018 would be:

January 1—grant date

The total compensation cost is determined at the grant date, but no journal entry is recorded on the grant date.

December 31, 2018 and 2019—record compensation expense:

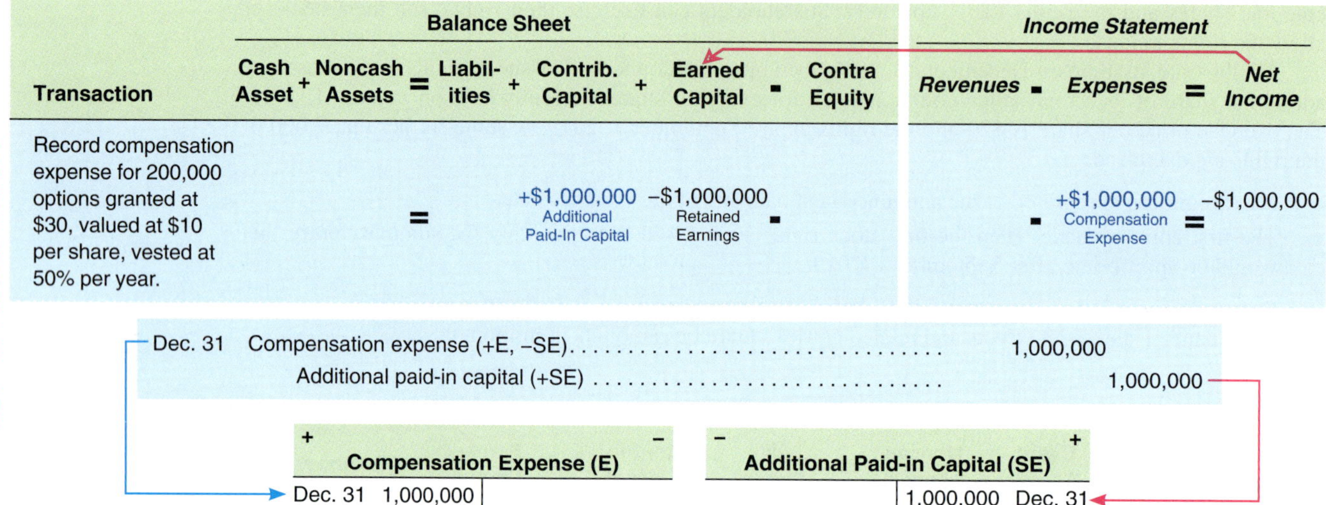

The two entries together bring the total stock-based compensation expense to $2 million. Once vested, the option will not be exercised unless the market price of the common stock exceeds the exercise price. Next, suppose that its stock price rises and all options are exercised on November 15, 2020, with the stock being issued from treasury shares purchased previously at $25. The accounting and financial statement effects follow. In effect, senior management has purchased these shares by contributing $2 million in employment services and $6 million in cash.

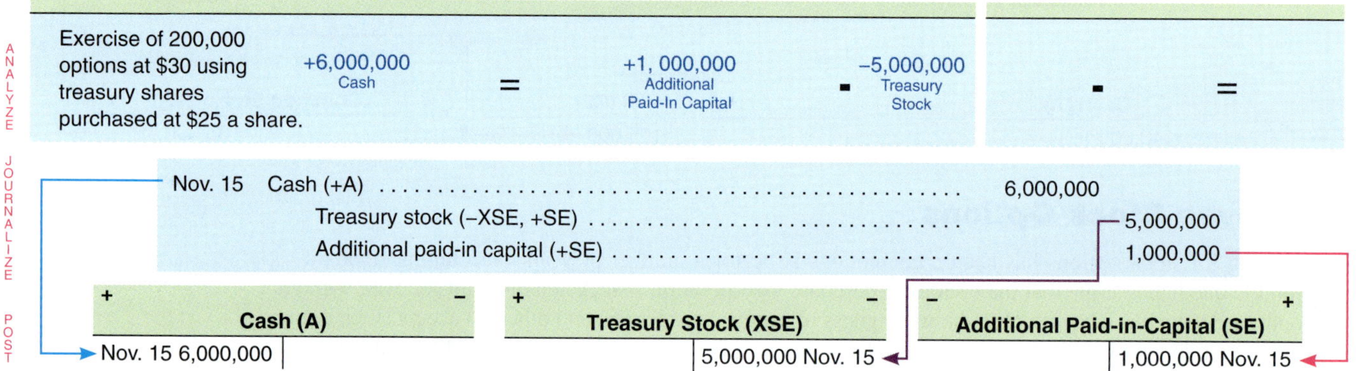

Restricted Stock

Companies are increasingly moving away from stock options and to other types of performance-based pay. One type that is commonly used is restricted stock, either in the form of restricted stock share awards or restricted stock unit awards (which we refer to hereafter as **restricted stock awards (RSAs)** and **restricted stock units (RSUs)** for convenience). Indeed, a recent study by Willis Watson Towers reports that in 2017, 71% of the S&P 600 granted restricted stock while only 35% granted stock options.[9] Indeed, Pfizer granted $5.6 million in options in 2017 while in 2014 the company granted almost $196 million in options. In 2017, Pfizer granted $301 million in value of RSUs.

Restricted stock plans give employees shares or rights to shares, but these are restricted (meaning the employee does not have full ownership) until the employee has satisfied vesting requirements. If the

[9] Michael Bowie, Robert Newbury, and Jang Han, "Executive Compensation Bulletin: Long-term incentives a major driver of S&P 1500 CEO compensation," Willis Towers Watson: Executive Pay Matters, November 9, 2018, https://www.towerswatson.com/en/Insights/Newsletters/Global/executive-pay-matters/2018/11/Executive-Compensation-Bulletin-Long-term-incentives-major-driver-S-P-1500-CEO-compensation

employee leaves before the awards vest, the shares or rights would be lost. Pfizer states that it has a three-year vesting period.

While unvested, both RSAs and RSUs are potentially dilutive securities in the calculation of diluted EPS. We note that, generally, unvested RSAs are not included in the calculation of basic EPS, even though as we will see below, the shares are outstanding. (However, sometimes they are considered participating securities and included in the calculation of basic EPS. For example, CISCO excludes them from basic EPS and Facebook includes them.) RSUs are not outstanding shares and are not included in the calculation of basic EPS. RSUs are considered potentially dilutive in the calculation of diluted EPS.

Restricted Stock Award (RSA)

An RSA is a form of equity compensation that transfers stock to the recipient on the date of the grant. It is not an option to buy shares but rather an award of shares. The recipient's rights in shares are restricted until the shares vest.

On the grant date of an RSA, the company increases (debits) a contra-equity account, Unearned Compensation—Equity (also called Deferred Compensation), for the fair value of the shares at the grant date. Common Stock at par and Paid-in Capital in Excess of Par are increased (credited). Over the vesting period, this Unearned Compensation-Equity amount is reversed to Compensation Expense using the straight-line method. Note that compensation is valued at the fair value of the shares at the grant date and is unaffected by any change in stock value during the vesting period.

To illustrate, suppose that on January 1, 2019 a company grants 1,000 shares (RSAs) with a total fair value of $30,000 and a 3-year vesting period. Common stock has a $1 per share par value. The accounting and financial statement effects and related entries would be:

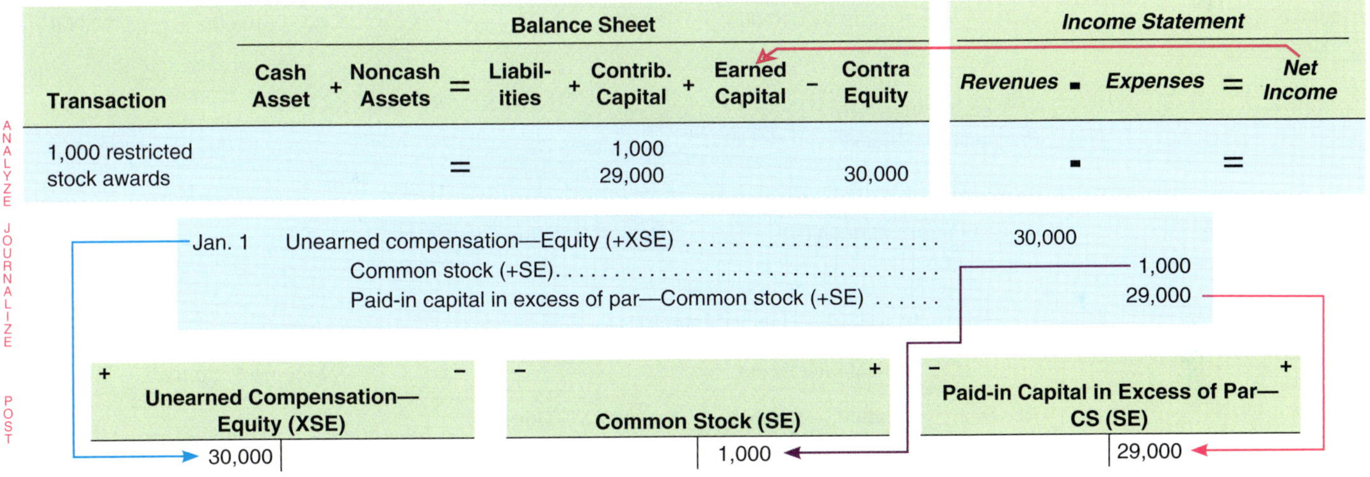

Transaction	Cash Asset	+ Noncash Assets	= Liabilities	+ Contrib. Capital	+ Earned Capital	− Contra Equity	Revenues	− Expenses	= Net Income
1,000 restricted stock awards			=	1,000 29,000		30,000		−	=

December 31, 2019, 2020, and 2021—To record compensation expense

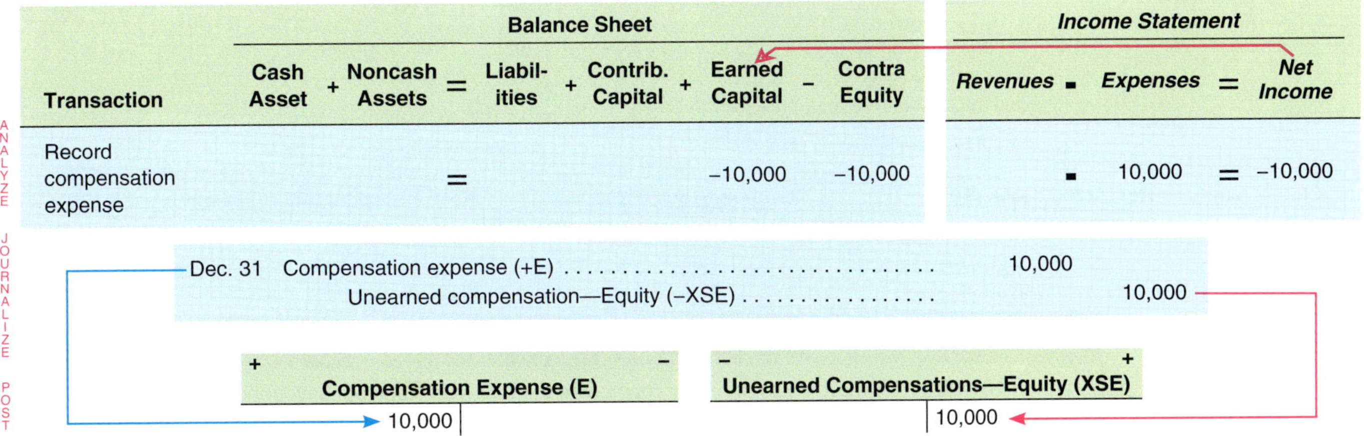

Transaction	Cash Asset	+ Noncash Assets	= Liabilities	+ Contrib. Capital	+ Earned Capital	− Contra Equity	Revenues	− Expenses	= Net Income
Record compensation expense			=		−10,000	−10,000		− 10,000	= −10,000

Restricted Stock Unit (RSU)

An RSU is not an actual transfer of stock on the grant date, but rather a commitment to transfer stock once vesting conditions are met. Thus upon the grant of an RSU, the employee is granted the right to receive a certain number of shares of stock at a future date under certain conditions. There is no issuance of shares on the grant date, in contrast to the RSA discussed above; thus, no accounting entry is required on the grant date. The compensation value is determined at the grant date, however. Over the vesting period as the compensation is earned, the company records Compensation Expense (debit) and increases (credits) an account called Paid-in Capital—Restricted Stock for the proportionate share of the value each reporting period (using the straight-line method). After the employee meets the vesting requirements (the restrictions lapse), the amount from Paid-in Capital—Restricted Stock is transferred to Common Stock at par and Paid-in Capital—Common Stock.

To illustrate, suppose that on January 1, 2019, a company grants 1,000 RSUs. Each RSU may be exchanged for 1 share of $1 par common stock. The fair value of the shares on the grant date is $30 and the requisite service period is 3 years. (Assume no forfeitures and no expectation of forfeitures.) The accounting and financial statement effects and related entries would be:

January 1, 2019—Grant of RSUs
No entry.

December 31, 2019, 2020, and 2021—To record compensation expense

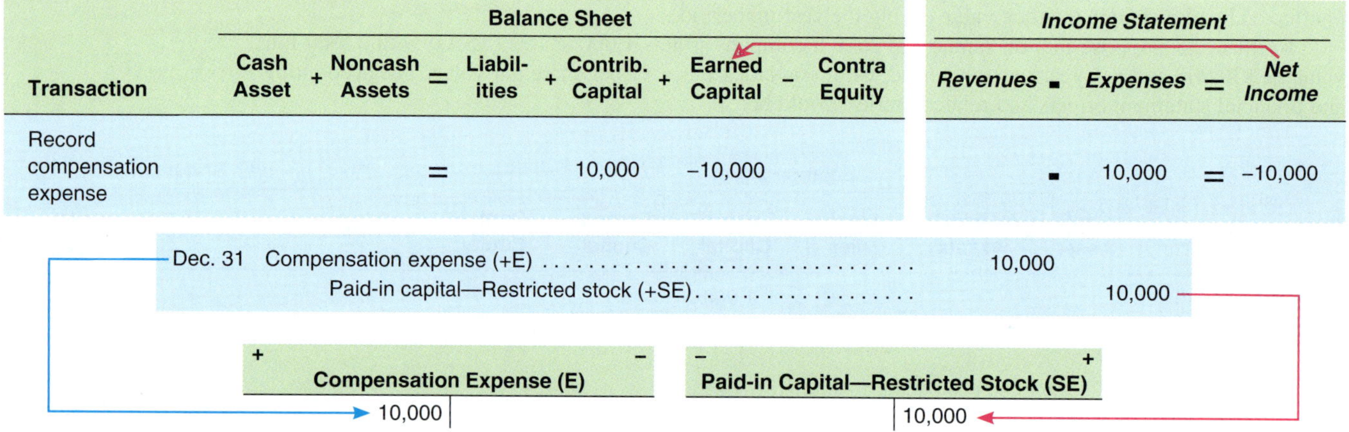

Transaction	Cash Asset	+ Noncash Assets	=	Liabilities	+ Contrib. Capital	+ Earned Capital	− Contra Equity	Revenues	−	Expenses	=	Net Income
Record compensation expense			=		10,000	−10,000			−	10,000	=	−10,000

		Debit	Credit
Dec. 31	Compensation expense (+E)	10,000	
	Paid-in capital—Restricted stock (+SE)		10,000

Compensation Expense (E): + 10,000 (debit)

Paid-in Capital—Restricted Stock (SE): 10,000 (credit)

January 1, 2022—To record issuance of stock

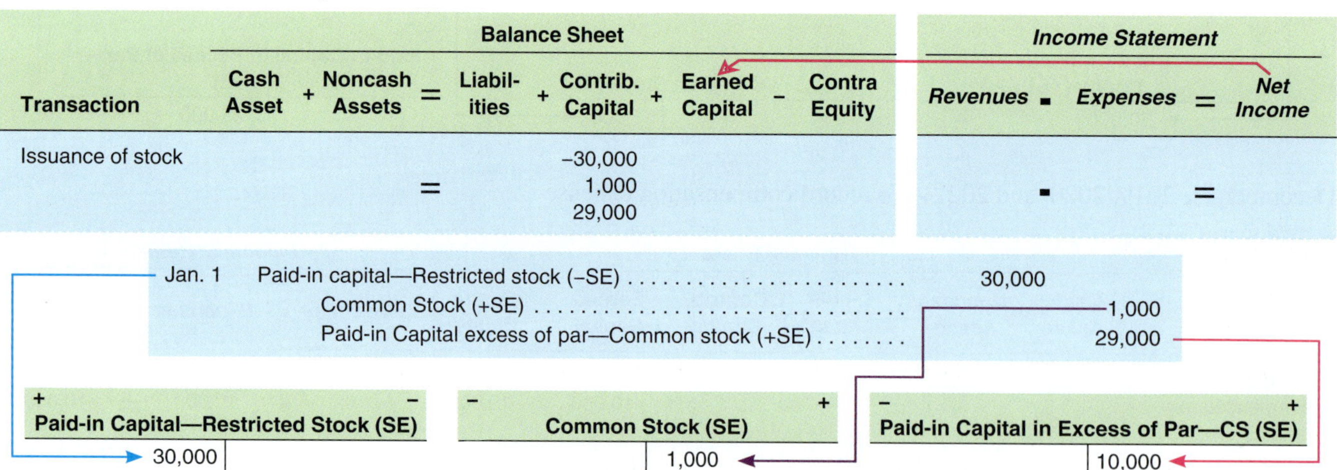

Transaction	Cash Asset	+ Noncash Assets	=	Liabilities	+ Contrib. Capital	+ Earned Capital	− Contra Equity	Revenues	−	Expenses	=	Net Income
Issuance of stock			=		−30,000 1,000 29,000				−		=	

		Debit	Credit
Jan. 1	Paid-in capital—Restricted stock (−SE)	30,000	
	Common Stock (+SE)		1,000
	Paid-in Capital excess of par—Common stock (+SE)		29,000

Paid-in Capital—Restricted Stock (SE): 30,000 (debit)

Common Stock (SE): 1,000 (credit)

Paid-in Capital in Excess of Par—CS (SE): 10,000 (credit)

BUSINESS INSIGHT

In their 2017 annual report, Tesla, Inc. reports the use of employee stock options, compensatory restricted stock units, and as having convertible debt. However, their basic and diluted EPS are equivalent at a negative $11.83 per share. The company states that roughly 10 million stock option awards, over 2 million convertible senior notes, and almost 600,000 warrants are excluded from the computation of diluted net income per share, because the effect is anti-dilutive. This is because in 2017, Tesla reported a loss; if the loss is spread out over more shares the effect is anti-dilutive.

APPENDIX 11A REVIEW

Kallapur, Inc., has issued convertible debentures: each $1,000 bond is convertible into 200 shares of $1 par common stock. Assume that the bonds were sold at a discount, and that each bond has a current unamortized discount equal to $150.

REQUIRED

1. Using the financial statement effects template, illustrate the effects of the conversion of one of its bonds.
2. Prepare journal entries for the transaction assuming conversion of one bond.
3. Post the journal entries to the related T-accounts.

The solution to this review problem can be found on page 579.

SUMMARY

Describe business financing through stock issuances. (p. 530) **LO1**

- Contributed capital represents the cumulative cash (or other asset) inflow that the company has received from the sale of various classes of stock, preferred and common.
- Preferred stock receives preference in terms of dividends before common and, if cumulative, receives all dividends not paid in the past before common dividends can be paid. Preferred stock can also be designated as convertible into common stock at the holder's option and at a predetermined conversion ratio. Voting privileges reside only with the common stock.

Explain and account for the issuance and repurchase of stock. (p. 533) **LO2**

- Common stock is often repurchased by the firm for use in stock award programs or to signal management confidence in the company or simply to return cash to shareholders. Repurchased stock is either cancelled or held for reissue. The repurchase is debited to a contra equity account titled treasury stock.

Describe how operations increase the equity of a business. (p. 538) **LO3**

- Earned capital includes retained earnings, which represents the cumulative profit that has been retained by the company. Earned capital is increased by income earned and decreased by losses and dividends declared by the firm. Earned capital also includes the effects of items included in other comprehensive income.

Explain and account for dividends and stock splits. (p. 538) **LO4**

- Dividends in the form of stock decrease retained earnings and increase contributed capital by an equivalent amount.
- A stock split is a proportionate distribution similar in substance to a stock dividend. The new number of shares outstanding must be disclosed. Otherwise, no further accounting is required unless the state of incorporation requires that the par value be proportionally adjusted.

Define and illustrate comprehensive income. (p. 543) **LO5**

- Comprehensive income includes several additional items not recognized in net income including: adjustments for changes in foreign exchange rates, unrealized changes in available-for-sale debt securities, and pension liability adjustments. The concept is designed to highlight impacts on net assets that are beyond management's control.

Describe and illustrate the basic and diluted earnings per share computations. (p. 546) **LO6**

- Earnings per share is a closely watched number reported for all publicly traded firms. Basic EPS is computed as the ratio of net income (less preferred dividends and noncontrolling interests) to the weighted average number of outstanding shares for the period. The value of this performance metric is subject to all the difficulties in measuring net income including the fact that net income can increase due to an acquisition or divestiture that can have no impact on the number of outstanding shares.
- Most analysts are more interested in what is termed diluted earnings per share. This conservative calculation, which, if reported, never exceeds basic EPS, reflects the maximum reduction in basic EPS possible assuming conversion of the convertible securities.
- Stock options that are "in the money" are always dilutive.
- Convertible securities that would be antidilutive are treated as if they were not converted.

LO7 Appendix 11A: Analyze the accounting for convertible securities, stock rights, stock options, and restricted stock. **(p. 549)**

- Convertible securities are debt and equity instruments, including stock rights, that allow these securities to be exchanged for other securities, typically common stock. The convertible feature adds value to the security to which it is attached.
- Stock options, one form of stock right, allow the holders to exchange them at a specified (strike) price for common stock. This right is valuable and should create an expense when granted to an employee or other individual. Expense recognition is appropriate, using the value obtained by applying an options-pricing model, even though the calculation is not precise. The option will not be exercised unless the market price of the common stock exceeds the strike price.
- Convertible preferred stock and convertible debt securities need to be considered in the calculation of DEPS to the extent conversion reduces reported BEPS.
- Restricted share awards and restricted unit awards are recorded as compensation expense as the vesting period expires (as the employee works over the vesting period).
- Generally, unvested restricted stock awards and restricted stock units are excluded from the denominator of basic EPS. If dilutive, they are taken into account in the calculation of diluted EPS. Once vested, the shares are included in the computation of basic EPS.

GUIDANCE ANSWERS . . . YOU MAKE THE CALL

You are the Chief Financial Officer Several points must be considered. (1) Treasury shares are likely to prop up earnings per share (EPS). While the numerator (earnings) is likely dampened by the use of cash for the stock repurchase (because the cash cannot be reinvested in operations), EPS is likely to increase because of the reduced shares in the denominator. (2) If the shares are sufficiently undervalued (in management's opinion), the stock repurchase and subsequent resale can provide a better return than some alternative investments. (3) Stock repurchases send a strong signal to the market that management feels its stock is undervalued. This is more credible than merely making that argument with analysts. On the other hand, company cash is diverted from other investments. This is bothersome if such investments are mutually exclusive either now or in the future.

KEY RATIOS

Net income available for common shareholders =
Net income − Net income attributable to noncontrolling interests − Preferred dividends

$$\text{Return on Common Equity (ROCE)} = \frac{\text{Net income available for common shareholders}}{\text{Average common shareholders' equity}}$$

$$\text{Basic earnings per share (BEPS)} = \frac{\text{Net income available for common shareholders}}{\text{Weighted average number of common shares outstanding}}$$

Diluted earnings per share (DEPS) =

$$\frac{\text{Net income available for common shareholders} + \text{Add-backs}}{\text{Weighted average number of common shares} + \text{Shares of convertible securities and stock options assumed to be converted}}$$

KEY TERMS

Accumulated other comprehensive income (AOCI) (p. 544)
Basic EPS (BEPS) (p. 547)
Book value per share (p. 546)
Call feature (p. 533)
Common stock (p. 531)
Complex capital structure (p. 546)
Comprehensive income (p. 543)
Contributed capital (p. 530)
Conversion feature (p. 533)
Convertible securities (p. 549)
Diluted EPS (DEPS) (p. 547)
Dilutive securities (p. 546)
Dividend preference (p. 532)
Earned capital (p. 531)
Liquidating value (p. 532)
Liquidation preference (p. 532)
Noncontrolling interest (p. 531)
Participation feature (p. 533)
Par value (p. 531)
Preferred stock (p. 532)
Restricted stock award (RSA) (p. 552)
Restricted stock unit (RSU) (p. 552)
Shares authorized (p. 531)
Shares issued (p. 531)
Shares outstanding (p. 531)
Simple capital structure (p. 546)
Stock dividends (p. 540)
Stock rights (p. 550)
Stock split (p. 542)
Stock warrant (p. 550)
Treasury stock (p. 536)
Vesting period (p. 551)

Assignments with the MBC logo in the margin are available in myBusinessCourse.
See the Preface of the book for details.

MULTIPLE CHOICE

1. Suppose Pfizer issues 100,000 shares of its common stock, $0.05 par value, to obtain a warehouse and the accompanying land when the price of the stock is $22.00. Which one of the following statements is not true?
   a. The newly acquired assets will increase total assets by $2.2 million.
   b. Retained earnings are unaffected.
   c. The common stock account increases by $5,000.
   d. Total shareholders' equity increases by $2,195,000.

2. Assume Pfizer resells 10,000 shares of its stock that were purchased when the market price of the stock was $25. If the shares are resold for $22, which one of the following statements holds?
   a. Additional paid-in capital decreases by $30,000.
   b. The treasury stock account increases by $30,000.
   c. Additional paid-in capital increases by $30,000.
   d. The treasury stock account decreases by $30,000.

3. Suppose Pfizer declares a 200,000 common stock dividend (par $0.05) when the market value of a share is $20.00. Which one of the following statements is true?
   a. The common stock account increases by $10,000.
   b. Additional paid-in capital decreases by $3.99 million.
   c. Retained earnings increases by $4 million.
   d. Additional paid-in capital increases by $4 million.

4. Which of the following statements is true?
   a. When a *large stock dividend* is paid, retained earnings are reduced by the market value of the shares distributed.
   b. Neither stock dividends nor stock splits affect basic earnings per share calculations.
   c. A three-for-one stock split increases the total outstanding shares by 300%.
   d. A stock split has no financial statement effects because it is not a monetary transaction.

5. Which of the following statements is not true in relation to diluted EPS (DEPS)?
   a. Stock options that are in the money will always cause DEPS to be less than basic EPS.
   b. Convertible bonds, if dilutive, will cause changes in both the numerator and the denominator of DEPS.
   c. Stock analysts tend to concentrate their attention on DEPS instead of basic EPS.
   d. A company's only equity contract that can lead to dilution is stock options.

Multiple Choice Answers
1. d 2. a 3. a 4. d 5. d

QUESTIONS

Q11-1. Define *par value stock.* What is the significance of a stock's par value from an accounting and analysis perspective?

Q11-2. What are the basic differences between preferred stock and common stock? What are the typical features of preferred stock?

Q11-3. What features make preferred stock similar to debt? Similar to common stock?

Q11-4. What is meant by dividend arrearage on preferred stock? If dividends are two years in arrears on $500,000 of 6% preferred stock, and dividends are declared at the end of this year, what amount of total dividends must preferred shareholders receive before any distributions are made to common shareholders?

Q11-5. Distinguish between authorized stock and issued stock. Why might the number of shares issued be more than the number of shares outstanding?

Q11-6. Describe the difference between contributed capital and earned capital. Specifically, how can earned capital be considered as an investment by the company's shareholders?

Q11-7. How does the account "additional paid-in capital" (APIC) arise? What inferences, if any, can you draw from the amount of APIC as reported on the balance sheet relative to the common stock amount in relation to the financial condition of the company?

Q11-8. Define *stock split.* What are the major reasons for a stock split?

Q11-9. Define *treasury stock.* Why might a corporation acquire treasury stock? How is treasury stock reported in the balance sheet?

Q11-10. If a corporation purchases 600 shares of its own common stock at $10 per share and resells them at $14 per share, where would the $2,400 increase in capital be reported in the financial statements? Why is no gain reported?

Q11-11. A corporation has total stockholders' equity of $4,628,000 and one class of $2 par value common stock. The corporation has 500,000 shares authorized; 300,000 shares issued; 260,000 shares outstanding; and 40,000 shares as treasury stock. What is its book value per share?

Q11-12. What is a stock dividend? How does a common stock dividend distributed to common shareholders affect their respective ownership interests?

Q11-13. What is the difference between the accounting for a small stock dividend and the accounting for a large stock dividend?

Q11-14. Employee stock options have a potentially dilutive effect on earnings per share (EPS) that is recognized in the diluted EPS computation. What can companies do to offset these dilutive effects and how might this action affect the balance sheet?

Q11-15. What information is reported in a statement of stockholders' equity?

Q11-16. What items are typically reported under the stockholders' equity category of other comprehensive income (OCI)?

Q11-17. What is a stock option vesting period? How does the vesting period affect the recognition of compensation expense for stock options?

Q11-18. Describe the accounting for a convertible bond. Would this accounting ever result in the recognition of a gain in the income statement?

MINI EXERCISES

LO1 **M11-19. Analyzing and Identifying Financial Statement Effects of Stock Issuances**

On June 1, Beatty Corp. issues (*a*) 8,000 shares of $50 par value preferred stock at $68 cash per share and it issues (*b*) 12,000 shares of $1 par value common stock at $10 cash per share.

a. Do these transactions increase contributed capital or earned capital?

b. What is the effect of these transactions on Beatty Corp.'s income statement?

c. What are the differences between the preferred stock and the common stock issued by Beatty Corp.?

LO2 **M11-20. Analyzing and Identifying Financial Statement Effects of Stock Issuances**

On September 1, Magliolo, Inc., (*a*) issues 18,000 shares of $10 par value preferred stock at $48 cash per share and (*b*) issues 120,000 shares of $2 par value common stock at $37 cash per share.

a. Using the financial statement effects template, illustrate the effects of these two issuances.

b. Prepare the journal entries for the two issuances.

c. Post the journal entries from *b* to the related T-accounts.

M11-21. Distinguishing between Common Stock and Additional Paid-in Capital LO2

Cisco Systems
NASDAQ :: CSCO

Following is the stockholders' equity section from the **Cisco Systems, Inc.**, balance sheet (in millions, except par value).

Shareholders' equity	July 28, 2018
Preferred stock, no par value: 5 shares authorized; none issued and outstanding	$ —
Common stock and additional paid-in capital, $0.001 par value: 20,000 shares authorized; 4,614 shares issued and outstanding at July 28, 2018	42,820
Retained earnings	1,233
Accumulated other comprehensive income (loss)	(849)
Total Cisco shareholders' equity	43,204
Noncontrolling interests	—
Total equity	$43,204

For the $42,820 million reported as "common stock and additional paid-in capital," what portion is common stock and what portion is additional paid-in capital? Explain.

M11-22. Identifying and Analyzing Financial Statement Effects of Stock Issuance and Repurchase LO2

On January 1, 2019, Bartov Company issues 5,000 shares of $100 par value preferred stock at $250 cash per share. On March 1, the company repurchases 5,000 shares of previously issued $1 par value common stock at $83 cash per share.

a. Using the financial statement effects template, illustrate the effects of these two transactions.

b. Prepare the journal entries for the two transactions.

c. Post the journal entries from *b* to the related T-accounts.

M11-23. Assessing the Financial Statement Effects of a Stock Split LO4

Aflac Incorporated
NYSE :: AFL

In its second quarter 2018 10-Q, **Aflac Incorporated** included the following information:

Stock split: On February 13, 2018, the Board of Directors of the Parent Company declared a two-for-one stock split of the Company's common stock in the form of a 100% stock dividend payable on March 16, 2018 to shareholders of record at the close of business on March 2, 2018. The stock split was payable in the form of one additional common stock share for every share of common stock held. All equity and share-based data, including the number of shares outstanding and per share amounts, have been adjusted to reflect the stock split for all periods presented in this Quarterly Report on Form 10-Q.

Aflac effected this stock split as a large stock dividend. What changes has Aflac made to its balance sheet as a result of this action?

M11-24. Computing Basic and Diluted Earnings per Share LO2, 6

Zeller Corporation began 2018 with 120,000 shares of common stock and 16,000 shares of convertible preferred stock outstanding. On March 1 an additional 10,000 shares of common stock were issued. On August 1, another 16,000 shares of common stock were issued. On November 1, 6,000 shares of common stock were acquired for the treasury. The preferred stock has a $2 per-share dividend rate, and each share may be converted into one share of common stock. Zeller Corporation's 2018 net income is $501,000.

a. Compute basic earnings per share for 2018.

b. Compute diluted earnings per share for 2018.

c. If the preferred stock were not convertible, Zeller Corporation would have a simple capital structure. How would this change Zeller's earnings per share presentation?

M11-25. Assessing Common Stock and Treasury Stock Balances LO2, 6

Toyota Motor Corporation (ADR)
NYSE :: TM

Following is the stockholders' equity section from the **Toyota Motor Corporation**'s balance sheet for the 2018 fiscal year, which ended on March 31, 2018.

Toyota Motor Corporation Shareholders' Equity (Millions of Yen)	March 31, 2018
Common stock, no par value: authorized 10,000,000,000 shares in 2017 and 2018; issued: 3,262,997,492 shares at March 31, 2018	¥ 397,050
Additional paid-in capital	487,502
Retained earnings	19,473,464
Accumulated other comprehensive income (loss)	435,699
Treasury stock, at cost: 353,073,500 shares at March 31, 2018	(2,057,733)
Total Toyota Motor Corporation shareholders' equity	¥18,735,982

a. Toyota has repurchased 353,073,500 shares that comprise its March 31, 2018, treasury stock account. Compute the number of outstanding shares as of March 31, 2018.

b. Assume that all of this treasury stock had been acquired in one purchase on July 1, 2017. What would have been the effect on the denominator of the basic EPS calculation?

LO4 **M11-26. Identifying and Analyzing Financial Statement Effects of Cash Dividends**

Freid Corp. has outstanding 6,000 shares of $50 par value, 6% preferred stock, and 40,000 shares of $1 par value common stock. The company has $328,000 of retained earnings. At year-end, the company declares and pays the regular $3 per share cash dividend on preferred stock and a $2.20 per share cash dividend on common stock.

a. Using the financial statement effects template, illustrate the effects of these two dividend payments.

b. Prepare the journal entries for the two dividend payments.

c. Post the journal entries from *b* to the related T-accounts.

LO4 **M11-27. Analyzing and Identifying Financial Statement Effects of Stock Dividends**

Dutta Corp. has outstanding 70,000 shares of $5 par value common stock. At year-end, the company declares and issues a 4% common stock dividend when the market price of the stock is $21 per share.

a. Using the financial statement effects template, illustrate the effects of this dividend declaration and payment.

b. Prepare the journal entries for the stock dividend declaration and payment.

c. Post the journal entries from *b* to the related T-accounts.

LO4 **M11-28. Analyzing, Identifying, and Explaining the Effects of a Stock Split**

On September 1, Weiss Company has 250,000 shares of $15 par value ($165 market value) common stock that are issued and outstanding. Its balance sheet on that date shows the following account balances relating to the common stock.

Common stock	$3,750,000
Paid-in capital in excess of par value	2,250,000

On September 2, Weiss splits its stock 3-for-2 and reduces the par value to $10 per share.

a. How many shares of common stock are issued and outstanding immediately after the stock split?

b. What is the dollar balance of the common stock account immediately after the stock split?

c. What is the likely reason that Weiss Company split its stock?

LO4 **M11-29. Distributing Cash Dividends to Preferred and Common Shareholders**

Dechow Company has outstanding 20,000 shares of $50 par value, 6% cumulative preferred stock, and 80,000 shares of $10 par value common stock. The company declares and pays cash dividends amounting to $160,000.

a. If no arrearage on the preferred stock exists, how much in total dividends, and in dividends per share, is paid to each class of stock?

b. If one year's dividend arrearage on the preferred stock exists, how much in total dividends, and in dividends per share, is paid to each class of stock?

LO3, 4 **M11-30. Analyzing and Preparing a Retained Earnings Reconciliation**

Use the following data to prepare the 2019 retained earnings reconciliation for Maffett Company.

Total retained earnings, December 31, 2018	$347,000
Stock dividends declared and paid in 2019	28,000
Cash dividends declared and paid in 2019	35,000
Net income for 2019	94,000

M11-31. Accounting for Large Stock Dividend and Stock Split LO4

Watts Corporation has 40,000 shares of $10 par value common stock outstanding and retained earnings of $820,000. The company declares a 100% stock dividend. The market price at the declaration is $17 per share.

a. Prepare the general journal entry for the stock dividend.

b. Assume that the company splits its stock two shares for one share and reduces the par value from $10 to $5 rather than declaring a 100% stock dividend. How does the accounting for the stock split differ from the accounting for the 100% stock dividend?

M11-32. Computing Basic and Diluted Earnings per Share LO6

During 2018, Park Corporation had 50,000 shares of $10 par value common stock and 10,000 shares of 8%, $50 par value convertible preferred stock outstanding. Each share of preferred stock may be converted into three shares of common stock. Park Corporation's 2018 net income was $440,000.

a. Compute the basic earnings per share for 2018.

b. Compute the diluted earnings per share for 2018.

M11-33. Computing Earnings per Share LO6

Kingery Corporation began the calendar (and fiscal) year with a simple structure consisting of 38,000 shares of common stock outstanding. On May 1, 10,000 additional shares were issued, and another 1,000 shares were issued on September 1. The company had a net income for the year of $234,000.

a. Compute the earnings per share of common stock.

b. Assume that the company also had 6,000 shares of 6%, $50 par value cumulative preferred stock outstanding throughout the year. Compute the basic earnings per share of common stock.

M11-34. Defining and Computing Earnings per Share LO6

Siemens AG (ADR)
OTCMKTS :: SIEGY

Siemens AG reports the following basic and diluted earnings per share in its 2018 annual report.

	Year Ended September 30,	
(shares in thousands; earnings per share in €)	2018	2017
Income from continuing operations attributable to shareholders of Siemens AG	€ 5,683	€ 5,908
Weighted average shares outstanding—basic	815,063	812,180
Effect of dilutive share-based payment	11,600	13,591
Effective of dilutive warrants	828,316	829,163
Weighted average shares outstanding—diluted	1,653	3,392
Basic earnings per share (from continuing operations)	€ 6.97	€ 7.27
Diluted earnings per share (from continuing operations)	€ 6.86	€ 7.13

a. Describe the accounting definitions for basic and diluted earnings per share.

b. Identify the Siemens numbers that make up both EPS computations.

c. What calculation limits the reported value of diluted EPS?

M11-35. Analyzing Stock Option Expense for Income LO7

Merck & Co.
NYSE :: MRK

Merck & Co., Inc., reported net income attributable to Merck & Co., Inc., of $2,394 million for the 2017 fiscal year. Its 2017 10-K report contained the following information regarding its stock options.

Employee stock options are granted to purchase shares of Company stock at the fair market value at the time of grant. These awards generally vest one-third each year over a three-year period, with a contractual term of 7-10 years . . . The weighted average exercise price of options granted in 2017 was $63.88 per option . . . The weighted average fair value of options granted in 2017 was $7.04 per option.

a. Merck granted 4,232,000 options to employees in 2017. Using a journal entry, show how the stock option grants would be recorded in 2017. (Assume all grants took place on January 1, 2017.)

b. How does the granting of stock options affect EPS?

c. Merck employees exercised 11,512,000 options in 2017, paying a total of $499 million in cash to the company. Using a summary journal entry, show how these option exercises would be recorded in 2017.

d. How does the exercise of stock options affect EPS?

LO2, 4, 6

M11-36. Examining the Effect of Stock Transactions

Year 1: Noreen Company issues 10,000 shares of its no-par common stock for $30/share in cash. Year 2: Noreen Company buys 1,000 shares of its no-par common stock for $28/share in cash. Year 3: Noreen Company declares but has not yet paid a dividend on its no-par common stock of $2 per share. The company's basic earnings per share were $10 in the third year.

Indicate the effect (increase, decrease, no effect) of each of these stock decisions for each year on the items listed.

Year	Total Assets	Total Liabilities	Total Stockholders' Equity	EPS	Operating Income
1					
2					
3					

LO1, 2, 3, 6

M11-37. Reporting Stockholders' Equity

Bonner Company began business this year and immediately sold 600,000 common shares for $18,000,000 cash and paid $1,000,000 in common dividends. At midyear, the firm bought back some of its own shares. The company reports the following additional information at year-end:

Net income	$5,000,000
Common stock, at par	$6,000,000
Retained earnings beginning of year	$ 0
Common shares authorized:	1,000,000
Common shares outstanding at year's end:	550,000

a. What was the average sales price of a common share when issued?

b. What is the par value of the common?

c. How much is in the Additional paid-in capital account at the end of the year?

d. Determine the retained earnings amount at the end of the year.

e. How many shares of stock are in the treasury at the end of the year?

f. Compute BEPS.

LO6

JetBlue
NASDAQ :: JBLU

M11-38. Analyzing Earnings Per Share Effects of Convertible Securities

JetBlue Airways Corporation reports the following data in its 2016 10-K. The data relate to the corporation's computation of its earnings per share calculations. (Dollar and share data are in millions.)

Numerator:	**2016**
Net income	$759
Effect of dilutive securities:	
Interest on convertible debt, net of income taxes and profit sharing.	2
Net income applicable to common stockholders after assumed conversions for diluted earnings per share	$761
Denominator:	
Weighted average shares outstanding for basic earnings per share	326.5
Effect of dilutive securities:	
Employee stock options and restricted stock units	2.1
Convertible debt	13.6
Adjusted weighted average shares outstanding and assumed conversions for diluted earnings per share	342.2

REQUIRED

a. What is the objective behind the calculation of diluted EPS?

b. Calculate JetBlue's basic EPS.
c. Calculate JetBlue's diluted EPS.
d. In 2014, JetBlue stated that it excluded 6.9 million stock options from the computation of diluted EPS. Under what circumstances would this be appropriate?

EXERCISES

E11-39. Identifying and Analyzing Financial Statement Effects of Stock Transactions LO2

Lipe Company reports the following transactions relating to its stock accounts.

Feb. 20 Issued 10,000 shares of $1 par value common stock at $25 cash per share.
Feb. 21 Issued 15,000 shares of $100 par value, 8% preferred stock at $275 cash per share.
Jun. 30 Purchased 2,000 shares of its own common stock at $15 cash per share.
Sep. 25 Sold 1,000 shares of the treasury stock at $21 cash per share.

a. Using the financial statement effects template, illustrate the effects of these transactions.
b. Prepare the journal entries for these transactions.
c. Post the journal entries from *b* to the related T-accounts.

E11-40. Analyzing and Identifying Financial Statement Effects of Stock Transactions LO2

McNichols Corp. reports the following transactions relating to its stock accounts.

Jan. 15 Issued 25,000 shares of $5 par value common stock at $17 cash per share.
Jan. 20 Issued 6,000 shares of $50 par value, 8% preferred stock at $78 cash per share.
Mar. 31 Purchased 3,000 shares of its own common stock at $20 cash per share.
June 25 Sold 2,000 shares of the treasury stock at $26 cash per share.
July 15 Sold the remaining 1,000 shares of treasury stock at $19 cash per share.

a. Using the financial statement effects template, illustrate the effects of these transactions.
b. Prepare the journal entries for these transactions.
c. Post the journal entries from *b* to the related T-accounts.

E11-41. Analyzing and Computing Average Issue Price and Treasury Stock Cost LO1, 2, 6

The Coca-Cola Company
NYSE :: KO

Following is the stockholders' equity section from the The Coca-Cola Company 2017 balance sheet. (All amounts in millions except par value.)

The Coca-Cola Company Shareowners' Equity	December 31, 2017
Common stock—$0.25 par value; authorized—11,200 shares; issued—7,040 shares	$ 1,760
Capital surplus	15,864
Reinvested earnings	60,430
Accumulated other comprehensive income (loss)	(10,305)
Treasury stock, at cost—2,781 shares	(50,677)
Equity attributable to shareowners of The Coca-Cola Company	$17,072

a. Compute the number of shares outstanding.
b. At what average price were the Coca-Cola shares issued?
c. At what average cost were the Coca-Cola treasury stock shares purchased?
d. How should treasury stock be treated in calculating EPS?

E11-42. Analyzing and Distributing Cash Dividends to Preferred and Common Stocks LO4

Moser Company began business on March 1, 2018. At that time, it issued 20,000 shares of $60 par value, 7% cumulative preferred stock, and 100,000 shares of $5 par value common stock. Through the end of 2020, there has been no change in the number of preferred and common shares outstanding.

a. Assume that Moser declared and paid cash dividends of $0 in 2018, $183,000 in 2019, and $200,000 in 2020. Compute the total cash dividends and the dividends per share paid to each class of stock in 2018, 2019, and 2020.

b. Assume that Moser declared and paid cash dividends of $0 in 2018, $84,000 in 2019, and $150,000 in 2020. Compute the total cash dividends and the dividends per share paid to each class of stock in 2018, 2019, and 2020.

LO6

E11-43. Computing Basic and Diluted Earnings per Share

Soliman Corporation began the year 2018 with 25,000 shares of common stock and 5,000 shares of convertible preferred stock outstanding. On May 1, an additional 9,000 shares of common stock were issued. On July 1, 6,000 shares of common stock were acquired for the treasury. On September 1, the 6,000 treasury shares of common stock were reissued. The preferred stock has a $4 per-share dividend rate, and each share may be converted into two shares of common stock. Soliman Corporation's 2018 net income is $230,000.

a. Compute earnings per share for 2018.

b. Compute diluted earnings per share for 2018.

c. If the preferred stock were not convertible, Soliman Corporation would have a simple capital structure. How would this change Soliman's earnings per share presentation?

LO4, 6

E11-44. Analyzing and Distributing Cash Dividends to Preferred and Common Stocks

Potter Company has outstanding 15,000 shares of $50 par value, 8% preferred stock, and 50,000 shares of $5 par value common stock. During its first three years in business, it declared and paid no cash dividends in the first year, $280,000 in the second year, and $60,000 in the third year.

a. If the preferred stock is cumulative, determine the total amount of cash dividends paid to each class of stock in each of the three years.

b. If the preferred stock is noncumulative, determine the total amount of cash dividends paid to each class of stock in each of the three years.

c. How should each type of preferred dividends be treated in calculating EPS?

LO1, 2

Chipotle Mexican Grill
NYSE :: CMG

E11-45. Analyzing and Computing Issue Price, Treasury Stock Cost, and Shares Outstanding

The following is the stockholders' equity section from **Chipotle Mexican Grill, Inc.**'s balance sheet (in thousands, except per share data).

Shareholders' Equity	December 31, 2017
Preferred stock, $0.01 par value, 600,000 shares authorized, no shares issued as of December 31, 2017	$ —
Common stock, $0.01 par value, 230,000 shares authorized, and 35,852 shares issued as of December 31, 2017	359
Additional paid-in capital	1,305,090
Treasury stock, at cost, 7,826 common shares at December 31, 2017	(2,334,409)
Accumulated other comprehensive income (loss)	(3,659)
Retained earnings	2,397,064
Total shareholders' equity	$1,364,445

a. Show the computation to derive the $359 thousand for common stock.

b. At what average price has Chipotle issued its common stock?

c. How many shares of Chipotle common stock are outstanding as of December 31, 2017?

d. At what average cost has Chipotle repurchased its treasury stock as of December 31, 2017?

e. Give three reasons why a company such as Chipotle would want to repurchase almost $2,350 million of its common stock.

LO4

E11-46. Analyzing and Distributing Cash Dividends to Preferred and Common Stocks

Skinner Company began business on June 30, 2018. At that time, it issued 18,000 shares of $50 par value, 6% cumulative preferred stock, and 90,000 shares of $10 par value common stock. Through the end of 2020, there has been no change in the number of preferred and common shares outstanding.

a. Assume that Skinner declared and paid cash dividends of $63,000 in 2018, $0 in 2019, and $378,000 in 2020. Compute the total cash dividends and the dividends per share paid to each class of stock in 2018, 2019, and 2020.

b. Assume that Skinner declared and paid cash dividends of $0 in 2018, $108,000 in 2019, and $189,000 in 2020. Compute the total cash dividends and the dividends per share paid to each class of stock in 2018, 2019, and 2020.

E11-47. Analyzing and Identifying Financial Statement Effects of Dividends LO4

Chaney Company has outstanding 25,000 shares of $10 par value common stock. It also has $405,000 of retained earnings. Near the current year-end, the company declares and pays a cash dividend of $1.90 per share and declares and issues a 4% stock dividend. The market price of the stock at the declaration date is $35 per share.

a. Using the financial statement effects template, illustrate the effects of these two separate dividends.
b. Prepare the journal entries for these two separate dividend transactions.
c. Post the journal entries from *b* to the related T-accounts.

E11-48. Identifying and Analyzing Financial Statement Effects of Dividends LO3, 4

Homework MBC

The stockholders' equity of Palepu Company at December 31, 2018, appears below.

Common stock, $10 par value, 200,000 shares authorized; 80,000 shares issued and outstanding	$800,000
Paid-in capital in excess of par value	480,000
Retained earnings	305,000

During 2019, the following transactions occurred:

May 12 Declared and issued a 7% stock dividend; the common stock market value was $18 per share.
Dec. 31 Declared and paid a cash dividend of 75 cents per share.

a. Using the financial statement effects template, illustrate the effects of these transactions.
b. Prepare the journal entries for these transactions.
c. Post the journal entries from *b* to the related T-accounts.
d. Prepare a retained earnings reconciliation for 2019 assuming that the company reports 2019 net income of $283,000.

E11-49. Analyzing and Identifying Financial Statement Effects of Dividends LO3, 4

The stockholders' equity of Kinney Company at December 31, 2018, is shown below:

5% preferred stock, $100 par value, 10,000 shares authorized; 4,000 shares issued and outstanding	$ 400,000
Common stock, $5 par value, 200,000 shares authorized; 50,000 shares issued and outstanding	250,000
Paid-in capital in excess of par value—preferred stock	40,000
Paid-in capital in excess of par value—common stock	300,000
Retained earnings	656,000
Total stockholders' equity	$1,646,000

The following transactions, among others, occurred during 2019.

Apr. 1 Declared and issued a 100% stock dividend on all outstanding shares of common stock. The market value of the stock was $11 per share.
Dec. 7 Declared and issued a 3% stock dividend on all outstanding shares of common stock. The market value of the stock was $14 per share.
Dec. 20 Declared and paid (1) the annual cash dividend on the preferred stock and (2) a cash dividend of 80 cents per common share.

a. Using the financial statement effects template, illustrate the effects of these transactions.
b. Prepare the journal entries for these transactions.
c. Post the journal entries from *b* to the related T-accounts.
d. Prepare a 2019 retained earnings reconciliation assuming that the company reports 2019 net income of $253,000.

E11-50. Analyzing, Identifying, and Explaining the Effects of a Stock Split LO4, 6

Homework MBC

On March 1 of the current year, Xie Company has 400,000 shares of $20 par value common stock that are issued and outstanding. Its balance sheet shows the following account balances relating to common stock.

Common stock	$8,000,000
Paid-in capital in excess of par value	3,400,000

On March 2, Xie Company splits its common stock 2-for-1 and reduces the par value to $10 per share.

a. How many shares of common stock are issued and outstanding immediately after the stock split?

b. What is the dollar balance in its common stock account immediately after the stock split?

c. What is the dollar balance in its paid-in capital in excess of par value account immediately after the stock split?

d. What is the effect of a stock split on the calculation of EPS?

LO3, 4

Intuit Inc.
NASDAQ :: INTU

E11-51. Analyzing and Computing Dividends and Effect of Options Exercises

Following is the stockholders' equity section of the **Intuit Inc.** balance sheet (dollars in millions, except par value; shares in thousands). Changes in the company's outstanding shares are due to (1) treasury share purchases by the company and (2) issues of treasury shares for employee stock options.

Stockholders' Equity ($ millions)	July 31, 2018	July 31, 2017
Preferred stock, $0.01 par value		
Authorized—1,345 shares total; 145 shares designated Series A; 250 shares designated Series B Junior Participating		
Issued and outstanding—none	$ —	$ —
Common stock, $0.01 par value		
Authorized—750,000 shares		
Outstanding—258,616 shares at July 31, 2018, and 255,668 shares at July 31, 2017	3	3
Additional paid-in capital	5,335	4,854
Treasury stock, at cost	(11,050)	(10,778)
Accumulated other comprehensive income (loss)	(35)	(22)
Retained earnings	8,101	7,297
Total stockholders' equity	**$2,354**	**$1,354**

a. In the fiscal year ended July 31, 2018, Intuit reported net income of $1,211 million. How much did Intuit pay in dividends to its common shareholders?

b. In the fiscal year ended January 31, 2018, Intuit repurchased 1,870 thousand of its common shares. How many shares were issued to employees under stock option plans?

c. Intuit's issuance of shares for stock option plans increased the Additional paid-in capital balance by $96 million. Was the (average) option exercise price greater or less than the (average) amount Intuit paid to acquire the treasury shares that were reissued?

LO2

Merck & Co.
NYSE :: MRK

E11-52. Analyzing and Computing Issue Price, Treasury Stock Cost, and Shares Outstanding

Following is the stockholders' equity section of the **Merck & Co., Inc.**, balance sheet.

Merck & Co., Inc. Stockholders' Equity ($ millions)	Dec. 31, 2017	Dec. 31, 2016
Common stock, $0.50 par value		
Authorized—6,500,000,000 shares		
Issued—3,577,103,522 shares in 2017 and 2016	$ 1,788	$ 1,788
Other paid-in capital	39,902	39,939
Retained earnings	41,350	44,133
Accumulated other comprehensive income (loss)	(4,910)	(5,226)
	78,130	80,634
Less treasury stock, at cost:		
880,491,914 shares in 2017 and 828,372,200 shares in 2016	43,794	40,546
Total Merck & Co., Inc. stockholders' equity	$34,336	$40,088

a. Explain the derivation of the $1,788 million in the common stock account.

b. Using December 31, 2017, balances, at what average issue price were the Merck common shares issued?

c. At what average cost was the Merck treasury stock as of December 31, 2017?

d. How many common shares are outstanding as of December 31, 2017?

E11-53. Analyzing the Accounting and Effects of Convertible Securities, Stock Options, and Restricted Stock

LO7

Facebook, Inc.
NASDAQ :: FB

A portion of Note 2: Earnings per Share from Facebook, Inc.'s 10-K is as follows:

	2018 Class A Stock	2017 Class A Stock
Basic EPS:		
Numerator		
Net income attributable to common shareholders.	$18,410	$13,022
Denominator		
Weighted ave. shares outstanding	2,406	2,375
Less: Shares subject to repurchase	—	2
Number of shares used for basic EPS calculation	2,406	2,373
Basic EPS.	$ 7.65	$ 5.49
Diluted EPS:		
Numerator		
Net income attributable to common shareholders.	$18,410	$13,022
Reallocation of income attributable to participating securities. . .	1	14
Reallocation of net income as a result of conversion of Class B to Class A common stock.	3,701	2,898
Net income attributable to common shareholders for diluted EPS	$22,112	$15,934
Denominator		
Number of shares used for basic EPS computation	2,406	2,373
Conversion of Class B to Class A common stock	484	528
Weighted average effect of dilutive securities:		
Employee stock options.	2	4
RSUs	29	49
Shares subject to repurchase and other	—	2
Number of shares used for diluted EPS computation	2,921	2,956
Diluted EPS	$ 7.57	$ 5.39

a. Explain why employee stock options and restricted stock units are adjustments to the denominator for diluted EPS.

b. Facebook computes EPS separately for its Class B shares (not shown here) and states that the computation of the diluted EPS for its Class A stock assumes the conversion of its Class B common stock to Class A common stock. Based on the table above, what were the effects of the assumed conversion?

E11-54. Interpreting Information in the Statement of Shareholders' Equity

LO2, 4

Walt Disney Co.
NYSE :: DIS

The 2018 statement of stockholders' equity for **Walt Disney Co.** is presented below. (Disney includes both par value and additional paid-in capital under the heading "Common Stock." Noncontrolling interests have been excluded for simplicity, so the rows may not add up to the total shown. All amounts in millions.)

	Equity Attributable to Disney					
	Shares	Common Stock	Retained Earnings	Accumulated Other Comprehensive Income (Loss)	Treasury Stock	Total Disney Equity
Balance at September 30, 2017. . . .	1,517	$36,248	$72,606	$(3,528)	$(64,011)	$41,315
Comprehensive income	—	—	12,598	431	—	13,029
Equity compensation activity	6	518	—	—	—	518
Common stock repurchases.	(35)	—	—	—	(3,577)	(3,577)
Dividends	—	14	(2,529)	—	—	(2,515)
Contributions	—	—	—	—	—	—
Distributions and other	—	(1)	4	—	—	3
Balance at September 29, 2018. . . .	1,488	$36,779	$82,679	$(3,097)	$(67,588)	$48,773

REQUIRED

a. Did Disney issue any additional common shares in fiscal year 2018 (ending on September 29, 2018)?

b. What was Disney's total comprehensive income in fiscal year 2018?

c. Show how Disney recorded the purchase of treasury shares in fiscal year 2018 using the financial statement effects template. Prepare the journal entry and post to the related T-accounts.

d. According to its statement of cash flows, Disney paid common dividends of $2,515 million in fiscal year 2018. What might be a possible explanation for the fact that dividends reduced retained earnings by $2,529 million?

PROBLEMS

LO2, 3, 6 **P11-55. Analyzing and Identifying Financial Statement Effects of Stock Transactions**
The stockholders' equity section of Gupta Company at December 31, 2018, follows.

8% preferred stock, $25 par value, 50,000 shares authorized; 6,800 shares issued and outstanding	$170,000
Common stock, $10 par value, 200,000 shares authorized; 50,000 shares issued and outstanding	500,000
Paid-in capital in excess of par value—preferred stock	68,000
Paid-in capital in excess of par value—common stock	200,000
Retained earnings	270,000

During 2019, the following transactions occurred:

Jan. 10 Issued 28,000 shares of common stock for $17 cash per share.
Jan. 23 Purchased 8,000 shares of common stock for the treasury at $19 cash per share.
Mar. 14 Sold one-half of the treasury shares acquired January 23 for $21 cash per share.
July 15 Issued 3,200 shares of preferred stock for $128,000 cash.
Nov. 15 Sold 1,000 of the treasury shares acquired January 23 for $24 cash per share.

REQUIRED

a. Using the financial statement effects template, illustrate the effects of each transaction.

b. Prepare the journal entries for these transactions.

c. Post the journal entries from *b* to the related T-accounts.

d. Indicate the impact of each transaction on the calculation of basic EPS.

e. Prepare the December 31, 2019, stockholders' equity section of the balance sheet assuming the company reports 2019 net income of $59,000.

LO2, 3, 4, 5, 6 **P11-56. Analyzing and Identifying Financial Statement Effects of Stock Transactions**
The stockholders' equity of Sougiannis Company at December 31, 2018, follows.

7% Preferred stock, $100 par value, 20,000 shares authorized; 5,000 shares issued and outstanding	$ 500,000
Common stock, $15 par value, 100,000 shares authorized; 40,000 shares issued and outstanding	600,000
Paid-in capital in excess of par value—preferred stock	24,000
Paid-in capital in excess of par value—common stock	360,000
Retained earnings	325,000
Total stockholders' equity	$1,809,000

The following transactions, among others, occurred during 2019.

Jan. 12 Announced a 3-for-1 common stock split, reducing the par value of the common stock to $5 per share. The authorized shares were increased to 300,000 shares.
Sept. 1 Acquired 10,000 shares of common stock for the treasury at $10 cash per share.
Oct. 12 Sold 1,500 treasury shares acquired September 1 at $12 cash per share.
Nov. 21 Issued 5,000 shares of common stock at $11 cash per share.
Dec. 28 Sold 1,200 treasury shares acquired September 1 at $9 cash per share.

REQUIRED

a. Using the financial statement effects template, illustrate the effects of each transaction.
b. Prepare the journal entries for these transactions.
c. Post the journal entries from *b* to the related T-accounts.
d. Indicate the impact of each transaction on the calculation of basic EPS.
e. Prepare the December 31, 2019, stockholders' equity section of the balance sheet assuming that the company reports 2019 net income of $83,000.
f. Compute return on common equity for 2019.

P11-57. Identifying and Analyzing Financial Statement Effects of Stock Transactions **LO2, 3, 6**

The stockholders' equity of Verrecchia Company at December 31, 2018, follows.

Common stock, $5 par value, 350,000 shares authorized; 150,000 shares issued and outstanding	$750,000
Paid-in capital in excess of par value	600,000
Retained earnings	346,000

During 2019, the following transactions occurred.

Jan. 5	Issued 10,000 shares of common stock for $12 cash per share.
Jan. 18	Purchased 4,000 shares of common stock for the treasury at $14 cash per share.
Mar. 12	Sold one-fourth of the treasury shares acquired January 18 for $17 cash per share.
July 17	Sold 500 shares of the remaining treasury stock for $13 cash per share.
Oct. 1	Issued 5,000 shares of 8%, $25 par value preferred stock for $35 cash per share. This is the first issuance of preferred shares from 50,000 authorized shares.

REQUIRED

a. Using the financial statement effects template, illustrate the effects of each transaction.
b. Prepare the journal entries for these transactions.
c. Post the journal entries from *b* to the related T-accounts.
d. Prepare the December 31, 2019, stockholders' equity section of the balance sheet assuming that the company reports net income of $72,500 for the year.
e. How will each transaction affect the calculation of basic EPS?

P11-58. Identifying and Analyzing Financial Statement Effects of Stock Transactions **LO2, 4**

Following is the stockholders' equity of Dennis Corporation at December 31, 2018.

8% preferred stock, $50 par value, 10,000 shares authorized; 7,000 shares issued and outstanding	$ 350,000
Common stock, $20 par value, 50,000 shares authorized; 25,000 shares issued and outstanding	500,000
Paid-in capital in excess of par value—preferred stock	70,000
Paid-in capital in excess of par value—common stock	385,000
Retained earnings	238,000
Total stockholders' equity	$1,543,000

The following transactions, among others, occurred during 2019.

Jan. 15	Issued 1,000 shares of preferred stock for $62 cash per share.
Jan. 20	Issued 4,000 shares of common stock at $36 cash per share.
May 18	Announced a 2-for-1 common stock split, reducing the par value of the common stock to $10 per share. The authorization was increased to 100,000 shares.
June 1	Issued 2,000 shares of common stock for $60,000 cash.
Sept. 1	Purchased 2,500 shares of common stock for the treasury at $18 cash per share.
Oct. 12	Sold 900 treasury shares at $21 cash per share.
Dec. 22	Issued 500 shares of preferred stock for $59 cash per share.

REQUIRED

a. Using the financial statement effects template, illustrate the effects of each transaction.
b. Prepare the journal entries for these transactions.
c. Post the journal entries from *b* to the related T-accounts.

LO1, 2, 5, 6, 7

Procter & Gamble
NYSE :: PG

P11-59. Analyzing and Interpreting Stockholders' Equity and EPS
Following is the stockholders' equity section of the balance sheet for **The Procter & Gamble Company** along with selected earnings and dividend data. For simplicity, balances for noncontrolling interests have been left out of income and shareholders' equity information.

($ millions except per share amounts)	2018	2017
Net earnings attributable to Procter & Gamble shareholders	$ 9,750	$15,326
Common dividends	7,057	6,989
Preferred dividends	265	247
Basic net earnings per common share	$ 3.75	$ 5.80
Diluted net earnings per common share	$ 3.67	$ 5.59
Shareholders' equity:		
Convertible class A preferred stock, stated value $1 per share (600 shares authorized)	$ 967	$ 1,006
Nonvoting class B preferred stock, stated value $1 per share	—	—
Common stock, stated value $1 per share (10,000 shares authorized) shares issued: 2018—4,009.2; 2017—4,009.2	4,009	4,009
Additional paid-in capital	63,846	63,641
Reserve for ESOP retirement	(1,204)	(1,249)
Accumulated other comprehensive income (loss)	(14,749)	(14,632)
Treasury stock, at cost (shares held: 2018—1,511.2, 2017—1,455.9)	(99,217)	(93,715)
Retained earnings	98,641	96,124
Shareholders' equity attributable to Procter & Gamble shareholders	$52,293	$55,184

a. Compute the number of shares outstanding at the end of each fiscal year. Estimate the average number of shares outstanding during 2018. How do these two computations compare?

b. Calculate the average cost per share of the shares held as treasury stock at the end of each fiscal year.

c. In 2018, preferred shareholders elected to convert 4.58 million shares of preferred stock ($39 million book value) into common stock. Rather than issue new shares, the company granted to the preferred shareholders 4.58 million common shares held in treasury stock with a total cost of $33 million. Prepare a journal entry to illustrate how this transaction would have been recorded.

d. P&G has no convertible debt outstanding. What could explain the reported diluted EPS?

e. Calculate P&G's return on common equity (ROCE) for fiscal 2018.

LO5, 7

Alphabet Inc.
NASDAQ :: GOOGL

P11-60. Analyzing and Interpreting Equity Accounts and Earnings per Share
The 2017 and 2018 statements of stockholders' equity for **Alphabet Inc.** are presented below along with portions on Notes 10 and 12 relating to stockholders' equity and equity-based compensation.

ALPHABET INC.
Consolidated Statements of Stockholders' Equity
(In millions, except per share amounts which are reflected in thousands)

	Class A and Class B Common Stock, Class C Capital Stock and Paid-in Capital		Accumulated Other Comprehensive Income (Loss)	Retained Earnings	Total Stock-holders' Equity
	Shares	Amount			
Balance at December 31, 2016	691,293	$36,307	$(2,402)	$105,131	$139,036
Cumulative effect of accounting change	0	0	0	(15)	(15)
Common and capital stock issued	8,652	212	0	0	212
Stock-based compensation expense	0	7,694	0	0	7,694
Tax withholding related to vesting of restricted stock units	0	(4,373)	0	0	(4,373)
Repurchases of capital stock	(5,162)	(315)	0	(4,531)	(4,846)
Sale of subsidiary shares	0	722	0	0	722
Net income	0	0	0	12,662	12,662
Other comprehensive income	0	0	1,410	0	1,410

continued

continued from previous page

	Class A and Class B Common Stock, Class C Capital Stock and Paid-in Capital		Accumulated Other Comprehensive Income (Loss)	Retained Earnings	Total Stock-holders' Equity
	Shares	Amount			
Balance as of December 31, 2017	694,783	40,247	(992)	113,247	152,502
Cumulative effect of accounting change	0	0	(98)	(599)	(697)
Common and capital stock issued	8,975	148	0	0	148
Stock-based compensation expense	0	9,353	0	0	9,353
Tax withholding related to vesting of restricted stock units and other	0	(4,782)	0	0	(4,782)
Repurchases of capital stock	(8,202)	(576)	0	(8,499)	(9,075)
Sale of subsidiary shares	0	659	0	0	659
Net income	0	0	0	30,736	30,736
Other comprehensive loss	0	0	(1,216)	0	(1,216)
Balance as of December 31, 2018	695,556	$45,049	$(2,306)	$134,885	$177,628

Note 10: Stockholders' Equity

Convertible Preferred Stock

Our board of directors has authorized 100 million shares of convertible preferred stock, $0.001 par value, issuable in series. As of December 31, 2017 and 2018, no shares were issued or outstanding.

Class A and Class B Common Stock and Class C Capital Stock

Our board of directors has authorized three classes of stock, Class A and Class B common stock, and Class C capital stock. The rights of the holders of each class of our common and capital stock are identical, except with respect to voting. Each share of Class A common stock is entitled to one vote per share. Each share of Class B common stock is entitled to 10 votes per share. Class C capital stock has no voting rights, except as required by applicable law. Shares of Class B common stock may be converted at any time at the option of the stockholder and automatically convert upon sale or transfer to Class A common stock.

Share Repurchases

In October 2016, the board of directors of Alphabet authorized the company to repurchase up to $7.0 billion of its Class C capital stock, which was completed during 2018. In January 2018, the board of directors of Alphabet authorized the company to repurchase up to $8.6 billion of its Class C capital stock. The repurchases are being executed from time to time, subject to general business and market conditions and other investment opportunities, through open market purchases or privately negotiated transactions, including through Rule 10b5-1 plans. The repurchase program does not have an expiration date.

During the years ended December 31, 2017 and 2018, we repurchased and subsequently retired 5.2 million shares of Alphabet Class C capital stock for an aggregate amount of $4.8 billion and 8.2 million shares of Alphabet Class C capital stock for an aggregate amount of $9.1 billion, respectively.

Note 12: Compensation Plans

Stock Plans

Under our 2012 Stock Plan, RSUs or stock options may be granted. An RSU award is an agreement to issue shares of our publicly traded stock at the time the award vests. Incentive and non-qualified stock options, or rights to purchase common stock, are generally granted for a term of 10 years. RSUs granted to participants under the 2012 Stock Plan generally vest over four years contingent upon employment or service with us on the vesting date.

As of December 31, 2018, there were 31,848,134 shares of stock reserved for future issuance under our Stock Plan.

Stock-Based Compensation

For the years ended December 31, 2016, 2017 and 2018, total stock-based compensation expense was $6.9 billion, $7.9 billion and $10.0 billion, including amounts associated with awards we expect to settle in Alphabet stock of $6.7 billion, $7.7 billion, and $9.4 billion, respectively.

For the years ended December 31, 2016, 2017 and 2018, we recognized tax benefits on total stock-based compensation expense, which are reflected in the provision for income taxes in the Consolidated Statements of Income, of $1.5 billion, $1.6 billion, and $1.5 billion, respectively.

For the years ended December 31, 2016, 2017 and 2018, tax benefit realized related to awards vested or exercised during the period was $2.1 billion, $2.7 billion and $2.1 billion, respectively. These amounts do not include the indirect effects of stock-based awards, which primarily relate to the research and development tax credit.

Stock-Based Compensation

The following table summarizes the activities for our options for our unvested RSUs for the year ended December 31, 2018:

	Number of Shares	Weighted-Average Grant-Date Fair Value
Unvested as of December 31, 2017	20,077,346	$ 712.45
Granted	12,669,251	$1,095.89
Vested	(12,847,910)	$ 765.45
Forfeited/canceled	(1,431,009)	$ 814.19
Unvested as of December 31, 2018	18,467,678	$ 936.96

As of December 31, 2018, there was $16.2 billion of unrecognized compensation cost related to unvested employee RSUs. The amount is expected to be recognized over a weighted-average period of 2.5 years.

Note 11. Net Income Per Share (in part)

We compute net income per share of Class A and Class B common stock and Class C capital stock using the two-class method. Basic net income per share is computed using the weighted-average number of shares outstanding during the period. Diluted net income per share is computed using the weighted-average number of shares and the effect of potentially dilutive securities outstanding during the period. Potentially dilutive securities consist of restricted stock units and other contingently issuable shares. The dilutive effect of outstanding restricted stock units and other contingently issuable shares is reflected in diluted earnings per share by application of the treasury stock method. The computation of the diluted net income per share of Class A common stock assumes the conversion of Class B common stock, while the diluted net income per share of Class B common stock does not assume the conversion of those shares.

REQUIRED

a. What is the difference between Alphabet's Class A common stock and its Class B common stock? Why do they have two different classes of common stock? In fiscal year 2014, Alphabet created shares of Class C capital stock, which participate in any common dividends, but have no voting rights. What might be the purpose of the Class C stock?

b. Alphabet repurchased some of their Class C shares in 2018. Prepare the journal entry to show the repurchase transaction.

c. Using the information in the notes, estimate the stock-based compensation expense for 2019 related to the 2018 grants of restricted stock units. Show the journal entry.

d. Alphabet states that there is $16.2 billion of unrecognized compensation cost related to unvested employee RSUs. What are these and why isn't this a liability on the balance sheet for Alphabet?

e. Alphabet reported net income of $30,736 million in 2018 and basic EPS of $44.22 per share. Estimate the weighted average number of shares used to calculate basic EPS.

f. Assume Alphabet has 15.0 million stock options outstanding at the end of 2018. If all outstanding stock options were exercised in 2018, what would be the impact on Alphabet's basic EPS?

g. Alphabet reported diluted EPS of $43.70 in 2018. What are the primary dilutive securities that Alphabet mentions?

CASES AND PROJECTS

LO7 Northrop Grumman NYSE :: NOC

C11-61. Interpreting Disclosure on Convertible Preferred Securities

Northrop Grumman Corporation reports the following in footnote 4 to its 2008 10-K related to its convertible preferred stock.

Conversion of Preferred Stock—On February 20, 2008, the company's board of directors approved the redemption of the 3.5 million shares of mandatorily redeemable convertible preferred stock on April 4, 2008. Prior to the redemption date, substantially all of the preferred shares were converted into common stock at the election of shareholders. All remaining unconverted preferred shares were redeemed by the company on the redemption date. As a result of the conversion and redemption, the company issued approximately 6.4 million shares of common stock.

REQUIRED

a. What do you believe is meant by the terms "mandatorily redeemable" prior to the words "preferred stock"?

b. Northrop's balance sheet at December 31, 2007, shows preferred stock of $350 million and $0 million on December 31, 2008. Northrop originally sold the preferred shares at par. What was the preferred par value per share?

c. The fair market value of a preferred share, as reported by Northrop on December 31, 2008, was $146. What could account for the substantial increase in the value per share?

d. How should preferred stock be treated in an analysis of a company?

e. Discuss the general effects of the April 4th conversion on Northrop Grumman's balance sheet.

C11-62. Identifying Corporate Takeover, Stock Ownership, and Managerial Ethics **LO1, 2**

Ron King, chairperson of the board of directors and chief executive officer of Image, Inc., is pondering a recommendation to make to the firm's board of directors in response to actions taken by Jack Hatcher. Hatcher recently informed King and other board members that he (Hatcher) had purchased 15% of the voting stock of Image at $12 per share and is considering an attempt to take control of the company. His effort to take control would include offering $16 per share to stockholders to induce them to sell shares to him. Hatcher also indicated that he would abandon his takeover plans if the company would buy back his stock at a price 50% over its current market price of $13 per share.

King views the proposed takeover by Hatcher as a hostile maneuver. Hatcher has a reputation of identifying companies that are undervalued (that is, their underlying net assets are worth more than the price of the outstanding stock), buying enough stock to take control of such a company, replacing top management, and, on occasion, breaking up the company (that is, selling off the various divisions to the highest bidder). The process has proven profitable to Hatcher and his financial backers. Stockholders of the companies taken over also benefited because Hatcher paid them attractive prices to buy their stock.

King recognizes that Image is currently undervalued by the stock market but believes that eventually the company will significantly improve its financial performance to the long-run benefit of its stockholders.

REQUIRED

What are the ethical issues that King should consider in arriving at a recommendation to make to the board of directors regarding Hatcher's offer to be "bought out" of his takeover plans?

C11-63. Understanding Shareholders' Meeting, Managerial Communications, and Financial Interpretations **LO1, 3**

The stockholders' equity section of Pillar Corporation's comparative balance sheet at the end of 2018 and 2019 is presented below. It is part of the financial data just reviewed at a stockholders' meeting.

	December 31, 2019	December 31, 2018
Common stock, $10 par value, 600,000 shares authorized; issued at December 31, 2019, 275,000 shares; 2018, 250,000 shares	$ 2,750,000	$2,500,000
Paid-in capital in excess of par	4,575,000	4,125,000
Retained earnings (see Note)	2,960,000	2,825,000
Total stockholders' equity	$10,285,000	$9,450,000

Note: Availability of retained earnings for cash dividends is restricted by $2,000,000 due to a planned plant expansion.

The following items were also disclosed at the stockholders' meeting: net income for 2019 was $1,220,000; a 10% stock dividend was issued December 14, 2019; when the stock dividend was declared, the market value was $28 per share; the market value per share at December 31, 2019, was $26; management plans to borrow $500,000 to help finance a new plant addition, which is expected to cost a total of $2,300,000; and the customary $1.54 per share cash dividend had been revised to $1.40 when declared and issued the last week of December 2019. As part of its investor relations program, during the stockholders' meeting management asked stockholders to write any questions they might have concerning the firm's operations or finances. As assistant controller, you are given the stockholders' questions.

REQUIRED

Prepare brief but reasonably complete answers to the following questions:

a. What did Pillar do with the cash proceeds from the stock dividend issued in December?

b. What was my book value per share at the end of 2018 and 2019?

c. I owned 7,500 shares of Pillar in 2018 and have not sold any shares. How much more or less of the corporation do I own at December 31, 2019, and what happened to the market value of my interest in the company?

d. I heard someone say that stock dividends don't give me anything I didn't already have. Why did you issue one? Are you trying to fool us?

e. Instead of a stock dividend, why didn't you declare a cash dividend and let us buy the new shares that were issued?

f. Why are you cutting back on the dividends I receive?

g. If you have $2,000,000 put aside in retained earnings for the new plant addition, which will cost $2,300,000, why are you borrowing $500,000 instead of just the $300,000 needed?

LO2, 3, 6

C11-64. Assessing Stock Buybacks, Corporate Accountability, and Managerial Ethics

Liz Plummer, vice president and general counsel, chairs the Executive Compensation Committee for Sunlight Corporation. Four and one-half years ago, the compensation committee designed a performance bonus plan for top management that was approved by the board of directors. The plan provides an attractive bonus for top management if the firm's earnings per share grows each year over a five-year period. The plan is now in its fifth year; for the past four years, earnings per share has grown each year. Last year, earnings per share was $1.95 (net income was $7,800,000 and the weighted average common shares outstanding was 4,000,000). Sunlight Corporation has no preferred stock and has had 4,000,000 common shares outstanding for several years. Plummer has recently seen an estimate that Sunlight's net income this year will decrease about 5% from last year because of a slight recession in the economy.

Plummer is disturbed by an item on the agenda for the board of directors meeting on June 20 and an accompanying note from Rob Lundy. Lundy is vice president and chief financial officer for Sunlight. Lundy is proposing to the board that Sunlight buy back 600,000 shares of its own common stock on July 1. Lundy's explanation is that the firm's stock is undervalued now and that Sunlight has excess cash available. When the stock subsequently recovers in value, Lundy notes, Sunlight will reissue the shares and generate a nice increase in contributed capital.

Lundy's note to Plummer merely states, "Look forward to your support of my proposal at the board meeting."

REQUIRED

Why is Plummer disturbed by Lundy's proposal and note? What possible ethical problem does Plummer face when Lundy's proposal is up for a vote at the board meeting?

LO2, 7

Restaurant Brands International Inc.
NYSE :: QSR

C11-65. Redeemable Preferred Shares

Restaurant Brands International, Inc. reports the following in footnote 13 to their financial statements in their 2017 10-K related to redeemable preferred stock.

Note 13

Redeemable Preferred Shares

On December 12, 2014 we issued 68,530,939 Class A 9.0% cumulative compounding perpetual voting preferred shares (the "Preferred Shares") to a subsidiary of Berkshire Hathaway, which were outstanding until the Redemption Date (as defined below). A 9.0% annual dividend accrued on the purchase price of $43.775848 per Preferred Share, and was payable quarterly in arrears, when declared and approved by our board of directors. The Preferred Shares were redeemable at our option on and after December 12, 2017. During 2014, we adjusted the carrying value of the Preferred Shares to their redemption price of $48.109657 per Preferred Share (the "redemption price"). The Preferred Shares were classified as temporary equity while outstanding because redemption was not solely within our control, as the Preferred Shares also contained provisions that allowed the holder to redeem the Preferred Shares for cash beginning in December 2024 or upon a change in control.

On December 12, 2017 (the "Redemption Date"), we redeemed all of the issued and outstanding Preferred Shares for aggregate consideration of $3,115.6 million (the "Redemption Consideration"), consisting of (i) $3,297.0 million, which is the redemption price of $48.109657 per Preferred Share multiplied by the number of Preferred Shares outstanding, plus (ii) $54.0 million of accrued and unpaid preferred dividends up to the Redemption Date, minus (iii) an adjustment of $235.4 million, . . . The $235.4 million adjustment, net of $1.6 million of related transaction costs, is reflected as a $233.8 million increase to net income attributable to common shareholders and common shareholder's equity. . . . Upon redemption, the Preferred Shares were deemed canceled, dividends ceased to accrue and all rights of the holder terminated.

The company's balance sheet, in part, reflected the following:

Restaurant Brands International Inc. and Subsidiaries
Excerpt from Consolidated Balance Sheet
December 31, 2017 and 2016 (millions of USD)
LIABILITIES, REDEEMABLE PREFERRED SHARES AND SHAREHOLDERS' EQUITY

	2017	2016
Current liabilities:		
Accounts and drafts payable	$ 412.9	$ 369.8
Other accrued liabilities	838.2	469.3
Gift card liability	214.9	194.4
Advertising fund liabilities	110.8	83.3
Current portion of long-term debt and capital leases	78.2	93.9
Total current liabilities	1,655.0	1,210.7
Term debt, net of current portion	11,800.9	8,410.2
Capital leases, net of current portion	243.8	218.4
Other liabilities, net	1,455.1	784.9
Deferred income taxes, net	1,508.1	1,715.1
Total liabilities	16,662.9	12,339.3
Redeemable preferred shares; no par value; 68,530,939 shares authorized, issued and outstanding at December 31, 2016	—	3,297.0
Shareholders' equity:		
Common shares, no par value; unlimited shares authorized at December 31, 2017, and December 31, 2016; 243,899,476 shares issued and outstanding at December 31, 2017; 234,236,678 shares issued and outstanding at December 31, 2016	2,051.5	1,955.1
Retained earnings	650.6	445.7
Accumulated other comprehensive income (loss)	(475.7)	(698.3)
Total Restaurant Brands International Inc. shareholders' equity	2,226.4	1,702.5
Noncontrolling interests	2,334.2	1,786.1
Total shareholders' equity	4,560.6	3,488.6
Total liabilities, redeemable preferred shares and shareholders' equity	$21,223.5	$19,124.9

a. Where were the redeemable preferred shares listed on the balance sheet before they were redeemed?

b. What was the aggregate sales price of the redeemable preferred shares in 2014?

c. When issued, $250 million of the issue price was allocated to warrants that were issued as part of the transaction in 2014. Later in 2014, the company adjusted the carrying value of the redeemable preferred shares to their redemption price of $3,297 million. What was the increase in the carrying value of the shares? Where would this have been reported, if at all?

d. If you were an analyst of the company, how would you have viewed these shares?

SOLUTIONS TO REVIEW PROBLEMS

Mid-Chapter Review 1

SOLUTION

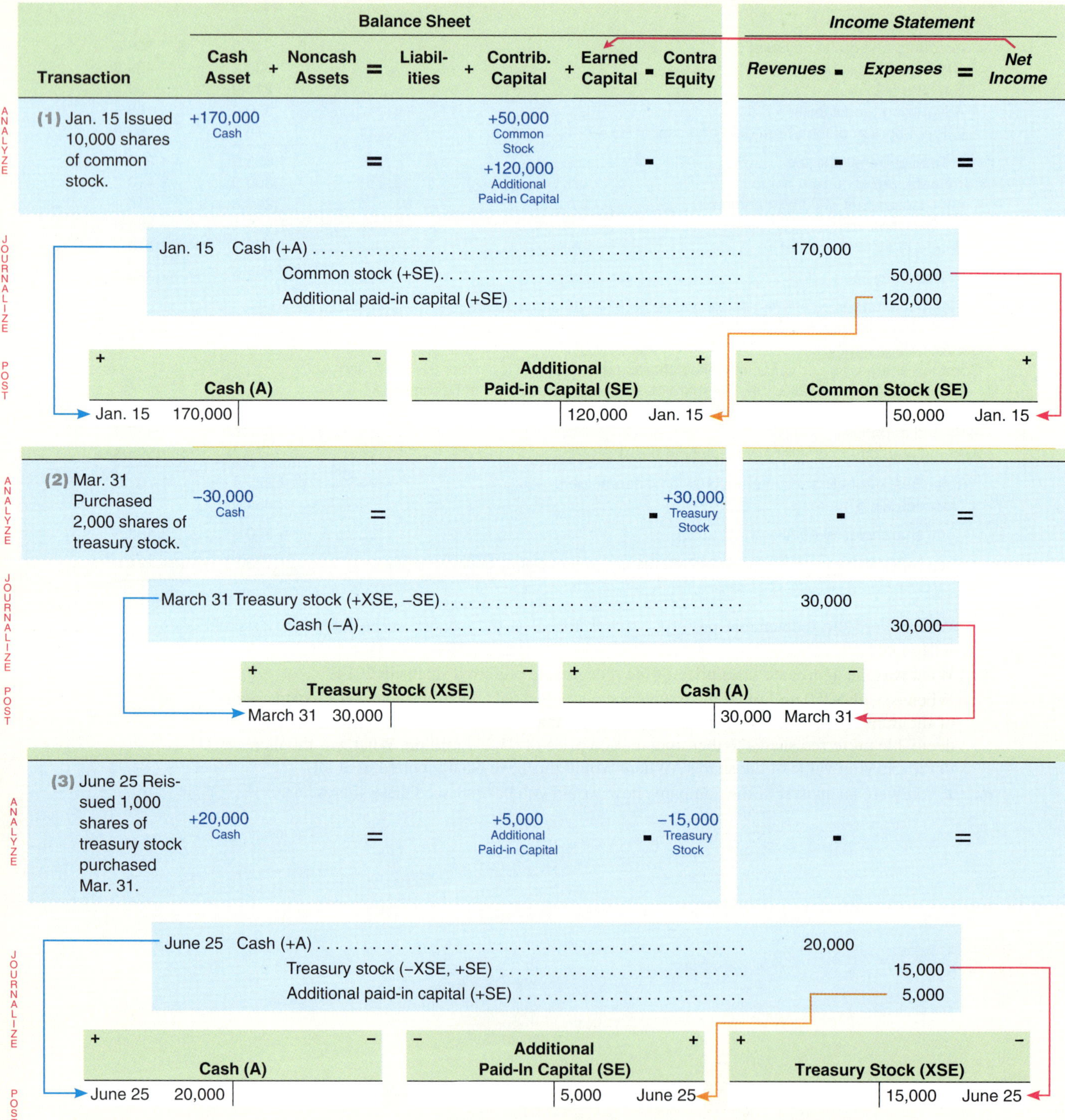

Mid-Chapter Review 2

SOLUTION

a.

	Preferred Stock	Common Stock
Year 1	$ 0	$ 0
Year 2		
Arrearage from Year 1 ($1,000,000 × 5%).	50,000	
Current-year dividend ($1,000,000 × 5%)	50,000	
Balance to common		200,000
Year 3		
Current-year dividend ($1,000,000 × 5%)	50,000	
Balance to common		30,000

b.

	Preferred Stock	Common Stock
Year 1	$ 0	$ 0
Year 2		
Current-year dividend ($1,000,000 × 5%)	50,000	
Balance to common		250,000
Year 3		
Current-year dividend ($1,000,000 × 5%)	50,000	
Balance to common		30,000

Mid-Chapter Review 3

SOLUTION

ANALYZE

Transaction	Cash Asset	+	Noncash Assets	=	Liabil-ities	+	Contrib. Capital	+	Earned Capital	Revenues	−	Expenses	=	Net Income
	Balance Sheet									**Income Statement**				
(1) Apr. 1 Declared a 100% stock dividend.				=			+250,000 Common Stock		−250,000[1] Retained Earnings		−		=	

JOURNALIZE

		Debit	Credit
(1) April 1	Retained earnings (−SE).	250,000	
	Common stock (+SE).		250,000

POST

− Retained Earnings (SE) +	
April 1 250,000	

− Common Stock (SE) +	
	250,000 April 1

1 This large stock dividend reduces retained earnings at the par value of shares distributed (50,000 shares × 100% × $5 par value = $250,000). Contributed capital (common stock) increases by the same amount.

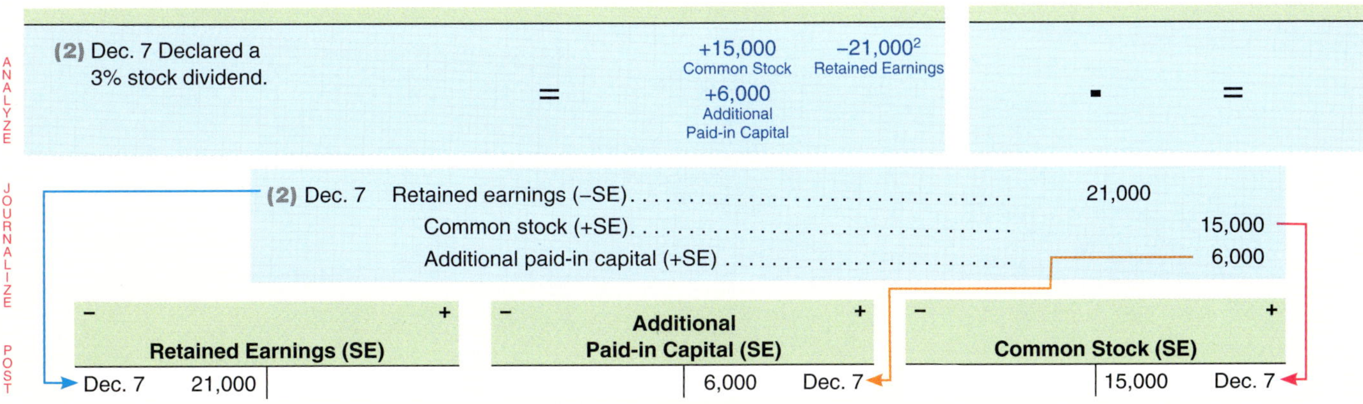

2 This small stock dividend reduces retained earnings at the market value of shares distributed (3% × 100,000 shares × $7 per share = $21,000). Contributed capital increases by the same amount ($15,000 to common stock and $6,000 to paid-in capital).

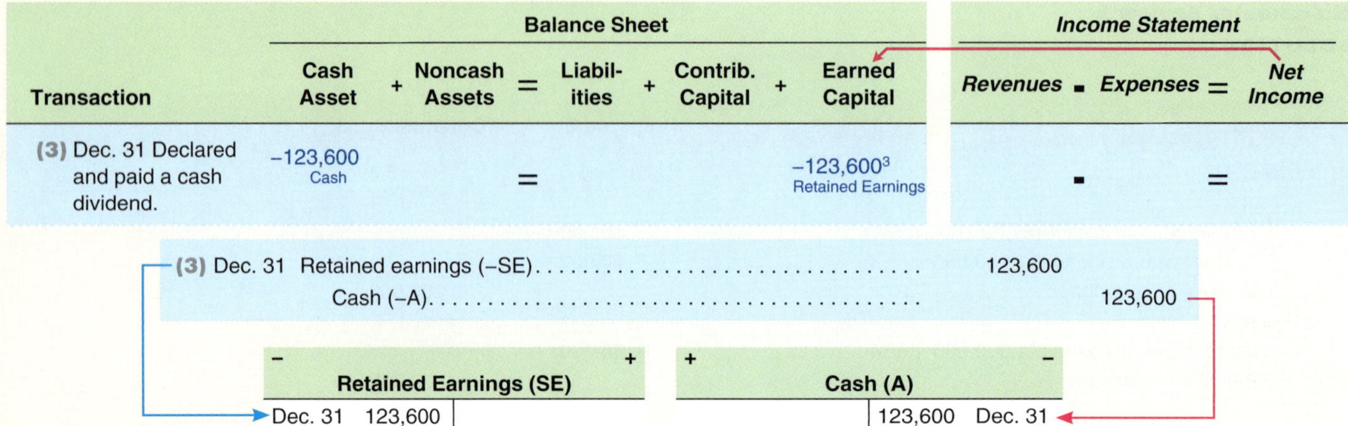

3 At the time of the cash dividend, there are 103,000 shares outstanding. The cash paid is, therefore, 103,000 shares × $1.20 per share = $123,600.

Mid-Chapter Review 4

SOLUTION

Retained Earnings Reconciliation For Year Ended December 31, 2019		
Retained earnings, December 31, 2018.		$513,000
Add: Net income		412,000
		925,000
Less: Cash dividends declared $1.25 × [160,000 + (0.10 × 160,000)]	$220,000	
Stock dividends declared $11 × (160,000 × 0.10)	176,000	396,000
Retained earnings, December 31, 2019.		$529,000

Chapter-End Review

SOLUTION

1. Basic EPS would be calculated as follows (millions, except per share amount):

$$\text{Basic EPS} = \frac{\$1{,}750 - \$40}{760 \text{ shares}} = \$2.25 \text{ per share}$$

2. Diluted EPS is calculated as follows (millions, except per share amounts):

$$\text{Diluted EPS} = \frac{\$1{,}750}{770 \text{ shares}} = \$2.27 \text{ per share}$$

3. Petroni would only report basic EPS on its income statement. Diluted EPS, as calculated in requirement 2, is actually higher than basic EPS because the convertible preferred stock is anti-dilutive. GAAP requires that reported diluted EPS must be lower than basic EPS. Consequently, Petroni would not report the diluted EPS number.

Apendix 11A Review

SOLUTION

ANALYZE

Transaction	Cash Asset	+	Noncash Assets	=	Liabil-ities	−	Contra Liabilities	+	Contrib. Capital	+	Earned Capital	Revenues	−	Expenses	=	Net Income
Conversion of an $850 book-value bond into 200 common shares of $1 par value.				=	−1,000 Bonds Payable	−	−150 Bond Discount		+200 Common Stock +650 Additional Paid-In Capital				−		=	

JOURNALIZE

Bonds payable (−L)	1,000	
Bond discount (−XL, +L)		150
Common stock (+SE)		200
Additional paid-in capital (+SE)		650

POST

Bonds Payable (L) (− / +): 1,000

Additional Paid-in Capital (SE) (− / +): 650

Bond Discount (XL) (+ / −): 150

Common Stock (SE) (− / +): 200

12 Reporting and Analyzing Financial Investments

LEARNING OBJECTIVES

1. Explain and interpret the three levels of investor influence over an investee—passive, significant, and controlling. (p. 582)
2. Describe the term "fair value" and the fair value hierarchy. (p. 584)
3. Describe and analyze accounting for passive investments. (p. 584)
4. Explain and analyze accounting for investments with significant influence. (p. 596)
5. Describe and analyze accounting for investments with control. (p. 600)
6. Appendix 12A: Illustrate and analyze accounting mechanics for equity method investments. (p. 609)
7. Appendix 12B: Apply consolidation accounting mechanics. (p. 611)
8. Appendix 12C: Discuss the reporting of derivative securities. (p. 612)

ALPHABET
www.Alphabet.com

When Sergey Brin and Larry Page, Stanford computer science students, started **Google Inc.**, in September, 1998, they were probably unaware that their fortune would be made in the advertising field that now generates nearly all its revenue.

Google went public in August, 2004, with an offering price below $100 a share. By the end of 2018, the comparable share price exceeded $2,000! In 2015, a holding company named **Alphabet, Inc.**, was formed with Google as its most significant business. However, the accompanying graph shows that Alphabet, Inc.'s spectacular returns occurred early in its life as a public company, and returns over the past six years have been more in line with market averages. Over these recent years, Alphabet, Inc., has met investor expectations (which are high), but has not exceeded them. Analysts point to the substantial challenge faced by the company to find investments that will allow Alphabet, Inc., to match its past returns of over 50%.

Alphabet, Inc., faces competition in general-purpose search engines from **Yahoo, Inc.**, and **Microsoft Corporation**, in vertical search engines and e-commerce websites from **Kayak.com**, **Monster Worldwide, Inc.**, **Amazon.com, Inc.**, and others, in social networks from **Facebook, Inc.**, and **Twitter, Inc.**, The company also competes fiercely with **Apple Inc.**, in the mobile applications market. In addition, the company faces legal challenges from competitors and anti-trust investigations in the United States and other countries. Alphabet, Inc., faces substantial competition and scrutiny as it attempts to build its presence in international markets. The company faces pressure from its employees' objections to some of its contracts with customers, from privacy concerns of users and regulators, and from customers who object to the placement of their advertisements in proximity to certain types of content.

Alphabet, Inc., addresses these growth challenges in several ways. More than 15% of Alphabet's 2018 revenue is spent on research and development to advance the company's provision of cutting-edge products and services to its users and its diversification away from advertising. In addition, Alphabet, Inc., acquires companies with technology that the company can leverage. Most of these acquisitions are small, but Alphabet, Inc., acquired **YouTube, Inc.**, in 2006 for $1.19 billion, **DoubleClick, Inc.**, in 2008 for $3.19 billion, **Motorola Mobility Holdings, Inc.**, in 2012 for $12.4 billion, **Nest Labs, Inc.**, in 2014 for $2.7 billion and an operation of **HTC Corporation**

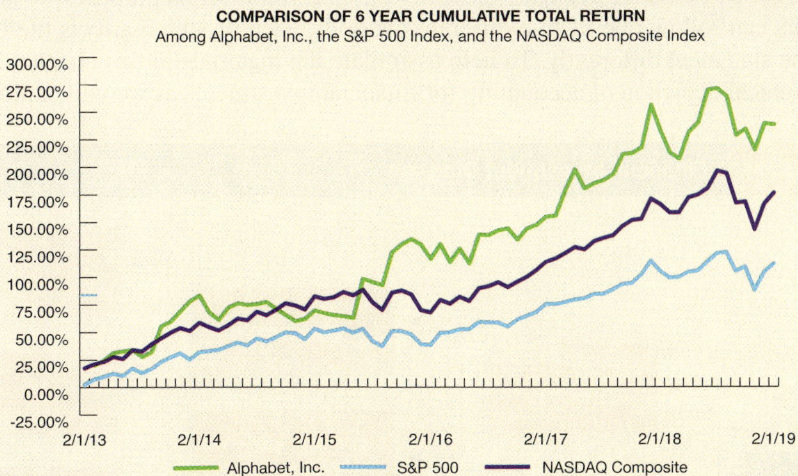

in 2018 for $1.1 billion to work on hardware development. In addition to these investments for operating growth, Alphabet, Inc.'s 2018 balance sheet shows that approximately 50% of its reported assets are cash and securities.

As we discuss in this chapter, the accounting method used to report investments depends on the investor company's purpose in making the investment and on the degree of influence or control that the investor company can exert over the investee company (the company whose securities are being purchased). One consequence of these accounting methods is that small changes in the amount invested can produce significant changes in the investor's financial statements.

Sources: Alphabet 2018 10-K report, *Wall Street Journal*, February 5, 2019.

CHAPTER ORGANIZATION

Reporting and Analyzing Financial Investments

Passive Investments	Investments with Significant Influence	Investments with Control	Further Considerations
• Trading Securities • Available-for-Sale Securities • Held-to-Maturity Securities	• Accounting and Reporting • Equity Method and Effects on Ratios	• Accounting and Reporting • Acquired Assets and Liabilities • Accounting for Goodwill • Noncontrolling Interest	• Equity Method Mechanics (Appendix 12A) • Consolidation Accounting Mechanics (Appendix 12B) • Reporting Derivative Securities (Appendix 12C)

INTRODUCTION

1

LO1 Explain and interpret the three levels of investor influence over an investee—passive, significant, and controlling.

Most companies invest in government securities or the securities of other companies. These investments often have the following strategic goals:

- **Short-term investment of excess cash.** Companies often generate excess cash for investment either during slow times of the year (after receivables are collected and before seasonal production begins) or for liquidity needs (such as to counter strategic moves by competitors or to quickly respond to acquisition opportunities).
- **Alliances for strategic purposes.** Companies often acquire an equity interest in other companies for strategic purposes, such as gaining access to their research and development activities, to supply or distribution markets, or to their production and marketing expertise.
- **Market penetration or expansion.** Acquisitions of controlling interests in other companies can achieve vertical or horizontal integration in existing markets or can be avenues to penetrate new and growing markets.

Investments in government securities and in the securities of other companies are usually referred to as **financial investments**. Firms make these investments for different purposes, so accounting for the investments can follow one of five different methods, each of which affects the balance sheet and the income statement differently. To help assimilate the materials in this chapter, **Exhibit 12.1** provides a graphical depiction of accounting for financial investments as we will explore it.

EXHIBIT 12.1 Financial Investment Diagram

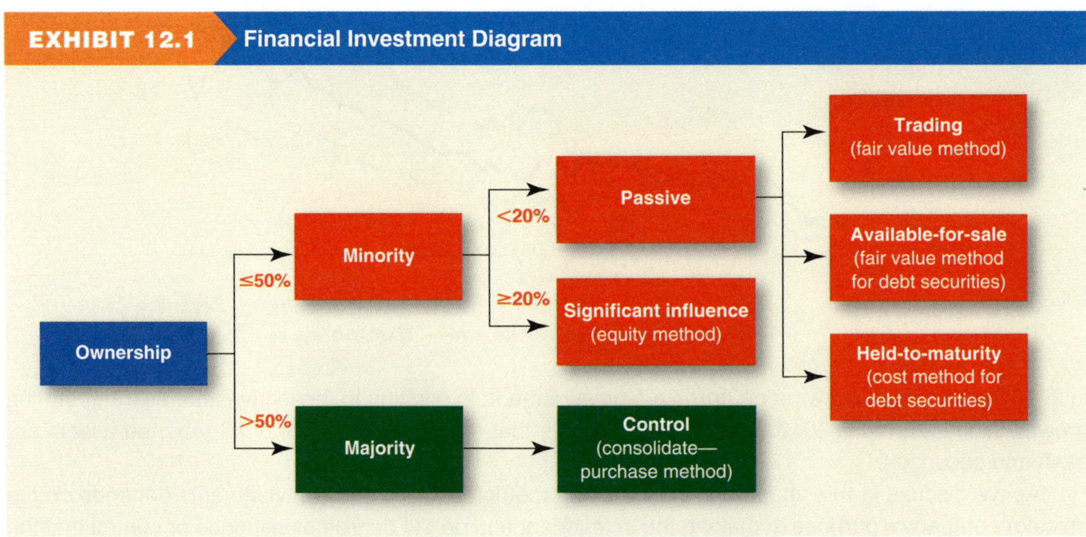

The degree of influence or control that the investor company (purchaser) can exert over the investee organization (the company or government whose securities are being purchased) determines the accounting method. U.S. GAAP identifies three levels of influence/control:

1. **Passive influence**. In this case, the purchasing company is merely an investor and cannot exert influence over the investee organization. The purchaser's goal for this investment is to realize interest, dividends, and capital gains. Generally, passive investor status is presumed if the investor company owns less than 20% of the outstanding voting stock of the investee. Investments in debt securities, such as bonds or notes of other organizations, are also classified as passive investments.
2. **Significant influence**. An investor company can sometimes exert significant influence over, but not control, the activities of an investee company. This level of influence can result from the percentage of voting stock owned. It also can result from legal agreements, such as a license to use technology, a formula, or a trade secret like production know-how. It also can occur when the investor company is the sole supplier or customer of the investee. Generally, significant influence is presumed if the investor company owns 20% to 50% of the voting stock of the investee.
3. **Controlling influence**. When a company has control over another, it has the ability to elect a majority of the board of directors and, as a result, the ability to determine its strategic direction and hiring of executive management. Control is generally presumed if the investor company owns more than 50% of the outstanding voting stock of the investee company. Control can sometimes occur at less than 50% stock ownership by virtue of legal agreements, technology licensing, or other contractual means.

Once the type of investment and the level of influence/control is determined, the appropriate accounting method is applied as outlined in **Exhibit 12.2**.

EXHIBIT 12.2 Investment Type, Accounting Treatment, and Financial Statement Effects

	Accounting	Balance Sheet Effects	Income Statement Effects	Cash Flow Effects
Passive	Trading (Debt or equity investments)	Investment balance reported as end-of-period fair value	Interest and dividend payments from investee are included in income Capital gain/loss recognized in the period in which it occurs	Purchase/sale of investee yields investing cash flows Interest and dividend payments received from investee are operating cash inflows
	Available-for-Sale (Debt investments only)	Investment balance reported as end-of-period fair value	Interest payments from investee are included in income Capital gain/loss recognized when investment sold; interim gain/loss reported as AOCI*	Purchase/sale of investee yields investing cash flows Interest payments received from investee are operating cash inflows
	Held-to-Maturity (Debt investments only)	Investment balance reported at adjusted acquisition cost	Interest payments from investee are included in income Capital gain/loss recognized when investment sold	Purchase/sale of investee yields investing cash flows Interest payments received from investee are operating cash inflows
Significant Influence	Equity Method	Investment balance reflects purchase price and subsequent changes in proportion owned of investee's earned equity	Investor reports income equal to percent owned of investee income Sale of investee yields gains/losses	Purchase/sale of investee yields investing cash flows Dividend payments received from investee are operating cash inflows
Control	Consolidation	Balance sheets of investor and investee are presented as if one entity	Income statements of investor and investee are presented as if one entity Sale of investee yields gains/losses	Purchase/sale of investee yields investing cash flows Cash flows of investor and investee are presented as if one entity

*AOCI (Accumulated Other Comprehensive Income) is defined on page 531 and discussed further in the following pages.

There are two basic reporting issues with investments: (1) how investment income should be recognized and (2) at what amount (cost or fair value) the investment should be reported on the balance sheet. We next discuss both of these issues under each of the three investment types.

FAIR VALUE: AN INTRODUCTION

2

LO2 Describe the term "fair value" and the fair value hierarchy.

The term **fair value** is finding increasing use in the language of accounting, but it is particularly prevalent in the accounting for financial investments. When an investor purchases a security for $100, the relevance of that acquisition cost fades rather quickly. If the investor considers selling the security a year later, the original $100 cost is much less meaningful than the current price for the security in the markets. Or, if we were to look at the balance sheet of a company, it would be useful to know how much its investments are worth today, rather than what was paid for them at various points in the past.

When accounting requires the use of fair value, U.S. GAAP defines fair value as the amount that an independent buyer would be willing to pay for an asset (or the amount that would need to be paid to discharge a liability) in an orderly transaction. For an asset that is actively traded on financial markets, fair value is the amount that we would receive by selling that asset at the balance sheet date. But fair value is also used when there is no active market for the asset. When Microsoft accounts for its acquisition of LinkedIn, it must report the fair value of the intellectual property that it obtained in that transaction. In such cases, fair value is not "mark-to-market," but rather "mark-to-model." For instance, fair value might be determined by a discounted cash flow analysis as in Chapter 9. U.S. GAAP allows various methods to be used in determining the "most representative" fair value at the appropriate date.

While fair values are often deemed to be more relevant than historical cost, they are also viewed as more subjective—particularly when fair value is determined by reference to a model rather than a liquid market. For this reason, U.S. GAAP requires that firms disclose the methods used to determine fair value for their assets using a **fair value hierarchy**.

Level 1: Values based on quoted prices in active markets for identical assets/liabilities. An example would be a common share of a company traded on an active exchange. For instance, Alphabet, Inc.'s class A common stock closed at a price of $1,035.61 per share on December 31, 2018. That price would be used to determine the fair value of another company's investment in Alphabet, Inc., stock.

Level 2: Values based on observable inputs other than Level 1 (e.g., quoted prices for similar assets/liabilities or interest rates or yield curves). An example would be a bond that is infrequently traded, but that is similar to bonds that are actively traded. Moody's rates Alphabet, Inc., bonds at Aa2. Other bonds with that rating would likely have a similar yield, which could be used to compute the present value of the bond payments to estimate the fair value of a bond investment.

Level 3: Values based on inputs observable only to the reporting entity (e.g., management estimates or assumptions). An example would be an operating asset that is judged to be impaired.

Alphabet, Inc.'s use of fair value to report its investments is presented in the coming pages. The purpose of the classification is to provide an assessment of the subjectivity that underlies the numbers in the balance sheet (and sometimes, the income statement), with Level 1 being the most reliable and Level 3 being the most subjective.

In addition, companies have a **fair value option** that provides them with the *option* of using fair value to measure the value of many financial assets and liabilities. This option extends the use of fair value to a wide range of financial assets and liabilities, including accounts and notes receivable, accounts and notes payable, and bonds payable. Other assets that *must* be reported at fair value include (1) investments in other companies' equity securities, (2) derivative securities, such as options, futures, and forward contracts, that are purchased to hedge price, interest rate, or foreign exchange rate fluctuations, (3) long-term assets that are impaired, and (4) inventories that have been written down to fair value based on the lower-of-cost-or-market rule.

PASSIVE INVESTMENTS IN DEBT SECURITIES

3

LO3 Describe and analyze accounting for passive investments.

The term "passive" refers to the investor's role in trying to influence the operations of the investee organization. So, short-term investments of excess cash are typically passive investments, usually in liquid, low-risk securities. In addition, investors seeking trading profits from short-term capital gains would be considered passive investors, even though their trading style may be active. Debt securities have no ownership interest, so they are always passive, and we leave the accounting for passive equity investments for the next section. Passive debt investments can be broadly grouped into two categories: those reported at cost and those reported at fair value. Furthermore, there are two methods for reporting investments at fair value. These alternative treatments are discussed below.

Acquisition of the Investment

When a debt investment is acquired, regardless of the amount purchased, the investment is initially recorded on the balance sheet at its fair value, that is, its price on the date of purchase. This accounting is the same as that for the acquisition of other assets such as inventories or plant assets. Subsequent to acquisition, investments are carried on the balance sheet as current or long-term assets, depending on management's expectations about their ultimate holding period (the assets are reported as current assets if management expects to dispose of them within one year).

When investments are sold, any recognized gain or loss on sale usually is equal to the difference between the proceeds received and the book (carrying) value of the investment on the balance sheet. However, there is one passive investment method where that is not true.

To illustrate entries for a passive debt investment, assume that—on January 1 of Year 1—Pownall Company wants to earn a return on a cash balance for which it has no immediate need. King Company has just issued high-quality bonds that mature in five years. Each bond has a face value of $1,000 and an annual coupon rate of interest equal to 10% (paid semi-annually on June 30 and December 31). The bonds have a current market price of $1,000, implying a 10% annual discount rate. At the start of the year, Pownall Company purchases 500 of King Company's bonds for $500,000. The financial statement effects of this transaction for Pownell are the following:

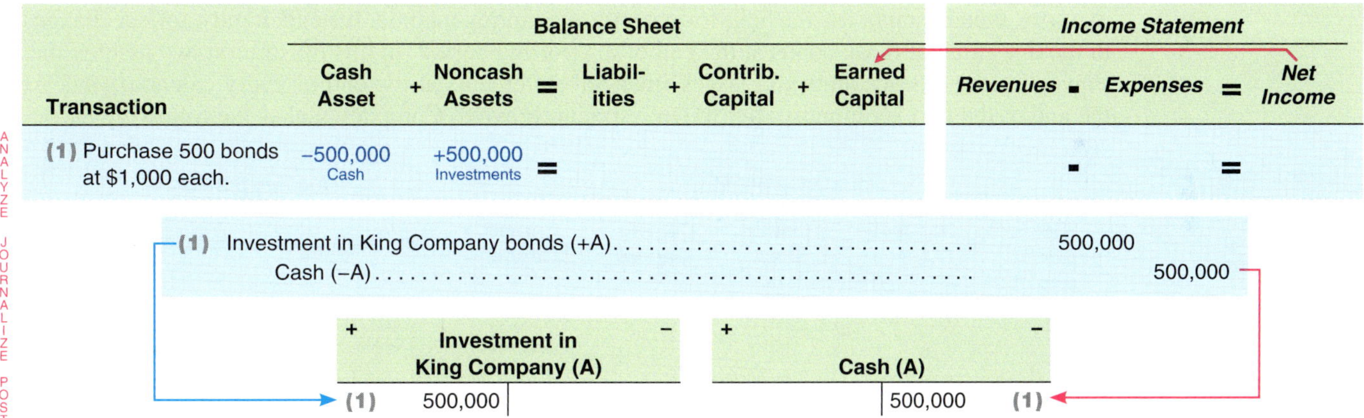

While accounting for the initial investment is straightforward, the subsequent reporting can follow one of three paths.

Investments Reported at Cost

When a company purchases a debt security, and it has the positive intent and the ability to hold that security until it matures, the value fluctuations between purchase and maturity are not relevant for financial statement readers. In such cases, these debt securities are classified as **held-to-maturity (HTM)**. **Exhibit 12.3** summarizes the reporting of these securities.

EXHIBIT 12.3

Investment Classification	Reporting of Fair Value Changes	Reporting Interest Received and Gains and Losses on Sale
Held-to-Maturity (HTM)	Fair value changes are not reported in either the balance sheet or income statement	Reported as other income in income statement

In our illustrative example, we assume (for the moment) that Pownall Company has the ability and the intent to hold the bonds until they mature. For the King Company bonds, Pownall Company's use of the held-to-maturity method would have the following interest income and book value pattern over the five years (mirroring the accounting for a bond from Chapter 9). At the end of each six-month period, Pownall would receive an interest payment of $25,000 and recognize investment income of the same amount. Fluctuations in the market value of King Company bonds are not reflected in the accounting for the investment. At the end of year 5, Pownall would also receive a principal repayment of $500,000.

Year	Beginning Book Value (A)	Interest Income	Interest Received	Principal Payment	Ending Book Value
	(a)	(b) = (a) × 10%/2	(c)		(d) = (a) + (b) − (c)
½	500,000	25,000	25,000	-0-	500,000
1	500,000	25,000	25,000	-0-	500,000
1½	500,000	25,000	25,000	-0-	500,000
2	500,000	25,000	25,000	-0-	500,000
2½	500,000	25,000	25,000	-0-	500,000
3	500,000	25,000	25,000	-0-	500,000
3½	500,000	25,000	25,000	-0-	500,000
4	500,000	25,000	25,000	-0-	500,000
4½	500,000	25,000	25,000	-0-	500,000
5	500,000	25,000	25,000	500,000	-0-

Investments Marked to Fair Value

If Pownall Company does not have the ability or the intent to hold the King Company bonds to maturity, then it cannot use the held-to-maturity accounting method. Instead, it must reflect changes in the fair value of those bonds at the end of a reporting period. In this illustration, we assume that Pownall closes its accounts and issues financial statements at the end of every calendar year. At the end of the first six months after the investment, Pownall Company makes the following entry:

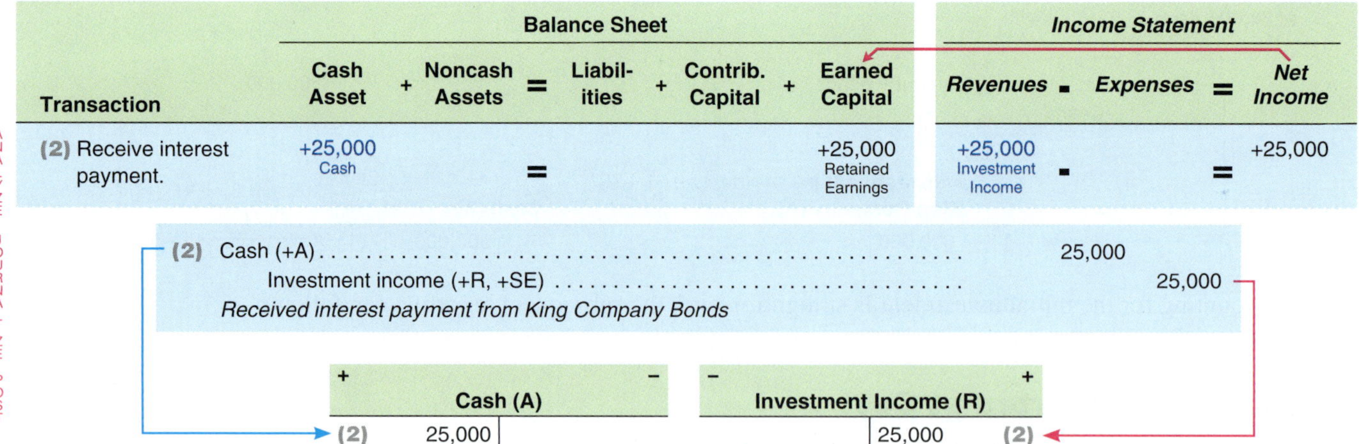

Transaction	Cash Asset	+	Noncash Assets	=	Liabilities	+	Contrib. Capital	+	Earned Capital	Revenues	−	Expenses	=	Net Income
(2) Receive interest payment.	+25,000 Cash			=					+25,000 Retained Earnings	+25,000 Investment Income	−		=	+25,000

(2) Cash (+A) 25,000
Investment income (+R, +SE) 25,000
Received interest payment from King Company Bonds

+ Cash (A) −		− Investment Income (R) +	
(2) 25,000			25,000 (2)

Sale of the Investment

On July 1, Year 1, an unexpected liquidity need causes Pownall to sell 100 of the 500 bonds for $950 cash per bond. The financial statement effects of this transaction and its related entries for Pownall follow.

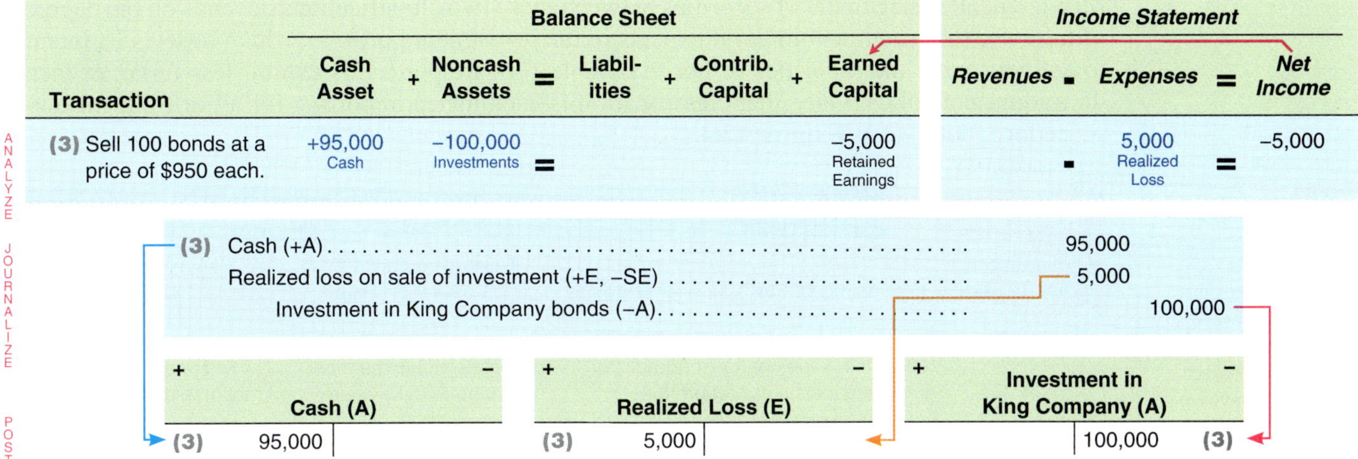

The gain or loss on sale is reported as a component of *other income,* which is commonly commingled with interest and dividend revenue in the income statement.

On the statement of cash flows, the $500,000 purchase (transaction 1) would be an investing cash outflow, and the $95,000 proceeds (transaction 2) would be an investing cash inflow. If Pownall Company presents its cash flows from operating activities using the indirect method, we would see an addition of the $5,000 loss on sale among the adjustments from net income to cash from operations.

Accounting for the purchase and sale of investments is similar to any other asset. Further, there is no difference in accounting for purchases and sales across the different types of passive investments when those purchases and sales occur in the same reporting period.

Pownall Company continues to receive interest payments from its remaining King Company bonds. On December 31, it would make the following entry:

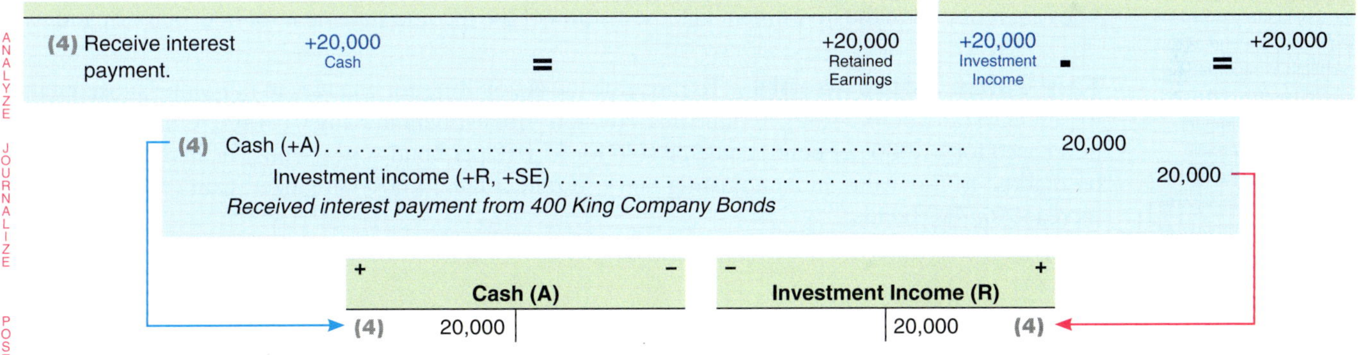

However, as Pownall Company reaches the end of its fiscal reporting period (a year-end), and the hold-to-maturity assumption is no longer valid, we can see that there are different ways in which we might determine the balance sheet value of the 400 bonds of King Company that Pownall Company still owns. And, that balance sheet value will be the asset's book value going forward, affecting gains and losses now and when the shares are ultimately sold.

Debt Investments Marked to Fair Value

The following two classifications of marketable debt securities require the investment to be reported on the balance sheet at current fair value:

1. **Trading (T) securities**. These are investments in debt securities that management intends to actively buy and sell for trading profits as market prices fluctuate.
2. **Available-for-sale (AFS) securities**. These are investments in debt securities that management intends to hold for interest income; although it may sell them if the price is right or if the organization needs cash.

Management's assignment of securities between these two classifications depends on the degree of turnover (transaction volume) it expects in the investment portfolio, which reflects its intent to actively trade the securities or not. Available-for-sale portfolios exhibit less turnover than do trading portfolios. Once that classification is established, reporting for a portfolio follows procedures detailed in **Exhibit 12.4**.

FYI GAAP permits companies to have multiple portfolios, each with a different classification. Management can change portfolio classification provided it adheres to strict disclosure and reporting requirements if its expectations of turnover change.

EXHIBIT 12.4 Accounting Treatment for Trading and Available-for-Sale Debt Investments

Investment Classification	Reporting of Fair Value Changes	Reporting Gains and Losses on Sale	Reporting Interest Income
Trading (T)	Balance sheet values are updated to reflect fair value changes; unrealized gains and losses are reported as investment income; affects equity via retained earnings	Gain or loss on sale equals proceeds minus the most recent book (fair) value	Reported as investment income in income statement
Available-for-Sale (AFS)	Balance sheet values are updated to reflect fair value changes; unrealized gains and losses bypass the income statement and are reported directly in the statement of comprehensive income and then in accumulated other comprehensive income (AOCI), a component of equity	Gain or loss on sale equals proceeds minus the original acquisition cost of the investment; any unrealized gains or losses in accumulated other comprehensive income must be eliminated	Reported as investment income in income statement

Both trading (T) and available-for-sale (AFS) investments are reported at fair values on the statement date. Whether the change in fair value affects current income depends on the investment classification: available-for-sale securities have no immediate income effect; trading securities have an income effect. The impact on shareholders' equity is similar for both classifications, with the only difference being whether the change is reflected in retained earnings or in accumulated other comprehensive income (AOCI) in equity. Interest income and any gains or losses on security sales are reported in the investment income section of the income statement for both classifications.

FYI When trading securities are marked-to-fair value, the unrealized gain/loss is recorded as income and reported in the income statement. For available-for-sale investments, unrealized gains/losses are reported as other comprehensive income.

Fair Value Adjustments To illustrate the accounting for changes in fair value subsequent to purchase (and before sale), assume that Pownall's investment in King Co. (400 remaining bonds purchased for $1,000 per bond) could be sold for $1,010 per bond at year-end. The investment must be marked to fair value in an adjusting entry to reflect the $4,000 unrealized gain ($10 per bond increase for 400 bonds).

If the investment is classified as trading securities (T) the entry would be:

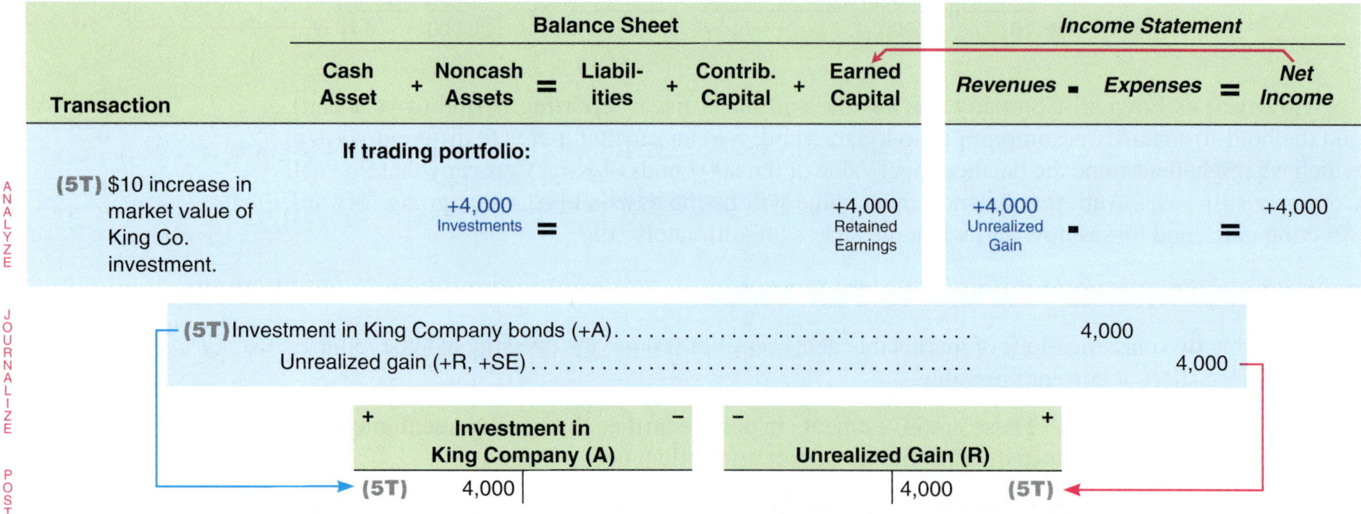

The investment account is increased by $4,000, making the end-of-year book value of Pownall's investment equal to $404,000, its fair value. Total investment income reported on Pownall's income statement would be $44,000, consisting of a realized holding loss of $5,000, interest income of $45,000 (= 500 × 10% × $1,000/2 + 400 × 10% × $1,000/2) and $4,000 in unrealized holding gains. If Pownall is actively trading to achieve capital gains, then this approach seems like the correct way to "keep score."

This entry to adjust the balance sheet to reflect the fair value of the securities is an adjusting entry. It would need to be made at the end of every fiscal period as financial reports are being prepared.

What happens when the securities are subsequently sold? Assume that Pownall Company sells its 400 bonds of King Company for $990 per bond on July 1 of Year 2. Pownall Company would receive the interest payment of $20,000 on June 30 of Year 2, as in transaction (4) above. On July 1, Year 2, Pownall receives $396,000 (= 400 × $990) in cash, and it no longer owns bonds of King Company. When the trading method is used, the accounting for the sale of shares is relatively simple:

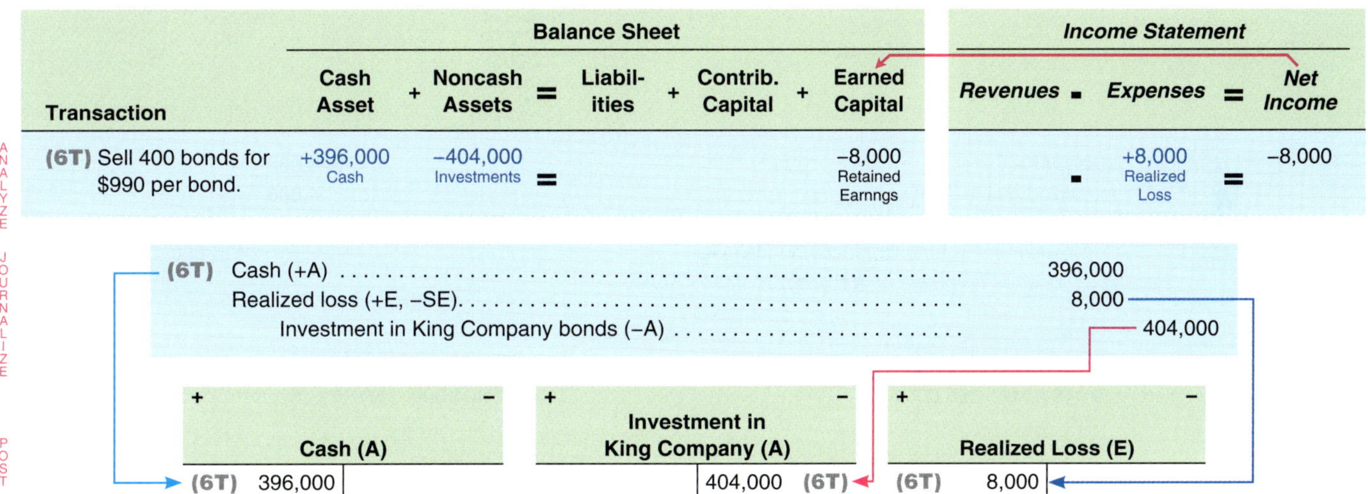

	Balance Sheet						Income Statement		
Transaction	Cash Asset	+ Noncash Assets	= Liabilities	+ Contrib. Capital	+ Earned Capital		Revenues	− Expenses	= Net Income
(6T) Sell 400 bonds for $990 per bond.	+396,000 Cash	−404,000 Investments	=		−8,000 Retained Earnngs			− +8,000 Realized Loss	= −8,000

(6T) Cash (+A) . . . 396,000
Realized loss (+E, −SE) . . . 8,000
Investment in King Company bonds (−A) . . . 404,000

Cash (A): (6T) 396,000 (debit)
Investment in King Company (A): 404,000 (6T) (credit)
Realized Loss (E): (6T) 8,000 (debit)

Under the trading securities method, holding gains and losses (both realized and unrealized) are recognized in income in the period in which they occur. Holding these 400 bonds caused a holding gain of $4,000 in Year 1 and a holding loss of $8,000 in Year 2. Again, if Pownall Company were actively seeking capital gains, we would say that they were less successful in Year 2 than they had been in Year 1.

Now let's assume that Pownall Company had classified its investment in King Company as available-for-sale (AFS) securities; the end-of-year adjusting entry would be the following:

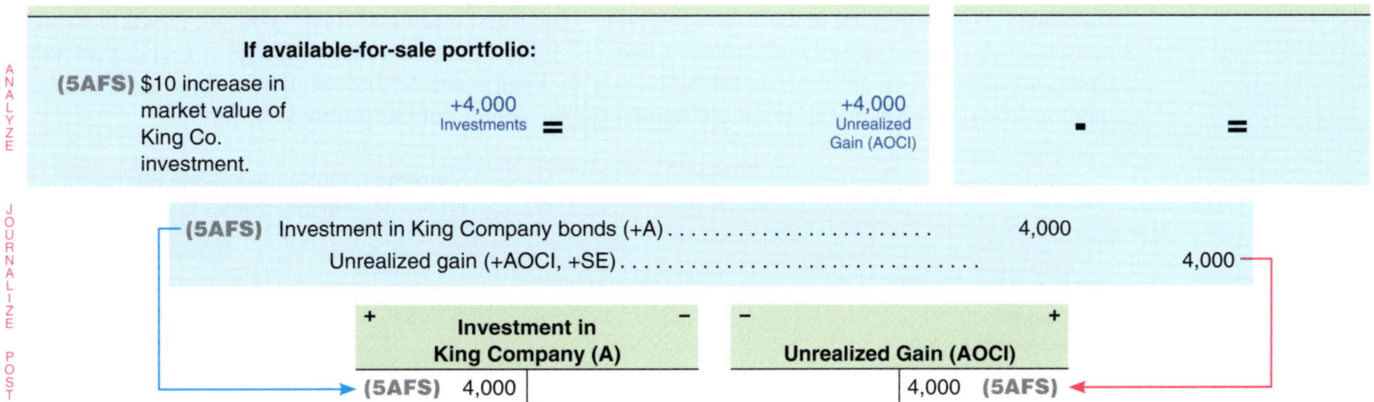

If available-for-sale portfolio:

Transaction	Cash Asset	+ Noncash Assets	= Liabilities	+ Contrib. Capital	+ Earned Capital		Revenues	− Expenses	= Net Income
(5AFS) $10 increase in market value of King Co. investment.		+4,000 Investments	=		+4,000 Unrealized Gain (AOCI)			−	=

(5AFS) Investment in King Company bonds (+A) . . . 4,000
Unrealized gain (+AOCI, +SE) . . . 4,000

Investment in King Company (A): (5AFS) 4,000 (debit)
Unrealized Gain (AOCI): 4,000 (5AFS) (credit)

As under the trading method, the investment account is increased by $4,000 (from $400,000 to $404,000) to reflect the increase in fair value of the shares owned at the end of Year 1. However, when accounted for as an AFS security, the unrealized gain (or loss) bypasses the income statement, is reported in the statement of other comprehensive income, and ends up in accumulated other comprehensive income (AOCI), a separate component of shareholders' equity. In contrast to the trading method, the increase in the investment does not result in an immediate income statement effect. Under AFS, Pownall Company's investment income for Year 1 would reflect only the $5,000 realized loss from the sale of 100 bonds, plus the interest income of $45,000. The $4,000 unrealized gain is reflected in stockholders' equity, but not reported on the income statement. In a sense, the balance sheet has been updated to reflect the current values, but the income statement has been left out of the picture for the time being.

When Pownall Company sells the 400 bonds for $396,000 in the subsequent period, the entry under AFS would be the following:

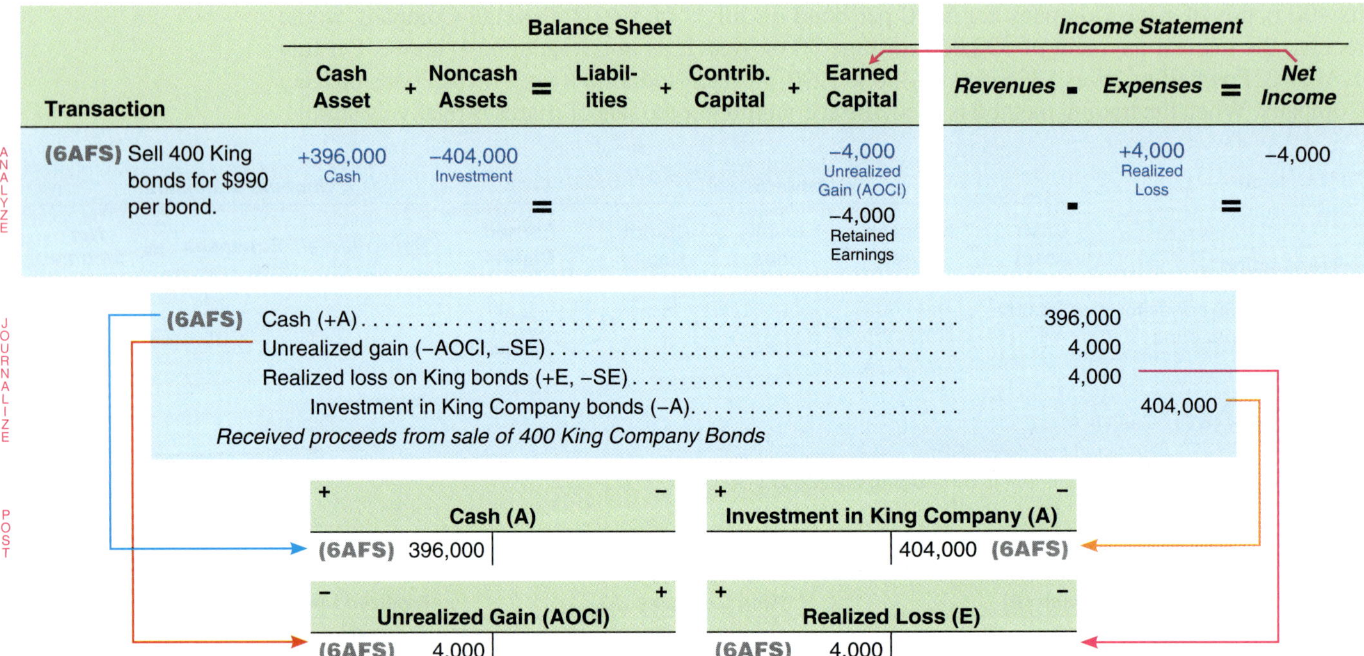

Under AFS, the realized gain (loss) goes into income when the security is sold, and the amount is determined by comparing the amount received when the shares are sold ($990 per bond) to the amount paid for the shares when originally purchased ($1,000 per bond). When the investment is sold, the entry must delete the investment (which was valued at $1,010 per bond at the end of last period) *and* the unrealized holding gain ($10 per bond) that was put into accumulated other comprehensive income when those shares were revalued. Both the Investment in King Company account and the AOCI for King Company have zero balances after this transaction.

The principal difference between trading and available-for-sale accounting is in the income statement, as summarized in the following table. Under the trading security method, Pownall Company records income of $44,000 in Year 1 and $12,000 in Year 2. Under available-for-sale, Pownall Company records income that is $4,000 lower in Year 1 and $4,000 higher in Year 2. The total income from the investment in King Company is the same, but the timing is different.

	Income Reported in Income Statement From Investment in King Company Bonds	
	Trading	**Available-for-Sale**
Year 1:		
Interest income	$45,000	$45,000
Realized holding loss	(5,000)	(5,000)
Unrealized holding gain	4,000	—
Total Year 1 investment income	$44,000	$40,000
Year 2:		
Interest income	$20,000	$20,000
Realized holding loss	(8,000)	(4,000)
Total year 2 investment income	12,000	16,000
Total investment income—Year 1 plus Year 2	$56,000	$56,000

Because of the difference in the way unrealized gains and losses are reported, the classification of investments as either trading or available-for-sale will have an effect on key ratios that might be used to evaluate the performance of a company. Ratios that use net income in the calculation are affected. Return on equity (ROE), return on assets (ROA), and profit margin (PM) are among those ratios affected. Return on net operating assets (RNOA), which is discussed in Appendix A at the end of Chapter 5, would not be affected by this classification because passive investments would be considered nonoperating assets and excluded from the calculation of net operating assets and the gains and losses would be excluded from net operating profit after taxes (NOPAT).

PASSIVE INVESTMENTS IN EQUITY SECURITIES

While passive investments in debt securities may be accounted for in three different ways, passive investments in equity securities should be reported based on the trading method. That is, passive equity investments should be marked to fair value and changes in fair value should be reported in the income statement in the period they occur. The available-for-sale method—which lets unrealized holding gains and losses go into AOCI until the security is sold—is not allowed for passive investments in equity securities.

When an equity security is purchased, the cost of purchase increases (debits) the investment asset. Dividends received are reported as income by the investing company. At the end of every reporting period, the investing company must adjust the investment asset's value to its current fair value. If the value has increased, the change produces an unrealized holding gain in the investing company's income statement. If the investment asset's value has decreased, then marking the assets value down to fair value produces an unrealized holding loss in the investing company's income statement. Fluctuations in the fair value of an equity security are presented as they occur in the investing company's balance sheet and income statement. When the equity security is sold, the realized holding gain or loss is determined by subtracting the fair value from the investing company's most recent balance sheet from the proceeds from the sale.

In the investing company's statement of cash flows, the original investment would be an investing cash outflow, and the sale proceeds would appear as an investing cash inflow (assuming that the purchase and sale were cash transactions). Cash dividends received would be operating cash inflows (under US GAAP). If the investing company uses the indirect method to report its operating cash flows, it would have to subtract any unrealized holding gain (or add back any unrealized holding loss) that was reporting in its income statement.

As an example, assume that Pownall Company used $50,000 cash to purchase 1,000 common shares of King Company on January 1, Year 1. One thousand shares represent 5% of King's outstanding common stock, so Pownall's investment is considered passive. During Year 1, King pays dividends to its common shareholders equal to $1.50 per share. Assume that King Company shares are traded actively on a national stock exchange. At the end of Year 1, the bid price for a common share of King Company is $55. Shortly after the end of Year 1, Pownall sells its investment and receives $52,000 in cash. These events would be accounting for in the following way:

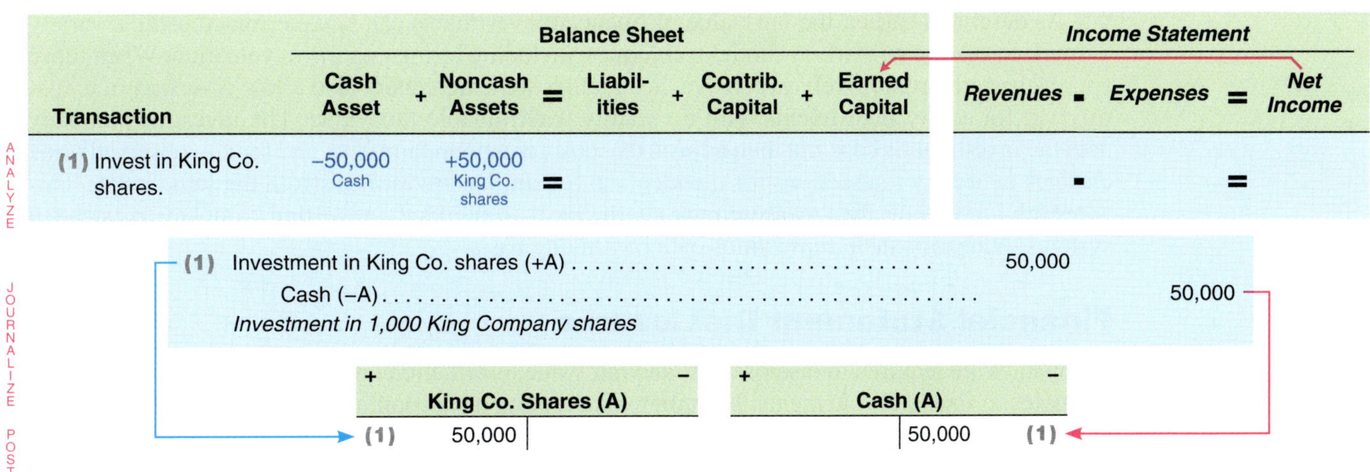

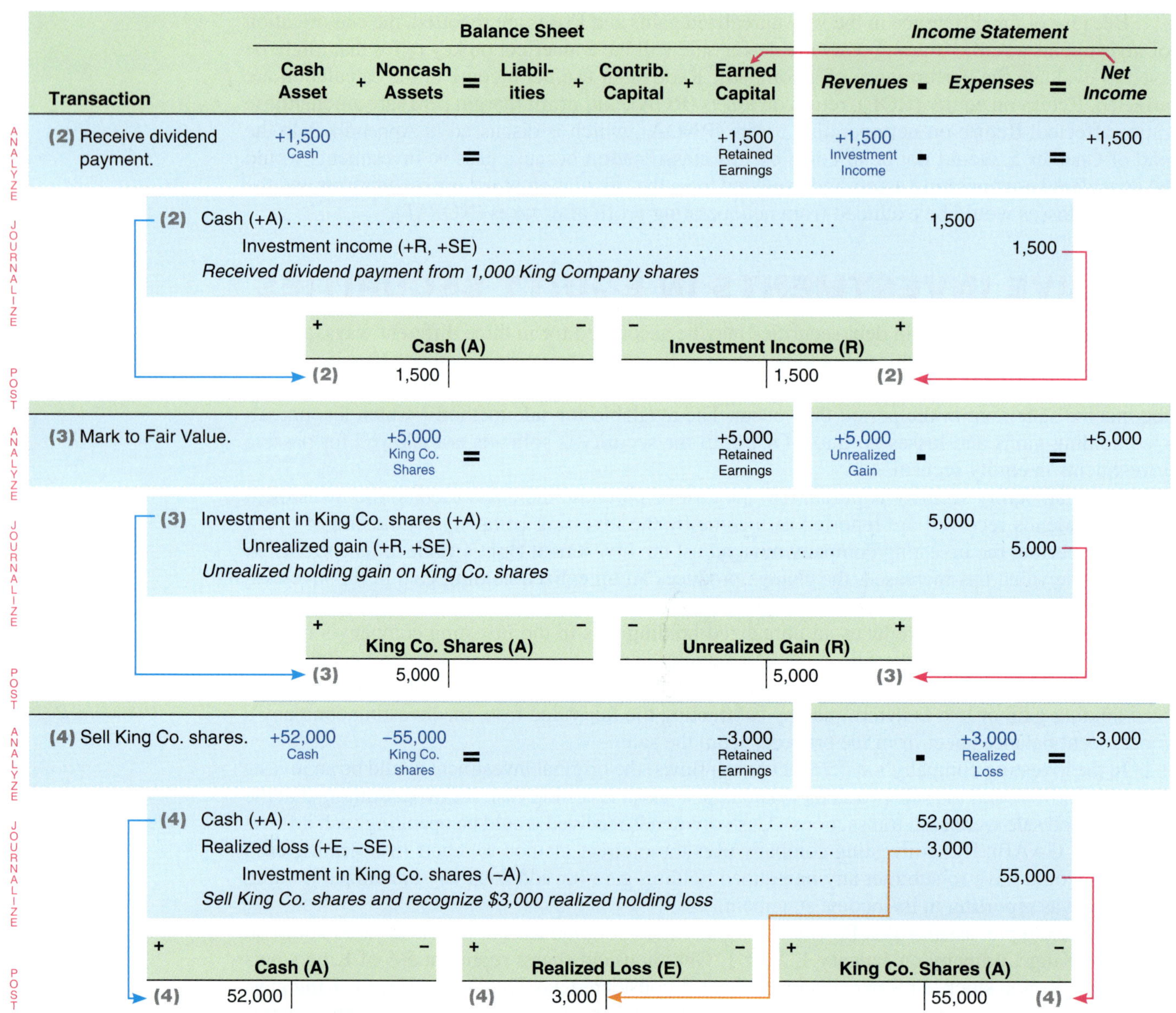

The available-for-sale method is not allowed for equity investments, so the holding gain/loss component of Pownall Company's investment income always reflects the events of that period. There is no opportunity for the investing company to "store up" holding gains or losses and to recognize them at a desired time.

As described earlier, the fair value of financial investments can be determined using a variety of mark-to-market or mark-to-model techniques, including hiring experts in valuation. When those approaches are prohibitively expensive, accounting standard setters also allow a version of a **cost method** for equity investments with no readily determinable fair value. The investing company uses the investment's cost, but then adjusts that cost for any impairments and for any observed price changes in orderly transactions for the identical (or similar) investment from the same issuer. This approach—known as the "measurement alternative"—requires the investing company to establish systems to identify such transactions on a continuing basis.

Financial Statement Disclosures

Companies are required to disclose cost and fair value information on their investment portfolios in footnotes to financial statements. **Alphabet, Inc.**, reports its accounting policies for its investments in note 1 to its 2018 10-K report:

Cash, Cash Equivalents, and Marketable Securities

We invest all excess cash primarily in government bonds, corporate debt securities, mortgage-backed and asset-backed securities, time deposits, and money market funds.

We classify all investments that are readily convertible to known amounts of cash and have stated maturities of three months or less from the date of purchase as cash equivalents and those with stated maturities of greater than three months as marketable securities.

We determine the appropriate classification of our investments in marketable securities at the time of purchase and reevaluate such designation at each balance sheet date. We have classified and accounted for our marketable debt securities as available-for-sale. After consideration of our risk versus reward objectives, as well as our liquidity requirements, we may sell these debt securities prior to their stated maturities. As we view these securities as available to support current operations, we classify highly liquid securities with maturities beyond 12 months as current assets under the caption marketable securities on the Consolidated Balance Sheets. We carry these securities at fair value, and report the unrealized gains and losses, net of taxes, as a component of stockholders' equity, except for unrealized losses determined to be other-than-temporary, which we record within other income (expense), net. We determine any realized gains or losses on the sale of marketable debt securities on a specific identification method, and we record such gains and losses as a component of other income (expense), net.

Non-Marketable Investments

We account for non-marketable equity investments through which we exercise significant influence but do not have control over the investee under the equity method. Beginning on January 1, 2018, our non-marketable equity securities not accounted for under the equity method are either carried at fair value or under the measurement alternative upon the adoption of ASU 2016-01. Under the measurement alternative, the carrying value is measured at cost, less any impairment, plus or minus changes resulting from observable price changes in orderly transactions for identical or similar investments of the same issuer. Adjustments are determined primarily based on a market approach as of the transaction date. We classify our non-marketable investments as non-current assets on the Consolidated Balance Sheets as those investments do not have stated contractual maturity dates.

We account for our non-marketable investments that meet the definition of a debt security as available-for-sale securities.

This footnote reveals that Alphabet, Inc., reports investments with maturities of three months or less as cash equivalents. These investments are most likely treated as trading securities and any changes in their fair value would result in a gain or loss that would be reported in the income statement. Because of the short maturity of these investments, the gains and losses due to changes in fair value are generally very small. Liquid investments with longer maturities are reported as marketable securities and classified as available-for-sale. Consistent with this accounting treatment, Alphabet, Inc., notes that its marketable securities are carried in the balance sheet at fair value and it reports the "unrealized gains and losses, net of taxes, as a component of stockholders' equity." The cash, cash equivalents, and marketable securities are presented under current assets in the balance sheet:

December 31 ($ millions)	2018
Cash and cash equivalents	$ 16,701
Marketable securities	92,439
Total cash, cash equivalents, and marketable securities	$109,140

In note 3 to its 10-K, Alphabet, Inc., provides further information about the composition of its investment portfolio starting with its investments in debt securities.

The following table summarizes Alphabet, Inc.'s debt securities by significant investment categories (in millions):

	As of December 31, 2018						
	Adjusted Cost	Gross Unrealized Gains	Gross Unrealized Losses	Fair Value	Cash and Cash Equivalents	Marketable Securities	Non-Marketable Securities
Level 2:							
Time deposits	$ 2,202	$ 0	$ 0	$ 2,202	$2,202	$ 0	$ 0
Government bonds	53,634	71	(414)	53,291	3,717	49,574	0
Corporate debt securities	25,383	15	(316)	25,082	44	25,038	0
Mortgage-backed and asset-backed securities	16,918	11	(324)	16,605	0	16,605	0
	98,137	97	(1,054)	97,180	5,963	91,217	0
Level 3:							
Nonmarketable securities	147	116	0	263	0	0	263
Total	$98,284	$213	$(1,054)	$97,443	$5,963	$91,217	$263

A large portion of Alphabet, Inc.'s investment in debt securities is in government securities, including U.S. government debt, foreign government bonds, and municipal securities. The various types of securities are divided into two groups, labeled "Level 2" and "Level 3." These labels refer to the method used to determine the fair value of each investment. The fair values of the investments listed as Level 2 are determined based on a combination of quoted prices for identical or similar instruments in active markets and models with significant observable market inputs. A small portion of Alphabet, Inc.'s debt investments are listed as Level 3. These represent preferred stock and convertible debt investments that are issued by private companies and have no quoted market prices.

For each type of investment, Alphabet, Inc., reports its cost, its fair value, and the gross unrealized gains and losses; the latter equaling the difference between the cost and fair value. Alphabet reports the cost of its debt investments at $98,284 million and its fair value at $97,443 million. The fair value total is then divided into cash and cash equivalents of $5,963 million, marketable securities of $91,217 million, and nonmarketable securities of $263 million.

In addition to information about its investments in debt securities, Alphabet must report on its equity investments. As seen in the table below, the investments in marketable equity securities are of a much smaller magnitude than the debt securities and are almost all reported using Level 1 fair values. There is no reporting of unrealized holding gains and losses, because equity investments are recorded at fair value, with gains and losses (both realized and unrealized) going through income as they occur.

	As of December 31, 2018	
	Cash and Cash Equivalents	Marketable Securities
Level 1:		
Money market funds	$3,493	$ 0
Marketable equity securities	0	994
	3,493	994
Level 2:		
Mutual funds	0	228
Total	$3,493	$1,222

Alphabet, Inc., has also invested in nonmarketable equity securities and, at the end of 2018, these securities had a Level 3 fair value of $12,275 million.

Potential for Earnings Management

When a company owns an asset with a disparity between its fair value and its book value, there is a potential for "real earnings management" or "transaction smoothing." Real earnings management refers to the use of transactions (rather than estimates) to arrive at an attractive earnings number. Examples from previous chapters would include the liquidation of LIFO inventory or the sale of a fully-depreciated physical asset with remaining life. Such transactions would increase reported income and—perhaps—disguise disappointing results in a company's fundamental operations.

These concerns are also relevant in the accounting for financial investments. Suppose financial investments were kept on the books at their original cost. Over time, some would appreciate in value while others would decline. Keeping the investments at cost reduces financial statement usefulness in two ways. First, it fails to keep financial statement readers informed about changes in the company's asset values. Second, it provides management with an earnings management tool. Selling off assets with accumulated gains (losses) would increase (decrease) reported earnings, thereby providing an income smoothing tool that might disguise the company's performance.

The reporting practices for passive investments are designed to limit this sort of problem. For instance, the requirement to mark equity securities to their fair value every reporting period means that holding gains and losses cannot build up over an extended time period. And, on the last day of a reporting period, the holding gain/loss reported in income would be the same—whether the security was sold or not. However, it is still useful for a financial statement reader to identify gains and losses to clarify a company's sources of income. For instance, Alphabet's nonmarketable equity securities' holding gains and losses accounted for a $4.1 billion increase in the company's investment income for 2018.

Fair value fluctuations are ignored for debt securities under the held-to-maturity method. But if a bond is held until its maturity, there will be no gain or loss at that point. The book value and the fair value will coincide. The requirements for using held-to-maturity are that the investing company has both the intent and ability to hold the debt instrument until it matures, and transfers to another accounting method are generally not permitted.

The available-for-sale method "disconnects" the balance sheet and the income statement, so the balance sheet reports up-to-date values for financial assets, but the unrealized holding gains and losses do not go through the income statement until realized in a transaction. This practice does provide an opportunity for management to affect the current period's income by selling selected securities. Alphabet, Inc., could sell the debt securities with accumulated unrealized holding gains of $213 million to increase pre-tax income or sell those with accumulated unrealized holding losses to decrease pre-tax income by $1,054 million. But limiting this method to debt securities reduces the potential magnitude of these effects, and the financial statement reader can look in the footnotes to find the realized holding gains and losses included in income.

MID-CHAPTER REVIEW 1

PART 1: AVAILABLE-FOR-SALE SECURITIES

Show the effects (amount and account) of the following four transactions involving investments in marketable securities classified as available-for-sale in the financial statement effects template, prepare the journal entries, and post the journal entries to the appropriate T-accounts. Assume that the investiing company's books are closed and financial reports issued semiannually on June 30 and December 31.

1. On January 1, 2019, purchased 500 Pincus Corporation bonds for $470,000 cash. The bonds have a face value of $1,000 each and an annual coupon rate of interest of 6% that is paid semi-annually on June 30 and December 31.
2. On June 30, 2019, receive interest of $15,000.
3. On June 30, 2019, the fair value of a Pincus Corporation bond is $920.
4. On July 31, 2019, all of the Pincus Corporation bonds are sold for $450,000 cash.

PART 2: TRADING SECURITIES

Using the same transaction information 1 through 4 from part 1, enter the effects (amount and account) relating to these transactions in the financial statement effects template, prepare the journal entries, and post the journal entries to the related T-accounts assuming that the investments are classified as trading securities.

The solution to this review problem can be found on pages 632–634.

4

LO4 Explain and analyze accounting for investments with significant influence.

INVESTMENTS WITH SIGNIFICANT INFLUENCE

Many companies make investments in other companies that yield them significant influence over those other companies. These intercorporate investments are usually made for strategic reasons including:

- **Prelude to acquisition.** Significant ownership can allow the investor company to gain a seat on the board of directors from which it can learn much about the investee company, its products, and its industry.
- **Strategic alliance.** One example of a strategic alliance is an investment in a company that provides critical inputs for the investor's production process or distribution of finished products. This relationship is closer than the usual supplier-buyer relationship, often because the investor company provides trade secrets or technical know-how of its production process.
- **Pursuit of research and development.** Many research activities in the pharmaceutical, software, and oil and gas industries are conducted jointly. The common motivation is to reduce risk or the amount of capital invested by the investor. The investor company's equity investment often carries an option to purchase additional shares or the entire company, which it can exercise if the research activities are fruitful.

A crucial feature in each of these investments is that the investor company has ownership sufficient to exert *significant influence* over the investee company. GAAP requires that such investments be accounted for using the *equity method.*

Significant influence is the ability of the investor to affect the financing or operating policies of the investee. Ownership levels of 20% to 50% of the outstanding common stock of the investee presume significant influence. Significant influence can also exist when ownership is less than 20%. Evidence of such influence can be that the investor company is able to gain a seat on the board of directors of the investee by virtue of its equity investment, or the investor controls technical know-how or patents that are used by the investee, or the investor is able to exert significant influence by virtue of legal contracts between it and the investee. There is growing pressure for determining significant influence by the facts and circumstances of the investment instead of the strict ownership percentage rule reflected in current corporate reporting.

Accounting for Investments with Significant Influence

Investments with significant influence must be accounted for using the **equity method**. The equity method of accounting for investments reports the investment on the balance sheet at an amount equal to the proportion of the investee's equity owned by the investor; hence the name equity method. (This accounting assumes acquisition at book value. Acquisition at an amount greater than book value is covered in Appendix 12A.) Contrary to passive investments that are reported at fair value, equity method investments increase (decrease) with increases (decreases) in the earned equity of the investee.

Equity method accounting is summarized as follows:

- Investments are initially recorded at their purchase cost.
- Dividends received are treated as a recovery of the investment and, thus, reduce the investment balance. (Unlike passive investments, dividends are *not* reported as income.)
- The investor reports income equal to its proportionate share of the reported income of the investee; the investment account is increased by that income or decreased by its share of any loss.
- The investment is *not* reported at fair value as is the case with most passive investments.

To illustrate the accounting for investments using the equity method, consider the following scenario: Assume that Alphabet, Inc., acquires a 30% interest in Mitel Networks, a company seeking to develop a new technology in a strategic alliance with Alphabet. At acquisition, Mitel reports $1,000 of stockholders' equity, the book values of its assets and liabilities equal their fair values, and Alphabet purchases its 30% stake for $300. At the first year-end, Mitel reports profits of $100 and pays $20 in cash dividends to its shareholders ($6 to Alphabet). Following are the financial statement effects for Alphabet (the investor company) for this investment using the equity method:

Transaction	Balance Sheet: Cash Asset	+ Noncash Assets	= Liabilities	+ Contrib. Capital	+ Earned Capital	Income Statement: Revenues	− Expenses	= Net Income
(1) Purchased 30% investment in Mitel for $300 cash.	−300 Cash	+300 Investment in Mitel						
(2) Mitel reports $100 income.		+30 Investment in Mitel			+30 Retained Earnings	+30 Investment Income		+30
(3) Mitel pays $20 cash dividends, $6 to Alphabet.	+6 Cash	−6 Investment in Mitel						
Ending balance of Alphabet's investment account.		324						

The related journal entries and T-accounts are:

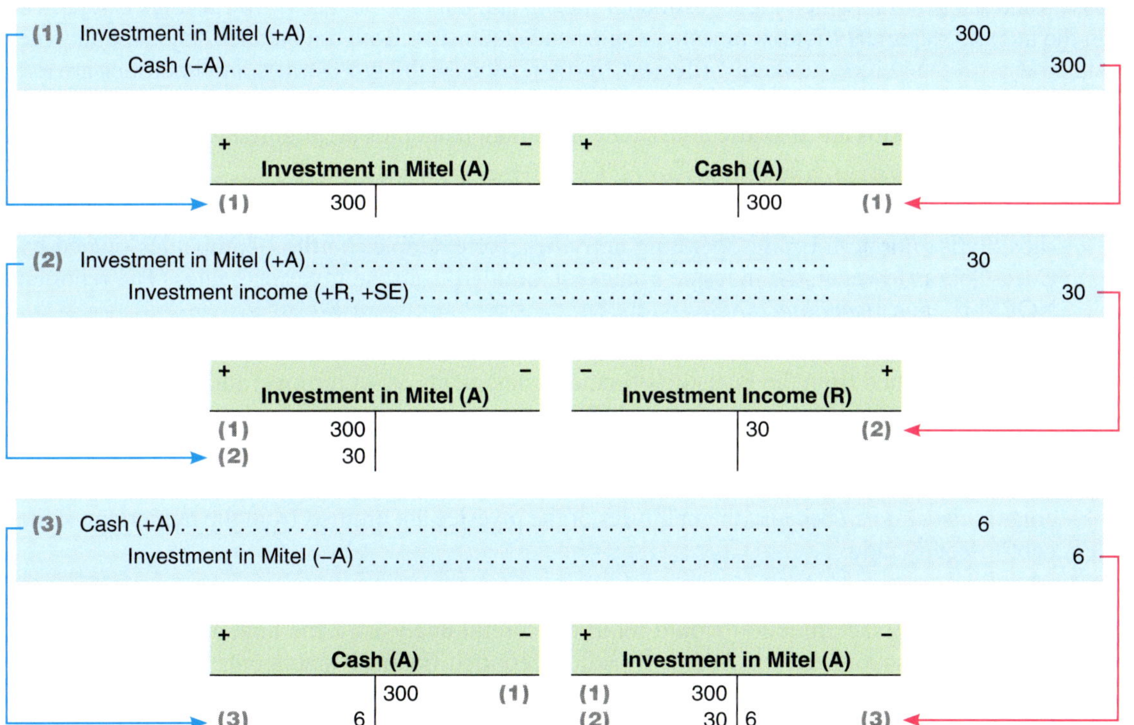

The investment is initially reported on Alphabet's balance sheet at its purchase price of $300, representing a 30% interest in Mitel's equity of $1,000. During the year, Mitel's equity increases to $1,080 ($1,000 plus $100 income and less $20 dividends). Likewise, Alphabet's investment increases by $30 to reflect its 30% share of Mitel's $100 income and decreases by $6 from Mitel's $20 of dividends (30% × $20). After these transactions, Alphabet's investment in Mitel is reported on Alphabet's balance sheet at 30% of $1,080, or $324. Appendix 12A covers the case in which Alphabet might have paid a premium over 30% of the fair value of Mitel's net assets.

FYI Investee dividend-paying ability can be (a) restricted by regulatory agencies or foreign governments, (b) prohibited under debt agreements for highly leveraged borrowers, and/or (c) influenced by directors that the investor does not control.

On the statement of cash flows, the original investment in Mitel would be seen as a $300 investing cash outflow. The $6 dividend received would be an operating cash inflow. However, the indirect method presentation would start with net income, which includes $30 in income from Mitel. Therefore, a negative $24 adjustment would be necessary (entitled something like "excess of equity income over dividends received") to arrive at the correct operating cash inflow.

Two final points about equity method accounting: First, just as the equity of a company is different from its fair value, so is the balance of the equity investment account different from its fair value. Indeed, there can be a substantial difference between the book value of an investment and its fair value. Second, if the investee company reports income, the investor company also reports income. Recognition of equity income by the investor, however, does not mean that it has received that income in cash. Cash is only received if the investee's directors declare a dividend payment.

RESEARCH INSIGHT

Equity Income and Stock Prices The equity method of accounting for investments does not recognize any dividends received from the investee or any fair value changes for the investee in the investor's income until the investment is sold. However, research has found a positive relation between investors' and investees' stock prices at the time of investees' earnings and dividend announcements. This relation suggests that the fair value includes information regarding investees' earnings and dividends when assessing the stock prices of investor companies. This finding implies the market looks beyond the book value of the investment account in determining stock prices of investor companies. The finding also reflects the fact that the earnings from the operations of subsidiaries are considered earnings of the parent corporation.

Equity Method Accounting and Effects on Ratios

Under equity method accounting, only the net equity owned is reported on the balance sheet (not the assets and liabilities to which the investment relates), and only the net equity in earnings is reported in the income statement (not the investee's sales and expenses). Both the balance sheet and income statements are, therefore, markedly affected. Further, because the gross assets and liabilities are left off the balance sheet, and because the sales and expenses are omitted from the income statement, several financial ratios are also affected. Some important examples are highlighted:

- **Net operating profit margin** (NOPM = NOPAT/Sales revenue). Most analysts include equity income (sales less expenses) in NOPAT because it relates to operating investments. (These subsidiaries are performing operating activities, for example, bottling companies owned by Coca-Cola.) However, the investee's sales are omitted from the investor's sales. The reported NOPM is, thus, *overstated*.
- **Asset turnover ratios** (Sales revenue/Average assets). Because the investee's sales and its assets are omitted from the investor's financial statements, asset turnover ratios such as inventory turnover, receivables turnover, and PPE turnover are affected. The direction of the effect is, however, *indeterminable*.
- **Financial leverage** (Debt-to-equity = Total liabilities/Total stockholders' equity). Financial leverage is *understated* because the liabilities of the investee are omitted from the numerator of the debt-to-equity ratio.

Profitability ratios like ROE and ROA are also affected by the use of equity method investments, though the exact direction would require a careful analysis of the noncontrolling interests described on page 606. Analysts frequently adjust reported financial statements for equity investments before conducting their analysis. One approach to adjusting the reported financial statements would be to consolidate the equity method investee with the investor company.

Financial Statement Disclosures

Coca-Cola Company reports its interest in three of its international affiliates using the equity method. It reported the following amounts in its 2017 and 2016 financial statements:

Coca-Cola—Financial Statement Effects of Equity Investments ($ millions)	2017	2016
Balance sheet:		
Equity method investments	$20,856	$16,260
Income statement:		
Equity income—net	$ 1,071	$ 835
Cash flow statement:		
Equity (income) loss, net of dividends	$ (628)	$ (449)

Coca-Cola's equity method investment of $20,856 million represents 23.7% of its total assets of $87,896 million. Its equity income of $1,071 million is 83.5% of its consolidated net income of $1,283 million. And, while Coca-Cola recognized $1,071 million in income from its equity investees, $628 million was not received in dividends, meaning that Coca-Cola received $443 million ($1,071 million – $628 million) in dividends.

Pertinent portions of note 6 from Coca-Cola's 2017 10-K report are presented below:

The Company's equity method investments include, but are not limited to, our ownership interests in CCEP, Monster, AC Bebidas, Coca-Cola FEMSA, S.A.B. de C.V. ("Coca-Cola FEMSA"), Coca-Cola HBC AG ("Coca-Cola Hellenic"), and Coca-Cola Bottlers Japan Inc., ("CCBJI"). As of December 31, 2017, we owned approximately 18 percent, 18 percent, 20 percent, 28 percent, 23 percent, and 17 percent, respectively, of these companies' outstanding shares. As of December 31, 2017, our investment in our equity method investees in the aggregate exceeded our proportionate share of the net assets of these equity method investees by $ 9,932 million. This difference is not amortized.

A summary of financial information for our equity method investees in the aggregate is as follows (in millions):

Year ended December 31,[1]	2017
Net operating revenues	$73,339
Cost of goods sold	42,867
Gross profit	30,472
Operating income	7,577
Consolidated net income	$ 4,545
Less: Net income attributable to noncontrolling interests	120
Net income attributable to common shareowners	$ 4,425
Equity income (loss)—net	$ 1,071

[1] The financial information represents the results of the equity method investees during the Company's period of ownership.

December 31,	2017
Current assets	$25,023
Noncurrent assets	66,578
Total assets	$91,601
Current liabilities	17,890
Noncurrent liabilities	29,986
Total liabilities	$47,876
Equity attributable to shareowners of investees	41,773
Equity attributable to noncontrolling interests	1,952
Total equity	43,725
Company equity investment	$20,856

One can see that there is a substantial amount of economic activity in these equity method investees relative to that of Coca-Cola. Coca-Cola reports 2017 revenues of $35.4 billion, which is less than half of the $73.3 billion in revenues reported by the equity method investees.

YOU MAKE THE CALL

You are the Chief Financial Officer A substantial percentage of your company's sales are made through a key downstream producer, who combines your product with other materials to make the product that is ultimately purchased by consumers. In the last two years, this downstream producer has been branching out into other products that limit the capacity that can be devoted to your product. As a result, the growth prospects for your company have been diminished. What potential courses of action can you consider? Explain. (Answer on page 615.)

MID-CHAPTER REVIEW 2

Show the effects (amount and account) relating to the following four transactions involving investments in marketable securities accounted for using the equity method in the financial statement effects template, prepare the journal entries, and post the journal entries to the related T-accounts.

1. Purchased 5,000 shares of Hribar common stock at $10 cash per share. These shares reflect 30% ownership of Hribar.
2. Received a $2 per share cash dividend on Hribar common stock.
3. Made an adjustment to reflect $100,000 income reported by Hribar.
4. Sold all 5,000 shares of Hribar common stock for $90,000.

The solution to this review problem can be found on pages 635–636.

5

LO5 Describe and analyze accounting for investments with control.

INVESTMENTS WITH CONTROL

If the investor company owns enough of the voting stock of the investee company such that it can exercise control over the investee, it must report **consolidated financial statements**. For example, in footnote 1 to its 2018 10-K describing its accounting policies, Alphabet, Inc., reports:

> **Basis of Consolidation**
> The consolidated financial statements of Alphabet include the accounts of Alphabet and entities consolidated under the variable interest and voting models. Noncontrolling interests are not presented separately as the amounts are not material. All intercompany balances and transactions have been eliminated.

This statement means that Alphabet, Inc.'s financial statements are an aggregation of those of the parent company and all its subsidiary companies to create the financial statements of the total economic entity. This process involves adding up the separate financial statements, while being careful to remove the effect of transactions between the separate entities.

Accounting for Investments with Control

Accounting for business combinations (acquisitions) can be thought of as requiring one additional step to equity method accounting. Under the equity method, the investment balance represents the proportion of the investee's equity owned by the investor, and the investor company income statement includes its proportionate share of the investee's income. Consolidation accounting (1) replaces the investment balance with the investee's assets and liabilities to which it relates, and (2) replaces the equity income reported by the investor with the investee's sales and expenses to which it relates. Specifically, the consolidated balance sheet includes the gross assets and liabilities of the investee company, and the income statement includes the gross sales and expenses of the investee.

To illustrate, consider the following scenario. Penman Company acquires all of the common stock of Nissim Company by exchanging $3,000 cash for all of Nissim's common stock. Nissim will continue to exist as a separate legal company—a subsidiary of Penman Company, the parent.

In this case, the $3,000 purchase price is equal to the book value of Nissim's stockholders' equity (contributed capital of $2,000 and retained earnings of $1,000), and we assume that the fair values of Nissim's assets and liabilities are the same as their book values. On Penman's balance sheet, the investment in Nissim Co. appears as a financial investment (GAAP only requires consolidation for financial statements issued to the public, not for the internal financial records of the separate companies). Penman records an initial balance in the investment account of $3,000, which equals the purchase price. The balance sheets for Penman and Nissim immediately after the acquisition, together with the required consolidating adjustments (or eliminations), and the consolidated balance sheet that the two companies report are shown in **Exhibit 12.5**.

EXHIBIT 12.5 Mechanics of Acquisition Accounting (Purchased at Book Value, where Book Values = Fair Values)

	Penman Company	Nissim Company	Consolidating Adjustments*	Consolidated
Current assets	$ 5,000	$1,000		$ 6,000
Investment in Nissim	3,000	0	$(3,000)	0
PPE, net	10,000	4,000		14,000
Total assets	$18,000	$5,000		$20,000
Liabilities	$ 5,000	$2,000		$ 7,000
Contributed capital	10,000	2,000	(2,000)	10,000
Retained earnings	3,000	1,000	(1,000)	3,000
Total liabilities and equity	$18,000	$5,000		$20,000

*The accounting equation remains in balance with these adjustments.

Penman controls the activities of Nissim, so GAAP requires consolidation of the two balance sheets. That is, Penman must report a balance sheet as if the two companies were one economic entity. For the most part, this process involves adding together the companies' resources and obligations. However, if one company has a claim on the other (e.g., a receivable) and the other company has an obligation to the first (e.g., a payable), the consolidation process must eliminate both the claim and the obligation. In the case of Penman Company and Nissim Company, the consolidated balances for current assets, PPE, and liabilities are the sum of those accounts on each balance sheet. Penman's asset investment in Nissim represents a claim on Nissim Company, and Nissim's stockholders' equity accounts represent an obligation that is held by Penman, and this intercompany claim/obligation must be eliminated to complete the consolidation. This elimination is accomplished by removing the financial investment of $3,000, and removing Nissim's equity to which that investment relates.

The consolidated balance sheet is shown in the far right column of **Exhibit 12.5**. It shows total assets of $20,000, total liabilities of $7,000, and stockholders' equity of $13,000. Consolidated equity equals that of the parent company—this is always the case when the parent owns 100% of the subsidiary's shares.

Comparing the first and last columns of **Exhibit 12.5** demonstrates the difference between the equity method and consolidation. In the left column, it appears that Penman spent $3,000 to acquire a financial asset. However, in the last column, it appears that Penman spent $3,000 to acquire a "bundle" of assets and liabilities consisting of $1,000 in cash plus $4,000 in PPE minus $2,000 in liabilities. The purchase of the financial asset was the means by which this bundle was acquired. The net value of this bundle is $3,000, so the net assets don't change. But the financial statement reader gets more information about what was acquired.

Penman Company's statement of cash flows would show an investing cash outflow for the acquisition of Nissim Company. However, the outflow is shown net of the cash received in the acquisition, which was $1,000. Therefore, the investing section would have a line item showing something like "Cash paid for acquisitions, net of cash acquired" with an outflow of $2,000.

In addition, the changes in Penman's operating assets and liabilities on this year's balance sheet from last year's balance sheet will no longer match the adjustments for operating assets and liabilities on the indirect method statement of cash flows from operations. For instance, the change in Penman's receivables will be changes due to its own operations (including Nissim after the acquisition) plus any receivables acquired in the Nissim acquisition.

The illustration above assumes that the purchase price of the acquisition equals book value and the fair values of the acquired company's assets and liabilities are equal to their book values. What changes, if any, occur when the purchase price and book value are different? To explore this case, consider an acquisition where purchase price exceeds book value (the typical scenario). This situation might arise, for example, if an investor company believes it is acquiring something of value that is not reported on the investee's balance sheet—such as tangible assets whose fair values have risen above book value, or unrecorded intangible assets like patents or corporate synergies. When an acquisition occurs, all assets and liabilties acquired (both tangible and intangible) must be recognized at their fair value on the consolidated balance sheet.

To illustrate an acquisition where purchase price exceeds book value, assume that Penman Company acquires 100% of Nissim Company for $4,000 instead of the $3,000 purchase price we used in the previous illustration. Also assume that in determining its purchase price, Penman feels that the additional $1,000 ($4,000 vs. $3,000) is justified because (1) Nissim's PPE is worth $300 more than its book value, and (2) Penman expects to realize $700 in additional value from corporate synergies.

The $4,000 investment account reflects two components: the book value acquired of $3,000 (as before) and an additional $1,000 of newly acquired assets. The post-acquisition balance sheets of the two companies, together with the consolidating adjustments and the consolidated balance sheet, are shown in **Exhibit 12.6**.

EXHIBIT 12.6 Mechanics of Acquisition Accounting (Purchased above Book Value)

	Penman Company	Nissim Company	Consolidating Adjustments	Consolidated
Current assets	$ 4,000	$1,000		$ 5,000
Investment in Nissim	4,000	0	$(4,000)	0
PPE, net	10,000	4,000	300	14,300
Goodwill			700	700
Total assets	$18,000	$5,000		$20,000
Liabilities	$ 5,000	$2,000		$ 7,000
Contributed capital	10,000	2,000	(2,000)	10,000
Retained earnings	3,000	1,000	(1,000)	3,000
Total liabilities and equity	$18,000	$5,000		$20,000

The consolidated balances for current assets, PPE, and liabilities are the sum of those accounts on each company's balance sheet. The investment account, however, includes newly acquired assets that must be reported on the consolidated balance sheet. The consolidation process in this case has two steps. First, the $3,000 equity of Nissim Company is eliminated against the investment account as before. Then, the remaining $1,000 of the investment account is eliminated through the adjustments for revised asset and liability balances on the consolidated balance sheet ($300 of PPE and $700 of goodwill not reported on Nissim's balance sheet). Thus, the consolidated balance sheet reflects the book value of Penman and the *fair value* (book value plus the excess of Nissim's fair value over book value) for Nissim Company at the acquisition date.

Reporting of Acquired Assets and Liabilities

Acquisitions are often made at a purchase price in excess of the book value of the acquired company's equity. The excess purchase price must be allocated to all of the assets and liabilities acquired, including those that do not currently appear on the balance sheet of the acquired company. This allocation can be done in three steps:

Step 1: Adjust the book value of all tangible assets acquired and all liabilities assumed to fair value. This adjustment addresses the issue of misvalued assets and liabilities on the acquired firm's balance sheet.

Step 2: Assign a fair value to any identifiable intangible assets. Recall from Chapter 8 that intangible assets are only reported on the balance sheet if they are purchased; internally created intangible assets (other than software) are not capitalized. This step requires the acquiring firm to assign a value to the acquired company's intangible assets, even if those assets are not reported on the acquired firm's balance sheet.

Step 3: Assign the residual amount to goodwill. Goodwill is the excess of the acquisition price over the fair value of identifiable net assets acquired. That is, whatever value cannot be assigned to identifiable tangible and intangible assets is considered goodwill.[1]

[1] What happens if goodwill is negative? Such a "bargain purchase" is uncommon, because it implies that the "whole" of the acquired company is worth less than the sum of its parts. Therefore, when an acquirer believes that it has made a bargain purchase, it must carefully check its valuation of all the components of the goodwill calculation. If that review confirms that the acquirer has made a bargain purchase, then it recognizes a gain in its income from continuing operations.

The acquiring company is required to disclose relevant information about the allocation of the purchase price in its footnotes.

For example, consider Alphabet's reported allocation of its total $1.1 billion purchase price in January 2018 for a business from HTC Corporation as reported in Note 7 to its 2018 10-K report:

Note 7. Acquisitions
2018 Acquisitions
HTC Corporation (HTC)
In January 2018, we completed the acquisition of a team of engineers and a non-exclusive license of intellectual property from HTC for $1.1 billion in cash. In aggregate, $10 million was cash acquired, $165 million was attributed to intangible assets, $934 million was attributed to goodwill, and $9 million was attributed to net liabilities assumed. Goodwill, which was included in the Google segment, is not deductible for tax purposes. We expect this transaction to accelerate Google's ongoing hardware efforts. The transaction was accounted for as a business combination.

Other Acquisitions
During the year ended December 31, 2018, we completed other acquisitions and purchases of intangible assets for total consideration of approximately $573 million. In aggregate, $10 million was cash acquired, $295 million was attributed to intangible assets, $293 million was attributed to goodwill, and $25 million was attributed to net liabilities assumed. These acquisitions generally enhance the breadth and depth of our offerings and expand our expertise in engineering and other functional areas. The amount of goodwill expected to be deductible for tax purposes is approximately $81 million. . . .

For all intangible assets acquired and purchased during the year ended December 31, 2018, patents and developed technology have a weighted-average useful life of 3.7 years, customer relationships have a weighted average useful life of 2.3 years, and trade names and other have a weighted-average useful life of 3.7 years.

Of the $1,673 billion paid for acquisitions, Alphabet assigned $1,227 million to goodwill. The remaining $446 million includes $20 million in cash plus $460 million in intangible assets, less $34 million in liabilities. The $460 million in intangible assets and the $34 million in liabilities were recorded at fair value at the time of the acquisition.

Alphabet reports its aggregated goodwill separately on its balance sheet, but combines its other intangible assets in its balance sheet under the title "Intangible assets, net." Goodwill can only be recognized as an asset in an acquisition and only then in the amount by which the purchase price exceeds the fair value of the net assets acquired, including all identifiable intangible assets.

For the acquisitions it made in 2018, Alphabet, Inc., estimates customer relationships have a weighted average useful life of 2.3 years. Patents and developed technology have a weighted average useful life of 3.7 years. Tradenames and other intangibles have a weighted average useful life of 3.7 years. The majority of these assets are not deductible for tax purposes. These estimated lives determine the annual amortization expense associated with these assets on the firm's financial books. Goodwill is not amortized under GAAP although it is subject to impairment write-down. The effect of this accounting treatment is to relieve the income statement of the annual amortization expense. The Securities and Exchange Commission is sufficiently concerned with the impact on the income statement that it scrutinizes acquisition accounting for excessive goodwill capitalization.

Reporting of Goodwill GAAP requires companies to test goodwill annually for impairment just like any other asset. To begin, the investor company can judge qualitatively—based on economic events and conditions—whether it is more likely than not that the fair value of the subsidiary is less than its book value. If that is not the case (i.e., if fair value exceeds book value), then no further testing is needed.

If it is more likely than not that the subsidiary's fair value is less than its book value, then the fair value of that subsidiary is determined and compared with the book value of the parent company's investment account.[2] If the fair value is greater than the investment balance, the investment's goodwill is deemed not to be impaired. If the subsidiary's book value exceeds its fair value, then

[2] The fair value of the subsidiary company can be determined using market comparables or another valuation method (such as the discounted cash flow model, residual operating income model, or P/E multiples).

its goodwill must be written down by the amount of the difference, resulting in an impairment loss that is reported in the consolidated income statement.

To illustrate the impairment computation, assume that a subsidiary's current book value is reported at $1 million on the parent company's balance sheet, but the subsidiary is found to have a current fair value of $900,000. Under these conditions, goodwill is impaired by $100,000, which is computed as follows.

Fair value of subsidiary	$ 900,000
Minus book value of net assets	(1,000,000)
Impairment loss	$ (100,000)

The financial statement effects and related journal entry and T-accounts are:

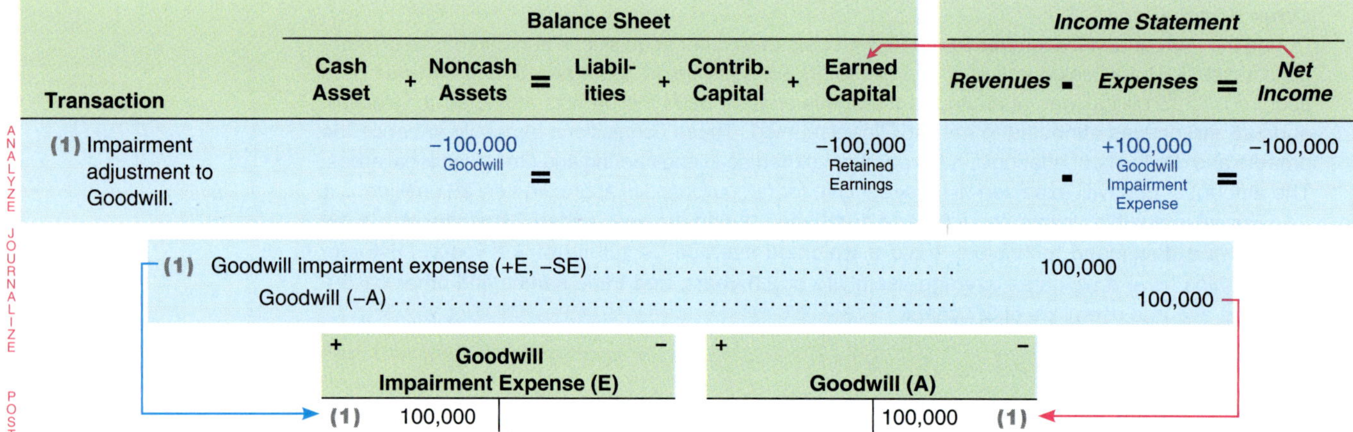

Transaction	Cash Asset	+ Noncash Assets	= Liabil-ities	+ Contrib. Capital	+ Earned Capital	Revenues	− Expenses	= Net Income
	Balance Sheet					**Income Statement**		
ANALYZE (1) Impairment adjustment to Goodwill.		−100,000 Goodwill			−100,000 Retained Earnings		+100,000 Goodwill Impairment Expense	−100,000

JOURNALIZE

(1) Goodwill impairment expense (+E, −SE) 100,000
Goodwill (−A) 100,000

POST

+ Goodwill Impairment Expense (E) −	
(1) 100,000	

+ Goodwill (A) −	
	100,000 (1)

This analysis of investee company implies that goodwill must be written down by $100,000. The impairment loss is reported as a separate line item in the consolidated income statement. The related footnote disclosure describes the reasons for the write-down.

General Electric reports the following goodwill impairment in excerpts from its third quarter 10-Q for 2018:

During the third quarter of 2018, we recognized a non-cash pre-tax goodwill impairment charge of $22.0 billion related to our Power Generation and Grid Solutions businesses within our Power segment. See Note 8 to the consolidated financial statements for further information . . .

NOTE 8. GOODWILL AND OTHER INTANGIBLE ASSETS
GOODWILL
CHANGES IN GOODWILL BALANCES

(In millions)	Balance at January 1, 2018	Acquisitions	Impairments	Dispositions, Currency Exchange and Other	Balance at September 30, 2018
Power	$25,269	$—	$(21,147)	$(2,255)	$ 1,868
Renewable Energy	4,093	—	—	13	4,106
Aviation	10,008	—	—	(38)	9,970
Oil & Gas	23,943	16	—	688	24,647
Healthcare	17,306	—	—	(40)	17,266
Transportation	902	—	—	(17)	885
Lighting	—	—	—	—	—
Capital	984	—	—	—	984
Corporate	1,463	—	(827)	15	651
Total	$83,968	$16	$(21,973)*	$(1,634)	$60,377

* Difference due to rounding.

continued

continued from previous page

Goodwill balances decreased primarily as a result of impairments (discussed below), the reclassification of the Distributed Power business within our Power segment to Assets of businesses held for sale and currency effects of a stronger U.S. dollar, partially offset by adjustments to the allocation of purchase price associated with our acquisitions of Baker Hughes and LM Wind Power . . .

Based on the results of our step one testing, the fair values of each of our reporting units exceeded their carrying values except for the Power Generation and Grid Solutions reporting units, within our Power segment. The majority of the goodwill in our Power segment was recognized as a result of the Alstom acquisition at which time approximately $15,800 million of goodwill was attributed to our Power Generation and Grid Solutions reporting units. As previously disclosed, the Power market as well as its operating environment continues to be challenging . . .

General Electric went on to describe additional analysis of its goodwill impairments. The FASB has simplified the steps that companies must use to determine these amounts, and General Electric will use that simpler method in future years. The company's goodwill impairment was significant for its financial reports. The $22.0 billion goodwill impairment increased the company's costs and expenses by 72% for the quarter, producing a loss from continuing operations of $22.9 billion for the quarter.

Reported goodwill across companies differs widely in total and as a percentage of company assets as the following fiscal 2017 and 2018 figures indicate ($ millions).

	Total Assets	Reported Goodwill	Goodwill Percentage
Alphabet, Inc.	$232,792	$17,888	7.7%
Facebook, Inc.	97,334	18,301	18.8%
Apple, Inc.	365,725	—	0.0%
Adobe Inc.	18,769	10,581	56.4%
PepsiCo, Inc.	79,804	14,744	18.5%
The Coca-Cola Company	87,896	9,401	10.7%
The Procter & Gamble Company	118,310	45,175	38.2%
Colgate-Palmolive Company	12,676	2,218	17.5%
Valeant Pharmaceuticals International, Inc.	37,497	15,593	41.6%
Bristol Myers Squibb Co.	33,551	6,863	20.5%

Reported goodwill is an indicator of whether a company has developed its business opportunities or purchased them and, in the same fashion, reported intangible assets are an indicator of whether a company has acquired its intellectual property in-house or by purchasing it. The purchase of intellectual properties and business opportunities allows a company to react quickly to conditions, but it is often a more expensive way to achieve growth.

BUSINESS INSIGHT

In competitive bidding situations, the winning bidder is likely to be the one who most overvalued the item, a phenomenon known as the "winner's curse." Therefore, acquisition goodwill is viewed with some skepticism by financial analysts. Does the goodwill represent synergies like future cost savings or business opportunities that are available only to the combined companies? Or, does it represent an overpayment?

A *Financial Times* article described multi-billion dollar goodwill impairment charges by General Electric and ascribes a significant portion of these charges to a 2015 acquisition of Alstom in which the $10.1 billion purchase price resulted in $17.3 billion in goodwill. The article said that "the company was so keen to get the deal done that it paid too much."

When companies record a goodwill impairment charge, they often emphasize that the impairment was a "non-cash charge," implying that it is therefore less important. That statement is true as far as the current period is concerned, but acquisitions involve cash or some other item of value. Goodwill impairment requires no current cash outflows, but it does reflect on the wisdom of past cash outflows.

Source: Ed Crooks, "GE's $23 Billion Writedown Is a Case of Goodwill Gone Bad," *Financial Times*, October 3, 2018.

Noncontrolling Interest

Noncontrolling interest represents the equity of shareholders who own a minority of the shares of one or more of the subsidiaries in a consolidated entity. When a company acquires a controlling interest in another company, it must consolidate that subsidiary when preparing its financial statements by reporting all of the subsidiary's assets and liabilities in the consolidated balance sheet and all of the subsidiary's revenues and expenses in the consolidated income statement. This is true even when the controlling parent company acquires less than 100% of the subsidiary. When less than 100% of the subsidiary's shares are acquired, there are two groups of shareholders: the parent company's shareholders and the noncontrolling shareholders who own a minority of the subsidiary's shares. These noncontrolling shareholders have a claim on the net assets and the earnings of the subsidiary company and this claim is considered part of the consolidated company's shareholders' equity.

To illustrate the reporting of noncontrolling interest, assume that Penman Company acquires 80% of Nissim Company for $2,400 (80% of $3,000). Because Penman must consolidate 100% of the assets and liabilities of Nissim, Penman's equity must increase to maintain the accounting equation. A new equity account titled noncontrolling interests is added to Penman's stockholders' equity. The consolidation worksheet is presented in **Exhibit 12.7**.

EXHIBIT 12.7 Mechanics of Consolidation Accounting (Less than 100% of Subsidiary Shares Purchased with Fair Values = Book Values)

	Penman Company	Nissim Company	Consolidating Adjustments	Consolidated
Current assets	$ 5,600	$1,000		$ 6,600
Investment in Nissim	2,400	0	$(2,400)	0
PPE, net	10,000	4,000		14,000
Total assets	$18,000	$5,000		$20,600
Liabilities	$ 5,000	$2,000		$ 7,000
Contributed capital	10,000	2,000	(2,000)	10,000
Retained earnings	3,000	1,000	(1,000)	3,000
Penman shareholders' equity	13,000			13,000
Noncontrolling interests			600	600
Total equity	13,000			13,600
Total liabilities and equity	$18,000	$5,000		$20,600

The contributed capital of the consolidated entity (common stock, additional paid-in capital, treasury stock, etc.) refers to the parent company's shareholders' equity (in this example, Penman Company). The net assets owned by the noncontrolling shareholders are represented in one account, labeled noncontrolling interests, which is considered to be part of shareholders' equity of the consolidated company. Each period, the noncontrolling interests equity account is increased by the noncontrolling shareholders' share of the subsidiary's net income, and decreased by any dividends paid to those shareholders.

The consolidated income statement lists total consolidated revenues and expenses and consolidated net income. After net income is computed, the portion of net income that is attributed to noncontrolling interests is subtracted. If the noncontrolling shareholders own 20% of the subsidiary's shares, then 20% of the earnings of the subsidiary are subtracted from the consolidated entity's income statement. (This is not 20% of the consolidated company's earnings, only 20% of the subsidiary's earnings.)

The stockholders' equity section of The Walt Disney Company's 2018 balance sheet is shown as an illustration of the presentation of noncontrolling interests in the balance sheet:

The Walt Disney Company Consolidated Balance Sheet (Stockholders' equity section only) ($ millions)	September 29, 2018
Equity	
Preferred stock	—
Common stock, $0.01 par value, authorized—4.6 billion shares, issued—2.9 billion shares	$ 36,779
Retained earnings	82,679
Accumulated other comprehensive income	(3,097)
Treasury stock, at cost, 1.4 billion shares	(67,588)
Total Disney shareholders' equity	48,773
Noncontrolling interests	4,059
Total equity	$ 52,832

Total Disney Company's shareholders' equity is listed at $48,773 million. This is the equity claim of those investors who own shares in Disney. Next, the $4,059 million of noncontrolling interests is listed. This amount represents the share of The Walt Disney Company subsidiaries' net assets that is owned by noncontrolling shareholders (e.g., Hong Kong Disneyland Resort and Shanghai Disney Resort). The final line lists the total equity, which is the sum of Disney's stockholders' equity and the noncontrolling interests.

The Walt Disney Company's income statement presents noncontrolling interests as follows:

The Walt Disney Company Consolidated Income Statement (excerpts) ($ millions)	Year ended September 29, 2018
Income before income taxes	$14,729
Income taxes	(1,663)
Net income	13,066
Less: Net income attributable to noncontrolling interests	(468)
Net income attributable to The Walt Disney Company (Disney)	$12,598

The Walt Disney Company presents net income of $13,066 million. This is income for the consolidated entity, including the share of income for Disney's shareholders as well as that portion that is for the noncontrolling interests. Next, the income attributable to noncontrolling interests ($468 million) is subtracted, leaving net income attributable to Disney's shareholders ($12,598 million).

A GLOBAL PERSPECTIVE

U.S. GAAP and IFRS are very similar in their treatment of the accounting for investments as covered in this chapter. IFRS defines the term fair value in the same way and requires disclosure of fair values according to their determination as Level 1, Level 2, or Level 3. Passive investments are classified as being for trading purposes or as being held-to-maturity, with all other passive investments accounted as available-for-sale. Unlike GAAP, IFRS allows equity investments to be accounted for under available-for-sale. Under this option, however, the unrealized holding gains and losses remain in AOCI and are never recognized in income.

GAAP uses the term "equity" or "affiliate" to describe an investment involving significant influence (usually between 20% and 50%). IFRS uses the term "associate" to describe such an investment, with the same 20% threshold. The investment balance is equal to the investor's cost plus the proportionate share of changes in the investee's net assets since the date of investment. If the investor's cost exceeds the proportionate book value, the excess is attributed to individual assets (including goodwill) and liabilities and subsequent earnings will include the appropriate amortizations of those value adjustments.

The process of accounting for an acquisition and issuing subsequent consolidated financial statements is very similar to that described in the previous section.

Limitations of Consolidation Reporting Consolidation of financial statements is meant to present a financial picture of the entire set of companies under control of the parent. Because investors typically purchase stock in the parent company and not in the subsidiaries, the view is more relevant than would be one of the parent company's own balance sheet with subsidiaries reported as equity investments. Still, we must be aware of certain limitations that the consolidation process entails:

1. Consolidated income does not imply that cash is received by the parent company and is available for subsidiaries. The parent can only receive cash via dividend payments, and dividend payments may trigger tax obligations. It is readily possible, therefore, for an individual subsidiary to experience cash flow problems even though the consolidated group has strong cash flows. Likewise, debts of a subsidiary are not obligations of the consolidated group. Thus, even if the consolidated balance sheet is strong, creditors of a failing subsidiary are often unable to sue the parent or other subsidiaries to recoup losses.
2. Consolidated balance sheets and income statements are a mix of the subsidiaries, often from different industries. Comparisons across companies, even if in similar industries, are often complicated by the different mix of subsidiary companies. Companies are required to report some financial results for their business segments. For instance, **General Electric** reports revenues, operating profits and assets for each of its eight operating segments—Power, Renewable Energy, Oil & Gas, Aviation, Healthcare, Transportation, Lighting, and GE Capital.
3. Segment disclosures on individual subsidiaries are affected by intercorporate transfer-pricing policies that can artificially inflate the profitability of one segment at the expense of another. Companies also have considerable discretion in the allocation of corporate overhead to subsidiaries, which can markedly affect segment and subsidiary profitability.

FINANCIAL STATEMENT ANALYSIS

This section introduces no new ratios, but the topics covered in Chapter 12 do have implications for ratios covered in other chapters. For instance, gains and losses on available-for-sale securities are not recognized in income until those securities are sold. Therefore, management can increase net income by selling securities on which it has gains or decrease net income by selling securities on which it has losses. As a result, management may have a means to smooth the variations in income over time, using gains and losses from previous periods that have nothing to do with current performance. As careful financial statement users, we can read the footnotes to find the realized gains and losses included in income for the period.

Financial ratio comparisons are also affected by the percentage ownership of affiliated companies. For instance, suppose Naughton Group has 50% ownership in the company that distributes its products. Chapman Enterprises, a competitor of Naughton, owns 55% of the shares of the company that distributes its products. While the difference between 50% and 55% ownership probably has little economic significance, the accounting reports for Naughton and Chapman will look very different. Naughton's income statement will report only its own revenues and expenses, while Chapman's income statement will report its own revenues and expenses *and* the revenues and expenses of the distribution company (less any intercompany adjustments). Naughton's balance sheet will report its own assets, including its 50% equity in the distributor, while Chapman's balance sheet will report its own assets and liabilities *plus* those of the distribution company. Financial statement readers should interpret comparisons of ratios like PPE Turnover in light of these effects.

A similar "quantum" change in accounting occurs at 20% ownership. There may appear to be little economic difference between owning 19% of a company's shares and owning 20% of those shares. But there is a significant difference in the accounting for those two alternatives, and this difference sometimes affects the choice between a 19% investment and a 20% investment. If the investee is a start-up earning losses, a 20% investment would require the investor to recognize 20% of those losses in its own income. A 19% investment would not recognize any share of the losses, though the fair value fluctuations of the investment will be recognized in income as they occur.

Finally, acquisitions disrupt the usual relationships between income statements and between the income statement and balance sheet items. When one company acquires another, the acquirer consolidates the acquired company as of the date that the deal closes. At that point, it includes the acquired company's assets and liabilities on the consolidated balance sheet, and it begins to report the acquired company's revenues and expenses from that time forward. So, if Hoskin Corp. acquires 100% of Lynch, Inc., on December 31, 2019, how will the inventory turnover ratio be affected? The 2019 cost of goods sold for Hoskin will reflect a year of Hoskin's COGS plus one day of Lynch's COGS. The beginning-of-year inventory will be 100% of Hoskin's inventory at that time, but the end-of-year inventory will be 100% of Hoskin's inventory plus 100% of Lynch's inventory. The inventory turnover ratio is likely to decrease significantly, but that decrease is due to the acquisition, not necessarily a decline in Hoskin's operating performance.

The acquisition's effect on reported sales growth should be carefully examined as well. Suppose that Hoskin Corp and Lynch, Inc., both have a December 31 fiscal year and that Hoskin acquired Lynch on June 30, 2018—halfway through the fiscal year for both companies. When looking at Hoskin's reported revenue and its growth, one should recognize that the 2017 revenues will be Hoskin's alone, and the 2018 revenues will reflect Hoskin's sales plus half a year of Lynch's sales. Finally, the 2019 revenues will reflect a full year of sales for the combined firms. A careful reader of the financial statements should use the footnotes to try to separate out the effects of the acquisition from the ongoing, organic performance of the combined company.

CHAPTER-END REVIEW

On January 1 of the current year, Bradshaw Company purchased all of the common shares of Dukes Company for $600,000 cash—this is $200,000 in excess of Dukes' book value of its equity. The balance sheets of the two firms immediately after the acquisition follow:

	Bradshaw (Parent)	Dukes (Subsidiary)	Consolidating Adjustments	Consolidated
Current assets	$1,000,000	$100,000		
Investment in Dukes	600,000	—		
PPE, net	3,000,000	400,000		
Goodwill	—	—		
Total assets	$4,600,000	$500,000		
Liabilities	$1,000,000	$100,000		
Contributed capital	2,000,000	200,000		
Retained earnings	1,600,000	200,000		
Total liabilities and equity	$4,600,000	$500,000		

During purchase negotiations, Dukes' PPE was appraised at $500,000, and all of Dukes' remaining assets and liabilities were appraised at values approximating their book values. Also, Bradshaw concluded that payment of an additional $100,000 was warranted because of anticipated corporate synergies. Show the impact of the transaction in the financial statement effects template, prepare the appropriate journal entry, post the journal entry to the related T-accounts, and prepare the consolidated balance sheet at acquisition.

The solution to this review problem can be found on pages 636–637.

APPENDIX 12A: Equity Method Mechanics

LO6 Illustrate and analyze accounting mechanics for equity method investments.

The appendix provides a comprehensive example of accounting for an equity method investment. Assume that Petroni Company acquires a 30% interest in the outstanding voting shares of Wahlen Company on January 1, 2019, for $234,000 in cash. On that date, Wahlen's book value of equity is $560,000. Petroni agrees to pay $234,000 for a company with a book value of equity equivalent to $168,000 ($560,000 × 30%) because it feels that (1) Wahlen's balance sheet is undervalued by $140,000 (Petroni estimates PPE is undervalued by $50,000 and that Wahlen has unrecorded patents valued at $90,000) and (2) the investment is expected to yield intangible benefits valued at $24,000. (The $140,000 by which the balance sheet is undervalued translates into an investment equivalent of $42,000 [$140,000 × 30%]. This, plus the intangible benefits valued at $24,000, comprises the $66,000 difference between the purchase price [$234,000] and the book value equivalent [$168,000].)

The effect of the investment on Petroni's books is to reduce cash by $234,000 and to report the investment in Wahlen for $234,000. The investment is reported at its fair value at acquisition, just like all other asset acquisitions, and it is reported as a noncurrent asset because the expected holding period of equity method investments is in excess of one year. Subsequent to this purchase there are three main aspects of equity method accounting:

1. Dividends received from the investee are treated as a return *of* the investment rather than a return *on* the investment (investor company records an increase in cash received and a decrease in the investment account).
2. When the investee company reports net income for a period, the investor company reports its proportionate ownership of that income. This amount is usually reported in the investment income section of its income statement. Thus, both income and the investment account increase from equity method income. If the investee company reports a net *loss* for the period, income of the investor company is reduced as well as its investment account by its proportionate share.
3. The investment balance is not marked-to-fair value (market) as with passive investments. Instead, it is recorded at its historical cost and is increased (decreased) by the investor company's proportionate share of investee income (loss) and decreased by any cash dividends received. Unrecognized gains (losses) can, therefore, occur if the fair value of the investment differs from this adjusted cost. (If a decline in value is deemed "other than temporary," then the investment would be written down.)

To illustrate these mechanics, let's return to our illustration and assume that subsequent to acquisition, Wahlen reports net income of $50,000 and pays $10,000 cash dividends. Petroni would reflect these events in the FSET as follows:

	Balance Sheet										Income Statement				
Transaction	Cash Asset	+	Noncash Assets	=	Liabil-ities	+	Contrib. Capital	+	Earned Capital		*Revenues*	−	*Expenses*	=	*Net Income*
(1) Purchase 30% of Wahlen Co. stock.	−234,000 Cash		+234,000 Investment in Wahlen	=								−		=	
(2) Recognize 30% of Wahlen net income.			+15,000 Investment in Wahlen						+15,000 Retained Earnings		+15,000 Investment Income				+15,000
(3) Receive 30% of Wahlen dividends.	+3,000 Cash		−3,000 Investment in Wahlen												

After these entries, the investment balance is $246,000. Petroni has an investing cash outflow of $234,000 and an operating cash inflow of $3,000. Retained earnings increase by $15,000 from recognizing the 30% share of Wahlen's net income.

However, Petroni must also account for the differential values that accounted for the purchase premium. If Wahlen's PPE is undervalued by $50,000 and has an expected remaining life of twenty years, Petroni must depreciate $750 (= 30%*$50,000/20 years) in value for each of the next twenty years. And, if the unrecorded patents have an expected useful life of nine years, Petroni must amortize $3,000 (= 30%*$90,000/9 years) of the investment's value for each of the coming nine years. These amortizations are deducted from the investment income recognized by Petroni. The entries are the following:

Transaction	Cash Asset	+	Noncash Assets	=	Liabil-ities	+	Contrib. Capital	+	Earned Capital		*Revenues*	−	*Expenses*	=	*Net Income*
(4) Depreciate additional PPE value.			−750 Investment in Wahlen	=					−750 Retained Earnings		−750 Investment Income	−		=	−750
(5) Amortize additional patent assets.			−3,000 Investment in Wahlen						−3,000 Retained Earnings		−3,000 Investment Income				−3,000

A part of the premium paid by Petroni is attributed to items that have definite lives (PPE and patents), and we must account for those amounts in judging the investment's performance. In this case, Petroni records income of $11,250 on its $234,000 investment – $15,000 for its share of Wahlen's income, minus the $3,750 amortization of the premiium paid for PPE and patents. The Investment in Wahlen asset has a value of $242,250 ($234,000 + 15,000 – 3,000 – 750 – 3,000) after all entries.

The amount attributed to goodwill is tested for impairment annually, but it is not subject to periodic amortization.

APPENDIX 12B: Consolidation Accounting Mechanics

LO7 Apply consolidation accounting mechanics.

This appendix is a continuation of the example we introduced in Appendix 12A, extended to the consolidation of a parent company and one wholly owned subsidiary. Assume that Petroni Company acquires 100% (rather than 30% as in Appendix 12A) of the outstanding voting shares of Wahlen Company on January 1, 2019. To obtain these shares, Petroni pays $420,000 cash and issues 20,000 shares of its $10 par value common stock. On this date, Petroni's stock has a fair value of $18 per share, and Wahlen's book value of equity is $560,000. Petroni is willing to pay $780,000 ($420,000 plus 20,000 shares at $18 per share) for this company with a book value of equity of $560,000 because it believes Wahlen's balance sheet is understated by $140,000 (its PPE is undervalued by $50,000 and it has unrecorded patents valued at $90,000). The remaining $80,000 of the purchase price excess over book value is ascribed to corporate synergies and other unidentifiable intangible assets (goodwill). Thus, the purchase price consists of the following three components:

Investment ($780,000)	Book value of Wahlen ($560,000)
	Excess fair value over book ($140,000)
	Goodwill ($80,000)

The investment in Wahlen appears as a financial asset on Petroni's books. This means that at acquisition, Petroni's assets increase by $360,000 (cash decreases by $420,000 and the investments account increases by $780,000) and its equity (contributed capital) increases by the same amount.

The balance sheets of Petroni and Wahlen at acquisition follow, including the adjustments that occur in the consolidation process and the ultimate consolidated balance sheet.

Accounts	Petroni Company	Wahlen Company	Consolidation Adjustments*		Consolidated Balance Sheet
			Entry S	Entry A	
Cash	$ 168,000	$ 80,000			$ 248,000
Receivables, net	320,000	180,000			500,000
Inventory	440,000	260,000			700,000
Investment in Wahlen	780,000	0	$(560,000)	$(220,000)	0
Land	200,000	120,000			320,000
PPE, net	1,040,000	320,000		50,000	1,410,000
Patents	0	0		90,000	90,000
Goodwill	0	0		80,000	80,000
Totals	$2,948,000	$960,000			$3,348,000
Accounts payable	$ 320,000	$ 60,000			$ 380,000
Long-term liabilities	760,000	340,000			1,100,000
Contributed capital	1,148,000	80,000	(80,000)		1,148,000
Retained earnings	720,000	480,000	(480,000)		720,000
Totals	$2,948,000	$960,000			$3,348,000

*Entry S refers to elimination of subsidiary stockholders' equity, and Entry A refers to adjustment of assets and liabilities acquired.

The initial balance of the investment account at acquisition ($780,000) reflects the $700,000 fair value of Wahlen's net tangible assets and patents ($560,000 book value + $140,000 undervaluation of assets) plus the goodwill ($80,000) acquired. Goodwill is the excess of the purchase price over the fair value of the net assets acquired. It does not appear on Petroni's balance sheet as an explicit asset at this point. It is, however, included in the investment balance and will emerge as a separate asset during consolidation.

The process of completing the initial consolidated balance sheet involves eliminating Petroni's investment account and replacing it with the assets and liabilities of Wahlen Company to which it relates. Recall the investment account consists of three items: the book value of Wahlen ($560,000), the excess of net asset fair value over book value ($140,000), and goodwill ($80,000). The consolidation process eliminates each item as follows:

Entry S: Elimination of Wahlen's book value of equity: Investment account is reduced by the $560,000 book value of Wahlen, and each of the components of Wahlen's equity ($80,000 common stock and $480,000 retained earnings) is eliminated.

7

Entry A: Elimination of the excess of purchase price over book value: Investment account is reduced by $220,000 to zero. The remaining adjustments increase assets (A) by the additional purchase price paid. PPE is written up by $50,000, and a $90,000 patent asset and an $80,000 goodwill asset are reported.

Stepping back from the consolidation process, we can see its effects by comparing the Petroni Company (parent) balance sheet to the consolidated balance sheet. The Petroni Company balance sheet shows a financial asset valued at $780,000. Consolidation gives us a different perspective. Rather than viewing this as a financial investment, consolidation views the financial investment as the *means* by which Petroni Company acquired a bundle of assets and liabilities. That is, the financial asset of $780,000 has been replaced by Cash ($80,000), Receivables ($180,000), Inventory ($260,000), Land ($120,000), PPE – net ($370,000), Patent ($90,000), Goodwill ($80,000), Payables ($60,000) and Long-term liabilities ($340,000). This bundle has a net value equal to the $780,000, but it provides much more detail about the transaction in which Petroni engaged.

The one part of the balance sheet that is not changed by the consolidation is the shareholders' equity section. The consolidated shareholders' equity accounts are the same as the parent company shareholders' equity accounts when the parent owns 100% of the subsidiary.

Consolidation is similar in successive periods. To the extent that the excess purchase price has been assigned to depreciable assets, or identifiable intangible assets that are amortized over their useful lives, the new assets recognized initially are depreciated. If the PPE value adjustment has an estimated life of 20 years, then the consolidated income statement would include depreciation of 1/20 of this $50,000 each year. Amortization of the $90,000 patent would also appear in the consolidated income statement. Finally, because goodwill is not amortized under GAAP, it remains at its carrying amount of $80,000 on the consolidated balance sheet unless and until it is impaired and written down.

8

LO8 Discuss the reporting of derivative securities.

APPENDIX 12C: Accounting for Investments in Derivatives

Derivatives refer to financial instruments that are utilized by companies to reduce various kinds of risks. Some examples follow:

- A company expects to purchase raw materials for its production process and wants to reduce the risk that the purchase price increases prior to the purchase.
- A company has an accounts receivable on its books that is payable in a foreign currency and wants to reduce the risk that exchange rates move unfavorably prior to collection.
- A company borrows funds on a floating rate of interest (such as linked to the prime rate) and wants to convert the loan to a fixed rate of interest.

Companies are commonly exposed to these and many similar types of risk. Although companies are generally willing to assume the normal market risks that are inherent in their business, many of these financial-type risks can add variability to income and are uncontrollable. Fortunately, commodities, currencies, and interest rates are all traded on various markets and, further, securities have been developed to manage all of these risks. These securities fall under the label of derivatives. They include forward contracts, futures contracts, option contracts, and swap agreements.

Companies use derivatives to manage many of these financial risks. The reduction of risk comes at a price: the fee that another party (called the counterparty) is charging to assume that risk. Most counterparties are financial institutions, and managing financial risk is their business and a source of their profits. Although derivatives can be used effectively to manage financial risk, they can also be used for speculation with potentially disastrous results. It is for this reason that regulators passed standards regarding their disclosure in financial statements.

Reporting of Derivatives Derivatives work by offsetting the gain or loss for the asset or liability to which they relate. Derivatives thus shelter the company from such fluctuations. For example, if a hedged receivable denominated in a foreign currency declines in value (due to a strengthening of the $US), the derivative security will increase in value by an offsetting amount, at least in theory. As a result, net equity remains unaffected and no gain or loss arises, nor is a loss reported in income.[3]

Although accounting for derivatives is complex, it essentially boils down to this: the derivative contract and the asset or liability to which it relates are both reported on the balance sheet at fair value. The asset and

[3] Unrealized gains and losses on derivatives classified as effective *cash flow hedges* (such as those relating to planned purchases and usage of commodities) are accumulated in other comprehensive income (OCI) and are not recognized in current income until the commodity is used (such as when both the purchase and sale of inventory occurs). Unrealized gains and losses on derivatives classified as *fair value hedges* (such as those relating to interest rate hedges and swaps, and the hedging of asset values such as relating to securities) as well as the changes in value of the hedged asset (liability) are recorded in current income on the same line as the hedged item.

liability are offsetting *if* the hedge is effective and, thus, net equity is unaffected. Likewise, the related gains and losses are largely offsetting, leaving income unaffected. Income is impacted only to the extent that the hedging activities are ineffective or result from speculative activities. It is this latter activity, in particular, that regulators were concerned about in formulating accounting standards for derivatives.

Disclosure of Derivatives Companies are required to disclose both qualitative and quantitative information about derivatives in notes to their financial statements and elsewhere (usually in Management's Discussion and Analysis section). The aim of these disclosures is to inform outsiders about potential risks underlying derivative securities.

Following is **Southwest Airlines Co.**'s disclosures from note 1 to its 2018 10-K report relating to its use of derivatives.

Financial Derivative Instruments

The Company accounts for financial derivative instruments at fair value and applies hedge accounting rules where appropriate. The Company utilizes various derivative instruments, including jet fuel, crude oil, unleaded gasoline, and heating oil-based derivatives, to attempt to reduce the risk of its exposure to jet fuel price increases. These instruments are accounted for as cash flow hedges upon proper qualification. The Company also has interest rate swap agreements to convert a portion of its fixed-rate debt to floating rates and has swap agreements that convert certain floating-rate debt to a fixed-rate. The majority of these interest rate hedges are appropriately designated as either fair value hedges or as cash flow hedges.

Since the majority of the Company's financial derivative instruments are not traded on a market exchange, the Company estimates their fair values. Depending on the type of instrument, the values are determined by the use of present value methods or option value models with assumptions about commodity prices based on those observed in underlying markets.

The Company adopted the New Hedging Standard as of January 1, 2018. See Note 2 for further information on this adoption.

All cash flows associated with purchasing and selling derivatives are classified as operating cash flows in the Consolidated Statement of Cash Flows, within Changes in certain assets and liabilities. The Company classifies its cash collateral provided to or held from counterparties in a "net" presentation on the Consolidated Balance Sheet against the fair value of the derivative positions with those counterparties. See Note 10 for further information.

Southwest Airlines' derivative use is mainly to hedge against fuel cost. Those hedges act to place a ceiling on fuel cost. The company reports that 79% of its 2018 fuel consumption was covered by hedging activity.

From a reporting standpoint, unrealized gains and losses on these derivative contracts are accumulated in the accumulated other comprehensive income (AOCI) portion of its stockholders' equity until the fuel is consumed. Once that fuel is consumed, those unrealized gains and losses are removed from AOCI and the gain (loss) on the option is used to offset the loss (gain) on fuel. In 2018, Southwest Airlines recognized a net gain on its hedging activities of $168 million, compared to total fuel and oil expense of $4,616 million.

Although the fair value of derivatives and their related assets or liabilities can be substantial, the net effect on earnings and stockholders' equity is usually minor because companies are mainly using them as hedges and not as speculative securities. The accounting standards for derivative instruments were enacted in response to a concern that speculative activities were not adequately disclosed. Subsequent to its passage, the financial effects have often appeared modest (with occasional exceptions such as **JP Morgan Chase**'s "London Whale" in 2012). Either these companies were not speculating to the extent expected, or they have since reduced their level of speculation in response to increased scrutiny from better disclosures.

SUMMARY

Explain and interpret the three levels of investor influence over an investee—passive, significant, and controlling. (p. 582) **LO1**

- Ownership of 20% or less in another corporation is presumed to be a passive investment by the investor.
- Significant influence is assumed to be available to the investor corporation if it owns more than 20% but not over 50% of the outstanding voting stock of the investee corporation.
- Control is generally presumed if the investing firm owns more than 50% of the outstanding voting stock of the investee corporation.

LO2 Describe the term "fair value" and the fair value hierarchy. (p. 584)

- Fair value is the amount that an independent buyer would be willing to pay for an asset (or the amount that would need to be paid to discharge a liability) in an orderly transaction.
- Fair value can be determined by reference to a market price when available, but it may also be determined by other methods (discounted cash flow analysis, pricing of comparable assets, etc.). GAAP defines three levels of fair value determination:
    - Level 1: Values based on quoted prices in active markets for identical assets/liabilities
    - Level 2: Values based on observable inputs other than Level 1 (e.g., quoted prices for similar assets/liabilities or interest rates or yield curves)
    - Level 3: Values based on inputs observable only to the reporting entity (e.g., management estimates or assumptions.)
- GAAP requires that companies disclose their fair value determinations in the footnotes of their financial statements.

LO3 Describe and analyze accounting for passive investments. (p. 584)

- Ownership of a debt security or 20% or less of the equity of another corporation is treated as a passive investment by the investor. Investing for returns is the objective rather than influencing another corporation's decisions. The investment is reported as a long-term asset only if the intention is to retain the asset for longer than a year. Investments in debt securities are segregated into three types—trading securities, held-to-maturity securities, or securities available-for-sale.
- Debt securities that management intends to hold to maturity are carried at (amortized) cost unless their value is considered impaired in which case the security is written down. Otherwise changes in fair value are not recognized on the balance sheet or the income statement.
- Debt securities treated as trading securities have an objective of short-term gain and will be converted into cash in a very short period of time. Any trading securities held at the end of an accounting period are marked to their fair value. The value change is recognized as an unrealized gain (or loss) in the income statement.
- Debt securities treated as available-for-sale securities are those which classify as neither held-to-maturity nor trading. Any securities held at the end of an accounting period are also marked to their fair value. However, the value change bypasses the income statement to become part of retained earnings called other comprehensive income. Holding gains and losses are recognized in income when the security is sold.
- Investments in equity securities are always marked to fair value, with holding gains and losses (both realized and unrealized) going through income in the period they occur.
- Gains and losses realized on sale, and dividends on passive investments are reported as other income in the income statement.

LO4 Explain and analyze accounting for investments with significant influence. (p. 596)

- Significant influence is assumed to be available to the investor corporation if it owns more than 20% but not over 50% of the outstanding voting stock of the investee corporation. Typically, the investment is initially recorded as a long-term asset at the purchase price.
- In the case of significant influence, the equity method of reporting is followed.
- Under the equity method, the investor recognizes its proportionate share of the investee's net income as income and an increase in the investment account. Any dividends received by the investor are treated as a recovery of the investment and reduce the investment balance.

LO5 Describe and analyze accounting for investments with control. (p. 600)

- If a corporation is considered to have control of another corporation, the financial statements of both firms are consolidated and reported as though they were a single entity.
- Control means that the investor has the ability to affect the strategic direction of the investee. Control is generally presumed if the investing firm owns more than 50% of the outstanding voting stock of the investee corporation.
- At the time of the acquisition, acquired assets and liabilities are restated at fair value in the consolidated balance sheet.
- If the purchase price exceeds the fair value of acquired net assets, the remainder is labeled "goodwill." Goodwill is not amortized, but tested for impairment annually.

LO6 Appendix 12A: Illustrate and analyze accounting mechanics for equity method investments. (p. 609)

- Under the equity method of accounting, neither the investee's assets nor its liabilities are reported on the investor's balance sheet. Only the proportionate investment is reported. Further, only the investor's net equity is reported in income; and the investee's sales and expenses are omitted.

- The result is that revenues and expenses, but not NOPAT, are understated; NOPM (NOPAT/Sales) is overstated; and net operating assets (NOA) are understated. Also, financial leverage is understated. ROE remains unaffected.

Appendix 12B: Apply consolidation accounting mechanics. (p. 611) **LO7**

- Identifiable intangible assets (such as patents, trademarks, customer lists) often result from the acquisition of one corporation by another. This is a situation in which the acquirer will have control and consolidation accounting is required.
- Intangibles are valued at the purchase date and then (unless indefinite-lived) amortized over their economic life. Any remaining purchase price not allocated to tangible or identifiable intangible assets is treated as goodwill.
- Goodwill and other indefinite-lived intangibles are not amortized but written down when and if considered impaired. The write-down is an expense of the period.
- Reports of consolidated corporations are often difficult to understand because they commingle the assets, liabilities, revenues, expenses, and cash flows of several businesses that can be very different. General Electric and its subsidiary provide an example.

Appendix 12C: Discuss the reporting of derivative securities. (p. 612) **LO8**

- Derivatives refer to financial instruments that are utilized by companies to reduce various kinds of risks.
- Derivatives work by offsetting the gain or loss for the asset or liability to which they relate.
- The accounting for derivatives boils down to this: the derivative contract and the asset or liability to which it relates are both reported on the balance sheet at fair value. The asset and liability are offsetting if the hedge is effective. Likewise, the related gains and losses are largely offsetting, leaving income unaffected.

GUIDANCE ANSWERS . . . YOU MAKE THE CALL

You are the Chief Financial Officer When a key component of a company's distribution process begins to turn its attention to other products, it can have a detrimental effect of the prospects for future growth. For instance, the soft-drink companies depend heavily on their bottling companies to get the product to the consumer. In these circumstances, companies may purchase enough shares in the distribution company to exert significant influence (or even control) over the key distributor.

KEY TERMS

Asset turnover ratios (p. 598)
Available-for-sale (AFS) securities (p. 587)
Consolidated financial statements (p. 600)
Controlling influence (p. 583)
Cost method (p. 592)
Derivatives (p. 612)
Equity method (p. 596)
Fair value (p. 584)
Fair value hierarchy (p. 584)
Fair value option (p. 584)
Financial investments (p. 582)
Financial leverage (p. 598)
Held-to-maturity (HTM) (p. 585)
Net operating profit margin (p. 598)
Passive influence (p. 583)
Significant influence (p. 583)
Trading (T) securities (p. 587)

Assignments with the  logo in the margin are available in myBusinessCourse.
See the Preface of the book for details.

MULTIPLE CHOICE

1. Corporation A owns 50% of corporation B. This is a case where:
   a. Corporation A controls corporation B.
   b. Corporation A does not control corporation B.
   c. Corporation A has significant influence on corporation B.
   d. Corporation A does not have a significant influence on corporation B.
   e. Both *a* and *c* are correct.

2. In accounting for available-for-sale debt securities, the
   a. securities are reported on the balance sheet at their fair value.

Multiple Choice Answers
1. c 2. e 3. a 4. b

b. securities are reported at cost.
c. increases in fair value are reported in income.
d. increases in fair value are not reported in income.
e. both *a* and *d* are correct.

3. Which of the following statements is true of investments accounted for under the equity method?
a. Investor reports its percentage share of the investee's income in its income.
b. Investor reports dividends received from the investee in its operating income.
c. Investment is reported at its fair value.
d. Investment is reported at cost plus any dividends received from the investee.
e. Investment is reported at fair value less any dividends received from the investee.

4. Which of the following statements is true about goodwill?
a. Current reporting standards require that goodwill be amortized over its economic life.
b. Goodwill is written down when the fair value of the investee is less than the book value.
c. Goodwill can be recognized only when the acquisition price does not exceed the value of the tangible and identifiable intangible assets acquired.
d. The recording of goodwill can be based on the acquisition of assets such as patents and trademarks.
e. Goodwill equals retained earnings.

Superscript A (B, C) denotes assignments based on Appendix 12A (12B, 12C).

QUESTIONS

Q12-1. For investments in debt securities, what measure (fair value or amortized cost) is used for the balance sheet to report (a) trading securities, (b) available-for-sale securities, and (c) held-to-maturity securities?

Q12-2. What is an unrealized holding gain (loss)? Explain. For passive investments in equity securities, how are unrealized holding gains (losses) treated?

Q12-3. Where are unrealized holding gains and losses related to trading securities reported in the financial statements? Where are unrealized holding gains and losses related to available-for-sale securities reported in the financial statements?

Q12-4. What does *significant influence* imply regarding financial investments? Describe the accounting procedures used for such investments.

Q12-5. On January 1 of the current year, Yetman Company purchases 40% of the common stock of Livnat Company for $250,000 cash. During the year, Livnat reports $80,000 of net income and pays $60,000 in cash dividends. At year-end, what amount should appear in Yetman's balance sheet for its investment in Livnat?

Q12-6. What accounting method is used when a stock investment represents more than 50% of the investee company's voting stock? Explain.

Q12-7. What is the underlying objective of consolidated financial statements?

Q12-8. Finn Company purchases all of the common stock of Murray Company for $750,000 when Murray Company has $300,000 of common stock and $450,000 of retained earnings. Book values of the assets and liabilities of Murray Company equal their fair values. If a consolidated balance sheet is prepared immediately after the acquisition, what amounts are eliminated in preparing it? Explain.

Q12-9.[B] Bradshaw Company owns 100% of Dee Company. At year-end, Dee owes Bradshaw $75,000. If a consolidated balance sheet is prepared at year-end, how is the $75,000 handled? Explain.

Q12-10. What are some limitations of consolidated financial statements?

MINI EXERCISES

LO1

M12-11. Classifying Investments as Passive, Significant, or Controlling
For each of the situations below, determine if the investment should be reported as a passive investment (P), an investment reflecting significant influence (SI), or a controlling interest (C).

a. ______ Griffin Company purchased 25% of the common stock of Wright, Inc., Griffin is one of several suppliers that Wright, Inc., relies on to supply subcomponents.

b. ______ Dye Corporation purchased 20% of the 2016 $40 million bond issue offered by Glover Company.

c. ______ Zhao, Inc., purchased 2,000 shares of Alphabet, Inc., common stock, paying $1.1 million.

d. ______ Watts Corporation purchased 65% of the common stock of Zimmerman, Inc., common stock for cash. Watts and Zimmerman had been engaged in several strategic alliances prior to the purchase.

e. ______ Shevlin, Inc., purchased 15% of Bowen Company's common stock. Shevlin is Bowen Company's largest customer, buying more than 60% of its output.

M12-12. Interpreting Disclosures of Available-for-Sale Securities

LO3

Cisco Systems, Inc.
NASDAQ :: CSCO

Use the following year-end footnote information from **Cisco Systems, Inc.**'s 10-K report to answer parts *a* and *b*.

($ millions)	2018
Cost of available-for-sale fixed income securities	$37,512
Gross unrealized gains	44
Gross unrealized losses	(547)
Fair value of available-for-sale fixed income securities	$37,009

a. At what amount is its available-for-sale investments reported on Cisco's 2018 balance sheet? Explain.

b. How is its net unrealized loss of $503 million ($44 million – $547 million) reported by Cisco in its financial statements?

M12-13. Accounting for Passive Investments in Equity Securities

LO3

Assume that Wasley Company purchases 6,000 common shares of Pincus Company for $12 cash per share. Shares of Pincus Company are actively traded. During the year, Wasley receives a cash dividend of $1.10 per common share from Pincus, and the year-end market price of Pincus common stock is $13 per share. How much income does Wasley report relating to this investment for the year?

M12-14. Analyzing Disclosures of Investment Securities

LO2

Microsoft Corporation
NASDAQ :: MSFT

In its June 30, 2018, balance sheet, **Microsoft Corporation** reports an investment in available-for-sale fixed-income (debt) securities with a value of $129,475. As available-for-sale securities, these investments are reported at their fair value, and Microsoft provides the following information in its footnotes.

June 30, 2018 (In $ millions)	Level 1	Level 2	Level 3	Gross Fair Value
Commercial paper	$ 0	$2,513	$ 0	$ 2,513
Certificates of deposit	0	2,058	0	2,058
U.S. government and agency securities	107,015	1,742	0	108,757
Foreign government bonds	22	5,054	0	5,076
Mortgage- and asset-backed securities	0	3,855	0	3,855
Corporate notes and bonds	0	6,894	15	6,909
Municipal securities	0	307	0	307

a. Explain the differences between the three columns labeled Level 1, Level 2, and Level 3.

b. Are all of these investments "marked-to-fair value"? If not, which ones are not marked-to-fair value? Which investment values do you regard as most subjective? Least subjective?

c. If Microsoft needed to raise cash to take advantage of an investment opportunity, which of these investments do you regard as most liquid (i.e., most easily turned into cash)? Least liquid?

M12-15. Analyzing and Interpreting Equity Method Investments

Stober Company purchases an investment in Lang Company at a purchase price of $1 million cash, representing 30% of the outstanding stock and book value of Lang. During the year, Lang reports net income of $100,000 and pays cash dividends of $40,000. At the end of the year, the fair value of Stober's investment is $1.2 million.

a. At what amount is the investment reported on Stober's balance sheet at year-end?

b. What amount of income from investments does Stober report? Explain.

c. Stober's $200,000 unrealized gain in investment fair value (choose one and explain):

(1) is not reflected on either its income statement or balance sheet.

(2) is reported in its current income.

(3) is reported on its balance sheet only.

(4) is reported in its other comprehensive income.

d. Prepare journal entries to record the transactions and events above.

e. Post the journal entries from *d* to their respective T-accounts.

f. Record each of the transactions from *d* in the financial statement effects template.

LO4 **M12-16. Calculating Income for Equity Method Investments**

Kross Company purchases an equity investment in Penno Company at a purchase price of $5 million, representing 40% of the outstanding stock and book value of Penno. During the current year, Penno reports net income of $600,000 and pays cash dividends of $200,000. At the end of the year, the market value of Kross's investment is $5.3 million. What amount of income does Kross report relating to this investment in Penno for the year? Explain.

LO5 **M12-17. Computing Consolidating Adjustments and Noncontrolling Interest**

Philipich Company purchases 80% of Hirst Company's common stock for $600,000 cash when Hirst Company has $300,000 of common stock and $450,000 of retained earnings, and the fair values of Hirst's assets and liabilities equal their book values. If a consolidated balance sheet is prepared immediately after the acquisition, what amounts are eliminated when preparing that statement? What amount of noncontrolling interest appears in the consolidated balance sheet? Where does it appear?

LO5 **M12-18. Computing Consolidated Net Income**

Benartzi Company purchased a 90% interest in Liang Company on January 1 of the current year. Benartzi Company had $600,000 net income for the current year *before* recognizing its share of Liang Company's net income. If Liang Company had net income of $150,000 for the year, what is the consolidated net income for the year? How would it be presented?

LO4, 5 **M12-19. Effect of Investing on Ratios**

DeFond Company wishes to secure a reliable supply of a key component for its production processes, and its management is considering two alternative investments. Verduzco Company produces exactly the supply that DeFond needs, so DeFond could use cash to purchase 100% of the common stock of Verduzco. Lin Company produces twice as much of the component that DeFond needs, but DeFond could form a joint venture with another company where each would purchase 50% of Lin Company's common stock and each take 50% of Lin Company's output.

The table that follows gives the balance sheet information for all three companies prior to any investment by DeFond. For the questions below, assume that DeFond would be able to purchase shares at the investee companies' book values and that the investee companies' assets and liabilities have fair values equal to their book values.

	DeFond Company	Verduzco Company	Lin Company
Cash	$ 800	$ 100	$ 200
Investment	—	—	—
Noncash assets	2,000	900	1,800
Liabilities	2,200	700	1,400
Shareholders' Equity	600	300	600

a. Suppose that DeFond purchases 100% of Verduzco's common stock for $300. Produce the consolidated balance sheet for DeFond immediately after the acquisition.

b. Suppose that DeFond purchases 50% of Lin's common stock for $300. Produce the balance sheet for DeFond immediately after the investment (using the equity method).

c. From a business perspective, either of these investments will accomplish the objective of obtaining a reliable supply of components. How will the financial ratios differ between the two alternatives?

M12-20. Reporting of and Analyzing Financial Effects of Trading (Debt) Securities LO3

Hartgraves Company had the following transactions and adjustments related to a bond investment that is a trading security.

2018

Oct. 1 Purchased $500,000 face value of Skyline, Inc.'s 7% bonds at 97 plus a brokerage commission of $1,000. The bonds pay interest on September 30 and March 31 and mature in 20 years. Hartgraves Company expects to sell the bonds in the near future.

Dec. 31 Made the adjusting entry to record interest earned on investment in the Skyline bonds.

31 Made the adjusting entry to record the current fair value of the Skyline bonds. At December 31, 2018, the fair value of the Skyline bonds was $490,000.

2019

Mar. 31 Received the semiannual interest payment on investment in the Skyline bonds.

Apr. 1 Sold the Skyline bond investment for $492,300 cash.

a. Prepare journal entries to record these transactions.
b. Post the journal entries from *a* to their respective T-accounts.
c. Record each of the transactions in the financial statement effects template.

M12-21. Reporting of and Analyzing Financial Effects of Investments in Equity Securities LO3

Blouin Company had the following transactions and adjustment related to a stock investment that is a trading security.

2018

Nov. 15 Purchased 10,000 shares of Lane, Inc.'s common stock at $17 per share plus a brokerage commission of $1,200. Blouin expects to sell the stock in the near future.

Dec. 22 Received a cash dividend of $1.00 per share of common stock from Lane.

31 Made the adjusting entry to reflect year-end fair value of the stock investment in Lane. The year-end fair value of the Lane common stock is $15.50 per share.

2019

Jan. 20 Sold all 10,000 shares of the Lane common stock for $150,000.

a. Prepare journal entries to record these transactions.
b. Post the journal entries from *a* to their respective T-accounts.
c. Record each of the transactions in the financial statement effects template.

M12-22. Reporting of and Analyzing Financial Effects of Available-for-Sale (Debt) Securities LO3

Refer to the data for Hartgraves Company in Mini Exercise 12-20. Assume that when the shares were purchased, management did not intend to sell the stock in the near future. Record the transactions and adjustments for Hartgraves Company as an available-for-sale security.

M12-23. Computing Stockholders' Equity in Consolidation LO5

On January 1 of the current year, Halen Company purchased all of the common shares of Jolson Company for $575,000 cash. On this date, the stockholders' equity of Halen Company consisted of $600,000 in common stock and $310,000 in retained earnings. Jolson Company had $350,000 in common stock and $225,000 in retained earnings. What amount of total stockholders' equity appears on the consolidated balance sheet?

EXERCISES

E12-24. Assessing Financial Statement Effects of Trading and Available-for-Sale (Debt) Securities LO1, 3

Four transactions involving investments in marketable debt securities classified as trading follow.

(1) On July 1, purchased US Treasury Bonds for $407,000 in cash. The bonds have a face value of $400,000 and pay interest semi-annually (June 30 and December 31) at an annual rate of 4.00%.
(2) Received cash interest payment of $8,000 on December 31.
(3) Year-end market price of bonds is $411,000.
(4) Received cash interest payment of $8,000 and sold all bonds on June 30 for $408,000.

a. Prepare journal entries to record the four transactions.
b. Post the journal entries from *a* to their respective T-accounts.

c. Record each of the transactions from *a* in the financial statement effects template.

d. Using the same transaction information as above and assuming the investments in marketable securities are classified as available-for-sale, (i) prepare journal entries to record the transactions, (ii) post the journal entries to their respective T-accounts, and (iii) record each of the transactions in the financial statement effects template.

LO1, 3

E12-25. Assessing Financial Statement Effects of Passive Investments in Equity Securities

For the following transactions involving investments in marketable securities, assume that:

(1) Ohlson Co. purchases 5,000 common shares of Freeman Co. at $16 cash per share.

(2) Ohlson Co. receives a cash dividend of $1.25 per common share from Freeman.

(3) Year-end market price of Freeman common stock is $17.50 per share.

(4) Ohlson Co. sells all 5,000 common shares of Freeman for $86,400 cash.

a. Prepare journal entries to record the four transactions.

b. Post the journal entries from *a* to their respective T-accounts.

c. Record each of the transactions from *a* in the financial statement effects template.

LO5

Microsoft Corporation
NASDAQ :: MSFT

E12-26. Acquisitions and Trend Analysis

In its 2018 10-K annual report, Microsoft Corporation reported the following revenues:

	Fiscal Year Ended June 30		
($ millions)	**2018**	**2017**	**2016**
Total revenues	$110,360	$96,571	$91,154

a. Calculate the yearly revenue growth for this period. Based on this trend, what revenue would you forecast for fiscal year 2019?

In December of 2016 (i.e., almost in the middle of fiscal year 2017, Microsoft completed its $27.0 billion acquisition of LinkedIn Corporation. In the 10-K footnotes for 2018, Microsoft reports

Following are the supplemental consolidated financial results of Microsoft Corporation on an unaudited pro forma basis, as if the acquisition had been consummated on July 1, 2015:

(In millions, except earnings per share) **Year Ended June 30,**	**2017**	**2016**
Revenue	$98,291	$94,490

b. How does the acquisition of LinkedIn affect your interpretation of the growth trend in part *a*?

c. Using the footnote information, revise the growth calculations to separate the measures of "organic growth" from "purchased growth."

LO1, 3

E12-27. Reporting of and Analyzing Financial Effects of Trading (Debt) Securities

Barclay, Inc., had the following transactions and adjustments related to a bond investment that is classified as a trading security.

2018

Nov. 1 Purchased $300,000 face value of Joos, Inc.'s 9% bonds at 102 plus a brokerage commission of $900. The bonds pay interest on October 31 and April 30 and mature in 15 years. Barclay expects to sell the bonds in the near future.

Dec. 31 Made the adjusting entry to record interest earned on investment in the Joos bonds.

31 Made the adjusting entry to record the current fair value of the Joos bonds. At December 31, 2018, the fair value of the Joos bonds was $301,500.

2019

Apr. 30 Received the semiannual interest payment on investment in the Joos bonds.

May 1 Sold the Joos bond investment for $300,900 cash.

a. Prepare journal entries to record these transactions.

b. Post the journal entries from *a* to their respective T-accounts.

c. Record each of the transactions in the financial statement effects template.

E12-28. Reporting of Stockholders' Equity in Consolidation

LO5

Baylor Company purchased 75% of the common stock of Reed Company for $600,000 in cash when the stockholders' equity of Reed Company consisted of $500,000 in common stock and $300,000 in retained earnings. On the acquisition date, the stockholders' equity of Baylor Company consisted of $900,000 in common stock and $440,000 in retained earnings. Prepare the stockholders' equity section in the consolidated balance sheet as of the acquisition date.

E12-29. Interpreting Footnote Disclosures for Investments

LO3

CNA Financial Corporation
NYSE :: CNA

CNA Financial Corporation provides the following information from its 2018 10-K report:

Investments

The Company classifies its fixed maturity securities as either available-for-sale or trading, and as such, they are carried at fair value. Changes in fair value of trading securities are reported within Net investment income on the Consolidated Statements of Operations. Changes in fair value related to available-for-sale securities are reported as a component of other comprehensive income. Losses may be recognized within Net realized investment gains (losses) on the Consolidated Statements of Operations when a decline in value is determined by the Company to be other-than-temporary.

December 31, 2018 ($ millions)	Cost or Amortized Cost	Gross Unrealized Gains	Gross Unrealized Losses	Estimated Fair Value
Fixed maturity securities available-for-sale:				
Corporate and other bonds	$18,764	$ 791	$395	$19,160
States, municipalities, and political subdivisions	9,681	1,076	9	10,748
Asset-backed:				
Residential mortgage-backed	4,815	68	57	4,826
Commercial mortgage-backed	2,200	28	32	2,196
Other asset-backed	1,975	11	24	1,962
Total asset-backed	8,990	107	113	8,984
U.S. Treasury and obligations of government-sponsored enterprises	156	3	—	159
Foreign government	480	5	4	481
Redeemable preferred stock	10	—	—	10
Total fixed maturity securities available-for-sale	38,081	1,982	521	39,542
Total fixed maturity securities trading	4	—	—	4
Total fixed maturity securities	$38,085	$1,982	$521	$39,546

a. At what amount is its investment portfolio reflected on its balance sheet? In your answer identify its fair value, cost, and any unrealized gains and losses.

b. How are its unrealized gains and/or losses reflected in CNA's balance sheet and income statement?

c. How are any impairment losses and the gains and losses realized from the sale of securities reflected in CNA's balance sheet and income statement?

E12-30. Assessing Financial Statement Effects of Equity Method Securities

LO4

The following transactions involve investments in marketable securities and are accounted for using the equity method.

(1) Purchased 12,000 common shares of Barth Co. at $9 cash per share; the shares represent 30% ownership in Barth.

(2) Received a cash dividend of $1.25 per common share from Barth.

(3) Recorded income from Barth stock investment when Barth's net income is $80,000.

(4) Sold all 12,000 common shares of Barth for $120,500.

a. Prepare journal entries to record these four transactions.

b. Post the journal entries from *a* to their respective T-accounts.

c. Record each of the transactions in the financial statement effects template.

E12-31. Assessing Financial Statement Effects of Equity Method Securities

The following transactions involve investments in marketable securities and are accounted for using the equity method.

(1) Healy Co. purchases 15,000 common shares of Palepu Co. at $8 cash per share; the shares represent 25% ownership of Palepu.
(2) Healy receives a cash dividend of $0.80 per common share from Palepu.
(3) Palepu reports annual net income of $120,000.
(4) Healy sells all 15,000 common shares of Palepu for $140,000 cash.

a. Prepare journal entries to record these four transactions.
b. Post the journal entries from *a* to their respective T-accounts.
c. Record each of the transactions in the financial statement effects template.

LO1, 3, 4

E12-32. Assessing Financial Statement Effects of Passive and Equity Method Investments
On January 1, 2019, Ball Corporation purchased, as a stock investment, 10,000 shares of Leftwich Company common stock for $15 cash per share. On December 31, 2019, Leftwich announced net income of $80,000 for the year and paid a cash dividend of $1.10 per share. At December 31, 2019, the market value of Leftwich's stock was $19 per share.

a. Assume that the stock acquired by Ball represents 15% of Leftwich's voting stock—a passive equity investment. For the following transactions, (1) prepare journal entries, (2) post those journal entries to their respective T-accounts, and (3) record each of the transactions in the financial statement effects template.
(1) Ball purchased 10,000 common shares of Leftwich at $15 cash per share; the shares represent a 15% ownership in Leftwich.
(2) Leftwich reported annual net income of $80,000.
(3) Received a cash dividend of $1.10 per common share from Leftwich.
(4) Year-end market price of Leftwich common stock is $19 per share.

b. Assume that Ball's $150,000 investment purchased 30% of Leftwich's voting stock and that Ball accounts for this investment using the equity method since it is able to exert significant influence. For the same four transactions as above, (1) prepare journal entries, (2) post those journal entries to their respective T-accounts, and (3) record each of the transactions in the financial statement effects template.

LO1, 3

Amazon.com, Inc.
NASDAQ :: AMZN

E12-33. Allocation of Acquisition Purchase Price
During 2017, **Amazon.com, Inc.**, made two significant acquisitions intending to expand the company's retail presence. On May 12, 2017, Amazon acquired Souq Group Ltd. ("Souq"), an e-commerce company, for approximately $583 million, net of cash acquired and on August 28, 2017, acquired Whole Foods Market, a grocery store chain, for approximately $13.2 billion, net of cash acquired. Other acquisitions were also made for consideration of $204 million making a total of $13,963 million (net of cash acquired) for the year.

From the footnote of its 2018 10-K, Amazon provides the following information:

The aggregate purchase price of these acquisitions was allocated as follows (in millions):

December 31,	2017
Purchase Price	
Cash paid, net of cash acquired	$13,963
Allocation	
Goodwill	?
Intangible assets:	
Marketing-related	1,987
Contract-based	440
Technology-based	166
Customer-related	54
	2,647
Property and equipment	3,810
Deferred tax assets	117
Other assets acquired	1,858
Long-term debt	(1,165)
Deferred tax liabilities	(961)
Other liabilities assumed	(1,844)
	$13,963

a. How are the values in the above table determined?

b. How much goodwill would Amazon.com recognize from these acquisitions? How will that goodwill be treated in subsequent periods?

c. Do you think Amazon.com shareholders would prefer to see an allocation that gives a lot of value to separately-identifiable assets or an allocation where most of the acquisition price goes to goodwill? Why?

E12-34. Allocation of Acquisition Purchase Price LO5

Intel Corporation
NASDAQ :: INTC

On August 21, 2017, upon the completion of a tender offer, Intel Corporation acquired 97.3% of the outstanding ordinary shares of Mobileye. This acquisition "combines Mobileye's leading computer vision expertise with Intel's high-performance computing and connectivity expertise to create automated driving solutions from car to cloud. The combination is expected to accelerate innovation for the automotive industry and position Intel as a leading technology provider in the fast-growing market for highly and fully autonomous vehicles."

Total consideration to acquire Mobileye was $14,875 million (net of $366 million of cash and cash equivalents acquired).

The fair values of the assets acquired and liabilities assumed in the acquisition of Mobileye, by major class, were recognized as follows:

Short-term investments and marketable securities	$ 370
Tangible assets	227
Goodwill	?
Identified intangible assets	4,482
Current liabilities	(69)
Deferred tax liabilities and other	(418)

a. How are the values in the above table determined?

b. How much goodwill would Intel recognize from this acquisition? How will that goodwill be treated in subsequent periods?

c. Do you think Intel's shareholders would prefer to see an allocation that gives a lot of value to separately-identifiable assets or an allocation where most of the acquistion price goes to goodwill? Why?

E12-35. Reporting of and Analyzing Financial Effects of Passive Equity Securities LO1, 3

Guay Company had the following transactions and adjustment related to a passive equity investment.

2019

Nov. 15 Purchased 5,000 shares of Core, Inc.'s common stock at $16 per share plus a brokerage commission of $900. Guay Company expects to sell the stock in the near future.

Dec. 22 Received a cash dividend of $1.25 per share of common stock from Core.

31 Made the adjusting entry to reflect year-end fair value of the stock investment in Core. The year-end market price of the Core common stock is $17.50 per share.

2020

Jan. 20 Sold all 5,000 shares of the Core common stock for $86,400.

a. Prepare journal entries to record these transactions.

b. Post the journal entries from *a* to their respective T-accounts.

c. Record each of the transactions in the financial statement effects template.

E12-36. Reporting of and Analyzing Financial Effects of Equity Securities Under International Standards LO1, 3

Refer to the data for Guay Company in Exercise 12-35. Assume that Guay Company reports under International Financial Reporting Standards (IFRS). Under IFRS, Guay can designate an equity investment for accounting based on FVOCI (fair value—other comprehensive income). While holding the equity investment, dividends are recorded in income and unrealized holding gains and losses go to AOCI, much like AFS securities. However, the difference is that these gains and losses are never recognized in income. Rather, they remain in AOCI. Assume that when the shares were purchased, management designated its investment in Core, Inc., for FVOCI treatment.

a. Record the transactions and adjustments for Guay Company under this assumption.

b. Why might the standard setters have allowed this option to companies reporting under IFRS?

LO1, 2, 3, 4

E12-37. Reporting and Interpreting Financial Investment Performance

Kasznik Company began operations on January 2, 2019, and by year-end (December 31) had made the following investments in financial securities. Year-end information on these investments follows.

Investment	Cost or End-of-Year Equity Basis (as appropriate)	Year-End Fair Value	Investment Classification
Common stock of Barth, Inc.	$ 68,000	$ 65,300	Fair value (Trading)
Common stock of Foster, Inc.. . . .	162,500	160,000	Fair value (Trading)
30-Year US Treasury Bond.	197,000	192,000	Available-for-sale
10-Year US Treasury Note	157,000	154,700	Available-for-sale
Ertimur, Inc.	100,000	102,400	Equity method
Soliman, Inc..	136,000	133,200	Equity method

a. At what total amount are the trading stock investments reported at in the December 31, 2019, balance sheet?

b. At what total amount are the available-for-sale debt investments reported at in the December 31, 2019, balance sheet?

c. At what total amount are the equity method stock investments reported at in the December 31, 2019, balance sheet?

d. What total amount of unrealized holding gains or unrealized holding losses related to the investments appears in the 2019 income statement?

e. What total amount of unrealized holding gains or unrealized holding losses related to the investments appears in the stockholders' equity section of the December 31, 2019, balance sheet?

f. What total amount of fair value adjustment to the investments appears in the December 31, 2019, balance sheet? Which category of investments does the fair value adjustment relate to? Does the fair value adjustment increase or decrease the financial statement presentation of these investments?

LO1, 4

Merck & Co., Inc.
NYSE :: MRK

E12-38. Analyzing Equity Method Investment Footnotes

Merck & Co., Inc., reports a December 31, 2016, balance of $715 million in "Investments in affiliates accounted for using the equity method" ("Investments in affiliates"). Provide the entries for the following events for fiscal year 2017:

a. Merck's share of income from its affiliates was $42 million.

b. Merck received dividends and distributions from its affiliates of $2 million during fiscal year 2017.

c. After these events, what should be the balance in Merck's investments in affiliates account at December 31, 2017? The actual balance was $767 million. What might explain any differences between these two values?

LO7

E12-39.[B] Constructing the Consolidated Balance Sheet at Acquisition

On January 1 of the current year, Healy Company purchased all of the common shares of Miller Company for $500,000 cash. Balance sheets of the two firms at acquisition follow.

	Healy Company	Miller Company	Consolidating Adjustments	Consolidated
Current assets	$1,700,000	$120,000		
Investment in Miller.	500,000	—		
Plant assets, net.	3,000,000	410,000		
Goodwill	—	—		
Total assets	$5,200,000	$530,000		
Liabilities.	$ 700,000	$ 90,000		
Contributed capital	3,500,000	400,000		
Retained earnings	1,000,000	40,000		
Total liabilities and equity	$5,200,000	$530,000		

During purchase negotiations, Miller's plant assets were appraised at $425,000; and all of its remaining assets and liabilities were appraised at values approximating their book values. Healy also concluded that an additional $45,000 (in goodwill) demanded by Miller's shareholders was warranted because Miller's earning power was better than the industry average. (1) prepare the consolidating adjustments, (2) prepare the consolidated balance sheet at acquisition, (3) prepare journal entries to record the transactions, (4) post the journal entries to their respective T-accounts, and (5) record each of the transactions in the financial statement effects template.

E12-40.[B] Constructing the Consolidated Balance Sheet at Acquisition **LO7**

Rayburn Company purchased all of Kanodia Company's common stock for cash on January 1, at which time the separate balance sheets of the two corporations appeared as follows:

	Rayburn Company	Kanodia Company	Consolidating Adjustments	Consolidated
Investment in Kanodia	$ 600,000	—		
Other assets	2,300,000	$700,000		
Goodwill	—	—		
Total assets	$2,900,000	$700,000		
Liabilities	$ 900,000	$160,000		
Contributed capital	1,400,000	300,000		
Retained earnings	600,000	240,000		
Total liabilities and equity	$2,900,000	$700,000		

During purchase negotiations, Rayburn determined that the appraised value of Kanodia's other assets was $720,000; and all of its remaining assets and liabilities were appraised at values approximating their book values. The remaining $40,000 of the purchase price was ascribed to goodwill. (1) prepare the consolidating adjustments, (2) prepare the consolidated balance sheet at acquisition, (3) prepare journal entries to record the transactions, (4) post the journal entries to their respective T-accounts, and (5) record each of the transactions in the financial statement effects template.

E12-41. Assessing Goodwill Impairment **LO5**

On January 1, 2019, Engel Company purchases 100% of Ball Company for $16.8 million. At the time of acquisition, Ball's stockholders' equity (and the fair value of its identifiable net assets) is reported at $10.2 million. Engel ascribes the excess of $6.6 million to goodwill. Assume that the fair value of Ball declines to $12.5 million.

a. Provide computations to determine if the goodwill has become impaired and, if so, the amount of the impairment.

b. What impact does the impairment of goodwill have on Engel's financial statements?

E12-42.[B] Constructing the Consolidated Balance Sheet at Acquisition **LO5, 7**

Easton Company acquires 100% of the outstanding voting shares of Harris Company on January 1, 2019. To obtain these shares, Easton pays $210,000 in cash and issues 5,000 of its $10 par value common stock. On this date, Easton's stock has a fair value of $36 per share, and Harris's book value of stockholders' equity is $280,000. Easton is willing to pay $390,000 for a company with a book value for equity of $280,000 because it believes that (1) Harris buildings are undervalued by $40,000, and (2) Harris has an unrecorded patent that Easton values at $30,000. Easton considers the remaining balance sheet items to be fairly valued (no book-to-fair value difference). The remaining $40,000 of the purchase price excess over book value is ascribed to corporate synergies and other general unidentifiable intangible assets (goodwill). The January 1, 2019, balance sheets at the acquisition date follow:

	Easton Company	Harris Company	Consolidating Adjustments	Consolidated
Cash	$ 84,000	$ 40,000		
Receivables	160,000	90,000		
Inventory	220,000	130,000		
Investment in Harris	390,000	—		
Land	100,000	60,000		
Buildings, net	400,000	110,000		
Equipment, net	120,000	50,000		
Total assets	$1,474,000	$480,000		

continued

continued from previous page

	Easton Company	Harris Company	Consolidating Adjustments	Consolidated
Accounts payable	$ 160,000	$ 30,000		
Long-term liabilities	380,000	170,000		
Common stock	500,000	40,000		
Additional paid-in capital	74,000	—		
Retained earnings	360,000	240,000		
Total liabilities & equity	$1,474,000	$480,000		

a. Show the breakdown of the investment into the book value acquired, the excess of fair value over book value, and the portion of the investment representing goodwill.

b. Prepare the consolidating adjustments and the consolidated balance sheet. Identify the adjustments by whether they relate to the elimination of stockholders' equity [S] or the excess of purchase price over book value [A].

c. How will the excess of the purchase price over book value acquired be treated in years subsequent to the acquisition?

LO6

E12-43.[A] Accounting for Equity Method Investments

Refer to the Easton Company acquisition described in E12-42. Instead of a 100% acquisition, assume that Easton purchased 40% of the outstanding shares of Harris Company on January 1, 2019, for $156,000 in cash. Also assume that the undervalued buildings have an estimated remaining useful life of 20 years and the unrecorded patent has a useful life of 5 years.

During 2019, Harris reported net income of $80,000 and paid cash dividends to shareholders totaling $40,000.

a. Prepare journal entries to record Easton Company's equity in the earnings of Harris Company, including any amortization of the excess of fair value over book value of assets acquired.

b. What is the value of the investment in Harris Company reported on Easton Company's balance sheet as of December 31, 2019?

LO8

Hewlett Packard Enterprise Company
NYSE :: HPE

E12-44.[C] Reporting and Analyzing Derivatives

Hewlett Packard Enterprise Company reports the following information on its cash-flow hedges (derivatives) in comprehensive income (net income plus other comprehensive income) in its 2018 10-K report:

($ millions)	Total
Net earnings	$1,908
Net unrealized gain/(loss) on available-for-sale securities	(12)
Net unrealized gain/(loss) on cash flow hedges	177
Net unrealized components of defined benefit pension plans	(210)
Net cumulative translation adjustment	(50)
Provision for income taxes	(42)
Comprehensive income	$1,771

a. Identify and describe the usual applications for derivatives.

b. How are derivatives and their related assets (and/or liabilities) reported on the balance sheet?

c. By what amount has the unrealized gain or loss on the HPE derivatives affected its current income? What are the analysis implications?

PROBLEMS

LO1, 2, 3

Metlife Inc.
NYSE :: MET

P12-45. Analyzing and Interpreting Available-for-Sale Securities Disclosures

Following is a portion of the investments footnote 8 from **MetLife Inc.**'s 2017 10-K report. Investment earnings are a crucial component of the financial performance of insurance companies such as MetLife, and investments comprise a large part of its assets. MetLife accounts for its bond investments as available-for-sale securities.

Fixed Maturity Securities Available-for-Sale

The following tables present the fixed maturity securities AFS by sector.

	December 31, 2017				
	Cost or Amortized Cost	Gross Unrealized			Estimated Fair Value
(in millions)		Gains	Temporary Losses	OTTI Losses	
Fixed Maturity Securities:					
U.S. corporate	$ 76,005	$ 7,007	$ 351	$ —	$ 82,661
Foreign government	55,351	6,495	312	—	61,534
Foreign corporate	52,409	3,836	676	—	55,569
U.S. government and agency	43,446	4,227	279	—	47,394
RMBS	27,846	1,145	233	(42)	28,800
State and political subdivision	10,752	1,717	13	1	12,455
ABS	12,213	116	39	(1)	12,291
CMBS	8,047	222	42	—	8,227
Total fixed maturity securities	$286,069	$24,765	$1,945	$(42)	$308,931

	December 31, 2016				
	Cost or Amortized Cost	Gross Unrealized			Estimated Fair Value
(in millions)		Gains	Temporary Losses	OTTI Losses	
Fixed Maturity Securities:					
U.S. corporate	$ 73,280	$ 6,027	$ 764	$—	$ 78,543
Foreign government	49,864	6,485	373	—	55,976
Foreign corporate	49,308	2,926	1,572	(1)	50,663
U.S. government and agency	41,294	3,682	543	—	44,433
RMBS	28,393	1,039	410	(10)	29,032
State and political subdivision	10,977	1,340	85	1	12,231
ABS	11,266	90	128	3	11,225
CMBS	7,294	237	71	—	7,460
Total fixed maturity securities	$271,676	$21,826	$3,946	$(7)	$289,563

REQUIRED

a. At what amount does MetLife report its bond investments on its balance sheets for 2017 and 2016?

b. What are its net unrealized gains (losses) for 2017 and 2016? By what amount did these unrealized gains (losses) affect its reported income?

c. What is the difference between *realized* and *unrealized* gains and losses? Are realized gains and losses treated differently in the income statement than unrealized gains and losses? MetLife's 2017 pre-tax income was $3,536 million. What is the maximum amount MetLife could have increased pre-tax income by selling available-for-sale securities on the last day of 2017?

d. Many analysts compute a *mark-to-market investment return* as follows: Net investment income + Realized gains and losses + Change in unrealized gains and losses. Do you think that this metric provides insights into the performance of MetLife's investment portfolio beyond that which is included in GAAP income statements? Explain.

P12-46.[B] Preparing the Consolidated Balance Sheet LO5, 7

On January 1, 2016, Gem Company purchased for $392,000 cash a 70% stock interest in Alpine, Inc., which then had common stock of $420,000 and retained earnings of $140,000. Balance sheets of the two companies immediately after the acquisition were as follows:

	Gem	Alpine
Current assets	$258,000	$160,000
Stock investment—Controlling (Alpine)	392,000	—
Plant and equipment (net)	265,000	460,000
Total assets	$915,000	$620,000

continued

continued from previous page

	Gem	Alpine
Liabilities	$ 50,000	$ 60,000
Common stock	700,000	420,000
Retained earnings	165,000	140,000
Total liabilities and stockholders' equity	$915,000	$620,000

At the time of Gem's investment, the fair values of Alpine's assets and liabilities were equal to their book values.

REQUIRED

Prepare the consolidated balance sheet on the acquisition date; include a column for consolidating adjustments (see **Exhibit 12.7** for guidance).

LO1, 2, 3, 4

P12-47. Analyzing and Reporting Debt Investment Performance

Columbia Company began operations in 2019 and by year-end (December 31) had made six bond investments. Year-end information on these bond investments follows.

Company	Face Value	Cost or Amortized Cost	Year-End Fair Value	Classification
Ling, Inc.	$100,000	$102,400	$105,300	Trading
Wren, Inc.	$250,000	$262,500	$270,000	Trading
Olanamic, Inc.	$200,000	$197,000	$199,000	Available for sale
Fossil, Inc.	$150,000	$154,000	$160,000	Available for sale
Meander, Inc.	$100,000	$101,200	$102,400	Held to maturity
Resin, Inc.	$140,000	$136,000	$137,000	Held to maturity

REQUIRED

a. At what total amount will the trading bond investments be reported in the December 31, 2019, balance sheet?

b. At what total amount will the available-for-sale bond investments be reported in the December 31, 2019, balance sheet?

c. At what total amount will the held-to-maturity bond investments be reported in the December 31, 2019, balance sheet?

d. What total amount of unrealized holding gains or unrealized holding losses related to bond investments will appear in the 2019 income statement?

e. What total amount of unrealized holding gains or unrealized holding losses related to bond investments will appear in the stockholders' equity section of the December 31, 2019, balance sheet?

f. What total amount of fair value adjustment to bond investments will appear in the December 31, 2019, balance sheet? Which category of bond investments does the fair value adjustment relate to? Does the fair value adjustment increase or decrease the financial statement presentation of these bond investments?

LO1, 4, 5, 6, 7
Caterpillar Inc.
NYSE :: CAT

P12-48.[A, B] Analyzing and Interpreting Disclosures on Consolidations

Caterpillar Inc., consists of two business units: the manufacturing company (parent corporation) and a wholly owned finance subsidiary. These two units are consolidated in Caterpillar's 2018 10-K report. Following is a supplemental disclosure that Caterpillar includes in its 10-K report that shows the separate balance sheets of the parent and its subsidiary, as well as consolidating adjustments and the consolidated balance sheet presented to shareholders. This supplemental disclosure is not mandated under GAAP, but is voluntarily reported by Caterpillar as useful information for investors and creditors.

	Consolidated	Supplemental Consolidating Data: Machinery, Energy & Transportation	Financial Products	Consolidating Adjustments
Assets				
Current assets				
Cash and short-term investments	$ 7,857	$ 6,968	$ 889	$ —
Receivables—trade and other	8,802	4,677	401	3,724
Receivables—finance	8,650	—	13,989	(5,339)
Prepaid expenses and other current assets	1,765	1,227	583	(45)
Inventories	11,529	11,529	—	—
Total current assets	38,603	24,401	15,862	(1,660)
Property, plant and equipment—net	13,574	9,085	4,489	—
Long-term receivables—trade and other	1,161	302	204	655
Long-term receivables—finance	13,286	—	13,951	(665)
Investments in Financial Products subsidiaries	—	3,672	—	(3,672)
Noncurrent deferred and refundable income taxes	1,439	2,015	116	(692)
Intangible assets	1,897	1,897	—	—
Goodwill	6,217	6,217	—	—
Other assets	2,332	886	1,446	—
Total assets	$78,509	$48,475	$36,068	$(6,034)
Liabilities				
Current liabilities				
Short-term borrowings	$ 5,723	$ —	$ 5,723	$ —
Short-term borrowings with consolidated companies	—	—	1,500	(1,500)
Accounts payable	7,051	6,972	194	(115)
Accrued expenses	3,573	3,212	361	—
Accrued wages, salaries, and employee benefits	2,384	2,350	34	—
Customer advances	1,243	1,243	—	—
Dividends payable	495	495	—	—
Other current liabilities	1,919	1,532	433	(46)
Long-term debt due within one year	5,830	10	5,820	—
Total current liabilities	28,218	15,814	14,065	(1,661)
Long-term debt due after one year	25,000	8,015	16,995	(10)
Liability for postemployment benefits	7,455	7,455	—	—
Other liabilities	3,756	3,111	1,336	(691)
Total liabilities	64,429	34,395	32,396	(2,362)
Stockholders' equity				
Common stock	5,827	5,827	919	(919)
Treasury stock	(20,531)	(20,531)	—	—
Profit employed in the business	30,427	30,427	3,543	(3,543)
Accumulated other comprehensive income (loss)	(1,684)	(1,684)	(943)	943
Noncontrolling interests	41	41	153	(153)
Total stockholders' equity	14,080	14,080	3,672	(3,672)
Total liabilities and stockholders' equity	$78,509	$48,475	$36,068	$(6,034)

REQUIRED

a. Does each individual company (unit) maintain its own financial statements? Explain. Why does GAAP require consolidation instead of providing the financial statements of individual companies (units)?

b. What is the balance of Investments in Financial Products Subsidiaries as of December 31, 2018, on the parent's balance sheet (Machinery, Energy & Transportation)? What is the equity balance of the financial products subsidiary to which this relates as of December 31, 2018? Do you see a relation? Will this relation always exist?

c. Refer to your answer for *a*. How does the equity method of accounting for the investment in the subsidiary company obscure the actual financial condition of the parent company that is revealed in the consolidated financial statements?

d. Refer to the Consolidating Adjustments column reported—it is used to prepare the consolidated balance sheet. Generally, what do these adjustments accomplish?

e. Compare the consolidated balance of stockholders' equity with the stockholders' equity of the parent company (Machinery, Energy & Transportation). Will the relation that is evident always hold? Explain.

f. Recall that the parent company uses the equity method of accounting for its investment in the subsidiary, and that this account is eliminated in the consolidation process. What is the relation between consolidated net income and the net income of the parent company? Explain.

g. What do you believe is the implication for the consolidated balance sheet if the fair value of the Financial Products subsidiary is greater than the book value of its stockholders' equity?

CASES AND PROJECTS

LO1, 3

Apple Inc.
NASDAQ :: AAPL

C12-49. Effect of Investment Accounting on Performance Ratios

Apple Inc., is one of the most successful enterprises of all time. Its computers, tablets, phones, and watches are all highly desired by consumers, and the company's product innovations keep arriving at a steady pace. Apple's financial success can also be attributed to its supply chain management and to its management of its income taxes. Historically, U.S. income taxes have been based on payments from Apple's international subsidiaries, so the company (and many others) could defer the payment of taxes by retaining profits in its international subsidiaries and investing in relatively safe, liquid financial assets. As a result, Apple's balance sheet reports substantial investments in marketable securities, as shown in the following:

($ millions)	September 29, 2018	September 30, 2017
Total assets	$365,725	$375,319
Marketable securities	211,187	248,606
Net operating assets (operating assets – operating liabilities)	10,443	1,121

The following information is taken from the company's fiscal 2018 income statement and footnotes:

($ millions)	Year Ended September 29, 2018
Operating income	$ 70,898
Interest and dividend income	5,686
Interest expense	(3,240)
Other expenses	(441)
Income before provision for income tax	72,903
Provision for income tax	(13,372)
Net income	$ 59,531

Finally, the following table is taken from Note 2 of Apple's 2018 10-K annual report. The reported numbers are slightly higher than those reported from Apple's balance sheet above because some AFS securities are classified as cash equivalents on the balance sheet, rather than marketable securities.

Fixed-income (debt) investments—AFS:

($ millions)	Adjusted cost	Unrealized gains	Unrealized losses	Fair value
2018	$220,723	$ 209	$(4,173)	$216,759
2017	253,084	1,278	(694)	253,668

REQUIRED

a. Calculate Apple's return on assets for fiscal year 2018. Assume an income tax rate of 25%.

b. Calculate Apple's RNOA for 2018. (Refer to Appendix A of Chapter 5 for further discussion.) What factors contribute to this RNOA?

c. What method does Apple use to account for its fixed-income investments? What value is included in its 2018 balance sheet?

d. From its balance sheet, it would appear that a significant portion of Apple's resources are devoted to investing in financial instruments. Calculate the after-tax return to Apple's financial assets. Apple's Statement of Other Comprehensive Income reports an after-tax unrealized holding loss on AFS investments equal to $3,407 million? What would have been Apple's return to financial investments if it had used the trading security method for these investments?

C12-50. Analyzing Financial Statement Effects of Passive and Equity Investments LO1, 3, 4

On January 2, 2019, Magee, Inc., purchased, as a stock investment, 20,000 shares of Dye, Inc.'s common stock for $21 per share, including commissions and taxes. On December 31, 2019, Dye announced a net income of $280,000 for the year and declared a dividend of 80 cents per share, payable January 15, 2020, to stockholders of record on January 5, 2020. At December 31, 2019, the market value of Dye's stock was $18 per share. Magee received its dividend on January 18, 2020.

REQUIRED

a. Assume that the stock acquired by Magee represents 10% of Dye's voting stock and is classified in the trading category. Prepare all journal entries appropriate for this investment, beginning with the purchase on January 2, 2019, and ending with the receipt of the dividend on January 18, 2020. (Magee recognizes dividend income when received.)

b. Post the journal entries from part *a* to their respective T-accounts.

c. Record each of the transactions from part *a* in the financial statement effects template.

d. Assume that the stock acquired by Magee represents 40% of Dye's voting stock. Prepare all journal entries appropriate for this investment, beginning with the purchase on January 2, 2019, and ending with the receipt of the dividend on January 18, 2020.

e. Post the journal entries from part *d* to their respective T-accounts.

f. Record each of the transactions from part *d* in the financial statement effects template.

C12-51. Assessing Management Interpretation of Consolidated Financial Statements LO1, 2, 3, 4, 5

Demski, Inc., manufactures heating and cooling systems. It has a 75% interest in Asare Company, which manufactures thermostats, switches, and other controls for heating and cooling products. It also has a 100% interest in Demski Finance Company, created by the parent company to finance sales of its products to contractors and other consumers. The parent company's only other investment is a 25% interest in the common stock of Knechel, Inc., which produces certain circuits used by Demski, Inc., A condensed consolidated balance sheet of the entity for the current year follows.

DEMSKI, INC., AND SUBSIDIARIES
Consolidated Balance Sheet
December 31, 2019

Assets		
Current assets		$19,300,000
Stock investment—Influential (Knechel)		2,600,000
Other assets		71,400,000
Excess of cost over equity acquired in net assets of Asare Company		1,700,000
Total assets		$95,000,000
Liabilities and shareholders' equity		
Current liabilities		$10,300,000
Long-term liabilities		14,200,000
Shareholders' equity		
Common stock	$50,000,000	
Retained earnings	16,700,000	
Demski, Inc., shareholders' equity	66,700,000	
Noncontrolling interests	3,800,000	
Total shareholders' equity		70,500,000
Total liabilities and shareholders' equity		$95,000,000

This balance sheet, along with other financial statements, was furnished to shareholders before their annual meeting, and all shareholders were invited to submit questions to be answered at the meeting. As chief financial officer of Demski, you have been appointed to respond to the questions at the meeting.

REQUIRED

Answer the following shareholder questions.

a. What is meant by *consolidated* financial statements?

b. Why is the investment in Knechel shown on the consolidated balance sheet, but the investments in Asare and Demski Finance are omitted?

c. Explain the meaning of the asset Excess of Cost over Equity Acquired in Net Assets of Asare Company.

d. What is meant by *noncontrolling interest* and to what company is this account related?

LO1, 2, 3, 4 **C12-52. Understanding Intercorporate Investments, Accounting Practices, and Managerial Ethics** Doug Stevens, controller of Nexgen, Inc., has asked his assistant, Gayle Sayres, for suggestions as to how the company can improve its reported financial performance for the year. The company is in the last quarter of the year and projections to the end of the year show the company will have a net loss of about $400,000 before tax.

"My suggestion," said Sayres, "is that we sell 1,000 of the 200,000 common shares of Heflin Company that we own. The 200,000 shares gives us a 20% ownership of Heflin, and we have been using the equity method to account for this investment. We have owned this stock a long time and the current market value of the 200,000 shares is about $750,000 above our book value for the stock."

"That sale will only generate a gain of about $3,750," replied Stevens.

"The rest of the story," continued Sayres, "is that once we sell the 1,000 shares, we will own less than 20% of Heflin. We can then reclassify the remaining 199,000 shares from the influential category to the passive equity/fair value category. Then we value the stocks at their current fair value, include the rest of the $750,000 gain in this year's income statement, and finish the year with a healthy net income."

"But," responded Stevens, "we aren't going to sell all the Heflin stock; 1,000 shares maybe, but certainly not any more. We own that stock because they are a long-term supplier of ours. Indeed, we even have representation on their board of directors. The 199,000 shares do not belong in the passive category."

Sayres rolled her eyes and continued, "The classification of an investment as passive or not depends on management's intent. This year-end we claim it was our intent not to exert influence over Heflin. Next year we change our minds and take the stock out of the trading category. Generally accepted accounting principles can't legislate management intent, nor can our outside auditors read our minds. Besides, why shouldn't we take advantage of the flexibility in GAAP to avoid reporting a net loss for this year?"

REQUIRED

a. Should generally accepted accounting principles permit management's intent to influence accounting classifications and measurements?

b. Is it ethical for Doug Stevens to implement the recommendation of Gayle Sayres?

SOLUTIONS TO REVIEW PROBLEMS

Mid-Chapter Review 1

SOLUTION TO PART 1

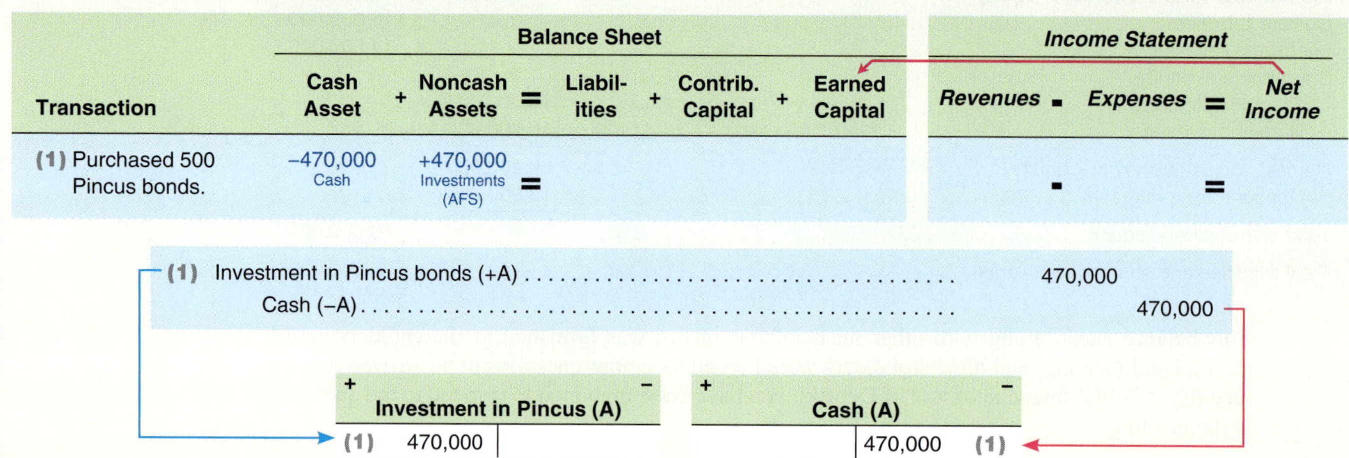

	Balance Sheet										Income Statement				
Transaction	Cash Asset	+	Noncash Assets	=	Liabil-ities	+	Contrib. Capital	+	Earned Capital		*Revenues*	-	*Expenses*	=	*Net Income*
(1) Purchased 500 Pincus bonds.	−470,000 Cash		+470,000 Investments (AFS)	=								-		=	

ANALYZE

JOURNALIZE

(1) Investment in Pincus bonds (+A)	470,000	
Cash (−A)		470,000

POST

+ Investment in Pincus (A) −	
(1) 470,000	

+ Cash (A) −	
	470,000 (1)

continued

continued from previous page

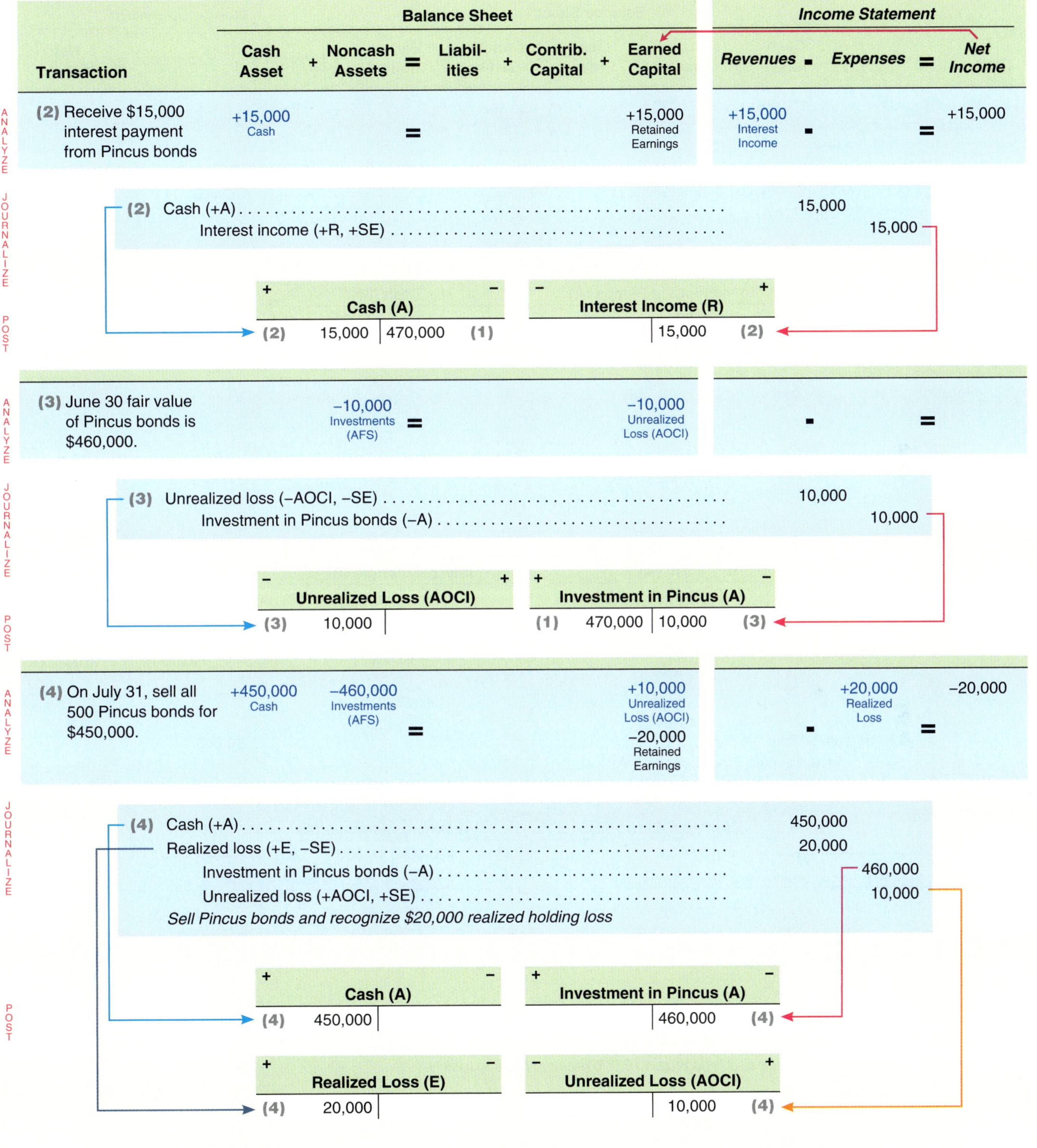

SOLUTION TO PART 2

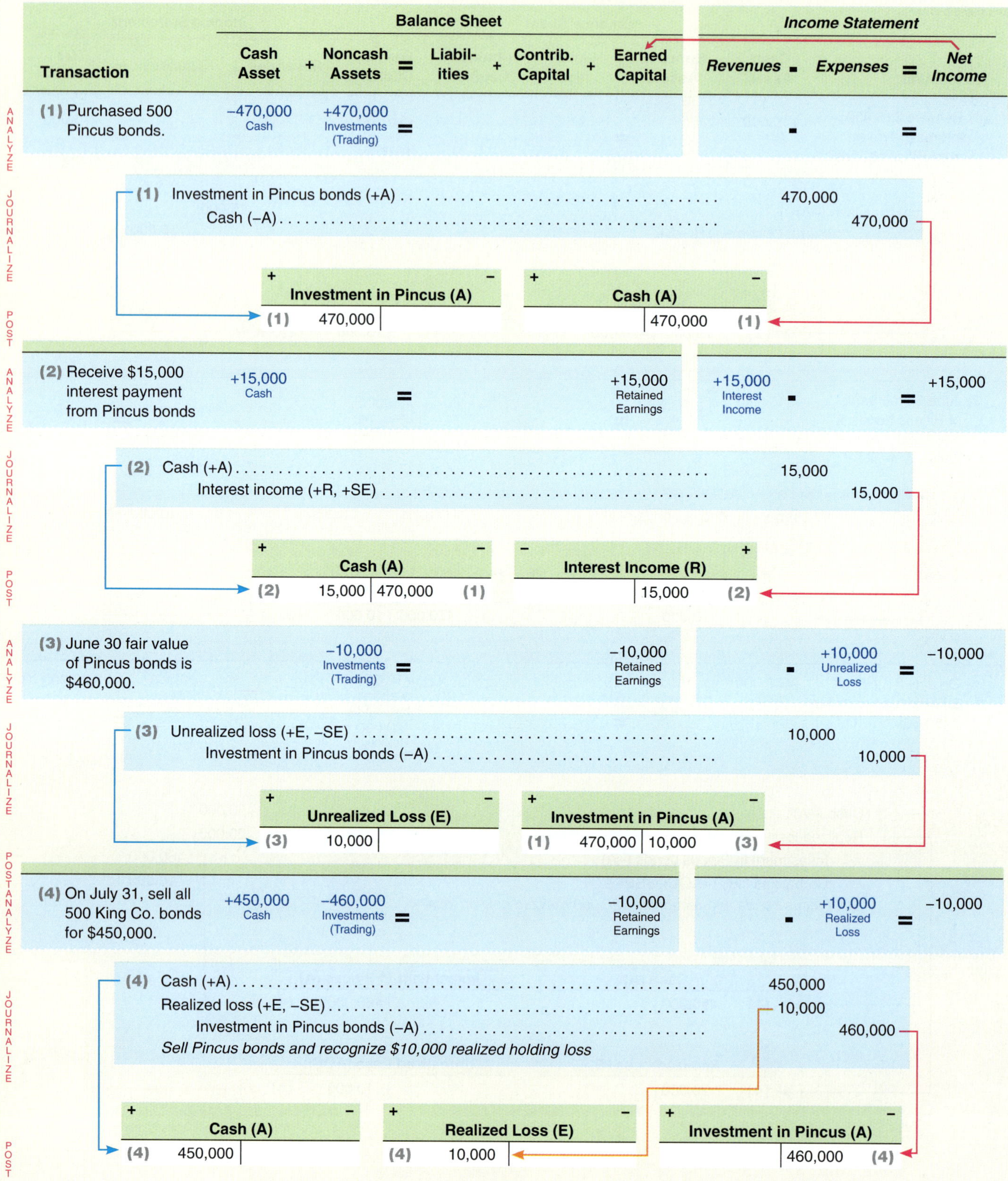

Mid-Chapter Review 2

SOLUTION

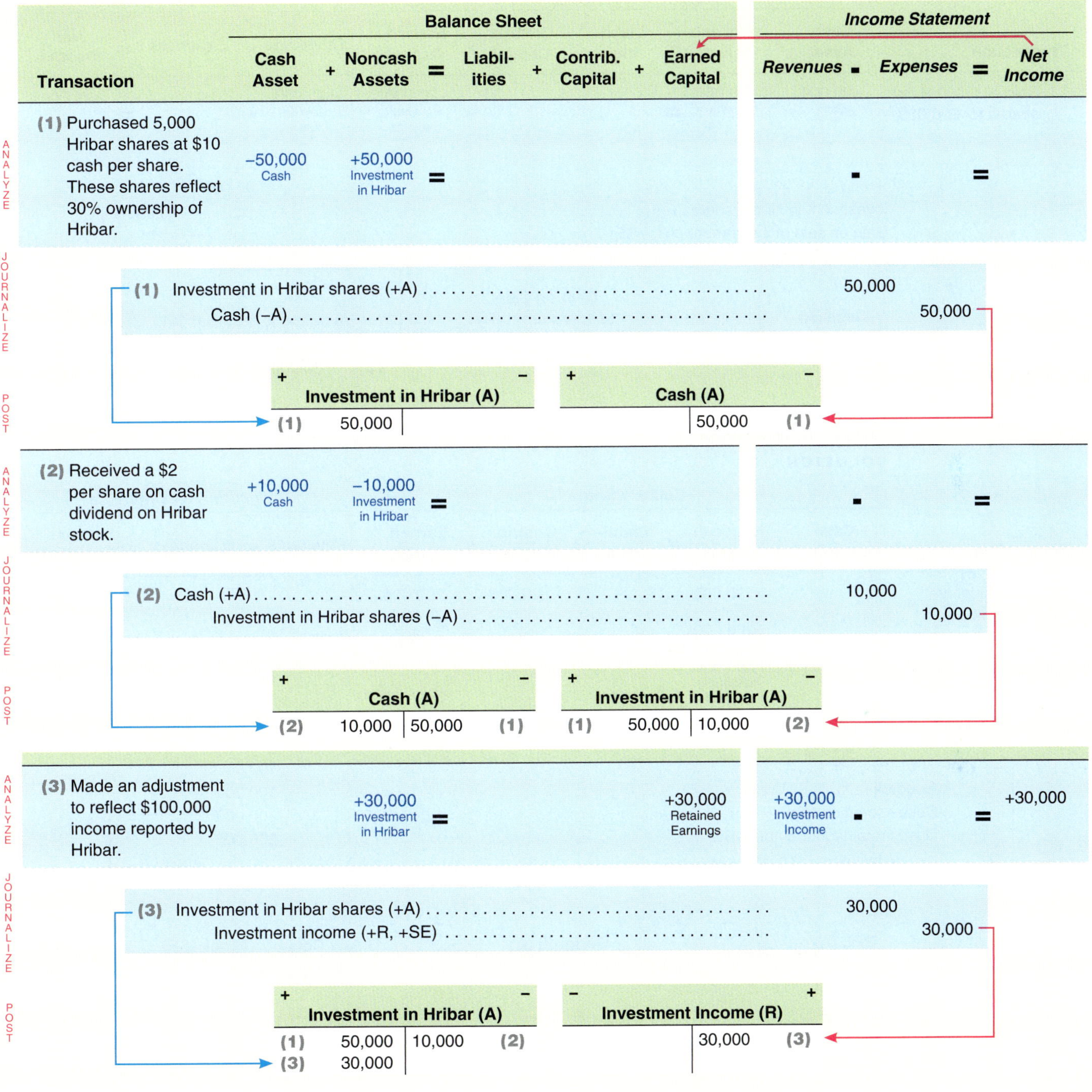

Transaction	Cash Asset	+	Noncash Assets	=	Liabilities	+	Contrib. Capital	+	Earned Capital	Revenues	−	Expenses	=	Net Income
(1) Purchased 5,000 Hribar shares at $10 cash per share. These shares reflect 30% ownership of Hribar.	−50,000 Cash		+50,000 Investment in Hribar	=							−		=	
(2) Received a $2 per share on cash dividend on Hribar stock.	+10,000 Cash		−10,000 Investment in Hribar	=							−		=	
(3) Made an adjustment to reflect $100,000 income reported by Hribar.			+30,000 Investment in Hribar	=					+30,000 Retained Earnings	+30,000 Investment Income	−		=	+30,000

Journal entry	Dr.	Cr.
(1) Investment in Hribar shares (+A)	50,000	
Cash (−A)		50,000
(2) Cash (+A)	10,000	
Investment in Hribar shares (−A)		10,000
(3) Investment in Hribar shares (+A)	30,000	
Investment income (+R, +SE)		30,000

Post (1):

+ Investment in Hribar (A) −		+ Cash (A) −	
(1) 50,000			50,000 (1)

Post (2):

+ Cash (A) −		+ Investment in Hribar (A) −	
(2) 10,000	50,000 (1)	(1) 50,000	10,000 (2)

Post (3):

+ Investment in Hribar (A) −		− Investment Income (R) +	
(1) 50,000	10,000 (2)		30,000 (3)
(3) 30,000			

continued

continued from previous page

ANALYZE

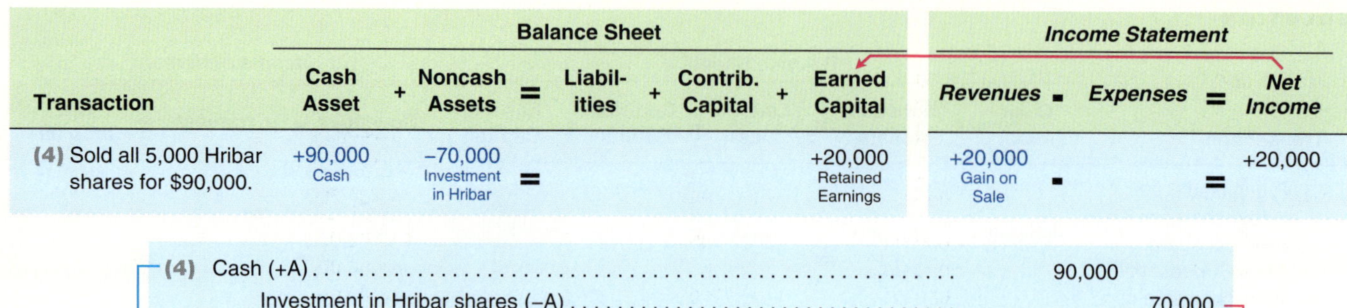

Transaction	Cash Asset	+	Noncash Assets	=	Liabil-ities	+	Contrib. Capital	+	Earned Capital	Revenues	−	Expenses	=	Net Income
	Balance Sheet									**Income Statement**				
(4) Sold all 5,000 Hribar shares for $90,000.	+90,000 Cash		−70,000 Investment in Hribar	=					+20,000 Retained Earnings	+20,000 Gain on Sale	−		=	+20,000

JOURNALIZE

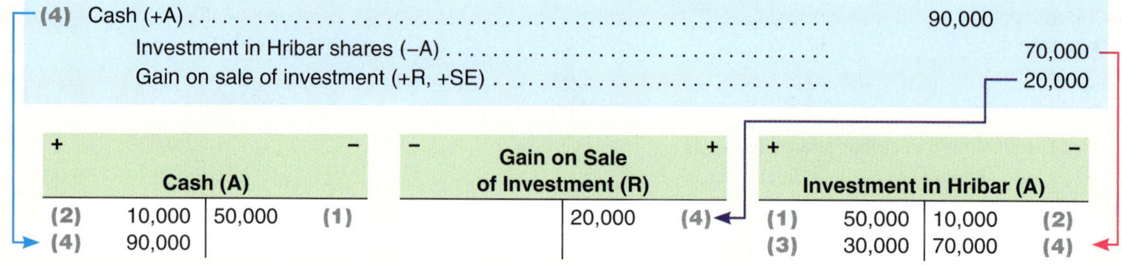

(4) Cash (+A)	90,000	
Investment in Hribar shares (−A)		70,000
Gain on sale of investment (+R, +SE)		20,000

POST

+ Cash (A) −			
(2)	10,000	50,000	(1)
(4)	90,000		

− Gain on Sale of Investment (R) +			
		20,000	(4)

+ Investment in Hribar (A) −			
(1)	50,000	10,000	(2)
(3)	30,000	70,000	(4)

Chapter-End Review

SOLUTION

ANALYZE

Transaction	Cash Asset	+	Noncash Assets	=	Liabil-ities	+	Contrib. Capital	+	Earned Capital	Revenues	−	Expenses	=	Net Income
	Balance Sheet									**Income Statement**				
(1) Consolidation adjustment for Bradshaw.			+100,000 PPE, net +100,000 Goodwill −600,000 Investment in Dukes	=			−200,000 Dukes Common Stock		−200,000 Dukes Retained Earnings		−		=	

JOURNALIZE

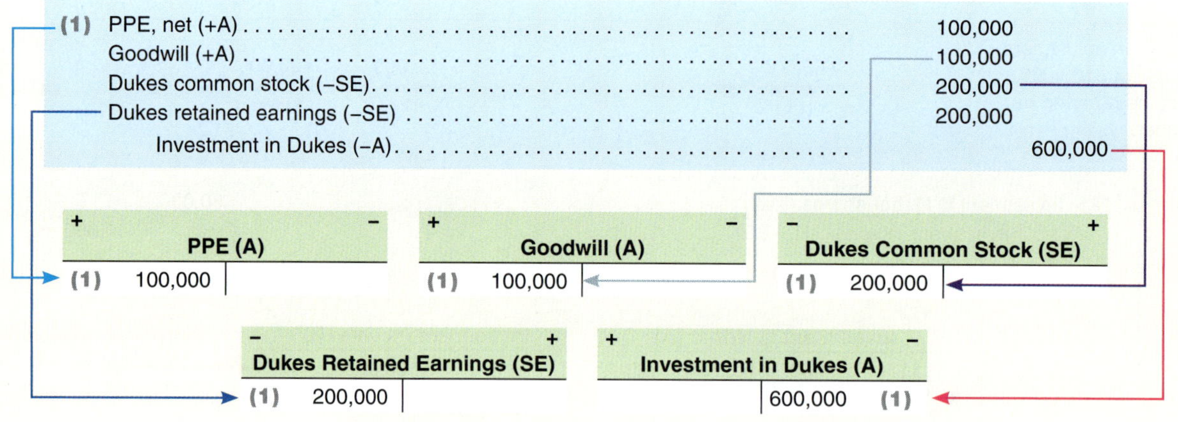

(1) PPE, net (+A)	100,000	
Goodwill (+A)	100,000	
Dukes common stock (−SE)	200,000	
Dukes retained earnings (−SE)	200,000	
Investment in Dukes (−A)		600,000

POST

+ PPE (A) −			
(1)	100,000		

+ Goodwill (A) −			
(1)	100,000		

− Dukes Common Stock (SE) +			
(1)	200,000		

− Dukes Retained Earnings (SE) +			
(1)	200,000		

+ Investment in Dukes (A) −			
		600,000	(1)

	Bradshaw (Parent)	Dukes (Subsidiary)	Consolidating Adjustments	Consolidated
Current assets	$1,000,000	$100,000		$1,100,000
Investment in Dukes	600,000	—	$(600,000)	
PPE, net	3,000,000	400,000	100,000	3,500,000
Goodwill	—	—	100,000	100,000
Total assets	$4,600,000	$500,000		$4,700,000
Liabilities	$1,000,000	$100,000		$1,100,000
Contributed capital	2,000,000	200,000	(200,000)	2,000,000
Retained earnings	1,600,000	200,000	(200,000)	1,600,000
Total liabilities and equity	$4,600,000	$500,000		$4,700,000

Notes: The $600,000 investment account is eliminated together with the $400,000 book value of Dukes' equity to which it mainly relates. The remaining $200,000 consists of the additional $100,000 in PPE assets and the $100,000 in goodwill from expected corporate synergies. Following these adjustments, the balance sheet items are summed to yield the consolidated balance sheet.

Compound Interest and the Time-Value of Money

Suppose you were lucky enough to hold a winning lottery ticket that allowed you to choose when you would receive your prize. Most of us would answer: Now! But let's say this ticket gave you the option of receiving $20,000 now, or $24,000 two years from now. Which would you choose?

Of course, $24,000 is better than $20,000. But the choice is not that simple. If you take the $20,000 today, you can buy a new car, pay next semester's tuition, or invest the money in the stock market. If you wait, you'll receive the larger prize, but you may have to take the bus for the next two years, postpone your college studies, or pass up on a great investment opportunity.

This is the essence of what is called the **time-value of money**. A dollar received today is worth more than a dollar received two years in the future. Having cash in our possession gives us the opportunity to spend or invest that cash today. Cash received in the future cannot be spent or invested today.[1]

The easiest way to illustrate the time-value of money is to assume that we collect the $20,000 cash prize today and invest it in a money-market account that guarantees a 10% return on your investment. In one year, the investment would be worth $22,000—which is the original $20,000 investment plus $2,000 interest ($20,000 × 10%). At the end of two years, the investment would be worth $24,200 [= $22,000 + ($22,000 × 10%) = $22,000 × 1.10].

In the second year, the investment earns a return of $2,200, which is $22,000 × 10%. The interest earned in the second year is greater than the interest earned in year one because the interest earned in the first year earns interest in year two. This interest earned on interest is called **compound interest**. As interest accumulates on an investment, both the original investment and the accumulated interest will earn a return in subsequent periods. Interest calculated on the original investment, but not on interest accrued in prior periods, is called **simple interest**.

This Appendix explains and illustrates the concepts of time-value of money and compound interest. It is divided into three sections. The first two address future value concepts and present value concepts, respectively. In the last section, we illustrate the use of spreadsheet software to compute present and future values.

[1] The time value of money is primarily due to lost opportunities. However, the risk associated with some future cash flows will influence our assessment of their time value. That is, there may be some uncertainty associated with a future payment. For instance, in our lottery ticket example, there may be a possibility that the payer could default on the $24,000 payment. Risk is reflected in time value calculations by using higher interest rates for risky cash flows.

FUTURE VALUE CONCEPTS

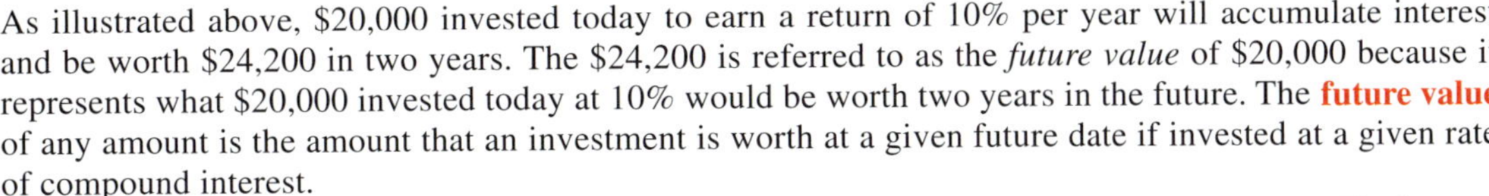

As illustrated above, \$20,000 invested today to earn a return of 10% per year will accumulate interest and be worth \$24,200 in two years. The \$24,200 is referred to as the *future value* of \$20,000 because it represents what \$20,000 invested today at 10% would be worth two years in the future. The **future value** of any amount is the amount that an investment is worth at a given future date if invested at a given rate of compound interest.

Assume that we allow our \$20,000 investment to continue to earn interest for three years. The interest will continue to compound and the future value will continue to grow. This is illustrated in **Exhibit A.1**.

EXHIBIT A.1 Future Value of \$20,000

Initial investment	\$20,000
Interest earned in year 1 (initial investment × 10%)	2,000
Investment plus accumulated interest (future value) in 1 year	22,000
Interest earned in year 2 (year 1 amount × 10%)	2,200
Investment plus accumulated interest (future value) in 2 years	24,200
Interest earned in year 3 (year 2 amount × 10%)	2,420
Investment plus accumulated interest (future value) in 3 years	\$26,620

As **Exhibit A.1** illustrates, the future value of \$20,000 invested for three years at 10% per year is \$26,620. This can be calculated as $\$26{,}620 = \$20{,}000 \times 1.10 \times 1.10 \times 1.10 = \$20{,}000 \times (1.10)^3$. Similarly, if the interest rate is 8%, the future value is $\$25{,}194 = \$20{,}000 \times (1.08)^3$. That is, to determine the future value of an amount n periods in the future, we multiply the present value by one plus the interest rate, raised to the nth power:

$$\textbf{Future Value} = \textbf{Present Value} \times (\mathbf{1} + \textbf{interest rate})^{n}$$

The future value of any amount depends on two factors: time and rate. That is, how many periods (e.g., years or months) into the future do we want to project the future value and what rate of return (or interest rate) do we use? There are two simple methods that we can use to obtain future values. The first method uses tables presented at the end of this Appendix. **Table A.1** presents the future value of a single amount. To use the table, move across the top of the table to choose the appropriate interest rate and then move down the column to choose the number of periods in the future. **Table A.1** shows that future value increases as the number of periods and as the interest rate increase.

For example, if we move across the top to the 10% column and then down to period 3, **Table A.1** provides a value of 1.33100. This is the future value of \$1 in three periods at 10% interest per period and is called the **future value factor**. If we want to calculate the future value of \$20,000, we multiply the *future value factor* from **Table A.1** by \$20,000:

Initial Amount	×	Future Value Factor	=	Future Value
\$20,000	×	**1.33100**	=	**\$26,620**

The future value can also be calculated using a financial calculator. Financial calculators require four inputs to calculate a fifth value, which is the solution. We illustrate the use of a calculator with the following graphic:

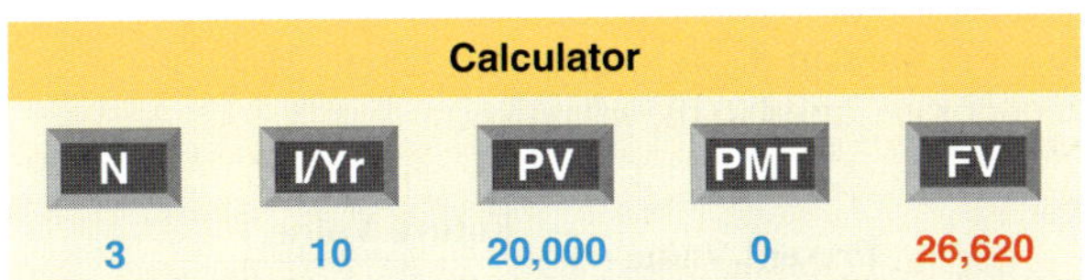

On the financial calculator, N is the number of periods (3), I/Yr is the interest rate per period (10), PV is the current, or present, value (\$20,000), PMT refers to a periodic payment (0 in our example) and FV is the future value. Because we are calculating the future value in this illustration, that value is highlighted in red as the solution.[2]

Whether we use the tables at the end of the Appendix or a financial calculator, it is important to recognize that these computations are based on an interest rate *per period*. Most interest rates are stated on an annual, or *per year*, basis. However, for compound interest calculations, a period need not be equal to a year.

[2] Actually, most calculators return a solution of −26,620. The calculator interprets the PV as an investment (cash out) and FV as the return (cash in). So, if PV is entered as a positive amount, then FV will come back negative, and vice versa.

Therefore, we must always be careful to adjust our interest rate *per year* to the appropriate interest rate *per period* and use the corresponding number of time periods in our calculations.

To illustrate, assume that our \$20,000 investment paid 8% annual interest, *compounded quarterly*. Although the interest rate is quoted as 8% *per year*, the rate is actually 2% every three-month *period* (=8%/4). Hence, in three years, we would have twelve periods. To determine the future value, we would go down the 2% column in **Table A.1** to the 12-period row to get a future value factor of 1.26824.

Initial Amount	×	**Future Value Factor**	=	**Future Value**
\$20,000	×	**1.26824**	=	**\$25,365**

Alternatively, using the financial calculator:

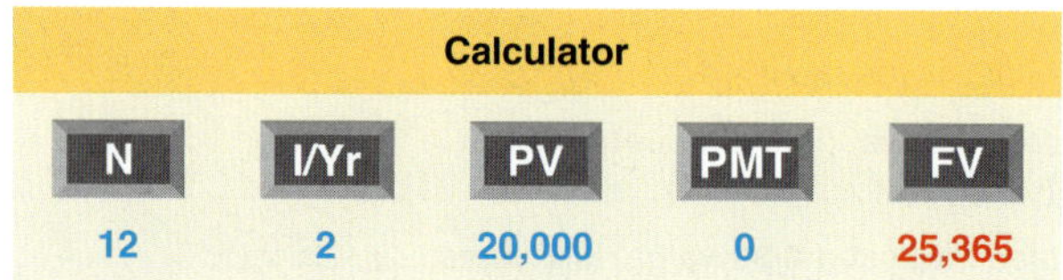

That is, the future value of \$20,000 invested for three years at 8%, compounded quarterly, is \$25,365.

PRESENT VALUE CONCEPTS

The concept of *present value* is the inverse of future value. Rather than determining how much an amount today is worth in the future, present value determines how much a future amount is worth today. The **present value** of an amount is the value *today* of a cash flow occurring at a future date given a rate of compound interest. As was the case with future value, present values depend on two factors: time and rate.

Present value is a particularly useful concept because it allows us to compare cash flows occurring at different times in the future. We can do this because we can calculate the value of each cash flow at a common point in time—today. For example, let's say we want to compare two investments. Investment A pays \$15,000 in two years. Investment B pays \$16,000 in three years. We cannot compare these two investments directly, because the payoffs occur in different amounts at different times in the future.[3] However, we can determine how much each payoff is worth today. If the appropriate interest rate is 8%, the present value of Investment A is \$12,860 and the present value of Investment B is \$12,701. (We demonstrate how to compute these amounts below.) Hence, Investment A is worth more today than Investment B. By determining the value of each cash payoff at the same point in time (today) we can easily compare the alternatives.

Present Value of a Single Amount

To determine the present value of a single cash payment occurring one period in the future, we simply divide the future cash flow by one plus the interest rate (the interest rate is also called the **discount rate**):[4]

$$\textbf{Present Value} = \frac{\textbf{Future Value}}{\textbf{(1 + discount rate)}}$$

If the cash flow occurs *n* periods in the future, we rearrange the equation from the previous page and divide by one plus the discount rate raised to the nth power:

$$\textbf{Present Value} = \frac{\textbf{Future Value}}{\textbf{(1 + discount rate)}^n}$$

[3] The reason that this comparison is difficult is that Investment A pays a return in two years while Investment B doesn't pay a return until year 3. One way to understand this complexity is to ask: What will happen to the cash earned on Investment A during the third year? Or, alternatively, if we invest the return on Investment A for an additional year, how much would we earn after three years? By comparing present values, we are implicitly assuming that any cash payoffs from either investment could be reinvested at the rate of return used to calculate the present value.

[4] The term "discount rate" is often used when referring to present values. This is because when future cash flows are valued using present value calculations, the present value is always less than the future cash amount. Hence, we say that the future value is "discounted" to the present value using the "discount rate."

There are two simple methods for obtaining the present value of a single cash flow occurring at any date in the future. The first method relies on **Table A.2** at the end of this Appendix. We use **Table A.2** in the same way we used **Table A.1** to calculate future values. First, we choose the column representing the appropriate discount rate, and then we move down the column to select the number of periods in the future. The value in the table is the **present value factor**, which decreases as the number of periods and the interest rate increase. We then multiply the future amount by the *present value factor* to get the present value.

For example, consider Investment A. From **Table A.2**, the present value factor for 8% and two periods is 0.85734. The present value of $15,000 received in two years, discounted at 8% per year is calculated as follows:

Future Amount	×	Present Value Factor	=	Present Value
$15,000	×	**0.85734**	=	**$12,860**

The present value can also be computed using a financial calculator. In this case, N=2; I/Yr = 8; PMT = 0; FV = 15,000 and PV is our answer (highlighted in red).

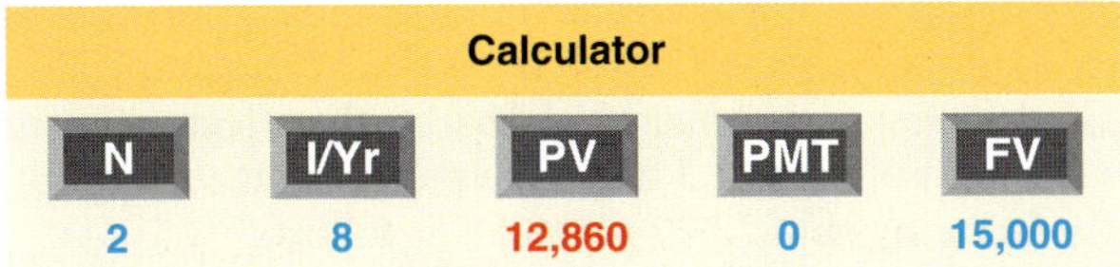

By similar means we can compute the present value of Investment B. The present value factor for 8%, and three periods is 0.79383. The present value of $16,000 received in three years, discounted at 8% per year is:

Future Amount	×	Present Value Factor	=	Present Value
$16,000	×	**0.79383**	=	**$12,701**

Or, using the financial calculator, we get the same answer as follows:

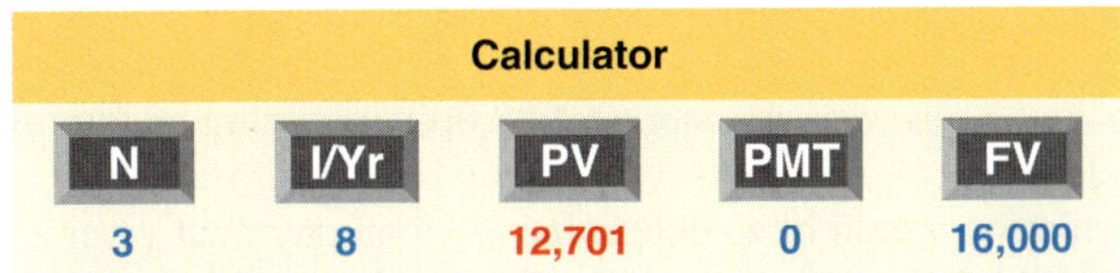

Present Value of an Annuity

Sometimes, we are faced with determining the present value of a series of regular, equal payments, called an **annuity**. For example, let's say we have an investment that pays $7,000 each year for the next three years. We can calculate the present value of each payment and then sum the results to get the present value of the entire annuity. Assume the appropriate discount rate is 6% per year. From **Table A.2**, the present value factors for a 6% discount rate are 0.94340 for one period, 0.89000 for two periods, and 0.83962 for three periods. The calculation of the present value is presented in **Exhibit A.2** (rounded to the nearest whole dollar):

EXHIBIT A.2 Present Value of an Annuity of 3 Payments of $7,000 Discounted at 6%

	Future Payment	×	Present Value Factor	=	Present Value
1	$7,000		0.94340		6,604
2	7,000		0.89000		6,230
3	7,000		0.83962		5,877
					$18,711

While this method of computing the present value of an annuity is accurate, it can be tedious for annuities with many cash payments. **Table A.3** at the end of this Appendix presents present value factors for annuities of various lengths. This table is used in the same way as **Table A.2**: first we choose the column reflecting our discount rate, and then we choose the row representing the number of payments. From **Table A.3**, the present value factor for an annuity of three payments discounted at 6% is 2.67301. To calculate the present value of an annuity, we multiply the periodic payment by the present value factor:

Payment	×	Present Value Factor	=	Present Value
$7,000	×	**2.67301**	=	**$18,711**

Or alternatively, using a financial calculator, we enter N=3, I/Yr=6, PMT=7,000, FV=0, and the solution is the PV, highlighted in red:

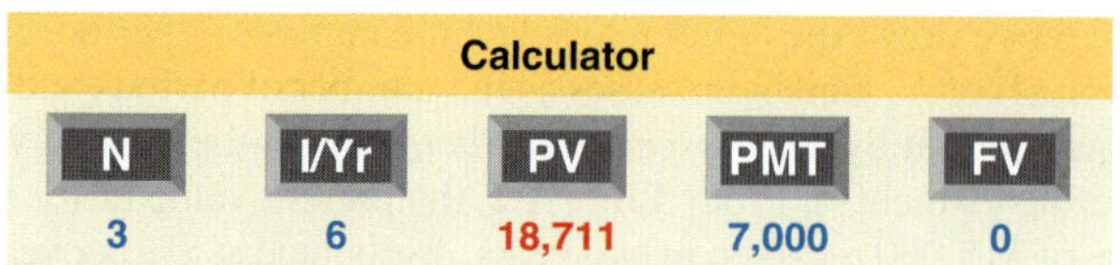

Installment Loans

One useful application of the present value of an annuity is to value an *installment loan*. An **installment loan** is a loan that requires a series of equal payments, or installments, each of which includes interest and some of the original principal. Assume that we take out a bank loan requiring 12 quarterly payments of $2,000 and an annual interest rate of 8%. When working with annuities, a period is the time between payments and the number of payments is the number of periods we use in our calculations. Because the payments are made quarterly, the 8% annual rate is compounded quarterly. That is, the effective interest rate is 2% per quarter. To calculate the loan amount, we use **Table A.3** to get the present value factor for 12 payments discounted at 2%, and then multiply the factor by our $2,000 payment, as follows:

Payment	×	Present Value Factor	=	Present Value
$2,000	×	**10.57534**	=	**$21,151**

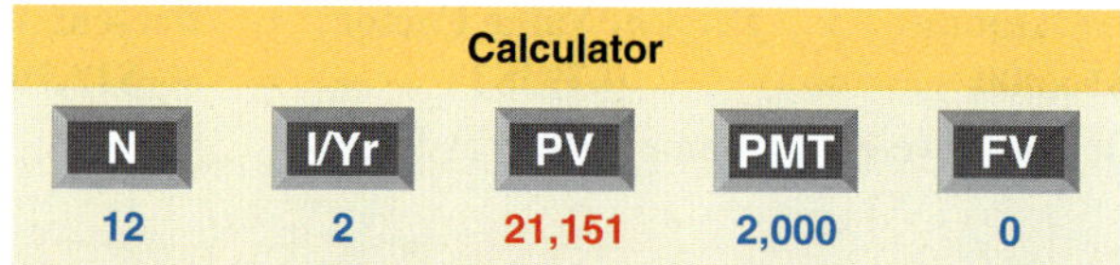

That is, if we agreed to make 12 quarterly payments of $2,000, including an interest charge of 2% per quarter, we could borrow $21,151.

A more common calculation would be to determine the loan payment given the amount borrowed. For example, if we borrow $30,000 and agree to repay the loan in 24 equal monthly payments at a 12% annual interest rate (1% per month), what monthly payment would we need to make to repay the loan plus interest? To compute the payment, we divide the present value (the loan amount) by the present value factor from **Table A.3** (1%, 24 periods) as follows:

Present Value	÷	Present Value Factor	=	Payment
$30,000	÷	**21.24339**	=	**$1,412.20**

Using a financial calculator, we can calculate the payment (PMT) directly, given the other inputs:

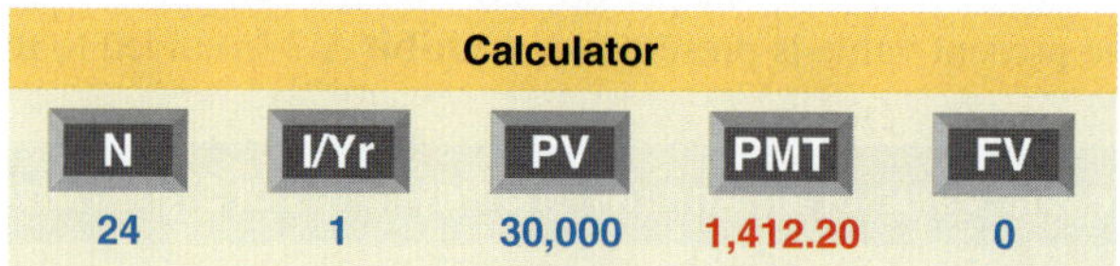

Bond Valuation

From Chapter 9, we know that a typical corporate bond has a face value of $1,000 and pays periodic interest payments every six months based on the stated (or coupon) interest rate. That is, the face value and the stated rate of a bond allow us to lay out the cash flows that will be paid to the bondholder. We also know that bonds are valued using the market interest rate, which may be different from the stated rate.

Bonds represent a combination of an annuity of the periodic interest payments and a single future payment of the face value, or principal payment, sometimes called a **balloon payment**. In order to value a bond, we must calculate the present value of each of these two components. Let's assume that we wish to value a $1,000, 5-year, 7% bond that pays a semi-annual coupon payment. The face value is $1,000 and the semi-annual payment is $35 (= $1,000 × 7%/2). Let's assume a market interest rate (yield) of 8% (which is 4% every six months). The bond is valued as the sum of two parts:

1. Use **Table A.2** to compute the value of the principal (balloon) payment.
2. Use **Table A.3** to compute the value of the annuity of interest (coupon) payments.

This calculation is illustrated in **Exhibit A.3**:

EXHIBIT A.3 Calculating a Bond Value Using Present Value Tables (4%, 10 periods)

	Cash Flow	×	Present Value Factor	=	Present Value
Face value: 1 payment of $1,000 at the end of 5 years (**Table A.2**—4%, 10 periods)	$1,000	×	0.67556	=	675.56
Semi-annual coupon payments: 10-payment annuity of $35 every six months (**Table A.3**—4%, 10 periods)	$35	×	8.11090	=	283.88
					$959.44

The bond value can also be calculated using a financial calculator, with the following inputs: N=10; I/Yr=4; PMT=35; FV=1,000. The solution is the PV:

Calculator

N	I/Yr	PV	PMT	FV
10	4	959.45	35	1,000

The calculator automatically adds the present value of the annuity (10 payments of $35) to the present value of the single amount ($1,000 principal value) to get the bond value. That is, the market is willing to invest $959.45 in a $1,000, 5-year, 7% bond that pays interest semi-annually, and this amount is what would be received in proceeds from issuing the bond. The difference between $1,000 and $959.45 can be attributed to the difference between the 7% coupon rate of interest and the 8% required by investors.

Calculating Bond Yields

Sometimes we know the future cash payments and the present value of those payments, but not the discount rate used to compute the present value. This would be useful, for example, if we knew the price of a bond but wanted to determine the yield.

To illustrate the calculation of a bond yield, assume that we have a $1,000, 8-year, 5% bond that is currently priced at 104 (104% of par value or $1,040). The semiannual interest payment is $25 (= $1,000 × 5%/2) and the principal amount of $1,000 is due in 8 years (16 semiannual periods). We input the following values: N=16; PV=1,040; PMT=25; FV=1,000. The solution is returned by pressing the I/Yr button:

Calculator

N	I/Yr	PV	PMT	FV
16	2.20	1,040	25	1,000

In this case, the calculator returns a solution of 2.20%. This is the interest rate *per period* that discounts the future payments on the bond to the present value of $1,040. Because each period is six months, we must double this rate to get the bond yield (or market rate of interest), which is always quoted on an annual basis. Thus, the yield on this bond is 4.4% (= 2.2% × 2).[5]

Future Value of Annuities

On occasion, we may have a future funding target that will be met by making period payments. For instance, we may wish to accumulate a down payment for a residence or accumulate a retirement balance to draw upon in future years. For this analysis, we must examine the future value created by an annuity, i.e., a series of payments.

Suppose we wish to accumulate a down payment by making quarterly payments into an account that earns 4% per year (1% per quarter). Payments of $2,000 would be made at the beginning of each quarter

[5] Technically, in order to obtain the result illustrated here, the amounts for PMT and FV must be entered with the same sign, but the PV amount must be entered with the opposite sign. For example, if we enter PV = −1,040, PMT = 25 and FV = 1,000, we would get the result above.

and would continue for five years. How much would accumulate over the five years? The future value of each payment can be determined using **Table A.1**, but **Table A.4** accumulates the amounts in a convenient format. An annuity of $2,000 per quarter for 20 quarters at 1% per period would produce a future value of:

Payment	×	Future Value Factor	=	Future Value
$2,000	×	**22.2392**	=	**$44,478.40**

This analysis would also allow for testing the sensitivity of the amount to various factors. For instance, making payments for 6 years, would increase the balance to $54,486.40. Investing in an account that provided 2% interest per quarter would accumulate $49,566.60 after five years.

USING EXCEL TO COMPUTE TIME VALUE

Spreadsheet software, such as Microsoft Excel© is extremely useful for performing a variety of time-value calculations. In this section, we illustrate a few of the features of Excel.

Future Value Calculations

Calculating future value in Excel is straightforward by using the formula for future value or using the function wizard feature. Assume we wish to compute the future value of $12,000 invested today at 6% interest for four years. The formula for this calculation is:

=12000*1.06^4

Excel returns the value 15149.72. An alternative method of making this calculation is by using the function wizard. The function wizard is accessed by clicking on the *fx* icon in the formula bar at the top of the spreadsheet.

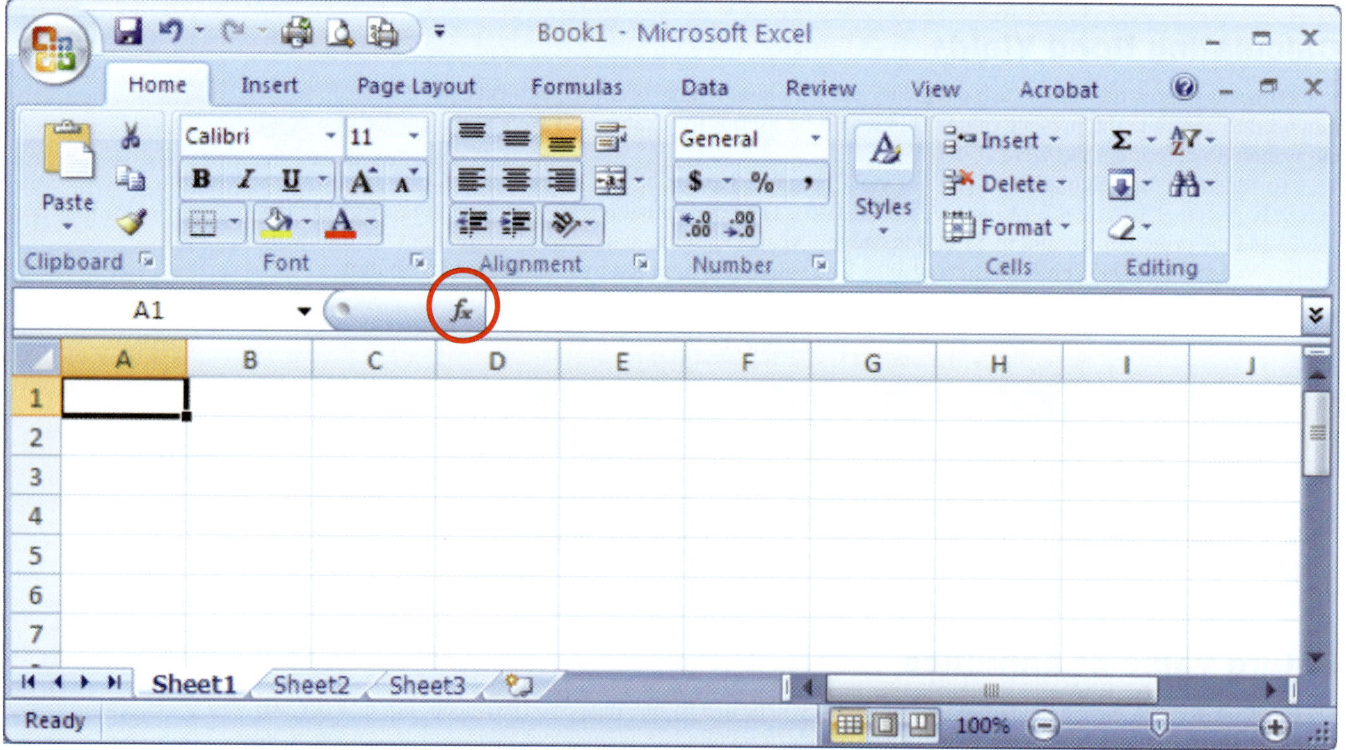

Clicking on the *fx* icon opens a dialog box that offers a variety of built-in functions. The dialog box appears as follows:

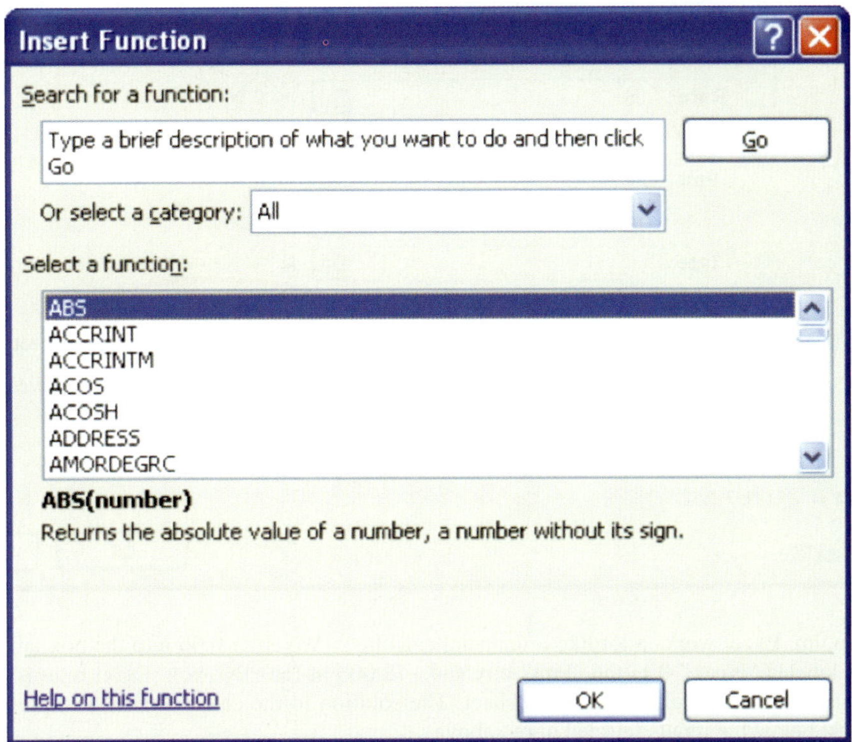

Now, the user can scroll through the long list of built-in Excel functions or customize the search by selecting a category of functions. In the screen shot below, the category of functions described as "Financial" is selected. Scrolling through the list, we select the FV function (for future value).

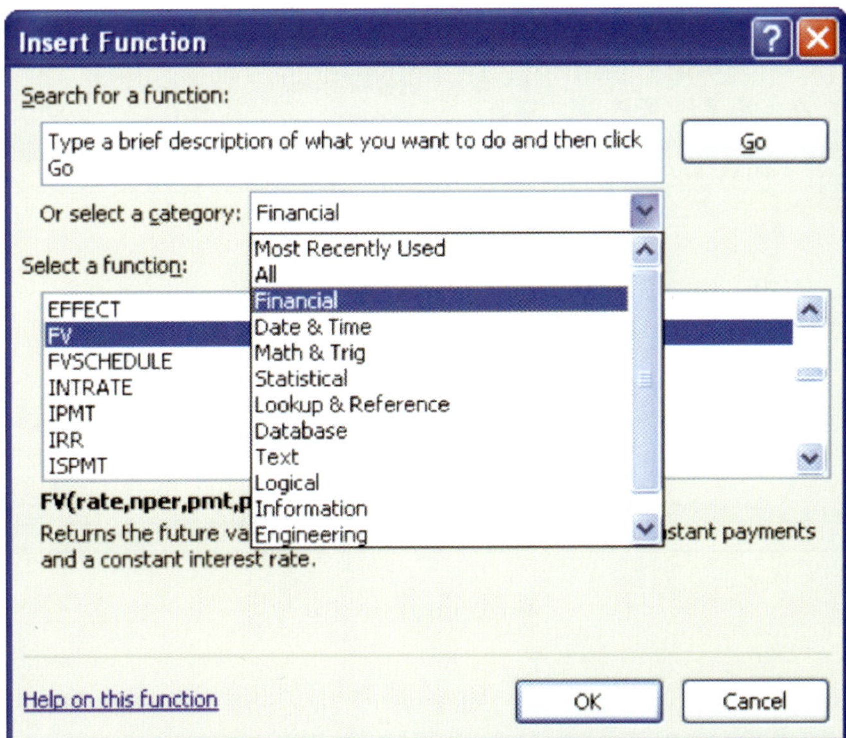

Once the FV function is selected, a new dialog box appears:

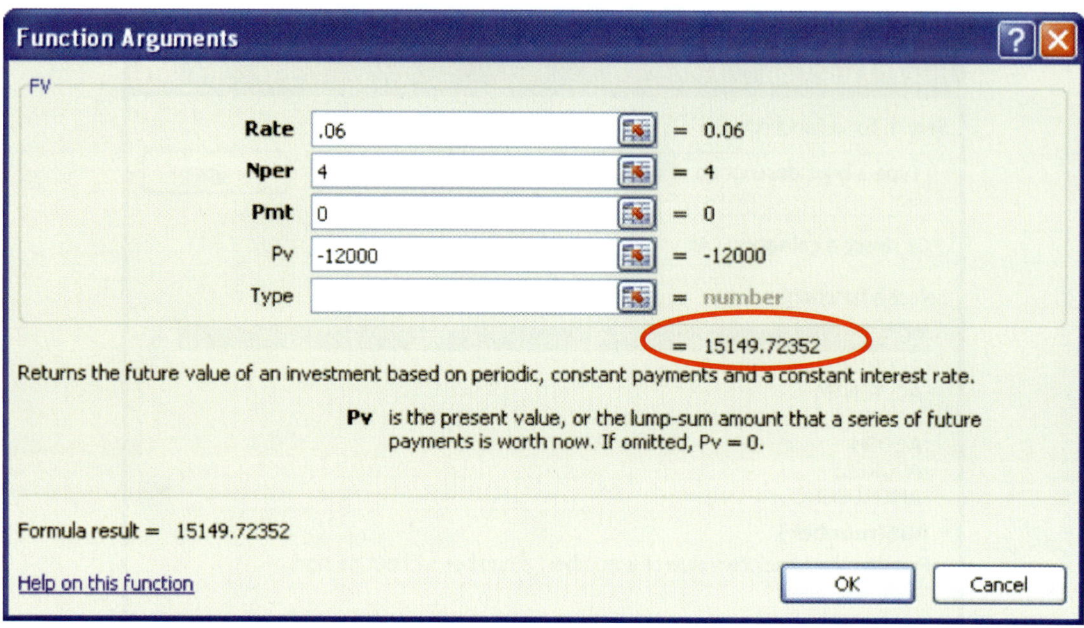

At this point, Excel works a lot like a financial calculator. We enter 0.06 into the box labeled "Rate," 4 in the box labeled "Nper," 0 in the "Pmt" box and −12,000 in the "Pv" box. Excel returns the value of $15,149.72 in the selected cell in the spreadsheet. The solution to the calculation is also presented in the dialog box just below the inputs (circled in red above).

One advantage of Excel, is that it allows the user to enter cell locations as function arguments in the dialog box. This can be useful if we wish to gauge the impact of changing an argument. For instance, we could enter the following in a spreadsheet:

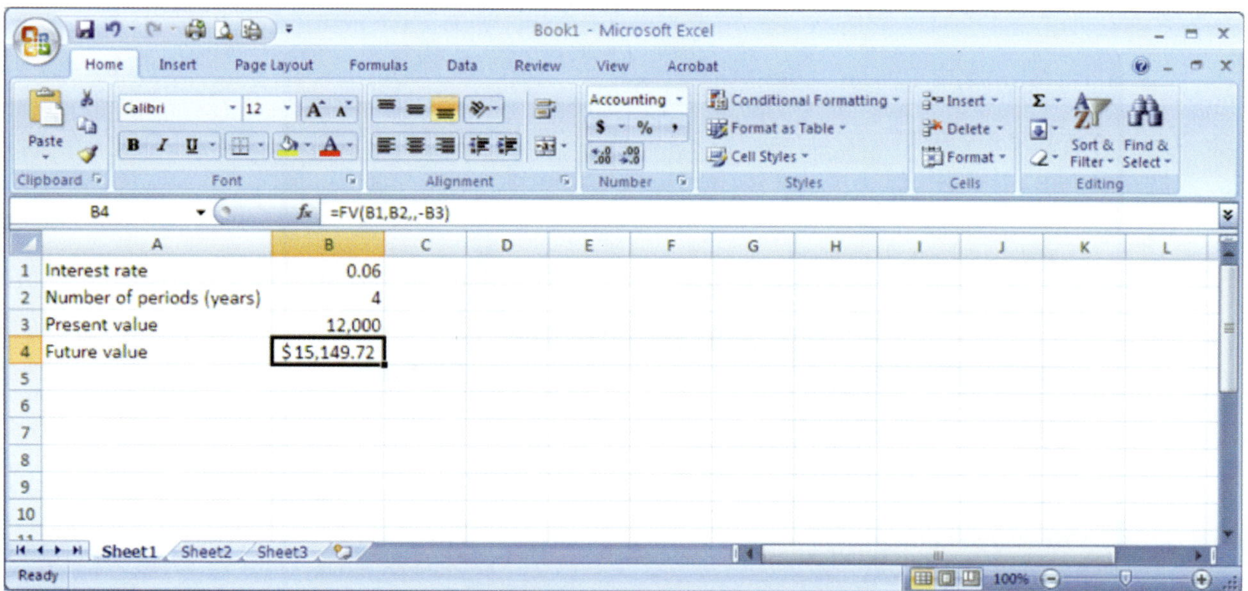

The amount presented as the "Future value" is actually returned by the dialog box below:

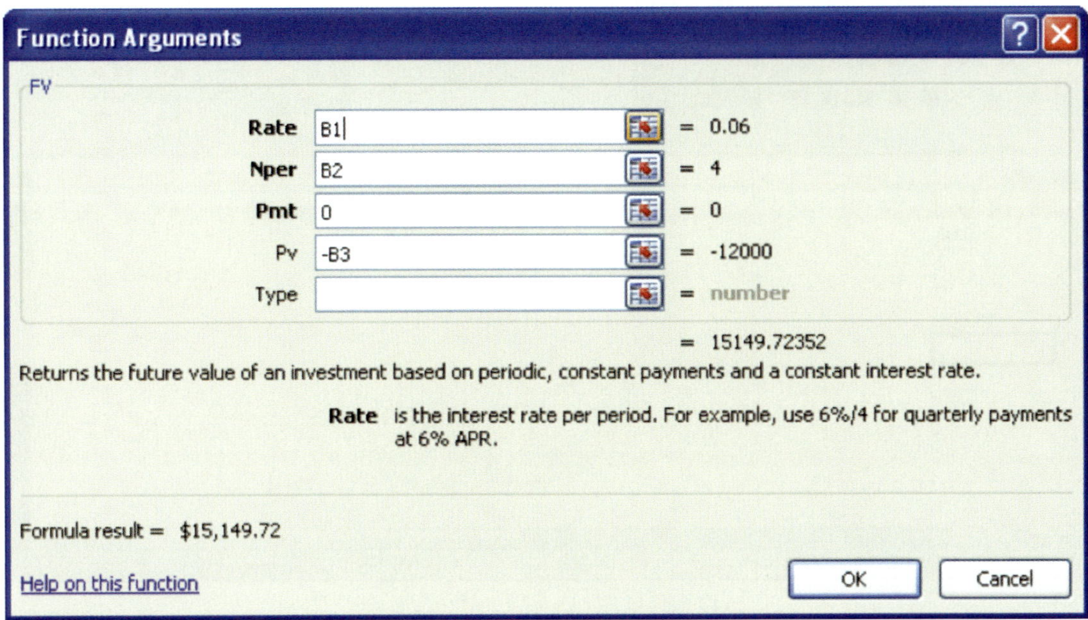

When we enter cell locations (e.g., "B1") in the boxes for function arguments, the function wizard uses the value in that cell as the argument. The benefit of this is that we can now change an argument and recalculate the future value without revisiting the function wizard dialog box. For example, let's say we wish to determine what the future value of our investment would be if we held our investment for five years instead of four years. We simply replace the "4" in cell B2 with a "5" as follows:

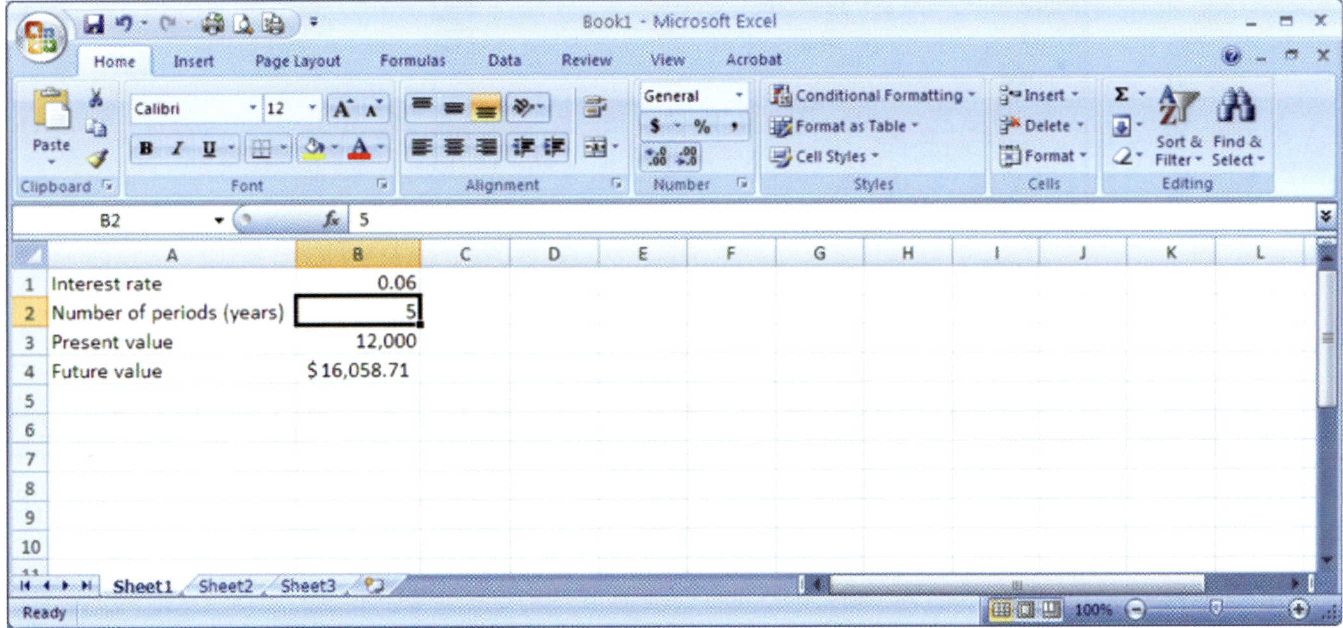

Excel automatically returns the value of $16,058.71 as the future value (cell B4).

Present Value Calculations

Computing present value is as straightforward as future value. The function to use is "PV" for present value. Let's assume we wish to calculate the present value of $15,000 that we expect to receive in two years discounted at 8% per year. Earlier, we determined that the present value is $12,860. To make this calculation using Excel, we enter each of the arguments in the spreadsheet as follows:

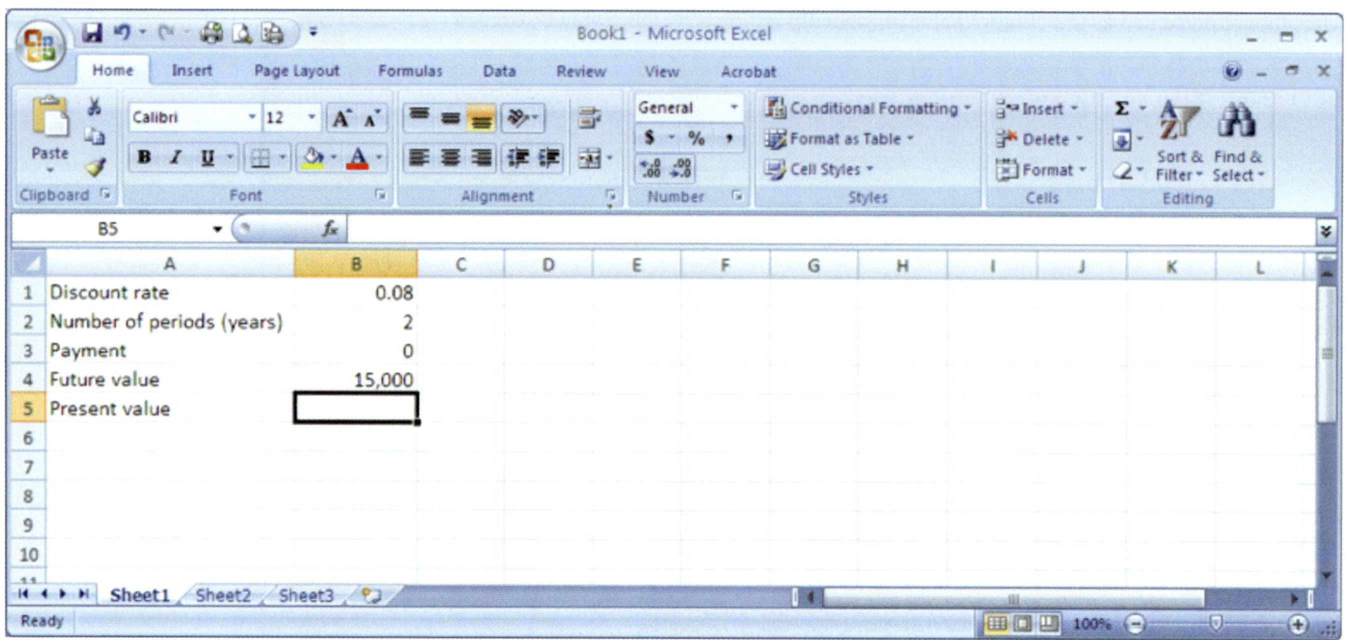

We then use the function wizard to access the "PV" function:

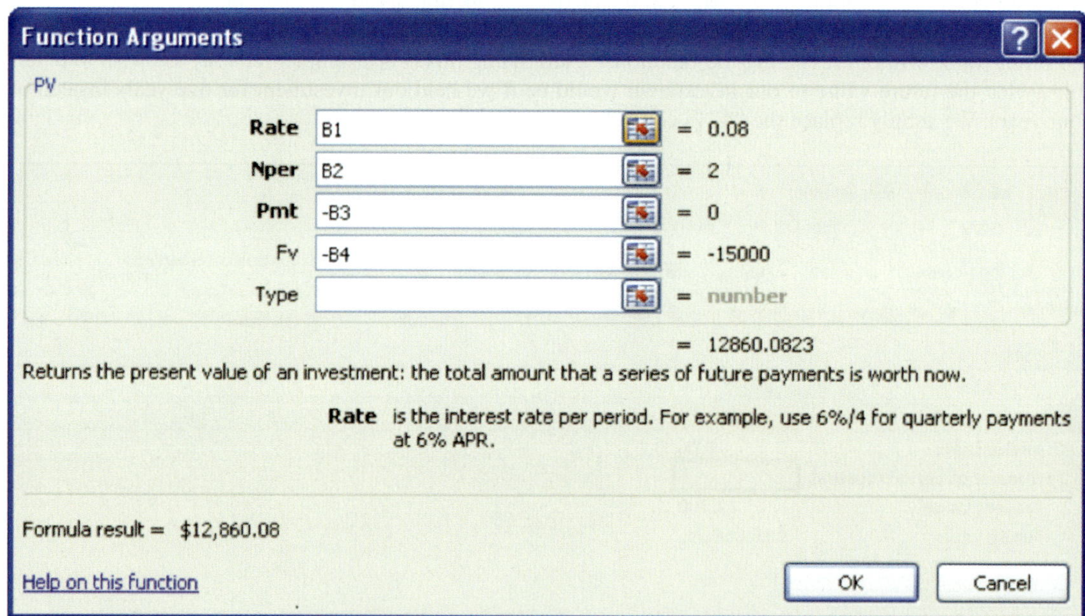

The PV function is similar to the FV function. The amount returned is the present value of $12,860.08. The "Pmt" argument in the PV function is used for annuity payments. In this example, we wanted the present value of a lump-sum amount paid in two years, so the payment was set to 0. However, we can use the same function to compute the present value of an annuity by entering the annuity payment as a negative amount in the "Pmt" argument or in the payment cell of our spreadsheet. Earlier, we determined that the present value of a series of $7,000 payments received annually for three years and discounted at 6% is $18,711. To compute this amount using Excel, we list the payment (Pmt) as 7,000 and the future value (FV) as 0:

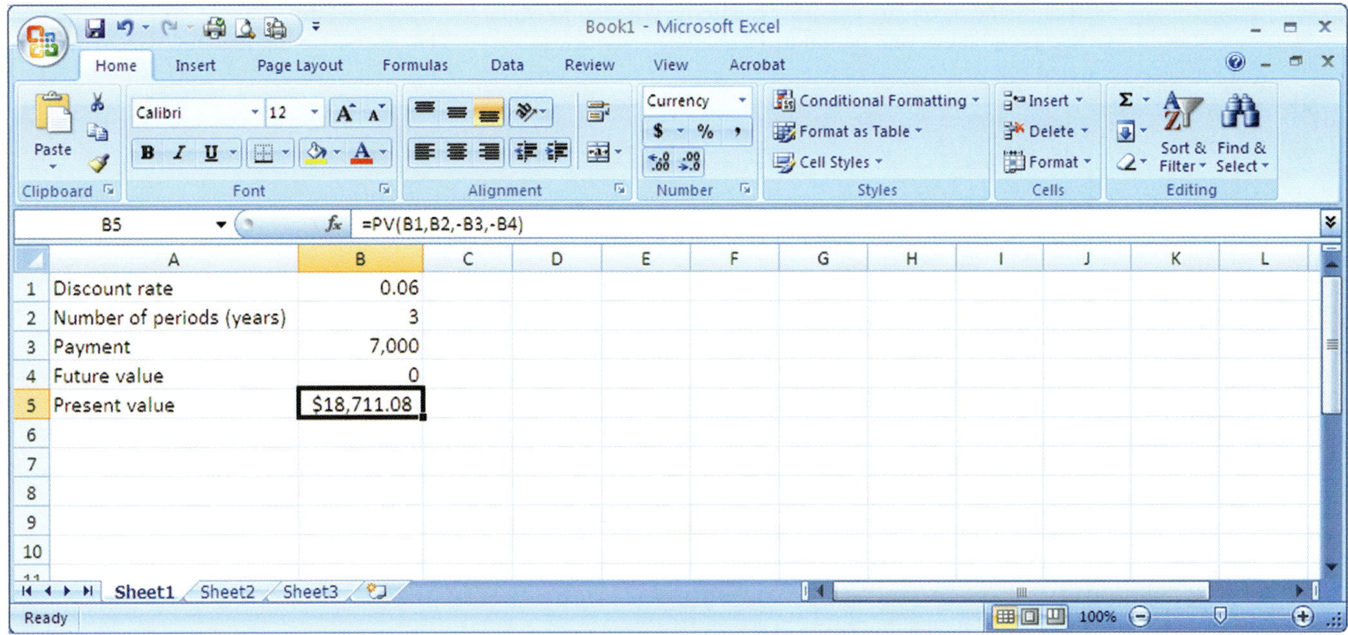

Similarly, our installment loan that requires 12 quarterly payments of $2,000 at 8% interest per year (2% per quarter) would have a present value of $21,150.68, which is computed as follows:

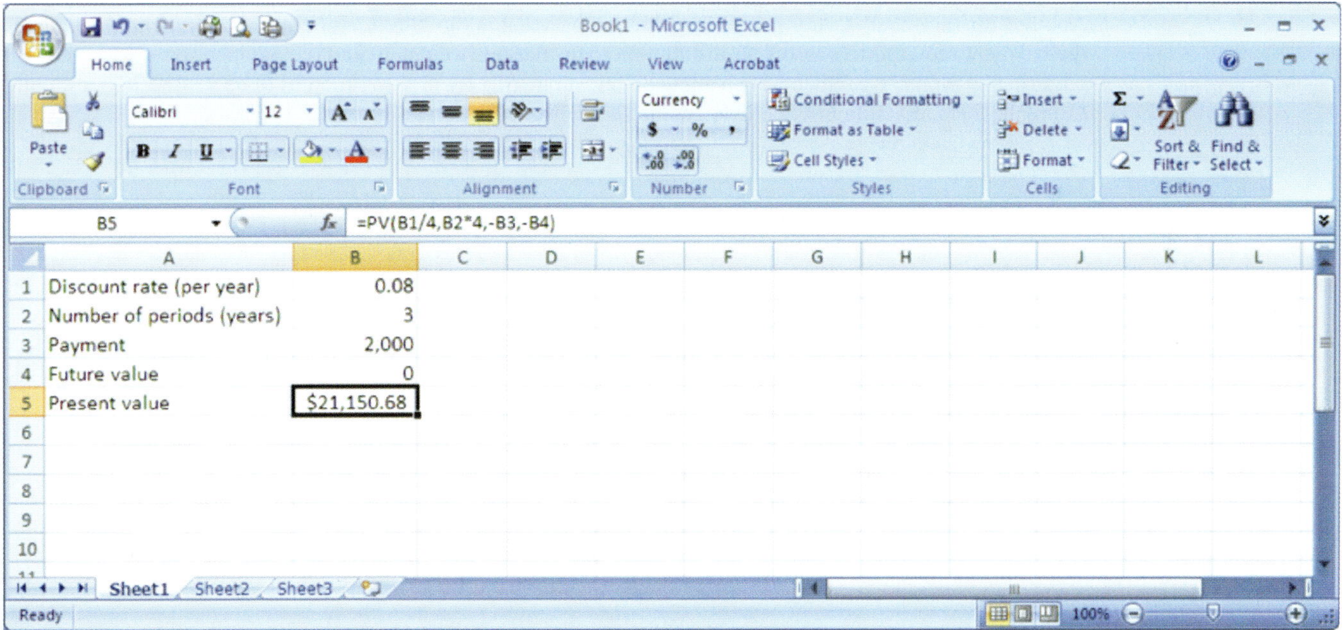

Because the payments are made quarterly, we need to adjust the 8% annual discount rate to 2% per quarter (8%/4) and the 3 year period to 12 quarterly payments (3 × 4). This is done in the function wizard as illustrated below:

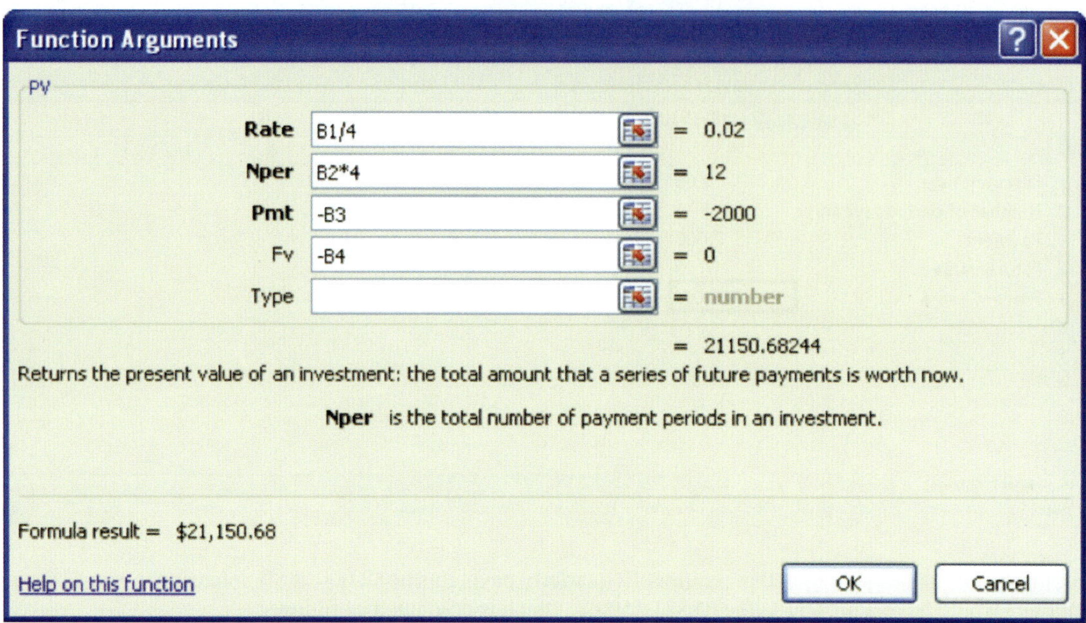

Another function that is very useful for installment loans is the "PMT" function. This function calculates the payment required to pay off an installment loan. Earlier, we calculated the payment on a $30,000 loan requiring 24 monthly payments at an annual interest rate of 12% (1% per month) to be $1,412.20 per month. Using the PMT function in Excel, we get the same result:

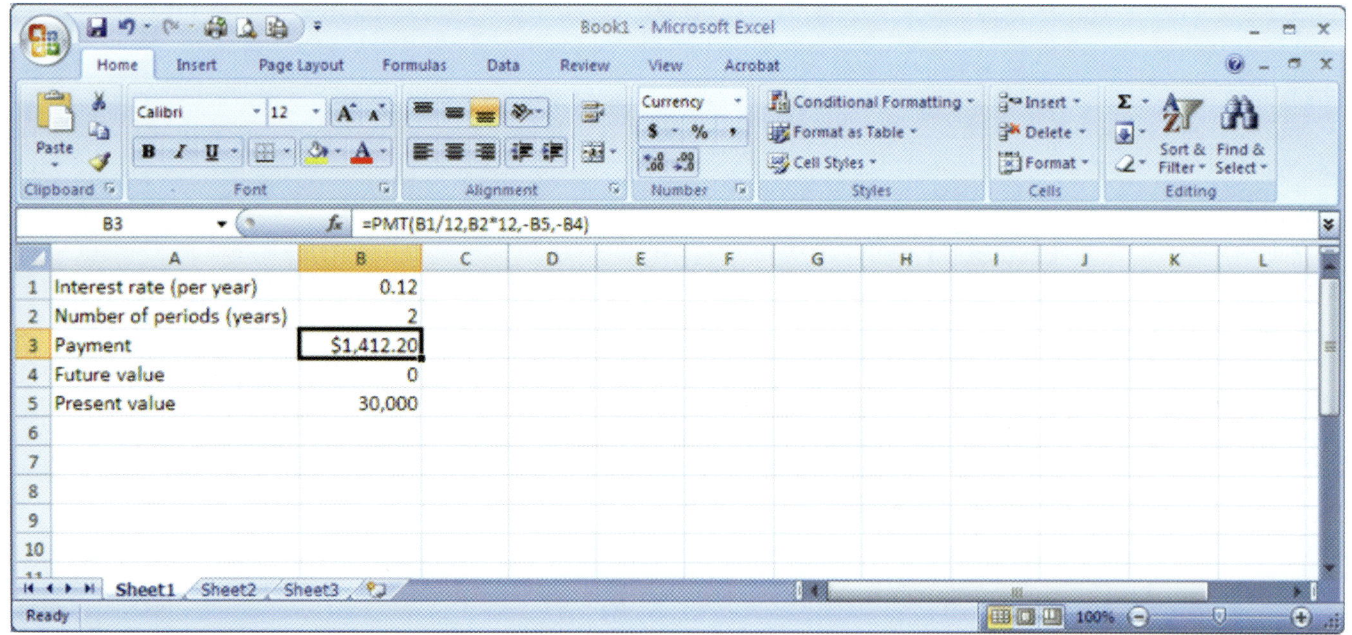

Here we need to divide the annual interest rate by 12 and multiply the number of years by 12 in order to allow for monthly compounding.

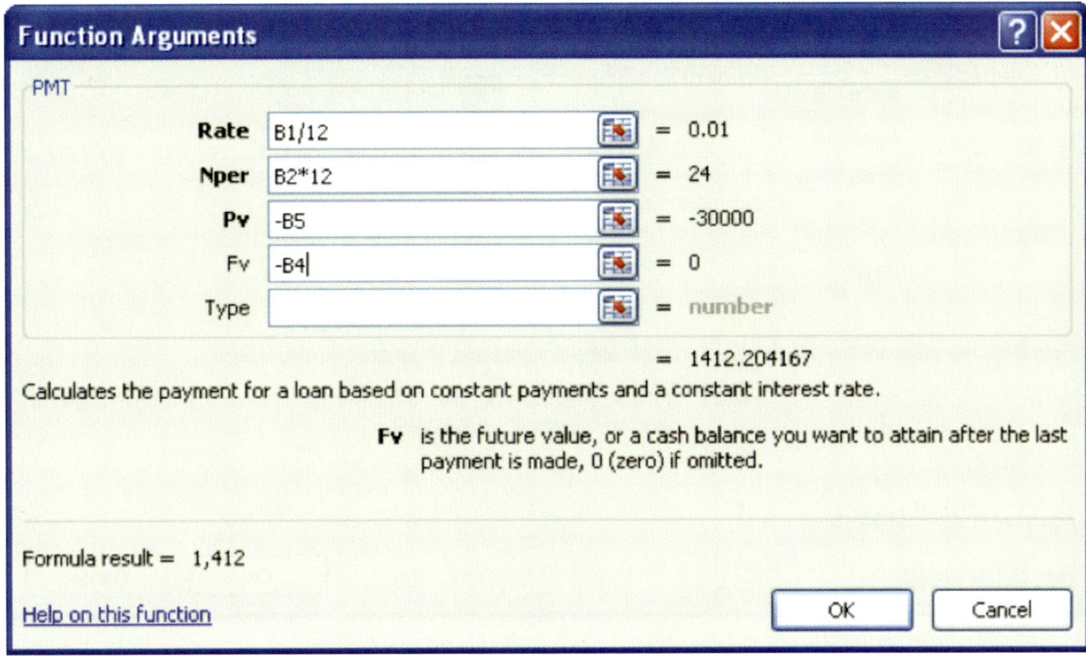

Excel is very useful for setting up loan amortization tables. These tables lay out the loan payments and calculate the interest and principal included in each payment. To illustrate, assume we borrow $5,000 at 4% annual interest, and agree to repay the loan in 8 quarterly payments (four payments per year for two years). The quarterly payment is $653.45 calculated as follows:

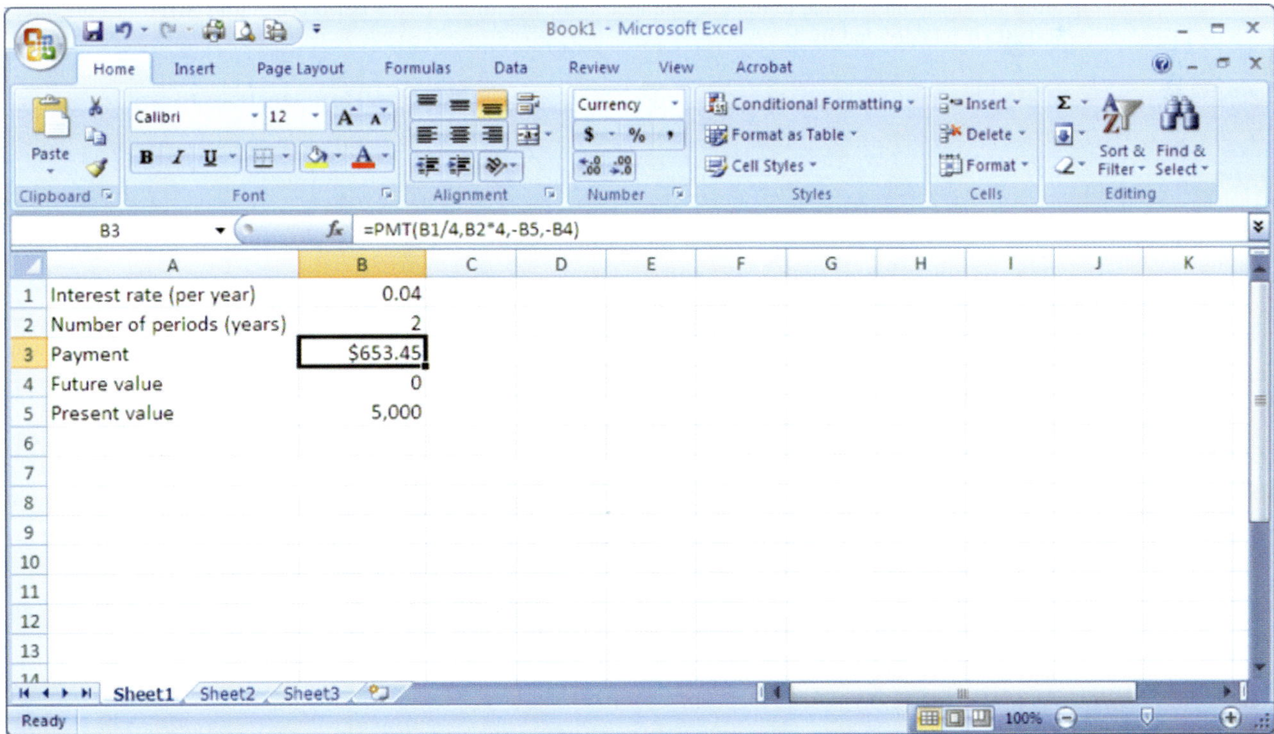

The function box appears as follows:

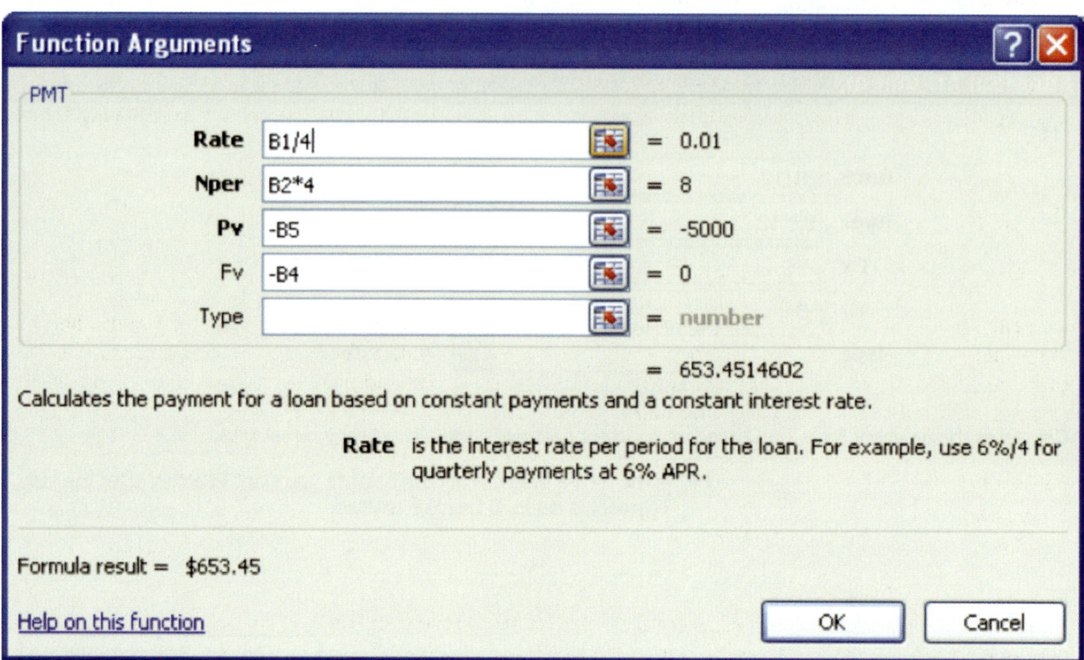

The loan amortization table can be set up on the same worksheet or in a separate sheet linked to the payment calculation. Here we use the same worksheet.

The first column [D] lists the period (1 through 8). In the second column [E], we list the loan balance at the beginning of each period. For the first period, the beginning balance is the loan amount of $5,000. Thereafter, the beginning balance is set equal to the ending balance from the previous period, which is in column [I]. Column [F] lists the quarterly payment of $653.45. In column [G], we compute the interest each quarter. This amount is equal to the loan balance at the beginning of the period (Column [E]) times the interest rate (cell B1) divided by 4.

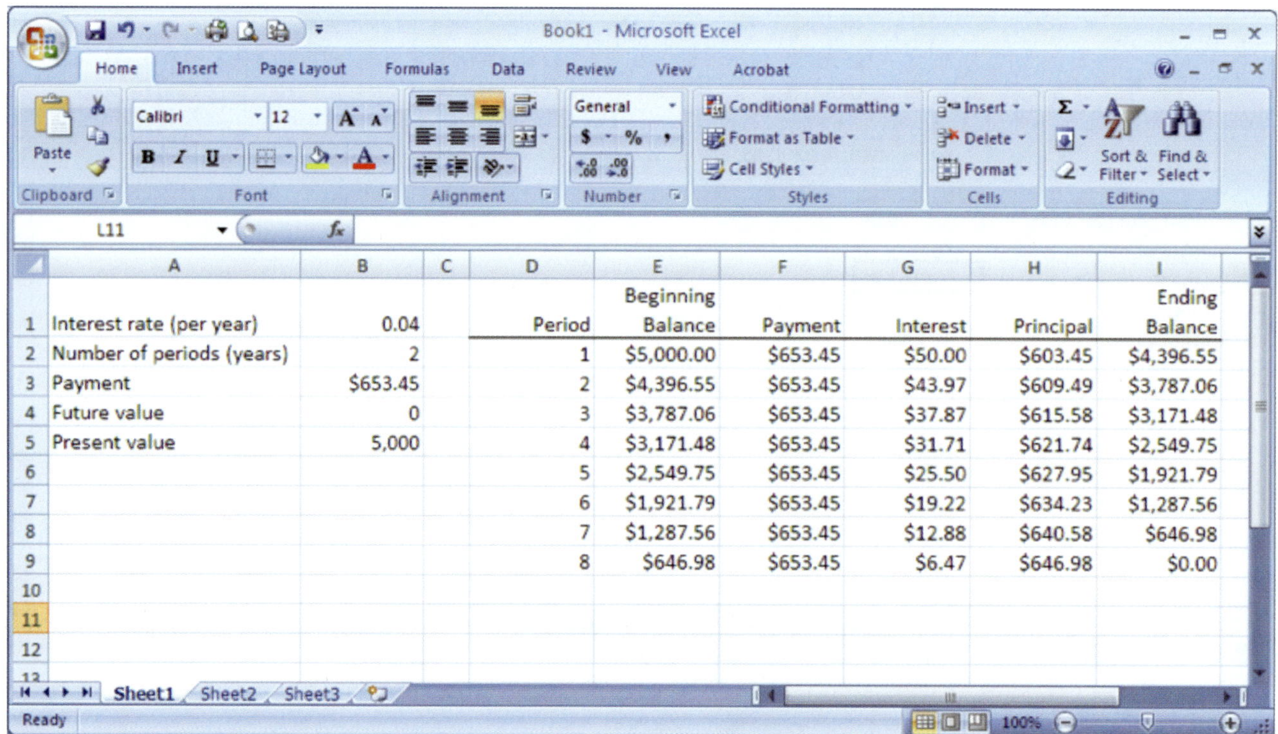

	A	B	C	D	E	F	G	H	I
1	Interest rate (per year)	0.04		Period	Beginning Balance	Payment	Interest	Principal	Ending Balance
2	Number of periods (years)	2		1	$5,000.00	$653.45	$50.00	$603.45	$4,396.55
3	Payment	$653.45		2	$4,396.55	$653.45	$43.97	$609.49	$3,787.06
4	Future value	0		3	$3,787.06	$653.45	$37.87	$615.58	$3,171.48
5	Present value	5,000		4	$3,171.48	$653.45	$31.71	$621.74	$2,549.75
6				5	$2,549.75	$653.45	$25.50	$627.95	$1,921.79
7				6	$1,921.79	$653.45	$19.22	$634.23	$1,287.56
8				7	$1,287.56	$653.45	$12.88	$640.58	$646.98
9				8	$646.98	$653.45	$6.47	$646.98	$0.00
10									
11									
12									

In column [H] we compute the principal component of each payment. This amount is the payment (column [F]) minus the interest (column [G]). Finally, the ending balance (column [I]) is the beginning balance (column [E]) minus the principal (column [H]). Note that the ending balance in period 8 is $0 (the loan has been completely paid off).

Loan amortization tables are especially useful for accountants because the table computes the amounts we enter for each payment. To illustrate, to record the original $5,000 loan, we make the following journal entry:

Cash (+A)	5,000.00	
Loan payable (+L)		5,000.00

Now, each period, we make a loan payment of $653.45 and that payment is part interest expense and part loan principal. To determine the split between interest and principal, we consult the loan amortization table. For instance, in period 1, the payment is split as $50.00 of interest and $603.45 of principal. To record this payment, we would make the following journal entry:

Interest expense (+E, −SE)	50.00	
Loan payable (−L)	603.45	
Cash (−A)		653.45

Finally, Excel allows us to easily compute the present value of a series of irregular cash flows. To do this we use the NPV function. (NPV stands for *Net Present Value.*) To compute NPV we need a series of cash flows at regular time intervals, such as one payment per year. If we skip a period, we must enter a 0 for that period. The cash flows can be a mixture of positive and negative cash flows (for instance receipts and payments). In the following spreadsheet, we present a series of seven cash flows and calculate the present value of these payments discounted at 5% using the NPV function.

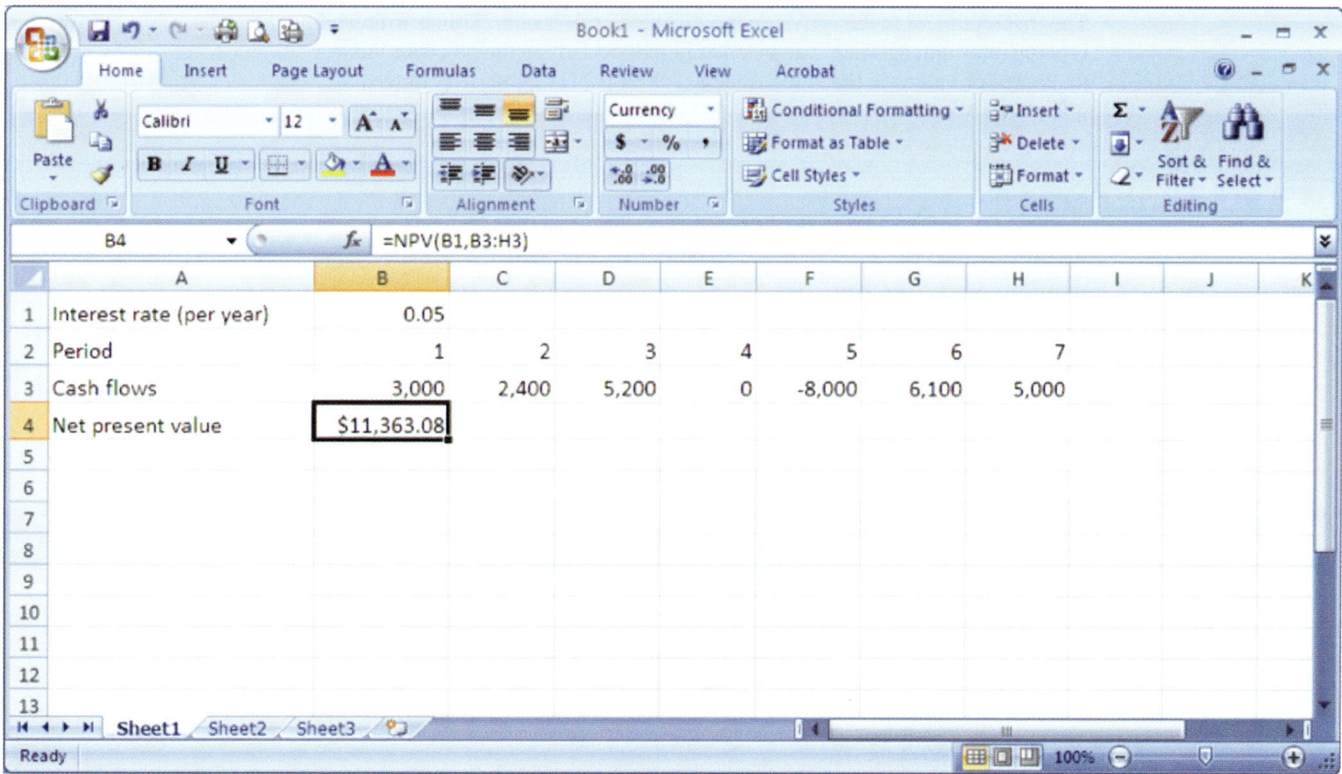

The spreadsheet shows a net present value of $11,363.08. The function wizard dialog box for the NPV function is presented below:

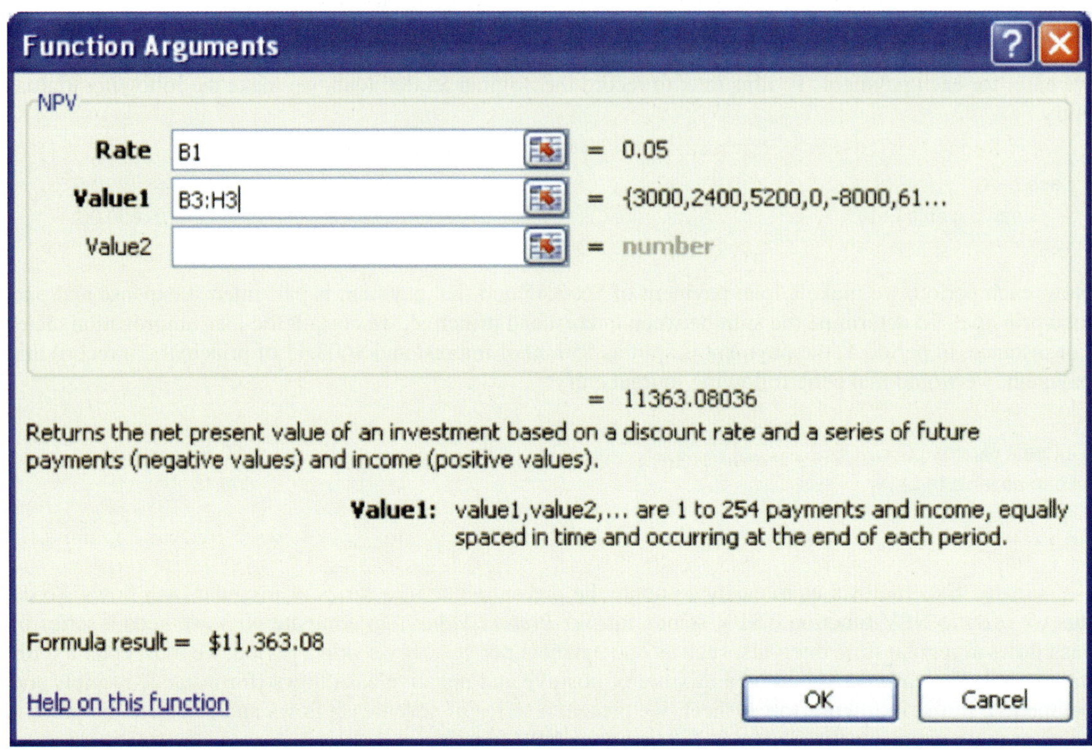

The first argument in the NPV function is the discount rate. This is followed by the series of cash flows that is being discounted. These can be entered individually in the box for "Value1," "Value2," etc. or by referring to a range of values in the spreadsheet, such as B3:H3, as shown above.

KEY TERMS

Annuity (p. 641)
Balloon payment (p. 642)
Compound interest (p. 638)
Discount rate (p. 640)
Future value (p. 639)
Future value factor (p. 639)
Installment loan (p. 642)
Present value (p. 640)
Present value factor (p. 641)
Simple interest (p. 638)
Time-value of money (p. 638)

Assignments with the MBC logo in the margin are available in myBusinessCourse. See the Preface of the book for details.

EXERCISES

EA-1. Dawn Riley deposited $4,000 in a money market account on January 2, 2019. How much will her savings be worth on January 2, 2025 if the money market account earns a return of

a. 4%?
b. 6%?
c. 8%?

EA-2. Jason Shields invested $7,500 in an account that pays a 12% return. How much will the account be worth in four years if the interest is compounded

a. annually?
b. quarterly?
c. monthly?

EA-3. Leslie Porter is planning a trip to Europe upon graduation in two years. She anticipates that her trip will cost $14,000. She would like to set aside an amount now to save for the trip. How much should she set aside if her savings earns 4% interest compounded quarterly?

EA-4. Matt Wilson has an investment opportunity that promises to pay him $24,000 in four years. He could earn 6% if he invested his money elsewhere. What is the maximum amount that he should be willing to invest in this opportunity?

EA-5. Robert Smith purchased a used car for $14,000. To pay for his purchase, he borrowed $12,500 from a local bank at 12%. The loan requires that Robert repay the loan by making 36 monthly payments. How much will Robert have to pay each month to repay the loan?

EA-6. Refer to Exercise EA-5. How much interest will Robert Smith pay as part of his first monthly payment?

EA-7. Sandy Nguyen just graduated from college and has $40,000 in student loans. The loans bear interest at a rate of 8% and require quarterly payments.

a. What amount should Sandy pay each quarter if she wishes to pay off her student loans in six years?

b. Sandy can only afford to pay $1,500 per quarter. How long will it take Sandy to repay these loans?

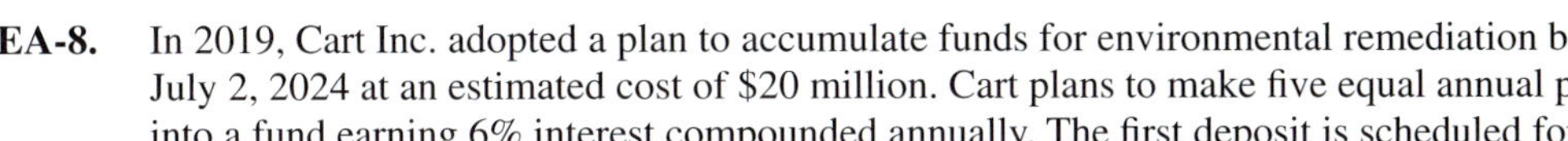

EA-8. In 2019, Cart Inc. adopted a plan to accumulate funds for environmental remediation beginning July 2, 2024 at an estimated cost of $20 million. Cart plans to make five equal annual payments into a fund earning 6% interest compounded annually. The first deposit is scheduled for July 1, 2019. Determine the amount of the required annual deposit.

EA-9. On May 1, 2019, Ott, Inc. sold merchandise to Fox Inc. Fox signed a noninterest bearing note requiring payment of $60,000 annually for 7 years. The first payment is due May 1, 2020. The prevailing rate for similar notes on that date is 9%. What amount should Ott, Inc. report as revenue in 2019 and 2020?

EA-10. Rex Corporation accepted a $10,000, 5% interest bearing note from Brooks Inc. on December 1, 2018 in exchange for machinery with a list sales price of $9,500. The note is payable on December 1, 2021. If the prevailing interest rate is 8%, what revenues should Rex report in its income statement for the year ended December 31, 2018?

EA-11. Rye Company is considering purchasing a new machine with a useful life of ten years, at which time its salvage value is estimated to be $50,000. Management estimates a net increase in operating cash inflow due to the new machine at $200,000 per year. What is the maximum amount the company should be willing to pay for the machine if the relevant cost of capital associated with this type of investment is 12%?

EA-12. Debra Wilcox won $7 million in the California lottery. She must choose how she wants the prize to be paid to her. First, Debra can elect to receive 26 annual payments, with the first payment due immediately. Second, she can elect to receive a single payment immediately for the entire amount. However, if she elects the single payment option, the winning prize is reduced to one-half the winnings ($3.5 million). Which option should Debra choose if her cost of capital (discount rate) is

a. 8%?

b. 4%?

c. What rate would make Debra indifferent between these two options?

EA-13. Linda Reed, an executive at VIP Inc. has earned a performance bonus. She has the option of accepting $60,000 now or $100,000 5 years from now. What would you advise her to do? Explain and support with calculations.

EA-14. On September 1, 2018, Luft, Inc. deposited $400,000 in a debt retirement fund. The company needs $955,000 cash to settle a maturing debt September 1, 2026. What is the minimal rate of compound interest required to assure the debt will be paid when due?

EA-15. Wolf Inc. establishes a construction fund on July 1, 2019, by making a single deposit of $360,000. At the end of each year, Wolf will deposit an additional $60,000. The fund guarantees a 12% return each year. How much will be in the fund on June 30, 2023?

EA-16. Sylvia Owen, owner of I-Haul Trucking is considering expanding operations from Seattle to the Portland area. Expansion is estimated to cost $10 million including the required new facilities and

additional trucks. Sylvia has elected to finance the expansion by borrowing from her local bank at a yearly interest rate of 10%. She has agreed to repay the loan in twenty equal payments over a 10-year period to begin in six months. (Payments will be made at the end of every half-year period.)

a. What will Sylvia periodic payments be?

b. How much of her first payment will be interest expense?

c. Assume that after five years, Sylvia decided to pay off the loan early. How much would she owe at that time?

Homework MBC **EA-17.** On November 1, 2018, Ybarra Construction Company issued $200,000 of 5-year bonds that pay interest at an annual rate of 5%. The interest payments are due every six months (that is, the interest is compounded semi-annually). At the end of the five-year period, Ybarra must pay the bond holders a balloon payment of $200,000.

a. What would the issue price of the bonds be if the prevailing interest rate is (i) 4%? (ii) 6%?

b. Compute the market price of these bonds on November 1, 2020 assuming that the prevailing market interest rate at that time is 8%.

Homework MBC **EA-18.** On August 1, 2019, Paradise Airlines agreed to lease a passenger jet from Boeing Corporation. The 20-year lease requires an annual payment of $450,000. If Paradise were to purchase the jet, it could borrow the necessary funds at a 9% interest rate.

a. What is the present value of the lease payments if the first payment is due on August 1, 2020?

b. What is the present value of the lease payments if the first payment is due on August 1, 2019?

Homework MBC **EA-19.** Burnham Corporation is comparing two alternatives for leasing a machine.

Alternative A is a lease that requires six annual payments of $8,000 with the first payment due immediately.

Alternative B is a lease that requires two payments of $11,000 and three payments of $9,000 with the first payment due one year from now.

a. Which alternative should Burnham choose if the relevant discount rate is 5%?

b. Which alternative should Burnham choose if the relevant interest rate is 7%?

Homework MBC **EA-20.** On January 2, 2019, DeSantis Company is comparing two alternatives for leasing a machine.

Alternative A is a lease that requires 24 quarterly payments of $3,000 with the first payment due on March 31, 2019.

Alternative B is a lease that requires five annual payments of $14,300 with the first payment due on December 31, 2019.

Which alternative should DeSantis choose if the appropriate discount rate is 8% compounded quarterly?

Homework MBC **EA-21.** Despite his relative youth, Samuel Hunter has started planning for his retirement. At present, he has $2,400 he can invest, and he believes that he will be able to invest that amount each year for the next 39 years—40 contributions in total.

a. If his investment earns 4% per year for the 40 years, how much will Samuel have accumulated at the end of 40 years?

b. If Samuel delays investing for 10 years, how will that affect the balance accumulated at the end of 40 years?

c. If Samuel begins investing now and finds an investment earning 5% per year for 40 years, how much more will he have accumulated than if he earns 4%?

Homework MBC **EA-22.** Janice Utley is saving for a real estate investment. If she invests $1,000 now and then at the beginning of each of the next 35 months (36 months in total) at an interest rate of 1% per month, what will be the investment balance at the end of month 36?

TABLE A.1 Future Value of Single Amount

$f = (1 + i)^t$

	Interest Rate											
Period	0.01	0.02	0.03	0.04	0.05	0.06	0.07	0.08	0.09	0.10	0.11	0.12
1	1.01000	1.02000	1.03000	1.04000	1.05000	1.06000	1.07000	1.08000	1.09000	1.10000	1.11000	1.12000
2	1.02010	1.04040	1.06090	1.08160	1.10250	1.12360	1.14490	1.16640	1.18810	1.21000	1.23210	1.25440
3	1.03030	1.06121	1.09273	1.12486	1.15763	1.19102	1.22504	1.25971	1.29503	1.33100	1.36763	1.40493
4	1.04060	1.08243	1.12551	1.16986	1.21551	1.26248	1.31080	1.36049	1.41158	1.46410	1.51807	1.57352
5	1.05101	1.10408	1.15927	1.21665	1.27628	1.33823	1.40255	1.46933	1.53862	1.61051	1.68506	1.76234
6	1.06152	1.12616	1.19405	1.26532	1.34010	1.41852	1.50073	1.58687	1.67710	1.77156	1.87041	1.97382
7	1.07214	1.14869	1.22987	1.31593	1.40710	1.50363	1.60578	1.71382	1.82804	1.94872	2.07616	2.21068
8	1.08286	1.17166	1.26677	1.36857	1.47746	1.59385	1.71819	1.85093	1.99256	2.14359	2.30454	2.47596
9	1.09369	1.19509	1.30477	1.42331	1.55133	1.68948	1.83846	1.99900	2.17189	2.35795	2.55804	2.77308
10	1.10462	1.21899	1.34392	1.48024	1.62889	1.79085	1.96715	2.15892	2.36736	2.59374	2.83942	3.10585
11	1.11567	1.24337	1.38423	1.53945	1.71034	1.89830	2.10485	2.33164	2.58043	2.85312	3.15176	3.47855
12	1.12683	1.26824	1.42576	1.60103	1.79586	2.01220	2.25219	2.51817	2.81266	3.13843	3.49845	3.89598
13	1.13809	1.29361	1.46853	1.66507	1.88565	2.13293	2.40985	2.71962	3.06580	3.45227	3.88328	4.36349
14	1.14947	1.31948	1.51259	1.73168	1.97993	2.26090	2.57853	2.93719	3.34173	3.79750	4.31044	4.88711
15	1.16097	1.34587	1.55797	1.80094	2.07893	2.39656	2.75903	3.17217	3.64248	4.17725	4.78459	5.47357
16	1.17258	1.37279	1.60471	1.87298	2.18287	2.54035	2.95216	3.42594	3.97031	4.59497	5.31089	6.13039
17	1.18430	1.40024	1.65285	1.94790	2.29202	2.69277	3.15882	3.70002	4.32763	5.05447	5.89509	6.86604
18	1.19615	1.42825	1.70243	2.02582	2.40662	2.85434	3.37993	3.99602	4.71712	5.55992	6.54355	7.68997
19	1.20811	1.45681	1.75351	2.10685	2.52695	3.02560	3.61653	4.31570	5.14166	6.11591	7.26334	8.61276
20	1.22019	1.48595	1.80611	2.19112	2.65330	3.20714	3.86968	4.66096	5.60441	6.72750	8.06231	9.64629
21	1.23239	1.51567	1.86029	2.27877	2.78596	3.39956	4.14056	5.03383	6.10881	7.40025	8.94917	10.80385
22	1.24472	1.54598	1.91610	2.36992	2.92526	3.60354	4.43040	5.43654	6.65860	8.14027	9.93357	12.10031
23	1.25716	1.57690	1.97359	2.46472	3.07152	3.81975	4.74053	5.87146	7.25787	8.95430	11.02627	13.55235
24	1.26973	1.60844	2.03279	2.56330	3.22510	4.04893	5.07237	6.34118	7.91108	9.84973	12.23916	15.17863
25	1.28243	1.64061	2.09378	2.66584	3.38635	4.29187	5.42743	6.84848	8.62308	10.83471	13.58546	17.00006
26	1.29526	1.67342	2.15659	2.77247	3.55567	4.54938	5.80735	7.39635	9.39916	11.91818	15.07986	19.04007
27	1.30821	1.70689	2.22129	2.88337	3.73346	4.82235	6.21387	7.98806	10.24508	13.10999	16.73865	21.32488
28	1.32129	1.74102	2.28793	2.99870	3.92013	5.11169	6.64884	8.62711	11.16714	14.42099	18.57990	23.88387
29	1.33450	1.77584	2.35657	3.11865	4.11614	5.41839	7.11426	9.31727	12.17218	15.86309	20.62369	26.74993
30	1.34785	1.81136	2.42726	3.24340	4.32194	5.74349	7.61226	10.06266	13.26768	17.44940	22.89230	29.95992
31	1.36133	1.84759	2.50008	3.37313	4.53804	6.08810	8.14511	10.86767	14.46177	19.19434	25.41045	33.55511
32	1.37494	1.88454	2.57508	3.50806	4.76494	6.45339	8.71527	11.73708	15.76333	21.11378	28.20560	37.58173
33	1.38869	1.92223	2.65234	3.64838	5.00319	6.84059	9.32534	12.67605	17.18203	23.22515	31.30821	42.09153
34	1.40258	1.96068	2.73191	3.79432	5.25335	7.25103	9.97811	13.69013	18.72841	25.54767	34.75212	47.14252
35	1.41660	1.99989	2.81386	3.94609	5.51602	7.68609	10.67658	14.78534	20.41397	28.10244	38.57485	52.79962
36	1.43077	2.03989	2.89828	4.10393	5.79182	8.14725	11.42394	15.96817	22.25123	30.91268	42.81808	59.13557
37	1.44508	2.08069	2.98523	4.26809	6.08141	8.63609	12.22362	17.24563	24.25384	34.00395	47.52807	66.23184
38	1.45953	2.12230	3.07478	4.43881	6.38548	9.15425	13.07927	18.62528	26.43668	37.40434	52.75616	74.17966
39	1.47412	2.16474	3.16703	4.61637	6.70475	9.70351	13.99482	20.11530	28.81598	41.14478	58.55934	83.08122
40	1.48886	2.20804	3.26204	4.80102	7.03999	10.28572	14.97446	21.72452	31.40942	45.25926	65.00087	93.05097

TABLE A.2 Present Value of Single Amount $p = 1/(1+i)^t$

Period	Interest Rate											
	0.01	0.02	0.03	0.04	0.05	0.06	0.07	0.08	0.09	0.10	0.11	0.12
1	0.99010	0.98039	0.97087	0.96154	0.95238	0.94340	0.93458	0.92593	0.91743	0.90909	0.90090	0.89286
2	0.98030	0.96117	0.94260	0.92456	0.90703	0.89000	0.87344	0.85734	0.84168	0.82645	0.81162	0.79719
3	0.97059	0.94232	0.91514	0.88900	0.86384	0.83962	0.81630	0.79383	0.77218	0.75131	0.73119	0.71178
4	0.96098	0.92385	0.88849	0.85480	0.82270	0.79209	0.76290	0.73503	0.70843	0.68301	0.65873	0.63552
5	0.95147	0.90573	0.86261	0.82193	0.78353	0.74726	0.71299	0.68058	0.64993	0.62092	0.59345	0.56743
6	0.94205	0.88797	0.83748	0.79031	0.74622	0.70496	0.66634	0.63017	0.59627	0.56447	0.53464	0.50663
7	0.93272	0.87056	0.81309	0.75992	0.71068	0.66506	0.62275	0.58349	0.54703	0.51316	0.48166	0.45235
8	0.92348	0.85349	0.78941	0.73069	0.67684	0.62741	0.58201	0.54027	0.50187	0.46651	0.43393	0.40388
9	0.91434	0.83676	0.76642	0.70259	0.64461	0.59190	0.54393	0.50025	0.46043	0.42410	0.39092	0.36061
10	0.90529	0.82035	0.74409	0.67556	0.61391	0.55839	0.50835	0.46319	0.42241	0.38554	0.35218	0.32197
11	0.89632	0.80426	0.72242	0.64958	0.58468	0.52679	0.47509	0.42888	0.38753	0.35049	0.31728	0.28748
12	0.88745	0.78849	0.70138	0.62460	0.55684	0.49697	0.44401	0.39711	0.35553	0.31863	0.28584	0.25668
13	0.87866	0.77303	0.68095	0.60057	0.53032	0.46884	0.41496	0.36770	0.32618	0.28966	0.25751	0.22917
14	0.86996	0.75788	0.66112	0.57748	0.50507	0.44230	0.38782	0.34046	0.29925	0.26333	0.23199	0.20462
15	0.86135	0.74301	0.64186	0.55526	0.48102	0.41727	0.36245	0.31524	0.27454	0.23939	0.20900	0.18270
16	0.85282	0.72845	0.62317	0.53391	0.45811	0.39365	0.33873	0.29189	0.25187	0.21763	0.18829	0.16312
17	0.84438	0.71416	0.60502	0.51337	0.43630	0.37136	0.31657	0.27027	0.23107	0.19784	0.16963	0.14564
18	0.83602	0.70016	0.58739	0.49363	0.41552	0.35034	0.29586	0.25025	0.21199	0.17986	0.15282	0.13004
19	0.82774	0.68643	0.57029	0.47464	0.39573	0.33051	0.27651	0.23171	0.19449	0.16351	0.13768	0.11611
20	0.81954	0.67297	0.55368	0.45639	0.37689	0.31180	0.25842	0.21455	0.17843	0.14864	0.12403	0.10367
21	0.81143	0.65978	0.53755	0.43883	0.35894	0.29416	0.24151	0.19866	0.16370	0.13513	0.11174	0.09256
22	0.80340	0.64684	0.52189	0.42196	0.34185	0.27751	0.22571	0.18394	0.15018	0.12285	0.10067	0.08264
23	0.79544	0.63416	0.50669	0.40573	0.32557	0.26180	0.21095	0.17032	0.13778	0.11168	0.09069	0.07379
24	0.78757	0.62172	0.49193	0.39012	0.31007	0.24698	0.19715	0.15770	0.12640	0.10153	0.08170	0.06588
25	0.77977	0.60953	0.47761	0.37512	0.29530	0.23300	0.18425	0.14602	0.11597	0.09230	0.07361	0.05882
26	0.77205	0.59758	0.46369	0.36069	0.28124	0.21981	0.17220	0.13520	0.10639	0.08391	0.06631	0.05252
27	0.76440	0.58586	0.45019	0.34682	0.26785	0.20737	0.16093	0.12519	0.09761	0.07628	0.05974	0.04689
28	0.75684	0.57437	0.43708	0.33348	0.25509	0.19563	0.15040	0.11591	0.08955	0.06934	0.05382	0.04187
29	0.74934	0.56311	0.42435	0.32065	0.24295	0.18456	0.14056	0.10733	0.08215	0.06304	0.04849	0.03738
30	0.74192	0.55207	0.41199	0.30832	0.23138	0.17411	0.13137	0.09938	0.07537	0.05731	0.04368	0.03338
31	0.73458	0.54125	0.39999	0.29646	0.22036	0.16425	0.12277	0.09202	0.06915	0.05210	0.03935	0.02980
32	0.72730	0.53063	0.38834	0.28506	0.20987	0.15496	0.11474	0.08520	0.06344	0.04736	0.03545	0.02661
33	0.72010	0.52023	0.37703	0.27409	0.19987	0.14619	0.10723	0.07889	0.05820	0.04306	0.03194	0.02376
34	0.71297	0.51003	0.36604	0.26355	0.19035	0.13791	0.10022	0.07305	0.05339	0.03914	0.02878	0.02121
35	0.70591	0.50003	0.35538	0.25342	0.18129	0.13011	0.09366	0.06763	0.04899	0.03558	0.02592	0.01894
36	0.69892	0.49022	0.34503	0.24367	0.17266	0.12274	0.08754	0.06262	0.04494	0.03235	0.02335	0.01691
37	0.69200	0.48061	0.33498	0.23430	0.16444	0.11579	0.08181	0.05799	0.04123	0.02941	0.02104	0.01510
38	0.68515	0.47119	0.32523	0.22529	0.15661	0.10924	0.07646	0.05369	0.03783	0.02673	0.01896	0.01348
39	0.67837	0.46195	0.31575	0.21662	0.14915	0.10306	0.07146	0.04971	0.03470	0.02430	0.01708	0.01204
40	0.67165	0.45289	0.30656	0.20829	0.14205	0.09722	0.06678	0.04603	0.03184	0.02209	0.01538	0.01075

TABLE A.3 Present Value of Ordinary Annuity $p = \{1 - [1/(1+i)^t]\}/i$

	Interest Rate											
Period	**0.01**	**0.02**	**0.03**	**0.04**	**0.05**	**0.06**	**0.07**	**0.08**	**0.09**	**0.10**	**0.11**	**0.12**
1	0.99010	0.98039	0.97087	0.96154	0.95238	0.94340	0.93458	0.92593	0.91743	0.90909	0.90090	0.89286
2	1.97040	1.94156	1.91347	1.88609	1.85941	1.83339	1.80802	1.78326	1.75911	1.73554	1.71252	1.69005
3	2.94099	2.88388	2.82861	2.77509	2.72325	2.67301	2.62432	2.57710	2.53129	2.48685	2.44371	2.40183
4	3.90197	3.80773	3.71710	3.62990	3.54595	3.46511	3.38721	3.31213	3.23972	3.16987	3.10245	3.03735
5	4.85343	4.71346	4.57971	4.45182	4.32948	4.21236	4.10020	3.99271	3.88965	3.79079	3.69590	3.60478
6	5.79548	5.60143	5.41719	5.24214	5.07569	4.91732	4.76654	4.62288	4.48592	4.35526	4.23054	4.11141
7	6.72819	6.47199	6.23028	6.00205	5.78637	5.58238	5.38929	5.20637	5.03295	4.86842	4.71220	4.56376
8	7.65168	7.32548	7.01969	6.73274	6.46321	6.20979	5.97130	5.74664	5.53482	5.33493	5.14612	4.96764
9	8.56602	8.16224	7.78611	7.43533	7.10782	6.80169	6.51523	6.24689	5.99525	5.75902	5.53705	5.32825
10	9.47130	8.98259	8.53020	8.11090	7.72173	7.36009	7.02358	6.71008	6.41766	6.14457	5.88923	5.65022
11	10.36763	9.78685	9.25262	8.76048	8.30641	7.88687	7.49867	7.13896	6.80519	6.49506	6.20652	5.93770
12	11.25508	10.57534	9.95400	9.38507	8.86325	8.38384	7.94269	7.53608	7.16073	6.81369	6.49236	6.19437
13	12.13374	11.34837	10.63496	9.98565	9.39357	8.85268	8.35765	7.90378	7.48690	7.10336	6.74987	6.42355
14	13.00370	12.10625	11.29607	10.56312	9.89864	9.29498	8.74547	8.24424	7.78615	7.36669	6.98187	6.62817
15	13.86505	12.84926	11.93794	11.11839	10.37966	9.71225	9.10791	8.55948	8.06069	7.60608	7.19087	6.81086
16	14.71787	13.57771	12.56110	11.65230	10.83777	10.10590	9.44665	8.85137	8.31256	7.82371	7.37916	6.97399
17	15.56225	14.29187	13.16612	12.16567	11.27407	10.47726	9.76322	9.12164	8.54363	8.02155	7.54879	7.11963
18	16.39827	14.99203	13.75351	12.65930	11.68959	10.82760	10.05909	9.37189	8.75563	8.20141	7.70162	7.24967
19	17.22601	15.67846	14.32380	13.13394	12.08532	11.15812	10.33560	9.60360	8.95011	8.36492	7.83929	7.36578
20	18.04555	16.35143	14.87747	13.59033	12.46221	11.46992	10.59401	9.81815	9.12855	8.51356	7.96333	7.46944
21	18.85698	17.01121	15.41502	14.02916	12.82115	11.76408	10.83553	10.01680	9.29224	8.64869	8.07507	7.56200
22	19.66038	17.65805	15.93692	14.45112	13.16300	12.04158	11.06124	10.20074	9.44243	8.77154	8.17574	7.64465
23	20.45582	18.29220	16.44361	14.85684	13.48857	12.30338	11.27219	10.37106	9.58021	8.88322	8.26643	7.71843
24	21.24339	18.91393	16.93554	15.24696	13.79864	12.55036	11.46933	10.52876	9.70661	8.98474	8.34814	7.78432
25	22.02316	19.52346	17.41315	15.62208	14.09394	12.78336	11.65358	10.67478	9.82258	9.07704	8.42174	7.84314
26	22.79520	20.12104	17.87684	15.98277	14.37519	13.00317	11.82578	10.80998	9.92897	9.16095	8.48806	7.89566
27	23.55961	20.70690	18.32703	16.32959	14.64303	13.21053	11.98671	10.93516	10.02658	9.23722	8.54780	7.94255
28	24.31644	21.28127	18.76411	16.66306	14.89813	13.40616	12.13711	11.05108	10.11613	9.30657	8.60162	7.98442
29	25.06579	21.84438	19.18845	16.98371	15.14107	13.59072	12.27767	11.15841	10.19828	9.36961	8.65011	8.02181
30	25.80771	22.39646	19.60044	17.29203	15.37245	13.76483	12.40904	11.25778	10.27365	9.42691	8.69379	8.05518
31	26.54229	22.93770	20.00043	17.58849	15.59281	13.92909	12.53181	11.34980	10.34280	9.47901	8.73315	8.08499
32	27.26959	23.46833	20.38877	17.87355	15.80268	14.08404	12.64656	11.43500	10.40624	9.52638	8.76860	8.11159
33	27.98969	23.98856	20.76579	18.14765	16.00255	14.23023	12.75379	11.51389	10.46444	9.56943	8.80054	8.13535
34	28.70267	24.49859	21.13184	18.41120	16.19290	14.36814	12.85401	11.58693	10.51784	9.60857	8.82932	8.15656
35	29.40858	24.99862	21.48722	18.66461	16.37419	14.49825	12.94767	11.65457	10.56682	9.64416	8.85524	8.17550
36	30.10751	25.48884	21.83225	18.90828	16.54685	14.62099	13.03521	11.71719	10.61176	9.67651	8.87859	8.19241
37	30.79951	25.96945	22.16724	19.14258	16.71129	14.73678	13.11702	11.77518	10.65299	9.70592	8.89963	8.20751
38	31.48466	26.44064	22.49246	19.36786	16.86789	14.84602	13.19347	11.82887	10.69082	9.73265	8.91859	8.22099
39	32.16303	26.90259	22.80822	19.58448	17.01704	14.94907	13.26493	11.87858	10.72552	9.75696	8.93567	8.23303
40	32.83469	27.35548	23.11477	19.79277	17.15909	15.04630	13.33171	11.92461	10.75736	9.77905	8.95105	8.24378

TABLE A.4 Future Value of Annuity Paid at Beginning of Period

	Interest Rate											
Period	**0.01**	**0.02**	**0.03**	**0.04**	**0.05**	**0.06**	**0.07**	**0.08**	**0.09**	**0.10**	**0.11**	**0.12**
1	1.0100	1.0200	1.0300	1.0400	1.0500	1.0600	1.0700	1.0800	1.0900	1.1000	1.1100	1.1200
2	2.0301	2.0604	2.0909	2.1216	2.1525	2.1836	2.2149	2.2464	2.2781	2.3100	2.3421	2.3744
3	3.0604	3.1216	3.1836	3.2465	3.3101	3.3746	3.4399	3.5061	3.5731	3.6410	3.7097	3.7793
4	4.1010	4.2040	4.3091	4.4163	4.5256	4.6371	4.7507	4.8666	4.9847	5.1051	5.2278	5.3528
5	5.1520	5.3081	5.4684	5.6330	5.8019	5.9753	6.1533	6.3359	6.5233	6.7156	6.9129	7.1152
6	6.2135	6.4343	6.6625	6.8983	7.1420	7.3938	7.6540	7.9228	8.2004	8.4872	8.7833	9.0890
7	7.2857	7.5830	7.8923	8.2142	8.5491	8.8975	9.2598	9.6366	10.0285	10.4359	10.8594	11.2997
8	8.3685	8.7546	9.1591	9.5828	10.0266	10.4913	10.9780	11.4876	12.0210	12.5795	13.1640	13.7757
9	9.4622	9.9497	10.4639	11.0061	11.5779	12.1808	12.8164	13.4866	14.1929	14.9374	15.7220	16.5487
10	10.5668	11.1687	11.8078	12.4864	13.2068	13.9716	14.7836	15.6455	16.5603	17.5312	18.5614	19.6546
11	11.6825	12.4121	13.1920	14.0258	14.9171	15.8699	16.8885	17.9771	19.1407	20.3843	21.7132	23.1331
12	12.8093	13.6803	14.6178	15.6268	16.7130	17.8821	19.1406	20.4953	21.9534	23.5227	25.2116	27.0291
13	13.9474	14.9739	16.0863	17.2919	18.5986	20.0151	21.5505	23.2149	25.0192	26.9750	29.0949	31.3926
14	15.0969	16.2934	17.5989	19.0236	20.5786	22.2760	24.1290	26.1521	28.3609	30.7725	33.4054	36.2797
15	16.2579	17.6393	19.1569	20.8245	22.6575	24.6725	26.8881	29.3243	32.0034	34.9497	38.1899	41.7533
16	17.4304	19.0121	20.7616	22.6975	24.8404	27.2129	29.8402	32.7502	35.9737	39.5447	43.5008	47.8837
17	18.6147	20.4123	22.4144	24.6454	27.1324	29.9057	32.9990	36.4502	40.3013	44.5992	49.3959	54.7497
18	19.8109	21.8406	24.1169	26.6712	29.5390	32.7600	36.3790	40.4463	45.0185	50.1591	55.9395	62.4397
19	21.0190	23.2974	25.8704	28.7781	32.0660	35.7856	39.9955	44.7620	50.1601	56.2750	63.2028	71.0524
20	22.2392	24.7833	27.6765	30.9692	34.7193	38.9927	43.8652	49.4229	55.7645	63.0025	71.2651	80.6987
21	23.4716	26.2990	29.5368	33.2480	37.5052	42.3923	48.0057	54.4568	61.8733	70.4027	80.2143	91.5026
22	24.7163	27.8450	31.4529	35.6179	40.4305	45.9958	52.4361	59.8933	68.5319	78.5430	90.1479	103.6029
23	25.9735	29.4219	33.4265	38.0826	43.5020	49.8156	57.1767	65.7648	75.7898	87.4973	101.1742	117.1552
24	27.2432	31.0303	35.4593	40.6459	46.7271	53.8645	62.2490	72.1059	83.7009	97.3471	113.4133	132.3339
25	28.5256	32.6709	37.5530	43.3117	50.1135	58.1564	67.6765	78.9544	92.3240	108.1818	126.9988	149.3339
26	29.8209	34.3443	39.7096	46.0842	53.6691	62.7058	73.4838	86.3508	101.7231	120.0999	142.0786	168.3740
27	31.1291	36.0512	41.9309	48.9676	57.4026	67.5281	79.6977	94.3388	111.9682	133.2099	158.8173	189.6989
28	32.4504	37.7922	44.2189	51.9663	61.3227	72.6398	86.3465	102.9659	123.1354	147.6309	177.3972	213.5828
29	33.7849	39.5681	46.5754	55.0849	65.4388	78.0582	93.4608	112.2832	135.3075	163.4940	198.0209	240.3327
30	35.1327	41.3794	49.0027	58.3283	69.7608	83.8017	101.0730	122.3459	148.5752	180.9434	220.9132	270.2926
31	36.4941	43.2270	51.5028	61.7015	74.2988	89.8898	109.2182	133.2135	163.0370	200.1378	246.3236	303.8477
32	37.8690	45.1116	54.0778	65.2095	79.0638	96.3432	117.9334	144.9506	178.8003	221.2515	274.5292	341.4294
33	39.2577	47.0338	56.7302	68.8579	84.0670	103.1838	127.2588	157.6267	195.9823	244.4767	305.8374	383.5210
34	40.6603	48.9945	59.4621	72.6522	89.3203	110.4348	137.2369	171.3168	214.7108	270.0244	340.5896	430.6635
35	42.0769	50.9944	62.2759	76.5983	94.8363	118.1209	147.9135	186.1021	235.1247	298.1268	379.1644	483.4631
36	43.5076	53.0343	65.1742	80.7022	100.6281	126.2681	159.3374	202.0703	257.3759	329.0395	421.9825	542.5987
37	44.9527	55.1149	68.1594	84.9703	106.7095	134.9042	171.5610	219.3159	281.6298	363.0434	469.5106	608.8305
38	46.4123	57.2372	71.2342	89.4091	113.0950	144.0585	184.6403	237.9412	308.0665	400.4478	522.2667	683.0102
39	47.8864	59.4020	74.4013	94.0255	119.7998	153.7620	198.6351	258.0565	336.8824	441.5926	580.8261	766.0914
40	49.3752	61.6100	77.6633	98.8265	126.8398	164.0477	213.6096	279.7810	368.2919	486.8518	645.8269	859.1424

TABLE A.5 Present Value of an Annuity Due of *n* Payments of 1 Each: $PVAD = \left[\frac{1-1(1+i)^n}{i}\right] \times (1+i)$

This table shows the present value of an annuity due of $1 at various rates of interest and for various time periods. It is used to compute the present value of a series of payments made at the beginning of each interest compounding period.

n	2%	3%	4%	5%	6%	7%	8%	9%	10%	11%	12%	15%
1	1.00000	1.00000	1.00000	1.00000	1.00000	1.00000	1.00000	1.00000	1.00000	1.00000	1.00000	1.00000
2	1.98039	1.97087	1.96154	1.95238	1.94340	1.93458	1.92593	1.91743	1.90909	1.90090	1.89286	1.86957
3	2.94156	2.91347	2.88609	2.85941	2.83339	2.80802	2.78326	2.75911	2.73554	2.71252	2.69005	2.62571
4	3.88388	3.82861	3.77509	3.72325	3.67301	3.62432	3.57710	3.53130	3.48685	3.44371	3.40183	3.28323
5	4.80773	4.71710	4.62990	4.54595	4.46511	4.38721	4.31213	4.23972	4.16987	4.10245	4.03735	3.85498
6	5.71346	5.57971	5.45182	5.32948	5.21236	5.10020	4.99271	4.88965	4.79079	4.69590	4.60478	4.35216
7	6.60143	6.41719	6.24214	6.07569	5.91732	5.76654	5.62288	5.48592	5.35526	5.23054	5.11141	4.78448
8	7.47199	7.23028	7.00205	6.78637	6.58238	6.38929	6.20637	6.03295	5.86842	5.71220	5.56376	5.16042
9	8.32548	8.01969	7.73274	7.46321	7.20979	6.97130	6.74664	6.53482	6.33493	6.14612	5.96764	5.48732
10	9.16224	8.78611	8.43533	8.10782	7.80169	7.51523	7.24689	6.99525	6.75902	6.53705	6.32825	5.77158
11	9.98259	9.53020	9.11090	8.72173	8.36009	8.02358	7.71008	7.41766	7.14457	6.88923	6.65022	6.01877
12	10.78685	10.25262	9.76048	9.30641	8.88687	8.49867	8.13896	7.80519	7.49506	7.20652	6.93770	6.23371
13	11.57534	10.95400	10.38507	9.86325	9.38384	8.94269	8.53608	8.16073	7.81369	7.49236	7.19437	6.42062
14	12.34837	11.63496	10.98565	10.39357	9.85268	9.35765	8.90378	8.48690	8.10336	7.74987	7.42355	6.58315
15	13.10625	12.29607	11.56312	10.89864	10.29498	9.74547	9.24424	8.78615	8.36669	7.98187	7.62817	6.72448
16	13.84926	12.93794	12.11839	11.37966	10.71225	10.10791	9.55948	9.06069	8.60608	8.19087	7.81086	6.84737
17	14.57771	13.56110	12.65230	11.83777	11.10590	10.44665	9.85137	9.31256	8.82371	8.37916	7.97399	6.95423
18	15.29187	14.16612	13.16567	12.27407	11.47726	10.76322	10.12164	9.54363	9.02155	8.54879	8.11963	7.04716
19	15.99203	14.75351	13.65930	12.68959	11.82760	11.05909	10.37189	9.75563	9.20141	8.70162	8.24967	7.12797
20	16.67846	15.32380	14.13394	13.08532	12.15812	11.33560	10.60360	9.95012	9.36492	8.83929	8.36578	7.19823
21	17.35143	15.87747	14.59033	13.46221	12.46992	11.59401	10.81815	10.12855	9.51356	8.96333	8.46944	7.25933
22	18.01121	16.41502	15.02916	13.82115	12.76408	11.83553	11.01680	10.29224	9.64869	9.07507	8.56200	7.31246
23	18.65805	16.93692	15.45112	14.16300	13.04158	12.06124	11.20074	10.44243	9.77154	9.17574	8.64465	7.35866
24	19.29220	17.44361	15.85684	14.48857	13.30338	12.27219	11.37106	10.58021	9.88322	9.26643	8.71843	7.39884
25	19.91393	17.93554	16.24696	14.79864	13.55036	12.46933	11.52876	10.70661	9.98474	9.34814	8.78432	7.43377

Data Analytics

This appendix can be downloaded from this book's website.

Index

Note: Exhibits included in the index with e following the page numbers.

Note: Exhibits included in the index with e following the page numbers.

Note: Exhibits included in the index with e following the page numbers.

Note: Exhibits included in the index with e following the page numbers.

Note: Exhibits included in the index with e following the page numbers.

G

Note: Exhibits included in the index with e following the page numbers.

Note: Exhibits included in the index with e following the page numbers.

Note: Exhibits included in the index with e following the page numbers.

M

N

Note: Exhibits included in the index with e following the page numbers.

O

P

Note: Exhibits included in the index with e following the page numbers.

Note: Exhibits included in the index with e following the page numbers.

Note: Exhibits included in the index with e following the page numbers.

T

Note: Exhibits included in the index with e following the page numbers.

U

Y

Z

Note: Exhibits included in the index with e following the page numbers.